Common Strategies of Anadromous
and Catadromous Fishes

Cover design by John E. Cooper

An International Symposium on
Common Strategies of Anadromous and Catadromous Fishes

Sponsor

Northeastern Division, American Fisheries Society

Steering Committee

Michael J. Dadswell, Chair

Kenneth L. Beal	Christine M. Moffitt
John E. Cooper	Stephen G. Rideout
David S. Crestin	Roger A. Rulifson
Ronald J. Klauda	Richard L. Saunders

Richard H. Schaefer

Cooperators

U.S. Fish and Wildlife Service
Department of Fisheries and Oceans, Government of Canada
National Marine Fisheries Service
National Science Foundation
Atlantic States Marine Fisheries Commission
Sport Fishery Research Foundation
International Association of Fish and Wildlife Agencies
Hudson River Foundation
New England Power Service Company
Philadelphia Electric Company
Northeast Utilities
Tidal Power Corporation
Le Boeuf, Lamb, Leiby and MacRae
New England Aquarium
Lawler, Matusky & Skelly Engineers
New England Fisheries Development Foundation
Connecticut River Salmon Association
Restoration of Atlantic Salmon in America
Point Judith Fishermen's Cooperative
BioSonics, Incorporated
Northwest Marine Technology, Incorporated
Smith-Root, Incorporated

Common Strategies of Anadromous and Catadromous Fishes

Edited by

Michael J. Dadswell

Ronald J. Klauda

Christine M. Moffitt

Richard L. Saunders

Roger A. Rulifson

John E. Cooper

Proceedings of an International Symposium
Held in Boston, Massachusetts, USA
March 9–13, 1986

American Fisheries Society Symposium 1

Bethesda, Maryland
1987

The American Fisheries Society Symposium series is a registered serial. Suggested citation formats follow.

Entire book

Dadswell, M. J., R. J. Klauda, C. M. Moffitt, R. L. Saunders, R. A. Rulifson, and J. E. Cooper, editors. 1987. Common strategies of anadromous and catadromous fishes. American Fisheries Society Symposium 1.

Article within the book

Gross, M. R. 1987. Evolution of diadromy in fishes. American Fisheries Society Symposium 1:14–25.

Library of Congress Catalog Card Number: 87-070241
ISSN 0892-2284   ISBN 0-913235-42-3

Address orders to
American Fisheries Society
5410 Grosvenor Lane, Suite 110
Bethesda, Maryland 20814, USA

CONTENTS

Ocean Migrations

Recruitment Mechanisms

Future Directions

Abstracts of Poster Papers

Preface

This International Symposium was attended by over 200 representatives of academia, industry, government, conservation organizations, and the private sector. Enthusiastic but congenial debate stimulated by 48 presentations and countless informal conversations took place against the dynamic setting of early spring in New England. Participants who journeyed to the Boston Park Plaza Hotel from 17 countries were greeted by a raging snow storm that rapidly degenerated to a cold rain. But we were all rewarded by blue skies and crisp sunshine as the gathering dispersed after four intensive days and two evening sessions. Important new acquaintances were struck that will hopefully lead to creative scientific collaborations and inspire future conferences to wrestle with this important topic.

The editors thank the following referees for their contributions to the scientific quality of this book.

Albert, R. C.
Delaware River Basin Commission
West Trenton, New Jersey, USA

Bates, K.
Department of Fisheries
Olympia, Washington, USA

Bjornn, T. C.
University of Idaho
Moscow, Idaho, USA

Blaber, S. J. M.
CSIRO Marine Laboratories
Cleveland, Queensland, Australia

Blake, R. W.
University of British Columbia
Vancouver, British Columbia, Canada

Bok, A.
University of Zimbabwe
Harare, Zimbabwe

Booke, H. E.
University of Massachusetts
Amherst, Massachusetts, USA

Bradley, T. M.
University of Rhode Island
Kingston, Rhode Island, USA

Brannon, E. L.
University of Washington
Seattle, Washington, USA

Bruton, M.
J. L .B. Smith Institute of Ichthyology
Grahamstown, South Africa

Cadwallader, P. L.
Department of Conservation, Forests and Lands
Alexandra, Victoria, Australia

Chadwick, M. P.
Department of Fisheries and Oceans
Moncton, New Brunswick, Canada

Charnov, E.
University of Utah
Salt Lake City, Utah, USA

Chittenden, M. E.
Virginia Institute of Marine Science
Gloucester Point, Virginia, USA

Clarke, W. C.
Department of Fisheries and Oceans
Nanaimo, British Columbia, Canada

Cooper, J. E.
East Carolina University
Greenville, North Carolina, USA

Cooper, E. L.
Pennsylvania State University
University Park, Pennsylvania, USA

Crecco, V. A.
Connecticut Department of Environmental
  Protection
Waterford, Connecticut, USA

Davis, T.
CSIRO Division of Fisheries
Hobart, Tasmania, Australia

Dickhoff, W. W.
University of Washington
Seattle, Washington, USA

Dodson, J. J.
Laval University
Ste. Foy, Quebec, Canada

Domermuth, R. B.
Pennsylvania Power and Light
Allentown, Pennsylvania, USA

Dunbar, M. J.
McGill University
Montreal, Quebec, Canada

Dutil, J.-D.
Department of Fisheries and Oceans
Mont-Joli, Quebec, Canada

Eriksson, L.-O.
University of Umeå
Umeå, Sweden

Evans, G. T.
Department of Fisheries and Oceans
St. John's, Newfoundland, Canada

Everest, F. H.
U.S. Forest Service
Corvallis, Oregon, USA

Fitzgerald, G. J.
Laval University
Ste. Foy, Quebec, Canada

Friars, G. W.
Atlantic Salmon Federation
St. Andrews, New Brunswick, Canada

Garrod, D. J.
Fisheries Laboratory
Sulfolk, England, UK

Gibson, R. J.
Department of Fisheries and Oceans
St. John's, Newfoundland, Canada

Glebe, B. D.
Huntsman Marine Laboratory
St. Andrews, New Brunswick, Canada

Godin, J. G.
Mount Allison University
Sackville, New Brunswick, Canada

Goodyear, C. P.
U.S. Fish and Wildlife Service
Kearneysville, West Virginia, USA

Greeley, M. S.
Oak Ridge National Laboratory
Oak Ridge, Tennessee, USA

Griffith, R. W.
Southeastern Massachusetts University
North Dartmouth, Massachusetts, USA

Hastings, R. W.
Rutgers University
Camden, New Jersey, USA

Healy, M. C.
Department of Fisheries and Oceans
Nanaimo, British Columbia, Canada

Helfman, G. S.
University of Georgia
Athens, Georgia, USA

Helle, J. H.
National Marine Fisheries Service
Auke Bay, Alaska, USA

Hocutt, C. H.
University of Zimbabwe
Harare, Zimbabwe

Hubbs, C.
University of Texas at Austin
Austin, Texas, USA

Hutchins, J.
Summit Technology
Seattle, Washington, USA

Jellyman, D. J.
Ministry of Agriculture and Fisheries
Christchurch, New Zealand

Jensen, A. L.
University of Michigan
Ann Arbor, Michigan, USA

Jessop, B. M.
Department of Fisheries and Oceans
Halifax, Nova Scotia, Canada

Johnson, L. J.
Department of Fisheries and Oceans
Winnipeg, Manitoba, Canada

Kedney, G.
Laval University
Ste. Foy, Quebec, Canada

Keenleyside, M. H. A.
Western University
London, Ontario, Canada

Kelley, D. W.
D. W. Kelley and Associates
Newcastle, California, USA

Kwain, W.
Ministry of Natural Resources
Maple, Ontario, Canada

LaBar, G. W.
University of Vermont
Burlington, Vermont, USA

Leggett, W. C.
McGill University
Montreal, Quebec, Canada

MacPhail, D.
University of British Columbia
Vancouver, British Columbia, Canada

Marshall, T. L.
Department of Fisheries and Oceans
Halifax, Nova Scotia, Canada

McAllister, D. E.
National Museum of Canada
Ottawa, Ontario, Canada

McCleave, J. D.
University of Maine
Orono, Maine, USA

McCormack, S. D.
University of California
Berkeley, California, USA

McDowall, R. M.
Ministry of Agriculture and Fisheries
Christchurch, New Zealand

Miller, R. R.
University of Michigan
Ann Arbor, Michigan, USA

Moffit, C. M.
University of Idaho
Moscow, Idaho, USA

Moriarity, C.
Fisheries Research Centre
Dublin, Ireland

Mullan, J. W.
U.S. Fish and Wildlife Service
Levenworth, Washington, USA

Neves, R. J.
Virginia Polytechnic Institute and State
   University
Blacksburg, Virginia, USA

Peterman, R. M.
Simon Fraser University
Burnaby, British Columbia, Canada

Pippy, J.
Department of Fisheries and Oceans
St. John's, Newfoundland, Canada

Power, G.
University of Waterloo
Waterloo, Ontario, Canada

Quinn, T. P.
University of Washington
Seattle, Washington, USA

Reddin, D.
Department of Fisheries and Oceans
St. John's, Newfoundland, Canada

Richkus, W. A.
Martin Marietta Environmental Systems
Columbia, Maryland, USA

Roff, D.
McGill University
Montreal, Quebec, Canada

Rourke, A. W.
University of Idaho
Moscow, Idaho, USA

Rulifson, R. A.
East Carolina University
Greenville, North Carolina, USA

Saila, S. B.
University of Rhode Island
Narragansett, Rhode Island, USA

Savidge, I. R.
University of Colorado
Boulder, Colorado, USA

Scarnecchia, D. L.
Iowa State University
Ames, Iowa, USA

Schreck, C. B.
Oregon State University
Corvallis, Oregon, USA

Setzler-Hamilton, E. M.
University of Maryland
Solomons, Maryland, USA

Sinclair, M.
Department of Fisheries and Oceans
Halifax, Nova Scotia, Canada

Skud, B. E.
National Marine Fisheries Service
Narragansett, Rhode Island, USA

Smith, R. J. F.
University of Saskatchewan
Saskatoon, Saskatchewan, Canada

Smoker, W. W.
University of Alaska
Juneau, Alaska, USA

Specker, J. L.
University of Rhode Island
Kingston, Rhode Island, USA

Talbot, C.
Department of Agriculture and Fisheries
Pitlochry, Scotland, UK

Thorpe, J. E.
Department of Agriculture and Fisheries
Pitlochry, Scotland, UK

Tremblay, M. J.
Department of Fisheries and Oceans
Halifax, Nova Scotia, Canada

Van Winkle, W.
Oak Ridge National Laboratory
Oak Ridge, Tennessee, USA

Ware, D. M.
Department of Fisheries and Oceans
Nanaimo, British Columbia, Canada

Watts, F. J.
University of Idaho
Moscow, Idaho, USA

Webb, P. W.
University of Michigan
Ann Arbor, Michigan, USA

Weisbart, M.
St. Francis Xavier University
Antigonish, Nova Scotia, Canada

Welch, D. W.
Department of Fisheries and Oceans
Nanaimo, British Columbia, Canada

Williams, G. C.
State University of New York
Stony Brook, New York, USA

Wood, C.
Department of Fisheries and Oceans
Nanaimo, British Columbia, Canada

Wright, S.
Washington Department of Game
Olympia, Washington, USA

Young, B. H.
New York Department of Environmental
    Conservation
Stony Brook, New York, USA

Introduction

Anadromous and catadromous (diadromous) fishes rely on freshwater, estuarine, and marine ecosystems to complete their life cycles. On a global scale, diadromous fishes encounter a suite of similar problems during their lifetimes such as osmoregulatory adjustment, food-web changes, and problems of long-distance navigation. In spite of these obstacles, life history strategies evolved which ensured survival of these species. If, as scientists, we agree with Darwinian evolutionary thinking, we should accept that the adaptive effort required for a fish to alternately exploit habitats of completely different osmotic character must confer a selective advantage. That this adaptive process exists and that evolution takes a similar course in taxonomically diverse fishes implies some fundamental commonality.

In 1983, several members of the Northeastern Division of the American Fisheries Society met and, after considerable animated discussion, concluded the time was appropriate to examine current knowledge about the biology of anadromous and catadromous fishes during critical phases of their life cycles. The goal of the symposium was to identify key similarities or differences in life history patterns and to examine these to assist our understanding of diadromy. We decided that an international group of researchers should gather and explore the possible existence of comparable evolutionary strategies among diadromous species on a global scale. We hoped that this exchange of different ideas and approaches would yield a broader perspective for the definition and solution of research and management problems.

We met at the Park Plaza Hotel in Boston, Massachusetts, between March 9 and 13, 1986. The 200 participants presented 48 papers, 44 of which are published here. In these, the reader will find that although we were searching for commonality in life histories, it was not clearly apparent (see papers by Randall et al. and Quinn and Leggett). Rather, it became evident that a commonality among diadromous species did exist for growth characteristics (see papers by Gross, Thorpe, and Power et al.). The participants heard that diadromous fishes exploit alternate habitats to enhance growth potential and that natural or induced changes in growth profoundly affected their life histories. Whether this is a strategy in the evolutionary sense or a tactic necessary to meet an objective remains unresolved. Perhaps future symposia will clarify the situation.

The symposium and this document were organized into a keynote and four topical sections. The keynote section serves to review the occurrence of diadromy and explore the possible evolutionary processes. The topical sections deal with possible critical life cycle periods and mechanisms—utilization of freshwater, transition to and from the sea, migration, and recruitment. Authors were encouraged to exchange ideas and discuss topic coverage before the symposium, and manuscripts were available for reference following the meeting. We think this approach fostered an exceptional degree of recognition and cooperation, resulting in a cohesive final publication. Interested participants also presented their ideas and findings in a poster session, the abstracts from which have been included here. An evening workshop was held to discuss future directions for research into diadromy, and it is summarized in these proceedings.

This was the first international symposium on diadromous fishes in general. The feeling during the meeting was very positive; whether or not we met our objectives will be judged by the future acceptance of this document. During our planning of this symposium, we urged the prospective participants to explore new ideas or reexamine old ones in light of new knowledge. To this end, we encouraged new thinking rather than a review of past findings. We believe we achieved this goal, and we thank the authors for their cooperation and hard work.

We thank Mr. Rubtchinsky, Karen D'Arcy and the staff of the Boston Park Plaza Hotel for making our stay so comfortable and productive. The attention we received and the excellent conference facilities they provided contributed greatly to a successful symposium.

We wish to thank our financial contributors for the support which made the symposium a reality, particularly the U.S. Fish and Wildlife Service, the U.S. National Marine Fisheries Service, the U.S. National Science Foundation, and the Department of Fisheries and Oceans, Canada. The editors are grateful for the time their agencies and institutions allowed them to devote to this project. We greatly appreciate the assistance given by

Stephen Rideout, Ken Beal, Dick Cutting, Dave Crestin, Dick Schaeffer, Lee Sochasky, Kevin Stokesbury, Jim Williams, Anna Reddin, Evelyn Walker, Rocky Perham, and Jay McMenemy in organizing and running this symposium. Fred Serchuk, the President of the Northeastern Division, supported us to the hilt even after experiencing the spirited exchanges of the committee meetings. For all of us, I believe it was a rewarding experience.

MICHAEL J. DADSWELL
Department of Fisheries and Oceans
Biological Station
St. Andrews, New Brunswick, Canada

American Fisheries Society Symposium 1:1–13, 1987

EVOLUTION AND IMPORTANCE OF DIADROMY

The Occurrence and Distribution of Diadromy among Fishes

ROBERT M. MCDOWALL

Fisheries Research Division, Ministry of Agriculture and Fisheries, Christchurch, New Zealand

Abstract.—Diadromy is a specialized migratory phenomenon of fishes involving regular, seasonal, more or less obligatory migrations between fresh and marine waters. It occurs in three distinct forms: anadromy, in which adult fish migrate from the sea to spawn in fresh water; catadromy, in which adult fish migrate from fresh water to spawn in the sea; and amphidromy, in which migrations involve larval or juvenile fishes not close to reproduction. Diadromous fish constitute less than 1% of the world fish fauna. Most diadromous species (54%) are anadromous; fewer are catadromous (25%) or amphidromous (21%). Diadromy tends to occur most frequently and consistently in certain primitive fish taxa (lampreys, sturgeons, diverse salmoniforms, anguillid eels). It is quite widespread in some others (mullets, herrings, gobies) and occurs sparsely and intermittently in diverse perciform families. Analysis of data on the geographical distribution of diadromy shows that anadromy predominates in cool to cold temperate regions but also occurs in the tropics, that catadromy predominates in the tropics and southern subtropics but also occurs widely into both the northern and southern cool temperate regions, and that amphidromy is known in both the northern and southern temperate regions but is probably much more widespread than present data imply.

Diadromy is a widely recognized phenomenon of fishes, one that has generated considerable interest amongst ichthyologists and fisheries biologists. This interest has diverse sources. First, many valuable fishes that have historically been exploited by humans are diadromous. Second, enormous numbers of fishes may participate in their migrations and they are easily observed and caught. Third, major physiological problems are involved when fishes abruptly move from one aquatic salinity to a very different one. Fourth, migrations are predictable on a seasonal basis, yet unpredictable from day to day—they are there, but not there. There are no doubt other reasons.

In spite of very evident fascination that diadromous fishes have held for humans, the phenomenon has never been reviewed generally. Two recent substantial books on fish, one on strategies and tactics in reproduction (Potts and Wootton 1984), the other on mechanisms of fish migration (McCleave et al. 1984), scarcely give diadromy in its various forms a mention. In this paper, I discuss the various forms of diadromy, give their definitions and applications, and briefly review their occurrences among fishes from phylogenetic and geographical perspectives. Diadromy has been studied very intensively for a select group of fishes—particularly for species of the Salmonidae and Anguillidae—to the extent that many accounts seem to regard these as almost the only

instances. For the most part, however, diadromy is quite poorly understood and described.

Terminology

This symposium has been titled "Strategies of Anadromous and Catadromous Fishes," but, up to this point, I have used the term diadromous and have done so deliberately. There are three distinct forms of diadromy: in addition to the well-discussed anadromy and catadromy, there is amphidromy. Clearly, most attention has been focussed on the first of these—anadromy—and some on the second—catadromy—but in terms of the frequency with which the three forms of diadromy occur in nature, the usual exclusion of amphidromy cannot be justified. As knowledge of fish migrations has grown, the number of species found to be amphidromous has also grown, and will probably continue to grow, faster than other forms of diadromy (Myers 1949b).

The terms anadromous and catadromous have their origins in nineteenth-century Russian literature and were drawn to the attention of English-speaking scientists by Meek (1916). However, it was Myers (1949b) who brought the terms into wide usage and applied rigorous definitions to them. There is some validity in the suggestion that Myers' definitions are somewhat different from those originally proposed (Shubnikov 1976). However, the original use, as presented by Meek (and much more recently by Shubnikov 1976), leaves us with terms that are more or less equivalent to denatant (catadromous) and contranatant (anadromous). As such, the terms are redundant, linguistically obscure, have little value, and in my view are better diverted to Myers' definitions, which make them very useful terms to describe distinctive migratory phenomena in fishes.

To the original terms anadromous and catadromous, Myers (1949b) added diadromous and amphidromous (as well as additional terms like oceanodromous and potamodromous that are not pertinent to this discussion). The essence of Myers' terms lies in his definition of diadromous, which follows.

Diadromous: truly migratory fishes which migrate between the sea and fresh water. This is a general and inclusive term, the key points of which are migration and the movement between saline and fresh waters. Thus diadromy is a specialized form of migration. This is not the occasion to become diverted into a dissertation on how migration should be defined, but I suggest that Northcote's (1979) definition be used: migration is

> movement resulting in an alternation between two or more habitats (i.e., a movement away from one habitat followed by a return again), occurring with regular periodicity (usually seasonal or annual), but certainly within the life span of an individual and involving a large fraction of the breeding population. Movement at some stage in this cycle is directed rather than a random wandering or passive drift, although these may form a part of one leg of migration.

Within the general term diadromous, Myers defined the following.

Anadromous: diadromous fishes which spend most of their lives in the sea and which migrate to fresh water to breed. Most anadromous species spend most of their life cycles in the sea. The key point here is the return migration to fresh water for the purpose of breeding, typified by the invasion of fresh water by mature to ripe adults.

Catadromous: diadromous fishes which spend most of their lives in fresh water and migrate to the sea to breed. Most catadromous species spend most of their life cycles in fresh water. Here, the key point is a return seawards migration of mature adults for the purpose of breeding.

Amphidromous: diadromous fishes whose migration from fresh water to the sea, or vice versa, is not for the purpose of breeding but occurs at some other regular phase of the life cycle. Amphidromous species divide their life cycles variously between freshwater and marine habitats. The key point here is that migration is not a breeding migration but is typified by the return migration of well-grown juveniles that continue to feed and grow for several months, or even years, after migration and prior to maturation.

Before I move on to some examples and an analysis of the occurrence of the various forms of diadromy, it is important to relate these terms to other categories into which fish are commonly placed.

Myers (1949a), Darlington (1948, 1957), and others have grouped freshwater fishes into primary species, found exclusively in fresh water, secondary species, occurring rarely in brackish or seawater, and peripheral species, commonly found in seawater. All diadromous fishes belong in the peripheral category, for obvious reasons, although not all peripheral fishes are diadromous.

Diadromous fishes are routinely described as euryhaline, this referring to the apparent ease with which they move between fresh and salt waters. Thus Evans (1984), in a review of gill physiology in fishes, tabulated the "euryhaline" families and included catadromous and anadromous families, though he ignored amphidromy. However, Black (1957), Fontaine (1975), and others have drawn an important distinction between euryhaline fishes, which can move between fresh and salt waters frequently, freely, and at any time, and amphihaline fishes, which can do so only at carefully regulated stages of life. Thus, the ability of amphihaline species to migrate may be both periodic and transient and be related to carefully mediated and timed physiological and hormonal changes connected with and usually preceding migration. Knowledge of fishes clearly shows that the distinction between amphihaline and euryhaline is applicable to various of the diadromous families. A careful analysis of the salinity-change tolerances of diadromous fish would, I believe, reveal that a great many fish customarily classified as euryhaline actually are amphihaline. I do not wish to suggest that there is a crisp distinction between euryhaline and amphihaline but rather to point out that both extremes certainly exist and that the difference needs to be recognized in understanding the behavior of diadromous fishes.

A final interesting series of relevant terms was suggested many years ago by Heape (1931) who noted that fish migrations may be gametic, related to reproduction; climatic, related to environmental changes; and alimental, related to feeding changes—to which Myers (1949a) added osmoregulatory, related to changes in aquatic salinities, a distinctive and general feature of diadromous migrations.

Occurrence of Diadromy

There is a substantial number of diadromous species. Cohen (1970) estimated the total number of species of fish as about 20,000 and considered that about 115 of these, or 0.6%, were diadromous. My estimate, from an intensive search of the literature, is nearer 160 diadromous species (about 0.8%) (Table 1). This is not far from Cohen's estimate and both numbers show that diadromy occurs in a small proportion of fishes yet is by no means rare. Of these 160 species, about 87 (54%) are anadromous, 41 (25%) are catadromous, and 34 (21%) are amphidromous.

Knowledge of diadromy in fishes is weakly presented in the fish literature, especially in general texts on ichthyology and fisheries biology. A typical representation defines anadromous and

TABLE 1.—Families of fishes known to be diadromous.

Family[a]	Diadromous species[b]	Total species	Percentage diadromous
Petromyzontidae *	6	33	18.1
Geotriidae *	1	1	100.0
Mordaciidae *	2	3	66.7
Acipenseridae *	8	27	29.6
Anguillidae †	15	15	100.0
Salmonidae *	28	68	41.2
Osmeridae *	6	12	50.0
Salangidae *	13	14	92.8
Plecoglossidae #	1	1	100.0
Retropinnidae *	3	4	75.0
Prototroctidae #	2	2	100.0
Aplochitonidae *#	3	3	100.0
Galaxiidae †#	7	36	19.4
Clupeidae *†#	16	180	8.8
Eugraulidae	1	110	0.9
Ariidae *	1	120	<1.0
Syngnathidae *	1	175	0.5
Gasterosteidae *	2	8	25.0
Gadidae *	1	55	1.8
Scorpaenidae †	1	300	0.3
Percichthyidae *†	3	40	7.5
Centropomidae †	1	30	3.3
Kuhliidae †	2	12	16.6
Mugilidae †	11?	70	15.7
Cottidae *#	3	300	1.0
Mugiloididae #	1	26	3.8
Bovichthyidae †	1	6	18.6
Gobiidae *#	14?	800	1.7
Eleotridae #	7?	150	4.6
Rhyacichthyidae	1	1	100.0
Pleuronectidae †	3	99	3.0
Soleidae †	1	117	0.8

[a] Key: * = anadromous; † = catadromous; # = amphidromous.
[b] ? = highly uncertain.

lists salmon and perhaps lampreys then defines catadromous and lists eels and perhaps galaxiids. Sometimes other species with which authors may be personally familiar may be mentioned, such as mullets or sticklebacks. Most accounts omit amphidromy altogether. Many accounts are highly inaccurate, such as McKeown's (1984): "Fish from the southern hemisphere such as some of the southern trout (*Galaxias* spp.) as well as certain smelt and grayling species also display catadromous behavior." In fact, although one galaxiid is marginally catadromous, most are amphidromous, as are the southern graylings (genus *Prototroctes*), whereas the southern smelts (genus *Retropinna*) are anadromous.

In looking at the occurrence of the various forms of diadromy in fishes, I intend first to briefly review each category on a worldwide basis. The various forms of diadromy are usually described from northern hemisphere fishes. In spite of statements that, for instance, "there are no anadromous fish in the southern hemisphere" (Day et al., 1981), all three forms of diadromy can be illustrated from the four much less widely known southern hemisphere salmoniform families Galaxiidae, Aplochitonidae, Retropinnidae, and Prototroctidae. I intend to use these as illustrations rather than the much more widely known and discussed northern families.

Anadromy

Anadromy is by far the best recognized form of diadromy, this being a consequence of its occurrence in important and well-known northern hemisphere groups such as lampreys (Petromyzontidae), sturgeons (Acipenseridae), and particularly salmonids (Salmonidae). Less well known are osmerids (Osmeridae) and salangids (Salangidae), diverse northern temperate and tropical shads (Clupeidae), plus an assortment of other families including possibly a pipefish (Syngnathidae), a cod (Gadidae), some sticklebacks (Gasterosteidae), sculpins (Cottidae), and basses (Percichthyidae). Amongst the southern salmoniform families, anadromy is seen in *Lovettia* (Aplochitonidae) and within both the retropinnid genera *Retropinna* and *Stokellia*, which very closely resemble the northern Osmeridae (Table 1).

Typical is the Tasmanian whitebait *Lovettia sealii* which has a very basic, simple, anadromous life cycle (Figure 1). It spawns during spring in rivers at or just above the limits of tidal influence. The larvae hatch and move immediately to sea where they spend just a year before returning to

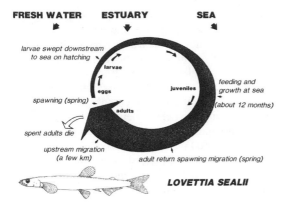

FIGURE 1.—Life history of *Lovettia seali*.

the rivers to spawn and die (Blackburn 1950). *Retropinna retropinna* from New Zealand has a somewhat more complex anadromous life cycle (Figure 2): Spawning takes place during spring and summer in flowing fresh waters, usually only a few kilometres above tidal influence. Development occurs where the eggs settle on river substrates and the larvae move to sea immediately on hatching. They live at sea normally for 2 years before returning to fresh water during the spring and summer to spawn and die. In some rivers, juvenile yearlings visit estuaries in the summer but seem to return to sea; a very small proportion fails to mature at age 2 but does so at age 3 (McDowall 1978). These and some other southern

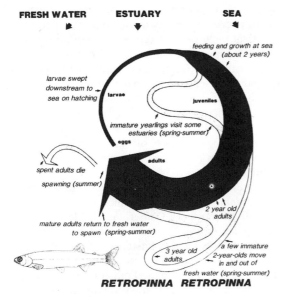

FIGURE 2.—Life history of *Retropinna retropinna*.

salmoniforms thus display the typical anadromous life history strategy.

The definition of anadromy requires that spawning is in fresh water. It may be just above the tidal zone, as it is for the Tasmanian whitebait and the retropinnid smelts as well as for various sturgeons, salmonids, osmerid smelts, shads, and sticklebacks. Or, it may be vast distances inland, as it is for other salmonids, sturgeons, and shads. In general, the spawning migration is associated with cessation of feeding until after spawning, when it may resume in iteroparous species. There are some examples of feeding by migratory adults in fresh water before spawning, e.g., *Salmo trutta* and *Retropinna retropinna*.

Catadromy

Catadromy, if we were to judge from most general published descriptions, appears to be almost exclusive to anguillid eels, mullets being also mentioned. Certainly the 15 species of anguillids are catadromous, as are several mullets (possibly up to about a dozen species), though their life histories are poorly detailed especially for tropical species. However, additional catadromous fishes include a galaxiid, two clupeids, two percichthyid basses, a centropomid, a bovichthyid, a scorpaenid, one or two kuhliids and cottids, and several flatfishes (Table 1). Life histories of many of these, too, are poorly known, although all of them undergo some sort of movement downstream and into the sea to spawn. Doubts about whether or not these fish are catadromous revolves around whether the movements into and life in fresh water are obligatory, rather than a facultative habit carried out by few, some, or perhaps most of the population.

Amongst fishes listed as catadromous, the southern family Galaxiidae is frequently cited. This is an erroneous generalization even though one species, the widely distributed inanga *Galaxias maculatus,* can be described as marginally catadromous (Figure 3). Spawning by this species takes place during autumn in brackish river estuaries under the influence of the tide. The eggs are deposited amongst terrestrial stream-bank vegetation when this is inundated by high spring tides. The eggs settle amongst the bases of the plants and develop out of the water in the humid air. Hatching is stimulated by a subsequent series of spring tides, about 2 weeks later, and the newly hatched larvae are swept out to sea. They grow and develop in the marine plankton for about 6 months and return the following spring as juve-

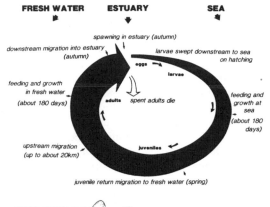

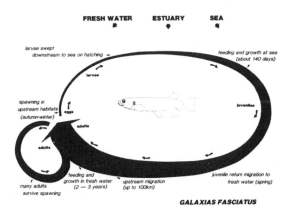

FIGURE 4.—Life history of *Galaxias fasciatus*.

FIGURE 3.—Life history of *Galaxias maculatus*.

niles about 50 mm long. These penetrate into river systems and feed and grow there for a further 6 months. A downstream spawning migration of the ripe adults into river estuaries follows to complete the cycle. Spent adults all die. Because the adults do not actually return to the sea, the cycle is barely catadromous. It lies at the margin between catadromy and amphidromy (McDowall 1968, 1978).

Amphidromy

Amphidromy is much less understood but it is a more widely occurring phenomenon than is generally reported. Various amphidromous groups are misreported as anadromous or catadromous. Amphidromy is a less explicit term than either andromy or catadromy and may be represented by species that spawn in fresh water (freshwater amphidromy) or the sea (marine amphidromy). Included in the category amphidromy is the plecoglossid ayu, several galaxiids, two aplochitonids (probably), both southern graylings (Prototroctidae) a mugiloidid, a cottid, and a diverse array of sleepers and gobies (Eleotridae and Gobiidae) (Table 1).

Although amphidromy is most often ignored by students of fish migration, it is well represented among the southern salmoniforms. Several species of *Galaxias* are representative (Figure 4). Spawning takes place during the autumn and winter in fresh water in or near typical adult habitat with little or no spawning migration. This may be at low elevations and near the sea but may also be at many hundreds of metres in altitude and a hundred or more kilometres inland. Egg devel-

opment is at the spawning site and the newly hatched larvae are swept to sea by the river flows. They live at sea for 4–6 months in the marine plankton and return to fresh water as slender juveniles. These penetrate upstream into the fluviatile habitats of the adults, where they resume feeding and grow to maturity over a period of 2–3 years. Unlike the semelparous cycle of the inanga, these species are repeat spawners and may live for many years (McDowall 1978).

The Australian genus *Prototroctes* (family Prototroctidae) and the South American *Aplochiton* (family Aplochitonidae) also appear likely to be amphidromous although they are little known.

Life History Stage at Migration

The life history stages at which diadromous fishes undertake migrations are variable. The stage at which the osmoregulatory transition between fresh and salt water (or the reverse) occurs is obviously of critical importance because this is a period of osmoregulatory stress.

There are no evident explicit instances of "migrating eggs," although the eggs of some species undergo a passive, rather haphazard, downstream movement during development. This has been described for several anadromous fishes, e.g., the striped bass *Morone saxatilis* (Talbot 1966). It is said to be true of European and North American shads (*Alosa fallax* and *A. sapidissima*), but not of the alewife *Alosa pseudoharengus* (Bagenal and Braun 1978). Lindroth (1957) considered that the eggs of *Coregonus lavaretus* are carried downstream, some lodging amongst the river gravels but some reaching coastal waters before hatching. There are a few described instances where the eggs of diadromous fishes are capable of coping with a wide range of salinities. The eggs of the catadromous inanga *Galaxias maculatus* tolerate estaurine salinities varying between fully fresh and fully marine waters; they develop and hatch satisfactorily in either extreme and in intermediate salinities (McDowall 1978). The eggs of the pink salmon *Oncorhynchus gorbuscha* may sometimes be deposited in estuarine circumstances and evidently hatch (Hanavan and Skud 1954).

Many species appear to be capable of migrating as larvae immediately or soon after hatching and prior to feeding. Again, this is mostly a passive denatant movement. This is true for at least some aplochitonids, galaxiids, retropinnids, prototroctids, osmerids, salmonids (but usually only after some weeks have been spent in the stream gravels after hatching), clupeids, gasterosteids, and some of the heterogeneous array of perciforms (a mugiloidid, eleotrids, gobiids). In these cases, newly hatched larvae are known or thought to go rapidly to sea. It is important to recognize this, in view of suggestions that early life history stages may be much less tolerant of salinity variation than older fish.

Movements of well-grown juveniles between marine and fresh waters (in both directions) are widely present and seem to occur in all groups in which there is diadromy. Such migrations can relate to either of two different strategies. There may be an initial outmigration in which the new cohort leaves the spawning habitat to move to a feeding habitat, as is true for lampreys, anguillid eels, salmonids, osmerids, sturgeons, clupeids, and others. Or, there may be a return migration of the juveniles from a feeding habitat to what is initially a further feeding habitat, as for galaxiids, prototroctids, eleotrids, a mugiloidid, etc.

Similarly, there are groups of fishes in which migration follows growth to adult maturity, such as lampreys, eels, sturgeons, salmonids, osmerids, retropinnids, some aplochitonids (*Lovettia*), gasterosteids, etc. In these fishes, too, the migration is a movement from a feeding habitat to a spawning habitat but, at this stage, feeding and growth of most species is complete or nearly so. Gonad development may be incomplete but will depend on transfer of energy from somatic to reproductive tissues without further food intake. Repeat-spawning (iteroparous) species typically display a dual alternation of habitats by the fully mature adult fish with each successive maturation of the gonads—a spawning migration by mature fish and a trophic migration by spent fish. The ripening fish cease feeding as the spawning period approaches and migrate into the spawning habitat.

Survivors then return to the normal feeding habitat where they resume feeding and growing in preparation for a further spawning. Growth in length after first spawning may be very restricted, especially in some salmonids.

In all these species, there is a dual or reciprocal migration pattern—sea to fresh water and the reverse—but the combination of stages within species at which migration takes place is also diverse. Fish may migrate initially as either eggs or newly hatched larvae and return as juveniles or adults, or they may migrate as juveniles and come back as adults. It needs to be well recognized that diadromy does not always involve the migration of mature or ripe adult fish.

Phylogenetic Distribution of Diadromy

The occurrence of diadromy among the orders and families of fishes reveals some interesting patterns. Diadromy is a very strongly represented, if not dominant, phenomenon of all the Petromyzontiformes—both the northern (Petromyzontidae) and southern lampreys (Geotriidae and Mordaciidae)—of the Acipenseridae in the Acipenseriformes and the Anguillidae in the Anguilliformes, and of a large number of salmoniform families—Osmeridae, Plecoglossidae, Salangidae, Retropinnidae, Galaxiidae, Salmonidae, Prototroctidae, and Aplochitonidae (Table 1). In all these families for which diadromy is a distinctive if not predominant and possibly primitive feature, species that are nondiadromous can in many instances be interpreted as landlocked derivatives of diadromous species.

Throughout the remainder of fish taxa, diadromy is, I believe, best regarded as an intermittently occurring phenomenon in diverse and unrelated groups. Thus there is one diadromous member of the Engraulidae (anchovies), one or a few ariid catfishes alone in the vast Ostariopysi, and one gadid amongst the whole Paracanthopterygii. In the Acanthopterygii, diadromy is shown by a couple of sticklebacks, a scorpaenid and a few cottids of diverse genera, and occasional representatives in several perciform families—one bovichthyid, one mugiloidid, a few percichthyids, a centropomid, etc. In none of these families could diadromy be described as a family feature.

In a few additional groups, notably the Clupeidae, Mugilidae, Gobiidae, and Eleotridae, diadromy seems to be a widely occurring phenomenon that appears in diverse genera (Table 1) and it is hard to determine whether it is a basic, perhaps primitive, feature of the family or has appeared independently in two or more lineages. I suspect the latter, although there are species groups within families that are characteristically diadromous such as the alosid shads (Clupeidae); the New Zealand eleotrid genus *Gobiomorphus;* and the aphyiine gobiid genera *Sicyopterus, Sicydium,* and others.

The type of diadromy represented by closely related fishes tends to be consistent. Thus, all diadromous lampreys are anadromous, as are all sturgeons, salmonids, osmerids, retropinnids, etc. Anguillid eels are consistently catadromous, as are mugilids and pleuronectids (Table 1). But there are also families in which various forms of diadromy are represented. In some instances, this may arise because species regarded as confamilial may actually be quite distantly related, or it may indicate that diadromy has evolved more than once and in different ways in that family. Examples include Clupeidae (anadromy, catadromy, and amphidromy), Percichthyidae (anadromy and catadromy), Cottidae (anadromy and amphidromy), and Gobiidae (catadromy and amphidromy). However, diverse forms of diadromy may indicate that one form of diadromy has evolved from another form. In the Galaxiidae, catadromy and amphidromy are expressed by closely related, congeneric species. This seems to be an instance in which an amphidromous life cycle has evolved towards catadromy (in *Galaxias maculatus*). There appears to have been neoteny, in which the adult retains the shoaling habitats and body form of the juveniles and in which the spawning habitat has moved from upstream habitats to estuaries. This seems to be an exception amongst all the families in which diadromy is recognized.

Families in which diadromy is most strongly represented tend to be very ancient. The lampreys, sturgeons, anguillid eels, and various salmoniform families probably date well back into the Mesozoic. By contrast, more modern groups, particularly the perciforms, generally have intermittent and erratic occurrences of diadromy. This is an important point in view of frequent suggestions that anadromy evolved in groups like the salmons during Pleistocene glacial times and in response to reduced sea salinities around ice margins. I think that it has to be recognized that diadromy is present in very widely dispersed and ancient groups and that its evolution in these groups was likely to be much longer ago than the Pleistocene. The consistent occurrence of diadromy in the lampreys and salmoniforms in both northern and southern hemispheres points, perhaps, to the existence of diadromous fishes on Pangaea during the Mesozoic.

There are many very primitive fish groups in which diadromy is not present. I do not imply that the widespread occurrence of diadromy in these various primitive groups necessarily indicates relationships—although close phylogenetic relationships may exist—amongst the lampreys (Hubbs and Potter 1971) or amongst several of the salmoniform families (McDowall 1969; Fink 1984), for instance.

Geographical Distribution of Diadromy

Interspecific Variation

Many published statements refer to differences in geographical distribution of the various forms of diadromy. Berg (1959) considered that anadromous fishes are peculiar to the temperature and, to some extent, the polar latitudes of both hemispheres, and that the tropics lack them. Day et al. (1981) concurred with this statement. Baker (1978) claimed that anadromy is greatest in polar–temperate environments and catadromy in the tropics; he suggested that only eels are catadromous in the tropics. Others have made similar generalizations.

What data these views were based on is not clear from the above accounts, and some of these assertions are manifestly untrue. Berg (1959) and Day et al. (1981) were wrong to say that there is no anadromy in the tropics, and Baker (1978) was wrong to claim that only eels are catadromous in the tropics. The validity of assertions about the distribution and relative abundance of anadromy and catadromy, in relation to latitude, depends on what the assertions actually mean. Arguments that anadromy is more abundant in the cooler and catadromy in the warmer regions could refer to changes in the actual number of species that are anadromous at various latitudes, to the relative frequency of anadromy and catadromy with change in latitude, or to the relative proportions of the faunas that are anadromous or catadromous, and to how these proportions vary with latitude. Each of these alternatives needs to be examined separately.

The most straight-forward of these issues concerns, simply, where do anadromy, catadromy, and amphidromy occur in relation to latitude, and how frequently? I have examined this by charting the latitudinal distribution (1° intervals) of fish species in each of the categories of diadromy and enumerating the species that are diadromous at

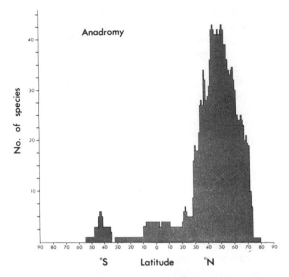

FIGURE 5.—Latitudinal distribution and frequency of anadromy among fishes.

each latitude. The data, by species number, clearly show the following.

(1) Anadromy (Figures 5, 6) is very strongly dominant in the northern subpolar and cool temperate regions (Petromyzontidae, Acipenseridae, Salmonidae, Osmeridae, Cottidae, etc.), declines to moderate representation in the northern warm temperate zone and tropics (particularly Clupeidae), is largely absent from the southern warm temperate zone, but occurs in the southern cool temperate region (Geotriidae, Retropinnidae, some Aplochitonidae).

(2) Catadromy (Figures 7, 8) is present though

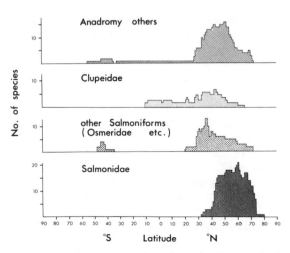

FIGURE 6.—Latitudinal distribution and frequency of anadromy within major anadromous fish families.

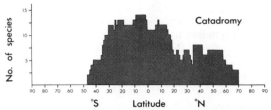

FIGURE 7.—Latitudinal distribution and frequency of catadromy among major fishes.

sparse in the northern cool temperate area (primarily Anguillidae, Mugilidae, Cottidae), rises southward to a peak in the southern subtropics and warm temperate region (primarily Anguillidae, plus more Mugilidae, Percichthyidae, Centropomidae), and declines rapidly in the southern cool temperate zone, where it is rare (Galaxiidae, Bovichthyidae).

(3) Amphidromy (Figure 9) is sparsely represented in the northern cool temperate zone (Plecoglossidae, Cottidae, Gobiidae), appears weakly in the northern subtropics and tropics (further Gobiidae, Eleotridae), and has its greatest manifestation in the southern cool temperate area (Galaxiidae, Prototroctidae, Mugiloididae, further Eleotridae). However, I am very dubious about the evident paucity of amphidromy through the tropics and northern temperate region and suspect that, once life histories are better known, a different picture of its latitudinal occurrence will emerge, particularly when gobioid taxonomy and life histories are elucidated.

The relative latitudinal frequencies of anadromy, catadromy, and amphidromy (Figure 10) support Baker's (1978) view that anadromy is mostly a cool temperate and catadromy mostly a tropical phenomenon. If the data are broken down by family, a somewhat altered perspective is obtained, although it does not negate the above generalization. This breakdown shows that lam-

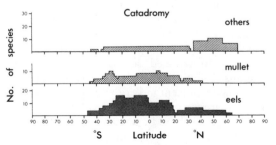

FIGURE 8.—Latitudinal distribution and frequency of catadromy within major catadromous fish families.

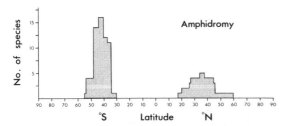

FIGURE 9.—Latitudinal distribution and frequency of amphidromy among fishes.

preys, sturgeons, and several salmoniform families are cool temperate anadromous fishes, but these families largely contain cool temperate fishes anyway. The distributions of diadromous members of the families do not differ profoundly from the distributions for the families as a whole. Clupeids are widely anadromous from the cool temperate zone to the tropics, and possibly this, too, is representative of their distribution as a family. The majority of catadromous fishes in temperate and tropical latitudes comprises anguillid eels, and the eels as a group are temperate to tropical in range. The same is true of the mullets. Thus, in arguing that anadromy is characteristic of colder areas and catadromy of the tropics, it seems to me that we are saying little more than that certain groups, which happen to be cool temperate, are anadromous, while others, which happen to be catadromous, are essentially temperate to tropical in range. Whether there is a causal connection in these relationships is a much more complex question that is not easily examined.

The question of the proportions of fish faunas that are anadromous, catadromous, and amphidromous, and how these proportions vary geographically, is also complex, and data to clarify the question are sparse. The freshwater and diadromous fish faunas of most areas of the world are surprisingly poorly documented in a way that makes calculation of the proportions that are diadromous possible. However, useful and interesting information on this matter can be obtained for the east and west coasts of North America from Lee et al. (1980), from which I have enumerated the number of species occurring at each degree of latitude. I included only those freshwater species that occupy coastal drainages between Point Barrow and Cape San Lucas (west coast) and between Cape Chidley and the tip of the Florida Peninsula (east coast). The species were

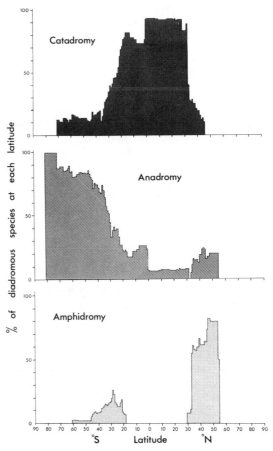

FIGURE 10.—Frequencies of catadromy, anadromy, and amphidromy, as proportions of total diadromous fish species at each degree of latitude.

classified according to whether they were diadromous or not, and diadromous species were separated into anadromous, catadromous, and amphidromous categories.

Along the Pacific (west) coast of North America, the faunal diversity varies widely but is quite low with a maximum of about 60 species at around latitude 42°N, and a broad peak between latitudes 35 and 50°N (Figure 11). The absolute abundance of anadromy along this coast is relatively stable, at about 10 to 15 species, from the limits of analysis at 70°N south to about latitude 38°N. Amongst these anadromous species, the proportion of salmoniforms (Salmonidae, Osmeridae) rises, though slightly, to the north and of other groups to the south; most northern anadromous species are salmoniforms. Thus anadromy is a strongly represented part of the fauna in subarctic and cool temperate latitudes and changes little as

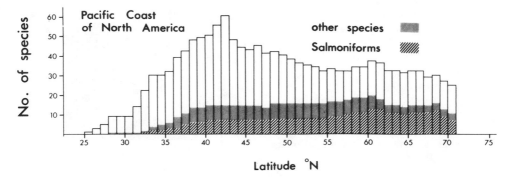

FIGURE 11.—Frequency of anadromy along the Pacific (west) coast of North America in relation to the total freshwater fish fauna at each latitude.

far south as 40°N, but the diversity of the fauna rises considerably so that the proportion of the fauna that is anadromous declines substantially. Catadromy is sparsely represented and shows slight reduction in frequency with increasing latitude. It is never a major constituent of the fauna. Amphidromy is represented by only the occasional species and no significant trend is evident.

On the east coast (Figure 12), overall diversity is much greater, reaching a peak of some 130 species around latitude 35°N, and declines much more sharply to the north and south than on the west coast. Diversity at 50°N, 20 to 30 species, is similar on the two coasts. Anadromous fishes contribute relatively sparsely to the total eastern fauna, and reach a peak of about 20 species at latitudes 40 to 45°N (where total diversity is about 90 species), distinctly north of the peak diversity for all species (35°N). Major contributors to anadromy are clupeids and salmoniforms (Salmonidae and Osmeridae), and these have overlapping but complementary distributions, clupeids being more southern and salmoniforms tending to

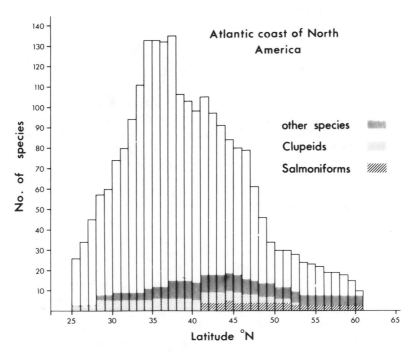

FIGURE 12.—Frequency of anadromy along the Atlantic (east) coast of North America in relation to the total freshwater fish fauna at each latitude.

replace them to the north. Catadromy in eastern North America is sparsely represented, as on the west coast, and declines with latitude; amphidromy is even rarer.

Taken together, these data suggest that through warm temperate to subpolar environments, anadromy is present in a small and relatively constant number of fish species but the relative contribution of anadromy to the biotas varies inversely with species diversity and is greatest towards the polar extremes of the region. Catadromy is so sparsely represented that it can scarcely be regarded as a significant phenomenon amongst North American freshwater fishes. Amphidromy can largely be discounted on the basis of present knowledge, but this view might change as the faunas become better known.

A comparable analysis of South American fish faunas would be very interesting, but data are insufficient to make it possible. However, there are enough data to show that in far southern Patagonia all the species present may be diadromous (Geotriidae, Galaxiidae, and Aplochitonidae, which are anadromous and amphidromous). However, the fauna itself is very sparse; Tierra del Fuego has no more than about five species, at least four of them diadromous. These southern groups extend northwards in range for varying distances, gradually disappearing as the fauna becomes augmented by additional, nondiadromous groups. These additions include two nondiadromous representatives of the southern diadromous families (the galaxiids *Galaxias globiceps* and *Brachygalaxias bullocki*), but they are primarily southern outliers of the vast ostariophysan faunas of the tropical–temperate Amazon basin and other large eastern South American river systems. Detailed analysis of these faunas and the occurrence of diadromy is not possible owing to the meagre knowledge of the fish faunas of northern Chile, Argentina, and areas to the north; however, diadromy in any form seems to be sparsely represented and not nearly as abundant as in either polar–temperate northern lands or in Australasia. What can be said is that both absolute abundance and relative abundance of diadromous fishes decline with decreasing latitude from far southern South America. Were similar data available for subarctic western Europe and eastern Asia, I have little doubt that a similar pattern would emerge.

Haedrich (1983) concluded that with a change in latitude there is a shift in the relative phylogenetic position of the dominant families, some of which are diadromous, that are found in estuaries. He suggested that this was in keeping with the general distribution of the world's fish faunas. The more primitive groups are found in estuaries at high latitudes and the more advanced groups nearer the tropics. A pattern of this sort cannot be recognized in the diadromous fishes and is upset primarily because the great majority of diadromous fishes have primitive origins. Most of them are cool temperate species, but some are warm temperate to tropical. More advanced groups have occasional diadromous representatives, but they are variously subpolar to tropical in occurrence—groups like cottids and sticklebacks are strongly represented in the colder, high latitudes, while mullets, gobies and others are more tropical in occurrence.

Intraspecific Variation

A further interesting aspect of geographical variation in the occurrence of diadromy is "within-group variation." Rounsefell (1958) summarized the situation for salmonids, writing that "different species inhabit different ranges of latitudes but within each species there seems to be a greater degree of anadromy towards the north." Kendall (1935) reported that "on each coast of both the Pacific and Atlantic Oceans there are certain extents of southwards projections of the anadromous *Salvelinus* zones. But these marine forms gradually disappear, becoming almost or quite exclusively freshwater inhabitants at the southern terminus of each range." Brook trout *Salvelinus fontinalis* in eastern North America are anadromous in Canada and the northern New England states of the USA, but become restricted to cool mountain streams in Pennsylvania, Virginia, and Georgia. Arctic char *S. alpinus* also tend to be more exclusively freshwater in habit in the southern parts of their range (Scott and Crossman 1973); Vladykov (1963) suggested that the species is anadromous across the Arctic north of Canada and becomes wholly freshwater in New England and along the north coast of the Gulf of St. Lawrence. Nordeng (1961) discussed the loss of anadromy in southern populations of Arctic (alpine) char in Scandinavia, and suggested that it disappears in areas that are warmed by the North Atlantic drift—at about 65°N along the coast of Norway. Loss of anadromy in southern populations of Dolly Varden *S. malma* is also likely (Scott and Crossman 1973). Similarly, in Europe, the brown trout *Salmo trutta* is widely although facultatively anadromous in the northern parts of its range—Scandinavia and the British Isles. But at the southern end, in the Mediterranean, no anadromous stocks of *S. trutta* are known. Outside its native range, in Australia and New Zealand at least, *S. trutta* is confined more sharply to fresh water in northern (warmer) regions and becomes increasingly "sea-run" in the south where "sea trout" constitute important angler fisheries (McDowall 1984). *Salmo trutta* also certainly runs to sea in southern Chile (Zama and Cardenas 1984), but I am unsure of its status further north in South America.

Ekman (1953) reported that the threespine stickleback *Gasterosteus aculeatus* becomes more strictly fluviatile (i.e., nonanadromous) as latitude decreases; McKeown (1984) described it as almost entirely marine, only entering fresh water to breed in northern parts of its range, whereas in the south it is almost entirely freshwater in habit. Dudley et al. (1977) said that the striped bass *Morone saxatilis* is similarly more anadromous in the northern part of its range.

There are also some instances in which diadromy is lost at northern (cold) extremes of species' ranges. This is reported, for instance, of the white perch *Morone americanus,* which is anadromous around Chesapeake Bay but not in the colder waters of the Canadian maritime provinces (Scott and Crossman 1973). Loss of anadromy was attributed to the cold temperatures. Dadswell (1979) considered that anadromy was less well developed in northern populations of the shortnosed sturgeon *Acipenser brevirostrum* along the Atlantic coast of North America.

Conclusions

From this review of the occurrence of diadromy in fishes, we can conclude (1) that it occurs in a small proportion of the world fish fauna (less than 1%); (2) that it predominates in some of the more primitive taxa of fishes; (3) that it occurs in three distinct forms—anadromy, catadromy and amphidromy; (4) that anadromy is more common in cooler waters and catadromy in the tropics; and (5) that anadromy (54% of diadromous species) is more widely present than catadromy (25%) and amphidromy (21%). However, important changes in this picture may emerge with increased knowledge of fishes.

This review raises a host of questions relating to diadromy as a phenomenon, about how it has evolved, about why the patterns discussed above have developed, and about the strategic life history or evolutionary values and advantages. Some of these will be addressed directly or indirectly later in this publication. All of them provide fruitful areas for investigation and discussion.

References

Bagenal, T. B., and E. Braun. 1978. Eggs and early life history. IBP (International Biological Programme) Handbook 3:165–201.

Baker, R. R. 1978. The evolutionary ecology of animal migration. Hodder and Stoughton, London, England.

Berg, L. S. 1959. Vernal and hiemal races among anadromous fishes. Journal of the Fisheries Research Board of Canada 16:515–537.

Black, V. S. 1957. Excretion and osmoregulation. Pages 163–205 *in* M. E. Brown, editor. The physiology of fishes. Academic Press, London, England.

Blackburn, M. 1950. The Tasmanian whitebait *Lovettia sealii* (Johnston), and the whitebait fishery. Australian Journal of Marine and Freshwater Research 1:155–198.

Cohen, D. M. 1970. How many recent fishes are there? Proceedings of the California Academy of Sciences 38:341–346.

Dadswell, M. J. 1979. Biology and population characteristics of the shortnose sturgeon, *Acipenser brevirostrum* Le Sueur 1818 (Osteichthyes: Acipenseridae) in the St. Johns River estuary, New Brunswick, Canada. Canadian Journal of Zoology 56:2186–2210.

Darlington, P. J. 1948. The geographical distribution of the cold-blooded vertebrates. Quarterly Review of Biology 23:1–26, 105–123.

Darlington, P. J. 1957. Zoogeography, the geographical distribution of animals. John Wiley & Sons, New York, New York, USA.

Day, J. H., S. J. M. Blaber, and J. H. Wallace. 1981. Estuarine fishes. Pages 197–221 *in* J. H. Day, editor. Estuarine ecology—with particular reference to southern Africa. Balkema, Rotterdam, The Netherlands.

Dudley, R. G., A. W. Miller, and J. W. Terrell. 1977. Movements of adult striped bass (*Morone saxatilis*) in the Savannah River, Georgia. Transactions of the American Fisheries Society 106:314–322.

Ekman, S. 1953. The zoogeography of the sea. Sidgwick and Jackson, London, England.

Evans, D. H. 1984. The role of gill permeability and transport mechanisms in euryhalinity. Pages 239–283 *in* W. S. Hoar and D. J. Randall, editors. Fish physiology, volume 10. Gills, part B. Ion and water Transfer. Academic Press, London, England.

Fink, W. L. 1984. Basal euteloests: relationships. American Society of Ichthyologists and Herpetologists Special Publication 1:202–206.

Fontaine, M. 1975. Physiological mechanisms in the migrations of marine and amphihaline fish. Advances in Marine Biology 13:241–355.

Haedrich, R. L. 1983. Estuarine fishes. Ecosystems of the World 26:183–207.

Hanavan, M. G., and B. E. Skud. 1954. Survival of pink

salmon spawning in an intertidal area with special reference to the influence of crowding. U.S. Fish and Wildlife Services Fisheries Bulletin 56(95): 167–176.

Heape, W. 1931. Emigration, migration and nomadism. Heffer, Cambridge, England.

Hubbs, C. L., and I. C. Potter. 1971. Distribution, phylogeny and taxonomy. Pages 1–65 in M. C. Hardisty and I. C. Potter, editors. The biology of lampreys. Academic Press, London, England.

Kendall, W. C. 1935. The fishes of New England. II. The salmons. Memoirs of the Boston Society for Natural History 9(1):1–166.

Lee, D. S., C. R. Gilbert, C. H. Howitt, R. E. Jenkins, D. E. McAllister, and J. R. Stauffer. 1980. Atlas of North American freshwater fishes. North Carolina State Museum of Natural History, Raleigh, North Carolina, USA.

Lindroth, A. 1957. A study of the whitefish (Coregonus) of the Sundsvall Bay district. Institute of Freshwater Research Drottningholm Report 38:70–110.

McCleave, J. D., G. P. Arnold, J. S. Dodgson, and W. H. Neill. 1984. Mechanisms in migration of fishes. Plenum, New York, USA.

McDowall, R. M. 1968. Application of the terms anadromous and catadromous to the southern hemisphere salmonoid fishes. Copeia 1968:176–178.

McDowall, R. M. 1969. Relationships of galaxioid fishes with a further discussion of salmoniform classification. Copeia 1969:796–824.

McDowall, R. M. 1978. New Zealand freshwater fishes—a guide and natural history. Heinemann Educational Books, Auckland, New Zealand.

McDowall, R. M. 1984. Trout in New Zealand waters. Wetland Press, Wellington, New Zealand.

McKeown, B. A. 1984. Fish migration. Croom Helm, Beckenham, England. (Also available from Timber Press, Beaverton, Oregon, USA.)

Meek, A. 1916. The migrations of fishes. Edward Arnold, London, England.

Myers, G. S. 1949a. Salt tolerance of freshwater fish groups in relation to zoogeographical problems. Bijdragen tot de Dierkunde 28:315–322.

Myers, G. S. 1949b. Usage of anadromous, catadromous and allied terms for migratory fishes. Copeia 1949:89–97.

Nordeng, M. 1961. On the biology of the char (Salvelinus alpinus Linnaeus) in Salangen, Norway. I. Age and spawning frequency determined from scales and otoliths. Nytt Magasin for Zoologi (Oslo) 10:67–123.

Northcote, T. G. 1979. Migratory strategies and production in fresh water. Pages 326–359 in S. D. Gerking, editor. Ecology of freshwater fish production. Blackwell Scientific Publications, Oxford, England.

Potts, G. W., and R. J. Wootton. 1984. Fish reproduction—strategies and tactics. Academic Press, London, England.

Rounsefell, G. A. 1958. Anadromy in North American Salmonidae. U.S. Fish and Wildlife Service Fisheries Bulletin 58(131):171–185.

Scott, W. B., and E. J. Crossman. 1973. Freshwater fishes of Canada. Fisheries Research Board of Canada Bulletin 184.

Subnikov, D. A. 1976. Types of migrations of diadromous and semidiadromous fishes. Journal of Icthyology 16:531–535.

Talbot, G. B. 1966. Estuarine environmental requirements and limiting factors for striped bass. American Fisheries Society Special Publication 3:37–49.

Vladykov, V. D. 1963. A review of salmonid genera and their broad geographical distribution. Transactions of the Royal Society of Canada, series 3 1:459–504.

Zama, A., and E. Cardenas. 1984. Introduction into Aysen, Chile, of Pacific salmon, number 9. Descriptive catalogue of marine and freshwater fishes from the Aysen region, southern Chile, with zoogeographical notes on the fish faunas. Ministerio de Economia, Fomenta y Reconstructions, Santiago, Chile, and Japan International Co-operative Agency.

American Fisheries Society Symposium 1:14–25, 1987
© Copyright by the American Fisheries Society 1987

Evolution of Diadromy in Fishes

Mart R. Gross[1]

Department of Biological Sciences, Simon Fraser University
Burnaby, British Columbia V5A 1S6, Canada

Abstract.—One of the major unresolved questions of diadromous fishes is how they evolved. In this paper, several issues in the evolution of diadromy are examined from the viewpoint of life history theory. The paper opens with a discussion of whether it is appropriate to use the term "strategy" in describing the biology of diadromous fishes since there is little evidence that diadromy arose through frequency-dependent intraspecific competition. Next, a comparison between diadromous and nondiadromous species reveals a similarity in their life history traits including egg size, fecundity, age at first maturity, and body size. Even comparisons between diadromous and nondiadromous populations within species reveals few life history differences. Thus, identification of fishes as "diadromous" is a subjective rather than an evolutionary classification. Third, one of the key questions for diadromy—when does natural selection favor habitat switching?—is addressed. The question is resolved through a life history model showing how natural selection operates on each component of a diadromous life cycle. To evolve, migration must maximize fitness or the lifetime product of reproductive success × survivorship. Diadromy, therefore, occurs when the gain in fitness from using a second habitat minus the migration costs of moving between habitats exceeds the fitness from staying in only one habitat. The most important biological variable in explaining the presence and direction of diadromous migration is apparently the relative availability of food in sea and freshwater habitats. Since seas are often more productive than fresh waters in the temperate zone, while the reverse occurs in the tropics, both anadromy and catadromy can evolve. Finally, amphidromy is hypothesized to be an ancestral state in the evolution of anadromy and catadromy. Amphidromy will be evolutionarily stable, however, if there is insufficient advantage to completing adult development in a second habitat. This and future studies of life history evolution can provide much insight into the biology and effective management of diadromous fishes.

Although diadromous fishes have been the subject of numerous ecological (Foerster 1968; Leggett 1977; Northcote 1978; Peterman 1984), physiological (Hoar 1976; McKeown 1984), migrational (Groot et al. 1975; Quinn 1982; Hasler and Scholz 1983), systematic (Thomas et al. 1986; McDowall 1987, this volume), and distributional studies (Baker 1978; McDowall 1987), little attention has been directed towards understanding how diadromy evolved through natural selection. This paper aims to use life history theory to examine the evolution of diadromy in fishes. Its purpose is not to extensively review literature nor to examine a single topic in detail; rather, it attempts to clarify several key issues central to understanding how and why diadromy evolved.

The paper has three parts. The first focuses on clarifying the meaning of "strategies" and "tactics" as terminology for understanding the evolution of diadromous life histories. These terms have been so often misapplied in the literature that their meaning now lacks substance (e.g., Kramer 1984). Since scientific progress and communication rely upon terminology (Ziman 1984; Cohen 1985), it is important to clarify the terms on which this symposium is based.

The second and major part of the paper addresses the evolution of diadromy by asking four questions. (1) What are diadromous fishes from a "life history" perspective rather than a "classification" perspective? (2) Why do fishes migrate? (3) What is the importance of sea and freshwater habitats in the evolution of diadromy? (4) What are the links between amphidromy, catadromy, and anadromy? A life history model is developed to help clarify how natural selection acts on the evolution of diadromy.

In the final part, some implications for the management of diadromous fishes arising from the study of their evolution are discussed.

Strategies and Tactics

The term strategy is so widely used without definition that its meaning is often in doubt. From

---

[1]Present address: Department of Zoology, University of Toronto, Toronto, Ontario M5S 1A1, Canada.

a life history perspective, strategy and tactic are defined as follows (Maynard Smith 1982; Gross 1984). A strategy is a genetically determined life history or behaviour program which has evolved because it maximizes fitness (lifetime reproductive success) under frequency-dependent intraspecific competition. Under intraspecific competition that is frequency-dependent, the fitness from a behaviour or life history depends upon the actions of others in the population. For example, if obtaining a territory were necessary for successful reproduction and depended upon body size, an individual's fitness at maturity would depend upon the size of other mature individuals in the population. In this case, size at maturity would evolve as a "strategy" because the optimal size for any individual would depend upon what size others in the population attained.

Strategies are composed of tactics: the ontogenetic stages of development or actions specifically used for achieving given life history or behaviour programs. Strategies therefore evolve through alterations in their tactics. For example, one tactic in a maturity strategy could involve an individual delaying maturity until it was larger in size than other members of the population. Should this tactic yield a higher fitness than other possible tactics, the maturity strategy which evolves in the population would include delaying maturity.

Not all genetic programs are strategic. Nonstrategic or "simple" life histories (Parker 1984) are those which evolve in the absence of frequency-dependent competition. For example, if fitness at maturity is not influenced by conspecific body size, then maturity will not be strategic; body size will evolve as a simple life history, independent of the size of conspecifics.[2]

Therefore, two very different kinds of life history evolution exist. On the one hand are strategic life histories which evolve to maximize fitness in response to competition among individuals sharing the same gene pool. On the other hand are simple life histories which evolve to maximize fitness in response to environmental conditions originating from outside the gene pool.

The distinction between simple and strategic life histories is an important one since simple life histories can be analyzed with optimization models (e.g., Alexander 1982; Jonsson et al. 1984),

while strategic life histories usually require more complex frequency-dependent or game theoretic models (e.g., Colman 1982; Gross and Charnov 1982; Maynard Smith 1982). Not only will the type of life history we expect to find influence our method of quantitative analysis, it will also affect our research hypothesis. As an example of why it is necessary to correctly distinguish between strategic and simple life history evolution, let us consider the case of precociously mature males in salmon populations. Precocious male salmon have long been viewed as a biological "mistake" because researchers were not aware of how precocity could evolve when all individuals were under the same environmental selection pressure. Recently, work analyzing precocity as a life history "strategy" (Gross 1984; 1985) has shown that precocious males can evolve as an alternative means for breeding. Through a combination of morphological and behavioural attributes, precocious males successfully circumvent the territorial defense of larger and older individuals.

At present, there is insufficient evidence to conclude whether diadromy has evolved as a simple or strategic life history in fishes. Some authors (e.g., Baker 1978; Northcote 1978; McDowall 1987) have summarized information which suggests that the migration of diadromous fishes may be a direct response to the environment (especially temperature, water level, or food availability). Others have suggested that migration behaviour may also be influenced by the actions of conspecific competitors (e.g., Gross 1985). Diadromy may, therefore, be a complex collection of life history traits, some of which are strategic and others simple in origin. Separating the relative contributions of competitive and environmental selection pressure should thus be an interesting direction for future studies of diadromy. Until the results of such studies are available, use of the term "strategy" to generally describe diadromous life histories is premature.

Evolution of Diadromous Habit

What are Diadromous Fishes?

The first question which should be addressed in a study of the evolution of diadromy is: What are diadromous fishes? In more detail: Are they different from other fishes? If so, in what way? Are diadromous fishes a real (biological) category, or an artificial category based on perceived needs to group and pigeonhole fishes?

---

[2]The term "simple" does not suggest triviality but designates that selection is from noncompetitive sources.

As defined by McDowall (1987), a diadromous fish is one which uses two habitats—specifically the sea and fresh water—during its life history. Use of these two habitats requires migration across a saline–freshwater boundary and thus the capability to osmoregulate in different salinities. While this provides a useful description of diadromous species, there are several problems with McDowall's definition.

First, multiple-habitat use, migration, and changes in osmoregulation are common to the biology of many fish species (Leggett 1977; Harden-Jones 1981; McKeown 1984). Desert pupfishes (*Cyprinodon* spp.), for example, cross salinity gradients in Arizona deserts that range from fresh water to several times the salinity of seawater (Hillyard 1981). Similarly, many fishes near inland saline lakes (e.g., the Great Salt Lake of Utah) regularly migrate between freshwater feeder streams and the lake's "estuaries" (Sigler and Miller 1963). Multiple habitat use and osmoregulatory changes during migration are, therefore, not unique biological features of diadromous fishes.

Second, crossing the sea–freshwater boundary is not an obligate but a facultative behaviour of many species labelled diadromous. For example, some populations of the brown trout *Salmo trutta* along the European coast migrate to the sea while others do not (Baker 1978). The same holds true for some Pacific salmon (*Oncorhynchus* spp.) in North America (e.g., kokanee *O. nerka*: Hanson and Smith 1967). An extreme form of facultative properties involves the coexistence within populations of both migratory and nonmigratory behaviour. In populations of Atlantic salmon *Salmo salar,* Arctic char *Salvelinus alpinus,* and brown trout, for example, some males and females may not take part in seaward migration at all (Jones 1959; Nordeng 1983; Jonsson 1985). Instead, they mature within fresh water. Since alternative migratory behaviours occur both among and within diadromous fish populations, crossing a sea–freshwater boundary is clearly not a biological requisite for being classified a diadromous species.

It is thus apparent that two of the three principal elements in McDowall's definition of diadromy—migration and the ensuing osmoregulatory changes—are not unique to diadromous fishes. Moreover, crossing the sea–freshwater boundary is only partially expressed in some species. While the key factor in defining diadromy may be crossing a geographical boundary, the biological importance of this remains open to question.

If diadromous fish species are a biological entity, uniquely different from other types of fishes, then a comparison of important life history traits such as egg size, fecundity, age at first maturity, and body size should reveal a significant general difference between diadromous and nondiadromous species. Past studies have shown that comparisons of such life history traits between evolutionary groupings invariably reveal differences (e.g., Stearns 1977). A comparison of representative diadromous and nondiadromous species from the same families reveals no generally significant differences (Table 1).[3] Diadromous species produce some of the smallest and largest egg sizes known, exhibit both early and late maturation, and are mature at both a small and large body size.

An even stronger test for differences in life history results from a comparison of diadromous and nondiadromous populations within species. The Salmoninae, a subfamily of the Salmonidae, has been selected for this analysis because a large, reliable data set is available. A comparison of eight life history traits between anadromous and nondiadromous populations of seven species reveals a significant difference in body size, with anadromous populations being larger for the same age at maturity (Table 2). As a consequence of this size difference, the anadromous form is more fecund (both in egg number and in ovary volume). However, this difference in growth rate is attributable to environmental differences (see below), and is not accompanied by changes in life history traits. Five of the eight traits examined, including age at maturity, maximum broods in lifetime, egg diameter, and hatching time, show no significant difference. Classifying fishes as diadromous or nondiadromous, therefore, provides little insight into their life history evolution. The answer to the question "Do diadromous fishes have unique life histories?" is no!

What then are diadromous fishes? They are a group of species which have been artificially (versus biologically) classified based largely on their habit of migrating between the sea and fresh water. This geographical boundary is a conceptual (rather than biological) distinction since similar osmoregulatory boundaries are crossed by land-locked fishes (e.g., desert pupfish). The classifi-

---

[3]Comparing species within the same families largely controls for complications of phylogeny (Harvey and Mace 1982).

TABLE 1.—A comparison of life history traits of representative diadromous and nondiadromous species (as classified by McDowall 1987). The mean ± 1 SD is given for species within each family (midvalues were used for each species). The number of species examined is in parentheses. Data are from Breder and Rosen (1966), Hart (1973), Scott and Crossman (1973), and Hutchings and Morris (1985). Two-tailed t-tests (Sokal and Rohlf 1981) are used to compare diadromous against nondiadromous species. The only significant difference is in salmonid egg size ($P < 0.05$*).

Diadromy status	Egg diameter (mm)	Age at maturity (years)	Maximum body length (mm)	Fecundity (1,000s of eggs)
	Petromyzontidae (lampreys)			
Diadromous	0.96±0.27 (3)	8.0±1.4 (2)	488±265 (5)	30.1±26.6 (5)
Nondiadromous	1.04±0.05 (4)	6.4±0.7 (5)	240±107 (5)	4.1±4.5 (4)
t_{df}	t_5=0.6	t_5=2.2	t_8=1.9	t_7=1.9
	Salmonidae (salmons)			
Diadromous	5.27±0.96 (13)	4.6±1.5 (13)	1,035±241 (13)	4.2±2.8 (13)
Nondiadromous	2.77±1.05 (8)	5.8±3.5 (8)	812±465 (8)	52.0±91.1 (8)
t_{df}	t_{19}=5.6*	t_{19}=1.1	t_{19}=1.5	t_{19}=1.9
	Osmeridae (smelts)			
Diadromous	0.95±0.05 (3)	2.7±0.6 (3)	185±31 (3)	24.1±5.7 (3)
Nondiadromous	1.00±0.00 (2)	1.5±0.7 (2)	203±56 (10)	34.0±21.7 (3)
t_{df}	t_3=1.3	t_3=2.1	t_{11}=0.5	t_4=0.8
	Clupeidae (herrings)			
Diadromous	0.95±0.07 (2)	4.0±1.4 (2)	296±89 (3)	102.6±31.9 (2)
Nondiadromous	1.31±0.36 (8)	2.7±0.8 (5)	230±158 (4)	110.8±153.5 (5)
t_{df}	t_8=1.4	t_5=1.6	t_5=0.6	t_5=0.1

cation of fishes as being either diadromous or nondiadromous is thus based on convenience rather than biology.

While the habit of crossing a sea–freshwater boundary appears to have little effect on life history traits, this migratory behaviour may still provide the key to understanding the so-called diadromous fishes. Three major evolutionary questions concerning migration in diadromous fishes are: Why migrate? What is the selection importance of the sea and freshwater habitats for migration? What are the evolutionary links among amphidromy, anadromy and catadromy?

Why Migrate?

Migration behaviour is widespread among fishes (e.g., Leggett 1977; Northcote 1978). When viewed from an evolutionary perspective, the only significant difference between the migration of diadromous species and that of nondiadromous species is the osmoregulatory cost associated with crossing the sea–freshwater boundary (but note the "landlocked" exceptions above). Diadromous migration is therefore part of the larger question of why any fish should migrate.

To answer this question, we need to consider how migration increases the evolutionary fitness of individuals that migrate relative to those that do

not. Fitness (W) can be quantified by the lifetime summation (Σx) of an individual's probability of surviving to reproduce at any age x (l_x) multiplied by its fecundity (or male fertility) and breeding success at that age (b_x):

$$W = \Sigma \, l_x \, b_x.$$

Because migration involves switching habitats, we need to understand the contribution of each habitat to l_x and b_x as well as the costs of moving between these habitats (also in terms of l_x and b_x). Migration costs include the energy and physiological mechanisms for osmoregulation, energetic demands of swimming, and exposure to predators or disease. Since the main characteristic of diadromy is alternation between habitats, a single migration model can be developed to explain the evolution of all three diadromous forms: amphidromy, anadromy, and catadromy (Figure 1).

The conditions for the evolution of diadromy in a nondiadromous population can be modeled as follows. In a nondiadromous population, individuals complete their entire life cycle in one habitat (H_1). By contrast, a diadromous life history includes the use of one habitat (H_1) for reproduction and early rearing, a juvenile removal migration (M_1) which involves crossing the sea–freshwater

TABLE 2.—A comparison of eight life history traits of anadromous (A) and nondiadromous (ND) forms of seven species of *Salmo* and *Salvelinus*. Data are from Hutchings and Morris (1985). Two-tailed sign tests (Siegel 1956) are used to test for significant differences between A and ND means ($P < 0.05$*).

Species or statistic	Age at maturity (years)		Maximum broods in lifetime		Egg diameter (mm)		Hatching time (d)	
	A	ND	A	ND	A	ND	A	ND
Salmo clarki	4.0	3.5	6.0	7.0	4.70	4.70	45.5	45.5
S. gairdneri	4.0	4.0	5.0	5.0	4.00	4.00	47.5	47.5
S. salar	5.0	5.0	11.0	10.0	6.00	5.25	175.0	175.0
S. trutta	4.0	3.5	10.0	11.0	4.50	4.25	89.5	115.0
Salvelinus alpinus	7.0	8.0	18.0	12.0	4.35	4.30	180.0	72.0
S. fontinalis	4.5	2.5	5.0	8.0	4.25	3.85	125.0	125.0
S. malma	8.0	5.5	11.0	12.0	4.50	3.55	225.0	225.0
Mean	5.2	4.6	9.4	9.3	4.61	4.27	126.8	115.0
SD	1.6	1.8	4.6	2.7	0.65	0.56	69.6	67.1
Sign test	$P=0.376$		$P=0.688$		$P=0.062$		[a]	

[a] Excessive ties; data not significantly different.

boundary,[4] a second habitat for adult rearing (H_2), and an adult return migration (M_2) to H_1 for reproduction. Thus the cost of the total migration M_T equals those of M_1 and M_2. For simplicity, the analysis will be restricted to females and will assume that b_x is linearly related to growth, that growth rate is independent of size but dependent upon habitat, and that the species is semelparous (breeds once and dies). Under such conditions, the diadromous life cycle (D) may evolve in a nondiadromous population (ND) if:

$$W(D) > W(ND) \qquad (1)$$

or

$$W(H_1 + H_2 + M_T)_D > W(H_1)_{ND}; \qquad (2)$$

$W(H_1)_{ND} = 1$;

g = growth rate of D relative to ND (D/ND);

s = survivorship rate of D relative to ND;

t = proportion of D spent in each life zone (i.e., for zones $H_1 + H_2 + M_T$, $t_1 + t_2 + t_m = 1$).

For a diadromous individual,

$$W(H_1) = t_1 W(H_1)_{ND} = t_1;$$
$$W(H_2) = t_2(g_2 \cdot s_2);$$

$$W(M_T) = t_m(g_m \cdot s_m).[5]$$

It follows from expression (2) that

$$t_2(g_2 \cdot s_2) + t_m(g_m \cdot s_m) > 1 - t_1, \qquad (3)$$

or

$$[t_2(g_2 \cdot s_2) + t_m(g_m \cdot s_m)]/[t_2 + t_m] > 1. \qquad (4)$$

Diadromous migration will therefore evolve in a nondiadromous population (if there are appropriate mutations) when expression (4) is satisfied.

I now digress and explain why growth (g_x) was substituted for the b_x benefit of migration. The answer is that fecundity in many species (Bagenal 1967), including diadromous fishes (Table 2), increases with body size and hence growth. Moreover, body size can also contribute to success during breeding since intrasexual fighting determines access to territories and mates in many species (Schroder 1982; Sargent et al. 1986; van den Berghe and Gross 1986). Finally, as will be shown later in this paper, growth is a key variable in diadromous migration.

This simple life history model specifies the growth and survivorship contribution of each habitat and can account for the migration costs between them. Substitution of appropriate values into expression (4) should allow us to calculate the fitness advantage of diadromy. Unfortunately, data appropriate for the model are not presently available because research on diadromous fishes

---

[4]Initial removal migration may be of eggs (rare), newly hatched larvae (common), or well-grown individuals (very common) (McDowall 1987). For simplicity, I consider the removal migration of well-grown individuals.

[5]Write $t_{m,1}(g_{m,1} \cdot s_{m,1}) + t_{m,2}(g_{m,2} \cdot s_{m,2})$ to consider removal (1) and return (2) migration separately.

TABLE 2.—Extended.

Species or statistic	Maximum length (cm)		Length at maturity (cm)		Fecundity (number of eggs)		Egg production (egg size × number)	
	A	ND	A	ND	A	ND	A	ND
Salmo clarki	99.0	99.1	39.3	20.0	2,323	1255	10,918	5,899
S. gairdneri	122.0	91.5	50.0	42.0	4,483	1500	17,932	6,000
S. salar	140.0	99.0	67.0	21.5	11,196	2384	67,176	12,516
S. trutta	102.0	82.6	51.5	29.0	1,510	738[b]	6,399	1,390
Salvelinus alpinus	96.0	55.0	63.0	27.7	4,582	1576	19,932	6,777
S. fontinalis	80.0	86.0	27.0	20.0	2,550	2550	10,838	9,818
S. malma	127.0	75.0	37.5	15.1	4,250	1412	19,125	5,013
Mean	109.4	84.0	47.9	25.0	4,413	1631	21,760	6,773
SD	20.9	15.5	14.3	8.9	3,223	635	20,657	3,552
Sign test	$P=0.454$		$P=0.016^*$		$P=0.016^*$		$P=0.016^*$	

[b] Calculated from the original reference (Lee 1971) to replace the value in Hutchings and Morris (1985), which is incorrect.

has proceeded without the theoretical and evolutionary direction necessary to understand why diadromy exists.

Some insight into the costs and benefits of diadromy from existing data may be provided by a comparison of diadromous and nondiadromous forms within species (Table 2). Egg production by anadromous forms is, on average, threefold greater than that of their nondiadromous conspecifics. Therefore, the fitness advantage of anadromy may be threefold through the enhancement

of b_x.[6] These data do not, however, indicate the l_x cost in obtaining the threefold b_x advantage. In our model, egg production must be devalued by the survivorship costs incurred as a consequence of migration. Moreover, mortality during maturation in the sea could exceed potential adult mortality in fresh water. Perhaps the only reasonable conclusion from these data is that diadromous fishes may have as much as a threefold higher mortality than nondiadromous fishes and still be favored in evolution.

Thus, one important use of the life history model is that it allows us to quantify the relationship between growth and mortality in the evolution of diadromy. The model also clarifies how growth and mortality may interact. The variables g, s, and t each have three or more values—one for each habitat and one for the costs of migration.[7] The combination of these independent variables can result in some surprising conclusions about fitness.

The effect of combining the variables is illustrated in the following example. Figure 2 has four time periods: (1) while fish are in the early rearing habitat (H_1); (2) during juvenile migration (M_1); (3) while adults are in the rearing habitat (H_2); and (4)

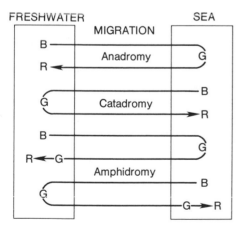

FIGURE 1.—The three life histories of diadromous fishes (McDowall 1987). Each life history includes occupation of freshwater and sea habitats and migration between them. Anadromous, catadromous, and amphidromous life histories are defined by the habitat in which birth (B), growth (G), and reproduction (R) take place. Some growth may occur in the habitat of birth.

[6]Threefold is probably a minimum estimate since the larger size of diadromous individuals will further increase b_x through increased success in breeding competition.

[7]The variables contribute independently in our model. "Dynamic optimization," however, would allow for interaction among the variables (see Mangel and Clark 1986).

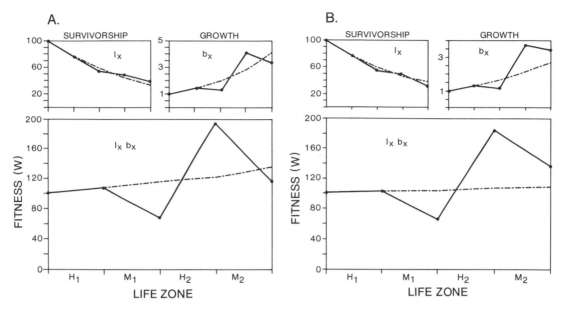

FIGURE 2.—Responses (A, B) of the fitness of diadromous fishes to growth and survivorship in the habitat for early rearing (H_1), during juvenile migration (M_1), in the habitat for adult rearing (H_2), and during adult migration (M_2). The solid line indicates the diadromous life history, the broken line the nondiadromous life history. In case B, H_1 survivorship has been increased 2.6% and growth rate decreased 7.0% from those of case A.

during adult return migration (M_2). For simplicity, the amount of time spent in each period is assumed equal ($t_1 = t_2 = t_m$), and the following values are held constant: $g_2 = 3.2$; $s_2 = 0.9$; $g_m = 0.9$; $s_m = 0.7$. These values mean that in H_2, a fish's growth is more than tripled and 90% of individuals survive. However, migration decreases body size by 10%, and survivorship during migration is only 70% (assumed the same for both juvenile and adult migration).

In Figure 2A, H_1 provides 76% survivorship ($s_1 = 0.76$) and 40% increase in body size ($g_1 = 1.4$). From survivorship considerations alone, a diadromous life history is favored because the enhanced survivorship in H_2 relative to that in H_1 is greater than the mortality costs of migration between the habitats. However, growth favors the nondiadromous life history even though the growth in H_2 exceeds that of H_1. The difference is simply not enough to allow for the costs of migration. Thus, while a survivorship advantage favors diadromy, growth does not. Which life history will evolve can be determined through a fitness calculation ($\Sigma\ l_x b_x$) and, in this case, a nondiadromous life history is favored (Figure 2A). Thus, even when the potential fitness gains in H_2 exceed those in H_1, migration will not be favored because of the costs in moving between these habitats.

Now imagine that a change in H_1 increases survivorship by 2.6% (s_1 now equals 0.78 rather than 0.76) and decreases growth by 7.0% ($g_1 = 1.3$ rather than 1.4) (Figure 2B). When survivorship alone is considered, a nondiadromous habit is favored. By contrast, the growth advantage realized in H_2 will favor a diadromous habit even when the migration costs are included. Here, the calculation of fitness shows that the growth advantage outweighs the survivorship costs and that a diadromous life history will evolve.

This example shows how even minor changes in g and s will have a major impact on the evolution of diadromous fishes. The sensitivity of the model's results may also explain why closely related species, and even populations within a species, have evolved different life histories.

In summary, our model shows that differences in growth rate alone or mortality alone between habitats will not predict migration behaviour. Furthermore, the difference in habitat quality, $W(H_2) - W(H_1)$ where $W(H_1) = 1$ by definition, must be positive for migration to evolve. That is, H_2 must give a greater growth rate × survival advantage if natural selection is to favor a migratory strategy. Finally, the costs of migration, $t_m(g_m \cdot s_m)$, including, the physiological costs of changing osmoregulation, increased predation, and the energetics of

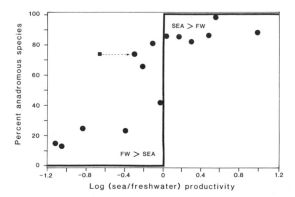

FIGURE 3.—The relationship between percent anadromous species, 100·(anadromous species)/(anadromous + catadromous species), and the relative productivity of neighbouring seas and fresh waters (FW). Productivity is grams carbon fixed per square meter per year (from Gross et al., unpublished). The point marked by the square would be further to the right, as indicated by the arrow, were it not for a single anomalous value for freshwater productivity.

moving between habitats, must be considered. Even if $W(H_2) - W(H_1) > 1$, fish will be favored to remain in H_1 when this difference is less than $t_m(g_m \cdot s_m)$.

What is the Importance of Sea and Freshwater Habitats?

The use of both sea and freshwater habitats is by definition the single pattern characteristic of diadromous species. Can the relative effects of these two habitats on b_x and l_x explain why diadromy evolves?

Baker (1978) and Northcote (1978) suggested several biological reasons why b_x and l_x could be enhanced by movement between sea and freshwater habitats. For example, b_x could be affected by differences in food resources or temperature conditions between the seas and fresh waters. Decreased predation, less disease, or favorable abiotic conditions could increase l_x. These authors could not determine, however, which of these selective factors was most critical to the evolution of diadromy.

Baker and Northcote also noted a latitudinal trend in the incidence of anadromy and catadromy. Conclusive evidence that anadromy is more frequent in cold temperate latitudes while catadromy is relatively more common in the tropics has been provided by McDowall (1987). In terms of life history theory (see also Baker 1978), the selection gradient for northern fishes must

therefore be positive in the sea direction while that for tropical fishes is in the freshwater direction.

Following Northcote (1978), Gross, R. M. McDowall, and R. C. Coleman (unpublished) assimilated existing data on primary productivity in freshwater and sea habitats to test the importance of food production in the evolution of diadromy. They found that in northern latitudes sea productivity exceeded that of fresh water, while in tropical latitudes freshwater productivity exceeded that of the sea. Moreover, the incidence of diadromy increased with the relative differences in freshwater and sea productivity. Finally, when relative productivity is plotted in relation to the frequency of anadromous and catadromous fishes, it becomes clear that differential productivity and thus growth resources are a key factor in the evolution of anadromy and catadromy (Figure 3). In short, diadromous migrations have evolved to track aquatic productivity.

Experimental evidence also supports this conclusion. Norwegian populations of Arctic char have both resident and anadromous individuals that belong to the same gene pool—that is, a single individual may become either anadromous or resident. Nordeng (1983) experimentally produced crosses between resident and anadromous individuals and reared the progeny under three feeding regimes: low, moderate and high. He found that increasing the amount of food significantly increased the proportion of resident individuals in his crosses at the expense of anadromous fish. The fish were thus able to facultatively adjust to the increased productivity of their freshwater habitat and respond by not migrating. In terms of our model, expression (4) was no longer satisfied, at least for some individuals, when Nordeng increased g_1 relative to g_2.

In summary, while survivorship considerations are important for understanding diadromy, the relative productivity or growth advantage of sea and freshwater habitats appears to be key to its evolution. The productivity differential can probably explain why fish migrate across the sea–freshwater boundary, predict their direction of movement, and account for where in the world diadromous species occur.

Amphidromy, Anadromy, and Catadromy

Considerable insight may be obtained into the phylogeny of amphidromous, anadromous, and catadromous fishes by analyzing their relationships in light of the above results. For example,

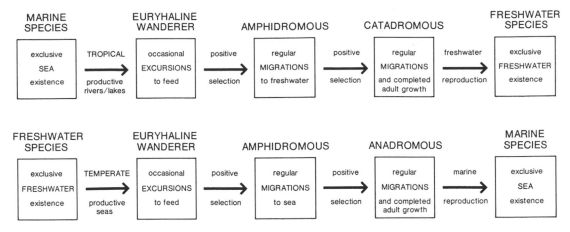

FIGURE 4.—Overview of the evolution of diadromy in fishes.

tropical marine fishes will be more likely to cross into fresh water as facultative wanderers than temperate marine fishes, because freshwater productivity often exceeds that of marine waters in the tropics. This would suggest that amphidromous fishes in the tropics are of marine origin. Moreover, continued residual selection after amphidromy, favoring adult specialization in the tropical freshwater habitat, will give rise to the evolution of catadromy (Figure 4). By contrast, freshwater fishes are more likely to cross into the sea as facultative wanderers in cold temperate and subpolar regions. Selection will first favor the evolution of an amphidromous habit. Continued selection will eventually give rise to an anadromous life history. Temperate amphidromous fishes may thus be of freshwater origin (Figure 4). Finally, selection may favor including the reproductive phase within the habitat of adult growth because this removes the costs of migration. Therefore, some marine fish species in temperate latitudes are probably of freshwater origin, while some freshwater species in tropical latitudes may be of marine origin (Figure 4).

Several lines of evidence support the above evolutionary hypothesis. First, several taxonomic groupings of fishes are known to include both marine and freshwater species (Nelson 1984). Second, the freshwater fauna of New Zealand, Australia, and the Hawaiian Islands is suspected to be of marine origin (McDowall 1978; Merrick and Schmida 1984). Third, some populations of pink salmon *Oncorhynchus gorbuscha* spawn in saline estuaries and spend the rest of their lives in the high seas (Morrow 1980), a behaviour suggesting that the pink salmon, classified as a diadromous freshwater species (McDowall 1987), could be evolving towards exclusive use of marine habitats.

Management Implications

Several implications for the management of diadromous fishes emerge from this study of their evolution.

(1) The life history model presented here and the experimental work of Nordeng (1983) demonstrate that growth perturbations can have profound and possibly deleterious effects on diadromous fish management. A case in point is the recent practice by North American hatcheries of releasing smolts of Pacific salmon (*Oncorhynchus* spp.) at a larger than natural size to increase survivorship. This practice resulted in a significant increase in precocious maturity among males (Bilton et al. 1982) and, as a consequence, a decrease in total fish biomass—an outcome contrary to management objectives.

We should thus expect any alteration in natural habitats which affects food resources to perturb the selective pressures for migration. The increasing eutrophication of freshwater habitats, for example, will likely result in some fresh populations no longer migrating to the sea. Continued "fertilization" of freshwater lakes to enhance the growth rate of juvenile sockeye salmon *Oncorhynchus nerka* (Hyatt and Stockner 1985) could well select for nonanadromous populations of this species. Without consideration of the life history consequences of migration, such management of diadromous fishes is an unscientific exercise.

(2) The increased growth, fecundity, and thus

biomass characteristic of diadromous species may suggest that they have robust life cycles. However, such logic is not sound from the perspective of life history theory. Consider, for instance, that evolutionarily "robust" species are often low in abundance (e.g., top-level predators), and that many species which were once abundant have been driven close to extinction by a slight alteration to their environment (Soule and Wilcox 1980). The absence of a relationship between abundance and robustness results because no species gets "ahead" in evolution—each evolutionary progression forward is eventually matched by a balanced cost (red queen hypothesis: Van Valen 1973).

Furthermore, because diadromous fishes do not have strikingly different life histories from nondiadromous fishes, it is unlikely that the stability of their recruitment process will differ. Therefore, no theoretical justification exists for proposing different stabilities of anadromous and marine stocks simply based on freshwater–sea migration behaviour.

(3) Because diadromous fishes depend upon the integrity of multiple habitats, their life histories may be more "fragile" than those of nonmigratory species. Imagine a 0.5 probability of habitat degradation by humans. If the degradation of habitats is an independent event, and the time spent by fishes in each habitat is equal, then the probability that two habitats remain suitable is 0.5 × 0.5 = 0.25. However, since destruction of any one habitat may prevent successful reproduction and survival of a diadromous fish, we must calculate the probability that either one or the other is degraded. This probability is 0.75 or 1 − (0.5 × 0.5). Thus, a fish using only one habitat has a 25% better chance of survival than one using two habitats.

Why then do fish species become dependent upon multiple habitats when this decreases their long-term probability of survivorship? The answer is that neither "foresight" nor "group selection" (where population rather than individual traits are favored: Williams 1966) is molding life history evolution in most fishes. What may be maladaptive in the long term is a natural consequence of fitness advantages at some point in an evolutionary history.

Conclusions

Whether or not diadromous life cycles have evolved as "strategies" remains open for question. Research directed at determining the relative contribution of conspecific "conflict" and environmental "opportunity" in the natural selection of diadromy may resolve this issue.

Diadromous species do not have life history traits which are uniquely different from nondiadromous species. A classification system which groups fishes as being either diadromous or nondiadromous is a subjective one, based on crossing a geographical boundary (sea–fresh water). It is not a biological or evolutionary one, based on life history theory.

The key to the evolution of diadromy lies in understanding natural selection for habitat switching. Switching habitats may impact on two important life history parameters: reproductive success (b_x) and survivorship (l_x). Since selection for diadromy will occur only if $\Sigma\, l_x b_x$ is maximized, increasing either reproductive success alone or survivorship may not favor diadromy. The migration model formulated here suggests that the necessary conditions for diadromy to evolve are:

$$[t_2(g_2 \cdot s_2) + t_m(g_m \cdot s_m)]/(t_2 + t_m) > 1,$$

where g and s are the measurements of b_x and l_x in alternative habitats, and t is the proportion of time spent in each part of the life cycle. Therefore the growth and survivorship advantages of utilizing a second habitat, plus the costs of moving between habitats, must exceed the advantages of staying in only one habitat ($=1$) for the same period of time. Even slight variations in these three variables may greatly influence natural selection for the evolution of diadromy. This model could be successfully used to direct future research into the biology of diadromous fishes.

The relative availability of food in sea and freshwater habitats appears to be the key factor driving the evolution of diadromy. Anadromy has evolved when food resources in the sea exceed those in fresh water while catadromy has evolved when freshwater food resources exceed those in the sea.

Selection for diadromy has probably been responsible for the colonization of tropical fresh waters by certain marine fishes. It may also have contributed to the marine fauna of temperate latitudes. Species of Pacific salmon (*Oncorhynchus* spp.) are an interesting example of the possible divergence of a freshwater genus into primarily marine, anadromous, and freshwater species (pink, coho, and "residual" sockeye salmon, respectively). Studies in fish phylogeny will gain considerable insight from a consideration of the evolution of diadromy.

The life histories of diadromous fishes are sensitive to changes in growth rate. Therefore, any management programs which impact on growth rate (e.g., hatcheries and lake fertilization) will perturb the behaviour of diadromous fishes. Examples include the overproduction of precociously mature males in salmon as a consequence of hatchery practices and the possible unintentional production, through lake fertilization, of freshwater populations from species which are presently anadromous.

Acknowledgments

I especially thank Robert McDowall for providing a prepublication copy of his work on diadromy. Ronald Coleman and Nancy Gerrish discussed many of the concepts that appear here, and Gerrish edited the manuscript. I thank Christine Moffitt, John Reynolds, and an anonymous referee for comments on the manuscript and Ron Ydenberg and Tom Quinn for discussions on life history evolution. Robin Baker's classical work (1978) on animal migration formed a basis for much of my thinking about diadromy.

References

Alexander, R. M. 1982. Optima for animals. Arnold, London, England.

Bagenal, T. B. 1967. A short review of fish fecundity. Pages 89–111 in S. D. Gerking, editor. The biological basis of freshwater fish production. Blackwell Scientific Publications, Oxford, England.

Baker, R. R. 1978. The evolutionary ecology of animal migration. Holmes and Meier, New York, New York, USA.

Bilton, H. T., D. F. Alderdice, and J. T. Schnute. 1982. Influence of time and size at release of juvenile coho salmon (Oncorhynchus kisutch) on returns at maturity. Canadian Journal of Fisheries and Aquatic Sciences 39:426–447.

Breder, C. M., and D. E. Rosen. 1966. Modes of reproduction in fishes. T.F.H. Publications, Neptune City, New Jersey, USA.

Cohen, I. B. 1985. Revolution in science. Belknap, Cambridge, England.

Colman, A. 1982. Game theory and experimental games: the study of strategic interaction. Pergamon, Oxford, England.

Foerster, R. E. 1968. The sockeye salmon (Oncorhynchus nerka). Fisheries Research Board of Canada Bulletin 162.

Groot, C., K. Simpson, I. Todd, P. D. Murray, and G. A. Buxton. 1975. Movements of sockeye salmon (Oncorhynchus nerka) in the Skeena River estuary as revealed by ultrasonic tracking. Journal of the Fisheries Research Board of Canada 32:233–242.

Gross, M. R. 1984. Sunfish, salmon, and the evolution of alternative reproductive strategies and tactics in fishes. Pages 55–75 in G. Potts and R. Wootton, editors. Fish reproduction: strategies and tactics. Academic Press, London, England.

Gross, M. R. 1985. Disruptive selection for alternative life histories in salmon. Nature (London) 313:47–48.

Gross, M. R., and E. L. Charnov. 1982. Alternative male life histories in bluegill sunfish. Proceedings of the National Academy of Sciences of the United States of America 77:6937–6940.

Hanson, A. J., and H. D. Smith. 1967. Mate selection in a population of sockeye salmon (Oncorhynchus nerka) of mixed age groups. Journal of the Fisheries Research Board of Canada 24:1955–1977.

Harden-Jones, F. R. 1981. Fish migration—strategies and tactics. Society for Experimental Biology Seminar Series 13:139–165.

Hart, J. L. 1973. Pacific fishes of Canada. Fisheries Research Board of Canada Bulletin 180.

Harvey, P. H., and G. M. Mace. 1982. Comparisons between taxa and adaptive trends: problems of methodology. Pages 343–362 in King's College Sociobiology Group, editors. Current problems in sociobiology. Cambridge University Press, Cambridge, England.

Hasler, A. C., and A. T. Scholz. 1983. Olfactory imprinting and homing in salmon. Springer-Verlag, New York, New York, USA.

Hillyard, S. D. 1981. Energy metabolism and osmoregulation in desert fishes. Pages 385–409 in R. J. Naiman and D. L. Soltz, editors. Fishes in North American deserts. John Wiley & Sons, New York, New York, USA.

Hoar, W. S. 1976. Smolt transformation: evolution, behavior and physiology. Journal of the Fisheries Research Board of Canada 33:1234–1252.

Hutchings, J. A., and D. W. Morris. 1985. The influence of phylogeny, size and behaviour on patterns of covariation in salmonid life histories. Oikos 45:118–124.

Hyatt, K. D., and J. G. Stockner. 1985. Response of sockeye salmon (Oncorhynchus nerka) to fertilization of British Columbia coastal lakes. Canadian Journal of Fisheries and Aquatic Sciences 42:320–331.

Jones, J. W. 1959. The salmon. Collins, London, England.

Jonsson, B. 1985. Life history patterns of freshwater resident and sea-run migrant brown trout in Norway. Transactions of the American Fisheries Society 114:182–194.

Jonsson, B., K. Hindar, and T. G. Northcote. 1984. Optimal age at sexual maturity of sympatric and experimentally allopatric cutthroat and Dolly Varden charr. Oecologia 1984:319–325.

Kramer, P. J. 1984. Misuse of the term strategy. BioScience 34:405.

Lee, S. H. 1971. Fecundity of four species of salmonid fishes in Newfoundland waters. Master's thesis. Memorial University of Newfoundland, St. John's, Canada.

Leggett, W. C. 1977. The ecology of fish migrations.

Annual Review of Ecology and Systematics 8:285–308.

Mangel, M., and C. W. Clark. 1986. Towards a unified foraging theory. Ecology 67:1127–1138.

Maynard Smith, J. 1982. Evolution and the theory of games. Cambridge University Press, Cambridge, England.

McDowall, R. M. 1978. New Zealand freshwater fishes: a guide and natural history. Heinemann Education Books, Auckland, New Zealand.

McDowall, R. M. 1987. The occurrence and distribution of diadromy among fishes. American Fisheries Society Symposium 1:1–13.

McKeown, B. A. 1984. Fish migration. Timber Press, Beaverton, Oregon, USA.

Merrick, J. R., and G. E. Schmida. 1984. Australian freshwater fishes. Griffen Press, Netley, Australia.

Morrow, J. E. 1980. The freshwater fishes of Alaska. Alaska Northwest Publications, Anchorage, Alaska, USA.

Nelson, J. S. 1984. Fishes of the world, 2nd edition. John Wiley & Sons, New York, New York, USA.

Nordeng, H. 1983. Solution to the "char problem" based on Arctic char (*Salvelinus alpinus*) in Norway. Canadian Journal of Fisheries and Aquatic Sciences 40:1372–1387.

Northcote, T. G. 1978. Migratory strategies and production in freshwater fishes. Pages 326–359 in S. D. Gerking, editor. Ecology of freshwater fish populations. John Wiley & Sons, New York, New York, USA.

Parker, G. A. 1984. Evolutionarily stable strategies. Pages 30–61 in J. R. Krebs and N. B. Davies, editors. Behavioural ecology: an evolutionary approach, 2nd edition. Sinauer Associates, Sunderland, Massachusetts, USA.

Peterman, R. M. 1984. Density-dependent growth in early ocean life of sockeye salmon (*Oncorhynchus nerka*). Canadian Journal of Fisheries and Aquatic Sciences 41:1825–1829.

Quinn, T. P. 1982. A model for salmon navigation on the high seas. Pages 79–85 in E. L. Brannon and E. O. Salo, editors. Proceedings of the salmon and trout migratory behavior symposium. University of Washington, College of Fisheries, Seattle, Washington, USA.

Sargent, R. C., M. R. Gross, and E. P. van den Berghe. 1986. Male mate choice in fishes. Animal Behaviour 34:545–550.

Schroder, S. L. 1982. The influence of intrasexual competition on the distribution of chum salmon in an experimental stream. Pages 275–285 in E. L. Brannon and E. O. Salo, editors. Proceedings of the salmon and trout migratory behavior symposium. University of Washington, College of Fisheries, Seattle, Washington, USA.

Scott, W. B., and E. J. Crossman. 1973. Freshwater fishes of Canada. Fisheries Research Board of Canada Bulletin 184.

Siegel, S. 1956. Nonparametric statistics. McGraw-Hill, New York, New York, USA.

Sigler, W. F., and R. R. Miller. 1963. Fishes of Utah. Utah State Department of Fish and Game, Salt Lake City, Utah, USA.

Sokal, R. R., and F. J. Rohlf. 1981. Biometry, 2nd edition. W. H. Freeman, San Francisco, California, USA.

Soule, M. E., and B. A. Wilcox, editors. 1980. Conservation biology: an evolutionary-ecological perspective. Sinauer Associates, Sunderland, Massachusetts, USA.

Stearns, S. C. 1977. The evolution of life history traits. Annual Review of Ecology and Systematics 8:145–171.

Thomas, W. K., R. E. Withler, and A. T. Beckenbach. 1986. Mitochondrial *DNA* analysis of Pacific salmonid evolution. Canadian Journal of Zoology 64:1058–1064.

van den Berghe, E. P., and M. R. Gross. 1986. Length of breeding life of coho salmon (*Oncorhynchus kisutch*). Canadian Journal of Zoology 64:1482–1486.

Van Valen, L. 1973. A new evolutionary law. Evolutionary Theory 1:1–30.

Williams, G. C. 1966. Adaptation and natural selection. Princeton University Press, Princeton, New Jersey, USA.

Ziman, J. 1984. An introduction to science studies: the philosophical and social aspects of science and technology. Cambridge University Press, Cambridge, England.

American Fisheries Society Symposium 1:26, 1987

UTILIZATION OF THE FRESHWATER HABITAT

Preamble

CHRISTINE M. MOFFITT

Idaho Cooperative Fish and Wildlife Research Unit, University of Idaho
Moscow, Idaho 83843, USA

The papers in this section explore the utilization of fresh water by diadromous species and examine the plasticity of life history strategies of many species. We compare variability in the length of freshwater residence; we look at how some introduced species have adapted and altered their life histories to accommodate an exotic environment; and we examine how some species partition use of their freshwater environment.

The freshwater environment provides an essential habitat for diadromous fishes. Anadromous species utilize fresh water for two distinct periods: early life and adult reproduction. Catadromous species generally have an extended rearing phase in fresh water. Diadromous species may spend as little as a few days or rather lengthy portions of their life in fresh water. Anadromous "B-run" steelhead *Salmo gairdneri* in Idaho spend 50–60% of their lifetimes in fresh water: 2–3 years as juveniles then, after 2 years at sea, another 8 months during late summer, fall, and winter before spawning in the spring. Catadromous anguillids spend from 20 to over 90% of their lifetimes in fresh water, depending on rearing location and sex.

One common theme of the papers in this section is that of human alteration or manipulation of the environment. In some cases, the modification is simply harvest of a stock or introduction of an exotic stock or species. Other alterations are a complex of activities that may include water diversion, flow modification or obstruction of fish passage, introduction of toxic compounds, and alterations of nutrient and trophic relationships.

As Mart Gross points out in his keynote paper, the probability that all of the environments used by diadromous species will remain unaltered is a multiple of the probabilities that each of them separately will be unaltered. Perturbation of the freshwater environment is widespread throughout the world. In southern Africa, where numerous dams have blocked migrations of fish and altered the quality and quantity of flow regimes, biologists are worried about the survival of several species of catadromous fishes, one of which *(Myxus capensis)* is now listed as threatened. In Pacific North America, the toll on anadromous fish from water development has been severe. The Pacific Northwest Electrical Power Planning and Conservation Act of 1980 mandated equal rights for fish and wildlife along with power and other water usages. However, because of mortality associated with fish passage at dams and habitat lost to fish production, the program goals of total fish produced can be met only with considerable hatchery supplementation, the effects of which are discussed in this section.

We must accept that we are going to live in a human-modified world. Through examination of the following papers, we can widen our understanding of the problems and become better able to propose compromises for management that will allow diadromous fish to adapt to the modifications and still thrive.

American Fisheries Society Symposium 1:27–41, 1987

Variability in Length of Freshwater Residence of Salmon, Trout, and Char

ROBERT G. RANDALL

Department of Fisheries and Oceans, Gulf Fisheries Centre, Post Office Box 5030
Moncton, New Brunswick E1C 9B6, Canada

MICHAEL C. HEALEY

Department of Fisheries and Oceans, Pacific Biological Station
Nanaimo, British Columbia V9R 5K6, Canada

J. BRIAN DEMPSON

Department of Fisheries and Oceans, Northwest Atlantic Fisheries Centre
Post Office Box 5667, St. John's, Newfoundland A1C 5X1, Canada

Abstract.—Length of freshwater residence varies considerably among and within anadromous species of the subfamily Salmoninae (salmons, trouts and chars) during both the juvenile and adult phases of the life cycles. The age of smolts can vary from less than 1 to 8 years, depending on species and population. Within populations, interannual variation in age of smolts can also be significant: for Atlantic salmon *Salmo salar* in one New Brunswick river, the proportion of each year class that smolted at age 2 ranged between 8% and 74% over a 17-year period. Both genetics and environment affect the age of smolts, but the relative importance of each factor has not been clearly identified. For individual species, biologists have traditionally attributed fluctuations in age of smolts to environmental factors affecting freshwater growth such as water temperature and population densities. However, genetic factors are also important. The duration of freshwater residence by adult Salmoninae preceding spawning is also under genetic and environmental control. The variability in length of freshwater residence has important implications for stock management. Fluctuations in the ages of smolts in an Atlantic salmon population alter egg-to-smolt survival by up to 50%. Chinook salmon *Oncorhynchus tshawytscha* that smolt at different ages can also have different migration routes at sea and are thus exposed to different commercial fisheries. Similarly, duration and timing of freshwater residence by adult salmonids preceding spawning can determine their exploitation rate by angling and commercial fisheries.

Comparative studies of anadromous salmonids usually emphasize the extreme variability in life history traits found among different species and populations (Rounsefell 1958a, 1962; Hoar 1976; Hutchings and Morris 1985). One such trait is length of freshwater residence, which varies during both the juvenile and adult phases of the life cycles. Arctic char, for instance, reside mainly in fresh water, making only relatively short feeding migrations to sea in summer, while chum salmon utilize freshwater only for spawning and egg incubation (Table 1 gives scientific names of these and other salmonine species). Between these two extremes, other species have been ranked according to their "degree of anadromy," depending (along with other traits) on how long they reside in fresh water (Rounsefell 1958a). Freshwater residence also varies within species, both among populations inhabiting different geographic areas and within populations over time.

Length of freshwater residence is determined by both genetics and environment (e.g. Jones 1959; Ricker 1972), but the relative importance of each factor has not been clearly established. Realizing the variability in freshwater residence and the factors that determine it, however, is important to managers because it can affect survival. Annual fluctuations in smolting age within populations, for example, affect freshwater survival rates from eggs to smolts (Foerster 1968; Drucker 1972; Buck and Hay 1984). Adult survival can also be affected; the length of time salmon spend in fresh water prior to spawning can determine their vulnerability to different fisheries.

The objectives of this paper are threefold: (1) to review the variability found in length of freshwater residence among and within species of the subfamily Salmoninae (salmons, trouts, and chars); (2) to identify and discuss the relative importance of environmental and genetic factors contributing to this variability; and (3) to identify the specific implications of this variability to managers. Our discussion will be restricted primarily, although not exclusively, to North American populations.

Length of Freshwater Residence among and within Species

Three genera of the subfamily Salmoninae—*Salvelinus, Salmo,* and *Oncorhynchus*—have representative anadromous populations in North America. In discussing length of freshwater residence, we proceed from the primarily freshwater species of the genus *Salvelinus,* which show the least degree of anadromy (Rounsefell 1958a), to the most specialized species of *Oncorhynchus,* where utilization of freshwater habitat is minimized. Geographic distributions of species within these three genera in North America are given by Scott and Crossman (1973).

Salvelinus

Anadromous populations of brook trout, Dolly Varden, and Arctic char often live sympatrically with resident forms. In contrast to Pacific and Atlantic salmon, anadromous chars have an extended but somewhat irregular period of freshwater residence. Chars generally do not overwinter at sea and maturing adults of Arctic char often remain in fresh water during the year in which they spawn. Migration to sea occurs in spring, and juveniles and adults reside in estuarine or coastal waters from 1 to 4 months before returning to fresh water (Armstrong and Morrow 1980; Johnson 1980; Power 1980). Duration of sea residence can be more extended in populations of brook trout in the southern portion of their range (Power 1980).

Because the life history of chars differs from Atlantic and Pacific salmon, Johnson (1980) cautioned use of accepted terminology when movements to and from the sea are discussed. Morphological and physiological changes associated with smolting in salmon are not as well defined for chars. McCormick et al. (1985) found that estuarine residence is required by brook trout to induce hypoosmoregulatory mechanisms needed for acclimation and subsequent seawater residence.

Populations of anadromous Arctic char and Dolly Varden frequently have bimodal length distributions (Armstrong 1974; Johnson 1980). The two modes can be loosely defined as adults and juveniles (smolts); the juvenile mode consists of immature individuals less than 300 mm in length while the adult mode may consist of both immature and mature fish. Juveniles can make a number of seaward migrations and a seaward "smolt" run will consist of both first-time and repeat migrants. Because the spatial extent of the seaward migration may be limited and small Arctic char do not necessarily migrate into areas of full-strength seawater (Johnson 1980), marine growth is variable and it is often difficult to distinguish first-time from repeat migrants. In this paper, the term smolts for *Salvelinus* species refers to fish within the juvenile size category.

Anadromous brook trout populations have smolt ages ranging from 1 to 7 years (Table 1). In the Maritime Region of Canada, most smolts are 2 and 3 years of age, whereas in Newfoundland, smolt ages 2 to 4 dominate (O'Connell 1982). Brook trout smolts from the Richmond Gulf of eastern Hudson Bay are mostly 3 and 4 years of age (Dutil and Power 1980). Thus, there is evidence of a latitudinal cline in age at smoltification of brook trout (Castonguay et al. 1982).

Dolly Varden in Alaska migrate to sea from 2 to 6 years of age, but most are age 3 and 4 (Armstrong 1970) (Table 1). Arctic char similarly show a wide variation in age at first seaward migration. Populations in Labrador migrate seaward at ages 1 to 8 but predominantly at ages 2 to 4 (Dempson and Green 1985; Dempson, personal observation). A similar range in smolt ages occurs in more western populations across North America (Johnson 1980).

Salmo

Anadromous species within the genus *Salmo* include cutthroat trout, brown trout, steelhead, and Atlantic salmon. In addition to anadromous populations, all four species have wholly freshwater populations occurring throughout their native ranges.

Anadromous cutthroat trout are similar to Arctic char in that their movements at sea are localized and they rarely stray far from their home streams. Cutthroat trout migrate to sea at ages 1 to 6 years but predominantly at ages 2 to 4 (Table 1; Johnston 1982). The majority of cutthroat trout return to fresh water to overwinter or mature (or both) in the same year they migrate to sea. High proportions of cutthroat trout that reenter fresh water survive spawning and return to the marine environment; Johnston (1982) estimated survival in a Washington stream averaged 41% (23–79%). Resident populations of cutthroat trout often occur in the same watersheds as anadromous populations.

TABLE 1.—Ages at migration to sea of species of Salmoninae throughout their natural ranges; + indicates that the age has been recorded; ++ indicates ages that dominate in many populations.

Species	Age								
	0	1	2	3	4	5	6	7	8
Brook trout (Salvelinus fontinalis)		+	++	++	++	+	+	+	
Arctic char (Salvelinus alpinus)		+	+	++	++	++	++	+	+
Dolly Varden (Salvelinus malma)			+	++	++	+	+		
Cutthroat trout (Salmo clarki)		+	++	++	++	+	+		
Brown trout (Salmo trutta)		+	++	++	+	+	+		
Rainbow trout, steelhead (Salmo gairdneri)		+	++	++	+				
Atlantic salmon (Salmo salar)		+	++	++	++	+	+	+	+
Sockeye salmon (Oncorhynchus nerka)	+	++	++	+	+				
Coho salmon (Oncorhynchus kisutch)	+	++	++	+					
Chinook salmon (Oncorhynchus tshawytscha)	++	++	+						
Chum salmon (Oncorhynchus keta)	++								
Pink salmon (Oncorhynchus gorbuscha)	++								

Throughout their native range in Europe and western Asia, anadromous brown trout are not as extensively distributed as resident forms (Frost and Brown 1967). Ages at migration to sea in British populations range from 1 to 6 years, but most juveniles become smolts at ages 2 and 3 (Table 1) (Fahy 1978, 1980). Depending on the population and location, many brown trout return to fresh water the same year they become smolts, most as immature fish (called finnock trout). Adult sea trout usually return to spawn after one to three winters at sea (Fahy 1978). Movements at sea are generally restricted to estuarine and coastal waters (Rounsefell 1958a; Mills 1971). Anadromous brown trout populations have been successfully introduced into eastern North America (MacCrimmon and Marshall 1968), but few studies have been published describing their life cycles.

Variability in length of freshwater residence among west coast steelhead populations was discussed by Withler (1966) and Ricker (1972). Juvenile steelhead spend 1 to 4 years in fresh water before migrating to sea, and the predominant smolt ages are 2 and 3 (Table 1). Unlike other species of Salmo, steelhead spawn in spring. Adult steelhead return to fresh water in summer (maturing in fresh water) or in winter (maturation occurs at sea) after residing at sea from 1 to 4

years (usually 2 or 3). Summer and winter migrants can occur in the same river. Because of the seasonal differences in adult returns, length of freshwater residence by adult steelheads prior to spawning varies considerably.

Within the genus Salmo, Atlantic salmon have the most consistently anadromous life cycle (Rounsefell 1958a). Most populations are anadromous; and where landlocked populations occur, they have probably been derived from local migratory stocks since the last glacial period (Power 1958; Behnke 1972). The age of smolts varies considerably among and within populations: smolt ages of 1 to 8 years have been recorded and ages 2, 3, and 4 are common (Table 1). Latitudinal clines in age at smoltification, with increasing smolt ages from south to north, have been reported from both the east (Dahl 1910; Svardson 1954) and west sides of the Atlantic (Power 1981). Adult Atlantic salmon return to fresh water to spawn in autumn after one, two, or (less commonly) three or more winters at sea. Seasonal timing of the adult run depends on the population and in most populations can occur from early spring to late autumn just prior to spawning. Early and late spawning runs can occur in the same river. In the Miramichi River, New Brunswick, for instance, Atlantic salmon enter the river in two main periods, May to July and August to

October (Saunders 1967); thus, residence in fresh water varies from 1 to 5 months prior to spawning. After spawning, kelts overwinter in the river and migrate to sea in the following early spring. The extent and timing of adult movements between marine (or estuary) and freshwater environments is much more variable in northern (Ungava) Atlantic salmon populations (Robitaille et al. 1986).

Oncorhynchus

Length of freshwater residence of adult Pacific salmon is determined by the length and speed of river migration and the time spent in a prespawning condition. Both factors vary among species and populations, particularly for chinook and sockeye salmon stocks, as reviewed in detail by Ricker (1972). Because all Pacific salmon are semelparous, adult use of freshwater habitat is limited to migration and spawning.

Sockeye salmon smolts range in age from 0 to 4, but most are 1 or 2 (Table 1). Yearling smolts predominate in the southern part of the range and 2-year-old smolts in the northern part, but this trend is not universal, as populations dominated by 1- or 2-year-old smolts may occur in close geographic proximity. Smolts aged 0, 3, or 4 occur incidentally throughout the range of sockeye salmon, except that age-3 smolts are common in a few populations (e.g., Ozernaia River and Karluk River populations, Hanamura 1966; Rounsefell 1958b).

Throughout their natural range, pink salmon and chum salmon migrate to sea almost immediately after emerging from gravel redds in the spring (Table 1). For populations that spawn a long distance from the sea (e.g., Asian and Yukon River chum salmon, Skeena River and Fraser River pink salmon), downstream migration may take several weeks. Length of freshwater residence also varies somewhat as a result of differences in length of incubation among years or among populations (e.g., Hunter 1959; Sano 1966). The incubation period is clearly thermally dependent (e.g., Alderdice and Velsen 1978); however, differences in thermal regime appear not to be a complete explanation for differences in length of incubation.

Chinook salmon migrate to sea either shortly after emerging from redds, after about 2.5 months of freshwater residence, or after a year or more in fresh water (Healey 1980, 1983; Carl and Healey 1984). Underyearling migrants predominate in North American populations at latitudes south of about 56°N, whereas yearling and older migrants predominate north of 56°N on the North American coast and in Asia (Table 1) (Healey 1983).

Coho salmon migrate to sea as smolts aged 0, 1, 2, or 3 years but most populations are dominated by age-1 or 2 smolts (Table 1) (Foerster and Ricker 1953; Shapovalov and Taft 1954; Drucker 1972; Yuen 1984; Huttunen 1985; Sharr et al. 1985). Yearling smolts predominate in the southern part of the coho salmon's range and 2-year-old smolts in the northern part, although, as with sockeye salmon, this is not a universal rule (Drucker 1972).

Sockeye salmon exhibit both landlocked (kokanee) populations and "residual" (nonanadromous) members of anadromous populations, but most are anadromous. Pink, chum, chinook, and coho salmon have no landlocked populations throughout their natural ranges, although residual coho salmon of both sexes do exist as lake dwellers (Foerster and Ricker 1953). The ability of three of these four species to develop landlocked populations, however, has been demonstrated by their successful introduction into the Laurentian Great Lakes (Ricker and Loftus 1968; Carl 1982; Kwain 1987, this volume).

Salmonid species that become smolts at more than one age can also show interannual variation in the age composition of seaward migrants (Figure 1). For Atlantic salmon in the Miramichi River, between 8% and 74% of the year classes from 1964 to 1979 were smolts at age 2.

Length of freshwater residence can be different for male than female salmonids. Males sometimes mature in fresh water, thus delaying or avoiding smoltification. "Precocious" males have been recorded in anadromous populations of chinook salmon (Rich 1920), sockeye salmon (Foerster 1968), rainbow trout (Shapovalov and Taft 1954), brown trout (Campbell 1977), Dolly Varden (Armstrong and Morrow 1980), brook trout (Power 1980), Arctic char (Dempson and Green 1985), and Atlantic salmon (Jones 1959). Proportions of males that mature in fresh water can vary extensively within and among populations (e.g., for Atlantic salmon, see Myers et al. 1985). Mortality or delayed smoltification resulting from freshwater maturation (Thorpe 1986) explains the preponderance of females often observed in smolt runs.

Causes of Variation in Freshwater Residence

Juveniles

Any attempt to explain the length of freshwater residence among juvenile salmonids must account

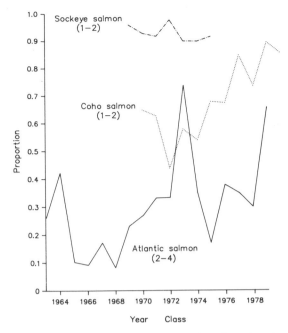

FIGURE 1.—Variation in the proportion of age-1 sockeye and coho salmon smolts and age-2 Atlantic salmon smolts over several year classes. The range of smolt ages for each population is given in parentheses. Data sources: sockeye salmon: LeBrasseur et al. (1978); coho salmon: Holtby and Hartman (1982); Atlantic salmon: Randall (unpublished).

for the degree of variation among species and for the variation between populations and between years within populations. While it is generally conceded that differences in freshwater residence among species have a genetic origin (these differences are, in part, regarded as species "characteristics"; Hoar 1958), differences in length of freshwater residence within species have usually been regarded as environmentally induced (Rich 1920; Elson 1957; Jones 1959; Hanamura 1966; Foerster 1968; Drucker 1972). Occasionally in the past (Rich and Holmes 1928) and more recently (Ricker 1972; Refstie et al. 1977; Thorpe and Morgan 1978; Healey 1983; Carl and Healey 1984), evidence has been put forward that variation in age of seaward migration within species is partly genetic as well.

Environmental influences.—The hypothesis that length of freshwater residence is environmentally controlled is based on evidence that smolt age is determined by growth conditions in fresh water. Physiological changes associated with smolting, including osmoregulatory competence, are related to size (McInerney 1964; Weisbart

1968; Hoar 1976; Wedemeyer et al. 1980; McCormick et al. 1985). In addition, marine survival following smoltification appears to be size dependent (Murray 1968; Walters et al. 1978; Bilton et al. 1982). These observations suggest there is a minimum size for a successful smolt (Elson 1957) and unless a fish reaches this size during a critical time window, it will remain in fresh water for another year (or until the next suitable time window) (Thorpe 1986). Where conditions for growth are time limited or poor, older smolt ages will occur. Hence, the increasing age of smolts with increasing latitude (referred to earlier) is explained by shorter growing seasons in northern areas. In addition to latitude, biologists have attempted to correlate smolt age with more specific environmental factors affecting growth, such as water temperature, discharge, nutrients, and population density (Table 2). The effect of environment on smolting age is best exemplified by

TABLE 2.—Examples of studies from which authors have related ages at migration to sea by young salmonids to environmental or genetic factors.

Factor	Species	References
Day length (growing season)	Atlantic salmon	Dahl (1910); Svardson (1954); Power (1981)
	Brown trout	Fahy (1980)
	Rainbow trout	Withler (1966)
	Chinook salmon	Healey (1983)
Temperature	Atlantic salmon	Chadwick (1981)
	Chinook salmon	Healey (1983)
	Coho salmon	Holtby and Hartman (1982)
Nutrients	Sockeye salmon	Foerster (1968); LeBrasseur et al. (1978)
	Coho salmon	Holtby and Hartman (1982)
Discharge rate	Atlantic salmon	Chadwick (1981); Marshall (1984)
	Coho salmon	Holtby and Hartman (1982)
Population density	Atlantic salmon	Chadwick (1981); Buck and Hay (1984)
	Sockeye salmon	Foerster (1968)
	Coho salmon	Holtby and Hartman (1982)
Genetic	Chinook salmon	Rich and Holmes (1928); Healey (1983); Carl and Healey (1984)
	Atlantic salmon	Refstie et al. (1977); Thorpe and Morgan (1978)
	Several species	Ricker (1972)

hatchery data. Native stocks of Atlantic salmon in
Maritime Canada, for instance, normally become
smolts at ages 2 to 5, but under optimum growth
conditions in hatcheries, age-1 smolts are produced.

Several deductions from the hypothesis that
smolt age is determined by growth conditions in
fresh water may be tested. First, we would expect
the range of smolt sizes to be relatively small if the
fish migrate to sea as soon as possible after they
reach their critical size. On the contrary, however, the range of smolt sizes among populations
is large (Figure 2), particularly for sockeye and
coho salmon. It seems reasonable to presume that
the smallest age-1 smolts represent the minimum
size required to become smolts and 60–80 mm is
the size at which these latter two species are
capable of osmoregulating in seawater, provided
other conditions are appropriate (Weisbart 1968).
The minimum smolt size is, therefore, 30–40 mm
longer than the size at which sockeye and coho
salmon emerge from redds. If the fish that failed to
migrate as age-1 smolts did so because they were
smaller than the minimum size, and also if their
growth during their second freshwater season was
equal to their growth during the first (an optimistic
assumption), then age-2 smolts should not exceed
100–120 mm fork length. Yet many do (Figure 2),
contrary to the hypothesis that age of smolting is
determined by the age at which the fish reaches
some minimum size.

Mean size of Atlantic salmon smolts does not
vary among populations to the degree it does in
sockeye and coho salmon populations (Figure 2),
perhaps indicating constant size at migration is
more characteristic of this species. Most smolts
are between 130 and 170 mm in length, regardless
of age, although Ungava stocks have larger and
older smolts than average (Power 1969). Even
with this relative consistency in size at seaward
migration, however, there is a lack of evidence for
a fixed size beyond which Atlantic salmon must
become smolts, even within populations (Thorpe
1986). To explain variability among year classes in
growth and smolt production in a Newfoundland
population of Atlantic salmon, Evans et al. (1984)
argued that the criterion length for smolting must
decrease with age.

A second deduction from the hypothesis that
smolt age is determined by growth conditions is
that smolt age should be negatively correlated
with freshwater growth. Scale analyses yielding
back-calculated lengths often have indicated that
young smolts within populations grew faster (at

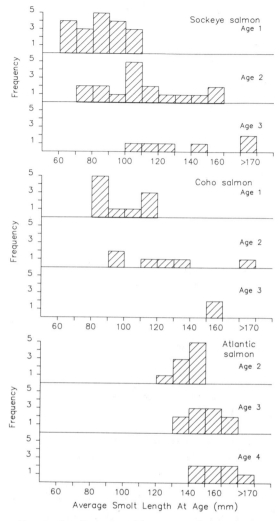

FIGURE 2.—Frequency histograms of average smolt
length at age for sockeye, coho, and Atlantic salmon
from different spawning populations. Data sources:
sockeye salmon: Foerster (1968); coho salmon: Foerster
and Ricker (1953), Shapovalov and Taft (1954), Drucker
(1972), Holtby and Hartman (1982); Atlantic salmon
Jones (1949, 1959), Forsythe (1967, 1968), Murray
(1968), Jessop (1975), Lear and Day (1977), Chadwick
(1981), Hesthagen and Garnas (1984), Piggins and Mills
(1985), Randall (unpublished).

the same age) than older smolts (e.g., Jones 1949).
However, comparisons of growth and age at smoltification among year classes show no consistent
relationships. Foerster (1968) argued that a negative correlation existed for sockeye salmon in
some British Columbia lakes, but he also reported
the proportion of 2-year-old smolts in Lake Dal-
nee, Kamchatka, increased when feeding condi-

tions were both poor and exceptionally good. Ricker (1972) found a significant negative correlation between the mean size of yearling sockeye salmon and the proportion of age-2 smolts in two lakes, but a positive correlation in another lake. Ricker concluded that even where negative correlations existed, they were weak and age at seaward migration was relatively insensitive to large changes in growth among year classes.

A further consequence of the above prediction is that age-1 sockeye salmon smolts in populations which also produce older smolts should be smaller, when averaged over populations, than age-1 smolts in populations which produce only (or virtually only) smolts of that age. In the former instance, most age-1 smolts would be near the critical size whereas, in the latter case, many smolts would be above critical size. Smolts from seven sockeye salmon populations that produced only age-1 smolts averaged 85.1 mm fork length whereas age-1 smolts from 13 populations that produced smolts aged 1, 2, and older averaged 86.5 mm fork length (Foerster 1968; LeBrasseur et al. 1978). These smolt data are, therefore, inconsistent with the prediction that smolt age is correlated with growth rate.

Finally, we would expect the size of smolts to be larger early in the smolt run whereas only those fish which had reached the critical size should be present toward the end. Furthermore, the fish remaining in fresh water after the smolt migration should be smaller than the smolt migrants. Both these predictions have been confirmed by observations in several smolt runs (Allen 1944; Krogius and Krokhin 1948; Shapovalov and Taft 1954; Parker and Vincent 1955; Rounsefell 1958b; Hartman et al. 1967; Foerster 1968; Osterdahl 1969). When there is more than one age-group present, the older fish tend to migrate first and, in general, the larger members of any year class are the first to migrate. There are many exceptions to these rules, however; at Little Kitoi, Alaska, Parker and Vincent (1955) noted that patterns of migration appeared to be influenced by age, growth, and racial characteristics, not merely by size.

The lack of consistent correlations between growth and smolt age and size may, in part, be a consequence of when the physiological commitment to smoltification is made. The latter deduction in particular, concerning characteristics of smolt runs, assumes this commitment is made just prior to seaward migration. Thorpe (1986), however, cited evidence that, for Atlantic salmon at least, the commitment is made much earlier.

Growth rate (more specifically, the rate of acquisition of surplus energy), according to Thorpe's hypothesis, must exceed a threshold level at a specific time in the summer before migration (July) when the fish are sensitive to photoperiodic stimulation before physiological changes associated with smolting are triggered. If this is the case, differential growth rates after this specific time window may account for some of the variation in smolt sizes at migration. Despite this possibility, it is difficult to account for all variation in smolt age or size characteristics solely on the basis of growth conditions in fresh water.

In some respects, therefore, the data are not consistent with the hypothesis that smolt age is wholly environmentally controlled. The contrary evidence may be explained, in part, if we assume that critical smolt sizes are population- and age-specific (Thorpe 1986). Such an assumption implies, however, a significant degree of underlying genetic control of age or size at smoltification.

Genetic influences.—An alternative to the hypothesis that age of smolting is determined by environmental conditions is the hypothesis that fish are genetically programmed to migrate at a certain age. As with the former hypothesis, several deductions from this hypothesis can be examined. First, we would expect migrants of different ages to differ genetically. Observations on polymorphic enzyme systems in chinook salmon that migrated seaward at different ages in the Nanaimo River demonstrated the existence of such genetic differences. In this system, chinook salmon that migrated to sea as fry in April and May, as fingerlings in June, or as yearlings in the spring following emergence from the spawning nest differed significantly in the frequency of alleles at certain loci as well as in body morphology (Carl and Healey 1984). Recently, Saxton et al. (1984) found high heritability for several measures of smolting success in coho salmon and strong genetic correlations between growth rate and smolting success. These latter correlations suggest that the commonly observed connection between size and smoltification may have a genetic basis. For chum salmon, whose freshwater residence is confined to the incubation period, there is evidence of significant variation in incubation period, apparently designed to ensure synchronous emergence of fry among local populations that spawned at different times (Figure 3). Subsequent investigation has confirmed that the differences in incubation rates are genetically determined (R. F. Tallman, Department of Fisheries

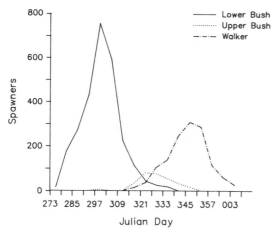

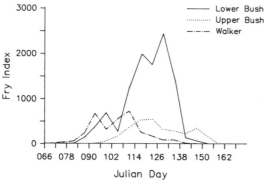

FIGURE 3.—Temporal occurrence of spawning chum salmon in three local populations and the temporal emergence of their fry, showing separation in spawning time but synchrony in emergence.

and Oceans, Nanaimo, British Columbia, personal communication). Thus, there is evidence to support the prediction that Pacific salmon which migrate at different ages differ genetically.

Second, we would expect the proportion of migrants of different freshwater ages in a population each year to be relatively constant, or at least not related in any simple way to environmental parameters. This prediction is based on the assumption that any population characteristic controlled by a stable polymorphism will behave conservatively in the presence of interannual environmental variation. Contrary to this prediction, as we pointed out before, some populations demonstrate large interannual fluctuations in age composition of seaward migrants (Figure 1). It is difficult to account for this variation if age of smolting is largely genetically determined.

Third, fish of different freshwater ages should breed true with regard to freshwater age of their

offspring. Rich and Holmes (1928) found that the progeny of chinook salmon migrated at the same freshwater age as their parents had, even though incubated in a hatchery and then transplanted to rearing streams where the resident population typically migrated at a different age. Similarly, among sockeye salmon from Cultus Lake, Ricker (1972) noted that progeny of age-2 smolts tended to migrate at the same age. In more recent experiments with Altantic salmon, genetic influences on age at smolting have been well documented (Refstie et al. 1977; Thorpe and Morgan 1978).

The obvious, and not surprising, conclusion from these observations is that age of migration must have a genetic component, but that it is also strongly influenced by environmental conditions. The relative importance of environmental and genetic influences undoubtedly differs between species and probably differs among populations of the same species. Genetic influences on age of smolting within species have been underestimated until recently, however. Each population can include several reproductively isolated stocks, and each stock can have unique life history traits, including age at smolting (e.g., Saunders 1981). The forces which maintain multiple freshwater ages in the same population are unknown but presumably have to do with the relative survival probabilities and growth rates in the freshwater and marine environments and with the ultimate reproductive success of individuals (Saunders and Schom 1985). These forces have been explored to some extent with respect to age and size at maturity of Pacific salmon (Gross 1984; Healey and Heard 1984; Hankin and Healey 1986; Healey 1986) but not, as yet, with respect to age at seaward migration.

Adults

Maturation of male salmon in fresh water, like age at smoltification, is controlled by both environmental and genetic factors. Maturation is positively correlated with growth, but it also differs among populations irrespective of their growth characteristics (for recent literature reviews, see Ricker 1972; Randall et al. 1986; Thorpe 1986). The adaptive significance of early sexual maturation of male salmon was discussed by Myers (1983; 1984) and Gross (1984). Demographic consequences of extended freshwater residence by males will be discussed later.

Seasonal patterns of adult salmon returns also have a genetic and environmental basis (Ricker 1972; Power 1981; Saunders 1981). When progeny of several species of salmon and trout were transplanted to nonnatal rivers, they returned at the same time as their parents and at different times from the endemic populations (Ricker 1972). Both Saunders (1967; 1981) and Elson (1973) felt that early- and late-running Atlantic salmon in the Miramichi River were genetically distinct stocks. Saunders (1967) documented that early-running salmon spawned in headwaters while late-running salmon spawned lower in the river; this spatial separation in spawning has recently been confirmed by sonic-tagging studies (T. G. Lutzac, Department of Fisheries and Oceans, Moncton, New Brunswick, personal communication). Similarly, different seasonal runs of steelhead and Pacific salmon are thought to be genetically distinct because of spatial and temporal differences in spawning (Withler 1966; Healey 1983; Leider et al. 1984).

Evidence of environmental factors affecting timing of river ascent is somewhat scarcer. Exact timing of upstream migrations depends on hydrographic conditions such as water flow and temperature (e.g., Jones 1959; Elson 1969; Power 1981). Thus, the length of time adult salmon spend in fresh water prior to spawning can vary somewhat from one year to the next depending on weather conditions.

Management Implications of Freshwater Residence

Several management implications are relevant to length of freshwater residence. Early writers emphasized the apparent loss in fishery production that resulted when fingerlings remained an extra year in fresh water; the additional year of mortality was not compensated by an increase in adult size (Krogius and Krokhin 1948; Foerster 1968). To illustrate and quantify the effect on adult yield of a salmon population that smoltifies at different ages, we use a salmonid life history model developed by Evans and Dempson (1986) for Atlantic salmon. The model is simple in structure (Figure 4); it has only one form of density dependence that allows the population to stabilize; the density-dependent term uses a Ricker function:

$$\phi(Bx) = Bx \exp(-Bx/R);$$

Bx is the potential number of eggs laid and $\phi(Bx)$ is the number that are successfully spawned. In each simulation, $R = 1.0 \times 10^6$. Biological statistics for proportion spawners of two different sea ages, proportion female, mean weight, and num-

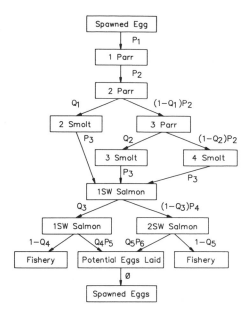

FIGURE 4.—Structure of a salmon population model (modified from Evans and Dempson 1986) used to estimate the effect on smolt and adult yield of varying smolt ages. Symbols are:

P_1: first-year survival; fraction of spawned eggs that become age-1 parr;

P_2: survival fraction for each subsequent river year;

Q_1: fraction of age-2 parr that become age-2 smolts which depends on stock type (Table 4);

Q_2: fraction of age-3 parr that become age-3 smolts which depends on stock type (Table 4);

P_3: survival fraction in the first year at sea;

Q_3: fraction of 1SW (one-sea-winter) fish that return as 1SW fish;

P_4: survival fraction in the second year at sea;

Q_4: fraction of 1SW salmon surviving the fishery;

P_5: number of eggs per 1SW salmon, the product of proportion of females in the 1SW population and the fecundity (mean weight × number of eggs per kilogram) of female 1SW salmon;

Q_5: fraction of 2SW salmon surviving the fishery;

P_6: number of eggs per 2SW salmon.

ber of eggs per kilogram were average values recorded for the Miramichi River, New Brunswick (Table 3). Survival from spawned egg to age-1 parr of 0.10 also has been reported or used in assessing the Miramichi salmon stock (Randall and Chadwick 1983). Four different stock types were used, among which mean smolt age varied from 2.4 to 3.0 years (Table 4).

Each simulation began with 250,000 spawned eggs. The model was run for 25 years to achieve stability. Comparative output values summarized in Figure 5 are average values for the following 10

TABLE 3.—Biological variables and survival values used in simulations of an Atlantic salmon population with various smolt age distributions. Symbols are defined in Figure 4; smolt age distributions given in Table 4.

Description	Symbol	Value		Reference
Model variables		Sea age		
		1SW	2SW	
Proportion spawners	Q_3	0.76	0.24	Randall (1985)
Proportion female	[a]	0.25	0.88	Randall (1985)
Mean weight (kg)	[a]	1.55	4.46	Randall and Chadwick (1983)
Eggs/kg	[a]	2,035	1,636	Randall (1985)
Survival rates				
Freshwater				
Egg to age-1 parr	P_1	0.10		Randall and Chadwick (1983)
Age 1 to age 2	P_2	0.40		Assumed
Age 2 to age 3	P_2	0.40		Assumed
Age 3 to age 4	P_2	0.40		Evans et al. (1984)
Marine				
Smolt to 1SW	P_3	0.165		Chadwick and Reddin (1985)
1SW to 2SW	P_4	0.60		Chadwick and Reddin (1985)
Fishing				
1SW	Q_4	0.45		Pippy (1982)
2SW	Q_5	0.15		Pippy (1982)

[a] These three variables yield P_5 for 1SW fish and P_6 for 2SW fish.

years (years 26 to 35). Coefficients of variation of output values were less than 0.6%. It is clear (Figure 5) that a reduction in smolt age increases survival from egg to smolt and increases adult production. As mean smolt age decreases from 3.0 to 2.4 years, the increase in adult yield becomes proportionately less. For example, a reduction in smolt age from 3.0 years to 2.8 years results in an increase in total production of adult 1SW salmon from 305 to 451 kg (48%). A further reduction in mean smolt age to 2.6 years only increases 1SW salmon production from 451 to 629 kg (39%). This effect is the result of the nonlinear density-dependent function regulating the number of spawned eggs. Nevertheless, the potential increase in yield of adult salmon with decreasing smolt ages is significant (Figure 5). Although our model uses parameters from an Atlantic salmon population, the results may be applicable to any salmonid species that has multiple smolt ages.

Whether or not these potential increases in smolt and adult yields actually occur in natural salmon populations is yet to be confirmed, but at least one study suggests they do. Buck and Hay (1984) found that, despite large annual fluctuations in egg deposition, smolt yield remained relatively constant in a Scottish Atlantic salmon population. Growth and survival of parr appeared density dependent, such that when densities were low, more parr migrated at a young age, thus increasing their survival to the smolt stage.

Because of the potential impact of varying age at migration on adult yield, management plans could be enhanced if smolt age could be predicted. This may become possible when density-dependent (Buck and Hay 1984) or such environmental influences on smolt age as discharge rate (Marshall 1984) are more clearly defined. Attempts to deliberately alter smolt ages, however, should be done with caution. It is conceivable that variation in smolt age represents an important genetic adaptation in some populations and overall fitness may be reduced if smolt age is manipulated too much (Carl and Healey 1984).

Arctic char may undergo several seaward migrations prior to reaching a size vulnerable to commercial exploitation. Their longevity is also much greater than it is for species of *Salmo* or *Oncorhynchus;* maximum Arctic char ages often exceed 15 to 20 years. Thus the fishable stock may be composed of a wide range of ages with various freshwater histories. As a result, the effect of lowered smolt age on potential adult yield would be less than that expected for Atlantic or Pacific salmon.

TABLE 4.—Assumed smolt age distributions of four stocks simulated in an Atlantic salmon population model.

Smolt age (years)	Stock			
	1	2	3	4
2	0.10	0.30	0.50	0.70
3	0.85	0.65	0.45	0.25
4	0.05	0.05	0.05	0.05
Mean	3.00	2.80	2.60	2.40

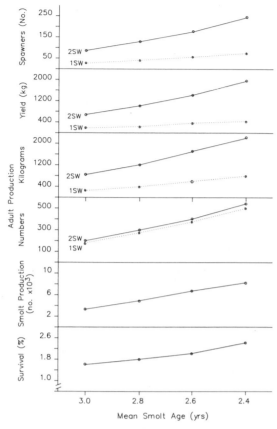

FIGURE 5.—Increases in freshwater survival (egg to smolt) and smolt production and in adult production, yield, and spawning escapement with decreasing smolt ages in a hypothetical Atlantic salmon population (Tables 3, 4; Figure 4); 1SW and 2SW represent one- and two-sea-winter fish, respectively.

Where alternative uses of freshwater habitats conflict with fish production, the manager may find extended freshwater residence of young salmon poses important problems. With pink and chum salmon that spend only the incubation period in fresh water, the river and its water are available for other purposes for about half the year without affecting fish production. When the species spends a year or more in fresh water, as do coho and Atlantic salmon for instance, river flows, water quality, and temperature must be maintained within tolerable limits throughout the year and important habitat configurations must also be protected. Since larger salmonids often occupy different habitats than smaller ones, the longer salmon spend in fresh water the greater the diversity of habitats that must be maintained for their benefit.

When freshwater age is a reflection of important stock differences, which may include ocean migratory behaviour, additional complications are introduced for the fishery manager. For example, chinook salmon that migrate to sea as yearlings or underyearlings appear to have quite different ocean migratory behaviour from chinook salmon that migrate at later ages (Healey 1983), and these differences profoundly affect the way in which the two types or "races" of chinook salmon are harvested. Harvesting Pacific salmon on a stock-by-stock basis poses severe problems for the manager, even at our present level of stock definition (Healey 1982), and it is doubtful that further subdivision of stocks could be incorporated into the design of management systems.

If we assume that length of freshwater residence reflects an important tradeoff between probabilities of freshwater and marine survival, it is possible that length of freshwater residence will be altered by intensive marine fisheries. The population, or some component of it (say males), may find it advantageous to lengthen their freshwater life and shorter their marine life, thereby reducing their size at maturity and their vulnerability to marine fisheries. This mechanism may apply, for instance, to male Atlantic salmon parr (Myers 1983, 1984) such that increasing fishing pressure may result in an increase in the proportion maturing in fresh water. Myers (1983, 1984) noted that increased proportions of maturing parr, because of high mortality following maturation, can strongly affect the yield to a fishery: up to 60% of the potential adult male production was lost in one Newfoundland river due to maturation in fresh water.

The duration of freshwater residence by adult salmonids preceding spawning can affect exploitation rates. Early-run Atlantic salmon in the Miramichi River, because of their prolonged stay in the river, are exploited by anglers (and poachers) more so than late-run salmon (Elson 1973). Similarly, early- and late-run salmon are exploited differentially at sea; in this case, late-run fish are the more heavily exploited (Elson 1973). For Maritime Atlantic salmon stocks in general, Power (1981) found a negative correlation between commercial catches and summer rainfall; he suggested low river discharges delayed adult migrations, thus exposing salmon to commercial fisheries for longer periods. For Pacific salmon, in areas where early- and late-run fish contribute to multistock fisheries (e.g., pink salmon returning to Fraser River), effective management is more difficult and overfishing weak stocks is always a possibility (Healey 1982). Realizing these stock-specific and environmental influences on length of freshwater residence is therefore paramount to sound management.

References

Alderice, D. F., and F. P. J. Velsen. 1978. Relation between temperature and incubation time for eggs of chinook salmon (Oncorhynchus tshawytscha). Journal of the Fisheries Research Board of Canada 35:69–75

Allen, K. R. 1944. Studies on the biology of the early stages of the salmon (Salmo salar). 4. The smolt migration in the Thurso River in 1938. Journal of Animal Ecology 13:63–85.

Armstrong, R. H. 1970. Age, food and migration of Dolly Varden smolts in southeastern Alaska. Journal of the Fisheries Research Board of Canada 27:991–1004.

Armstrong, R. H. 1974. Migration of anadromous Dolly Varden (Salvelinus malma) in southeastern Alaska. Journal of the Fisheries Research Board of Canada 31:435–444.

Armstrong, R. H., and J. E. Morrow. 1980. The Dolly Varden char, Salvelinus malma. Pages 99–140 in E. K. Balon, editor. Charrs: salmonid fishes of the genus Salvelinus. Dr. W. Junk, The Hague, The Netherlands.

Behnke, R. J. 1972. The systematics of salmonid fishes of recently glaciated lakes. Journal of the Fisheries Research Board of Canada 29:639–671.

Bilton, H. T., D. F. Alderdice, and J. T. Schnute. 1982. Influence of time and size at release of juvenile coho salmon (Oncorhynchus kisutch) on returns at maturity. Canadian Journal of Fisheries and Aquatic Sciences 39:426–447.

Buck, R. J. G., and D. W. Hay. 1984. The relation between stock size and progeny of Atlantic salmon, Salmo salar L., in a Scottish stream. Journal of Fish Biology 23:1–11.

Campbell, J. S. 1977. Spawning characteristics of brown trout and sea trout Salmo trutta L. in Kirk Burn, River Tweed, Scotland. Journal of Fish Biology 11:217–229.

Carl, L. M. 1982. Natural reproduction of coho salmon and chinook salmon in some Michigan streams. North American Journal of Fisheries Management 2:375–380.

Carl, L. M., and M. C. Healey. 1984. Differences in enzyme frequency and body morphology among three juvenile life history types of chinook salmon (Oncorhynchus tshawytscha) in the Nanaimo River, British Columbia. Canadian Journal of Fisheries and Aquatic Sciences 41:1070–1077.

Castonguay, M., G. J. Fitzgerald, and Y. Côté. 1982. Life history and movements of anadromous brook charr, Salvelinus fontinalis, in the St-Jean River, Gaspé, Québec. Canadian Journal of Zoology 60:3084–3091.

Chadwick, E. M. P. 1981. Biological characteristics of Atlantic salmon smolts in Western Arm Brook, Newfoundland. Canadian Technical Report of Fisheries and Aquatic Sciences 1024.

Chadwick, E. M. P., and D. G. Reddin. 1985. Fishing and natural mortality rates for 1SW Atlantic salmon (Salmo salar L.). International Council for the Exploration of the Sea, CM 1985/M:18, Copenhagen, Denmark.

Dahl, K. 1910. The age and growth of salmon and trout in Norway as shown by their scales. Salmon and Trout Association, London, England.

Dempson, J. B., and J. M. Green. 1985. Life history of anadromous Arctic charr, Salvelinus alpinus, in the Fraser River, northern Labrador. Canadian Journal of Zoology 63:315–324.

Drucker, B. 1972. Some life history characteristics of coho salmon of the Karluk River system, Kodiak Island, Alaska. U.S. National Marine Fisheries Service Fishery Bulletin 70:79–94.

Dutil, J. D., and G. Power. 1980. Coastal populations of brook trout, Salvelinus fontinalis, in Lac Guillaume-Delisle (Richmond Gulf) Québec. Canadian Journal of Zoology 58:1828–1835.

Elson, P. F. 1957. The importance of size in the change from parr to smolt in Atlantic salmon. Canadian Fish Culturist 21:1–6.

Elson, P. F. 1969. High temperature and river ascent by Atlantic salmon. International Council for the Exploration of the Sea, CM 1969/M:12, Copenhagen, Denmark.

Elson, P. F. 1973. Genetic polymorphism in Northwest Miramichi salmon, in relation to season of river ascent and age at maturation and its implication for management of the stocks. International Commission for the Northwest Altantic Fisheries, Research Document 73/76, Dartmouth, Canada.

Evans, G. T., and J. B. Dempson. 1986. Calculating the sensitivity of a salmonid population model. Canadian Journal of Fisheries and Aquatic Sciences 43:863–868.

Evans, G. T., J. C. Rice, and E. M. P. Chadwick. 1984. Patterns in growth and smolting of Atlantic salmon (Salmo salar) parr. Canadian Journal of Fisheries and Aquatic Sciences 41:783–797.

Fahy, E. 1978. Variation in some biological characteristics of British sea trout, Salmo trutta L. Journal of Fish Biology 13:123–138.

Fahy, E. 1980. Growing season as a factor in sea trout production. Journal of Fish Biology 17:541–546.

Foerster, R. E. 1968. The sockeye salmon, Oncorhynchus nerka. Fisheries Research Board of Canada Bulletin 162.

Foerster, R. E., and W. E. Ricker. 1953. The coho salmon of Cultus Lake and Sweltzer Creek. Journal of the Fisheries Research Board of Canada 10:293–319.

Forsythe, M. G. 1967. Analysis of the 1965 smolt run in the Northwest Miramichi River, New Brunswick. Fisheries Research Board of Canada Technical Report 4.

Forsythe, M. G. 1968. Analysis of the 1966 smolt run in the Northwest Miramichi River, New Brunswick.

Fisheries Research Board of Canada Technical Report 91.

Frost, W. E., and M. E. Brown. 1967. The trout. Collins, London, England.

Gross, M. 1984. Sunfish, salmon and the evolution of alternative reproductive strategies and tactics in salmon. Pages 55–75 in C. W. Potts and R. J. Wootton, editors. Fish reproduction, strategies and tactics. Academic Press, London, England.

Hanamura, N. 1966. Sockeye salmon in the far east. International North Pacific Fisheries Commission Bulletin 18:1–28.

Hankin, D. G., and M. C. Healey. 1986. Dependence of exploitation rates for maximum yield and stock collapse on age and sex structure of chinook salmon (Oncorhynchus tshawytscha) stocks. Canadian Journal of Fisheries and Aquatic Sciences 43: 1746–1759.

Hartman, W. L., W. R. Heard, and B. Drucker. 1967. Migratory behavior of sockeye salmon fry and smolts. Journal of the Fisheries Research Board of Canada 24:2069–2099.

Healey, M. C. 1980. Utilization of the Nanaimo River estuary by juvenile chinook salmon, Oncorhynchus tshawytscha. U.S. National Marine Fisheries Service Fishery Bulletin 77:653–668.

Healey, M. C. 1982. Multispecies, multistock aspects of Pacific salmon management. Canadian Special Publication of Fisheries and Aquatic Sciences 59: 119–126.

Healey, M. C. 1983. Coastwide distribution and ocean migration patterns of stream- and ocean-type chinook salmon, Oncorhynchus tshawytscha. Canadian Field-Naturalist 97:427–433.

Healey, M. C. 1986. Optimum size and age at maturity in Pacific salmon and the effects of size-selective fisheries. Canadian Special Publication of Fisheries and Aquatic Sciences 89:39–52.

Healey, M. C., and W. R. Heard. 1984. Inter- and intrapopulation variation in the fecundity of chinook salmon (Oncorhynchus tshawytscha) and its relevance to life history theory. Canadian Journal of Fisheries and Aquatic Sciences 41:476–483.

Hesthagen, T., and E. Garnas. 1984. Smolt age and size of Atlantic salmon Salmo salar L. and sea trout Salmo trutta L. in a Norwegian river. Fauna Norvegiae Series A 5:46–49.

Hoar, W. S. 1958. The evolution of migratory behaviour among juvenile salmon of the genus Oncorhynchus. Journal of the Fisheries Research Board of Canada 15:391–428.

Hoar, W. S. 1976. Smolt transformation: evolution, behavior and physiology. Journal of the Fisheries Research Board of Canada 33:1233–1252.

Holtby, L. B., and G. F. Hartman. 1982. The population dynamics of coho salmon (Oncorhynchus kisutch) in a west coast rain forest stream subjected to logging. Pages 308–347 in G. F. Hartman, editor. Proceedings of the Carnation Creek workshop, a 10-year review. Department of Fisheries and Oceans, Pacific Biological Station, Nanaimo, Canada.

Hunter, J. G. 1959. Survival and production of pink and chum salmon in a coastal stream. Journal of the Fisheries Research Board of Canada 16:835–886.

Hutchings, J. A., and D. W. Morris. 1985. The influence of phylogeny, size and behaviour on patterns of covariation in salmonid life histories. Oikos 45:118–124.

Huttunen, D. C. 1985. Abundance, age, sex, and size of salmon (Oncorhynchus sp.) catches and escapements in the Kuskokwim area, 1983. Alaska Department of Fisheries and Game, Technical Data Report 133, Juneau, Alaska, USA.

Jessop, B. M. 1975. Investigation of the salmon (Salmo salar) smolt migration of the Big Salmon River, New Brunswick, 1966–72. Canada Fisheries and Marine Service Technical Report MAR/T-75-1.

Johnson, L. 1980. The Arctic charr, Salvelinus alpinus. Pages 15–98 in E. K. Balon, editor. Charrs: salmonid fishes of the genus Salvelinus. Dr. W. Junk, The Hague, The Netherlands.

Johnston, J. M. 1982. Life histories of anadromous cutthroat with emphasis on migratory behaviour. Pages 123–127 in E. L. Brannon and E. O. Salo, editors. Proceedings of the salmon and trout migratory behaviour symposium. University of Washington, School of Fisheries, Seattle, Washington, USA.

Jones, J. W. 1949. Studies of the scales of young salmon (Salmo salar L.) in relation to growth migration and spawning. Fisheries Investigations, Series I, Salmon and Freshwater Fisheries, Great Britain Ministry of Agriculture Fisheries and Foods 5:1–23.

Jones, J. W. 1959. The salmon. Collins, London, England.

Krogius, F. V., and E. M. Krokhin. 1948. On the production of young sockeye salmon (Oncorhynchus nerka Walb.). Fisheries Research Board of Canada, Translation Series 109, 1958, Ottawa, Canada.

Kwain, W. 1987. Biology of pink salmon in the North American Great Lakes. American Fisheries Society Symposium 1:57–65.

Lear, W. H., and F. A. Day. 1977. An analysis of biological and environmental data collected at North Harbour River, Newfoundland, during 1959–75. Canada Fisheries and Marine Service Technical Report 697.

LeBrasseur, R. J., and six coauthors. 1978. Enhancement of sockeye salmon (Oncorhynchus nerka) by lake fertilization in Great Central Lake: summary report. Journal of the Fisheries Research Board of Canada 35:1580–1596.

Leider, S. A., M. W. Chilcote, and J. J. Loch. 1984. Spawning characteristics of sympatric populations of steelhead trout (Salmo gairdneri): evidence for partial reproductive isolation. Canadian Journal of Fisheries and Aquatic Sciences 41:1454–1462.

MacCrimmon, H. R., and T. L. Marshall. 1968. World distribution of brown trout, Salmo trutta. Journal of the Fisheries Research Board of Canada 25: 2527–2548.

Marshall, T. L. 1984. Tobique River discharge as an index of the percentage of 1-SW salmon which smoltified at age 2 and returned to Mactaquac. Canadian Atlantic Fisheries Scientific Advisory Committee, Research Document 84/95, Dartmouth, Canada.

McCormick, S. D., R. J. Naiman, and E. T. Montgomery. 1985. Physiological smolt characteristics of anadromous and non-anadromous brook trout *(Salvelinus fontinalis)* and Atlantic salmon *(Salmo salar)*. Canadian Journal of Fisheries and Aquatic Sciences 42:529–538.

McInerney, J. E. 1964. Salinity preference: an orientation mechanism in salmon migration. Journal of the Fisheries Research Board of Canada 21:995–1018.

Mills, D. 1971. Salmon and trout: a resource, its ecology, conservation and management. Oliver and Boyd, Edinburgh, Scotland.

Murray, A. R. 1968. Smolt survival and adult utilization of Little Codroy River, Newfoundland, Atlantic salmon. Journal of the Fisheries Research Board of Canada 25:2165–2218.

Myers, R. A. 1983. Evolutionary change in the proportion of precocious parr and its effect on yield in Atlantic salmon. International Council for the Exploration of the Sea, CM 1983/M:13, Copenhagen, Denmark.

Myers, R. A. 1984. Demographic consequences of precocious maturation of Atlantic salmon *(Salmo salar)*. Canadian Journal of Fisheries and Aquatic Sciences 41:1349–1353.

Myers, R. A., J. A. Hutchings, and R. J. Gibson. 1985. Variation in precocious maturation within and among populations of Atlantic salmon. International Council for the Exploration of the Sea, CM 1985/M:9, Copenhagen, Denmark.

O'Connell, M. F. 1982. The biology of anadromous *Salvelinus fontinalis* (Mitchill, 1815) and *Salmo trutta* Linnaeus, 1758 in river systems flowing into Placentia Bay and St. Mary's Bay, Newfoundland. Doctoral dissertation. Memorial University of Newfoundland, St. John's, Canada.

Osterdahl, L. 1969. The smolt run of a small Swedish river. Pages 205–215 *in* T. G. Northcote, editor. Symposium of salmon and trout in streams. H. R. MacMillan Lectures in Fisheries, University of British Columbia, Vancouver, Canada.

Parker, R. R., and R. E. Vincent. 1955. Progress reports on research studies at the Kitoi Bay research station. Pages 25–67 *in* Alaska Department of Fisheries and Game Annual Report 1955, Juneau, Alaska, USA.

Piggins, D. J., and C. P. R. Mills. 1985. Comparative aspects of the biology of naturally produced and hatchery-reared Atlantic salmon smolts *(Salmo salar* L.). Aquaculture 45:321–333.

Pippy, J. 1982. Report of the working group on the interception of mainland salmon in Newfoundland. Canadian Manuscript Report of Fisheries and Aquatic Sciences 1654.

Power, G. 1958. The evolution of freshwater races of the Atlantic salmon *(Salmo salar* L.). Journal of the Arctic Institute of North America 11:86–92.

Power, G. 1969. The salmon of Ungava Bay. Arctic

Institute of North America Technical Paper 22.

Power, G. 1980. The brook charr, *Salvelinus fontinalis*. Pages 141–203 *in* E. K. Balon, editor. Charrs: salmonid fishes of the genus *Salvelinus*. Dr. W. Junk, The Hague, The Netherlands.

Power, G. 1981. Stock characteristics and catches of Atlantic salmon *(Salmo salar)* in Québec, and Newfoundland and Labrador in relation to environmental variables. Canadian Journal of Fisheries and Aquatic Sciences 38:1601–1611.

Randall, R. G. 1985. Spawning potential and spawning requirements of Atlantic salmon in the Miramichi River, New Brunswick. Canadian Atlantic Fisheries Scientific Advisory Committee, Research Document 85/68, Dartmouth, Canada.

Randall, R. G., and E. M. P. Chadwick. 1983. Assessment of the Miramichi River salmon stock in 1982. Canadian Atlantic Fisheries Scientific Advisory Committee, Research Document 83/21, Dartmouth, Canada.

Randall, R. G., J. E. Thorpe, R. J. Gibson, and D. G. Reddin. 1986. Biological factors affecting age at maturity in Atlantic salmon *(Salmo salar)*. Canadian Special Publication of Fisheries and Aquatic Sciences 89:90–96.

Refstie, T., T. A. Steine, and T. Gjedrem. 1977. Selection experiments with salmon. II. Proportion of Atlantic salmon smoltifying at 1 year of age. Aquaculture 10:231–242.

Rich, W. H. 1920. Early history and seaward migration of chinook salmon in the Columbia and Sacramento rivers. U.S. Bureau of Fisheries Bulletin 37:1–74.

Rich, W. H., and H. B. Holmes. 1928. Experiments in marking young chinook salmon on the Columbia River, 1916 to 1927. U.S. Bureau of Fisheries Bulletin 44:215–264.

Ricker, W. E. 1972. Hereditary and environmental factors affecting certain salmonid populations. Pages 19–160 *in* R. C. Simon and P. A. Larkin, editors. The stock concept in Pacific salmon. H. R. MacMillan Lectures in Fisheries, University of British Columbia, Vancouver, Canada.

Ricker, W. E., and K. H. Loftus. 1968. Pacific salmon move east. Pages 37–39 *in* Fisheries Council of Canada Annual Review 43, Ottawa, Canada.

Robitaille, J. E., Y. Côté, G. Shooner, and G. Hayeur. 1986. Growth and maturation patterns of Atlantic salmon, *Salmo salar,* in the Koksoak River, Ungava, Quebec. Canadian Special Publication of Fisheries and Aquatic Sciences 89:62–69.

Rounsefell, G. A. 1958a. Anadromy in North American Salmonidae. U.S. Fish and Wildlife Service Fishery Bulletin 58(131):171–185.

Rounsefell, G. A. 1958b. Factors causing decline in sockeye salmon of Karluk River, Alaska. U.S. Fish and Wildlife Service Fishery Bulletin 58:79–169.

Rounsefell, G. A. 1962. Relationships among North American Salmonidae. U.S. Fish and Wildlife Service Fishery Bulletin 62:235–269.

Sano, S. 1966. Chum salmon in the far east. International North Pacific Fisheries Commission Bulletin 18:41–57.

Saunders, R. L. 1967. Seasonal pattern of return of Atlantic salmon in the Northwest Miramichi River, New Brunswick. Journal of the Fisheries Research Board of Canada 24:21–32.

Saunders, R. L. 1981. Atlantic salmon *(Salmo salar)* stocks and management implications in the Canadian Atlantic provinces and New England, USA. Canadian Journal of Fisheries and Aquatic Sciences 38:1612–1625.

Saunders, R. L., and C. B. Schom. 1985. Importance of the variation in life history parameters of Atlantic salmon *(Salmo salar)*. Canadian Journal of Fisheries and Aquatic Sciences 42:615–618.

Saxton, A. M., W. K. Hershberger, and R. N. Iwamoto. 1984. Smoltification in the net-pen culture of coho salmon: quantitative genetic analysis. Transactions of the American Fisheries Society 113:339–347.

Scott, W. B., and E. J. Crossman. 1973. Freshwater fishes of Canada. Fisheries Research Board of Canada Bulletin 184.

Shapovalov, L., and A. C. Taft. 1954. The life histories of the steelhead rainbow trout *(Salmo gairdneri gairdneri)* and silver salmon *(Oncorhynchus kisutch)* with special reference to Waddell Creek, California, and recommendations regarding their management. California Department of Fish and Game, Fish Bulletin 98.

Sharr, S., D. R. Bernard, D. N. McBride, and W. Goshert. 1985. Catch and escapement statistics for Copper River, Bering River, and Prince William Sound sockeye, chinook, coho and chum salmon, 1983. Alaska Department of Fisheries and Game, Technical Data Report 135, Juneau, Alaska, USA.

Svardson, G. 1954. Salmon stock fluctuations in the Baltic Sea. Institute of Freshwater Research Drottningholm Report 36:226–262.

Thorpe, J. E. 1986. Age at first maturity in Atlantic salmon, *Salmo salar*: freshwater period influences and conflicts with smolting. Canadian Special Publication of Fisheries and Aquatic Sciences 89:7–14.

Thorpe, J. E., and R. I. G. Morgan. 1978. Parental influence on growth rate, smolting rate and survival in hatchery reared juvenile Atlantic salmon, *Salmo salar*. Journal of Fish Biology 13:549–556.

Walters, C. J., R. Hilborn, R. M. Peterman, and M. J. Staley. 1978. Model for examining early ocean limitation of Pacific salmon production. Journal of the Fisheries Research Board of Canada 35:1303–1315.

Wedemeyer, G. A., R. L. Saunders, and W. C. Clarke. 1980. Environmental factors affecting smoltification and early marine survival of anadromous salmonids. U.S. National Marine Fisheries Service Marine Fisheries Review 42(6):1–14.

Weisbart, M. 1968. Osmotic and ionic regulation in embryos, alevins and fry of the five species of Pacific salmon. Canadian Journal of Zoology 46:385–397.

Withler, I. L. 1966. Variability in life history characteristics of steelhead trout *(Salmo gairdneri)* along the Pacific coast of North America. Journal of the Fisheries Research Board of Canada 23:365–393.

Yuen, H. J. 1984. Bristol Bay salmon *(Oncorhynchus* sp.)—1981, a compilation of catch, escapement, and biological data. Alaska Department of Fisheries and Game, Technical Data Report 129, Juneau, Alaska, USA.

American Fisheries Society Symposium 1:42–56, 1987

Reproductive Ecology of the American Eel

GENE S. HELFMAN, DOUGLAS E. FACEY, L. STANTON HALES, JR.,
AND EARL L. BOZEMAN, JR.

Zoology Department and Institute of Ecology
University of Georgia, Athens, Georgia 30602, USA

Abstract.—Male and female American eels *Anguilla rostrata* differ in several life history attributes. Females are distributed across the range of the species, occurring in all appropriate estuarine and freshwater habitats. Females mature at lengths greater than 45 cm. Both length and age at maturity appear to correlate with latitude and distance from the Sargasso Sea spawning grounds. Males are generally restricted to estuarine habitats and are most abundant in the southeastern United States. They seldom exceed 45 cm in length. No latitudinal cline in length at maturity is evident. We propose that male and female American eels experience different selection pressures, resulting in different evolutionary solutions. Males occur in highly productive habitats close to the spawning grounds, grow rapidly, and mature at a small size. Females, which increase in fecundity with increasing size, may be selected for large size at maturity. Costs associated with slow-growth (freshwater and high-latitude) habitats may be lower for females since slow growth also leads to larger size at maturity. Differences in distribution between males and females may result from male larvae settling earlier from the plankton, differential larval mortality, or a sex change to female induced by long larval intervals. Panmictic (random) spawning at a localized, upcurrent site promotes broad geographic distribution of larvae capable of surviving in many habitat types.

By any ecological measure, the American eel *Anguilla rostrata* is a successful species. The native range of the species encompasses more than 10,000 km of coastline from Greenland and Iceland to Venezuela, including many offshore islands (Boëtius 1985). Distribution is probably limited only by the vagaries of currents carrying larvae from the presumed tropical west Atlantic spawning locale and by a lack of fresh water. American eels also occur naturally in perhaps the broadest diversity of habitats of any fish species in the world. These habitats include clear, small, unproductive headwater streams dependent on allochthonous inputs; large, turbid, productive rivers; blackwater swamps and rivers; clear, subterranean springs and caves; clear and turbid, deep and shallow, vegetated and barren lakes and ponds, including bodies covered seasonally by ice; and fresh, brackish, and saltwater marshes. In many of these systems, American eels are among the numerical dominants (e.g., Smith and Saunders 1955; Ogden 1970).

Most aspects of the ecology and behavior of the species are also characterized by variability. Anguillid eels are dietary generalists, eating live and recently dead matter; the only apparent limitation on the diversity of their food is set by its availability (see Tesch 1977 and Moriarty 1978 for reviews). Variability also applies to life history traits: differences exist even within drainage systems with respect to several life history attributes, including distribution and growth of sexes and age and size at maturity (Helfman et al. 1984b).

The literature on life history attributes of American eels contains many apparent contradictions. Explanations of life history phenomena have often overlooked the substantial ecological and behavioral plasticity of anguillid eels. The view adopted here is that the American eel has evolved a mixed, generalist strategy with respect to life history traits of males and females. The intent of this paper is to propose a life history that is consistent with the information from the sometimes confusing literature on population attributes of the species, including information on breeding locale, larval distribution, genetic makeup, population structure, size, age, sex, sexual determination, differentiation, and maturation at different locales. The hypotheses developed from this review suggest that (1) males have a shorter larval period than females; (2) males have more distinct habitat preferences than females because males can benefit more from fast-growth habitats; and (3) male maturation is primarily size dependent, whereas female maturation is determined by a larger set of conditions.

Summary of Life History Information

Spawning and Larval Dispersal

American eels apparently spawn on the warm side of a thermal front in 22–25°C water in the Sargasso Sea (23–26°N, 69–74°W, February–March 1981) at less than 350 m depth (Kleckner and McCleave 1982, 1985; Kleckner et al. 1983; see McCleave et al. 1987, this volume). Leptocephali are carried northwestward and then northward via the Florida Current and Gulf Stream, the majority of individuals entering the Gulf Stream north of 30°N (approximately opposite Jacksonville, Florida). Both numbers and sizes of larvae increase between St. Augustine, Florida, and Cape Hatteras, North Carolina, perhaps because large numbers of larger leptocephali arrive directly from the western Sargasso Sea, rather than because individuals grow as they move northward with the primary currents (Kleckner and McCleave 1982). Computer simulations of larval drift indicate a broad, surprisingly uniform distribution of larvae along the North American coast (Power and McCleave 1983), rather than a substantial reduction in numbers of larvae with time and distance.

Larvae drift northward and eastward with these major currents for about 1 year before they metamorphose into glass eels, the time depending on latitude: glass eels from the Altamaha River, Georgia, estuary are 250–300 d old, which is younger than glass eels from New England and Canada (Helfman et al. 1984b; E. B. Brothers, Ithaca, New York, personal communication). In contrast, larvae of the European eel are presumed to drift for up to 6 years prior to metamorphosis (van Utrecht and Holleboom 1985). Movement shoreward is poorly understood and may involve active swimming, selective tidal-stream transport, and transport by Gulf Stream intrusions and longshore currents (e.g., Kleckner and McCleave 1982, 1985; Power and McCleave 1983; Williams and Koehn 1984). Glass eels are attracted to rivers, perhaps via olfaction (Sorensen 1986), where they transform into elvers.

Genetic evidence for panmixis.—Genetic evidence to date supports the concept of a single panmictic (randomly breeding) population of American eels. Electrophoretic studies of allozymic variation have documented relative genetic homogeneity among elvers sampled from five locales between Florida and Newfoundland, indicating dispersal from a panmictic population (Williams et al. 1973; Koehn and Williams 1978; Williams and Koehn 1984). Weak but significant geographic variation at three loci in juvenile (yellow) American eels (Williams and Koehn 1984) is believed to result from intense local selection that occurs primarily after recruitment of elvers to rivers (selection at one locus in elvers was evident). The magnitude of genetic variation in yellow American eels was remarkably small, given the vast geographic range and diversity of habitats sampled, further supporting panmixis.

Information from studies of mitochondrial DNA (mtDNA) genotypes allows even closer scrutiny of degrees of relatedness among conspecific populations. This technique (Avise and Lansman 1983; Brown 1983) has advantages over allozymic studies for distinguishing populations and providing estimates of intraspecific genealogy. In contrast to allozymes, mtDNA is inherited maternally and, therefore, is not segregated and recombined during each generation of sexual reproduction; further, mtDNA evolves rapidly and is apparently not under direct environmental selection but changes via random mutation and drift.

Avise et al. (1986) compared mtDNA genotypes of American eels at seven locales along the North American coastline from Maine to Louisiana. A characteristic mtDNA genotype predominated at all locales and was identical in 73 of the 109 individuals assayed. The remaining individuals showed minor heterogeneity; no more than two mutation steps distinguished them from the common pattern. As additional evidence of minimal divergence among samples, variant genotypes observed in two or more individuals were not confined to specific locales, and one strong polymorphism was geographically widespread and not significantly different in frequency among collections. Overall mean sequence divergence, p (Nei and Li 1979), was $\cong 0.1\%$.

Mitochondrial DNA diversity in American eels is remarkably low. Restriction-enzyme surveys of mtDNA typically indicate extensive sequence differences among conspecific but allopatric samples of other species, p being an order of magnitude higher than the values for American eels (range, 0.4–8.0%; mean, 2.1%; $N = 15$ species; Avise and Lansman 1983; Avise et al. 1984; Saunders et al. 1986). The American eel species, or lineage, can therefore be considered effectively homogeneous with respect to mtDNA. If genetic differences among locales had occurred, the data would suggest separate breeding stocks (e.g., Kleckner and McCleave 1982) in which new mtDNA genotypes had drifted to fixation. The observed homogeneous pattern suggests a panmictic population within which random mating and passive larval dispersal prevent population subdivision.

Age and Size at Maturity

In contrast to fishing practices in Europe, fisheries targeted at migrating adult (silver) American eels in North America are limited (e.g., Eales 1968), and details of the migrations are poorly known. Trends in timing, ages, sizes, and sexual differences have been summarized by Facey and Helfman (in press). These trends indicate greater ages and sizes at maturity in northern than in southern stocks, and progressively later migration times from north to south along the Atlantic coast of North America (Table 1).

In the absence of information from many regions on age, size, and sexual characteristics of silver eels, general population data can be used instead for inference. When values for mean and maximum ages from various studies of yellow eels (Table 2) are combined with information on silver eels (Table 1), the magnitude of age and size differences among regions becomes striking. At northern locales, mean and maximum ages of yellow eels range from 10 to 16 years and 18 to 23 years, respectively (Gray and Andrews 1970; Ogden 1970; Hurley 1972; Facey and LaBar 1981). In contrast, mean and maximum ages of 2.7–6.2 years and 5–15 years observed in southerly stocks (Boëtius and Boëtius 1967; Harrell and Loyacano 1982; Hansen and Eversole 1984; Helfman et al.

1984b; Ross et al. 1984) suggest that reproductive migrations occur at younger ages in the south than at northern latitudes. Size distributions in northern versus southern stocks differ similarly: individuals longer than 700 mm are rare at lower latitudes, whereas individuals longer than 800 mm are common at many northern locales.

A misleading aspect of these general comparisons is a failure to distinguish between sexes; the latitudinal trends in age and size apply primarily to females (Table 1). The total range in age of migrating male American eels, based on limited published data, is 3 to 10 years (means, 5.1–5.5 years). Ages of yellow male American eels vary from 1 to 6 years (means, 2.8–5.8 years; Gray and Andrews 1970; Hansen and Eversole 1984; Helfman et al. 1984b; Ross et al. 1984). In contrast, female silver American eels range in age from 4 to 18 years (means, 8.6–12.3 years) and female yellow eels range from 2 to 23 years (e.g., Facey and LaBar 1981; Helfman et al. 1984b). The limited data on male silver eels indicate similarities in size and perhaps age at migration across a broad region of North America, whereas sizes and ages of females generally increase with latitude.

Age and length at maturity can also be determined from frequency distributions at different locales. Several authors have interpreted a relatively sharp decline in numbers at a particular size- or age-class as representing the loss of animals due to spawning migrations (Gray and Andrews 1971; Facey and LaBar 1981; Harrell

TABLE 1.—Months of capture, lengths, and ages of migrating adult (silver) American eels caught along the Atlantic coast of North America; lengths and ages are means (ranges). Modified from Facey and Helfman (in press).

Capture locality (listed north to south)	Months of capture	Males		
		N	Length (mm)	Age (years)
Newfoundland	Aug–Sep			
Gibson Lake, New Brunswick	Autumn			
St. John River, New Brunswick	Early Autumn			
Lower St. Lawrence River	Mid Sep–late Oct			
St. Lawrence River	Aug–Oct			
St. Lawrence estuary	Aug–Oct			
Rhode Island	Sep–Nov	87	≈334 (280–400)	
Rhode Island	Sep–Nov	380	323 (304–355)	
Southeast of Cape Cod	Early Nov	1	373	
East of Assateague Island	Late Dec			
Cape Charles	Nov	52	372 (339–438)	
Upper Chesapeake Bay	Oct	84	≈306 (275–360)	≈5.1 (3–10)
Chesapeake Bay	Nov		(395–438)	
Southeast of Chesapeake Bay	Early Dec			
Cooper River, South Carolina	Aug	6	≈277 (214–322)	3.0
Georgia	Oct–Mar	73	329 (282–375)	5.5 (3–10)

[a] Ages estimated by Hurley (1972) were based on length of specimens.
[b] Means but not ranges were provided from four rivers; standard deviations: males, ±27.2 mm; females, ±73.9 mm.
[c] Five of six "silver" eels (criteria not given) were caught in August; capture date of the sixth was not given.

and Loyacano 1982; Hansen and Eversole 1984; Helfman et al. 1984b). By applying this interpretation to investigations lacking complete data on age and length of silver eels, we calculate that females mature at approximately 10 to 12 years (470–547 mm) in the Chesapeake Bay area (Foster and Brody 1982), at 11 to 13 years (490–640 mm) in New Jersey streams (Ogden 1970), and at 18 to 20 years (800–900 mm) in Lake Champlain (Facey and LaBar 1981). This indirect comparison suggests that American eels mature at larger sizes and older ages as one proceeds northward along the North American coastline. In Lake Champlain (Facey and LaBar 1981), distance from the sea may be an added variable in the relationship between latitude and age and size at maturity, although Gray and Andrews (1971) reported age and size differences in adjacent lake and river stocks in Newfoundland. Correlation analysis of life history traits with geographic variables (Table 1) supports the qualitative impressions. Average female length at maturity is significantly correlated with both latitude ($r = 0.643$; $P < 0.05$) and distance to the Sargasso Sea ($r = 0.801$; $P < 0.01$; df = 8). Male length correlates with neither factor (latitude, $P > 0.50$; distance, $P > 0.20$, df = 5). Average age at maturity in females is positively correlated with distance to the Sargasso ($r = 0.866$; $P < 0.05$) but only weakly correlated with latitude ($r = 0.633$; $P < 0.20$; df = 4). Data on male ages are too sparse to allow analysis. Whether latitude or distance have direct effects on

life history traits is unknown. The possible effect is complicated by a strong positive relationship between the two geographic variables ($r = 0.972$; $P < 0.001$).

Although differences occur in population structure as a function of latitude, variation also exists in several life history attributes on a much smaller geographic scale. Within the same river system, age of females at maturity differs. For example, Helfman et al. (1984b) found that female yellow American eels in the estuary of the Altamaha River, Georgia, seldom attained ages greater than 7 years and lengths greater than 470 mm, whereas, 80 km upriver, maximum ages and sizes for females of 13 years and 700 mm, occurred. Age distributions of males did not differ between the two sites, although estuarine males apparently grew larger. Freshwater American eels were on average older, longer, and heavier, had higher condition factors, and grew more slowly than estuarine animals.

The only other direct comparison of estuarine and freshwater American eels from the same river system and time period is that of Gray and Andrews (1971). Female, presumably silver, eels migrating from freshwater Topsail Pond, Newfoundland, grew faster and attained greater maximum ages (18 years) and sizes (931 mm) than did females from nearby brackish Topsail Barachois, where none were older than 12 years or longer than 760 mm. Hurley (1972) documented markedly different sizes, ages, and growth rates of

TABLE 1.—Extended.

Capture locality (listed north to south)	Females			Reference
	N	Length (mm)	Age (years)	
Newfoundland	92	694 (535–931)	12.3 (9–18)	Gray and Andrews (1970, 1971)
Gibson Lake, New Brunswick				Smith and Saunders (1955)
St. John River, New Brunswick				Jessop (1982)
Lower St. Lawrence River	36	(832–918)	(13–14)[a]	Hurley (1972)
St. Lawrence River	80	805 (600–1,000)		Dutil et al. (1987)
St. Lawrence estuary	91	908 (660–1,000)		Dutil et al. (1987)
Rhode Island	54	≈537 (410–800)		Winn et al. (1975)
Rhode Island	110	525 (495–588)[b]		Bianchini et al. (1983)
Southeast of Cape Cod	1	642		Wenner (1973)
East of Assateague Island	6	636 (609–658)		Wenner (1973)
Cape Charles	46	633 (418—845)		Wenner and Musick (1974)
Upper Chesapeake Bay				Foster and Brody (1982)
Chesapeake Bay		(366–452)		Wenner (1973)
Southeast of Chesapeake Bay	3	551 (512–579)		Wenner (1973)
Cooper River, South Carolina				Harrell and Loyacano (1982)[c]
Georgia	7	584 (413–682)	8.6 (4–13)	Facey and Helfman (in press)

TABLE 2.—Frequencies of occurrence of juvenile (yellow) male American eels in relation to latitude and distance from spawning site. Data are for differentiated animals and are drawn only from studies that used histological techniques for assessing sex.

Locale	% male	Total number sexed	Latitude (°N)	Approximate distance from spawning site (km)[a]	Reference
Matamek River, Quebec					
Freshwater	<1	571	51°	4,430+	Dolan and Power (1977)
Estuarine	5	40	51°	4,430	Dolan and Power (1977)
Newfoundland					
Freshwater	<1	184	47°	4,170+	Gray and Andrews (1970)
Estuarine	0	170	47°	4,170	Gray and Andrews (1970)
Lake Champlain, Vermont					
Freshwater	0	356	44°	5,200	Facey and LaBar (1981)
Chesapeake Bay, Maryland					
Freshwater–estuarine[b]	0	315	39°	2,330	Foster and Brody (1982)
Cooper River, South Carolina					
Freshwater	0	415	33°12'	1,520	Harrell and Loyacano (1982)
Estuarine	4	458	32°48'	1,470	Hansen and Eversole (1984)
Savannah River, Georgia					
Freshwater	15	65	33°16'	1,450	Helfman and Bozeman (unpublished)
Estuarine	58	111	32°8'	1,400	Helfman and Bozeman (unpublished)
Ogeechee River, Georgia					
Freshwater	26	132	32°8'	1,400	
Estuarine	25	172	31°54'	1,380	
Freshwater pond	4	22	32°47'	1,650	Facey and Helfman (in press)
Altamaha River, Georgia					
Freshwater	6	212	31°38'	1,410	Helfman et al. (1984b)
Estuarine	36	203	31°21'	1,350	Helfman et al. (1984b)
Satilla River, Georgia					
Freshwater	0	27	31°13'	1,360	Helfman and Bozeman (unpublished)
Estuarine	33	150	30°58'	1,320	Helfman and Bozeman (unpublished)
Mississippi, Alabama					
Estuarine[c]	5	82	30°15'	2,050	Ross et al. (1984)

[a] Distance was measured along straight-line segments. Larvae headed for Atlantic coast locales were assumed to enter the Gulf Stream from the Sargasso Sea at 30°N, 80°W (Kleckner and McCleave 1982). Larvae headed for Gulf of Mexico locales were assumed to follow the shortest straight lines.

[b] "Tidal freshwater."

[c] Four estuarine sites; gear bias may have excluded small males.

American eels in Lake Ontario and in the Ottawa River, 120 km north. Smith and Saunders (1955) looked at American eels from 15 locales in the Maritime Provinces of Canada and found different maximum lengths (520–870 mm) but similar maximum ages.

Sex Ratios

Juveniles.—Although American eels occur throughout the river drainages of eastern North America, sex ratios vary considerably in different geographic locales (Table 2). Males are noticeably lacking from collections of juvenile (yellow) American eel stocks made throughout most of the northern portion of the species' range. Juvenile males have been found abundantly only in four Georgia rivers; even at these locales, females constituted more than 60% of the local stock (only investigations employing histological analysis of sex are discussed here, for reasons outlined in Dolan and Power 1977; the trends discussed are also generally supported by studies employing macroscopic examination, e.g., Vladykov 1966).

Sex ratios differ not only regionally, but also within a given drainage system. Where males are numerous, they are relatively abundant in estuaries (Table 2), and are often absent from collections made in upriver habitats. At northern latitudes, males are rare but slightly more abundant in brackish than in fresh water (Gray and Andrews 1970; Dolan and Power 1977). Comparative data from intermediate latitudes (33°N to 47°N) are unavailable.

Although a latitudinal cline in the distribution of males is suggested, rivers close to one another are likely to support different sex ratios (Table 2). For example, the Altamaha, Ogeechee, and Savannah rivers flow into the Atlantic Ocean within an 80 km stretch of Georgia coastline, and the mouths of the Ogeechee and Savannah River are less than 15 km apart. Yet male American eels in those three rivers constitute 6–26% of the freshwater stocks and 25–58% of the estuarine stocks. Samples of yellow eels from the Cooper River estuary, 150 km north of the Savannah River, contained only 4% males, and no males were captured in samples taken upriver. Conditions favoring the existence of males may differ over relatively short distances.

Another sex-related difference involves mobility and home range. The widespread distribution of American eels attests to the animals' mobility; much of this movement occurs in the yellow eel phase (see Williams and Koehn 1984). Studies of seasonal migration patterns and home ranges of juvenile American eels indicate that animals in riverine or lacustrine habitats tend to be relatively mobile, engaging in seasonal movements and having relatively large home ranges (e.g., Smith and Saunders 1955; Hurley 1972; LaBar and Facey 1983; but see Gunning and Shoop 1962). Estuarine American eels tend to be relatively sedentary, exhibiting little evidence of seasonal movements and having relatively restricted home ranges (Helfman et al. 1983, 1984a; Ross et al. 1984; Bozeman et al. 1985; Ford and Mercer 1986). Although such a difference may be habitat- rather than sex-dependent, estuarine stocks, which typically include more males, tend to be relatively less mobile in both the short and long term. Higher productivity in estuaries (Odum 1971) may preclude the necessity for extensive foraging and seasonal movements (Hansen and Eversole 1984; Helfman et al. 1984b).

Adults.—Sex ratios of American eels are also confusing because the ratios may differ between samples of silver and yellow eels at the same locale. For example, only one of 22 yellow eels captured in a pond on the Ogeechee River, Georgia, was male, whereas all nine silver eels captured during the same period were male; 91% of all silver eels caught in Georgia over 3 years were male, whereas males never constituted more than 58% of the stock—usually much less—at any one locale (Helfman et al. 1984b; Facey and Helfman, in press; see Table 2). Similarly, no males were found among 415 yellow eels from the Cooper River, South Carolina (Table 2), but all six silver eels captured were male (Harrell and Loyacano 1982). No males occurred among more than 1,000 yellow eels from various locales around Chesa-

peake Bay, but 84 male (and no female) silver eels were taken in one October collection at one locale (Foster and Brody 1982). Wenner and Musick (1974) obtained 52 male and 46 female silver eels from commercial fishermen in the Chesapeake Bay, further indicating an unexpectedly high proportion of migrating males. Males predominated among silver eels captured in Rhode Island (Winn et al. 1975; Bianchini et al. 1983), although histological assessment of sex ratios of yellow eels has not been reported for that area.

Sexual Determination and Differentiation

The topic of sexual determination in anguillids has been debated actively in the European literature for more than 75 years (e.g., Bellini 1907; see Parsons et al. 1977 and Wiberg 1983 for reviews). Several major questions remain unanswered. Is determination genetic or phenotypic? If determination is phenotypic, what conditions trigger it? Are all eels equipotentially male and female and, if so, for how long?

Evidence for genetic determination of sex has been drawn from decreasing male abundance with increasing latitude and elver size (Vladykov 1966) and from observations of sex chromosomes in European eels, females being the heteromorphic sex (reviewed in Wiberg 1983). Vladykov (1966) found smaller elvers in southern North America where juvenile males were more abundant, and concluded that smaller elvers became males, whereas larger elvers became females. European eels may develop similarly (e.g., Bellini 1907; Kuhlmann 1975). Although Vladykov (1966) may have overestimated male abundance (Sinha and Jones 1966; Dolan and Power 1977), his observations regarding distribution of male American eels have been partially confirmed (Helfman 1984b; see below). Increasing larval size with increasing latitude has also been reported by Kleckner and McCleave (1982).

The hypothesis of genetic determination (Vladykov 1966) was tested by Vladykov and Liew (1982), who stocked elvers from different sources in the same pond during different years. The resulting proportions of males varied from 27 to 71% between studies. Vladykov and Liew (1982) felt these results demonstrated that sex of *A. rostrata* was determined upon fertilization and not influenced by environment. However, more males were produced in the trial that began with 30% more elvers, and these elvers came from a locale nearer to the sea than in the other trial. The source of elvers may have influenced sex ratios, or differences in elver densities between trials could have affected growth conditions, resulting in different sex ratios (see below). The results of their study therefore appear inconclusive.

Studies of presumed sex chromosomes in European eels have also led to alternative interpretations. Inaccuracies in most earlier studies were pointed out by Wiberg (1983), who concluded that no consistent heteromorphism occurred that could be interpreted as sex chromosomes. H-Y antibody studies (Wiberg 1982) indicate females are in fact heterogametic, despite lacking definitive sex chromosomes (see Wachtel and Koo 1981). Wiberg (1983) proposed that sex determination was largely phenotypic and that higher developmental temperatures favor maleness, perhaps via protogynous sex reversal. Colombo et al. (1984) proposed that, based on histological evidence, differentiated female gonads are irreversible once eels exceed 175–200 mm in length. They found that complete male sexual differentiation did not occur until the beginning of sexual maturation to silver eels; testes of many smaller males included oocytes and, therefore, would not be irreversibly differentiated, leaving the possibility of phenotypic control of sex. Wiberg's (1982) H-Y antigen studies indicate considerable sexual plasticity, perhaps in the form of protandrous (male first) sex change. Additional study is needed to establish the stage at which sex reversal or determination occurs.

A positive correlation between elver or juvenile density and frequency of males in stocks of European eels is the primary evidence for phenotypic determination of sex (see Sinha and Jones 1975, Parsons et al. 1977, and Tesch 1977 for reviews). Application of these ideas to American eels is difficult because little data exist on elver densities (Sorensen and Bianchini 1986). An indirect measure might be abundance of yellow eels in estuarine regions, which presumably reflects the densities of previously recruited elvers. Sex ratios of yellow eels are unknown for most estuarine locales for which density estimates exist (e.g., Bianchini et al. 1982; Ford and Mercer 1986). Appropriate data are available only for Biloxi Bay, Mississippi (Ross et al. 1984), and the Altamaha River, Georgia (Helfman et al. 1984b; Bozeman et al. 1985). Biloxi Bay contained 200–500 eels/hectare, whereas the Georgia site contained 180–230 eels/hectare. If the two studies were similarly accurate, the density–sex determination hypothesis would predict males to be more common at the Mississippi locale. Ross et al. (1984) reported 5% males there, although sampling bias may have caused male abundance to be underestimated; Helfman et al. (1984b) found 36% males at the Georgia site. These findings do not confirm the presumed positive correlation between density and frequency of males. A fishery-based, regional analysis of eel densities (Kleckner and McCleave 1985) indicated that the St. Lawrence estuary and New Jersey-to-Virginia region have the densest American eel populations, whereas the southeastern Atlantic and Gulf of Mexico regions have the lowest densities. Their findings suggest an inverse relationship between American eel density and male abundance. Consequently, no viable explanation exists for determination of sex or distribution of sexes in American eels.

Sexual differentiation in American eels is more straightforward than determination, but is still complicated. Differentiation does not occur until the yellow eel phase, generally at lengths between 250 and 300 mm (e.g., Gray and Andrews 1970; Dolan and Power 1977; Hansen and Eversole 1984; Helfman et al. 1984b). Considerable overlap in length between differentiated and undifferentiated animals is common, however; females as small as 166 mm and males as small as 209 mm co-occur with undifferentiated animals 320–350 mm long. Ages also overlap; some undifferentiated animals are 2–4 years older than some differentiated animals, at least in the southeastern United States (Hansen and Eversole 1984; Helfman et al. 1984b). In Canada, differentiated American eels may be typically older than undifferentiated animals (e.g., Gray and Andrews 1970). Other anguillids apparently follow a similar pattern, differentiating at lengths of about 250–300 mm (e.g., Satoh et al. 1962; Colombo et al. 1984).

The Life History Scenario

Male versus Female Solutions

Life history characteristics of male and female American eels (Table 3) suggest sexually dimorphic life histories: differences in distribution produce skewed sex ratios, males being common only in estuaries of the southeastern United States; ages and sizes at maturity differ, these sizes overlapping little; males appear to vary much less in size at maturity than females; age and size at maturity correlate more strongly with latitude for females than for males; the timing of spawning migrations, correlated with latitude, may differ between sexes.

TABLE 3.—Known and postulated life history characteristics of American eels. Characteristics marked with an asterisk (*) are extrapolated from studies of European eels. Parenthetical numbers following postulated traits refer to the respective characteristics listed first in the table.

Known or generally assumed characteristics

(1) Panmictic breeding (random mating) in Sargasso Sea (approximately 25°N, 70°W)
(2) Semelparity—breed once and die
(3) Random larval dispersal via major currents
(4) Initial sex ratios close to equality
(5) Larval size increases with latitude
(6) Variable larval interval prior to settling
(7) Overlap in size and age between differentiated and undifferentiated fish, at least at low latitudes
(8) Phenotypic control of sex*
(9) Females heterogametic, without sex chromosomes*
(10) Experimental induction of maleness in dense populations*
(11) Juveniles are habitat and trophic generalists
(12) Female-dominated juvenile (and operational?) sex ratios throughout geographic and habitat range
(13) Males most common in southeastern United States and in estuaries
(14) Estuarine growth rates faster, at least in southeastern United States
(15) Females larger and older than males, with little overlap of size of mature fish and narrower variance in length (and age?) of males (300–400 mm) than of females (500–900 mm)
(16) Female growth rates faster
(17) Latitudinal cline in timing of reproductive migrations
(18) "Spontaneous" appearance of mature males, with largest males migrating earlier in the season*

Postulated determinants, selection pressures, and life history characteristics

Males time, energy, and risk minimizers; females size maximizers (5, 13–16)
Larval duration differs between sexes, with male interval shorter (3–6, 8, 13), or male larvae change to female after some given interval (4–6, 8, 9, 12)
Male distribution minimizes transit costs to and from spawning grounds (1, 3, 6, 13, 14)
Male size at maturation relatively fixed, female relatively open (7, 15, 18)
Female maturation determined by combination of size, energetic stores, environmental conditions, and distance to spawning grounds; male maturation determined primarily by size (14, 15, 18)
Male reproductive migrations widespread temporally, females pulsed (18)
Size-dependent fecundity encourages upriver or high-latitude occurrence and slow growth in females (11–15).

Males and females, therefore, may have evolved different life history solutions in response to different selection pressures. Males mature rapidly and at a small size. This time-constrained strategy contrasts with that of females, which increase their fecundity through increased size and thus are selected to reproduce at the largest size possible. In the size-advantage models of Ghiselin (1969) and Warner (1975), large body size has little relative effect on male fitness, provided that size-related social interactions do not affect spawning success. Females, however, are generally constrained by energetic costs of gamete production. In eels as well as other fishes, egg production is directly related to body size: larger females produce more eggs (Wenner and Musick 1974; Wootton 1984). These conditions promote the evolution of small body size in males and large body size in females.

Unique to American eels is not that males are smaller than females, but that males also differ in habitat choice and geographic distribution. Are the selection pressures favoring small size in males related to the pressures determining habitat, geography, and the tactics through which males achieve their different life history? Male American eels appear to minimize many costs associated with achieving reproductive size. They mature at younger ages and smaller sizes than females. They occur primarily in southeastern United States estuaries, the closest region to the spawning area, thus minimizing distances of both larval and reproductive migrations. They reduce intraspecific predation by remaining downriver while still elvers, thereby avoiding areas with highly cannibalistic, large females (e.g., Moriarty 1978, 1987 [this volume]). They may avoid seasonal migrations that characterize female stocks in upriver locales. They settle and remain in estuarine areas of relatively high, constant productivity compared with upriver habitats of females. Males may, therefore, mature when they attain some minimum size, perhaps related to a swimming-speed–body-size relationship and the energy stores needed to migrate to the spawning region. Whenever an individual male attains that size, it should migrate, it being assumed that females will occur on the breeding grounds.

Few advantages accrue to a small female, however; benefits instead increase directly with increasing size. To achieve the largest size possible, females probably incur greater energetic and temporal costs. They engage in extensive postlarval and seasonal migrations, dispersing over a wide geographic and habitat range. The greater energetic stores of larger eels (Tesch 1977) may promote survival during unfavorable periods or seasons of slow growth. Females can afford to wait through bad years of minimal growth because all growth increases fecundity. The waiting game of achieving large size does, however, entail costs. An individual can be killed at any size and age, but large size reduces this probability (e.g., Paine 1976; Werner and Gilliam 1984; see also Gibbons et al. 1981). Hence, larger females probably experience minimal predation and may also be relatively successful competitors (see Moriarty 1987).

The size at which males should mature can then be predicted from the size range of females. We assume that maturation size depends on energetic stores needed for migration to the Sargasso Sea, and that females also invest more in gametes. Because males generally occur closer to the Sargasso Sea than females, they can afford to be smaller than females. If too small, however, costs associated with predation and the swimming-speed–body-size relationship again become substantial. Hence, males would be expected to mature at a smaller size than the minimum at which females mature; females further from the spawning grounds would be expected to mature at larger sizes than females that are closer. The average size at which males mature is 300–400 mm, whereas females mature at average sizes of 500–800 mm (Table 1).

Rather than males preferring estuaries and females preferring riverine habitats (e.g., Moriarty 1978), females may prefer neither estuaries nor upriver habitats. Estuaries are productive regions that promote rapid growth. Rapid growth apparently mandates rapid maturation in many fishes (see Stearns and Crandall 1984 for review), such that rapidly growing females seldom achieve large size (e.g., Vladykov and Liew 1982). Latitudinal clines in size and age at maturity in other fish species (e.g., Loesch 1987, this volume) suggest a general physiological process whereby long growing seasons cause relatively rapid maturation. Females in estuaries mature faster (younger) than upriver females, but at a smaller size (Helfman et al. 1984a, 1984b), thereby incurring a fitness cost due to the direct relationship between body size and fecundity. Consequently, in contrast to male American eels, which inhabit estuaries where they grow and mature rapidly, some females inhabit estuaries and mature rapidly at small size whereas others move upriver and grow slowly but mature at larger sizes.

Sexually dimorphic strategies might explain differences in timing of reproductive migrations between sexes within a given river system. (Latitudinal differences in dates of migrations probably serve to synchronize arrival of silver eels from different regions on the spawning grounds: see Wenner 1973; Facey and Helfman, in press; Table 2). In many places, male silver eels are relatively abundant, even though immature males are apparently absent in that region (e.g., Winn et al. 1975;

Foster and Brody 1982; Facey and Helfman, in press). This might result if strong differences in both the frequency and duration of reproductive migrations occurred between sexes, perhaps reflecting differences in the internal and external cues that prompt spawning migrations. Migration of females may be governed by the synchrony of complex internal cues (length, weight, age, gonad size, fat or energy reserves), and external cues (climate, rainfall and river height, distance to the spawning grounds, social factors). Female migration could then be delayed until such cues occurred in concert, resulting in temporally pulsed, simultaneous migration of many females. The probability that an investigator will encounter migrating females is low, therefore, unless sampling is extensive and continuous.

If migration of males occurs according to a relatively fixed, size-dependent schedule, such movement could be spread over a migrational season, the duration of which would be determined largely by when different individuals attained threshold size. Some migrating males would probably be captured in a periodic sampling protocol. The idea that males mature on a relatively fixed, size-dependent basis could be tested indirectly by monitoring sizes of males that migrated on different dates. Males that reached migration size prior to the usual migration season should delay migration; they would presumably continue to grow until they migrated. This buildup of maturing animals should then migrate during the first migratory waves of the season and should consist of larger animals than those that reach appropriate size during the season itself. Such a pattern would also account for the observed size range of migrating males, which does not correlate as well with latitude as it does for females. No data relevant to this hypothesis are available for American eels, although some support exists from studies on European eels. Deelder (1970) reported that the largest male silver eels of *A. anguilla* migrate first in Dutch waters; average lengths then decrease during a migratory season.

Sex Determination

Both genotype and environment probably combine to determine sex (see also Williams and Koehn 1984). But when and why does genetic control give way to environmental influence? We propose that sex determination and differentiation in American eels depend on events during two phases: the planktonic larval period and the period shortly after metamorphosis and settlement in the juvenile habitat. Short planktonic periods and rapid initial growth favor maleness, whereas extended larval periods and slow growth favor femaleness. This hypothesis, an extension of the conservative male versus size-maximizing female strategies, is supported by the distribution of sexes in North America (Table 2) and the growth conditions encountered where the two sexes are found.

Evidence of the influence of duration of the larval period on sex determination includes the greater abundance of male American eels closer to the Sargasso Sea (Table 2) and the species' ability to vary the length of its larval interval; southeastern elvers are younger than more northerly individuals. The latitudinal distribution of sexes could then arise if males have either a larval phase that cannot be extended as it can be for females or a varied larval interval that, when extended beyond some period, results in sex change to females. Cohorts of larvae carried longer by currents would become increasingly female, and the proportion of males among the juvenile population should be greatest in habitats closest to the spawning region.

Latitudinal differences in larvae and elvers support the larval duration hypothesis. Small elvers were found at southerly locales by Vladykov (1966), and smaller (but not necessarily younger) larvae were found off eastern Florida than occurred further north (Kleckner and McCleave 1982). Relatively small larvae may spend less time in the plankton. Vladykov (1966) proposed that small elvers became males, whereas larger elvers found further north became females. A similar mechanism has been suggested for European eels (e.g., Bellini 1907; Kuhlmann 1975).

Environmental conditions after larval settlement may also influence sexual determination. For European eels, population density in estuaries has been reported to affect sexual determination, maleness resulting from negative effects of crowding (Tesch 1977). Experimental results suggesting a positive correlation between elver density and male abundance have failed to control for differential mortality between sexes, or may have used founder populations with skewed sex ratios (e.g., Parsons et al. 1977; see Sinha and Jones 1966 and Vladykov and Liew 1982 for additional critiques). We instead view estuaries as favorable environments for anguillid eels. Male American eels are most abundant in southeastern salt marshes characterized by high productivity and long growing seasons (Turner 1976; Linthurst and Reimold 1978; Gallagher et al. 1980). American eels in Georgia, South Carolina, and Bermuda estuaries (31–33°N) grow faster than more northerly animals and animals in upriver habitats in the same river (Boëtius and Boëtius 1967; Hansen and Eversole 1984; Helfman et al. 1984a, 1984b; no upriver data are available for Bermuda). If male American eels are most abundant where eel density is highest, it seems logical that favorable growth conditions promote rather than proscribe maleness.

An apparent contradiction to the above argument is the observation that females grow faster among American, European, African, and Japanese anguillids (Tesch 1977; Helfman et al. 1984b). Slow overall growth of male anguillids could reflect a decrease in growth after differentiation or with the onset of maturation (Smith and Saunders 1955; Gray and Andrews 1971; Egusa 1979; Hurley and Christie 1982; Helfman et al. 1984a, 1984b), suggesting a shift of energy from somatic to gonadal compartments (e.g., Iles 1984). In contrast to males, females generally differentiate at considerably smaller sizes and younger ages than those at which they mature; they could continue growing at relatively fast rates until maturation. Hence, sex differences in growth rate between sexes may have little bearing on the possible effects of growing conditions on sex determination.

We therefore view locales with naturally dense populations as a reflection of advantageous living conditions. Males might choose such habitats to maximize growth rates and minimize time required to reach maturity. Males need travel no further than southeastern estuaries to find appropriate habitat. This male strategy dictates settlement in the nearest appropriate habitat from the spawning grounds, and would also explain low male abundance at high latitudes. Females, however, could pursue a variable strategy with respect to habitat choice. Many females remain in estuaries where they are numerically dominant; density-dependent sex determination does not adequately explain why females predominate and grow well in estuarine habitats where males occur. One possible caveat in this discussion concerns instantaneous or initial versus population or operational (breeding) sex ratios. Although sampling at a given time may indicate few males, rapid maturation and turnover of males, or greater mortality of females during maturation and migration, could produce an operational sex ratio closer to parity. An understanding of the possible interaction of life history differences and sex ratios requires accurate calculation of life table variables for American eels (e.g., Trivers 1985).

A prematuration sex reversal, rather than differential mortality, could also explain the observed distribution patterns. Biochemical and histological evidence suggests that animals born female remain so, whereas some males may be able to change to females (Wiberg 1982; Colombo et al. 1984). Long larval periods might favor such change in sexually labile individuals. Females at southerly latitudes could be genetic females carried directly by ocean currents, plus males entrained off southern coastlines and induced to change sex to females. Postsettlement conditions, such as favorable estuarine habitats, might discourage sex reversal. The small size at which males mature means high vulnerability to predators. If males spend a prolonged period as small individuals, as would occur in the slow-growth conditions of upriver habitats, these costs could become extreme (Werner et al. 1983). Some undifferentiated males upriver might therefore benefit by switching to female. Females could even shorten the time spent as small fish by residing initially in fast-growth estuaries and then moving upriver to slow-growth environments.

Tests of the Hypotheses

The influences of larval duration and estuarine growth conditions on sexual determination are testable. Both influences could be investigated by reciprocal transplantation of larvae or recently transformed glass eels to different estuarine habitats. Larvae should be captured offshore at different latitudes or distances from the spawning grounds. Densities would have to be controlled throughout such trials; density dependence and Wiberg's (1983) hypothesis of temperature-dependent determination could be tested simultaneously. Electron microscopic analysis of the chemical composition of different annuli in an otolith (T. J. Mulligan and F. D. Martin, unpublished) could indicate if females spend an initial period in rapid-growth habitats (estuaries) prior to moving upriver, thereby minimizing time spent as small, predator-vulnerable individuals (e.g., Haro 1987, this volume). Although logistically difficult, such experiments would prove invaluable.

The larval duration hypothesis could also be tested by assessing the frequency of males among samples of juvenile eels at different distances from the spawning region. Sampling must include all appropriate size classes and employ histology for

determining sex. If rapid growth alone favors maleness, regardless of larval duration (as suggested by G. W. LaBar, University of Vermont, personal communication), stocks in the northern Gulf of Mexico should contain higher frequencies of males than stocks at similar latitudes but closer to the spawning region (e.g., Georgia, north Florida). Sex ratios have not been determined over most of the range of the species. Critical areas for such sampling are the northeastern Gulf of Mexico, both coasts of Florida, the middle Atlantic United States, Bermuda, and Iceland. Bermuda would also provide a test of the growth condition hypothesis. Bermuda is roughly the same distance from the spawning region as Rhode Island but, because of latitude and the Gulf Stream, should have a longer growing season and, therefore, more males than Rhode Island (provided that larvae destined for Bermuda enter the Gulf Stream at about 30°N, 70°W before being transported northeastward; see Kleckner and McCleave 1982; Power and McCleave 1983).

Panmixis, Ecological Plasticity, and Life History

Panmixis, as indicated from genetic investigations of American eels, represents an extreme breeding strategy along a continuum, the other extreme being inbreeding. Inbreeding permits rapid fixation of beneficial traits in a population, but has the presumed cost of a reduced ability to adapt to environmental change. In panmixis, each adult has a high probability of combining genes with a mate that experienced different selection pressures, which would maximize adaptability to changing environments but limit directional selection.

The primary advantages of panmixis lie in its extreme bet-hedging nature (Stearns 1977). In a large population with unpredictable larval dispersal to many habitats, assortative mating would be risky. Assume mating by two American eels from a headwater stream in the Canadian Maritimes. Their offspring would be best adapted to cold water of low productivity, relatively few predators and competitors, and extreme winter temperatures (e.g., Smith 1966; Scott and Crossman 1973). Larvae from such a spawning might be transported to the Maritimes, but are also likely to settle in a highly productive, turbid, predator- and competitor-dense, tepid southeastern United States river. Most larvae from such a spawning probably would be unsuccessful in many of the habitat types in which American eels occur. Alternatively, promiscuous, random mating would, over generations, cause constant reshuffling and recombining of the gene pool, producing individuals genetically prepared for most habitat types (see Vrijenhoek and Lerman 1982). One result would be considerable genetic similarity among larvae despite strong selection in different juvenile habitats (e.g., Williams and Koehn 1984). This scenario parallels the observed and presumed conditions of breeding and genetic differentiation by American eels.

The apparent spawning locale of American eels then becomes an integral part of a panmictic life history strategy. An organism adapted to a broad variety of habitat types and with a long-lived planktonic larva that can extend its larval period while drifting with ocean currents would be expected to spawn where currents maximized larval dispersal to the range of appropriate habitat types. In this manner, panmixis, passive larval dispersal, diverse juvenile habitats, and sexual and ecological plasticity all serve to reinforce each other as selection pressures producing a highly successful, widespread, generalist species.

Acknowledgments

The ideas presented here have developed in the course of discussions with and assistance from J. C. Avise, E. B. Bermingham, H. S. Horn, J. L. Meyer, J. Pickering, H. R. Pulliam, and N. C. Saunders. G. W. LaBar, J. D. McCleave, and G. C. Williams critiqued an earlier draft. This work is a result of research sponsored by the National Oceanic and Atmospheric Administration's Office of Sea Grant under grants NA80AA-D-00091 and NA84AA-D-00072.

References

Avise, J. C., G. S. Helfman, N. C. Saunders, and L. S. Hales. 1986. Mitochondrial DNA differentiation and life history pattern in North Atlantic eels. Proceedings of the National Academy of Sciences of the United States of America 83:4350–4354.

Avise, J. C., and R. A. Lansman. 1983. Polymorphism of mitochondrial DNA in populations of higher animals. Pages 147–164 in M. Nei and R. K. Koehn, editors. Evolution of genes and proteins. Sinauer, Sunderland, Massachusetts, USA.

Avise, J. C., J. E. Neigel, and J. Arnold. 1984. Demographic influences on mitochondrial DNA lineage survivorship in animal populations. Journal of Molecular Evolution 20:99–105.

Bellini, A. 1907. Experiences sur l'elevage de l'anguille en stabulation a comacchio. Bulletin de la Société Centrale d'Aquiculture et de Pêche, Paris III-x:1–40.

Bianchini, M., P. W. Sorensen, and H. E. Winn. 1982. Stima dell'abbondanza e schemi di movimento a breve raggio della anguilla Americana, Anguilla rostrata, nel Narrow River, Rhode Island, USA. Naturalista Siciliano (supplement 4) 6(2):269–277. (Translated by P. W. Sorensen.)

Bianchini, M., H. E. Winn, and P. W. Sorensen. 1983. Differences among populations of American eels from adjacent river basins. Nova Thalassia 6 (supplement):701–703.

Boëtius, I., and J. Boëtius. 1967. Eels, Anguilla rostrata LeSueur, in Bermuda. Videnskabelige Meddelelser fra Dansk Naturhistorisk Forening i Khobenhavn 130:63–84.

Boëtius, J. 1985. Greenland eels, Anguilla rostrata LeSueur. Dana 4:41–48.

Bozeman, E. L., G. S. Helfman, and T. Richardson. 1985. Population size and home range of American eels in a Georgia tidal creek. Transactions of the American Fisheries Society 114:821–825.

Brown, W. M. 1983. Evolution of animal mitochondrial DNA. Pages 62–88 in M. Nei and R. K. Koehn, editors. Evolution of genes and proteins. Sinauer, Sunderland, Massachusetts, USA.

Colombo, G., G. Grandi, and R. Rossi. 1984. Gonad differentiation and body growth in Anguilla anguilla L. Journal of Fish Biology 24:215–228.

Deelder, C. L. 1970. Synopsis of biological data on the eel Anguilla anguilla (Linnaeus) 1758. FAO (Food and Agricultural Organization of the United Nations) Fishery Synopsis 80.

Dolan, J. A., and G. Power. 1977. Sex ratio of American eels, Anguilla rostrata, from the Matamek River system, Quebec, with remarks on problems in sexual identification. Journal of the Fisheries Research Board of Canada 34:294–299.

Dutil, J.-D., M. Besner, and S. D. McCormick. 1987. Osmoregulatory and ionoregulatory changes and associated mortalities during the transition of maturing American eels to a marine environment. American Fisheries Society Symposium 1:175–190.

Eales, J. G. 1968. The eel fisheries of eastern Canada. Fisheries Research Board of Canada Bulletin 166.

Egusa, S. 1979. Notes on the culture of the European eel (Anguilla anguilla L.) in Japanese eel-farming ponds. Rapports et Procès-Verbaux des Rèunions, Council Internationale pour l'Exploration de la Mer 174:51–58.

Facey, D. E., and G. S. Helfman. In press. Reproductive migrations of American eels in Georgia. Proceedings of the Annual Conference Southeastern Association of Fish and Wildlife Agencies 39.

Facey, D. E., and G. W. LaBar. 1981. Biology of American eels in Lake Champlain, Vermont. Transactions of the American Fisheries Society 110:396–402.

Ford, T. E., and E. Mercer. 1986. Density, size distribution and home range of American eels, Anguilla rostrata, in a Massachusetts salt marsh. Environmental Biology of Fishes 17:309–314

Foster, J. W. S., III, and R. W. Brody. 1982. Status report: the American eel fishery in Maryland, 1982.

Maryland Tidewater Administration, Tidal Fisheries Division, Annapolis, Maryland, USA.

Gallagher, J. L., R. J. Reimold, R. A. Linthurst, and W. J. Pfeiffer. 1980. Aerial production, mortality, and mineral accumulation—export dynamics in *Spartina alterniflora* and *Juncus roemerianus* plant stands. Ecology 61:303–312.

Ghiselin, M. T. 1969. The evolution of hermaphroditism among animals. Quarterly Review of Biology 44:189–208.

Gibbons, J. W., R. D. Semlitsch, J. L. Greene, and J. P. Schubauer. 1981. Variation in age and size at maturity of the slider turtle *(Pseudemys scripta)*. American Naturalist 117:841–845.

Gray, R. W., and C. W. Andrews. 1970. Sex ratio of the American eel *Anguilla rostrata* (LeSueur) in Newfoundland waters. Canadian Journal of Zoology 48:483–487.

Gray, R. W., and C. W. Andrews. 1971. Age and growth of the American eel *Anguilla rostrata* (LeSueur) in Newfoundland waters. Canadian Journal of Zoology 49:121–128.

Gunning, G. E., and C. R. Shoop. 1962. Restricted movements of the American eel, *Anguilla rostrata* (LeSueur) in freshwater streams, with comments on growth rate. Tulane Studies in Zoology 9:265–272.

Hansen, R. A., and A. G. Eversole. 1984. Age, growth, and sex ratio of American eels in brackish water portions of a South Carolina river. Transactions of the American Fisheries Society 113:744–749.

Haro, A. J. 1987. Pigmentation, size, and upstream migration of elvers and young American eels in a coastal Rhode Island stream. American Fisheries Society Symposium 1:558.

Harrell, R. M., and H. H. Loyacano, Jr. 1982. Age, growth and sex ratio of the American eel in the Cooper River, South Carolina. Proceedings of the Annual Conference Southeastern Association of Fish and Wildlife Agencies 34:349–359.

Helfman, G. S., E. L. Bozeman, and E. B. Brothers. 1984a. Comparison of American eel growth rates from tag returns and length–age analyses. U.S. National Marine Fisheries Service Fishery Bulletin 82:519–522.

Helfman, G. S., E. L. Bozeman, and E. B. Brothers. 1984b. Size, sex, and age of American eels in a Georgia river. Transactions of the American Fisheries Society 113:132–141.

Helfman, G. S., D. L. Stoneburner, E. L. Bozeman, P. A. Christian, and R. Whalen. 1983. Ultrasonic telemetry of American eel movements in a tidal creek. Transactions of the American Fisheries Society 112:105–110.

Hurley, D. A. 1972. The American eel *(Anguilla rostrata)* in eastern Lake Ontario. Journal of the Fisheries Research Board of Canada 29:535–543.

Hurley, D. A., and W. J. Christie. 1982. A reexamination of statistics pertaining to growth, yield and escapement in the American eel *(Anguilla rostrata)* stocks of Lake Ontario. Pages 83–85 *in* K. H. Loftus, editor. Proceedings of the 1980 North

American eel conference. Ontario Ministry of Natural Resources, Ontario Fisheries Technical Report Series 4, Toronto, Canada.

Iles, T. D. 1984. Allocation of resources to gonad and soma in Atlantic herring, *Clupea harengus*. Pages 331–348 *in* G. W. Potts and R. J. Wootton, editors. Fish reproduction: strategies and tactics. Academic Press, New York, New York, USA.

Jessop, B. M. 1982. A review of the status and management of commercial fisheries for American eels *(Anguilla rostrata)* in the maritime provinces. Pages 28–32 in K. H. Loftus, editor. Proceedings of the 1980 North American eel conference. Ontario Ministry of Natural Resources, Ontario Fisheries Technical Report Series 4, Toronto, Canada.

Kleckner, R. C., and J. D. McCleave. 1982. Entry of migrating American eel leptocephali into the Gulf Stream system. Helgoländer Wissenschaftliche Meeresuntersuchungen 35:329–339.

Kleckner, R. C., and J. D. McCleave. 1985. Spatial and temporal distribution of American eel larvae in relation to North Atlantic ocean current systems. Dana 4:67–92.

Kleckner, R. C., J. D. McCleave, and G. S. Wippelhauser. 1983. Spawning of American eel, *Anguilla rostrata,* relative to thermal fronts in the Sargasso Sea. Environmental Biology of Fishes 9:289–293.

Koehn, R. C., and G. C. Williams. 1978. Genetic differentiation without isolation in the American eel, *Anguilla rostrata.* II. Temporal stability of geographic patterns. Evolution 32:624–637.

Kuhlmann, H. 1975. The influence of temperature, food, size, and origin on the sexual differentiation of elvers *(Anguilla anguilla)*. Helgoländer Wissenschaftliche Meeresuntersuchungen 27:139–155. (In German with English abstract.)

LaBar, G. W., and D. E. Facey. 1983. Local movements and inshore population sizes of American eels in Lake Champlain, Vermont. Transactions of the American Fisheries Society 112:111–116.

Linthurst, R. A., and R. J. Reimold. 1978. Estimated net aerial primary productivity for selected estuarine angiosperms in Maine, Delaware, and Georgia. Journal of Applied Ecology 15:919–931.

Loesch, J. G. 1987. Overview of life history aspects of anadromous alewife and blueback herring in freshwater habitats. American Fisheries Society Symposium 1:89–103.

McCleave, J. D., R. C. Kleckner, and M. Castonguay. 1987. Reproductive sympatry of American and European eels and implications for migration and taxonomy. American Fisheries Society Symposium 1:286–297.

Moriarty, C. 1978. Eels—a natural and unnatural history. Universe Books, New York, New York, USA.

Moriarty, C. 1987. Factors influencing recruitment of the Atlantic species of anguillid eels. American Fisheries Society Symposium 1:483–491.

Nei, M., and W. H. Li. 1979. Mathematical models for studying genetic variation in terms of restriction endonucleases. Proceedings of the National Academy of Sciences of the United States of America 76:5269–5273.

Odum, E. P. 1971. Fundamentals of ecology, 3rd edition. W. B. Saunders, Philadelphia, Pennsylvania, USA.

Ogden, J. C. 1970. Relative abundance, food habits, and age of the American eel, *Anguilla rostrata* (LeSueur), in certain New Jersey streams. Transactions of the American Fisheries Society 99:54–59.

Paine, R. T. 1976. Size-limited predation: an observational and experimental approach with the *Mytilus–Pisaster* interaction. Ecology 57:858–873.

Parsons, J., K. U. Vickers, and Y. Warden. 1977. Relationship between elver recruitment and changes in the sex ratio of silver eels, *Anguilla anguilla* L. migrating from Lough Neagh, Northern Ireland. Journal of Fish Biology 10:211–229.

Power, J. H., and J. D. McCleave. 1983. Simulation of the North Atlantic Ocean drift of *Anguilla* leptocephali. U.S. National Marine Fisheries Service Fishery Bulletin 81:483–500.

Ross, S. T., M. S. Peterson, and J. R. Brent. 1984. Fishery potential of American eels in the northern Gulf of Mexico. The Gulf and South Atlantic Fisheries Development Foundation, Tampa, Florida, USA.

Satoh, H., N. Nakamura, and T. Hibiya. 1962. Studies on the sexual maturation of the eel. I. On the sex differentiation and the maturing process of the gonads. Bulletin of the Japanese Society of Scientific Fisheries 28:579–584.

Saunders, N. C., L. G. Kessler, and J. C. Avise. 1986. Genetic variation and geographic differentiation in mitochondrial DNA of the horseshoe crab, *Limulus polyphemus*. Genetics 112:613–627.

Scott, W. B., and E. J. Crossman. 1973. Freshwater fishes of Canada. Fisheries Research Board of Canada Bulletin 184.

Sinha, V. R. P., and J. W. Jones. 1966. On the sex and distribution of the freshwater eel *(Anguilla anguilla)*. Journal of Zoology (London) 150:371–385.

Sinha, V. R. P., and J. W. Jones. 1975. The European freshwater eel. Liverpool Press, Liverpool, England.

Smith, M. W. 1966. The Atlantic provinces of Canada. Pages 521–534 *in* D. G. Fry, editor. Limnology in North America. University of Wisconsin Press, Madison, Wisconsin, USA.

Smith, M. W., and J. W. Saunders. 1955. The American eel in certain freshwaters of the maritime provinces of Canada. Journal of the Fisheries Research Board of Canada 12:238–269.

Sorensen, P. W. 1986. Origins of the freshwater attractant(s) of migrating elvers of the American eel, *Anguilla rostrata*. Environmental Biology of Fishes 17:185–200.

Sorensen, P. W., and M. L. Bianchini. 1986. Environmental correlates of the freshwater migration of elvers of the American eel in a Rhode Island brook. Transactions of the American Fisheries Society 115:258–268.

Stearns, S. C. 1977. The evolution of life-history traits: a critique of the theory and a review of the data. Annual Review of Ecology and Systematics 8:145–171.

Stearns, S. C., and R. E. Crandall. 1984. Plasticity for age and size at sexual maturity: a life history response to unavoidable stress. Pages 13–33 *in* G. W. Potts and R. J. Wootton, editors. Fish reproduction: strategies and tactics. Academic Press, New York, New York, USA.

Tesch, F.-W. 1977. The eel: biology and management of anguillid eels. Translated from German by J. Greenwood. Chapman and Hall/John Wiley & Sons, New York, New York, USA.

Trivers, R. 1985. Social evolution. Benjamin/Cummings, Menlo Park, California, USA.

Turner, R. E. 1976. Geographic variation in salt marsh macrophyte production: a review. Contributions in Marine Science 20:47–68.

van Utrecht, W. L., and M. A. Holleboom. 1985. Notes on eel larvae (*Anguilla anguilla* Linnaeus, 1758) from the central and eastern North Atlantic and on glass eels from the European continental shelf. Bijdragen tot de Dierkunde 55:259–262.

Vladykov, V. D. 1966. Remarks on the American eel (*Anguilla rostrata* LeSueur): size of elvers entering streams; the relative abundance of adult males and females; and present economic importance of eels in North America. Internationale Vereinigung für Theoretische und Angewandte Limnologie Verhandlungen 16:1007–1017.

Vladykov, V. D., and P. K. L. Liew. 1982. Sex of adult American eels *(Anguilla rostrata)* collected as elvers in two different streams along the eastern shore of Canada, and raised in the same freshwater pond in Ontario. Pages 88–93 *in* K. H. Loftus, editor. Proceedings of the 1980 North American eel conference. Ontario Ministry of Natural Resources, Ontario Fisheries Technical Report Series 4, Toronto, Canada.

Vrijenhoek, R. C., and S. Lerman. 1982. Heterozygosity and developmental stability under sexual and asexual breeding systems. Evolution 36:768–776.

Wachtel, S. S., and G. C. Koo. 1981. H-Y antigen in gonadal differentiation. Pages 255–299 *in* C. R. Austin and R. G. Edwards, editors. Mechanisms of sex differentiation in animals and man. Academic Press, New York, New York, USA.

Warner, R. R. 1975. The adaptive significance of sequential hermaphroditism in animals. American Naturalist 109:61–82.

Wenner, C. A. 1973. Occurrence of American eels, *Anguilla rostrata*, in waters overlying the eastern North American continental shelf. Journal of the Fisheries Research Board of Canada 30:1752–1755.

Wenner, C. A., and J. A. Musick. 1974. Fecundity and gonad observations of the American eel, *Anguilla rostrata*, migrating from Chesapeake Bay, Virginia. Journal of the Fisheries Research Board of Canada 31:1387–1391.

Werner, E. E., and J. F. Gilliam. 1984. The ontogenetic

niche and species interactions in size-structured populations. Annual Review of Ecology and Systematics 15:393–425.

Werner, E. E., J. F. Gilliam, D. J. Hall, and G. G. Mittelbach. 1983. An experimental test of the effects of predation risk on habitat use in fish. Ecology 64:1540–1548.

Wiberg, U. 1982. Serological cross-reactivity to rat anti H-Y antiserum in the female European eel (Anguilla anguilla). Differentiation 21:206–208.

Wiberg, U. H. 1983. Sex determination in the European eel (Anguilla anguilla, L.): a hypothesis based on cytogenetic results, correlated with the findings of skewed sex ratio. Cytogenetics and Cell Genetics 36:589–598.

Williams, G. C., and R. K. Koehn. 1984. Population genetics of North Atlantic catadromous eels (Anguilla). Pages 529–560 in B. J. Turner, editor. Evolutionary genetics of fishes. Plenum, New York, New York, USA.

Williams, G. C., R. K. Koehn, and J. B. Mitton. 1973. Genetic differentiation without isolation in the American eel, Anguilla rostrata. Evolution 27:192–204.

Winn, H. E., W. A. Richkus, and L. K. Winn. 1975. Sexual dimorphism and natural movements of the American eel (Anguilla rostrata) in Rhode Island streams and estuaries. Helgoländer Wissenschaftliche Meeresuntersuchungen 27:156–166.

Wootton, R. J. 1984. Introduction: strategies and tactics in fish reproduction. Pages 1–12 in G. W. Potts and R. J. Wootton, editors. Fish reproduction: strategies and tactics. Academic Press, New York, New York, USA.

Note Added in Proof

P. R. Todd (New Zealand Ministry of Fisheries, Christchurch, personal communication) has offered the following explanation for the "spontaneous" appearance of males among migrating silver eels from locales where males were apparently lacking as juveniles (yellow eels). If males mature shortly after differentiation, they would not appear in collections of juveniles but would be represented in collections of migrating adults. Females, with a longer interval between differentiation and maturation, would be regularly represented in collections of juveniles. Such an explanation does not account fully for numerical dominance of males in some samples of migrating adults, but is a simple explanation for the apparent lack of males in many areas where they might be expected from the larval duration hypothesis. This explanation is also consistent with the general time-minimization strategy proposed for males above.

American Fisheries Society Symposium 1:57–65, 1987

Biology of Pink Salmon in the North American Great Lakes[1]

W. Kwain[2]

Lake Superior Fisheries Research Unit, Ontario Ministry of Natural Resources
875 Queen Street East, Box 130, Sault Ste. Marie, Ontario P6A 5L5, Canada

Abstract.—In 1956, approximately 21,000 pink salmon *Oncorhynchus gorbuscha* juveniles from the Skeena River of British Columbia were inadvertently released into Thunder Bay of Lake Superior by the Ontario government during a transplant of pink salmon to Hudson Bay. Mature pink salmon were first reported in Lake Superior in 1959. By 1971, they were reported as abundant and widespread. Since then, pink salmon have expanded into all the Great Lakes: Lake Huron by 1969; Lake Michigan by 1973; Lakes Erie and Ontario by 1979. These pink salmon form the only known self-perpetuating populations of the species in fresh water and are now regarded as established exotics in the Great Lakes. Furthermore, in Lake Superior, 3-year-old pink salmon have not been uncommon, and their occurrence appears to have allowed establishment of an even-year spawning stock in Lake Superior in addition to the odd-year stock originally introduced. The plasticity of the pink salmon life history in the Great Lakes clearly denies the hypothesis that the species has an obligatorily 2-year life cycle. This plasticity, moreover, may provide the potential for genetic engineering and the opportunity to establish the long-awaited off-year pink salmon runs in northwestern North America and a new stock along the Atlantic coast.

The purpose of this paper is to summarize the literature on pink salmon *Oncorhynchus gorbuscha* of the North American Great Lakes; to provide further information on the species' migratory behaviour, population size, meristics, feeding, etc., in the Great Lakes; and to compare and contrast these freshwater populations with anadromous forms from the Pacific coast.

The Great Lakes have the first and only self-sustaining population of freshwater pink salmon in the world. The introduction of pink salmon into the Great Lakes was an accidental by-product of an attempt to establish a sport and commercial fishery for the native peoples of the Hudson Bay and James Bay areas. In 1954, the Ontario government investigated the Winisk and the Attawapiskat rivers to determine if Pacific salmon could be introduced there. In the fall of 1954, 1,000,000 eyed eggs of chum salmon *Oncorhynchus keta* were received from Washington state. In January 1955, half of these eggs were planted through the ice into prepared artificial nests. The remainder were planted as juveniles in late May and early June. In the fall of 1955, 787,000 pink salmon eggs

were collected from the Skeena River in British Columbia, incubated to the eyed stage in the Horsefly Lake Hatchery on the Fraser River near Vancouver, British Columbia, and then shipped to the Port Arthur Hatchery to be further cultured. In January 1956, 513,000 eyed eggs and yolk-sac larvae were planted in the Goose Creek, which flows into Hudson Bay. The following spring, an additional 224,112 juveniles were planted.

In 1957 and 1958, the rivers were surveyed intensively for the spawning adults but none were found. While these futile attempts were carried out in the Hudson and James bay areas in 1959, pink salmon were successfully spawning in tributaries of Lake Superior.

Two pink salmon were caught in the fall of 1959 by U.S. anglers in or just above the mouths of two Minnesota streams flowing into Lake Superior (Schumacher and Eddy 1960). The capture of two mature pink salmon at different places in the Lake Superior drainage raised an interesting question concerning their origin and probability of survival. Inquiries revealed that when the last aircraft load of juvenile pink salmon was flown to the Hudson Bay area in 1956, three troughs of some 7,000 juveniles each remained in the hatchery. These juveniles were released into a drain leading into the Current River a few meters away. The Current River drains to Lake Superior (Figure 1).

For years, pink salmon appeared to be confined to Lake Superior but, in 1969, a spent pink salmon

[1]Contribution 86-06 of the Research Section, Fisheries Branch, Ontario Ministry of Natural Resources, Box 50, Maple, Ontario, L0J 1E0, Canada.
[2]Present address: Ontario Ministry of Natural Resources, Post Office Box 50, Maple, Ontario, L0J 1E0, Canada.

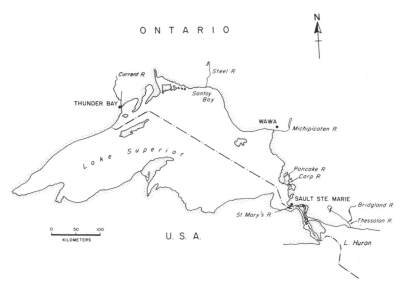

FIGURE 1.—Study areas along Lakes Superior and Huron.

female was collected in the Carp River, a Michigan tributary of Lake Huron (not the Carp River shown in Figure 1). A pink salmon was collected in Lake Michigan in 1973 (Wagner and Stauffer 1975). In 1976, a small group of even-year spawning pink salmon was found in the Steel River, Lake Superior (Kwain and Chappel 1978), and another in the Chocolay River, Michigan (Wagner 1978). These were the first reported incidences of pink salmon spawning in even years in the Great Lakes. By 1979, the species had expanded farther into the lower Great Lakes; pink salmon were caught in both Lake Erie and Lake Ontario that year (Emery 1981; Kwain and Lawrie 1981). The pink salmon is now regarded as an established exotic species in the Great Lakes, having expanded not only its distribution but also the numbers of both its odd- and its even-year spawners.

Pink salmon on the west coast of North America have been considered obligatorily anadromous fish that cannot reproduce, or at least cannot maintain a natural population, without residing for some time in a marine environment (Rounsefell 1958). Hart (1973) stated that the return migration takes place during the second summer with extremely few exceptions. The 2-year life cycle is so invariable that runs in odd-numbered years are effectively isolated from even-year runs so that there is no gene flow between them. The contrasting biologies of Pacific pink salmon, which are consistently anadromous, with those of the Great

Lakes, which show variable life cycles and widespread straying behaviour, make study of the latter particularly interesting.

Methods

Much of this study was conducted on the north shore of Lake Superior, Ontario, from 1971 to 1985 (Figure 1). From 1971 to 1979, sampling efforts were concentrated in the Steel River and vicinity; they included fall experimental fishing in Santoy Bay, study of spawning runs in the river, excavation of redds, and observation of the springtime downstream migration of the fry. The spawning population of the Michipicoten River, eastern Lake Superior, was studied in 1977 and again in 1985. Populations in two tributaries near Sault Ste. Marie (Carp and Pancake rivers) were monitored from 1981 onward for sizes of run, sex ratios, timing of entrances into the river, and downstream migrations.

Downstream migration of juvenile pink salmon was monitored in the Pancake and Carp rivers during April and May of 1980. In previous experiments to determine when the newly hatched larvae start to move downstream, an artificial stream was simulated in the laboratory. A 120 × 240-cm plywood box was divided into eight 15-cm-wide channels connected at alternate ends to allow continuous flow through each channel in sequence. Each end was equipped with a trap so that fish could move in but not out. Water velocity ranged between 3.5 and 4.5 cm/s, and water temperature was maintained at 5–6°C. Experiments were carried out daily (February 3–April 21, 1978) except for weekends and holidays. During each trial, 10 randomly selected juveniles were placed in the centre of the stream for 30 min acclimation before release. The juveniles in each trap were counted and removed every morning, before a new group of fish was introduced.

The saltwater tolerance of pink salmon fry soon after they emerged from the gravel was tested by standard 96-h bioassay procedures (APHA et al. 1976). Tests were conducted weekly between December 17, 1979, and February 29, 1980, with 10 randomly selected juveniles per test solution. The experiment was completed when 100% of the fry survived in full-strength salt water.

In July and August 1981, the stomach contents of 441 pink salmon captured in Lake Superior and tributaries were examined. Stomachs containing food were preserved in 10% formalin for later examination in the laboratory, where food organisms were sorted and identified. Twenty stomachs from Lake Huron fish (unknown capture dates) also were examined. The number of stomachs in which each item occurred was recorded and the volume of food contents was recorded for each fish.

Pink salmon were collected from several locations in the Great Lakes for a study of meristic characters. The samples were of fish from Lake Superior (Carp and Pancake rivers), Lake Huron (Brunt Island, Ontario, and Albany Creek, Michigan), Lake Michigan (Black River, Michigan), Lake Erie (Fisher and Young creeks), and research laboratory stock. The meristic characteristics counted were numbers of branchiostegal rays; gill rakers; pectoral, pelvic, dorsal, and anal fin rays; vertebrae; pyloric caeca; and lateral line scales. The length and weight of each fish were measured and scales were taken for age determinations.

Results

Adult Migration

Spawning migrations of pink salmon occur from late August to early October in several large tributaries of Lake Superior (Kwain and Lawrie 1981) and Lake Erie (Emery 1981). This timing is similar to that of sea-run pink salmon on the Pacific coast (Pritchard 1937).

In 1981, pink salmon were first observed in nearshore areas of Pancake Bay on August 18. In Batchawana and Pancake bays, 621 pink salmon were caught; 486 were marked and released alive. These fish were caught almost exclusively near the water surface and on the northwest side of nets set within 200 m of the shoreline (in water depths less than 10 m). Nets set concurrently but farther than 200 m from the shoreline caught few fish (<1 fish/100 m · h effort). Recaptures of fish that were fin-clipped in near- and offshore areas were made exclusively to the southeast of the tagging sites.

Mature migrating adults appeared occasionally in late August at the mouths of the Pancake and Carp rivers. The numbers of fish moving into both rivers increased dramatically after September 1, peaked on approximately September 10, then decreased to nearly zero by September 30.

Spawning behaviour is similar to that described for Pacific coast anadromous stocks of pink salmon (Scott and Crossman 1973). The female digs a redd and is attended by several males. After shedding her eggs, she digs gravel from upstream to cover the fertilized eggs. At preferred spawning areas, the same redd site is dug many times by different females. Previously laid eggs are dislodged and drift downstream. Most dislodged eggs probably die or are eaten.

Some pink salmon deposit their eggs at the first patch of suitable gravel in the stream. In Lake Erie, on September 25, 1979, pink salmon were seen along the lake shore within inner Long Point Bay (D. Reid, Ontario Ministry of Natural Resources, personal communication). They were located in 1 m of water, up to 6 m from the shore. The two specimens collected were ripe and ready to spawn. This seemed unusual as pink salmon do not normally spawn on shoals, although spawning within the tidal areas of some west coast streams has been documented (Helle et al. 1964). Spawning activity had also been found near the river mouth of the Carp River, along the lake shore, in 1983.

In 1981, several hundred fish that had not spawned were recaptured in the Carp and Pancake rivers attempting to return to the lake. Some of these fish were caught and placed back upstream several times. A few of these fish were subsequently caught in nearshore areas of the lake; 19 fish were from the Carp River and 13 from the Pancake River (Kwain and Rose 1986).

Population sizes at various tributaries of Lake Superior were estimated by mark–recapture methods in several years (Table 1). The Michipicoten River was surveyed in 1977 and 1985. Although the results show some difference, the

TABLE 1.—Population estimates for spawning populations of pink salmon in four tributaries of Lake Superior during 1977–1985.

Year	River	Number marked	Number examined	Number recaptured	Population estimate	95% confidence limits
1977	Michipicoten	386	716	3	85,000	36,242–133,758
1979	Steel	1,817	1,155	259	95,308	40,675–149,147
1981	Carp	1,526	387	78	7,500	6,046–9,257
1981	Pancake	1,103	1,134	171	7,285	6,265–8,466
1985	Michipicoten	159	1,895	116	61,326	51,134–73,551

1977 estimate was based on only three recaptures compared with 116 in the latter survey. Bagdovitz et al. (1986) reported that the abundance of pink salmon had declined precipitously in Lake Superior since the large runs seen in 1979. They speculated that the large numbers of adults combined with the low flows in the spawning tributaries during the fall of 1979 contributed to the collapse by inducing severe egg and larva mortality. However, the dramatic decline of pink salmon was not observed on the north shore of Lake Superior.

Population Structure

The size of pink salmon varied with location; their average weight in the Great Lakes was 630 g. The largest fish caught in Lake Superior weighed 2.3 kg and in Lake Huron, 5.0 kg. The latter fish measured 760 mm total length and appears to be a record for the species in the Great Lakes. Pink salmon over 3 kg frequently occur in both Lakes Huron and Erie.

The original planting of pink salmon in Lake Superior (1956) was from an odd-year stock (one spawning in odd-numbered years) taken from the Skeena River, British Columbia. Odd-year runs of pink salmon still dominate in the Great Lakes, but even-year runs now occur—the first was reported in 1976 (Kwain and Chappel 1978)—primarily in Lake Superior. Since there were no known introductions of even-year pink salmon to the Great Lakes, the even-year runs were thought to have started when a few 3-year-old spawners produced progeny that followed the usual 2-year life cycle. In Lake Superior, at least 21 3-year-old pink salmon were found in the 1978 run (Wagner and Stauffer 1980). Since then, 3-year-old pink salmon have been found in odd-year runs in most tributaries (Nicolette 1984).

In September 1977, 32,000 pink salmon eggs from the Michipicoten River of Lake Superior and 900 newly hatched yolk-sac larvae from Bridgeland Creek of northern Lake Huron were raised in the Sault Ste. Marie research laboratory. In September 1979, 76% of the survivors from two lots matured, spawned, and died. During maturation, the coloration darkened on their backs, large black dots appeared on both lobes of the tails, and the silvery sheen of the bellies diminished. Males did not develop the characteristic pink salmon hump on their backs. The remaining fish did not mature and retained their bright green backs and silvery sides. Among those that matured, males outnumbered females 2:1. Among those that did not spawn, all were females except one. Some of these survived and matured in 1980 as 3-year-olds, others in 1981 as 4-year-olds. Though these laboratory-reared pink salmon were small (Table 2), they did produce viable eggs and the second generation exhibited the same slow growth in the laboratory as their parents.

Pink salmon can live up to 4 years, and maturation can be delayed for 1 or 2 years because of low water temperature and poor growth (Kwain 1982). On the other hand, in September 1981, five of 304 age-1 pink salmon examined from the Michipicoten River were sexually mature males (Kwain and Kerr 1984). No annuli were present on their scales.

Few differences among the five lake stocks are detectable (Table 3) but, in most characteristics, a definite difference exists between the lake stocks and the laboratory stock (fish were taken from the wild lake stocks and incubated and raised in the laboratory). Differences were noted in the numbers of gill rakers, pectoral and pelvic fins, vertebrae, and pyloric caeca.

The meristic counts of the Great Lakes pink

TABLE 2.—Mean length and weight of laboratory-reared pink salmon maturing in each of three consecutive years.

Year of maturation	Age	Fork length (mm)			Weight (g)		
		Mean	SD	N	Mean	SD	N
1979	2	231	37	51	108	62	51
1980	3	265	19	35	162	38	38
1981	4	302	30	43	215	97	43

TABLE 3.—Mean counts for meristic characters of pink salmon collected from five locations and a laboratory stock.[a]

		Lake Huron				
Meristic character	Lake Superior (N=54)	Albany Creek (N=20)	Burnt Island (N=25)	Lake Michigan (N=20)	Lake Erie (N=22)	Laboratory stock (N=30)
Branchiostegal rays	12.46 z	12.55 z	12.68 z	12.75 zy	12.64 z	13.07 y
Dorsal fin rays	12.88 z	12.90 z	12.84 z	12.80 z	12.86 z	
Pectoral fin rays	15.63 z	15.75 z	15.60 z	15.70 z	15.82 z	16.67 y
Pelvic fin rays	10.82 z	10.75 z	10.80 z	10.85 z	10.77 z	11.22 y
Anal fin rays	16.57 zy	16.25 z	16.24 z	16.30 zy	16.64 y	
Lateral line scales	171.10 z	176.47 z	177.20 z	177.11 z	178.59 z	
Gill rakers	30.11 z	30.70 z	30.68 z	30.30 z	30.46 z	29.40 y
Vertebrae	67.78 y	68.25 zy	68.44 z	68.50 z	68.23 zy	67.03 x
Pyloric caeca	140.20 x	149.60 zy	141.56 yx	156.00 z	149.27 zy	128.20 w
Fork length (mm)	36.99 y	35.80 y	38.44 z	40.08 z	42.65 z	25.97 x

[a] Values along a row without a letter in common are significantly different at $P < 0.05$ (Duncan's multiple-range test).

salmon were within the ranges for sea-run pink salmon (Hart 1973; Scott and Crossman 1973): branchiostegal rays, 10–15; pyloric caeca, 121–195; gill rakers on the first gill arch, 26–34; lateral line scales, 150–205; dorsal fin rays, 10–15; anal fin rays, 13–17; pectoral fin rays, about 15; pelvic fin rays, about 10; vertebrae, 63–72. Beacham (1985) suggested that patterns of meristic and morphometric variability reflect genetic differences. He further stated that meristic characteristics appear less likely to be modified by selection in response to local environmental conditions than morphometric ones.

Fry Emigration

The percentage of juveniles trapped in a downstream trap of the artificial stream was positively related to their age (Figure 2). Three weeks after emerging from the bottom, 50% of the juveniles moved downstream. This percentage increased with age and, at 8 weeks, all fish had completed their emigration. Juveniles moved downstream only at night, even when the artificial stream was covered by a dark plastic sheet by day.

Salinity tolerance was used as an index of when the newly hatched larvae were fully adapted for downstream migration, which would take them to seawater in their native range. One month after emergence, half of the stock of pink salmon fry were ready to live in seawater and juveniles were fully adapted to the seawater at the age of 9 weeks (Figure 2).

In 1980, pink salmon juveniles started to move down the Carp and Pancake rivers during the first week of May. The run peaked early in the month and emigration was complete at the end of May.

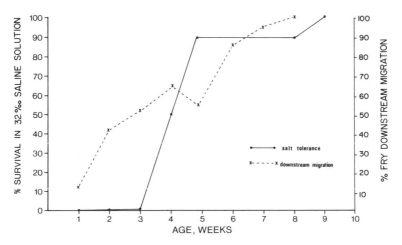

FIGURE 2.—Percentages of pink salmon juveniles that survived in full-strength salt water (32 ‰) and that were caught in downstream laboratory traps at various ages.

On May 12, trap nets were checked at half-hour intervals from 1000 to 1600 hours and no fry were captured. Juveniles were caught during the overnight setting, thus confirming our laboratory observations of movement. There was no significant difference in size between early and late season migrants.

No pink salmon juveniles were found during trawling, beach seining, or scuba diving. This is somewhat different from the west coast stock; Hart (1973) reported that juveniles there moved to deep water in September. The disappearance of Great Lakes pink salmon juveniles from nearshore areas might be attributed to their avoidance of unfavourable nearshore water temperatures (>20°C) and their movement to cooler water at deeper depths (Kwain 1982).

Feeding Behaviour

Generally, just prior to or during spawning, salmon do not feed, but 15% of the 635 stomachs of maturing pink salmon collected in 1979 at Santoy Bay and Steel River contained food (Kwain 1982). The fullness of the stomachs was negatively correlated with the progress of the spawning run; as the fish moved close to the spawning ground, the percentage of stomachs with food decreased.

During the 1981 exploratory fishing survey, 461 stomachs were examined; 90 contained food (Table 4; Withler and Kwain 1984). During early and middle August, while they still occupied the open lake waters, pink salmon fed on a wide variety of organisms, but mainly on aquatic crustacea (mysids), fish (rainbow smelt *Osmerus mordax*), and terrestrial insects (presumably taken from the surface). Late in August and during September, as they matured and congre-

gated near the spawning rivers, pink salmon fed mainly on rainbow smelt. In the pooled data, fish (rainbow smelt) and insects (moths, flies, mosquitoes, and others) showed the greatest frequency of occurrence. Zooplankton (Cladocera and Copepoda) were next most frequently eaten. The pink salmon had fed at or near the water surface because almost all identifiable insects were terrestrial. There was little evidence that adult pink salmon fed on benthic organisms.

Pink salmon juveniles move downstream soon after they emerge, and on their way downstream, they usually do not feed; therefore, there is no competition for nursery space and food in the stream. On the contrary, their small size made young juveniles, moving into the open water, vulnerable to heavy predation in Michipicoten Bay, Lake Superior. In 1984, a juvenile pink salmon was found in a stomach of a lake trout *Salvelinus namaycush,* and identified by the Michigan Department of Natural Resources (MDNR) research staff at Marquette Research Station, Marquette, Michigan (J. Peck, MDNR, personal communication). This is the first positive evidence that fish predators in the open lake use pink salmon as prey.

Discussion

Pink salmon originating from a single introduction of juveniles in 1956 have reproduced successfully in Lake Superior for the past 30 years, and recently have expanded into all of the Great Lakes. These pink salmon form the only known self-perpetuating population of the species in fresh water. Their increase and spread has been remarkable, and they are now regarded as one of the established exotics in the Great Lakes.

During the period of that spread, an even-year

TABLE 4.—Numbers of pink salmon stomachs containing various prey items, Lakes Superior and Huron, 1981 (from Withler and Kwain 1984).

	Open water			Bays and rivers		
Prey or statistic	Lake Superior, Jul 30–Aug 13	Lake Superior, Aug 17–28	Lake Huron Burnt Island, unknown	Pancake Bay, Aug 23–Sep 4	Pancake and Carp rivers, Aug 26–Sep 3	Total
Crustacea	7	33	0	0	0	40
Fish	3	23	10	9	7	52
Terrestrial insects	6	33	1	2	0	42
Aquatic insects						
Adult	0	6	0	0	0	6
Immature	2	6	0	0	0	8
Stomachs examined	25	260	20	115	41	461
Stomachs with food	8	54	11	10	7	90
Volume of contents (mL)	2.8	4.0	3.9	5.0	5.0	

run was observed in the Steel River of Lake Superior in 1976 (Kwain and Chappel 1978). It was believed that the even-year run resulted from slow growth and late maturation of pink salmon in the low water temperatures and nutrient concentrations of Lake Superior. Later a 3-year-old female pink salmon was found in Michigan waters (Wagner and Stauffer 1980). Since then, the spawning of pink salmon in even years has gradually increased and expanded into other geographic areas. However, the number of even-year spawners is not as large as it is in odd years.

In the Pacific range of the pink salmon, their 2-year life cycle is so invariant that genetic divergences between spawning stocks are apparent (Aspinwall 1974). One spawning stock is usually numerically dominant over another, although reversals of dominance are not uncommon (Royce 1962).

Most of the 3-year-old pink salmon known from the west coast have been taken from the Skeena River (Anas 1959); since the Skeena River was the source of the stock planted into Lake Superior, the Great Lakes pink salmon may have inherited the traits of late maturation. One other 3-year-old west coast pink salmon was found in the Gulf of Alaska by Turner and Bilton (1968), but they did not give its origin.

The presence of mature yearling pink salmon in the Michipicoten River, Lake Superior, is unusual. Only one natural occurrence of precocious pink salmon has been reported previously. Five yearling, sea-run pink salmon were captured in Chamber Creek, Puget Sound, Washington, in September 1978 (Foster et al. 1981). Artificially induced precocity in male pink salmon was accomplished by elevating the temperature of seawater in outside tanks to 12°C (MacKinnon and Donaldson 1976). The five precocious 1-year-old males and one 3-year-old fish found together during the odd-year run in the Michipicoten River demonstrate the plasticity of the pink salmon life cycle in the freshwater environment and suggest that the stereotypic perception of this species' rigid 2-year life cycle is inappropriate.

The reverse migration from the spawning rivers may have resulted from an excess of fish for available spawning sites. Such behaviour suggests that overcrowding may lead pink salmon to expand their range in search of alternative spawning sites, rather than to die without issue in the overpopulated stream. Exiting from rivers also has been reported for Pacific stocks of pink salmon (Helle 1966). Semko (1954) displaced

salmon from Karymaisky Spring to the river below the mouth of the spring. Returns for pink, chum, and sockeye salmon *Oncorhynchus nerka* were 13.9, 21.2, and 35.0%, respectively. This order of return would be expected if the length of association with freshwater and estuarine nursery areas by the young were proportional to the precision of return as adults to the natal stream.

Russian biologists released 48.4 million pink salmon juveniles in the years 1956–1959. In 1960, pink salmon with well-developed sexual products entered almost all the rivers of northern Murmansk, the White Sea, and further to the east as far as the Karataikha River. Entries of pink salmon were noted also beyond the boundaries of the USSR, in the rivers of Norway, Iceland, and Scotland (Yu and Ustyugov 1977). The Russians have said that when fry were released into four rivers in 1960, 66,110 pink salmon entered 23 rivers (Berg 1961).

The success of transplantation of pink salmon both in Russia and in the Great Lakes has proved that pink salmon not only thrive well in the planted rivers, but also stray quickly into adjacent areas.

Quinn (1984) hypothesized that straying is an evolutionary alternative to homing and that these two life history strategies are in dynamic equilibrium. He also said that straying should be relatively common in populations spawning in unstable streams, and in species with little variation in age at maturity. If straying is a genetically maintained strategy, then genotypes expressing this characteristic should be selected for when homing is detrimental to survival. Great Lakes pink salmon are the descendants of 21,000 juveniles released into the Current River. Homing fish would have perished without spawning, vainly trying to locate either the Skeena River or the hatchery. In time, as rivers are colonized, selection may again favour homing, because straying within territory already colonized may be redundant at best and destructive of river-specific stocks at worst (Bams 1976).

Fraser and Fedorenko (1983) found that sea-run pink salmon juveniles in Jones Creek usually migrated from the spawning channel during April and May, the peak run being 50% completed on May 3 (range, April 10 to May 23). They also found that pink salmon juveniles largely migrated from the channel after dusk, but daytime migration also occurred when creek flows were high and waters were turbid. The Great Lakes pink salmon juveniles exhibit similar emigration behaviour.

The Great Lakes pink salmon feed on a wide variety of organisms when they occupy the open water but, when they approach the nearshore areas, they feed exclusively on rainbow smelt. Many biologists wonder if the pink salmon will affect the survival of other predators that also use rainbow smelt as their main diets.

Hart (1973) stated that eggs, alevins, fry of pink salmon are eaten by a wide variety of organisms including Dolly Varden *Salvelinus malma,* cutthroat trout *Salmo clarki,* coho salmon *Oncorhynchus kitsuch,* sculpins *Cottus* spp., and aquatic birds, mammals, and insect larvae. He also suggested that this predation probably does not have important effects on pink salmon populations in years of high abundance.

Stauffer (1971) found that age-0+ salmonids ate salmon eggs in Michigan. Johnson and Ringler (1979) found that Pacific salmon eggs accounted for at least 90% of the October diet of juvenile steelhead *Salmo gairdneri,* coho salmon, adult brook trout *Salvelinus fontinalis,* and brown trout *Salmo trutta* in a tributary of Lake Ontario. In November, salmon eggs made up 38–95% of the diets of these species. Therefore, a large population of pink salmon in the Great Lakes is not necessarily having an adverse impact on the existing fish populations. On the contrary, pink salmon might provide another prey species in the system.

The first effort to introduce the Pacific pink salmon into the northwestern Atlantic was made during 1906–1908 (Lear 1980); later, a serious effort was made in Maine during 1913–1917 and again in 1921–1925 (Bigelow and Schroeder 1953). Also, an introduction of pink salmon from British Columbia to Newfoundland was begun in 1958. These direct transplantation efforts have been unsuccessful. The great success of pink salmon in the Great Lakes, however, suggests that this stock could be used as a donor for the Atlantic region. It may already have become one. Pink salmon were caught near the mouth of the St. Lawrence River (Emery 1981) and one was captured in the Miramichi River, New Brunswick, which drains to the Gulf of St. Lawrence (Randall 1984); perhaps these fish were derived from the Lake Ontario population. In any case, freshwater pink salmon have a convincing potential to support both commercial and sport fisheries in the Great Lakes.

Acknowledgments

I thank J. A. MacLean, W. J. Christie, C. M. Moffitt, M. H. A. Keenleyside, B. E. Skud, and J. H. Helle for their critical comments and reviews. I also thank the staff of Lake Superior Fisheries Research Unit for their technical assistance.

References

Anas, R. E. 1959. Three-year-old pink salmon. Journal of the Fisheries Research Board of Canada 16:91–92.

APHA (American Public Health Association), American Water Works Association, and Water Pollution Control Federation. 1976. Standard methods for the examination of water and waste water, 14th edition. APHA, Washington, D.C., USA.

Aspinwall, N. 1974. Genetic analysis of North American populations of the pink salmon, *Oncorhynchus gorbuscha,* possible evidence for the neutral mutation–random drift hypothesis. Evolution 28:295–305.

Bagdovitz, M. S., W. W. Taylor, W. C. Wagner, J. P. Nicolette, and G. P. Spangler. 1986. Pink salmon populations in the U.S. waters of Lake Superior, 1981–1984. Journal of Great Lakes Research 12:72–81.

Bams, R. A. 1976. Survival and propensity for homing as affected by presence or absence of locally adapted genes in two transplanted populations of pink salmon (*Oncorhynchus gorbuscha*). Journal of the Fisheries Research Board of Canada 33:2716–2725.

Beacham, T. D. 1985. Meristic and morphometric variation in pink salmon (*Oncorhynchus gorbuscha*) in southern British Columbia and Puget Sound. Canadian Journal of Zoology 63:366–372.

Berg, M. 1961. Pink salmon (*Oncorhynchus gorbuscha*) in north Norway in the year 1960. Acta Borealia A: Scientia 17.

Bigelow, H. B., and W. C. Schroeder. 1953. Fishes of the Gulf of Maine. U.S. Fish and Wildlife Service Fishery Bulletin 53(74).

Emery, L. 1981. Range extension of pink salmon in the lower Great Lakes. Fisheries (Bethesda) 6(2):7–10.

Foster, R. W., C. Bagatell, and H. J. Fuss. 1981. Return of one-year-old pink salmon to a stream in Puget Sound. Progressive Fish-Culturist 43:31.

Fraser, F. J., and A. Y. Fedorenko. 1983. Jones Creek pink salmon spawning channel: a biological assessment, 1954–1982. Canadian Technical Report of Fisheries and Aquatic Sciences 1188.

Hart, T. L. 1973. Pacific fishes of Canada. Fisheries Research Board of Canada Bulletin 180.

Helle, J. H. 1966. Behavior of displaced adult pink salmon. Transactions of the American Fisheries Society 95:188–195.

Helle, J. H., R. S. Williamson, and J. E. Bailey. 1964. Intertidal ecology and life history of pink salmon at Olsen Creek, Prince William Sound, Alaska. U.S. Fish and Wildlife Service Special Scientific Report Fisheries 483.

Johnson, J. H., and N. H. Ringler. 1979. Predation on Pacific salmon eggs by salmonids in a tributary of Lake Ontario. Journal of Great Lakes Research 5:177–181.

Kwain, W. 1982. Spawning behavior and early life history of pink salmon (*Oncorhynchus gorbuscha*) in the Great Lakes. Canadian Journal of Fisheries and Aquatic Sciences 39:1353–1360.

Kwain, W., and J. A. Chappel. 1978. First evidence of even-year spawning pink salmon, *Oncorhynchus gorbuscha*, in Lake Superior. Journal of the Fisheries Research Board of Canada 35:1373–1376.

Kwain, W., and S. J. Kerr. 1984. Return of 1-year-old pink salmon in Michipicoten River, eastern Lake Superior. North American Journal of Fisheries Management 4:335–337.

Kwain, W., and A. H. Lawrie. 1981. Pink salmon in the Great Lakes. Fisheries (Bethesda) 6(2):2–6.

Kwain, W., and G. A. Rose. 1986. Spawning migration of Great Lakes pink salmon (*Oncorhynchus gorbuscha*): size and sex distributions, river entrance and exit. Journal of Great Lakes Research 12:101–108.

Lear, W. H. 1980. The pink salmon transplant experiment in Newfoundland. Pages 213–243 *in* J. E. Thorpe, editor. Salmon ranching. Academic Press, London, England.

MacKinnon, C. W., and E. M. Donaldson. 1976. Environmentally induced precocious sexual development in the male pink salmon, *Oncorhynchus gorbuscha*. Journal of the Fisheries Research Board of Canada 33:2602–2605.

Nicolette, J. P. 1984. A 3-year-old pink salmon in an odd-year run in Lake Superior. North American Journal of Fisheries Management 4:130–132.

Pritchard, A. L. 1937. Variation in the time of run, sex proportions, size and egg content of adult pink salmon (*Oncorhynchus gorbuscha*) at McClinton Creek, Masset Inlet, B.C. Journal of the Biological Board of Canada 3:403–416.

Quinn, T. P. 1984. Homing and straying in Pacific salmon. Pages 357–362 *in* J. D. McCleave, G. P. Arnold, J. J. Dodson, and W. H. Neill, editors. Mechanisms of migration in fishes. Plenum, New York, New York, USA.

Randall, R. G. 1984. First record of a pink salmon *Oncorhynchus gorbuscha*—new record in the Miramichi River, New Brunswick, Canada. Naturaliste Canadien (Quebec) 111:455–457.

Rounsefell, G. A. 1958. Anadromy in North American

Salmonidae. U.S. Fish and Wildlife Service Fishery Bulletin 58(131):171–185.

Royce, W. F. 1962. Pink salmon fluctuations in Alaska. Pages 15–33 *in* N. J. Wilimovsky, editor. Symposium on pink salmon. H. R. MacMillan Lectures in Fisheries, University of British Columbia, Vancouver, Canada.

Schumacher, R. E., and S. Eddy. 1960. The appearance of pink salmon, *Oncorhynchus gorbuscha* (Walbaum), in Lake Superior. Transactions of the American Fisheries Society 89:371–373.

Scott, W. B., and E. J. Crossman. 1973. Freshwater fishes of Canada. Fisheries Research Board of Canada Bulletin 184.

Semko, R. L. 1954. [The stock of west Kamchatka salmon and their commercial utilization.] Izvestiya Tikhookeanskogo Nauchino-Issledovateliskoso Instituta Rybnogo Khozyaistva i Okeanografii 41:3–109. Translated from Russian: Fisheries Research Board of Canada, Translation Series 288, Ottawa, Canada.

Stauffer, T. M. 1971. Salmon eggs as food for stream salmonids and sculpins. Michigan Department of Natural Resources, Research Development Report 233, Lansing, Michigan, USA.

Turner, C. E., and H. T. Bilton. 1968. Another pink salmon (*Oncorhynchus gorbuscha*) in its third year. Journal of the Fisheries Research Board of Canada 25:1993–1996.

Wagner, W. C. 1978. A three-year-old pink salmon from Lake Superior. Michigan Department of Natural Resources, Fisheries Research Report 1861, Lansing, Michigan, USA.

Wagner, W. C., and T. M. Stauffer. 1975. Occurrence of pink salmon in Michigan, 1963–1973. Michigan Department of Natural Resources, Technical Report 75-3, Lansing, Michigan, USA.

Wagner, W. C., and T. M. Stauffer. 1980. Three-year-old pink salmon in Lake Superior tributaries. Transactions of the American Fisheries Society 109:458–460.

Withler, F. C., and W. Kwain. 1984. Survey of pink salmon in eastern Lake Superior, 1981. Canadian Technical Report of Fisheries and Aquatic Sciences 1317.

Yu, G. K., and A. F. Ustyugov. 1977. The pink salmon, *Oncorhynchus gorbuscha*, in the rivers of the north of Krasnoyarsk Territory. Journal of Ichthyology 17:320–322.

American Fisheries Society Symposium 1:66–78, 1987

American Shad and Striped Bass in California's Sacramento–San Joaquin River System

Donald E. Stevens and Harold K. Chadwick

California Department of Fish and Game, Bay–Delta Fishery Project
Stockton, California 95205, USA

Richard E. Painter

California Department of Fish and Game, Inland Fisheries Division
Oroville, California 95965, USA

Abstract.—American shad *Alosa sapidissima* and striped bass *Morone saxatilis* were introduced to the Sacramento–San Joaquin river system, which includes a large inland delta, during the 1870s. Both species supported commercial fisheries by the turn of the century. Legislative action terminated the commercial striped bass fishery in 1935 and the American shad fishery in 1957; thus, only sportfishing is legal now. American shad runs in 1976 and 1977 were about 3×10^6 fish. The present (1982) stock of adult (≥ 40.6 cm) striped bass is about 1×10^6 fish, down from about 1.7×10^6 in the early 1970s. Previous striped bass stock estimates are not available, but peak catches occurred in the early 1960s. Both species are spring spawners and their spawning grounds overlap, but American shad make greater use of the upper reaches of the Sacramento River system and striped bass make greater use of the delta. In summer, the main American shad nursery includes the lower Feather River, much of the Sacramento River, and the northern delta. Most young American shad leave the rivers and estuary by year's end, though some remain in the estuary for more than 1 year and may not go to sea. River flows transport essentially all young striped bass to the estuary within a few days after spawning occurs. By summer, peak concentrations of young striped bass are in the fresh–saltwater mixing zone. Year-class strengths of young American shad and striped bass vary widely, and high river flows during the spawning and early nursery periods have a positive effect on both species. However, since 1977, abundance of young striped bass has consistently been below expected levels. Populations of American shad and striped bass obviously have declined from their initial peaks in the early 1900s, probably largely in response to habitat degradation associated with human activities. Hatchery propagation and stocking are being tested as means of mitigating losses of striped bass to water projects and power plants. Despite some potential adverse impacts on native species, we believe that the introductions of American shad and striped bass have been beneficial to California.

The Sacramento River and San Joaquin River, the major streams in California's Central Valley, drain about 153,000 km² and form a tidal estuary from their junction in an inland delta to San Francisco Bay (Figure 1). The delta has large cultivated islands that were reclaimed from marsh in the latter part of the nineteenth and the early twentieth centuries. These islands are surrounded by approximately 1,130 km of interlaced channels varying in width from about 50 m to 1.5 km and generally less than 15 m deep. Suisun, San Pablo, and San Francisco bays to the west cover an area of about 1,125 km². More than 50% of Suisun and San Pablo bays is less than 2 m deep at low tide. In San Francisco Bay, shallows are somewhat less extensive partly because of landfill practices that have been associated with development of urban and industrial areas along the shore. Important marshes remain in the estuary, particularly

around Suisun Bay, northern San Pablo Bay, and southern San Francisco Bay.

The historical annual flow from the rivers entering the estuary averaged about 1,100 m³/s, but now only about one-half that amount passes through the estuary due to local use along the rivers and exports to the San Joaquin Valley and southern California (Chadwick 1977). Dams regulate flow in the major tributaries of the Sacramento–San Joaquin watershed. Seasonal flow patterns are modified by water storage behind these dams in winter and spring with subsequent release for diversion in summer and fall. Roughly 85% of the inflow to the delta originates in the Sacramento River, 10% is from the San Joaquin River, and 5% is from miscellaneous eastern valley streams. Water is diverted, primarily for agriculture, all along the rivers and in the delta. Largest diversions are by the U.S. Bureau of Reclamation's

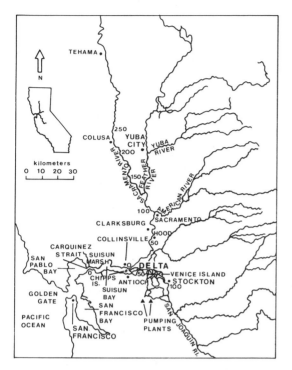

FIGURE 1.—Sacramento–San Joaquin River system. Numbers indicate locations in river kilometers as defined by Turner (1976).

Central Valley Project (CVP) and California's State Water Project (SWP) in the southern delta. Combined diversion rate by these projects averaged 190 m³/s in 1978 and could increase to about 270 m³/s in 25 years under present authorizations (Chadwick 1977).

American Shad

Introduction and Fisheries

American shad *Alosa sapidissima* were first introduced into the Sacramento–San Joaquin river system in 1871 when it was still largely unchanged by humans. Initially, about 10,000 young of the year were transported from New York and released into the Sacramento River near Tehama. An additional 819,000 young fish were stocked from 1873 to 1881 (Skinner 1962).

The American shad population exploded and soon supported a major commercial gill-net fishery in the estuary during the spawning runs. American shad were sold in San Francisco markets by 1879. Catches regularly exceeded 450,000 kg from 1900 to 1945, and about 2.5 million kg were taken in 1917. After 1945, the fishery dimin-

ished and, in 1957, it was terminated by legislation due to public concerns about the impact of the gill nets on striped bass *Morone saxatilis* (Skinner 1962).

Although American shad were commercially important, enthusiasm for sportfishing did not begin until the 1950s when a major fishery developed on the spawning grounds in the upper Sacramento River system (Radovich 1970), particularly the mainstem Sacramento and the American, Feather and Yuba rivers. Once established, the popularity of fishing for American shad grew and, by the mid-1960s, an estimated 100,000 angler-days were expended (California Department of Fish and Game 1965). More recently, however, angler interest has declined. In 1977 and 1978, about 35,000 and 55,000 angler-days were expended to catch 79,000 and 140,000 American shad, respectively (Meinz 1981). The present bag limit is 25 fish/d, but most anglers typically release all or most of their catch.

An interesting, but secondary, means of catching American shad called "bumping" is practiced by sport fishermen at night in the delta (Radovich 1970). A long-handled chicken-wire dip net is fished in the prop wash of a slowly moving boat and when a shad bumps the net, the "bumper" quickly attempts to flip it into the boat. Essentially all fish caught are males, which apparently are attracted to the prop wash as they would be to a spawning female.

Spawning

From 1975 to 1978, based on analysis of scales, 92% of the male American shad spawned for the first time in the Sacramento–San Joaquin river system as 3- or 4-year-olds and 79% of the females initially spawned as 4- or 5-year-olds (Wixom 1981). For both sexes, spawning appeared to occur for the first time as early as age 2 and as late as age 7. Once a fish spawned, it continued to do so annually.

American shad spawn from the tidal basin upstream into fresh water in both the Sacramento and San Joaquin rivers, although the primary spawning area is the Sacramento River system upstream from Hood (Hatton 1940; Stevens 1966a; Painter et al. 1977; Table 1).

Adults returning from the ocean begin passing through the delta in late March or April (Stevens 1966a). In fyke traps (Hallock et al. 1957) set in the Sacramento River at Clarksburg, American shad catches increase substantially through April and peak from the first to latter third of May

TABLE 1.—Life history strategies of American shad and striped bass in the Sacramento–San Joaquin river system.

Feature	American shad	Striped bass
Migration to fresh water	Mar–May	Sep–May
Major spawning locations	Upper Sacramento River and major tributaries	Delta, mainstem Sacramento River
Major spawning period	May–early Jul	Apr–Jun
Temperatures during peak spawning	17–24°C	17–20°C
Major nursery areas of young fish	Lower Feather River, Sacramento River from Colusa downstream, delta	Delta, Suisun Bay
Usual environment after first year	Ocean, but a few fish remain in the estuary	Estuary, but many of the larger fish migrate to the ocean for several months each year

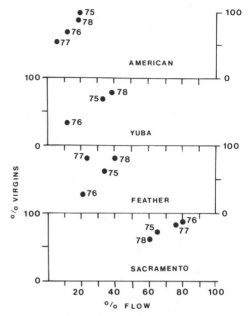

FIGURE 2.—Percentage of American shad spawning runs formed by virgins and percentage contribution of streams in the Sacramento River system to the flow downstream from their confluences with adjacent river branches.

(Table 2). River temperatures during May generally range from about 14°C to 21°C.

River flow may affect the distribution of American shad during their initial spawning runs in the Sacramento River system (Painter et al. 1980). Although this hypothesis is unproven, it is supported by some crude measures of the distribution of virgin spawners in the American, Yuba, and mainstem Sacramento rivers where percentages of the runs formed by virgins (Wixom 1981) tend to increase with the contribution of these streams to the flow immediately downstream from their confluences with adjacent river branches (Figure 2). Similar results were not obtained for the Feather River; however, this may reflect a longer residence period for young fish in that tributary allowing them to become imprinted for homing on their maiden runs. Sampling with beach seines reveals that many young American shad remain in the Feather River through summer, whereas few reside in the Sacramento River above Colusa, and the Yuba and American rivers (Table 3).

TABLE 2.—Catch of adult American shad in fyke traps set in the Sacramento River at Clarksburg. Open cells mean no sampling.

Period		Year								Mean
		1974	1975	1976	1979	1980	1982	1983	1984	
Mar	21–31	0	0	7	10	7	1		2	3.9
Apr	1–10	0	8	8	62	16	3		7	14.9
	11–20	50	38	65	56	19			29	42.8
	21–30	380	174	59	213	30	153	120	68	149.6
May	1–10	594	264	133	181	20	303		178	239.0
	11–20	389	427	168	220	122	356		92	253.4
	21–30	433	498	28	105	32	197	582	151	253.2
May 31–Jun 9		137	109	30	14	3	149	538	23	125.4
Jun	10–19	116	38	4	2	4	6	96	20	35.8
	20–29	16	2					41		19.7
Annual index[a]		2,115	1,558	502	863	242	1,216	2,811	570	

[a] Sum of catches from April 1 to June 9. In years when traps were not fished during some periods, catches were adjusted upward based on mean percentage of catch during those periods in years with complete data.

TABLE 3.—Mean catch per seine haul of young American shad in the Sacramento–San Joaquin river system. Sampling was almost weekly from July through September. Numbers of samples are in parentheses.[a]

	Year		
Area	1976	1977	1978
Sacramento River above Colusa	0.0 (18)	0.1 (38)	0.1 (12)
Feather River above Yuba River	0.0 (9)	0.0 (8)	(0)
Feather River below Yuba River	7.7 (18)	7.2 (26)	7.2 (8)
Yuba River	1.1 (18)	0.4 (15)	0.0 (8)
Sacramento River from Colusa to Sacramento	8.6 (15)	3.6 (37)	0.7 (13)
American River	(0)	0.1 (11)	3.9 (12)
North delta[b]	3.0 (62)	1.9 (43)	8.5 (30)
South delta[c]	0.2 (13)	0.0 (10)	0.0 (10)

[a] Data from M. Meinz, California Department of Fish and Game.
[b] Rivers and sloughs north from San Joaquin River upstream to Sacramento.
[c] San Joaquin River and rivers and sloughs to the south.

Most repeat spawners in the Sacramento River system probably home to the tributary where they have spawned previously. During 1978, about 6,000 American shad were tagged on the spawning grounds. During subsequent years, 12 tags were returned from these fish. Nine of these returns were from the river of tag origin. Of the remainder, only one was an obvious stray from routes that led to the river where the fish were tagged (Table 4).

TABLE 4.—Distribution of tag recoveries during 1979 and subsequent years for American shad that were tagged while on their spawning grounds in the Sacramento River system in 1978.

	Spawning ground 1978			
Recovery location	American River	Feather River	Yuba River	Upper Sacramento River
Delta and Sacramento River below American River	0	1	0	1
American River	0	1[a]	0	0
Feather River above Yuba River	0	2	0	0
Sacramento River above Feather River	0	0	0	7
Total recoveries	0	4	0	8
Number tagged	312	1,211	199	4,242

[a] Obvious stray from route back to 1978 spawning ground.

Sampling of American shad eggs with nets set in the Feather River indicates that spawning occurs predominantly from May to July at temperatures of 17–24°C (Painter et al. 1977).

Nursery

The location of the summer nursery of American shad may be discerned from a combination of seine surveys (M. Meinz, California Department of Fish and Game, personal communication), trawling in the delta (Stevens 1966a), and catches at the fish screens in front of the SWP diversion in the southern delta. The flow in most of the spawning areas is swift enough that the eggs are washed downstream before they hatch. During the seine surveys, few young American shad were ever captured in the Sacramento River above Colusa, in the Feather River above the Yuba River, in the Yuba River, in the American River except at its mouth in 1978, and in the south delta (Table 3). Young American shad were more numerous in the Feather River below the mouth of the Yuba River, in the Sacramento River from Colusa to Sacramento, and in the north delta. Despite the virtual absence of fish in seine hauls from the south delta, catches in trawls (Stevens 1966a) and at the SWP fish screens (Figure 3) reveal that young American shad are present in the south delta in summer. Increasing catches in trawls in the fall and at the fish screens in October and November are consistent with the seining data in demonstrating that many young American shad do not enter the delta until their out-migration. Thus, the main summer nursery of American shad appears to include the lower Feather River and to extend from Colusa on the Sacramento River to the north delta; modest numbers of fish also use the south delta.

In 1978, a wet year, the seine catches were notably lower in the Sacramento River and higher

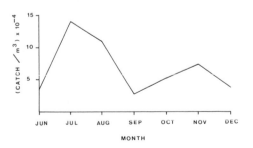

FIGURE 3.—Mean monthly catch of young American shad at the State Water Project fish screens in the Sacramento–San Joaquin Delta, 1968–1980 (Bay–Delta Fishery Project 1981).

in the northern delta than in 1976 and 1977, which were dry years. This difference probably reflects the transport of young fish by river flow, and suggests that annual flow differences cause the precise location of major concentrations of juvenile fish to vary.

During their out-migration, young American shad typically range in fork length from about 5 to 15 cm (Stevens 1966a). Most young American shad leave the estuary by year's end (Ganssle 1966; Stevens 1966a); however, some remain for more than 1 year and perhaps do not go to sea. Ganssle (1966) reported catching American shad in their second year of life in trawl tows in San Francisco, San Pablo, and Suisun bays. More recently, California Department of Fish and Game biologists have captured some yearling (about 20–30 cm fork length) American shad in these areas during trawl surveys in the spring and fall (1967 to 1985) and in gill nets fished in Suisun Bay (fall 1973) and the tidal sloughs of the Suisun Marsh (February, June, and October 1977 and 1978). In the Suisun Marsh, more than 30 of these fish (22–35 cm fork length) were taken during February when they were almost 2 years old.

Little is known about American shad at sea along the Pacific coast. The recapture of three of our tags by commercial bottom-fish trawlers from 1975 to 1977 has revealed that some Sacramento–San Joaquin fish inhabit the ocean off the northern California coast.

Abundance

We estimated adult American shad abundance in 1976 and 1977 from mark–recapture data. Fish were captured in gill nets in the delta downstream from the sportfishing areas. Only those fish that appeared in good condition were tagged. Floy anchor tags (Dell 1968) were inserted into the musculature below the dorsal fin so the tag became anchored behind the neural spines of the vertebrae and pterygiophores that support the fin rays. About half of the tags offered a $5 reward. Each fish was categorized as a male or female by presence or absence of milt when finger pressure was applied in a squeezing motion near the urogenital area.

We did not observe many tags during sampling for recaptures. Thus, instead of the usual Petersen method, we divided annual estimates of catch by estimates of exploitation rates. Catches were estimated by multiplying estimates of angler effort, based on instantaneous-use counts, by catch per unit effort (Meinz 1981). These catch estimates were stratified according to sex ratios observed during Meinz's creel census. Mailed tag returns corrected for nonresponse were used to estimate exploitation rates (Table 5). The tags were conspicuous and the program was well publicized; therefore, we believe that tag recognition was high and tag returns accurately depicted the fraction of the population caught by anglers.

Due to the "catch-and-release" nature of the fishery, some fish in the catches were potentially recounted, which would lead to overestimates of abundance; since anglers only caught about 1 to 4% of the population, this bias was inconsequential.

The American shad run in 1976 was estimated to be 3.04×10^6 fish, consisting of 1.44×10^6 males and 1.60×10^6 females (Table 5). In 1977 the population estimate was 2.79×10^6 fish and consisted of 1.25×10^6 males and 1.54×10^6 females.

TABLE 5.—American shad mark–recapture, catch, and abundance estimates for the Sacramento–San Joaquin river system.

Year	Sex	Number of tags released		Number of tags recovered		Exploitation rate[c]	Catch[d]	Abundance estimate (10^6)[e]
		Reward	No reward	Reward[a]	No reward[b]			
1976	Male	1,789	1,904	69	74	0.039	56,165	1.44
	Female	939	937	15	15	0.016	25,562	1.60
1977	Male	2,437	2,226	95	91	0.040	49,853	1.25
	Female	1,305	1,260	27	22	0.019	29,325	1.54

[a] Mailed tag returns were corrected for nonresponse. Response rate was 0.59 based on return of 10 of 17 $5 reward tags observed during 1976–1977 creel census.

[b] Mailed tag returns were corrected for nonresponse. Response rate was 0.40 based on overall 1976–1977 nonreward tag return rate (0.013) divided by reward tag return rate (0.019) times reward tag response rate (0.59).

[c] Total tags recaptured divided by total tags released.

[d] From Meinz (1981).

[e] Catch divided by exploitation rate.

Numbers of spawners may be less than our estimates of the total runs. Scale analyses suggest not all American shad in the delta migrate upstream to spawn or enter the fishery. A small sample of 15 shad was recovered in 1977 after being tagged in 1976. Six of those fish lacked spawning checks on their scales.

While our data indicate that American shad are abundant, past populations probably were larger. We speculate that in 1917, at an average weight of 1.4 kg/shad, almost 2×10^6 fish were caught in the 2.6×10^6-kg commercial fishery. While we do not know the efficiency of the early fishery, it is reasonable to speculate that the total shad population was several times the number landed, and perhaps two to three times greater than current runs.

Abundance of young American shad in the Sacramento–San Joaquin Estuary varies annually by more than an order of magnitude, and the strongest year classes occur in the years with the highest river flows during the spawning and nursery periods (Stevens and Miller 1983). There are two abundance indices. One is based on catches of out-migrants at the fish screens of the CVP and SWP diversions in the delta (1959–1984); the other is calculated from catches of out-migrants during a fall midwater trawl survey at 87 sampling stations scattered from San Pablo Bay through the delta (1967–1984, except 1974 and 1979). Logarithms (base 10) of the abundance indices are directly correlated with the volume of river inflow to the delta during various combinations of months in spring and summer. For example, $r = 0.77$ for $\log_{10}$(midwater trawl index) versus mean April-to-June flows ($P < 0.001$). Several factors may cause abundance to increase with river flow, including decreased predation and decreased losses to diversions. However, our preferred hypothesis is that high river flows increase availability of nursery habitat by dispersing spawners and young fish (Stevens and Miller 1983).

The value of the correlations between young American shad abundance and river flow would be enhanced if a similar correlation existed between the year-class strength of adult American shad and flow in the natal year. We looked for such a correlation, using catches of adult American shad in striped bass fyke traps set in the Sacramento River during 8 years from 1974 to 1984. We standardized the annual catch of American shad to a trapping effort of 70 d (April 1–June 9). This standardized catch ranged from 242 fish in 1980 to 2,811 fish in 1983 (Table 2). Although the age composition of these American shad was not directly estimated, ages 3–5 generally form the bulk of the spawning run (Wixom 1981); thus, we correlated $\log_{10}$(catch) against 3-year means of April–June inflow to the delta 3 to 5 years earlier. The results were not conclusive. The correlation coefficient, 0.56, indicated a positive association between the catch and flow, but it was not statistically significant. Numerous factors, including variations in the age structure of the population (Wixom 1981), could have confounded this correlation. Alternatively, mortality may vary after the out-migration.

Striped Bass

Introduction and Fisheries

In 1879, 8 years after the American shad was introduced, 132 young striped bass from the Navesink River, New Jersey, were released into Carquinez Strait. A second plant of 300 fish from the Shrewsbury River, New Jersey, followed in 1882.

Like the American shad, striped bass experienced a population explosion soon after their introduction. Commercial harvesting started in the early 1880s and, by the turn of the century, exceeded 450,000 kg annually. The greatest recorded catch, over 900,000 kg, occurred in 1903. Subsequently, annual catches declined due to increased restrictions on the fishery (Craig 1928).

In 1935, the commercial fishery for striped bass was closed although the stock was not depleted (Craig 1930; Clark 1932, 1933). The closure stemmed largely from a social conflict between sport and commercial fishing interests which culminated with the closure of the commercial gillnet fisheries for chinook salmon Oncorhynchus tshawytscha and American shad in 1957. Thousands of striped bass were killed annually in the nets and could not be marketed legally. Closure of the chinook salmon and American shad fisheries reduced fishing mortality for striped bass, but the magnitude of the reduction cannot be estimated, because the precise magnitude of that incidental harvest is unknown and some illegal netting continues.

The striped bass sport fishery has become the most important fishery in the estuary and one of the most important fisheries on the Pacific coast. From 1969 to 1979, the annual catch varied from 107,000 fish (1978) to 403,000 fish (1975) (White 1986), and the annual recreational value is estimated to exceed 45 million dollars (Meyer Resources 1985).

Striped bass angling occurs the year around, but fishing localities vary seasonally in accordance with the striped bass migratory pattern (Stevens 1980). Tag recoveries (Chadwick 1967; Orsi 1971; White 1986) indicate that currently most adults inhabit salt water—San Pablo Bay, San Francisco Bay, and the Pacific Ocean—in the summer. The proportion entering the ocean varies from year to year, perhaps in response to water temperature (Radovich 1963). These fish begin returning to the delta in the fall although many overwinter in the bay area.

The distribution of fishing effort has shifted since the late 1950s as postspawning striped bass generally have migrated farther downstream and stayed there longer. Thus, fishing has improved in San Francisco Bay and the Pacific Ocean and declined in the delta. Also, the use of the Sacramento River as a spawning area appears to have increased, improving fishing there in the spring (Chadwick 1967). While significant environmental changes have occurred, data are insufficient to develop conclusions regarding causes of the changes in striped bass migrations.

Present fishing regulations include a 45.7 cm minimum length and a daily bag limit of two fish. From 1956 to 1981, the minimum length was 40.6 cm and the bag limit was three fish. Prior to 1956, regulations were more liberal: a 30.5 cm minimum length and five-fish bag limit generally was in effect.

Exploitation rates have been estimated almost annually since 1958. They have varied from 12 to 28% except for 37% in 1958 (Chadwick 1968; Miller 1974; White 1986) and are lower than those for Atlantic coast stocks (Kohlenstein 1981) that are fished commercially.

Spawning

The majority of striped bass spawning, 62% on the average, occurs in the Sacramento River, the remainder in the delta (Farley 1966; Turner 1976; California Department of Fish and Game, unpublished data). Unlike the American shad, relatively few striped bass spawn in the Sacramento River tributaries. Striped bass migrate to the reach of the Sacramento River from Sacramento to Colusa in April and May just before spawning. The geographical center of spawning there has varied from river km 148 in 1966 to km 200 in 1963 (Turner 1976).

Tag returns provide evidence of strong homing by striped bass which spawn in the upper Sacramento River, but it is unknown if the pattern is inherited by progeny of fish that spawned there or if it evolves later in life (Chadwick 1967).

In the delta, Turner (1976) found that the bulk of spawning occurred in the San Joaquin River between Antioch (river km 34) and Venice Island (river km 61). A moderate amount of spawning apparently occurred below Antioch in 1967 and 1969, although high flows in those years may have transported eggs farther seaward.

The migration farther up the San Joaquin is blocked in many years by a reverse salinity gradient that results from the use of the interior delta channels to carry Sacramento River water, characteristically low in dissolved solids, to the CVP–SWP pumping plants, and relatively high concentrations of dissolved solids coming from the upper San Joaquin River due to agricultural drainage. Total dissolved solids (TDS) of about 350 mg/L appear to repel the upstream migrants (Radtke and Turner 1967).

The striped bass and American shad spawning seasons overlap (Table 1). As for American shad, the time of striped bass spawning varies annually depending on water temperature, which is a function of weather (Turner 1976). Both species begin spawning at about 17°C, but since many striped bass spawn in the delta, which warms earlier than the upper Sacramento River system, striped bass begin spawning earlier than the American shad. Striped bass spawning also ends earlier; few fish spawn at temperatures exceeding 20°C.

Based on 7 years of data, the middle of the striped bass spawning period in the delta averaged 15 d earlier than in the Sacramento River. Most striped bass spawning occurred in the delta between April 23 and May 25. In the Sacramento River, most spawning occurred between May 10 and June 12. The greatest deviations from this period in the Sacramento River were in 1966 and 1972 when 20–25% of the striped bass spawned before May 10, and in 1969 when about 25% spawned after June 12. The difference between the spawning periods was greatest when river flows, as estimated at Chipps Island in May, were high ($r = 0.85$) reflecting an increased lag in the warming of the Sacramento River as flows increased (Turner 1976).

Total dissolved solids generally are low where the striped bass spawn. In 7 of the 9 years in which eggs were sampled in the delta, more than 80% of all newly spawned eggs were collected where TDS were less than 200 mg/L. However, in 1968 and 1972, salinity intruded into the spawning area and sizable numbers of eggs were spawned at higher TDS levels with no obvious effect on year-class strength. In the Sacramento River, TDS levels were always less than 200 mg/L (Turner 1976).

Nursery

The striped bass nursery overlaps that of the American shad, but it is predominantly farther downstream because the eggs and larvae from the Sacramento River drift to tidewater, where they coexist with larvae that were spawned in the delta.

By midsummer, flow patterns created by CVP–SWP operations have carried many of the young fish to the south delta, where they are lost through the water project export pumps. Other fish have drifted westward, as they did historically, to the fresh–saltwater mixing zone.

This mixing zone, or "entrapment zone" (Arthur and Ball 1979), is generally more productive than areas up or downstream, and its location varies annually. In high-flow summers, it is generally located in Suisun Bay; at low flows, it is in the delta (Turner and Chadwick 1972; Arthur and Ball 1979; Conomos 1979). Hence, the summer distribution of juvenile striped bass is correlated with river flow (Turner and Chadwick 1972; $r = -0.64$, $P < 0.01$, for percentage of the population in the delta versus log_{10}[mean May–July delta outflow], 1959–1985).

Midwater trawl catches (Stevens 1977a) indicate that young striped bass remain concentrated in and around the entrapment zone until river flows increase due to fall or winter storms. At that time, they disperse throughout the estuary.

During their second and third years, striped bass are spread throughout the estuary and the rivers above the delta. Male striped bass mature when they are 2 or 3 years old, whereas females mature at 4 or 5 years. Once striped bass mature, they take up the adult migratory pattern.

Abundance

The striped bass population has been declining since the 1960s and is now at its lowest level since measures have been available. Adult striped bass (total length ≥ 40.6 cm) abundance is being measured with Petersen population estimates and the catch per effort (CPE) of fish captured during tagging studies (Stevens et al. 1985). Petersen estimates have been calculated annually from

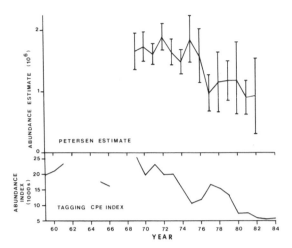

FIGURE 4.—Trends in abundance of adult striped bass (≥40.6 cm total length) in the Sacramento–San Joaquin estuary. Vertical bars for the Petersen estimates are 95% confidence intervals; CPE is catch per effort. (From Stevens et al. 1985.)

1969 through 1982, and the CPE measurements are available for 1959 to 1961, 1965 to 1966, and 1969 to 1984.

According to the Petersen estimates, the striped bass population was around 1.7×10^6 fish and stable between 1969, when the estimates began, and 1976 (Figure 4). It then declined to about 1×10^6 fish and remained near this lower level through 1982. The CPE index indicates that the striped bass population declined steadily from the late 1960s to a low level in 1975. It then rose briefly, but declined to even lower levels by 1984 (Figure 4). Thus, the population of adult striped bass in the estuary has definitely fallen to a low level—much lower than when estimates were first available 20 years ago. However, the precise timing and magnitude of the decline are uncertain.

Catch records from the charter boat fishery suggest that peak striped bass abundance in recent years occurred in the early 1960s. Charter boat operators are required to report catches to the California Department of Fish and Game. Although these boats presently take only about 14% of the total catch (White 1986) and their fishing locations and methods have varied over the years, their reports are the best long-term striped bass catch records available (Stevens 1977b). In the late 1950s and early 1960s, success on charter boats exceeded two fish per angler-day. After 1963, success dropped and, while fluctuating irregularly, was frequently less than one fish per angler-day from 1969 to 1982 (Figure 5).

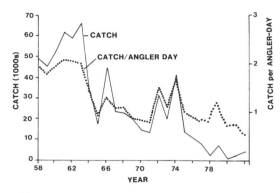

FIGURE 5.—Trend in striped bass catch on charter boats in the Sacramento–San Joaquin estuary.

Total catches on charter boats are affected by the number of anglers willing to pay for a day's fishing. Not surprisingly, fishing effort varies according to angler success (Miller 1974). Thus, decreased effort associated with the generally low success in the late 1970s and early 1980s caused total catch to decline even more severely than catch per angler-day. In 1980, the total catch on charter boats was only about 1,400 fish, substantially lower than the 47,000 to 67,000 striped bass landed each year from 1958 to 1963 (Figure 5).

The recent decline in adult striped bass abundance has been accompanied by below-average recruitment and an increase in annual angler harvest from about 15% of the population in 1970 to about 27% in 1976. Generally, these exploitation rates would be considered safe, but increased survival or recruitment obviously are needed to reverse the population trend (Stevens et al. 1985). Increased survival potentially could be attained by reducing exploitation or other mortality factors.

Abundance of young-of-the-year striped bass has been measured annually, except for one year, since 1959. The population is sampled every second week from late June to late July or early August throughout the nursery habitat. When their mean fork length reaches 38 mm, a young-of-the-year index is calculated on the basis of catch per net tow weighted by the volume of water in the areas where the fish are caught (Turner and Chadwick 1972; Stevens et al. 1985).

The index of young striped bass abundance has varied from 6.3 to 117.2 during the 26 survey years. From 1959 to 1976, variations in spring and early summer river flow and water diversion rates largely accounted for the annual variations in young striped bass abundance, high river flows

being beneficial and high diversion rates being detrimental (Turner and Chadwick 1972; Chadwick et al. 1977; Stevens et al. 1985). Thus, in the Sacramento–San Joaquin river system, high river flows benefit both young striped bass and American shad.

Since 1977 the abundance of young striped bass has been considerably lower than predicted by regressions based on the 1959–1976 data. Several factors have been identified as probable major contributors to the decline of young striped bass (Stevens et al. 1985): (1) the adult population, reduced by a combination of lower recruitment and higher mortality rates, produces fewer eggs; (2) production of food for young striped bass has declined; (3) large numbers of striped bass eggs and young have been removed from the estuary by diversion of water needed for agriculture, power plant cooling, and other uses; (4) toxicants may cause mortality of adults, reduce their ability to reproduce, or reduce the survival of their eggs and young.

Correlations indicate a positive association between indices of young striped bass abundance and subsequent recruitment to the adult population. This suggests that past losses of young striped bass have contributed to the decline of the adult stock and that the recent decline in young striped bass abundance is leading to a further reduction of adults (Stevens et al. 1985).

Discussion

The explosion and spread of the populations of American shad and striped bass shortly after their introductions reveals that environmental conditions formerly were nearly ideal for these species in the Sacramento–San Joaquin river system. At the time of the introductions, although the rivers and delta were largely leveed, the rest of the system was relatively undeveloped by humans. There were hundreds of kilometers of rivers suitable for spawning; no major dams blocked the runs and reduced the freshwater flows that disperse the young. California agriculture and industry were just beginning, so losses of young fish to water diversions and toxic wastes would have been minimal. Also, the native fish fauna contained few top predators in those areas used extensively by the young of both species.

The American shad and striped bass populations have declined since the early 1900s. Striped bass, in particular, have not coped well recently. Available evidence indicates that neither population has been overfished, but there is substantial evidence that the favorable environment initially experienced by both species has become less friendly due to human activities.

American shad and striped bass have similar spawning strategies and early life histories and also overlapping nurseries; thus, both species are vulnerable to many of the same environmental disturbances. The most obvious of these have been the construction of dams in the upper reaches of the rivers; water diversions by water projects, power plants, and farms along the rivers and in the delta; and discharges and accidental spills of toxic substances by municipalities, industries, and agriculture. Specifically, these perturbations have had the following adverse effects.

(1) River flows have been reduced in quantity and quality. Year-class strengths of both American shad (Stevens and Miller 1983) and striped bass (Turner and Chadwick 1972; Chadwick et al. 1977; Stevens 1977b; Stevens et al. 1985) correlate positively with river flow during the spawning and nursery periods. Flows must be ample to attract American shad spawners into Sacramento River tributaries, transport and disperse the young of both species to suitable nursery habitat, repel salinity intrusions in the striped bass spawning area in the western delta, dilute the salinity of the upper San Joaquin River that repels striped bass spawners, and reduce the probability of entrainment of young fish and their food organisms in water diversions. Water project dams and pumps have reduced flows during the spring and early-summer periods, which are most critical in this respect.

In regard to the quantity of flow, abundance of not only American shad and striped bass, but also the abundance of other anadromous fishes in the Sacramento–San Joaquin river system, specifically chinook salmon and longfin smelt *Spirinchus thaleichthys,* is known to benefit from high flows (Stevens and Miller 1983). In contrast, our American shad results are in discord with Crecco and Savoy's (1984) results for the Connecticut River, where American shad year-class strength and flow are inversely correlated.

(2) Food supplies for young fish have been reduced. An adequate supply of zooplankton must be available at the time and place that the young fish initially feed. A decline in zooplankton has coincided with the recent decline in young striped bass abundance and provides one of the most likely explanations for the recent low abundance of young striped bass (Stevens et al. 1985). Considerable evidence exists that populations of phytoplankton, zooplankton, opossum shrimp *Neomysis mercedis,* and other organisms in the estuarine food web have been reduced through effects of water project operations on the quantity of flows of the Sacramento and San Joaquin rivers, the location of the entrapment zone, and the growing use of the delta channels as conduits to carry water south to the CVP and SWP pumps (Turner 1966; Turner and Heubach 1966; Heubach 1969; Arthur and Ball 1979; Knutson and Orsi 1983; Stevens et al. 1985).

(3) Fish have been entrained in water diversions and lost. The magnitude of entrainment losses of both species to diversions by water projects, local agriculture, power plants, and other industry have been on the order of 10^6 to 10^9 fish annually since the 1950s. Screens help save the larger individuals, but only operational constraints can save larval fish. The recent decline of the adult striped bass population began in the 1960s, lagging the onset of major water project operations by only a few years. This pattern suggests that entrainment losses and other impacts of water diversions have contributed substantially to the decline and that striped bass losses, at least, are not materially compensated by subsequent reductions in density-dependent mortality.

(4) Pollution is a potentially important stressor. We cannot define the overall effect of pollution because the data base is inadequate, but we do know that large quantities of potentially toxic substances reach the river system. Major waste treatment facilities discharge into the delta and bays; although they have been much improved in the last decade, other important sources of pollution still exist. Much of the watersheds of the Sacramento and San Joaquin rivers are treated with pesticides, a variety of toxicants enter the rivers and bays with runoff from industrial and urban areas whenever it rains, and accidental spills of all sorts commonly occur (Stevens et al. 1985). Recent studies of the health of adult striped bass from the Sacramento–San Joaquin system have revealed that gonads, liver, and muscles have accumulated toxic substances, primarily monocyclic aromatic hydrocarbons (MAH), chlorinated hydrocarbons, and heavy metals (Whipple 1984). Health, as measured by liver, gonad, and egg condition, is inversely correlated with concentrations of MAH and Zn in the tissues. High tissue concentrations of MAH and Zn also are associated with greater parasite infestations. Quantities of Hg in striped bass flesh have been

sufficient to trigger health warnings regarding its consumption by humans.

While American shad and striped bass have similarities in their life history strategies, there are also differences that appear to benefit the American shad, which has not had a recent decline paralleling that of the striped bass. Two differences in their life history strategies may be relevant.

(1) The major striped bass nursery is in the estuary (Chadwick 1964; Turner and Chadwick 1972), whereas the American shad nursery is partly upstream. Perhaps American shad have not suffered the same fate because the upstream environment has not been degraded as much as that of the estuary.

(2) American shad spend most of their lives in the ocean. In contrast, striped bass live mostly in the estuary; only the larger fish go to sea and only for a few months each year. Thus, due to various sources of pollution in the region surrounding the estuary, striped bass probably are exposed to more toxicity. Toxic exposure of American shad has not received the same attention that Whipple (1984) has given to adult striped bass, however.

All identified adverse changes in habitat quality are associated with human activities. The California Department of Fish and Game has been attempting to counter these changes by working with water development agencies during project planning and with control agencies such as the State Water Resources Control Board and regional water quality control boards.

Mitigation for striped bass losses in the form of annual stocking of about 200,000 yearling hatchery fish is currently required of the Pacific Gas and Electric Company by the water quality control boards. Hatchery production is also being negotiated between the Departments of Fish and Game and Water Resources to mitigate effects of the State Water Project. Additionally, the Department of Fish and Game is experimentally stocking about 500,000 marked yearling striped bass annually. This stocking and the evaluation of its effectiveness are funded by a $3.50 stamp that must be purchased by every striped bass angler.

There has been no attempt to mitigate or restrict American shad losses other than by fish screens on diversions and indirectly through constraints placed by the control agencies on water project and power plant operations for protection of striped bass and chinook salmon.

Subsequent to the introductions of striped bass and American shad, two native fishes experienced disastrous declines. One, the thicktail chub *Gila crassicauda,* once common, apparently is now extinct (Shapovalov et al. 1981); another, the Sacramento perch *Archoplites interruptus,* formerly the major top predator, now is very rare in the delta. However, assessments of the impacts of American shad and striped bass on these and other natives are precluded by introductions of numerous other fishes, particularly centrarchids and ictalurids in the late 1800s, and by vast environmental changes such as the construction of levees that eliminated delta tidal marshes and flood plains of the rivers upstream, dams that blocked spawning runs, the various water diversions, and toxic discharges. American shad, being plankton feeders and spending most of their lives in the ocean, undoubtedly have had less impact than striped bass, which are more estuarine and prey on both introduced and native species (Stevens 1966b; Thomas 1967). Considering that even with the present depleted stock, the annual recreational value of the Sacramento–San Joaquin striped bass population is estimated to exceed $45 million (Meyer Resources 1985), and that American shad also support a popular fishery, we believe that the introductions of these species have been of substantial benefit to California.

Acknowledgments

The striped bass research has involved numerous biologists associated with the Bay–Delta Fishery Project and other units of the California Department of Fish and Game over the years. This work has largely been supported by Federal Aid in Fish Restoration funds, the California Department of Water Resources, and the U.S. Bureau of Reclamation. Some of the American shad results are a by-product of the striped bass research. However, much work specifically directed toward American shad was performed by the California Department of Fish and Game with funding from the California Department of Water Resources and the Anadromous Fish Conservation Act. R. Painter was project leader for these studies, and M. Meinz and L. Wixom developed many of the results that we have described. K. Odenweller drew the figures for this paper.

References

Arthur, J. F., and M. D. Ball. 1979. Factors influencing the entrapment of suspended material in the San Francisco Bay–Delta estuary. Pages 143–174 *in* T. J. Conomos, editor. San Francisco Bay: the urbanized estuary. American Association for the

Advancement of Science, Pacific Division, San Francisco, California, USA.

Bay–Delta Fishery Project. 1981. The John E. Skinner Delta Fish Protective Facility 1968–1980—a summary of the first 13 years of operation. California Department of Fish and Game, Anadromous Fisheries Branch, Administrative Report 81-5. Sacramento, California, USA.

California Department of Fish and Game. 1965. California fish and wildlife plan. Sacramento, California, USA.

Chadwick, H. K. 1964. Annual abundance of young striped bass (Roccus saxatilis) in the Sacramento–San Joaquin Delta, California. California Fish and Game 50:69–99.

Chadwick, H. K. 1967. Recent migrations of the Sacramento–San Joaquin River striped bass population. Transactions of the American Fisheries Society 96:327–342.

Chadwick, H. K. 1968. Mortality rates in the California striped bass population. California Fish and Game 54:228–246.

Chadwick, H. K. 1977. Effects of water development on striped bass. Marine Recreational Fisheries 2:123–130.

Chadwick, H. K., D. E. Stevens, and L. W. Miller. 1977. Some factors regulating the striped bass population in the Sacramento–San Joaquin estuary, California. Pages 18–35 in W. Van Winkle, editor. Proceedings of the conference on assessing the effects of power-plant-induced mortality on fish populations. Pergamon, New York, New York, USA.

Clark, G. H. 1932. The striped bass supply, past and present. California Fish and Game 18:297–298.

Clark, G. H. 1933. Fluctuations in the abundance of striped bass in California. California Department of Fish and Game, Fish Bulletin 39.

Conomos, T. J. 1979. Properties and circulation of San Francisco Bay waters. Pages 47–84 in T. J. Conomos, editor. San Francisco Bay: the urbanized estuary. American Association for the Advancement of Science, Pacific Division, San Francisco, California, USA.

Craig, J. A. 1928. The striped bass supply of California. California Fish and Game 14:265–272.

Craig, J. A. 1930. An analysis of the catch statistics of the striped bass (Roccus lineatus) fishery in California. California Department of Fish and Game, Fish Bulletin 24.

Crecco, V. A., and T. F. Savoy. 1984. Effects of fluctuations in hydrographic conditions on year-class strength of American shad (Alosa sapidissima) in the Connecticut River. Canadian Journal of Fisheries and Aquatic Sciences 41:1216–1223.

Dell, M. B. 1968. A new fish tag and rapid, cartridge-fed applicator. Transactions of the American Fisheries Society 97:57–59.

Farley, T. C. 1966. Striped bass, Roccus saxatilis, spawning in the Sacramento–San Joaquin river systems during 1963 and 1964. California Department of Fish and Game, Fish Bulletin 136:28–43.

Ganssle, D. 1966. Fishes and decapods of San Pablo and Suisun bays. California Department of Fish and Game, Fish Bulletin 133:64–94.

Hallock, R. J., D. H. Fry, Jr., and D. A. LaFaunce. 1957. The use of wire fyke traps to estimate runs of adult salmon and steelhead in the Sacramento River. California Fish and Game 43:271–298.

Hatton, S. R. 1940. Progress report on Central Valley fisheries investigation, 1939. California Fish and Game 26:335–373.

Heubach, W. 1969. Neomysis awatschensis in the Sacramento–San Joaquin estuary. Limnology and Oceanography 14:533–546.

Knutson, A. C., and J. J. Orsi. 1983. Factors regulating abundance and distribution of the shrimp Neomysis mercedis in the Sacramento–San Joaquin estuary. Transactions of the American Fisheries Society 112:476–485.

Kohlenstein, L. C. 1981. On the proportion of the Chesapeake Bay stock of striped bass that migrates into the coastal fishery. Transactions of the American Fisheries Society 110:168–179.

Meinz, M. 1981. American shad, Alosa sapidissima, sport fishery in the Sacramento River system, 1976–1978: catch and effort. California Department of Fish and Game, Anadromous Fisheries Branch, Administrative Report 81-1, Sacramento, California, USA.

Meyer Resources. 1985. The economic value of striped bass, Morone saxatilis, chinook salmon, Oncorhynchus tshawytscha, and steelhead trout, Salmo gairdneri, of the Sacramento and San Joaquin river systems. California Department of Fish and Game, Anadromous Fisheries Branch, Administrative Report 85-3, Sacramento, California, USA.

Miller, L. W. 1974. Mortality rates for California striped bass (Morone saxatilis) from 1965–1971. California Fish and Game 60:157–171.

Orsi, J. J. 1971. The 1965–1967 migrations of the Sacramento–San Joaquin estuary striped bass population. California Fish and Game 57:257–267.

Painter, R. E., L. H. Wixom, and M. Meinz. 1980. Management plan for American shad (Alosa sapidissima) in central California. California Department of Fish and Game, Anadromous Fish Conservation Act, Job 5, AFS-17, Final Report, Sacramento, California, USA.

Painter, R. E., L. H. Wixom, and S. N. Taylor. 1977. An evaluation of fish populations and fisheries in the post-Oroville Project Feather River. Report to the California Department of Water Resources in accordance with Federal Power Commission License 2100, Sacramento, California, USA.

Radovich, J. 1963. Effect of ocean temperature on the seaward movements of striped bass, Roccus saxatilis, on the Pacific coast. California Fish and Game 49:191–206.

Radovich, J. 1970. How to catch, bone, and cook a shad. California Department of Fish and Game, Sacramento, California, USA.

Radtke, L. D., and J. L. Turner. 1967. High concentrations of total dissolved solids block spawning migration of striped bass *(Roccus saxatilis)* in the San Joaquin River, California. Transactions of the American Fisheries Society 96:405–407.

Shapovalov, L., A. J. Cordone, and W. A. Dill. 1981. A list of the freshwater and anadromous fishes of California. California Fish and Game 67:4–38.

Skinner, J. E. 1962. An historical review of the fish and wildlife resources of the San Francisco Bay area. California Department of Fish and Game, Water Project Branch, Report 1, Sacramento, California, USA.

Stevens, D. E. 1966a. Distribution and food habits of the American shad, *Alosa sapidissima,* in the Sacramento–San Joaquin Delta. California Department of Fish and Game, Fish Bulletin 136:97–107.

Stevens, D. E. 1966b. Food habits of striped bass, *Roccus saxatilis,* in the Sacramento–San Joaquin Delta. California Department of Fish and Game, Fish Bulletin 136:68–96.

Stevens, D. E. 1977a. Striped bass *(Morone saxatilis)* monitoring techniques in the Sacramento–San Joaquin estuary. Pages 91–109 *in* W. Van Winkle, editor. Proceedings of the conference on assessing the effects of power-plant-induced mortality on fish populations. Pergamon, New York, New York, USA.

Stevens, D. E. 1977b. Striped bass *(Morone saxatilis)* year class strength in relation to river flow in the Sacramento–San Joaquin estuary, California. Transactions of the American Fisheries Society 106:34–42.

Stevens, D. E. 1980. Factors affecting the striped bass fisheries of the west coast. Marine Recreational Fisheries 5:15–28.

Stevens, D. E., D. W. Kohlhorst, L. W. Miller, and D. W. Kelley. 1985. The decline of striped bass in the Sacramento–San Joaquin estuary, California. Transactions of the American Fisheries Society 114:12–30.

Stevens, D. E., and L. W. Miller. 1983. Effects of river flow on abundance of young chinook salmon, American shad, longfin smelt, and delta smelt in the Sacramento–San Joaquin river system. North American Journal of Fisheries Management 3:425–437.

Thomas, J. L. 1967. The diet of juvenile and adult striped bass, *Roccus saxatilis,* in the Sacramento–San Joaquin river system. California Fish and Game 53:49–62.

Turner, J. L. 1966. Seasonal distribution of crustacean plankters in the Sacramento–San Joaquin Delta. California Department of Fish and Game, Fish Bulletin 133:95–104.

Turner, J. L. 1976. Striped bass spawning in the Sacramento and San Joaquin rivers in central California from 1963 to 1972. California Fish and Game 62:106–118.

Turner, J. L., and H. K. Chadwick. 1972. Distribution and abundance of young-of-the-year striped bass, *Morone saxatilis,* in relation to river flow in the Sacramento–San Joaquin estuary. Transactions of the American Fisheries Society 101:442–452.

Turner, J. L., and W. Heubach. 1966. Distribution and concentration of *Neomysis awatschensis* in the Sacramento–San Joaquin Delta. California Department of Fish and Game, Fish Bulletin 133:105–112.

Whipple, J. A. 1984. The impact of estuarine degradation and chronic pollution on populations of anadromous striped bass *(Morone saxatilis)* in the San Francisco Bay–Delta, California: a summary for managers and regulators. National Marine Fisheries Service, Southwest Fisheries Center, Administrative Report T-84-01, Tiburon, California, USA.

White, J. R. 1986. The striped bass sport fishery in the Sacramento–San Joaquin estuary, 1969–1979. California Fish and Game 72:17–37.

Wixom, L. H. 1981. Age and spawning history of American shad *(Alosa sapidissima)* in central California, 1975–1978. California Department of Fish and Game, Anadromous Fisheries Branch, Administrative Report 81-3, Sacramento, California, USA.

American Fisheries Society Symposium 1:79–88, 1987

Increased Spawning by American Shad Coincident with Improved Dissolved Oxygen in the Tidal Delaware River

KEITH R. MAURICE, ROBERT W. BLYE, AND PAUL L. HARMON

RMC-Environmental Services
Fricks Lock Road, Rural Delivery 1, Pottstown, Pennsylvania 19464, USA

DOUGLAS LAKE

C. T. Main, Incorporated
Southeast Tower, Prudential Building, Boston, Massachusetts 02199, USA

Abstract.—Prior to 1900, American shad *Alosa sapidissima* spawned throughout freshwater reaches of the Delaware River, and the principal spawning ground was in tidal fresh water near Philadelphia, Pennsylvania. The principal spawning grounds were eliminated during the early 1900s and only a remnant population spawned upstream of the Delaware Water Gap. Elimination of spawning downstream was coincident with a rapid decline in the size of the American shad runs in the Delaware River and was attributed to severe pollution of tidal waters from Wilmington, Delaware, to Philadelphia. Ichthyoplankton collections from 1944 through 1978 between Wilmington and the Delaware Water Gap indicated minimal spawning of American shad, but recent surveys near Hutchinson, New Jersey, and Point Pleasant, New Hope, and Yardley, Pennsylvania, found a much greater density of eggs and larvae. The increased spawning is likely due to recently improved dissolved oxygen in tidal waters. Seasonal deterioration in dissolved oxygen, thought to have once blocked much of the late segment of the spring spawning run, is now less severe and occurs later. This may allow a greater number of late-season migrants to reach the nontidal region downstream of the Delaware Water Gap, where they spawn when water temperatures are suitable.

Prior to 1900, American shad *Alosa sapidissima* used most of the freshwater areas of the Delaware River as spawning grounds, including the East and West branches and many tributaries (Figure 1). The principal spawning ground was in tidal fresh water near Philadelphia, Pennsylvania (Mansueti and Kolb 1953; Walburg and Nichols 1967; Chittenden 1976).

The principal spawning grounds were eliminated during the early 1900s and only a remnant population spawned upstream of the Delaware Water Gap (km 345) primarily from Port Jervis, New York (km 410), to Hancock, New York (km 532), and into the lower East Branch (Cable 1945; Sykes and Lehman 1957; Chittenden 1976). This rapid decline in the size of the American shad runs in the Delaware River was attributed to severe pollution of the tidal Delaware from Wilmington, Delaware (km 116), to Philadelphia (km 146 to 180) (Ellis et al. 1947; Sykes and Lehman 1957; Chittenden 1969; Miller et al. 1982).

This paper compares the present incidence of spawning by American shad in the nontidal Delaware River downstream of the Delaware Water Gap to previous studies and relates the observed increase to improved dissolved oxygen concentrations in tidal waters.

Methods

Ichthyoplankton collections were made in the Delaware River near Hutchinson, New Jersey (km 309), from 1981 through 1984, and near Point Pleasant, Pennsylvania (km 253), from 1982 through 1985 (Figure 1) to determine what species of fishes spawned at the sites and their spawning periods, relative abundances, and distributions. Additional exploratory collections were made near New Hope, Pennsylvania (km 240), and Yardley, Pennsylvania (km 220), in 1984 to determine the downstream limits of spawning by American shad.

Near Hutchinson, ichthyoplankton were collected during both day and night from April 27 to June 29 in 1981, April 12 to July 8, 1982, May 9 to July 15, 1983, and only at night from April 24 to June 6, 1984. Samples were collected twice per week at nine stations in 1981 and at 14 stations in 1982 and once per week at 14 stations in 1983 and at nine stations in 1984. Collection gear was a 0.5-m, 505-μm-mesh, 3:1 ratio ichthyoplankton net with a General Oceanics Model 2030 digital flow meter mounted off-center in the mouth. Oblique tows from near bottom to surface were made in an upstream direction until approximately 100 m³ of water were filtered.

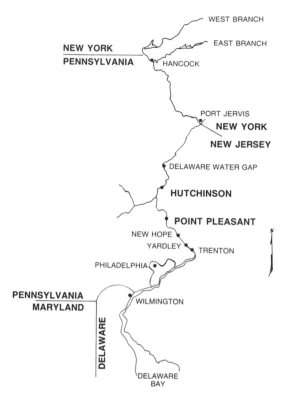

FIGURE 1.—Location of historical spawning grounds of American shad and ichthyoplankton collection stations in the Delaware River.

Near Point Pleasant, ichthyoplankton was collected both day and night at four stations from April 16 to July 21, 1982, March 17 to July 21, 1983, March 26 to July 6, 1984, and April 9 to July 18, 1985. Samples were collected weekly in May and June and biweekly in July. Collections were made irregularly in March and April, weather permitting. Collection gear comprised two 114-cm-long cylinder cone nets of 505-μm mesh attached to a bongo frame whose cylinders were 28 cm long and 20 cm in diameter. A General Oceanics Model 2030 flow meter was centered in the right cylinder. Stationary sets or oblique tows from bottom to surface were conducted in an upstream direction at three stations until at least 33 m^3 of water per replicate were filtered. At the fourth station, a 10-min surface tow was done in an oval pattern.

Ichthyoplankton was collected at night at two stations near New Hope and at three stations near Yardley on June 21 and 26, 1984, with the same gear and sampling techniques as at Point Pleasant.

Ichthyoplankton tows were made with an outboard-powered johnboat fitted with a sidearm boom and winch to minimize avoidance by larval fish. An 18.2-kg batwing depressor attached to each apparatus ensured that it was deployed to the bottom and stable during tows.

The contents of each sample were concentrated into labeled jars and preserved with 10% formalin containing rose bengal dye. Sorted specimens were identified to the lowest possible taxon and developmental stage.

Results

We collected 18,555 eggs and 7,033 larvae from American shad in 1,289 ichthyoplankton collections made near Hutchinson from April through July, 1981–1984 (Table 1). Spawning of American shad was observed on numerous occasions and began in late April at water temperatures of 8–15°C. Peak spawning activity at Hutchinson occurred between late May and the third week of June when mean water temperatures were 16.9–26.5°C (Tables 2, 3). Peak abundance of larvae occurred 8–15 d later depending on the time of year and water temperature. Abundance of eggs in samples declined rapidly near mid-June, although a few eggs were occasionally collected in early July. Eggs were collected as late as July 6, 1982, at a mean water temperature of 22.4°C. The highest mean temperature at which eggs were collected was 27.1°C.

At Hutchinson, American shad larvae were first collected between May 7 and 24 and were most abundant in June. In all years, by late June to mid-July the abundance of larval American shad decreased, although occasionally substantial numbers of larvae were still taken.

American shad were never observed spawning at Point Pleasant; however, 1,732 shad larvae and 58 eggs were taken in 417 ichthyoplankton samples collected during April through July in 1982–1985 (Table 1). The majority of eggs were collected at low densities during the day and were in an advanced stage of embryological development, suggesting downstream drift from upstream spawning grounds (Tables 4–6). Two eggs collected at night on May 30, 1985, were in an early stage of embryological development and were probably spawned nearby. Eggs were collected as early as April 17 in 1985 and as late as June 25 in 1984 at mean temperatures from 12.8 to 26.7°C.

At Point Pleasant, larvae were present in much greater densities than were eggs and generally were more abundant at night. Larvae were first

TABLE 1.—Summary of collections of eggs and larvae of American shad at Hutchinson, New Jersey, Point Pleasant, Pennsylvania, New Hope, Pennsylvania, and Yardley, Pennsylvania, 1981–1985.

Station	Year	Life stage	Period of occurrence[a]	Range of water temperatures (°C)[b]	Minimum and maximum number per 100 m³	Total number collected
Hutchinson	1981	Eggs	Apr 30–Jun 11	15.0–24.9	0.4–142.6	437
		Larvae	May 7–Jun 26	15.7–26.5	0.4–12.9	126
Hutchinson	1982	Eggs	Apr 16–Jul 6	10.5–22.4	0.8–124.4	1,941
		Larvae	May 6–Jul 8	15.5–25.3	0.2–300.2	2,814
Point Pleasant	1982	Eggs	Apr 28–May 13	13.7–19.5	1.1–3.7	5
		Larvae	May 19–Jul 7	17.3–24.4	1.0–339.5	387
Hutchinson	1983	Eggs	May 10–Jul 5	12.8–27.1	0.9–2122.0	13,024
		Larvae	May 17–Jul 19	14.2–28.1	0.8–635.0	1,880
Point Pleasant	1983	Eggs	May 4–Jun 16	12.8–26.7	1.0–11.6	35
		Larvae	May 26–Jun 30	18.1–26.7	1.0–947.6	715
Hutchinson	1984	Eggs	Apr 24–Jun 27	8.0–25.7	0.9–468.8	3,153
		Larvae	May 24–Jun 27	18.0–25.7	0.9–672.7	2,213
Point Pleasant	1984	Eggs	May 10–Jun 25	12.8–21.9	1.0–1.3	4
		Larvae	Jun 8–Jul 11	21.9–24.8	1.3–465.2	384
New Hope	1984	Larvae	Jun 21–Jun 26	22.0–24.0	1.3–20.2	18
Yardley	1984	Larvae	Jun 21–Jun 26	20.7–24.0	1.4–15.4	15
Point Pleasant	1985	Eggs	Apr 17–May 30	13.6–22.4	1.3–5.1	14
		Larvae	May 9–Jun 26	18.0–22.8	1.3–169.3	246

[a] Some of the dates for Hutchinson represent collections made during the day. They will not correspond to those in Table 3, which presents only night collections.
[b] These are the lowest and highest mean daily temperatures for all samples in which the life stage was collected.

collected as early as May 9 in 1985 and as late as July 11 in 1984 and were most abundant in June.

In 10 exploratory samples collected June 21 and 26, 1984, at New Hope and Yardley, Pennsylvania, we collected 33 American shad larvae (1.3/100 m³ to 20.2/100 m³).

Discussion

To compare collections made at Hutchinson and Point Pleasant with previous work, we summarized all known collections of ichthyoplankton made between Wilmington and the Delaware Water Gap since 1944 (Table 7). Minimal spawning occurred downstream of the Delaware Water Gap

TABLE 2.—Densities (number per 100 m³) of eggs and larvae of American shad collected at night from the Delaware River at Hutchinson, New Jersey, 1981–1984.[a] Zeros indicate collection efforts were made but no eggs or larvae were captured.

	1981		1982		1983		1984	
Date	Eggs	Larvae	Eggs	Larvae	Eggs	Larvae	Eggs	Larvae
Apr 15–20			0	0				
21–25			<1	0			1	0
26–30	13	0	7	0				
May 1–5	4	0	18	0				
6–10	<1	<1	3	<1	22	0	28	0
11–15	0	0	7	<1				
16–20	<1	0	1	3	12	0		
21–25	21	<1	<1	2	381	2	49	3
26–31	4	1	3	2	186	11		
Jun 1–5	2	1	14	<1				
6–10	0	<1	12	<1	206	30	138	1
11–15	0	3	0	<1	110	32	52	5
16–20	0	<1	14	1			65	111
21–25	0	<1	2	30	4	16	15	99
26–30	0	<1	<1	58	<1	<1	2	29
Jul 1–5			2	15	<1	16		
6–10			<1	8				
11–15					0	15		
16–20					0	3		

[a] Daytime densities were generally less than 1.

TABLE 3.—Mean water temperatures (°C) during ichthyoplankton sampling in the Delaware River at Point Pleasant, 1982–1985, and Hutchinson, 1981–1984.

	Point Pleasant				Hutchinson			
Date	1982	1983	1984	1985	1981	1982	1983	1984
Apr 15–20	11.0			13.6		10.5		
21–25				16.2		11.0		8.0
26–30	13.7		11.7		15.0	13.7		
May 1–5		14.2	14.5	20.9		15.5		
6–10	17.5		12.8	18.0	15.7	15.5	12.8	12.1
11–15	19.5	12.8	14.3			18.7		
16–20	20.5	14.5		20.7	15.6	22.5	14.2	
21–25			16.6	18.9	16.9	17.0	18.1	18.0
26–31	19.8	18.1		22.4	22.2	20.0	15.5	
Jun 1–5	17.3	19.5		20.8	20.4	19.5		
6–10	19.1	19.3	21.9		24.9	17.0	19.7	18.1
11–15			24.1	21.3	24.9	16.0	23.6	25.7
16–20	21.0	26.7		22.6	26.5	20.0		20.0
21–25	21.3	23.5	21.9		24.0	21.5	23.1	22.8
26–30	22.4	23.4		21.6	24.8	25.3	22.4	23.2
Jul 1–5			24.8	22.8		22.0	27.1	
6–10	24.4	24.8				22.4[a]		
11–15			21.6				27.8	
16–20				26.6			28.1	

[a] Temperature on July 6; temperature on July 8 was 25.3°C.

through the mid 1970s. Cable (1945) documented spawning from Bordentown, New Jersey, to Equinunk, Pennsylvania, in collections made during early May through early June 1944. She found few eggs at any station and most eggs below Milford, Pennsylvania, were dead; normal survival occurred only at Lackawaxen and Equinunk. No information on densities of eggs and larvae sampled was available.

Barker (1965) collected at Belvidere, New Jersey, Easton, Pennsylvania, and Milford, New Jersey, in May and early June 1963 and at Easton, Milford, and Lumberville, Pennsylvania, and West Trenton, New Jersey, in May and early June 1964 (Table 7). He did not express data for densities of eggs and larvae but, based on his gear,

TABLE 4.—Densities (number/100 m³) of eggs and larvae of American shad collected during daylight from the Delaware River at Point Pleasant, Pennsylvania, 1982–1985. Zeros indicate collection efforts were made but no eggs or larvae were captured.

	1982		1983		1984		1985	
Date	Eggs	Larvae	Eggs	Larvae	Eggs	Larvae	Eggs	Larvae
Apr 15–20	0	0					<1	0
21–25							0	0
26–30	<1	0			0	0		
May 1–5			2	0	0	0	0	0
6–10	0	0			<1	0	0	0
11–15	0	0	<1	0	0	0		
16–20	0	0	0	0			0	4
21–25					0	0	0	10
26–31	0	<1	5	1			1	9
Jun 1–5	0	17	0	9			0	10
6–10	0	21	1	4	0	30		
11–15					0	102	0	<1
16–20	0	20	<1	121			0	3
21–25	0	0	0	3	<1	10		
26–30	0	3	0	10			0	0
Jul 1–5					0	5	0	0
6–10	0	0	0	0				

TABLE 5.—Density (number/100 m³) of American shad eggs and larvae collected at night from the Delaware River at Point Pleasant, Pennsylvania, 1982–1985. Zeros indicate collection efforts were made but no eggs or larvae were collected.

Date	1982 Eggs	1982 Larvae	1983 Eggs	1983 Larvae	1984 Eggs	1984 Larvae	1985 Eggs	1985 Larvae
Apr 15–20	0	0					<1	0
21–25							0	0
26–30	0	0			0	0		
May 1–5			0	0	0	0	<1	0
6–10	<1	0					0	<1
11–15	<1	0	0	0	0	0		
16–20	0	16	0	0			<1	8
21–25					0	0	0	12
26–31	0	13	<1	2			2	42
Jun 1–5	0	3	<1	63			0	33
6–10	0	85	0	8	<1	6		
11–15					0	32	0	28
16–20	0	16	<1	238			0	4
21–25	0	32	0	71	0	117	0	0
26–30	0	62	0	9	0	7	0	4
Jul 1–5					0	0	0	0
6–10	0	3	0	0				
11–15					0	<1		

flow rate, and length of collection, we estimated that densities in 1963 were 1–13 eggs/100 m³ and 2–20 larvae/100 m³ at Belvidere. At Easton, we estimated densities of 1–6 eggs/100 m³ and 1–5 larvae/100 m³. At Milford, no eggs were collected; however, we estimated larval density as 1–2/100 m³. Twenty eggs collected at Belvidere and 15 collected at Easton were at a one-cell stage of embryonic development, equivalent to an age of 2 h, which suggests they were spawned nearby. In 1964, only eight eggs were collected at Easton. Apparently, the downstream terminus of spawning in the early 1960s was near Easton, Pennsylvania.

More recently, Didun (1978) collected eggs and larvae at densities of 7–23/100 m³ and 5–23/100 m³, respectively, near Portland, Pennsylvania, in May–August 1977 (Table 7). He collected no eggs or larvae from April 13 to May 18, 1978. Weston (1977) reported no eggs or larvae were collected April 12–June 29, 1976, near Martins Creek, Pennsylvania. Willis and Harmon (1977) collected eggs at densities of 2–15/100 m³ and larvae at a density of 3/100 m³ at Gilbert generating station during April–August 1976. Numerous collections of ichthyoplankton made in tidal waters from Wilmington to near Trenton, New Jersey, during the 1970s yielded virtually no American shad eggs or larvae. The low spawning intensity during the 1960s downstream of the Delaware Water Gap apparently continued through the mid-1970s. During this period, as mentioned earlier, the main spawning grounds were north of Port Jervis (Sykes and Lehman 1957; Chittenden 1976).

In our study, we usually collected far greater numbers and densities of American shad eggs and larvae than previous researchers did, indicating greater spawning recently between Trenton and the Delaware Water Gap. We found far greater numbers and densities of eggs and larvae at Hutchinson than did Barker (1965) at the nearby areas at Belvidere and Easton in the mid-1960s and Weston (1975) at Martins Creek in 1976.

Spawning was not documented near Point Pleasant in the mid-1960s and occurred no closer than Easton, 47 km upstream (Barker 1965). The findings of Willis and Harmon (1977) suggest that spawning occurred 23 km upstream of Point

TABLE 6.—Embryonic development (based on Marcy 1976) of American shad eggs collected at Point Pleasant during 1982–1985.

Approximate state of embryonic development	Development time (h)	Number of eggs	Percentage of total eggs collected
Morula	1–2	2	3.4
Blastula	3–5	6	10.3
Gastrula	5–14	18	31
Primitive streak	14–25	6	10.3
Early embryo	25–33	13	22.4
Tail-free embryo	33–35	1	1.7
Indeterminate		12	20.6

TABLE 7.—Summary of surveys for eggs and larvae of American shad downstream of the Delaware Water Gap 1944–1983. Surveys conducted after 1944 are listed in order of river kilometer from the mouth.

Study area	Approximate river kilometer	Year	Total number collected		Source
			Eggs	Larvae	
Bordentown, New Jersey, to Equinunk, Pennsylvania	206–520	1944	Spawning occurred throughout the study area; however, most eggs collected below Milford, Pennsylvania (km 398), were dead when taken. Normal survival occurred only at Lackawaxen, Pennsylvania (km 447), and at Equinunk, Pennsylvania.		Cable (1945)
Edge Moor, Delaware	116	1974	0	0	Preddice (1974); Molzahn et al. (1975)
		1975	0	0	Morrisson et al. (1976)
Chester, Pennsylvania	130	1973	0	0	Potter et al. (1974a)
		1974	0	0	Didun and Harmon (1976)
		1976	0	0	Philadelphia Electric Company (1977a)
Eddystone, Pennsylvania	137	1973	0	0	Potter et al. (1974b)
		1974	0	0	Harmon and Smith (1975)
		1976–1977	0	0	Philadelphia Electric Company (1977c)
Schuylkill River	149[a]	1975–1976	0	0	Philadelphia Electric Company (1977e)
Philadelphia, Pennsylvania	156–167	1976	0	0	Philadelphia Electric Company (1977b, 1977d, 1977f)
Burlington, New Jersey	189	1972	0	0	Anselmini (1974a)
		1973	0	1	Anselmini (1974b)
		1978	0	0	Ichthyological Associates (1979a)
Newbold Island, New Jersey	194–210	1971	0	0	Anselmini (1976)
Mercer Generating Station, New Jersey	210	1971	0	0	Anselmini (1974c)
		1972	6	0	Anselmini (1974c)
		1973	0	0	Anselmini (1974c)
		1978	0	0	Ichthyological Associates (1979b)
Tidal boundary, Trenton, New Jersey	215				
West Trenton, New Jersey	225	1964	0	0	Barker (1965)
Lumberville, Pennsylvania	251	1964	0	0	Barker (1965)
Point Pleasant, Pennsylvania	253	1983	16	4	Brundage et al. (1983)
Milford, New Jersey	270	1963	0	4	Barker (1965)
		1964	0	0	Barker (1965)
Gilbert Generating Station, New Jersey	275	1976	80	3	Willis and Harmon (1977)
Easton, Pennsylvania	300	1963	27	10	Barker (1965)
		1964	8	0	Barker (1965)
Martins Creek, Pennsylvania	314	1976	0	0	Weston (1977)
Belvidere, New Jersey	319	1963	27	67	Barker (1965)
Portland, Pennsylvania	332	1977	4	9	Didun (1978)
		1978	0	0	Didun (1978)

[a] Schuylkill River mouth—this study was conducted in the tidal section of the Schuylkill River approximately 10.5 km upstream of its junction with the Delaware River.

Pleasant near Gilbert generating station; however, the embryological development of the eggs was not determined and there is no way of knowing if they had been spawned nearby or had drifted from upstream spawning grounds. We, as well as Brundage et al. (1983), collected small numbers and densities of eggs at Point Pleasant. Two of the specimens we collected at night on May 30, 1985, were no more than 2 h old, suggesting they were spawned nearby. The large density of larvae there also suggests that spawning now occurs upstream of Point Pleasant. Our collection of 33 larvae at densities of 1–20/100 m^3 near New Hope and Yardley suggests some spawning may now occur as far downstream as Trenton.

The increased spawning we found downstream of the Delaware Water Gap probably reflects recent improvements in tidal dissolved oxygen concentrations, as was predicted by several earlier researchers. The decline of American shad stocks in the Delaware River and the drastic reduction in spawning downstream of the Delaware Water Gap were attributed to the seasonally low dissolved oxygen in tidal waters from Wilmington to Philadelphia (Ellis et al. 1947; Sykes and Lehman 1957; Chittenden 1969; Miller et al. 1982).

The dissolved-oxygen requirements of American shad are based primarily on laboratory studies of juveniles. Ellis et al. (1947) found that levels less than 5 mg/L were lethal to juveniles; how-

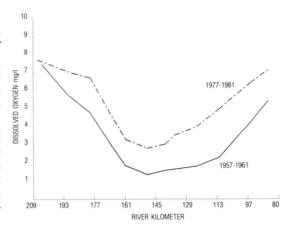

FIGURE 3.—Mean concentrations of dissolved oxygen (mg/L) during June–October 1957–1961 and 1977–1981 along the tidal Delaware River (Albert 1984).

ever, Chittenden (1973) believed these findings were biased by handling stress. Burdick (1954) collected apparently healthy juveniles in the Hudson River when dissolved oxygen was 4–5 mg/L and Tagatz (1961) found that respiratory movements became more rapid as dissolved oxygen was reduced below 4 mg/L. Bradford et al. (1968) reported successful hatches of healthy larvae at 4 mg/L, but lower values produced many deformed larvae. Chittenden (1973) found some sublethal effects began at approximately 3.5 mg/L and Miller et al. (1982) found that less than 3 mg/L blocked migration in the Delaware River. Dorfman (1970) found 33% mortality at 2–3 mg/L and Tagatz (1961) and Chittenden (1969) found high mortality at less than 2 mg/L.

Dissolved oxygen values of 3 mg/L or less occurred from early spring through late fall in much of the region from Wilmington to Philadelphia between the early 1900s and the early 1970s (Ellis et al. 1947; Sykes and Lehman 1957; Keighton 1965; Chittenden 1969; Kiry 1974; Thurston-Rogers and Baren 1978; Albert 1984). Consequently, tidal waters became unsuitable as spawning grounds for American shad and the latter segment of the adult spawning migration was blocked to varying degrees each year from reaching nontidal spawning grounds (Sykes and Lehman 1957; Chittenden 1969; Miller et al. 1971; Thurston-Rogers and Baren 1978). In some years, large numbers of American shad were killed (Cable 1945; Sykes and Lehman 1957; Chittenden 1969) or blocked from migrating upstream and forced to spawn downstream or in other river systems (Chittenden 1969; Miller et al. 1971;

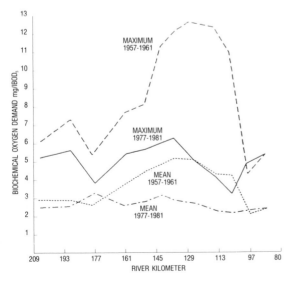

FIGURE 2.—Mean and maximum 5-d biochemical oxygen demand during June–October 1957–1961 and 1977–1981 along the tidal Delaware River (Albert 1984).

Delaware Division of Fish and Wildlife 1978).

Point-source pollution entering tidal waters of the Delaware River has greatly decreased since the late 1950s and dissolved oxygen has increased recently. Daily pollution loadings, evaluated as 5-d biochemical oxygen demand, have decreased by half between 1957–1961 and 1977–1981 (Figure 2), so 113 km of tidal waters have shown increased dissolved oxygen levels (Figure 3). Mean dissolved oxygen content of river water samples collected from June through October has risen more than 1 mg/L at most locations and 2 mg/L below river km 142 near Eddystone, Pennsylvania. Dissolved oxygen has increased the most since the late 1970s; water quality improved noticeably in 1980 and 1981 after Philadelphia's Southwest Water Pollution Control Plant was upgraded (Albert 1984).

Increased levels of dissolved oxygen in tidal waters have shortened the time that dissolved oxygen content below 3 mg/L blocks the upstream migration of American shad. During the 1950s and 1960s, dissolved oxygen content of tidal waters declined to less than 3 mg/L as early as the beginning of April and did not rise above that level until late November to early December (Sykes and Lehman 1957; Chittenden 1969; Thurston-Rogers and Baren 1978; R. Albert, personal communication, 1985). Since 1976, levels of dissolved oxygen have not declined below 3.0 mg/L until early to late June and have risen above that level by early to late October (Thurston-Rogers and Baren 1978; R. Albert, personal communication, 1985).

Spawning migrations of American shad peak at Trenton about mid-April and are nearly complete by early May (Chittenden 1969; Friedersdorff 1976), so most of the spawning adults probably now successfully reach the nontidal region, and the run may include more late migrants than in previous years. Glebe and Leggett (1981) found that late-season migrants in the Connecticut River encountered warmer temperatures and spawned much closer to the river mouth than did earlier migrants. Chittenden (1969) found that, of 250 females examined near New Hope, most had minimal ovarian development and only one, a late-season migrant collected on May 15, 1963, was near spawning condition. This suggests that late-season migrants in the Delaware River also spawn closer to the river mouth than do earlier ones. The postponed decline in dissolved oxygen concentration below 3 mg/L, caused by improved water quality, allows a longer period of safe migration through tidal waters, and more late-season migrants can spawn in the nontidal river downstream of the Delaware Water Gap.

Our observations of increased spawning of American shad coincident with improved dissolved oxygen in the tidal Delaware River confirm the predictions of earlier researchers, especially Chittenden (1969). The correlation provides impetus to further clean up the tidal Delaware River near Philadelphia by showing a positive benefit of the millions of dollars already spent.

Acknowledgments

Public Service Electric and Gas of New Jersey provided funding for the work at Hutchinson. Dilip Mathur and Chris Frese critically reviewed an early draft of the manuscript. Beverly Maximenko typed the paper.

References

Albert, R. 1984. Water pollution control—progress on the Delaware River. Water Pollution Control Association of Pennsylvania Magazine 17(1):10–17. (Water Pollution Control Association of Pennsylvania, Locust Grove, Virginia, USA.)

Anselmini, L. D. 1974a. An ecological study of the Delaware River in the vicinity of Burlington, New Jersey in 1972. Report to the Public Service Electric and Gas Company, Newark, New Jersey, USA.

Anselmini, L. D. 1974b. An ecological study of the Delaware River in the vicinity of Burlington, New Jersey in 1973. Report to the Public Service Electric and Gas Company, Newark, New Jersey, USA.

Anselmini, L. D. 1974c. An ecological study of the Delaware River in the vicinity of the Mercer generating station, Trenton, New Jersey. Report to Public Service Electric and Gas Company, Newark, New Jersey, USA.

Anselmini, L. D. 1976. An ecological study of the Delaware River in the vicinity of Newbold Island. Progress report for the period January–December 1971 to Public Service Electric and Gas Company, Newark, New Jersey, USA.

Barker, J. 1965. Observations on some areas of the Delaware River between Belvidere and Scudders Falls, New Jersey in respect to their utilization by American shad, *Alosa sapidissima* (Wilson), for spawning purposes in 1963 and 1964. New Jersey Department of Conservation and Economic Development, Bureau of Fisheries Laboratory, Miscellaneous Report 28, Lebanon, New Jersey, USA.

Bradford, A. D., J. G. Miller, and K. Buss. 1968. Bioassays of eggs and larval stages of American shad, *Alosa sapidissima*. Pages 52–60 *in* Suitability of the Susquehanna River for restoration of shad. U.S. Department of the Interior, Washington, D.C., USA.

Brundage, H. M., A. L. Maiden, and S. J. Beck. 1983. First progress report of pre-operational biological monitoring studies for the Point Pleasant pumping station. Report to Neshaminy Water Resources Authority, County of Bucks, Pennsylvania, USA.

Burdick, G. E. 1954. An analysis of the factors, including pollution, having possible influence on the abundance of shad in the Hudson River. New York Fish and Game Journal 1:189–205.

Cable, L. E. 1945. The pollution problem in the Delaware River in relation to restoration of the shad fishery. U.S. Fish and Wildlife Service, Washington, D.C., USA. (Not seen; cited in Mansueti and Kolb 1953.)

Chittenden, M. E. 1969. Life history and ecology of the American shad, *Alosa sapidissima,* in the Delaware River. Doctoral dissertation, Rutgers University, New Brunswick, New Jersey, USA.

Chittenden, M. E. 1973. Effects of handling on oxygen requirements of American shad *(Alosa sapidissima).* Journal of the Fisheries Research Board of Canada 30:105–110.

Chittenden, M. E. 1976. Present and historical spawning grounds and nurseries of American shad, *Alosa sapidissima,* in the Delaware River. U.S. National Marine Fisheries Service Fishery Bulletin 74: 343–352.

Delaware Division of Fish and Wildlife. 1978. Restoration of shad runs in the Brandywine Creek and its tributaries January 1, 1976–December 31, 1978. Dover, Delaware, USA.

Didun, A. 1978. A study of the fishes of the Delaware River in the vicinity of the Portland generating station of Metropolitan Edison Company. Report to Metropolitan Edison Company, Reading, Pennsylvania, USA.

Didun, A., and P. L. Harmon. 1976. An ecological study of the Delaware River in the vicinity of Chester generating station. Chester Progress Report 2 to Philadelphia Electric Company, Philadelphia, Pennsylvania, USA.

Dorfman, D. 1970. Responses of some anadromous fishes to varied oxygen concentrations and increased temperatures. Doctoral dissertation. Rutgers University, New Brunswick, New Jersey, USA.

Ellis, M. M., B. A. Westfall, D. K. Meyer, and W. S. Platner. 1947. Water quality studies of the Delaware River with reference to shad migration. U.S. Fish and Wildlife Service Special Scientific Report 38.

Friedersdorff, J. W. 1976. Population estimates and relative abundance work on adult American shad stocks in the Delaware River 1969–1976. Pages 305–320 *in* Proceedings of a workshop on American shad, December 14–16, 1976. U.S. Government Printing Office, Washington, D.C., USA.

Glebe, B. D., and W. C. Leggett. 1981. Temporal, intrapopulation differences in energy allocation and use by American shad *(Alosa sapidissima)* during the spawning migration. Canadian Journal of Fisheries and Aquatic Sciences 38:795–805.

Harmon, P. L., and D. C. Smith. 1975. An ecological study of the Delaware River in the vicinity of

Eddystone generating station. Eddystone Progress Report 4 to Philadelphia Electric Company, Philadelphia, Pennsylvania, USA.

Ichthyological Associates. 1979a. Burlington generating station demonstration for Section 316(b) of the Federal Water Pollution Control Act Amendments of 1972. Effect of the cooling water intake structure entrainment and impingement of fishes. Report to the Public Service Electric and Gas Company, Newark, New Jersey, USA.

Ichthyological Associates. 1979b. Mercer generating station demonstration for Section 316(b) of the Federal Water Pollution Control Act Amendments of 1972. Effect of the cooling water intake structure entrainment and impingement of fishes. Report to Public Service Electric and Gas Company, Newark, New Jersey, USA.

Keighton, W. B. 1965. Delaware River water quality Bristol to Marcus Hook, Pennsylvania. August, 1949–December, 1963. U.S. Geological Survey, Water-Supply Paper 1809-0.

Kiry, P. R. 1974. An historical look at the water quality of the Delaware River estuary to 1973. Contributions from the Department of Limnology Academy of Natural Sciences of Philadelphia 4:1–28.

Mansueti, R., and W. Kolb. 1953. A historical review of the shad fisheries of North America. University of Maryland, Chesapeake Biological Laboratory, Publication 97, Solomons, Maryland, USA.

Marcy, B. C., Jr. 1976. Early life history studies of American shad in the lower Connecticut River and the effects of the Connecticut Yankee Plant. American Fisheries Society Monograph 1:141–168.

Miller, J. P., F. R. Griffiths, and P. A. Thurston-Rogers. 1982. The American shad *(Alosa sapidissima)* in the Delaware River basin. U.S. Fish and Wildlife Service, Rosemont, New Jersey, USA.

Miller, J. P., W. M. Zarback, J. W. Friedersdorff, and R. W. Marshall. 1971. Annual progress report Delaware River basin anadromous fish project. U.S. Fish and Wildlife Service AFS-2-4, Rosemont, New Jersey, USA.

Molzahn, R. F., and associates. 1975. An ecological study of the Delaware River in the vicinity of Edge Moor power station. Progress report for the period June–November, 1974, to Delmarva Power and Light Company, Wilmington, Delaware, USA.

Morrison, N. J., and associates. 1976. An ecological study of the Delaware River in the vicinity of Edge Moor power station. Progress report for the period December 1974–September 1975 to Delmarva Power and Light Company, Wilmington, Delaware, USA.

Philadelphia Electric Company. 1977a. Chester generating station, materials prepared for 316(b) report to the Environmental Protection Agency, Philadelphia, Pennsylvania, USA.

Philadelphia Electric Company. 1977b. Delaware generating station, materials prepared for 316(b) report to the Environmental Protection Agency, Philadelphia, Pennsylvania, USA.

Philadelphia Electric Company. 1977c. Eddystone generating station, materials prepared for 316(b) report to the Environmental Protection Agency, Philadelphia, Pennsylvania, USA.

Philadelphia Electric Company. 1977d. Richmond generating station, materials prepared for 316(b) report to the Environmental Protection Agency, Philadelphia, Pennsylvania, USA.

Philadelphia Electric Company. 1977e. Schuylkill generating station, materials prepared for 316(b) report to the Environmental Protection Agency, Philadelphia, Pennsylvania, USA.

Philadelphia Electric Company. 1977f. Southwark generating station, materials prepared for 316(b) report to the Environmental Protection Agency, Philadelphia, Pennsylvania, USA.

Potter, W. A., D. C. Smith, and P. L. Harmon. 1974a. An ecological study of the Delaware River in the vicinity of Chester generating station. Chester Progress Report 1 to Philadelphia Electric Company, Philadelphia, Pennsylvania, USA.

Potter, W. A., D. C. Smith, and P. L. Harmon. 1974b. An ecological study of the Delaware River in the vicinity of Eddystone generating station. Eddystone Progress Report 3 to Philadelphia Electric Company, Philadelphia, Pennsylvania, USA.

Preddice, T. L. 1974. An ecological study of the Delaware River in the vicinity of Edge Moore power station. Progress report for the period January–May, 1974, to Delmarva Power and Light Company, Wilmington, Delaware, USA.

Sykes, J. E., and B. A. Lehman. 1957. Past and present Delaware River shad fishery and considerations for its future. U.S. Fish and Wildlife Service Research Report 46.

Tagatz, M. E. 1961. Reduced oxygen tolerance and toxicity of petroleum products to juvenile American shad. Chesapeake Science 2:65–71.

Thurston-Rogers, P. A., and C. F. Baren. 1978. Present configuration of the Delaware River pollution block and its relationship to shad migrations. U.S. Fish and Wildlife Service, Special Report of the Delaware River basin anadromous fishery project, Rosemont, New Jersey, USA.

Walburg, C. H., and P. R. Nichols. 1967. Biology and management of the American shad and status of the fisheries, Atlantic Coast of the United States, 1960. U.S. Fish and Wildlife Service Special Scientific Report Fisheries 550.

Weston (Incorporated). 1977. An ecological study of the effects of the Martins Creek steam electric station cooling water intake. Report to Pennsylvania Power and Light Company, Allentown, Pennsylvania, USA.

Willis, T., and P. Harmon. 1977. Final report Gilbert generating station biological monitoring program April 1976–March 1977. Report to Central Jersey Power and Light Company, Morristown, New Jersey, USA.

American Fisheries Society Symposium 1:89–103, 1987

Overview of Life History Aspects of Anadromous Alewife and Blueback Herring in Freshwater Habitats[1]

JOSEPH G. LOESCH

Virginia Institute of Marine Science, School of Marine Science, College of William and Mary
Gloucester Point, Virginia 23062, USA

Abstract.—Anadromous alewives (*Alosa pseudoharengus*) and blueback herring (*A. aestivalis*) are sympatric from New Brunswick and Nova Scotia to upper South Carolina. Alewives range allopatrically north to Labrador and Newfoundland, while blueback herring are found south to Florida. The two species are collectively referred to as alewife, gaspereau, or river herring because of similarities in appearance, time of spawning, methods of capture, and uses of the commercial catches. Despite their similarities, there are important life history differences. Alewives select lentic areas for spawning. Blueback herring spawn in lotic sites in the sympatric distribution, but primarily use lentic sites in their allopatric range. The differential selection of spawning sites by blueback herring reduces competition with alewives for spawning grounds in sympatry. River herring return to natal streams for spawning, but they also readily colonize new streams or ponds and reoccupy systems from which they had been extirpated. Negative phototropic behavior is exhibited by juvenile river herring in the nursery areas and by adults in the coastal waters. Alewives remain deeper in the water column than blueback herring in both locations. The vertical separation, and the choice of different spawning sites by adults, could reduce interspecific feeding competition between juveniles of the two species. The phototropic behavior can affect estimates of species composition, relative abundance, and feeding chronology and intensity. All life stages of both landlocked and anadromous river herring provide forage for many freshwater and marine predators. The mortality of anadromous alewives provides an important source of nutrients for headwater ponds.

The alewife *Alosa pseudoharengus* and the blueback herring *A. aestivalis* are anadromous members of the family Clupeidae. Collectively, they are referred to as alewife or gaspereau in Canada and as river herring in the United States. In both countries, the commercial landings are reported as alewife. Collective reference to the two species stems from similarities in their appearance (Figure 1), times of spawning, methods of capture, and the frequent juxtaposition of spawning grounds. The commercial catches are used primarily for bait, pet food, and fish meal; in Canada, a substantial portion of the catch also is salted and exported for human consumption. Small, local markets exist for smoked river herring and fresh or canned roe.

The objectives herein are to address some temporal and spatial uses of freshwater habitats by adult and juvenile anadromous alewives and blueback herring, to examine some conflicting research findings, and to consider the fishes' ecological role in fresh water. Detailed life histories are not presented, since such compilations already exist (e.g., Bigelow and Welsh 1925; Hildebrand and Schroeder 1928; Bigelow and Schroeder 1953; Hildebrand 1963; Leim and Scott 1966; PSEG 1982, 1984; Fay et al. 1983). However, some basic life history aspects are given for readers not familiar with the two species.

Adults

Geographical Distribution and Morphological Comparisons

The alewife and the blueback herring have a largely sympatric distribution (Figure 2). Alewives occur from Labrador and Newfoundland to South Carolina (Berry 1964; Winters et al. 1973; Burgess 1978), while blueback herring range from Nova Scotia and northeastern New Brunswick to Florida (Smith 1898; Bigelow and Schroeder 1953; Alexander 1984a, 1984b).

Adults are generally distinguished at capture on the basis of eye diameter, body depth, and peritoneum color. The diameter of the alewife eye is generally larger than the distance from the tip of the snout to the forward edge of the eye, but the two measurements are about equal for blueback herring (Figure 1) (Bigelow and Schroeder 1953; Hildebrand 1963). The alewife peritoneum is pale (pearl grey to pinkish white), sometimes with-

[1]Contribution 1327 of the Virginia Institute of Marine Science, School of Marine Science, College of William and Mary, Gloucester Point, Virginia, USA.

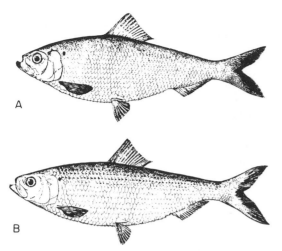

FIGURE 1.—Alewife (A) and blueback herring (B). (Source: Fay et al. 1983.)

dusky spots (melanophores); in contrast, the blueback herring peritoneum is generally black but sometimes soot grey with darker spots. With a modest amount of magnification, the two species can also be separated by scale imbrication patterns and positioning of the scale baseline and dividing line: the baseline is anterior of the dividing line in blueback herring, but the lines coincide in alewife (O'Neill 1980; MacLellan et al. 1981). On fresh specimens, the dorsal coloration also differs: greyish green on alewives, but bluish on blueback herring (Bigelow and Schroeder 1953). However, color soon fades after capture and MacLellan et al. (1981) reported substantial variation in dorsal coloration with ambient lighting changes. Neves (1981) associated the greenish dorsal coloration of the alewife with its deeper vertical distribution (56–110 m) relative to the blueback herring (27–55 m) in coastal waters where green light penetrates deeper than blue light.

The two species can be separated by other characteristics not readily used in the field. Otoliths of alewives and blueback herring differ in shape (Scott and Crossman 1973; Price 1978; O'Neill 1980). The electrophoretic patterns of muscle myogen for the two species are different and species-specific, but there is no intraspecific variation (McKenzie 1973). Differences between meristic characteristics have been shown for the two species, but with the exception of lower gill raker counts, differences are small and overlap occurs in the ranges of each characteristic (Hildebrand 1963; Messieh 1977). Myomere counts,

however, were reported to be a reliable characteristic for separating larval alewives and blueback herring (Chambers et al. 1976). Differences between both unfertilized eggs and fertilized eggs of the two species also have been shown (Kuntz and Radcliffe 1917; Norden 1967).

Migratory Behavior

The onset of river herring spawning is related to water temperature; thus, it varies with latitude, and it may vary annually by 3 to 4 weeks in a given locality. There is considerable overlap in the spawning seasons of the two species. Alewife spawning generally begins between 5 and 10°C and blueback herring spawning between 10 and 15°C (Belding 1920; Bigelow and Schroeder 1953; Havey 1961; Kissil 1969; Saila et al. 1972; Richkus 1974; Loesch and Lund 1977; Wang and Kernehan 1979). Alewives begin to spawn 3–4 weeks earlier than blueback herring in the sympatric distribution, but their peaks of spawning differ by only 2–3 weeks (Hildebrand and Schroeder 1928). Both species return to sea shortly after spawning (Belding 1920; Hildebrand and Schroeder 1928).

In North Carolina, alewives begin spawning in late February (Holland and Yelverton 1973; Tyus 1974; Frankensteen 1976); in the Chesapeake Bay region, the onset of spawning is in March (Hildebrand and Schroeder 1928), generally about mid-March in Virginia tributaries to the bay. In the mid-Atlantic and lower New England states, alewives commence spawning in late March or early April (Cooper 1961; Kissil 1969; Marcy 1969; Smith 1971; Saila et al. 1972; Richkus 1974; Zich 1978; Wang and Kernehan 1979). The onset of spawning in Massachusetts is generally from early to mid-April (Belding 1920; Bigelow and Schroeder 1953), but is delayed until late April to mid-May in Maine (Rounsefell and Stringer 1943; Bigelow and Schroeder 1953; Havey 1961; Libby 1981). Alewife spawning runs in tributaries to the Bay of Fundy begin in late April or early May, but the runs are a month later in the colder tributaries to the Gulf of St. Lawrence (Leim and Scott 1966; Dominy 1971, 1973).

The onset of spawning by blueback herring has been reported as December in Florida (McLane 1955). Blueback herring are present in the Santee River, South Carolina, in February (Bulak and Christie 1981), but spawning commences in early March (Christie 1978; Meador 1982). In the Chesapeake Bay region, a few blueback herring are caught in pound nets during March, but the primary spawning runs begin in early April in the

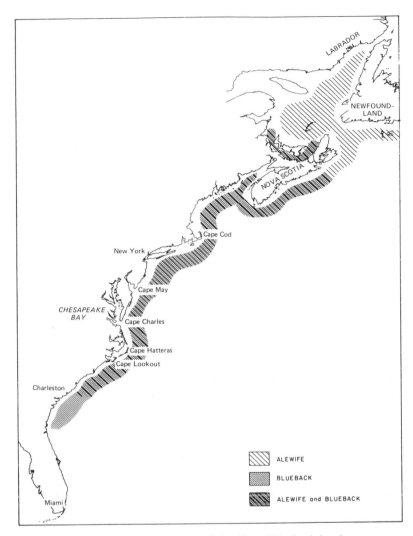

FIGURE 2.—Distributions of alewife and blueback herring.

lower tributaries and in late April in the upper reaches of the Bay (Hildebrand and Schroeder 1928). In the mid-Atlantic region, spawning occurs in late April (Smith 1971; Zich 1978; Wang and Kernehan 1979). Blueback herring have been collected in mid-April in the lower Connecticut River, but spawning commences about mid-May (Loesch and Lund 1977). In tributaries to the Saint John River, New Brunswick, blueback herring are present in May (Messieh 1977; Jessop et al. 1982) but spawn in June (Leim and Scott 1966).

Selection of Spawning Habitat

Spawning alewives and blueback herring are, to a large degree, spatially isolated within their sympatric range. Alewives spawn in slow-flowing lower tributaries and in late April in the upper sections of streams or enter ponds and lakes (Smith 1907; Belding 1920; Bigelow and Welsh 1925; Bigelow and Schroeder 1953; Leim and Scott 1966; Kissil 1969; Havey 1973; Richkus 1974). In contrast, blueback herring in the sympatric range prefer to spawn where the flow is relatively swift, avoiding lentic sites (Bigelow and Welsh 1925; Loesch and Lund 1977). The differential selection of spawning grounds is well demonstrated in Connecticut waters. The slow-flowing Bride Brook in East Lyme attracts large alewife runs which enter Bride Lake (Kissil 1974), but blueback herring do not utilize the system. In the Connecticut River system, blueback herring select such fast-moving waters as the upper Salmon River and Roaring Brook but avoid the slow-flowing waters of Higganum and Mill creeks, sites of alewife runs (Loesch and Lund 1977). The two species may occur together at locations where further upstream migration is barred by dams. At such sites, alewives favor shore-bank eddies or deep pools for spawning while blueback herring concentrate in the main stream flow (Loesch and Lund 1977). Stream partitioning has been reported for other anadromous fishes, e.g., the salmonids (Gibson 1966, 1978; Cunjak and Green 1983). Nilsson (1967) reviewed the ecology and behavior of anadromous and nonandromous interacting species.

Alewives are the dominant ($\geq 90\%$) river herring species in New England, except in the upper Connecticut River (DiCarlo 1981; Gibson 1982; Greenwood 1982; Flagg and Squires 1983). The dominance occurs, in part, because alewives, but not blueback herring, spawn in the freshwater ponds which form the headwaters of most coastal streams in New England. Alewives also dominate in the Atlantic coastal ponds and streams of Nova Scotia (B. M. Jessop, personal communication). However, proportions of blueback herring are much higher in the larger tributaries of the Saint John River estuary, although alewives remain in the dominant species with a seasonal ratio of 7:3 (Messieh 1977; Jessop et al. 1982). In the Gulf of Saint Lawrence region, where there are few lakes, as in the West River, Nova Scotia, and the Miramichi River, New Brunswick, blueback herring often exceed alewives (Alexander 1984b; B. M. Jessop, personal communication).

In the Carolinas where alewives are few and further south where they are absent, blueback herring exhibit more variety in the selection of spawning grounds (Street 1970; Frankensteen 1976; Christie 1978). Studies of egg, larval, and adult densities in South Carolina and Georgia show that blueback herring choose seasonally flooded rice fields, cypress swamps, and oxbows in preference to the adjoining streams (Adams and Street 1969; Godwin and Adams 1969; Adams 1970; Street 1970; Curtis et al. 1982; Meador et al. 1984). This change in habitat preference reflects an ability of blueback herring to adapt to the substantial environmental changes encountered from the Canadian maritime provinces and New England southward to the broad coastal plains of the southern United States.

The selection by blueback herring of lotic spawning sites in the north but lentic sites in the south suggests a clinal spawning pattern that reduces competition with alewives for spawning grounds when the two species are sympatric. Blueback herring spawning behavior has not been studied in the middle portion of the species range to help confirm this, however. Although the northern stocks do not generally spawn in ponds, they have the ability to do so. Blueback herring captured at the base of the Mactaquac Dam in the Saint John River system successfully spawn after release into the head pond (B. M. Jessop, personal communication) and blueback herring, not alewives, occur in Lake Champlain.

River herring return to natal streams for spawning. This theory has been supported by morphometric and meristic differences among fish from different systems (Messieh 1977), the establishment or reestablishment of spawning runs after gravid fish are placed in ancestral or new systems lacking runs (Belding 1920; Bigelow and Welsh 1925; Havey 1961), and olfaction experiments (Thunberg 1971). Alewife and blueback herring will also occupy new systems or increase in abundance within systems when changes in physical or hydrological conditions permit or enhance entry. This behavior was exemplified by the invasion of the Great Lakes by the alewife through the Welland Canal system and the huge increase in numbers of blueback herring passed above the Holyoke Dam on the Connecticut River after improvements to the lift facilities (Moffitt et al. 1982).

It has been stated, and also erroneously attributed to this author (Jones et al. 1978), that blueback herring do not ascend fresh water as far as alewives (Smith 1898; Hildebrand and Schroeder 1928; Bigelow and Schroeder 1953; Hildebrand 1963; Scott and Crossman 1973). There is only contrary evidence for this premise. Blueback herring spawn 150–200 km upstream in the Carolinas (Davis and Cheek 1967; Adams and Street 1969; Adams 1970; Street 1970). Gravid alewives and blueback herring are captured in pound nets at river km 85 in the Rappahannock River in Virginia, about 175 km from the mouth of the Chesapeake Bay. Blueback herring migrate to the Holyoke Dam, 136 km from the Connecticut River mouth, and continue upstream when the fish lift operates (Loesch 1969; Loesch and Lund 1977; Moffitt et al. 1982). Crecco (1982) concluded that it is the blueback herring, not the alewife, that travels farther up the Connecticut River. Both species occur at the Mactaquac Dam, 148 km from the mouth of the Saint John River (Messieh 1977; Jessop et al. 1982), and some fish passed upstream of the dam proceed another 100 km.

Distributions of young of the year further substantiate that blueback herring migrate far upstream (Massmann 1953; Davis and Cheek 1967; Perlmutter et al. 1967; Loesch 1969; Crecco et al. 1981; Crecco and Blake 1983). Loesch and Lund (1977) concluded that the upstream distribution of gravid blueback herring is a function of habitat suitability and hydrological conditions permitting access to such sites. I believe the premise of a shorter spawning migration by blueback herring developed because early studies were primarily on northern streams where alewives entered the head ponds.

Fecundity and Maturity

Fecundity of river herring is related to age and size, but is highly variable (e.g., Street 1969; Scherer 1972; Loesch and Lund 1977; PSEG 1984). Estimates of fecundity for anadromous alewives range from about 100,000 to 467,000 eggs (PSEG 1984). A nonlandlocked but resident alewife population in upper Chesapeake Bay produces only 60,000–100,000 eggs per mature female (Foerster and Goodbred 1978). Fecundity estimates for anadromous blueback herring range from about 33,000 to 400,000 eggs (PSEG 1982). The large range is primarily due to age and size, but differences in methods also contribute to the variability. Only river herring ovaries that were ripe but not extruding eggs (stage IV as described by Nikolsky 1963), were used by Kissil (1969) and Loesch (1969, 1981) to estimate fecundity. In contrast, Scherer (1972) did not separate stage-IV from partially spawned ovaries in blueback herring. With alewives from the Parker River, Massachusetts, Mayo (1974) counted all ova, but Huber (1978) counted only yolked eggs 0.58 mm and larger.

The relationship of fecundity to age or size is generally presented as a monotonic linear or curvilinear function. However, Mayo (1974) and Huber (1978) found that maximal alewife fecundity occurred between ages 5 and 7, then declined for older fish. Similarly for blueback herring, weights of both unspawned (stage-IV) and spawned (stage-VI) ovaries increased with total fish length through the 296–305-mm interval, then declined (Loesch 1969). Loesch and Lund (1977) concluded that maximum fecundity occurs at about age 6, and suggested that a "fecundal senility" may occur in chronologically or physiologically older blueback herring.

First spawning by river herring occurs from ages 3 to 6, but the composition of virgin spawners is strongly dominated by age-4 fish (Loesch 1969; Marcy 1969; Street and Adams 1969; Tsimenides 1970; Scherer 1972; Pate 1974; Loesch and Lund 1977; PSEG 1982, 1984). In general, spawning stocks of river herring are made up primarily of 3–8-year-old fish. Males tend to dominate age-classes 3–5; females live longer and, thus, dominate the older age-classes. Recruitment to the matured population by both species is essentially completed by age 5. From a synthesis of available information and their own studies, PSEG (1982, 1984) reported that typically 82–100% of male alewives and 60–95% of the females mature by age 4. Similarly, they reported that about 54–99% of male blueback herring and 41–98% of the females mature by age 4. The modal age for all spawning river herring is generally 4 or 5; however, modality is readily affected by the presence of a strong year class or by recruitment failure.

Sex Ratio

Sex ratios of river herring have been compiled by PSEG (1982, 1984). They concluded that the male:female ratio throughout a season or over several years is either 1:1 or favors males. Male domination of the sex ratio is probably due to a greater proportion of males maturing at ages 3 and 4. Males tend to dominate in the early runs, but the proportion of females increases (sometimes significantly) in the later runs (Cooper 1961; Dominy 1971; Kissil 1974; Loesch and Lund 1977). Estimates of sex ratio are, however, readily affected by spatiotemporal differences. Samples collected in the lower portion of an estuary may contain immature females that do not migrate to the spawning grounds (Loesch and Lund 1977). The proportion of male blueback herring on the spawning grounds after the day of arrival can change because males tend to remain longer than females and, after exiting, some males may return in the succeeding wave (Loesch 1969). In addition, female alewives and blueback herring in the process of spawning generally attract several males (Loesch and Lund 1977; Wang and Kernehan 1979; PSEG 1982, 1984). Belding (1920) reported that as many as 25 male alewives may follow a female. Libby (1981) suggested that physical aspects of the alewife migration route could also affect sex ratio estimates.

Length and Age

There is considerable variation in the mean lengths at age reported for river herring. Part of the variation is undoubtedly natural, but part is due to different methods of back-calculating lengths at age from analysis of scale annuli. Most investigators (e.g., Messieh 1977; Kornegay 1978) used the aging method described by Cating (1953) and Marcy (1969), but Lipton (1979) and Travelstead (1980) followed Beal's (1968) method in which an additional annulus is placed at or near the scale zone representing the initial freshwater residence. In most studies, 1 January has been used as the birthdate for *Alosa*; in contrast, PSEG (1982, 1984) used 1 April for alewives and 1 May for blueback herring. Different methods of measuring lengths at capture also confound apparent and real variation. Fork length is used in the southern Atlantic coastal states, total length in the northern states, and both measurements in Canada. Standard length has also been used (Huber 1978). Furthermore, total length has been measured either with the upper lobe of the caudal fin depressed parallel to the long axis of the body (e.g., Kissil 1969; Loesch 1969; Jessop et al. 1982) or with the lobe in its normal position (e.g., Messieh 1977). Thus, the suggestion of a latitudinal trend of increasing length from south to north (Marcy 1969; Richkus and DiNardo 1984) may be more apparent than real.

Mean lengths of alewives in New England ponds were observed to decrease during the spawning season (Cooper 1961; Kissil 1974; Rideout 1974), but the trend was not noted for blueback herring (Loesch 1969). Libby (1982) reported alewife lengths at age decreased during the spawning migration; however, little of the total variation in length was explained by his linear regression analyses (weighted mean r^2 values were only 6.7 and 7.2% for males and females, respectively).

Jessop et al. (1982, 1983) derived linear functions for interconverting fork and total lengths of river herring in New Brunswick, but their applicability to other regions is not known. In general, females of both species are larger than males, and alewives are somewhat larger than blueback herring. A maximum total length of 380 mm was attributed to both species (Hildebrand and Schroeder 1928; Hildebrand 1963), but most reported maximum total lengths range from 310 to 350 mm (PSEG 1982, 1984).

Juveniles

Stream Distribution

When spawned in flowing streams, river herring

eggs (after the loss of adhesiveness) and larvae are transported downstream (Wang and Kernehan 1979; PSEG 1982, 1984). In Chesapeake Bay tributaries, juveniles (young of the year) are distributed widely throughout tidal freshwater nursery areas in spring and early summer, but subsequently move upstream in summer with the encroachment of saline water (Warinner et al. 1970). With decreasing water temperatures in the fall or early winter, the juveniles move downstream as a first stage of their seaward migration. Some juvenile *Alosa* will remain in deep estuarine waters through the winter (Hildebrand and Schroeder 1928).

Prior to a general exodus from tidal fresh water, larger juvenile *Alosa* move to saline water (Loesch 1969; Marcy 1976; Loesch and Kriete 1980). This emigration affects estimates of growth and mortality derived from changes in mean size and relative abundance. The somewhat protracted river herring spawning periods (in all but the northern ranges) also affect estimates of growth and mortality. When juveniles produced at peak spawning become susceptible to capture, there is an apparent decrease in the growth rate and often an actual decrease in mean length estimates. This apparent "negative growth" was noted for juvenile river herring in the Connecticut River and Chesapeake Bay tributaries (Loesch 1969; Loesch and Kriete 1980) and it is also apparent in growth estimates for juvenile blueback herring in the Susquehanna River (Whitney 1961) and juvenile American shad *Alosa sapidissima* in the Connecticut River (Marcy 1976). Crecco et al. (1984) and Essig and Cole (1986) avoided the growth distortions associated with new recruits by determining age of larval river herring from daily growth rings on otoliths.

Vertical Distribution

Woodhead (1966) and Blaxter (1975) reviewed the extensive research regarding the role of light in the vertical migrations of marine fishes, but few studies have addressed this movement by anadromous *Alosa*. One study in Virginia waters (Loesch et al. 1982) was initiated because annual surveys showed different ratios for adults and juveniles: blueback herring constituted about 70% of the commercial river herring landings, but accounted for 95% of the juveniles collected in surface waters of tidal freshwater nurseries. This indicated either differential mortality of alewives and blueback herring or differential availability of juveniles to surface trawls. The latter premise was investigated by day and night sampling with paired bottom and surface trawls (Loesch et al. 1982). The data indicated diel migratory activities by alewives and blueback herring (Table 1). Bottom catches were significantly greater during the day than at night; conversely, surface catches were significantly greater at night than during the day. Net avoidance in the daytime could explain decreased catches by the surface gear, but not the decreased bottom catches at night. The concentration of alewives in bottom water during the day and their upward migration at night has been reported for landlocked stocks (Lindenberg 1976; Brandt 1980; Janssen and Brandt 1980; Kelso and Ney 1985). Meador (1982) found that the density of larval anadromous blueback herring at the surface gradually increased from day through dusk and night and was maximum at dawn. The general pattern of vertical migration by marine clupeids is an upward movement at night followed by a spreading out of the fish (Balls 1951; Blaxter and Holliday 1963). Often, diel activities of fishes account for more variability in catch than does gear type and vessel (Sissenwine and Bowman 1978).

A partial spatial separation of juvenile alewife and blueback herring stocks also was evident (Table 1): catches with the bottom trawl during the daytime were 76.5% alewives and 23.5% blueback herring; catches with the surface trawl at night were 1.4% alewives and 98.6% blueback herring. This is the same vertical pattern reported by Neves (1981) for adult river herring in coastal waters, i.e., alewives were deeper in the water column than blueback herring. Because juvenile alewife and blueback herring diets are identical (Davis and Cheek 1967; Burbidge 1974; Watt and Duerden 1974; Weaver 1975), the vertical separation of juveniles and the different spawning sites selected by the adults could reduce interspecific feeding competition by juveniles.

Distributions determined from the surface trawls (Table 1) were confirmed by samples of juveniles obtained with a push net (Table 2). The highest densities of blueback herring, and the only catches of alewives, occurred at night. The occurrence of blueback herring in the push-net samples was also inversely related to available light (as indicated by opacity indexes) during the daytime. The greater daytime catches of *Alosa* with the bottom trawl, and the greater night catches at the surface with both trawl and push net, indicate diel migratory activities. The inverse association between push-net catches and opacity index values indicates that the diel activity, at least of blueback herring, is an expression of a general negative phototropic behavior by the fish or by the prey they follow. Janssen and Brandt (1980) reported that the extent and timing of vertical migrations of landlocked alewives in Lake Michigan coincided with those of *Mysis relicta*, their major food item.

Warinner et al. (1970) also reported a diel vertical migration by juvenile river herring, but the movement was toward the surface in daylight hours. Possibly, this contradictory finding resulted from reduced insolation and a high degree of light attentuation during the daytime in the surface waters of the Potomac River. On 29 October 1968, when Warinner sampled, the opacity index was zero (clear sky) from 0700 to 1000 hours, then increased throughout the day. The index reached a maximal value of 10 (completely overcast) at 1600 hours and remained there until 1 h after sunset (about 1800 hours). In addition to the reduction in insolation, there were dense phytoplankton blooms in the river (J. E. Warinner, personal communication). Blooms of bluegreen algae were often so massive in the Potomac River in that era that the tidal freshwater to mesohaline reach was described as a putting green (Lear and Smith 1976).

There are, of course, ramifications of phototropic behavior which affect fisheries research. The paired trawl data (Table 1) show that an estimate of the ratio of alewives to blueback herring is dependent upon both the choice of gear and the

TABLE 1.—Day and night catches and geometric mean catches (numbers/5-min tow) of juvenile alewife and blueback herring in the Mattaponi River, Virginia, 26–28 September 1977. Effort: 56 paired bottom and surface day tows, and 34 paired night tows. (Modified from Loesch et al. 1982.)

	Alewife				Blueback herring			
	Bottom		Surface		Bottom		Surface	
Time	Total	Mean	Total	Mean	Total	Mean	Total	Mean
Day	2,229	7.4	0	0	684	2.0	20	0.2
Night	3	0.1	34	0.7	35	0.7	2,459	71

TABLE 2.—Pushnet catches and geometric mean catches (numbers/5-min sample) of alewife and blueback herring in surface waters of the James River, Virginia, under various light conditions, 18–20 October 1978. Each mean is based on 20 samples. National Weather Service opacity index: 1 completely clear; 10 completely overcast. (Modified from Loesch et al. 1982.)

Light condition	Opacity index	Alewife		Blueback herring	
		Total catch	Mean catch	Total catch	Mean catch
Night		378	14	23,786	1,082
Overcast day	10	0		14,979	752
Clear day	3	0		7,713	293

time of day. Errors in estimating abundance due to vertical migration have been reported for marine fishes (e.g., Boerema 1964; Hempel 1964; Konstantinov 1964; Parrish et al. 1964; Woodhead 1964). Because of the negative phototropic behavior of river herring, serious errors in estimates of juvenile abundance could occur with changes in insolation and attentution. It is also unlikely that abundance indexes for juveniles will be obtained annually under seasonably similar average conditions of insolation and attenuation, unless the frequency of the sampling is high. Frequent sampling is particularly important in the period when availability and catchability are high. Turner and Chadwick (1972) reported deficiencies in their annual index of juvenile striped bass when the index was developed from catch data collected at 2-week intervals. In addition, Heimbuch et al. (1983) analyzed juvenile striped bass catch data and found a significant season-by-sampling-site interaction.

The results of feeding studies could also be influenced by phototropic behavior. Feeding chronology and feeding intensity by juvenile river herring were investigated by Burbidge (1974) and Weaver (1975). Feeding intensity was measured as the ratio of stomach weight to body weight. Burbidge reported that active feeding by juvenile blueback herring began at dawn, increased through the day to a maximum at dusk, and then declined from dusk to dawn. Weaver found diurnal feeding by juvenile alewife, but the activity was bimodal. Peak feeding occurred from about 1 to 3 h before sunset and a minor increase in feeding about 2 h after sunrise.

Burbidge's and Weaver's findings indicate different feeding chronologies for juvenile alewives

and blueback herring, and present an apparent contradiction to the paired trawl data (Table 1) that indicated upward migration at night, presumably to feed. Phototropism can be used for one possible explanation of these inconsistencies. Within populations of species that exhibit phototropic behavior, some individuals will be more responsive and others less responsive to the stimulus. Thus, some juvenile river herring would rise in the water column before sunset and linger there after sunrise. With a greater dispersion of prey at night, or a limited amount of prey when juvenile density is maximum, the biomodal peaks of alewife feeding activity reported by Weaver (1975) could be observed since the measure of feeding intensity did not consider the proportion of the population feeding. Burbidge's (1974) observations of increased feeding activity during the daytime by blueback herring were made in the Potomac River on 25 July and 29 October 1968. These data can be related to the degree of sky opacity recorded hourly by the National Weather Service at Quantico, Virginia. On 25 July, the index value was 1 at 0600 hours; from 0700–1400 hours, it increased to 4 (mean, 3); from 1500 hours to sunset (about 1900 hours), it varied from 7 to 10 (mean, 9). The opacity index of 29 October (previously discussed) followed a similar increasing trend. Thus, increasing feeding activity and increasing daytime sky opacity appear correlated.

Ecological Considerations

Concerns about introducing river herring into closed freshwater systems, particularly when predator stocks are low, include uncontrolled population growth, competition for food and space, selective feeding on zooplankton, piscivority, and growth beyond an acceptable prey size (Brooks and Dodson 1965; Lackey 1969; Hutchinson 1971; Smith 1971; Brown 1972; Kohler and Ney 1980; Prince and Barwick 1981). Few of these misgivings have been stated about the presence, or establishment of anadromous runs of river herring. Watt and Duerden (1974) estimated that juvenile river herring in the Mactaquac impoundment consumed about 73% of the total zooplankton produced from July to October, but no negative consequences were reported. McCaig (1980) found that when gravid, sea-run alewives and yearling trout were stocked in reclaimed ponds in Massachusetts, growth of yearling trout was repressed but, by age 2, the trout appeared to benefit from the juvenile alewives that served as forage. The apparent competition between the adult alewives and the younger trout could have been induced since rotenone, which was used to remove all fish species prior to stocking, also decimates zooplankton populations (Kiser et al. 1963; Anderson 1970; Neves 1975). Richkus (1975) concluded that zooplankton density and juvenile alewife growth in two Rhode Island ponds were inversely related to juvenile abundance. Vigerstad and Cobb (1978) found that although the zooplankton in two Rhode Island ponds, one of which hosted anadromous alewife runs, were taxonomically alike, the relative abundance and population cycles of the zooplankton differed; a lower density and an earlier peak in total zooplankton was attributed to the presence of juvenile alewives. Marcy (1976) concluded that juvenile American shad in the Connecticut River grew slower below the Enfield Dam than upriver of it, and attributed the slower growth primarily to strong competition with juvenile river herring for food and space. However, diets of juvenile American shad (Walburg 1957; Massmann 1963; Davis and Cheek 1967; Levesque and Reed 1972; Domermuth and Reed 1980) do not suggest this species competes with juvenile river herring for food. Crecco and Blake (1983) found very obvious differences in the diets of coexisting larvae of American shad and blueback herring and concluded that intraspecific competition for food may be more severe than interspecific competition. There are many reports of cannibalism by landlocked alewives (e.g., Morsell and Norden 1968; Lackey 1970; Kohler and Ney 1980; Wells 1980), but only two reports of cannibalism by anadromous river herring (PSEG 1982, 1984)—probably because studies of these fish in open systems have been limited and because adults return to sea shortly after spawning.

Very positive contributions to freshwater ecosystems can result from the presence of river herring. All life stages of both anadromous and landlocked river herring are important forage for many freshwater and marine fishes; in addition, birds, amphibians, reptiles, and mammals have also been documented as predators (Table 3). Durbin et al. (1979) estimated the total nutrient input to a pond in Rhode Island from anadromous adult alewife mortality amounted to 0.43 g P, 2.7 g N, and 16.8 g C per square meter over a 2-month period, an input per unit of lake volume at least comparable to that from mortalities during large salmon migrations in Alaska. In contrast, the loss in biomass due to the seaward migration of juvenile alewives was insignificant. Thus, Durbin et al.

TABLE 3.—Reported predators on anadromous and landlocked river herring (all life stages).[a]

Fish predators	
American eel	*Anguilla rostrata*
Bluefish	*Pomatomus saltatrix*
Largemouth bass	*Micropterus salmoides*
Pumpkinseed	*Lepomis gibbosus*
Redfin pickerel	*Esox americanus americanus*
Salmon (chinook; coho)	*Oncorhynchus tshawytscha; O. kisutch*
Shiner (emerald; spottail)	*Notropis atherinoides; N. hudsonius*
Silver hake	*Merluccius bilinearis*
Striped bass	*Morone saxatilis*
Trout (brown; lake)	*Salmo trutta; Salvelinus namaycush*
Walleye	*Stizostedion vitreum vitreum*
Weakfish	*Cynoscion regalis*
White bass	*Morone chrysops*
White perch	*Morone americana*
Yellow perch	*Perca flavescens*
Other predators	
Snapping turtle	*Cheldydra serpentina*
Northern water snake	*Nerotea sipedon*
Fish hawk	*Pandion haliaetus*
Heron (green; great blue; night)	*Butorides virescens virescens; Ardea herodias; Nycticorsx nycticorsx*
Herring gull	*Larus argentatus*
Mink	*Mustella vision*

[a] Sources: Belding (1920); Welsh and Breder (1924); Hollis (1952); Foye (1956); Stevens (1958); Hay (1959); Schaefer (1960); Cooper (1961); Edsal (1964); Trent and Hassler (1966); Kissel (1969); Bennett and Gibbons (1972); Manooch (1972); Shirey (1972); Tyus (1972); Richards (1976); Bulak and Christie (1980); Wells (1980); Kohler and Ney (1981); Hatch et al. (1981); Stewart et al. (1981); Ech and Wells (1983); personal observations.

noted that anadromous alewives are a nutrient source to a system rather than just a mechanism for nutrient regeneration. From in situ incubation of autumn leaf litter, Durbin et al. (1979) also concluded that alewife mortality provided the N and P that stimulated the microbial breakdown of the leaf litter. The energy released from the litter breakdown, for the most part, passed into the detrital food chain rather than to the plankton. They suggested that by hastening the breakdown of the leaf litter, alewife mortality could reduce the sedimentation rate of lakes.

Acknowledgments

I thank the reviewers of earlier drafts for their critical readings and constructive comments. I also thank the many fishery biologists who shared their knowledge and unpublished findings with me.

References

Adams, J. G. 1970. Clupeids in the Altamaha River, Georgia. Georgia Game and Fish Commission, Coastal Fisheries Division, Contribution Series 20,

Brunswick, Georgia, USA.

Adams, J. G., and M. W. Street. 1969. Notes on the spawning and embryological development of blueback herring (*Alosa aestivalis* Mitchill) in the Altamaha River, Georgia. Georgia Game and Fish Commission, Marine Fisheries Division, Contribution Series 16, Brunswick, Georgia, USA.

Alexander, D. R. 1984a. Status of the Margaree River gaspereau fishery (1983). Department of Fisheries and Oceans, Canadian Atlantic Fisheries Scientific Advisory Committee Research Document 84/17, Moncton, Canada.

Alexander, D. R. 1984b. Status of the Miramichi River estuary gaspereau fishery (1983). Department of Fisheries and Oceans, Canadian Atlantic Fisheries Scientific Advisory Committee Research Document 84/23, Moncton, Canada.

Anderson, R. S. 1970. Effects of rotenone on zooplankton communities and a study of their recovery patterns in two mountain lakes in Alberta. Journal of the Fisheries Research Board of Canada 27:1335–1356.

Balls, R. 1951. Environmental changes in herring behavior. A theory of light avoidance as suggested by echosounding observations in the North Sea. Journal du Conseil, Conseil International pour l'Exploration de la Mer 17:274–298.

Beal, K. L. 1968. Age and growth of the blueback herring *Alosa aestivalis* (Mitchill). Master's thesis. College of William and Mary, Williamsburg, Virginia, USA.

Belding, D. L. 1920. A report upon the alewife fisheries of Massachusetts. Department of Conservation, Division of Fisheries and Game, Boston, Massachusetts, USA.

Bennett, D. H., and J. W. Gibbons. 1972. Food of the largemouth bass (*Micropterus salmoides*) from a South Carolina reservoir receiving heated effluent. Transactions of the American Fisheries Society 101:650–654.

Berry, F. H. 1964. Review and emendation of: family Clupeidae. Copeia 1964:720–730.

Bigelow, H. B., and W. C. Schroeder. 1953. Fishes of the Gulf of Maine. U.S. Fish and Wildlife Service Fishery Bulletin 53(74).

Bigelow, H. B., and W. W. Welsh. 1925. Fishes of the Gulf of Maine. U.S. Bureau of Fisheries Bulletin 40(1):1–567.

Blaxter, J. H. S. 1975. The role of light in the vertical migration of fish—a review. British Ecological Society Symposium 16:189–210.

Blaxter, J. H. S., and F. G. T. Holliday. 1963. The behavior and physiology of herring and other clupeids. Pages 261–393 *in* F. S. Russell, editor. Advances in marine biology, volume 1. Academic Press, London, England.

Boerema, L. K. 1964. Some effects of diurnal variation in the catches upon estimates of abundance of plaice and sole. Rapports et Procès-Verbaux des Réunions, Conseil International pour l'Exploration de la Mer 155:52–57.

Brandt, S. B. 1980. Spatial segregation of adult and young-of-the-year alewives across a thermocline in Lake Michigan. Transactions of the American Fisheries Society 109:469–478.

Brooks, J. L., and S. I. Dodson. 1965. Predation, body size, and composition of plankton. Science (Washington, D.C.) 150:28–35.

Brown, E. H., Jr. 1972. Population biology of alewives (*Alosa pseudoharengus*) in Lake Michigan, 1949–1970. Journal of the Fisheries Research Board of Canada 29:477–500.

Bulak, J. S., and R. W. Christie. 1980. The importance of blueback herring to the forage base of Lake Marion and Moultrie. South Carolina Wildlife and Marine Resources Department, Completion Report SCR 1–4, Columbia, South Carolina, USA.

Bulak, J. S., and R. W. Christie. 1981. Santee–Cooper blueback herring studies. South Carolina Wildlife and Marine Resources Department, Annual Progress Report SCR 1–5, Columbia, South Carolina, USA.

Burbidge, R. G. 1974. Distribution, growth, selective feeding, and energy transformation of young-of-the-year blueback herring, *Alosa aestivalis* (Mitchill), in the James River, Virginia. Transactions of the American Fisheries Society 103:297–311.

Burgess, G. H. 1978. *Alosa pseudoharengus* (Wilson), alewife. Page 65 *in* D. S. Lee, C. R. Gilbert, C. H. Hocutt, R. E. Jenkins, D. E. McAllister, and J. R. Stauffer, Jr., editors. Atlas of North American freshwater fishes. North Carolina State Museum of Natural History, Raleigh, North Carolina, USA.

Cating, J. P. 1953. Determining age of Atlantic shad from their scales. U.S. Fish and Wildlife Service Fishery Bulletin 54:187–199.

Chambers, J. R., J. A. Musick, and J. Davies. 1976. Methods of distinguishing larval alewife from larval blueback herring. Chesapeake Science 17:93–100.

Christie, R. W. 1978. Spawning distributing of blueback herring, *Alosa aestivalis* (Mitchill) in abandoned rice fields and tributaries of the west branch of the Cooper River, South Carolina. Master's thesis. Clemson University, Clemson, South Carolina, USA.

Cooper, R. 1961. Early life history and spawning migration of the alewife, *Alosa pseudoharengus*. Master's thesis. University of Rhode Island, Kingston, Rhode Island, USA.

Crecco, V. 1982. Overview of alewife and blueback herring runs in Connecticut. Report to Atlantic States Marine Fisheries Commission, Alosid Scientific and Statistical Committee, Washington, D.C., USA.

Crecco, V. A., and M. M. Blake. 1983. Feeding ecology of coexisting larvae of American shad and blueback herring in the Connecticut River. Transactions of the American Fisheries Society 112:498–507.

Crecco, V., L. Gunn, and T. Savoy. 1981. Population dynamics studies of American shad, *Alosa sapidissima*, in the Connecticut River. Connecticut Department of Environmental Protection, Marine Fisheries Office, Annual Progress Report AFC 13:1, Waterford, Connecticut, USA.

Crecco, V., L. Gunn, and T. Savoy. 1984. Population dynamics studies of American shad, *Alosa sapidissima*, in the Connecticut River. Connecticut Department of Environmental Protection, Marine Fisheries Office, Completion Report AFC 13:1–3, Waterford, Connecticut, USA.

Cunjak, R. A., and J. M. Green. 1983. Habitat utilization by brook trout char (*Salvelinus fontinalis*) and rainbow trout (*Salmo gairdneri*) in Newfoundland streams. Canadian Journal of Zoology 61:1214–1219.

Curtis, T. A., R. W. Christie, and J. S. Bulak. 1982. Santee–Cooper blueback herring studies. South Carolina Wildlife and Marine Resources Department, Annual Progress Report SCR 1–6, Columbia, South Carolina, USA.

Davis, J. R., and R. P. Cheek. 1967. Distribution, food habits, and growth of young clupeids, Cape Fear river system, North Carolina. Proceedings of the Annual Conference Southeastern Association of Game and Fish Commissioners 20:250–260.

DiCarlo, J. S. 1981. Overview of alosid stocks of Massachusetts. Report to Atlantic States Marine Fisheries Commission, Alosid Scientific and Statistical Committee, Washington, D.C., USA.

Domermuth, R. B., and R. J. Reed. 1980. Food of juvenile American shad, *Alosa sapidissima*, juvenile blueback herring, *A. aestivalis*, and pumpkinseed, *Lepomis gibbosus*, in the Connecticut River below Holyoke Dam, Massachusetts. Estuaries 3:65–68.

Dominy, C. L. 1971. Evaluation of a pool and weir fishway for passage of alewives (*Alosa pseudoharengus*) at White Rock, Gaspereau River, Nova Scotia. Canada Department of Fisheries and Forestry, Resource Development Branch, Progress Report 3, Halifax, Canada.

Dominy, C. L. 1973. Effects of entrance pool weir elevation and fish density on passage of alewives in a pool and weir fishway. Transactions of the American Fisheries Society 102:398–404.

Durbin, A. G., S. W. Nixon, and C. A. Oviatt. 1979. Effects of the spawning migration of alewife, *Alosa pseudoharengus*, on a freshwater ecosystem. Ecology 60:8–17.

Ech, G. W., and L. Wells. 1983. Biology, population structure, and estimated forage requirements of Lake Trout in Lake Michigan. U.S. Fish and Wildlife Service Technical Paper 111.

Edsall, T. A. 1964. Feeding by three species of fishes on the eggs of spawning alewives. Copeia 1964:226–227.

Essig, R. J., and C. F. Cole. 1986. Methods of estimating larval fish mortality from daily increments in otoliths. Transactions of the American Fisheries Society 115:34–40.

Fay, C. W., R. J. Neves, and G. B. Pardue. 1983. Species profiles: life histories and environmental requirements of coastal fisheries and invertebrates (mid-Atlantic)—alewife/blueback herring. U.S. Fish and Wildlife Service Biological Services Program FWS/OBS-82/11.9.

Flagg, L., and T. Squires. 1983. Status of alewife stocks in the state of Maine. Report to Atlantic States Marine Fisheries Commission, Alosid Scientific and Statistical Committee, Washington, D.C., USA.

Foerster, J. W., and S. L. Goodbred. 1978. Evidence for a resident alewife population in the northern Chesapeake Bay. Estuarine and Coastal Marine Science 7:437–444.

Foye, R. E. 1956. Reclamation of potential trout ponds in Maine. Journal of Wildlife Management 20:389–398.

Frankensteen, E. D. 1976. Genus *Alosa* in a channelized and unchannelized creek of the Tar River Basin, North Carolina. Master's thesis. East Carolina University, Greenville, North Carolina, USA.

Gibson, R. J. 1966. Some factors influencing the distribution of brook trout and young Atlantic salmon. Journal of the Fisheries Research Board of Canada 23:1977–1980.

Gibson, R. J. 1978. The behavior of juvenile Atlantic salmon (*Salmo salar*) and brook trout (*Salvelinus fontinalis*) with regard to temperature and to water velocity. Transactions of the American Fisheries Society 107:703–712.

Gibson, M. R. 1982. State of Rhode Island, overview of alosid stocks. Report to Atlantic States Marine Fisheries Commission, Alosid Scientific and Statistical Committee, Washington, D.C., USA.

Godwin, W. F., and J. G. Adams. 1969. Young clupeids of the Altamaha River, Georgia. Georgia Game and Fish Commission, Marine Fisheries Division, Contribution Series 15, Brunswick, Georgia, USA.

Greenwood, J. C. 1982. Shad and river herring abstract. Report to Atlantic States Marine Fisheries Commission, Alosid Scientific and Statistical Committee, Washington, DC, USA.

Hatch, R. W., P. M. Haack, and E. H. Brown Jr. 1981. Estimation of alewife biomass in Lake Michigan 1967–1978. Transactions of the American Fisheries Society 110:575–584.

Havey, K. A. 1961. Restoration of anadromous alewives at Long Point, Maine. Transactions of the American Fisheries Society 90:281–286.

Havey, K. A. 1973. Production of juvenile alewives, *Alosa pseudoharengus*, Love Lake, Washington County, Maine. Transactions of the American Fisheries Society 102:434–437.

Hay, J. 1959. The run. W. W. Norton, New York, New York, USA.

Heimbuch, D. G., P. W. Jones, and B. J. Rothschild. 1983. An analysis of Maryland's juvenile striped bass index of abundance. University of Maryland, Chesapeake Biological Laboratory, Technical Memorandum 6, UMCEES 83-51, Solomons, Maryland, USA.

Hempel, G. 1964. Diurnal variations in catch, feeding and swimming activity in plaice (*Pleuronectes platessa*). Rapports et Procès-Verbaux des Réunions, Conseil International pour l'Exploration de la Mer 155:58–64.

Hildebrand, S. F. 1963. Family: Clupeidae. Pages

257–452 *in* Y. H. Olsen, editor. Fishes of the western North Atlantic, volume 1 (part 3). Memoirs of the Sears Foundation for Marine Research, New Haven, Connecticut, USA.

Hildebrand, S. F., and W. C. Schroeder. 1928. Fishes of Chesapeake Bay. U.S. Bureau of Fisheries Bulletin 43 (part 1).

Holland, B. F., and G. F. Yelverton. 1973. Distribution and biological studies of anadromous fishes offshore North Carolina. North Carolina Department of Natural and Economic Resources, Division of Commercial and Sport Fisheries, Special Scientific Report 24, Beaufort, North Carolina, USA.

Hollis, E. H. 1952. Variations in the feeding habits of the striped bass *Roccus saxatilis* (Walbaum) in Chesapeake Bay. Bulletin of the Bingham Oceanographic Collection Yale University 14(1):111–131.

Huber, M. E. 1978. Adult spawning success and emigration of juvenile alewives (*Alosa pseudoharengus*) from the Parker River, Massachusetts. Master's thesis. University of Massachusetts, Amherst, Massachusetts, USA.

Hutchinson, B. P. 1971. The effect of fish predation on the zooplankton of ten Adirondack lakes with particular reference to the alewife, *Alosa pseudoharengus*. Transactions of the American Fisheries Society 100:325–335.

Janssen, J., and S. B. Brandt. 1980. Feeding ecology and vertical migration of adult alewives (*Alosa pseudoharengus*) in Lake Michigan. Canadian Journal of Fisheries and Aquatic Sciences 37:177–184.

Jessop, B. M., W. E. Anderson, and A. H. Vromans. 1983. Life-history data on the alewife and blueback herring of the Saint John River, New Brunswick, 1981. Canadian Data Report of Fisheries and Aquatic Sciences 426.

Jessop, B. M., A. H. Vromans, and W. E. Anderson. 1982. Life-history data on alewife and blueback herring, Mactaquac Dam, 1975–81. Canadian Data Report of Fisheries and Aquatic Sciences 367.

Jones, P. W., F. D. Martin, and J. D. Hardy, Jr. 1978. Development of fishes of the mid-Atlantic bight, volume 1. Acipenserida through Ictaluridae. U.S. Fish and Wildlife Service Biological Services Program FWS/OBS-78/12.

Kelso, W. E., and J. J. Ney. 1985. Nocturnal foraging by alewives in reservoir coves. Proceedings of the Annual Conference Southeastern Association of Fish and Wildlife Agencies 36:125–134.

Kiser, R. W., J. R. Donaldson, and P. R. Olson. 1963. The effects of rotenone on zooplankton populations in freshwater lakes. Transactions of the American Fisheries Society 92:17–24.

Kissil, G. W. 1969. Contributions to the life history of the alewife, *Alosa pseudoharengus* (Wilson), in Connecticut. Doctoral dissertation. University of Connecticut, Storrs, Connecticut, USA.

Kissil, G. W. 1974. Spawning of the anadromous alewife, *Alosa pseudoharengus*, in Bride Lake, Connecticut. Transactions of the American Fisheries Society 103:312–317.

Kohler, C. C., and J. J. Ney. 1980. Piscivority in a land-locked alewife (*Alosa pseudoharengus*) population. Canadian Journal of Fisheries and Aquatic Sciences 37:1314–1317.

Kohler, C. C., and J. J. Ney. 1981. Consequences of an alewife die-off to fish and zooplankton in a reservoir. Transactions of the American Fisheries Society 110:360–369.

Konstantinov, K. G. 1964. Diurnal, vertical migrations of dermersal fish and their possible influence on the estimation of fish stocks. Rapports et Procès-Verbaux des Réunions, Conseil International pour l'Exploration de la Mer 155:23–26.

Kornegay, J. W. 1978. Comparison of aging methods for alewife and blueback herring. North Carolina Department of Natural Resources and Community Development, Division of Marine Fisheries, Special Scientific Report 30, Morehead City, North Carolina, USA.

Kuntz, A., and L. Radcliffe. 1917. Notes on the embryology and larval development of twelve teleostean fishes. U.S. Bureau of Fisheries Bulletin 35:89–134.

Lackey, R. T. 1969. Food interrelationships of salmon, trout, alewives, and smelt in a Maine lake. Transactions of the American Fisheries Society 98:641–646.

Lackey, R. T. 1970. Observations on newly introduced landlocked alewives in Maine. New York Fish and Game Journal 17:110–116.

Lear, D. W., and S. K. Smith. 1976. Phytoplankton of the Potomac estuary. Pages 70–74 *in* W. T. Mason and K. C. Flynn, editors. The Potomac estuary: biological resources, trends and options. Interstate Commission on the Potomac River Basin, Technical Publication 76–2, Rockville, Maryland.

Leim, A. H., and W. B. Scott. 1966. Fishes of the Atlantic coast of Canada. Fisheries Research Board of Canada Bulletin 155.

Levesque, R. C., and R. J. Reed. 1972. Food availability and consumption by young Connecticut River shad *Alosa sapidissima*. Journal of the Fisheries Research Board of Canada 29:1495–1499.

Libby, D. A. 1981. Difference in sex ratios of the anadromous alewife, *Alosa pseudoharengus*, between the top and bottom of a fishway at Damariscotta Lake, Maine. U.S. National Marine Fisheries Service Fishery Bulletin 79:207–211.

Libby, D. A. 1982. Decrease in length at predominant ages during a spawning migration of the alewife, *Alosa pseudoharengus*. U.S. National Marine Fisheries Service Fishery Bulletin 80:902–905.

Lindenberg, J. G. 1976. Seasonal depth distribution of landlocked alewives, *Alosa pseudoharengus* (Wilson), in a shallow, eutrophic lake. Transactions of the American Fisheries Society 105:395–399.

Lipton, D. W. 1979. Comparison of scales and otoliths for determining age and growth of the alewife (*Alosa pseudoharengus*, Wilson). Master's thesis. College of William and Mary, Williamsburg, Virginia, USA.

Loesch, J. G. 1969. A study of the blueback herring, *Alosa aestivalis* (Mitchill) in Connecticut waters. Doctoral dissertation. University of Connecticut,

Storrs, Connecticut, USA.

Loesch, J. G. 1981. Weight relation between paired ovaries of blueback herring. Progressive Fish-Culturist 43:77–79.

Loesch, J. G., and W. H. Kriete, Jr. 1980. Anadromous fisheries research program, Virginia. Virginia Institute of Marine Science, School of Marine Science, Annual Report AFC 10:1, Gloucester Point, Virginia, USA.

Loesch, J. G., W. H. Kriete Jr., and E. J. Foell. 1982. Effects of light intensity on the catchability of juvenile anadromous *Alosa* species. Transactions of the American Fisheries Society 111:41–44.

Loesch, J. G., and W. A. Lund, Jr. 1977. A contribution to the life history of the blueback herring, *Alosa aestivalis*. Transactions of the American Fisheries Society 106:583–589.

MacLellan, P., G. E. Newsome, and P. A. Dill. 1981. Discrimination by external features between alewife and blueback herring. Canadian Journal of Fisheries and Aquatic Sciences 38:544–546.

Manooch, C. S. 1972. Food habits of yearling and adult striped bass, *Morone saxatilis* (Walbaum), from Albemarle Sound, North Carolina. Master's thesis. North Carolina State University, Raleigh, North Carolina, USA.

Marcy, B. C., Jr. 1969. Age determination from scales of *Alosa pseudoharengus* (Wilson) and *Alosa aestivalis* (Mitchill) in Connecticut waters. Transactions of the American Fisheries Society 98:622–630.

Marcy, B. C., Jr. 1976. Early life history studies of American shad in the lower Connecticut River and the effects of the Connecticut Yankee plant. American Fisheries Society Monograph 1:141–168.

Massmann, W. H. 1953. Relative abundance of young fishes in Virginia estuaries. Transactions of the North America Wildlife Conference 18:439–449.

Massmann, W. H. 1963. Summer food of juvenile American shad in Virginia waters. Chesapeake Science 4:167–171.

Mayo, R. K. 1974. Population structure, movement, and fecundity of the anadromous alewife, *Alosa pseudoharengus* (Wilson), in the Parker River, Massachusetts. Master's thesis. University of Massachusetts, Amherst, Massachusetts, USA.

McCaig, R. S. 1980. Effects of sea-run alewives on rainbow trout and brown trout in reclaimed ponds. Progressive Fish-Culturist 42:59–63.

McKenzie, J. A. 1973. Comparative electrophoresis of tissues from blueback herring and gaspereau. Comparative Biochemistry and Physiology B, Comparative Biochemistry 44:65–68.

McLane, W. M. 1955. The fishes of the St. Johns River system. Doctoral dissertation. University of Florida, Gainesville, Florida, USA.

Meador, M. R. 1982. Occurrence and distribution of larval fish in the Santee River system. Master's thesis. Clemson University, Clemson, South Carolina, USA.

Meador, M. R., A. G. Eversole, and J. S. Bulak. 1984. Utilization of portions of the Santee River system by spawning blueback herring. North American Journal of Fisheries Management 4:155–163.

Messieh, S. N. 1977. Population structures and biology of alewives (*Alosa pseudoharengus*) and blueback herring (*Alosa aestivalis*) in the St. John River, New Brunswick. Environmental Biology of Fishes 2:195–210.

Moffitt, C. M., B. Kynard, and S. G. Rideout. 1982. Fish passage facilities and anadromous fish restoration in the Connecticut River basin. Fisheries (Bethesda) 7(6):2–11.

Morsell, J. W., and C. R. Norden. 1968. Food habits of the alewife, *Alosa pseudoharengus* (Wilson), in Lake Michigan. Proceedings, Conference on Great Lakes Research 11:96–102.

Neves, R. J. 1975. Zooplankton recolonization of a lake cove treated with rotenone. Transactions of the American Fisheries Society 104:390–393.

Neves, R. J. 1981. Offshore distribution of alewife, *Alosa pseudoharengus*, and blueback herring, *Alosa aestivalis*, along the Atlantic coast. U.S. National Marine Fisheries Service Fishery Bulletin 79:473–485.

Nikolsky, G. V. 1963. The ecology of fishes. Academic Press, New York, New York, USA.

Nilsson, N.-A. 1967. Interactive segregation between fish species. Pages 293–313 *in* S. D. Gerking, editor. The biological basis of freshwater fish production. Blackwell Scientific Publications, Oxford, England.

Norden, C. R. 1967. Development and identification of the larval alewife, *Alosa pseudoharengus* (Wilson), in Lake Michigan. Proceedings, Conference on Great Lakes Research 10:70–78.

O'Neill, J. T. 1980. Aspects of the life histories of anadromous alewife and the blueback herring, Margaree River and Lake Aninsle, Nova Scotia, 1978–1979. Master's thesis. Acadia University, Wolfville, Canada.

Parrish, B. B., J. H. S. Blaxter, and W. B. Hall. 1964. Diurnal variations in size and composition of trawl catches. Rapports et Procès-Verbaux des Réunions, Conseil International pour l'Exploration de la Mer 155:27–34.

Pate, P. P., Jr. 1974. Age and size composition of commercial catches of blueback herring and alewife in Albemarle Sound, North Carolina and its tributaries. Proceedings of the Annual Conference Southeastern Association of Game and Fish Commissions 27:560–568.

Perlmutter A., E. E. Schmidt, and E. Leff. 1967. Distribution and abundance of fish along the shores of the lower Hudson River during the summer of 1965. New York Fish and Game Journal 14:46–75.

Price, W. S. 1978. Otolith comparison of *Alosa pseudoharengus* and *Alosa aestivalis*. Canadian Journal of Zoology 56:1216–1218.

Prince, E. D., and D. H. Barwick. 1981. Landlocked blueback herring in two South Carolina reservoirs: reproduction and suitability as stocked prey. North American Journal of Fisheries Management 1:41–45.

PSEG (Public Service Electric and Gas Company). 1982. blueback herring (*Alosa aestivalis*): a synthesis of information on natural history, with reference to occurrence in the Delaware River and estuary and involvement with Salem nuclear generating station. Salem Nuclear Generating Station 316 (b) Appendix VI, Newark, New Jersey, USA.

PSEG (Public Service Electric and Gas Company). 1984. Alewife (*Alosa pseudoharengus*): a synthesis of information on natural history, with reference to occurrence in the Delaware River and estuary and involvement with Salem nuclear generating station. Salem Nuclear Generating Station 316 (b) Appendix V, Newark, New Jersey, USA.

Richards, S. W. 1976. Age, growth, and food of bluefish (*Pomatomus saltatrix*) from east central Long Island Sound from July through November, 1975. Transactions of the American Fisheries Society 105:523–525.

Richkus, W. A. 1974. Factors influencing the seasonal and daily patterns of alewife (*Alosa pseudoharengus*) migration in a Rhode Island river. Journal of the Fisheries Research Board of Canada 31:1485–1497.

Richkus, W. A. 1975. Migratory behavior and growth of juvenile anadromous alewives, *Alosa pseudoharengus*, in a Rhode Island drainage. Transactions of the American Fisheries Society 104:483–493.

Richkus, W. A., and G. DiNardo. 1984. Current status and biological characteristics of the anadromous alosids stocks of the eastern United States: American shad, hickory shad, alewife, and blueback herring. Phase I in interstate management planning for migratory alosids of the Atlantic coast. Atlantic States Marine Fisheries Commission, Interstate Fisheries Management Program, Washington, D.C., USA.

Rideout, S. G. 1974. Population estimate, movement, and biological characteristics of anadromous alewives, *Alosa pseudoharengus* (Wilson) utilizing the Parker River, Massachusetts in 1971–1972. Master's thesis. University of Massachusetts, Amherst, Massachusetts, USA.

Rounsefell, G. A., and L. D. Stringer. 1943. Restoration and management of the New England fisheries with special reference to Maine. Transactions of the American Fisheries Society 86:97–111.

Saila, S. B., T. T. Polgar, D. J. Sheehy, and J. M. Flowers. 1972. Correlations between alewife activity and environmental variables at a fishway. Transactions of the American Fisheries Society 101:583–594.

Schaefer, R. H. 1960. Growth and feeding habits of the whiting or silver hake in the New York Bight. New York Fish and Game Journal 7:85–98.

Scherer, M. D. 1972. The biology of the blueback herring, *Alosa aestivalis* (Mitchill), in the Connecticut River above the Holyoke Dam, Holyoke, Massachusetts. Master's thesis. University of Massachusetts, Amherst, Massachusetts, USA.

Scott, W. B., and E. J. Crossman. 1973. Freshwater fishes of Canada. Fisheries Research Board of Canada Bulletin 84:1–966.

Shirey, C. A. 1972. Food habits of bluefish, *Pomatomus*

saltatrix, in the vicinity of Artificial Island, New Jersey. Ichthyological Associates, Middletown, Delaware, USA.

Sissenwine, M. P., and E. W. Bowman. 1978. An analysis of some factors affecting the catchability of fish by bottom trawls. International Commission for the Northwest Atlantic Fisheries, Research Bulletin 13.

Smith, B. A. 1971. The fishes of four low-salinity tidal tributaries of the Delaware River estuary. Master's thesis. Cornell University, Ithaca, New York, USA.

Smith, H. M. 1898. Notes on the extent and condition of the alewife fisheries of the United States in 1896. Pages 31–43 *in* U.S. House of Representatives Document 221, part 24. Report of the Commissioner for the year ending June 30, 1898. Washington, D.C., USA.

Smith, H. M. 1907. The fishes of North Carolina. North Carolina geological and economic survey, volume 2, E. M. Uzzell, Raleigh, North Carolina, USA.

Stevens, R. E. 1958. The striped bass of the Santee–Cooper reservoir. Proceedings of the Annual Conference Southeastern Association of Game and Fish Commissioners 11:253–264.

Stewart, D. J., J. F. Kitchell, and L. B. Crowder. 1981. Forage fishes and their salmonid predators in Lake Michigan. Transactions of the American Fisheries Society 110:751–763.

Street, M. W. 1969. Fecundity of the blueback herring in Georgia. Georgia Game and Fish Commission, Marine Fisheries Division, Contribution Series 17, Brunswick, Georgia, USA.

Street, M. W. 1970. Some aspects of the life histories of hickory shad, *Alosa mediocris* (Mitchill), and blueback herring, *Alosa aestivalis* (Mitchill), in the Altamaha River, Georgia. Master's thesis. University of Georgia, Athens, Georgia, USA.

Street, M. W., and J. G. Adams. 1969. Aging of hickory shad and blueback herring in Georgia by the scale method. Georgia Game and Fish Commission, Marine Fisheries Division, Contribution Series 18, Brunswick, Georgia, USA.

Thunberg, B. E. 1971. Olfaction in parent stream selection by the alewife (*Alewife pseudoharengus*). Animal Behaviour 19:217–225.

Travelstead, J. G. 1980. Age determination and growth of the blueback herring, *Alosa aestivalis*. Master's thesis. College of William and Mary, Williamsburg, Virginia, USA.

Trent, L., and W. H. Hassler. 1966. Feeding behavior of the adult striped bass, *Roccus saxatilis*, in relation to stages of sexual maturity. Chesapeake Science 7:189–192.

Tsimenides, N. C. 1970. Mortality rates and population size of the alewife *Alosa pseudoharengus* (Wilson) in the Rappahannock and Potomac rivers. Master's thesis. College of William and Mary, Williamsburg, Virginia, USA.

Turner, J. L., and H. K. Chadwick. 1972. Distribution and abundance of young-of-the-year striped bass, *Morone saxatilis*, in relation to river flow in the

Sacramento–San Joaquin estuary. Transactions of the American Fisheries Society 101:442–452.

Tyus, H. M. 1972. Note on the life history of the alewife, *Alosa pseudoharengus*, in North Carolina. Journal of the Elisha Mitchell Scientific Society 88:241–243.

Tyus, H. M. 1974. Movements and spawning of anadromous alewives, *Alosa pseudoharengus* (Wilson) at Lake Mattamuskeet, North Carolina. Transactions of the American Fisheries Society 103:392–395.

Vigirstad, T. J., and J. S. Cobb. 1978. Effects of predation by sea-run juvenile alewives (*Alosa pseudoharengus*) on the zooplankton community at Hamilton Reservoir, Rhode Island. Estuaries 1:36–45.

Walburg, C. H. 1957. Observations on the food and growth of juvenile American shad, *Alosa sapidissima*. Transactions of the American Fisheries Society 86:302–306.

Wang, J. C. S., and R. J. Kernehan. 1979. Fishes of the Delaware estuaries: a guide to early life histories. Ecological Analysts, Towson, Maryland, USA.

Warinner, J. E., J. P. Miller, and J. Davis. 1970. Distribution of juvenile river herring in the Potomac River. Proceedings of the Annual Conference Southeastern Association of Game and Fish Commissioners 23:384–388.

Watt, W. D., and F. C. Duerden. 1974. Aquatic ecology of the Saint John River, volume 2. The Saint John River Basin Board, report 15g., Fredericton, Canada.

Weaver, J. E. 1975. Food selectivity, feeding chronology, and energy transformations of juvenile alewife (*Alosa pseudoharengus*) in the James River near Hopewell, Virginia. Doctoral dissertation. University of Virginia, Charlottesville, Virginia, USA.

Wells, L. 1980. Food of alewives, yellow perch, spottail shiners, trout-perch, and slimy and fourhorn sculpins in southeastern Lake Michigan. U.S. Fish and Wildlife Service Technical Paper 98:1–12.

Welsh, W. W., and C. M. Breder, Jr. 1924. Contributions to the life histories of Sciaenidae of the eastern United States coast. U.S. Bureau of Fisheries Bulletin 39(945):141–201.

Whitney, R. R. 1961. The Susquehanna fishery study, 1957–1960. A report on the desirability and feasibility of passing fish at Conowingo Dam. Maryland Department of Research and Education, Contribution 169, Solomons, Maryland, USA.

Winters, G. H., J. A. Moores, and R. Chaulk. 1973. Northern range extension and probable spawning of gaspereau (*Alosa pseudoharengus*) in the Newfoundland area. Journal of the Fisheries Research Board of Canada 30:860–861.

Woodhead, P. M. J. 1964. Diurnal changes in trawl catches of fishes. Rapports et Procès-Verbaux des Réunions, Conseil International pour l'Exploration de la Mer 155:35–44.

Woodhead, P. M. J. 1966. The behavior of fish in relation to light in the sea. Oceanography and Marine Biology: an Annual Review 4:337–403.

Zich, H. E. 1978. Existing information on anadromous clupeid spawning in New Jersey. New Jersey Department of Environmental Protection, Division of Fish, Game and Shellfish, Bureau of Fisheries, Miscellaneous Report 41, Lebanon, New Jersey, USA.

American Fisheries Society Symposium 1:104–121, 1987

Life History Styles of Diadromous Fishes in Inland Waters of Southern Africa

MICHAEL N. BRUTON

J. L. B. Smith Institute of Ichthyology, Grahamstown 6140, South Africa

ANTON H. BOK

Cape Department of Nature and Environmental Conservation, East London 5200, South Africa

MARTIN T. T. DAVIES

*Department of Ichthyology and Fisheries Science, Rhodes University
Grahamstown 6140, South Africa*

Abstract.—Southern Africa has only five catadromous fish species (four anguillid eels *Anguilla bengalensis labiata, A. bicolor bicolor, A. marmorata marmorata,* and *A. mossambica* and one mullet *Myxus capensis*) and no anadromous forms except introduced trout. The reason for the paucity of diadromous fishes is probably the unstable nature of rivers in the region due to low or erratic rainfalls, high soil moisture deficits, and unreliable availability of resources such as food and space compared with that in the ocean. Human manipulation of inland waters through the construction of impoundments and the abstraction of water has further reduced water availability in rivers and introduced barriers to migration. The mullet and eels show various adaptations for life in the unpredictably perturbed inland waters of southern Africa. The mullet shows a predominance of females in older and larger size-classes (which increases population fecundity), delayed gonadal development in fresh water, an extended spawning season, a wide range of sizes at first maturity and semelparity. The anguillid eels show the same saltatory development as their congeners in the northern hemisphere whereby each developmental stage is matched to the requirements of the environment. Glass eel migrations into fresh water occur mainly in midsummer but differ in magnitude between years. Adaptations for life in fresh water include the presence of specialist migratory life history stages (glass eel and elver), a predominance of females in larger and older size-classes (to increase population fecundity), delayed gonadal maturation in fresh water and semelparity. The catadromous fishes of southern Africa are highly vulnerable to human manipulations of inland waters due to their obligate migrations. Management options available to ensure their survival include water flow manipulation to provide minimum base flows for migrations, translocation of fish over barriers to migration, construction of fish passes, and artificial propagation to enhance wild stocks.

Fishes typically undertake cyclical migrations if the habitat which is optimal for feeding by adults is not optimal for breeding or for feeding by the young. As a result, they alternate between two or more habitats. In the case of diadromous fishes, a habitat in an inland water and one in the ocean have been chosen for feeding or breeding, and migrations take place between the two systems. For diadromous fishes to be present, therefore, inland water systems must offer a resource to the species concerned which is not as readily available in the ocean.

Although southern Africa has a diverse fish fauna, there are few diadromous fishes in the subcontinent. In this paper, we describe the nature of lotic systems in southern Africa in order to explain the paucity of diadromous forms, and discuss the freshwater biology of two groups of

catadromous fishes. Recommendations for the conservation and management of diadromous fishes are also made.

Southern Africa is defined here as that part of Africa south of and including the Cunene and Zambezi catchments, i.e., south of about 17°S latitude. There are 2,200 species of marine fishes (to a depth of 2,000 m) in southern Africa (Smith and Heemstra 1986) and 231 species of primary and secondary freshwater fishes (Skelton et al., in press). McDowall (1987, this volume), following Myers (1949), defined diadromous fish as "truly migratory fishes which migrate between the sea and fresh water." By this definition, there are five species of catadromous fishes in southern Africa (Table 1) and no truly anadromous or amphidromous forms. The catadromous species include all four anguillid eels known from southern Africa

TABLE 1.—Catadromous fishes of southern Africa.

Anguillidae	
Anguilla mossambica Peters, 1852	Longfin eel
Anguilla bengalensis labiata Peters, 1852	African mottled eel
Anguilla marmorata marmorata Quoy and Gaimard, 1824	Madagascar mottled eel
Anguilla bicolor bicolor McClelland, 1844	Shortfin eel
Mugilidae	
Myxus capensis (Valenciennes in C and V, 1836)	Freshwater mullet

(*Anguilla bengalensis labiata, A. bicolor bicolor, A. marmorata marmorata,* and *A. mossambica*) and one of the 15 mullet species *(Myxus capensis).* A second mullet, *Mugil cephalus,* commonly enters fresh waters but is more common in estuaries and the ocean. The five truly catadromous species represent only 0.2% of the total number of fish species in the region, below the world average of 0.6% (McDowall 1987).

Several species are on the fringe of diadromy and may be so classified when their life cycles are better known. At least seven species have established breeding populations in both marine–estuarine and freshwater habitats in southern Africa and may migrate to the other biome to feed (questionably amphidromous; Table 2). An additional 24 species of marine and estuarine fishes sporadically or frequently enter fresh waters in the region (Table 3) but this movement does not involve a large portion of the population. These species may be regarded as facultatively amphidromous species and consist of euryhaline marine fishes which enter rivers and freshwater lagoons, mainly on the warm east coast, for nonbreeding purposes. They are derived mainly from families which are widely known to be diadromous, i.e., Clupeidae, Syngnathidae, Centropomidae, Kuhliidae, Gobiidae, and Eleotridae (McDowall 1987),

TABLE 2.—Fishes which have established breeding populations in both marine–estuarine and fresh waters in southern Africa (data from Bruton and Kok 1980; Smith and Heemstra 1986).

Clupeidae	
Gilchristella aestuaria (Gilchrist, 1916)	Estuarine roundherring
Gobiidae	
Awaous aeneofuscus (Peters, 1852)	Freshwater goby
Croilia mossambica Smith, 1955	Burrowing goby
Glossogobius callidus (Smith, 1936)	River goby
Glossogobius giuris (Hamilton-Buchanan, 1822)	Tank goby
Silhouettea sibayi Farquharson, 1970	Spinnaker goby
Redigobius dewaali (Weber, 1897)	Checked goby

as well as some which are less commonly known to enter fresh waters, i.e., Carcharinidae, Pristidae, Elopidae, Sparidae, and Lutjanidae.

A single species of megalopid, the oxeye tarpon *Megalops cyprinoides,* occurs in southern Africa and frequently enters freshwater lakes and rivers (e.g., Lake Mgobezeleni: Bruton and Appleton 1975; Pongolo River: Bruton and Kok 1980), some as far as 300 km from the ocean (Jubb 1967). Megalopids have leptocephalus larvae similar to those of eels, but with a forked tail (Smith and Heemstra 1986), and they spawn in the ocean. The freshwater populations could, therefore, be regarded as catadromous but they probably represent a small fraction of the total population, which is abundant in brackish lagoons and estuaries and also occurs in the ocean.

Five species of estuarine–lagoonal fishes are known to make short movements into fresh waters where at least two species (*Eleotris fusca* and *Hypseleotris dayi*) may breed (Table 4). Introduced brown trout *Salmo trutta* and rainbow trout *S. gairdneri* have been reported to enter the sea sporadically in False Bay and to return to the Eerste River in the western Cape Province, South Africa (Harrison 1958, 1958–1959; Anonymous 1959–1960). They cannot, however, be regarded as anadromous as the bulk of their populations remain in fresh water throughout life. R. M. McDowall (personal communication) has found that *S. trutta* is facultatively anadromous in Australasia; it is confined to fresh waters in the warmer northern regions but increasingly enters the ocean further south. He also reported that *S. trutta* runs to sea in southern Chile. These trends are, therefore, confirmed in southern Africa. The lack of anadromous fishes in southern Africa, and their apparent paucity in Africa as a whole, is in contrast to the situation in the inland African Great Lakes. Here numerous species of ostariophysan fishes migrate from the giant inland seas up the rivers to spawn (e.g., Whitehead 1959). Catadromy, however, appears to be rare or absent.

Lotic Environments of Southern Africa

In the semiarid to arid areas characteristic of low-latitude southern hemisphere land masses, such as southern Africa, the proportion of the mean annual precipitation (MAP) which is converted to river flow varies from less than 25% in high rainfall zones to 0% in deserts and averages less than 10%. This is in contrast to the high rainfall areas characteristic of northern hemi-

TABLE 3.—Marine and estuarine fish species which sporadically or frequently enter fresh waters in southern Africa but are not known to breed there (data from Jubb 1967; Bruton and Kok 1980; Smith and Heemstra 1986).

Carcharhinidae	
Carcharhinus leucas	Zambezi shark
(Valenciennes in Muller and	
Henle, 1884)	
Pristidae	
Pristis microdon Latham, 1794.	Smalltooth sawfish
Megalopidae	
Megalops cyprinoides	Oxeye tarpon
(Broussonet, 1782)	
Hemirhamphidae	
Hyporhamphus (Hyporhamphus)	Shortfin halfbeak
improvisus	
(Smith, 1933)	
Belonidae	
Strongylura leiura (Bleeker, 1851)	Yellowfin needlefish
Atherinidae	
Atherinomorus lacunosus (Forster,	Hardyhead silverside
1801)	
Atherina breviceps Valenciennes,	Cape silverside
1835	
Syngnathidae	
Microphis fluviatilis (Peters, 1852)	Freshwater pipefish
Microphis brachurus (Bleeker,	Shorttail pipefish
1853)	
Haemulidae	
Pomadasys commersonnii	Spotted grunter
(Lacepède, 1801)	
Sparidae	
Acanthopagrus berda (Forsskål,	Riverbream
1775)	
Monodactylidae	
Monodactylus argenteus	Natal moony
(Linnaeus, 1758)	
Monodactylus falciformis	Cape moony
Lacepède, 1800	
Mugilidae	
Mugil cephalus Linnaeus, 1758	Flathead mullet[a]
Liza macrolepis (Smith, 1846)	Largescale mullet
Liza richardsoni (Smith, 1846)	Southern mullet
Gobiidae	
Caffrogobius nudiceps	Barehead goby
(Valenciennes, 1827)	
Glossogobius biocellatus	Sleepy goby
(Valenciennes, 1837)	
Mugilogobius durbanensis	Durban goby
(Barnard, 1927)	
Ambassidae	
Ambassis gymnocephalus	Bald glassy
(Lacepède, 1801)	
Ambassis natalensis Gilchrist and	Slender glassy
Thompson, 1908	
Ambassis productus Guichenot,	Longspine glassy
1866	
Lutjanidae	
Lutjanus argentimaculatus	River snapper
(Forsskål, 1775)	
Kuhliidae	
Kuhlia rupestris (Lacepède, 1802)	Rock flagtail

[a]Called striped mullet in North America.

TABLE 4.—Estuarine fishes which may perform a short migration into fresh water to breed (questionably anadromous).

Eleotridae	
Eleotris fusca (Bloch and Schneider, 1801)	Dusky sleeper
Eleotris mauritianus Bennett, 1831	Widehead sleeper
Eleotris melanosoma Bleeker, 1852	Broadhead sleeper
Hypseleotris dayi Smith, 1950	Golden sleeper
Ophiocara porocephala (Valenciennes, 1837)	Flathead sleeper

intensity of solar radiation combine to exhaust soil moisture. Subsequent precipitation has to satisfy soil moisture deficits before surface runoff takes place. Subsurface flow is also reduced and contributes little or nothing to flow stability. For example, Australia, South Africa, and Canada all have a MAP of 500 mm but a much smaller proportion of the MAP is converted into river flow in Australia (9.0%) and South Africa (8.6%) than in Canada (65.7%) (Alexander 1985).

Evaporation potential plays an important role in the hydrological processes of semiarid southern continents. In these areas of low, sporadic rainfall, an increasingly large proportion of soil moisture is returned to the atmosphere between rainfall events via direct evaporation or transpiration from plants. The rain thus falls on dry soil that inhibits surface runoff. Over most of southern Africa, potential evaporation exceeds precipitation (mainly rain) by factors of two to 25 (Alexander 1985). MacMahon (1979) has shown that river flow becomes increasingly more variable the more arid the climate; the coefficient of variability for river flow is 1.14 for southern Africa and 0.65 for North America where the MAP is less than 500 mm. The global value for the arid zones is 0.99.

The relatively unstable flows of rivers in the semiarid southern continents have prompted the construction of storage reservoirs, which dampen downstream water-level fluctuations. Furthermore, these reservoirs have to be proportionately larger (with capacities as large as five times the mean annual river flow) than those in the northern hemisphere in order to provide a reliable water supply and store large inputs from occasional floods. Flow regimes downstream of these reservoirs are drastically altered and, except for occasional floods, may be totally dependent on the operating criteria for the reservoirs (Ward and Stanford 1979; Alexander 1985). Where river channels are used for the conveyance of water to downstream users, flows are lower but less variable than under natural conditions. Where river

sphere land masses where the range is 25–75% (Alexander 1985). In the more arid southern hemisphere continents, precipitation events are less frequent, and the lessened cloud cover plus higher channels are not used for water conveyance, they are dry more frequently and for longer periods than before.

Alexander (1985) has estimated that the point of maximum economic utilization of surface and groundwater resources in South Africa will be reached early next century, which means that increasing demands on water resources will have to be met. Clearly, fishes which are adapted to natural cycles of river flow in southern Africa will be impacted by these developments. A thorough understanding of the ecology of these fish species is, therefore, required in order to manage their populations effectively.

Biology of Diadromous Mullets in Southern Africa

Distribution, Growth, and Breeding

Myxus capensis, the freshwater mullet, is endemic to the south and southeast coast of South Africa from Kosi Bay (27°S) to the Bree River (about 34°S) and occurs in the freshwater reaches of rivers and lagoons throughout its range (Crass 1964; Jubb 1967). Recent reports (e.g., Bok 1980)

have suggested that the natural range of this species has been sharply reduced by human changes to riverine environments. A study was carried out by Bok (1979, 1980, 1983, 1984a,b) on aspects of the species' breeding biology, migrations, relative abundance, and demography, which is summarized here. The study concentrated mainly on three eastern Cape rivers, the Kowie, Great Fish, and Swartkops (Figure 1). These rivers have physical and biotic characteristics that represent the typical habitat of *M. capensis* in the eastern Cape. In addition, all larger rivers from the Kromme to the Great Kei (Figure 1) were surveyed to determine the presence and extent of freshwater mullet in habitats further upstream.

A full range of sizes of juvenile mullet was collected in the upper, middle, and lower estuarine reaches as well as in the freshwater reaches of the rivers with gill and seine nets, traps, fyke nets, rotenone, and hook and line (Bok 1979). In order to catch ripe-running adults, seine netting was conducted in the surf zone off the mouth of the Great Fish River. Comparative data were also collected on the flathead mullet *Mugil cephalus,*

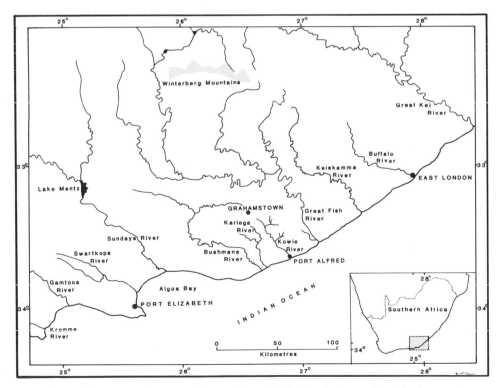

FIGURE 1.—Map of the eastern Cape area, South Africa, showing localities mentioned in the text. Insert: map of southern Africa showing the position of the eastern Cape area.

which frequently enters eastern Cape rivers. Further details on the methods used are provided by Bok (1979, 1983). The study on the mullet species was conducted over 8 years (1975–1982).

The demography, sex ratio, growth rates, and longevity of *Myxus capensis* clearly reflect this species' adaptation, at a life history level, to strong selection pressures in its environment. The sampled populations were predominantly females, particularly in larger size-classes and older age-groups (Figures 2, 3). Males over 3 years old were very rare, while older females were relatively common and some individuals reached 5 years. Female *M. capensis* grow faster than males after the second year (Figure 4); the predominance of females in the larger size-classes may reflect the faster growth rate of females or higher rates of mortality or emigration of males.

The age structure of *Myxus capensis* in fresh water is markedly different from that of *Mugil cephalus,* a fish which seldom reaches 2 years of age in fresh water in southern Africa (Figure 5).

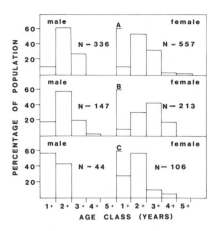

FIGURE 3.—The age structures of *Myxus capensis* in the Kowie (A), Swartkops (B), and Great Fish (C) rivers, excluding the 0+ year class. Values were calculated from length–age keys (Ricker 1975). (From Bok 1983.)

Even in estuarine areas, the number of 3-year-old and older *M. cephalus* was markedly lower than for *M. capensis*. Large numbers of age-0 and 1-year-old *M. cephalus* were captured in the freshwater reaches of the Great Fish and other rivers, but most juveniles migrated downstream to the estuaries before the maximum size and age were reached.

The limited numbers of older *M. cephalus* captured in fresh water did not allow accurate growth curves to be calculated but, using samples from estuaries, we found that females grew faster than males, as in *M. capensis*. However, in contrast to estuarine populations where a 1:1 sex ratio was found, *M. cephalus* in rivers showed a preponder-

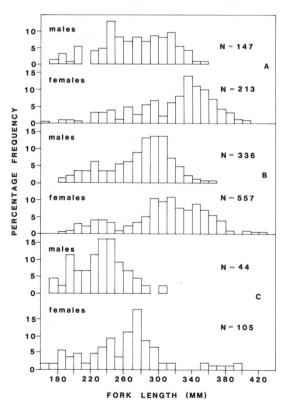

FIGURE 2.—Length frequencies of male and female *Myxus capensis* from the freshwater areas of the Swartkops (A), Kowie (B), and Great Fish (C) rivers. (From Bok 1983.)

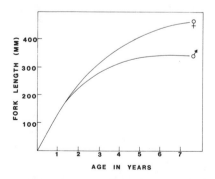

FIGURE 4.—Growth in fork length (*L*, mm) over time (*t*, years) of male and female *Myxus capensis* from the Kowie River calculated from the von Bertalanffy growth equation (from Bok 1983):
males, $L_t = 353 [1 - e^{-0.585(t - 0.182)}]$;
females, $L_t = 521 [1 - e^{-0.316(t - 0.055)}]$.

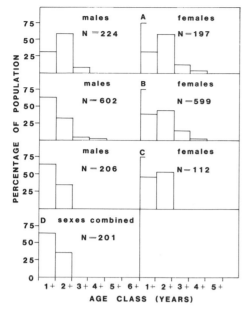

FIGURE 5.—The age structure of *Mugil cephalus* in the Kowie (A) and Great Fish (B) estuaries and in the Swartkops (C) and Kowie (D) rivers. The 0+ year classes are excluded. Values were calculated from length–age keys (Ricker 1975). (From Bok 1983.)

ance of males (Bok 1983).

M. capensis spawns throughout the year with a peak in spring. *M. cephalus,* in contrast, has a well-defined winter spawning period from April to October with peak spawning from June to September (Bok 1983). Numerous South African estuarine fishes have protracted spawning periods, and hence recruitment periods, which may act as a buffer against recruitment failure and as a result of short-term adverse climatic or hydrological conditions (Wallace 1975).

The continuous spawning of *M. capensis* has additional advantages related to its catadromous behaviour in an unstable riverine environment.

Continuous spawning would allow the adult fish to migrate downstream to the ocean for spawning during irregular periods of high river flow at any time of the year. Furthermore, the numerous rapids impeding the upstream migration of early juveniles may only be negotiable at certain levels of river flow. The extended recruitment period found in this species would, therefore, counteract detrimental effects due to short-term adverse river conditions.

An understanding of the selection pressures associated with the evolution of spawning at any time of the year, as opposed to seasonal spawning, may indicate the importance of these tactics in the two mullet species. A short well-defined spawning period would be associated with high rates of survival of progeny during a particular spawning period, whereas all-year spawning would suggest that there is no advantage for this species to spawn at any particular time; i.e., survival of eggs, embryos, larvae, and juveniles responds to unpredictable environmental conditions. As it is likely that the eggs and young fry of the two mullet species have similar developmental requirements, differences in the lengths of the spawning periods may be due to different selection pressures on the older juveniles. The extended spawning periods of *M. capensis* may, therefore, be associated with the obligatory need of this species to recruit into an unpredictable freshwater habitat. The relatively seasonal spawning period of *M. cephalus* indicates this species is not similarly constrained in the estuarine environment.

The gonads of *M. capensis* attained limited development in fresh water, where a maximum gonadosomatic index (GSI = 100 [gonad weight/body weight]) of 0.77 and stage III of development (Nikolskii 1963) was reached (Table 5). The gonads developed further in estuaries (stage IV; GSI

TABLE 5.—Gonadal development of adult female *Myxus capensis* (fork length > 250 mm) from freshwater, estuarine, and marine areas of the eastern Cape, South Africa. Gonads termed "active" are those in developmental stage III and above (from Bok 1983). The GSI (gonadosomatic index) is 100(ovary weight)/(body weight).

Area	Locality	Total number caught	% with "active gonads"	Maximum GSI
Kowie River	Freshwater	451	13.3	0.73
	Estuary	60	40.0	2.70
Great Fish River	Freshwater	65	6.2	0.77
	Estuary	311	47.3	12.77
Swartkops River	Freshwater	185	31.4	0.68
Surf zone	Great Fish River beach	14	71.4	15.9

= 12.8) but ripe-running fishes (stage V) were only captured in the sea. Only one spent female was captured in fresh water, indicating that few fish return to the rivers after spawning and that spawning normally occurs once in a life cycle (semelparity).

In contrast, *M. cephalus* undergoes considerable gonadal development in fresh water. Although few mature adult fish were caught in rivers during this study, a 4-year-old *M. cephalus* held in an 8-hectare impoundment developed ripe gonads weighing up to 101.5 g and had a GSI of 3.08. Five-year-old *M. capensis* in the same impoundment showed limited gonadal development with GSI values of less than 0.6. In studies elsewhere, female *M. cephalus* have been reported from fresh water with ripe gonads and GSI values of over 12 (Shireman 1975) and over 19 (Abraham et al. 1966).

Limited gonadal development in fresh waters holds a distinct adaptive advantage for catadromous fishes. The risk of isolation in a river subject to erratic flows means that energy diverted to gonadal development would be wasted if the fish cannot reach the ocean to spawn. In addition, fish heavy in roe may not be able to undertake long downstream migrations in shallow water. Instead, *M. capensis* only reaches sexual maturity in estuaries where there is a clear passage to the marine

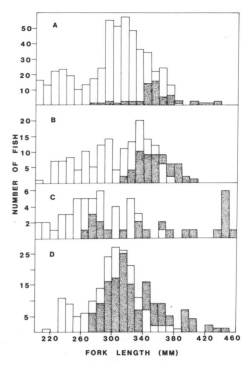

FIGURE 7.—Length frequencies of sexually active (shaded bars) and sexually inactive (open bars) female *Myxus capensis* (fork length > 200 mm) caught in the freshwater areas of the Kowie (A) and Swartkops (B) rivers and in the Kowie estuary (C) and Great Fish estuary (D). (From Bok 1983.)

spawning areas (Figure 6).

The absolute fecundity *(AF)* of *M. capensis* increases as a cube of its fork length *(FL)*: $AF = 0.0127 \, FL^{2.898}$; $r^2 = 0.93$; $N = 21$). Female *M. capensis* become sexually mature at about 260 mm FL, whereas males mature at about 210 mm FL. Females show a wide range of size (and age) at first maturity (Figure 7).

The relatively larger size of females is a strategy to maximize egg production, as total population fecundity is approximately proportional to the total weight of mature females present (Weatherley 1972). A sex ratio in favour of females (as in *M. capensis*) will also increase population fecundity. The size of male fish does not appear to influence spawning success greatly, as there is normally more than sufficient sperm in fish which engage in external fertilization, especially group spawners (Nikolskii 1969). *Myxus capensis* move offshore to breed but the act of spawning has not as yet been observed. *Mugil cephalus* is known to be polygynous (Arnold and Thompson 1958); in the case of *Crenimugil crenilabis,* the release of

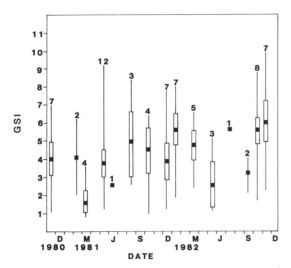

FIGURE 6.—Gonadosomatic indexes (GSI = 100 [ovary weight/body weight]) (GSI) of female *Myxus capensis* with "active" gonads caught at station 3 in the Great Fish estuary. The data are given as means (squares), standard errors (rectangles), and ranges (vertical lines) of monthly catches. Numerals indicate sample sizes. (From Bok 1984b.)

milt and eggs occurs when the whole school "erupts in a frenzy of jumping, thrashing fish" (Helfrich and Allen 1975).

The wide range of size (and age) at sexual maturity of *M. capensis* (Figure 7) is an important adaptation to unstable riverine environments. As discussed above, adult fish migrate into seawater to spawn and few return to fresh water. If all the fish matured (and migrated downstream) at ages 2 and 3, there would only be two or three year classes in fresh water, and the population would be vulnerable to prolonged adverse environmental conditions.

During droughts, when rivers in the eastern Cape may cease to flow for 2 years or more, recruitment stocks would be unable to migrate into fresh water and may suffer heavy mortalities. In addition, breeding migrations would be prevented and the cycle of spawning and recruitment interrupted. If all potential spawners participated in a spawning migration at the first opportunity after a drought, the river would be virtually depopulated until recruitment from this postdrought spawning took place. In the absence of ranges of size and age at first maturity, these fish would

reach maturity at the same time and the cycle would be repeated. This cycle of population peaks and troughs would result in (a) insufficient utilization of the freshwater habitat and (b) vulnerability to adverse environmental conditions. By having a wide range of size and age at first sexual maturity, the reproductive effort of the population is spread over several years and recruitment failure can be compensated for.

A similar strategy was recorded by Nikolskii (1969) for Pacific salmon: *Oncorhynchus keta* breeds at ages 2–7 in unstable spawning conditions whereas *O. gorbuscha* breeds at ages 1–2 under stable conditions.

Life History Style

Young *M. capensis* migrate into fresh water at a small size (15–40 mm FL) and return to the sea when sexually mature. Virtually all growth takes place in the freshwater feeding areas. The movement into fresh water therefore represents a feeding migration to enhance abundance through increased growth, fecundity, and survival, as is typical of catadromous fish (Northcote 1978). A sex ratio in favour of females and a marked

TABLE 6.—Life history traits of *Myxus capensis* which may enhance size, fecundity, and abundance in freshwater reaches of eastern Cape rivers, South Africa, as well as their possible adaptive significances and comparisons with traits of *Mugil cephalus*.

Myxus capensis		*Mugil cephalus* trait
Trait	Adaptive significance	
Reduced gonadal development in fresh water, advanced development only once in estuary	Improved migratory ability; reduces risk of energy wastage if ripe fish are isolated in freshwater reaches	Advanced gonadal development in fresh water, fully ripe specimens reported in fresh water elsewhere
Downriver spawning migration at large size and when sufficient energy reserves have been accumulated	Enables full exploitation of food reserves available in fresh water to increase growth and hence fecundity	In most rivers, migrate downriver as subadults
Spawning and recruitment at any time of the year	Buffering effect against short-term adverse conditions for egg, embryo, or larval survival, recruitment into estuary and, particularly, recruitment into fresh water; enables infrequent floods to be used at any time for downriver spawning migration	Seven-month spawning season, with pronounced 2–3 month peak
Sex ratio in favour of females, predominance of females in large size-classes	Maximizes egg production and ensures high population fecundity	Sex ratio in fresh water in favour of males
Relatively wide range in size and age (2+ to 5+ years) at first sexual maturity	Insurance against loss of breeding and recruitment in consecutive poor years due to isolation in fresh water during droughts	Few fish older than age 2+ in fresh water; nearly all spawning fish 2+ and 3+ years old
Relatively constant first year growth, possibly "fixed" upper growth limit	Optimize superior upriver migratory ability of small mullet under low-flow (normal) conditions	Can drastically increase growth in first year under favourable conditions

predominance of females in the larger size-classes are typical of diadromous fishes (Northcote 1978). The strategies evolved by *M. capensis* to survive in an unstable riverine habitat are summarized in Table 6, where their adaptive significance is emphasized by comparison with the tactics of *M. cephalus,* which is not as well adapted for unstable riverine conditions in the eastern Cape.

In terms of *r* and *K* selection, *M. capensis* has mainly *r*-selected characters, i.e., early maturity, small body size, high fecundity, semelparity, and a short life span. The theory of *r* and *K* selection has, however, been shown to have limited value for aquatic organisms (Pianka 1970; Mann and Mills 1979; Balon 1981, 1984; Noakes and Balon 1982). For example, where there is a wide fluctuation in juvenile mortality and relatively stable adult mortality, Murphy (1968) proposed that selection would be for long life and iteroparity, i.e., *K* rather than *r* characteristics would be selected for, despite the unstable habitats occupied by juveniles. The important factor determining adaptive response may be the age specificity of the mortality, whether density dependent or density independent (Schaffer 1974). For a semelparous species with a widely fluctuating juvenile mortality, it may be advantageous for only a fraction of the adults to breed every year. *Myxus capensis* probably fits into this category as their wide range of age at first (and final) maturity and prolonged spawning season allow them to retain the advantages of iteroparity without sacrificing high individual fecundity. Similar advantages of bethedging traits (sensu Stearns 1976) have been postulated for Atlantic salmon *Salma salar* (Murphy 1968; Mann and Mills 1979).

Biology of Diadromous Eels in Southern Africa

Distribution, Migration, and Biology in Fresh Water

Four anguillid eel species are found in southern Africa (Table 1). All have similar life history cycles, although some are more tropical in distribution than others (Figure 8). The proposed spawning area in the Indian Ocean is based upon samples of larvae taken by the Dana expedition to the western Indian Ocean in 1929 and 1930. Jespersen (1942) noted that the leptocephali caught were small (37 mm) and this led Jubb (1961) to postulate that the spawning grounds were near the African continent between latitudes 10° and 20°S and longitudes 60° and 65°E, where there is a zone

of warm water at great depth (Tesch 1977). Larvae carried from the hypothetical spawning ground in the westward flow of the south equatorial current would be taken northwards up the east coast of Africa and also southwards in the Mocambique and Agulhas currents. The discovery of small "elvers" (43–54 mm total length) of *Anguilla mossambica* in the Uvongo River mouth in Natal (Jubb 1960) is evidence of this southerly distribution. The freshwater distribution of southern African eels has subsequently been documented in greater detail (Figure 8).

The five principal phases of the life cycle of *Anguilla anguilla* in the northern hemisphere (leptocephalus, glass eel, elver, yellow eel, silver eel: Bertin 1956) are also present in the four anguillid species in southern Africa (Jubb 1961). The metamorphosis of the leptocephalus larva into the glass eel (Strubberg 1913) precedes entry into fresh water. Through successive changes in pigmentation, the glass eel becomes an elver and then develops into a pigmented young eel (Tesch 1977). Sampling over 7 years (1973–1979) in the ebb and flow reaches of southern African rivers has revealed that the upstream migrations of the glass eels there vary in extent seasonally and reach a peak in midsummer (November–January). Glass eels were caught throughout the winter in these rivers but in low numbers, less than 1% of the annual total (Figure 9; M. T. T. Davies, unpublished).

Many of the glass eels entering fresh water were slightly pigmented on the head with a caudal spot and some rostral pigment, indicating that they had probably remained in the estuary for a short period before entering fresh water (Deelder 1958; Jellyman 1977). These glass eels showed a strong rheotactic response, as also recorded by Deelder (1958), Creutzberg (1961), and Jellyman (1977), and usually swam in shoals near the river bank. The largest migrations were recorded in association with high spring tides during above-average river flow following a flood and at night (Davies, unpublished). Peak juvenile anguillid migrations during spring tides have also been noted by Lowe (1952), Tesch (1977), and Jellyman (1977); photophobic responses have been reported by Tesch (1977) but not by Jellyman (1979). There was no apparent correlation between water temperature and the size of the glass eel migration (Davies, unpublished), a finding also reported by Jellyman (1977) but not by Matsui (1952) or Deelder (1952) for Japanese and European glass eels, respectively.

The size of juvenile eel migrations into southern

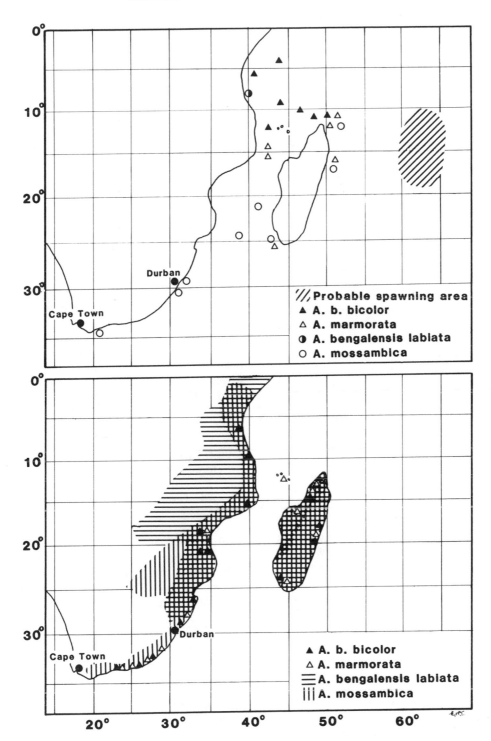

FIGURE 8.—Distribution of the South African eel species. Above: larval distributions and probable spawning area. Below: coastal and inland distributions. (Modified after Tesch 1977.)

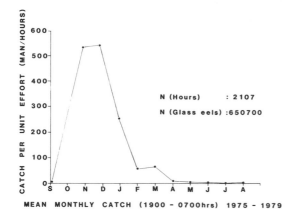

MEAN MONTHLY CATCH (1900 - 0700hrs) 1975 - 1979

FIGURE 9.—The monthly variation of catch per unit effort of glass eels (mainly *Anguilla mossambica*) from the Keiskamma River in the eastern Cape, South Africa (M. T. T. Davies, unpublished).

African rivers is substantially smaller than in other regions of the world (Lowe 1952; Jellyman 1979; Sloane 1984), where several hundred tonnes have been recorded in one season (Tesch 1977). The reason for this is unknown but may be related to the relatively low mean annual runoff of most southern African rivers (Alexander 1985).

A subsample of 164 glass eels taken from catches made during 1975–1978 in the Umkomaas River in Natal Province, the Umtata River in Transkei, and the Sundays River in the eastern Cape consisted of 86% *A. mossambica,* 9.7% *A. marmorata,* 3.7% *A. bengalensis labiata,* and 0.6% *A. bicolor bicolor;* the length range was 41.3–54.9 mm (Davies, unpublished). These glass eels are smaller than those reported by Tesch (1977) in Europe and by Jellyman (1979) in New Zealand at similar migratory stages.

The young eels employ a series of migrations to move into the upstream reaches of rivers. When a body size of 25–30 cm is reached, the rheotactic response diminishes and the eels become more sedentary. This phase of the life cycle is termed the "yellow eel" stage. Jubb (1961) demonstrated that the diet of southern African anguillids is similar but size dependent. *Anguilla mossambica* up to 20 cm long feed entirely on aquatic insects and the aquatic larvae and nymphs of insects. From 20 to 50 cm total length (TL), the proportion of these food items declines and crustacea (mainly the freshwater crab *Potamon sidneyi*) and fish increase in importance. Above 50 cm TL, the diet consists of fish, crabs, and frogs. The bulk of the *A. mossambica* population measures between 25

and 45 cm TL; the largest eels (>50 cm TL) make up less than 10% of the total population (Jubb 1961; McEwan and Hecht 1984) and are nearly all females (Jubb 1961). The maximum size recorded for *A. bengalensis labiata* and *A. marmorata* in southern Africa is 185 cm and 18 kg, whereas *A. bicolor bicolor* is the smallest local species, the largest specimen being a mature female of 64 cm and 500 g (Jubb 1961).

Jubb (1970) estimated the length of residency in fresh water of *A. mossambica* males to be 8–10 years and for females 15–20 years. Males reached a length of 35–60 cm, whereas females were larger at first maturity and attained 122 cm TL. The residency in fresh water of immature male and female *A. bengalensis labiata* in Kenyan rivers has been reported as 6–8 years and 9–19 years, respectively (Jubb 1961). In Lake Kariba on the middle Zambezi River, juveniles surmount the dam wall in their second year of life and then spend approximately 7 years in streams of the lake drainage (Balon 1975).

The earlier maturation of males ensures that different year classes will interbreed, which may increase genetic variability. Furthermore, by investing more energy in early somatic growth, females increase their fecundity. Jubb (1964) found that males of *A. marmorata* and *A. b. bicolor* were absent or rare in fresh waters in southern Africa.

Before migrating back to the ocean, yellow eels undergo morphological and physiological changes. The colouration changes from mottled yellow–green, yellow, or brown to silver, and the size of the eye more than doubles (Jubb 1961). In addition, the head elongates (Jubb 1964) and substantial body reserves are accumulated (Jubb 1970). Full maturity with advanced gut degeneration has not been observed in fresh water. These preparations for spawning are very similar to those recorded for northern hemisphere eels (Tesch 1977; Boëtius and Boëtius 1980) and suggest that the southern African forms also undertake a long migration to the spawning grounds. Boëtius and Boëtius (1980) have estimated that the protein and lipid reserves built up by *A. anguilla* would provide sufficient energy for a 4,000-km migration as well as for full sexual development.

Southern African anguillids are slow-growing and long-lived. *A. mossambica* has the slowest growth rate of several anguillids studied, reaching only 49 cm after 10 years and 74 cm after 18 years in fresh water (McEwan and Hecht 1984). In Lake

Kariba, male and female *A. bengalensis* reached 75–77 cm TL after 10 years (Balon 1975) and 18 was the maximum age (132 cm) in the sample collected. Growth studies under culture conditions in southern Africa have provided further evidence that southern African anguillids are slow-growing (Davies, unpublished). Slow growth and great longevity are also characteristic of other anguillid species (Tesch 1977; Moriarty 1978); one species attains 60 years (Todd 1980).

We propose that slow growth and small initial size allows anguillids to take maximum advantage of unpredictable river conditions in southern Africa. Many east and south coast rivers in southern Africa originate in mountainous regions over 1,500 m above sea level and descend rapidly onto the coastal plain via numerous waterfalls and rapids. Small eels may be better able to negotiate steep inclines than larger eels. Skead (1959) found that *A. mossambica* of 15 cm TL climbed the 33-m wall of the Laing Dam on the Buffalo River, whereas 20-cm-TL eels were unable to do so. Although Jubb (1961, 1964, 1967) concluded that eels would not be able to negotiate the 128-m high wall of Kariba Dam, which is 1,050 km from the Indian Ocean, Balon (1975) showed that an abundant population of *A. bengalensis* occurs in the lake, mostly at depths from 25 to 40 m. Balon (1973) also showed that this species occurs in the Kalomo River at Siengwazi Falls, 300 km upstream of Kariba Dam. Eels have not, however, been reliably reported to have surmounted the 60–100-m barrier of Victoria Falls, the 37-m vertical rock face of the Siengwazi Falls, or the 14-m-high waterfalls of the Kafue Gorge (Jubb 1964; Bell-Cross 1968; Balon 1974, 1975). On the other hand, there are reports of anguillids climbing the 70-m falls on the Lunsemfuna River, a tributary of the Luangwa River in Zambia (Frost 1957), as well as major waterfalls on the Pungwe River (Turnbull-Kemp 1958). As eels rely on surface tension to climb moist surfaces, their ratios of surface area to volume will determine how efficiently they climb. As surface area increases by the square and mass by the cube, the larger the eel becomes, the less effective its adhesive surface area will be. Jubb (1964) has also noted that small eels are capable of wriggling up wet moss and crevices but, once they reach a size of about 18 cm, a vertical surface becomes a physical barrier.

Size and possibly different climbing ability cause a separation of eel species in the same river system. Jubb (1960) found *A. mossambica* to be the most common eel above the Laing Dam wall on the Buffalo River, whereas *A. marmorata* and *A. b. bicolor* were only found downstream from the dam. *Anguilla mossambica* was likewise the only eel species above the walls of Lake Mentz (104 km inland) and Churchill Dam (30 km inland) on the Sundays and Kromme rivers, respectively, whereas the other species were only found downstream.

Sloane (1984) has shown that *Anguilla australis australis* in Tasmania exhibits 5–10 years of slow initial growth in fresh water followed by several years of faster growth once the eels have migrated into the headwaters. Miller (1979) has furthermore pointed out that the retention of a small body size by fish facilitates feeding on individual small prey items and the exploitation of space-restricted habitats. Southern African elvers utilize cryobenthic habitats such as gravel, stony riffles, and sand interstices for feeding and shelter, and thus exploit a niche which is not available to larger eels or to most small, nonelongated fishes. In headwater streams, the relatively low population density and relative abundance of food may provide suitable conditions for accelerated growth.

Life History Styles

Anguilla mossambica and *A. bengalensis labiata,* the most numerous anguillids in southern Africa, have a mixture of *r*- and *K*-selected life history traits, i.e., high fecundity and semelparity on the one hand but slow growth, eventual large body size, and a long life span on the other.

The life cycle of anguillid eels is, however, better interpreted in terms of saltatory development and altricial–precocial life styles, as proposed by Balon (1981, 1984, 1985) and Noakes and Balon (1982). The hypothesis of saltatory development predicts that species should respond to environmental conditions by heterochronous rates of development. These rates will provide a more appropriate "match" to existing environmental conditions by moving the individual either to the altricial or the precocial life style. Heterochrony provides the ability to adapt to a fluctuating environment by shifting the timing of appearance of structures and functions. Balon (1981) and Noakes and Balon (1982) used the terms altricial (generalist) and precocial (specialist) in the general ecological sense: altricial young are relatively small and incompletely developed, whereas precocial young are relatively larger and more completely developed, at a particular time in ontogeny. Paedomorphosis is the process available for "retracing" phylogeny and prolonging early ontogeny, with its concomitant flexibility and adaptability, as occurs in eels and tarpons. In general, the trend in evolution will be from altricial to precocial (Balon 1985) as communities will tend towards a more mature, competitive condition through ecological succession. Eels are an excellent example of altricial fishes which produce small, incompletely developed young and colonize unstable environments. The need for dispersal may, however, be responsible for the extreme extension of the larval period through "reverse" specialization (e.g., Balon 1985).

Implications of Habitat Changes for Catadromous Fishes

The obligate catadromous life cycles of *Myxus capensis* and the four anguillid eels in the erratic rivers of southern Africa have made these species particularly vulnerable to human alterations of the freshwater environment (Figure 10). The most detrimental impacts are the construction of barriers to migration and the regulation of water flow downstream of impoundments. These actions interfere with the ability of the fishes to exploit fully the freshwater environment in which they are obliged to spend their nonbreeding lives. Physical

or hydrological barriers to migration can severely limit these species from colonizing more upstream portions of rivers and force them to live in suboptimal regions of rivers nearer the estuary. This impact will reduce the abundance of anguillids, which may have commercial importance, and of the freshwater mullet *Myxus capensis,* which is listed in the South African Red Data Book as a threatened species (Skelton 1987).

Various other proposals for the conservation of indigenous freshwater fishes have been made by Crass (1969), Gaigher et al. (1980), and Skelton (1983). Options available for the management of catadromous fishes include water-flow manipulation, translocation of stocks, construction of fishways, and artificial propagation.

Base flow levels and simulated flood peaks have to be established in the regulated rivers to ensure adequate water depths and flow regimes for eel and mullet migration. Furthermore, Creutzberg (1961) has shown that glass eels in Europe are strongly attracted to flowing rivers where olfactory stimuli from mature eels are present. A reduction in the mean annual runoff from a river may reduce the olfactory stimuli necessary to attract eels from the ocean. Controlled releases of relatively large volumes of water for short periods

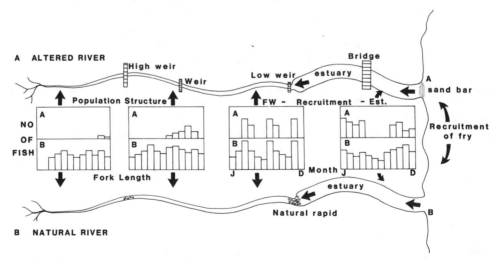

FIGURE 10.—Diagrammatical representation of the factors affecting the survival, distribution, and abundance of *Myxus capensis* in rivers in the eastern Cape, South Africa (after Bok 1983). The natural river has more reliable water flow with no abstraction whereas the altered river has an unreliable flow due to water abstraction, artificial barriers, and an eroded catchment. Bridge construction over the estuary reduces tidal exchange and causes the river mouth to close, thus inhibiting migration. Impoundment construction dampens flood peaks and reduces scouring. As a result, pools become shallower and more turbid due to siltation, which reduces the fish-holding capacity of the river. Fish recruitment in the altered river is inhibited by these changes but is continuous in the natural river. As a result, the population structure of fishes in the upper reaches of the altered river is changed to include only large fishes which are able to survive and negotiate barriers to migration.

during midsummer (November–February) may thus be an effective management strategy.

Myxus capensis has been successfully translocated to points above barriers to migration. The translocation of elvers within river systems can be achieved as large numbers periodically accumulate below barriers and can easily be hand-netted or trapped.

The construction of fish ladders on the many artificial barriers to migration of eels and mullet would be relatively costly but could be achieved on the majority of weirs that are less than 2 m high. Fish ladders in the northern hemisphere have been designed mainly for use by large fish with better swimming ability than *M. capensis*. Knowledge of the swimming ability of the mullet will be needed in order to effect a practical design. The entrance to the fish ladder should be at the base of the barrier, which usually requires a zigzagging stepped structure. The location of the fish ladder on the river will also influence its design, as different-sized fish will have different requirements.

Eel ladders usually have a different design and take advantage of the eel's ability to climb. Strong water flows are broken by bristle, brushwood, or sacking so that the eels can negotiate their way through the moist material without being swept away by the current. Recently developed Hidrostal pumps (Patrick and Sim 1985; Rodgers and Patrick 1985) may serve the same purpose as fish ladders.

Artificial propagation of mullet will permit the large-scale restocking of rivers without the potentially detrimental effects of netting wild populations. *Myxus capensis* have recently been artificially propagated by administering hormone injections to adults captured in estuaries prior to their migration to the ocean to spawn. Improved techniques for raising the delicate larvae are, however, required before mass propagation will be possible. Anguillid eels have rarely been spawned and have not as yet been reared in captivity, so this is not a practical option.

There are several further threats to catadromous fishes in southern African inland waters, of which high sediment loads and alien fishes are particularly important. The weathering and decomposition of rocks, soil, and dead plant material and their transport into inland waters is a natural phenomenon which creates a background of suspended and dissolved material. There is, however, widespread evidence that rates of erosion have been increased by human activities

(e.g., Balek 1977), especially in arid and semiarid areas where variation in the hydrological cycle is extreme and plant cover is reduced. Unnaturally high sediment loads may reduce food availability, feeding efficiency, and growth rates of fishes and reduce habitat diversity (Bruton 1985). These effects are particularly marked in the larger rivers which penetrate far inland into geologically young, erodable sediments (Branch and Grindley 1979; Plumstead 1984). Begg (1978) has shown that over 60% of the estuaries in Natal Province have excessive silt loads.

One beneficial effect of impoundments is that they act as sediment traps and reduce downstream turbidity levels, as found by Mayekiso (1986) in the eastern Cape. Excessive turbidity levels can be controlled by conventional measures of combating soil erosion as well as by techniques such as stream-bank stabilization and instream sediment traps (Hansen et al. 1983). Naturally high sediment loads in low-latitude southern hemisphere rivers could explain the paucity of anadromous fishes in the region, as the blanketing of the substratum by sediment would create unfavourable conditions for spawning by salmoniform fishes. Increased turbidities also interfere with the feeding efficiencies of iliophagous fishes (Whitfield and Blaber 1978; Bruton 1985).

Twenty alien fish species have been introduced into southern African inland waters (Bruton and Merron 1985), but only rainbow trout, brown trout, and black bass *Micropterus* spp. are likely to compete with the anguillid eels. Common carp *Cyprinus carpio* may detrimentally affect *Myxus capensis* by increasing turbidity levels as a result of their benthic foraging habit (Bruton 1985).

Summary

The five catadromous fish species in southern Africa have survived variable freshwater environments by adopting life cycles which are flexible and retain as many options as possible. Their basic strategy is to make optimal use of two different water bodies, the ocean for breeding and fresh waters for feeding, but their need to move between the two makes them vulnerable to natural or artificial changes in their migration routes. Catadromous fish do not guard their young or bear them alive, but afford them some protection by choosing a spawning area where conditions for early development, especially with respect to predation rates and food availability, are better than encountered in fresh waters.

The reason for the paucity of diadromous fishes in southern Africa must, therefore, be that the inland waters, at present, do not provide reliable resources which improve on conditions in the ocean. The lack of anadromous fishes in the subcontinent may, however, not be entirely the result of present environmental conditions but may be due to historical events. Diadromy occurs most strongly in the ancestral fish groups (lampreys, sturgeons, eels, salmoniforms, clupeids), which are relatively uncommon in southern Africa compared to high-latitude, northern hemisphere subcontinents. The salmoniform fishes, which form an important component of northern hemisphere anadromous stocks, did not colonize southern Africa naturally. Those species that have been introduced have, however, survived and at least two species show signs of anadromy. Another alternative is that anadromous species previously existed in southern Africa but have died out as a result of the semiarid conditions which prevail during the present hot, dry interpluvial period.

Hutchings and Morris (1984) have suggested that the life style of a fish (e.g., anadromy) has an influence on covariation in life history traits. Anadromy (or catadromy) could, for instance, have evolved as an adaptive strategy to enhance age-specific survival. Neave (1958) and Hoar (1976) have argued that anadromy could have been imposed on primitive salmonid-like fish because of large-scale environmental disruptions and resultant deterioration of freshwater habitats, which forced the fishes to migrate to the ocean to breed and feed. Life history traits which favoured a migratory life cycle would therefore have been selected. The leptocephalus larva of anguillids and megalopids is an example of a life history option, gained through paedomorphosis (sensu Balon 1985), which enhances the survival of a migratory species. Pfeiler (1986) has recently shown that the leaf-like premetamorphic leptocephali obtain a significant fraction of their nutritional needs by absorbing dissolved organic matter across surface epithelia using a system similar to that in certain marine invertebrates. This adaptation allows the elopomorphs to exploit extra food resources in the ocean during the planktonic larval stage before they metamorphose into more actively swimming, exogenously feeding, upstream migrators. Genetic, physiological, and developmental pathways constrain, to some extent, the range of tactics which can be acquired in any given phylogenetic lineage, so that each group of taxa has a limited number of reproductive and survival alternatives (Stearns 1980, 1983; Brown 1983; Hutchings and Morris 1984). In southern Africa, only the anguillids, mugilids, and megalopids have the necessary traits to exploit inland waters and the ocean by way of a diadromous life cycle.

It is surprising, however, that no anadromous fishes have evolved on the west coast of southern Africa where large, permanent rivers occur (Olifants, Orange, Cunene) and the nutrient-rich, cold, upwelling Benguella Current provides apparently suitable conditions for feeding and early development of fishes. McDowall (1987) and Gross (1987, this volume) have demonstrated that anadromy occurs most frequently in high latitudes, or off cold west coasts, where the productivity of the ocean greatly exceeds that of fresh water, which is the case off the west coast of southern Africa. The establishment of sea-run rainbow trout populations on this coast is therefore of some interest (Harrison 1958, 1958–1959; Anonymous 1959–1960).

It is likely that further study will reveal that some of the fishes listed in Tables 2–4 are amphidromous, but the fact remains that southern Africa possesses few diadromous fishes. There is, therefore, an even greater need to study and understand the few species which do exist so that their long-term survival can be ensured.

Acknowledgments

We are grateful to E. K. Balon, S. J. M. Blaber, T. Hecht, P. C. Heemstra, P. B. N. Jackson, R. A. Jubb, C. M. Moffitt, A. J. Ribbink, C. J. Skead, and P. H. Skelton for useful comments on the manuscript, to R. E. Stobbs and Elizabeth Tarr for technical assistance, and to Huibre Tomlinson and Jean Pote for processing the manuscript.

References

Anonymous. 1959–1960. Sea-run rainbow trout, lower Eerste River. Piscator 47:93.

Abraham, M., N. Blanc, and A. Yashouv. 1966. Oogenesis in five species of grey mullets (Teleostei, Mugilidae) from natural and landlocked habitats. Israel Journal of Zoology 15:155–172.

Alexander, W. J. R. 1985. Hydrology of low latitude southern hemisphere land masses. Hydrobiologia 125:75–83.

Arnold, E. L., and V. R. Thompson. 1958. Offshore spawning of the striped mullet Mugil cephalus in the Gulf of Mexico. Copeia 1958:130–132.

Balek, J. 1977. Hydrology and water resources in tropical Africa. Elsevier, New York, New York, USA.

Balon, E. K. 1973. The eels of Siengwazi Falls (Kalomo River, Zambia) and their significance. Journal of the National Museum of Zambia 2:65–82.

Balon, E. K. 1974. Fishes from the edge of Victoria Falls, Africa: demise of a physical barrier for downstream invasions. Copeia 1974:643–660.

Balon, E. K. 1975. The eels of Lake Kariba: distribution, taxonomic status, age, growth and density. Journal of Fish Biology 7:797–815.

Balon, E. K. 1981. Saltatory processes and altricial to precocial forms in the ontogeny of fishes. American Zoologist 21:573–596.

Balon, E. K. 1984. Patterns in the evolution of reproductive styles in fishes. Pages 35–53 in C. W. Potts and R. J. Wootton, editors. Fish reproduction: strategies and tactics. Academic Press, London, England.

Balon, E. K. 1985. Early life histories of fishes: new developmental, ecological and evolutionary perspectives. Developments in Environmental Biology of Fishes 5:1–280.

Begg, G. 1978. The estuaries of Natal. Natal Town and Regional Planning Report 41, Pietermaritzburg, South Africa.

Bell-Cross, G. 1968. Physical barriers separating the fishes of the Kafue and middle Zambezi River systems. Zambia Department of Game and Fisheries, Fisheries Research Bulletin 4:97–98.

Bertin, L. 1956. Eels, a biological study. Cleaver-Hume, London, England.

Boëtius, I., and J. Boëtius. 1980. Experimental maturation of female silver eels, Anguilla anguilla. Estimates of fecundity and energy reserves for migration and spawning. Dana 1:1–28.

Bok, A. H. 1979. The distribution and ecology of two mullet species in some freshwater rivers in the eastern Cape, South Africa. Journal of the Limnological Society of Southern Africa 5:97–102.

Bok, A. H. 1980. Freshwater mullet in the eastern Cape. Eastern Cape Naturalist 69:12–14.

Bok, A. H. 1983. The demography, breeding biology and management of two mullet species (Pisces: Mugilidae) in the eastern Cape, South Africa. Doctoral dissertation. Rhodes University, Grahamstown, South Africa.

Bok, A. H. 1984a. Extensive culture of two mullet species in freshwater impoundments in the eastern Cape. South African Journal of Zoology 19:31–36.

Bok, A. H. 1984b. Freshwater mullet in the eastern Cape—a strong case for fish ladders. The Naturalist (Port Elizabeth) 28:31–35.

Branch, G. M., and J. R. Grindley. 1979. Ecology of southern African estuaries. Part XI. Mngazana: a mangrove estuary in Transkei. South African Journal of Zoology 14:149–170.

Brown, K. M. 1983. Do life history tactics exist at the intraspecific level? Data from freshwater snails. American Naturalist 121:871–879.

Bruton, M. N. 1985. The effects of suspensoids on fish. Hydrobiologia 125:221–241.

Bruton, M. N., and C. C. Appleton. 1975. Survey of the Mgobezeleni lake system in Zululand, with a note on the effect of a bridge on the mangrove swamp. Transactions of the Royal Society of South Africa 41:282–294.

Bruton, M. N., and H. M. Kok. 1980. The freshwater fishes of Maputaland. Pages 210–224 in M. N. Bruton and K. H. Cooper, editors. Studies on the ecology of Maputaland. Rhodes University, Grahamstown, South Africa.

Bruton, M. N., and S. V. Merron. 1985. Alien and translocated aquatic animals in southern Africa: a general introduction, checklist and bibliography. South African National Scientific Programmes, Report 113, Pretoria, South Africa.

Crass, R. S. 1964. Freshwater fishes of Natal. Shuter & Shooter, Pietermaritzburg, South Africa.

Crass, R. S. 1969. The effects of land use on freshwater fish in South Africa, with particular reference to Natal. Hydrobiologia 34:38–56.

Creutzberg, F. 1961. On the orientation of migratory elvers (Anguilla vulgaris Turt.) in a tidal area. Netherlands Journal of Sea Research 1:257–338.

Deelder, C. L. 1952. On the migration of the elver (Anguilla vulgaris Turt.) at sea. Journal du Conseil, Conseil Permanent International pour l'Exploration de la Mer 18:187–218.

Deelder, C. L. 1958. On the behaviour of elvers (Anguilla vulgaris Turt.) migrating from the sea into fresh water. Journal du Conseil, Conseil Permanent International pour l'Exploration de la Mer 24:135–146.

Frost, W. E. 1957. A note on eels (Anguilla spp.). Piscator 38:104–106.

Gaigher, I. G., K. C. D. Hamman, and S. C. Thorne. 1980. The distribution, conservation status and factors affecting the survival of indigenous fishes in the Cape Province. Koedoe 23:57–88.

Gross, M. 1987. The evolution of diadromy in fishes. American Fisheries Society Symposium 1:14–25.

Hansen, E. A., G. R. Alexander, and W. H. Dunn. 1983. Sand sediment in a Michigan trout stream. Part I. A technique for removing sand bedload from streams. North American Journal of Fisheries Management 3:355–364.

Harrison, A. C. 1958. Sea-run trout of the Eerste River. Piscator 43:44–53.

Harrison, A. C. 1958–1959. Sea-run rainbow trout of the Eerste River. Part II: further captures in salt water. Piscator 44:83–84.

Helfrich, P., and P. M. Allen. 1975. Observations on the spawning of mullet, Crenimugil crenilabis (Forsskal) at Enewetak, Marshall Islands. Micronesica 11:219–225.

Hoar, W. S. 1976. Smolt transformation: evolution, behaviour and physiology. Journal of the Fisheries Research Board of Canada 33:1234–1252.

Hutchings, J. A., and D. W. Morris. 1984. The influence of phylogeny, size and behaviour on patterns of covariation in salmonid life histories. Oikos 45:118–124.

Jellyman, D. J. 1977. Summer upstream migration of juvenile freshwater eels in New Zealand. New

Zealand Journal of Marine and Freshwater Research 11:61–71.

Jellyman, D. J. 1979. Invasion of a New Zealand freshwater stream by glass-eels of two *Anguilla* spp. New Zealand Journal of Marine and Freshwater Research 11:193–209.

Jespersen, P. 1942. Indo-Pacific leptocephalids of the genus *Anguilla*. Dana-Report Carlsberg Foundation 22:1–128.

Jubb, R. A. 1960. Elvers and post-elvers of the freshwater eels of South Africa. Piscator 49:68–76.

Jubb, R. A. 1961. The freshwater eels (*Anguilla* spp.) of southern Africa. An introduction to their identification and biology. Annals of the Cape Provincial Museums, Natural History 1:15–48.

Jubb, R. A. 1964. The eels of South African rivers and observations on their ecology. Monographiae Biologicae 14:186–205.

Jubb, R. A. 1967. Freshwater fishes of South Africa. Balkema, Cape Town, South Africa.

Jubb, R. A. 1970. Freshwater eels: *Anguilla* species. Eastern Cape Naturalist 39:10–15.

Lowe, R. H. 1952. The influence of light and other factors on the seaward migration of the silver eel (*Anguilla anguilla* L.). Journal of Animal Ecology 21:275–309.

MacMahon, T. A. 1979. Hydrological characteristics of arid zones. Proceedings of the Canberra Symposium, December 1979. International Association of Hydrological Sciences Publication 128:105–123.

Mann, R. H., and C. A. Mills. 1979. Demographic aspects of fish fecundity. Symposia of the Zoological Society of London 44:161–177.

Matsui, I. 1952. Studies on the morphology, ecology and pond culture of the Japanese eel (*Anguilla japonica* Temminck and Schlegel). Journal of Shimonosiki College of Fisheries 2:1–245.

Mayekiso, M. 1986. Some aspects of the ecology of the eastern Cape rocky *Sandelia bainsii* (Pisces: Anabantidae) in the Tyume River, eastern Cape, South Africa. Masters thesis. Rhodes University, Grahamstown, South Africa.

McDowall, R. M. 1987. The occurrence and distribution of diadromy among fishes. American Fisheries Society Symposium 1:1–13.

McEwan, A., and T. Hecht. 1984. Age and growth of the longfin eel, *Anguilla mossambica* Peters, 1852 (Pisces: Anguillidae) in Transkei rivers. South African Journal of Zoology 4:280–285.

Moriarty, C. 1978. Eels: a natural and unnatural history. David and Charles, London, England.

Miller, P. J. 1979. A concept in phenology. Symposia of the Zoological Society of London 44:263–306.

Murphy, G. I. 1968. Pattern in life history and the environment. American Naturalist 102:390–404.

Myers, G. S. 1949. Usage of anadromous, catadromous and allied terms for migratory fishes. Copeia 1949:89–97.

Neave, F. 1958. The origin and speciation of *Oncorhynchus*. Transactions of the Royal Society of Canada 52:25–39.

Nikolskii, G. V. 1963. The biology of fishes. Academic Press, London, England.

Nikolskii, G. V. 1969. Fish population dynamics as the biological background for rational exploitation and management of fishery resources. Oliver and Boyd, Edinburgh, Scotland.

Noakes, D. L. G., and E. K. Balon. 1982. Life histories of tilapias: an evolutionary perspective. Pages 61–82 *in* R. S. V. Pullin and R. H. Lowe-McConnell, editors. The biology and culture of tilapias. ICLARM (International Center for Living Aquatic Resources Management), Manila, Philippines.

Northcote, T. G. 1978. Migratory strategies and production in fresh water. Pages 326–359 *in* S. D. Gerking, editor. Ecology of freshwater fish production. Blackwell Scientific Publications, Oxford, England.

Patrick, P. H., and B. Sim. 1985. Effectiveness of a hidrostal pump in the live transfer of American eels. Hydrobiologia 128:57–60.

Pfeiler, E. 1986. Towards an explanation of the developmental strategy in leptocephalous larvae of marine fishes. Environmental Biology of Fishes 15:3–13.

Pianka, E. R. 1970. On r- and K-selection. American Naturalist 104:592–597.

Plumstead, E. E. 1984. The occurrence and distribution of fish in selected Transkei estuaries. Department of Foreign Affairs and Information, Report N8/2/1/3/2, Pretoria, South Africa.

Ricker, W. E. 1975. Computation and interpretation of biological statistics of fish populations. Fisheries Research Board of Canada Bulletin 191.

Rodgers, D. W., and P. H. Patrick. 1985. Evaluation of a hidrostal pump fish return system. North American Journal of Fisheries Management 5:393–399.

Schaffer, W. M. 1974. Optimal reproductive effort in fluctuating environments. American Naturalist 108:783–790.

Shireman, J. V. 1975. Gonadal development of striped mullet (*Mugil cephalus*) in fresh water. Progressive Fish-Culturalist 37:205–208.

Skead, C. J. 1959. The climbing of juvenile eels. Piscator 46:74–86.

Skelton, P. H. 1983. Perspectives on the conservation of threatened fishes in southern Africa. The Naturalist (Port Elizabeth) 77:3–12.

Skelton, P. H. 1987. South African red data book—fishes, revised edition. South African Council for Scientific and Industrial Research, National Scientific Programmes Report, Pretoria, South Africa.

Skelton, P. H., M. N. Bruton, and P. H. Greenwood. In press. The freshwater fishes of southern Africa: an annotated checklist. J. L. B. Smith Institute of Ichthyology, Special Publication.

Sloane, R. D. 1984. Upstream migration by young pigmented freshwater eels (*Anguilla australis australis* Richardson) in Tasmania. Australian Journal of Marine and Freshwater Research 36:61–73.

Smith, M. M., and P. C. Heemstra, editors. 1986. Smiths' sea fishes. Macmillan, Johannesburg, South Africa.

Stearns, S. C. 1976. Life history tactics: a review of the ideas. Quarterly Review of Biology 51:3–47.

Stearns, S. C. 1980. A new view of life-history evolution. Oikos 35:266–281.

Stearns, S. C. 1983. The influence of size and phylogeny on patterns of covariation among life-history traits in the mammals. Oikos 41:173–187.

Strubberg, A. 1913. The metamorphosis of elvers as influenced by outward conditions. Meddelelser fra Kommissioner for Havundersogelser. Serie: Fiskeri 4:1–11.

Tesch, F.-W. 1977. The eel. Biology and management of anguillid eels. Chapman and Hall, London, England.

Todd, P. R. 1980. Size and age of migrating New Zealand eels (*Anguilla* sp.). New Zealand Journal of Marine and Freshwater Research 14:283–293.

Turnbull-Kemp, P. S. J. 1958. Eels in Rhodesia trout streams. Piscator 41:210–212.

Wallace, J. H. 1975. The estuarine fishes of the east coast of South Africa. Part III. Reproduction. Oceanographic Research Institute (Durban) Investigational Report 41:1–48.

Ward, J. V., and J. A. Stanford. 1979. Ecology of regulated streams. Plenum, New York, New York, USA.

Weatherley, A. H. 1972. Growth and the ecology of fish populations. Academic Press, London, England.

Whitehead, P. J. P. 1959. The anadromous fishes of Lake Victoria. Revue de Zoologie et de Botanique Africaines 59:329–363.

Whitfield, A. K., and S. J. M. Blaber. 1978. Resource segregation among iliophagous fish at Lake St Lucia, Zululand. Environmental Biology of Fishes 3:293–296.

American Fisheries Society Symposium 1:122–130, 1987
© Copyright by the American Fisheries Society 1987

Fishways—Historical Assessment of Design Practices

John F. Orsborn

Albrook Hydraulics Laboratory, Department of Civil and Environmental Engineering
Washington State University, Pullman, Washington 99164, USA

Abstract.—Fishway design has evolved in a conservative fashion. Initial costs or practicality have limited the development of some innovative structures. Conservative design stems from (1) a lack of hard data on fish swimming and leaping capabilities, (2) a lack of integration of fluid mechanics with fish capabilities, and (3) designs based on fish responses rather than on stimuli. This paper summarizes the state of the art in fishway design and the development of several more efficient fishway designs. The efficiencies are derived from a combination of more expeditious fish passage, maximization of the instream flow operating range, and less costly construction. When competing or conflicting water uses are present, such as in the development of small hydropower, the minimization of water use in the fishway can become a fourth consideration.

When John Muir was on the McCloud River in California in 1874, he noted that prior to gold dredging the Tuolumne River had "abounded in salmon." He noted also that the Connecticut River was a salmon stream before dams were constructed and we had poisoned the Connecticut and other rivers with our "strangely complicated filths for which our civilization is peculiar." Muir concluded by stating that our "migratory food fishes, such as shad and salmon, will again become abundant" after we make the paths clear and clean from the oceans to the spawning grounds by treating our sewage and by constructing fish ladders over dams (Engberg 1984).

The successful design, construction, and operation of fishways has been curtailed at times due to inadequate bioengineering information. In some instances, the completion of successful fishways is hindered by other constraints including biases, unproven fish swimming and leaping capabilities, and some conservative design criteria perpetuated through time without being tested.

Much of what T. R. Pryce-Tannatt (1938) said 50 years ago is still valid.

The designing of a fish pass is fraught with uncertainty, because it is almost impossible to prophesy the behavior of fish and quite impossible to anticipate the vagaries of water. The subject involves a working knowledge of hydraulics; and, while hydraulic engineers conversant with the habits and requirements of fish are rarely to be found, the rules and assumptions of hydraulics themselves are apt to be disconcertingly upset when applied to the functioning of a fishpass. The subject is by no means within sight of finality. There is indeed much about it yet to be learnt—and unlearnt.

Four general elements of fishway efficiency are important in the design of fishways. The respective goals are to (1) optimize speed and success of fish passage to minimize delay, stress, damage, and fallback of fish; (2) minimize water use while achieving element (1) where there are competing water uses; (3) maximize the range of stream flow under which the fishway is operable by matching fishway operation to flows during the period of desired fish passage; and (4) minimize construction (and operation and maintenance) costs by using construction methods and materials appropriate to the remoteness and geometric, hydrologic, and geologic characteristics of the site.

This paper traces the development of the hydraulic and biomechanical design features of several types of fishways and includes a short glossary of fish passage terms in an appendix.

Historical Development of Fishways

Some of the earliest fishways designed and constructed were of the weir-and-pool type (Figure 1). Termed fish ladders, they have been in existence since at least 1853, as evidenced by the Ballysodare fish ladder in Ireland (Pryce-Tannat 1938). The British Salmon Fishery Act of 1861 required that fish passes be installed and maintained "in an efficient state" at new dam sites on salmon rivers (Pryce-Tannatt 1938). But, many fishways were unsuccessful (Calderwood 1930). Early design efforts were based more on intuition than on scientific and engineering endeavor.

Before the early 1900s, fishway development included detailed plans but little scientific and engineering methodology. Numerous patent ap-

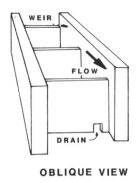

OBLIQUE VIEW

FIGURE 1.—Schematic diagram of a full-width weir fishway.

PLAN VIEW   CROSS SECTION

FIGURE 3.—Plan view and section of Landmark's forerunner to the slotted fishway (Norway, circa 1890).

plications were filed. The objective of these designers was to retard the velocity enough in a steep channel to allow fish to pass. In 1879, Marshall MacDonald from Virginia invented a fish pass consisting of a timber trough with a slope of 1:3 (Figure 2). The flow was deflected upstream by bucket-shaped deflectors to reduce the velocity. MacDonald's fishway was an outstanding idea, but his design analysis was incomplete and his fishway was abandoned.

At the same time in Norway, Landmark built pool and weir ladders to pass fish over waterfalls by blasting chains of pools in rock formations. Landmark also developed a forerunner of the slotted fishway by installing weir walls obliquely to one side wall of a channel, but not joining the opposite side wall (Figure 3). Simple jet deflectors were placed on the opposite side wall, creating a slot which extended the full height of the weir wall (McLeod and Nemenyi 1940).

Five major developments in fishway research

occurred in this century: (1) research by G. Denil from Brussels, Belgium, 1908–1939; (2) research by the British Institution of Civil Engineers, Committee on Fish Passes in England, 1936–1938; (3) studies by McLeod and Nemenyi at the University of Iowa, 1939–1940; (4) development of the vertical slot fishway for use at Hell's Gate on the Fraser River in British Columbia by Bell and others, 1943–1946; and (5) research at the Bonneville Fisheries-Engineering Research Laboratory in Washington, 1951–1972.

Denil's first scientific investigation of fishway design began in 1908 in Belgium (McLeod and Nemenyi 1940). His work culminated in the development of a chute fishway with many roughness elements (Denil 1909, 1937). Variations of his original design are still used today. Denil's designs showed a marked scientific advance but, more importantly, they stimulated research into fish behavior and the application of hydraulic engineering to fisheries problems. Denil was the first person to assess the mechanical capabilities of fish, and to match them to the opposing hydraulic forces within a fishway (British Institution of Civil Engineers 1942).

The British Institution of Civil Engineers (1942), Committee on Fish Passes, launched a comprehensive investigation into numerous aspects of fishway design just prior to World War II. The appendix of the committee's report described hydraulic research by White and Nemenyi on jet dispersion; pool overfalls; fish swimming resistance; relations among depth, slope, and flow in channels; flow in roughened steep channels; lateral spreading of a submerged jet; and the upward deflection of a submerged jet. The committee simplified Denil's design to the one which is commonly used today (Katopodis and Rajaratnam 1983) (Figure 4).

The first systematic American investigation of fishways occurred at the University of Iowa; McLeod and Nemenyi (1940) were the first to use fish as research subjects. Interestingly, one of their comments was that "it appeared that the fish learned to climb." They tested five fishways: pool and overfall, pool and submerged orifice, paired-

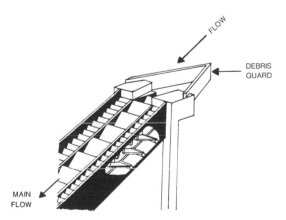

FIGURE 2.—MacDonald's 1879 steep-slope fishway in Virginia.

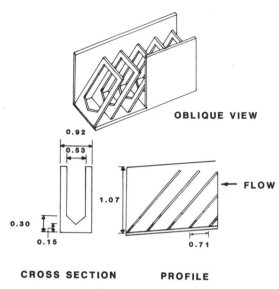

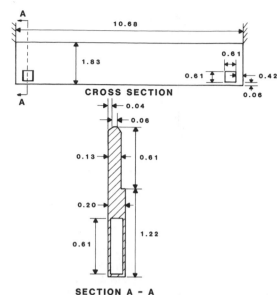

FIGURE 4.—Three views of a commonly used variation of Denil's fishway concept (British Institution of Civil Engineers 1942). Units are in meters.

FIGURE 5.—Initial Bonneville fishway overflow weir and submerged-orifice fish ladder. Units are in meters.

obstacle baffled fishways, alternate-obstacle baffled fishways, and modified Denil fishways. New designs and concepts concerning energy dissipation resulted from these studies.

Fish behavior was beginning to emerge as a consideration for fishway design. The following excerpt was taken from the report by the Committee on Fish Passes (British Institution of Civil Engineers 1942).

Migratory fish have certain definite habits and well-marked preferences, which are displayed in their journey to their spawning grounds. One pass may prove entirely successful, whilst for another the fish may show a definite distaste. In designing a fish-pass, therefore, the problem is not merely an engineering and hydraulic one.

This notion of fish behavior and preference was not widely accepted. Even within the same report it is written, "the fish is not a conscious being, able to act in anticipation of difficulties ahead." Construction of the Bonneville Dam on the Columbia River in 1937–1938 accelerated the development of new types of fish passage facilities. The initial Bonneville ladders were 10.7 m wide with full-width overflow weirs and submerged orifices on a line adjacent to each wall (Figure 5). McLeod and Nemenyi (1940) suggested that submerged jets should be staggered. But in the McLeod and Nemenyi study, the orifice openings were 40–50% of the chamber width. At the Bon-

neville ladder, the orifice widths are only about 10% of the chamber width.

During 1945–1946, after extensive hydraulic model tests, a major fishway was constructed at Hell's Gate on the Fraser River in British Columbia. This new design was a double vertical slot fishway (Figure 6). Vertical slot fishways work well where large fluctuations in river stage occur and the fishway flows are unregulated. This fishway was designed so that the flow from the two slots met in the center to reduce velocity. The design decreased the length of pool needed to

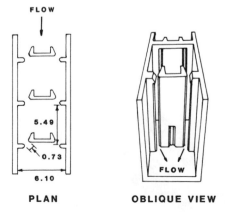

FIGURE 6.—Hell's Gate double-slotted fishway chambers developed for the Fraser River in British Columbia. Units are in meters.

dissipate the kinetic energy. Hell's Gate fishway was the first recorded instance in which fishway size was based on the number of fish anticipated in peak runs; a volume of 0.06 m³ was allowed for each fish. To apply this new slotted fishway to smaller fish runs, the design was halved along the centerline, and the baffle dimensions were modified to adjust for the tendency of the jet to turn directly downstream towards the next slot.

The biological studies of the Hell's Gate fishway are noteworthy because the possibility of biological fishway failure was openly considered. Factors such as "a trailing rope, the odor of a man, or some other disturbing factor" were mentioned as potential deterrents to passage of fish through an otherwise physically passable ladder (Jackson 1950). Even "psychological factors" governing the motivation of the fish were mentioned. These fishway designers were sensitive to conditions that might provoke an avoidance reaction by fish.

The need for fishway design criteria for large dam systems on the Columbia River prompted the U.S. Army Corps of Engineers and Bureau of Commercial Fisheries to initiate a fisheries research program in 1951. This program used the ethology of fish, the objective analysis of behavior, to examine the "stimulation of their sensory mechanisms" (Hoar 1958). Joint research by biologists and engineers increased at the Bonneville laboratory. Among the factors explored were the effects on fish passage rates of darkness (Long 1959), fishway capacity (Elling and Raymond 1959), fishway slope (Gauley 1960), and flow velocity (Weaver 1963). In 1962, researchers developed a new fish ladder for Ice Harbor Dam on the Snake River (Figure 7). This design has been used at numerous dams on the Columbia–Snake river system. These ladders use a vertically extended center portion of the weir wall, with short wing walls projecting upstream, to dampen oscillations which produced transverse waves across the full-width weirs at Bonneville Dam (Figure 5).

The first fishway design manual was published by Clay in 1961. He defined a fishway as "essentially a water passage around or through an obstruction, so designed as to dissipate the energy in the water in such a manner as to enable fish to ascend without undue stress." This definition served to characterize both the current and historical approaches to fishway development and was originally stated by the Committee on Fish Passes (British Institution of Civil Engineers 1942). The term "undue" has yet to be defined.

A fishway for use at remote sites was developed by Ziemer (1962) of the Alaska Department of Fish and Game. This roughened chute (called the Alaska steeppass), based on the work of Denil, was constructed of aluminum to meet the needs of fish passage in areas where access is by trail or by air (Figure 8).

Recently, a spiral fishway has been developed in Canada (Aeroceanics Fish Corporation 1976). It is constructed of fiberglass-reinforced plastic with alternating vertical baffles projecting 0.23 m into the channel (Figure 9). Like the Alaska steeppass fishway, the Aeroceanics fishway consists of sections which are light enough to be flown into remote areas. The Alaska steeppass and spiral fishway are examples of the search for a low-cost, light-weight fishway. Another circular fishway is under development which uses slots for flow control. One of the major construction benefits of circular fishways is that they are space-

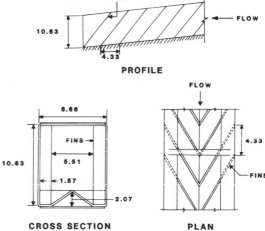

FIGURE 8.—Type-A Alaska steeppass fishway, similar to Denil number 6. Units are in meters.

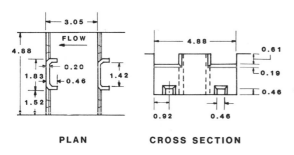

FIGURE 7.—The Ice Harbor type of fish ladder design with double weirs directly above double ports. Units are in meters.

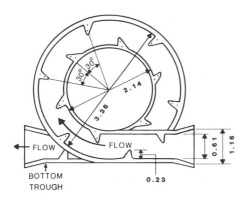

PLAN VIEW

FIGURE 9.—Aeroceanics fiberglass spiral fishway. Units are in meters.

and foundation-efficient.

Rather than a self-initiated, active movement, fish can be lifted passively by means of fish locks and lifts. Such systems are limited by their intermittent mode of operation and the failure of mechanical parts (Moffitt et al. 1982; Bell 1984). Consideration was given to the use of atmospheric pressure locks and fish elevators as alternatives for the fish passage facilities developed at Vernon, Bellows Falls, and Wilderdams on the Connecticut River system (Rizzo 1968–1970), but standard concrete fishway designs were used. One of the most effective fish elevators appears to be the

FIGURE 10.—Warner fishlift installed in the 1982–1985 test arrangement at Cariboo Dam on the Brunette River near Burnaby, British Columbia.

Warner fishlift (Figure 10) at Cariboo Dam on the Brunette river near Burnaby, British Columbia. The fishlift system operates by raising and lowering a column of water; the fish are supported in the upper part of the water column by a mesh floor (Warner, personal communication).

Fishway design has evolved rapidly over the past 75 years. Biological data are now documented and swimming speeds have been determined (Beamish 1978; Bell 1984). Many current fishway applications are trending towards smaller facilities. Part of this impetus has come from the recent increase in small-scale hydroelectric projects. An economic incentive is present in all design considerations, but the most important design objective for any fishway should be the expeditious transport of fish past the barrier.

Two New Developments in Fishway Design

Weir, Baffle, and Pool Fish Ladder Design Study

Step size is fundamental to fish ladder design. Everhart and Youngs (1981) and Bell (1984) suggested that the maximum drop in water surface between pools should be about 0.30 meters. The reason cited is "to provide for as rapid and easy a migration as possible." They acknowledged that fish are capable of leaping higher. The key words are rapid and easy. This ideology is in harmony with Clay's (1961) objective of allowing fish to ascend "without undue stress," as was stated also by the British Institution of Civil Engineers (1942). The recurrent theme is the facility of passage. It is likely that facility of passage was defined empirically. After many observations of fish moving through fish ladders, step sizes were probably selected because the fish passage conditions looked good. Such decisions have been tempered with the desire to pass the weaker fish to perpetuate a gene pool. It is possible that a factor of safety was included. The result is that many fishways have been designed based on criteria that underestimated fish capabilities.

Stuart (1962) offered an explanation of why migrating salmon and trout show preference for certain flow conditions. The stimulus for leaping appeared to be the "force of the impact of falling water" (Stuart 1962). This stimulus occurs when a standing wave is formed in the plunge pool just downstream of the place where the jet from a waterfall or weir strikes the plunge pool. Fish could be stimulated to leap when confronted with certain hydraulic conditions. It had been and is still widely believed that fish prefer swimming to leaping. For this reason, as noted by Clay (1961), fishway designs were focused on providing water passages for swimming. Bell (1984) noted that jumping behavior, although not fully understood, is known to be triggered by shadow patterns and upwelling. Upwelling is analogous to the standing wave described by Stuart, and it occurs as a distracting stimulus in the corners and along the walls of some fishway chambers.

Observations of fish behavior substantiate the stimulus premise. Fish sense the momentum and pressure fluctuations in the flow, much as we can sense these conditions by placing our hands in the path of a water jet. Leaps as high as 3.50 meters for salmon have been reported in the literature (Calderwood 1930). Mills (1971) showed a photograph of an Atlantic salmon *Salmo salar* leaping 3.65 meters. Others have reported leaps by steelhead *Salmo gairdneri* of 4–5 m when the fish were assisted by standing waves and could swim the last distance to the crest (Orsborn and Powers 1985). When compared with current design recommendations suggesting only about 0.30 meters of drop between pools (Bell 1984), the potential for increasing the pool-step height for capable species is obvious. Based on the capabilities of some species, and the disparity between criteria and capabilities, it seems that a large factor of safety is involved in current design practice.

A different definition of a weir-and-pool fishway might read "a hydraulic environment so constructed as to dissipate the energy in the water in such a manner as to stimulate fish to ascend by leaping." The objectives of my and my colleagues' study, established in the spirit of this definition, were to (1) determine the physical mechanism and magnitude of Stuart's standing wave and extend his ideas, (2) develop a fishway configuration based on the concept that fish can be stimulated to leap, and (3) assess the performance of the new weir, baffle, and pool fishway in the field (Aaserude and Orsborn 1985). We decided to capitalize on leaping behavior and explore some new principles of weir-and-pool fish ladder design.

In developing a new weir-and-pool fish ladder, we tested hydraulic models in the laboratory to determine the weir geometry with the best hydraulic conditions to stimulate fish leaping—the largest standing wave, no pulsing flow, the most vertical trajectory, and the pool depth and volume required for energy dissipation. Field tests were required to develop information on the leaping

success of coho salmon *Oncorhynchus kisutch* and chum salmon *O. keta* for different leaping heights.

We conducted field studies to provide hydraulic conditions which allowed these Pacific salmon to pass through a weir-and-pool fishway at various rates of ascent. Shorter pools were developed by incorporating baffles (Figure 11) into the design to dissipate the energy in the falling flow and in the pool velocities (Aaserude and Orsborn 1985).

A major result of our field tests was the demonstration of how important and multifunctional the baffles were. In the laboratory we concentrated on developing baffles to dissipate kinetic energy and to guide the fish to the standing wave through which they leap to the next pool. Baffles doubled the leaping success of coho salmon attempting leaps of 0.70 from about 28% to over 60%. A detailed discussion of these tests was presented in Aaserude and Orsborn (1985).

The results of laboratory experimentation guided the development of a new weir–baffle–pool fish ladder configuration based on the concept that fish can be stimulated to leap. Field tests to assess the performance of the new fishway provided

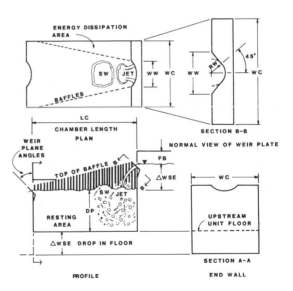

Nomenclature

WW – Top Weir Width	SW – Standing Wave
WC – Chamber Width	DP – Depth of pool
RW – Radius of Weir	FB – Freeboard
LC – Chamber Length	WSE – Change in Water Surface Elevation

FIGURE 11.—Nomenclature sketch for weir, baffle and pool fish ladder (Orsborn 1985).

insight into fish response which served to further refine the design. From these studies we concluded the following.

(1) The physical mechanism governing the formation of the standing wave, as described by Stuart (1962), is the buoyancy of entrained air bubbles.

(2) The magnitude of the vertical velocity in the standing wave is a function of air bubble size. A typical upward velocity is 0.32 m/s. Standing waves assist leaping fish.

(3) Perforated or slotted baffles improve fishway pool hydraulics by dissipating energy, directing flow, providing resting zones, and guiding fish. Slotted baffles with 50% open space are better. The baffles should extend to the top of the weir wall (Figure 11).

(4) The required depth of the fishway pool is a function of the jet entrance velocity and geometry. The amount of flow and fall height are the dominant factors influencing fishway pool depth requirements.

(5) A weir opening of 60 cm at the top is adequate for salmon and trout. A semicircular weir with 45° flaring sides, placed at a 45° downstream vertical angle, worked best.

(6) Fish often leap from the standing wave. It is uncertain whether they do so because they are stimulated or because standing waves coincidentally occur where fish would naturally initiate a leap.

(7) A methodology to match fish capabilities with differential elevations of fishway pools shows promise as a design methodology (Aaserude and Orsborn 1985).

(8) Fish capabilities are often underestimated in the design of fishway pool step sizes.

(9) A comparative analysis of energy expended by fish while swimming or leaping showed that, once the differential elevation exceeds about 0.7 meters, leaping is more efficient than swimming (Orsborn and Powers 1985).

Thus, we recommend the geometry of the new weir, baffle, and pool fishway unit (Figure 11) according to the following design criteria.

(1) Leave an opening at bottom of baffles just downstream of the jet for fish to exit in case they fall behind baffles.

(2) Use the baffle arrangement in Figure 11 to minimize the chance of fish falling behind the baffles.

(3) Use perforated plate baffles with round holes of less than 5-cm diameter to keep from gilling smaller fish.

(4) Use a vertical weir angle of $\theta = 45°$; 0° is adequate, but $-20°$ upstream causes the low flow to cling to the weir wall.

(5) Use 0.06–0.17 m³/s for flow through the weir (Figure 11), depending on how anxious the fish are to move.

(6) The ladder can be operated at higher flows (0.3 m³/s) because the excess weir flow falls behind baffles where energy is dissipated.

(7) Use a flared weir rather than a semicircular weir to give better clearance for leaping fish, wider discharge range, and better jet shape.

(8) Test water surface drops were up to 1.0 m and pool depths to 1.3 m.

(9) Use a weir width not greater than 40% of chamber width; the ratio of chamber length to chamber width is about 8:5, or 8:6, or 6:4 in smaller ladders for resident trout (Orsborn 1985).

Chute-and-Pool Fishway Design

During the testing of the new weir, baffle, and pool fishway, some tests were run on smooth plywood chutes 40 cm wide to develop swimming performance curves as a function of fish condition (Powers and Orsborn 1985). Following these experiments, it was decided to apply some simple roughness strips (3.8 cm × 3.8 cm), 15 cm apart, on the floor of the steepest smooth channel which the fish could not negotiate.

After the strips were added, 100% of the chum salmon negotiated a 25% slope in a chute 2.40 m long. These preliminary results indicate that (1) the expensive and sometimes dangerous vanes on the floor and side walls of Denil and Alaska steeppass fishways may not be necessary to pass fish up a chute fishway efficiently, and (2) all that may be required is a more turbulent boundary layer in the wakes of the roughness elements provided by an adequately roughened floor. This finding is in contrast to one of Denil's designs in which he removed the floor baffles because they contributed a small percentage of the total flow resistance compared with the length of the wall baffles (Denil 1937). The benefits of the simple roughened chute and pool fishway are reduced air entrainment and turbulence, better attraction flow, fish can swim to pass, better debris passage, low expense, small flow (about 1/3 of slotted fishway), and the ease of adding attraction flow with a false floor conduit (Powers and Orsborn 1985).

Further tests are being conducted in our laboratory to determine the best floor baffle system. Field tests will be run with several species of fish to determine performance curves for the design factors of slope, discharge, depth, fish speed, and limiting conditions. If resources allow, we plan to run comparative tests among the new simple chute, a Denil fishway, and an Alaska steeppass.

References

Aaserude, R. G., and J. F. Orsborn. 1985. New concepts in fishladder design. Bonneville Power Administration, Project 82-14, Final Report, part 2, Portland, Oregon, USA.

Aeroceanics Fish Corporation. 1976. The Aeroceanics fishway—a new concept, product brochure. Scarborough, Canada.

Beamish, F. W. H. 1978. Swimming capacity. Pages 101–187 in W. S. Hoar and D. J. Randall, editors. Fish physiology, volume 7. Locomotion. Academic Press, New York, New York, USA.

Bell, M. C. 1984. Fisheries handbook of engineering requirements and biological criteria. U.S. Corps of Engineers, Fisheries Engineering Research Program, Portland, Oregon, USA.

British Institution of Civil Engineers. 1942. Report of the committee on fish-passes. William Clowes and Sons, London, England. (Reprinted 1948.)

Calderwood, W. L. 1930. Salmon and sea trout. Edward Arnold, London, England.

Clay, C. H. 1961. Design of fishways and other facilities. Department of Fisheries of Canada, Ottawa, Canada.

Denil, G. 1909. La genès e d'une échelle a poissons nouvelle. Bulletin Populaire de la Pisciculture et des Améliorations de la Pêche, Deuxième Année, 9 (September–October). (Brussels, Belgium.)

Denil, G. 1937. La mécanique du poisson de riviere. Chapitre X. Les Capacites mécaniques de la truite et du saumon. Annales des Travaux Publics de Belgique 38:411–433.

Elling, C. H., and H. L. Raymond. 1959. Fishway capacity experiment. U.S. Fish and Wildlife Service Special Scientific Report Fisheries 299.

Engberg, R. 1984. John Muir summering in the Sierra. University of Wisconsin Press, Madison, Wisconsin, USA.

Everhart, W. H., and W. D. Youngs. 1981. Principles of fishery science. Cornell University Press, Ithaca, New York, USA.

Gauley, J. R. 1960. Effect of fishway slope on rate of passage of salmonids. U.S. Fish and Wildlife Service Special Scientific Report Fisheries 350.

Hoar, W. S. 1958. The analysis of behaviour of fish. Pages 99–111 in The investigation of fish-power problems. H. R. MacMillan Lectures in Fisheries,

University of British Columbia, Vancouver, Canada.

Jackson, J. R. 1950. Variations in flow patterns at Hell's Gate and their relationships to the migration of sockeye salmon. International Pacific Salmon Fisheries Commission Bulletin 3.

Katopodis, C., and N. Rajaratnam. 1983. A review and laboratory study of the hydraulics of Denil fishways. Canadian Technical Report of Fisheries and Aquatic Sciences 1145.

Long, C. W. 1959. Passage of salmonids through a darkened fishway. U.S. Fish and Wildlife Service Special Scientific Report Fisheries 300.

McLeod, A. M., and P. Nemenyi. 1940. An investigation of fishways. University of Iowa Studies in Engineering Bulletin 24, Iowa City, Iowa, USA.

Mills, D. 1971. Salmon and trout. Oliver and Boyd, Edinburgh, Scotland.

Moffitt, C. M., B. Kynard, and S. Rideout. 1982. Fish passage facilities and anadromous fish restoration in the Connecticut river basin. Fisheries (Bethesda) 7(6):2–11.

Orsborn, J. F. 1985. Summary report—development of new concepts in fishladder design. Bonneville Power Administration, Project 82-14, Final Report, part 1, Portland, Oregon, USA.

Orsborn, J. F., and P. D. Powers. 1985. Fishways—an assessment of their development and design. Bonneville Power Administration, Project 82-14, Final Report, part 3, Portland, Oregon, USA.

Powers, P. D., and J. F. Orsborn. 1985. Analysis of barriers to upstream fish migration. Bonneville Power Administration, Project 82-14, Final Report, part 4, Portland, Oregon, USA.

Pryce-Tannatt, T. C. 1938. Fish passes in connection with obstructions in salmon rivers. The Buckland Lectures for 1937. Edward Arnold, London, England.

Rizzo, B. 1968–1970. Fish passages facilities design parameters for Connecticut river dams. Vernon Dam, Bellows Dam, and Wilder Dam. Massachusetts Bureau of Sport Fisheries and Wildlife, Boston, Massachusetts, USA.

Stuart, T. A. 1962. The leaping behaviour of salmon and trout at falls and obstructions. Department of Agriculture and Fisheries for Scotland, Report 28, Her Majesty's Stationary Office, Edinburgh, Scotland.

Weaver, C. R. 1963. Influence of water velocity upon orientation and performance of adult migrating salmonids. U.S. Fish and Wildlife Service Bureau of Commercial Fisheries Fishery Leaflet 63:97–121.

Ziemer, G. L. 1962. Steeppass fishway development. Alaska Department of Fish and Game, Information Leaflet 12, Juneau, Alaska, USA.

Appendix: Short Glossary of Fishway Terms
(Refer to Figure 12 for general layout of fishways)

Alaska steeppass: Denil fishway developed for use in remote areas of Alaska. It consists of prefabricated metal in sections with vanes on the floor and sides; there is high air content in the flow, which has low attractiveness in competition with other flows.

Attraction flow: flow from the fishway entrance. Fishway flow sometimes is augmented by auxiliary flow to form the attraction flow.

Baffle: any protrusion or device on the floor, walls, or both of a chute or channel used to create kinetic energy loss (velocity reduction). Large baffles provide a wake where fish can rest.

Barriers (to upstream migration): may be physical or chemical, natural or artificial in nature; for example, debris and log jams, chutes, falls, culverts, and temperature.

Denil: a fishway chute with roughness elements (baffles, vanes) on the sides, or floor (or both) which cause the average water velocity to be reduced.

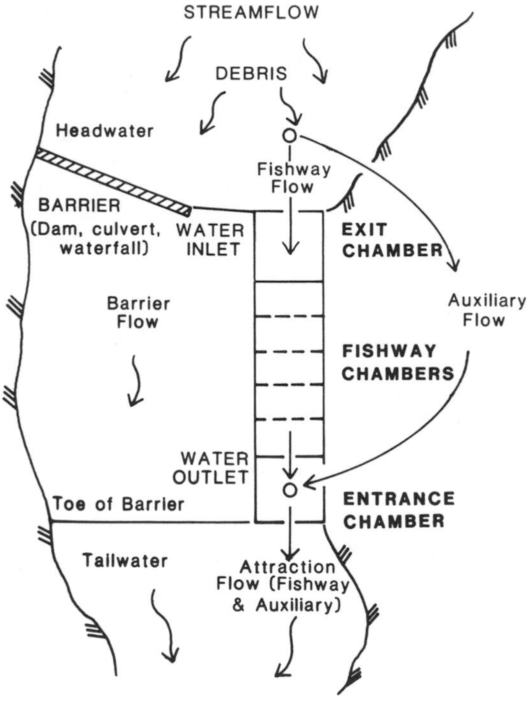

Fish ladder: a type of fishway consisting of a series of drops for dissipating kinetic energy in eddies in pools.

Fish speeds (velocity): defined in three ranges: sustained, prolonged, and burst speeds (formerly called cruising, sustained, and burst speeds).

Fishway: general term for any flow passage which fish negotiate by swimming or leaping; it can be a high-velocity chute, a cascade or vertical waterfall, or an artificial structure such as a culvert, a series of low walls across a channel (weir-and-pool fishway), or merely a chute up which the fish swim.

Fishway chamber or unit: one of the parts of a fishway which governs the type of flow through the fishway chute, weir and pool, or lock chamber.

Fishway entrance: downstream opening in the fishway structure through which fish enter the fishway; the outlet for the attraction flow.

Fishway exit: upstream end of the fishway from which fish exit the structure; the intake for the fishway flow.

Flow: the amount of water passing a point (or cross section) in a fishway; discharge (measured in cubic meters per second).

Flow control: the means (ports, slots, baffles, weirs, gates) whereby the amount of flow and the drop in water surface pool elevations are controlled, or the roughness and clear space in chutes.

Kinetic energy: the energy due to the velocity of the flow.

Momentum: the discharge multiplied by the net change in velocity when the flow changes direction, or when the velocity is dissipated in a large pool, such as with attraction flow.

Relative velocity: speed at which a fish moves relative to the water or to the fishway.

Stream: any moving body of water; all rivers are streams, but not all streams are rivers.

Stress: can be caused by repeated expenditures of energy (such as unsuccessful jumping at a barrier), chemicals, abnormal temperature and oxygen levels, prolonged swimming at a taxing rate, swimming from a lower- to higher-velocity region, or environmental changes.

Velocity: speed of water through a cross-sectional flow passage area; local velocities can be considerably higher or lower than the average.

Velocity profile: values of velocity at different depths in a channel; higher velocities near the water surface reduce to zero at the bottom and at the sides.

FIGURE 12.—Nomenclature sketch for a general fishway site.

American Fisheries Society Symposium 1:131–136, 1987
© Copyright by the American Fisheries Society 1987

Use of Hatcheries in the Management of Pacific Anadromous Salmonids

JAMES A. LICHATOWICH

Oregon Department of Fish and Wildlife, 303 Ballard Extension Hall, Oregon State University
Corvallis, Oregon 97331, USA

JOHN D. MCINTYRE

Seattle National Fishery Research Center, Building 204, Naval Station
Seattle, Washington 98115, USA

Abstract.—Confidence in the use of hatcheries for managing Pacific anadromous salmonids has waxed and waned several times in the past 100 years. Now that many of the technological problems have been solved, other problems associated with integration of hatchery fish into natural ecosystems are being identified. The Oregon coho salmon *Oncorhynchus kisutch* fishery is used as an example to point out the kinds of problems confronting managers—problems that include (1) the overharvest of wild stocks by fisheries geared up to harvest the more productive hatchery stocks, (2) density-dependent survival in both freshwater and marine environments that may be associated with large releases of smolts from hatcheries, and (3) outplanting of hatchery fish to supplement natural spawning that can, if not carefully implemented, reduce survival of the natural and hatchery juveniles. Managers will have to give thoughtful considerations to these problems so that hatcheries are effective tools of management.

Propagation and stocking of anadromous salmonids has been used as a management tool in the northwestern United States for more than a century. The role of hatcheries has increased to a point that hatchery fish make up the majority of the fish harvested by some fisheries. In recent years, 75% of the coho salmon *Oncorhynchus kisutch* landed in Oregon, for example, had been released from hatcheries (Oregon Department of Fish and Wildlife 1982).

The primary purpose for the artificial propagation and stocking of anadromous salmonids clearly is to produce fish that ultimately will be captured by a commercial fishery or used for recreation. It was always the hope, but not always fact, that hatcheries would meet the demand for fish. Many of the technological problems associated with early fish culture efforts have been solved, but it is not always clear what sizes and quality of fish to produce or how these fish can be incorporated into the natural ecosystems of which they become a part after they are stocked. We briefly describe the history of hatcheries in the management of anadromous salmonids in western North America and use the case history of the Oregon coho salmon fishery to exemplify some of the problems that need resolution as enhancement programs for Pacific salmon and steelhead *Salmo gairdneri* expand. Finally, we describe our view of the emerging role of hatcheries in management of Pacific anadromous salmonids.

Historical Perspective

Most early attempts to propagate salmon were characterized by a great deal of enthusiasm but little understanding of salmonid life histories (Hume 1893). The first hatcheries were intended to rebuild and stabilize a declining salmon fishing industry (Fish Commission of Oregon 1921). Once early culturists learned to spawn salmon and to incubate eggs, they rapidly developed large hatchery stations to provide fish for the commercial fishery. The salmon canning industry often opposed conservation measures to protect salmon, but advocated more hatchery programs that were, in effect, direct subsidies to the industry (De-Loach 1939). By 1929, 72 hatcheries for salmon and steelhead were annually stocking 500 million fry and fingerlings in the northwestern USA (Cobb 1930).

Differences in stocks and their habitat requirements generally were ignored by early fish culturists. Bonneville Hatchery on the lower Columbia River, for example, received eggs of chinook salmon *Oncorhynchus tshawytscha* from as far away as Alaska as well as from Idaho, eastern Washington, and southern Oregon. Fry were redistributed to watersheds throughout the region with little regard for their origin (Wallis 1964). Through the 1930s, as the problems that hatcheries were supposed to address became more acute, no detectable change was being produced by hatchery operation and the program began to decline (McNeil and Bailey 1975).

The present era of anadromous fish culture in the northwestern USA dates from the late 1950s, when the release of smolts became accepted as the standard. Hatchery biologists made important advances in the treatment and prevention of disease and improved diets became generally available at reasonable costs. These advances in culture technology improved postrelease survival and rekindled enthusiasm for hatchery programs (E. R. Jeffries, paper read at 26th Annual Northwest Fish Culture Conference, 1975). This renewed enthusiasm coincided with a period of rapid degradation of habitats and the development of hydroelectric power stations along migratory pathways. Given their new successes, hatcheries were perceived to be a means by which the region could continue to develop its water resources for power, irrigation, and industrial or domestic uses and, at the same time, maintain the salmon fishery at historic levels. As a result, the productivity of many natural habitats for salmon was destroyed.

Enactment of strong environmental legislation and vigorous enforcement of existing laws helped to overcome many of the worst abuses. Many irrigation ditches were screened, logging practices were improved, and effluents from industrial and municipal sources were treated. Harvest rates are being regulated to rebuild natural production, and federal, state, and private programs for habitat restoration are improving. In conjunction with improving freshwater habitats and the emphasis on restoration of wild salmon and steelhead populations, the role of hatcheries is also changing. In addition to producing fish for a fishery (enhancement) or producing fish to replace those formerly produced in habitats now lost (mitigation), fish are being produced for release (outplanting) in rehabilitated or underseeded habitat. Even in their traditional mitigation and enhancement roles, hatcheries are being managed with a greater awareness of salmonid breeding structure and of the need to ensure that hatchery-produced fish are integrated into the ecosystem in ways that minimize impacts on wild populations.

Oregon's Coho Salmon: A Case History

Consistent with the knowledge of their time, early salmon culturists in Oregon assumed salmon abundance could be increased by stocking unfed fry because they believed natural populations were prevented from expansion by insufficient spawning gravel and excessive mortality during incubation. In 1910, the fishery was declining in spite of the stocking of unfed fry, so hatcherymen began experimenting with the release of fed fry (Johnson 1984). Catch increased during the next 5 years—a result that fishermen and culturists attributed to the new hatchery methods. Based on this initial success, many people concluded that the new method would permit hatcheries to bring Oregon's rivers back to full production (Fish Commission of Oregon 1921).

In spite of annual releases of 4–31 million coho salmon fingerlings (Johnson 1984), the catch continued to decline through the 1920s and 1930s and remained depressed through the 1950s (Figure 1). Because efforts to improve diets and pathology services were unsuccessful, and production continued to decline, management biologists became disillusioned with hatchery programs (E. R. Jeffries, unpublished, 1975).

Coincident with the development of the Oregon moist pellet, and with significant reductions of hatchery losses due to bacterial kidney disease, coho salmon production began to increase in the early 1960s (Fish Commission of Oregon 1962). Increased returns of coho salmon to the hatcheries of origin encouraged the production of greater numbers of smolts (Figure 2). Biologists and hatcherymen once again believed that another technological breakthrough was in hand that would allow for the sustained production of coho salmon at levels capable of supporting a growing fishery (Oregon Department of Fish and Wildlife 1982). In

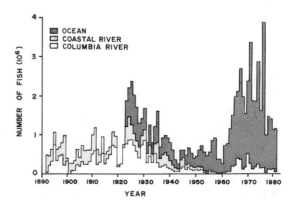

FIGURE 1.—Number of coho salmon landed in the Oregon Production Index Area and Columbia River, 1892–1982. (From Johnson 1983.)

FIGURE 2.—Comparison of coho salmon hatchery smolts released and wild and hatchery adults produced (landed) in the Oregon Production Index Area one year later. (From Nickelson and Lichatowich 1983.)

response to the growing hatchery program, the number of adult coho salmon harvested continued to increase to a peak in 1976 followed by a steep decline to less than half the average number landed in the late 1960s and early 1970s (Figures 1, 2). Although hatchery fish have made up 75% of the coho salmon catch in recent years (Oregon Department of Fish and Wildlife 1982), hatchery technology could not sustain the fishery that had developed.

The decline in the number of coho salmon did not discourage investment by private sea-ranching corporations. Encouraged by the high survival and hatchery surpluses of previous years, private sea-ranching corporations were bringing their newly completed facilities into full production. Even though the number of coho salmon continued to decline, the release of hatchery smolts continued to increase after 1977 (Figure 2) largely as a result of production by these corporations (Cummings 1983).

Several hypotheses to explain the collapse of Oregon's coho salmon stocks after 1976 have been examined (Oregon Department of Fish and Wildlife 1982), and it now appears that it was related to a change in upwelling off the Oregon coast. Nickelson and Lichatowich (1983) showed

that survival of hatchery-reared coho salmon was more than twice as high during strong upwelling periods (average 8.5%) than during low-upwelling times (average 3.5%). Improved diets and disease control in the late 1950s contributed to increased survival, but the climatic patterns and their effect on the nearshore ecosystem exerted a greater influence on survival than did improvements in technology.

The rapid increase in numbers of adult coho salmon in the 1960s stimulated growth in the fishing fleet. The number of licenses issued to individual commercial fishermen for all fisheries increased from 2,565 in 1960 to 8,566 in 1978 (Carter 1981). Since many more surviving offspring are produced by a female spawned in a hatchery than by a female spawning in the wild, hatchery stocks were able to withstand a growing fishery and higher harvest rates. The increasing harvest rates, however, caused a sharp decline in the escapement of wild coho salmon in coastal streams and Columbia River tributaries in the late 1960s, i.e., in the number of adults that escaped the oceanic and downstream fisheries and reached spawning grounds (Figure 3). To offset the overharvest of wild stocks, surplus fish at hatcheries were used to supplement spawning in natural habitats. Between 1981 and 1985, about 16 million coho salmon presmolts (0.44 g) were stocked at densities of 3.9 fish/m² in streams judged to have too few spawners.

Unlike the earlier experiments with fed fry in 1910, the new program of stocking presmolts was extensively evaluated. Three broods of coho

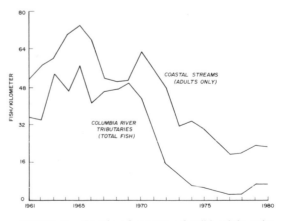

FIGURE 3.—Trends of counts of wild adult coho spawning in Oregon coastal and Columbia River index streams, 1961–1980 (moving average of three). (From Oregon Department of Fish and Wildlife 1982.)

salmon in 15 control and 15 treatment streams were each monitored through a complete life cycle. Although the stocking of presmolts increased the density of juvenile coho salmon in the treatment streams, hatchery presmolts displaced 40–50% of the wild juveniles rearing in the stream (Solazzi et al. 1983). The number of adults returning to treatment and control streams did not differ significantly (Nickelson et al. 1985). Adult coho salmon originating from hatcheries as presmolts produced few surviving progeny. Even though hatchery fish were no longer being released and were not present in treatment streams, subsequent densities of naturally spawned juveniles in treatment streams (which had received presmolts) were about 50% less than densities of juveniles in control streams (Nickelson et al. 1985)

The relatively high percentage of hatchery fish in the landings (75%) may be viewed as the result of highly successful hatchery programs. As we discussed, however, when fishing intensity expanded to take advantage of the increasing number of hatchery fish, it caused a decline in the escapement of natural spawners. We have also shown evidence that hatchery coho salmon outplanted into coastal streams as presmolts displaced naturally produced fry and that progeny from adults of hatchery origin have low survival in the natural environment. As a consequence, one has to consider the possibility that at least part of the program's apparent success was because of negative effects produced by the program on natural stocks of coho salmon.

Whatever the shortcomings of the past, hatcheries now play an important role in compensating for lost freshwater habitats, and the commercial and sport fisheries depend on hatchery fish. We are confident that future hatchery programming will be increasingly directed to more effective use of both natural and hatchery fish and to levels of production that are consistent with limitations imposed by the habitat and other desirable species—topics that are the subject of the next section.

Emerging Role of Hatcheries

Management agencies in the northwestern USA are beginning to recognize the need to integrate hatcheries into the total fish production system. The Northwest Power Planning Council, for example, comprises state representatives directed to implement the Northwest Power Act. The council insisted that hatchery fish from their program be used in such a way to complement natural fish production (Northwest Power Planning Council 1984). Similar program elements have been prepared by the states of Washington, Oregon, Idaho, and Alaska; by Canada; and by the U.S. Fish and Wildlife Service. Success in meeting these commitments depends on the ingenuity of managers in overcoming the problems that often result from the use of hatchery fish to supplement natural populations of anadromous salmonids. We here attempt to describe some of the problems confronting managers who are attempting to develop programs consistent with these commitments.

As shown earlier in the example of the coho salmon fishery, when mixed-stock fisheries harvest excess hatchery fish, they tend to overharvest the relatively unproductive natural populations. This problem tends to increase as the proportion of hatchery fish increases. Overharvest of natural populations may be the most important problem of concern in protecting the genetic diversity that remains in anadromous fishes. The problem may be acute for populations whose reproductive rate has been reduced by the degradation of habitats.

The problems generated by a fishery on mixed hatchery and wild stocks can be avoided if it is possible to harvest the hatchery and wild stocks at different rates. For example, hatchery stocks may be selected to return to the river for spawning at a time sufficiently different from the wild stock so that harvest in fresh water can be regulated to protect the wild fish while fully exploiting the harvestable surplus of the hatchery fish. Also, if the hatchery stock were differentially marked by removal of a fin, regulations could permit selective harvest of hatchery fish and release of wild fish. Both of these methods can be applied in some circumstances where the harvest of salmon or steelhead takes place in fresh water. However, mixed-stock fisheries in the ocean cannot be regulated as just described.

In systems dominated by hatchery fish, another emerging strategy is to use fry from hatcheries to stock natural habitats (outplanting), thus enabling the maintenance of high harvest rates and production from both hatchery and natural components of the system. That juvenile hatchery fish do not substitute one-for-one for naturally produced fish was indicated by the data of Reisenbichler and McIntyre (1977), Solazzi et al. (1983), Chilcote et al. (1984), and Nickelson et al. (1985). The basis for these results is not entirely clear, but it appears that the purposeful and inadvertent selection that occurs in a hatchery can result in hatchery fish that are maladapted for life in streams. Successful outplanting, consequently, depends partly on a hatchery operator's ability to produce fish that are qualitatively similar to the fish produced naturally in the stream to be stocked.

In the absence of data describing the breeding relationships of the population in question to other populations in the local area, one must assume that the population to be supplemented is a separate stock. Brood fish from that stock can be expected to produce progeny with a higher potential for survival once they are outplanted than can be expected for progeny of fish from a remote brood stock. Even when hatchery fish produced from brood fish in the endemic stock are used, changes in the gene pool will probably occur in hatchery fish (Reisenbichler and McIntyre 1986). Actions can be taken to mitigate the tendency for selective breeding in hatcheries, but some selection and adaptation to hatchery conditions seems inevitable.

Increasing the rearing density of fry and fingerlings in a stream through stocking can increase mortality rates of juvenile fish produced from natural reproduction through competition for food and space. Mortality associated with these interactions increases as density increases in an environment with limited food and space. This problem may be exacerbated for fish from natural reproduction because hatchery fish are likely to be larger—a condition that can result in displacement of the wild fish in agonistic encounters. Stocking has the potential, therefore, for eliminating fish from natural reproduction. The most common existing strategy for managing hatchery fish is to rear them to the smolt stage and release them with the expectation that they will emigrate directly to the ocean.

Density-dependent effects in fresh water are usually presumed to be negligible when smolts are released, but Royal (1972) showed that rates of survival from smolt to adult were inversely related to the numbers of steelhead smolts released from hatcheries several kilometers inland from the ocean. Since survival rates of steelhead from hatcheries near the ocean did not decline as the number of smolts increased, a density-related mortality factor may have reduced smolt numbers when distances to the ocean were great. Any such density-dependent effect for hatchery fish presumably would also influence smolts from natural production. It appears that successful integration of hatchery and natural components of a fish production system requires the development of smolt release schedules that will minimize any density-related mortality in the receiving waters.

Density of salmonid populations may also influence growth (Peterman 1984) and survival (J. Ames, Washington Department of Fisheries, Olympia, Washington, unpublished) in marine environments; and, as in the Oregon experience described earlier, ocean productivity may be a limiting variable for salmonid enhancement programs.

Intensive fishing, habitat alteration, manipulation of population density, and genetic alteration all characterize the anadromous salmonid production systems that evolve as demand increases. We can find no compelling reason to believe that conditions will change substantially in the future; thus, it seems that we can expect more and more systems to have both natural and hatchery components. Fishing is likely to exceed the intensity that is consistent with a desirable yield from natural production, especially from those populations dependent on degraded habitat, and hatcheries will be used to compensate for both habitat alteration and overharvest.

The role of hatcheries in these systems is to provide the quantity and quality of fish needed to create an equilibrium among the artificial and natural system components and harvest rate. Once an acceptable harvest rate is negotiated, and an escapement goal is established that is consistent with production in the available habitat, the artificial rearing space that is required to supplement natural production can be identified (McIntyre and Reisenbichler 1986). Because some of the fish produced in the hatchery are to be used for supplementing natural production, they should be produced from local brood fish and reared under conditions that, to the extent possible, do not favor survival of some individuals over others. To do otherwise results in relatively low survival of fish produced by a hatchery and deleterious effects on the supplemented population (Reinsenbichler and McIntyre 1986).

Integration of hatchery and wild components of a production system requires more information than is now available or is used in management programs. Some of the important prerequisites to the integration of hatchery and wild production are better definitions of stock differences, especially in relation to habitat requirements; more information on optimal escapements and the natural capacity of streams to rear juveniles at different life history stages; and disease histories and resistances of hatchery and supplemented wild stocks.

Anadromous salmonids produced in combined systems of natural and artificial production will differ from fish produced under the natural conditions of the past. The course of these changes in populations of anadromous salmonids is impossible to predict and, at best, difficult to detect. Speculation as to their significance for conservation and management can proceed unimpeded by facts. Nevertheless, change in anadromous fish populations appears to be an inevitable consequence of human interference with the ecosystems of which these fish are a part. Understanding the character and significance of these changes requires thoughtful speculation on the part of resource managers and the interested public.

Acknowledgments

Reg Reisenbichler, Harry Wagner, and Mark Wade read early drafts of this paper and improved its content through many helpful suggestions.

References

Carter, N. C. 1981. Multi-fishery activity in Oregon commercial fishing fleets: an economic analysis of short-run decision-making behavior. Doctoral dissertation. Oregon State University, Corvallis, Oregon, USA.

Chilcote, M. W., S. A. Leider, J. J. Loch, and R. F. Leland. 1984. Kalama River salmonid studies. 1982 progress report. Washington State Game Department, Fisheries Research Report 83-3, Olympia, Washington, USA.

Cobb, J. N. 1930. Pacific salmon fisheries. U.S. Bureau of Fisheries, Document 1092, Washington, D.C., USA.

Cummings, T. E. 1983. Private salmon hatcheries in Oregon. Oregon Department of Fish and Wildlife, Portland, Oregon, USA.

DeLoach, D. B. 1939. The salmon canning industry. Oregon State College, Oregon State Monograph, Economic Studies. 1. Corvallis, Oregon, USA.

Fish Commission of Oregon. 1921. Biennial report of the Fish Commission of the State of Oregon. Portland, Oregon, USA.

Fish Commission of Oregon. 1962. Biennial report. Portland, Oregon, USA.

Hume, R. D. 1893. Salmon of the Pacific coast. Schmidt Label and Lithographic, San Francisco, California, USA.

Johnson, K. 1983. A history of coho fisheries management in Oregon through 1982. Oregon Department of Fish and Wildlife, Information Report 84-12, Portland, Oregon, USA.

Johnson, S. L. 1984. Freshwater environmental problems and coho production in Oregon. Oregon Department of Fish and Wildlife, Information Report 84-11, Portland, Oregon, USA.

McIntyre, J. D., and R. R. Reisenbichler. 1986. A model for selecting harvest fraction for aggregate populations of hatchery and wild anadromous salmonids. Pages 179–189 in R. H. Stroud, editor. Fish culture in fisheries management. American Fisheries Society, Fish Culture Section and Fisheries Management Section, Bethesda, Maryland, USA.

McNeil, W. J., and J. E. Bailey. 1975. Salmon ranchers manual. U.S. National Marine Fisheries Service, Northwest Fisheries Center, Processed Reports, Seattle, Washington, USA.

Nickelson, T. E., and J. A. Lichatowich. 1983. The influence of the marine environment on the interannual variation in coho salmon abundance: an overview. Pages 24–36 in W. G. Pearcy, editor. The influence of ocean conditions on the production of salmonids in the north Pacific. Oregon State University, Corvallis, Oregon, USA.

Nickelson, T. E., L. A., Van Dyke, and D. L. Bottom. 1985. Coastal coho production factors. Oregon Department of Fish and Wildlife, Progress Report AFS-74-4, Portland, Oregon, USA.

Northwest Power Planning Council. 1984. Columbia River basin fish and wildlife program. Northwest Power Planning Council, Portland, Oregon, USA.

Oregon Department of Fish and Wildlife. 1982. Comprehensive plan for production and management of Oregon's anadromous salmon and trout. Part II. Coho salmon plan. Oregon Department of Fish and Wildlife, Portland, Oregon, USA.

Peterman, R. M. 1984. Density-dependent growth in early ocean life of sockeye salmon (Oncorhynchus nerka). Canadian Journal of Fisheries and Aquatic Sciences 41:1825–1829.

Reisenbichler, R. R., and J. D. McIntyre. 1977. Genetic differences in growth and survival of juvenile hatchery and wild steelhead trout, Salmo gairdneri. Journal of the Fisheries Research Board of Canada 34:123–128.

Reisenbichler, R. R., and J. D. McIntyre. 1986. Requirements for integrating natural and artificial production of anadromous salmonids in the Pacific northwest. Pages 365–374 in R. H. Stroud, editor. The role of fish culture in fisheries management. Fish Culture Section and Fisheries Management Section, American Fisheries Society, Bethesda, Maryland, USA.

Royal, L. A. 1972. An examination of the anadromous trout of the Washington Game Department. Washington Department of Game, Olympia, Washington, USA.

Solazzi, M. F., S. L. Johnson, and T. E. Nickelson. 1983. The effectiveness of stocking hatchery coho presmolts to increase the rearing density of juvenile coho salmon in Oregon coastal streams. Oregon Department of Fish and Wildlife, Information Report 83-1, Portland, Oregon, USA.

Wallis, J. 1964. An evaluation of the Bonneville salmon hatchery. Fish Commission of Oregon, Portland, Oregon, USA.

American Fisheries Society Symposium 1:137, 1987

TRANSITION TO AND FROM THE MARINE ENVIRONMENT

Preamble

RICHARD L. SAUNDERS

Department of Fisheries and Oceans, Biological Station
St. Andrews, New Brunswick E0G 2X0, Canada

Diadromous fishes have developed a variety of physiological and behavioral mechanisms to prepare them for the often demanding transition from fresh water to the marine environment and vice versa. This transition must be made twice, once on leaving the spawning–nursery habitat and again to return to the appropriate spawning place; some fishes repeatedly cross the tenuous marine–freshwater barrier. Osmotic and ionic regulation must adapt quickly to contrasting salinities so as to maintain the appropriate internal environment for organs and tissues to function properly. This regulation must be at minimum energetic cost; otherwise, there might be little advantage to making the transition. However, some fishes may accept high energetic costs in order to take advantage of special conditions such as feeding opportunities and spawning–nursery requirements during short-term residence in the environment to which they immigrate. Several papers in this section emphasize the seasonal and developmental changes in organ systems involved with osmoregulation and metabolic adjustments that are often necessary to prepare the emigrants for changing ionic strength, new thermal regimes, and great changes in quality and quantity of food in the new environment. Most diadromous migrations are opportunistic, allowing fishes to realize a growth potential not easily reached in the primary environment. Physiological changes allow fishes not only to tolerate diverse environments but also to thrive under a wide range of life styles.

Diadromous migrations often involve drastic changes in behavior. Some anadromous salmonids quit their feeding territories in streams and form aggregations or schools during their migrations to and after reaching the sea; eels arrive at the mouths of streams in great numbers and make their way upriver where they spend several years and accomplish nearly all of their growth.

Gonad development of various diadromous fishes is timed in accordance with bioenergetic demands of food searching and migration and the requirement to move into or away from the sea at specific stages of sexual maturation. Some fishes, notably the salmonids, exercise flexibility in age and size at maturity to improve long-term reproductive success; some live and mature in fresh water while others mature after diadromous migrations. Evolution and adaptive radiation have allowed diadromous fishes to move through and to live in contrasting environments, not only to tolerate diverse environments but also to thrive and gain long-term reproductive advantage, which is the ultimate measure of the success of a species.

The authors of papers in this section give clear examples of the mechanisms by which fishes are able to practice diadromy and to benefit through this widespread evolutionary development. Contributions dealing with a variety of species have come from Sweden, Scotland, Canada, and the United States.

American Fisheries Society Symposium 1:138–150, 1987

Behavioral Aspects of Selective Tidal Stream Transport in Juvenile American Eels

JAMES D. MCCLEAVE AND GAIL S. WIPPELHAUSER

Department of Zoology and Migratory Fish Research Institute, University of Maine
Orono, Maine 04469, USA

Abstract.—Selective tidal stream transport is a major behavioral mechanism of migration for a variety of juvenile and adult fishes, including the catadromous eels *Anguilla* spp. A fish accomplishes such a migration by entering the water column when the tide is flowing in the migratory direction and leaving the water column to hold position on the bottom when the tide is flowing in the opposite direction. Results of field, laboratory, and simulation research lead us to conclude that this mechanism, used by juvenile American eels *A. rostrata* (glass eels) migrating up estuaries, is influenced by an endogenous biological clock somehow entrained to the local tidal cycle. Series of 10-min or 15-min tows of 0.5-m-diameter nets were made throughout 20 flood tides in salinity-stratified, partially stratified, and tidal freshwater portions of the Penobscot River estuary, Maine, USA. A profile of temperature, salinity, and water current velocity accompanied each tow. American eels tended to enter the water column well after low slack tide and leave it well before high slack in stratified conditions, but they tended to enter the water before low slack and leave after high slack in tidal fresh water. However, the length of time glass eels were in the water column was statistically similar (about 190 min) in all three hydrographic conditions. In the laboratory, locomotor activity of groups of glass eels collected in salinity-stratified tidal waters, tidal fresh water, and nontidal fresh water was measured for periods of six tidal cycles (75 h) in 1-m-diameter annular tanks in gently flowing natural water in constant dim light. Groups from tidal waters generally showed rhythmic bouts of activity of circa-tidal periodicity, while groups from above head of tide did not. Transport of glass eels through a 30-km portion of the estuary was simulated for various flow regimes and behaviors. Optimum time for transport (about 250 min) was much shorter than a full flood tide (about 370 min) under all hydrographic conditions. At low and moderate discharges there was a broad range of times glass eels could be in the water column, and of times they could start on the flood tide, that resulted in rapid and successful upstream transport. Increased freshwater discharge decreased successful transport for both long and short sojourns in the water column. A clock-controlled sojourn of 190–280 min in the water column provided successful upstream transport under a variety of estuarine circumstances.

Selective tidal stream transport (Greer Walker et al. 1978) is an important mechanism of migration for a variety of juvenile and adult fishes, including the up-estuary migration of glass eels of the catadromous European eel *Anguilla anguilla* (Creutzberg 1958, 1961), American eel *A. rostrata* (McCleave and Kleckner 1982; Sheldon and McCleave 1985), and probably the shortfinned and longfinned eels *A. australis* and *A. diefenbachii* of New Zealand (Jellyman 1977). Adult European eels also exhibit the behavior associated with selective transport (Arnold and Cook 1984; J. D. McCleave, M. Greer Walker, and G. P. Arnold, unpublished data), but its role in adult migration is unclear.

In this behavior, the fishes make a semidiurnal vertical migration in phase with the tidal flow to accomplish a horizontal migration. They enter the water column while the tidal flow is in the direction of migration and leave the water column while the tidal flow is in the opposite direction.

This behavior is utilized, for example, by larval plaice *Pleuronectes platessa* to migrate from the open North Sea into estuarine nursery areas (Creutzberg et al. 1978; Rijnsdorp et al. 1985), by juvenile plaice to reenter these areas after overwintering offshore (de Veen 1978), and by adult plaice to migrate back and forth between feeding and spawning areas (Greer Walker et al. 1978; Harden Jones et al. 1979). Selective tidal stream transport has also been reported for juvenile sole *Solea solea* and juvenile European flounder *Platichthys flesus* (de Veen 1987), adult sole and spotted dogfish *Scyliorhinus canicula* (Greer Walker et al. 1980), and Atlantic cod *Gadus morhua* (Harden Jones 1977).

It should be recognized that selective tidal stream transport involves a subset of a larger suite of behaviors in which depth choice or vertical migration by fishes modulates their horizontal drift in tidally dynamic areas. Fishes can be flushed rapidly from an estuary by actively selecting near-surface waters, as do capelin larvae *Mallotus villosus* (Fortier and Leggett 1982, 1983) and smolts of the anadromous Atlantic salmon *Salmo salar* (Fried et al. 1978). It can also result in retention in the estuarine areas of fishes that cross the pycnocline on a semidiurnal or diurnal basis, as do larvae of Atlantic herring *Clupea harengus harengus* (Graham 1972; Fortier and Leggett 1982, 1983, 1984) following an initial passive drift on the deep, landward, residual currents.

Research on the cues that trigger the behavioral components of selective tidal stream transport is largely lacking except for the pioneering work of Creutzberg (1961), which showed that European glass eels could discriminate the odor of ebb and flood waters and would alter their swimming behavior in response to such odor changes. McCleave and Kleckner (1982) discussed the behavioral discrimination problems confronting fishes during their migration through coastal regions and estuaries. How do glass eels, in this case, choose when to enter the water column at the beginning of the flood tide? How do they choose when to leave it at the end of the flood tide? The latter question is not trivial in view of the fact that a fish drifting in open water has no fixed visual or tactile reference against which to judge the direction of water flow, a point recognized by Creutzberg (1961) and others (e.g., Tesch 1965; Harden Jones 1968; Rommel and McCleave 1973). How do glass eels position themselves vertically in a stratified water column to take advantage of rapid upriver currents? How do glass eels synchronize their sojourn in the water column with the flood tide, rather than the ebb tide; i.e., how do they "lock on" to the appropriate tide?

McCleave and Kleckner (1982) felt that American glass eels responded to local hydrographic conditions and suggested that cues such as differences in odor between flood and ebb tides, flow reversals, and changes in turbulence or electrical fields might play roles in the selective behavior of glass eels. They noted that a circa-tidal clock, known for many coastal fishes (Gibson 1982), might be effective as a timer for the duration of the transporting tide in unstratified coastal areas but argued that such a clock might be ineffective in estuaries where the duration of the flooding or ebbing tide varies greatly with vertical and horizontal position in the estuary. In contrast, Tesch (1965) speculated that an endogenous clock is an appropriate control mechanism for tidal transport of glass eels.

This paper addresses the question: just how selective is selective tidal stream transport in the upriver migration of catadromous eels? We present evidence that the view of McCleave and Kleckner (1982) may have been naive and that a circa-tidal clock may indeed be the mechanism controlling the duration of the active and inactive phases of glass eel tidal transport. We consider (1) field experiments on American glass eels to define the precision with which ascents into the water column and descents from the water column are timed relative to low and high slack water, (2) laboratory experiments on the locomotor rhythmicity of American glass eels, and (3) a simple simulation model of the flexibility of the transport system in a complex estuary. We comment on vertical positioning in the water column but do not consider the question of how the appropriate tide for transport is chosen.

Tidal Stream Transport of Glass Eels

McCleave and Kleckner (1982) used systems of buoyed and anchored plankton nets at four depths to determine vertical distribution of glass eels at night on ebb and flood tides at a salinity-stratified (lower) station and at an unstratified, tidal, freshwater (upper) station in the middle of the channel of the Penobscot River estuary, Maine, USA (Figure 1). The distributions were compared with concurrently made profiles of water current velocity and salinity. Under stratified conditions, glass eels remained on or near the bottom on ebb tides and moved into the water column in or below the halocline on flood tides, where they were transported up the estuary. On ebb tides, catches were largest in the deepest net and much smaller or zero in the other three nets; on flood tides, catches were always greatest in the third net down and second greatest in the deepest net. Under tidal freshwater conditions also, the glass eels remained on or near bottom on ebb tides and moved into all depths on flood tides. Under both conditions, catch rates were always 8 to 30 times greater on flood tides than on ebb tides. A thorough statistical analysis, which took into account the possibility of oriented horizontal swimming, has essentially confirmed the earlier conclusion that modulated drift can account for the observed catches (McCleave et al., in press).

Timing of Ascents and Descents

The objectives of our study of the precision of the behavior of glass eels utilizing selective tidal stream transport under different hydrographic regimes were to determine (1) the relationships

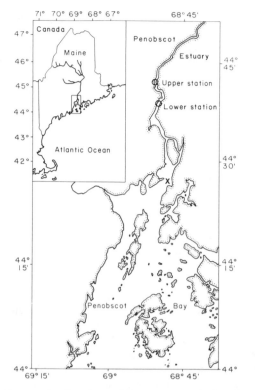

FIGURE 1.—Penobscot River estuary, Maine, from near head of tide to the Atlantic Ocean showing stations where American glass eels and hydrography (O) or hydrography only (X) was sampled by McCleave and Kleckner (1982) and by us. Reproduced from McCleave and Kleckner (1982), with permission.

between times of ascent from the bottom and times of flow reversal on the bottom, and between the times of descent from the water column and the times of flow reversal at typical American eel swimming depth, (2) the current velocities during ascents and descents, and (3) the length of time that glass eels remain in the water column on a given flood tide.

Methods

We conducted field studies in April and May 1983–1985 at two locations in the riverine portion of the Penobscot River estuary (Figure 1). The lower station normally provided salinity stratification (0–28‰) and two-layered flow, while the upper station normally provided unstratified freshwater (<1‰) tidal flow. High or low river discharge sometimes created partial stratification (0–7‰) at either station or even tidal freshwater conditions at the lower station. Tides in the estuary are semidiurnal and the average range is about 4 m.

Glass eels were collected by towing one or two side-by-side pairs of plankton nets in an arrangement which sampled a constant depth relative to the surface, even under difficult conditions of two-layered flow (Figure 2). A pressure-sensitive ultrasonic transmitter on the net vane allowed us to monitor and adjust depth of fishing. Depth of fishing was 6–10 m, 1–3 m, or both, depending on whether one or two sets of nets were used. A flowmeter in the mouth of each net allowed us to estimate volume of water filtered. Sampling was in midchannel and usually began before scheduled low tide, i.e., before glass eels were in the water column, and continued through flood tide until glass eels were again scarce or absent in the water column. Fourteen flood tides were sampled during evening–night and six were sampled during daylight. On each of 17 flood tides, 12–23 tows of 10 min each were made in rapid succession; on three flood tides 10–13 tows of 15 min each were made. The 10-min tows filtered an average of about 265 m^3 of water and the 15-min tows about 415 m^3. The catches of glass eels per 100 m^3 of water filtered were averaged for the pair of nets in each tow. Each mean catch was converted to percent of the total catch for that tide.

During each tow, measurements of water-current speed and direction, salinity, and temperature were made at 1-m intervals of depth from another boat. From these profiles, the times of

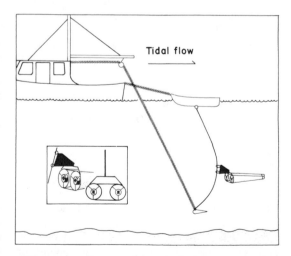

FIGURE 2.—System of towed plankton nets used to sample American glass eels in the Penobscot River estuary during 1983 and 1984. In 1985, two pairs of nets were sometimes attached to the cable. Inset shows detail of the vane which oriented the net into the water flow. Nets were 0.5 m in diameter, 2 m long, and had 0.75-mm mesh.

low and high slack water (i.e., flow reversal) were determined as accurately as possible for 1 m below the surface, the fishing depth, and 1 m above the bottom.

On the basis of the profiles, water conditions were classified as stratified (0–28‰ salinity), partially stratified (>1‰ only during latter half of flood tide), or fresh water (<1‰). The duration of flood tide was longest in stratified conditions and shortest in freshwater conditions. Current speed and direction in stratified conditions were not uniform from surface to bottom. At the beginning and end of flood tide, for example, surface water was ebbing while bottom water was flooding. Speed and direction in the other two conditions were more nearly uniform from surface to bottom.

During each tide, the time intervals were determined when (1) eels initially ascended into the water column, (2) catches initially increased by 5% or more of the total catch for a tide, (3) catches finally decreased by 5% or more of the total catch, and (4) eels finally became scarce or disappeared from the water column. Both the time of the tow and the period of uncertainty (time to previous tow for ascents, time to subsequent tow for descents) were included in the time intervals. Times of ascents were compared with time of slack water 1 m from the bottom. Times of descents were compared with the time of slack water at depth of fishing. Durations of time between first ascent and final descent and between first 5% or more increase and final 5% or more decrease in catch were computed for each tide. Single-classification analysis of variance and Tukey–Kramer multiple-comparisons tests for unequal sample sizes were used to compare fish behavior in the three water conditions.

Results

Three trends provide strong evidence that glass eels do not time their sojourn in the water column precisely to local hydrographic conditions but rather rely on an endogenous clock to time the vertical migration.

First, the times of initial ascents occurred after low slack water in stratified conditions, clustered about slack water in partially stratified conditions, and occurred (with one exception) before slack water in freshwater conditions (Figure 3; Table 1); all pairs of means were significantly different ($P < 0.05$). The same trend was present in the times of initial 5% or more increases in catch, but the increases in fresh water approximated the time of slack water (Table 1). For this measure of ascents,

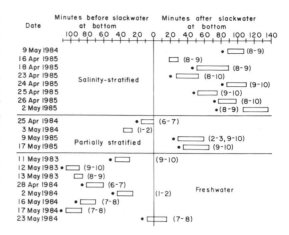

FIGURE 3.—Time intervals during which initial ascents of American glass eels occurred (open bars) relative to the time of low slack water at the bottom in three tidal conditions, Penobscot River estuary. Numbers in parentheses are depths of fishing in meters. Dots indicate tow was preceded by at least one tow which did not catch any glass eels.

the mean times in salinity-stratified and partially stratified conditions were significantly different ($P < 0.05$) from mean times in tidal fresh water but not from each other. By both measures, ascents occurred in stratified conditions when bottom water was already flooding at up to 16 cm·s^{-1}. Initial ascents occurred in tidal fresh water while bottom water was still ebbing at up to 12 cm·s^{-1}.

TABLE 1.—Times (min) of ascent of American glass eels before (−) or after (+) low slack water at the bottom and times (min) of descent before (−) or after (+) high slack water at depth of fishing for glass eels in three tidal conditions. Times for individual ascents and descents are the midpoints of the interval of uncertainty. Data are means ± SDs (N). Values along a row without a letter in common are significantly different ($P < 0.05$).

Measure	Tidal conditions		
	Salinity-stratified	Partially stratified	Fresh water
Relative to low slack water			
Initial ascent	+75±32 (8) z	+20±37 (5) y	−62±36 (8) x
Initial ≥5% increase in catch[a]	+92±35 (8) z	+44±32 (5) z	−14±50 (8) y
Relative to high slack water			
Final ≥5% decrease in catch[a]	−49±61 (7) z	0±35 (6) z	0±26 (8) z
Final descent	+11±63 (6) z	+53±34 (6) z	+55±42 (8) z

[a] Relative to total catch for the tidal cycle.

Second, the opposite trend occurred in descents as measured by final 5% or more decreases in catch and by final descent, though without statistical significance. Decreases in catch of 5% or more occurred generally before high slack water in stratified conditions and clustered about high slack water in the other two conditions (Table 1). Final descents occurred around high slack water in stratified conditions and after high slack in the other two conditions.

Third, and as a consequence of the first two trends, the length of time glass eels were present in the water column on a flood tide was similar for all three water conditions ($P > 0.05$) whether measured as the time between initial ascents and final descents (about 280 min) or the time between initial increase and final decrease of 5% or more (about 190 min: Table 2). The time is substantially less than the full duration of a flood tide (about 370 min).

The trends are quite clear, but the data are characterized by considerable variability (Figure 3; Tables 1, 2). Some of the variability is attributable to the sampling method because of tow duration and the interval between tows. However, much of the variation is biological in nature.

Locomotor Rhythmicity

Concurrently with our field study, we undertook a laboratory study to determine whether glass eels collected from salinity-stratified water, from tidal fresh water, and from nontidal fresh water exhibit rhythmic locomotor activity of circa-tidal periodicity in constant conditions. Sixteen species of intertidal fishes are known to exhibit endogenous activity rhythms of circa-tidal

TABLE 2.—Times (min) between initial ascents and final descents and between initial 5% or more increase and final 5% or more decrease in catches of American glass eels in three tidal conditions, Penobscott River estuary. Times for individual tides are measured between midpoints of the initial and final intervals of uncertainty. Data are means ± SDs (*N*). There are no significant differences among means within each measure.

Measure	Tidal conditions		
	Salinity-stratified	Partially stratified	Fresh water
Initial ascent to final descent	286±45 (8)	271±43 (5)	275±63 (8)
Initial ≥5% increase to final ≥5% decrease	217±43 (8)	187±74 (5)	171±42 (8)

periodicity (Gibson 1982), including plaice (Gibson 1973), which also utilize selective tidal stream transport (Harden Jones et al. 1979; Rijnsdorp et al. 1985).

Methods

The locomotor activity of glass eels in groups of 32–128 was recorded in annular tanks filled with gently flowing (3–9 cm·s^{-1}) natural water in constant, very dim light. The diameters of the inner and outer stainless-steel rings forming the annulus were 57.5 cm and 97.5 cm. The plexiglass base was covered with about 3 cm of gravel except for one wedge left clear. Two pairs of vertical polyvinyl chloride pipes with vertical slits were connected to pumps to create a gentle clockwise current. Water was also pumped through a cooling unit to maintain temperature, usually within a 3°C range during an experiment. However, temperature of the experiments varied with time of season.

Activity was recorded on videotape by the technique of shadow cinematography (Arnold and Nuttall-Smith 1974). One Fresnel lens was placed above and one below the clear-wedge portion of the annual tank. An underrun 12-V tungsten–halogen lamp was placed below the lower lens and a video camera above the upper lens. Such a system allows nearly transparent fishes to appear as dark silhouettes against a light background with only a glowing lamp filament as the light source.

American glass eels were collected with pushed or towed plankton nets during flood tides from tidal areas of the Penobscot River estuary or with a dip net from a freshwater stream which empties into the estuary. Water was collected from the same locations and depths as the fish. Glass eels and water were placed in the annular tanks within 8 h.

Activity was videotaped for 2.5 min of each 5.0 min interval for at least 75 h (six tidal cycles). The number of glass eels swimming with the current and the number swimming against the current across the camera's field of view were counted for each 2.5-min interval. Actograms of hourly sums were plotted. Half-hourly sums were analyzed for periodicity with both autocorrelation and maximum entropy spectral analysis (MESA) as outlined by Dowse et al. (1987). Our criteria for rhythmicity were rigorous. Locomotor activity was considered significantly rhythmic only if significant periods ($P < 0.05$) occurred in the correlogram *and* if the dominant peak in the MESA occurred at a similar periodicity *and* if these

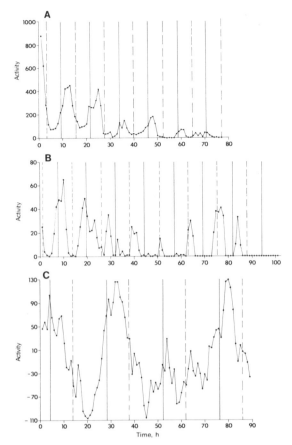

FIGURE 4.—(A) Actogram of American glass eels, collected 18 April 1985 on flood tide from salinity-stratified water, which were swimming with the current when tested in the laboratory in an annular tank with constant clockwise current and constant very dim light. Activity axis is hourly sum of glass eels passing with the current through the camera's field of view. Solid vertical lines indicate scheduled times of high water and dashed lines the times of low water at the collection site. (B) Actogram of glass eels, collected 2 May 1984 on flood tide from tidal fresh water, which were swimming against the current when tested in the laboratory. Activity axis is hourly sum of glass eels passing against the current through the camera's field of view. Vertical lines are as in A. (C) Actogram of glass eels, collected 12 May 1984 from nontidal fresh water, which were swimming against the current when tested in the laboratory. Solid vertical lines indicate scheduled times of sunset and dashed lines the times of sunrise at the collection site. Activity axis is as in B. Negative activity values occur because a regression analysis was applied to remove a long-term trend from the data.

periods were evident in visual inspection of the actogram. We also considered activity to be rhythmic if nonsignificant peaks occurred in the correlogram that matched the period lengths from

the other two criteria. Otherwise, activity was considered arrhythmic.

Results

Rhythmic patterns of activity of circa-tidal periodicity, some statistically significant and some not, were detected for American eels collected from tidal salinity-stratified water and tidal fresh water, but not for those from nontidal fresh water, when the fish were tested in continuous current and constant very dim light. Only one experiment was conducted with glass eels from salinity-stratified waters ($N = 47$ eels). In that experiment, glass eels swimming against the current were scored as rhythmic even though rhythmicity was nonsignificant by our criteria; the period length of the rhythmicity as determined by MESA was 10.4 h. Activity bouts were mostly centered on the times of scheduled high tide for the collection site. Glass eels swimming with the current showed a similar pattern, but their bouts of activity mostly followed the times of scheduled high tide (Figure 4A). Period length was about 11.2 h.

In two of the three experiments ($N = 32, 61, 88$ eels) with glass eels from tidal fresh water, significant periodicity was found both for those swimming with and against the current (Figure 4B). Period lengths ranged from 10.3 h to 12.6 h. In one experiment, there was no evident rhythmicity, but the water-circulation pipes had clogged and greatly reduced the current speed.

Glass eels which were collected in a freshwater stream just above the head of tide showed no evidence of circa-tidally rhythmic activity in three experiments ($N = 90, 100, 128$ eels). In one experiment there was weak evidence for circadian rhythmicity, with eels most active generally between scheduled times of sunset and sunrise (Figure 4C). Period length was approximately 30 h.

Thus glass eels from estuarine situations exhibited circa-tidal locomotor rhythms. These rhythms, though variable, were evident even though the fish were tested in groups. The variability was expected both because the glass eels were tested in groups and because circa-tidal rhythms of marine organisms in general have been found to be highly variable compared with terrestrial animals (Rawson and DeCoursey 1976).

Simulation of Tidal Stream Transport

The field and laboratory evidence for biological-clock control of the semidiurnal vertical migration of glass eels prompted us to develop a simple simulation model of tidal transport of glass eels. With this model we could investigate how flexible such a control mechanism might be in a complex estuary. Our objectives were to examine how the degree of success and time of transport through the study area were affected by the interaction of variables associated with the eels' behavior (duration of time in water column, time of entry into and exit from water column, vertical position) and variables associated with the transporting system (neap or spring tide, amount of river discharge).

The Model

Movement through a 30-km long section of "estuary" was simulated. Current velocity and salinity profiles obtained at three stations in the Penobscot River estuary (Figure 1) provided the basic hydrographic data. The upper two stations (those used for our field studies) were about 7.5 km apart and the lower two about 22.5 km apart. Profiles were obtained in midchannel at each station at least hourly through a complete tidal cycle (ebb and flood) during neap-tide, low-runoff conditions during 6–8 May 1980. The profiles nearest the time of scheduled low tide and scheduled high tide and the five most evenly spaced profiles between them were used in the model.

Salinity stratification occurred at the lower two stations. The depth of the halocline at each profile was defined as the 1-m depth of water over which the greatest salinity change occurred. The average

current speed (upriver or downriver) for each profile was calculated (1) above the halocline, (2) below the halocline, (3) above middepth, and (4) below middepth. The first two sets of values were used to simulate situations in which the glass eels, when off the bottom, "chose" a depth in the water column above or below the halocline, and the second two sets were used in situations in which the glass eels "chose" simply the upper or lower half of the water column. Only values for above and below middepth were used wherever no stratification occurred.

These sets of values, derived from actual measurements, were assumed representative of neap tides and low river discharge (Table 3). Spring-tide values were estimated by increasing all current speeds (both upriver and downriver) by 20%. Medium river-discharge values were estimated by increasing the downriver speeds by 20% and decreasing the upriver speeds by 20%. The procedures were combined to estimate values for spring tide plus medium-discharge conditions. Saltwater penetration does not reach the middle station of our three hydrographic stations during conditions of very high discharge. To simulate high-discharge, neap-tide conditions, we modified the medium-discharge, neap-tide data set. Values for the lowest station (X, Figure 1) were unchanged. Values from the "upper" station were transferred to the "lower" station. Values from the upper station were increased by 20% on ebb

TABLE 3.—Water current speeds (cm·s^{-1}) for neap-tide, low-discharge conditions derived from seven profiles made at three stations in the Penobscot River estuary (Figure 1) at approximately equal time intervals between scheduled low and high tides 6–8 May 1980. Positive values denote upriver current.

Station	Depth	Low tide	1	2	3	4	5	High tide
		Profile						
		Relative to depth of halocline						
Upper	Above halocline	−32	−4	1	5	36	−2	−42
	Below halocline	−26	−5	2	7	29	−1	−34
Lower	Above halocline	−10	6	1	14	42	13	−69
	Below halocline	27	36	37	36	44	18	−15
X	Above halocline	−45	−27	−10	−2	20	7	−22
	Below halocline	7	15	21	30	32	27	1
		Relative to middepth						
Upper	Top half	−32	−4	1	5	36	−2	−42
	Bottom half	−26	−5	2	7	29	−1	−34
Lower	Top half	−23	0	−5	17	40	16	−50
	Bottom half	11	24	29	39	45	16	−7
X	Top half	−17	−5	7	20	24	22	−5
	Bottom half	9	16	21	30	35	26	2

and decreased by 20% on flood to form the new upper-station values. Comparisons with actual profiles made during various flood tides in association with our field work suggest that these estimated values are reasonable.

The distance between the lowest two stations was divided into 20 cells of 1,125 m each and the distance between the upper two stations into 20 cells of 375 m. The duration of time the simulated fish spent in the water column on each tide was specified for each simulation run and was divided into 20 increments, l, of duration I. The proportion of time spent high and low in the water column (see above) was specified for each run. Thus the average transporting current speed $\bar{V}_l$, to which the glass eel was subject during any time increment was linearly interpolated as the sum of eight products:

$$\bar{V}_l = \sum_{ijk} H_i X_j T_k V_{ijk};\ i = 1, 2; j = 1, 2; k = 1, 2;$$

H_i is the proportion of time spent high or low in the water column, X_j is the proportion of distance the eel-containing cell was to the next upriver or downriver hydrographic station, T_k is the proportion of time the increment was to the time of the previous or subsequent current profile, and V_{ijk} is the current speed at the appropriate vertical–horizontal–time positions. Speeds and distances traveled were appropriately modified when eels passed from one cell to another during a time increment. The distance traveled during each tide was then

$$D = \sum_{l=1}^{20} \bar{V}_l\, I.$$

Eels were "released" at various times during a flood tide at the upper end of cell 2, i.e., 2,250 m above the lower station. The model calculated minimum, maximum, and final positions and elapsed time tide-by-tide and accumulated the results. A run was terminated when the eel reached the upper end of the 30-km portion of estuary (success) or 40 transporting tides had passed without the eel attaining the 30-km distance (failure). Eels generally either passed through the 30 km or reached an obvious equilibrium point within the 30 km in fewer than 40 tides, in most cases far fewer.

Four assumptions should be made explicit. It was assumed that eels entered the water column

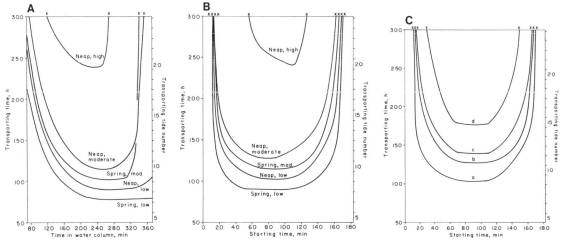

FIGURE 5.—(A) Effects of time spent in water column and conditions of low, moderate, and high discharge and of neap and spring tides on time to complete a simulated 30-km selective tidal stream transport by American glass eels. Time in the water column is centered on midpoint of flood tide; eels are assumed to spend 90% of this time below and 10% above the halocline. X indicates transport failure. (B) Effects of starting time after scheduled low tide and conditions of low, moderate, and high discharge and of neap and spring tides on time for American glass eels to complete a simulated 30-km selective tidal stream transport. Time of eels in the water column is 190 min, time is assumed to be spent 90% below and 10% above the halocline. (C) Effects of proportion of time spent by glass eels above and below the halocline or in the upper and lower halves of the water column and of starting time after scheduled low tide on time to complete a simulated 30-km selective tidal stream transport. Time in the water column is 190 min. Curve a—10% of time above the halocline or above middepth (curves the same), neap tide, low discharge. Curve b—50% of time above middepth, neap tide, low discharge. Curve C—50% of time above halocline, neap tide, low discharge. Curve d—50% of time above halocline, neap tide, moderate discharge.

every flood tide, that they remained there for the duration of the selected time in water column, and that there was a negligible number of eels in the water column on ebb tide. The first two assumptions are untested, the third is reasonable based upon previous field studies (McCleave and Kleckner 1982). It was further assumed that current profiles made in midchannel were representative of the transporting system. However, we know that glass eels are even more abundant near shore than in midchannel (Sheldon and McCleave 1985). Because of the assumptions, the conclusion drawn in the following section should be reasonable when considered as relative among the groups, i.e., the trends should be correct. However, absolute transport rates through the estuary would be correct only if our assumptions were correct and our manipulations of current speeds were representative of actual estuarine conditions.

Results of Simulations

The amount of time a glass eel needs to spend in the water column to achieve fastest upriver transport is far less than the full 372.5 min of an average flood tide. The time providing fastest transport was about 250 min under various tidal and runoff conditions, provided that the time in the water column was centered about the midpoint of the flood tide (Figure 5A).

At low and moderate discharges, transport time through the 30 km varied little over a rather wide range of time in the water column. Two trends were apparent. First, passing from neap- to spring-tide phases of the lunar cycle speeded transport by about the time of one transporting tide over a broad range of times in the water column (Figure 5A). Second, passing from low- to moderate-runoff conditions delayed transport by about two tides near the optimum and also narrowed the range of times in the water column over which rapid transport occurred. Thus, remaining in the water column much less or, especially, much more than the optimum made little difference under conditions of low discharge but resulted in a significant delay or even a failure of transport under moderate discharge.

At very high discharge, transport time more than doubled and the range of times leading to successful transport narrowed further. The curves (Figure 5A) are not symmetrical because the actual current speeds are not a simple sinusoidal function with maximum speed at the midpoint of the time between scheduled low and high tides, as

often modeled (e.g., Dodson and Dohse 1984). Rather, speeds increased gradually, peaked about 4 h into the cycle, and then decreased rapidly (Table 3).

For a given modest time in the water column (e.g., 190 min[1] at low and moderate discharges, transport time varied little over a rather wide range (window) of starting times after scheduled low tide (Figure 5B). However, transport failed in all cases when eels ascended at the time of scheduled low tide. Likewise, transport failed if they delayed their sojourn until the final 190 min of the scheduled flood tide. Passing from neap to spring tides speeded transport by about one tide and slightly widened the window for successful transport. Passing from low to moderate discharge slowed transport by about two tides and slightly narrowed the window. Again, extreme discharge greatly slowed transport and greatly narrowed the window of successful start times.

If most of the time during transport was spent lower in the water column, say more than 90%, as seems the case in stratified conditions, it made little difference whether the halocline or simply the lower half of the water column was used as the depth reference (Figure 5C). As expected, transport was slowed as a greater proportion of time was spent above the depth reference, an effect heightened by increased discharge. Furthermore, and less expectedly, the delay was greater when the halocline was chosen as the depth reference. Reducing the time spent above the depth reference from 10 to 0% made less than an hour's difference in transport time.

Discussion

The simulations suggest that a vertical migration of circa-tidal periodicity controlled by a biological clock is a flexible mechanism for achieving up-estuary transport. Successful and rapid transport occurs within rather broad limits on time spent in the water column, starting time on the flood tide, and, to some extent, vertical position.

While the fairly short sojourn times of glass eels

---

[1]In subsequent simulations, the time in the water column was assumed to be 190 min. This time was based upon the time between initial and final 5% or greater changes in catches obtained in the field (Table 2). This seemed more realistic than the time based upon first and last eels caught (280 min, Table 2) or the optimum based upon the simulation (250 min, Figure 5A). Use of the latter two would change the times of transport slightly but not the relative trends.

we estimated from field data (Table 2) initially seemed quite surprising, results of the simulations show the adaptive nature of the behavior. Sojourn times longer than our estimated range of 190–280 min make little difference in transport time under low discharge conditions. However, they impose a substantial delay or even failure at moderate or high discharges. Over much of the species' geographic range, migration of American glass eels occurs during spring when discharges are generally high and variable due to rains and snowmelt.

Even under the best transport circumstances (low discharge, spring tides) (Figure 5A), a short sojourn time seems adaptive, because negatively buoyant glass eels (Hickman 1981) must expend energy to remain in the water column. However, our simulations show that energy expenditure beyond the short sojourn time would not result in any transport gain. On the other hand, risk of predation may be proportional to amount of time in the water column.

Given a particular sojourn time, there is a point, still in the tidal portion of an estuary, at which the selective tidal stream transport system will no longer operate because net up-estuary transport equals net down-estuary transport. The location of that point depends upon the behavior of the glass eels, but the upper limit is set by hydrographic conditions, which vary greatly with discharge. The simulations indicate that a short sojourn time, probably less than 250 min, allows the farthest penetration up the estuary before active upstream swimming must replace tidal transport. This can be seen in Figure 5A if one considers high discharge to be roughly the equivalent of far up the estuary.

Various authors have observed that glass eels halt their inward migration for some time near the upper limit of saltwater penetration: Deelder (1958, 1960) and Tesch (1971) for European eels; Jellyman (1977, 1979) and Sloane (1984) for shortfinned and longfinned eels; McCleave and Kleckner (1982) for American eels. Morphological (Jellyman 1979), behavioral (Deelder 1958; Jellyman 1979), and unspecified physiological changes (Deelder 1960; Tesch 1971) are said to occur during this delay in migration. A change in behavior from a semidiurnal vertical migration to a positively rheotactic horizontal migration must occur at some point in the estuary to allow penetration of freshwater streams. However, it is interesting to speculate that the delay might occur at the point where the semidiurnal vertical migra-

tion ceases to result in net up-estuary transport, rather than where glass eels choose to halt their migration for physiological reasons. Deelder (1958) attributed a long delay during one year to exceptionally heavy freshwater discharge. Sloan (1984) noted a decline in catches when increased discharge moved the freshwater–estuarine interface seaward. McCleave and Kleckner (1982) described what they believed to be a breakdown of the transport system following a long period of rain.

This is not to say that behavioral and physiological changes need not occur. We suggest that these changes may occur at a location specified by the tidal regime rather than at a particular salinity or temperature. Glass eels may continue to exhibit a semidiurnal vertical migration, spending, say, 190 min in the water column during each tidal cycle. Because at some location in the estuary the tide floods for substantially less than 190 min, the glass eels may simply oscillate at that location until a behavioral switch is made. Such oscillations occurred under several circumstances in our simulations.

In considering whether there are common migratory strategies among juveniles of anadromous and catadromous fishes migrating through the transition zone between the sea and fresh water, the obvious answer is no, because one migration is downstream and the other upstream. However, it is tempting to speculate that the control over expression of positive rheotaxis may be by the same mechanism with opposite sign. Seaward migration of salmonids seem to occur when thyroid hormones are suppressed (Thorpe 1982; Ewing et al. 1984; Birks et al. 1985). It is known that the rheotactic response of older elvers of the European eel is lost when they are exposed to a thyroid inhibitor (Fontaine 1954). Perhaps active upstream migration of glass eels occurs when thyroid activity is stimulated (Fontaine 1975); such stimulation might be the key to the transition from vertical to horizontal migration.

In contrast, the type of genetic control of migratory behavior is surely not common among catadromous eels and anadromous salmonids and clupeids. Anadromous species, because of their homing tendencies, readily develop genetically based, population-specific, adaptive life history strategies, such as time of downstream migration by juvenile Atlantic salmon (Riddell and Leggett 1981; Riddell et al. 1981) or time and frequency of upstream spawning migration by American shad *Alosa sapidissima* (Leggett and Carscadden

1978). However, reproduction of Atlantic eels, at least, is essentially panmictic (Williams and Koehn 1984; Avise et al. 1985; Helfman et al. 1987, this volume). As a result, the genetic basis of the selective tidal stream transport is the same throughout the geographic range of each species; there is no stock of glass eels specifically adapted for migration in the Penobscot River estuary. Given this, perhaps control by an endogenous, labile (Rawson and DeCoursey 1976), circa-tidal clock is effective in the great variety of hydrographic and tidal regimes invaded each spring by glass eels over their geographic range.

Several fundamental questions remain for future work. The generality of the mechanism suggested above needs to be tested in a variety of hydrological conditions. Furthermore, despite speculation (McCleave and Kleckner 1982; Arnold and Cook 1984), there is still no direct evidence for what serves as the entraining cue (sensu Harden Jones 1984) to ensure that the sojourn in the water column remains in phase with the tide. Gibson (1984) has shown that cycles of hydrostatic pressure can elicit cycles of locomotor activity in plaice, Atlantic cod, and sand gobies *Pomatoschistus minutus*. Such a pressure cycle is a potential entraining cue, but its magnitude as a proportion of ambient hydrostatic pressure decreases rapidly offshore. There is also little evidence on what the clue is that allows the eels to select the appropriate tide for transport. Olfaction may well play a role (Creutzberg 1959, 1961). In other species, such as plaice, the situation is more complex because one tidal phase is chosen by maturing adults for transport to the spawning ground, and the other tidal phase is chosen by spent adults a month or two later for transport back to the feeding ground (Harden Jones et al. 1979; Arnold and Cook 1984).

In considering the transition from oceanic leptocephalus to freshwater elver, two broader categories of questions remain. (1) What causes the change in behavior from diurnal vertical migrations by leptocephali (Castonguay and McCleave 1987) to semidiurnal vertical migrations by glass eels? Is this change in behavior coupled with metamorphosis or does it occur later when glass eels are closer to the mouths of estuaries? (2) What causes the change in behavior from semidiurnal vertical migrations by glass eels to active horizontal migrations by the eels (which may again become active during the scotophase of a circadian rhythm)? Does this change occur where the selective tidal stream transport system is no longer effective?

Acknowledgments

This research was supported by the National Science Foundation (grant BNS-8122116). The paper was written while the senior author was a visiting professor in the Department of Biology, McGill University, Montreal, Quebec, Canada. The counsel of William C. Leggett and the financial support of the Natural Sciences and Engineering Research Council of Canada, the McGill University Faculty of Graduate Studies and Research, the University of Maine Center for Marine Studies, the Leopold Schepp Foundation, and the Eppley Foundation for Research are gratefully acknowledged. We thank Chris Chambers and William C. Leggett for their reviews of the manuscript.

References

Arnold, G. P., and P. H. Cook. 1984. Fish migration by selective tidal stream transport: first results with a computer simulation model for the European continental shelf. Pages 227–261 *in* J. D. McCleave, G. P. Arnold, J. J. Dodson, and W. H. Neill, editors. Mechanisms of migration in fishes. Plenum, New York, New York, USA.

Arnold, G. P., and P. B. N. Nuttall-Smith. 1974. Shadow cinematography of fish larvae. Marine Biology (Berlin) 28:51–53.

Avise, J. C., G. S. Helfman, N. C. Saunders, and L. S. Hales. 1985. Mitochondrial DNA analysis of population genetic structure in catadromous eels (*Anguilla*). Genetics (supplement) 110:S43.

Birks, E. K., R. D. Ewing, and A. R. Hemmingsen. 1985. Migratory tendency in juvenile steelhead trout, *Salmo gairdneri* Richardson, injected with thyroxine and thiourea. Journal of Fish Biology 26:291–300.

Castonguay, M., and J. D. McCleave. 1987. Vertical distributions, diel and ontogenetic vertical migrations and net avoidance of leptocephali of *Anguilla* and other common species in the Sargasso Sea. Journal of Plankton Research 9:195–214.

Creutzberg, F. 1958. Use of tidal streams by migrating elvers (*Anguilla vulgaris* Turt.). Nature (London) 181:857–858.

Creutzberg, F. 1959. Discrimination between ebb and flood tide in migrating elvers (*Anguilla vulgaris* Turt.) by means of olfactory perception. Nature (London) 184:1961–1962.

Creutzberg, F. 1961. On the orientation of migrating elvers (*Anguilla vulgaris* Turt.) in a tidal area. Netherlands Journal of Sea Research 1:257–338.

Creutzberg, F., A. T. G. W. Eltink, and G. J. van Noort. 1978. The migration of plaice larvae *Pleuronectes platessa* into the western Wadden Sea. Pages 243–251 *in* D. S. McLusky and A. J. Berry, editors. Physiology and behavior of marine organisms. Pergamon, Oxford, England.

Deelder, C. L. 1958. On the behaviour of elvers (*Anguilla vulgaris* Turt.) migrating from the sea into fresh water. Journal du Conseil Permanent International pour l'Exploration de la Mer 24:135–146.

Deelder, C. L. 1960. Ergebnisse der holländischen Untersuchungen über den Glasaalzug. Archiv für Fischereiwissenschaft 11:1–10.

de Veen, J. F. 1978. On selective tidal transport in the migration of North Sea plaice (*Pleuronectes platessa*) and other flatfish species. Netherlands Journal of Sea Research 12:115–147.

Dodson, J. J., and L. A. Dohse. 1984. A model of olfactory-mediated conditioning of directional bias in fish migrating in reversing tidal currents based on the homing migration of American shad (*Alosa sapidissima*). Pages 263–281 in J. D. McCleave, G. P. Arnold, J. J. Dodson, and W. H. Neill, editors. Mechanisms of migration in fishes. Plenum, New York, New York, USA.

Dowse, H. B., J. C. Hall, and J. M. Ringo. 1987. Circadian and ultradian rhythms in *period* mutants of *Drosophila melanogaster*. Behavior Genetics 17:19–35.

Ewing, R. D., M. D. Evenson, E. K. Birks, and A. R. Hemmingsen. 1984. Indices of parr–smolt transformation in juvenile steelhead trout (*Salmo gairdneri*) undergoing volitional release. Aquaculture 40:209–221.

Fontaine, M. 1954. Du determinisme physiologique des migrations. Biological Reviews of the Cambridge Philosophical Society 29:390–418.

Fontaine, M. 1975. Physiological mechanisms in the migration of marine and amphihaline fish. Advances in Marine Biology 13:241–355.

Fortier, L., and W. C. Leggett. 1982. Fickian transport and the dispersal of fish larvae in estuaries. Canadian Journal of Fisheries and Aquatic Sciences 39:1150–1163.

Fortier, L., and W. C. Leggett. 1983. Vertical migrations and transport of larval fish in a partially mixed estuary. Canadian Journal of Fisheries and Aquatic Sciences 40:1543–1555.

Fortier, L., and W. C. Leggett. 1984. Small-scale covariability in the abundance of fish larvae and their prey. Canadian Journal of Fisheries and Aquatic Sciences 41:502–512.

Fried, S. M., J. D. McCleave, and G. W. LaBar. 1978. Seaward migration of hatchery-reared Atlantic salmon, *Salmo salar,* smolts in the Penobscot River estuary, Maine: riverine movements. Journal of the Fisheries Research Board of Canada 35:76–87.

Gibson, R. N. 1973. Tidal and circadian activity rhythms in juvenile plaice, *Pleuronectes platessa*. Marine Biology (Berlin) 22:379–386.

Gibson, R. N. 1982. Recent studies on the biology of intertidal fishes. Oceanography and Marine Biology an Annual Review 20:363–414.

Gibson, R. N. 1984. Hydrostatic pressure and the rhythmic behaviour of intertidal marine fishes. Transactions of the American Fisheries Society 113:479–483.

Graham, J. J. 1972. Retention of larval herring within the Sheepscot estuary of Maine. U.S. National Marine Fisheries Service Fishery Bulletin 70:299–305.

Greer Walker, M., F. R. Harden Jones, and G. P. Arnold. 1978. The movements of plaice (*Pleuronectes platessa* L.) tracked in the open sea. Journal du Conseil, Conseil International pour l'Exploration de la Mer 38:58–86.

Greer Walker, M., J. D. Riley, and L. S. Emerson. 1980. On the movements of sole (*Solea solea*) and dogfish (*Scyliorhinus canicula*) tracked off the East Anglian coast. Netherlands Journal of Sea Research 14:66–77.

Harden Jones, F. R. 1968. Fish migration. Edward Arnold, London, England.

Harden Jones, F. R. 1977. Performance and behaviour on migration. Pages 145–170 in J. H. Steele, editor. Fisheries mathematics. Academic Press, London, England.

Harden Jones, F. R. 1984. A view from the ocean. Pages 1–26 in J. D. McCleave, G. P. Arnold, J. J. Dodson, and W. H. Neill, editors. Mechanisms of migration in fishes. Plenum, New York, New York, USA.

Harden Jones, F. R., G. P. Arnold, M. Greer Walker, and P. Scholes. 1979. Selective tidal stream transport and the migration of plaice (*Pleuronectes platessa* L.) in the southern North Sea. Journal du Conseil, Conseil International pour l'Exploration de la Mer 38:331–337.

Helfman, G. S., D. E. Facey, L. S. Hales, and E. L. Bozeman, Jr. 1987. Reproductive ecology of the American eel. American Fisheries Society Symposium 1:42–56.

Hickman, R. A. 1981. Densities and swimbladder development of juvenile American eels, *Anguilla rostrata* (Lesueur), as related to energetics of migration. Journal of Fish Biology 18:507–517.

Jellyman, D. J. 1977. Invasion of a New Zealand freshwater stream by glass-eels of two *Anguilla* spp. New Zealand Journal of Marine and Freshwater Research 11:193–209.

Jellyman, D. J. 1979. Upstream migration of glass-eels (*Anguilla* spp.) in the Waikato River. New Zealand Journal of Marine and Freshwater Research 13:13–22.

Leggett, W. C., and J. E. Carscadden. 1978. Latitudinal variation in reproductive characteristics of American shad (*Alosa sapidissima*): evidence for population specific life history strategies in fish. Journal of the Fisheries Research Board of Canada 35:1469–1478.

McCleave, J. D., J. J. M. Bedaux, P. G. Doucet, J. C. Jager, J. T. L. Jong, W. J. van der Steen, and B. Voorzanger. In press. Statistical methods for analysis of plankton and nekton distribution, with applications to selective tidal stream transport of juvenile American eels. Journal du Conseil, Conseil International pour l'Exploration de la Mer.

McCleave, J. D., and R. C. Kleckner. 1982. Selective tidal stream transport in the estuarine migration of glass eels of the American eel (*Anguilla rostrata*). Journal du Conseil, Conseil International pour l'Exploration de la Mer 40:262–271.

Rawson, K. S., and P. J. DeCoursey. 1976. A comparison of the rhythms of mice and crabs from intertidal and terrestrial habitats. Pages 33–52 *in* P. J. DeCoursey, editor. Biological rhythms in the marine environment. University of South Carolina Press, Columbia, South Carolina, USA.

Riddell, B. E., and W. C. Leggett. 1981. Evidence of an adaptive basis for geographic variation in body morphology and time of downstream migration of juvenile Atlantic salmon (*Salmo salar*). Canadian Journal of Fisheries and Aquatic Sciences 38: 308–320.

Riddell, B. E., W. C. Leggett, and R. L. Saunders. 1981. Evidence of adaptive polygenic variation between two populations of Atlantic salmon (*Salmo salar*) native to tributaries of the S. W. Miramichi River, N.B. Canadian Journal of Fisheries and Aquatic Sciences 38:321–333.

Rijnsdorp, A. D., M. van Stralen, and H. W. van der Veer. 1985. Selective tidal transport of North Sea plaice larvae *Pleuronectes platessa* in coastal nursery areas. Transactions of the American Fisheries Society 114:461–470.

Rommel, S. A., Jr., and J. D. McCleave. 1973. Prediction of oceanic electric fields in relation to fish migration. Journal du Conseil, Conseil International pour l'Exploration de la Mer 35:27–31.

Sheldon, M. R., and J. D. McCleave. 1985. Abundance of glass eels of the American eel, *Anguilla rostrata*, in mid-channel and near shore during estuarine migration. Naturaliste canadien (Québec) 112: 425–430.

Sloane, R. D. 1984. Invasion and upstream migration by glass-eels of *Anguilla australis australis* Richardson and *A. reinhardtii* Steindachner in Tasmanian freshwater streams. Australian Journal of Marine and Freshwater Research 35:47–59.

Tesch, F.-W. 1965. Verhalten der Glasaale (*Anguilla anguilla*) bei ihrer Wanderung in den Ästuarien deutscher Nordseeflüsse. Helgoländer wissenschaftliche Meeresuntersuchungen 12:404–419.

Tesch, F.-W. 1971. Aufenthalt der Glasaale (*Anguilla anguilla*) an der südlichen Nordseeküste vor dem Eindringen in das Süsswasser. Vie et Milieu (supplement) 22:381–392.

Thorpe, J. E. 1982. Migration in salmonids, with special reference to juvenile movements in fresh water. Pages 86–97 *in* E. L. Brannon and E. O. Salo, editors. Proceedings of the salmon and trout migratory behavior symposium. University of Washington, Seattle, Washington, USA.

Williams, G. C., and R. K. Koehn. 1984. Population genetics of North Atlantic catadromous eels (*Anguilla*). Pages 529–560 *in* B. J. Turner, editor. Evolutionary genetics of fishes. Plenum, New York, New York, USA.

American Fisheries Society Symposium 1:151–161, 1987

The Reproductive Ecology of Threespine Sticklebacks Breeding in Fresh and Brackish Water

G. I. KEDNEY, V. BOULÉ, AND G. J. FITZGERALD

Département de biologie, L'Université Laval, Ste. Foy, Québec G1K 7P4, Canada

Abstract.—We compared the reproductive success of threespine sticklebacks *Gasterosteus aculeatus* spawning in fresh and brackish water. There were no evident genotypic differences between the two spawning groups, both of which overwinter in the St. Lawrence estuary. However, males spawning in fresh water took longer to hatch their eggs and had higher egg mortality than fish spawning in brackish tide pools. There were significant differences in male parental behavior and aggression between the two habitats. River males were less aggressive and fanned their eggs less than pool males. The pool males were subjected to greater egg cannibalism and higher bird predation than river males. We suggest that migratory and nonmigratory strategies occur because upstream migration to spawn in fresh water is relatively inexpensive and any physiological disadvantage of spawning in fresh water is offset by reduced risk of predation upon eggs or adults.

Fish migration remains a topic of intense interest as shown by the number of recent reviews (e.g., McCleave et al. 1984; McKeown 1984; Smith 1985). Current hypotheses to explain why fish migrate include feeding optimization, avoidance of unfavorable conditions, and possibly habitat colonization (e.g., Leggett 1977; Northcote 1978). Presumably the advantages of migration outweigh the costs in terms of individual fitness, as individuals are positioned into the best location for a given biological activity (Bond 1979); i.e., individuals that migrate should have a greater reproductive success than those that do not. However, evidence for the adaptive significance of fish migration remains elusive. In most cases the reproductive success of individual migrants cannot be compared to nonmigrants, either because the whole population migrates or because necessary data on nonmigrants have not been collected.

The threespine stickleback *Gasterosteus aculeatus* is found on the shores of all northern continents in both fresh and salt water (Wootton 1976, 1984). Its distribution results from repeated and successful colonizations of the freshwater habitat from a marine base (Bell 1984). Anadromous populations generally consist entirely or largely of the form "trachurus," which is morphologically distinct from the freshwater form "leiurus." This distinction is based mainly on the number and arrangement of lateral plates. Trachurus fish are considered to be genetically adapted to an anadromous lifestyle due to their larger size, more streamlined form, and ability to nest in currents (Hagen 1967; Taylor and McPhail

1986).

Here we report the results of a field study which compared the reproductive success of individual threespine sticklebacks, form trachurus, that migrate from the St. Lawrence estuary to spawn in fresh water with that of individuals that spawn in brackish-water tide pools directly adjacent to the estuary. This unique situation, where individuals overwintering in the St. Lawrence estuary choose to migrate to spawn in fresh water or remain downstream to breed in brackish water, provides an excellent opportunity to examine the adaptive significance of migration. Our primary objective was to determine if individuals spawning in fresh water differed in their reproductive success from fish spawning in the tide pools.

Reproductive success usually means the number of offspring that survive to reproduce but, in the field, this usually cannot be measured directly. The most useful index of reproductive success of a male stickleback in the field is the number of eggs he obtains in his nest (FitzGerald and Wootton 1986). Important proximate factors affecting reproductive success of male sticklebacks include obtaining a territory, territory size, choice of a nest site, supply of females (sex ratios), and time spent on the breeding grounds (FitzGerald and Wootton 1986). The reproductive success of a male may also depend upon the most efficient allocation of time spent between fanning his eggs, aggressively defending his territory, and feeding during the parental phase. The reproductive biology of sticklebacks is characterized by the division of roles between the sexes. Apart from courtship, the female is free to forage for food and so increase her fecundity during the breeding season.

In many populations of threespine sticklebacks, few if any fish survive to a second breeding season (Coad and Power 1973; Wootton 1976; Craig and FitzGerald 1982). However, in the laboratory, males and females can complete a number of breeding cycles within a reproductive season (Wootton 1976). Life history theory (e.g., Horn and Rubenstein 1984) predicts that animals having a single reproductive season should invest most of their time and energy into reproduction; thus we predicted that individuals would remain on the breeding grounds as long as possible.

Our second objective was to determine if there were morphological, meristic, or behavioral differences between the fish in the two habitats. Our approach was to compare results obtained from river fish over two seasons to those obtained from fish breeding in the tide pools. Most data on tide pool fish were taken from previous studies conducted at the site from 1977 to 1985 (e.g., Fitz-Gerald 1983; Whoriskey 1984; FitzGerald and Whoriskey 1985).

Methods

Study site.—The study was conducted in a salt marsh at the Isle Verte National Wildlife Reserve situated along the southern shore of the St. Law- rence estuary approximately 20 km east of Rivière du Loup, Québec (Figure 1). The salt marsh is a semiopen system where fish are able to move from the estuary to tide pools or from pool to pool only during bimonthly flooding of the marsh. The threespine stickleback overwinters in the St. Lawrence estuary; in early May, individuals either migrate into Rivière des Vases, a tidal river, to spawn 2.5 km upstream in fresh water or into a series of adjacent tide pools (maximum distance 250 m from the estuary), where they spawn in brackish water (range 14.0–26.7‰). Upstream migration of threespine sticklebacks is blocked by a waterfall approximately 2.5 km from the river mouth. Below this natural barrier, threespine sticklebacks occur all along the river, but the principal freshwater spawning site is just below the waterfall. Additional details of the two study sites have been given elsewhere (Reed and Moisan 1971; Lambert and FitzGerald 1979; Worgan and FitzGerald 1981a, 1981b; Ward and FitzGerald 1983a, 1983b).

The study was carried out in a 100-m stretch of river situated approximately 100 m downstream of the impassable waterfall and in the salt marsh tide pools. At the river breeding site, the water is always fresh (0‰). Daily water temperatures, measured continuously over 24 h during May and June 1985, averaged a minimum of 7.1°C (range

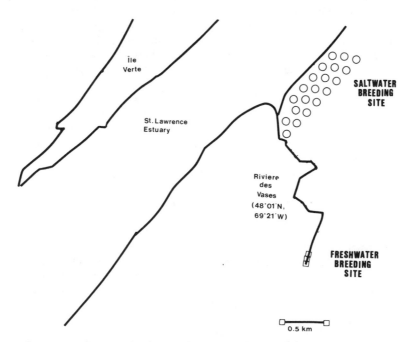

FIGURE 1.—Study region in the Isle Verte National Wildlife Reserve, Québec.

0–13.0°C) and a maximum of 15.7°C (range 5.0–21.0°C). Surface current speed, except during occasional flooding, never exceeded 0.6 m/s and was usually less than 0.3 m/s; pH was usually 7.0 and dissolved oxygen values ranged from 8.5 to 12.0 mg/L with little diel variation. River width averaged 2.85 m with midchannel water depth ranging from 3.0 to 35.0 cm. The river bed consisted of a sand–clay–mud mixture with scattered rocky areas. The river flows through a ditch approximately 3.0 m deep and cover is provided by overhanging bushes. The only other fish species found are ninespine sticklebacks *Pungitius pungitius,* brook sticklebacks *Culaea inconstans,* brook trout *Salvelinus fontinalis,* and central mudminnows *Umbra limi.* The latter three species are rare.

Although tide pools in the salt marsh range in area from 1 to 1,000 m², only those ranging in size from 10 to 30 m² in the *Spartina patens* zone were used in this study. The pools are shallow (<0.5 m) with mud bottoms. Water temperatures measured in May and June 1985 attained a mean minimum value of 9.7°C (range, 1.0–17.0°C) and a mean maximum value of 20.7°C (range, 6.0–27.5°C). Oxygen levels in the pools usually range from 3.3 to 16.6 mg/L, but can drop below 1 mg/L (Reebs et al. 1984). Salinity varied little during the sampling periods (May 25–31 and June 23–29; mean, 23.46‰; range, 21.59–26.23‰) as pools remained unflooded; pH varied between 7.0 and 9.5. Other fish species found in the pools were blackspotted sticklebacks *Gasterosteus wheatlandi,* ninespine sticklebacks, and, rarely, mummichogs *Fundulus heteroclitus* and fourspine sticklebacks *Apeltes quadracus.*

Morphometrics and meristics.—An analysis of selected morphometric and meristic characters was undertaken to determine whether river and pool fish are from the same stock. Subsamples of 50 fish (25 males, 25 females) from each total sample ($N = 72$, $N = 101$ river fish; $N = 89$, $N = 347$ pool fish; 1984 and 1985, respectively) of the river and pool fish were used in the analysis. For each individual, the following data were recorded: total length, standard length, number of lateral plates, number of gill rakers, number of dorsal and anal fin rays, body depth, head length, length of dorsal and pelvic spines, and length and depth of caudal peduncle. All measurements and counts were taken from the left flank of the fish, which had been previously stained with alizarin red for lateral plate enumeration (Bell 1984). Counts of lateral plates, including those contributing to the

caudal keel, were made using a binocular microscope. All body measurements were made with Helios vernier calipers accurate to 0.05 mm, except dorsal and pelvic spine lengths which were measured with the aid of a calibrated eyepiece (10× magnification). Total length, standard length, head length, caudal peduncle length, and caudal peduncle depth were recorded following Hubbs and Lagler (1958). Body depth, dorsal spine length, and pelvic spine length were measured following Hagen and Gilbertson (1972). Gill rakers, including rudimentary ones, were counted on the entire left first arch after removal of the operculum. Dorsal and anal fin ray counts followed Coad and Power (1973, 1974).

Residence time and population size.—Immigration–emigration patterns in Rivière des Vases were determined in 1985 by marking and recapturing fish. Fish were trapped in two unbaited minnow traps placed in midstream on the breeding grounds. All fish caught were sexed (see Wootton 1976), marked with pieces of colored plastic slipped over a dorsal spine (Kynard 1978), and then released. This procedure, which allowed recognition of individuals and date of first marking, has been used previously for movement and behavior studies of sticklebacks in the tide pools (e.g., FitzGerald and van Havre 1985; Whoriskey et al. 1986) with no obvious effects on fish behavior. Traps were checked once daily from May 11 to July 8, 1985, and the number of marked individuals of each sex was recorded. All recaptured individuals were multiple-marked in order to determine if the same fish were reentering the traps. Altogether, 225 fish were captured.

This method assumes that the area surrounding each trap represents a pool of marked and unmarked fish that is subsequently sampled by trapping (e.g., Lotrich 1975). If marked and unmarked fish behave similarly, a stable ratio of both groups implies that no immigration, emigration, or mortality is occurring during the trapping period. However, if movement into and out of the area is occurring, changes in the ratio of marked to unmarked fish should reflect this. One known bias with this method is that we probably "lose" those marked males that become territorial and do not enter traps after initial capture. However, any effect of these males on the ratio of marked to unmarked fish should occur at the onset of the breeding season and thus be easily recognizable.

The capture–recapture method allowed us to estimate the river population by applying a modified Schnabel method (Ricker 1975) where $N = [CtMt/(R + 1)]$; N is the size of the population at the time of marking, Ct is the total catch in the sample, Mt is the number of fish marked, and R is the number of recaptured marked fish in the sample. Our behavioral observations of marked fish indicated that maximum dispersion was 100 m on either side of the minnow traps. Thus we considered the area sampled to be a 200-m stretch of river. Additional data on population size was obtained in 1984. Four hundred sixty-three individuals were captured between May 17 and July 27, 1984, and were spine-clipped to allow individual recognition. Unfortunately we did not distinguish the number of recaptures per individual so these data could not be used to determine residence patterns.

Nest location.—To determine the location of nests in the river, the following data were collected on 26 nests in 1984 and 27 nests in 1985: nest depth, distance to the nearest conspecific nest (index of territory size), distance to the river bank, and degree of cover (rocks and woody debris). Cover was classified as (1) open: cover absent; (2) 25%: nest covered on one side; (3) 50%: nest covered on two sides; (4) 75%: nest covered on three sides; and (5) 100%: nest entirely in cover but visible to an overhead observer (see FitzGerald 1983).

Male behavior.—To obtain data on river-male time budgets, we observed 53 males chosen because they had been showing fanning behavior and had well-constructed nests. These data were the duration, frequency, and percentage of time the male was (1) at nest: within an estimated 20 cm of his nest; (2) away from nest: farther than 20 cm from his nest; (3) fanning: pushed water into his nest using the pectoral fins; (4) being aggressive: a pooled measure of the aggressive behaviors—chases, bites, and threat displays—directed toward a conspecific. Behavioral observations were made for 10 min/male between 0900 and 1700 hours when visibility was best from vantage points on the banks of the pools and river. Observations were recorded on a Datamyte 800 event recorder (Electrogeneral Corporation, Minnetonka, Minnesota). No data could be collected on rainy days or on the day following rain because of turbid water conditions. All data were collected in June 1984 and 1985.

Nest contents and egg-hatching times.—To estimate the reproductive success of males breeding in the river and pools, we counted the number of eggs obtained from 53 nests mentioned above and

from a sample of 85 nests (1984) obtained from the tide pools as reported by FitzGerald and Whoriskey (1985). Eggs from an additional 31 river nests were collected in 1985. Eggs in nests were classified as dead or alive (dead eggs become opaque when preserved in formalin). Nests in the pools were surveyed on the last day of an interflood period. This is the latest time that eggs can be collected as many individuals leave the pools during tidal flooding and others enter to begin another round of spawning (Whoriskey et al. 1986). Eggs in the river nests were collected toward the end of the breeding season to ensure that nest contents were a reliable index of reproductive success.

The time taken for eggs to hatch in the river and two pools was determined (1985 only) by following the daily activities of nesting males. Seven males in the river and 11 from the pools, whose spawning times were known accurately to within 1 d, were checked daily until their eggs hatched and fry were seen around the nests.

Physical and reproductive conditions.—To determine if the physical condition of river and pool fish (both sexes) differed, we measured in the laboratory the total length and wet weight of 173 river and 436 pool fish. These data were used to calculate the physical condition factor: $PCF = 100(\text{wet weight, g})/(\text{total length, cm})^3$. This index measures fish robustness (Bagenal 1978). To compare clutch sizes and egg diameters, ovaries from 263 females were collected and placed in Gilson's fluid to separate the eggs from gonadal tissue. The number of mature eggs per clutch was later determined. Eggs larger than 1.0 mm in diameter were considered mature (Wallace and Selman 1979). The diameters of 20 eggs, arbitrarily subsampled from each specimen, were measured to the nearest 0.05 mm with a calibrated microscope eyepiece.

Sex ratios.—Female sticklebacks may, in certain circumstances, be a limiting resource for males (e.g., Whoriskey 1984; Whoriskey et al. 1986). To determine if females were limiting for males in the river, the male-to-female sex ratios at the river breeding site were estimated by counting fish obtained from May to July in 1984 and 1985. Fish were obtained from the two minnow traps (see above), counted, and released once daily at low tide. These periods cover the breeding season of threespine sticklebacks at Isle Verte. Individuals were sexed according to secondary sexual characteristics (see Wootton 1976): cryptic coloration and swollen abdomens for females and nuptial coloration for males. Sex ratio data calculated from fish collected in the river were compared to similar data obtained for pool fish in 1982 and 1983 by Whoriskey (1984). We justify this comparison because relative abundances and sex ratios of fish in the pools have been relatively stable since we began working at the site in 1977 (see FitzGerald 1983; Whoriskey 1984; Whoriskey et al. 1986).

Egg predation.—An important feature of the reproductive biology of sticklebacks is nest raiding and egg eating (Whoriskey and FitzGerald 1985b). To evaluate the frequency of egg cannibalism in the river compared with that in the pools, we examined 52 (35 male, 17 female) stomachs from river fish collected between May 31 and June 14 in both 1984 and 1985 when breeding was most important in the river and pools. Comparable data on fish from the pools were taken from Whoriskey and FitzGerald (1985b). We did not control for differences in digestion rates or diel feeding activity (e.g., Worgan and FitzGerald 1981a; Walsh and FitzGerald 1984; Whoriskey et al. 1985) but we did note the frequency of nest raiding at both sites, so our data should provide a rough indication of the occurrence of egg predation in the two habitats.

Statistical analysis.—Our authorities for statistical tests were Steel and Torrie (1980) and Zar (1974). We used nonparametric procedures when data failed to meet the assumptions of parametric tests. Sample sizes and tests varied depending on the parameter being analyzed and are given throughout the text. All computations were calculated by Statistical Analysis System (SAS) programs (Ray and Sall 1982).

Results

Morphometrics and Meristics

There were no differences for any of the selected meristic and morphometric traits between river and pool fish (Table 1). River males were significantly longer than pool males in 1985 but not in 1984 (Table 2). River and pool females showed no significant differences in length in 1984 and 1985 (Table 3).

Residence Time and Population Size

The ratio of marked to unmarked fish varied little during the study period, indicating that very little immigration or emigration occurred (Figure 2). By mid-July fish had ceased breeding and moved downstream to the estuary. The sharp

TABLE 1.—A morphometric and meristic comparison of threespine sticklebacks breeding in tide pools and in Rivière des Vases, Isle Verte, Québec. Values are means (SD). Data were pooled for the two sample years 1984 and 1985, and represent 100 river fish (50 male, 50 female) and 100 pool fish (50 male, 50 female). No means differed significantly between river and pool fish (Mann–Whitney U-tests; $P > 0.05$).

Characteristic	River	Pool
Number of lateral plates	28.09 (3.38)	28.15 (3.03)
Number of gill rakers	15.04 (1.45)	15.09 (1.29)
Number of dorsal fin rays	11.82 (0.72)	11.56 (0.71)
Number of anal fin rays	8.85 (0.56)	8.75 (0.54)
Body depth[a]	11.72 (0.59)	11.51 (0.71)
Head length[a]	15.91 (0.99)	15.58 (0.85)
1st dorsal spine length[a]	5.62 (0.57)	5.53 (0.74)
2nd dorsal spine length[a]	5.70 (0.54)	5.64 (0.72)
3rd dorsal spine length[a]	1.61 (0.33)	1.67 (0.40)
Pelvic spine length[a]	7.83 (0.89)	7.44 (0.82)
Caudal peduncle length[a]	6.49 (0.77)	6.27 (0.80)
Caudal peduncle depth[a]	2.03 (0.22)	1.94 (0.23)

[a] Measurements (mm) were adjusted to a 50.0 mm standard length. The adjustment technique followed Hagen and Gilbertson (1972) and McPhail (1984) and is outlined in Steel and Torrie (1980).

decrease in the ratio of marked to unmarked fish that occurred between May 28 and June 3 and between June 11 and June 17 was probably because some marked males became territorial. The stability of the mark–recapture ratios suggests that most fish remained on the breeding grounds from late May to early July. Multiple recaptures of individuals during this period support this contention (Figure 3).

The population of threespine sticklebacks in the river was estimated at 882 (95% confidence intervals: 759–1,038) and 466 (95% confidence intervals: 374–598) in 1984 and 1985, respectively. Estimates of the number of adults on the breeding grounds were 6.0 and 3.0 fish/m^2 in 1984 and 1985, respectively. Although it is obvious that the population of river fish is much less than that of pool

TABLE 2.—Mean total lengths and physical condition factors (PCF) for threespine stickleback males caught in Rivière des Vases and tide pools, Isle Verte, Québec, in May and June 1984 and 1985. Values are means (SD). The river mean is marked with an asterisk if it differs significantly from the pool mean that year. (Mann–Whitney U-test; $P < 0.05$*).

	1984		1985	
Measure	River	Pools	River	Pools
Total length (cm)	6.80 (0.50)	6.86 (0.38)	6.70 (0.53)*	6.39 (0.57)
PCF	1.14 (0.11)*	1.09 (0.12)	1.24 (0.11)*	1.13 (0.15)
N	47	43	77	179

TABLE 3.—Reproductive data for threespine stickleback females caught in Rivière des Vases and tide pools, Isle Verte, Québec, in May and June 1984 and 1985. Values for the first four measures are means (SD). The river entry is marked with an asterisk if it differs from the pool entry for that year (Mann–Whitney U-test of means or covariance analysis of regressions; $P < 0.05$*).

	1984		1985	
Measure	River	Pools	River	Pools
Total length (cm)	7.40(0.40)	7.41(0.45)	7.45(0.53)	7.32(0.61)
PCF[a]	1.11(0.13)	1.19(0.16)	1.33(0.16)*	1.22(0.56)
Egg diameter (mm)	1.02(0.24)	1.15(0.19)	1.20(0.20)	1.29(0.23)
Number of mature eggs	169(154.0)*	260(140.0)	346(150.5)*	282(140.9)
Length–fecundity[b] regression	$Y = 8.78X - 5.24$*	$Y = 1.01X + 1.52$	$Y = 4.95X - 1.60$*	$Y = 2.10X + 0.35$
Weight–fecundity[b] regression	$Y = 0.07X - 1.92$	$Y = 0.08X + 1.94$	$Y = 1.38X - 1.58$*	$Y = 1.12X + 1.76$
N	25	46	24	168

[a] PCF = physical condition factor.
[b] $Y = \log_{10}$ (eggs/clutch); $X = \log_{10}$ (total length, cm) or $\log_{10}$ (weight, g).

fish (one 30-m pool may contain as many fish as occur on the entire breeding grounds in the river), it is problematic to compare densities of threespine sticklebacks in the two habitats because of immigration and emigration during flooding in the pools during the breeding season.

Nest Location

There were significant differences between nest locations in the river and pools. River males built their nests farther from the bank and in deeper water, and used more cover, than did pool males (Table 4). Males avoiding nesting in the middle of the pools, as seen from diagrams in FitzGerald (1983), Whoriskey (1984), and Gaudreault and FitzGerald (1985). Nesting densities were similar in the river in 1984 and 1985, averaging 0.47 nests/m². This contrasts with the lowest nesting densities recorded for threespine sticklebacks

breeding in allopatry in the pools (0.80 nests/m²: Whoriskey 1984). Although overall nesting densities were different on the two spawning grounds, mean internest distances did not differ between the two sites because of aggregation of spawning males.

Male Behavior

River males spent significantly less time fanning eggs than pool fish and were much less aggressive (Table 5). There were no significant differences in either time at or time away from nests between the two groups.

Nest Contents and Egg Hatching Times

Many nests in both the river and pools were empty. However, no difference between the percentages of empty nests in the two habitats was

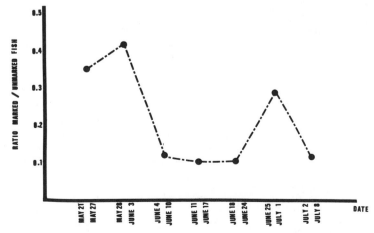

FIGURE 2.—Ratio of marked to unmarked threespine sticklebacks collected at the freshwater breeding site in Rivière des Vases from May 21 to July 8, 1985. Total number of fish marked was 225; 71 marked fish and 876 unmarked fish were captured during the sampling period.

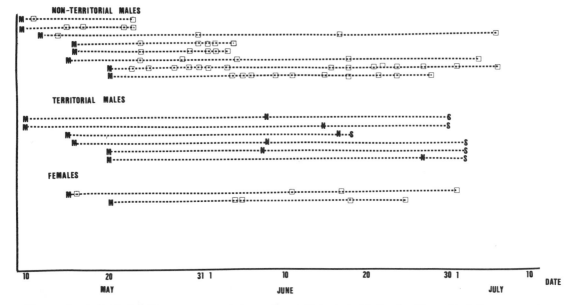

FIGURE 3.—Individual residence patterns of threespine sticklebacks in Rivière des Vases. Each line represents an individual. M = date of first marking; N = date a male was first observed with a territory; S = date eggs were collected from the nest; □ = date of recapture.

noted (Table 6). There were significant differences in the mean numbers of eggs per nest between the two habitats, but these differences were not consistent for the 1984 and 1985 seasons (Table 6). In 1985 (1984 pool data are unavailable), there was a significantly higher egg mortality in the river nests than in the pool nests. The mean time to hatch was significantly longer in the river than the pools in 1985 (Table 6).

Physical and Reproductive Conditions

River males were in better condition than pool males in both years (Table 2), whereas the condition factor was higher for river females only in 1985 (Table 3). Egg diameters were similar for females in the two habitats but the mean number of eggs per clutch showed a significant interyear

TABLE 4.—Nest site variables for male threespine sticklebacks breeding in Rivière des Vases and in tide pools. Tide pool data are from Whoriskey (1984). Values are means (SD). The river value is marked with an asterisk if it differs from the pool value in that year (Mann–Whitney U-test; $P < 0.01*$).

Measurement	River	Pools
Distance to bank (cm)	80.5 (50.0)*	49.1 (26.4)
Nest depth (cm)	44.0 (60.3)*	8.3 (6.4)
Internest distance (cm)	44.6 (35.4)	37.0 (27.4)
Percent cover	41.8 (29.5)*	2.4 (12.4)
N	53	78

variation (Table 3). Length–fecundity regressions suggest a higher relative fecundity for river females, i.e., river females of a given length have

TABLE 5.—Behavior data[a] for 106 nesting male threespine sticklebacks in Rivière des Vases and tide pools. Data are means (SD). Pool data are from Whoriskey (1984). River values are marked with an asterisk if they differ from the respective pool means (Mann–Whitney U-test; $P < 0.05$).

Behavior and measure	River	Pools
At nest		
Frequency	12.09 (8.73)	16.55 (9.34)
Duration[b]	6.34 (2.49)	7.00 (2.08)
% time[c]	63.04 (25.00)	69.37 (20.50)
Away from nest		
Frequency	12.30 (10.40)	15.33 (9.44)
Duration[b]	2.68 (2.28)	2.83 (1.94)
% time[c]	26.77 (22.75)	28.36 (19.51)
Fanning		
Frequency	10.28 (8.31)*	15.06 (7.41)
Duration[b]	1.93 (1.87)*	3.06 (1.66)
% time[c]	19.17 (18.68)*	29.51 (15.31)
Aggression		
Frequency	2.96 (4.17)*	14.53 (13.97)
Duration[c]	0.11 (0.16)*	0.26 (0.23)
% time[c]	1.21 (1.80)*	2.45 (2.31)

[a]Data are based on 10-min samples for each of 53 river and pool fish.

[b]Total duration (min) in either habitat may not add up to 10 min as some behavior patterns can occur concurrently: e.g., "at nest" and "fanning."

[c]Total percentage time in either habitat may not add up to 100% as some behavior patterns can occur concurrently: e.g., "at nest" and "fanning."

TABLE 6.—Reproductive success of male threespine sticklebacks in Rivière des Vases and tide pools. Values are means±SD (N); empty cells mean no data. The river mean is marked with an asterisk if it differs from the pool mean in that year (Mann–Whitney U-test; P < 0.05).

Measure	1984		1985	
	River	Pools[a]	River	Pools[a]
% empty nests	58	48	43	48
Mean number of eggs per nest[b]	224.0±507.5* (47)	183.0±300.7 (85)	471.7±847.7* (31)	526.6±665.6 (37)
Mean number of eggs per nest[c]	619.1±693.2* (17)	335.5±339.0 (44)	860.2±996.2* (17)	1025.5±588.2 (19)
% dead eggs per nest	55.5±49.9 (17)		17.5±30.9* (17)	2.0±6.7 (19)
Mean hatch time (d)			17.1±2.8* (7)	11.4±5.1 (11)

[a] Data from FitzGerald and Whoriskey (1985).
[b] Includes empty nests.
[c] Only nests with eggs.

more eggs per clutch than pool females of similar length (Table 3). However, weight–fecundity regressions indicate a higher fecundity of river females only in 1985.

Sex Ratios

Males outnumbered females at the freshwater river site over the breeding season (Figure 4). This contrasted with the situation in the pools (1982 and 1983), where males significantly outnumbered females only late in the breeding season. FitzGerald (1983) reported a significant male-biased sex ratio in one pool in early May 1981.

Egg Predation

Both river male and female threespine stickle-

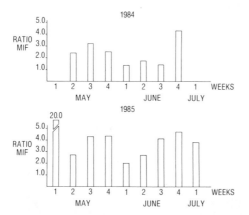

FIGURE 4.—Sex ratios (males/females, M/F) of threespine sticklebacks in Rivière des Vases during the breeding seasons of 1984 and 1985. Ratios for all sample dates were significantly different from 1:1 (chi-square tests, P < 0.05; N = 589 in 1984 and 947 in 1985).

backs consumed fewer eggs than did a comparable sample of pool fish. In the river, there were no sex differences in cannibalism, while in the pools, females ate more eggs than did males (Table 7). Percentage occurrence data yielded similar results and thus are not included here.

Discussion

In the spring, threespine sticklebacks have the option of migrating upstream to spawn in fresh water or to forego this movement and spawn in brackish-water pools. The key question is: why do some fish migrate 2.5 km upstream if they can spawn in tide pools close to the estuary? Suitable space for nest sites did not appear to be limiting either in the river or in the pools (Whoriskey and FitzGerald 1985a). The animals of both sites appear to be of the same stock, as evidenced by the meristic and morphological data. Furthermore,

TABLE 7.—Comparison of the mean number of eggs eaten by male and female threespine sticklebacks captured in Rivière des Vases and in tide pools. River data were collected between May 31 and June 14, 1984 and 1985. Tide pool data were collected between May 31 and June 9, 1982 and 1983 by Whoriskey (1984). Values are means±SD (N). The river value is marked with an asterisk if it differs from the pool value for the same sex (Mann–Whitney U-test; P < 0.01).

Sex	River	Pools
Male	3.58±13.59* (35)	4.28±8.70 (191)
Female	4.30±14.66* (17)	6.78±11.46 (197)[a]

[a] Mann–Whitney U-test, P < 0.01, differences are between sexes within pools.

the condition factor and fecundity data indicate that movement upstream is not energetically costly.

The only previous investigation of which we are aware that compared migratory and nonmigratory forms of the threespine stickleback is Hagen's (1967) classic study. He showed that anadromous (trachurus) fish are bigger and more fecund than resident (leiurus) fish in the Little Campbell River, British Columbia. The anadromous fish migrated from the sea to spawn 2.4 km upstream in fresh water. These fish were, on average, larger and twice as fecund as the nonmigratory fish. Wootton (1984) argued that this increased fecundity has probably evolved to balance the inevitable costs of a migration. The potential rate of increase of the anadromous population should equal that of the resident population and thus the two would have equal mean fitnesses. While Isle Verte fish and Hagen's fish migrated similar distances, the former showed no compensatory increase in fecundity (clutch size). This is surprising because of the increased costs of spawning in fresh water at Isle Verte (i.e., greater egg mortality, longer hatch times). It is possible that females produce more clutches in fresh water than in the pools because individuals remain longer in the river than in the pools. Data are needed on the total seasonal and lifetime egg production of migrants and nonmigrants and on the fecundities of fish that migrate much greater distances, as they do in the Fraser River, British Columbia (Taylor and McPhail 1986).

The length of the breeding season is similar at the two sites, but individual fish remain longer upstream than in the pools. Although mature fish occur in the river in May and June, the first nests are not built until early June. In the pools, some nesting occurs in May but most reproduction takes place in June. Thus, most males in both habitats probably complete only one breeding cycle because of the time necessary to build a nest, court females, hatch eggs, and care for fry. A complete breeding cycle may take close to 3 weeks.

Although there were significant differences in nest location at the two sites, there was no evidence that these differences were related to individual reproductive success. Male behavior during the parental phase may directly affect the time to hatch and the number of eggs hatching (Wootton 1976). River males fanned significantly less often and for shorter bouts than did pool males. It is interesting that this reduction in fan-

ning time was not because of increased aggressiveness by parental males. River males were significantly less aggressive than pool males; perhaps river males are inherently less aggressive. An alternative hypothesis is that river males fan less and are less aggressive because of some environmental difference between the two habitats, such as the presence of a current in the river. We can exclude the possibility that river fish are less aggressive than pool fish because of temperature differences between the two habitats. Aggression by territorial males toward an intruder was similar over a 15–25°C temperature range in standardized laboratory tests (FitzGerald et al. 1986).

Although there were significant differences in the number of eggs in nests in both habitats, these differences were not consistent from year to year, so the biological significance of this result, if any, remains unknown. The higher egg mortality for river fish may have been due to reduced fanning levels of the males, as fanning behavior is directly related to hatching success (Wootton 1976). The lower water temperatures in the river may also slow egg development. Although the higher egg mortality and the longer hatch times may reduce the success of males spawning in the river, in certain situations river males could leave more offspring than pool males. For example, many pools dry out leaving both eggs and adults stranded (personal observations).

It seems likely that rates of predation on eggs and young fish are lower in fresh water at our site. Predation upon a male's eggs by schools of females is significantly higher in the pools than in the river. We never saw females form schools to raid nests in the river as occurs in the pools (Whoriskey and FitzGerald 1985b), perhaps because of the presence of fewer females at the freshwater site. Also we have seen, but not yet quantified, heavy predation by fish lice (*Argulus* sp.) upon stickleback fry in the pools but not in the river. Fish in the pools are also subjected to heavy bird predation (Whoriskey and FitzGerald 1985c). While we did not quantify this predation for the river site, our casual observations suggest that it is probably much less important than it is in the pools.

In conclusion, we suggest that migration upstream into fresh water is physiologically inexpensive and any disadvantages of spawning in fresh water (e.g., osmoregulation, less food) are offset by the lower risk of predation on eggs and fry and of possible bird predation on breeding adults.

Acknowledgments

This research was supported by the National Science and Engineering Research Council of Canada and Les Fonds pour la formation de chercheurs et l'aide à la recherche (FCAR, Québec). We thank J. J. Dodson, H. Guderley, P. Magnan, and F. G. Whoriskey for helpful discussion and comments on the manuscript. Special thanks go to R. Poulin, P. Picard, F. Bolduc, and S. Berubé for field assistance. The Canadian Wildlife Service gave permission to work on the ecological reserve at Isle Verte.

References

Bagenal, T. 1978. Methods for assessment of fish populations in freshwater. IBP (International Biological Programme) Handbook 3.

Bell, M. A. 1984. Evolutionary phenetics and genetics. Pages 431–528 in B. J. Turner, editor. Evolutionary genetics of fishes. Plenum, New York, New York, USA.

Bond, C. E. 1979. Biology of the fishes. Saunders College Publishing, Philadelphia, Pennsylvania, USA.

Coad, B. W., and G. Power. 1973. Observations on the ecology and meristic variation of the threespine stickleback, *Gasterosteus aculeatus* L., 1758, and the blackspotted stickleback, *G. wheatlandi* Putnam, 1867, (Osteichthyes: Gasterosteidae) in Amory Cove, Québec. Canadian Field-Naturalist 87:113–122.

Coad, B. W., and G. Power. 1974. Meristic variation in the threespine stickleback, *Gasterosteus aculeatus,* in the Matamek River system, Quebec. Journal of the Fisheries Research Board of Canada 31:1155–1157.

Craig, D., and G. J. FitzGerald. 1982. Reproductive tactics of four sympatric sticklebacks (Gasterosteidae). Environmental Biology of Fishes 4:369–375.

FitzGerald, G. J. 1983. The reproductive ecology and behaviour of three sympatric sticklebacks (Gasterosteidae) in a saltmarsh. Biology of Behaviour 3:67–79.

FitzGerald, G. J., H. Guderley, and A. Blouin. 1986. The effect of temperature upon the aggressive behaviour of male sticklebacks (Gasterosteidae) Naturaliste canadien (Québec) 113:235–240.

FitzGerald, G. J., and N. van Havre. 1985. Flight, fright and shoaling in sticklebacks (Gasterosteidae). Biology of Behaviour, 10:321–331.

FitzGerald, G. J., and F. G. Whoriskey. 1985. The effects of interspecific interactions upon male reproductive success in two sympatric sticklebacks, *Gasterosteus aculeatus* and *G. wheatlandi.* Behaviour 93:112–126.

FitzGerald, G. J., and R. J. Wootton. 1986. The behavioural ecology of sticklebacks. Pages 409–432 in T. J. Pitcher, editor. The behaviour of teleost fish.

Croom Helm, London, England.

Gaudreault, A., and G. J. FitzGerald. 1985. Field observations of intraspecific and interspecific aggression among sticklebacks (Gasterosteidae). Behaviour 93:203–211.

Hagen, D. W. 1967. Isolating mechanisms in three-spine sticklebacks (Gasterosteidae). Journal of the Fisheries Research Board of Canada 24:1637–1692.

Hagen, D. W., and L. G. Gilbertson. 1972. Geographical variation and environmental selection in *Gasterosteus aculeatus* L. in the Pacific Northwest, America. Evolution 26:32–51.

Horn, H. S., and D. I. Rubenstein. 1984. Behavioral adaptation and life history. Pages 279–298 in J. R. Krebs and N. B. Davies, editors. Behavioural ecology: an evolutionary approach. Blackwell Scientific Publications, Oxford, England.

Hubbs, C. L., and K. F. Lagler. 1958. Fishes of the Great Lakes region. University of Michigan Press, Ann Arbor, Michigan, USA.

Kynard, B. E. 1978. Breeding behavior of a lacustrine population of threespine sticklebacks (*Gasterosteus aculeatus* L.). Behaviour 67:178–207.

Lambert, Y., and G. J. FitzGerald. 1979. Summer food and movements of the Atlantic tomcod, *Microgadus tomcod* (Walbaum) in a small tidal creek. Naturaliste canadien (Québec) 106:555–559.

Leggett, W. C. 1977. The ecology of fish migrations. Annual Review of Ecology and Systematics 8:282–308.

Lotrich, V. A. 1975. Summer home range and movements of *Fundulus heteroclitus* (Pisces: Cyprinodontidae) in a tidal creek. Ecology 56:191–198.

McCleave, J. D., G. P. Arnold, J. J. Dodson, and W. H. Neill, editors. 1984. Mechanisms of migrations of fishes. Plenum, New York, New York, USA.

McKeown, B. A. 1984. Fish migration. Timber Press, Beaverton, Oregon, USA.

McPhail, J. D. 1984. Ecology and evolution of sympatric sticklebacks (*Gasterosteus*): morphological and genetic evidence for a species pair in Enos Lake, British Columbia. Canadian Journal of Zoology 62:1402–1408.

Northcote, T. G. 1978. Migratory strategies and production in freshwater fishes. Pages 326–369 in S. D. Gerking, editor. Ecology of freshwater fish production. John Wiley & Sons, New York, New York, USA.

Ray, A. A., and J. P. Sall, editors. 1982. SAS user's guide: statistics. SAS Institute, Cary, North Carolina, USA.

Reebs, S. G., F. G. Whoriskey, Jr., and G. J. FitzGerald. 1984. Diel patterns of fanning activity, egg respiration, and nocturnal behavior of male threespine sticklebacks, *Gasterosteus aculeatus* L. (f. trachurus). Canadian Journal of Zoology 62:329–334.

Reed, A., and G. Moisan. 1971. The *Spartina patens* tidal marshes of the St. Lawrence estuary and their importance to aquatic birds. Naturaliste canadien (Québec) 98:905–922.

Ricker, W. E. 1975. Computation and interpretation of biological statistics of fish populations. Fisheries Research Board of Canada Bulletin 191.

Smith, R. J. F. 1985. The control of fish migration. Springer-Verlag, New York, New York, USA.

Steel, R. G., and J. H. Torrie. 1980. Principles and procedures in statistics. McGraw-Hill, New York, New York, USA.

Taylor, E. B., and J. D. McPhail. 1986. Prolonged and burst swimming in anadromous and freshwater threespine sticklebacks, *Gasterosteus aculeatus*. Canadian Journal of Zoology 64:416–420.

Wallace, R. A., and K. Selman. 1979. Physiological aspects of oogenesis in two species of sticklebacks, *Gasterosteus aculeatus* L. and *Apeltes quadracus* (Mitchill). Journal of Fish Biology 14:551–564.

Walsh, G., and G. J. FitzGerald. 1984. Resource utilization and coexistence of three species of sticklebacks (Gasterosteidae) in tidal salt-marsh pools. Journal of Fish Biology 25:405–420.

Ward, G., and G. J. FitzGerald. 1983a. Fish predation on the macrobenthos of tidal salt marsh pools. Canadian Journal of Zoology 61:1358–1361.

Ward, G., and G. J. FitzGerald. 1983b. Macrobenthic abundance and distribution in tidal pools of a Quebec salt marsh. Canadian Journal of Zoology 61:1071–1085.

Whoriskey, F. G. 1984. Le rôle de facteurs biotiques et abiotiques selectionnées dans la structuration d'une communauté d'épinoche (Pisces: Gasterosteidae). Doctoral dissertation. Université Laval, Ste. Foy, Québec, Canada.

Whoriskey, F. G., and G. J. FitzGerald. 1985a. Nest sites of the threespine stickleback: can site charac-

ters alone protect the nest against egg predators and are nest sites a limiting resource? Canadian Journal of Zoology 63:1991–1994.

Whoriskey, F. G., and G. J. FitzGerald. 1985b. Sex, cannibalism and sticklebacks. Behavioural Ecology and Sociobiology 18:15–18.

Whoriskey, F. G., and G. J. FitzGerald. 1985c. The effects of bird predation on an estuarine stickleback (Pisces: Gasterosteidae) community. Canadian Journal of Zoology 63:301–307.

Whoriskey, F. G., G. J. FitzGerald, and S. G. Reebs. 1986. The breeding-season population structure of three sympatric, territorial sticklebacks (Pisces: Gasterosteidae). Journal of Fish Biology 29: 635–648.

Whoriskey, F. G., A. Gaudreault, N. Martel, S. Campeau, and G. J. FitzGerald. 1985. The activity budget and behavior patterns of female threespine sticklebacks, *Gasterosteus aculeatus* (L.), in a Québec tidal salt marsh. Naturaliste canadien (Québec) 112:113–118.

Wootton, R. J. 1976. Biology of the sticklebacks. Academic Press, London, England.

Wootton, R. J. 1984. A functional biology of the sticklebacks. Croom Helm, London, England.

Worgan, J. P., and G. J. FitzGerald. 1981a. Diel activity and diet of three sympatric sticklebacks (Gasterosteidae) in a tidal salt marsh. Canadian Journal of Zoology 12:2375–2379.

Worgan, J. P., and G. J. FitzGerald. 1981b. Habitat segregation in a salt marsh among adult sticklebacks (Gasterosteidae). Environmental Biology of Fishes 6:105–109.

Zar, J. H. 1974. Biostatistical analysis. Prentice-Hall, Englewood Cliffs, New Jersey, USA.

American Fisheries Society Symposium 1:162–174, 1987

Oocyte Development in Striped Bass: Factors Influencing Estimates of Age at Maturity[1]

JENNIFER L. SPECKER, DAVID L. BERLINSKY, AND HAROLD D. BIBB

Department of Zoology, University of Rhode Island, Kingston, Rhode Island 02881, USA

JOHN F. O'BRIEN

Rhode Island Division of Fish and Wildlife, West Kingston, Rhode Island 02892, USA

Abstract.—The striped bass *Morone saxatilis* is an anadromous fish capable early in life of adapting to brackish and marine waters and having a potential lifespan surpassing 20 years. From a larger, ongoing study of seasonal changes in oocyte populations of the striped bass ovary, we contribute in this paper detailed information on histological and histochemical properties of oocytes taken in the summer and in the autumn from striped bass caught in nets off Rhode Island and from fish impounded in Cat Cove (salinity, 23–32‰), Massachusetts. Frequency distributions of oocyte diameters were obtained from stained tissue sections examined by light microscopy in order to relate our descriptions to previous studies. Migrant females caught in June contained a distribution of oocytes whose diameters ranged from 0.02 to 0.23 mm, with mode and median at 0.07 mm. Some of the oocytes from ovaries that appeared granular contained ooplasm with cortical vesicles, suggesting that these females had recruited a clutch of oocytes into the pituitary-dependent phase of oocyte growth. Migrant females caught in November were categorized into two groups. The first group was similar to the group in June in which oocytes were invisible to the unaided eye; oocyte diameters ranged from 0.02 to 0.17 mm, with mode and median at 0.07 mm. The second group contained a distribution of oocytes ranging in diameter from 0.02 to 0.36 mm, with a mode at 0.07 mm and a median at 0.08 mm; granule-filled vacuoles appeared at the periphery of oocytes that were 0.22–0.36 mm in diameter. The histochemistry of ovaries from striped bass at Cat Cove suggests that the oocytes of these females undergo the same developmental processes as those in migrant female striped bass. Variability among available estimates of age at maturity for female striped bass was examined.

Maturity schedules derived for female striped bass *Morone saxatilis* are quite variable. The proportion of age-class IV females judged to be sexually mature range from 0 to 97%; estimates of the proportion of mature age-class V females range from 17 to 100% (Figure 1). These differences can be important because the estimated proportion of spawning stock at each age affects the predicted outcome that fishing pressure will have on the population and, consequently, influences management policy (Anonymous 1980; Goodyear 1984; Goodyear et al. 1985).

Discrepancies among the seven available maturity schedules may reflect true differences between stocks, artifactual differences due to the application of dissimilar criteria, or a combination of these two probable sources of variability. To make clear the difficulties of deriving a uniform maturity schedule for all female striped bass, we begin with a brief review of their life history and the known elements of their reproductive cycle. Currently available maturity schedules are reviewed in terms of the stock under study and the criteria used to discern mature from immature females. Because measurements of oocyte diameters have been used as a major indicator of sexual maturity, the available information about oocyte growth during the annual reproductive cycle is presented. Finally, we address the need for more precise criteria by which to evaluate sexual maturity by presenting detailed information on the histology and histochemistry of ovaries collected from impounded fish and migrant fish collected in the summer and in the autumn. This work is in progress and is part of our larger effort to discover early indicators of the onset of sexual maturity in striped bass and to characterize oocyte development in mature females throughout the year.

Life History

The migratory range of the striped bass originally extended the length of the Atlantic coast of North America from the Gulf of St. Lawrence to

---

[1]We dedicate this paper to our friend Charles E. Wilde, Jr., Professor and Chair of Zoology, University of Rhode Island, on the occasion of his retirement.

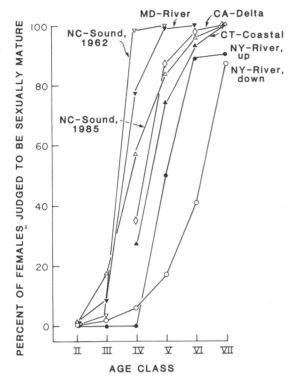

FIGURE 1.—Estimates of maturity schedules for female striped bass. Data are from collections taken in Albemarle Sound, North Carolina (NC-Sound, 1985: Harris et al. 1985; NC-Sound, 1962: Lewis 1962), the Potomac River, Maryland (MD-River: Wilson et al. 1975), the Sacramento–San Joaquin delta system, California (CA-Delta: Scofield 1931), the coastal waters, Connecticut (CT-Coastal: Merriman 1941), and two locations on the Hudson River, New York (NY-River, up and NY-River, down: McLaren et al. 1981).

the Gulf of Mexico (Merriman 1941). The population introduced on the Pacific coast extends at least from Los Angeles to the Columbia River (Scofield 1931; Chadwick 1967). The major spawning grounds are the Roanoke River in North Carolina, the tributaries of the Chesapeake Bay in Virginia and Maryland, the Hudson River in New York, and the Sacramento–San Joaquin delta system of California. The major stocks of migratory striped bass spawn between April and June (Setzler et al. 1980). Juveniles are quite adaptable to brackish water and seawater shortly after hatching (Doroshev 1970; Lal et al. 1977). Until the end of their second year, juvenile striped bass seem to remain within their natal freshwater or estuarine system (Vladykov and Wallace 1938; Merriman 1941; Raney 1952; Mansueti 1961). At least on the Atlantic coast, the male striped bass

tend to remain on the coast near their natal and spawning grounds even after they mature (Raney 1952), whereas female striped bass tend to migrate much greater distances than males (Merriman 1941; Raney 1952). Both sexes remain near the coast even during longer migrations. Striped bass can be quite long-lived, reaching, in one known occasion, 30 years (Merriman 1941) and attaining weights of greater than 45 kg.

The migrations of striped bass in the Chesapeake Bay, Hudson River, and Sacramento–San Joaquin delta stocks do not seem to be closely tied to reproductive activity (Merriman 1941; Raney 1952; Mansueti 1961; Chadwick 1967). In fact, Vladykov and Wallace (1952) concluded from their tagging studies of striped bass in the Chesapeake Bay that most of the stock remains in the bay and does not undertake coastal migrations. In the Hudson River, there is a population of striped bass that overwinters prior to spawning in late spring (Raney et al. 1954; Clark 1968). Clearly, migration into the marine environment is not a necessary prerequisite to spawning, since striped bass impounded in the Santee–Cooper Reservoir in South Carolina are known to spawn (Scruggs 1957). There is also some indication that striped bass are capable of spawning in brackish water as well as fresh water (Scofield 1931; Setzler et al. 1980).

Maturity Schedules

Scofield (1931) sampled fish at the spawning grounds of the Sacramento delta system. These west coast striped bass are known to undergo annual migrations (Chadwick 1967). Scofield (1931) measured the diameters of about 200 oocytes from 150 to 200 fish for each month of the year, around 205,000 oocyte diameters altogether. He preserved ovarian tissue in 10% formalin and the oocytes that he measured were those that floated free from midsections of the ovary following mechanical teasing of the ovarian tissue. In this way, Scofield identified two populations of oocytes. He found an ever-present population whose mean diameter and mode was 0.125 mm and whose maximum was 0.29 mm; these he called immature oocytes. He found that a second population of oocytes seemed to grow larger than 0.29 mm in diameter beginning in January. By May these oocytes had a diameter whose mode was about 0.8 mm and by June the mode was about 1.4 mm. There were no intermediate-sized oocytes in these fish in the final 2 months before spawning.

Merriman (1941) caught migrant striped bass off the south coast of New England. This migrant population consisted primarily of females whose predominant origin was probably Chesapeake Bay (Setzler et al. 1980; Fabrizio 1985). The migratory component of the Chesapeake Bay striped bass tends to be mostly females age-class II and older (Kohlenstein 1981) with the larger females migrating farther north (Mansueti 1961). Merriman (1941) evaluated the reproductive condition of 109 female striped bass caught between April and November. Of these, he fixed tissue from 46 in Bouin's, stained them with hematoxylin and eosin, and estimated oocyte diameter using an ocular micrometer. The other 63 ovaries were preserved in 10% formalin. Samples from the midsection of these preserved ovaries were macerated and the oocytes that floated free were measured using a dissecting microscope with an ocular micrometer. Merriman concluded that the two methods gave him similar results, but the comparison is not available. Merriman identified two populations of oocytes. The diameters of the first averaged 0.07 mm and were as large as 0.18 mm. Ovaries which contained only this population were designated immature. The diameters of the second population of oocytes averaged 0.22 mm with a maximum at 0.58 mm. Merriman designated ovaries containing both populations as mature.

Lewis (1962) took his ovarian fragments from the commercial catch of a striped bass population in Albemarle Sound, North Carolina (salinity range from 0.5 to 5‰). From June to December, this population consists primarily of sexually immature striped bass which have never spawned and which probably never left the sound; from December to May, these "resident" females are joined by repeat spawners probably from the offshore migratory population (Harrel Johnson, North Carolina Division of Marine Fisheries, personal communication, 1986). Lewis (1962) tabulated both size and appearance of oocytes obtained from a total of 946 female striped bass collected in every month except June. Ovarian tissue was obtained by extracting gonad fragments with ear forceps and the tissue was preserved in 10% formalin. From each fragment of ovarian tissue, at least 100 oocytes were randomly selected and measured on a grid-etched slide with a dissecting microscope (45×) and an ocular micrometer. Lewis described three populations of oocytes. Type-1 oocytes were 0.03–0.23 mm in diameter with a mode at 0.10 mm and were

translucent; these were present in all ovaries. Type-2 oocytes were 0.16–0.30 mm and were opaquely speckled. Type-2 oocytes were present all year but not in all fish. Some type-2 oocytes appeared to develop into type-3 oocytes during the summer. Type-3 oocytes ranged from 0.33–1 mm. These type-3 oocytes grew rapidly in the spring and were found in fish which were at least in age-group III and were greater than 432 mm in length.

Harris et al. (1985) reexamined the striped bass from Albermarle Sound about 20 years after Lewis (1962). In their sample of 177 females, "If the largest type-2 or type-3 ovum found was equal to or greater than the minimum size of ova for a given month the fish was considered mature and expected to spawn the following spring." Although maturity was evaluated somewhat as in Lewis's study (1962), more females were estimated to be mature at an earlier age (Figure 1).

Wilson et al. (1975) examined ovaries from 159 striped bass from the Potomac River spawning stock. Females were classified as mature if their ovaries appeared granulated (analogous to Lewis's type-2 oocytes), enlarged, or spent. In their data set, the mature ovaries accounted for 3.95 to 11.45% of the female's entire body weight; that is, the gonadosomatic index (GSI) of mature females was at least 3.95%.

McLaren et al. (1981) examined ovaries from 479 female striped bass collected from mid-March until late June in the Hudson River between river kilometers 11 and 81, measured from the mouth. The migratory behavior of the Hudson River striped bass seems to differ from that of fish from the Chesapeake Bay in that both females and males might leave the river after spawning but most remain near the river mouth (McLaren et al. 1981). The criterion used to designate a female as mature ultimately was a ratio of ovarian weight to body weight greater than 1:70; that is, a GSI greater than 1.43%. This criterion was based on the distributions of GSIs among fish classified, from visual inspection of the ovary, as obviously mature and among fish classified as obviously immature. After the criterion was determined, the obviously mature and immature fish were reclassified and the fish whose stage of maturity had been indeterminable were classified.

Oocyte Growth and Development

Only one complete annual cycle of oocyte growth has been documented for striped bass (Scofield 1931). This complete cycle, along with the other partial cycles described, generally suggests that oocyte growth occurs from late fall through spring (Figure 2). Oocyte growth appears to differ from one geographical location to another, although these differences may reflect different methods of obtaining measurements (e.g., from fresh or fixed material or after alternative types of fixation). Significantly, reproductive maturity in female striped bass is now primarily evaluated on the basis of oocyte size and this criterion would seem from figure 2 to be applicable during only part of the year.

Wallace and Selman (1981) described four general stages of oocyte development among teleosts. These general stages or phases are distinguished by specific differences in physiological events and the regulation of these events. Within these broad stages are specific stages that have been used in devising staging systems such as that adapted by Groman (1982) for striped bass from a previous

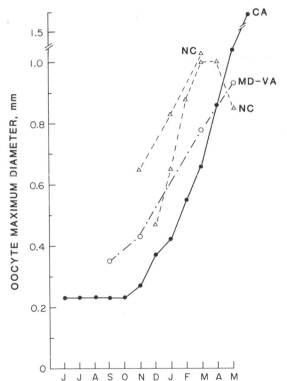

FIGURE 2.—Available measurements of annual changes in the diameter of the largest oocytes in mature striped bass. Data are taken from Lewis (1962) for North Carolina (left NC curve), Scofield (1931) for California (CA), Jackson and Tiller (1952) for Maryland–Virginia (MD–VA), and Harris et al. (1985) for North Carolina (right NC curve).

system for Gulf menhaden *Brevoortia patronus* (Combs 1969).

Only the first of these general stages is independent of the pituitary; the rest require gonadotropin to proceed. The teleostean oocyte initially contains little cytoplasm and the nucleus contains a single nucleolus. During the gonadotropin-independent primary growth phase, multiple nucleoli appear at the periphery of the nucleus (germinal vesicle), lampbrush chromosomes become apparent, and basophilic material, possibly ribonucleoprotein particles, accumulates around the germinal vesicle (Wallace and Selman 1981).

During the first of the three gonadotropin-dependent stages, the yolk vesicles form. Although these structures have been designated yolk vesicles, it is not clear that they play a role in yolk formation. Rather, it has been suggested that they migrate to the periphery of the oocyte where they play a role in the cortical reaction of the ovum at the time of fertilization (Wallace and Selman 1981). Thus these structures are also called cortical alveoli. During true vitellogenesis, the third stage of oocyte growth, oocytes sequester vitellogenin from the maternal circulation. This serum protein contains phosphorus, lipid, carbohydrate, calcium, and iron (de Vlaming et al. 1980) and is the precursor of yolk. In many teleosts, vitellogenin is packaged into granules that eventually fuse into a fluid phase which is surrounded by cytoplasm containing the cortical alveoli. At the onset of the maturation phase, the final stage of oocyte development, the oocyte is nearly full size except for increases due to some variable amount of final water and protein uptake (Wallace and Selman 1985).

Although Groman (1982) has provided photomicrographs depicting stages of striped bass oocyte development based on Combs's (1969) staging system for the Gulf menhaden, no classification system based on detailed histochemistry and physiological correlates now exists for striped bass. In this report, we provide detailed histochemical descriptions of striped bass oocytes contained in ovaries collected in the summer and in the autumn. This study is part of our larger effort to provide criteria for evaluating the reproductive status of female striped bass throughout the year.

Histochemistry of Striped Bass Oocytes

Methods

Sampling and collection.—Striped bass were collected from offshore Rhode Island in June and in October–November (shortened to November in text) of 1985, and were collected from Cat Cove, Massachusetts, in August and November of 1985. From the ocean-caught striped bass at both times of the year, ovaries were selected for further analysis in such a way that at each time half ($N = 5$) appeared granular to the unaided eye and half ($N = 5$) appeared translucent and void of oocytes. Of the striped bass from Cat Cove, most that were caught in June were analyzed ($N = 5$) and the only two females caught in November were both included in our analyses.

The striped bass at Cat Cove consist of two groups of fish of Hudson River origin received from the consulting firm of Stone and Webster: one group from the 1978 year class was transferred to Cat Cove as 1-year-olds and a second group from the 1979 year class was transferred as 3-month-olds. Cat Cove is a 3.6-hectare tidal flat contained by a dike and maintained by the Massachusetts Division of Marine Fisheries. The salinity of Cat Cove ranges from 23 to 32‰ and the temperature ranges from 0 to 27°C over the year (Paul Diodati, Massachusetts Division of Marine Fisheries, personal communication). All striped bass from Cat Cove were caught with a purse seine and were transferred within 5 min to a holding tank in the on-site laboratory. The fish were stunned by a blow to the head, blood was collected for other analyses, total lengths and weights were measured, and the gonads were removed. In November, the fish were anesthetized in 2-phenoxyethanol (0.03%) for about 5 min prior to blood collection.

The striped bass sampled in the coastal waters off Rhode Island were captured as part of a stock identification project conducted by the Rhode Island Division of Fish and Wildlife. Striped bass were collected with floating pound nets and anchored gill nets. Within 6 h of capture, the fish were brought to the laboratory where they were weighed and their fork-lengths were measured. The gonads were removed through a mid-ventral incision and their weights and lengths were recorded. Age was determined for each striped bass by examination of scales collected from above the lateral line (Raney 1952).

Histology.—Ovarian tissue for histological and histochemical analyses was always removed from the midlength of the ovary even though we confirmed an earlier report (Scofield 1931) that oocyte development in the striped bass ovary is uniform throughout its length. Tissue was cut from the ovaries in a radial fashion that resulted in the collection of tissue from the ovarian surface into the lumen. Standard histological procedures were used (Humason 1979). Briefly, the tissues were fixed in Bouin's solution for a minimum of 3 d, dehydrated in a graded series of alcohols, and cleared in methyl salicylate prior to paraffin infiltration. The tissue was sectioned at 10 μm using a rotary microtome and stained with hematoxylin and eosin.

The presence of carbohydrates, specifically acid mucopolysaccharides, was visualized by the alcian blue method for carbohydrates with free acidic groups (Humason 1979). The presence of proteins was indicated through the use of the mercuric bromphenol blue method for staining proteins and peptides (Humason 1979).

The diameters of all germ cells in histological sections of ovaries from these fish were measured in three fields either directly with an ocular micrometer and a binocular microscope (200×) or indirectly from camera lucida drawings which gave the same results. Diameters of approximately 150 oocytes were obtained for each fish. The smallest interval we could measure was 0.005 mm.

Frequency Distributions of Oocyte Diameters

Distributions of oocyte diameters varied with the time of year. Fish caught in June from offshore Rhode Island contained oocytes that ranged in diameter from 0.02 to 0.23 mm, with both the mode and the median at 0.07 mm (Figure 3). Fish caught from offshore Rhode Island in November were separated into two categories on the basis of the sizes of oocytes present in the ovaries (Figure 3). The first of these was made up of fish that contained oocytes 0.02–0.17 mm in diameter, with both mode and median at 0.07 mm. The second category comprised fish whose ovaries contained oocytes ranging in diameter from 0.02 to 0.36 mm, with a mode of 0.07 mm and a median of 0.08 mm. While the distribution of oocyte diameters in this second category was continuous in the material we examined, its appearance gives some suggestion of bimodality (Figure 3).

The diameters of oocytes from striped bass caught in August at Cat Cove ranged from 0.02 to 0.21 mm with a median of 0.10 mm (Figure 3). In November, the distribution of oocyte sizes from Cat Cove fish ranged from 0.02 to 0.45 mm. This distribution was discontinuous and more clearly bimodal than that from fish taken from offshore Rhode Island.

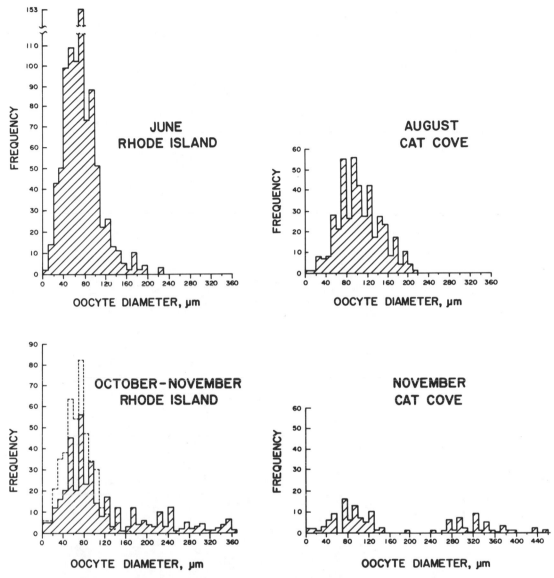

FIGURE 3.—Frequency distributions of oocyte diameters measured in histological sections of ovaries from striped bass caught in coastal waters off Rhode Island in June and October–November 1985 and from striped bass caught in Cat Cove, Massachusetts, in August and November 1985. Dashed line in the distribution for Rhode Island, October–November, represents those ovaries without visible oocytes; solid line represents ovaries in which oocytes were visible; this distinction is not made in other panels.

Striped Bass from Offshore Rhode Island: June

The smallest oocytes included in our counts and measurements were approximately 0.02 mm in diameter and contained a nucleus that was large (roughly 0.01 mm in diameter) relative to the diameter of the cell. These small oocytes contained scant cytoplasm that was intensely basophilic and homogeneous in appearance (Figure 4A). Most oocytes of this and slightly larger sizes contained one or two nucleoli, although larger numbers were present in some oocytes in this size group. Oocytes of this type correspond to those desribed as stage II by Groman (1982).

In oocytes that were somewhat larger and that measured approximately 0.04–0.05 mm in diameter, multiple nucleoli were present and appeared to be distributed randomly in the nucleus. In

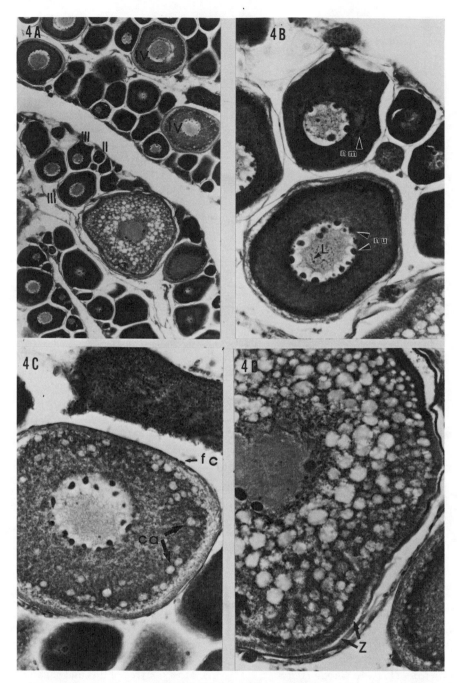

FIGURE 4.—Oocytes from the ovary of a striped bass caught in June off the coast of Rhode Island; sections are stained with hematoxylin and eosin. All stages are those of Groman (1982) and are indicated by Roman numerals. **A:** Various stages of oocytes present in an ovary in June. **B:** Stage-III oocytes. In the larger and more highly developed stage-III oocyte, an intensely basophilic ring is located near the periphery of the oocyte, and lampbrush chromosomes (L) are present within the nucleus. Several nucleoli (nu) may be seen near the nuclear membrane. In the smaller stage-III oocyte, ''nuage'' material (nm) is present. **C:** Stage-IV oocyte shortly after yolk vesicles, or cortical alveoli (ca), have begun to form. Note the flattened nuclei of follicle cells (fc). **D:** Late stage-IV oocyte; Z marks the zona radiata. Panel A is 26× magnification; panels B, C, and D are 106×.

oocytes of this size, the nucleus stained less darkly in hematoxylin and eosin and in bromphenol blue; darkly staining filamentous strands of chromatin occasionally were distributed in the lightly staining karyoplasm in favorable material. Although "nuage" material that may comprise ribonucleoprotein particles (Wallace and Selman 1981) sometimes was seen in perinuclear locations, the basophilic ooplasm in these oocytes was also generally homogeneous in appearance.

Considerable differences could be observed between oocytes ranging in diameter from 0.06 to 0.10 mm and those of the previous two size groups. Whereas the ooplasm continued to stain uniformly basophilic, the nuclei had grown considerably, attaining diameters of roughly 0.04 mm and had become true germinal vesicles as a result of their large size. The nucleoli in these oocytes were more numerous (approximately 11 per plane when sectioned through the center) and most had migrated to the periphery of the nuclear membrane, although some still maintained a central location. Among the other differences between oocytes of this group and those described earlier were the presence of lampbrush chromosomes that were quite apparent in germinal vesicles of favorable material, the much more obvious presence of follicular cells that surrounded the oocytes, and the presence of an intensely basophilic ring near the periphery of the ooplasm (Figure 4B). Although follicle cells were present around the smaller oocytes described earlier, they became much more apparent with increasing oocyte size. Oocytes of both these types are similar to those referred to as stage III by Groman (1982).

The types of oocytes that have been described to this point were present in all ovaries from fish caught during June and were in the gonadotropin-independent phase of growth as described by Wallace and Selman (1981). In some ovaries, additional types of larger oocytes were also observed (Figure 4C, D). These larger oocytes were seen in all ovaries with oocytes visible to the unaided eye, and were entering the gonadotropin-dependent phase of growth (Wallace and Selman 1981). These oocytes ranged in diameter from approximately 0.12 to 0.22 mm. The germinal vesicle was considerably larger, averaging approximately 0.05 mm in diameter, and stained less basophilically than at earlier stages. Nearly all the nucleoli were located along the internal surface of the nuclear membrane.

Striped Bass from Offshore Rhode Island: October–November

Ovaries from fish caught during the autumn tended to fall into one of two groups based on the oocytes they contained. The first group contained oocytes which were indistinguishable from the types previously described for the fish caught in June. However, the largest oocytes in this group were measured at 0.17 mm in diameter rather than 0.22 mm as in June.

The second group of ovaries seen in autumn fish were distinguished from the first by the obvious presence of much larger oocytes (0.22–0.36 mm in diameter) in addition to the types previously described (Figure 5A). The germinal vesicle had undergone considerable development, attaining a diameter of 0.09 mm, and lampbrush chromosomes could be readily visualized in a number of these. After oocytes in this group had begun the production of cortical alveoli, the ooplasm began to stain positively for acid mucopolysaccharides with alcian blue (late stage IV), and during this period of cortical alveolar growth and development, alcian blue staining became increasingly intense. Cortical alveoli also appear to have increased in diameter during this period (to 0.015 mm). As has been discussed by Wallace and Selman (1981), these cortical alveoli appeared to make up two different populations. One group contained granular structures that stained with metanil yellow, whereas the other contained more amorphous material that stained intensely with alcian blue (Figure 5D).

Striped Bass from Cat Cove: August and November

The types of oocytes previously described in fish caught offshore during June were also seen in fish caught at Cat Cove during August (Figure 5B).

Oocytes present in fish caught at Cat Cove in November were similar to those present in fish caught off the Rhode Island coast during the same month (Figure 5C, D). Although the largest of the oocytes present in the Cat Cove fish were larger than their counterparts in offshore fish, the histological appearance of oocytes in the two groups of November fish was not greatly different.

Age-Class and Ovarian Status

We chose ovaries for inclusion in this study based on the visibility of oocytes on gross inspection. In June, the maximum diameters of oocytes present in ovaries without macroscopically visible

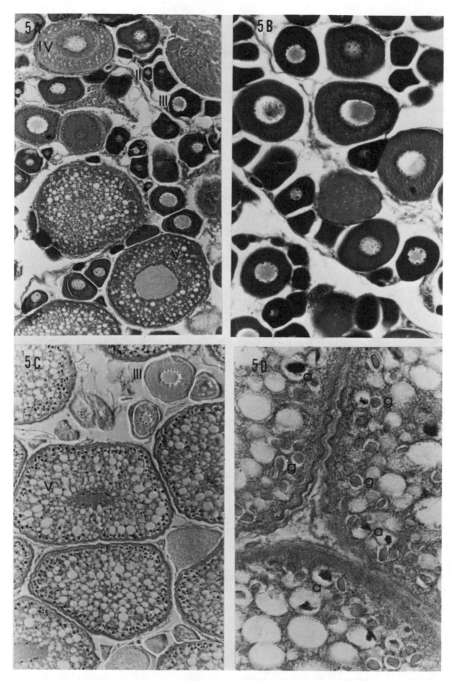

FIGURE 5.—**A:** Oocytes from the ovary of a striped bass caught in November 1985 off the coast of Rhode Island. Oocytes of stages II, III, and IV are present. (Hematoxylin and eosin.) **B:** Oocytes from the ovary of a striped bass caught in June 1985 at Cat Cove. (Bromphenol blue.) **C:** Oocytes from the ovary of a striped bass caught in November 1985 at Cat Cove. The large stage-V oocytes have stained with alcian blue, while the stage-III oocytes have not. (Alcian blue and metanil yellow.) **D:** Area near the peripheries of three oocytes from a striped bass caught in November 1985 at Cat Cove. Some cortical alveoli contain granules (g) that stain with metanil yellow while others contain a more amorphous material (a) that stains with alcian blue. Panels A, B, and C are 26× magnification; panel D is 106×.

oocytes ranged from 0.10 to 0.13 mm (Table 1). The maximum diameters of oocytes in ovaries that appeared granulated ranged from 0.13 to 0.22 mm. This suggests that deposition of opaque material begins in oocytes that reach about 0.13 mm in diameter. Oocytes with opaque material ranged in diameter from 0.12 to 0.22 mm in the material we examined. Our histochemical analyses showed that the cytoplasm of these oocytes does not stain uniformly, as earlier developmental stages of oocytes do, and that vesicles appear in the ooplasm. The presence of these yolk vesicles or cortical alveoli suggests further that ovaries containing macroscopically visible oocytes in June are recruiting a clutch of oocytes into the gonadotropin-dependent phase of growth.

In our analysis of ovaries from coastal migrants in June, females with oocytes entering the pituitary-dependent growth phase were from age-classes V to X, whereas females without such oocytes were from age-classes IV and V.

In October–November, ovaries of coastal migrants without macroscopically visible oocytes contained oocytes whose largest diameters ranged from 0.09 to 0.16 mm (Table 1). The female striped bass sampled were from age-classes III and IV. Ovaries with visible oocytes had oocytes whose largest diameters ranged from 0.28 to 0.37 mm, and the ovaries came from females in age-classes V–VII.

Discussion

The ovary can be usefully described as following one of three patterns of dynamic organization (Marza 1938). The pattern of synchronous oocyte development is exemplified by the anadromous *Oncorhynchus* species of salmon and the catadromous eels (Anguillidae). In these fish, which spawn once and die, all oocytes grow and ovulate in a single wave. In ovaries that undergo an asynchronous pattern of development, all stages of oocyte development are present and no domi-

TABLE 1.—Vital statistics for female striped bass examined for ovarian histochemistry in 1985; nd = not done.

Date	Macroscopically visible oocytes	Age (years)	Weight (kg)	Length (mm)	Ovary weight (g)	Maximum oocyte diameter (mm)
		Offshore Rhode Island: June				
11 Jun	No	4	2.3	550	8.8	0.11
12 Jun	No	?	2.0	540	9.1	0.13
12 Jun	No	?	2.3	570	8.4	0.10
6 Jun	No	5	2.5	575	10.7	0.12
21 Jun	No	5	2.3	580	9.3	0.11
6 Jun	Yes	5	1.8	515	14.4	0.22
10 Jun	Yes	5	2.0	570	13.7	0.19
4 Jun	Yes	5	1.8	530	10.1	0.18
21 Jun	Yes	6	3.5	690	20.4	0.13
24 Jun	Yes	10	7.2	845	94.5	0.20
		Offshore Rhode Island: October–November				
4 Nov	No	3	1.5	495	5.0	0.09
18 Oct	No	4	3.0	610	12.6	0.16
4 Nov	No	4	2.5	565	10.4	0.16
4 Nov	No	4	2.5	565	9.1	0.12
4 Nov	No	4	1.8	520	8.4	0.10
1 Nov	Yes	5	4.0	670	55.4	0.31
21 Oct	Yes	6?	4.0	677	33.8	0.28
1 Nov	Yes	6	5.0	700	76.6	0.28
21 Oct	Yes	6	5.8	760	64.0	0.32
21 Oct	Yes	7	7.0	805	79.3	0.37
		Cat Cove: August				
28 Aug	nd	6	1.8	550	21.5	0.20
28 Aug	nd	6	2.2	590	18.3	0.18
28 Aug	nd	6	1.7	530	16.4	0.21
28 Aug	nd	7	2.5	605	17.9	0.18
28 Aug	nd	7	1.9	555	22.8	0.20
		Cat Cove: November				
13 Nov	Yes	7	2.6	600	60.5	0.45
13 Nov	Yes	7	2.7	595	55.9	0.38

nant population which could be called a clutch is apparent. The third pattern, group synchrony, is most common among teleosts. Ovaries presenting this dynamic organization contain a heterogeneous population of smaller oocytes and a group of fairly synchronized developing oocytes.

The pattern of oocyte development and growth that is exhibited in the striped bass material we have examined to date is consistent with group synchrony. Most oocytes present in striped bass caught off the Rhode Island coast during June, and at Cat Cove in August, were part of a heterogeneous group of small oocytes (mode = 0.07 mm). These smaller oocytes were present in all the striped bass that we examined and appeared to be in the gonadotropin-independent phase of development. However, among the fish caught in November at both locations were those whose ovaries contained both a heterogeneous group of smaller oocytes and a second group of larger oocytes. Oocytes of this second group were of relatively uniform developmental stages and appeared to be oocytes recruited into the next clutch. On the basis of work completed, it remains unclear whether any of the oocytes examined in this study had begun true vitellogenesis.

Our observations on 20 migrant striped bass are inadequate to propose a new maturity schedule. However, our histochemical identification of oocytes in the cortical alveolar stage suggests that the gonadotropin-dependent phase of growth begins as early as June. We found that ovaries that appeared granular to the unaided eye were those in which oocytes that were forming cortical alveoli (yolk vesicles) first appeared. These oocytes in the cortical alveolar stage fit Lewis's (1962) description of type-2 oocytes.

Overall, given previous criteria which, in part, relied on the gross appearance of oocytes in the ovary, our data at this time tend to match Merriman's (1941) earlier maturity schedule in that most female striped bass were found to contain these growing oocytes beginning during their sixth year (age-class V). We cannot, however, rule out the possibility that more than one year is required for oocytes recruited into pituitary-dependent developmental phases to reach the final maturation phase.

The possibility that striped bass containing Lewis's (1962) type-2 oocytes may not spawn the following spring was first raised by Chadwick (1965). Chadwick (1965) examined striped bass in San Francisco and San Pablo bays using the morphometric and visual criteria proposed by Lewis (1962). He was unable to distinguish mature and immature females as Scofield (1931) had done for those fish collected more than 48 km upstream on the spawning grounds in the Sacramento delta. Instead of observing a simple dichotomy between immature and maturing oocytes in the spring, Chadwick found substantial numbers of females (457–762 mm in length, so age-classes IV–VII: Scofield 1931) whose ovaries in April did not contain oocytes greater than 0.29 mm. Neither Scofield nor Lewis had observed this type of ovary in females near the spawning grounds at that time of year. Given Scofield's (1931) and Lewis's (1962) findings that oocytes grew from 0.3 mm to about 1.0 mm beginning in early October (Roanoke River) or December (Sacramento delta) until May, Chadwick proposed that "these fish are at least a year away from maturation [and] some bass must develop type-2 eggs more than a year before spawning." Scofield, in fact, had aborted his attempt to distinguish "immature and maturing" oocytes in ovaries from fish taken in San Francisco and San Pablo bays and had concluded that "[in the] spawning migrants [found in the bays] the ovaries . . . had not ripened sufficiently to make possible an accurate determination of the degree of maturity."

Finally, a comparison of oocyte growth in striped bass caught offshore with striped bass from Cat Cove suggests that oocyte growth can occur at different rates in females in different locations. The striped bass impounded in Cat Cove appeared to contain a clutch of oocytes in November whose overall diameters were slightly larger than oocytes in the females collected off Rhode Island. The potential capability of striped bass contained in tidal ponds to undergo complete reproductive cycles merits further attention.

The migratory behavior of striped bass and differences in the migratory behavior among populations of striped bass (Setzler et al. 1980) both contribute to difficulties in calculating good estimates of age at maturity. Nearness of sampling to the spawning grounds probably greatly affects estimates of age at maturity. Overall, maturity schedules should seem to be more accelerated if fish are sampled near the spawning grounds than if they are sampled during migration.

Merriman's (1941) maturity schedule is the one used in current models of striped bass population dynamics that affect management policies (Goodyear et al. 1985). Only Merriman has composed a maturity schedule for coastal migrants. However, Merriman examined only 109 females and many of these seem to have been collected during the time of year (postspawning to November) when it would have been most difficult to judge maturity from size frequencies of oocytes. The development of criteria that could be used equally well at all times of year to assess sexual maturity awaits full descriptions of the stages of oocyte development and seasonal changes in the composition of the ovary. Potential real differences in maturity schedules among the major east coast stocks warrant further consideration.

Acknowledgments

We acknowledge and appreciate the efforts and cooperation of Phil Coates, Paul Diodati, and their staff from the Massachusetts Division of Marine Fisheries; the efforts and cooperation of the Rhode Island Division of Fish and Wildlife; the advice of Mary Fabrizio-Wilde, Saul Saila, Howard Bern, and Graham Young; the expertise of Timothy Whitesel; and the skillful assistance of Steven Parker and Dung My Nguyen. This work was supported by the National Sea Grant College Program under grant NA85AA-D-SG094 (to J.L.S.) and by the California Department of Fish and Game Striped Bass Project (contract 85/86 C-1184 to H. A. Bern, University of California).

References

Anonymous. 1980. Interstate fisheries management plan for the striped bass of the Atlantic coast from Maine to North Carolina. Atlantic States Marine Fisheries Commission, Washington, D.C., USA.

Chadwick, H. D. 1965. Determination of sexual maturity in female striped bass (Roccus saxatilis). California Fish and Game 51:202–206.

Chadwick, H. D. 1967. Recent migrations of the Sacramento–San Joaquin striped bass population. Transactions of the American Fisheries Society 96:327–342.

Clark, J. 1968. Seasonal movements of striped bass contingents of Long Island Sound and the New York Bight. Transactions of the American Fisheries Society 97:320–343.

Combs, R. M. 1969. Embryogenesis, histology and organology of the ovary of Brevoortia patronus. Gulf Research Reports 2:333–434.

de Vlaming, V. L., H. S. Wiley, G. Delahunty, and R. A. Wallace. 1980. Goldfish (Carassius auratus) vitellogenin: induction, isolation, properties and relationship to yolk proteins. Comparative Biochemistry and Physiology B, Comparative Biochemistry 67:613–623.

Doroshev, S. I. 1970. Biological features of the eggs, larvae and young of the striped bass [Roccus saxatilis (Walbaum)] in connection with the problem of its acclimatization in the USSR. Journal of Ichthyology 10:235–248.

Fabrizio, M. C. 1985. Discrimination and classification of striped bass stocks. Doctoral dissertation. University of Rhode Island, Kingston, Rhode Island, USA.

Goodyear, C. P. 1984. Analysis of potential yield per recruit for striped bass produced in Chesapeake Bay. North American Journal of Fisheries Management 4:488–496.

Goodyear, C. P., J. E. Cohen, and S. W. Christensen. 1985. Maryland striped bass: recruitment declining below replacement. Transactions of the American Fisheries Society 114:146–151.

Groman, D. B. 1982. Histology of the striped bass. American Fisheries Society Monograph 3.

Harris, R. C., Jr., B. L. Burns, H. B. Johnson, and R. A. Rulifson. 1985. An investigation of size, age, and sex of North Carolina striped bass. Completion Report, Project AFC-18 to U.S. National Marine Fisheries Service, Washington, D.C., USA.

Humason, G. L. 1979. Animal tissue techniques, 4th edition. W. H. Freeman, San Francisco, California, USA.

Jackson, H. W., and R. E. Tiller. 1952. Preliminary observations on spawning potential in the striped bass (Roccus saxatilis Walbaum). Maryland Department of Research and Education, Publication 93, Annapolis, Maryland, USA.

Kohlenstein, L. C. 1981. On the proportion of the Chesapeake Bay stock of striped bass that migrates into the coastal fishery. Transactions of the American Fisheries Society 110:168–179.

Lal, K., R. Lasker, and A. Kuljis. 1977. Acclimation and rearing of striped bass larvae in seawater. California Fish and Game 63:210–218.

Lewis, R. M. 1962. Sexual maturity as determined from ovum diameters in striped bass from North Carolina. Transactions of the American Fisheries Society 91:279–282.

Mansueti, R. J. 1961. Age, growth, and movements of the striped bass, Roccus saxatilis, taken in size-selective fishing gear in Maryland. Chesapeake Science 2:9–36.

Marza, V. D. 1938. Histophysiologie de l'ovogenese. Hermann, Paris, France. (Not seen; cited in Wallace and Selman 1981.)

McLaren, J. B., J. C. Cooper, T. B. Hoff, and V. Lander. 1981. Movements of Hudson River striped bass. Transactions of the American Fisheries Society 110:158–167.

Merriman, D. 1941. Studies of the striped bass (Roccus saxatilis) of the Atlantic coast. U.S. Fish and Wildlife Service Fishery Bulletin 50(35):1–77.

Raney, E. C. 1952. The life history of the striped bass, Roccus saxatilis (Walbaum). Bulletin of the Bingham Oceanographic Collection, Yale University 14(1):5–97.

Raney, E. C., W. S. Woolcott, and A. G. Mehring. 1954. Migratory pattern and racial structure of Atlantic coast striped bass. Transactions of the North American Wildlife Conference 19:376–396.

Scofield, E. C. 1931. The striped bass of California

(Roccus lineatus). California Division of Fish and Game, Fish Bulletin 29:1–82.

Scruggs, G. D., Jr. 1957. Reproduction of resident striped bass in Santee–Cooper Reservoir, South Carolina. Transactions of the American Fisheries Society 85:144–159.

Setzler, E. M., and eight coauthors. 1980. Synopsis of biological data on striped bass, *Morone saxatilis* (Walbaum). NOAA (National Oceanic and Atmospheric Administration) Technical Report NMFS (National Marine Fisheries Service) Circular 433.

Vladykov, V. D., and D. H. Wallace. 1938. Is the striped bass *(Roccus lineatus)* of Chesapeake Bay a migratory fish? Transactions of the American Fisheries Society 67:67–86.

Vladykov, V. D., and D. H. Wallace. 1952. Studies of striped bass, *Roccus saxatilis* (Walbaum), with special reference to the Chesapeake Bay region during 1936–1938. Bulletin of the Bingham Oceanographic Collection, Yale University 14(1):132–177.

Wallace, R. A., and K. Selman. 1981. Cellular and dynamic aspects of oocyte growth in teleosts. American Zoologist 21:325–343.

Wallace, R. A., and K. Selman. 1985. Major protein changes during vitellogenesis and maturation of *Fundulus* oocytes. Developmental Biology 110:492–498.

Wilson, J. S., R. P. Morgan II, P. W. Jones, H. R. Lunsford, Jr., J. Lawson, and S. Murphy. 1975. Potomac River fisheries study: striped bass spawning stock assessment. University of Maryland, Chesapeake Biological Laboratory, UMCESS 76-14 CBL, Solomons, Maryland, USA.

American Fisheries Society Symposium 1:175–190, 1987

Osmoregulatory and Ionoregulatory Changes and Associated Mortalities during the Transition of Maturing American Eels to a Marine Environment

J.-D. Dutil

Ministére de Pêches et des Océans, C. P. 1000, 850, route de la Mer
Mont-Joli, Québec G5H 3Z4, Canada

M. Besner

Institut National de la Recherche Scientifique, 310 des Ursulines
Rimouski, Québec G5L 3A1, Canada

S. D. McCormick[1]

Department of Fisheries and Oceans, Biological Station
St. Andrews, New Brunswick E0G 2X0, Canada

Abstract.—Serum Na^+, Cl^-, and K^+ concentrations, branchial chloride cells and Na^+,K^+-ATPase activity, and pollutant levels were examined in maturing American eels *Anguilla rostrata* migrating down the St. Lawrence River estuary. The purpose was to investigate physiological changes that normally occur during seaward migration and their reversibility, and to determine the cause(s) of heavy annual mortalities of eels that occur in the freshwater portion of the St. Lawrence. Serum ion and osmotic concentrations were slightly lower in healthy eels collected in fresh water than in salt water. Freshwater eels and saltwater eels kept 96 h in salt- and fresh water, respectively, had similar concentrations as controls. The number of chloride cells increased during the transition to the marine environment, within 96 h in eels collected in fresh water and transferred to salt water, but the number of chloride cells did not regress in eels collected in salt water and transferred to fresh water for 96 h. Gill Na^+,K^+-ATPase activity increased as the eels moved to salt water in the estuary. Freshwater eels kept in salt water 96 h also showed a marked increase, but saltwater eels maintained high though reduced gill Na^+,K^+-ATPase activity when kept 96 h in fresh water. Diseased eels had much lower serum ion and osmotic concentrations than healthy eels, but they recovered to near normal concentrations when kept 96 h in salt water. Branchial chloride cells and Na^+,K^+-ATPase activity followed the same trend as in freshwater eels. Diseased eels had similar heavy metal and pesticide loads as healthy eels. Pathological conditions of their gills, however, suggested that diseased eels migrated through highly polluted areas. The results indicate that maturing eels in fresh water possess significant hypoosmoregulatory ability. Increases in chloride cells and gill Na^+,K^+-ATPase activity occur upon exposure to salt water. Maturing American eels may rely on two different mechanisms to maintain relatively constant serum ion and osmotic concentrations as they migrate through the estuaries. Mortalities are associated with ion loss in fresh water, perhaps as a result of increased permeability of the branchial membrane due to damage caused by pollution in the St. Lawrence.

Physiological control of osmotic balance in teleosts has been the focus of much research particularly on those species migrating between fresh and salt water (reviewed by Evans 1979, 1980). Teleosts maintain the osmotic concentrations of their bodies within narrow limits as they migrate between fresh water and salt water, Na^+ and Cl^- contributing most to the limited changes in the ion content of the blood (Parry 1966). Members of the family Anguillidae are no exception (Boucher-Firly 1935; Sharratt et al. 1964; Munroe and Poluhowich 1974; Schmidt-Nielsen and Renfro 1975); migrating eels face the problems of penetration of salts and osmotic loss of water as they move into the marine environment. Transfer of eels from fresh water to salt water causes the eels to ingest salt water (Smith 1930, 1932; Keys 1933), causes a decrease in the production of urine (Sharratt et al. 1964; Schmidt-Nielsen and Renfro 1975), and causes an increase in the volume of water reabsorbed passively (preadaptive in maturing *Anguilla japonica*), following NaCl transport through the intestinal mucosa (Oidé and Utida 1967a, 1967b; Utida et al. 1967; Skadhauge 1969). Monovalent ions are not excreted renally (Evans

[1]Present address: Department of Zoology, University of California, Berkeley, California 94720, USA.

1979), and an extrarenal structure is needed to maintain a constant osmotic concentration.

Gill chloride cells and Na^+,K^+-ATPase have been widely implicated in the branchial mechanisms of osmotic regulation. Chloride cells are located on the primary lamellae of the gills (reviewed by Laurent 1984). Transfer of eels to salt water results in the proliferation of gill chloride cells (Shirai and Utida 1970; Doyle and Epstein 1972), an increase in gill Na^+,K^+-ATPase activity (Epstein et al. 1967, 1971; Kamiya and Utida 1968, 1969; Bornancin and DeRenzis 1972; Butler and Carmichael 1972; Sargent and Thomson 1974; Sargent et al. 1975), and the formation of accessory cells (Dunel-Erb and Laurent 1980; Laurent and Dunel 1980) and leaky junctions (Sardet et al. 1979, 1980). Sodium ions (Mizuhira et al. 1970), Cl^- ions (Petrik 1968), and gill Na^+,K^+-ATPase (Mizuhira et al. 1970; Maetz and Bornancin 1975; Karnaky et al. 1976) are localized in association with the network of tubular smooth-surfaced endoplasmic reticulum of the chloride cells in saltwater-acclimated eels.

Increases in the number of branchial chloride cells and in activity of branchial Na^+,K^+-ATPase also occur in *Anguilla anguilla* and *A. japonica* in fresh water coincident with seaward migration but prior to saltwater entry (Utida et al. 1971; Thomson and Sargent 1977). Similar changes accompany the parr–smolt transformation in anadromous salmonids (see reviews by Hoar 1976; Wedemeyer et al. 1980; McCormick and Saunders 1987, this volume). During this transformation, osmoregulatory organs undergo structural and functional changes, while the fish are still in fresh water, that result in increased salinity tolerance. This process is under photoperiodic control (Wedemeyer et al. 1980) and can be triggered by migration (Zaugg et al. 1985) and water quality (Saunders et al. 1983). By analogy, environmental changes may influence the development of osmoregulatory organs prior to or during the downstream migration of eels.

Like most members of the genus *Anguilla*, American eels *A. rostrata* spend most of their life in lakes and rivers. They migrate out of fresh water at the onset of sexual maturation to reach the ocean, spawn, and die. This catadromous migration takes place throughout summer and autumn, and in the St. Lawrence River, Canada, results in heavy mortalities. Hundreds of dead eels are stranded on the shoreline. High mortalities date back to at least 1960. In the bad years of 1972 and 1973, losses were estimated to have been 100 metric tons. This rate has considerably decreased in recent years but losses still take place.

This study examines changes in serum Na^+, Cl^-, and K^+ concentrations, numbers of branchial chloride cells, and Na^+,K^+-ATPase activity that occur in healthy and diseased maturing American eels as they migrate down the St. Lawrence estuary and also in the laboratory following transfer from fresh water to salt water and from salt water to fresh water. The disease is shown to result from damage to the branchial membranes that cause disorders in the ionic and osmotic regulatory performance and in the rate of maturation, and is indicative of the bad conditions that maturing eels face as they migrate in the St. Lawrence.

Methods

The material collected in the period 1981–1985 is examined. Some of the 1981–1982 data have been published (Dutil 1984; Dutil and Lallier 1984). Some American eels were collected in 1983, 1984, and 1985 for histological examination of gills. Those eels collected in 1984 were also examined for heavy metals and pesticide contamination. Finally, Na^+, Cl^-, and K^+ contents and gill Na^+,K^+-ATPase activity were measured in eels collected in 1985.

Stations and collections.—Migrating eels were collected in commercial weirs in the St. Lawrence estuary near St. Nicolas (freshwater site, located 50 km above the highest point of penetration of salt water), and near Kamouraska (saltwater site, located 100 km downstream from the highest point of penetration of salt water) (Figure 1). Periods of sampling changed between locations, St. Nicolas eels being collected earlier than Kamouraska eels in general. The period extended from early August to late October. Conditions were homogeneous horizontally and vertically at St. Nicolas, but the circulation was very complex downstream where temperature and salinity varied horizontally and vertically. Temperature decreased from more than 20°C in mid-August to less than 10°C in mid-October. Salinity ranged between 0‰ at St. Nicolas to about 18–24‰ at Kamouraska. For information on the ion concentrations of the St. Lawrence River, refer to Cossa and Tremblay (1983).

Diseased eels referred to in this study were found exclusively in fresh water, mainly downstream from Lake St. Pierre, and were collected in St. Nicolas. There was no means of recognizing early stages in the disease; diseased eels collected

FIGURE 1.—Location of the collecting sites for American eels in the St. Lawrence River estuary.

in this study were sometimes moribund. They were distinguished from normal eels by their mottled pattern of skin pigmentation, their lack of any reaction to manipulations, their tendency to stay near the surface, and sometimes their incapacity to maintain vertical position as they moved. For details on the history of the disease, see Dutil and Lallier (1984).

Treatments.—Transportation to our laboratory took 15 min from the freshwater site and 2 h from the saltwater site. The eels were transported in river water from St. Nicolas and in moist air from Kamouraska. They were either killed immediately upon their arrival at our laboratory (no treatment) or assigned to one of two treatments: either 4 d in fresh water or 4 d in saltwater (20‰ chloride). The ion content of water in freshwater tanks fluctuated around these values: Na^+, 580 $\mu eq \cdot L^{-1}$; Cl^-, 800 $\mu eq \cdot L^{-1}$; K^+, 32 $\mu eq \cdot L^{-1}$; Ca^{++}, 950 $\mu eq \cdot L^{-1}$; Mg^{++}, 200 $\mu eq \cdot L^{-1}$. Mean annual concentrations in the St. Lawrence in St. Nicolas were: Na^+, 460 $\mu eq \cdot L^{-1}$; Cl^-, 590 $\mu eq \cdot L^{-1}$; K^+, 30 $\mu eq \cdot L^{-1}$; Ca^{++}, 1.4 $meq \cdot L^{-1}$; Mg^{++}, 600 $\mu eq \cdot L^{-1}$ (Cossa and Tremblay 1983). Saltwater was made by adding to tap water: NaCl, 16.1 $g \cdot L^{-1}$; $CaCl_2$, 1.0 $g \cdot L^{-1}$; KCl, 0.5 $g \cdot L^{-1}$; $NaHCO_3$, 0.1 $g \cdot L^{-1}$; $MgCl_2$, 3.1 $g \cdot L^{-1}$; $MgSO_4$, 3.8 $g \cdot L^{-1}$. Ion concentrations in the saltwater tanks were: Na^+, 260 $meq \cdot L^{-1}$; Cl^-, 300 $meq \cdot L^{-1}$; K^+, 6.8 $meq \cdot L^{-1}$; Ca^{++}, 14 $meq \cdot L^{-1}$; Mg^{++}, 64 $meq \cdot L^{-1}$. These are similar to concentrations in brackish water at Kamouraska, measured on occasion: Na^+, 230–

310 $meq \cdot L^{-1}$; Cl^-, 280–360 $meq \cdot L^{-1}$; K^+, 4.8–6.6 $meq \cdot L^{-1}$ (Ca^{++} and Mg^{++} were not measured). The eels were kept at 15.0°C in 500-L tanks and received no food. They were killed by a blow on the head, decerebrated, measured (± 1 mm), and weighed (± 1 g). Though the length-distribution for the pooled samples (1981–1985) looks homogeneous (Figure 2), there was a difference in mean length and mean weight between healthy eels collected in fresh water (hereafter referred to as FW eels) and healthy eels collected in salt water (hereafter referred to as SW eels) ($P < 0.05$) (Figure 2). The distribution for the diseased eels was also different from those of the FW and the SW eels ($P < 0.05$). However, based on histological examination of the gonads, the samples were homogeneous in that they were exclusively maturing females. This is not an unusual situation in the St. Lawrence (Dutil et al. 1985).

Histology.—Part of the gonad was dissected out, fixed in Bouin's solution 2 d, and dehydrated in alcohol (Miles Scientific Tissue Tek V.I.P. 1000). Tissues were embedded in paraffin (Paraplast +) and 8-μm sections were cut and mounted, stained in hematoxylin, and counterstained in eosine (Shandon Varistain 24-3). The slides were examined microscopically for sex and maturity based on the mean value of the maximum diameter of 10 randomly selected oocytes showing a nucleus.

Branchial filaments, taken from any gill arch, were cut longitudinally. Sections (6 μm) made through the afferent side were stained as above. The cytoplasm of chloride cells shows a strong reaction to eosine (Keys and Willmer 1932). Some of the tissues fixed in Bouin's solution were stained with PAS (periodic acid–Shiff) and PIC (picro–indigo–carmine) methods (Gabe 1968) to make sure that mucous cells had not been mistaken for chloride cells. Finally, the identification of chloride cells was corroborated by the use of osmium tetroxide. This chemical blackens chloride cells on a pale yellow background (Gabe 1968; Garcia-Romeu and Masoni 1970).

Branchial sections were examined for the relative abundance of chloride cells on primary and secondary lamellae. Relative abundance was scaled into four classes based on the examination of numerous interlamellar spaces on four or five primary lamellae: (1) sections showing less than one chloride cell per interlamellar space (i.e., between two secondary lamellae on the primary lamellae); (2) sections showing regularly one or two chloride cells per space and scattered cells

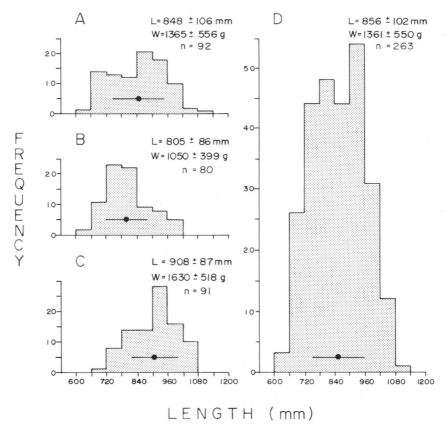

FIGURE 2.—Length-frequency distributions of diseased American eels (A), freshwater eels (B), saltwater eels (C), and pooled distribution (D). Mean lengths (L and solid circles), mean weights (W), standard deviations (± and horizontal lines), and numbers of fish (n) are shown.

near the arch; (3) sections showing regularly three to five chloride cells per space and numerous cells near the arch; (4) sections showing regularly three to five chloride cells per space plus a few cells located on the lower third of secondary lamellae, and numerous cells on secondary lamellae near the arch. The presence or absence of isolated chloride cells on secondary lamellae of individuals in classes 1 and 2 was also noted as were the pathological conditions.

Blood analysis.—Blood samples were collected from the posterior cardinal vein, allowed to clot for 5–10 min, and centrifuged at 4,000 revolutions/min for 5 min. The serum was stored at 4°C for less than 5 d prior to determinations of Na^+, Cl^-, and K^+ concentrations by flame spectrophotometry and of osmolality by freezing point depression measurement. The results are expressed in $meq \cdot L^{-1}$ and $mOsmol \cdot kg^{-1}$.

Gill Na^+,K^+-ATPase.—The Na^+,K^+-ATPase activity of branchial tissue samples (150–200 mg)

stored at −80°C for less than 40 d was determined following Zaugg (1982). Modifications were made to Zaugg's method, based on characteristics of the enzyme in eels, following Butler and Carmichael (1972) and Thomson and Sargent (1977). Solution A was modified to 100 mM NaCl, 20 mM KCl, 6 mM $MgCl_2 \cdot 6H_2O$, and 40 mM imidazole. The pH of solution A and that of ATP was adjusted to 7.2. Centrifugation times were prolonged to 10 min.

Heavy metals and pesticides.—Carcasses stored at −20°C for 6 months were deheaded, eviscerated, and homogenized and their heavy metal (9 variables), pesticide (16 variables), and PCB contents were measured following the methods outlined in the Chemical Methods Manual of the Inspection Branch of the Department of Fisheries and Oceans.

Statistical tests.—Analysis of variance was used to test for significant differences in mean lengths and mean weights (one fixed factor), serum ion concentrations, serum osmolality, and branchial Na^+,K^+-ATPase activity (two fixed factors, unbalanced design). Chloride cell counts were tested by median tests (Siegel 1956). Pairwise tests were made a posteriori following the Student–Newman–Keuls procedure (Sokal and Rohlf 1969) when the analysis of variance detected significant differences among means. Those tests were run only on distributions having homogeneous variances and at the same probability level as tests of homogeneity of variances (Underwood 1981). Homogeneity of variances was checked using Cochran's C-test (Winer 1971). Homogeneity of regression lines was tested by analysis of covariance (Snedecor and Cochran 1967).

Results

Na^+, Cl^-, and K^+ Concentrations

Sodium ion concentrations (Tables 1, 2) in untreated FW eels (147.4 meq·L^{-1}) were lower by 20 meq·L^{-1} than in untreated SW eels (167.7 ± 5.3). They were also lower in eels kept 4 d in fresh water than in eels kept 4 d in salt water, both for FW eels (144.8 meq·L^{-1} in fresh water versus 154.8 in salt water, NS) and SW eels (149.6 meq·L^{-1} in fresh water versus 157.9 in salt water). Saltwater eels tended to maintain slightly higher concentrations than FW eels in both treatments (NS). Freshwater eels and SW eels kept in fresh water also maintained a similar sodium concentration (144.8 and 149.6 meq·L^{-1}, respectively) to the untreated FW eels (147.4) but the concentration was lower in FW eels and in SW eels kept 4 d in salt water (154.8 and 157.9 meq·L^{-1}) than in the untreated SW eels (167.7).

The diseased eels had consistently lower Na^+ concentrations (117.4 meq·L^{-1}) than either FW or SW eels in the St. Lawrence (147.4 and 167.7 meq·L^{-1}). They behaved similarly to FW eels when transferred to fresh water for 4 d: their Na^+ concentration did not change. Transfer to salt water, however, resulted in a greater increase in Na^+ concentrations in diseased eels (117.4–136.0 meq·L^{-1}) than in FW eels (147.4–154.8 meq·L^{-1}, NS). Though the mean concentration was still lower than in FW eels, some individuals had recovered to near-normal levels as indicated by the range in concentrations.

The results for Cl^- (Tables 1, 2) were very similar to those for Na^+: the concentrations were much lower in untreated FW eels (110.0 meq·L^{-1}) than in untreated SW eels (122.2), and in fresh water (118.8 meq·L^{-1} for FW eels and 121.7 for SW eels) than in saltwater (132.2 meq·L^{-1} for FW

TABLE 1.—Mean Na^+, Cl^-, and K^+ concentrations and their standard deviations (meq·L^{-1}), in the sera of freshwater, saltwater, and diseased American eels subjected to 4-d treatments in fresh water or salt water or to no treatment. The range is shown in parentheses.

Ion and treatment	Freshwater eels	Saltwater eels	Diseased eels
Na^+			
Fresh water-4 d	144.8±8.8 (132–154) $N=5$	149.6±2.8 (144–152) $N=7$	114.8±8.3 (109–129) $N=5$
Salt water-4 d	154.8±3.2 (150–157) $N=5$	157.9±3.4 (151–160) $N=7$	136.0±12.5 (126–150) $N=3$
None	147.4±8.6 (135–156) $N=5$	167.7±5.3 (158–172) $N=6$	117.4±6.3 (106–125) $N=8$
Cl^-			
Fresh water-4 d	118.8±10.5 (107–129) $N=5$	121.7±7.7 (106–128) $N=7$	66.4±17.1 (53–96) $N=5$
Salt water-4 d	132.2±3.5 (128–136) $N=5$	133.4±4.2 (129–139) $N=7$	97.0±31.3 (61–118) $N=3$
None	110.0±14.3 (98–134) $N=5$	122.2±7.4 (109–131) $N=6$	72.9±11.8 (56–89) $N=8$
K^+			
Fresh water-4 d	4.23±1.96 (2.15–6.34) $N=5$	4.81±1.36 (3.30–6.70) $N=7$	7.49±2.97 (4.21–12.16) $N=5$
Salt water-4 d	3.71±0.96 (2.60–4.74) $N=5$	4.56±0.99 (3.11–5.96) $N=7$	4.20±0.23 (3.94–4.34) $N=3$
None	6.03±1.12 (4.33–7.05) $N=5$	4.67±1.37 (2.80–5.88) $N=6$	6.41±2.00 (4.09–10.44) $N=8$

eels and 133.4 for SW eels). There were also some dissimilarities; concentrations were higher in both FW and SW eels kept 4 d in fresh water than in untreated FW eels. Freshwater and SW eels kept 4 d in salt water maintained higher Cl^- concentrations than untreated SW eels.

Serum Cl^- concentrations in diseased eels followed the same trend as those for Na^+, but the gap between healthy eels and diseased eels was even wider and ranged from 30 to 50 meq·L^{-1}. Most interesting was the recovery of some individuals in salt water as indicated by an overlap in the range between the diseased eels in salt water (61–118 meq·L^{-1}) and the untreated SW eels (109–131 meq·L^{-1}), and the variability in the data for the diseased eels in salt water.

TABLE 2.—Results of pairwise tests on mean serum Na^+ concentrations, serum osmolality, and gill Na^+,K^+-ATPase activity in healthy American eels taken from freshwater (FW eels) or saltwater (SW eels) portions of the St. Lawrence River estuary and subjected to 4 d in fresh or salt water, or to no treatment, and in diseased eels. Asterisks denote significant differences.

Comparison by treatment				Comparison by status			
					Fresh water 4 d	Salt water 4 d	No treatment
Comparison	Diseased	FW eels	SW eels	Comparison			
Na (statistical threshold: $P = 0.01$)							
Fresh water-4 d × no treatment			*	Diseased eels × FW eels	*	*	*
Saltwater-4 d × no treatment	*		*	Diseased eels × SW eels	*	*	*
Fresh water-4 d × saltwater-4 d	*		*	FW eels × SW eels			*
Osmolality (statistical threshold: $P = 0.05$)							
Fresh water-4 d × no treatment			*	Diseased eels × FW eels	*	*	*
Saltwater-4 d × no treatment			*	Diseased eels × SW eels	*	*	*
Fresh water-4 d × saltwater-4 d				FW eels × SW eels		*	*
Na^+,K^+-ATPase (statistical threshold: $P = 0.05$)							
Fresh water-4 d × no treatment		*[a]	*	Diseased eels × FW eels			
Saltwater-4 d × no treatment				Diseased eels × SW eels	*	*	*
Fresh water-4 d × saltwater-4 d		*[a]	*	FW eels × SW eels	*	*	*

[a] Diseased eels and FW eels combined.

Results for serum K^+ (Tables 1, 2) are not so conclusive but they tend to confirm results on Na^+ and Cl^- for diseased eels kept 4 d in salt water. Plots of mean Na^+ and Cl^- concentrations against mean K^+ concentrations (Figure 3) both indicate extreme values for diseased eels kept in fresh water and for diseased eels that received no treatment, whereas the mean K^+ concentration of diseased eels kept in salt water does not show such an extreme and has by far the smallest coefficient of variation (6%).

Heterogeneity in the data was revealing in that it was associated with variability in the results for the diseased eels (Table 1). Variances in the Na^+ data were heterogeneous at the 5% level but not at the 1% level; those of Cl^- and K^+ proved heterogeneous at both the 1% and 5% levels. This suggests there was a biological basis for heterogeneity and may explain that transformations failed to restore the homogeneity of variances. The analysis of variance was run on Na^+ concentrations and not on Cl^- and K^+ concentrations. The interaction between the two factors (categories and treatments) turned out to be significant ($P = 0.002$) but much smaller than the main effects, particularly the categories of eels (mean square, categories = 6,320; mean square, treatments = 546; mean square, interaction = 298).

Serum Osmolality

Serum osmolality (Tables 2, 3) was lower in untreated FW eels (323.6 mOsmols·kg^{-1}) than in untreated SW eels (392.8). Freshwater eels in fresh water had a lower serum osmolality than FW eels in salt water (303.0 versus 319.0 mOsmol·kg^{-1}, NS). There was a similar and significant increase between SW eels kept in fresh water and SW eels kept in salt water (323.9 to 335.0 mOsmol·kg^{-1}), but transfer of SW eels to either fresh water or salt water resulted in a sharp decline in osmolality, not unlike the decrease in Na^+ (not Cl^-) concentration. These results, on the other hand, differ from those on Na^+ and Cl^- in that mean osmolality in SW eels kept 4 d in fresh water (323.9) was still higher than the mean osmolality of FW eels kept 4 d in salt water (319.0); the ranges overlap substantially.

TABLE 3.—Mean osmolality and standard deviations (mOsmol·kg^{-1}), in the sera of freshwater, saltwater, and diseased American eels subjected to 4-d treatments in fresh water or salt water or to no treatment. The range is shown in parentheses.

Treatment	Freshwater eels	Saltwater eels	Diseased eels
Fresh water-4 d	303.0±17.9 (272–317) N=5	323.9±4.0 (320–329) N=7	270.2±29.6 (235–300) N=5
Salt water-4 d	319.0±4.5 (313–324) N=5	335.0±3.6 (330–339) N=7	280.0±27.4 (259–311) N=3
None	323.6±22.5 (297–349) N=5	392.8±30.0 (355–422) N=6	257.1±16.4 (236–281) N=8

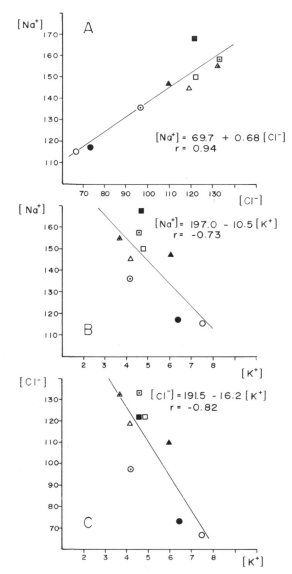

FIGURE 3.—Linear regressions of mean concentrations (meq · L^{-1}) of Na$^+$ on Cl$^-$ (A), Na$^+$ on K$^+$ (B), and Cl$^-$ on K$^+$(C) for American eels. ● Diseased eels with no treatment; ○ diseased eels in freshwater tanks; ⊙ diseased eels in saltwater tanks. ▲ Freshwater eels with no treatment; △ freshwater eels in freshwater tanks; ⬚ freshwater eels in saltwater tanks. ■ Saltwater eels with no treatment; □ saltwater eels in freshwater tanks; ⊡ saltwater eels in saltwater tanks.

Diseased eels had very low osmolalities compared with FW eels and SW eels for all treatments, reaching a low value of 235 mOsmol·kg^{-1}. Transfer of the diseased eels to either fresh water or salt water resulted in an increase in mean osmolality. Though the normal condition was restored in some individuals following transfer to fresh water and more particularly to salt water, where values as high as 310 mOsmol·kg^{-1} were reached, treatments did not restore normal concentrations in all individuals.

The analysis of variance showed that interaction was highly significant between the two factors (Figure 4) ($P < 0.0001$; mean square = 3,490) and that mean osmotic concentrations differed between categories ($P < 0.0001$; mean square = 32,096) and between treatments ($P = 0.001$; mean square = 2,915). Variances were not heterogeneous ($P > 0.05$).

Branchial Na$^+$,K$^+$-ATPase

Branchial Na$^+$,K$^+$-ATPase activity was similar in the diseased eels to that in the FW eels (Tables 2, 4), indicating that the low serum NaCl and osmotic concentrations observed in the diseased eels could not be associated with increased branchial enzymatic activity. Diseased eels and FW eels were pooled to test treatments (Table 2). The

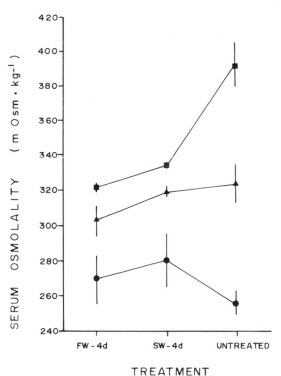

FIGURE 4.—Interaction between categories (freshwater or saltwater) and treatments (4 d in fresh or salt water, or no treatment) on mean serum osmolality in diseased American eels (●), freshwater eels (▲), and saltwater eels (■). Standard errors are shown as vertical bars.

TABLE 4.—Mean branchial Na$^+$,K$^+$-ATPase activity and standard deviations (μmol P$_i$·mg protein^{-1}·h^{-1}) of freshwater, saltwater, and diseased American eels subjected to 4-d treatments (fresh water or salt water or to no treatment). The range is shown in parentheses.

Treatment	Freshwater eels	Saltwater eels	Diseased eels
Fresh water-4 d	5.56±2.62 (3.3–9.6) $N=5$	29.06±9.99 (12.0–41.5) $N=7$	10.28±6.14 (4.3–19.6) $N=5$
Salt water-4 d	20.98±8.31 (12.9–33.9) $N=5$	45.00±9.32 (28.0–55.3) $N=7$	20.98±9.63 (10.3–32.6) $N=4$
None	19.24±13.61 (4.6–34.8) $N=5$	46.53±9.54 (37.7–61.8) $N=6$	14.98±5.40 (6.7–26.3) $N=10$

variances were not heterogeneous ($P > 0.05$) and the means differed between categories and treatments ($P < 0.0001$), but there was no interaction ($P = 0.4266$). The gill Na$^+$,K$^+$-ATPase activity (μmol P$_i$·mg protein^{-1}·h^{-1}) of untreated FW eels (including the diseased individuals) decreased upon transfer to fresh water (16.40 to 7.92) and increased (NS) upon transfer to salt water (20.98). Similarly, untreated SW eels transferred to fresh water showed a sharp decline in enzymatic activity (46.53 to 29.06), but no change when transferred to salt water (45.00). Gill Na$^+$,K$^+$-ATPase activity was also much higher in untreated SW eels transferred to fresh water than in untreated FW eels transferred to salt water. Finally, the level of activity in SW eels in any treatment was much higher than in the FW eels.

TABLE 5.—Frequency of occurrence of chloride cells, expressed as classes of relative abundance, observed in the gill sections of 94 American eels collected in 1983, 1984, and 1985 from the St. Lawrence River.

Category, treatment	Class of relative abundance[a]			
	1	2	3	4
Diseased eels + freshwater eels				
Fresh water-4 d	5	4	1	0
Salt water-4 d	1	3	5	2
Saltwater eels				
Fresh water-4 d	0	1	2	2
Salt water-4 d	0	0	5	2
No treatment				
Diseased eels	2	5	9	4
Freshwater eels	5	5	5	5
Saltwater eels	0	2	9	10

[a] Relative abundance of chloride cells increases with class number.

Gill Histology and Contamination

The number of chloride cells (Table 5) in the diseased eels was similar to that in FW eels ($\chi^2 = 0.41$). This observation is consistent with the results obtained for the branchial Na$^+$,K$^+$-ATPase activity. Diseased eels and FW eels also had fewer chloride cells than SW eels ($\chi^2 = 8.83$). Transfer of FW eels to salt water brought about proliferation of the chloride cells ($P < 0.02$), but the number of chloride cells was not reduced by transferring SW eels to fresh water for 4 d ($P = 0.42$) (Figures 5, 6). Median tests were performed on chloride cell abundance data after pooling of classes 1 and 2 and of classes 3 and 4.

The incidence of pathological conditions in the branchial tissues, however, differed markedly between diseased and healthy eels. Diseased eels had the highest incidence (86%), but some of the FW (28%) and SW eels (18%) also had similar damage (Table 6). Pathological conditions of the gills were so common when sections were examined for the relative abundance of chloride cells that the number of slides showing gill damage was assessed. Damage was not local and could sometimes be detected on macroscopic examination, particularly in 1985. Most common conditions included hypertrophic and hyperplastic cells, necrotic tissues, and some cases of aneurisms (Figure 6c). Interestingly, many diseased eels also had isolated chloride cells on the secondary lamellae (Table 6).

However, diseased eels did not have higher concentrations of contaminants than healthy eels collected in fresh water or in salt water (Table 7).

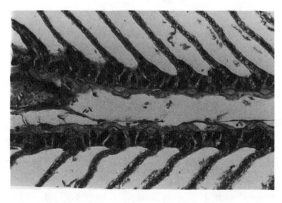

FIGURE 5.—Chloride cells, stained black by osmium tetroxide, in the branchial lamellae of an American eel. This eel was collected at the saltwater site in the St. Lawrence River and shows a moderately high number of chloride cells.

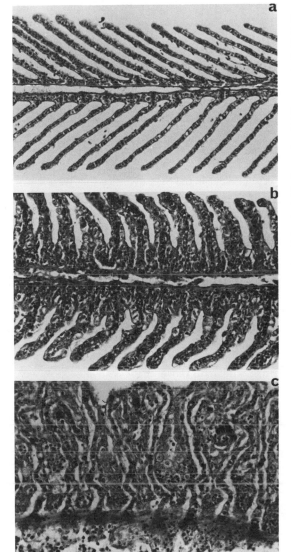

FIGURE 6.—Normal and pathological conditions of gill lamellae in American eels from the St. Lawrence River. **A:** Normal condition of primary and secondary lamellae. **B:** Reduction of the interlamellar space due to swelling of the gill lamellae. **C:** Thickening of membranes and fusion of secondary lamellae; the interlamellar space becomes nonexistent in such an extreme condition.

Generally, heavy metal, PCB, and pesticide concentrations were actually higher in SW eels than in FW eels and diseased eels. Mean heavy metal concentrations were slightly lower in diseased than in FW eels, and those of PCB and pesticides higher in diseased than in FW eels, but in those instances where they were higher than in FW

TABLE 6.—Frequency of occurrence of pathological conditions observed in the gill sections of 94 American eels collected in 1983, 1984, and 1985 from the St. Lawrence River, and occurrence of lamellar chloride cells.

Feature	Diseased eels $N=29$	Freshwater eels $N=32$	Saltwater eels $N=33$
Pathological conditions	25	9	6
Isolated chloride cells in secondary lamellae	17	2	1

eels, they were still lower than in SW eels. This rules out the possibility that the disease is related to contamination. The data indicate that the eels had spent part of their freshwater residence in polluted areas. Dutil et al. (1985) have shown that 70% of the eels caught in the St. Lawrence estuary came from Lake Ontario.

Maturation

Maturation rate, measured as change in the

TABLE 7.—Mean concentrations and standard deviations ($\mu g \cdot g^{-1}$, wet-weight basis) of heavy metals, PCBs, and pesticides in American eels collected in 1984 from the St. Lawrence River.

Chemical	Diseased eels, $N=16$	Freshwater eels, $N=15$	Saltwater eels, $N=20$
Hg	0.34 ± 0.21	0.36 ± 0.15	0.39 ± 0.21
Cd	0.03 ± 0.01	0.04 ± 0.04	0.02 ± 0.02
Co	<0.05	<0.05	<0.05
Cr	0.05 ± 0.04	0.06 ± 0.06	0.06 ± 0.02
Cu	0.77 ± 0.19	0.90 ± 0.28	0.93 ± 0.22
Mn	1.06 ± 0.28	1.14 ± 0.35	0.82 ± 0.24
Ni	<0.10	<0.10	<0.10
Pb	0.33 ± 0.12	0.36 ± 0.08	0.31 ± 0.05
Zn	34.78 ± 7.42	37.97 ± 7.36	34.34 ± 5.73
α-hexachlorocyclohexane	0.017 ± 0.004	0.016 ± 0.004	0.029 ± 0.041
γ-hexachlorocyclohexane	0.003 ± 0.001	0.003 ± 0.001	0.004 ± 0.001
Heptachlor	0.022 ± 0.020	0.013 ± 0.018	0.031 ± 0.025
Heptachlor epoxide	0.017 ± 0.013	0.012 ± 0.004	0.023 ± 0.013
Oxychlordane	0.016 ± 0.014	0.010 ± 0.006	0.022 ± 0.013
α-chlordane	0.058 ± 0.064	0.032 ± 0.028	0.062 ± 0.040
γ-chlordane	0.020 ± 0.019	0.015 ± 0.012	0.021 ± 0.011
Aldrin	0.007 ± 0.004	0.006 ± 0.002	0.008 ± 0.002
Dieldrin	0.061 ± 0.062	0.034 ± 0.020	0.103 ± 0.068
Endrin	0.011 ± 0.008	0.007 ± 0.004	0.015 ± 0.011
P-P^1-DDD	0.144 ± 0.102	0.103 ± 0.082	0.196 ± 0.111
P-P^1-DDE	0.261 ± 0.230	0.155 ± 0.156	0.412 ± 0.270
P-P^1-DDT	0.061 ± 0.054	0.037 ± 0.027	0.126 ± 0.085
DDD + DDE + DDT	0.460 ± 0.346	0.296 ± 0.196	0.734 ± 0.450
Hexachlorobenzene	0.054 ± 0.047	0.026 ± 0.016	0.099 ± 0.055
PCB	5.323 ± 4.415	3.030 ± 2.156	6.688 ± 3.673
Mirex	0.189 ± 0.185	0.056 ± 0.090	0.301 ± 0.222

natural logarithm of the mean diameter (μm) of 10 oocytes *(Y)* versus date *(X)*, was slower in diseased than healthy eels.

Healthy: $Y = 3.6936 + 0.0058X$;   (1)
          $N = 524$; $r^2 = 0.72$.

Diseased: $Y = 4.4274 + 0.0026X$;   (2)
           $N = 125$; $r^2 = 0.16$.

In a 2-month period (mid-August to mid-October), the diameter of oocytes increased from 149 to 174 μm in diseased eels and from 151 to 214 μm in healthy eels. The sections of gonadal tissues were as reported by Wenner and Musick (1974) for migrating American eels caught in Chesapeake Bay in late November; the oocytes were smaller but the mean diameter in some individuals caught late in October reached 250 μm. There was a great deal of variability in the data for diseased eels, but the variances were not significantly heterogeneous ($P > 0.05$). The slopes were significant ($P < 0.05$) and differed ($F = 20.05$; $P < 0.05$). The relationship between the diameter of oocytes and time in maturing American eels has not been reported in the literature. Data in an earlier study showed that immature eels had a mean oocyte diameter of 65 ± 7 μm that did not increase in the summer period ($P = 0.60$; Dutil et al. 1985). Maturing eels in equation (1) were collected between 1981 and 1985 from May to mid-October. Diseased eels in equation (2) were also collected between 1981 and 1985 but over a shorter period, mid-August to mid-October. However, the conclusions remained unchanged when eels collected before mid-August were excluded from the analysis.

Discussion

The changes in serum Na^+, Cl^-, K^+ and osmotic concentrations, and in branchial chloride cells and Na^+,K^+-ATPase activity measured in this study in maturing American eels migrating down the St. Lawrence estuary and in maturing eels transferred directly into fresh water or salt water may have been influenced by maturity. Some of the control mechanisms involved in the transition of eels to salt water are preparatory, i.e., they are set up when maturing eels are still in fresh water (Oidé and Utida 1967a, 1967b; Utida et al. 1967; Thomson and Sargent 1977). The eels in the present study varied in length and weight between locations but they were all females and their gonads were maturing. The changes may

also have been influenced by variations in water quality, as they are in Atlantic salmon *Salmo salar* (Saunders et al. 1983), and there are some indications that conditions in the tanks did not reflect natural conditions precisely. Saltwater eels kept in saltwater tanks had lower Na^+ concentrations than SW eels in nature. Freshwater eels kept in freshwater tanks also had higher Cl^- concentrations than FW eels in nature. There were lower calcium and magnesium concentrations in the freshwater tanks than in the St. Lawrence at St. Nicolas, and no doubt many more divalent ions were present in the St. Lawrence that were not in freshwater and saltwater tanks. Stress, associated with handling, is most likely to have occurred in SW eels as they were transported in moist air for 2 h before they were processed. This may have resulted in increases in the concentrations of metabolic by-products such as NH_4^+ and HCO_3^-. Bradley and Rourke (1985) recently demonstrated that decreased NH_4^+ excretion, associated with low environmental Na^+ concentrations, could result in elevated branchial NH_4^+, which causes edema and hyperplasia in rainbow trout *Salmo gairdneri*. Finally, the experimental salinities, while similar to those of the saltwater site, were also significantly less than the 35‰ that migratory eels would eventually encounter.

Migrating anadromous and catadromous fishes rely on two strategies to survive changes in salinity. Motais (1967) made the observation that contradictions in findings concerning the euryhaline mummichog *Fundulus heteroclitus* and European eel *Anguilla anguilla* should make us aware that the same mechanisms may not necessarily be common to all teleosts. Folmar and Dickhoff (1980) concluded that species such as mummichog might not have the same mechanisms of gill Na^+,K^+-ATPase regulation as salmonids. The number of ouabain binding sites is a function of external salinity in mummichogs, suggesting that these animals can react instantaneously to variations in salinity (Towle et al. 1977). The mechanism of short-term control has been modeled by Towle et al. (1977) and Sardet et al. (1979). Salmonids require a longer time to react to changes in salinity. Turnover rates of DNA measured in gill filaments of coho salmon *Oncorhynchus kisutch* indicated that protein synthesis required 4–6 d (Conte and Lin 1967). This is the time required to increase branchial Na^+,K^+-ATPase activity in coho salmon transferred to salt water (Folmar and Dickhoff 1979). Numerous reviews have been published recently on the role of chloride cells (Kirschner 1977; Payan et al. 1984), branchial Na^+,K^+-ATPase (Cantley 1981; Schuurmans Stekhoven and Bonting 1981; De-Renzis and Bornancin 1984), and branchial mechanisms of osmotic regulation (Evans 1979, 1980; Evans et al. 1982; Hoar and Randall 1984a, 1984b).

The results in this study indicate that maturing American eels migrating down the estuary might rely on a strategy based on both short-term and long-term mechanisms to maintain relatively constant serum ionic and osmotic concentrations in salt water. Maturing eels in nature exhibited the same mechanisms as used by salmonids (long-term control). The number of chloride cells increased markedly and gill Na^+,K^+-ATPase activity more than doubled in salt water. This resulted in relatively small increases in Na^+, Cl^-, and osmotic concentrations. The increases in serum Na^+ and Cl^- concentrations were much the same as observed in an earlier study (Dutil 1984). However, serum K^+ and osmolality were higher. These changes probably took place over a 4-week period because commercial landings peak 4 weeks earlier in St. Nicolas than in Kamouraska.

Transfer of FW eels to salt water demonstrated that maturing eels had the ability to maintain relatively constant ionic and osmotic concentrations without increasing their gill Na^+,K^+-ATPase activity (short-term control). Freshwater eels transferred to salt water maintained similar serum ionic and osmotic concentrations as SW eels in nature, and their serum osmotic concentration remained close to that of FW eels in nature, indicating that seaward-migrating eels in fresh water possess significant salinity tolerance and hypoosmoregulatory ability. The increase in ionic and osmotic concentrations reported in this study for FW eels (maturing) transferred to salt water are smaller than those reported for immature eels (Sharratt et al. 1964; Munroe and Poluhowich 1974) and similar to those reported for maturing eels (Sharratt et al. 1964; Butler 1966). Chloride cells proliferated over the 4-d period but there was no detectable change in gill Na^+,K^+-ATPase activity. The number of chloride cells had increased significantly in 4 d and peaked 10 d later in immature *A. japonica* transferred to salt water (Shirai and Utida 1970). Proliferation of chloride cells in immature European eels also preceded the change in gill Na^+,K^+-ATPase activity and a maximum was reached in less than 10 d but, in our study with American eels, there was no proliferation of chloride cells in fresh water such as

reported in maturing European eels (Thomson and Sargent 1977).

Transfer of SW eels to fresh water also points to the existence of a short-term mechanism enabling maturing eels to maintain osmotic integrity as salinity conditions change over a short period. Na^+, Cl^-, and K^+ concentrations returned in 4 d to the same level as in FW eels in fresh water, but there was no reduction in the number of chloride cells. Gill Na^+,K^+-ATPase activity decreased 30% but remained higher than in FW eels kept 4 d in salt water. The slight reduction of osmotic concentration can be explained by the increased permeability of the gills of SW eels in fresh water, resulting in the rapid passage of water through the membrane (Isaia 1984). These results suggest the existence of a mechanism to react to short-term variations in salinity. This is vital in such a situation and may also be vital during migration through estuaries. However, the reversibility of these mechanisms is not total in that ionic and osmotic concentrations in SW eels, though they tended to get near those of FW eels in both treatments, always remained higher than in FW eels.

The contradiction in the results, indicating that the number of chloride cells increased while gill Na^+,K^+-ATPase activity remained unchanged 4 d after transfer of maturing eels to salt water, may also have been due to the great variability in initial (untreated) ATPase levels. This variability was perhaps a reflection of variations in developmental stages of migratory eels. Both the variability and absolute levels of gill Na^+,K^+-ATPase activity were reduced following a 4-d exposure to fresh water. Levels of gill Na^+,K^+-ATPase activity of FW eels kept 4 d in fresh water were significantly lower than those of FW eels kept 4 d in salt water. If the low levels of gill Na^+,K^+-ATPase activity after 4 d in fresh water are considered "basal" levels, then higher and more variable levels in untreated FW eels may reflect a preparatory adaptation for their marine migration.

Since no mortality took place in eels that reached the brackish section of the estuary, the "disease" is likely to be linked to osmoregulatory failure. Bacterial and viral pathogens have been ruled out as potential causes of the mortality (Dutil and Lallier 1984; Robin, unpublished). The present study also rules out the possibility that mortalities are linked to higher concentrations of heavy metals and pesticides in the tissues of diseased eels through a delayed action of the chemicals on the changing eel physiology, such as described by Kerswill (1967). Dutil (1984) indicated that diseased eels had unusually low Na^+ and, more particularly, low Cl^- concentrations in their serum. Their serum osmotic concentrations were among the lowest recorded in the literature (as low as 217 $mOsmol \cdot kg^{-1}$ in extreme cases). The present study corroborates the earlier observations, i.e., low Na^+, low Cl^-, and extremely low osmotic concentrations (mean, 257 ± 16 $mOsmol \cdot kg^{-1}$) and suggests that iono- and osmoregulatory failure could also have resulted in a decrease in the rate of maturation. This failure to maintain constant ionic and osmotic concentrations is similar to that reported in maturing eels by Callamand and Fontaine (1940a, 1940b). Fontaine and Koch (1950) explained this by the fact that eels, unlike most teleosts, cannot absorb Cl^- from fresh water (Krogh 1937; Kirsch 1972). Normally, the eels receive minerals from their food but they stop feeding at the onset of maturation. Starvation might also be the reason for low Cl^- values reported, for instance, by Schmidt-Nielsen and Renfro (1975).

Developmental changes that are part of the preparatory adaptations for life of eels in the sea may be subject to interference. Schreck (1982) has reviewed the increased susceptibility of salmonids to stress during the parr–smolt transformation. McCormick and Saunders (1987) have argued that ion losses sometimes observed in fresh water during transformation are not solely the result of differentiation of osmoregulatory organs, but are due to a synergy between differentiation and environmental change. Perhaps a similar condition may explain ion losses and mortality in diseased eels. This explanation, however, is not supported by the results of Utida et al. (1967) showing that maturing eels had lower branchial ion losses than immature eels.

The high incidence of pathological conditions in gill sections of diseased American eels suggests that iono- and osmoregulatory failure result from a change in permeability of branchial membranes that might have been caused by pollution in the St. Lawrence estuary. Low Na^+, Cl^-, and osmotic concentrations cannot be explained by the proliferation of chloride cells and enhanced Na^+,K^+-ATPase activity in diseased eels in fresh water. Chloride loss through intact branchial membranes of eels is very slow, particularly in maturing individuals (Kirsch 1972), and cannot explain the lower Cl^- concentrations in diseased eels. However, high K^+ concentrations in diseased eels indicate that cells were being damaged.

Pathological conditions of the gills in this study included necrosis and a high incidence of hypertrophy and hyperplasia. Heavy metals injected into the blood of rainbow trout did not alter gill structure and function (Skidmore 1970), but pesticides and heavy metals in the environment do alter the gill structure of fishes (reviewed by Mallatt 1985). Alterations can be localized to any of the gill arches or some of the lamellae (Gardner and Yevitch 1970). Hypertrophy and hyperplasia are among the most common alterations (Gardner and Yevitch 1970; Temmink et al. 1983), and are considered initial reactions to membrane damage (Trump et al. 1981). In this study, there were also many instances of isolated chloride cells budding out in the secondary lamellae. Instances of increases in the number of chloride cells have been reported occasionally (Baker 1969; Matthiessen and Brafield 1973; Crespo et al. 1981; Tuurala and Soivio 1982). Laurent and Dunel (1980) concluded that skin damage and transfer of eels into deionized water induced the proliferation of chloride cells in the secondary lamellae and suggested that chloride cells in secondary lamellae may provide a mechanism for increasing net ion gain. Fishes experiencing such structural damage showed characteristic behaviors such as those observed in this study. They swam erratically, lost equilibrium, stayed close to the surface, and showed no reactions to manipulations (Lewis and Lewis 1971; Skidmore and Tovell 1972; Walsh and Ribelin 1975).

Structural alterations in gills have been shown to bring about respiratory distress (Skidmore 1970; Skidmore and Tovell 1972; Tuurala and Soivio 1982; Van Der Putte et al. 1982), and to perturb the acid–base balance resulting in iono- and osmoregulatory failure (McKim et al. 1970; Lewis and Lewis 1971; McCarty and Houston 1976; Lock et al. 1981; Tuurala and Soivio 1982; Van Der Putte et al. 1982; Spry and Wood 1985). The relative incidence of these two mechanisms is debatable, but results so far indicate that respiratory distress might occur in cases of acute toxicities and iono- and osmoregulatory problems might occur in cases of chronic sublethal toxicities (Spry and Wood 1985). Three factors may make eels more vulnerable to osmoregulatory problems than nonmigratory species in the St. Lawrence River. First, maturing eels cannot avoid moving through highly polluted, presumably fishless areas in order to reach the estuary and so are liable to damages resulting in increased permeability and loss of minerals through the branchial membranes, such as described in this study (though the causative pollutant has not been detected). Second, maturing eels do not feed as they migrate in fresh water, so they cannot make up for loss of minerals by food intake. Third, eels, in contrast to most teleosts, cannot absorb Cl^- through the gills in a freshwater environment (Krogh 1937; Kirsch 1972). These factors may act in synergy to produce the observed ion losses and, unless fish reach the marine environment in time, mortality.

Transferring diseased eels to salt water did not prevent mortality in all instances but the condition of some individuals became less critical. Iono- and osmoregulatory problems can be prevented by adding NaCl to experimental tanks (Lewis and Lewis 1971; see also references in Lock et al. 1981). The increase in serum Na^+ concentration was greater in diseased eels than in healthy individuals upon transfer to salt water (8 meq·L^{-1} and 20 meq·L^{-1} for healthy and diseased eels, respectively). Serum Cl^- concentrations followed the same trend, the increase being 24 meq·L^{-1}. Serum K^+ was reduced and stabilized; the coefficient of variation decreased from 30 to 6%. Similarly, there was an increase in serum osmotic concentration. Some diseased individuals died during the experiment, so these results should also be considered in terms of their variability. The ranges indicate that some individuals recovered to normal ion concentrations, based on untreated FW eels. For instance, the range in Na^+ concentrations in untreated diseased eels was 106–125 meq·L^{-1}. This became 126–150 meq·L^{-1} in diseased eels kept 4 d in salt water compared with 135–156 meq·L^{-1} in untreated FW eels and 150–157 meq·L^{-1} in FW eels kept 4 d in salt water. Two of the diseased individuals survived to the end of the 4-d period in salt water. Serum Na^+, Cl^-, and osmotic concentrations of those individuals were 132 and 150 meq·L^{-1}, 112 and 118 meq·L^{-1}, and 270 and 311 mOsmol·kg^{-1}, respectively.

Acknowledgments

The authors wish to thank J. D. McCleave for his helpful comments on the manuscript; J. M. Coutu, A. Giroux, G. Gosselin, B. Légaré, and D. Pelletier for their technical assistance; and F. Gingras and M. Ouellet, fishermen, for the collection of eels in St. Nicolas and Kamouraska. Pesticide and heavy metal contents were measured by the Laboratoire Régional de Longueuil of the Department of Fisheries and Oceans (Canada) and serum ion concentrations were measured by the Laboratoire d'Analyse Médicale L.B., Incorporated (Montréal, Canada). S. D. McCormick received financial support from the Natural Sciences and Engineering Research Council and the Department of Fisheries and Oceans.

References

Baker, J. T. P. 1969. Histological and electron microscopical observations on copper poisoning in the winter flounder (*Pseudopleuronectes americanus*). Journal of the Fisheries Research Board of Canada 26:2785–2793.

Bornancin, M., and G. DeRenzis. 1972. Evolution of the branchial sodium outflux and its components especially the Na/K exchange and the Na–K dependent ATPase activity during adaptation to sea water in *Anguilla anguilla*. Comparative Biochemistry and Physiology A, Comparative Physiology 43:577–591.

Boucher-Firly, S. 1935. Recherches biochimiques sur les Téléostéens Apodes. Annales de l'Institut Océanographique de Monaco 15:219–327.

Bradley, T. M., and A. W. Rourke. 1985. The influences of addition of minerals to rearing water and smoltification on selected blood parameters of juvenile steelhead trout, *Salmo gairdneri*. Physiological Zoology 58:312–319.

Butler, D. G. 1966. Effect of hypophysectomy on osmoregulation in the European eel (*Anguilla anguilla*). Comparative Biochemistry and Physiology 18:773–781.

Butler, D. G., and F. J. Carmichael. 1972. Na^+,K^+-ATPase activity in eel (*Anguilla rostrata*) gills in relation to changes in environmental salinity: role of adrenocortical steroids. General and Comparative Endocrinology 19:421–427.

Callamand, O., and M. Fontaine. 1940a. La chlorémie de l'anguille femelle au cours de son développement. Comptes Rendus de l'Académie des Sciences 211:298–300.

Callamand, O., and M. Fontaine. 1940b. Sur le déterminisme biochimique du retour à la mer de l'anguille femelle d'avalaison. Comptes Rendus de l'Académie des Sciences 211:357–359.

Cantley, L. C. 1981. Structure and mechanism of the (Na–K)-ATPase. Current Topics in Bioenergetics 11:201–237.

Conte, F. P., and D. Lin. 1967. Kinetics of cellular morphogenesis in gill epithelium during seawater adaptation of *Oncorhynchus*. Comparative Biochemistry and Physiology 23:945–957.

Cossa, D., and G. Tremblay. 1983. Major ions composition of the St. Lawrence River: seasonal variability and fluxes. Mitteilungen aus dem Geologisch–Paleontologischen Institut der Universitaet Hamburg 55:253–259.

Crespo, S., E. Soriano, C. Sampera, and J. Balasch. 1981. Zinc and copper distribution in excretory organs of the dogfish *Scyliorhinus canicula* and chloride cell response following treatment with zinc sulphate. Marine Biology (Berlin) 65:117–123.

DeRenzis, G., and M. Bornancin. 1984. Ion transport and gill ATPase. Pages 65–104 in Hoar and Randall (1984b).

Doyle, W. L., and F. H. Epstein. 1972. Effects of cortisol treatment and osmotic adaptation on the chloride cells in the eel, Anguilla rostrata. Cytobiologie 6:58–73.

Dunel-Erb, S., and P. Laurent. 1980. Ultrastructure of marine teleost gill epithelia: SEM and TEM study of the chloride cell apical membrane. Journal of Morphology 165:175–186.

Dutil, J.-D. 1984. Electrolyte changes of serum and muscle, and related mortalities in maturing Anguilla rostrata migrating down the St. Lawrence estuary (Canada). Helgoländer Meeresuntersuchungen 37:425–432.

Dutil, J.-D., and R. Lallier. 1984. Testing bacterial infection as a factor involved in the mortality of catadromous eels (Anguilla rostrata) migrating down the St. Lawrence estuary (Canada). Naturaliste canadien (Québec) 111:395–400.

Dutil, J.-D., B. Légaré, and C. Desjardins. 1985. Discrimination d'un stock de poisson, l'anguille (Anguilla rostrata), basée sur la présence d'un produit chimique de synthèse, le mirex. Canadian Journal of Fisheries and Aquatic Sciences 42:455–458.

Epstein, F. H., M. Cynamon, and W. McKay. 1971. Endocrine control of Na–K-ATPase in seawater adaptation in Anguilla rostrata. General and Comparative Endocrinology 16:323–328.

Epstein, F. H., A. I. Katz, and G. E. Pickford. 1967. Sodium and potassium activated adenosine triphosphatase of gills: role in adaptation of teleosts to seawater. Science (Washington, D.C.) 156:1245–1247.

Evans, D. H. 1979. Fish. Pages 305–390 in G. M. O. Maloy, editor. Comparative physiology and osmoregulation in animals. Academic Press, London, England.

Evans, D. H. 1980. Osmotic and ionic regulation by freshwater and marine fishes. Pages 93–122 in M. A. Ali, editor. Environmental physiology of fishes. Plenum, New York, New York, USA.

Evans, D. H., J. B., Claiborne, L. Farmer, C. Mallery, and E. J. Krasny. 1982. Fish gill ionic transport: methods and models. Biological Bulletin (Woods Hole) 163:108–130.

Folmar, L. C., and W. W. Dickhoff. 1979. Plasma thyroxine and gill (Na+K)-ATPase changes during seawater acclimation of coho salmon, Oncorhynchus kisutch. Comparative Biochemistry and Physiology A, Comparative Physiology 63:329–332.

Folmar, L. C., and W. W. Dickhoff. 1980. The parr-smolt transformation (smoltification) and seawater adaptation in salmonids. A review of selected literature. Aquaculture 21:1–37.

Fontaine, M., and H. Koch. 1950. Les variations d'euryhalinité et d'osmorégulation chez les poissons. Journal de Physiologie (Paris) 42:287–318.

Gabe, M. 1968. Techniques histologiques. Masson et Cie, Paris, France.

Garcia-Romeu, F., and A. Masoni. 1970. Sur la mise en évidence des cellules à chlorures de la branchie des poissons. Archives d'Anatomie Microscopique et de Morphologie Expérimentale 59:289–294.

Gardner, G. R., and P. P. Yevich. 1970. Histological and hematological responses of an estuarine teleost to cadmium. Journal of the Fisheries Research Board of Canada 27:2185–2196.

Hoar, W. S. 1976. Smolt transformation: evolution, behavior, and physiology. Journal of the Fisheries Research Board of Canada 33:1233–1252.

Hoar, W. S., and D. J. Randall, editors. 1984a. Fish physiology, volume 10. Gills, part A. Anatomy, gas transfer and acid–base regulation. Academic Press, Orlando, Florida, USA.

Hoar, W. S., and D. J. Randall, editors. 1984b. Fish physiology, volume 10. Gills, part B. Ion and water transfer. Academic Press, Orlando, Florida. USA.

Isaia, J. 1984. Water and nonelectrolyte permeation. Pages 1–38 in Hoar and Randall (1984b).

Kamiya, M., and S. Utida. 1968. Changes in activity of sodium–potassium-activated adenosinetriphosphatase in gills during adaptation of the Japanese eel to sea water. Comparative Biochemistry and Physiology 26:675–685.

Kamiya, M., and S. Utida. 1969. Sodium–potassium-activated adenosinetriphosphatase activity in gills of freshwater, marine, and euryhaline teleosts. Comparative Biochemistry and Physiology 31:671–674.

Karnaky, K. J., L. B. Kinter, W. B. Kinter, and C. E. Stirling. 1976. Teleost chloride cell. II. Autoradiographic localization of gill Na–K-ATPase in killifish Fundulus heteroclitus adapted to low and high salinity environments. Journal of Cell Biology 70:157–177.

Kerswill, C. J. 1967. Studies on effects of forest sprayings with insecticides, 1952–63, on fish and aquatic invertebrates in New Brunswick streams: introduction and summary. Journal of the Fisheries Research Board of Canada 24:701–708.

Keys, A. B. 1933. The mechanism of adaptation to varying salinity in the common eel and the general problem of osmotic regulation in fishes. Proceedings of the Royal Society of London Series B, Biological Sciences 112:184–199.

Keys, A., and E. N. Willmer. 1932. Chloride secreting cells in the gills of fishes, with special reference to the common eel. Journal of Physiology (London) 76:368–378.

Kirsch, R. 1972. The kinetics of peripheral exchanges of water and electrolytes in the silver eel (Anguilla anguilla) in fresh water and in sea water. Journal of Experimental Biology 57:489–512.

Kirschner, L. B. 1977. The sodium chloride excreting cells in marine vertebrates. Pages 427–452 in B. L. Gupta, R. B. Moreton, J. L. Oschman, and B. J. Walls, editors. Transport of ions and water in animals. Academic Press, London, England.

Krogh, A. 1937. Osmotic regulation in fresh water fishes by active absorption of chloride ions. Zeitschrift fuer Vergleichende Physiologie 24:656–666.

Laurent, P. 1984. Gill internal morphology. Pages 73–183 *in* W. S. Hoar and D. J. Randall, editors. Fish physiology, volume 10. Gills, part A. Anatomy, gas transfer and acid–base regulation. Academic Press, Orlando, Florida, USA.

Laurent, P., and S. Dunel. 1980. Morphology of gill epithelia in fish. American Journal of Physiology 238:R159.

Lewis, S. D., and W. M. Lewis. 1971. The effect of zinc and copper on the osmolality of blood serum of the channel catfish, *Ictalurus punctatus,* and golden shiner, *Notemigonus crysoleucas.* Transactions of the American Fisheries Society 100:639–643.

Lock, R. A. C., P. M. J. M. Cruijsen, and A. Van Overbeeke. 1981. Effects of mercuric chloride and methylmercuric chloride on the osmoregulatory function of the gills in rainbow trout, *Salmo gairdneri.* Comparative Biochemistry and Physiology C, Comparative Pharmacology 68:151–159.

Maetz, J., and M. Bornancin. 1975. Biochemical and biophysical aspects of salt excretion by chloride cells in teleosts. Fortschritte der Zoologie 23:322–362.

Mallatt, J. 1985. Fish gill structural changes induced by toxicants and other irritants: a statistical review. Canadian Journal of Fisheries and Aquatic Sciences 42:630–648.

Matthiessen, P., and A. E. Brafield. 1973. The effects of dissolved zinc on the gills of the stickleback *Gasterosteus aculeatus.* Journal of Fish Biology 5:607–613.

McCarty, L. S., and A. H. Houston. 1976. Effects of exposure to sublethal levels of cadmium upon water-electrolyte status in the goldfish *(Carassius auratus).* Journal of Fish Biology 9:11–19.

McCormick, S. D., and R. L. Saunders. 1987. Preparatory physiological adaptations for marine life of salmonids: osmoregulation, growth and metabolism. American Fisheries Society Symposium 1:211–229.

McKim, J. M., G. M. Christensen, and E. P. Hunt. 1970. Changes in the blood of brook trout *(Salvelinus fontinalis)* after short-term and long-term exposure to copper. Journal of the Fisheries Research Board of Canada 27:1883–1889.

Mizuhira, V., T. Amakawa, S. Yamashina, N. Shirai, and S. Utida. 1970. Electron microscopic studies on the localization of sodium ions and sodium–potassium activated adenosinetriphosphatase in chloride cells of eel gills. Experimental Cell Research 59:346–348.

Motais, R. 1967. Les mécanismes d'échanges ioniques branchiaux chez les téléostéens. Annales de l'Institut Océanographique (Paris) 45:1–84.

Munroe, V. R., and J. J. Poluhowich. 1974. Ionic composition of the plasma and whole blood of marine and fresh water eels, *Anguilla rostrata.* Comparative Biochemistry and Physiology A, Comparative Physiology 49:541–544.

Oidé, M., and S. Utida. 1967a. Changes in intestinal absorption and renal excretion of water during adaptation to sea water in the Japanese eel. Marine Biology (New York) 1:172–177.

Oidé, M., and S. Utida. 1967b. Changes in water and ion transport in isolated intestines of the eel during salt adaptation and migration. Marine Biology (New York) 1:102–106.

Parry, G. 1966. Osmotic adaptation in fishes. Biological Reviews of the Cambridge Philosophical Society 41:392–444.

Payan, P., J. P. Girard, and N. Mayer-Gostan. 1984. Branchial ion movements in teleosts: the roles of respiratory and chloride cells. Pages 39–63 *in* W. S. Hoar and D. J. Randall (1984b).

Petrik, P. 1968. The demonstration of chloride ions in the chloride cells of the gills of eels *(Anguilla anguilla)* adapted to sea-water. Zeitschrift fuer Zellforschung und Mikrosopische Anatomie 92:422–427.

Sardet, C., M. Pisam, and J. Maetz. 1979. The surface epithelium of teleostean fish gills: cellular and functional adaptations of the chloride cell in relation to salt adaptation. Journal of Cell Biology 80:96–117.

Sardet, C., M. Pisam, and J. Maetz. 1980. Structure and function of gill epithelium of euryhaline teleost fish. Pages 59–68 *in* B. Lahlou, editor. Epithelial transport in lower vertebrates. Cambridge University Press, London, England.

Sargent, J. R., and A. J. Thomson. 1974. The nature and properties of the inducible sodium-plus-potassium ion-dependent adenosine triphosphatase in the gills of eels *(Anguilla anguilla)* adapted to freshwater and seawater. Biochemical Journal 144:69–75.

Sargent, J. R., A. J. Thomson, and M. Bornancin. 1975. Activities and localization of succinic dehydrogenase and Na^+/K^+-activated adenosine triphosphatase in the gill of eels *(Anguilla anguilla)* adapted to freshwater and seawater. Comparative Biochemistry and Physiology B, Comparative Biochemistry 51:75–79.

Saunders, R. L., E. B. Henderson, P. R. Harmon, C. E. Johnston, and J. G. Eales. 1983. Effects of low environmental pH on smolting of Atlantic salmon *(Salmo salar).* Canadian Journal of Fisheries and Aquatic Sciences 40:1203–1211.

Schmidt-Nielsen, B., and J. L. Renfro. 1975. Kidney function of the American eel *Anguilla rostrata.* American Journal of Physiology 228:420–431.

Schreck, C. B. 1982. Stress and rearing of salmonids. Aquaculture 28:241–249.

Schuurmans Stekhoven, F., and S. L. Bonting. 1981. Transport adenosine triphosphatases: properties and functions. Physiological Reviews 61:1–76.

Sharratt, B. M., I. Chester Jones, and D. Bellamy. 1964. Water and electrolyte composition of the body and renal function of the eel *(Anguilla anguilla).* Comparative Biochemistry and Physiology 11:9–18.

Shirai, N., and S. Utida. 1970. Development and degeneration of the chloride cell during seawater and freshwater adaptation of the Japanese eel, *Anguilla japonica.* Zeitschrift fuer Zellforschung und Mikroskopische Anatomie 103:247–264.

Siegel, S. 1956. Nonparametric statistics for the behavioral sciences. McGraw-Hill, New York, New York, USA.

Skadhauge, E. 1969. The mechanism of salt and water absorption in the intestine of the eel *(Anguilla anguilla)* adapted to waters of various salinities. Journal of Physiology (London) 204:135–158.

Skidmore, J. F. 1970. Respiration and osmoregulation in rainbow trout with gills damaged by zinc sulphate. Journal of Experimental Biology 52:481–494.

Skidmore, J. F., and P. W. A. Tovell. 1972. Toxic effects of zinc sulphate on the gills of rainbow trout. Water Research 6:217–230.

Smith, H. W. 1930. The absorption and excretion of water and salts by marine teleosts. American Journal of Physiology 93:480–505.

Smith, H. W. 1932. Water regulation and its evolution in fishes. Quarterly Review of Biology 7:1–26.

Snedecor, G. W., and W. G. Cochran. 1967. Statistical methods. Iowa State University Press, Ames, Iowa, USA.

Sokal, R. R., and F. J. Rohlf. 1969. Biometry. W. H. Freeman, San Francisco, California, USA.

Spry, D. J., and C. M. Wood. 1985. Ion flux rates, acid–base status, and blood gases in rainbow trout, *Salmo gairdneri,* exposed to toxic zinc in natural soft water. Canadian Journal of Fisheries and Aquatic Sciences 42:1332–1341.

Temmink, J. H. M., P. J. Bouwmeister, P. de Jong, and J. H. J. van den Berg. 1984. An ultrastructural study of chromate-induced hyperplasia in the gill of rainbow trout *(Salmo gairdneri).* Aquatic Toxicology (Amsterdam) 4:165–179.

Thomson, A. J., and J. R. Sargent. 1977. Changes in the levels of chloride cells and (Na^+–K^+)-dependent ATPase in the gills of silver and yellow eels adapting to seawater. Journal of Experimental Zoology 200:33–40.

Towle, D. W., M. E. Gillman, and J. D. Hempel. 1977. Rapid modulation of gill Na^+–K^+ dependent ATPase activity during acclimation of killifish *Fundulus heteroclitus* to salinity change. Journal of Experimental Zoology 202:179–186.

Trump, B. J., I. K. Berezesky, and A. R. Orsonio-Vargas. 1981. Cell death and the disease process: the role of calcium. Pages 209–242 *in* I. D. Bowen and R. A. Lockshin, editors. Cell death in biology and pathology. Chapman and Hall, London, England.

Tuurala, H., and A. Soivio. 1982. Structural and circulatory changes in the secondary lamellae of *Salmo gairdneri* gills after sublethal exposures to dehydroabietic acid and zinc. Aquatic Toxicology (Amsterdam) 2:21–29.

Underwood, A. J. 1981. Techniques of analysis of variance in experimental marine biology and ecology. Oceanography and Marine Biology an Annual Review 19:513–605.

Utida, S., M. Kamiya, and N. Shirai. 1971. Relationship between the activity of Na^+–K^+-activated adenosinetriphosphatase and the number of chloride cells in eel gills with special reference to sea-water adaptation. Comparative Biochemistry and Physiology A, Comparative Physiology 38:433–447.

Utida, S., M. Oidé, S. Saishu, and M. Kamiya. 1967. Préétablissement du mécanisme d'adaptation à l'eau de mer dans l'intestin et les branchies isolés de l'anguille argentée au cours de sa migration catadrome. Comptes Rendus des Seances de la Societe de Biologie et des ses Filiales 161:1201–1204.

Van Der Putte, I., M. B. H. M. Laurier, and G. J. M. Van Eÿk. 1982. Respiration and osmoregulation in rainbow trout *(Salmo gairdneri)* exposed to hexavalent chromium at different pH values. Aquatic Toxicology (Amsterdam) 2:99–112.

Walsh, A. H., and W. E. Ribelin. 1975. The pathology of pesticide poisoning. Pages 515–558 *in* W. E. Ribelin and G. Migaki, editors. The pathology of fishes. University of Wisconsin Press, Madison, Wisconsin, USA.

Wedemeyer, G. A., R. L. Saunders, and W. C. Clarke. 1980. Environmental factors affecting smoltification and early marine survival of anadromous salmonids. U.S. National Marine Fisheries Service Marine Fisheries Review 42(6):1–14.

Wenner, C. A., and J. A. Musick. 1974. Fecundity and gonad observations of the American eel, *Anguilla rostrata,* migrating from Chesapeake Bay, Virginia. Journal of the Fisheries Research Board of Canada 31:1387–1391.

Winer, B. J. 1971. Statistical principles in experimental design, 2nd edition. McGraw-Hill, Tokyo, Japan.

Zaugg, W. S. 1982. A simplified preparation for adenosine triphosphatase determination in gill tissue. Canadian Journal of Fisheries and Aquatic Sciences 39:215–217.

Zaugg, W. S., E. F. Prentice, and F. W. Waknite. 1985. Importance of river migration to the development of seawater tolerance in Columbia River anadromous salmonids. Aquaculture 51:33–48.

American Fisheries Society Symposium 1:191–196, 1987

Osmoregulation in White Sturgeon: Life History Aspects

MARYANN MCENROE AND JOSEPH J. CECH, JR.

Department of Wildlife and Fisheries Biology, University of California, Davis
Davis, California 95616, USA

Abstract.—The white sturgeon *Acipenser transmontanus* is one of 29 extant species of Acipenseriformes. The acipenseriforms are the oldest and most primitive of the actinopterygians and are believed to have evolved at least 200 million years ago. Many of the extant species of sturgeons, including white sturgeon, are anadromous or semianadromous. The limited investigations of osmoregulation in white sturgeons have shown that they, like anadromous teleosts, are hypoosmotic in seawater and hyperosmotic in fresh water. Regulation of plasma electrolytes appears slower than in anadromous teleosts. Also, comparisons of urine electrolyte concentrations indicate fundamental differences in ionic regulation between North American and Eurasian sturgeon species.

All modern sturgeons spawn in fresh water, but the environment in which they reside during most of their adult life may differ. The adults of several species (*Acipenser medirostris*, *A. oxyrhynchus*, and *A. sturio*) live in oceanic environments; the adults of others (*Huso huso*, *H. dauricus*, *A. guldenstadti*, *A. stellatus*, and *A. nudiventris*) live in brackish water. Several species of sturgeon (*A. baeri*, *A. ruthens*, *A. fulvescens*, and *Scaphirynchus* spp.) spend their entire lives in fresh water. Doroshov (1985) has divided many of the extant sturgeon species into three categories according to their life history: anadromous, semianadromous, and landlocked. By this classification, the white sturgeon *Acipenser transmontanus* is a semianadromous fish: it spends most of its adult life in coastal marine environments and migrates into fresh water to spawn.

White sturgeons occur along the Pacific coast of North America from British Columbia to California (Lee et al. 1980), and migrate up the larger rivers (e.g., Fraser, Columbia, Umpqua, and Sacramento rivers) in the fall or winter. Sturgeon fry and juveniles remain in fresh water from several months to several years, depending on the species (Doroshov 1985). Juvenile Atlantic sturgeons (*Acipenser oxyrhynchus*) remain in fresh water for 1–6 years (Smith 1985). It is not known how long white sturgeon juveniles remain in a freshwater environment or when they migrate to sea. McEnroe and Cech (1985) found that the tolerance of juvenile white sturgeons to hyperosmotic environments increases with increasing age and size. The plasma electrolyte composition of white sturgeons acclimated to fresh water and seawater has also been determined (Potts and Rudy 1972; McEnroe and Cech 1985), and found to be similar to that of

teleosts. McEnroe and Cech (1985) also found significant increases in sodium and chloride concentrations and in osmolality 3 d after freshwater-acclimated fish were moved to seawater (33–35‰). The object of the present study was to determine the dynamics of white sturgeon plasma and urine electrolyte concentrations during changes in environmental salinity. It was hoped that light would be shed on the species' osmoregulatory mechanisms and its life history relationships with other sturgeon species.

Methods

In previous studies of blood electrolyte concentrations in white sturgeon, either blood samples were obtained from stressed fish and the water salinity was not reported (Urist and Van de Putte 1967) or the fish were not sufficiently acclimated to test salinities (Potts and Rudy 1972). We decided to repeat these studies using unstressed cannulated (ventral aorta) white sturgeons that were fully acclimated to either fresh, brackish, or seawater. Methods of capture, transport, and cannulation, the protocol for increasing the salinity of tank water, and blood sampling techniques were described by McEnroe and Cech (1985). Several of these fish were gradually returned to fresh water over an 8-h period and plasma samples were taken daily for several days. Blood samples were also obtained from juvenile white sturgeons, 1½–2 years old, by caudal venipuncture (McEnroe 1986). A single fish acclimated to brackish water (24‰) was transferred to fresh water by dilution of brackish San Francisco Bay water with fresh water. Plasma samples were taken for 2 d following transfer.

We collected urine samples from adult and

juvenile white sturgeons by inserting a cannula (PE 50) into the urinary papilla. Urine was sampled via syringe from the "urinary bladder" formed by the junction of the two archinephric ducts. Although this technique does not allow for estimates of water reabsorption in the kidney and "urinary bladder," it does provide an estimate of overall ion transport in the kidney.

Results and Discussion

Plasma Electrolytes

We found that adult white sturgeons acclimated to either fresh water or seawater have very similar blood electrolyte compositions and osmotic concentrations (Table 1). This is in agreement with the findings of Urist and Van de Putte (1967) on white sturgeon in fresh and brackish waters. The pattern of osmoregulation, as well as the ion concentrations in the blood of sturgeons acclimated to these two environments, is very similar to that of anadromous teleosts (Urist and Van de Putte 1967), except that the plasma concentration of all ions is slightly less in sturgeons acclimated to fresh water and seawater than in anadromous teleosts. White sturgeons differ from most teleosts

in their low concentration of plasma calcium in both fresh and seawater (Table 1). This was also observed in white sturgeons by Urist and Van de Putte (1967), but Potts and Rudy (1972) reported higher plasma calcium concentrations in green sturgeons *A. medirostris* transferred to fresh water (2.6–7.0 meq Ca^{++}/L) or seawater (3.6–10.0 meq Ca^{++}/L).

Juvenile freshwater white sturgeons had blood ion concentrations similar to, but higher than, those of freshwater-acclimated adults (Table 1). However, when the juveniles were gradually acclimated to seawater over several weeks and then held in seawater for several months, they exhibited significantly higher plasma ion concentrations than did the seawater-acclimated adults (Table 1). The ion concentrations observed in the plasma of these juvenile fish were in the ranges of those found in seawater-acclimated teleosts. This difference between the blood ionic concentrations of juveniles and adults acclimated to seawater may be due, in part, to the different blood-sampling techniques. These fish were later killed for gill histology and had abundant chloride cells on the primary lamellae of the gills (McEnroe 1986).

When cannulated white sturgeons were ex-

TABLE 1.—Electrolytes in plasma and urine of white sturgeons acclimated to fresh or seawater. Fish were sampled in different years and held either in Davis or at the Bodega Marine Laboratory (BML). Data are means (SD).

Life stage or water sample	Sample	Na$^+$ (meq/L)	K$^+$ (meq/L)	Cl$^-$ (meq/L)	Ca^{++} (meq/L)	Osmolality (mosmol/kg H$_2$O)
			Fish in fresh water			
Adults (Davis; N = 5)	Plasma	134.2 (6.9)	2.67 (0.79)	111.6 (3.4)		263.4 (9.1)
Adults (BML; N = 5)	Plasma	132.8 (12.2)	2.92 (0.43)	104.1 (4.6)	3.18 (0.16)	243.0 (5.0)
Juveniles (Davis; N = 11)	Plasma	140.3 (6.9)	3.53 (0.26)	116.6 (4.8)	3.91 (0.25)	268.3 (8.3)
Adults (BML; N = 6)	Urine	9.88 (9.76)	1.98 (0.43)	<25.0	0.53 (0.53)	36.5 (20.1)
Fresh water		22.5		0.10	0.93	
			Fish in seawater			
Adults (BML; N = 4)	Plasma	141.9 (5.7)	2.83 (0.16)	118.4 (7.3)	3.02 (0.69)	268.0 (12.1)
Juveniles (BML; N = 4)	Plasma	163.2 (10.1)	3.45 (0.46)	145.8 (8.8)	4.89 (0.16)	316.0 (11.8)
Adults (BML; N = 6)	Urine	4.9 (5.7)	1.68 (0.99)	150.8 (5.3)	18.2 (3.4)	276.0 (2.8)
Pacific Ocean seawater		509 (20)	30 (1)	540 (30)	10.0 (0.1)	

TABLE 2.—Mean (SD) plasma electolyte concentration in white sturgeon either acclimated to fresh water, transferred to seawater (33–35%), and returned to fresh water or acclimated to brackish water (24%) and transferred to fresh water.

Water	Days in water	N	Na+ (meq/L)	K+ (meq/L)	Cl− (meq/L)	Osmolality (mosmol/kg H₂0)
			Fresh to sea to fresh water			
Fresh	>21	3	131.6 (1.2)	2.18 (0.63)	110 (3)	262 (9)
Sea	3	3	204.5 (21.5)	4.03 (0.76)	173 (17)	393 (32)
Fresh	1	2	176.8 (55.4)	2.98 (1.02)	149 (41)	356 (96)
Fresh	4–5	2	131 (0.8)	2.54 (1.64)	112 (4)	267 (2)
			Brackish to fresh water			
Brackish	>21	1	131.7	2.70	117	260
Fresh	<1	1	129.1	1.89	113	228
Fresh	1	1	137.4	2.41	107	228
Fresh	2	1	118	2.09	104	211

posed to salinities that increased to full-strength artificial seawater (Instant Ocean) over several days, they showed a gradual rise in plasma electrolytes (McEnroe and Cech 1985). The electrolyte values in fish exposed 3 d to seawater were much greater than those of the seawater-acclimated white sturgeons at Bodega Marine Laboratory. When fish were transferred back to fresh water, plasma electrolyte values returned to freshwater-acclimated values after 4–5 d. Freshwater acclimation was incomplete after 1 d (Table 2). The single fish acclimated to brackish water (24‰) displayed freshwater-acclimation electrolyte values after less than 1 d in fresh water. After 2 d in fresh water, both sodium and osmotic concentrations appeared lower than freshwater-acclimation values.

Urine Electrolytes

Juvenile and adult white sturgeons in fresh water produced a very dilute urine which was low in Na+, Cl−, Ca++, and osmotic concentrations. Adult white sturgeon which had been acclimated to seawater for several months produced a urine which was isosmotic with the blood and contained high concentrations of Cl− and Ca++ (Table 1).

Ionic Relationships among Sturgeon Species

Previous studies (Magnin 1962; Urist and Van de Putte 1967; Potts and Rudy 1972; McEnroe and Cech 1985) have indicated that sturgeons, like anadromous teleosts, are hypoosmotic in fresh water. Magnin (1962) captured several species of sturgeon (*Acipenser transmontanus, A. sturio,* and *A. fulvescens*) and found little difference in the plasma ion concentration in fish from fresh and brackish waters. In the present study, we found that white sturgeons acclimated to fresh and seawater had very similar plasma electrolyte values (Table 1). Potts and Rudy (1972) reported blood and urine electrolyte concentrations from several green sturgeons and one white sturgeon from the Umpqua River estuary in Oregon. They obtained blood samples several days after transferring these fish to seawater or fresh water and showed evidence of elevated plasma electrolyte values in green sturgeons 2 d after transfer from brackish to sea water (Table 3). After the green sturgeons had been 3 d in seawater, their plasma values had declined to approach those of seawater-acclimated white sturgeons (Table 1). In contrast, plasma values in white sturgeons transferred from fresh water to seawater were still rising after 3 d exposure to seawater (Table 2; McEnroe and Cech 1985). Upon return to fresh water, their plasma values returned to those of freshwater-acclimated fish in 4–5 d. Potts and Rudy (1972) also investigated ion fluxes and gill water permeability in these species and found that sturgeons seem to require longer than euryhaline teleosts to decrease gill efflux of ions when transferred from brackish to fresh water. The one white sturgeon which we transferred from brackish to fresh water showed low sodium and osmotic concentrations even after 2 d in fresh water (Table 2). Sea-run brown trout *Salmo trutta* reach stable plasma electrolyte levels 24 h after transfer from fresh water to seawater (Hogstrand and Haux 1985).

Since the urine produced by white sturgeon in fresh water is low in Na+, Cl−, and Ca++, it is very likely that the fish reabsorb these ions from the filtrate, as do freshwater teleosts (Hickman and Trump 1969). Seawater-acclimated white sturgeon appear very much like marine teleosts in that Na+ excretion is extrarenal but some Cl− is

TABLE 3.—Mean (SD) plasma and urine electrolyte concentrations from green sturgeon or white sturgeon after transfer from brackish water to seawater or to fresh water; data are from Potts and Rudy (1972).

Sturgeon species	N	Days after transfer	Sample	Na$^+$ (meq/L)	K$^+$ (meq/L)	Cl$^-$ (meq/L)	Ca^{++} (meq/L)	Mg^{++} (meq/L)
				Brackish to seawater				
Green	3	2	Plasma	208 (22)	5.0[a]	189 (7)	9.6 (0.5)	
Green	2	2	Urine	28 (18)	1.2 (0.1)	118 (69)	5.1 (3.5)	
Green	3	3	Plasma	146 (17)	2.1 (0.4)	151 (16)	4.0 (0.4)	3.2 (1.0)
Green	3	3	Urine	12 (8)	1.9 (2.0)	100 (54)	7.5 (8.4)	45.8 (2.0)
				Brackish to fresh water				
Green	3	1	Plasma	119 (43)	4.8[a]	96 (43)	5.1 (1.1)	3.7 (0.5)
Green	4	3	Plasma	122 (12)	2.7 (1.9)	106 (6)	3.4 (0.6)	1.1 (0.3)
White	1	5	Plasma	125	5.5		6.8	

[a] Solitary datum.

lost in the urine. Divalent ions such as Ca^{++} are most likely excreted in the urine (Table 1). Green sturgeons show a similar urine electrolyte pattern when transferred from brackish to seawater (Table 3), emphasizing the similarities between these two North American species.

Natochin et al. (1985) have reported the plasma and urine electrolyte concentrations from several species of Russian sturgeon (*A. guldenstadti, A. stellatus, Huso huso,* and *A. persicus*) which live either in fresh water or in brackish water as adults (Table 4). While Natochin et al. found that these fish have plasma concentrations of Na$^+$ and K$^+$ similar to those in white sturgeons (Potts and Rudy 1972; Urist and Van de Putte 1972; McEnroe and Cech 1985), these Eurasian species have higher plasma levels of Ca^{++} (Table 4).

These Eurasian sturgeons also differ from white sturgeon in their urine ion composition: while white sturgeon in fresh water have very low amounts of Na$^+$ and Ca$^+$ in their urine (Table 1), the Eurasian sturgeons have appreciable concentrations of these ions in their urine when they are in fresh water (Table 4). It appears as if the Eurasian species can maintain plasma ion concentrations of Na$^+$ and Ca^{++} similar to those of the freshwater North American species while losing more of these ions in the urine. Potts and Rudy (1972) showed that green sturgeons caught in brackish water and transferred to seawater several days prior to sampling had relatively low urine concentrations of Na$^+$ and K$^+$ and high (much greater than plasma) concentrations of Mg^{++} (Table 3).

The regulation of magnesium may also differ between the Eurasian and North American sturgeons. Green sturgeons transferred to seawater have very low plasma Mg^{++} concentrations

(Table 3) and urine Mg^{++} concentrations 10 times higher (Potts and Rudy 1972). Whereas green sturgeons show no plasma magnesium differences between fresh water and seawater (Table 3), most of the Eurasian species have higher concentrations in brackish environments than in fresh water (Table 4). In all the studies mentioned, urine was sampled by basically the same technique, so there may be fundamental differences in the way that various sturgeon species regulate ions. Further studies on sturgeons, preferably on fish with cannulated "urinary bladders," could resolve this dilemma.

Sturgeons have been separated from the main line of teleostean evolution for at least 200 million years. However, anadromous sturgeons share with anadromous teleosts a similar life history strategy. Our research indicates that white sturgeons osmoregulate and respond to increases in salinity in a manner similar to that of the anadromous teleosts. However, sturgeons appear slower than teleosts in regulating plasma electrolytes after environmental salinity changes. Perhaps the ionic differences observed between white and Eurasian sturgeons are due to the different ionic compositions of the waters these fish inhabit. During its life cycle, the white sturgeon lives in the sea, in brackish estuaries, and in freshwater rivers. The Eurasian species studied by Natochin et al. live in the brackish Caspian Sea and in the fresh Volga River. The Caspian Sea had a Mg^{++} concentration of 29.2 meq/L (Natochin et al. 1985), considerably less than that of sea water (106 meq/L). Thus, the relatively high Mg^{++} concentration in the urine of the Caspian Sea sturgeons seems unusual. The differences among the various sturgeon species may mean that conclusions drawn from research on one species may not

TABLE 4.—Mean (SE) ionic composition (meq/L) of plasma (P) and urine (U) in Russian sturgeons; data are from Natochin et al. (1985).

Environment and species	N	Sample	Na$^+$	K$^+$	Ca^{++}	Mg^{++}
			Freshwater environments			
Lake Baikal						
Acipenser baeri	4	P	126.0 (4.0)	4.1 (0.8)	4.8 (0.2)	6.4 (1.6)
		U	20.0	2.1	1.6	1.4
Lake Balkhash						
A. nudiventris	1	P	140.0	3.9		3.1
Volga River						
A. guldenstadti	11	P	132.0 (1.0)	2.0 (1.0)	4.8 (0.3)	2.0 (0.2)
		U	85.0 (12.0)	6.1 (0.8)	4.9 (0.6)	1.5 (0.1)
A. stellatus	9	P	144.0 (1.0)	2.0 (0.2)	5.6 (0.8)	2.1 (0.2)
A. ruthens	6	P	128.0 (1.0)	2.2 (0.3)	5.0 (1.3)	1.8 (0.1)
		U	29.0 (1.0)	0.7 (0.2)	1.7 (0.6)	1.4 (0.3)
Huso huso	11	P	136.0 (1.0)	1.2 (0.1)	4.4 (0.2)	2.1 (0.1)
		U	50.0 (6.0)	2.0 (0.6)	2.4 (0.2)	1.2 (0.2)
			Brackish-water environments			
Northern Caspian Sea						
A. guldenstadti	10	P	132.1 (1.0)	4.2 (0.2)	5.3 (0.1)	3.6 (0.3)
		U	60.0 (3.0)	10.8 (0.9)	5.1 (0.4)	6.1 (0.7)
Southern Caspian Sea						
A. guldenstadti	11	P	144.0 (1.0)	2.9 (0.2)	7.9 (1.1)	9.7 (1.1)
		U	101.0 (7.0)	17.8 (2.3)	11.7 (1.1)	20.5 (3.0)
A. stellatus	10	P	146.0 (2.0)	2.7 (0.2)	6.1 (0.4)	8.2 (0.8)
		U	82.0 (8.0)	27.7 (3.1)	9.6 (1.3)	17.5 (2.8)
A. persicus	17	P	144.0 (2.0)	2.5 (0.2)	5.5 (0.4)	9.7 (0.9)
		U	99.0 (6.0)	16.6 (1.5)	8.6 (0.6)	16.0 (1.1)
H. huso	13	P	149.0 (1.0)	2.9 (0.3)	6.1 (0.5)	7.5 (1.0)
Black Sea						
A. guldenstadti	21	P	155.0 (1.0)	2.8 (0.1)	6.0 (0.2)	7.7 (0.7)
colchicus		U	83.0 (7.0)	19.7 (2.9)	10.4 (2.2)	25.7 (3.6)

be applicable to other sturgeon species.

Acknowledgments

We thank G. Cherr, A. and A. Cuanang, S Doroshov, P. Lutes, G. Monaco, E. Tavasieff, and the captain and crew of the R. V. *Stephanie K* for assistance in collecting specimens. We also thank N. Abramson, B. Jarvis, and J. Whipple of the National Marine Fisheries Service; C. Hand, P. Siri, and the staff at the University of California's Bodega Marine Laboratory; and the Aquaculture and Fisheries Program and the Institute of Ecology at the University of California, Davis, for space and technical support. The manuscript was improved by the comments of R. Griffith, R. Saunders, J. Specker, and an unknown referee and expertly processed by C. Lucido and A. Chamberlain. This work is a result of research sponsored in part by the National Sea Grant College Program, Department of Commerce, under grant NA80AA-D-00120, project R/F-90, through the California Sea Grant College Program, and in part by the California State Resources Agency.

References

Doroshov, S. I. 1985. Biology and culture of sturgeon, Acipenseriformes. Pages 251–274 *in* J. F. Muir and R. J. Roberts, editors. Recent advances in aquaculture, volume 2. Croom Helm, London, England.

Hickman, C. P., and B. F. Trump. 1969. The kidney. Pages 92–240 *in* W. S. Hoar and D. J. Randall, editors. Fish physiology, volume 1. Excretion, Ionic Regulation, and Metabolism. Academic Press, New York, New York, USA.

Hogstrand, C., and C. Haux. 1985. Evaluation of the sea-water challenge test on sea trout, *Salmo trutta.*

Comparative Biochemistry and Physiology A, Comparative Physiology 82:261–266.

Lee, D. S., C. R. Gilbert, C. H. Hocutt, R. E. Jenkins, D. E. McAllister, and J. E. Stauffer, Jr. 1980. Atlas of North American freshwater fishes. North Carolina State Museum of Natural History, Raleigh, North Carolina, USA.

Magnin, E. 1962. Reserches sur la systematique et la biologie des Acipenserides. Annales de la Station Centrale de Hydrobiologie Appliquee 9:7–244. (Ministere de l'Agriculture, Paris, France.)

McEnroe, M. 1986. Aspects of osmoregulation and its endocrine control in the white sturgeon. *Acipenser transmontanus*. Doctoral dissertation. University of California, Davis, California, USA.

McEnroe, M., and J. J. Cech. 1985. Osmoregulation in juvenile and adult white sturgeon, *Acipenser transmontanus*. Environmental Biology of Fishes 14:23–40.

Natochin, Y. V., V. I. Lukianenko, V. I. Kirsanov, E. A. Lavrova, G. F. Metallov, and E. I. Shakhmatova. 1985. Features of osmotic and ion regulation in Russian sturgeon (*Acipenser guldenstadti* Brandt). Comparative Biochemistry and Physiology A, Comparative Physiology 80:297–302.

Potts, W. T. W., and P. P. Rudy. 1972. Aspects of osmotic and ion regulation in the sturgeon. Journal of Experimental Biology 56:703–715.

Smith, T. I. J. 1985. The fishery, biology, and management of the Atlantic sturgeon *Acipenser oxyrhynchus* in North America. Environmental Biology of Fishes 14:61–72.

Urist, M. E., and K. A. Van de Putte. 1967. Comparative biochemistry of the blood of fishes. Pages 271–285 *in* P. W. Gilbert, R. W. Mathenson, and D. P. Hall, editors. Sharks, skates, and rays. Johns Hopkins Press, Baltimore, Maryland, USA.

American Fisheries Society Symposium 1:197–210, 1987

Involvement of the Thyroid Gland in Smoltification, with Special Reference to Metabolic and Developmental Processes

WALTON W. DICKHOFF

School of Fisheries WH-10, University of Washington, Seattle, Washington 98195, USA
and
National Marine Fisheries Service, Northwest and Alaska Fisheries Center
2725 Montlake Boulevard East, Seattle, Washington 98112, USA

CRAIG V. SULLIVAN

School of Fisheries WH-10, University of Washington

Abstract.—Thyroid hormones have been implicated in control of salmonid smoltification for over half a century, yet the role of thyroid hormones in coordinating this developmental event, which allows young salmonids to change from fresh- to seawater habitation, remains poorly understood. In this paper we review the evidence for thyroidal control of metabolic and developmental processes during smoltification, including recent research in our and other laboratories. We discuss the potential problems in interpreting in vivo responses of juvenile salmonids to exogenously administered thyroid hormones, and we develop some hypotheses concerning how thyroid hormones may act to promote smolt development, in order to provide a conceptual framework for future studies.

Hoar (1939) detected the activation of the thyroid gland of the anadromous Atlantic salmon *Salmo salar* during the parr-to-smolt transformation. He suggested that thyroid hormone may be involved in the rapid growth of fish in the spring, in the biochemical changes in tissues, and in the behavioral modifications that favor downstream migration and residence in the sea. Encouraged by his histological findings of thyroid activation in smolts, Hoar tried but failed to induce smolting in Atlantic salmon parr by feeding the fish desiccated thyroid gland or by injecting them with iodides or thyroid-stimulating hormone (Hoar 1965). Shortly after Hoar's attempts, Landgrebe (1941) reported inducing smoltification in Atlantic salmon and brown trout *Salmo trutta* by injecting the fish with extracts of bovine thyroid glands. Robertson (1949) reported that a silvery "smolt-like" steelhead *Salmo gairdneri* could be produced by injections of mammalian thyroid extract or thyrotropic hormone. Piggins (1962) reported that feeding yearling Atlantic salmon a diet containing 20% beef thyroid resulted in an 80% increase in production of yearling smolts (versus 2-year-old smolts) in the population. The migratory pattern and survival of the smolts "induced" by thyroid hormone were normal up until the time of seawater entry. These early studies, in which stimulatory effects on smoltification were observed after treatment with thyroid hormones or other thyroactive preparations, must be inter-

preted with caution since "smoltification" was defined as the acquisition of a silvery integumentary coat due to dermal purine deposition. Changes in body color are not necessarily correlated with other aspects of smoltification such as acquisition of the ability to osmoregulate in seawater.

Subsequent research has focused on identifying the physiological, morphological, and behavioral changes that constitute smoltification and determining whether thyroid hormones (or other hormones) play a part in directing those changes (see reviews by Fontaine 1975; Hoar 1976; Folmar and Dickhoff 1980). Interest in the involvement of the thyroid gland in smoltification has been renewed by the demonstration of an elevation in the blood plasma concentration of thyroid hormones during smoltification of Pacific salmon *Oncorhynchus* spp. and Atlantic salmon (Dickhoff et al. 1978, 1982; Nishikawa et al. 1979; Grau et al. 1981, 1982; Nagahama et al. 1982; Lindahl et al. 1983; Sullivan et al. 1983; Sower et al. 1984; Boeuf and Prunet 1985; Virtanen and Soivio 1985). Furthermore, it has been shown that smolt status is achieved in populations of coho salmon *Oncorhynchus kisutch* in fresh water when plasma thyroid hormone has returned to basal levels following a rise in the level during spring (Folmar and Dickhoff 1981). Despite the large amount of evidence for a correlation between thyroid activity and smolting, treatment of salmon parr with thyroid hormones in order to induce smolting generally has been only partly successful. For example, in several studies, treatment of the fish with thyroid hormones successfully induced pigmentary changes associated with smoltification, or increased growth rates, without apparent stimulation of the ability of the fish to osmoregulate in seawater (Fagerlund et al. 1980; Miwa and Inui 1983). An example of the results of two such experiments is shown in Table 1. Growth in length and weight and pigmentary changes were enhanced in yearling and in underyearling coho salmon that were fed triiodothyronine (T_3: 12 mg/kg of feed) ad libitum for several weeks before and during the period of elevated thyroid hormone levels associated with smoltification. The growth enhancement implies an anabolic effect of thyroid hormones since food conversion efficiency increased without a corresponding increase in food consumption (Table 1). Previous reports of similar effects of thyroid hormones on salmonid development have been summarized by Donaldson et al. (1979). In our experiments, a seawater challenge test (Clarke and Blackburn 1977) conducted at the

TABLE 1.—Final mean fork length, wet weight, food consumption, gross food conversion efficiency, and plasma sodium concentration for groups of coho salmon which were fed ad libitum with either a control diet or a diet containing 12 mg T_3/kg from January 9 to June 1 (yearlings) or from March 29 to June 1 (underyearlings). Plasma sodium concentration was determined after a 24-h seawater (28‰) challenge test conducted on June 1 (Clarke and Blackburn 1977). The initial mean length, weight, and percent smolt of the fish were, respectively, 6.3 cm, 3.1 g, and 0% (underyearlings) or 9.1 cm, 9.1 g, and 0% (yearlings). Rearing conditions were given by Sullivan et al. (1985). Underyearlings exhibited slight elongation of the operculum and attenuation of the rostral cartilages (see Higgs et al. 1982) on June 1. Asterisks indicate values that are significantly different from control values at $P \leq 0.05*$.

	Underyearlings		Yearlings	
Treatment	Control	T_3 (12mg/kg)	Control	T_3 (12mg/kg)
Fork length (cm)	10.9	11.4*	12.6	13.1*
Wet weight (g)	15.9	18.0*	23.8	27.9*
Food consumption[a]			26.8	26.0
Food conversion[b]			45.1	59.1*
Percent smolt[c]	73.0	81.0*	64.0	90.7*
Plasma sodium (meq/L)	205.0	246.0*	174.0	168.3

[a] Mg food/g fish·d.
[b] (Weight gain/weight of food fed) × 100.
[c] Morphological criteria (Gorbman et al. 1982).

normal time of seawater entry of these fish indicated no significant effect of hormonal treatment on the ability of yearlings to regulate their plasma sodium levels 24 h after transfer from fresh water to seawater; the ability of underyearlings to regulate plasma sodium levels was reduced by T_3 treatment (Table 1). This inhibition of seawater tolerance was apparent after 2 months of T_3 treatment. The relative ineffectiveness of exogenously administered thyroid hormones in stimulating all aspects of smoltification may be due to several factors. One possible reason is that many of the physiological processes of smoltification are probably controlled by other hormones that may function to a large extent independently of thyroid hormones (Bern 1978). Another important consideration is that the operation of the thyroid endocrine system and its control in fishes is poorly understood, and experiments attempting to demonstrate thyroid influences on smoltification have been done without adequate knowledge of appropriate dosages of hormone or the proper timing or duration of hormone treatment (reviewed by Donaldson et al. 1979; Higgs et al. 1982). The aim of this paper is to present some information and to develop some hypotheses concerning the developmental and metabolic effects of thyroid hormones in young salmon and to discuss how the thyroid system may be involved in smoltification.

Metabolism

The effects of thyroid hormones can be classified as being of short or long term. Short-term effects (hours to days) are likely due to direct action of the hormones on gene expression or enzyme activity and may involve synergistic and permissive action with other hormones. The long-term effects (months to years) probably occur through similar molecular mechanisms, although they are most likely indirect actions that involve the nervous system and other endocrine factors. For the purposes of this discussion, the long-term effects will be considered developmental or maturational actions of the thyroid hormones, while the short-term actions will be classified as metabolic. In mammals and birds, the metabolic actions of thyroid hormones are usually considered to be associated with regulation of metabolic rate for maintenance of body temperature. During cold-stress of a mammal, for example, the thyroid is activated (along with the sympathoadrenal medullary system) to increase metabolic heat production and maintain body temperature. In contrast with the situation in homeotherms, most evidence suggests that thyroid activity in fishes parallels ambient temperature (Gorbman 1969; Eales 1979), and there is no convincing evidence that thyroid hormones regulate resting metabolic rate. Apparently, the thyroidal regulation of metabolic rate evolved in conjunction with the evolution of homeothermy. Although thyroid hormones do not appear to regulate rates of metabolism for control of body temperature in fishes, there are important adaptations of intermediary metabolism that may be directed by thyroid hormones.

During smoltification of juvenile salmonids, growth typically increases, guanine is deposited in the skin and scales to impart a silver coloration, the forms of hemoglobin change, and mobilization of lipid stores increases. All of these events coincide with increases in the blood concentrations of thyroid hormones and all of these events can be promoted by administration of thyroid hormone to the fish prior to or during smoltification (Koch et al. 1964; Hoar 1976; Donaldson et al. 1979; Folmar and Dickhoff 1980; Sullivan et al. 1985).

Relatively few studies have been done to determine whether thyroid hormones have direct action on the physiological processes of smoltification. As an example of a short-term direct effect of thyroid hormone, T_3 stimulates incorporation of radiactive amino acids into trichloroacetic acid (TCA)-precipitable protein of salmon hepatocytes in vitro (Figure 1; Bhattacharya et al. 1985). Triiodothyronine (T_3) appeared to stimulate protein synthesis by liver cells during 24 h of incubation at hormone concentrations from 10^{-9} to 10^{-5} M. The typical concentration of T_3 in the blood of juvenile salmon is near 10^{-8} M, so the stimulation observed was a response to normal physiological concentrations of the hormone. A principal mechanism for the action of thyroid hormones is stimulation of nuclear gene transcription (reviewed by Oppenheimer 1985), so it is most likely that the observed increase in hepatocyte protein synthesis is due in part to gene activation. The cell nuclei of salmon and trout liver contain receptors for thyroid hormones (Van Der Kraak and Eales 1980; Darling et al. 1982; Bres and Eales 1985). These data show clearly that thyroid hormones have the potential to influence protein synthesis (and fish growth) directly during smoltification. Most other studies of thyroid hormones during smoltification have involved relatively high doses in vivo, making it difficult to determine whether the observed effects are physiologically relevant and whether they are due to indirect action of the hormone.

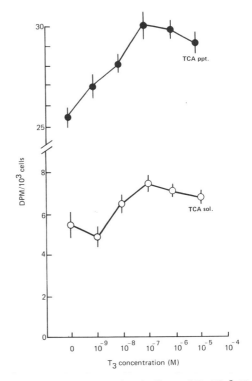

FIGURE 1.—The dose-related effects of T_3 (10^{-9}–10^{-5} M) on the levels of radioactivity in trichloroacetic acid (TCA)-precipitable (ppt.) and TCA-soluble (sol) fractions of salmon hepatocytes incubated for 24 h in the presence of [^{14}C]serine. DPM is disintegrations per minute. (Data from Bhattacharya et al. 1985.)

Thyroid hormones appear to promote lipid mobilization during smoltification. Elevation of blood levels of thyroxine (T_4) occurs coincidently with decreases in body lipids (Woo et al. 1978; Sheridan et al. 1983). Treatment of salmon parr with T_4 reduces the lipid concentration of liver and the size of the mesenteric fat stores. Part of the mechanism of lipid mobilization by T_4 appears to be enhancement of triacylglycerol lipase activity in some tissues (Sheridan et al. 1985). Another change in fat metabolism that occurs during smoltification, and therefore coincides with a period of elevated thyroid hormone levels, is an increase in the proportion of polyunsaturated fatty acids. This change in body fat composition was first reported by Lovern (1934) and more recently confirmed by Sheridan et al. (1985). The potential involvement of thyroid hormones in the change in fatty acid composition remains to be investigated.

The increase in general levels of activity during smoltification is undoubtedly associated with increases in metabolism, particularly along aerobic

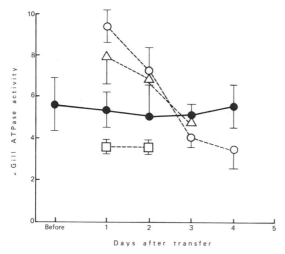

FIGURE 2.—Changes in gill Na^+,K^+-ATPase activity (μmol Pi/mg protein · h) of coho salmon after transfer to fresh water containing T_4 at 0.01 μg/mL (○), 0.10 μg/mL (△), or 1.00 μg/mL (□), or to water containing no T_4 (●). Symbols represent the mean values for 10 fish. Vertical bars indicate standard errors. (Data from Dickhoff et al. 1983).

pathways. Salmon smolts appear to consume more oxygen than do salmon parr (Power 1959; Withey and Saunders 1973). Both cytochrome-c oxidase and succinic dehydrogenase enzymes involved in aerobic metabolism in liver mitochondria are higher in Atlantic salmon smolts than in parr (Blake et al. 1984). Whether the changes in these enzyme activities depend on changes in thyroid hormones during smoltification of salmon remains to be shown. It is possible that thyroid hormones play a role in regulating these enzymes since Massey and Smith (1968) have shown that T_4 treatment of brown trout elevates the specific activities of oxidating enzymes for the substrates succinate, glutamate, and beta-hydroxybutyrate in the liver. However, additional studies of specific enzymes are needed in which salmon parr tissues are treated in vitro with physiological levels of thyroid hormones.

A topic of particular interest to researchers of thyroid hormone function in mammals is the ouabain-sensitive Na^+,K^+-adenosinetriphosphatase (ATPase) enzyme (Ismail-Beigi and Edelman 1970). It has been suggested that the operation of this ion-pumping enzyme is part of a mechanism for generating heat in homeothermic animals. Thyroid hormones would increase the activity or synthesis (or both) of Na^+,K^+-ATPase and, at the same time, increase the permeability of the cell to

sodium ions. Increased ion-pumping activity of the cell would be balanced by increased diffusion of sodium back into the cell so that no net transfer of sodium ions would occur. A by-product of this ion transport would be the heat generated from the continuous dissociation of ATP to ADP. Although this heat-generating mechanism appears to have no adaptive value in salmon, it has been suggested that thyroid hormone regulation of Na^+,K^+-ATPase activity may also have evolved in salmonids (Folmar and Dickhoff 1980). The ouabain-sensitive Na^+,K^+-ATPase activity of the gills of salmonids (gill ATPase) increases in fish during smoltification in fresh water (Zaugg and McLain 1970). The peak in gill ATPase activity coincides with maximal downstream migratory activity of Pacific salmon (Zaugg 1982). During smoltification of fish in fresh water, plasma levels of T_4 usually reach their peak values before the peak in gill ATPase activity. In some cases, however, the peaks of thyroid hormone and gill ATPase activity occur simultaneously. The lack of consistent correlation between blood T_4 levels and gill ATPase activity suggests that they are regulated independently (Folmar and Dickhoff 1981). A direct examination of T_4 influence on gill ATPase activity is shown in Figure 2. Juvenile coho salmon were immersed in fresh water containing T_4 (0.01, 0.1, or 1.0 μg/mL). Blood levels of T_4 in fish held in these T_4 solutions were in the physiological range (Table 2). The blood levels of T_4 were not elevated in fish immersed in the lowest concentration of T_4. Blood levels in fish at the higher doses of T_4 were similar to those observed at intermediate and peak times of the normal seasonal elevation of T_4 during smoltification (Dickhoff et al. 1978). It could be assumed that gill tissue levels of T_4 in fish treated with the lowest dose of T_4 were higher than those in control fish, since T_4 could enter the gill epithelium both from the blood and from the external medium bathing the tissues. The gill ATPase

TABLE 2.—Average plasma thyroxine concentration of coho salmon 24 h after transfer to fresh water containing thyroxine. Plasma thyroxine concentration values did not change significantly in the fish from day 1 to day 7 of hormone treatment.

Thyroxine treatment (μg/mL)	Plasma thyroxine (ng/mL $\pm$ SE)
Control	15.1±1.1
0.01	12.1±1.0
0.10	23.5±1.6
1.00	45.4±1.2

activity was elevated within 1 d of exposure to the lower doses of T_4 but decreased by days 3–4 of exposure to a level slightly lower than control values. The highest dose of T_4 resulted in a significantly depressed gill ATPase activity on days 1–2 of exposure. These data show a biphasic dose–response relationship between T_4 and gill ATPase activity. It is difficult to interpret the physiological significance of this relationship. Based on these data, it could be hypothesized that, during smoltification, increasing T_4 levels initially stimulate the increase in gill ATPase activity then, after elevated plasma T_4 levels are maintained for several weeks, these levels may inhibit gill ATPase and cause the observed decline in gill enzyme activity. This proposed mechanism for thyroid hormone regulation of gill ATPase activity is probably too simplistic since other hormones (prolactin, cortisol) have been implicated in control of gill ATPase in salmonids (reviewed by Foskett et al. 1983).

Another example of a physiological process upon which thyroid hormones may exert both an inhibitory and a stimulatory effect is the switch from the juvenile to the adult hemoglobin pattern that coincides with smoltification in several species of anadromous salmonids (Hashimoto and Matsura 1960; Vanstone et al. 1964; Wilkins 1968; Iuchi and Yamagami 1969; Koch 1972, 1982; Giles 1973; Giles and Vanstone 1976; Sullivan et al. 1985). Thyroid hormones have the potential to affect erythrocyte function directly since nuclear receptors for thyroid hormones, which display hormone-binding characteristics that are essentially identical to those of rainbow trout *Salmo gairdneri* or coho salmon hepatic T_3 receptors (Darling et al. 1982; Bres and Eales 1985), have been identified in rainbow trout erythrocytes (Sullivan et al. 1987a). Horizontal starch gel electrophoresis (pH 8.5) of hemolysates taken from coho

salmon fry indicates that there are three anodally migrating hemoglobins; during later developmental stages, two additional anodally migrating hemoglobins and five cathodally migrating hemoglobins appear and increase in concentration (Giles and Vanstone 1976). The hemoglobins that are present in adults but not in fry can be considered to be "adult hemoglobins." The increase in adult hemoglobin coincides in part with the period of parr–smolt transformation and may parallel changes in blood oxygen equilibria due to the reduced sensitivity to temperature, pH, and pCO_2 of adult hemoglobins relative to fry hemoglobins. It has been suggested that the changes in hemoglobin synthesis may act to ensure efficient oxygen transport during rapid changes in environmental temperature or pH and during metabolic acidosis that may occur during migration (Giles and Randall 1980). The change in hemoglobin pattern is truly ontogenetic. The sequence of hemoglobin patterns is species-specific (not polymorphic) and does not appear to be affected directly by variation in environmental temperature, pH, or dissolved oxygen (Giles 1973). Furthermore, unlike the seasonal nature of some other physiological components of smoltification such as increased growth rate, gill ATPase activity, or body silvering, the change in hemoglobin pattern is not reversible in normal, healthy individuals. As can be seen in Table 3, treatment of yearling coho salmon parr with dietary T_3 (12 mg/kg) inhibits increases in the proportion of adult hemoglobins during the first month of treatment and later accelerates the attainment of the high levels (30–45%) of adult hemoglobins found in smolts. Underyearlings respond similarly to T_3 treatment. However, in underyearlings, T_3 treatment does not result in attainment of the high levels of adult hemoglobins found in yearlings. Furthermore, T_3 treatment does not result in an

TABLE 3.—Changes in content of the adult forms of hemoglobin (as a percent of total hemoglobin) in hemolysates from yearling and underyearling coho salmon which were fed ad libitum with either a control diet or a diet containing 12 mg T_3/kg. Asterisks indicate values that are significantly different from control values at $P \leq 0.05$*. For details on rearing conditions, sampling, and analyses see Sullivan et al. (1985).

1980 yearlings			1982 yearlings			1982 underyearlings		
Date	Control	T_3	Date	Control	T_3	Date	Control	T_3
Jan 9	21.7	21.7	Feb 2	32.2	32.2	Mar 29	18.7	18.7
Feb 18	22.9	19.7*	Feb 25	35.2	33.7*	Apr 12	26.6	24.5
Mar 16	24.4	21.8	Mar 18	36.1	37.5	Apr 26	26.8	30.7
Apr 12	28.0	33.9*	Apr 29	39.5	43.8*	May 10	27.9	33.4*
Apr 27	31.6	34.3*	May 13	41.0	44.4*	May 24	29.7	32.9*
May 13	31.0	34.5	May 27	43.7	44.8			
May 29	30.6	32.1	Jul 19	42.6	41.5			

increase in the proportion of adult hemoglobins beyond that normally attained in yearling or underyearling controls. It follows that if one were to obtain a single blood sample from the fish in our experiments (Sullivan et al. 1985) to determine hemoglobin proportions after 1–3 weeks or 3 months of treatment, or at the end of the experiment in smolts, one could obtain three different results of hormonal treatment, subject to three mutually exclusive interpretations (inhibition, no effect, or enhancement of the proportion of adult hemoglobins). The results of our experiments, in which the effects of thyroid hormone treatment on gill ATPase activity and on adult hemoglobin expression were evaluated, demonstrate the difficulty in interpreting the effects of thyroid hormone treatment of fish. The effects of thyroid hormones may be reversed, depending on the dosage and timing or duration of treatment. This fact among others may be a basis for many of the conflicting reports on the function of thyroid hormones in salmonid physiology.

Development

Thyroid hormones promote the general development of vertebrates. It has been suggested that this role for thyroid hormones evolved early in vertebrate phylogeny because thyroid activity is a signal of the general well-being of an animal (Eales 1979; Dickhoff and Darling 1983). When food is plentiful and other environmental conditions (temperature, photoperiod) are favorable, the thyroid system is activated to promote developmental changes in growth, metamorphosis, reproduction, etc. In contrast, when conditions are generally unfavorable, the activity of the thyroid

system is reduced and the animal ceases growth and reproduction and may enter a phase of hibernation or estivation. One measure of the activity of the thyroid system is the blood plasma concentration of thyroid hormones; other important indicators include T_4 conversion to T_3, hormone clearance rates, hormone distribution to peripheral tissues, hormone kinetics, and concentration of thyroid hormone receptors in target tissues. Circulating levels of T_4 and T_3 in the blood of coho salmon have been determined throughout most of the life cycle (Figure 3). Elevations of blood T_3 in coho salmon occur after hatching and during yolk absorption in the embryo, during the first and second spring of life in fresh water, and during early stages of sexual maturation. These times represent periods of critical growth and developmental change of coho salmon in which thyroid hormones are likely to play a coordinating role. For example, treatment of developing salmon embryos with thyroid hormones increases development rate, yolk absorption, and the final differentiation of the alevin (Pickford 1957; Baker-Cohen 1961; Dodd and Matty 1964). The increase in plasma T_4 at later developmental stages may be due to changes in feedback sensitivity of the hypothalamus–pituitary axis which normally maintains blood thyroid hormone levels at some relatively constant value. Furthermore, these increases are probably due to an endogenous rhythm entrained by environmental cues; they are timed precisely so that increases in thyroid hormone occur in harmony with changes in other hormones. After a developmental surge, blood thyroid hormone returns to the basal levels determined by negative feedback mechanisms accord-

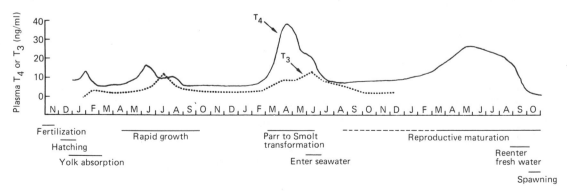

FIGURE 3.—Changes in the blood plasma concentrations of thyroxine (T_4) and 3,5,3′-triiodo-L-thyronine (T_3) of coho salmon throughout most of the life cycle. (Data from Dickhoff et al. 1982; Sower and Schreck 1982; Sullivan and Dickhoff 1985; Sullivan et al. 1987b.)

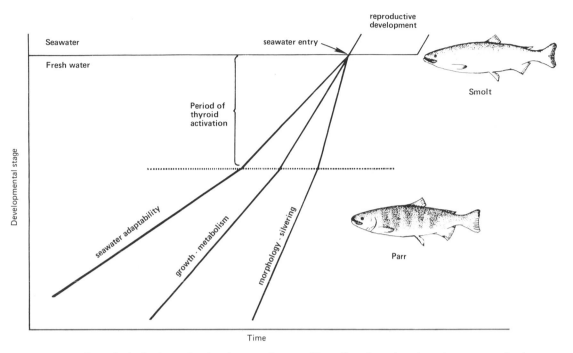

FIGURE 4.—Hypothetical scheme for developmental rates of juvenile salmon based on the concept of saltatory ontogeny. Various physiological and morphological systems may develop slowly in parr. At some critical time, a threshold is reached (smoltification) and the thyroid is activated to accelerate and synchronize development.

ing to some particular, perhaps new, set point. These critical periods of thyroid activation and the intervening periods of relative quiescence may be considered against the background of the thresholds and steps according to the theory of saltatory ontogeny in fishes (reviewed by Balon 1984). Physiological and morphological changes that are characteristic of smolts (in seawater adaptability, metabolism, and morphology) may occur at relatively slow rates in parr long before smoltification (Figure 4). Many of these physiological processes may be influenced by thyroid hormones. When development of parr reaches a critical point (threshold) and environmental conditions are favorable, the thyroid becomes activated to accelerate and coordinate the developmental rates of a variety of physiological systems so that they reach the next step (smolt stage) at the same time. Basal levels of thyroid hormones during intervening periods of thyroid activation (Figure 3) may determine, in part, rates of physiological and morphological development between steps. However, these processes also depend on other hormones so that there is a limit to the extent of influence by the thyroid. A hypothetical model (Figure 4) showing the effects of thyroid

hormone on smoltification can be used to illustrate characteristics of hormone action and explain some of the mixed results of experiments in which attempts are made to influence smoltification by treating fish with thyroid hormones.

One interesting aspect of the model concerns the relative rates of development of the various processes and the degree to which they may be influenced by thyroid hormones. The rates at which various systems develop are not equal (denoted by nonparallel lines in the model) either in the periods before or during thyroid activation. During normal development, all systems converge to their optimal developmental stage at the time when smoltification is complete. If the rates of development of individual systems during the period of thyroid activation are the maximal achievable rates or are characteristic of a given hormone concentration, then treatment of fish with thyroid hormones long before the normal period of thyroid activation could cause asynchronous development. For example, such treatment could cause complete silvering of the fish's skin long before the complete development of seawater adaptability. Asynchronous development could also occur if some of the developing systems were less sensitive to thyroid hormones or more dependent on other endocrine factors. Asynchronous smolt development could be the basis for the term "pseudosmolt" that is used to describe fish that have the morphological but not the physiological properties of smolts (Kubo 1974; Fontaine 1975).

Recent studies attempting to regulate smoltification by administration of thyroid hormones have yielded mixed results. Fagerlund et al. (1980) were able to stimulate growth of underyearling coho salmon with dietary T_3 fed at rates of 4 and 20 mg/kg. Seawater survival was also enhanced by T_3 feeding when fish were transferred to seawater in February but not in May. Somewhat similar results were reported by Refstie (1982) who fed T_3 (5 and 10 mg/kg) to underyearling and yearling Atlantic salmon. In Refstie's study, growth and seawater tolerance were enhanced in 7-month-old fish but not in 19-month-old fish. Saunders et al. (1985) found that feeding Atlantic salmon T_3 at rates of 10 to 100 mg/kg stimulated growth and enhanced seawater survival of both yearling and underyearling fish, but considerable morphological disfiguration was observed at the higher doses of T_3. Sullivan et al. (1985) treated underyearling and yearling coho salmon with dietary T_3 at rates of 4 and 12 mg/kg and found increased silvering, advanced development of adult hemoglobins, and more rapid growth with the higher dose of T_3, but survival in seawater was not significantly affected (Table 1). In contrast to these positive data, T_4 (250 mg/kg) fed to underyearling amago salmon *Oncorhynchus rhodurus* induced skin silvering but had no effect on growth or seawater tolerance (Miwa and Inui 1983). Ikuta et al. (1985) fed T_4 (250 mg/kg) to underyearling masu salmon *Oncorhynchus masou* and found increased silvering but no effects on growth or seawater survival. Lin et al. (1985) fed diets containing 8 mg T_3/kg to steelhead and found no advance in the timing of the thyroid hormone surges during smoltification; they did not examine other indicators of smolting. Some of the differences in results reported in these studies could be due to species differences, the use of T_4 or T_3 at different doses, and the timing and duration of treatment, among other variables. Fagerlund et al. (1980) treated underyearling coho salmon with T_3 at a time when endogenous thyroid activity was low (October to February) and found enhanced seawater survival within a few months prior to the normal time for seawater entry. Refstie (1982) treated Atlantic salmon at a time when thyroid

activity was low and found enhanced seawater survival of underyearling but not of yearling fish 4–6 months before the normal time for seawater entry. Saunders et al. (1985) treated both underyearling and yearling Atlantic salmon for about 6 months during periods when endogenous thyroid activity was estimated to be low for underyearlings and both low and high for underyearlings; better overall seawater survival was observed for underyearlings (which entered seawater near a normal time for smoltification) than for yearlings (which entered seawater at an abnormal time, in winter). Sullivan et al. (1985) treated both underyearling and yearling coho salmon with T_3 a few months before (yearlings) and during (yearlings and underyearlings) periods of high thyroid activity. Lin et al. (1985) treated steelhead (age not specified) with dietary T_3 shortly before and during the period of endogenous thyroid activation. In the studies on underyearling amago salmon (Miwa and Inui 1983) and masu salmon (Ikuta et al. 1985), treatment with dietary T_4 (250 mg/kg) was used during periods when it would be assumed that thyroid activity would be low. In both cases, the fish were subjected to seawater 4–6 months before the normal time for seawater entry.

Given the variables in all these experimental designs and the results of these thyroid hormone feeding experiments, several points can be made regarding the role of the thyroid system in smoltification and how fish respond to exogenously administered thyroid hormone. Dietary administration of T_3 at levels ranging from 5 to 20 mg/kg seems to be more effective both quantitatively and qualitatively than dietary administration of T_4. High levels of dietary T_3 (greater than 20 mg/kg) or prolonged exposure to lower doses may produce anomalies in growth and inhibit seawater survival. Younger fish (underyearlings) seem to be more responsive to hormone treatment than older fish. Treatment of fish during periods of low endogenous thyroid activity appears to be more effective than treatment when the thyroid is highly active. Significantly enhanced seawater survival is more likely to be observed in treated groups when seawater survival is low in control groups. Treated fish are more likely to survive well (greater than 70%) if they are transferred to seawater within a few months of smoltification than if they are transferred 4–6 months before (or after) smoltification. Some of these points have been stated previously (Higgs et al. 1982; McBride et al. 1982); they may provide some insight into the

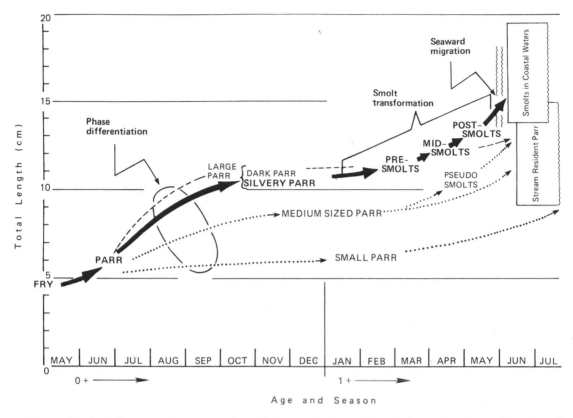

FIGURE 5.—Semidiagrammatic representation of body growth, phase differentiation, and smolt transformation of masu salmon (from Kubo 1974). Note that several types of parr differentiate during their first year of development. The parr have different developmental potentials which are expressed during smolt transformation (or lack or delay of it) during their second year.

ontogeny of smoltification and thyroid influence on this process.

It has been suggested in informal discussions that smoltification may begin during the year preceding migration to sea and that the changes observed in the spring of migration represent the completion of smoltification. Until recently, smolting has been most often defined as a modification of morphology and behavior (e.g., downstream migration of silvery salmon) that is usually limited to the spring. The need for a more precise definition has led people to include criteria based on identifiable biochemical and physiological transformations, which may begin changing much before spring. Earlier developmental changes influence the potential for smolting during the spring. In other words, smoltification is part of a developmental continuum of salmon in fresh water. In masu salmon, morphological changes during early development may later influence smolting. Kubo (1974, 1980) has made a thorough study

of the developing features of masu salmon during smoltification. He found considerable phenotypic polymorphism in parr as well as smolt stages and identified two important periods during salmon development (Figure 5). During the summer and early autumn, masu salmon went through a "phase differentiation" which separated the parr into two major groups. One group, the large or silvery parr, achieved the developmental potential to undergo complete smoltification during the following spring. The other group, the small to medium-sized parr, lacked the potential for full smoltification but some went through a partial morphological and physiological development (pseudosmolt) during the following spring.

Thorpe and colleagues have studied the bimodality in growth rate and smolting occurrence of young Atlantic salmon (Thorpe 1977; Thorpe and Morgan 1978, 1980; Thorpe et al. 1980, 1982; Langdon and Thorpe 1985). They showed that Atlantic salmon parr have different developmental potentials and may go through smoltification either as 1- or 2-year-old fish. The critical time at which developmental potentials are determined occurs approximately during the first summer and autumn that parr are in fresh water. The studies of Atlantic salmon by Thorpe and those of masu salmon by Kubo suggest that the summer, autumn, or both are periods when the fish "decide" whether or not to smoltify the following spring. Although, for both species, this decision may be influenced by development of the reproductive system (Thorpe et al. 1982; Miwa and Inui 1985), it is quite possible that the thyroid system is involved. The basal levels of thyroid hormones during the "phase differentiation" period may determine, in part, what proportion of a population may be in the upper modes of development and likely to smoltify the following spring. If this hypothesis is correct, treatment of parr with thyroid hormones during the summer should increase the proportion of the smolts the subsequent spring. In the normal operation of the thyroid system, abundant food and high ambient temperatures during the summer would elevate basal levels of thyroid hormones and promote growth so that a critical size for smoltification would be achieved. Smoltification would not be completed, however, until increasing photoperiod and water temperatures in the subsequent spring provide the environmental signals for the activation of other endocrine factors responsible for smoltification.

Another consideration which has been lacking in previous studies of hormone-induced smoltification is that the developmental changes influenced by thyroid hormones during naturally occurring smoltification may require a gradual or programmed increase in hormone levels during development; usually thyroid hormones have been applied abruptly and at a constant dose. It has been suggested (Eales 1985) that, in salmonids, the hypothalamic–hypophyseal–thyroid axis may function largely to ensure adequate amounts of T_4 as the substrate for production of the more biologically potent thyroid hormone T_3; a peripheral 5'-monodeiodinase enzyme converts T_4 to T_3. According to this view, control of biological responses to thyroid hormones would be achieved by regulating the extent of T_3 production from T_4 and the availability of T_3 receptors in the target tissues. In salmon and trout liver, as in most vertebrate tissues that have been examined, nuclear receptors specifically bind T_3 with several times higher affinity than T_4 (Darling et al. 1982; Bres and Eales 1985). Physiological adjustment of

other peripheral mechanisms involved in control of thyroid function, such as those involved in tissue distribution and rates of hormonal clearance, may also help to fine-tune responses to thyroid hormones and have been reported to occur during parr–smolt transformation (Specker et al. 1985). Application of Eales's hypothesis to the kinetics of plasma thyroid hormones during smoltification would suggest that the 10-fold increase in plasma T_4 levels that has repeatedly been observed in smolting salmon may correspond to an approximate doubling of basal levels of plasma T_3 in terms of biological potency. Following the increase in plasma T_4 levels, plasma T_3 levels also increase severalfold. The physiological mechanisms underlying the increase in plasma T_3 levels have not been identified in smolting salmon but they could result from induction of the peripheral 5'-deiodinase system in response to the increased plasma T_4 levels early in smoltification. A similar hypothesis has been proposed to explain increases in plasma T_3 during metamorphosis of anuran amphibians (Galton et al. 1982). In view of the greater biological responsiveness of vertebrate tissues to T_3 than to T_4 (Frieden 1967; Koerner et al. 1974; Jorgensen 1976) the changes in plasma thyroid hormone levels observed during smoltification suggest that increases in the thyroid hormonal signal, in terms of its biological potency, may progressively rise during this developmental period. Thus, a reasonable hypothesis might be that developmental change during smoltification may require a progressive increase in thyroidal stimulation. For example, in a study by Kollros (1961) of hypophysectomized *Rana pipiens* tadpoles immersed in T_4-containing solutions, progressive increases in hormone dose were required to stimulate developmental change from one stage to the next. In tadpoles treated with thyroid hormones at inappropriate doses for a particular developmental stage, the ensuing development was uncoordinated, resulting in uncoupled (asynchronous) rates of change of various metamorphic processes and in production of abnormal individuals (Kollros 1959). A similar situation has been observed in juvenile salmonids treated with thyroid hormones; treatment with hormone doses inappropriate to developmental stage may promote uncoordinated growth of various skeletal elements including rostral and opercular cartilages and fin rays (Higgs et al. 1982; Saunders et al. 1985). Furthermore, as discussed above, thyroid hormone treatment may stimulate some developmental processes, such as increases in growth, body silvering or adult hemoglobin synthesis without a concomitant increase in seawater tolerance even in the absence of obvious physical deformity (Table 1, yearlings). Thus, a kind of "pseudo-smoltification" can be induced by treatment with inappropriate doses of thyroid hormones relative to developmental stage.

In summary, thyroid hormones are strongly implicated in control of metabolic and developmental changes during salmonid smoltification. However, an adequate understanding of the role of thyroid hormones in controlling smoltification will require pursuit of several lines of investigation, some of which have been largely neglected in the past. These can be outlined as follows.

(1) Identify direct effects of thyroid hormones in vitro based on physiologically relevant doses and conditions.

(2) Evaluate in vivo responses to thyroid hormones at appropriate doses and duration of hormonal treatment relative to each developmental stage.

(3) Investigate multihormonal regulation of developmental processes during smoltification.

(4) Determine the extent to which early periods of thyroid activation or basal levels of thyroid hormones in the intervening periods may influence the degree and timing of subsequent thyroid activation and associated developmental processes.

Acknowledgments

During the preparation of this review, we were supported by the National Science Foundation under grant DCB-8416224, by Washington Sea Grant through project R/A-42, and by the U.S. Department of Agriculture (Science and Education—Aquaculture) under agreement 85-CRSR-2-2603.

References

Baker-Cohen, D. F. 1961. The role of the thyroid in the development of platyfish. Zoologica (New York) 46:181–223.

Balon, E. K. 1984. Patterns in the evolution of reproductive styles in fishes. Pages 35–54 in G. W. Potts and R. J. Wootton, editors. Fish reproduction: strategies and tactics. Academic Press, New York, New York, USA.

Bern, H. A. 1978. Endocrinological studies on normal and abnormal smoltification. Pages 97–100 in P. J. Gaillard and H. H. Boer, editors. Comparative endocrinology. Elsevier/North Holland Biomedical Press, Amsterdam, The Netherlands.

Bhattacharya, S., E. Plisetskaya, W. W. Dickhoff, and A. Gorbman. 1985. The effects of estradiol and triiodothyronine on protein synthesis by hepatocytes of juvenile coho salmon (Oncorhynchus kisutch). General and Comparative Endocrinology 57:103–109.

Blake, R. L., F. L. Roberts, and R. L. Saunders. 1984. Parr–Smolt transformation of Atlantic salmon (Salmo salar): activities of two respiratory enzymes and concentrations of mitochondria in the liver. Canadian Journal of Fisheries and Aquatic Sciences 41:199–203.

Boeuf, G., and P. Prunet. 1985. Measurements of gill (Na^+,K^+)-ATPase activity and plasma thyroid hormones during smoltification in Atlantic salmon (Salmo salar). Aquaculture 45:111–120.

Bres, O., and J. G. Eales. 1985. Thyroid hormone binding to isolated trout (Salmo gairdneri) liver nuclei in vitro: binding affinity, capacity and chemical specificity. General and Comparative Endocrinology 61:29–39.

Clarke, W. C., and J. Blackburn. 1977. A seawater challenge test to measure smolting of juvenile salmon. Canada Fisheries and Marine Service Technical Report 705.

Darling, D. S., W. W. Dickhoff, and A. Gorbman. 1982. Comparison of thyroid hormone binding to hepatic nuclei of the rat and a teleost (Oncorhynchus kisutch). Endocrinology 111:1936–1943.

Dickhoff, W. W., and D. S. Darling. 1983. Evolution of thyroid function and its control in lower vertebrates. American Zoologist 23:697–707.

Dickhoff, W. W., D. S. Darling, and A. Gorbman. 1983. Thyroid function during smoltification of salmonid fish. Gunma Symposia on Endocrinology 19:45–61.

Dickhoff, W. W., L. C. Folmar, and A. Gorbman. 1978. Changes in plasma thyroxine during smoltification of coho salmon (Oncorhynchus kisutch). General and Comparative Endocrinology 36:229–232.

Dickhoff, W. W., L. C. Folmar, J. L. Mighell, and C. V. W. Mahnken. 1982. Plasma thyroid hormones during smoltification of yearling and underyearling coho salmon and yearling chinook salmon and steelhead trout. Aquaculture 28:39–48.

Dodd, J. M., and A. J. Matty. 1964. Comparative aspects of thyroid function. Pages 303–356 in R. Pitt-Rivers and W. R. Trotter, editors. The thyroid gland, volume 1. Butterworths, London, England.

Donaldson, E. M., U. H. M. Fagerlund, D. A. Higgs, and J. R. McBride. 1979. Hormonal enhancement of growth. Pages 456–597 in W. S. Hoar and D. J. Randall, editors. Fish physiology, volume 8. Bioenergetics and Growth. Academic Press, New York, New York, USA.

Eales, J. G. 1979. Thyroid function in cyclostomes and fishes. Pages 341–436 in E. J. W. Barrington, editor. Hormones and evolution, volume 1. Academic Press, New York, New York, USA.

Eales, J. G. 1985. The peripheral metabolism of thyroid hormones and regulation of thyroidal status in poikilotherms. Canadian Journal of Zoology 63:1217–1231.

Fagerlund, U. H. M., D. A. Higgs, J. R. McBride, M. D. Plotnikoff, and B. S. Dosanjh. 1980. The potential for using the anabolic hormones 17 alpha-methyltestosterone and (or) 3,5,3'-triiodo-L-thyronine in the fresh water rearing of coho salmon (Oncorhynchus kisutch) and the effects on subsequent seawater performance. Canadian Journal of Zoology 58:1424–1432.

Folmar, L. C., and W. W. Dickhoff. 1980. The parr–smolt transformation (smoltification) and seawater adaptation in salmonids: a review of selected literature. Aquaculture 21:1–37.

Folmar, L. C., and W. W. Dickhoff. 1981. Evaluation of some physiological parameters as predictive indices of smoltification. Aquaculture 23:309–324.

Fontaine, M. 1975. Physiological mechanisms in the migration of marine and amphihaline fish. Advances in Marine Biology 13:241–355.

Foskett, J. K., H. A. Bern, T. E. Machen, and M. Conner. 1983. Chloride cells and the hormonal control of teleost fish osmoregulation. Journal of Experimental Biology 106:255–281.

Frieden, E. 1967. Thyroid hormones and the biochemistry of amphibian metamorphosis. Recent Progress in Hormone Research 23:139–194.

Galton, V. A., J. S. Cohen, and K. Munck. 1982. T_4 5'-monodeiodinase: the acquisition and significance of this enzyme system in the developing Rana catesbeiana tadpole. Gunma Symposia on Endocrinology 19:75–90.

Giles, M. A. 1973. The multiple hemoglobins of coho salmon (Oncorhynchus kisutch). Doctoral dissertation. University of British Columbia, Vancouver, Canada.

Giles, M. A., and D. J. Randall. 1980. Oxygenation characteristics of the polymorphic hemoglobins of coho salmon (Oncorhynchus kisutch) at different developmental stages. Comparative Biochemistry and Physiology A, Comparative Physiology 65:265–271.

Giles, M. A., and W. E. Vanstone. 1976. Ontogenetic variation in the multiple hemoglobins of coho salmon (Oncorhynchus kisutch) and the effect of environmental factors on their expression. Journal of the Fisheries Research Board of Canada 33:1144–1149.

Gorbman, A. 1969. Thyroid function and its control in fishes. Pages 241–274 in W. S. Hoar and D. J. Randall, editors. Fish Physiology, volume 2. The endocrine system. Academic Press, New York, New York, USA.

Gorbman, A., W. W. Dickhoff, J. L. Mighell, E. F. Prentice, and F. W. Waknitz. 1982. Morphological indices of developmental progress in the parr–smolt coho salmon, Oncorhynchus kisutch. Aquaculture 28:1–19.

Grau, E. G., W. W. Dickhoff, R. S. Nishioka, H. A. Bern, and L. C. Folmar. 1981. Lunar phasing of the thyroxine surge preparatory to seawater migration of salmonid fish. Science (Washington, D.C.) 211:607–609.

Grau, E. G., J. L. Specker, R. S. Nishioka, and H. A. Bern. 1982. Factors determining the occurrence of the surge in thyroid activity in salmon during smoltification. Aquaculture 28:49–57.

Hashimoto, K., and F. Matsura. 1960. Comparative studies of two hemoglobins of salmon. V. Change in proportion of two hemoglobins with growth. Bulletin of the Japanese Society of Scientific Fisheries 26:931–937.

Higgs, D. A., U. H. M. Fagerlund, J. G. Eales, and J. R. McBride. 1982. Application of thyroid and steroid hormones as anabolic agents in fish culture. Comparative Biochemistry and Physiology B, Comparative Biochemistry 73:143–176.

Hoar, W. S. 1939. The thyroid gland of the Atlantic salmon. Journal of Morphology 65:257–295.

Hoar, W. S. 1965. The endocrine system as a chemical link between the organism and its environment. Transactions of the Royal Society of Canada (Series 4) 3:175–200.

Hoar, W. S. 1976. Smolt transformation: evolution, behavior and physiology. Journal of the Fisheries Research Board of Canada 33:1234–1252.

Ikuta, K., K. Aida, N. Okumoto, and I. Hanyu. 1985. Effects of thyroxine and methyltestosterone on smoltification of masu salmon (Oncorhynchus masou). Aquaculture 45:289–304.

Ismail-Beigi, F., and I. S. Edelman. 1970. The mechanism of thyroid calorigenesis: role of active sodium transport. Proceedings of the National Academy of Sciences of the United States of America 67:1071–1078.

Iuchi, I., and K. Yamagami. 1969. Electrophoretic patterns of larval hemoglobins of the salmonid fish (Salmo gairdneri irridieus). Comparative Biochemistry and Physiology 28:977–979.

Jorgensen, E. C. 1976. Structure activity relationships of thyroxine analogs. Pharmacology and Therapeutics B, General and Systematic Pharmacology 2:661–682.

Koch, H. J. 1972. The shift in the proportions of the hemoglobins during growth of Salmo salar L. International Atlantic Salmon Foundation Special Publication Series 4:111–117.

Koch, H. J. 1982. Hemoglobin changes with size in the Atlantic salmon (Salmo salar L.). Aquaculture 28:231–240.

Koch, H. J. A., Bergstrom, E., and J. C. Evans. 1964. The microelectrophoretic separation on starch gel of the haemoglobins of Salmo salar L. Mededelingen van de Koninklijke Academie voor Wetenschappen Letteren en Schone Kunsten van Belgie, Klasse der Wetenschappen 26:3–32.

Koerner, D., M. I. Surks, and J. H. Oppenheimer. 1974. In vitro demonstration of specific triiodothyronine binding sites in rat liver nuclei. Journal of Clinical Endocrinology and Metabolism 38:706–709.

Kollros, J. J. 1959. Thyroid gland function in developing cold-blooded vertebrates. Pages 340–350 in A. Gorbman, editor. Comparative endocrinology. John Wiley & Sons, New York, New York, USA.

Kollros, J. J. 1961. Mechanisms of amphibian metamorphosis. American Zoologist 1:107–114.

Kubo, T. 1974. [Notes on the phase differentiation and smolt transformation of juvenile masu salmon *(Oncorhynchus masou)*.] Scientific Reports of the Hokkaido Salmon Hatchery 28:9–26. (In Japanese.)

Kubo, T. 1980. Studies on the life history of the "masu" salmon *(Oncorhynchus masou)* in Hokkaido. Scientific Reports of the Hokkaido Salmon Hatchery 34:1–95.

Landgrebe, F. W. 1941. The role of the pituitary and the thyroid in the development of teleosts. Journal of Experimental Zoology 18:162–169.

Langdon, J. S., and J. E. Thorpe. 1985. The ontogeny of smoltification: developmental patterns of gill $Na^+/K^+ATPase$, SDH, and chloride cells in juvenile Atlantic salmon, *Salmo salar* L. Aquaculture 45:83–96.

Lin, R. J., R. J. Rivas, R. S. Nishioka, and E. G. Grau. 1985. Effects of feeding triiodothyronine (T_3) on thyroxine (T_4) levels in the steelhead trout *(Salmo gairdneri)*. Aquaculture 45:133–142.

Lindahl, K., H. Lundqvist, and M. Rydevik. 1983. Plasma thyroxine levels and thyroid gland morphology in the Baltic salmon *(Salmo salar* L.) during smoltification. Canadian Journal of Zoology 61:1954–1958.

Lovern, J. A. 1934. Fat metabolism in fishes. V. The fat of the young salmon in its freshwater stages. Biochemical Journal 28:1961–1963.

Massey, B. D., and C. L. Smith. 1968. The action of thyroxine on mitochondrial respiration and phosphorylation in the trout *(Salmo trutta fario* L.) Comparative Biochemistry and Physiology 25:241–255.

McBride, J. R., D. A. Higgs, U. H. M. Fagerlund, and T. J. Buckley. 1982. Thyroid and steroid hormones: potential for control of growth and smoltification in salmonids. Aquaculture 28:201–210.

Miwa, S., and Y. Inui. 1983. Effects of thyroxine and thiourea on the parr–smolt transformation of amago salmon *(Oncorhynchus rhodurus)*. Bulletin of the National Research Institute of Aquaculture 4:41–52.

Miwa, S., and Y. Inui. 1985. Effects of L-thyroxine and ovine growth hormone on smoltification of amago salmon *(Oncorhynchus rhodurus)*. General and Comparative Endocrinology 58:436–442.

Nagahama, Y. S., S. Adachi, F. Tashiro, and E. G. Grau. 1982. Some endocrine factors affecting the development of seawater tolerance during the parr–smolt transformation of the amago salmon *(Oncorhynchus rhodurus)*. Aquaculture 28:81–90.

Nishikawa, K., T. Hirashima, S. Suzuki, and M. Suzuki. 1979. Changes in circulating L-thyroxine and L-triiodothyronine of the masu salmon *(Oncorhynchus masou)* accompanying the smoltification, measured by radioimmunoassay. Endocrinologica Japonica 26:731–735.

Oppenheimer, J. H. 1985. Thyroid hormone action at the nuclear level. Annals of Internal Medicine 102:374–384.

Pickford, G. E. 1957. The thyroid and thyrotropin.

Pages 130–134 *in* G. E. Pickford, editor. The physiology of the pituitary gland of fishes. New York Zoological Society, New York, New York, USA.

Piggins, D. J. 1962. Thyroid feeding of salmon parr. Nature (London) 195:1017–1018.

Power, G. 1959. Field measurements of basal oxygen consumption of Atlantic salmon parr and smolts. Arctic 12:195–202.

Refstie, T. 1982. The effects of feeding thyroid hormones on saltwater tolerance and growth rate of Atlantic salmon. Canadian Journal of Zoology 60:2706–2712.

Robertson, O. H. 1949. Production of the silvery smolt stage in rainbow trout by intramuscular injection of mammalian thyroid extract and thyrotropic hormone. Journal of Experimental Biology 110:337–355.

Saunders, R. L., S. D. McCormick, E. B. Henderson, J. G. Eales, and C. E. Johnston. 1985. The effect of orally administered 3,5,3'-triiodo-L-thyronine on growth and salinity tolerance of Atlantic salmon *(Salmo salar)*. Aquaculture 45:143–156.

Sheridan, M. A., W. V. Allen, and T. H. Kerstetter. 1983. Seasonal variation in the lipid composition of the steelhead trout, *Salmo gairdneri,* associated with the parr–smolt transformation. Journal of Fish Biology 23:125–134.

Sheridan, M. A., W. V. Allen, and T. H. Kerstetter. 1985. Changes in the fatty acid composition of the steelhead trout, *Salmo gairdneri,* associated with the parr–smolt transformation. Comparative Biochemistry and Physiology B, Comparative Biochemistry 80:671–676.

Sower, S. A., and C. B. Schreck. 1982. Steroid and thyroid hormones during sexual maturation of coho salmon *(Oncorhynchus kisutch)* in seawater or fresh water. General and Comparative Endocrinology 47:42–53.

Sower, S. A., C. V. Sullivan, and A. Gorbman. 1984. Changes in plasma estradiol and effects of triiodothyronine on plasma estradiol during smoltification of coho salmon *(Oncorhynchus kisutch)*. General and Comparative Endocrinology 54:486–492.

Specker, J. L., J. J. DiStephano III, E. G. Grau, R. S. Nishioka, and H. Bern. 1985. Development associated changes in thyroxine kinetics in juvenile salmon. Endocrinology 115:399–406.

Sullivan, C. V., Darling, D. S., and W. W. Dickhoff. 1987a. Nuclear receptors for L-triiodothyronine in trout erythrocytes. General and Comparative Endocrinology 65:149–160.

Sullivan, C. V., and W. W. Dickhoff. 1985. Thyroid hormones, gill $(Na^+,K^+)ATPase$ and seawater tolerance in salmon embryos. American Zoologist 25:80A. (Abstract.)

Sullivan, C. V., W. W. Dickhoff, S. D. Brewer, and G. P. Johnston. 1983. Plasma thyroid-hormone concentrations and gill (Na+K)-ATPase activities in postemergent pink salmon. Transactions of the American Fisheries Society 112:825–829.

Sullivan, C. V., W. W. Dickhoff, C. V. M. Mahnken, and W. K. Hershberger. 1985. Changes in the hemoglobin system of the coho salmon *(Oncorhynchus kisutch)* during smoltification and triiodothyronine and propylthiouracil treatment. Comparative Biochemistry and Physiology A, Comparative Physiology 81:807–813.

Sullivan, C. V., Iwamoto, R. N., and W. W. Dickhoff. 1987b. Thyroid hormones in blood plasma of developing salmon embryos. General and Comparative Endocrinology 65:337–345.

Thorpe, J. E. 1977. Bimodal distribution of length of juvenile Atlantic salmon *(Salmo salar)* under artificial rearing conditions. Journal of Fish Biology 11:175–184.

Thorpe, J. E., and R. I. G. Morgan. 1978. Parental influence on growth rate, smolting rate and survival in hatchery reared juvenile Atlantic Salmon, *Salmo salar*. Journal of Fish Biology 13:549–556.

Thorpe, J. E., and R. I. G. Morgan. 1980. Growth-rate and smolting-rate of male Atlantic salmon parr, *Salmo salar* L. Journal of Fish Biology 17:451–459.

Thorpe, J. E., R. I. G. Morgan, E. M. Ottaway, and M. S. Miles. 1980. Time of divergence of growth between potential 1+ and 2+ smolts among sibling Atlantic salmon. Journal of Fish Biology 17:13–21.

Thorpe, J. E., C. Talbot, and C. A. Villarreal. 1982. Bimodality of growth and smolting in Atlantic salmon, *Salmo salar*. Aquaculture 28:123–132.

Van Der Kraak, G. J., and J. G. Eales. 1980. Saturable 3,5,3′-triiodo-L-thyronine binding sites in liver nuclei of rainbow trout *(Salmo gairdneri* Richardson). General and Comparative Endocrinology 42: 437–448.

Vanstone, W. E., E. Roberts, and H. Tsuyuki. 1964. Changes in the multiple hemoglobin patterns of some Pacific salmon, genus *Oncorhynchus,* during the parr smolt transformation. Canadian Journal of Physiology and Pharmacology 42:697–703.

Virtanen, E., and A. Soivio. 1985. The patterns of T_3, T_4, cortisol and Na^+-K^+-ATPase during smoltification of hatchery reared *Salmo salar* and comparison with wild smolts. Aquaculture 45:97–111.

Wilkins, N. P. 1968. Multiple hemoglobins of the Atlantic salmon *(Salmo salar)*. Journal of the Fisheries Research Board of Canada 25:2651–2663.

Withey, K. G., and R. L. Saunders. 1973. Effects of a reciprocal photoperiod regime on standard rate of oxygen consumption of postsmolt Atlantic salmon *(Salmo salar)*. Journal of the Fisheries Research Board of Canada 30:1898–1900.

Woo, N. Y. S., H. A. Bern, and R. S. Nishioka. 1978. Changes in body composition associated with smoltification and premature transfer to seawater in coho salmon *(Oncorhynchus kisutch)* and king salmon *(O. tschawytscha* [sic]). Journal of Fish Biology 13:421–428.

Zaugg, W. S. 1982. Some changes in smoltification and seawater adaptability of salmonids resulting from environmental and other factors. Aquaculture 28:143–151.

Zaugg, W. S., and L. R. McLain. 1970. Adenosine triphosphatase activity in gills of salmonids; seasonal variations and salt water influence in coho salmon *(Oncorhynchus kisutch)*. Comparative Biochemistry and Physiology 35:587–596.

American Fisheries Society Symposium 1:211–229, 1987

Preparatory Physiological Adaptations for Marine Life of Salmonids: Osmoregulation, Growth, and Metabolism

STEPHEN D. McCORMICK[1] AND RICHARD L. SAUNDERS

Department of Fisheries and Oceans, Biological Station
St. Andrews, New Brunswick E0G 2X0, Canada

Abstract.—Atlantic salmon *Salmo salar,* steelhead *S. gairdneri,* and several species of Pacific salmon *Oncorhynchus* spp. undergo transformation from stream-dwelling parr to seaward-migrating smolts. Physiological, behavioral, morphological, and biochemical changes occur in fresh water in preparation for marine life. The preparatory nature of these adaptations is reviewed and discussed with particular emphasis on osmoregulation, metabolism, and growth. Functional changes in gill, kidney, gut, and urinary bladder result in increased salinity tolerance and hypoosmoregulatory ability. Some or all of these preparatory physiological changes may reverse in the absence of exposure to seawater. Changes in lipid, protein, and carbohydrate metabolism, oxygen consumption, and aerobic respiratory enzyme activity suggest increased catabolism during parr–smolt transformation. These transient changes in catabolism may reflect energetic demands of the extensive differentiation occurring during transformation. Although there is increased growth during parr–smolt transformation, evidence for a hypothesized increase in scope for growth after transformation is not convincing. We suggest that different aspects of the transformation have different developmental patterns, the timing of which is species-dependent and responsive to environmental change. Phylogenetic comparison of the differentiation of salmonid hypoosmoregulatory mechanisms and migratory behavior suggests that their evolution has occurred through heterochrony.

Transformation of the stream-dwelling parr to the seaward-migrating smolt is a significant life history event in many salmonids. Various morphological, physiological, and behavioral changes occur seasonally (usually in spring), develop over a period of 1–2 months, and are presumably adaptive for downstream migration and residence in the marine environment (see Table 1 and reviews by Hoar 1976; Folmar and Dickhoff 1980; Wedemeyer et al. 1980). Parr–smolt transformation has for some time been of interest as a developmental process (Hoar 1939; Bern 1978) and recently has come under more intense scrutiny as an important factor in the performance of hatchery-reared salmonids in ocean ranching and intensive aquaculture (Wedemeyer et al. 1980).

In the present undertaking, we review changes in osmoregulation, metabolism, and growth that occur during the parr–smolt transformation and that are to some degree interrelated. Substantial information exists concerning changes in salinity tolerance and metabolism, though much remains to be done in this area. Less is known concerning growth, and our discussion centers on what is not known. By stating hypotheses concerning the interrelationships of physiological changes during

the parr–smolt transformation, we hope to spur more focused research in this most fascinating and important area. In reviewing each of these areas we develop a common hypothesis: physiological changes during the parr–smolt transformation are preparatory adaptations, preparatory because they anticipate a change in environment and adaptive because they increase survival and fitness in a new environment.

Experiments conducted on the parr–smolt transformation have, of necessity, examined isolated aspects of development. Evidence for developmental changes are then unified under the single term "smoltification." This has often led to two disparate views that are equally wrong: that the transformation is a single and common process, or that it is a series of unconnected changes. Simpson (1985) stated the problem the following way:

Perhaps we should also be concerned lest our use of the term "smoltification" encourages a predilection to the belief that the process is a single one with a single or organically linked set of effectors. Smolting ought rather to be seen as the result of a large number of distinct processes—the change to particular patterns of growth, the elaboration of neurons associated with long-term memory, the development of different patterns of behaviour, major changes in metabolism and, finally, those changes in gill structure which permit the fish to pass from a hypo- to a hypertonic

[1]Present address: Department of Zoology, University of California, Berkeley, California 94720, USA.

environment. There seems to me no *a priori* reason for supposing that these processes evolved simultaneously, or for supposing that they are linearly interdependent or have functionally linked endocrine mediators.

If we are successful in this review, we shall have shown or suggested both the distinction between these processes and their interrelations. By adopting a comparative view, we hope to establish that different aspects of the parr–smolt transformation are present in different salmonid species and that their presence and developmental pattern are related to the timing and duration of anadromy of a population or species.

Osmoregulation

Ontogeny of Salinity Tolerance

Ontogenetic changes in salinity tolerance (defined here as the ability to survive seawater >30‰) have been found in virtually all salmonid species investigated. Whereas salmonid eggs cannot survive more than a few days in seawater, the posthatch alevin has even poorer survival, presumably due to loss of the chorion (Weisbart 1968). Salinity tolerance of Atlantic salmon *Salmo salar* alevins decreases as the water-impermeable vitelline membrane decreases in favor of a water-permeable epithelium (Parry 1960; Talbot et al. 1982). In contrast, salinity tolerance of chum salmon *Oncorhynchus keta* increases during development of the alevin (Kashiwagi and Sato 1969).

After resorption of the yolk sac, salinity tolerance of all salmonids increases with size and age, and is closely tied to, and probably caused by, increased ability to regulate plasma ions and osmolarity following exposure to seawater[2] (Parry 1958, 1960; Houston 1961; Conte and Wagner 1965; Conte et al. 1966; Wagner 1974b; McCormick and Naiman 1984b; Ouchi 1985). Conte and Wagner (1965) and McCormick and Naiman (1984b) concluded that size, not age, is the primary determinant of increased seawater survival for steelhead *Salmo gairdneri* and brook trout *Salvelinus fontinalis,* respectively. Size-dependent salinity tolerance may be due to a more

favorable surface-area-to-volume ratio for larger fish, or to a progressive development of hypoosmoregulatory mechanisms with size, or to both. By comparing studies of similar design, McCormick and Naiman (1984b) concluded that salinity tolerance was also related to genus: the size at which seawater survival occurs is smallest for *Oncorhynchus* species, larger for *Salmo* species, and largest for *Salvelinus* species. This phylogenetic relationship follows closely the duration of marine residence (shortest for *Salvelinus* species) characteristic of each genus, as pointed out by Rounsefell (1958) and Hoar (1976).

There is substantial evidence indicating that size-dependent changes in salinity tolerance are distinct from the more rapid, seasonally occurring changes in salinity tolerance associated with the parr–smolt transformation. Salinity tolerance of seasonally migrating Atlantic salmon, rainbow trout *Salmo gairdneri* and coho salmon *Oncorhynchus kisutch* increases rapidly over a period of 1–2 months, coinciding with the normal period of migration and visible smolt characteristics (Conte and Wagner 1965; Komourdjian et al. 1976; Clarke et al. 1978; Saunders et al. 1983, 1985; McCormick et al. 1987). These changes are independent of temperature (except as it affects developmental rate), and are responsive to photoperiodic cues (Saunders and Henderson 1970; Wagner 1974a; Komourdjian et al. 1976; Clarke et al. 1978; Johnston and Saunders 1981; Clarke et al. 1985; Saunders et al. 1985; McCormick et al. 1987).

Although some seasonal periodicity in salinity tolerance may occur at all life stages (Hoar 1965; Wagner 1974a), the ability to manifest large seasonal changes in salinity tolerance is size-dependent. Rainbow trout do not respond to seasonal cues with increased salinity tolerance until they are at least 10 cm long (Conte and Wagner 1965). Similar size-related limitations in the expression of parr–smolt transformation have been found for coho salmon (Clarke et al. 1978) and Atlantic salmon (Elson 1957; Parry 1960).

In distinguishing between size-dependent changes in salinity tolerance and the size-dependent parr–smolt transformation, the *degree* of salinity tolerance becomes important. Atlantic and coho salmon parr of 10–12 cm can routinely tolerate (i.e., survive for many days) a salinity of 30‰ (Saunders and Henderson 1969; Clarke and Nagahama 1977). These fish may begin to die after several weeks, however, and growth is inevitably poor. Such differences in the degree of salinity

---

[2]Chinook salmon (*O. tshawytscha*) are an apparent exception to this rule. Whereas other *Oncorhynchus* species develop increased salinity tolerance through increased ability to regulate plasma ions, chinook salmon develop an increased tolerance of elevated plasma ions (Weisbart 1968).

tolerance are not limited to the parr stage. Smolt-size (14–17 cm) Atlantic salmon that are denied seasonal cues through exposure to continuous light can adapt to 30‰ seawater, but cannot survive in 40‰ as can normal smolts, and exhibit poor feeding and growth in seawater (Saunders et al. 1985; McCormick et al. 1987). This distinction between the merely adequate or short-term sea-water survival of parr and the complete adaptability of smolts is an important one. Its basis lies in the increased hypoosmoregulatory ability of smolts (Parry 1960; Conte and Wagner 1965; Clark et al. 1978; Boeuf et al. 1978; Saunders and Henderson 1978; Hogstrand and Haux 1985) and perhaps other transport-related phenomena such as food conversion efficiency. Since parr can survive in seawater for extended periods of time, however, one can justifiably ask what the adaptive basis of increased salinity tolerance is at the time of smolting. Rapid acclimation to higher salinities with fewer osmotic perturbations may permit rapid movement through estuaries (Chernitsky 1983; McCormick et al. 1985), and immediate resumption of physiological and behavioral processes that might otherwise result in increased predation and interrupted feeding and growth.

The developmental processes that result in seasonally increased salinity tolerance and hypoosmoregulatory ability are apparently reversible if fish remain in fresh water. Rapid summer decreases in salinity tolerance have been observed in rainbow trout (Conte and Wagner 1965), coho salmon (Mahnken et al. 1982), and Atlantic salmon (Evropeytseva 1962). Generally known as "desmolting," this process may also result in reversion to a parr-like appearance (see Folmar et al. 1982). Whether or not "desmolting" results in a reversal of all physiological changes associated with the parr–smolt transformation will be discussed below.

Functional Changes in Osmoregulatory Organs

Teleosts normally maintain their plasma osmolarity within a narrow range (290–340 mOsmol/L) irrespective of the salinity of the external medium, and failure to do so for prolonged periods results in death. The transition from fresh water to seawater requires a reversal from net ion influx to net ion efflux which is regulated primarily by the gills but also involves the kidney, gut and urinary bladder (for a review of osmoregulation in teleosts, see Evans 1979; Foskett et al. 1983). In most teleosts this reversal is initiated by exposure

to a hyperosmotic environment. As the following discussion should demonstrate, seasonal changes in structure or function (differentiation) of the osmoregulatory machinery, which occur prior to and in anticipation of exposure to seawater, are responsible for increased salinity tolerance during the parr–smolt transformation. This seasonal differentiation is likely to be the result of qualitative and quantitative changes in gene expression, the hormonal control of which has yet to be elucidated (Dickhoff and Sullivan 1987, this volume).

In considering the mechanisms of osmoregulatory change (as well as metabolism and growth), we shall consider only those salmonid species which show a rapid (1–2 month), reversible, seasonally cued increase in salinity tolerance. In this group, Atlantic, coho, and masu salmon *Oncorhynchus masou* and steelhead have received the greatest attention. There are, however, inherent difficulties in conducting and comparing studies on a developmental phenomenon that occurs over many weeks but which has no absolute morphological criterion (Gorbman et al. 1982). Many researchers have used appearance (often the degree of silvering or fin darkening) as a sole criterion to distinguish smolts from nonsmolts. In addition to the subjective nature of this criterion, it has proved to be highly variable under artificial culture conditions and is often "uncoupled" from other aspects of the parr–smolt transformation (Wedemeyer et al. 1980). Seasonal changes in temperature may introduce physiological changes independent of developmental phenomena (Virtanen and Oikari 1984). Differences in methodology, species, and size further increase the difficulties of assessing experimental results. In most cases, the developmental process is clear enough (or the experimental condition controlled enough) in spite of these confounding factors. We shall attempt to point out the exceptions, particularly when conflicting results are apparent.

Gills.—For a variety of euryhaline teleosts, gill Na^+,K^+-ATPase activity increases after transfer from fresh water to seawater (Epstein et al. 1967; Kirschner 1980). Ionic and electrical gradients generated by this enzyme are central to current models of branchial ion fluxes (Maetz and Garcia-Romeau 1964; Silva et al. 1977). Increases in gill Na^+,K^+-ATPase occur in several salmonid species in freshwater *prior* to seawater entry. Such increases in coho salmon (Zaugg and McLain 1970; Giles and Vanstone 1976a; Lasserre et al. 1978), chinook salmon (Hart et al. 1981; Buckman and Ewing 1982), rainbow trout (Zaugg and Wagner 1973), and Atlantic salmon (McCartney 1976; Saunders and Henderson 1978; Boeuf et al. 1985; McCormick et al. 1987) occur seasonally and in phase with migration and increased salinity tolerance (Figure 1). Most of the gill Na^+,K^+-ATPase activity and ion transport capacity resides in mitochondria-rich chloride cells (Epstein et al. 1980; Foskett and Scheffey 1982). Chloride cells increase in number in gill opercular epithelium (Loretz et al. 1982) and change morphology in gill filaments (Richman 1985) of freshwater coho salmon smolts. Langdon and Thorpe (1985) found increased size and number of chloride cells in Atlantic salmon in early spring just before attainment of maximum salinity tolerance.

D. R. N. Primmett, F. B. Eddy, M. S. Miles, C. Talbot, and J. E. Thorpe (personal communication) measured whole-body Na^+ fluxes in juvenile Atlantic salmon; these fluxes are generally assumed to reflect the function of gill epithelium. During parr–smolt transformation, Na^+ flux changed from net influx (characteristic of freshwater teleosts) to net efflux. However, net Na^+ efflux is not an absolute requirement for increased salinity tolerance since maximum salinity tolerance was achieved after Na^+ flux had returned to a net influx. Iwata et al. (in press) found developmental changes in whole-animal transepithelial potential (TEP) of coho salmon. The TEP of coho

salmon in fresh water decreased gradually from 6 mV in early February to -12 mV in mid-April. In fish transferred to seawater for 12 h, TEP was 5 mV in February and increased to 16–18 mV in April through August. Taken together, these results indicate that developmental changes in mechanisms for ion transport found in freshwater-adapted smolts are important for seawater adaptation.

Kidney and urinary bladder.—The urine flow and water excretory rates of rainbow trout smolts in fresh water decrease relative to those in both pre- and postsmolts and are due entirely to a reduction in glomerular filtration rate (Holmes and Stainer 1966). Urine excretory rates of sodium and potassium and total osmolarity are also reduced in smolts. (Decreased urine flow and glomerular filtration occur in euryhaline teleosts after exposure to seawater [Hickman and Trump 1969], and the results of Holmes and Stainer may be interpreted as a preparatory adaptation.) However, the "seasonal" temperatures, variable timing of measurements, and use of appearance as the sole smolt criterion make it difficult to interpret these results. Recent work by Eddy and Talbot (1985) indicates that urine production by juvenile Atlantic salmon (>15 cm) increases during spring coincident with increasing gill Na^+,K^+-ATPase activity. These conflicting results con-

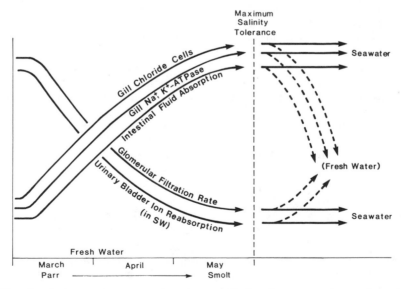

FIGURE 1.—Functional changes in osmoregulatory organs during the parr–smolt transformation. Functional changes normally associated with osmoregulation in seawater occur in fresh water and result in increased hypoosmoregulatory ability and salinity tolerance. In the absence of exposure to seawater, these changes are reversible.

cerning alteration of kidney function during parr–smolt transformation are, at present, unexplained.

Declines in kidney Na^+,K^+-ATPase activity in juvenile Atlantic salmon in spring were reported by McCartney (1976). Virtanen and Soivio (1985) reported that kidney Na^+,K^+-ATPase activity of juvenile Atlantic salmon raised in brackish water fluctuates considerably during spring, falling in early spring then rising to high levels in mid spring and falling again in late spring. S. D. McCormick and R. L. Saunders (unpublished data) found no seasonal change in kidney Na^+,K^+-ATPase activity in freshwater-reared Atlantic salmon, nor was the activity level of this enzyme different from that in fish exposed to continuous light (conditions that inhibit physiological changes associated with transformation). It should be noted that, unlike gill Na^+,K^+-ATPase activity, kidney Na^+,K^+-ATPase activity of Atlantic salmon changes slightly or not at all following increases in environmental salinity (Virtanen and Oikari 1984; McCormick et al., unpublished data).

Loretz et al. (1982) found that Na^+ and Cl^- reabsorption by the urinary bladder of freshwater-adapted coho salmon did not change between March and June. However, developmental changes in the urinary bladder were detected when coho salmon were experimentally adapted to seawater over this same period. In May, when seawater survival was low, Na^+ and Cl^- reabsorption by the urinary bladder of seawater-adapted fish was at high levels characteristic of salmon in fresh water. In June, when seawater survival was high, Na^+ and Cl^- reabsorption was abolished. While no functional differentiation of the urinary bladder was apparent in fresh water, a clear increase in its capacity to respond to sea water had occurred.

Gastrointestinal tract.—Increased drinking rate and absorption of water and salts across gut epithelia occur following adaptation of euryhaline telosts to seawater. Collie and Bern (1982) found that the capacity for net fluid absorption of the intestine increased twofold in freshwater-adapted juvenile coho salmon between March and May, and that high values in May were similar to those of salmon adapted to seawater. Reversion of intestinal net fluid absorption to prespring levels occurred in early autumn in fish held in fresh water. Developmental changes in drinking rate associated with the parr–smolt transformation have yet to be investigated.

Consequences of Developmental Changes on Osmoregulation in Fresh Water

The previous section has established that seasonal increases in salinity tolerance and hypoosmoregulatory ability occur in conjunction with increases in gill Na^+,K^+-ATPase activity, quantity of gill chloride cells, intestinal net fluid absorption and other osmoregulatory changes that are characteristic of seawater-adapted teleosts but which occur prior to seawater entry (Figure 1). If these mechanisms are detectable in smolts in fresh water, are they also fully functional in vivo, and do they, therefore, produce osmoregulatory difficulties (water gain and ion loss) for smolts in fresh water? D. N. R. Primmett, F. B. Eddy, M. S. Miles, C. Talbot, and J. E. Thorpe (personal communication) have recently argued that increases in ion fluxes across the body surface, which are presumably hormone-induced, precede and are responsible for increases in gill Na^+,K^+-ATPase activity and other osmoregulatory changes during transformation. Whereas we have stressed the adaptive nature of these changes, these researchers suggest they are primarily a consequence of the loss of freshwater osmoregulatory capacity (see also Langdon and Thorpe 1985; Simpson 1985). It should be stressed, however, that in each of these scenarios a seasonal differentiation occurs that results in increased salinity tolerance, which is clearly adaptive for a seaward-migrating fish. It is still unclear that all the osmoregulatory changes portrayed in Figure 1 are functional in the freshwater smolt (e.g., Na^+,K^+-ATPase increases may be demonstrable by enzymological assay of gill homogenates but the enzyme may not be functionally active in vivo), or whether they require induction by exposure to seawater. In either event, we emphasize that the physiological mechanisms necessary for long-term survival in seawater take several days to develop in euryhaline species (Foskett et al. 1983); in smolts, these adaptations are already in place and may be rapidly induced to become functional upon exposure to seawater.

Decreases in plasma chloride (in the late parr stage: Houston and Threadgold 1963) and muscle chloride (in migrating smolts: Fontaine 1951) occur in Atlantic salmon in fresh water. Plasma osmolarity has been reported to decrease during smolting of masu salmon (Kubo 1953), to be more variable in smolting Atlantic salmon (Koch and Evans 1959), and to increase absolutely in postsmolt Atlantic salmon (Parry 1961). On the other hand, a number of studies failed to find significant changes in plasma or muscle ions coincident with the parr–smolt transformation (see Folmar and Dickhoff 1980).

The variety and conflict of results in the investigations cited above suggest that environmental, experimental, and species differences may have influenced the results. Indeed, regulation of plasma and cellular ions of salmonids in fresh water can be affected by temperature (Kubo 1955), size (McCormick and Naiman 1984a), activity (Wood and Randall 1973), water quality (Eddy 1982), pH (Saunders et al. 1983), and stress (Schreck 1982). We have recently conducted a study in which rearing temperature for Atlantic salmon was held constant (5–8°C) from February to August (McCormick and Saunders, unpublished data). The interaction of seasonal and developmental phenomena was controlled by examining fish under both a simulated natural photoperiod and continuous light. (Atlantic salmon raised under continuous light grow normally but do not undergo a parr–smolt transformation: Saunders et al. 1985; McCormick et al. 1987.) A slight ($<5\%$) decrease in plasma Na^+, Cl^-, and osmolarity occurred in each group between March and April. No change in plasma Na^+, Cl^-, Mg^{++}, K^+, or osmolarity occurred during the period when salinity tolerance and gill Na^+,K^+-ATPase activity increased (May and June) and subsequently decreased (August) in Atlantic salmon reared under natural photoperiod; nor were the levels of plasma ions and osmolarity different from those in fish reared under continuous light, in which increases in gill Na^+,K^+-ATPase activity and salinity tolerance did not occur. These results indicate that changes in plasma ions are not a necessary consequence of differentiation in osmoregulatory organs during the parr–smolt transformation.

The above conclusion does not imply, however, that changes in plasma or muscle ions do not occur *in response to* environmental change during the parr–smolt transformation. Several authors have suggested a direct connection between downstream migration and osmoregulatory dysfunction in fresh water caused by preparatory differentiation (Fontaine 1975; D. R. N. Primmett, M. S. Miles, C. Talbot, and J. E. Thorpe, personal communication). We suggest that preparatory physiological changes followed by environmental change (such as increased temperature or water flow) may be required for osmoregulatory perturbation, which may, in turn, be connected to migratory behavior. Strong correlations exist be-tween downstream migration and water temperature for Atlantic salmon (Fried et al. 1978; Jonsson and Rudd-Hansen 1985). Kubo (1955) found that depression of plasma osmolarity during the parr–smolt transformation of masu salmon closely paralleled increases in water temperature.

Since a variety of other physiological and behavioral changes such as buoyancy, swimming ability, and orientation also occur during the parr–smolt transformation (Table 1), it seems likely that a variety of factors will be important in initiating migration. While we have supplied some suppositions, it is clear that the primary cue(s) of downstream migration and their relationship to osmoregulatory differentiation have yet to be established. In salmonid populations which undergo prolonged downstream migration there is evidence that migratory behavior and osmoregulatory differentiation do not occur together (Ewing et al. 1980; Bradley and Rourke 1984). This phenomenon may be due to the length and variability of migration, which might preclude accurate anticipation of seawater entry.

Metabolism

There is substantial evidence of a metabolic reorganization during the parr–smolt transformation. This evidence is derived primarily from

TABLE 1.—Some behavioral and physiological changes coincident with the parr–smolt transformation in salmonids.

Behavioral or physiological change	Reference
Increased deposition of guanine and hypoxanthine in skin and scales (silvering)	Johnston and Eales (1967)
Increased buoyancy due to increased air volume of swimbladder	Saunders (1965); Pinder and Eales (1969)
Alterations in blood hemoglobins (rapid increase in adult forms)	Vanstone et al. (1964); Giles and Vanstone (1976b); Koch (1982); Sullivan et al. (1985)
Increased schooling behavior	Kalleberg (1958)
Increased salinity preference	Baggerman (1960); McInerney (1964)
Negative rheotaxis	Wagner (1974b); Eriksson and Lundqvist (1982); Lundqvist and Eriksson (1985)
Decreased swimming ability	Glova and McInerney (1977); Smith (1982)

observations on changes in body composition, oxygen consumption, and mitochondrial enzyme activity. We wish to address two general hypotheses during the review of this evidence. First, does a metabolic increase occur during the parr–smolt transformation? Second, is such a metabolic increase due to energetic requirements of differentiation or to increased anabolism associated with growth or to both (Figure 2)?

Changes in Body Composition

Several changes in carbohydrate metabolism are concurrent with the parr–smolt transformation. Reduction of liver and muscle glycogen occurs in spring in Atlantic and coho salmon in both the presence and absence of migratory activity (Fontaine and Hatey 1953; Malikova 1957; Wendt and Saunders 1973; Woo et al. 1978). Blood glucose has been reported to increase in Atlantic salmon (Wendt and Saunders 1973) and to decrease in coho salmon (Woo et al. 1978) at

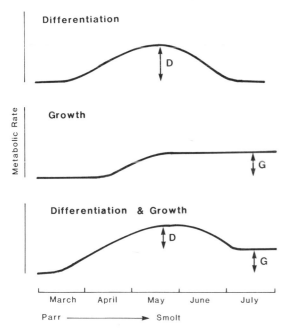

FIGURE 2.—Possible causes of metabolic increase during the parr–smolt transformation. Increases in metabolic rate due to differentiation and growth can be associated with catabolism and anabolism, respectively. Increased growth rate (which occurs in both parr and smolts in spring) will, a priori, result in increased metabolic rate. There also is evidence for increased metabolic rate due to differentiation. Arrows suggest the magnitudes of the influence on metabolic rate exerted by differentiation (D) and growth (G) acting separately or together.

the time of the parr–smolt transformation. Fontaine et al. (1963) reported that the powerful hyperglycemic agents adrenaline and noradrenaline are at their highest levels in Atlantic salmon during the final stages of smolting in April–May.

With the exception of decreased blood glucose, the above changes are often associated with short-term stress (Schreck 1981). The increased susceptibility of smolts to stress has been noted by several authors (Wendt and Saunders 1973; Schreck 1982). Seasonal changes in enzyme activity associated with glycogenolysis and glycogenesis, however, suggest a more permanent change that is unrelated to stress. Sheridan et al. (1985b) found that liver phosphorylase-*a* activity (glycogenolysis) of coho salmon increases by 64% between March and April, while uridine phosphate formation (glycogenesis) decreases by 54% from March to June.

Total body protein decreased by 10% between February and April in large (>14 cm) juvenile rainbow trout, but not in smaller fish under the same conditions (Fessler and Wagner 1969). In contrast, Woo et al. (1978) found no change in liver and muscle protein content of coho salmon parr and smolts. Serum protein content of coho salmon smolts was 15% lower than in parr or postsmolts (Woo et al. 1978). Cowey and Parry (1963) found a 30% increase in muscle content of nonprotein nitrogenous constituents of smolts over that in parr, due almost entirely to increased creatine content. The authors suggested that increased creatine may be due to greater availability of N-phosphoryl creatine for endergonic reactions or to increased metabolism of several amino acids for which creatine is an end product.

Cowey and Parry (1963) and Fontaine and Marchelidon (1971) could find no differences in total amino acid content of the brain or muscle between Atlantic salmon parr and smolts (they were able to sample both laboratory-reared and wild fish). The levels of particular amino acids did change, however. Threonine and glutamine contents of the brains of smolts increased, while muscle glycine and taurine decreased (Fontaine and Marchelidon 1971). Decreased muscle taurine content of Atlantic salmon smolts was also found by Cowey and Parry (1963). Fontaine and Marchelidon (1971) explained these changes as ramifications of several physiological changes during the parr–smolt transformation. Glycine (a precursor of purines) may be involved in events leading to deposition of guanine and hypoxanthine in skin and scales, which results in silvering (Johnston and Eales

1967). Taurine is important for intracellular isosmotic regulation in teleosts (increasing when plasma osmolarity increases: King and Goldstein 1983) and may be lowered in response to osmoregulatory changes in fresh water or be distributed to other more sensitive tissues in preparation for hyperosmotic regulation. Increases in threonine in the brain, which is under insulin control in mammals (Okumura et al. 1959), may be a by-product of increased insulin concentration resulting from glycemic fluctuations. While these intriguing suppositions have yet to be given experimental support, they underline the importance of distinguishing cause and effect in this complex developmental process.

Total body and muscle lipid decreases markedly in spring in juvenile Atlantic, coho, and masu salmon and in rainbow trout coincident with other parr–smolt changes (Vanstone and Markert 1968; Fessler and Wagner 1969; Saunders and Henderson 1970, 1978; Ota and Yamada 1974a, 1974b; Komourdjian et al. 1976; Farmer et al. 1978; Woo et al. 1978; Sheridan et al. 1983). These changes do not occur in small juveniles (parr), are not dependent on changes in activity or temperature, and return to prespring levels by late summer when fishes are retained in fresh water (Malikova 1957; Fessler and Wagner 1969; Ota and Yamada 1974a, 1974b; Farmer et al. 1978; Saunders and Henderson 1978; Woo et al. 1978). Moisture content of muscle varies inversely with lipid content (Farmer et al. 1978; Saunders and Henderson 1978; Woo et al. 1978) though this appears to be a common feature of teleosts and not peculiar to the parr–smolt transformation (Phillips 1969).

Sheridan and co-workers (Sheridan et al. 1983, 1985a, 1985b; Sheridan and Allen 1983) have examined lipid dynamics of coho salmon and rainbow trout in some detail. Lipid content of serum, liver, and muscle (white and red) is depleted by up to 60% in spring. Mesenteric fat does not fluctuate. Large amounts of triacylglycerol (normally used as energy storage) in muscle and liver are reduced more than other lipid classes. A reorganization of the fatty acid composition also occurs. Increased amounts of long-chain polyunsaturated fatty acids and decreased linoleic acid, characteristic of marine teleosts, occur in fresh water during the parr–smolt transformation. Similar changes in lipid composition coincident with the migratory period were observed in juvenile Atlantic and masu salmon (Lovern 1934; Ota and Yamada 1974a, 1974b). The adaptive value of these changes is as yet unknown, though sugges-

tions for a role in osmoregulation have been made (Sheridan et al. 1985a).

The biochemical bases of changes in lipid metabolism have also been investigated (Sheridan et al. 1985b). Lipolytic rate (measured by the release of ^{14}C-oleic acid from ^{14}C-triolein) increases one- to three-fold in liver, red muscle, and mesenteric fat in coho salmon over a 4-month period in spring. During this same period ^3H_2O incorporation into fatty acids of liver and mesenteric fat was halved, though no difference in lipogenesis of neutral lipids was detected. These results suggest both a reorganization of lipid composition for a marine existence and increased catabolism associated with the parr–smolt transformation.

Oxygen Consumption

Direct measurement of oxygen consumption is difficult to assess because of the relatively high individual variation, dependence on temperature and size (often requiring use of regressions, which can obscure data), effects of various activity levels, and differential response to handling stress or confinement. Baraduc and Fontaine (1955) found resting, weight-specific oxygen consumption of wild Atlantic salmon parr at 8°C was 25% lower than for wild smolts. Power (1959), working with Atlantic salmon from an Arctic environment, found a temperature divergence in oxygen consumption: smolts had lower oxygen consumption than parr below 13.5°C, but higher oxygen consumption above this temperature. This may be the result of increased activity in response to temperature. Higgins (1985) reported oxygen consumption as a function of differential growth and the parr–smolt transformation in Atlantic salmon. When oxygen consumption per animal was regressed to a common size, rapidly growing fish had higher oxygen consumption at 7.5°C than slower growing fish. Smolts (based on external appearance), however, had lower weight-specific oxygen consumption than nonsmolts. In one of the few reported studies in which activity levels were taken into account, Withey and Saunders (1973) found that postsmolt Atlantic salmon had higher rates of oxygen consumption than nonsmolts. Without more critical studies taking activity level into consideration, it is difficult to arrive at a firm conclusion concerning changes in oxygen consumption during the parr–smolt transformation.

Respiratory Enzymes

Mitochondrial enzyme activities are indicative of tissue respiratory rate or respiratory potential, though some enzymes are more representative than others (Ericinska and Wilson 1982). Succinate dehydrogenase (Chernitsky and Shterman 1981; Langdon and Thorpe 1985), citrate synthase and cytochrome-*c* oxidase activities (S. D. McCormick and R. L. Saunders, unpublished data) increase in gill homogenates of Atlantic salmon concurrent with the parr–smolt transformation. At first glance, these results would appear to coincide with the observed increase in numbers of mitochondria-rich chloride cells discussed earlier. Although chloride cells have greater respiratory enzyme activity than other gill cells (Sargent et al. 1975), whole-gill homogenates of fish which are acclimated to seawater do not have different respiratory enzyme activities (Epstein et al. 1967; Conte 1969; McCormick et al., unpublished data; for exceptions, see Sargent et al. 1975; Langdon and Thorpe 1984). Increases in gill respiratory enzyme activity observed during the parr–smolt transformation appear to go beyond what may be required for steady-state osmoregulation once seawater acclimation has occurred. The increase may be required for preparatory differentiation of the gills, or perhaps may aid in seawater adaptation during initial acclimation.

Blake et al. (1984) found up to 50% increases in mitochondrial concentration, and in the activities of succinate dehydrogenase and cytochrome-*c* oxidase, in the livers of large (>16 cm), silvery Atlantic salmon relative to those of parr. Similarly, McCormick and Saunders (unpublished data) found that liver citrate synthase activity of smolt-size Atlantic salmon increased 25% between March and June (coincident with increases in gill Na^+,K^+-ATPase activity) and subsequently declined to basal levels in August. These results, in combination with increased lipolytic and glycogenolytic enzyme activities in coho salmon livers, suggest that increased catabolism occurs in the liver during the parr–smolt transformation.

The evidence summarized here indicates that there is both reorganization and enhancement of metabolic activity during the parr–smolt transformation. Unfortunately, there is relatively little information on the reversibility of these changes. Metabolic alterations which are adaptations for seawater entry, such as changes in lipid composition, are analogous to preparatory osmoregulatory changes and are probably lost if the animals are maintained in fresh water. Metabolic increases appear to be at least partly catabolic, owing possibly to the energetic demands of differentiation. Recovery of pretransformation body

composition (Malikova 1957; Woo et al. 1978) and return of liver respiratory enzyme activity to presmolt level in summer indicate that increased catabolism subsides after the transformation, irrespective of the environmental salinity.

Growth

The apparent size threshold of the parr–smolt transformation may rule out growth rate as the primary stimulus for differentiation. Yet patterns of growth will undoubtedly affect the year of occurrence of the parr–smolt transformation and perhaps also its timing and intensity (Clarke 1982). The bimodal growth pattern of Atlantic salmon is a good example of the complex relationship between growth and transformation. Bimodal length-frequency distributions of laboratory-reared Atlantic salmon can be distinguished during the first autumn following hatching and have been attributed to an increase in growth rate of upper-mode fish (Kristinsson et al. 1985) and to a decline in growth rate owing to reduced appetite of lower-mode fish (Thorpe et al. 1982; Higgins 1985; Thorpe 1987a). Though these distinctions are controversial, it is clear that upper- and lower-mode fish do not further subdivide even after the fish in each mode are placed in separate tanks (Thorpe 1977). Upper-mode fish invariably become smolts in 1 year, while lower-mode males undergo a high rate of sexual maturation during their first autumn and normally require another year to achieve smolt size. Existence in the lower mode, however, does not preclude undergoing transformation; elevated early winter temperature resulting in higher growth and a greater size in early spring will result in normal smolt appearance and performance (Saunders et al. 1982; Kristinsson 1984). The relationship between high growth rates of upper-mode fish and the parr–smolt transformation may be indirect, coupled only by the size dependence of the transformation (Thorpe et al. 1982). Alternatively, bimodality may be an early manifestation of parr–smolt transformation such that changes taking place in spring are the climax of processes which have been proceeding since the previous autumn (Thorpe 1986).

Under natural conditions, juvenile Atlantic salmon may begin seaward migration at 2–4 years of age, and at weights of 30–50 g. They frequently attain weights of 1.5–2.5 kg in their first year at sea. Increased growth is undoubtedly due in large part to increased quantity and quality of food and more favorable year-round temperatures (Gross

1987, this volume). It is presently unclear whether smolts undergo a physiological change resulting in increased scope for growth (maximum food intake minus that necessary for maintenance: Brett 1979) at temperature and ration levels characteristic of the marine environment.

Increased growth of juvenile salmon occurs in spring concurrent with other transformation-related changes and in direct response to increasing photoperiod (Saunders and Henderson 1970; Knutsson and Grav 1976; Komourdjian et al. 1976; Clarke et al. 1978; Johnston and Saunders 1981; Higgins 1985). Though evidence for a common growth response of all salmonids to increasing photoperiod is lacking (Brett 1979), increased growth under increasing photoperiod also occurs in Atlantic salmon parr (Higgins 1985). One peculiar aspect of growth during the parr–smolt transformation is a decrease in condition factor ($100 \cdot$ weight/length^3; see Wedemeyer et al. 1980). This may be the result of a relative weight loss due to catabolism, or to an increased growth in length, such that increase in length outstrips growth in weight. Several authors have suggested an adaptive change in morphology to explain the latter hypothesis (Thorpe 1982).

In the absence of salinity effects, are parr and smolt distinguishable in their scope for growth either during or after the parr–smolt transformation? Higgins (1985) found that, at maximum ration and identical thermal regimes, Atlantic salmon in the upper size mode (incipient smolts) had a higher instantaneous growth rate in spring than lower-mode fish (parr), despite the smaller size of lower-mode fish which would, other things being equal, result in higher instantaneous growth rates (Brett 1979). It is unclear, however, whether this result is a function of the bimodal-growth pattern, the parr–smolt transformation, or both. We have recently compared the summer growth in fresh water of Atlantic salmon smolts (50 g) with juveniles (50 g) exposed to continuous light that inhibited at least the osmoregulatory aspects of the transformation (McCormick et al. 1987). Instantaneous growth rate of smolts and of fish in continuous light over a 6-week period at constant temperature (13°C) was the same (1.8%/d). We have concluded that either continuous-light treatment does not inhibit all aspects of the parr–smolt transformation, or that an increase in scope for growth (at maximum ration and at 13°C) does not accompany transformation in Atlantic salmon. This limited evidence does not favor either acceptance or rejection of an increased scope for

growth accompanying the parr–smolt transformation. If it does indeed occur, it is likely to be large and more easily detected in species such as Atlantic salmon which spend longer periods (2–5 years) in fresh water. Environmental effects on growth and scope for growth may also change after transformation. There is indirect evidence that the optimum temperature for marine growth of Atlantic salmon is lower than that for presmolt growth in fresh water (Reddin and Shearer 1987, this volume; Saunders 1987). Many fishes show reduced thermal optima for growth after the early juvenile stage (Hokanson 1977; Brett 1979; McCauley and Huggins 1979; Jobling 1981). Photoperiodic response may also change. Whereas growth of Atlantic salmon parr drops sharply in early autumn (decreasing photoperiod), despite favorable temperature and ration levels (R. L. Saunders, unpublished data), postsmolts in sea cages appear to continue growing rapidly in autumn until temperatures fall below 4°C (Sutterlin et al. 1981). Such an alteration in growth response to photoperiod has been observed in the bimodal growth pattern of juvenile Atlantic salmon (Kristinsson 1984; Higgins 1985; Kristinsson et al. 1985; Thorpe 1987a). Substantiation or rejection of these suppositions could greatly increase our understanding of ontogenetic and environmental influences on growth in teleosts.

Comparative Aspects of the Parr–Smolt Transformation

The variety of differentiative processes which occur and their responsiveness to photoperiodic cues underline the developmental nature of the parr–smolt transformation. This development has often been viewed as a single, size-related event which occurs seasonally and is reversible in the absence of sea water (Figure 3A). Although this may be true for some aspects of the transformation, other aspects, such as silvering, salinity tolerance, and gill Na$^+$,K$^+$-ATPase activity, often display slight but significant seasonal rhythms in the absence of "real" or "total" changes associated with transformation (Hoar 1965, 1976; Saunders and Henderson 1978; Langdon and Thorpe 1985; McCormick et al. 1987). Perhaps we can more correctly view these developmental processes as an interaction or synergism (Figure 3D) between prior development (Figure 3B) and seasonal rhythms (Figure 3C) which manifests itself in a critical size and season for transformation. Each component of the parr–smolt transformation may possess a different gradient of these developmental types. The existence of different developmental patterns emphasizes the adaptive value of temporal orchestration of the many changes that occur during the transformation. Otherwise, they may occur as isolated events or physiological developments which fall short of the attributes required for long-term marine residence.

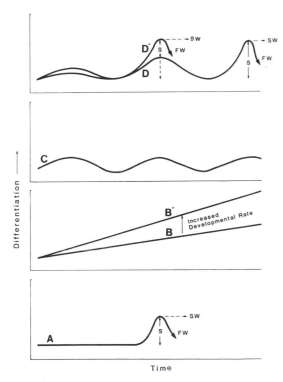

FIGURE 3.—Developmental patterns that may occur for different aspects of the parr–smolt transformation. **A**: Seasonal occurrence of physiological change that is dependent on seasonal cues and prior development (a critical size). **B**: Differentiation that is independent of season. A change from B to B′ may represent a change in ontogeny (i.e., increased growth rate resulting in increased differentiation at any time) or phylogeny (i.e., a different rate of differentiation relative to size resulting in increased salinity tolerance at any given size). **C**: Seasonal change that is independent of size, such as a photoperiod-cued increase in growth rate. **D**: Interaction of season and developmental rate. In this pattern, aspects of the parr–smolt transformation are an intensification and synchronization of seasonal changes that are also dependent on prior development. D and D′ represent, for instance, segments of a population that will undergo the parr–smolt transformation in the years n and $n + 1$, respectively. Analogous changes in developmental timing may have occurred in the course of salmonid evolution (see Figure 4). S represents physiological differences between parr and smolt; SW is seawater and FW is fresh water.

Analysis of the parr–smolt transformation as a developmental process consisting of numerous components can facilitate comparisons among salmonid species. Osmoregulatory physiology has received the most attention and can be more thoroughly explored. Brook trout, a member of the genus *(Salvelinus)* that has the least-developed capacity for marine residence in the subfamily Salmoninae (Rounsefell 1958; Hoar 1976), migrates into seawater at a relatively large size (>17 cm) and shows variability in the season of migration (White 1940; Wilder 1952; Castonguay et al. 1982; Montgomery et al. 1983). The development of salinity tolerance and hypoosmoregulatory ability in brook trout occurs at a larger size than in species of *Salmo* or *Oncorhynchus* (e.g., Figure 3, B versus B′; see also McCormick and Naiman 1984b). The osmoregulatory aspect of the parr–smolt transformation, as characterized by seasonal differentiation of osmoregulatory organs resulting in increased salinity tolerance, is undeveloped in brook trout (McCormick and Naiman 1984b; McCormick et al. 1985a). It should be noted, however, that seasonal silvering occurs in anadromous brook trout populations (though this is not necessarily associated with seawater entry: Black 1981), indicating that different physiological changes associated with the parr–smolt transformation can occur independently of one another.

Pink salmon *Oncorhynchus gorbuscha* and chum salmon represent the opposite end of the salmonid spectrum, often spending as little as a month or two in fresh water after hatching before migrating to sea. Salinity tolerance in these two species is incomplete in the posthatch alevin stage but increases rapidly, permitting survival in sea water at sizes less than 5 cm long (Weisbart 1968). It seems probable that such a rapid attainment of salinity tolerance will preclude a photoperiodically cued differentiation typical of other *Oncorhynchus* and *Salmo* species which undergo transformation and migrate at larger sizes. With the exception of changes in gill Na^+,K^+-ATPase activity (Sullivan et al. 1983) and kidney morphology (Ford 1958), little is known of the differentiation of osmoregulatory organs in pink and chum salmon. As in seasonally transforming salmonids, prolonged rearing of pink and chum salmon in fresh water results in substantial loss of salinity tolerance (Kashiwagi and Sato 1969; Iwata et al. 1982).

A phylogenetic comparison of the minimum size at which seawater entry occurs in salmonid species is presented in Figure 4. The developmen-

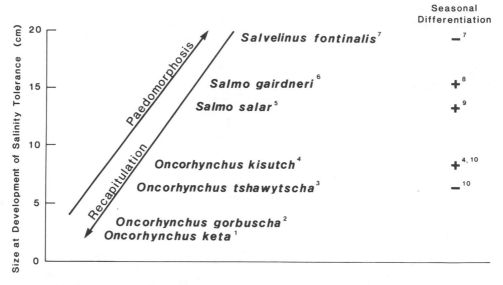

FIGURE 4.—Phylogenetic comparison of the minimum size at which the development of salinity tolerance occurs in the subfamily Salmoninae. Salinity tolerance is defined as greater than 75% survival in seawater (29‰ for at least 14 d. Seasonal differentiation (+) is defined as a photoperiod-controlled differentiation of osmoregulatory organs resulting in increased salinity tolerance. With the exception of brook trout, reversible ontogenetic differentiations have been shown to occur in the depicted species. Phylogenetic relationships suggest that heterochrony has occurred either through paedomorphosis (increasing size at differentiation) or recapitulation (decreasing size at differentiation). This hypothesis should not imply existence of a linear salmonid lineage but rather that, in the course of salmonid evolution, heterochrony has occurred in differentiation of osmoregulatory organs. References (superscripts): 1, Kashiwagi and Sato (1969); 2, Weisbart (1968); 3, Wagner et al. (1969); 4, Conte et al. (1966); 5, Johnston and Saunders (1981); 6, Conte and Wagner (1965); 7, McCormick and Niaman (1984a, 1984b); 8, Wagner (1974b); 9, Saunders and Henderson (1970); 10, Clarke et al. (1978).

tal nature of the attainment of salinity tolerance and the correspondence of this phylogeny to morphometrically and genetically based phylogenies of the subfamily Salmoninae (especially in that *Salmo* is intermediate between *Salvelinus* and *Oncorhynchus;* see Neave 1958 for review) leads us to conclude that heterochrony[3] in differentiation of hypoosmoregulatory capacity (and its underlying physiological mechanisms) has occurred during the evolution of these species (Figure 4; see Balon 1979, 1980 and Thorpe 1982 for earlier discussions of heterochrony in salmonids). The direction of heterochrony, either paedomorphic (increased size at attainment of salinity tolerance with advancing phylogeny) or recapitulatory (decreased size at attainment of salinity tolerance) has yet to be established. It seems likely that paedomorphosis would be associated with an ancestral seawater origin for salmonids,

and recapitulation with a freshwater origin. Arguments based on fossil and extant species have been given for freshwater (Tchernavin 1939; Hoar 1976) and seawater (Day 1887; Regan 1911; Balon 1968; Thorpe 1982) origins of salmonids. Developmental conflict between transformation and maturation, argued by Thorpe (1987, this volume) underlines the importance of changes in the timing of development in establishing a life history pattern. Viewing the parr–smolt transformation as a developmental process subject to changes in timing during the course of salmonid evolution should facilitate species comparison and help generate hypotheses concerning the adaptive mechanisms for seawater entry and their hormonal control. Indeed, it seems likely that changes in the timing of expression of endocrine mechanisms controlling the transformation are responsible for the observed heterochrony.

In a "common strategies" symposium, a final statement on comparative physiological tactics may seem inappropriately brief, yet a longer one is precluded by the limited state of our knowledge

---

[3]Heterochrony is defined as changes in the timing of development, following the terminology of Gould (1978).

concerning the osmoregulatory physiology of diadromous fishes which, with the exception of salmonids and anguillids, have been little studied. The seaward migration of salmon and eels, despite the many differences between these fishes, is accompanied by morphological change (such as silvering) and increases in salinity tolerance and gill Na^+,K^+-ATPase activity (Fontaine 1975; Thomson and Sargent 1977). The common "strategy" of these two groups is to make a single, seasonal seaward migration during their lifetime, and they display a "tactic" of undergoing preparatory physiological adaptations. This is in contrast to euryhaline species (such as *Fundulus* spp.) which make repeated, less predictable movements into seawater. These fishes must have the capacity to alter osmoregulatory physiology more frequently, and it is generally believed that these changes are induced by environmental salinity (Karnaky 1986). One might predict, therefore, that preparatory physiological adaptations for seawater entry entailing ontogenetic differentiation would occur in species which make a single seaward migration. Conversely, diadromous or nondiadromous fishes which make repeated seawater entries seem less likely to display such a tactic and may rely more heavily on induction by external salinity of a perpetual hypoosmoregulatory capacity.

Acknowledgments

This paper was greatly improved by the critical comments of Howard A. Bern, Richard S. Nishioka, Arthur W. Rourke, Robert L. Stephenson, Clive Talbot, John E. Thorpe, and Graham Young. William McMullon and Franklin Cunningham drew the figures, and Jeanine Hurley typed the manuscript. S. D. McCormick was supported by a postdoctoral fellowship from the Natural Sciences and Engineering Research Council of Canada and the Department of Fisheries and Oceans.

References

Baggerman, B. 1960. Salinity preference, thyroid activity and the seaward migration of four species of Pacific salmon *(Oncorhynchus)*. Journal of the Fisheries Research Board of Canada 17:295–322.

Balon, E. K. 1968. Notes to the origin and evolution of trouts and salmons with special reference to the Danubian trouts. Vestnik Ceskolovenske Spolecnosti Zoologicke 32:1–21.

Balon, E. K. 1979. The juvenilization process in phylogeny and the altricial to precocial forms in the ontogeny of fishes. Environmental Biology of Fishes 4:193–198.

Balon, E. K. 1980. Comparative ontogeny of charrs. Pages 703–720 *in* E. K. Balon, editor. Charrs:salmonid fishes of the genus *Salvelinus*. Dr. W. Junk, The Hague, The Netherlands.

Baraduc, M. M., and M. Fontaine. 1955. Etude comparée du métabolisme respiratoire du jeune saumon sédentaire (parr) et migrateur (smolt). Compte Rendu des Seances de la Société de Biologie Paris 149:1327–1329.

Bern, H. A. 1978. Endocrinological studies on normal and abnormal salmon smoltification. Pages 77–100 *in* P. J. Gaillard and H. H. Boer, editors. Comparative endocrinology. Elsevier/North-Holland Biomedical Press, Amsterdam, The Netherlands.

Black, G. A. 1981. Metazoan parasites as indicators of movements of anadromous brook charr *(Salvelinus fontinalis)* to sea. Canadian Journal of Zoology 59:1892–1896.

Blake, R. L., F. L. Roberts, and R. L. Saunders. 1984. Parr–smolt transformation of Atlantic salmon *(Salmo salar)*:activities of two respiratory enzymes and concentrations of mitochondria in the liver. Canadian Journal of Fisheries and Aquatic Sciences 41:199–203.

Boeuf, G., P. Lasserre, and Y. Harache. 1978. Osmotic adaptation of *Oncorhynchus kisutch* Walbaum. II. Plasma osmotic and ionic variations, and gill Na^+,K^+-ATPase activity of yearling coho salmon transferred to seawater. Aquaculture 15:35–52.

Boeuf, G., A. LeRoux, J. L. Gaignon, and Y. Harache. 1985. Gill (Na^+,K^+)-ATPase activity and smolting in Atlantic salmon *(Salmo salar)* in France. Aquaculture 45:73–81.

Bradley, T. M., and A. W. Rourke. 1984. An electrophoretic analysis of plasma proteins from juvenile *Oncorhynchus tshawytscha* (Walbaum). Journal of Fish Biology 24:703–709.

Brett, J. R. 1979. Environmental factors and growth. Pages 599–677 *in* W. S. Hoar, D. J. Randall, and J. R. Brett, editors. Fish physiology, volume 8. Bioenergetics and growth. Academic Press, New York, New York, USA.

Buckman, M., and R. D. Ewing. 1982. Relationship between size and time of entry into the sea and gill $(Na^+\text{-}K^+)$-ATPase activity for juvenile spring chinook salmon. Transactions of the American Fisheries Society 111:681–687.

Castonguay, M., G. J. Fitzgerald, and Y. Côté. 1982. Life history movements of anadromous brook charr, *Salvelinus fontinalis*, in the St. Jean river, Gaspé, Québec. Canadian Journal of Zoology 60:3084–3091.

Chernitsky, A. G. 1983. Adaptive significance of smoltification in the Atlantic salmon, *Salmo salar*. Journal of Evolutionary Biochemistry and Physiology 19:186–190.

Chernitsky, A. G., and L. Ya. Shterman. 1981. Peculiarities of osmoregulation in the migrating juvenile Atlantic salmons. Voprosy Ikhtiologii 21:497–502.

Clarke, W. C. 1982. Evaluation of the seawater challenge test as an index of marine survival. Aquaculture 28:177–183.

Clarke, W. C., H. Lundqvist, and L.-O. Eriksson. 1985. Accelerated photoperiod advances seasonal cycle of seawater adaptation in juvenile Baltic salmon, *Salmo salar* L. Journal of Fish Biology 26:29–35.

Clarke, W. C., and Y. Nagahama. 1977. Effect of premature transfer to sea water on growth and morphology of the pituitary, thyroid, pancreas, and interrenal in juvenile coho salmon *(Oncorhynchus kisutch)*. Canadian Journal of Zoology 54: 1620–1630.

Clarke, W. C., J. E. Shelbourn, and J. R. Brett, Jr. 1978. Growth and adaptation to sea water in underyearling sockeye *(Oncorhynchus nerka)* and coho *(O. kisutch)* salmon subjected to regimes of constant or changing temperature and daylength. Canadian Journal of Zoology 56:2413–2421.

Collie, N. L., and H. A. Bern. 1982. Changes in intestinal fluid transport associated with smoltification and seawater adaptation in coho salmon, *Oncorhynchus kisutch* (Walbaum). Journal of Fish Biology 21:337–348.

Conte, F. P. 1969. The biochemical aspects of salt secretion. Pages 105–120 in O. W. Neuhaus and J. E. Halver, editors. Fish in research. Academic Press, New York, New York, USA.

Conte, F. P., and H. H. Wagner. 1965. Development of osmotic and ionic regulation in juvenile steelhead trout *Salmo gairdneri*. Comparative Biochemistry and Physiology 14:603–620.

Conte, F. P., H. H. Wagner, J. Fessler, and C. Gnose. 1966. Development of osmotic and ionic regulation in juvenile coho salmon *(Oncorhynchus kisutch)*. Comparative Biochemistry and Physiology 18:1–15.

Cowey, C. B., and G. Parry. 1963. The non-protein nitrogen constituents of the muscle of parr and smolt stages of the Atlantic salmon *(Salmo salar)*. Comparative Biochemistry and Physiology 8:47–51.

Day, F. 1887. British and Irish salmonidae. Williams and Norgate, London, England.

Dickhoff, W. W., and C. Sullivan. 1987. Involvement of the thyroid gland in smoltification with special reference to metabolic and developmental processes. American Fisheries Society Symposium 1:197–210.

Eddy, F. B. 1982. Osmotic and ionic regulation in captive fish with particular reference to salmonids. Comparative Biochemistry and Physiology B, Comparative Biochemistry 73:125–141.

Eddy, F. B., and C. Talbot. 1985. Urine production in smolting Atlantic salmon, *Salmo salar* L. Aquaculture 45:67–72.

Elson, P. F. 1957. The importance of size in the change from parr to smolt in Atlantic salmon. Canadian Fish Culturist 21:1–6.

Epstein, F. H., A. I. Katz, and G. E. Pickford. 1967. Sodium and potassium-activated adenosine triphosphatase of gills: role in adaptation of teleosts to salt water. Science (Washington, D.C.) 156:1245–1247.

Epstein, F. H., P. Silva, and G. Kormanik. 1980. Role of Na-K-ATPase in chloride cell function. American Journal of Physiology 238:R246–R250.

Ericinska, M., and F. F. Wilson. 1982. Regulation of cellular energy metabolism. Journal of Membrane Biology 70:1–14.

Eriksson, L.-O., and H. Lundqvist. 1982. Circannual rhythms of growth and smolting in Baltic salmon. Aquaculture 28:113–122.

Evans, D. H. 1979. Fish. Pages 305–390 in G. M. O. Maloiy, editor. Osmotic and ionic regulation in animals, volume 1. Academic Press, London, England.

Evropeytseva, N. V. 1962. [Comparative analysis of the desmoltification process among the young of different ecological forms of Atlantic salmon.] Uchenye Zapiski Leningradskogo Gosudarstrennogo Universiteta 311:46–76. Translated from Russian: Fisheries Research Board of Canada Translation Series 431, Ottawa, Canada.

Ewing, R. D., C. A. Fustich, S. L. Johnson, and H. J. Pribble. 1980. Seaward migration of juvenile chinook salmon without elevated gill (Na+K)-ATPase activities. Transactions of the American Fisheries Society 109:349–356.

Farmer, G. J., J. A. Ritter, and D. Ashfield. 1978. Seawater adaptation and parr–smolt transformation of juvenile Atlantic salmon, *Salmo salar*. Journal of the Fisheries Research Board of Canada 35:93–100.

Fessler, J. L., and H. H. Wagner. 1969. Some morphological and biochemical changes in steelhead trout during the parr–smolt transformation. Journal of the Fisheries Research Board of Canada 26: 2823–2841.

Folmar, L. C., and W. W. Dickhoff. 1980. The parr–smolt transformation (smoltification) and seawater adaptation in salmonids. A review of selected literature. Aquaculture 21:1–37.

Folmar, L. C., W. W. Dickhoff, C. V. M. Mahnken, and F. W. Waknitz. 1982. Stunting and parr-reversion during smoltification of coho salmon *(Oncorhynchus kisutch)*. Aquaculture 28:91–104.

Fontaine, M. 1951. Sur la diminution de la teneur en chlore du muscle des jeunes saumons (smolts) lors de la migration d'avalaison. Comptes Rendus Hebdomadaires des Séances de l'Académie des Sciences 232:2477–2479.

Fontaine, M. 1975. Physiological mechanisms in the migration of marine and amphihaline fish. Advances in Marine Biology 3:241–355.

Fontaine, M., and J. Hatey. 1953. Contribution à l'étude du métabolisme glucidique du saumon *(Salmo salar* L.) à diverses étapes de son dévelopment et de ses migrations. Physiologia Comparata et Oecologia 3: 36–52.

Fontaine, M., and J. Marchelidon. 1971. Amino acid contents of the brain and the muscle of young salmon *(Salmo salar* L.) at parr and smolt stages. Comparative Biochemistry and Physiology A, Comparative Physiology 40:127–134.

Fontaine, M., M. Mazeaud, and F. Mazeaud. 1963. L'adrénalinémie du *Salmo salar* L. à quelques étapes de son cycle vital et de ses migrations. Comptes Rendus Hebdomadaires des Séances de l'Académie des Sciences 256:4562–4565.

Ford, P. 1958. Studies on the development of the kidney of the Pacific pink salmon (*Oncorhynchus gorbuscha* (Walbaum). II. Variation in glomerular count of the kidney of the Pacific salmon. Canadian Journal of Zoology 36:45–47.

Foskett, J. K., H. A. Bern, T. E. Machen, and M. Conner. 1983. Chloride cells and the hormonal control of teleost fish osmoregulation. Journal of Experimental Biology 106:255–281.

Foskett, J. K., and C. Scheffey. 1982. The chloride cell: definitive identification as the salt-secretory cell in teleosts. Science (Washington, D.C.) 215:164–166.

Fried, S. M., J. D. McCleave, and G. W. LaBar. 1978. Seaward migration of hatchery-reared Atlantic salmon, *Salmo salar*, smolts in the Penobscot River estuary, Maine:riverine movements. Journal of the Fisheries Research Board of Canada 35:76–87.

Giles, M. A., and W. E. Vanstone. 1976a. Changes in ouabain-sensitive adenosine triphosphatase activity in gills of coho salmon (*Oncorhynchus kisutch*) during parr–smolt transformation. Journal of the Fisheries Research Board of Canada 33:54–62.

Giles, M. A., and W. E. Vanstone. 1976b. Ontogenetic variation in the multiple hemoglobins of coho salmon (*Oncorhynchus kisutch*) and the effect of environmental factors on their expression. Journal of the Fisheries Research Board of Canada 33:1144–1149.

Glova, G. J., and J. E. McInerney. 1977. Critical swimming speeds of coho salmon (*Oncorhynchus kisutch*) fry to smolt stages in relation to salinity and temperature. Journal of the Fisheries Research Board of Canada 34:151–154.

Gorbman, A., W. W. Dickhoff, J. L. Mighell, E. F. Prentice, and F. W. Waknitz. 1982. Morphological indices of developmental progress in the parr–smolt coho salmon, *Oncorhynchus kisutch*. Aquaculture 28:1–19.

Gould, S. J. 1978. Ontogeny and phylogeny. Harvard University Press, Cambridge, Massachusetts, USA.

Gross, M. A. 1987. Evolution of diadromy in fishes. American Fisheries Society Symposium 1:14–25.

Hart, C. E., G. Concannon, C. A. Fustish, and R. D. Ewing. 1981. Seaward migration and gill (Na+K)-ATPase activity of spring chinook salmon in an artificial stream. Transactions of the American Fisheries Society 110:44–50.

Hickman, C. P., and B. F. Trump. 1969. The kidney. Pages 91–239 *in* W. S. Hoar and D. J. Randall, editors. Fish physiology, volume 1. Excretion, ionic regulation, and metabolism. Academic Press, New York, New York, USA.

Higgins, P. J. 1985. Metabolic differences between Atlantic salmon (*Salmo salar*) parr and smolts. Aquaculture 45:33–54.

Hoar, W. S. 1939. The thyroid gland of the Atlantic salmon. Journal of Morphology 65:257–295.

Hoar, W. S. 1965. The endocrine system as a chemical link between the organism and its environment. Transactions of the Royal Society of Canada 3: 175–200.

Hoar, W. S. 1976. Smolt transformation:evolution, behavior and physiology. Journal of the Fisheries Research Board of Canada 33:1233–1252.

Hogstrand, C., and C. Haux. 1985. Evaluation of the seawater challenge test on sea trout, *Salmo trutta*. Comparative Biochemistry and Physiology A, Comparative Physiology 82:261–266.

Hokanson, K. E. F. 1977. Temperature requirements of some percids and adaptations to the seasonal temperature cycle. Journal of the Fisheries Research Board of Canada 34:1524–1550.

Holmes, W. N., and I. M. Stainer. 1966. Studies on the renal excretion of electrolytes by the trout *Salmo gairdneri*. Journal of Experimental Biology 44: 33–46.

Houston, A. H. 1961. Influence of size upon the adaptation of steelhead trout (*Salmo gairdneri*) and chum salmon (*Oncorhynchus keta*) to sea water. Journal of the Fisheries Research Board of Canada 18:401–415.

Houston, A. H., and L. T. Threadgold. 1963. Body fluid regulation in smolting Atlantic salmon. Journal of the Fisheries Research Board of Canada 20: 1355–1369.

Iwata, M., S. Hasegawa, and T. Hirano. 1982. Decreased seawater adaptability of chum salmon (*Oncorhynchus keta*) fry following prolonged rearing in freshwater. Canadian Journal of Fisheries and Aquatic Sciences 39:509–514.

Iwata, M., R. S. Nishioka, and H. A. Bern. In press. Whole animal transepithelial potential (TEP) of coho salmon during the parr–smolt transformation and effects of thyroxine, prolactin and hypophysectomy. Fish Physiology and Biochemistry.

Jobling, M. 1981. Temperature tolerance and the final preferendum—rapid methods for the assessment of optimum growth temperatures. Journal of Fish Biology 19:439–455.

Johnston, C. E., and J. G. Eales. 1967. Purines in the integument of the Atlantic salmon (*Salmo salar*) during parr–smolt transformation. Journal of the Fisheries Research Board of Canada 24:955–964.

Johnston, C. E., and R. L. Saunders. 1981. Parr–smolt transformation of yearling Atlantic salmon (*Salmo salar*) at several rearing temperatures. Canadian Journal of Fisheries and Aquatic Sciences 38: 1189–1198.

Jonsson, B., and J. Rudd-Hansen. 1985. Water temperature as the primary influence of timing of seaward migrations of Atlantic salmon (*Salmo salar*) smolts. Canadian Journal of Fisheries and Aquatic Sciences 42:593–595.

Kalleberg, H. 1958. Observations in a stream tank of territoriality and competition in juvenile salmon and trout (*Salmo salar* L. and *S. trutta* L.). Institute of Freshwater Research Drottningholm Report 39: 55–98.

Karnaky, K. J. 1986. Structure and function of the chloride cell of *Fundulus heteroclitus* and other teleosts. American Zoologist 26:209–224.

Kashiwagi, M., and R. Sato. 1969. Studies of the osmoregulation of chum salmon, *Oncorhynchus keta* (Walbaum). I. The tolerance of eyed period of eggs, alevins and fry of the chum salmon to seawater. Tohoku Journal of Agricultural Research 20: 41–47.

King, P. A., and L. Goldstein. 1983. Organic osmolytes and cell volume regulation in fish. Molecular Physiology 4:53–66.

Kirschner, L. B. 1980. Comparison of vertebrate salt-excreting organs. American Journal of Physiology 238:R219–R223.

Knutsson, S., and T. Grav. 1976. Seawater adaptation in Atlantic salmon *(Salmo salar)* at different experimental temperatures and photoperiods. Aquaculture 8:169–187.

Koch, H. J. 1982. Hemoglobin changes with size in the Atlantic salmon *(Salmo salar* L.). Aquaculture 28: 231–240.

Koch, H. J., and J. C. Evans. 1959. Sodium regulation in the blood of parr and smolt stages of the Atlantic salmon. Nature (London) 184:283–284.

Komourdjian, M. P., R. L. Saunders, and J. C. Fernwick. 1976. Evidence for the role of growth hormone as a part of a 'light-pituitary axis' in growth and smoltification of Atlantic salmon *(Salmo salar)*. Canadian Journal of Zoology 54:544–551.

Kristinsson, J. B. 1984. Factors influencing the growth of juvenile Atlantic salmon. Doctoral dissertation. University of New Brunswick, Fredericton, Canada.

Kristinsson, J. B., R. L. Saunders, and A. J. Wiggs. 1985. Growth dynamics during the development of bimodal length-frequency distribution in juvenile Atlantic salmon *(Salmo salar* L.). Aquaculture 45: 1–20.

Kubo, T. 1953. On the blood of salmonid fishes of Japan during migration. I. Freezing point of blood. Bulletin of the Faculty of Fisheries Hokkaido University 4:138–148.

Kubo, T. 1955. Changes of some characteristics of blood of smolts of *Oncorhynchus masou* during seaward migration. Bulletin of the Faculty of Fisheries Hokkaido University 6:201–207.

Langdon, J. S., and J. E. Thorpe. 1984. Response of the gill Na$^+$–K$^+$ ATPase, succinic dehydrogenase activity and chloride cells to saltwater adaptation in Atlantic salmon, *Salmo salar* L., parr and smolt. Journal of Fish Biology 24:323–331.

Langdon, J. S., and J. E. Thorpe. 1985. The ontogeny of smoltification:developmental patterns of gill Na$^+$/K$^+$-ATPase, SDH, and chloride cells in juvenile Atlantic salmon, *Salmo salar* L. Aquaculture 45:83–96.

Lasserre, P., G. Boeuf, and Y. Harache. 1978. Osmotic adaptation of *Oncorhynchus kisutch* Walbaum. I. Seasonal variations of gill Na$^+$–K$^+$ ATPase activity in coho salmon, 0+-age and yearling, reared in freshwater. Aquaculture 14:365–382.

Loretz, C. A., N. L. Collie, N. H. Richman, and H. A. Bern. 1982. Osmoregulatory changes accompanying smoltification in coho salmon. Aquaculture 28: 67–74.

Lovern, J. A. 1934. Fat metabolism in fishes. V. The fat

of the salmon in its young freshwater stages. Biochemical Journal 28:1961–1963.

Lundqvist, H., and L.-O. Eriksson. 1985. Annual rhythms of swimming behavior and seawater adaptation in young Baltic salmon, *Salmo salar,* associated with smolting. Environmental Biology of Fishes 14:259–267.

Maetz, J., and F. Garcia-Romeau. 1964. The mechanism of sodium and chloride uptake by the gills of a freshwater fish, *Carassius auratus*. II. Evidence for NH$_4$$^+$/Na$^+$ and HCO$_3$$^-$/Cl$^-$ exchanges. Journal of General Physiology 47:1209–1227.

Mahnken, C., E. Prentice, W. Waknitz, G. Moran, C. Sims, and J. Williams. 1982. The applicability of recent smoltification research to public hatchery releases:an assessment of size/time requirements for Columbia River hatchery coho salmon *(Oncorhynchus kisutch)*. Aquaculture 28:251–268.

Malikova, E. M. 1957. Biochemical analysis of young salmon at the time of their transformation to a condition close to the smolt stage and during retention of smolts in fresh water. Trudy Latviiskovo Otdeleniia VNIRO 2:241–255.

McCartney, T. H. 1976. Sodium–potassium dependent adenosine triphosphatase activity in gills and kidneys of Atlantic salmon *(Salmo salar)*. Comparative Biochemistry and Physiology A, Comparative Physiology 53:351–353.

McCauley, R. W., and N. W. Huggins. 1979. Ontogenetic and non-thermal seasonal effect on thermal preferenda of fish. American Zoologist 19:267–271.

McCormick, S. D., and R. J. Naiman. 1984a. Osmoregulation in the brook trout, *Salvelinus fontinalis*. I. Diel, photoperiod and growth related physiological changes in freshwater. Comparative Biochemistry and Physiology A, Comparative Physiology 79: 7–16.

McCormick, S. D., and R. J. Naiman. 1984b. Osmoregulation in the brook trout, *Salvelinus fontinalis*. II. Effects of size, age and photoperiod on seawater survival and ionic regulation. Comparative Biochemistry and Physiology A, Comparative Physiology 79:17–28.

McCormick, S. D., R. J. Naiman, and E. T. Montgomery. 1985. Physiological smolt characteristics of anadromous and non-anadromous brook trout *(Salvelinus fontinalis)* and Atlantic salmon *(Salmo salar)*. Canadian Journal of Fisheries and Aquatic Sciences 42:529–538.

McCormick, S. D., R. L. Saunders, E. B. Henderson, and P. R. Harmon. 1987. Photoperiod control of parr–smolt transformation in Atlantic salmon *(Salmo salar):* changes in salinity tolerance, gill Na$^+$,K$^+$-ATPase and plasma thyroid hormones. Canadian Journal of Fisheries and Aquatic Sciences 44:1462–1468.

McInerney, J. E. 1964. Salinity preference:an orientation mechanism in salmon migration. Journal of the Fisheries Research Board of Canada 21:995–1018.

Montgomery, W. L., S. D. McCormick, R. J. Naiman, F. G. Whoriskey, and G. A. Black. 1983. Spring migratory synchrony of salmonid, catostomiol and cyprinid fishes in Rivière a là Truite, Québec. Canadian Journal of Zoology 61:2495–2502.

Neave, F. 1958. The origin and speciation of *Oncorhynchus*. Transactions of the Royal Society of Canada, Section 5:Biological Sciences 52:25–39.

Okumura, N., S. Otsuki, and H. Nasu. 1959. The influences of hypoglycaemic coma, repeated electroshocks and chlorpromazine or β-phenylisopropylmethylamine administration on the free amino acids in the brain. Journal of Biochemistry 47:207–247.

Ota, T., and M. Yamada. 1974a. Lipids of masu salmon. II. Seasonal variations in the lipids of masu salmon parr during the life in freshwater. Bulletin of the Japanese Society of Scientific Fisheries 40:699–706.

Ota, T., and M. Yamada. 1974b. Lipids of masu salmon. III. Differences in the lipids of residual type and seaward migration type of masu salmon parr during the period of seaward migration. Bulletin of the Japanese Society of Scientific Fisheries 40:707–713.

Ouchi, K. 1985. Effect of cortisol on the salinity tolerance of masu salmon *(Oncorhynchus masou)* parr adapted to different salinities. Bulletin of the National Research Institute of Aquaculture 7:21–27.

Parry, G. 1958. Size and osmoregulation in salmonid fishes. Nature (London) 181:1218–1219.

Parry, G. 1960. The development of salinity tolerance in the salmon, *Salmo salar* (L.), and some related species. Journal of Experimental Biology 37:425–434.

Parry, G. 1961. Osmotic and ionic changes in blood and muscle of migrating salmonids. Journal of Experimental Biology 38:411–427.

Phillips, A. M. 1969. Nutrition, digestion and energy utilization. Pages 391–432 *in* W. S. Hoar and D. J. Randall, editors. Fish Physiology, volume 1. Excretion, ionic regulation, and metabolism. Academic Press, New York, New York, USA.

Pinder, L., and J. G. Eales. 1969. Seasonal buoyance changes in Atlantic salmon *(Salmo salar)* parr and smolt. Journal of the Fisheries Research Board of Canada 26:2093–2100.

Power, G. 1959. Field measurement of the basal oxygen consumption of Atlantic salmon parr and smolts. Arctic 12:195–202.

Reddin, D. G., and W. M. Shearer. 1987. Sea-surface temperature and distribution of Atlantic salmon in the northwest Atlantic Ocean. American Fisheries Society Symposium 1:262–275.

Regan, C. T. 1911. The freshwater fishes of the British Isles. Methuen, London, England.

Richman, N. H. 1985. Hormones and osmoregulation in developing coho salmon *(Oncorhynchus kisutch)*. Doctoral dissertation. University of California, Berkeley, California, USA.

Rounsefell, G. A. 1958. Anadromy in North American Salmonidae. U.S. Fish and Wildlife Service Fishery Bulletin 58(131):171–185.

Sargent, J. R., A. J. Thompson, and M. Bornancin. 1975. Activities and localization of succinic dehydrogenase and Na⁺/K⁺-activated adenosine triphosphatase in the gills of freshwater and seawater

eels *(Anguilla anguilla)*. Comparative Biochemistry and Physiology B, Comparative Biochemistry 51:75–79.

Saunders, R. L. 1965. Adjustment of buoyancy in young Atlantic salmon and trout by changes in swimbladder volume. Journal of the Fisheries Research Board of Canada 22:335–352.

Saunders, R. L. 1987. The thermal biology of Atlantic salmon:influence of temperature on salmon culture with particular reference to constraints imposed by low temperature. Institute of Freshwater Research Drottningholm Report 65.

Saunders, R. L., and E. B. Henderson. 1969. Survival and growth of Atlantic salmon parr in relation to salinity. Fisheries Research Board of Canada Technical Report 147.

Saunders, R. L., and E. B. Henderson. 1970. Influence of photoperiod on smolt development and growth of Atlantic salmon *(Salmo salar)*. Journal of the Fisheries Research Board of Canada 27:1295–1311.

Saunders, R. L., and E. B. Henderson. 1978. Changes in gill ATPase activity and smolt status of Atlantic salmon *(Salmo salar)*. Journal of the Fisheries Research Board of Canada 35:1542–1546.

Saunders, R. L., E. B. Henderson, and B. D. Glebe. 1982. Precocious sexual maturation and smoltification in male Atlantic salmon *(Salmo salar)*. Aquaculture 28:211–229.

Saunders, R. L., E. B. Henderson, and P. R. Harmon. 1985. Effects of photoperiod on juvenile growth and smolting of Atlantic salmon and subsequent survival and growth in sea cages. Aquaculture 45:55–66.

Saunders, R. L., E. B. Henderson, P. R. Harmon, C. E. Johnston, and J. G. Eales. 1983. Effects of low environmental pH on smolting of Atlantic salmon *(Salmo salar)*. Canadian Journal of Fisheries and Aquatic Sciences 40:1203–1211.

Schreck, C. B. 1981. Stress and compensation in teleostean fishes:response to social and physical factors. Pages 295–321 *in* A. D. Pickering, editor. Stress and fish. Academic Press, New York, New York, USA.

Schreck, C. B. 1982. Stress and rearing of salmonids. Aquaculture 128:241–249.

Sheridan, M. A., and W. V. Allen. 1983. Wax esters in the liver and serum of steelhead trout, *Salmo gairdneri* Richardson. Comparative Biochemistry and Physiology B, Comparative Biochemistry 74:251–253.

Sheridan, M. A., W. V. Allen, and T. H. Kerstetter. 1983. Seasonal variations in the lipid composition of the steelhead trout, *Salmo gairdneri* Richardson, associated with the parr–smolt transformation. Journal of Fish Biology 23:125–134.

Sheridan, M. A., W. V. Allen, and T. H. Kerstetter. 1985a. Changes in the fatty acid composition of steelhead trout, *Salmo gairdneri* Richardson, associated with parr–smolt transformation. Comparative Biochemistry and Physiology B, Comparative Biochemistry 80:671–676.

Sheridan, M. A., N. Y. S. Woo, and H. A. Bern.

1985b. Changes in the rates of glycogenesis, glycogenolysis, lipogenesis and lipolysis in selected tissues of the coho salmon *(Oncorhynchus kisutch)* associated with parr–smolt transformation. Journal of Experimental Zoology 236:35–44.

Silva, P., R. Solomon, K. Spokes, and F. H. Epstein. 1977. Ovabain inhibition of gill Na–K-ATPase relationship to active chloride transport. Journal of Experimental Zoology 199:419–426.

Simpson, T. H. 1985. Epilogue. Salmonid Smoltification Workshop. Aquaculture 45:395–398.

Smith, L. S. 1982. Decreased swimming performance as a necessary component of the smolt migration in salmon in the Columbia River. Aquaculture 28:153–162.

Sullivan, C. V., W. W. Dickhoff, S. D. Brewer, and G. P. Johnston. 1983. Plasma thyroid-hormone concentrations and gill (Na+K)-ATPase activities in postemergent pink salmon. Transactions of the American Fisheries Society 112:825–829.

Sullivan, C. V., W. W. Dickhoff, C. V. W. Mahnken, and W. K. Hershberger. 1985. Changes in hemoglobin system of the coho salmon *(Oncorhynchus kisutch* during smoltification and triiodothyronine and prophthiouracil treatment. Comparative Biochemistry and Physiology A, Comparative Physiology 81:807–813.

Sutterlin, A. M., E. B. Henderson, S. P. Merrill, R. L. Saunders, and A. A. MacKay. 1981. Salmonid rearing trials at Deer Island, New Brunswick, with some projections of economic viability. Canadian Technical Report of Fisheries and Aquatic Sciences 1011.

Talbot, C., F. B. Eddy, and J. Johnston. 1982. Osmoregulation in salmon and sea trout alevins. Journal of Experimental Biology 101:61–70.

Tchernavin, V. 1939. The origin of salmon. Salmon and Trout Magazine 95:120–140.

Thomson, A. J., and J. R. Sargent. 1977. Changes in the levels of chloride cells and (Na+,K+)-dependent ATPase in the gills of yellow and silver eels adapting to seawater. Journal of Experimental Zoology 200:33–40.

Thorpe, J. E. 1977. Bimodal distribution of length of juvenile Atlantic salmon (*Salmo salar* L.) under artificial rearing conditions. Journal of Fish Biology 11:175–184.

Thorpe, J. E. 1982. Migration in salmonids, with special reference to juvenile movements in freshwater. Pages 86–97 in E. L. Brannon and E. O. Salo, editors. Proceedings of the salmon and trout migratory behavior symposium. University of Washington, School of Fisheries, Seattle, Washington, USA.

Thorpe, J. E. 1986. Age at first maturity in Atlantic salmon, *Salmo salar:*freshwater period influences and conflicts with smolting. Canadian Special Publication of Fisheries and Aquatic Sciences 89:7–14.

Thorpe, J. E. 1987a. Environmental regulation of growth patterns in juvenile Atlantic salmon. Pages 463–474 in R. C. Summerfelt and G. E. Hall, editors. Age and growth in fishes. Iowa State University Press, Ames, Iowa, USA.

Thorpe, J. E. 1987b. Smolting versus residency: developmental conflict in salmonids. American Fisheries Society Symposium 1:244–252.

Thorpe, J. E., C. Talbot, and C. Villareal. 1982. Bimodality of growth and smolting in Atlantic salmon, *Salmo salar* L. Aquaculture 28:123–132.

Vanstone, W. E., and J. R. Markert. 1968. Some morphological and biochemical changes in coho salmon, *Oncorhynchus kisutch,* during the parr–smolt transformation. Journal of the Fisheries Research Board of Canada 25:2403–2418.

Vanstone, W. E., E. Roberts, and H. Tsuyuki. 1964. Changes in the multiple hemoglobin patterns of some Pacific salmon, genus *Oncorhynchus,* during the parr–smolt transformation. Canadian Journal of Physiology and Pharmacology 42:697–703.

Virtanen, E., and A. Oikari. 1984. Effects of low acclimation temperature on salinity adaptation in the presmolt salmon, *Salmo salar* L. Comparative Biochemistry and Physiology A, Comparative Physiology 78:387–392.

Virtanen, E., and A. Soivio. 1985. The patterns of T_3, T_4, cortisol and Na+–K+-ATPase during smoltification of hatchery-reared *Salmo salar* and comparison with wild smolts. Aquaculture 45:97–109.

Wagner, H. H. 1974a. Photoperiod and temperature regulation of smolting in steelhead trout *(Salmo gairdneri)*. Canadian Journal of Zoology 52:219–234.

Wagner, H. H. 1974b. Seawater adaptation independent of photoperiod in steelhead trout *(Salmo gairdneri)*. Canadian Journal of Zoology 52:805–812.

Wagner, H. H., F. P. Conte, and J. L. Fessler. 1969. Development of osmotic and ionic regulation in two races of chinook salmon *O. tshawytscha.* Comparative Biochemistry and Physiology 29:325–341.

Wedemeyer, G. A., R. L. Saunders, and W. C. Clarke. 1980. Environmental factors affecting smoltification and early marine survival of anadromous salmonids. U.S. National Marine Fisheries Service Marine Fisheries Review 42(6):1–14.

Weisbart, M. 1968. Osmotic and ionic regulation in embryos, alevins, and fry of the five species of Pacific salmon. Canadian Journal of Zoology 46:385–397.

Wendt, C. A. G., and R. L. Saunders. 1973. Changes in carbohydrate metabolism in young Atlantic salmon in response to various forms of stress. International Atlantic Salmon Foundation Special Publication Series 4:55–82.

White, H. C. 1940. Life-history of sea-running brook trout *(S. fontinalis)* of Moser River, N. S. Journal of the Fisheries Research Board of Canada 5:176–186.

Wilder, D. G. 1952. A comparative study of anadromous and freshwater populations of brook trout (*Salvelinus fontinalis* (Mitchell)). Journal of the Fisheries Research Board of Canada 9:169–202.

Withey, K. G., and R. L. Saunders. 1973. Effect of a reciprocal photoperiod regime on standard rate of oxygen consumption of postsmolt Atlantic salmon

(Salmo salar). Journal of the Fisheries Research Board of Canada 30:1898–1900.

Woo, W. Y. S., H. A. Bern, and R. S. Nishioka. 1978. Changes in body composition associated with smoltification and premature transfer to seawater in coho salmon *(Oncorhynchus kisutch)* and king salmon *(O. tschawytscha)*. Journal of Fish Biology 13: 421–428.

Wood, C. M., and D. J. Randall. 1973. The influence of swimming activity on sodium balance in the rainbow trout *(Salmo gairdneri)*. Journal of Comparative Physiology 82:207–233.

Zaugg, W. S., and L. R. McLain. 1970. Adenosine triphosphatase activity in gills of salmonids: seasonal variations and salt water influences in coho salmon, *Oncorhynchus kisutch*. Comparative Biochemistry and Physiology 35:587–596.

Zaugg, W. S., and H. H. Wagner. 1973. Gill ATPase activity related to parr–smolt transformation and migration in steelhead trout *(Salmo gairdneri):* influence of photoperiod and temperature. Comparative Biochemistry and Physiology B, Comparative Biochemistry 45:955–965.

American Fisheries Society Symposium 1:230–235, 1987

Changes in Hepatic Mitochondrial Proteins of Steelhead during the Parr–Smolt Transformation

TERENCE M. BRADLEY

Department of Fisheries, Aquaculture and Pathology, University of Rhode Island
Kingston, Rhode Island, 02881, USA

Abstract.—The liver is a highly dynamic and metabolically active organ which may play a role in the parr–smolt transformation of anadromous salmonids. To investigate this possibility, hepatic mitochondrial proteins were examined at regular intervals during smoltification of juvenile steelhead *Salmo gairdneri*, i.e., February through May. Hepatic tissue was excised at regular intervals and processed to obtain a subcellular fraction highly enriched in mitochondria. The mitochondrial proteins were resolved by two-dimensional polyacrylamide gel electrophoresis. Polypeptides specific to early (parr), transitional, and late (smolt) stages were observed. The most pronounced changes include the appearance of a prominent polypeptide with an isoelectric point (pI) of 4.9 and apparent molecular weight (MW) of 51 kilodaltons which was found only in smolts. In addition, a series of high-MW polypeptides (>92 kilodaltons) became less prominent as time progressed and was no longer present in fish sampled in late May. Several additional quantitative and qualitative changes were noted. The changes observed in the protein profiles suggest alterations in enzymatic or structural components, or both. Modifications in the population of mitochondrial proteins may function in adaptation to a new environment and a shift in nutritional status.

The parr–smolt transformation of anadromous salmonids is a series of morphological, physiological, and behavioral changes that culminates in successful adaptation to the marine environment (Hoar 1976). Numerous physiological, biochemical, and endocrinological modifications occur during smoltification including: increased osmoregulatory ability (Folmar and Dickhoff 1980); elevation of branchial Na^+,K^+-ATPase activity (Zaugg and McLain 1972, 1976; Zaugg 1982); increased circulating thyroxine levels (Grau et al. 1981; Dickhoff et al. 1982); changes in hemoglobin fractions (Wilkins 1968; Sullivan et al. 1985); alterations in body composition (Johnston and Saunders 1981); and changes in the rates of glycogenesis, glycogenolysis, lipogenesis, and lipolysis in several tissues (Sheridan et al. 1985).

The liver is involved in the metabolism of carbohydrates, proteins, and lipids, the synthesis of most plasma proteins, and the clearance of steroid and thyroid hormones (Guyton 1981). Several recent findings indicate that the liver might have a central role in the smoltification process. Indeed, Blake et al. (1984) reported that the number of hepatic mitochondria and the activities of cytochrome-*c* oxidase and succinate dehydrogenase within mitochondria increase in Atlantic salmon *Salmo salar* during smoltification. In addition, hepatic receptors for thyroid hormones that have a major role in this process have been found in salmonids (Darling et al. 1982). Plasma proteins, a large percentage of which are synthesized in the liver, also change during smoltification (Bradley and Rourke 1984). Consequently, this study was designed to test the hypothesis that changes in the population of hepatic mitochondrial proteins occur during the parr–smolt transformation in steelhead *Salmo gairdneri*. To assess the validity of this hypothesis, liver tissue was excised from juvenile steelhead at regular intervals during smoltification, i.e., February through May. The tissue samples were processed to obtain hepatic mitochondrial proteins, which were subsequently analyzed by two-dimensional polyacrylamide gel electrophoresis.

Methods

Two-year-old steelhead (Clearwater strain, Idaho) were reared from eggs at the Aquaculture Center, University of Rhode Island, and maintained under simulated natural photoperiod with fluorescent lights. A natural temperature regimen with a range of 6–13°C was maintained also. Fish were fed a dry commercial ration to satiation four times daily.

Sampling was conducted biweekly from early February through May. The mean lengths (±SD) of fish sampled in February and May were 188 ± 7 mm and 230 ± 6 mm, respectively. After a 14-h fast, fish (*N* = 6) were lightly anesthetized at 0800 hours with tricaine (MS-222, 75 mg/L) and decapitated. The liver was rapidly excised, gall bladder removed, and hepatic tissue placed in ice-cold homogenization buffer (0.3 M sucrose, 10 mM tris-HCl, 0.1 mM ethylene glycol bis(β-aminoethyl ether)-N,N,N',N'-tetraacetic acid [EGTA]; pH 7.4). The excised tissue was diced into small cubes and homogenized in five volumes of buffer with a tissumizer (Tekmar Company, Cincinnati, Ohio) for two 5-s pulses. Homogenization time was determined initially by examination of the homogenate by light microscopy. The homogenate was filtered through six layers of buffer-soaked gauze to remove debris and unhomogenized tissue. The filtrate was then centrifuged at 700 × gravity for 10 min at 4°C. The pellet, containing unlysed cells, erythrocytes, cellular debris, and nuclei, was discarded, and the supernatant was centrifuged at 4,000 × gravity for 10 min (Brucker and Cohen 1976). The upper tan portion of the pellet was resuspended in 10 mL homogenization buffer and recentrifuged at 4,000 × gravity for 10 min. This washing procedure was repeated four times or until the supernatant was clear. The final supernatant was then discarded, and the mitochondria-rich pellet was resuspended in 1.0 mL deionized water, frozen at −70°C, and lyophilized. Protein concentrations were assayed by the method of Bradford (1976).

Between three and six mitochondrial fractions were analyzed for each sample date by two-dimensional polyacrylamide gel electrophoresis conducted as described by Bradley and Rourke (1984) with two exceptions. The zwitterionic detergent, CHAPS (Sigma Chemical Company, St. Louis, Missouri), was substituted for NP-40 in sample preparation and in first-dimension gels, and narrow-range pH 4–6.5 ampholytes (Pharmacia, Piscataway, New Jersey) were used. One hundred fifty micrograms of protein was loaded onto each isoelectric focussing (IEF) gel and electrophoresed for a total of 6,400 V·h. The second-dimension sodium dodecyl sulfate 8–15% linear-gradient slab gels were silver stained (GEL-CODE, Health Products, South Haven, Michigan). Molecular weight standards were coelectrophoresed on slab gels for determination of the apparent molecular weights (MW) of resolved mitochondrial proteins. Silver-stained gels were analyzed by dividing the gels into four regions based on MW: region 1, MW > 92 kilodaltons (kd), region 2, MW = 92–66 kd, region 3, MW = 65–35 kd, and region 4, MW < 35 kd.

The condition factor (100 × weight/length^3) and

TABLE 1.—The condition factors[a] of 2-year-old steelhead ($N = 6$) sampled for hepatic proteins from February through May

Month	Condition factor±SE
February	0.98±0.02
March	0.90±0.02
April	0.86±0.02
Early May	0.84±0.03
Late May	0.89±0.03

[a] Condition factor = 100 × weight/length^3.

degree of silvering were monitored throughout the sampling period.

Results

Condition factors decreased from February (0.98 ± 0.02) through early May (0.84 ± 0.03) and late May (0.89 ± 0.03) (Table 1). By mid-May, parr marks were no longer visible and all fish had the silvery appearance of smolts. These results indicate grossly that the fish underwent morphological changes known to occur during smoltification.

Significant changes in hepatic mitochondrial protein profiles were observed during parr–smolt transformation. These alterations were seen in both the number and quantity of proteins resolved. Although a large number of polypeptides were resolved (>200), only a limited number of representative protein changes are discussed. A representative pH gradient of a first-dimension IEF gel is depicted in Table 2. Typical protein profiles of fish sampled in February, March, April, early May, and late May are illustrated in Figures 1–3.

Several profile differences can be seen in region 1, containing polypeptides of the highest MW. In general, a trend toward a decrease in the number of polypeptides with MW > 92 kd was observed from February through May. Several polypep-

TABLE 2.—A pH profile of a typical first-dimension isoelectric focussing gel used to separate mitochondrial proteins. The values indicate the pH of sequential 10-mm sections of the gel.

Gel position	pH
Basic end	6.55
	6.20
	5.85
	5.65
	5.40
	5.10
	4.80
	4.50
Acidic end	4.15

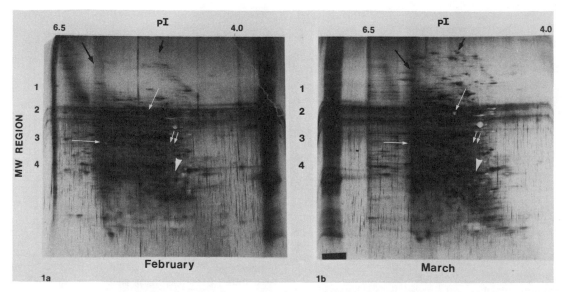

FIGURE 1.—Two-dimensional polyacrylamide gels of hepatic mitochondrial proteins from 2-year-old steelhead. Protein profiles are from fish sampled in February and March. The isoelectric points (pI) of a typical first-dimension gel are indicated at the top and the molecular-weight (MW) regions of the second-dimension gel on the left side. Arrows and triangles indicate sites at which the occurrence of polypeptides changed over time.

tides present in fish sampled in March were no longer visible in profiles from late May (Figures 1b, 3: dark arrows). One of four fish analyzed in early May had a larger number of high-molecular-weight polypeptides than any other fish sampled during this period (Figure 2b: dark arrows). However, this fish lacked several region 1 polypeptides present in parr in March. High-molecular-weight polypeptides were not readily resolved during the earliest sampling period.

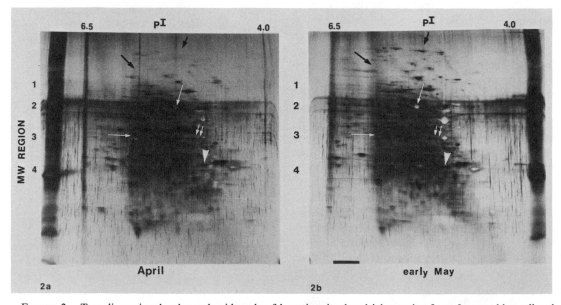

FIGURE 2.—Two-dimensional polyacrylamide gels of hepatic mitochondrial proteins from 2-year-old steelhead sampled in April and early May. The isoelectric points (pI) are indicated at the top and the molecular-weight (MW) regions at the left of each gel. Arrows and triangles indicate sites at which the occurrence of polypeptides changed over time.

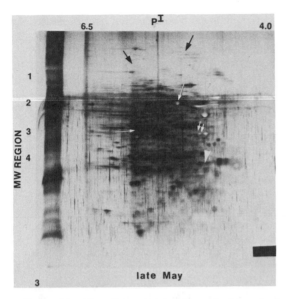

FIGURE 3.—Two-dimensional polyacrylamide gel of hepatic mitochondrial proteins from a 2-year-old steelhead sampled in late May. The molecular-weight (MW) regions are indicated at the left and the isoelectric points (pI) at the top of the gel. The arrows and triangles indicate sites at which the occurrence of polypeptides changed over time.

In region 2, a progressive increase in the quantity of two prominent, light-colored spots was observed (Figures 2, 3: vertical long white arrows). The two polypeptides (isoelectric point pI = 5.3, MW = 67 kd), barely visible in fish sampled in February, were readily apparent in most fish by late March and continued to increase until May. An increase in the quantity of these polypeptides was observed in all fish as smoltification progressed.

Two interesting alterations occurred in region 3. A cluster of light-colored polypeptides present from February became less visible by late May (Figures 1a, 3: horizontal white arrow). In addition, a more acidic polypeptide (pI = 4.9, MW = 51 kd) was prominent only in smolts sampled in late May (Figures 1–3: double white arrows). This polypeptide was present in two of five fish sampled in April but at very low concentrations.

A large percentage of the polypeptides in region 4 was diffuse and difficult to analyze. However, one change in protein profiles was readily apparent. A set of darkly staining polypeptides (pI = 4.6–4.9, MW = 33 kd) was observed in fish from March until the termination of sampling (Figures 1a–3, white triangles). These polypeptides were absent in fish sampled during February.

Discussion

The protein profiles indicate that alterations in the population of hepatic mitochondrial proteins occur during the parr–smolt transformation. Proteins specific to early stages (cluster of proteins in region 3) and late stages (pI = 5.3, MW = 67 kd; pI = 4.9, MW = 51 kd; pI = 4.6–4.9, MW = 33kd) of smoltification were observed. Transitional proteins (MW > 92 kd) present for only a limited time were observed also. Four of the five protein changes described were qualitative and one was quantitative. Limited variation in protein profiles occurred among individuals at any given sampling date. A minor deviation from the normal protein profile was observed in three fish. A "profile" from one fish in early May exhibited a greater than typical number of high-MW proteins in region 1 (Figure 2b: dark arrows). In addition, profiles from two fish in April contained a polypeptide (pI = 4.9, MW = 51 kd) in extremely low concentrations that was present in high concentrations in fish only during late May. Accordingly, the low degree of individual variability allowed analysis of qualitative or quantitative trends, or both, in representative proteins.

These findings are consistent with previous studies of amphibian metamorphosis, a differentiative period analogous in some respects to smoltification. Brucker and Cohen (1976) observed that the liver mitochondria are subject to pronounced modification during metamorphosis that is induced by thyroxine (T_4) in the bullfrog *Rana catesbeiana*. These changes include a rapid increase in the rate of mitochondrial DNA synthesis, a two-fold increase in mitochondrial protein mass, and increases in the concentration of cytochrome $a + a_3$ (complex IV) and cytochrome b (complexes II and III).

Changes in the hepatic proteins of other species can be induced by administration of thyroid hormones. In teleosts, the effect of triiodothyronine (T_3) on hepatocytes has been demonstrated. Bhattacharya et al. (1985) found that T_3 stimulated protein synthesis in dispersed hepatocytes of juvenile coho salmon *Oncorhynchus kisutch*. Similar effects on mitochondria have been induced by T_3 administration in the rat (Katyare et al. 1970). The quantity of mitochondrial protein fractions decreased by 40% after thyroidectomy and increased 160% upon treatment with T_3 in vivo. In addition, the turnover patterns of mitochondrial protein fractions were altered significantly by T_3 treatment.

The increase in plasma T_4 concentrations and subsequent physiological effects during smoltification in anadromous salmonids are well documented (Folmar and Dickhoff 1980; Grau et al. 1981; Dickhoff et al. 1982; Specker et al. 1984). Based upon the studies cited, it seems probable that the protein changes observed in the mitochondria of steelhead during smoltification are associated with the elevated plasma T_4 concentrations during this period.

The alterations in mitochondrial proteins might have adaptive significance in anadromous salmonids. Differences in hepatic mitochondria of Atlantic salmon parr and smolts have been observed (Blake et al. 1984). Smolts had higher quantities of mitochondria and significantly greater levels of cytochrome-c oxidase activity. These changes and those described herein indicate that the hepatic mitochondria may be involved in the transformation of freshwater parr to marine smolt. The polypeptide changes described in the results are only a few of the many that may be discerned by careful scrutiny of the gels. In the present study, the gels were slightly overloaded in order to attain resolution of proteins present in very low quantities; the sensitivity of the silver stain is approximately 1 ng.

The most interesting finding in the present study is that both qualitative and quantitative changes in proteins were observed in hepatic mitochondria. The appearance or disappearance of polypeptides in the gel profiles might be ascribed to several causes: (1) the qualitative changes might actually be quantitative, i.e., a change in concentration of the polypeptides above or below the sensitivity of the silver staining procedures; (2) alterations in translation, post-translational modification, or transport of the polypeptides; or (3) the expression of new genes. It is not possible to ascertain from the data in the present study whether the polypeptides in question are enzymes or structural proteins. The protein changes might be transitory, e.g., the polypeptides in region 1 (Figures 1–3, dark arrows), or they might be maintained with transfer to the marine environment. However, preliminary data from an ongoing study in this laboratory indicate that mitochondrial polypeptides specific to marine and freshwater environments are present in juvenile Atlantic salmon. In addition, oral administration of T_3 appears to induce synthesis of several polypeptides (Bradley, unpublished data).

Hepatic mitochondria play an integral role in carbohydrate and fat metabolism. These organelles contain a full complement of enzymes for the tricarboxylic acid cycle, fatty acid oxidation, oxidative phosphorylation and various shuttle-transport systems (Alberts et al. 1983). In rats, hepatic mitochondria have a relatively short half-life of 8.5 d (Beattie et al. 1967). If salmon have a similar mitochondria turnover pattern, the population of mitochondrial proteins and the metabolic pathways could be altered at relatively rapid rates throughout the parr–smolt transformation and serve as a sensitive adaptation mechanism. A metabolic advantage might be conveyed upon fish capable of adjusting structural components and specific enzyme activities and concentrations to best meet nutritional status and environmental conditions. Such hepatic changes have been observed in coho salmon during smoltification (Sheridan et al. 1985) and in sockeye salmon *Oncorhynchus nerka* during spawning migrations (French et al. 1983). Alterations in mitochondrial proteins, enzymatic or structural, may have a similar effect.

Acknowledgments

I thank R. C. Rhodes III for his critical review of the manuscript. I also thank F. Edgar and C. Wentworth for technical assistance in fish husbandry and M. Mann and S. Polofsky for help in preparing the manuscript. This work was supported, in part, by the National Sea Grant College Program, under grant NA85AA-D-SG094, project R/A-21, through the Rhode Island Sea Grant College Program. This is Rhode Island Agricultural Experiment Station Contribution 2326.

References

Alberts, B., D. Bray, J. Lewis, M. Raff, K. Roberts, and J. D. Watson. 1983. Molecular biology of the cell. Garland, New York, New York, USA.

Beattie, D. S., R. E. Basford, and S. B. Koritz. 1967. The turnover of the protein components of mitochondria from rat liver, kidney, and brain. Journal of Biological Chemistry 242:4584–4586.

Bhattacharya, S., E. Plisetskaya, W. W. Dickhoff, and A. Gorbman. 1985. The effects of estradiol and triiodothyronine on protein synthesis by hepatocytes of juvenile coho salmon (*Oncorhynchus kisutch*). General and Comparative Endocrinology 57:103–109.

Blake, R. L., F. L. Roberts, and R. L. Saunders. 1984. Parr-smolt transformation Atlantic salmon (*Salmo salar*): activities of two respiratory enzymes and concentrations of mitochondria in the liver. Canadian Journal of Fisheries and Aquatic Sciences 41:199–203.

Bradford, M. M. 1976. A rapid and sensitive method for

the quantitation of microgram quantities of protein utilizing the principle of dye binding. Analytical Biochemistry 72:248–254.

Bradley, T., and A. W. Rourke. 1984. An electrophoretic analysis of plasma proteins from juvenile *Oncorhynchus tshawytscha* (Walbaum). Journal of Fish Biology 24:703–709.

Brucker, R. F., and P. P. Cohen. 1976. Alterations in enzyme and cytochrome profiles of *Rana catesbeiana* liver organelles during thyroxine-induced metamorphosis. Science (Washington, D.C.) 168:533–543.

Darling, D. S., W. W. Dickhoff, and A. Gorbman. 1982. Comparison of thyroid hormone binding to hepatic nuclei of the rat and a teleost (*Oncorhynchus kisutch*). Endocrinology 111:1936–1941.

Dickhoff, W. W., L. C. Folmar, J. L. Mighell, and C. V. W. Mahnken. 1982. Plasma thyroid hormones during smoltification of yearling and under yearling coho salmon and yearling chinook salmon and steelhead trout. Aquaculture 28:39–48.

Folmar, L. C., and W. W. Dickhoff. 1980. The parr–smolt transformation (smoltification) and seawater adaptation in salmonids. Aquaculture 21:1–37.

French, C. J., P. W. Hochachka, and T. P. M. Mommsen. 1983. Metabolic organization of liver during spawning migration of sockeye salmon. American Journal of Physiology 245:R827–R830.

Grau, E. G., W. W. Dickhoff, R. S. Nishioka, H. A. Bern, and L. C. Folmar. 1981. Lunar phasing of the thyroxine surge preparatory to seaward migration of salmonid fish. Science (Washington, D.C.) 211:607–609.

Guyton, Arthur C. 1981. Textbook of medical physiology. W. B. Saunders, Philadelphia, Pennsylvania, USA.

Hoar, W. S. 1976. Smolt transformation: evolution, behavior, and physiology. Journal of the Fisheries Research Board of Canada 33:1234–1252.

Johnston, C. E., and R. L. Saunders. 1981. Parr–smolt transformation of yearling Atlantic salmon (*Salmo salar*) at several rearing temperatures. Canadian Journal of Fisheries and Aquatic Sciences 38:1189–1198.

Katyare, S. S., P. Fatterpaker, and A. Sreenivasan. 1970. Heterogeneity of rat liver mitochondrial fractions and the effect of tri-iodothyronine on their protein turnover. Biochemical Journal 118:111–121.

Sheridan, M. A., N. Y. S. Wood, and H. A. Bern. 1985. Changes in the rates of glycogenesis, glycogenolysis, lipogenesis, and lipolysis in selected tissues of the coho salmon (*Oncorhynchus kisutch*) associated with parr–smolt transformation. Journal of Experimental Zoology 236:35–44.

Specker, J. L., J. J. Distefano III, E. G. Grau, R. S. Nishioka, and H. A. Bern. 1984. Development-associated changes in thyroxine kinetics in juvenile salmon. Endocrinology 115:399–406.

Sullivan, C. V., W. W. Dickhoff, C. V. W. Mahnken, and W. K. Hershberger. 1985. Changes in the hemoglobin system of the coho salmon *Oncorhynchus kisutch* during smoltification and triiodothyronine and propylthiouracil treatment. Comparative Biochemistry and Physiology A, Comparative Physiology 81:807–813.

Wilkins, N. P. 1968. Multiple hemoglobins of the Atlantic salmon (*Salmo salar*). Journal of the Fisheries Research Board of Canada 25:2651–2663.

Zaugg, W. S. 1982. Some changes in smoltification and seawater adaptability of salmonids resulting from environmental and other factors. Aquaculture 28:143–151.

Zaugg, W. S., and L. R. McLain. 1972. Changes in gill adenosine triphosphatase activity associated with parr–smolt transformation in steelhead trout, coho, and spring chinook salmon. Journal of the Fisheries Research Board of Canada 29:161–171.

Zaugg, W. S., and L. R. McLain. 1976. Influence of water temperature on gill sodium–potassium stimulated ATPase activity in juvenile coho salmon (*Oncorhynchus kisutch*). Comparative Biochemistry and Physiology A, Comparative Physiology 54:419–421.

American Fisheries Society Symposium 1:236–243, 1987

Adaptive Flexibility in Life History Tactics of Mature Male Baltic Salmon Parr in Relation to Body Size and Environment[1]

T. Eriksson, L.-O. Eriksson, and H. Lundqvist

Department of Ecological Zoology, University of Umeå, S-901 87 Umeå, Sweden

Abstract.—The importance of size and early life history (sexually mature parr versus immature parr) on the behavior, growth, and survival of individually tagged two-summer-old Baltic (Atlantic) salmon *Salmo salar* has been studied in two stocks from northern Sweden. Data on growth, sexual maturation, and recapture rate have been gathered from fish released in the river at the time of the normal smolt run, from fish transferred to brackish water at time of smolting and subsequently released, and from fish transferred to brackish water at time of smolting and subsequently reared in net-pens for one summer. Recapture rates of previously mature males released in the river were low, about one-fifth those of immature fish of similar sizes. Electrofishing in autumn in the hatchery-release stream indicated that a majority of the previously released 2-year-old parr remaining in the stream were sexually mature males. Recapture rates of previously mature parr released in brackish water were indistinguishable from those of immature fish. Among fish retained in brackish water, only a small fraction of males matured sexually after the first summer in net-pens. The incidence of sexual maturation was highest among those males that had been previously mature at a small size. Growth rates were comparatively high among previously mature, precocious males that did not remature sexually. These males showed a higher instantaneous growth rate than immature fish. A discrete size-dependent relationship with sexual rematuration among previously mature males strongly affected their life histories. Many small, previously mature males showed a nonmigrant appearance and were unable to respond to shifts in the environment. At larger sizes, the choice to become sexually mature or to express a high growth rate depended largely on the environment the fish experienced. If they reached the sea, the majority of fish allocated their energetic resources to somatic growth. On the other hand, when retained in fresh water, males showed a capacity to mature at all sizes, indicating a flexibility in the choice of life history tactics.

Evolutionary history has formed a menu of tactical options allowing individuals of Baltic (Atlantic) salmon *Salmo salar* to become spawning residents in the riverine environment at small sizes or anadromous fish at large sizes (Jones 1959; Lundqvist 1983; Hutchings and Myers 1985). Since rivers generally are poor habitats for rapid growth to large size, the option of sexual maturation as a large fish is usually related to an extended migration to more productive environments in the sea.

When approaching the time for seaward migration, young Baltic salmon adjust their behaviour. They lose their territorial behaviour, form schooling groups, and leave the riverine environment. The migrating fish are termed smolts. The behavioural changes are connected with physiological, biochemical, and morphological changes (Hoar 1976; Wedemeyer et al. 1980). However, not all parr complete the transformation to smolt. A varying proportion of the male parr stay in the

river and participate in spawning (Österdahl 1969; Myers 1984).

Smolting itself is a dynamic process. Eriksson and Lundqvist (1982) and Lundqvist and Eriksson (1985) demonstrated the seasonality in smolting, expressed in the smoltification–desmoltification cycle. They also discussed the conflicting choices between migration and residency within individual fish at the time of the smolt run. The behavioural output throughout a Baltic salmon's lifetime is a result of both the underlying internal machinery and the individual's interpretation of the environmental information it receives. Obviously, an individual choice of life-style will be more or less successful and the alternatives are thereby subject to natural selection.

There is only limited information available regarding environmental influence on the life history components of Baltic salmon. This study focuses on the adaptive flexibility in life history tactics of precocious, sexually mature male parr of Baltic salmon. We discuss the importance of fish size and sex on the growth, survival, and behaviour of Baltic salmon in relation to their environment.

---

[1]Report 5 from the Norrby Laboratory, S-910 20 Hörnefors, Sweden.

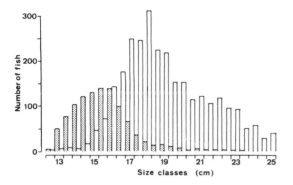

FIGURE 1.—Size-frequency distribution of immature Baltic salmon (unfilled columns) and previously mature males (filled columns) at time of tagging in May 1982, about 2 weeks before transfer to brackish water.

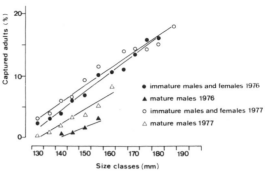

FIGURE 2.—Percentage recaptures of tagged Baltic salmon in relation to size at release in the Ume River. Two categories of smolts, sexually immature fish (circles) and previously mature males (triangles), are indicated for each year of release.

Methods

The riverine environment.—We have conducted release experiments with hatchery-reared Baltic salmon designed to assess the importance of size as a factor in determining the adult returns of precociously mature males compared with immature smolts (H. Lundqvist, W. C. Clarke, and H. Johansson, unpublished). Two-year-old Baltic salmon parr from the Ume River hatchery stock (63°50'N, 20°05'E) were used. In each of 3 years, 1975, 1976, and 1977, fish were sampled from an ungraded stock and individually tagged with external Carlin tags (Carlin 1955) after being anaesthetized in tricaine (MS-222, Sandoz). About 14,000 fish were tagged each year, of which 8–16% were mature males. Data from the release years 1976 and 1977 have been used in this study to demonstrate the relation between smolt size, category of fish, and recapture rate. Tagging was done in October–November, about 7 months prior to release. At tagging, fork length was measured to the nearest 0.5 cm and sexually mature, running-ripe males were noted. The mortality rate among tagged fish from month of tagging to release was less than 1% and did not differ between brood years. Fish less than 13 cm in fork length at the time of tagging were not included in the study. Fish were released in late May at the normal time of migration of wild smolts in the area.

The frequency of sexually mature three-summer-old males was determined in the Ume River, the stream into which hatchery fish were released, to get a random sample of resident three-summer-old salmon parr. Qualitative electrofishing was done in a 200-m-long part of the stream. The study covered a 5-year period (1979–1983) and was done

in early September each year, i.e., at the time Baltic salmon begin spawning in this part of Sweden. Numbers of sexually immature and early-maturing male parr of hatchery origin were noted.

The sea environment.—Size-dependent survival in the sea was studied in nonriver release experiments with 2-year-old Baltic salmon smolts. Information on growth and maturation during the first summer in the sea was obtained by keeping postsmolts in sea cages. In each of 3 years (1980–1982), about 6,000 individually tagged 2-year-old hatchery-reared smolts from the Ångerman River were used. Recapture data from release year 1981 have been omitted in this study since the number of captured fish originating from mature males was too low (less than five recoveries per size class). Fish were measured for length and classified as immature males and females or mature males while in fresh water. In late May, they were transferred to brackish water. Compared with fish from the Ume River stock, individuals from the Ångerman River stock have similar growth and maturation patterns (Lund-

TABLE 1.—Three-summer-old Baltic salmon parr sampled in autumn by electrofishing in the Ume River, in which hatchery fish were released.

Year	Females caught	Males caught	Percent males	Percent of males that were ripe
1979	2	14	87	100
1980	8	18	69	67
1981	4	30	88	100
1982	2	14	87	100
1983	2	69	97	100

qvist and Fridberg 1982) as well as similar meristic and morphometric characteristics (MacCrimmon and Claytor 1985).

The fish were kept in 50-m³ net-pens at a brackish water site at Ulvön (63°4'N, 18°40'E) in the Bothnian Sea, about 30 km north of the river mouth. A commercial dry salmon food (Ewos) was offered the fish at a rate of 2–3% of body weight/d. Releases of fish ($N = 1,700$–2,000) were done on three occasions. Smolts, acclimated to the brackish water (4‰) for 10–14 d and subsequently released, served as controls (Eriksson and Eriksson 1985). The two other groups were released with a 2–6 month delay.

One-way analysis of variance (ANOVA) was used in testing differences in percent adult recovery between years for each category. Covariance analysis was used to test differences among smolt categories and years adjusted for smolt size at time of release (Dixon 1981). The analysis was also carried out on arcsine-transformed values; the results were unchanged and thus not presented here. Data were considered as valid observations if more than five recoveries per size class

were made.

A separate study on the relation between sexual maturation and growth rate was done in 1982. For this purpose, we examined the fish kept in net-pens at Ulvön for later release. Figure 1 illustrates the size-frequency distribution of the two categories of fish, immature and previously mature males, used in this experiment. Fish from this experimental group were again sampled on September 23, measured in length, and examined for sexual maturity. All fish that were running-ripe were defined as sexually mature. The specific growth rate in length was calculated by the formula

$$100 \frac{\log_e l_1 - \log_e l_0}{t_1 - t_0};$$

l_0 is the mean length of the fish at time of tagging (t_0) and l_1 is the mean length after one summer in the sea (t_1).

Results

The Riverine Environment

Sexually immature smolts released in the river

TABLE 2.—Recaptures of Baltic salmon, both of immature fish and of previously mature (precocious) males, after they had been transferred to brackish water and released at Ulvön (Bothnian Sea). Slopes indicate increases in recapture rate per centimeter increase in fork lengths of fish.

		Fish release				
Year	Month	Number of fish	Category	Mean fork length ±SE (cm)	Percent recaptured[a]	Slope (%)
1980	Jun	1,453	Immature	16.8±0.08	12.2	0.9
		541	Precocious	15.1±0.1	9.8	3.6
	Aug	1,402	Immature		27.3	2.2
		587	Precocious		22.0	4.7
	Sep	1,190	Immature		32.2	0.6
		560	Precocious		21.4	1.1
1981	Jun	1,755	Immature	17.8±0.08	6.7	
		238	Precocious	15.3±0.2	3.4[b]	
	Aug	1,754	Immature		14.0	1.5
		237	Precocious		10.1	3.9
	Sep	1,498	Immature		20.6	1.0
		226	Precocious		20.2	4.9
1982	Jun	1,445	Immature	18.9±0.1	14.9	1.6
		542	Precocious	15.5±0.1	10.1	−0.2
	Sep	1,389	Immature		19.1	1.6
		455	Precocious		11.6	0.3
	Dec	1,255	Immature		20.6	1.2
		519	Precocious		16.8	1.8

[a] Recapture rates for immature fish did not differ significantly from those for precocious males within any release group ($P > 0.05$).
[b] Fewer than five precocious males were recaptured within each length group and no statistical analysis of this release group was done.

showed a significantly higher recapture rate ($P <$ 0.01) than smolts of previously mature males. The recapture rate was about five times higher for immature fish, 10.2% compared with 2.4% for previously mature males. In general, for both categories of smolts, survival to the adult stage was positively correlated with fish size at the time of release (Figure 2).

In autumn of the years 1979–1983, between 16 and 71 three-summer-old resident Baltic salmon were caught by electrofishing in the stream where they had been released. Most (69–97%) of these resident parr were males (Table 1). In four of the five years studied, all males captured were sexually mature. In 1980, an exceptionally low proportion of males was noted, 69%. There was also a low frequency of sexual maturation among these males (Table 1).

The Sea Environment

In the nonriver release experiment, there was no statistically significant difference in percent recapture between smolts of sexually immature fish and previously mature males released in June (Table 2). Delayed releases gave similar results. This similarity in recapture rates remained when adjustments were made for smolt size at release. Thus, in contrast with results obtained among river-released fish, previously mature males released in brackish water were taken at a similar rate as sexually immature fish of the same sizes

(Figure 3). Recapture rate increased with size of the released fish. The increase averaged 1.7%/cm increase in fork length for fish released in early June. Overall recapture rates for fish released in June (previously mature males and immature fish pooled) ranged from 6.3 to 13.6%. There were significant differences in survival between release times within years for both categories of fish ($P <$ 0.05). For later releases of fish, the rate of recapture steadily increased. Recapture rates for fish released in September were 16.0–28.7%.

The study evaluating the relation between body size at tagging and growth for mature males and immature fish after the first summer at sea showed large differences between categories in the incidence of sexually mature fish (Figure 4). Of all fish, 7.5% became sexually mature. Only males were found in this group. The majority of these maturing males (78.6%) had been mature as two-summer-old fish in fresh water. Among these previously mature males, 21.4% were sexually rematuring after about 4 months in brackish water. A small fraction (about 2.4%) of the fish classified as immature in fresh water matured sexually during the first summer in the sea.

The proportion of previously mature males that became sexually mature again was strongly related to size of the fish in spring (Figure 5). Small males rematured more frequently than large males. About 40% of all males that were previously mature in fresh water and had a body length of 13.0 cm at transfer to brackish water rematured. With increasing initial size, the proportion of rematuring males decreased. At fish sizes greater than 16 cm, this proportion was generally 10% or less.

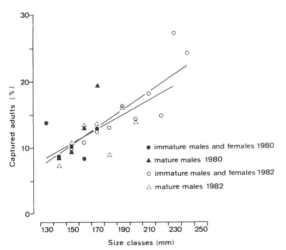

FIGURE 3.—Percentage recaptures of tagged Baltic salmon in relation to size at release from sea cages at Ulvön. Two smolt categories, sexually immature fish (circles) and previously mature males (triangles), are indicated for each year of release. Each regression line represents one year's data.

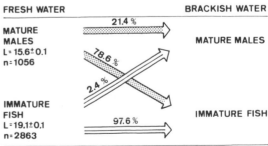

FIGURE 4.—Different life history patterns expressed by previously mature male and immature male and female Baltic salmon smolts after one summer in sea cages in brackish water. Fish were individually tagged in fresh water and transferred to brackish water at the normal time of smolt migration. L is fork length in mm±SE; n is number of fish.

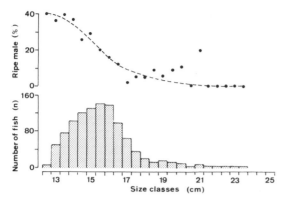

FIGURE 5.—Below: size-frequency distribution of previously mature male Baltic salmon at time of tagging in May 1982, about 2 weeks prior to transfer to brackish water. Above: size-dependent sexual rematuration among males (%) after one summer in the sea.

Thus, in autumn, there were four life history types distinguished by their sexual maturation patterns (Table 3). Within our study population, mature males in fresh water gave rise to sexually rematuring fish and immature postsmolts; previously immature fish yielded both immature postsmolts and a small fraction of mature males. The initial size and the relative growth rate during the first summer in the sea differed among the different life history types. Maturing male fish from both previously mature males and immature fish had a slow growth compared with immature fish coming from the same initial category of parr (Table 3). Thus, a high growth rate was noted among individuals that did not develop sexually. Previously mature males that did not mature in autumn showed a tendency for a higher growth rate, and attained the same final size, as immature fish that developed sexually. The process of sexual maturation obviously reduced the growth rate.

TABLE 3.—Maturation statuses and instantaneous growth rates of Baltic salmon following one summer in brackish water. Their previous maturation statuses in fresh water are indicated.

Reproductive status in		Growth rate (%/d)
Fresh water	Brackish water	
Mature males	Rematuring males	0.17
Mature males	Immature males	0.34
Immature fish	Maturing males	0.17
Immature fish	Immature males and females	0.28

Discussion

This study illustrates the plasticity of the life history patterns that Baltic salmon can express in response to different environments. It was demonstrated that previously mature males released in the river had a poor rate of survival compared with immature smolts. Corresponding males released in brackish water behaved differently and had a survival rate similar to that of immature smolts. This association between early life history option and survival of fish released in different environments has not been considered in detail earlier. A strong positive relationship between survival and smolt size is commonly observed among releases of hatchery-reared smolts of Baltic and Atlantic salmon (Carlin 1959; Isaksson and Bergman 1978). However, to our knowledge, no data on this relationship for early maturing males has previously been published. The reasons for this difference in survival among mature males released at different sites cannot be readily explained. We suggest that many small males follow a life history pattern aimed for residence in the river, i.e., sexual maturation. The dominance of mature males found among the resident age-2+ fish in the river in autumn supports these suggestions. Since sexual maturation and smolting are suggested as mutually exclusive processes (Evropeytseva 1960; Thorpe and Morgan 1980; Lundqvist 1983; Langdon and Thorpe 1985), the capacity of early-maturing males to smoltify seems to depend on the individual's gonadal state. As assessed by seawater challenge tests (Lundqvist et al. 1986), mature males with nonregressed gonads have a low ability to withstand high salinities compared with immature smolts. There is a close association between seawater tolerance and seaward migration (Lundqvist and Eriksson 1985). Thus, it is reasonable to suggest that previously mature males, due to internal factors, were not fully prepared for seaward migration at time of release. The relatively higher mortality among previously mature males compared with immature male and female fish would then follow due to high predation in the river. Most males that successfully migrated seawards originated from the larger size-groups of the population. Smaller males would become sexually mature again and not respond to environmental shifts while larger males would mature sexually only if retained in fresh water but not if reaching brackish water. A change in salinity in the water at the time of the smolt run has earlier been shown to affect the annual cycles of swimming behaviour among juvenile Baltic salmon (Eriksson 1984) and may thus be a possible cue for a decision between sexual maturation or growth. All males retained in fresh water beyond the normal time of seaward migration rematured sexually (Eriksson et al. 1979; Lundqvist and Fridberg 1982).

A flexible genetic system interacting with the environment would thus lead to different ages for maturity among individual male parr of different size. Leonardsson and Lundberg (in press) speculated that an evolutionary adjustment of genetic material, sustained as a mixed evolutionarily stable strategy, would allow individuals to respond with different tactics in a more stochastic manner depending on the external milieu.

Males with different life history strategies will obviously coexist in the river and give rise to a complex network of breeding phenotypes. Saunders and Schom (1985), in their study of life history features of Atlantic salmon, provided an illustration of the variability of reproductive tactics that can be seen at spawning. Jones and King (1952) described the sneaking spawning behaviour of male Atlantic salmon parr expressed when they compete with sea-run male adults for females at the spawning site. Hutchings and Myers (1985) and Myers and Hutchings (in press) demonstrated matings between male parr and sea-run females. Gross (1984) suggested disruptive selection as a primary cause for the coexistence of alternative mating tactics among different size-groups of male spawners. The significant number of males that rematured sexually in our study population in brackish water provided evidence for discrete size-groups of male phenotypes. Small male parr would only be successful in adopting a sneaking tactic if they were small enough to avoid direct conflicts with sea-run males. In our study, the demographic consequences of such behaviour is obvious since we found only small mature parr in early fall at the spawning site in the river.

Irrespective of environmental differences, most small mature males would remature sexually and transfer energy to gonadal tissue for reproduction. Since the risk of predation during migration at small sizes is extremely high, it would be a better strategy to stay in the river and try to reproduce. Similar findings were noted by Jonsson and Hindar (1982) in field observations aimed at evaluating the importance of size at sexual maturation in a population of Arctic char *Salvelinus alpinus*. Males of relatively small sizes were more or less forced to mature as early as possible. Sexual maturation would thus ensure a proper readaptation to the riverine environment as suggested by Lundqvist and Eriksson (1985).

Thorpe (1986) suggested that a fish's growth performance in early spring would determine whether or not it matured that year. In contrast, our results indicate a flexibility in the decision process between sexual maturation and growth that seems more closely dependent on the environment at time of the smolt run. Our different interpretation of the time for a final decision could be explained by the differences in water temperature regimes. In northern Swedish salmon rivers, the water temperature remains at 0.01–0.1°C during winter and it does not rise before the end of April. The low ambient river temperature in spring at our latitude will obviously depress the metabolic activity of the fish, resulting in poor growth and slow gonadal resorption during the spring period.

The present study also demonstrates an inverse relationship between growth rate and sexual maturation among fish transferred to brackish water. Previously mature males with a large body size at the sea site had a high growth rate and a significantly lower incidence of sexual rematuration, whereas small fish had a high incidence of sexually mature individuals. Thus, it would seem that a high growth rate blocked the gonadal cycle in these males. In addition, Eriksson and Lundqvist (1982) noted that mature male parr with a high gonadosomatic index (ratio of gonad weight to body weight) had a higher growth rate than immature fish of the same age and size when placed under constant photoperiod (12 h light:12 h darkness) and temperature (10°C). The compensatory growth shown by our large males would then be accompanied by resorption of gonads. In contrast, it is generally accepted that sexual maturity will be attained earlier by the faster-growing individuals in a parr population (Saunders et al. 1982; Thorpe 1986). Further, we have observed that large, previously immature male smolts with a comparatively high growth rate are likely to return as sexually mature, one-sea-winter-old spawners (grilse) (T. Eriksson, unpublished; H. Lundqvist, W. C. Clarke, and H. Johansson, unpublished). Our findings on the relation between size, growth, and sexual maturation of previously mature males and their tendency to become sea-run postsmolts seem thus to indicate a different physiological mechanism affecting this relationship during the different parts of the salmon's life cycle.

In conclusion, our data illustrate the variability in salmonid life history patterns. In northern Swedish salmon stocks, this flexibility seems to be influenced by the size of the fish. A proportion of the small fish follow a life history pattern aimed for residency in the river and have no possibility of responding to the environment. This is explained by the observation that these small fish have a chance to reproduce as "sneakers" if they stay in the river and that they face a very high risk of mortality if they migrate. The proportion of males that migrate increases with size. On reaching the sea, the fish allocate their energetic resources to growth. On the other hand, if retained in fresh water, the males remature, indicating a flexibility in the choice depending on environmental stimuli. In contrast, immature female Baltic salmon are obligated to a life history pattern that includes migration to achieve fast growth to large size. Our findings on differing survival values between immature and previously mature males released in fresh water could then be a result of different life history traits shown by Baltic salmon living in a seasonally fluctuating environment.

Acknowledgments

This work was sponsored by funds from the County Council of Västernorrland, the Swedish Council for Forestry and Agricultural Research, and the Swedish Natural Science Research Council. The Salmon Research Institute covered tagging costs for the delayed-release experiments. G. W. Friars, B. D. Glebe, J. E. Thorpe, and R. L. Saunders made valuable comments on an earlier draft of this manuscript. We thank The American Fisheries Society (Northeastern Division) for the invitation to present this paper at the symposium on "Common Strategies of Anadromous and Catadromous Fishes," Boston, Massachusetts, USA, March 9–13, 1986.

References

Carlin, B. 1955. Tagging of salmon smolts in the river Lagan. Institute of Freshwater Research Drottningholm Report 36:57–74.

Carlin, B. 1959. Results of salmon smolts tagging in the Baltic area. Rapports et Procés-Verbaux des Rèunions, Counseil International pour l'Exploration de la Mer 147:89–96.

Dixon, W. J., editor. 1981. BMDP statistical software 1981. University of California Press, Berkeley, California, USA.

Eriksson, L.-O, and T. Eriksson. 1985. Non river based sea-ranching experiments and net-pen rearing of Baltic salmon (*Salmo salar* L.) in the Bothnian Sea.

Preliminary report of the salmonid workshop on biological and economical organization of smolt production. Government of Japan, Ministry of Agriculture, Forestry and Fisheries, Tokyo, Japan.

Eriksson, L.-O., and H. Lundqvist. 1982. Circannual rhythms and photoperiod regulation of growth and smolting in Baltic salmon (*Salmo salar* L.) parr. Aquaculture 28:113–121.

Eriksson, L.-O., H. Lundqvist, and H. Johansson. 1979. On the normality of size distribution and the precocious maturation in a Baltic salmon, *Salmo salar* L., parr population. Aquilo Ser Zoologica 19:81–86.

Eriksson, T. 1984. Adjustments in annual cycles of swimming behaviour in juvenile Baltic salmon in fresh and brackish water. Transactions of the American Fisheries Society 113:467–471.

Evropeytseva, N. V. 1960. Correlation between the processes of early gonad ripening and transformation to the seaward migrating stage among male Baltic salmon (*Salmo salar* L.) held in ponds. Zoologicheskii Zhurnal 39:777–779. Translated from Russian: Fisheries Research Board of Canada, Translations Series 430, 1963, Ottawa, Canada.

Gross, M. 1984. Sunfish, salmon and the evolution of alternative reproductive strategies and tactics in fishes. Pages 55–75 *in* G. W. Potts and R. J. Wootton, editors. Fish reproduction: strategies and tactics. Academic Press, London, England.

Hoar, W. S. 1976. Smolt transformation: evolution, behaviour and physiology. Journal of the Fisheries Research Board of Canada 33:1234–1252.

Hutchings, J. A., and R. A. Myers. 1985. Mating between anadromous and nonanadromous Atlantic salmon, *Salmo salar*. Canadian Journal of Zoology 63:2219–2221.

Isaksson, A., and P. K. Bergman. 1978. An evaluation of two tagging methods and survival rates of different age and treatment groups of hatchery-reared Atlantic salmon smolts. Journal of Agricultural Research in Iceland 10:74–99.

Jones, J. W. 1959. The salmon, Collins, London, England.

Jones, J. W., and G. M. King. 1952. The spawning of male salmon parr (*Salmo salar* Linn., Juv.). Proceedings of the Zoological Society of London 122:615–619.

Jonsson, B., and K. Hindar. 1982. Reproductive strategy of dwarf and normal Arctic char (*Salvelinus alpinus*) from Vagnsvatnet Lake, western Norway. Canadian Journal of Fisheries and Aquatic Sciences 39:1404–1413.

Langdon, J. S., and J. E. Thorpe. 1985. The ontogeny of smoltification: developmental patterns of gill Na/K-ATPase, SDH, and chloride cells in juvenile Atlantic salmon, *Salmo salar*. Aquaculture 45:43–95.

Leonardsson, K., and P. Lundberg. In press. The choice of reproductive tactic as a mixed evolutionary stable strategy: the case of male Baltic salmon. Institute of Freshwater Research Drottningholm Report.

Lundqvist, H. 1983. Precocious sexual maturation and smolting in Baltic salmon (*Salmo salar* L.): photoperiodic synchronization and adaptive significance of annual biological cycles. Doctoral dissertation. University of Umeå, Umeå, Sweden.

Lundqvist, H., W. C. Clarke, L.-O. Eriksson, P. Funnegård, and B. Engström. 1986. Seawater adaptability in three different river stocks of Baltic salmon (*Salmo salar*) during smolting. Aquaculture 52:219–229.

Lundqvist, H., and L.-O. Eriksson. 1985. Annual rhythms of swimming behaviour and seawater adaptability in young Baltic salmon (*Salmo salar* L.) associated with smolting. Environmental Biology of Fishes 14:259–267.

Lundqvist, H., and G. Fridberg. 1982. Sexual maturation versus immaturity: different tactics with adaptive values in Baltic salmon (*Salmo salar* L.) male smolts. Canadian Journal of Zoology 60:1822–1827.

MacCrimmon, H. R., and R. R. Claytor. 1985. Meristic and morphometric identity of Baltic stocks of Atlantic salmon (*Salmo salar*). Canadian Journal of Zoology 63:2032–2037.

Myers, R. A. 1984. Demographic consequences of precocious maturation of Atlantic salmon (*Salmo salar*). Canadian Journal of Fisheries and Aquatic Sciences 41:1349–1353.

Myers, R. A., and J. A. Hutchings. In press. Mating of anadromous Atlantic salmon, *Salmo salar,* with mature male parr. Journal of Fish Biology.

Österdahl, L. 1969. The smolt run of a small Swedish river. Pages 205–215 *in* T. G. Northcote, editor. Salmon and trout in streams. H. R. MacMillan Lectures in Fisheries, University of British Columbia, Vancouver, Canada.

Saunders, R. L., E. B. Henderson, and B. D. Glebe. 1982. Precocious sexual maturation and smoltification in male Atlantic salmon (*Salmo salar*). Aquaculture 28:211–229.

Saunders, R. L., and C. B. Schom. 1985. Importance of the variation in life-history parameters of Atlantic salmon (*Salmo salar*). Canadian Journal of Fisheries and Aquatic Sciences 42:615–618.

Thorpe, J. E. 1986. Age at first maturity in Atlantic salmon, *Salmo salar* L.: freshwater period influences and conflicts with smolting. Canadian Special Publication of Fisheries and Aquatic Sciences 89:7–14.

Thorpe, J. E., and R. I. G. Morgan. 1980. Growth-rate and smolting-rate of progeny of male Atlantic salmon parr, *Salmo salar* L. Journal of Fish Biology 17:451–460.

Wedemeyer, G. A., R. L. Saunders, and W. C. Clarke. 1980. Environmental factors affecting smoltification and early marine survival of anadromous salmonids. U.S. National Marine Fisheries Service Marine Fisheries Review 42(6):1–14.

American Fisheries Society Symposium 1:244–252, 1987

Smolting versus Residency: Developmental Conflict in Salmonids

J. E. THORPE

Freshwater Fisheries Laboratory, Pitlochry PH16 5LB, Scotland, United Kingdom

Abstract.—Migration allows animals to find greater food resources and improve long-term reproductive success. Within salmonid species, however, both anadromy and residency are found almost universally as alternative life history patterns, which implies flexibility in methods of ensuring successful reproduction. When individual fish inhabit both the marine and the freshwater environments at some stage of development, contrasting adaptations are needed to permit success in each environment. Experimentally, the developmental conversions of smolting and maturation have been shown to be mutually incompatible, requiring abandonment or retention of freshwater adaptations, respectively. Maturation rates and growth rates have been found to be heritable and positively correlated. Conditions which favour very rapid development in fresh water lead to early maturity, which may occur before smolting, and so result in completion of the life cycle entirely in fresh water. Examples are given from sockeye salmon *Oncorhynchus nerka* and Atlantic salmon *Salmo salar* populations which have responded this way following severe density reductions under heavy exploitation. Such a mechanism may have permitted the evolution of entirely freshwater populations of otherwise anadromous salmonids, and ultimately the radiation of specialized species restricted to fresh water.

Salmonid fishes generally spawn in cool freshwater streams, burying their relatively few large yolky eggs (30–20,000 of 4–8 mm diameter) in gravel nests, in which the alevins hatch and complete their yolk-dependent development before they emerge into the open-water environment. Thereafter, they spend a variable proportion of their lives in the freshwater nursery environment before migrating to sea, where the greater part of growth takes place. The species are subdivided into discrete stocks, functioning as temporally or spatially separate breeding units (Billingsley 1981).

However, in each major salmonid genus there are species in which emigration to sea occurs incompletely, varying in proportion both within and between stocks; in some species emigration apparently does not occur at all (Thorpe 1982). The Pacific salmon *Oncorhynchus* species can be ranked in series according to their use of the freshwater environment:

pink salmon *O. gorbuscha* occupy it for reproduction and embryonic development only;

chum *O. keta* and chinook salmon *O. tshawytscha* feed as fry in rivers for days, weeks, or months during their migration to sea;

coho salmon *O. kisutch* defend fry feeding stations in rivers over 1–2 years before migrating to sea;

masu salmon *O. masou* behave like coho salmon except that 80–100% of the males do not migrate to sea, but complete their life cycle in fresh water (I follow T. Okazaki, Far Seas Fishery

Research Laboratory, Tokyo, personal communication, 1985, in considering amago salmon *O. rhodurus* as a physiological race of masu salmon on the grounds of biochemical identity);

sockeye salmon *O. nerka* may spend only days, or 1–4 years, in freshwater lakes before migration, or have entirely freshwater stocks of so-called kokanee.

The flexibility of life history patterns seen in masu and sockeye salmon is characteristic of the genera *Salmo* and *Salvelinus,* most of whose species possess both anadromous (i.e, migrant) and landlocked (i.e., nonmigrant) stocks (Ward 1932). However, there are also species that are wholly landlocked: the trouts of southwestern USA and Mexico, *Salmo aguabonita, S. apache, S. chrysogaster,* and *S. gilae* (R. Behnke, Colorado State University, Fort Collins, Colorado, personal communication, 1981); and the lake trout *Salvelinus namaycush* (Martin 1952). The biology of the genus *Hucho* has been documented recently (Holcik et al. 1984) and appears to contain at least one migrant species, *H. perryi,* and one nonmigrant, *H. hucho.* Migration has been defined as a fundamental biological response to adversity (Taylor and Taylor 1977). It allows animals to find greater food resources and improve long-term reproductive success. The present paper represents an attempt to understand the variety of salmonid life history patterns by focusing on reproduction as the key; in particular, it considers the developmental mechanisms which could have led to the evolution of restricted migration (residency or "landlocking") in the group.

Adaptation

Balon (1977) has documented the advantages for fish of burying eggs in the substrate. This general behaviour pattern of salmonids is shared with a number of other groups of fishes, in particular with other salmonoids such as the capelin *Mallotus villosus* (Templeman 1947), some smelts *Hypomesus* spp. (Frank and Leggett 1984), and the atherinoid grunions *Leuresthes* spp. (Walker 1952). Capelin spawning occurs from depths of 60 m, at which the eggs are broadcast on the seabed, through shallower coastal regions, and right up onto the shingle, where the eggs are buried in the beach largely through wave action. Grunion eggs are spawned at the high tide line and nest construction is limited to depressions in the sand caused by the bodily contortions of the fish swimming up the beach.

The salmonids are distinguished from their osmeroid relatives by spawning chiefly in rivers and streams rather than on the open coast or estuarine shores. Some primitive salmonids, such as the lenok *Brachymystax lenok* of Siberia (Smolanov 1961), broadcast their eggs over the streambed. All others excavate a hollow in the substrate, the female lifting the gravel by cavitation and the male fertilizing the eggs as the female deposits them in this hollow. She then excavates more gravel immediately upstream, which the river current carries into the nest, so covering the fertilized eggs (Greeley 1932; Fabricius 1953; Jones 1959; Blackett 1968; McCart 1970; Leggett 1980). The egg broadcasters produce relatively large numbers of small eggs (Smolanov 1961), while the egg buriers produce fewer larger eggs (Rounsefell 1957; Balon 1975, 1984; Bagenal 1978). The evolution of sophisticated protective spawning techniques have been paralleled by the evolution of reduced fecundity (Balon 1975, 1977, 1984). Greater maternal investment is made in each egg, from which the juvenile fish enters the open-water environment as a predator at the relatively large size of 2–3 cm and 100–250 mg.

In earlier papers (Thorpe 1982, 1984) I have argued that the freshwater salmonid habitat is relatively unproductive compared with the coastal marine environment and, by virtue of this low productivity, it does not support large prey or predator populations. Consequently, it is a relatively protected environment for the early developmental stages of these fishes (Kryzhanovskii 1949). However, there may come a point at which these protective advantages would be outweighed by the disadvantages of low food availability for the progeny. At that point, seaward migration would carry the progeny to a more rewarding habitat, in which growth to a larger size might procure competitive advantage for gene contribution to subsequent generations.

Success of this reproductive strategy has depended on the possession of two critical characteristics during the freshwater stage: behavioural adaptations permitting maintenance of station against a constantly flowing environment and physiological adaptations permitting hydromineral balance in a relatively dilute medium. Unless the behavioural mechanisms ensuring site attachment break down or are abandoned, the fish will never leave the river system. Similarly, unless the physiological mechanisms supporting life in fresh water are abandoned, the fish will not survive and grow in the sea. The characteristic emigration of juvenile salmonids from rivers is accompanied by just such a group of changes, together known as smolting (Hoar 1976; Bern and Mahnken 1982; Langdon 1985; Thorpe et al. 1985; D. R. M. Primmett et al., unpublished). Smolting may then be regarded as a collection of negative events, bringing to an end the adaptations which have allowed the fish to live in fresh water and resulting in emigration. However, reproduction takes place in fresh water, and so requires retention or reestablishment of these essential adaptations. Hence smolting and maturation must be physiologically opposed processes. Some experimental evidence supporting this hypothesis is reviewed below.

Smolting versus Maturation

Policansky (1983) concluded that fish mature as soon as they are developmentally able to do so; Stearns and Crandall (1984) suggested that stressed organisms delay maturity and thus gain fecundity or reduce juvenile mortality. Growth is an organism's means of reaching this reproductive state (Calow and Townsend 1981), and individuals that grow most rapidly in a population mature earliest. This positive correlation between growth rate and maturation rate has been shown for almost every salmonid species (Alm 1959; Thorpe 1986). However, in sibling populations of Atlantic salmon *Salmo salar*, relatively large individuals smolting at age 1 year did not mature until at least age 2.5 years, while in the same populations some smaller fish, which did not smolt at age 1 year, matured 6 months later without emigrating to sea

(Thorpe 1982). Smolting appeared to inhibit maturation.

Conversely, those fish which matured at age 1.5 years, failed to undergo changes at smolting at age 2 years as completely and effectively as did their immature siblings, having lower gill Na^+,K^+-ATPase and whole-cell sorbitol dehydrogenase activities than smolting fish (Langdon and Thorpe 1985). Maturation appeared to inhibit smolting. Sutterlin and MacLean (1984) also found that maturing female Atlantic salmon of a landlocked stock could not adapt to seawater in spring, when immature fish could do so. Among wild Atlantic salmon, Myers (1984) found that the proportion of age-1+ male parr that matured at age 2+ was high in the Little Codroy River, Newfoundland, when the proportion of immature age-1+ fish smolting at age 2+ was low.

In amago salmon, Nagahama (1985) found that plasma levels of the sex steroids testosterone and 11-ketotestosterone were high in maturing males before spawning, nondetectable or very low in smolting fish, and increased in desmolting fish. Miwa and Inui (1985) fed sterilized amago methyltestosterone or estradiol-17β. This resulted in reduced gill Na^+,K^+-ATPase activity, reduced number and size of gill chloride cells, and thicker skin and gill epithelium compared with smolting controls, and prevented epidermal silvering and seawater tolerance. Similarly, in the related masu salmon, Ikuta et al. (1985) found that feeding methyltestosterone in February–April prevented silvering, seawater adaptation, and change of caudal shape, whereas all these changes occurred in smolting fish. In the reverse experiment, Aida et al. (1984) castrated maturing masu, which then smolted, whereas the sham-operated controls did not. McCormick and Naiman (1985) found that maturation in male brook trout *Salvelinus fontinalis* had a negative influence on salinity tolerance.

Hence there is experimental evidence that smolting and maturation are mutually inhibitory processes, and at least some of the endocrine regulatory mechanisms have been revealed. But how are they initiated?

Regulation of Development

The developmental programme is genetically defined, but runs under environmental instruction. Smolting and maturation are developmental conversions (Smith-Gill 1983) which, like metamorphosis and maturity in amphibians, require seasonal environmental signals for their initiation.

The rate and direction of photoperiod change has been shown to influence the onset of both smolting and maturation in many salmonids (Lundqvist 1980; Eriksson and Lundqvist 1982; Clarke et al. 1985; Saunders et al. 1985; Thorpe 1986). In particular, Saunders and Henderson (1970) found that Atlantic salmon smolting could be accelerated or delayed by exposure to increasing or decreasing photoperiods, respectively. Scott et al. (1984) reviewed photoperiod effects on maturation in salmonids, concluding that increasing (or long) photoperiods are necessary for the initiation of gonadal recrudescence. Saunders et al. (1982) accelerated hatching and early rearing of Atlantic salmon by heating their water and found that a proportion of rapidly developing males matured as underyearlings, in their first autumn, while slower developers maintained growth and smolted the following spring. They also noted that by moderating growth rate it was possible to reduce the incidence of maturing parr. I have suggested (Thorpe 1986) that salmon are aware of their rate of acquisition of surplus energy through hormone kinetics associated with its storage. I postulated that provided this rate is above a genetically determined level in the early spring, when the fish are sensitive to photoperiodic stimulation of their gonadotrophic hormone systems (Scott and Sumpter 1983; Scott et al. 1984), maturation will be triggered. Similarly, Dutil (1986) has suggested that in Arctic char *Salvelinus alpinus* the decision to mature depends on internal perception of energy reserves in the spring. Pauly (1984) postulated the same general hypothesis for maturation in fish, expressing it in terms of the oxygen consumption required for such energy storage, rather than that storage itself. The contention, then, is that the developmental route taken by the fish—either to smolt or to mature—depends on the trophic opportunities available to them at the seasonally critical times.

Developmental rates (growth, smolting, maturation) in salmon have been shown to be heritable (Donaldson 1970; Ricker 1972; Thorpe 1975; Thorpe and Morgan 1978; Piggins 1979; Naevdal 1983; Thorpe et al. 1983). In particular, the incidence of maturity among male Atlantic salmon in fresh water before smolting has been shown experimentally to increase from 6.8 to 30.1% in three generations when rapidly developing fish were selected as brood stock (Thorpe et al. 1983). Since not all the members of a sibling population mature in the same year, it is suggested that the threshold levels of the biochemical indices which determine the maturation trigger vary throughout the population. Given the existence of such genetic variation in developmental potential and the wide geographic and climatic ranges occupied by salmonid species, it is not surprising to find great flexibility in the timing of maturation both within and between populations of the same species. In particular, there exists, in almost every salmonid species studied, maturation of fish at the freshwater stage before smolting among rapidly developing, miniature forms (Table 1). In many cases, these forms have been described as slow-growing dwarfs. This seems to arise from a confusion of size and rate. Under identical environmental conditions, it has been shown that these miniature fish grow as rapidly as, or more so than, the anadromous forms at first and then mature much sooner (Alm 1959; Murphy 1980; Thorpe et al. 1983; Sutterlin and MacLean 1984). They are thus faster, not slower, developers, especially during the critical sensitive season when maturation can be induced.

Demographic Consequences

Rates of growth are dependent on the rate of acquisition of surplus energy. Conditions which favour very rapid growth, especially at times when the fish are sensitive to triggering of the maturation switch, favour early maturation and particularly maturation before smolting (Figure 1). When food is abundantly available and, simultaneously, photoperiod is increasing and temperature is optimal, growth rate should be rapid. Culturists attempt to create such conditions, and

TABLE 1.—Representative records of salmonid maturation at small size before smolting.

Genus	Species	Authority
Hucho	*perryi*	Gritsenko et al. (1974)
Oncorhynchus	*masou*	Smirnov (1965)
	nerka	Ricker (1938)
	rhodurus	Kato (1973)
	tshawytscha	Robertson (1957)
Salmo	*gairdneri*	Schmidt and House (1979)
	ishchan	Vladimirov (1944)
	salar	Shaw (1836)
	trutta	Barach (1952)
Salmothymus	*obtusirostris*	Svetovidov (1975)
Salvelinus	*alpinus*	Frost (1965)
	fontinalis	Power (1980)
	leucomaenis	Gritsenko (1969)
	malma	Maekawa (1977)
	neiva	Volobuev (1977)

salmonids developing in hatcheries normally grow faster than their counterparts in the wild; here, parr maturation is commonplace. Trophic condi-

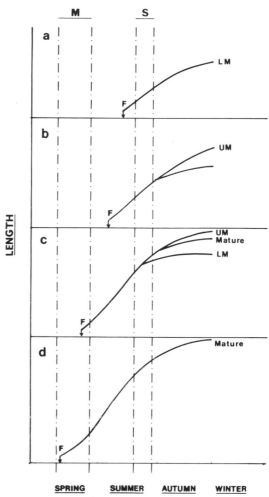

FIGURE 1.—Hypothetical growth curves for Atlantic salmon (from Thorpe 1986). M: sensitive period for maturation trigger. S: sensitive period for growth-arrest trigger. F: first feeding. UM: upper modal growth group. LM: lower modal growth group. (a) Poor developmental conditions: F late; growth rate low during S; whole population arrests growth. (b) Moderate developmental conditions: F early summer; growth rate higher during S; faster part of population maintains growth, remainder arrests. (c) Good developmental conditions: F late spring; growth rates in both S and M high; fastest part of male population maintains growth but then slows as the individuals mature; faster part of female population, and average part of male population, maintain growth; slower part of population (both sexes) arrest growth. (d) Exceptionally good developmental conditions: F early spring; growth rate of whole population high in both sensitive periods; all males mature, and females mature 1 year later.

tions may also be improved for individuals if population densities decrease, thereby reducing competition for food. Populations then respond by increasing individual growth and maturity rates, as in the following examples.

From 1930 to 1968 the population of sea-run sockeye salmon spawners entering Lake Uyeginsk, USSR, fell from about 100,000 to 300 (Nikulin 1970). In parallel with this decrease, the growth rate of juveniles in the lake increased. However, more dramatically, the proportion of the population which matured before smolting rose from 12.8% (all males) in 1930 to 86.7% (5% females) in 1968. Similarly, from 1935 to 1976 the sockeye salmon run into Lake Dalneye, Kamchatka, fell from 62,600 to 1,600 (Krogius 1979). Output of smolting fish decreased by 86% and the proportion of mature parr in the spawning population of males increased 20-fold from 0.35:1 to 7.93:1.

Such changes are noticeable first among males, for which costs of production of gonads are presumably lower than in females. Bagliniere and Maisse (1985) found that frequencies of occurrence of mature Atlantic salmon parr in rivers of Brittany, France, varied from 0 to 100% among males and were variable but low among females. Among masu and amago salmon, 80–100% of males and up to 20% of females do not smolt but mature as parr (Shirahata 1985).

Osterdahl (1969) suggested that large sea-run female Atlantic salmon required the presence of a large male to complete spawning satisfactorily. Myers and Hutchings (in press) have shown that this is not so, as sea-run females in the Exploits River, Newfoundland, spawned successfully when mature parr were the only males present. McCart (1970) recorded similar spawning patterns for sockeye salmon, Armstrong and Morrow (1980) for Dolly Varden *Salvelinus malma,* and Jonsson (1985) for brown trout *Salmo trutta.* Such pairings have been shown to yield fully viable offspring (Shaw 1836; Jones 1959), which tend to develop relatively fast, maintaining high incidence of parr maturity (Thorpe and Morgan 1980; Thorpe et al. 1983). Caswell et al. (1984) suggested that the increase from 31 to 75% in male parr maturation of Atlantic salmon in the Matamek River, Québec, was a consequence of selection in response to increased fishing pressure at sea. However, Myers et al. (1985) have shown that this increase could be explained by increases in growth rate alone.

Whatever the causes of environmental change,

it appears that salmonids are physiologically capable of capitalizing on improved feeding opportunities in fresh water and that this increases the proportion of the population which matures there before emigration. Since developmental rates are heritable, and selection for parr maturity can be rapid, the evolutionary avenue towards the total abandonment of the seawater phase in salmonid life history is clearly open. Wholly freshwater populations of Atlantic salmon are widespread in Newfoundland (Dalley et al. 1983), and in northeastern Europe (Berg 1985). It is likely that many arose originally by gradual physical isolation from the sea, due to isostatic rebound of the earth's crust in those regions following recession of the ice sheet some 8,000–10,000 years ago. Sutterlin and MacLean (1984) have found that the life span of the fish in Newfoundland populations is relatively short compared with anadromous fish from the same localities, which implies relatively high rates of development to maturity in such landlocked populations, even though the fish do not reach large size. By implication then, these survivors of originally anadromous populations have succeeded in the freshwater environment by virtue of their inherently high developmental rate.

Landlocked populations of sockeye salmon may have arisen in similar ways. Coexistence of sea-run sockeye salmon and wholly freshwater kokanee populations has been reported frequently, and McCart (1970) noted that interbreeding of the two forms occurred in the Babine Lake catchment, British Columbia. Ricker (1938) found that the fastest-growing members of the Cultus Lake sockeye salmon population matured early and became "residuals" rather than emigrating to sea.

In Japan, experiments are in progress (Shirahata 1985; T. Kobayashi, Hokkaido Salmon Hatchery, Sapporo, Japan, personal communication, 1985) attempting to induce hime salmon (landlocked sockeye salmon) to smolt and emigrate to sea by slowing down their freshwater development. Likewise, masu salmon growth is being retarded to increase the number of fish which smolt rather than mature and stay in fresh water. Zalewski et al. (1985), using brown trout from a resident nonmigratory population, made experimental plantings in a range of separate habitats in an upland stream in Poland. He found that growth rates were directly correlated with stream temperature and trophic status. However, the fish planted in the least productive habitat did not mature there, but smolted (M. Zalewski, University of Lodz, Poland, personal communication, 1985).

Balon (1980b) has argued that salmonid evolution has progressed by alteration of the proportion of the life span devoted to particular developmental stages (Figure 2). Burial of eggs in a protected gravel nest and provision of a relatively large yolk supply have permitted the skipping of the larval stage altogether. The fish progress directly from the yolk-dependent embryonic stage to the juvenile stage, at which point they are dependent entirely on exogenous foods. Compression of developmental stages is taken a step further when maturation is achieved without the necessity of an extended period of somatic growth. Once such compression has occurred, the way is open for radiation into even more extreme and specialized habitats. Cultivation experiments with rainbow trout *Salmo gairdneri* have shown that the timing of maturation and spawning can be altered by genetic selection to produce "strains" which spawn at almost any time of the year and even spawn twice per year (Whitehead et al. 1980; Breton et al. 1983). This experimental demonstration of broad adaptive capacity is mirrored in the wild. Whereas the majority of Arctic char stocks

spawn in autumn in cold clear streams (Johnson 1980), McCart and Bain (1974) found a population flourishing in hot springs in the Northwest Territories of Canada which spawned in late winter at a temperature of 14–16°C. Similarly, the majority of wild stocks of the rainbow trout complex live in cool clear waters, but R. J. Behnke (Colorado State University, Fort Collins, Colorado, USA; personal communication, 1981) reported redband trout (putatively derived from the *S. gairdneri* complex: Wilmot 1974) living in Chino Creek, northern Nevada, in a series of intermittent pools at a water temperature of 28°C, normally considered lethal for this species. Hokanson (1977) has shown that the temperature preferenda of fishes change ontogenetically. In general, the highest temperatures are favoured at juvenile stages (Figure 2).

Evolution through paedomorphosis (juvenilization) of the form proposed by Balon, with the speeding up of all developmental processes as occurs among the miniature forms of anadromous species, would permit the opportunity first to complete the life cycle in fresh water, and then to colonize more extreme habitats. The work reviewed above provides evidence of physiological and ecological bases for this evolutionary development, which allows primary development of wholly freshwater forms. Balon (1980b) has shown how subsequent radiation of larger, later-maturing forms may arise in *Salvelinus* species from the initial invaders.

References

Aida, K., T. Kato, and M. Awaji. 1984. Effects of castration on the smoltification of precocious male masu salmon *Oncorhynchus masou*. Bulletin of the Japanese Society of Scientific Fisheries 50:565–571.

Alm, G. 1959. Connection between maturity, size and age in fishes. Institute of Freshwater Research Drottningholm Report 40:5–145.

Armstrong, R. H., and J. E. Morrow. 1980. The Dolly Varden charr, *Salvelinus malma*. Pages 99–140 *in* Balon (1980a).

Bagenal, T. B. 1978. Aspects of fish fecundity. Pages 75–101 *in* S. D. Gerking, editor. Ecology and freshwater fish production. John Wiley & Sons, New York, New York, USA.

Bagliniere, J.-L., and G. Maisse. 1985. Precocious maturation and smoltification in wild Atlantic salmon in the Armorican Massif, France. Aquaculture 45: 249–263.

Balon, E. K. 1975. Reproductive guilds of fishes: a proposal and definition. Journal of the Fisheries Research Board of Canada 32:821–864.

Balon, E. K. 1977. Early ontogeny of *Labeotrophus* Ahl, 1927 (Mbuna, Cichlidae, Lake Malawi), with a

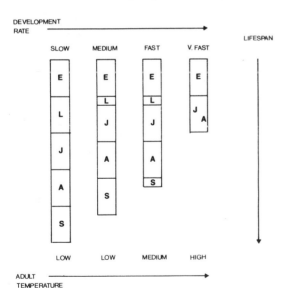

FIGURE 2.—Evolution of life history strategies in salmonids (simplified, after Balon 1980). Developmental periods are E: embryonic; L: larval; J: juvenile; A: adult; S: senescent. With increasing developmental rate, life span is shortened, and first the larval, and then the senescent periods are shortened and disappear.

discussion on advanced protective styles in fish reproduction and development. Environmental Biology of Fishes 2:147–176.

Balon, E. K., editor. 1980a. Charrs: salmonid fishes of the genus *Salvelinus*. Dr. W. Junk, The Hague, The Netherlands.

Balon, E. K. 1980b. Early ontogeny of the lake charr, *Salvelinus (Cristivomer) namaycush*. Pages 485–562 *in* Balon (1980a).

Balon, E. K. 1984. Patterns in the evolution of reproductive styles in fishes. Pages 35–53 *in* G. W. Potts and R. J. Wootton, editors. Fish reproduction. Academic Press, London, England.

Barach, G. P. 1952. [The significance of the brown trout on the resource origin of the Black Sea salmon.] Zoologicheskii Zhurnal 31:906–915. (In Russian.)

Berg, O. K. 1985. The formation of non-anadromous populations of Atlantic salmon, *Salmo salar* L., in Europe. Journal of Fish Biology 27:805–815.

Bern, H. A., and C. V. W. Mahnken, editors. 1982. Salmonid smoltification. Aquaculture 28:1–270.

Billingsley, L. W., editor. 1981. Stock concept international symposium. Canadian Journal of Fisheries and Aquatic Sciences 38:1457–1923.

Blackett, R. F. 1968. Spawning behavior, fecundity and early life-history of anadromous Dolly Varden char in southeast Alaska. Alaska Department of Fisheries and Game, Research Report 6, Juneau, Alaska, USA.

Breton, B., G. Maisse, and E. Lemenn. 1983. Controle photoperiodique de la saison de reproduction en salmoniculture: un experience pilote en Bretagne. Bulletin Francais de Pisciculture 288:35–45.

Calow, P., and C. R. Townsend. 1981. Resource utilisation in growth. Pages 220–244 *in* C. R. Townsend and P. Calow, editors. Physiological ecology. Blackwell Scientific Publications, Oxford, England.

Caswell, H., R. J. Naiman, and R. Morin. 1984. Evaluating the consequences of reproduction in complex salmonid life-cycles. Aquaculture 43:123–134.

Clarke, W. C., H. Lundqvist, and L.-O. Eriksson. 1985. Accelerated photoperiod advances seasonal cycle of seawater adaptation in juvenile Baltic salmon, *Salmo salar* L. Journal of Fish Biology 26:29–35.

Dalley, E. L., C. W. Andrews, and J. M. Green. 1983. Precocious male Atlantic salmon parr *Salmo salar* in insular Newfoundland. Canadian Journal of Fisheries and Aquatic Sciences 40:647–652.

Donaldson, L. R. 1970. Selective breeding of salmonoid fishes. Pages 65–74 *in* W. J. McNeil, editor. Marine aquiculture. Oregon State University Press, Corvallis, Oregon, USA.

Dutil, J.-D. 1986. Energetic constraints and spawning interval in the anadromous Arctic charr *(Salvelinus alpinus)*. Copeia 1986:945–955.

Eriksson, L.-O., and H. Lundqvist. 1982. Circannual rhythms and photoperiod regulation of growth and smolting in Baltic salmon *Salmo salar* L. Aquaculture 28:113–121.

Fabricius, E. 1953. Aquarium observations on the spawning behavior of the char, *Salmo alpinus*. Institute of Freshwater Research Drottningholm Report 31:57–99.

Frank, K. T., and W. C. Leggett. 1984. Selective exploitation of capelin *Mallotus villosus* eggs by winter flounder *Pseudopleuronectes americanus:* capelin egg mortality rates and contribution of egg energy to the annual growth of flounder. Canadian Journal of Fisheries and Aquatic Sciences 41: 1294–1302.

Frost, W. E. 1965. Breeding habits of Windermere char, *Salvelinus willughbii* (Gunther) and their bearing on speciation in these fish. Proceedings of the Royal Society of Edinburgh Section B (Biological Sciences) 63:232–284.

Greeley, J. R. 1932. The spawning habits of the brook, brown and rainbow trout and the problem of egg predators. Transactions of the American Fisheries Society 62:239–248.

Gritsenko, O. F. 1969. Dwarf males of the Kundzha or Siberian char (*Salvelinus leucomaenis* (Pall.)). Journal of Ichthyology 9:913–914.

Gritsenko, O. F., Ye. A. Malkin, and A. A. Churikov. 1974. Sakhalinskiyi taimen *Hucho perryi* (Brevoort) reki Bogatoyi (vostochnoye poberezhiye Sakhalina). Izvestia Tikhookeasnkogo Nauchno-Issledovatel'skogo Instituta Rybnogo Khozyaistva i Okeanografii 93:91–100.

Hoar, W. S. 1976. Smolt transformation: evolution, behaviour and physiology. Journal of the Fisheries Research Board of Canada 33:1234–1252.

Hokanson, K. E. F. 1977. Temperature requirements of some percids and adaptations to the seasonal temperature cycle. Journal of the Fisheries Research Board of Canada 34:1524–1550.

Holcik, J., K. Hensel, J. Nieslanik, and L. Skacel. 1984. Hlavatka: *Hucho hucho* (Linnaeus, 1758). The Huchen. Veda, Bratislava, Czechoslovakia. (In Slovak.)

Ikuta, K., K. Aida, N. Okumoto, and I. Hanyu. 1985. Effects of thyroxine and methyltestosterone on smoltification of masu salmon *Oncorhynchus masou*. Aquaculture 45:289–303.

Johnson, L. 1980. The Arctic charr, *Salvelinus alpinus*. Pages 15–98 *in* Balon (1980a).

Jones, J. W. 1959. The salmon. Collins, London, England.

Jonsson, B. 1985. Life history patterns of freshwater resident and sea-run migrant brown trout in Norway. Transactions of the American Fisheries Society 114:182–194.

Kato, F. 1973. Ecological study of the sea-run form of *Oncorhynchus rhodurus*, found in Ise Bay, Japan. Japanese Journal of Ichthyology 20:225–234.

Krogius, F. V. 1979. O vzaimosvyazi presnovodnogo i morskogo period zhizni krasnoi nerki ozera Dalnego. Biologiya Morya (Vladivostok) 3:24–29.

Kryzhanovskii, S. G. 1949. [Ecomorphological principles of development of carps, loaches and catfishes.] Trudy Instituta Morfologii Zhivotnykh Akademii Nauk SSSR 1:5–332. (In Russian.)

Langdon, J. S. 1985. Smoltification physiology in the culture of salmonids. Pages 79–118 *in* J. F. Muir and R. J. Roberts, editors. Recent advances in aquaculture. Croom Helm, London, England.

Langdon, J. S., and J. E. Thorpe. 1985. The ontogeny of smoltification: developmental patterns of gill Na-K-ATPase, SDH, and chloride cells in juvenile Atlantic salmon *Salmo salar* L. Aquaculture 45: 83–95.

Leggett, J. W. 1980. Reproductive ecology and behaviour of Dolly Varden charr in British Columbia. Pages 721–737 *in* Balon (1980a).

Lundqvist, H. 1980. Influence of photoperiod on growth in Baltic salmon parr *Salmo salar* L. with special reference to the effect of precocious sexual maturation. Canadian Journal of Zoology 58:940–944.

Maekawa, K. 1977. Studies on the variability of the landlocked miyabe charr, *Salvelinus malma miyabei* Oshima: I. Development and early life history. Japanese Journal of Ecology 27:91–102.

Martin, N. V. 1952. A study of the lake trout, *Salvelinus namaycush,* in two Algonquin Park, Ontario, lakes. Transactions of the American Fisheries Society 81:111–137.

McCart, P. 1970. A polymorphic population of *Oncorhynchus nerka* at Babine Lake, B.C. involving anadromous (sockeye) and non-anadromous (kokanee) forms. Doctoral dissertation. University of British Columbia, Vancouver, Canada.

McCart, P., and H. Bain. 1974. An isolated population of arctic char *(Salvelinus alpinus)* inhabiting a warm mineral spring above a waterfall at Cache Creek, Northwest Territories. Journal of the Fisheries Research Board of Canada 31:1408–1414.

McCormick, S. D., and Naiman, R. 1985. Hypoosmoregulation in an anadromous teleost: influence of sex and maturation. Journal of Experimental Zoology 234:193–198.

Miwa, S., and Y. Inui. 1985. Inhibitory effects of 17α-methyltestosterone and oestradiol-17β on smoltification of sterilised amago salmon *Oncorhynchus rhodurus.* Aquaculture 45:383.

Murphy, T. 1980. Studies on precocious maturity in artificially reared 1+ Atlantic salmon parr *Salmo salar* L. Doctoral dissertation. University of Stirling, Stirling, Scotland.

Myers, R. A. 1984. Demographic consequences of precocious maturation of Atlantic salmon *(Salmo salar).* Canadian Journal of Fisheries and Aquatic Sciences 41:1349–1353.

Myers, R. A., and J. A. Hutchings. In press. Mating of anadromous Atlantic salmon, *Salmo salar* L., with mature male parr. Journal of Fish Biology.

Myers, R. A., J. A. Hutchings, and R. J. Gibson. 1985. Variation in precocious maturation within and among populations of Atlantic salmon. International Council for the Exploration of the Sea, C.M. 1985/M:8, Copenhagen, Denmark.

Naevdal, G. 1983. Genetic factors in connection with age at maturation. Aquaculture 33:97–106.

Nagahama, Y. 1985. Involvement of endocrine systems in smoltification in the amago salmon, *Oncorhynchus rhodurus.* Aquaculture 45:383–384.

Nikulin, O. A. 1970. O svyazi mezhdu snizheniem absolyutnoi chislennosti krasnoi *Oncorhynchus nerka*

(Walb.) i uvelicheniem otnositelnoi chislennosti karlikov sredi nagulivayushcheisya molodi v ozere Uyeginskom (Okhotskii raion). Izvestiya Tikhookeanskogo Nauchno-Issledovatel'skogo Instituta Rybnogo Khozyaistva i Okeanografii 71:205–217.

Osterdahl, L. 1969. The smolt run of a small Swedish river. Pages 205–215 *in* T. G. Northcote, editor. Salmon and trout in streams. H. R. MacMillan Lectures in Fisheries, University of British Columbia, Vancouver, Canada.

Pauly, D. 1984. A mechanism for the juvenile-to-adult transition in fishes. Journal du Conseil, Conseil International pour l'Exploration de la Mer 41: 280–284.

Piggins, D. J. 1979. Annual report: 24. Salmon Research Trust of Ireland, Dublin, Ireland.

Policansky, D. 1983. Size, age and demography of metamorphosis and sexual maturation in fishes. American Zoologist 23:57–63.

Power, G. 1980. The brook charr, *Salvelinus fontinalis.* Pages 141–203 *in* Balon (1980a).

Ricker, W. E. 1938. "Residual" and kokanee salmon in Cultus Lake. Journal of the Fisheries Research Board of Canada 4:192–218.

Ricker, W. E. 1972. Hereditary and environmental factors affecting certain salmonid populations. Pages 27–160 *in* R. C. Simon and P. A. Larkin, editors. The stock concept in Pacific salmon. H. R. MacMillan Lectures in Fisheries, University of British Columbia, Vancouver, Canada.

Robertson, O. H. 1957. Survival of precociously mature king salmon male parr *O. tshawytscha* juv. after spawning. California Fish and Game 43:121–127.

Rounsefell, G. W. 1957. Fecundity of North American salmonidae. U.S. Fish and Wildlife Service Fishery Bulletin 57(122):451–468.

Saunders, R. L., and E. B. Henderson. 1970. Influence of photoperiod on smolt development and growth in Atlantic salmon *Salmo salar.* Journal of the Fisheries Research Board of Canada 27:1295–1311.

Saunders, R. L., E. B. Henderson, and B. D. Glebe. 1982. Precocious sexual maturation and smoltification in male Atlantic salmon *Salmo salar.* Aquaculture 28:211–229.

Saunders, R. L., E. B. Henderson, and P. R. Harmon. 1985. Effects of photoperiod on juvenile growth and smolting of Atlantic salmon and subsequent survival and growth in sea cages. Aquaculture 45:55–66.

Schmidt, S. P., and E. W. House. 1979. Precocious sexual development in hatchery-reared and laboratory maintained male steelhead trout *Salmo gairdneri.* Journal of the Fisheries Research Board of Canada 36:90–93.

Scott, A. P., S. M. Baynes, O. Skarphedinsson, and V. J. Bye. 1984. Control of spawning time in rainbow trout, *Salmo gairdneri,* using constant long daylengths. Aquaculture 43:225–233.

Scott, A. P., and J. P. Sumpter. 1983. The control of trout reproduction: basic and applied research on hormones. Pages 200–220 *in* J. C. Rankin, T. J. Pitcher, and R. T. Duggan, editors. Control processes in fish physiology. Croom Helm, London, England.

Shaw, J. 1836. An account of some experiments and observations on the parr, and on the ova of the salmon, proving the parr to be the young of the salmon. Edinburgh New Philosophy Journal 21:99–110.

Shirahata, S. 1985. Present status of salmonid smolt production in Japan. Pages 47–54 in S. Shirahata, editor. Preliminary report of the salmonid workshop on biological and economic optimization of smolt production. Ministry of Agriculture, Forestry, and Fisheries, Tokyo, Japan.

Smirnov, A. I. 1965. Nerestovyi etap i ego spetsifika v razvitii ryb. Pages 147–154 in Teoreticheskiye osnovy rybovodstva. Izvestia Nauk, Moscow, USSR.

Smith-Gill, S. J. 1983. Developmental plasticity: developmental conversion versus phenotypic modulation. American Zoologist 23:47–55.

Smolanov, I. I. 1961. Razvitiye lenka Brachymystax lenok (Pallas). Voprosy Ikhtiologii 1:136–148.

Stearns, S. C., and R. E. Crandall. 1984. Plasticity for age and size at sexual maturity: a life-history response to unavoidable stress. Pages 13–33 in G. W. Potts and R. J. Wootton, editors. Fish reproduction. Academic Press, London, England.

Sutterlin, A. M., and D. MacLean. 1984. Age at first maturity and the early expression of oocyte recruitment processes in two forms of Atlantic salmon (Salmo salar) and their hybrids. Canadian Journal of Fisheries and Aquatic Sciences 41:1139–1149.

Svetovidov, A. N. 1975. Sravnitelno-osteologicheskoye izucheniye balkanskogo endemichnogo roda Salmothymus v svyazi s klassifikatsiye. Zoologicheskii Zhurnal 54:1174–1190.

Taylor, L. R., and R. A. J. Taylor. 1977. Aggregation, migration and population mechanics. Nature (London) 265:415–421.

Templeman, W. 1947. Life history of the capelin Mallotus villosus O. F. Muller in Newfoundland waters. Bulletin of the Newfoundland Government Laboratory, Newfoundland Research Bulletin 17. St. Johns, Canada.

Thorpe, J. E. 1975. Early maturity in male Atlantic salmon. Scottish Fisheries Bulletin 42:15–17.

Thorpe, J. E. 1982. Migration in salmonids, with special reference to juvenile movements in freshwater. Pages 86–97 in E. L. Brannon and E. O. Salo, editors. Proceedings of the salmon and trout migratory behaviour symposium. University of Washington, School of Fisheries, Seattle, Washington, USA.

Thorpe, J. E. 1984. Downstream movements of juvenile salmonids: a forward speculative view. Pages 387–396 in J. D. McCleave, G. P. Arnold, J. J. Dodson, and W. H. Neill, editors. Mechanisms of migration in fishes. Plenum, New York, New York, USA.

Thorpe, J. E. 1986. Age at first maturity in Atlantic salmon, Salmo salar L.: freshwater period influence and conflicts with smolting. Canadian Special Publication of Fisheries and Aquatic Sciences 89:7–14.

Thorpe, J. E., H. A. Bern, R. L. Saunders, and A. Soivio, editors. 1985. Salmonid smoltification II. Aquaculture 45:1–404.

Thorpe, J. E., and R. I. G. Morgan. 1978. Parental influence on growth rate, smolting rate and survival in hatchery reared juvenile Atlantic salmon, Salmo salar. Journal of Fish Biology 13:549–556.

Thorpe, J. E., and R. I. G. Morgan. 1980. Growth-rate and smolting-rate of progeny of male Atlantic salmon parr, Salmo salar L. Journal of Fish Biology 17:451–460.

Thorpe, J. E., R. I. G. Morgan, C. Talbot, and M. S. Miles. 1983. Inheritance of developmental rates in Atlantic salmon. Aquaculture 33:123–132.

Vladimirov, V. I. 1944. [The river form of the Sevan trout Salmo ishchan gegarkuni Kessler, morpha alabalach nova.] Izvestiya Akademii Nauk Armyanskoi SSR Biologicheskie Nauki 3:61–72. (In Russian.)

Volobuev, V. V. 1977. [On the dwarf form of Salvelinus neiva (Salmoniformes, Salmonidae) from the Korral Lake (Okhota River basin).] Zoologicheskii Zhurnal 56:405–411. (In Russian.)

Walker, B. W. 1952. A guide to the grunion. California Fish and Game 38:409–420.

Ward, H. B. 1932. The origin of the landlocked habit in salmon. Proceedings of the National Academy of Sciences of the United States of America 18:569–580.

Whitehead, C., N. Bromage, R. Harbin, and A. Matty. 1980. Oestradiol 17-β calcium and vitellogenin interrelationships during accelerated and biannual spawnings in the rainbow trout. General and Comparative Endocrinology 40:329–330.

Wilmot, R. L. 1974. A genetic study of the red-band trout Salmo sp. Doctoral dissertation. Oregon State University, Corvallis, Oregon, USA.

Zalewski, M., P. Frankiewicz, and B. Brewinska. 1985. The factors limiting growth and survival of brown trout, Salmo trutta m. fario L., introduced to different types of streams. Journal of Fish Biology 27 (supplement A):59–73.

American Fisheries Society Symposium 1:253, 1987

OCEAN MIGRATIONS

Preamble

MICHAEL J. DADSWELL

Department of Fisheries and Oceans, Biological Station
St. Andrews, New Brunswick E0G 2X0, Canada

Where fishes went during their ocean migrations was a mystery that intrigued humans for centuries. Anadromous and catadromous fishes were particularly mysterious since they would disappear and then reappear suddenly in vast numbers. It was only 60 years ago that the ocean spawning site of European and American eels was discovered and 30 years ago that one of the major ocean feeding areas of Atlantic salmon was found. Through a continuing combination of chance and scientific sleuthing, the ocean pathways and migration destinations of diadromous fishes are being described, but it is a slow process. Much remains unknown. In this section, diadromous species are discussed at all levels of the knowledge spectrum. For some it is the near-to-final resolution; for others, the beginning.

We find that ocean migrations of diadromous fishes are highly variable both in duration and distance. Duration of ocean residence varies from short periods of weeks or months (Arctic char, galaxids) to periods of many years (barramundi, American shad). Species which spend short periods at sea may remain close to natal habitats; those spending long periods often migrate many thousands of kilometers. What is obvious from our review of life history patterns is that no rule governs oceanic migration strategy. Rather, there is a continuum of life history characteristics that is unconfined by taxonomic type. Among populations of certain species, some migrate long distances while others remain close to the reproductive site (striped bass). Among generic and family groups, some species migrate only short distances at sea while others migrate thousands of kilometers (Pacific salmon).

Why species evolve a particular migration type is unknown but factors controlling the choice now appear to be better defined. As descriptive information accumulates, researchers will be better able to synthesize data and formulate hypotheses. I hope the information contained herein will enhance this process.

American Fisheries Society Symposium 1:254–261, 1987

Hydromechanics of Fish Migration in Variable Environments

DANIEL WEIHS

Department of Aeronautical Engineering, Technion–Israel Institute of Technology
Haifa 32000, Israel

Abstract.—Migrations of fish species are often very long (in both time and space) and costly in terms of energy. Thus, efficient use of available energy is of great importance and various adaptations of morphology and behavior have resulted. These are especially significant for diadromous species, which encounter large variations in buoyancy, salinity, temperature, and flow conditions during their life cycles, which include large-scale migrations. A mathematical approach to fish migratory adaptations is utilized to analyze observed behavioral patterns and to predict effects of changing environmental pressures. The study is based on the hydrodynamical and mechanical principles of fish locomotion, feeding, and predator–prey interactions. Existing work is reviewed with the goal of identifying areas of future observational and theoretical research applicable to the understanding of the behavioral strategies of these species, many of which are commercially important.

Anadromous and catadromous fish have, by definition, the common characteristic of migration. In many cases, migration is the most catabolically significant behavior during their life history. Therefore, any attempt to understand the factors involved in behavioral strategies chosen by diadromous species must include an analysis of the energy required for locomotion.

Fish migration is characterized by directed and sustained motion over extremely large distances relative to fish length. If the total length of the fish is taken as the spatial scale factor, migrations can be defined as behavioral patterns that move a fish over distances of thousands to millions of fish lengths within a limited time period. The migratory behavior as a whole includes the sensory timing cues (zeitgebers) for the individual or school, the physical movements, and the inputs indicating arrival at the target. Migrations can be further separated into short- and long-term patterns based on the time spent performing them. Short-term migration has a diurnal basis and can include both horizontal and vertical motions; the long-term category deals with seasonal or annual migrations.

Horizontal and upwelling currents in the ocean permit at least some of the motions described above to be performed "for free" by the fish being swept along. This is especially characteristic of planktonic creatures (and is actually one definition of plankton) but can also apply to much larger fish. Indeed, the high cost of locomotion in water causes all aquatic life to be very sensitive to local currents and velocity changes and to make use of them (Arnold 1974). Spectacular examples of this

occur when cetaceans ride a ship's bow wave; more relevant to diadromy, salmon make use of fine variations in water flow caused by bottom topography during their upstream spawning migrations.

Hydrodynamics of Motion

Water is a dense, somewhat viscous, liquid so that moving through it requires the expenditure of significant amounts of energy. The energetic cost of directed motion can be 10 times the basal metabolic rate for sustained motion (Brett 1983) and up to three orders of magnitude larger for sprints by efficient swimmers (Puckett and Dill 1984) (data are for Pacific salmon *Oncorhynchus* spp.). Thus, understanding the forces involved in locomotion and obtaining estimates of their magnitude are of paramount importance in studying the energy balances associated with migration strategies.

To simplify the analysis presented here, consider only motion in a vertical plane *x, y* at constant forward speed[1] at an angle δ to the horizontal (Figure 1; Table 1). The equations of motion can then be written as

$$\Sigma_i(F)_{xi} = 0, \tag{1a}$$

$$\Sigma_i(F)_{yi} = 0, \text{ and} \tag{1b}$$

$$\Sigma_i(C)_{zi} = 0; \tag{1c}$$

F is a force, *C* is a couple (first moment of the

---

[1]Strictly speaking, all active fish-swimming is periodic because of the oscillatory manner in which fish propel themselves. Thus we actually have to discuss time-averaged speed (Weihs and Webb 1983).

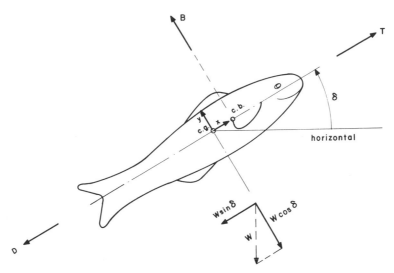

FIGURE 1.—The forces and couples acting on a fish in deep water. Symbols: c.g. is center of gravity and c.b. is center of buoyancy; others are defined in Table 1.

force), the subscripts x and y stand for coordinates opposite to the direction of motion and normal to it, respectively, and i denotes the various contributions to each of the equations. Equations (1a) to (1c) state that the sums of the forces and couples have to be zero for nonaccelerated motion. Three additional equations of this kind exist, summing the forces in the z direction and couples around the x and y axes and equating them to zero also; for motion in a vertical plane, these can be shown to be independent of equations (1) to (3) (no cross-interactions) and thus need not be considered here. For a neutrally buoyant fish, the force balance in the direction of motion is (Figure 1)

$$T - D - W \sin\delta = 0 \qquad (2a)$$

and in the y direction it is

$$N - W \cos\delta = 0. \qquad (2b)$$

When $\delta = 0$ (horizontal motion), these two equations reduce to

$$T = D \text{ and } N = W; \qquad (3)$$

i.e., the thrust T exactly counterbalances the drag D, and the normal force N is equal to the submerged weight W. When thrust and drag are not equal or, alternatively, when the fish is not neutrally buoyant, linear acceleration or deceleration occurs.

Hydrodynamic analysis is required to describe the forces in equations (2a) and (2b) in terms of measurable geometrical and kinematical parameters. Each of the forces T, D, and N is a function of the relative speed, the fish's shape and propulsive motions, and the water density. For fish of size over 5 cm and volume V_0 moving at one body length per second or more, each of these forces is roughly proportional to the velocity U squared and can be written as

$$F_j = \tfrac{1}{2} \rho V_o^{2/3} U^2 C_{F_j}; \qquad (4)$$

$F_j = T$, D, and N, respectively. (For smaller fish moving more slowly, the velocity exponent gradually goes down to unity, as has been obtained for larvae of 2–4 mm total length.) Estimation of the coefficients C_D, C_T, and C_N for various shapes and motions is done by the techniques of hydrodynamics. This has been extensively discussed in the literature (Webb and Weihs 1983) and will not be further elaborated here. However, the pitching motions defined by equation (1c) need also to be considered. This effect, which has not yet been adequately covered in the literature, is of special importance for fish that move between freshwater and marine environments due to the density differences encountered.

It has been commonly assumed that fish of neutral buoyancy do not require any hydrodynamic lift in order to move horizontally. This, however, is an oversimplification; although no *net* force is required in the direction perpendicular to the motion of the center of gravity (which will be assumed to be horizontal for simplicity, without loss to the generality of the argument), it does not mean that no forces are needed in that direction.

TABLE 1.—Symbols used in the analysis of fish hydromechanics.

B	buoyancy force
C	couple
C_{F_j}	nondimensional coefficients defined by equation (4)
D	drag force
E	total energy required for migration
$\dot{E}$	rate of energy expenditure
F	force
h	distance fish is swept normal to its initial direction of motion
H	width of current
K	defined in equation (6)
L	distance
l	fish total length
M	standard metabolic rate
N	upward force
Q	absolute velocity of fish
S_1	defined in equation (13)
T	thrust
t	time
U	relative speed between fish and the water surrounding it
V	current speed
V_o	volume of fish
W	weight (submerged)
x	horizontal coordinate opposite to direction of motion of fish
y	horizontal coordinate normal to direction of motion
z	vertical coordinate
β	angle between current and direction of swimming
γ	angle between direction of fish motion in current and initial direction of motion
δ	angle between horizon and direction of motion (positive when moving upwards)
ρ	density of water
τ	time for migration in still waters

Superscripts and Subscripts

c	see equation (9)
j	index
s	submerged
o	see equation (7)
1–5	migration path legs defined in Figure 2

In order for the fish to be able to control its orientation, the sum of all moments (couples) also has to be zero (equation 1c). Specifically, in this case, the total pitching moment around the center of gravity has to be zero, otherwise rotation around the pitching axis (Figure 1) will ensue.

One needs now to ask what will cause pitching moments in the first place for neutrally buoyant fish. These occur in part because the center of buoyancy usually does not coincide with the center of mass (Aleyev 1977). This problem can be especially important for diadromous species whose changes in buoyancy are potentially great due to the changes in environment.

In many species, buoyancy is controlled hydrostatically by expansion and collapse of a swim bladder. More generally, all fish are of nonuniform density throughout their structure. Thus, the centers of buoyancy and mass will not coincide in the general case (Aleyev 1977), and one can expect to find pitching moments produced. This question was reexamined recently at my request separately by P. W. Webb and J. J. Videler (personal communications). They found that in practically all species tested, significant pitching couples are produced by the misalignment of buoyancy and weight, as evidenced by measurement of the angles from the horizontal at which anesthetized and freshly dead fish are orientated in midwater.

The pitching couple produced by the distance between the centers of mass and buoyancy must be compensated for by hydrodynamic means. Stationary fish can so compensate by positioning the paired fins or the body at some angle of incidence to currents or by producing local flow and forces by fin motions. Moving fish can produce the couples required either by placing the paired fins at some angle of attack or by making asymmetric caudal fin motions that produce a net vertical force in addition to the thrust (thrust vectoring). For fish that propel themselves by pectoral fin motions, rotation of the fin-beat axis to produce a mean angle of incidence can achieve an analogous situation.

All of the techniques for producing couples described result in increasing the fish's energy expenditure by increasing drag (induced by lift) when speed is reduced for a given thrust or by increasing the total thrust required so that its component in the direction of motion provides the propulsive force, maintaining a given speed. Thus, if the balance of couples is ignored, the thrust required for directed forward motion will be underestimated. This problem is better known for non-neutrally buoyant fish, which usually compensate for the difference between submerged weight and buoyancy by hydrodynamic means—i.e., by producing lift with the pectoral fins (Magnuson 1978), causing additional drag (the so-called induced drag). This component of drag is proportional to the lift squared and is inversely proportional to the fin aspect ratio, so that negatively buoyant pelagic fish tend to have long and narrow pectoral fins. Magnuson (1978) has shown that induced drag produced in this manner is 30% of the total drag of a skipjack tuna *Euthynnus pelamis* swimming at a cruising speed of 1.5 body lengths per second. A 30% increment is probably greater than that required by neutrally buoyant fish for couple cancellation, but still indicates the order of magnitude of energy cost, even when the fish have attained buoyancy equilibrium in the new medium. This can be seen from the fact that the average distance between the center of buoyancy and center of gravity is 2.5% of total length (Aleyev 1977). Thus the couple produced is $C = 0.025lW$. The countering couple is most easily produced by the fin furthest away from the center of gravity, the caudal fin. This will be at least $0.5l$ distant, so that the lift force required to produce a couple C is $(0.025/0.5)W = 0.05W$ or 5% of submerged weight. Most negatively buoyant scombroids are about 6% negatively buoyant so that the lift force they require is almost the same.

Extra energetic costs due to induced drag produced by the necessity of countering vertical forces are also encountered during the process of density equilibration. This acclimatization process occurs when diadromous fish move between the river and marine environments. A 1% difference in density, for a fish of 30 cm length moving at 1–2 lengths per second, can cause a drag increase of over 14% (i.e., a 20% increase in energy required: Webb and Weihs 1983).

Energetic Constraints on Migratory Motions

As mentioned above, directed migration is an extremely costly behavior from the energetic point of view. Energetic requirements may limit migration in some cases. The greatest part of this requirement is expended on overcoming the drag produced by the water's resistance to the fish motion. Therefore, there is a major incentive for migrating fish to lower their drag. Adaptations for drag reduction are common to most types of fish, starting from the usually streamlined shape of most fish species. These had already been suggested by Sir George Cayley (in the 19th century) to be indicative of the solid of least resistance. In addition, scales, mucus, and gill efflux have been suggested as possible drag-reducing mechanisms (Aleyev 1977).

The main problem in estimating the drag on migrating fish is that a swimming fish needs to move parts of its body actively for at least part of the locomotory cycle. This includes the sideways oscillation of the body in axial locomotion and movements of fins. All these motions cause increases in the instantaneous resistance of the fish up to a factor of 5 (Weihs and Webb 1983). Analyses and measurements of the drag of an unmoving or even passively fluttering fish can, therefore, be completely irrelevant and even misleading. The difficulties of measuring or calculat-

ing the drag on an actively thrusting fish have yet to be overcome. Even the separation into drag and thrust produced by a given motion is not well defined. I shall not discuss the intricacies of this yet unsolved question, but use available results to go on directly to the immediate problem facing the migrating fish, that of producing the required thrust with minimum accompanying increase in drag. The simplest way of doing this is to make use of existing currents and, in the case of nearshore and river migrations, ground topography to minimize the need for swimming motions. For example, selective tidal transport (Harden Jones et al. 1978) is very energy efficient in many cases (Weihs 1978). In this behavior, fish migrating in an area with tidal currents move into midwater during the periods of favorable tides, swim with or are swept along by the tidal flow, and retire to the bottom when the current direction reverses. The gain in energy from the lessened need to swim actively more than compensates for the energy required for resting metabolism during the waiting periods in many cases. Bottom topography can cause zones of reduced water velocity, stagnant water, and even locally reversed flow, all helpful to the upstream migrant (Brett 1983).

In open nonmoving waters, the principle of minimizing the drag penalty of swimming motions results in various forms of two-phase, beat-and-coast swimming (Weihs and Webb 1983) in which the fish performs active swimming motions only part of the time, interspersing these bouts with coasting periods. These types of behavior, which include nage filée, alternate diving and climbing of negatively buoyant species, and high-speed intermittent bursts, all result in lower energy expenditure per unit distance crossed.

All migrations, no matter how carefully timed (to fit tidal currents, for example), or laid out spatially, will require some active swimming. The migrant faces an additional choice, that of trading off efficiency against power. This dilemma occurs at two different levels, the local (tactical) and the strategic (over the entire migration). The local problem is similar to the one discussed previously: minimizing the drag penalty. The most efficient way of slipping through the water is by moving no part of the body unnecessarily (sideways motions) as these extra (usually recoil) motions require energy, causing the increase in drag. This implies moving very limited parts of the body, such as the caudal fin or paired or dorsal fins only. However, overcoming drag requires a finite amount of energy so that the smaller the thrusting surfaces, the larger and faster their motions must be to achieve a given swimming speed. However, one of the basic principles of propulsors shows that it is more efficient to accelerate large masses of water slightly to produce a given force than to accelerate smaller masses to a higher speed; recall that the kinetic energy imparted to the water (and lost) is proportional to the velocity difference squared and to the mass to the first power. Thus, a trade-off is required between power required and efficiency, especially when having to move through nonuniform flows such as eddies.

On the strategic level, a problem occurs when, due to external constraints, the migration has to include swimming at average speeds above the optimum speed (Weihs and Webb 1983). This may happen when a fish encounters currents (Trump and Leggett 1980) that are close to the optimum swimming speed, thus forcing the migrant to raise its speed to inefficient levels. It can also happen when the total time available for completion of a migration is limited so that high speeds are needed to cross a given distance. Other external effects include geographical changes in the areas frequented by a species such as riverbed motions, variations in ocean currents, ocean-bed volcanic activity, etc. They also include such human influences as water pollution or overfishing of species that have a predator–prey relationship with the migrants. Other human-caused changes result from dam building, which not only changes the swimming conditions but can also cause cueing difficulties by changing the chemical constitution of the water reaching the sea.

Internal constraints, mainly involving the fishes' sensory and locomotory systems, also act on migrants. The sensors that trigger the start and end of migration need to be tuned to external cues. The development and maintenance of such sensors will, therefore, be influenced by changes in the strength of signals that need to be measured. A more sensitive cueing system is more difficult to develop and operate, but it can save a great deal of energy over the complete migratory pattern by allowing the fish to operate under conditions close to optimum. Assume, for example, that an individual does not start migration on time due to missed cues. It then needs to move faster during at least part of the motion phase in order to reach its target on time or miss out altogether, both outcomes bearing a heavy penalty. Locomotory system changes may include adaptations for more efficient swimming either by

morphological or behavioral means (Weihs and Webb 1983).

Migration in External Currents

Optimization of locomotion under uniform conditions has been rather thoroughly examined (see Weihs and Webb 1983 for a review). This is usually defined as motion in a uniform, nonmoving medium or motion in a constant current. The ocean environment includes many causes of nonuniformity such as layers of different temperature, salinity, particle concentrations, and currents, all of which can influence the choice of energy-minimizing trajectory. For example, it may be energetically advantageous for the fish to lengthen its journey in order to move through warmer waters where the muscular force is higher.

As a simple case of migration in nonuniform conditions, consider a generalization of the case studied by Trump and Leggett (1980). They examined the effects of a uniform current collinear with the fish's direction of motion; here, I study the case of a fish encountering a current at an oblique angle to its required direction of motion.[2] This current is assumed to be of uniform strength and covers a fraction H/L of the total distance to be crossed. The problem is to determine what the fish should do in order to minimize the energy cost of moving across the current from point A to B under these conditions (Figure 2). The optimization task is complicated by the fish's difficulty in establishing the speed and direction of the current instantaneously (it could presumably notice long-range effects of being swept downstream).

If the fish takes no special action, it will not reach point D on the intended trajectory (Figure 2) but will be swept by the current and find itself at point E, having then to swim towards B. For a fish swimming the whole migration horizontally at fixed speed U relative to the water, the total energy expenditure is increased because the distance EB is greater than DB and the time required for the leg CE may be greater than the time needed to traverse CD. To establish the quantitative difference, the route AB is divided into three parts: the track to the current (AC), the track through the current (CD or CE), and the track

---

[2]The optimization task here is more complicated because the motion is influenced not only by the current but also by the requirement of returning to the original objective.

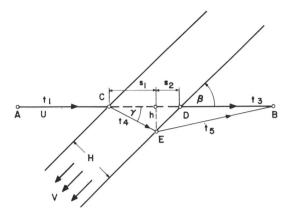

FIGURE 2.—Schematic representation of a fish's migratory motion with (track ACEB) and without (track ACDB) a current oblique to the migratory path. Symbols are defined in Table 1.

from the current (DB or GB).

Swimming horizontally at a constant speed U, a neutrally buoyant fish requires energy at the rate

$$\dot{E} = TU + M; \qquad (5)$$

T is the thrust and M is the standard metabolic rate (energy expended unrelated to swimming). Weihs (1973) showed that minimum energy expenditure at constant speed is obtained when $TU \simeq M$; i.e., $\dot{E} \simeq 2M$.

It is reasonable to assume that fish will swim voluntarily at this speed (and many species actually do: Weihs and Webb 1983). This assumption is not required at the present stage but will be used later on.

The thrust is proportional to velocity squared (equation 4) so for horizontal swimming,

$$\dot{E} = KU^3 + M \text{ (for which } K = \tfrac{1}{2}\rho V_0^{2/3}\, C_D), \quad (6)$$

and the total energy required for migration from A to B, with no currents encountered, is

$$E_0 = (KU^3 + M)\tau = (KU^3 + M)\frac{L}{U}; \qquad (7)$$

τ is the time required and

$$L = L_1 + L_2 + L_3 \qquad (8)$$

is the total distance traversed ($L_1 = AC$; $L_2 = CD$; $L_3 = DB$). Again, it is assumed that the fish swims continuously. Any periods of rest, feeding, etc., require further energy, but this will not be included because only costs of moving in different paths are being compared.

When a uniform current of speed V and width H, moving at an angle $180° + \beta$ from the direction of migration, is encountered at point C, the energy required for motion from A to B (along the trajectory ACEB) is

$$E_c = (KU^3 + M)\left(\frac{L_1}{U} + t_4 + t_5\right); \qquad (9)$$

t_4 and t_5 are the times spent in the current (traversing $CE = L_4$) and recovering from it (along track $EB = L_5$), respectively. This trajectory is obtained if the fish is swept essentially passively by the current and then has to correct his trajectory to get back to the original objective.

The absolute velocity Q of the fish while moving in the current at relative velocity U is

$$Q = [U - (V\cos\beta)^2 + (V\sin\beta)^2]^{1/2}$$

$$= U\left[1 - 2\frac{V}{U}\cos\beta + \left(\frac{V}{U}\right)^2\right] \qquad (10)$$

and

$$t_4 = \frac{L_4}{V} = \frac{L_2\sin\beta}{V\cos(\beta - \gamma)}; \qquad (11)$$

$$\gamma = \tan^{-1}\frac{V\sin\beta}{U - V\cos\beta}. \qquad (12)$$

The time spent moving from point E to point B is

$$t_5 = \frac{[(L_3 + S_1)^2 + h^2]^{1/2}}{U}; \qquad (13)$$

$$S_1 = \frac{L_2\sin\beta\cos\gamma}{\cos(\beta - \gamma)}$$

and

$$h = \frac{L_2\sin\beta\sin\gamma}{\cos(\beta - \gamma)} \text{ (Figure 2)}.$$

From equation (12), it can be seen that if $(V/U)\cos\beta = 1$, t_4 becomes infinite. This is because the component of current velocity in the direction opposite to the migratory route is equal to the swimming speed and so the migration cannot be completed. Thus, only cases where $(V/U)\cos\beta < 1$ are of interest here. Substitution of equations (10) to (13) into equation (9) gives the energy required to traverse the trajectory ACEB; from equations (9) and (7),

$$\frac{E_c - E_0}{E_0} = \frac{U}{L}[(t_4 - 1) + (t_5 - 1)]$$

$$= \frac{L_2}{L} \cdot$$

$$\left\{ \left[\frac{\sin\beta}{\cos(\beta - \gamma)} \cdot \frac{1}{1 - 2(V/U)\cos\beta + (V/U)^2} \right] - 1 \right\}$$

$$+ \frac{L_3}{L}\left\{ 1 + 2\frac{L_2}{L_3}\left[1 - \frac{\sin\beta\cos\gamma}{\cos(\beta - \gamma)} \right] + \left(\frac{L_2}{L_3}\right)^2 \cdot \right.$$

$$\left. \left[\left(1 - \frac{\sin\beta\cos\gamma}{\cos(\beta - \gamma)}\right)^2 + \left(\frac{\sin\beta\sin\gamma}{\cos(\beta - \gamma)}\right)^2 - 1 \right] \right\}. \quad (14)$$

When $V = 0$, we obtain, as expected, $E_c = E_0$. Also, for all $\beta \leq 90°$, this ratio is greater than unity, showing that traversing this current requires extra energy. It is useful to examine this ratio, as the only parameter in it specific to the fish (and under its control) is the velocity U. All the shape-specific factors and metabolic rate have cancelled out. The fish will probably seek to optimize the difference in energy (i.e., spend the least additional amount), and the ratio above represents this difference also. Thus, while the actual value of the excess energy required is not found, one still can obtain the optimal behavior by minimizing the ratio $(E_c - E_0)/E_0$ for any given set of parameters.

Typical results of such analyses show that the ratio of energies $(E_0 - E_c)/E_0$ for currents of velocity $V = U$ (the optimum swimming speed in undisturbed waters) increases with increasing current width (Figure 3). The current velocities considered typically are tens of centimeters per second, well within the range of oceanic currents. The effect of increasing the width of the current is almost linear when all other parameters are kept constant. Increases up to 50% in the energy required are illustrated in Figure 3, but much larger increments of energy are required as β approaches zero (when the current directly opposes the direction of swimming). The position of the current relative to the starting and end points of the migration path is also significant as can be seen from the full and dotted curves for $\beta = 45°$.

The energy ratio declines with increasing current angle β (Figure 4). For current speed $V = U$, the curves go to infinity for $\beta = 0°$ (when the fish move into the oncoming current) and gradually decrease as the angle β grows. Similar decreases, but from a finite value, occur for smaller velocities.

The results shown are just sample calculations

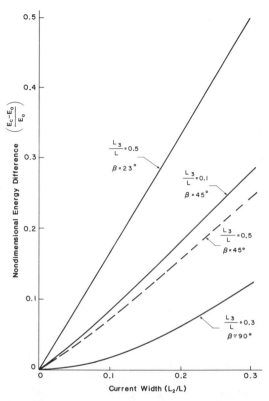

FIGURE 3.—The nondimensionalized difference in a fish's energy expenditure due to a current at angle 180° + β to the direction of migration versus normalized slant current width for various current angles along the migration trajectory. Current speed is equal to fish swimming speed.

of equation (14). It is not worthwhile to go into many more such calculations on a hypothetical basis. This equation is easy to apply to observed data, and the next step is to obtain experimental data for such deflected migrations.

Having shown that deflections due to currents can cause a significant increase in the energy required, one could now try to predict behavioral changes that would minimize this added expenditure. However, such optimization calculations, including directional and speed changes (moving into the current or changing relative speed), are premature. The problem is that any such computation requires prior knowledge (by the fish) of the current's width, speed, and direction and of the proportional part of the migration the current represents. Some of these parameters may be measurable. For example, current speed can be estimated if the fish has external references. If the fish can tell the actual azimuthal angle, it may also

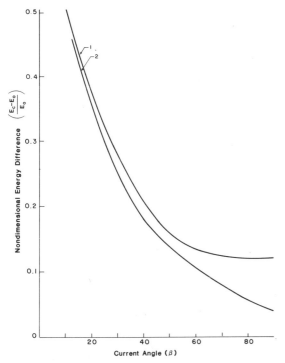

FIGURE 4.—The nondimensional energy difference versus current angle for a normalized slant current width of 20% of the total migration distance centered at 80% of the total distance (curve 1) and 40% of the distance (curve 2).

be able to figure out the angle β by knowing speed and measuring the actual angle γ. The placement of the current within the migration trajectory might be estimated by time elapsed since the migration started, but it is highly improbable that current width can be known in advance. Thus, optimization calculations can be done, but would have questionable predictive value. On the other hand, this method can be used to analyze observed behavior. Again, the next step is up to the observers.

Concluding Remarks

A theoretical framework for the analysis of migration in currents and otherwise variable environments has been presented. Due to the large number of input parameters this has only limited predictive value, but it may be of use in analyzing observed behavior and in suggesting behavioral patterns to look for in oceanic migrations. The importance of the position of a fish's center of mass for the animal's energetic balance has been emphasized, again with the purpose of encouraging further investigation into this subject, which has not been studied previously.

Acknowledgment

This study was partially supported by the Fund for Promotion of Research at Technion.

References

Aleyev, Y. G. 1977. Nekton. Dr. W. Junk, The Hague, The Netherlands.

Arnold, G. P. 1974. Rheotropism in fishes. Biological Reviews of the Cambridge Philosophical Society 49:515–576.

Brett, J. R. 1983. Life energetics of sockeye salmon *Oncorhynchus nerka*. Pages 29–63 *in* W. P. Aspey and S. I. Lustick, editors. Behavioral energetics: the cost of survival in vertebrates. Ohio State University Press, Columbus, Ohio, USA.

Harden Jones, F. R., G. P. Arnold, M. Greer Walker, and P. Scholes. 1978. Selective tidal stream transport and the migration of plaice (*Pleuronectes platessa* L.) in the southern North Sea. Journal du Conseil, Conseil International pour l'Exploration de la Mer 38:331–337.

Magnuson, J. J. 1978. Locomotion by scombrid fishes: hydromechanics, morphology and behavior. Pages 230–313 *in* W. S. Hoar and D. J. Randall, editors. Fish physiology, volume 7. Academic Press, New York, New York, USA.

Puckett, K. J., and L. M. Dill. 1984. Cost of sustained and burst swimming of juvenile coho salmon (*Oncorhynchus kisutch*). Canadian Journal of Fisheries and Aquatic Sciences 41:1511–1546.

Trump, C. L., and W. C. Leggett. 1980. Optimum swimming speeds in fish: the problem of currents. Canadian Journal of Fisheries and Aquatic Sciences 37:1076–1092.

Webb, P. W., and D. Weihs, editors. 1983. Fish biomechanics. Praeger, New York, New York, USA.

Weihs, D. 1973. Optimal fish cruising speed. Nature (London) 245:48–50.

Weihs, D. 1978. Tidal stream transport as an efficient method of migration. Journal du Conseil, Conseil International pour Exploration de la Mer 38:92–99.

Weihs, D., and P. W. Webb. 1983. Optimization of locomotion. Pages 339–371 *in* P. W. Webb and D. Weihs, editors. Fish biomechanics. Praeger, New York, New York, USA.

American Fisheries Society Symposium 1:262–275, 1987

Sea-Surface Temperature and Distribution of Atlantic Salmon in the Northwest Atlantic Ocean

D. G. Reddin

Science Branch, Department of Fisheries and Oceans, Post Office Box 5667
St. John's, Newfoundland A1C 5X1, Canada

W. M. Shearer

Freshwater Fisheries Laboratory Field Station, 16 River Street
Montrose, Scotland, United Kingdom

Abstract.—The objectives of this study were to investigate the seasonal distribution of Atlantic salmon *Salmo salar* in the northwest Atlantic Ocean in relation to sea-surface temperature and the influence of environmental conditions in the region on the abundance of Atlantic salmon off western Greenland. Research vessel catches indicated that Atlantic salmon of all sea ages occurred seasonally over most of the northwest Atlantic. The fish were concentrated throughout the year in the Labrador Sea gyre, in summer and fall off west Greenland, and in the spring near the eastern slope of the Grand Bank of Newfoundland. These areas had, in common, seasonal sea-surface temperatures between 4 and 8°C. The recapture sites of Atlantic salmon tagged and released as smolts in the Sand Hill River, Labrador, indicated that the fish modified their movements depending on sea-surface temperature. A multiple linear regression showed that environmental conditions in the northwest Atlantic during January and August influenced the abundance of Atlantic salmon off west Greenland. It was concluded that colder sea-surface temperatures in 1983 and 1984 may have been partly responsible for the low catches at Greenland in those years.

Before the advent of the high seas fisheries for Atlantic salmon *Salmo salar,* little was known about the location of their feeding areas in the north Atlantic Ocean. Menzies (1949) speculated that a possible site would be in the Irminger Current region southwest of Iceland (Figure 1) because of its ideal water temperatures and abundant food resources. Huntsman (1938), on the other hand, postulated that Atlantic salmon remained close by the mouths of the rivers in which they had hatched. During the 1960s, however, the capture of tagged Atlantic salmon of both European and North American origin in the high-seas fisheries off Greenland, in the northern Norwegian Sea, and around the Faroe Islands indicated that the fish make quite lengthy migrations at sea (Jensen 1980b; Anonymous 1981). May (1973) summarized information on the distribution and migration of Atlantic salmon in the northwest Atlantic and, showed that multi-sea-winter fish (those that had spent more than one winter at sea) occurred seasonally over most of the region including the Grand Bank of Newfoundland, the Labrador Sea, and off west Greenland. Recently, Lear (1976) and Reddin and Burfitt (1984) showed that Atlantic salmon are abundant east of the Grand Bank.

Migration and distribution of Atlantic salmon in the sea are related to reproductive strategies.

Since sea age at maturity controls the length of time spent at sea, the older a salmon is when it matures the longer it remains at sea and the farther it can move from its home river. Gross (1984) defined a strategy as a genetically determined life history or behavior program which dictates the course of development or action throughout an organism's life. Atlantic salmon exhibit several alternative life history strategies and can return from the sea at ages of 1 sea-winter (1SW), 2 sea-winters (2SW), 3 sea-winters (3SW), and, infrequently, 4 sea-winters (4SW) and older (Gardner 1976). These alternative strategies have a genetic basis (Naevdal 1983) that can be modified by interaction with the environment (Saunders et al. 1983; Gjerde 1984). The benefits of different strategies may be that older Atlantic salmon have higher fecundities and may be better able to utilize large river systems (Schaffer and Elson 1975) whereas grilse, which mature after one winter at sea, have a higher survival rate than older Atlantic salmon as a consequence of their earlier maturity. Geographic variations have also been noted. For example, Atlantic salmon stocks in Maine are almost exclusively 2SW salmon (Anonymous 1985b), while in Newfoundland many stocks are almost entirely grilse (O'Connell et al. 1985). Because of these variations, migra-

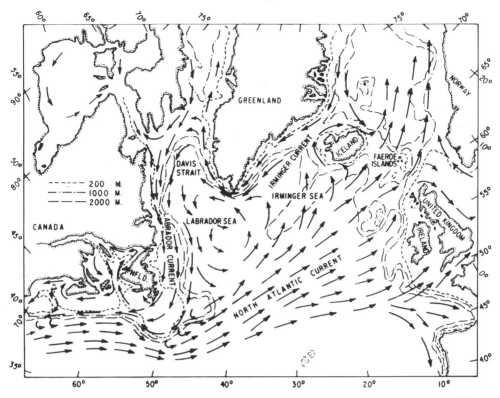

FIGURE 1.—Areas investigated for seasonal distributions of Atlantic salmon and general directions of flow of main surface currents in the northern Atlantic Ocean, adapted from Templeman (1967) and Stasko et al. (1973).

tion routes and distributions of Atlantic salmon will also vary geographically.

The commercial Atlantic salmon fishery at west Greenland began in 1960 with a modest catch of 60 tonnes caught entirely by Greenlandic fishing boats. The catch increased dramatically to 1,539 tonnes in 1965; in the following years vessels from Norway, Faroes, Sweden, and Denmark also participated. The catch peaked at 2,689 tonnes in 1971. Because of concern for the Atlantic salmon stocks contributing to these catches, a quota of 1,190 tonnes was imposed in 1976 and the participation of all foreign fishing vessels was phased out. In 1984 and 1985, the quota was reduced to 870 tonnes and 852 tonnes, respectively. Since 1968 the main gear used in this fishery has been monofilament drift gill nets. The results of tagging adults at Greenland and smolts in home rivers have shown that the salmon caught off west Greenland originated in rivers of Scotland, England, Ireland, Norway, Iceland, France, Spain, Sweden, Canada, and the United States (Parrish 1973; Jensen 1980a). These studies also showed that the age of the salmon on return to natal rivers

would be 2SW or older. No potential grilse of non-Greenlandic origin have been identified in catches taken off west Greenland. The landings have shown that Atlantic salmon are typically distributed along the entire west coast of Greenland from Cape Farewell north to Disko Bay, although some between-year differences have been noted (Christensen and Lear 1980). In 1983 and 1984, reported catches were 74% and 66% lower, respectively, than the quota. These low catches and the possibility of an environmental link led us into the present study.

The objectives of this paper are two-fold. First, we examine the relationship between sea-surface temperature and the distribution of Atlantic salmon in the northwest Atlantic. In particular, we are interested in discovering if Atlantic salmon adjust their movements to water temperature. Secondly, we examine the hypothesis that environmental conditions in the northwest Atlantic have influenced the abundance of Atlantic salmon and the quality of the fishery at west Greenland. To do this, we use data from the following sources. (1) Catch–effort data from Canadian research vessels fishing in the northwest Atlantic will be used to show the seasonal distribution of Atlantic salmon. (2) Sea temperatures and catch-effort data from west Greenland reported by Smed (1980) will be used to infer the depth at which Atlantic salmon are located in the water column. (3) Research vessel catch rates and sea-surface temperatures (SSTs) collected during cruises off west Greenland, in the Labrador Sea, and on the Grand Bank of Newfoundland will be examined to show the relationship between Atlantic salmon abundance and water temperature. (4) Environmental conditions in the northwest Atlantic, together with qualitative estimates of the abundance of Atlantic salmon at west Greenland based on catches taken during the fishery and the recapture sites of Atlantic salmon tagged as smolts at a counting fence facility on the Sand Hill River, Labrador, will be used to demonstrate that Atlantic salmon modify their distribution in response to water temperature.

Methods

The study area encompasses the northwest Atlantic including the Davis Strait, the Labrador Sea, the Grand Bank, and the Irminger Sea (Figure 1). The terminology used to describe life stages of Atlantic salmon is that recommended by Allan and Ritter (1977).

Seasonal distribution.—May (1973) described and reported the results of research vessel surveys in the northwest Atlantic from latitudes 43 to 70°N, 1965–1972. Data from research surveys since 1972, including studies in the areas of the Grand Bank (Reddin and Burfitt 1984; Reddin 1985) and the Irminger Sea (Jensen and Lear 1980) have been combined with that of May (1973; Figure 2). Most fishing consisted of repetitive surface sets at single stations in conjunction with tagging experiments. Drift gill nets constructed from multi- and monofilament twine of various mesh sizes between 114 mm and 155 mm and approximately 3 m in depth were used. In the years when surveys were conducted, stations were fished each month from February to October. Seasons were defined as follows: spring—22 March to 21 June; summer to autumn—22 June to 22 December; winter—23 December to 21 March. Catch rates were expressed as numbers of Atlantic salmon caught per nautical mile of net fished per hour.

Depth.—In order to investigate the relationship between Atlantic salmon and the environment, it is necessary to know the depth in the water column that Atlantic salmon inhabit. Obviously,

they spend a considerable amount of time in the upper few meters of the water column or they would not be susceptible to capture by surface gill nets. Furthermore, all commercial salmon fishing gear, including that fished off the Faroes, off west Greenland, and in home-water fisheries of North America and Europe, is set to fish near the surface. Moreover, stomach contents of Atlantic salmon primarily consist of organisms found in surface waters (Stasko et al. 1973). More direct evidence on swimming depths of Atlantic salmon in the open sea is scarce.

The depth Atlantic salmon inhabit at sea can also be inferred from catch rates and subsurface temperatures at Greenland. If Atlantic salmon are found only in the warm surface water, then catch rates from surface-set gill nets should fluctuate with the depth of warm water as Atlantic salmon spread themselves through it. Information on subsurface temperatures near west Greenland is available from the bathythermograph and Nansen bottle casts made by the research vessels involved in the 1972 international tagging experiment (Smed 1980). Atlantic salmon catch and effort data from research and commercial vessels are also available for 1972 (Christensen and Lear 1980). The thickness of the homogeneous upper layer, measured from the surface to the mixed-layer depth (MLD), was compared to estimates of catch per effort for the 1972 fishing season. Smed (1980) considered the water was mixed if the approximate vertical temperature gradient was less than 0.1°C in any 15 m. The data were grouped into three periods to facilitate comparison of MLD and catch rates: period 1 extended from 30 July to 19 August, period 2 from 20 August to 2 September, and period 3 from 3 September to 23 September (Table 1). These periods were chosen to reduce the effects of immigration and emigration (Andersen et al. 1980).

Sea temperature and food abundance.—Information on catch rates and SSTs was obtained from research vessels fishing at west Greenland in 1972 (Christensen and Lear 1980), in the Labrador Sea from 1965 to 1985, and in the area of the Grand Bank in 1979 and 1980 (Reddin 1985). In each case, the gear fished was similar to that used in the Labrador Sea (May 1973). The SSTs were recorded at each station with either bathythermograph or Nansen bottle casts or thermometers. The technique used to determine the abundance of prey, i.e., stomach contents (g) per unit weight of fish (kg), was described by Reddin (1985).

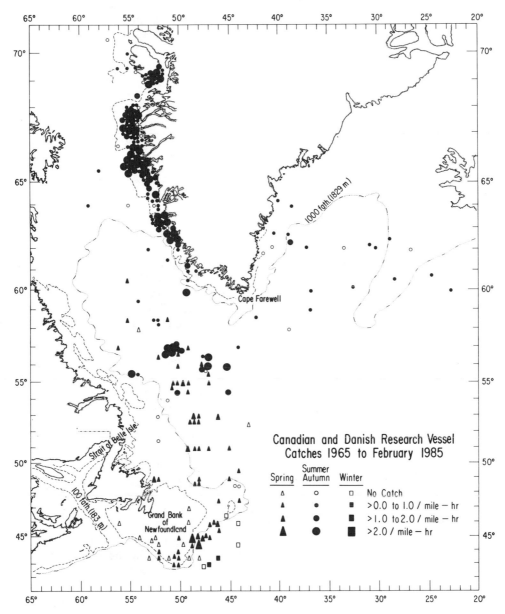

FIGURE 2.—Research vessel catches of Atlantic salmon in the northwest Atlantic Ocean, 1965–1985.

Environmental conditions.—An environmental factor was suggested as a possible cause of low catches at west Greenland (Anonymous 1985a) because poor catches in 1983 and 1985 were associated with cold winters in 1982–1983 and 1983–1984. This low abundance could have occurred if the low sea temperatures affected catch rates (Christensen and Lear 1980) or the distribution of salmon in the northwest Atlantic (Dunbar and Thomson 1979; May 1973), or both. This portion of our paper attempts to quantify changes in the environment in the northwest Atlantic Ocean and relate these changes to salmon abundance at west Greenland.

Environmental conditions in the northwest Atlantic were interpreted from the British Meteorological Office's ice charts issued monthly from Bracknell, England. Sea-surface temperatures were based on 15,000 reports from ships of opportunity and air–surface temperatures (ASTs) came

TABLE 1.—Estimates of the mixed-layer depth (MLD) and catch per unit effort (CPUE) of Atlantic salmon from selected commercial vessels, research vessels, and all commercial vessels fishing in 1972 at west Greenland. Values for MLD are from Smed (1980) and CPUE data are from Christensen and Lear (1980).

| Period | Dates | Mixed-layer depth (m) | | | Catch per unit effort | | | | | | | | |
| | | | | | Commercial vessels | | | Research vessels | | | All commercial vessels | | |
		Mean	SD	N	Mean[a]	SD	N	Mean[a]	SD	N	Mean[b]	SD	N
1	30 Jul–19 Aug	10.42	11.25	19	31.15	17.90	34	13.57	12.59	23	46.58	30.60	19
2	20 Aug–2 Sep	31.00	25.39	21	19.58	14.29	20	5.42	7.50	20	35.45	12.43	11
3	3 Sep–23 Sep	37.33	15.70	21	9.36	6.23	31	4.12	2.99	19	24.21	16.05	24

[a] Mean number of Atlantic salmon caught per nautical mile of net fished.
[b] Mean number of Atlantic salmon caught per 100 nets.

from ships of opportunity and land-based weather stations. Means of SSTs and ASTs were plotted for every 1° square, and isotherms were drawn at 4°C intervals for SST and at the 0°C isotherm for AST. The isotherms represent the mean SST and AST distributions for 10 d prior to the end of the month for which the chart was issued.

Analyses were done by the Statistical Analysis System procedures MEANS, STEPWISE, RANK, and REG (SAS 1982a, 1982b). The stepwise selection procedure was chosen because, for each step at which a variable is entered, all other variables in the model are tested and removed if they do not meet the selection criteria (Draper and Smith 1966). The 0.15 significance level was chosen for entry to and removal from the model. Analyses were performed on ranked data to avoid problems of nonnormality as some of the variables were not continuous (Conover 1980).

The environmental variables for analysis (Table 2) were

(a) the latitude of the northward extent in January of the 4°C water isotherm west of 45°W longitude (RJWAT-N);
(b) a measure of spring warming calculated as the difference between the area (km²) covered by 4°C water (or warmer) in January and that in March north of 50°N and west of 40°W (R-SPR);
(c) the latitude of the northward extent in August of the 4°C water isotherm west of 45°W longitude (RAWAT-N);
(d) the extent (%) of the west Greenland coast covered by the 4°C water isotherm north of 60°N latitude (R-AC);
(e) an estimate of smolt-class strength of Atlantic salmon which would contribute to the west Greenland fishery. Since most of the west

Greenland catches are 1SW fish that would return to home waters as 2SW fish and are largely from Canada and Scotland, the sum of MSW (multi-sea-winter) Atlantic salmon catches (tonnes) in Canada and Scotland in the year following the west Greenland fishery was used (SM-CL) (Anonymous 1985a).

For this analysis, the 4°C isotherm was chosen because the 3°C isotherm was not on the British Admiralty chart. However, temperature gradients between the warmer waters of Atlantic origin and the colder subpolar waters are well defined for much of the year; because of this, the 4°C isotherm is a convenient indicator of the transition zone between these two regions.

The dependent variable was Atlantic salmon abundance at west Greenland but a quantitative estimate was lacking since there are no effort values for the fishery at Greenland. Qualitative statements of the Greenlandic component of the fishery, as found in the annual reports of the Greenland Fisheries and Environmental Research Institute (Anonymous 1985a), were used (ABUND). These estimates were made by the scientific staff of Greenland Fisheries and Environmental Research Institute from reports of fishermen and fish plant managers. They are

category 1 (exceptionally poor): 1983, 1984;
category 2 (below average): 1970, 1972, 1976, 1978;
category 3 (average): 1973, 1974, 1977;
category 4 (above average): 1975, 1981, 1982;
category 5 (exceptionally good): 1971, 1979, 1980.

Annual sea temperature variations.—The results of smolt-tagging experiments that were car-

TABLE 2.—Environmental conditions in the northwest Atlantic Ocean and Atlantic salmon catches off west Greenland, 1969–1985. Asterisks denote $P \leq 0.01$**; other t values are nonsignificant ($P > 0.05$).

Year (n)	Latitude of 4°C isotherm in Jan (°N) (RJWAT-N)	Spring warming area of 4°C water (km²) (R-SPR)		Latitude of 4°C isotherm in Aug (°N) (RAWAT-N)	Extent of Greenland coast covered by 4°C water (%) (R-AC)	Sum of Canada + Scotland multi-sea-winter catches in year n+1 (tonnes) (SM-CL)	West Greenland	
		Jan	Mar				Catch (tonnes)	Quota (tonnes)
Environmental conditions and catches								
1969	60.0	98	92	76.0	50	2,065	2,210	
1970	59.0	73	50	68.5	5	1,978	2,146	
1971	61.5	102	55	72.5	60	1,789	2,689	
1972	51.0	19	36	71.5	40	2,312	2,113	
1973	58.0	83	57	68.5	50	2,167	2,341	
1974	58.0	59	70	74.5	80	2,242	1,917	
1975	57.0	49	84	74.5	25	2,049	2,030	
1976	56.5	54	36	71.5	65	2,252	1,175	1,190
1977	58.0	64	52	74.5	80	2,006	1,420	1,190
1978	52.0	37	79	70.0	60	1,303	984	1,190
1979	60.5	88	60	72.5	100	2,614	1,395	1,190
1980	55.5	41	49	75.0	100	2,462	1,194	1,190
1981	52.0	45	54	75.0	40	1,678	1,264	1,265
1982	55.5	46	45	75.0	15	1,575	1,077	1,253
1983	55.0	45	50	66.0	0	1,135	310	1,190
1984	47.0	20	6	64.0	0	[a]	297	870
1985	55.5	[a]	[a]	76.0	30	[a]	852	852
1969–1982								
Mean	56.8	61	58	72.8	55	2,035	1,711	
SD	3.26	24.7	17.0	2.51	29.0	355.4	552	
t-values: 1969–1982 versus 1983								
	−2.01	−2.53**	−1.84	−10.2**	−7.09**	9.48**	−9.49**	
t-values: 1969–1982 versus 1984								
	−11.2**	−6.21**	11.5**	−13.2**	−7.09**		−9.56**	
t-values: 1969–1982 versus 1985								
	−1.49			4.77**	−3.23**		−5.82**	

[a] Area measurements and catches not available.

ried out at a counting fence facility on the Sand Hill River, Labrador, from 1969 to 1971 (Pratt et al. 1974) were used to determine if Atlantic salmon can adjust their movements to the temperature of the water that they must swim through. Altogether, 25,075 Atlantic salmon smolts were tagged and released from 1969 to 1971, 16% of the smolts descending the river in those years. The tag used was a Carlin-type with a wire attachment applied below the dorsal fin of the fish.

Results

Seasonal Distribution

In spring Atlantic salmon have been found in surface waters of the northwest Atlantic from the southern edge of the Grand Bank to slightly south of Cape Farewell, Greenland (Figure 2). As May (1973) observed, the most westerly positions where Atlantic salmon are caught in spring coincide with the edge of the Arctic pack ice in water that is relatively cool, 3–8°C. Also, there are two locations where Atlantic salmon are particularly abundant in spring. One of them is about 480 km east of the Strait of Belle Isle. The other is slightly east of the 200-m isobath along the eastern edge of the Grand Bank. In these two locations, catch rates rival those at west Greenland in late summer, suggesting that Atlantic salmon are as abundant there per unit area as at west Greenland. Reddin and Burfitt (1984) have presented evidence suggesting that the stocks in the Labrador Sea may be separate from those along the eastern edge of the Grand Bank.

In late summer and autumn, Atlantic salmon are concentrated along the west Greenland coast from the inner coastal fiords to between 45 and 60 km offshore. Relatively good catches have also occurred in the Labrador Sea north of latitude 55°N. Atlantic salmon have also been caught by research vessels in the Irminger Sea although catch rates were not nearly as high as those off Greenland or in the Labrador Sea (Jensen and Lear 1980). In August 1985, an experimental fishery was conducted within the coastal fiords of east Greenland in latitudes 62–63°N; in 8 d of fishing, 400 Atlantic salmon were caught (A. L. Meister, Maine Sea Run Salmon Commission, Bangor, Maine, personal communication). Some of these fish were undoubtedly of North American origin since salmon tagged as smolts in North America have been caught in this area (Jensen and Lear 1980). No sets have been made in summer or autumn in the Grand Bank area.

Few sets have been made for Atlantic salmon in the northwest Atlantic during winter; those made were all in 1985 and east of the Grand Bank. The low catch rates suggest that the fish were elsewhere at this time. Since Atlantic salmon have been found in the Labrador Sea in the fall and

then in the following spring, it is possible that they also overwinter there.

The sea ages of Atlantic salmon caught during experimental fishing in the northwest Atlantic show that MSW fish range over much of the northwest Atlantic while those 1SW fish that would mature as grilse (potential grilse) do not. Virtually all the Atlantic salmon caught in the Labrador Sea were MSW. In sets on and east of the Grand Bank, however, both MSW and potential grilse were caught. At Greenland and in the Irminger Sea, only Atlantic salmon that would mature as 2SW and older fish have been caught.

Depth

Smed (1980) reported that there is a deepening of the homogeneous layer from period 1 (early August) through period 3 (September: Table 1). Comparison by t-test showed that the mean MLDs were significantly different between the

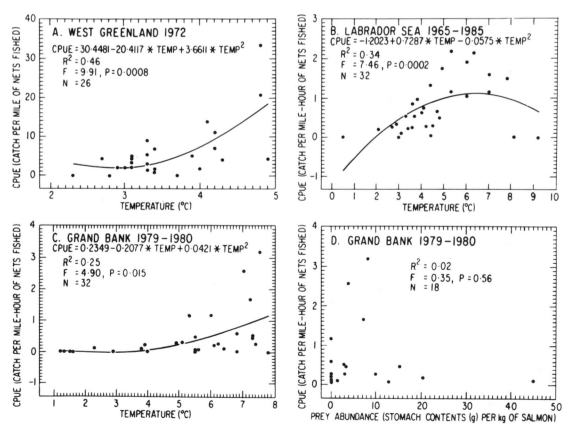

FIGURE 3.—Relationships between catch of Atlantic salmon per unit effort (CPUE) and temperature and food abundance at west Greenland, 1972; in the Labrador Sea, 1965–1985; and near Grand Bank, Newfoundland, 1979–1980.

TABLE 3.—Results of analysis of variance of ranked variables modeled against estimated abundances of Atlantic salmon off west Greenland as the dependent variable. Variables are defined in Table 2.

Variable	df	F	P
RJWAT-N	1, 13	2.220	0.16
R-SPR	1, 13	0.970	0.34
RAWAT-N	1, 13	12.200	0.01
R-AC	1, 13	3.310	0.09
SM-CL	1, 13	1.460	0.25

three periods at the 5% level of significance. As the homogeneous layer deepened, catch rates from research and commercial vessels decreased significantly from period 1 through period 3 (Table 1). As MLD increased in depth, Atlantic salmon probably spread throughout more of the water column, below the depth of nets that fished only the top 3 m of the water column. Although other factors such as wind, by-catch, and gear saturation also influence Atlantic salmon catch rates (Christensen and Lear 1980), this analysis suggests that, in the area of west Greenland, Atlantic salmon are found in the upper region of the water column from the surface to the MLD.

Sea Temperature and Food Abundance

The relationship between salmon abundance and SST was examined by relating catch rates to SSTs during research vessel cruises at west Greenland in 1972, in the Labrador Sea in 1965–1985, and in the area of the Grand Bank of Newfoundland in 1979–1980 (Figure 3A–C). In all three situations, catch rates were significantly correlated with SST: R^2 was 0.46 for west Greenland, 0.34 for the Labrador Sea, and 0.25 for the Grand Bank. Quadratic equations gave significantly better fits than linear ones. Catch rates typically increased at temperatures above 3°C; in the Labrador Sea, they declined above about 8°C. There were no sets made at SSTs higher than 5°C

at west Greenland or 8°C on the Grand Bank, but the available data suggest that Atlantic salmon are relatively abundant where water temperatures are 3–8°C.

Stomach contents from Atlantic salmon caught during the Grand Bank study (Reddin and Burfitt 1984) were used to examine the relationship between catch rate and prey abundance. The authors assumed that fish caught in gill nets did not regurgitate food and that stomach content per unit predator weight was an index of abundance of Atlantic salmon prey. They found no relationship between catch rate and prey abundance ($F = 0.35$; df $= 1, 17$; $P = 0.56$: Figure 3D). They then compared catches in two different locations, one of which had abundant prey and low SSTs, the other had less prey but higher SSTs. Catch rates were five times higher in the location with less prey and higher SSTs. From this, the authors concluded that SST has a stronger influence on Atlantic salmon distribution in the marine environment than prey abundance.

Environmental Conditions

Analysis of variance of ranked 1970–1983 environmental data indicated that only variables RAWAT-N and R-AC made significant contributions ($P < 0.15$) to modeled abundances of Atlantic salmon at west Greenland (dependent variable: Table 3). This suggested that the abundance of Atlantic salmon at west Greenland was significantly influenced by environmental conditions in August, i.e., the extent of warm water in the Davis Strait area and the length of the west Greenland coast covered by 4°C water.

Analysis by stepwise multiple linear regression of 1970–1983 data against abundances of Atlantic salmon at west Greenland indicated that RAWAT-N entered the model first ($r^2 = 0.50$; $F = 12.18$; $P = 0.005$) and RJWAT-N second ($F = 13.16$; $P = 0.0012$), given that RAWAT-N was in

TABLE 4.—Results of stepwise multiple linear regression of environmental variables against estimated abundances of Atlantic salmon. Only two variables contributed significantly to the model, for which $r^2 = 0.7052$. Variables are defined in Table 2.

Term	df	Sum of squares	Mean square	B value	SE	Type-II sum of squares	F	P
Regression	2	15.77	7.88				13.16	0.0012
Error	11	6.59	0.60					
Total	13	22.36						
Intercept				0.3805	0.6073			
RJWAT-N				0.1421	0.0518	4.52	7.52	0.0192
RAWAT-N				0.2358	0.0521	12.27	20.49	0.0009

the model (Table 4). Variable selection halted after step 2 since none of the other variables contributed significantly to the relationship. The r² was 0.71, indicating that much of the variance in abundance of Atlantic salmon at west Greenland could be explained by the northward extent of warm water in the Davis Strait in August and the northward extent of warm water in the Labrador Sea in January.

Data from the 1984 and 1985 fisheries at west Greenland were not used in the model and, therefore, can be used as an independent test of our hypothesis that environmental conditions in the northwest Atlantic control availability of Atlantic salmon to that fishery. Summers were colder in 1984 than in 1983 because of the very cold 1983–1984 winter (Rosenørn et al. 1984). Consequently, the 4°C isotherm in January was south of the Davis Strait and even in August did not extend very far north. The model predicted that the 1984 fishery would be poor and this was the case. Environmental conditions were much warmer in 1985 than in either 1983 or 1984, probably because of the mild 1984–1985 winter. Consequently, the 4°C isotherm in January, as well as in August, extended well up into the Davis Strait. This suggested that the 1985 fishery at west Greenland would be above average. The high 1985 landings during the first 2 weeks of fishing indicated that Atlantic salmon were again abundant at west Greenland as predicted (Anonymous 1986).

In conclusion, this analysis suggests that environmental conditions in the northwest Atlantic have had a significant effect on catches of Atlantic salmon at west Greenland, possibly by affecting marine mortality rates or distribution of the fish. The cold waters in 1983 and 1984 may have been partly responsible for the low catches off Greenland in those years.

Annual Sea Temperature Variations

Corroborative evidence that Atlantic salmon change their distribution at sea according to thermal conditions can be discerned from the sites of recapture of MSW Atlantic salmon tagged as smolts in the Sand Hill River, Labrador, during 1969–1971 (Pratt et al. 1974). Some of the fish from this stock were harvested in the general vicinity of the home river in Labrador as well as in Newfoundland (Figure 4). However, when plotted with the June 4°C isotherm, the distribution of tag recaptures suggested that some of the annual variability in the location of the harvest of these fish was related to environmental conditions

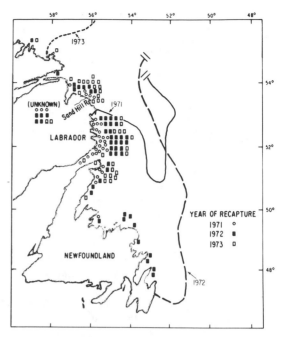

FIGURE 4.—Distribution of recapture sites for multi-sea-winter Atlantic salmon that were tagged as smolts at the Sand Hill River counting fence, Labrador (from Pratt et al. 1974). Also shown are the approximate locations of the 1971, 1972, and 1973 4°C isotherms in June.

(Figure 4). In 1972, for example, MSW fish were recaptured considerably farther south than in either 1971 or 1973. The 4°C surface isotherm for June extended much farther southward in 1972 than in 1971 and 1973. This probably occurred because of a more southerly distribution of ice in 1972 than in 1971 and 1973 (Reddin and Day 1980). We suggest, therefore, that the more abundant ice and concomitant lower water temperature in 1972 caused the MSW fish heading towards the coast to migrate much farther south than in 1971 and 1973. No such distributional change was noted for 1SW fish, which migrated towards coastal areas about a month later when the 4°C isotherm was north of Sand Hill River.

General Discussion and Conclusions

The results of our study of the relationship between the depth of the mixed layer and catch rates of Atlantic salmon in the commercial fishery at west Greenland indicate that the fish most commonly inhabit the upper portion of the water column. This agrees with the results from acoustic tagging experiments on Atlantic salmon in coastal waters by Westerberg (1982a, 1982b) and in the open sea by Jakupsstovu et al. (1985). In their experiments, Atlantic salmon remained mostly in the upper 5 m of the water column although, in both cases, short-term vertical movements to greater depths were noted.

There are two main sea-age classes of Atlantic salmon in the northwest Atlantic, grilse that mature after one winter at sea and older fish that mature after two or more sea winters (Allan and Ritter 1977). Atlantic salmon smolts with the potential to become MSW in age enter surface waters of the northwest Atlantic from the Connecticut River, USA, in the south to the Kapisigdlit River, Greenland, in the north. The immature postsmolts from rivers south of Labrador migrate northward throughout the summer and eventually reach the Labrador Sea, as has been shown for Maine and Quebec stocks (Caron 1983; Meister 1984). These fish spend much of their time feeding on abundant resources (Templemen 1967) in water temperatures suitable for growth in the eddy system bounded by the Labrador, North Atlantic, Irminger, and West Greenland currents (Figure 1). During their second summer in the sea, they move northward to an area extending from the northern Labrador Sea up into the Davis Strait and Irminger Sea. Tagging studies, both of smolts in natal rivers and of adults at Greenland, have shown that the majority of Atlantic salmon recovered at Greenland originated in rivers mainly in Canada, Norway, Scotland, and Ireland and are mostly 1SW fish that would not mature until the following year (Anonymous 1981; Jensen 1980a, 1980b). Reddin et al. (1979) have shown that Atlantic salmon of both North American and European origin occur in the Labrador Sea and Jensen and Lear (1980) have reported that Atlantic salmon of North American and European origin occurred in the summer–autumn period in the Irminger Sea. Although catch rates in the Irminger Sea were low compared to those at west Greenland, Jensen and Lear speculated that, because the area involved was so large, the total number of Atlantic salmon in the Irminger Sea could also be large but widely distributed. Because suitable oceanograhpic conditions exist each year in these areas (Reddin 1985), we suggest that Atlantic salmon also inhabit these areas annually. Although no research vessels have fished in the Labrador Sea in winter, we suggest that, since the appropriate conditions exist there, Atlantic salmon overwinter there as well.

In the fall, Atlantic salmon move south either through the Labrador Sea or along the Labrador coast (Reddin and Dempson 1986) to occupy an area in winter and spring about 480 km east of the Strait of Belle Isle. In the spring, Atlantic salmon are also found concentrated to the east of the Grand Bank (Reddin 1985). Reddin (1985) reported catch rates in 1980 for Atlantic salmon stocks east of the Grand Bank that were similar to those at west Greenland in some years. Atlantic salmon were also found in lower abundance over the Grand Bank and along its southwest edge, suggesting that some may migrate to home rivers over the southern Grand Bank. Seasonal oceanographic conditions suggest that Atlantic salmon do not overwinter in the Grand Bank area since the area covered by warm water is small and variable (Reddin 1985).

Until Reddin (1985) reported catching substantial numbers of potential grilse to the east of the Grand Bank, only potential MSW Atlantic salmon had previously been recorded in catches at sea in the northwest Atlantic. However, the routes taken to and from this area still remain largely unknown. May (1973) and Templeman (1967) had previously reported that no potential grilse were found in the Labrador Sea.

One is tempted to speculate, as suggested by May (1973), that movements of Atlantic salmon to and from Greenland are related to patterns of oceanic circulation in the north Atlantic (Figure 1). Fish from both Europe and North America could reach Greenland by drifting in the eddy system of the Labrador Sea, provided that European fish take a circuitous detour to the south and east going home and that North American fish move to the east en route to Greenland (May 1973). The environment, however, seems to lack the necessary stability to provide a reliable, constant directional cue from year to year, particularly as some of the current systems can be complex. Finally, it should be noted that, in light of present knowledge of the multisensory nature of fish migration (McCleave et al. 1984), fish may require a whole mosaic of environmental stimuli to orient in any meaningful way.

Leggett (1984) discussed the role of the ocean environment, especially of temperature, as a major influence on the distribution and movements of many fish species, including Atlantic salmon. For example, American shad (*Alosa sapidissima*) are most frequently caught in waters of 7–13°C (Neves and Depres 1979). Templeman (1966) explained how hydrographic conditions influence the inshore migration of Atlantic cod (*Gadus morhua*). Swordfish (*Xiphias gladius*) are found abundantly where surface temperatures exceed 16°C (Tibbo t al. 1961).

As Atlantic salmon spend much of their time in the surface water, and because temperature controls so many physiological processes (Harden Jones 1968; Saunders, in press), it is not surprising to find statistically significant relationships between catch rate and water temperature. Furthermore, data from the Sand Hill River experiment show that Atlantic salmon adjust their movements in relation to water temperature.

We have shown that the abundance of Atlantic salmon at west Greenland is related to hydrographic conditions in the northwest Atlantic, particularly in January and August. This hypothesis agrees with that of Dunbar and Thomson (1979), who discussed how global atmospheric change could influence the presence and abundance of Atlantic salmon at west Greenland. They suggested that Atlantic salmon are abundant there when the marine climate is cooling after a warming phase. Specifically, they related the latitude of the Icelandic low-pressure center to the warming and cooling of the West Greenland Current, which results from the relative influences of its two component currents—the warm Irminger Current and the cold East Greenland Current. They suggested that, during the cooling phases, the Labrador Sea gyre expands into the Davis Strait and, together with intensification of the Irminger and East Greenland currents into the West Greenland Current, shifts the distribution of Atlantic salmon into this area.

The low catches off west Greenland in 1983 and 1984 were shown to be related to colder than normal water temperatures in the northwest Atlantic. However, these low catches could have been caused by a shift in distribution patterns or an increased marine mortality, because both would result in decreased catches at west Greenland. Sutcliffe et al. (1977), Martin et al. (1984), Scarnecchia (1984), Martin and Mitchell (1985), and others have related abundances of Atlantic salmon and other marine species to environmental factors, indicating that fluctuations in abundance of various fish species are directly related to ocean climate and, in particular, to ocean temperature. Porter and Ritter (1984) and Anonymous (1985a) showed that the 1982 and 1983 smolt classes of Atlantic salmon from Mactaquac Fish Culture Station on the Saint John River experienced a higher than average marine mortality. Since the return rate to that hatchery is significantly correlated with the total Canadian catch, it can be used as an index of the survival of Cana-

dian stocks (Porter and Ritter 1984). Therefore, the lower return rate suggests decreased survival of Canadian stocks in 1983 and 1984. But, if the low 1983 catch had resulted solely from a shift in distribution and hence reduced abundance at west Greenland, then catches in home waters in Canada in 1984 should have been above normal, having been augmented by fish not caught at west Greenland. However, the 1984 Canadian catch of MSW Atlantic salmon (632 tonnes) was the worst recorded, being only 44% of the 1970–1983 mean of 1,426 tonnes (Anonymous 1985a). Reduced effort at Greenland and low spawning escapement in some rivers may also have contributed to these low catches (Porter and Ritter 1984; Anonymous 1985a).

Our results show a marked relation between catch rates and the 4°C isotherm. Also, where Atlantic salmon prey organisms occurred at equal densities at different temperatures, Atlantic salmon abundance, measured in terms of catch rate, was higher where temperatures were higher. Water of low surface temperature appeared not only capable of deflecting Atlantic salmon from their recognized migratory pathway but of curtailing their movements in the sea, as the fish were disinclined to pass through cold water even though warmer water was beyond. Since most gear set to catch Atlantic salmon is passive and depends on the fish coming towards it, any changes in the recognized migratory pathway of the fish can have a major influence on catch rates.

Since it has been shown that Atlantic salmon are mainly located in water between 4 and 8°C, it is possible to locate areas of probable abundance in the northwest Atlantic. For example, the major marine feeding area for North American stocks is in the Labrador Sea, where water of 4–8°C occurs seasonally and annually. In spring, Atlantic salmon are also common in the area of the Grand Bank. In the summer, Atlantic salmon move northward into the Davis Strait off west Greenland, where the appropriate water temperatures can again be normally found. Productivity of North American Atlantic salmon may be related to changes in the area covered by 4–8°C water in the northwest Atlantic since the size of this area varies annually.

Additional evidence on the relationship between water temperature and Atlantic salmon abundance is available from the northeast Atlantic. Areas of highest catch rate in the Faroese fishery were closely associated with SSTs above 4°C in 1984. In 1984, the highest catch rates occurred further north, coinciding with the more northerly position of the 4°C isotherm that year (Hjalti i Jakupsstovu, Fiskirannsóknarstovan, Tórshavn, Faroe Islands, personal communication). It was also reported that 1SW Atlantic salmon also moved north and thus became available to the fishery. At west Greenland in 1983 and 1984, lower SSTs were associated with a catch of higher mean sea age, mainly because of a decline in the proportion of 1SW fish (Anonymous 1985a). The present data do not allow the effect of a lowering of the SST on catch rate to be entirely separated from the effect of temperature on marine survival, since the end result, the availability of fish, is the same in both instances.

In summary, the results of this study indicate that (1) the distribution of Atlantic salmon varied seasonally in the northwest Atlantic, (2) growing Atlantic salmon were commonly found in water from 4 to 8°C, (3) much of the variation in abundance of Atlantic salmon at west Greenland may be environmentally induced, (4) Atlantic salmon alter their movements in response to water temperature, and (5) the poor 1983 and 1984 fisheries off west Greenland were related to colder than normal water temperatures.

Acknowledgments

This paper is based largely on information collected during research vessel cruises directed by Art May, Henry Lear, and Wilfred Templeman. We are grateful for their careful work and meticulous record keeping. We also thank Jens Møller Jensen and Sv. Aa. Horsted of Greenland Fisheries and Environmental Research Institute for their encouragement and for providing the abundance estimates for the Greenland fishery. We are also most grateful to David Ellett, Dunstaffnage Marine Research Laboratory, who was kind enough to critically review the hydrography. Constructive criticism of this and an earlier manuscript was provided by Rex Porter, Brian Dempson, Tony Hawkins, and two anonymous reviewers.

References

Allan, I. R. H., and J. A. Ritter. 1977. Salmonid terminology. Journal du Conseil, Conseil International pour l'Exploration de la Mer 37:293–299.

Andersen, K. P., Sv. Aa. Horsted, and J. M. Jensen. 1980. Estimation of some important population parameters based on the analysis of recaptures from the salmon tagging experiment at west Greenland in 1972. Rapports et Procès-Verbaux des Réunions, Conseil International pour l'Exploration de la Mer 176:136–141.

Anonymous. 1981. Report of meeting of north Atlantic salmon working group. Conseil International pour l'Exploration de la Mer, C.M. 1981/M:10, Copenhagen, Denmark.

Anonymous, 1985a. Report of meeting of the working group on north Atlantic salmon. Conseil International pour l'Exploration de la Mer, C.M. 1985/Assess:11, Copenhagen, Denmark.

Anonymous, 1985b. Report of meeting of the working group on north Atlantic salmon. Conseil International pour l'Exploration de la Mer, C.M. 1985/Assess:19, Copenhagen, Denmark.

Anonymous. 1986. Report of the working group on north Atlantic salmon. Conseil International pour l'Exploration de la Mer. C.M. 1985/Assess:17, Copenhagen, Denmark.

Caron, F, 1983. Migration vers L'Atlantique des post-saumoneaux (*Salmo salar*) du Golfe du Saint-Laurent. Naturaliste Canadien (Québec) 110:223–227.

Christensen, O., and W. H. Lear. 1980. Distribution and abundance of salmon at west Greenland. Rapports et Procès-Verbaux des Réunions, Conseil International pour l'Exploration de la Mer 176:22–35.

Conover, W. J. 1980. Practical nonparametric statistics. John Wiley & Sons, New York, New York, USA.

Draper, W. R., and H. Smith. 1966. Applied regression analysis. John Wiley & Sons, New York, New York, USA.

Dunbar, M. J., and D. H. Thomson. 1979. West Greenland salmon and climatic change. Meddelelser om Grønland 202(4):1–19.

Gardner, M. L. G. 1976. A review of factors which may influence the sea-age and maturation of Atlantic salmon, *Salmo salar* L. Journal of Fish Biology 9:289–327.

Gjerde, B. 1984. Response to individual selection for age at sexual maturity in Atlantic salmon. Aquaculture 38:229–240.

Gross, M. R. 1984. Sunfish, salmon, and the evolution of alternative reproductive strategies and tactics in fish. Pages 55–75 *in* G. W. Potts and R. J. Wootton, editors. Fish reproduction: strategies and tactics. Academic Press, London, England.

Harden Jones, F. R. 1968. Fish migration. Edward Arnold, London, England.

Huntsman, A. G. 1938. Sea behaviour in salmon. Salmon and Trout Magazine 90:24–28.

Jakupsstovu, S. H. i., P. T. Jorgensen, R. Mouritsen, and A. Nicolajsen, 1985. Biological data and preliminary observations on the spatial distribution of salmon within the Faroese fishing zone in February 1985. Conseil International pour l'Exploration de la Mer, C.M. 1985/M:30, Copenhagen, Denmark.

Jensen, J. M. 1980a. Recaptures from international tagging experiments at west Greenland. Rapports et Procès-Verbaux des Réunions, Conseil International pour l'Exploration de la Mer 176;122–135.

Jensen, J. M. 1980b. Recaptures of salmon at West Greenland tagged as smolts outside Greenland waters. Rapports et Proces-Verbaux des Reunions,

Conseil International pour l'Exploration de la Mer 176:114–121.

Jensen, J. M., and W. H. Lear. 1980. Atlantic salmon caught in the Irminger Sea and at east Greenland. Journal of Northwest Atlantic Fishery Science 1:55–64.

Lear, W. H. 1976. Migrating Atlantic salmon (*Salmo salar*) caught by otter trawl on the Newfoundland continental shelf. Journal of the Fisheries Research Board of Canada 33:1202–1205.

Leggett, W. C. 1984. Fish migrations in coastal and estuarine environments: a call for new approaches to the study of an old problem. Pages 159–178 in J. D. McCleave, G. P. Arnold, J. J. Dodson, and W. H. Neill, editors. Mechanisms of migration in fishes. Plenum, New York, New York, USA.

Martin, J. H. A., H. D. Dooley, and W. Shearer. 1984. Ideas on the origin and biological consequences of the 1970's salinity anomaly. Conseil International pour l'Exploration de la Mer, C.M. 1984/Gen:18, Copenhagen, Denmark.

Martin, J. H. A., and K. A. Mitchell. 1985. Influence of sea temperature upon the numbers of grilse and multi-sea-winter Atlantic salmon (*Salmo salar*) caught in the vicinity of the River Dee (Aberdeenshire). Canadian Journal of Fisheries and Aquatic Sciences 42:1513–1521.

May, A. W. 1973. Distribution and migrations of salmon in the northwest Atlantic. International Atlantic Salmon Foundation Special Publications Series 4:373–382.

McCleave, J. D., G. P. Arnold, J. J. Dodson, and W. H. Neill, editors. 1984. Mechanisms of migration in fishes. Plenum, New York, New York, USA.

Meister, A. L. 1984. The marine migrations of tagged Atlantic salmon (*Salmo salar* L.) of U.S.A. origin. Conseil International pour l'Exploration de la Mer, C.M. 1984/M:27, Copenhagen, Denmark.

Menzies, W. J. M. 1949. The stock of salmon. Its migrations, preservation and improvement. Edward Arnold, London, England.

Naevdal, G. 1983. Genetic factors in connection with age at maturation. Aquaculture 33:97–106.

Neves, R. J., and L. Depres. 1979. The oceanic migration of American shad, *Alosa sapidissima*, along the Atlantic coast. U.S. National Marine Fisheries Service Fishery Bulletin 77:199–212.

O'Connell, M. F., J. B. Dempson, D. G. Reddin, and E. G. M. Ash. 1985. Status of Atlantic salmon (*Salmo salar* L.) stocks of the Newfoundland Region, 1984. Canadian Atlantic Fisheries Scientific Advisory Committee, Research Document 85/15, Dartmouth, Canada.

Parrish, B. B. 1973. A review of the work of the ICES/ICNAF joint working party on north Atlantic salmon. International Atlantic Salmon Foundation Special Publication Series 4:383–396.

Porter, T. R., and J. A. Ritter. 1984. Possible causes of low abundance of Atlantic salmon in Canada— 1983. Conseil International pour l'Exploration de la Mer, C.M. 1984/M:28, Copenhagen, Denmark.

Pratt, J. D., G. M. Hare, and H. P. Murphy. 1974. Investigation of production and harvest of an Atlantic salmon population, Sand Hill River, Labrador. Fisheries and Marine Services, Resource Development Branch, Technical Report Series NEW/T-74-1, St. John's, Canada.

Reddin, D. G. 1985. Atlantic salmon (*Salmo salar* L.) on and east of the Grand Bank of Newfoundland. Journal of Northwest Atlantic Fishery Science 6:157–164.

Reddin, D. G., and R. F. Burfitt. 1984. A new feeding area for Atlantic salmon (*Salmo salar* L.) to the east of the Newfoundland continental shelf. Conseil International pour l'Exploration de la Mer, C.M. 1984/M:13, Copenhagen, Denmark.

Reddin, D. G., R. F. Burfitt, and W. H. Lear. 1979. The stock composition of Atlantic salmon caught off west Greenland and in the Labrador Sea in 1978 and a comparison to other years. Canadian Atlantic Fisheries Scientific Advisory Committee, Research Document 79/3, Dartmouth, Canada.

Reddin, D. G., and F. A. Day, 1980. 1969–72 Newfoundland and Labrador Atlantic salmon (*Salmo salar*) commercial catch data. Canadian Data Report of Fisheries and Aquatic Sciences 220.

Reddin, D. G., and J. B. Dempson. 1986. Origin of Atlantic salmon (*Salmo salar* L.) caught at sea near Nain, Labrador. Naturaliste Canadien (Québec) 113:211–218.

Rosenørn, J., J. S. Fabricius, E. Buch, and Sv. Aa. Horsted. 1984. Isvintre ved Vestgrønland. Forskining/ tusaut i Grønland 2:2–19.

SAS (Statistical Analysis System). 1982a. SAS user's guide: basics. SAS Institute, Cary, North Carolina. USA.

SAS (Statistical Analysis System). 1982b, SAS user's guide: statistics. SAS Institute, Cary, North Carolina, USA.

Saunders, R. L. In press. Thermal biology of Atlantic salmon. Institute of Freshwater Research Drottningholm Report 76.

Saunders, R. L., E. B. Henderson, B. D. Glebe, and E. J. Loudenslager. 1983. Evidence of a major environmental component in determination of the grilse:larger salmon ratio in Atlantic salmon (*Salmo salar*). Aquaculture 33:107–118.

Scarnecchia, D. L. 1984. Climatic and oceanic variations affecting yield of Icelandic stocks of Atlantic salmon (*Salmo salar*). Canadian Journal of Fisheries and Aquatic Sciences 41:917–935.

Schaffer, W. M., and P. F. Elson. 1975. The adaptive significance of variations in life history among local populations of Atlantic salmon in North America. Ecology 56:577–590.

Smed, J. 1980. Temperature of the waters off southwest and south Greenland during the ICES/ICNAF salmon tagging experiment in 1972. Rapports et Procès-Verbaux des Réunions, Conseil International pour l'Exploration de la Mer 176:18–21.

Stasko, A. B., A. M. Sutterlin, S. A. Rommel, Jr., and P. F. Elson. 1973. Migration-orientation of Atlantic salmon (*Salmo salar* L.). International Atlantic

Salmon Foundation Special Publication Series 4:119–137.

Sutcliffe, W. H., Jr., K. Drinkwater, and B. S. Muir. 1977. Correlations of fish catch and environmental factors in the Gulf of Maine. Journal of the Fisheries Research Board of Canada 34:19–30.

Templeman, W. 1966. Marine resources of Newfoundland. Fisheries Research Board of Canada Bulletin 154.

Templeman, W. 1967. Atlantic salmon from the Labrador Sea and off west Greenland, taken during *A. T. Cameron* cruise, July–August 1965. International Commission for the Northwest Atlantic Fisheries,

Research Bulletin 4:4–40.

Tibbo, S. N., L. R. Day, and W. F. Doucet. 1961. The swordfish (*Xiphias gladius* L.), its life-history and economic importance in the northwest Atlantic. Fisheries Research Board of Canada Bulletin 130.

Westerberg, N. 1982a. Ultrasonic tracking of Atlantic salmon (*Salmo salar* L.)—I. Movements in coastal regions. Institute of Freshwater Research Drottningholm Report 60:81–101.

Westerberg, H. 1982b. Ultrasonic tracking of Atlantic salmon (*Salmo salar* L.)—II. Swimming depth and temperature stratification. Institute of Freshwater Research Drottningholm Report 60:102–120.

American Fisheries Society Symposium 1:276–285, 1987

Review of the Marine Life History of Australasian Temperate Species of *Anguilla*

D. J. JELLYMAN

Fisheries Research Division, Ministry of Agriculture and Fisheries, Post Office Box 8324
Riccarton, Christchurch, New Zealand

Abstract.—Australasia has two temperate freshwater eel species—a longfinned eel *Anguilla dieffenbachii* endemic to New Zealand and a shortfinned eel *A. australis* which is separated into two subspecies according to whether it is found in New Zealand (*A. australis schmidtii*) or Australia (*A. australis australis*). These subspecies are differentiated by very small but consistent differences in number of vertebrae, although the taxonomic validity of this differentiation is open to question. From a review of vertebral counts, electrophoretic studies, species distributions, and features of adult and larval migration, it is tentatively concluded that both shortfinned subspecies are derived from a common gene pool which has partial geographic separation into eastern and western stocks. Differences in vertebral numbers probably reflect temperature differences across the spawning ground. Larvae from both stocks follow different migratory routes to their respective destinations. Spawning grounds of both species are unknown. To demark possible spawning areas, I examined the very limited larval material, ocean hydrology, size of glass eels and their arrival times in fresh water, zonation of glass eel otoliths, the degree of maturity of seaward migrating adults, and the seasonality in *Anguilla* spp. biology. Accordingly, the spawning ground of *A. australis* is proposed as being northeast of Samoa while that of *A. dieffenbachii* may lie east of Tonga. For both species, a larval life averaging 15 months is proposed, although the length of larval life of *A. australis* arriving in Australia seems quite variable.

Worldwide there are 15 species of freshwater eel, genus *Anguilla* (Castle and Williamson 1974), of which five are recognized as temperate species. Australia and New Zealand contain two of these temperate species, the longfinned eel *Anguilla dieffenbachii* Gray and the shortfinned eel *A. australis* Richardson. The longfinned eel is endemic to New Zealand, while the shortfinned eel occurs in New Zealand, southeast Australia and Tasmania, New Caledonia, Norfolk Island, and Lord Howe Island (Figure 1). During a study of Australasian eels, Schmidt (1928) proposed that the Australian and New Zealand populations of shortfinned eel should be classified as distinct subspecies on the basis of small but consistent differences in vertebral numbers. Griffin (1936), in turn, revised the nomenclature to the current usage, i.e., *A. australis australis*, Australian shortfinned eel, and *A. australis schmidtii*, New Zealand shortfinned eel. Given that the difference in mean vertebral number between these two populations is less than one vertebra, the validity of this taxonomic differentiation is open to question.

Although the freshwater biology of both species is reasonably well known (e.g., Jellyman and Todd 1982), the sea life is largely unknown. A single migratory longfinned eel caught at sea has been described (Todd 1973) and only four shortfinned leptocephali have been caught (Jespersen

1942; Castle 1963). Accordingly the sea-life phase of the eels' life history must be deduced from such information as the very limited larval data, oceanic hydrology, sizes and arrival times of glass eels, glass eel meristics and electrophoresis, and the timing and maturity of seaward migrating adults. This paper is primarily concerned with an evaluation of these features.

Marine Life History

Adult Eel Migration

A number of authors (Cairns 1941; Hobbs 1947; Burnet 1969; Todd 1981c) have noted definite sequences in the timing of the seaward migration of maturing adult eels in New Zealand. Migrations of shortfinned eel males and females take place from February to April, those of longfinned eel males during April and those of longfinned eel females from late April to May. Males precede females, and shortfinned eels precede longfinned eels. Fewer data are available for Australian eels but Sloane (1982) recorded migratory shortfinned eels (sex unspecified) from January to March, the latter month being the most important. These data suggest that Australian shortfinned eels commence their oceanic migration up to a month in advance of their New Zealand counterparts.

In both New Zealand and Australia, the extent

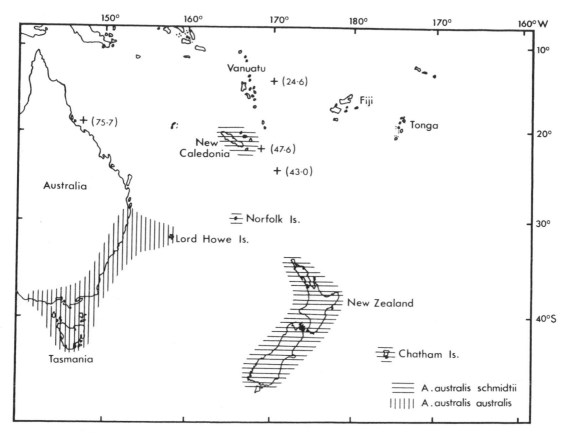

FIGURE 1.—Distribution of shortfinned eels *Anguilla australis australis* and *A. australis schmidtii*. Locations of single *A. australis* larvae reported by Jespersen (1942) and Castle (1963) are also indicated by + signs; their respective lengths are in parentheses.

of gonad development of migratory eels has been ranked by the gonadosomatic ratio (GSR), i.e., weight of gonads × 100/total weight of eel (Table 1). Comparison of Australian and New Zealand shortfinned females shows that the New Zealand eels have the greater GSR values. This may, in part, be because the Australian shortfinned eels were collected well inland. All indexes of gonad development in the longfinned eel (GSR, histological examination, egg diameters) exceed those of the shortfinned eel. Also, in a series of hormone treatment experiments on migratory eels, Todd (1979, 1981a) found that longfinned eels became sexually mature in a shorter time than did shortfinned eels. Based on GSR values, the longfinned eel is the most sexually mature of all the temperature *Anguilla* species at migration (Todd 1981a). Consistent with other *Anguilla* species, females of these two are substantially larger than males (Table 1). Of interest is the much larger size attained by Australian than by New Zealand shortfinned females.

TABLE 1.—Sizes and mean gonadosomatic ratios of migrating shortfinned eels *Anguilla australis* and longfinned eels *A. dieffenbachii* (Todd 1980, 1981b; Sloane 1982).

	Males			Females		
	Length (cm)		Gonadosomatic ratios (N)	Length (cm)		Gonadosomatic ratio (N)
Species	Mean	Range (N)		Mean	Range (N)	
A. australis						
New Zealand	43.2	38.1–59.8 (12,205)	0.27 (39)	62.3	48.3–102.4 (859)	3.49 (153)
Australia				94.5	80.4–110.0 (189)	2.35 (65)
A. dieffenbachii	62.4	48.2–73.5 (374)	1.43 (75)	114.6	73.7–156.0 (198)	8.12 (37)

Larval Life

In contrast to the American and European species of *Anguilla*, few larvae of the southern temperate species have been collected. Jespersen (1942) recorded a single *A. australis* larva and Castle (1963) recorded three. On the basis of proximity to the known range of adults, Castle tentatively assigned the two smaller larvae, 24.6 mm and 47.6 mm, to the New Zealand subspecies and the largest specimen, 75.7 mm, to the Australian subspecies. The latter larva was collected over the continental shelf of northeast Australia; the remaining three larvae came from the central southwest Pacific Ocean (Figure 1).

Despite the paucity of samples, the available specimens do allow some deductions to be made about likely spawning seasons and areas. Assuming similar growth rates to those proposed for larvae of the European eel *A. anguilla* and American eel *A. rostrata* by Harden Jones (1968) and Kleckner and McCleave (1985), the smallest of Castle's larvae was possibly about 3 months old. As the collection date was the end of September, this would give a birthdate at the end of June. The approximate hatching dates of the shortfinned eel larvae can be estimated as follows: 24.6-mm larva, late June; 43-mm larva, late June; 47.6-mm larva, late September. Accordingly, a spawning season of June to September is suggested.

Biology of Glass Eels

Several aspects of glass eel biology could provide further clues to the marine life history. For example, the size of glass eels and the timing of their freshwater invasions over a north-to-south range may indicate the general route of migration. Further, the length of sea life could be deduced from otolith zonation.

The arrival times of New Zealand glass eels in fresh water are August to November for the shortfinned eel and August to September–October for the longfinned eel (Jellyman 1977). Arrival times in the North Island are earlier than in the South Island. Thus, analysis of collection dates of 54 separate samples of glass eels from throughout New Zealand indicates that September is the main month in the North Island and October in the South Island. The season of arrival of shortfinned glass eels in Australia is more prolonged; migrations have been recorded from February to November (Sloane 1984b). Catches in Tasmania peaked in May–June and September–November; low catches for July and August were attributed to cool water temperatures (Sloane 1984b).

Length-frequency distributions of glass eels from various areas within New Zealand have been examined in some detail. Although no account could be taken of annual variations in size, the trend of a seasonal decrease in size (Jellyman 1977) was minimized by selecting only samples from September and October; as shrinkage accompanies pigmentation (Jellyman 1977), only glass eels at similar stages of pigmentation were considered. Analysis of variance indicated that South Island glass eels were significantly larger ($P < 0.05$) than North Island glass eels but differences from east to west coasts within either the North or South Island were not generally significant. Similarly, Sloane (1984b) noted that larger glass eels arrived in Tasmania than in New South Wales, Australia.

Otolith reading is used extensively to determine the freshwater age of *Anguilla* species and both Jellyman (1979) and Sloane (1984a) have validated this technique for *A. australis*. As otoliths from invading glass eels show consistent patterns (e.g., Liew 1974) the question arises whether or not this zonation is seasonal and can be used to calculate the length of sea life. If Matsui (1952) is correct in concluding that otolith formation in the Japanese eel (*A. japonica*) commences at 1.3 cm, then the potential for this record of sea life exists.

Viewed under reflected light, otoliths from glass eels show a transparent outer margin. To be consistent with zone formation in adult eels, this transparent zone would need to represent winter growth and hence be laid down during September–October. As Australian glass eels arrive from February to November (Sloane 1984b) they provide the opportunity to record zone formation over this extended period (summer–spring). However, data from Sloane (1984b) indicate that, for glass eels arriving in April, this transparent zone is already well differentiated and occupies 12% of otolith radius. Accordingly, it is concluded that, for Australasian glass eels at least, otolith zonation is not seasonal and cannot be used to determine the length of larval life.

Vertebral counts are the most important character used to separate otherwise similar species of *Anguilla*. Schmidt (1928) proposed the subspecific designation of New Zealand and Australian shortfinned eels on the basis of mean vertebral counts of 111.64 and 112.68, respectively. A more extensive survey by Ege (1939) confirmed these results and he too considered the difference to represent geographical separation of spawning stocks.

Given that this difference is one of mean values only and that there is a similar range in vertebral number of both "subspecies," it was decided to examine vertebral number of glass eels throughout their arrival season to see whether these differences were constant throughout this period. No shift in mean vertebral number took place throughout the season (Table 2).

The relationship between vertebral number (V) and length (L) of glass eels (both measurements determined from X rays) was also investigated. Although not strongly predictive, a positive linear relationship was established for these factors, for both the total sample in Table 2 (covering 145 d) and large subsamples for which temporal variation was much less, e.g., 10 d. For example, for the total sample,

$$V = 107.56 + 0.073L; \tag{1}$$
$$r = 0.18; P < 0.05 \text{ (df = 1, 686)}.$$

When the date of capture (as Julian date, J) was added, the resulting multiple regression was also significant:

$$V = 105.22 + 0.096L + 0.0037J; \tag{2}$$
$$R = 0.21; P < 0.05 \text{ (df = 2, 686)}.$$

Comparison of the results for equations (1) and (2) indicated that the inclusion of Julian date provided a significant improvement in the relationship of vertebral number and length ($F = 7.0064; P < 0.05$). Thus, for a given length there was a tendency for vertebral number to increase throughout the arrival season. Over the appropriate Julian dates, this seasonal increase for a given length was calculated as 0.42 vertebrae. This contrasts with a predicted seasonal decline of 0.31 vertebrae, calculated from substituting the appropriate mean lengths of early- and late-season glass eels into equation 1.

Electrophoresis

The technique of gel electrophoresis has been widely used to examine genetic variation or integrity in teleosts including that of European and American eels (e.g., De Ligny and Pantelouris (1973). A recent electrophoretic study of *Anguilla* larvae from the Sargasso Sea indicated that there were two distinct and genetically isolated groups of larvae which could be identified meristically as European or American eels (Comparini and Schoth 1982).

To investigate whether there are any biochemical differences between Australian and New Zealand shortfinned eels, muscle tissue of 40 eels from both Tasmania and Wellington (New Zealand) were tested. Results (Table 3) indicate that, for the proteins investigated, there was no evidence of genetic differences between the two eel samples.

Hydrology

Surface circulation in the south Pacific is an

TABLE 2.—Vertebral counts of glass eels of the New Zealand shortfinned eel *Anguilla australis* by month of arrival in fresh water.

Number of vertebrae or statistic	Jul	Aug	Sep	Oct	Nov	Dec	Total
			Number of fish				
115		2		1	1		4
114		3	7	5	4		19
113	1	14	25	29	31	1	101
112	8	25	64	59	76	3	235
111	5	29	47	56	60	5	202
110	3	10	19	21	17		70
109		1	3	1	3		8
108		1					1
Total	17	85	165	172	192	9	640
			Number of vertebrae				
Mean	111.59	111.65	111.67	111.66	111.68	111.56	111.66
SD	0.84	1.22	1.06	1.04	1.00	0.68	1.05

TABLE 3.—Results of a preliminary electrophoretic survey of some proteins in samples of shortfinned eels *Anguilla australis* from Wellington, New Zealand, and Tasmania. Numbers in parentheses are international reference numbers (IUBNC 1984).

Protein	Result
Esterase (3.1.1)	One monomorphic locus fixed for same allele in New Zealand and Tasmania
Glucose-6-phosphate isomerase (5.3.1.9)	One polymorphic locus with shared alleles in New Zealand and Tasmania
Glycerol-3-phosphate dehydrogenase (1.1.1.8)	One locus with streaky bands, similar in New Zealand and Tasmania
L-Lactate dehydrogenase (1.1.1.27)	Two monomorphic loci fixed for the same alleles in New Zealand and Tasmania
Malate dehydrogenase (1.1.1.37)	One polymorphic locus with shared alleles in New Zealand and Tasmania and one monomorphic locus fixed for same alleles in New Zealand and Tasmania
Phosphoglucomutase (5.4.2.2)	One polymorphic locus with shared alleles in New Zealand and Tasmania
Phosphogluconate dehydrogenase (1.1.1.44)	One monomorphic locus fixed for the same allele in New Zealand and Tasmania
Protein (not applicable)	One monomorphic locus fixed for the same allele in New Zealand and Tasmania

anticlockwise wind-driven gyre. The main features are the west-flowing South Equatorial Current, the East Australian Current (a western boundary current), and an eastward zonal flow north of the Subtropical Convergence (Figure 2). Current patterns within this general system are complicated by a complex series of bathymetric features including ridges, rises, land masses, shelves, and islands. In addition, current strength is influenced by the strength of equatorial westerly winds. Overall, surface circulation is characterized by a high degree of seasonal and annual variation (T. Murray, Fisheries Research Division, Wellington, personal communication).

If, like those of the three northern hemisphere temperate eel species, breeding areas of Australasian temperate eels are in the vicinity of the tropics, then the currents of interest are those which convey subtropical water to New Zealand and Australia. Most of the subtropical water around New Zealand is derived from the East Australian Current (Heath 1985). With passage of this current south along the Australian coast, an

eastward flow departs from it in the vicinity of latitude 31°S (Stanton 1981). The position of this zonal jet flow, which transports water across the Tasman Sea to east of New Zealand, is indicated by the Tasman Front (Heath 1985). The Tasman Current is a weak eastward zonal flow about as broad as the latitudinal extent of New Zealand. It intensifies in higher latitudes, and flow along the west coast of New Zealand is southwards south of about 44°S and northwards to the north of this latitude. Along the east coast of New Zealand, north- and south-moving flows converge to the north of the Subtropical Convergence and contribute to the eastward flow of the south Pacific gyre.

There is thought to be a further entry of subtropical water to the northeast of New Zealand (Heath 1985) from a southerly flow of a branch of the South Equatorial Current (Tchernia 1980). Part of the South Equatorial Current turns southwest between 140 and 180°W and, at a latitude of 20–30°S, this flow divides with one branch going due west to the Coral Sea and the other branch

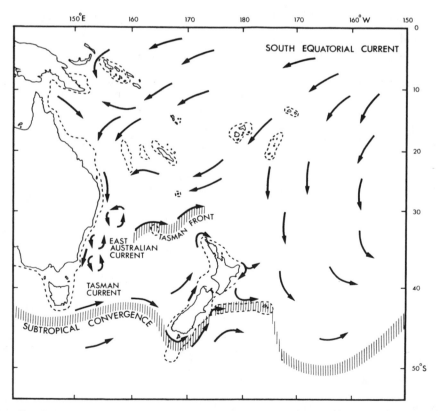

FIGURE 2.—Circulation patterns in the southwestern Pacific Ocean and Tasman Sea (after Tchernia 1980; Heath 1985). The dotted lines are 500-m isobaths.

flowing south to the east of New Zealand (Figure 2). With passage towards New Zealand, flow in this south-moving branch weakens and broadens.

Seasonality of Life History Events

As indicated by Tesch (1977), interspecific comparisons of seasonal events among the various species of temperate *Anguilla* are difficult because of the large intraspecific differences. Although migration times of adults of all five temperate species is late summer–autumn, the arrival times of glass eels is much more variable. Presumably, the latter variability reflects the proximities of the spawning grounds.

The Atlantic species of *Anguilla* spawn during late winter and spring of the northern hemisphere, i.e., February to April. Spawning season of the Japanese eel is unknown, although Moriarty (1978) mentioned collection of "small larvae" in February. If a similar seasonality of spawning is assumed for Australasian species, this would give August to October as the appropriate months. This is a little later than the June–September season suggested earlier.

Discussion

The discussion focuses on three questions. First, do the data suggest separate spawning areas for Australian and New Zealand shortfinned eels? Second, where are the likely breeding areas of shortfinned and longfinned eels? Third, what can be deduced about the length of marine life?

Discreetness of Shortfinned Eel Spawning Grounds

Although limited, the electrophoretic data do not suggest separate gene pools for Australian and New Zealand shortfinned eels. If there is some geographic separation of spawning grounds of both "subspecies," as suggested by Schmidt (1928), this separation may be incomplete and some genetic interchange may occur. Overlapping migration periods for adult shortfinned eels from Australia and New Zealand preclude the possibility of temporal separation of spawning.

Vertebral counts in the present study and those of Sloane (1984b) are in good agreement with previously published data of Schmidt (1928) and Ege (1939). Although mean differences between the Australian and New Zealand shortfinned eels are small (e.g., 0.94 vertebra: Ege 1939), the differences are statistically significant ($P < 0.05$). Further, the differences are geographically and seasonally constant. Thus, shortfinned eels popu-

lating land masses in the western Tasman Sea (Australia, Tasmania, Lord Howe Island) have average vertebral counts greater than shortfinned eels of the eastern Tasman Sea (New Caledonia, Norfolk Island, New Zealand, Chatham Islands). This geographic consistency of vertebral number suggests that separate larval migratory routes to the eastern and western Tasman Sea are likely. Hence some spatial separation of breeding areas is implied.

The seasonal consistency of vertebral counts for both eastern and western stocks is a further indicator that distinct and separate larval migratory routes are involved. There is no evidence of samples with mean vertebral number intermediate between the two stocks. Intermediates would be expected if considerable mixing of stocks took place either on the spawning grounds or during subsequent larval migration.

Both the present study and that of Boetius (1976) revealed a positive linear relationship between vertebral number and total length for glass eels of *A. australis* and *A. anguilla*, respectively, the largest glass eels having the most vertebrae and vice versa. This relationship, pleomerism, is widespread among fishes (Lindsey 1975) but, for both the above studies, it becomes necessary to explain why no decrease in mean vertebral number accompanies the observed decrease in mean length of glass eels throughout the season of arrival (Jellyman 1977).

For European eels, Harding (1985) proposed that glass eels arriving at a particular location comprise mixtures of distinct groups. Within each group, length is independent of vertebral number; the proportions of the groups vary seasonally such that, over the arrival season, vertebral number remains relatively constant but mean length changes. In the present study, a somewhat simpler answer is suggested. That is, the tendency for vertebral number to decrease with the seasonal decrease in size of glass eels is offset by a trend for vertebral number for a glass eel of given length to increase slightly throughout the arrival season. As temperature changes are known to affect vertebral number in fish (e.g., Taning 1952), this latter trend could be due to changing water temperatures during the spawning season. The net effect is for the two trends to cancel each other out, resulting in relatively constant mean vertebral number throughout the glass eel arrival season.

From the above review of vertebral count data and preliminary electrophoretic examination, it is suggested that a single breeding population of shortfinned eels exists but that there is a strong likelihood of partial geographic separation into eastern and western stocks. It is unlikely that this spatial separation is complete as there is a biochemical uniformity between Tasmanian (western) and New Zealand (eastern) stocks. Probably, both spawning stocks experience slightly different hydrological conditions at their respective spawning grounds with the result that larvae hatching in either area have slight differences in average myomere counts. These phenotypically different larvae are then conveyed to the eastern and western Tasman Sea by different current patterns.

Location of Spawning Grounds

The spawning grounds of the European and American eels were discovered through the location of successively smaller larvae. The virtual lack of larval material means this method cannot yet be used to delimit spawning areas of Australasian eels. However, some indication of the general location of the spawning grounds of the shortfinned eel may be possible from consideration of the smallest larva described by Castle (1963) and from surface hydrology.

It was previously suggested that the 24.6-mm larva was approximately 3 months old. Surface hydrology of the southwest Pacific (Figure 2) indicates that it is likely that this larva and the two larvae from the vicinity of New Caledonia would have arrived from the northeast. Given the high variability in surface circulation in the southwest Pacific, it is difficult to calculate how far larvae could drift in 3 months.

Donguy and Henin (1975) calculated a maximum mean velocity of 20 cm/s for the South Equatorial Current between the Solomon Islands and New Caledonia, but also suggested that velocities of twice this were possible. The average speed of the South Equatorial Current is given by Tchernia (1980) as 50–60 cm/s although this will decrease westward. Based on these data, a passively transported larva could cover 1,600–4,600 km in 3 months. When it is also considered that the distributions of 25–30-mm larvae of the European eel (Tesch 1978) and the American eel (Kleckner and McCleave 1985) cover areas of approximately 2,000 km in latitude and 3,500 km in longitude, further speculation on the origin of the smallest larva is of little use.

For both species of Atlantic eel, it has been shown that the further the arrival point of glass eels is from the breeding area, the later the arrival

time and the larger the glass eels (e.g., Vladykov 1966). From analysis of the average length and arrival times of Australian and New Zealand glass eels, it is concluded that arrival is from the north. There is no evidence to support the suggestion of Cairns (1941) that arrival of glass eels in New Zealand is from the west. The record of Ege (1939) for newly pigmented glass eels occurring in New Caledonia from April to July conforms more closely to the New Zealand arrival season (July to November) than to the Australian (March to November). Again, this suggests a reasonably direct route to New Zealand.

Examination of currents provides two alternative routes for larvae originating north of 10°S to reach the western Tasman Sea via the South Equatorial Current: a northern route between the Solomon Islands and Vanuatu and a more southerly one between New Caledonia and the Tasman Front (Figures 1, 2). Although not conclusive, the data suggest that the northern route is the more likely. For instance, New Caledonia and Norfolk Island are populated by the eastern Tasman Sea stock of shortfinned eels and not by the western stock as would be anticipated if the latter used the route south of New Caledonia. Also, the location of the largest of the larvae described by Castle (1963) is consistent with arrival of larvae in the Coral Sea from the north.

If the above route is correct, the spawning grounds of both stocks of shortfinned eel must lie somewhere to the east of where the westward branch of the South Equatorial Current divides from the south moving branch. Should the overall spawning area lie across the area of divergence of these currents, then larvae hatching in the northern part of the spawning ground would tend to be transported to the western Tasman Sea while those hatching in the southern part would tend to be transported to the central Tasman Sea or to the east of New Zealand. This would place the spawning area of shortfinned eels in the vicinity of 150–170°W and 5–15°S. If correct, this would be closer to the equator than spawning areas of the Atlantic species and would lie to the north of Castle's (1963) proposed area between Fiji and Tahiti, which was supported by Tesch (1977). Schmidt (1928) placed the breeding area the furthest west of all researchers, presuming that Australian shortfinned eels breed on the western side of the New Caledonian submarine ridge and New Zealand eels on the eastern side.

Dispersal of larvae in the open ocean is considered to be by passive transport on near-surface currents. Logically, transport of larval short-finned eels to the western Tasman Sea is via the East Australian Current, a brief period of active swimming being required to detrain from this current. It is of interest that glass eel arrival in Australian waters is over an extended period and up to 4 months before the earliest arrivals in New Zealand. Tesch (1977) assumed that the prolonged period indicated the lack of a distinct seasonal spawning. This is not supported from knowledge of the migration of adults, which takes place on a seasonal basis. A further possibility is that spawning is seasonal but transport time is highly variable. As transport to the western Tasman Sea is via a stronger and more directed current system than is transport to New Zealand, arrival times of glass eels in Australia and Tasmania would be predicted to precede arrival times in New Zealand, even though the distance to the spawning ground is greater. Glass eels arriving in Tasmania from September to November may have had their migration time lengthened by being caught in the gyres which characterize the southern extension of the East Australian Current. Lord Howe Island is probably populated by larvae transported by these gyres.

It is suggested that larvae arriving in the eastern Tasman Sea are transported on the southwest flowing portion of the South Equatorial Current. This current in turn subdivides, transporting some of these larvae west to New Caledonia and Norfolk Island while the remaining larvae continue south to arrive in the offshore waters northeast of New Zealand. Active swimming would be required to detrain from this current in a similar manner to that proposed by Kleckner and McCleave (1985) for the exit of American eel larvae from the Gulf Stream.

As detrainment from this current may take place several hundred kilometres off the continental shelf of New Zealand, the question arises, how are the larvae aware of the proximity and direction of land? Several suggestions may be advanced to answer this. For example, the larvae may encounter "inshore" water which leaves the New Zealand continental shelf to the northeast and east. Such water would almost certainly contain specific odours derived from fresh water which could act as olfactory cues similar to the way that tidal waters may contain odours attractive to migrating glass eels (Creutzberg 1961). Alternatively, some endogenous sense of destination and the ability to "navigate" may be involved. However, although there is evidence that

Pacific salmon are able to "navigate" to their natal waters by routes they have not travelled as juveniles (e.g., Healey and Groot 1987, this volume) there is, as yet, no evidence of inherited memory in fish.

As no larvae of the longfinned eel have been recorded, any indication of likely spawning areas must be deduced from the species' distribution and freshwater life history. Tesch (1977) considered that the freshwater distribution of longfinned eels implied that they have a longer journey to the spawning ground than do shortfinned eels. This is not supported by either the time of adult migration or the relative maturity of migratory eels, and Todd (1981b) suggested the reverse, i.e., the longfinned eels spawn closer to New Zealand than do shortfinned eels. As longfinned glass eels are larger than shortfinned glass eels, Tesch (1977) considered this as further evidence of a more distant spawning ground. Alternatively this size difference could reflect a genotypic difference (as adult longfinned eels are much larger than shortfinned eels: Table 1) or indicate a longer larval life resulting from earlier spawning at a closer site but with a slower migration of larvae.

As longfinned eels do not occur at New Caledonia or Norfolk Island, it is possible that they share the same larval life route as shortfinned larvae destined for New Zealand. If the spawning ground of longfinned eels has a latitude similar to that of Atlantic eels, then a location east of Tonga is suggested.

Length of Marine Life

Finally, some deductions can be made on the length of the marine phase of the life history of both eel species. For shortfinned eels, the theoretical minimum time available for migratory adults to attain sexual maturity and reach the spawning grounds is 4 months for eels migrating in February and spawning in June. Alternatively, spawning could take place the year following migration, 16 months after the fish leave fresh water. In a direct line, the distance from southern Australia or central New Zealand to the suggested spawning area is about 5,000 km. To cover this distance within 4 months would require an average swimming speed of 41 km/d. European silver eels have been found to swim at a speed equivalent to 44 km/d (Tesch 1978). At this rate, it is feasible for shortfinned eels to reach an area northeast of Samoa within 4 months.

With hormone treatment, migratory shortfinned and longfinned eels held at 20°C can achieve sexual maturity within 3–6 weeks and 3–4 weeks, respectively (Todd 1979, 1981a). It is not known how these laboratory data compare with rates of development in the wild, but they do indicate that it is possible for eels to reach maturity within the 4-month minimum time period. Accordingly, it is proposed that shortfinned eels spawn in the same year they migrate from fresh water.

It then remains to determine whether larvae hatching during June to September in any year arrive in Australia and New Zealand as glass eels the following year, or the year after that. In the case of a September-to-November arrival period for glass eels arriving in New Zealand, the minimum and maximum lengths of larval life (from a June-to-September spawning the previous year) would be 11–18 months. For passive movement by currents during an entire direct return journey of 5,000 km, an average migration speed of 10.6–17.3 cm/s is indicated. These speeds are less than the current speeds of 20 cm/s measured by Donguy and Henin (1975) north of New Caledonia and considerably less than the 50–60 cm/s given by Tchernia (1980) as the speed of the South Equatorial Current. It seems reasonable, then, to assume that glass eels arrive in New Zealand the year following spawning.

For Australian shortfinned glass eels, the most rapid migration rate would be required by the small numbers of glass eels arriving in Tasmania in March of any year. A July-to-September spawning period allows a maximum larval life of 9 months, which, in turn, implies a growth rate equivalent to that calculated for American eel larvae (Kleckner and McCleave 1985). The distance from Tasmania to the suggested spawning area via the route suggested is approximately 7,000 km. To cover this distance in 9 months would require an average migration speed of 29.6 cm/s, which is feasible given that velocities of the East Australian Current average 30 cm/s (Bramwell 1977) and have been recorded at 52 cm/s (Wyrtki 1962).

Little can be said about the larval life of the longfinned eel. It is assumed that, like the shortfinned eel, adults spawn the same year they migrate and that the progeny of spawning in a given year arrive in New Zealand the following year. As adult longfinned eels migrate later and at a more mature stage than do adult shortfinned eels, the spawning grounds may be closer. A winter spawning is assumed, which would give a length of larval life equivalent to that of shortfinned eels migrating to New Zealand.

Acknowledgments

I wish to thank Peter Smith, Fisheries Research Division, Wellington, for providing the electrophoretic data, and Ken Minns (visiting National Research Advisory Council senior fellow from Department of Fisheries and Oceans, Toronto) for computer assistance. Helpful comments on the manuscript were received from Robert McDowall and Peter Todd, Fisheries Research Division, Christchurch, and Peter Castle, Victoria University, Wellington. In particular, I wish to gratefully acknowledge the financial assistance of the American Fisheries Society's Northeastern Division, which enabled me to attend the symposium on Common Strategies of Anadromous and Catadromous Fishes.

References

Boetius, J. 1976. Elvers, *Anguilla anguilla* and *Anguilla rostrata* from two Danish localities. Size, body weight, developmental stage and number of vertebrae related to time of ascent. Meddelelser fra Danmarks Fiskeri-og Havundersogelser 7:199–220.

Bramwell, M., editor. 1977. The atlas of the oceans. Mitchell Beazley, London, England.

Burnet, A. M. R. 1969. Migrating eels in a Canterbury river, New Zealand. New Zealand Journal of Marine and Freshwater Research 3:230–244.

Cairns, D. 1941. Life-history of the two species of New Zealand fresh-water eel. Part I—taxonomy, age and growth, migration and distribution. New Zealand Journal of Science and Technology 23:53–72.

Castle, P. H. J. 1963. Anguillid leptocephali in the southwest Pacific. Zoology Publications from Victoria University of Wellington 33.

Castle, P. H. J., and G. R. Williamson. 1974. On the validity of the freshwater eel species *Anguilla ancestralis* Ege, from Celebes. Copeia 1974:569–570.

Comparini, A., and M. Schoth. 1982. Comparison of electrophoretic and meristic characters of 0-group eel larvae from the Sargasso Sea. Helgoländer Meeresuntersuchungen 35:289–299.

Creutzberg, F. 1961. On the orientation of migrating elvers (*Anguilla vulgaris* Turt.) in a tidal area. Netherlands Journal of Sea Research 1:257–338.

De Ligny, W., and E. M. Panterlouris. 1973. Origin of the European eel. Nature (London) 246:518–519.

Donguy, J. R., and C. Henin. 1975. Evidence of the south tropical counter-current in the Coral Sea. Australian Journal of Marine and Freshwater Research 26:405–409.

Ege, J. 1939. A revision of the genus *Anguilla* Shaw. A systematic, phylogenetic and geographical study. Dana-Report Carlsberg Foundation 16.

Griffin, L. T. 1936. Revision of the eels of New Zealand. Transactions of the Royal Society of New Zealand 66:12–26.

Harden Jones, F. R. 1968. Fish migration. Edward Arnold, London, England.

Harding, E. F. 1985. On the homogeneity of the European eel population (*Anguilla anguilla*). Dana 4:49–66.

Healey, M. C., and C. Groot. 1987. Marine migration and orientation of ocean-type chinook and sockeye salmon. American Fisheries Symposium 1:298–312.

Heath, R. A. 1985. A review of the physical oceanography of the seas around New Zealand—1982. New Zealand Journal of Marine and Freshwater Research 19:79–124.

Hobbs, D. 1947. Migrating eels in Lake Ellesmere. Transactions of the Royal Society of New Zealand 77:228–232.

IUBNC (International Union of Biochemistry, Nomenclature Committee). 1984. Enzyme nomenclature 1984. Academic Press, London, England.

Jellyman, D. J. 1977. Invasion of a New Zealand freshwater stream by glass-eels of two *Anguilla* spp. New Zealand Journal of Marine and Freshwater Research 11:193–209.

Jellyman, D. J. 1979. Scale development and age determination in New Zealand freshwater eels (*Anguilla* spp.). New Zealand Journal of Marine and Freshwater Research 13:23–30.

Jellyman, D. J., and P. R. Todd. 1982. New Zealand freshwater eels: their biology and fishery. New Zealand Ministry of Agriculture and Fisheries, Fisheries Research Division Information Leaflet 11, Christchurch, New Zealand.

Jespersen, P. 1942. Indo-Pacific leptocephalids of the genus *Anguilla*. Dana-Report Carlsberg Foundation 22.

Kleckner, R. C., and J. D. McCleave. 1985. Spatial and temporal distribution of American eel larvae in relation to north Atlantic Ocean current systems. Dana 4:67–92.

Liew, P. K. L. 1974. Age determination of American eels based on the structure of their otoliths. Pages 124–136 *in* T. B. Bagenal, editor. Proceedings of an international symposium on the ageing of fish. FAO (Food and Agriculture Organization of the United Nations), European Inland Fisheries Advisory Commission, Rome, Italy.

Lindsey, C. C. 1975. Pleomerism, the widespread tendency among related fish species for vertebral number to be correlated with maximum body length. Journal of the Fisheries Research Board of Canada 32:2453–2469.

Matsui, I. 1952. Studies on the morphology, ecology and pond-culture of the Japanese eel (*Anguilla japonica* Temminck and Schlegel). Journal of the Shimonoseki College of Fisheries 2(2):1–245.

Moriarty, C. 1978. Eels. A natural and unnatural history. David and Charles, London, England.

Schmidt, J. 1928. The freshwater eels of Australia with some remarks on the short-finned species of *Anguilla*. Records of the Australian Museum 16:179–210.

Sloane, R. D. 1982. A biological basis for the Tasmanian freshwater eel fishery. Doctoral dissertation. University of Tasmania, Hobart, Australia.

Sloane, R. D. 1984a. Distribution, abundance, growth and food of freshwater eels (*Anguilla* spp.) in the Douglas River, Tasmania. Australian Journal of Marine and Freshwater Research 35:325–339.

Sloane, R. D. 1984b. Invasion and upstream migration by glass-eels of *Anguilla australis australis* Richardson and *A. reinhardtii* Steindachner in Tasmanian freshwater streams. Australian Journal of Marine and Freshwater Research 35:47–59.

Stanton, B. R. 1981. An oceanographic survey of the Tasman Front. New Zealand Journal of Marine and Freshwater Research 15:289–297.

Taning, A. V. 1952. Experimental study of meristic characters in fishes. Biological Reviews of the Cambridge Philosophical Society 27:169–193.

Tchernia, P. 1980. Descriptive regional oceanography. Translated by C. D. Desmore. Pergamon Marine Series 3. Pergamon, Oxford, England.

Tesch, F.-W. 1977. The eel. Biology and management of anguillid eels. Chapman and Hall, London, England.

Tesch, F.-W. 1978. Telemetric observations on the spawning migration of the eel (*Anguilla anguilla*) west of the European continental shelf. Environmental Biology of Fishes 3:203–209.

Todd, P. R. 1973. First record of the freshwater eel *Anguilla dieffenbachii* Gray to be caught at sea. Journal of Fish Biology 5:231–232.

Todd, P. R. 1979. The hormone-induced maturation of New Zealand freshwater eels. Rapports et Procès-Verbaux des Réunions, Conseil Permanent International pour l'Exploration de la Mer 174:91–97.

Todd, P. R. 1980. Size and age of migrating New Zealand freshwater eels (*Anguilla* spp.). New Zealand Journal of Marine and Freshwater Research 14:283–293.

Todd, P. R. 1981a. Hormone-induced maturation in male New Zealand freshwater eels (*Anguilla* spp.). New Zealand Journal of Marine and Freshwater Research 15:237–246.

Todd, P. R. 1981b. Morphometric changes, gonad histology, and fecundity estimates in migrating New Zealand freshwater eels (*Anguilla* spp.). New Zealand Journal of Marine and Freshwater Research 15:155–170.

Todd, P. R. 1981c. Timing and periodicity of migrating New Zealand freshwater eels (*Anguilla* spp.). New Zealand Journal of Marine and Freshwater Research 15:225–235.

Vladykov, V. D. 1966. Remarks on the American eel (*Anguilla rostrata* Le Sueur). Sizes of elvers entering streams; the relative abundance of adult males and females; and present economic importance of eels in North America. Internationale Vereinigung für Theoretische und Angewandte Limnologie Verhandlungen 16:1007–1017.

Wyrtki, K. 1962. Geopotential topographies and associated circulation in the western south Pacific Ocean. Australian Journal of Marine and Freshwater Research 13:89–105.

American Fisheries Society Symposium 1:286–297, 1987

Reproductive Sympatry of American and European Eels and Implications for Migration and Taxonomy

JAMES D. MCCLEAVE, ROBERT C. KLECKNER,[1] AND MARTIN CASTONGUAY[2]

Department of Zoology and Migratory Fish Research Institute, University of Maine
Orono, Maine 04469, USA

Abstract.—Analysis of distribution records of leptocephali 10 mm or less long obtained from Johannes Schmidt's classical studies, from other historical sources, and from recent cruises in the Sargasso Sea leads us to conclude that (1) European eels *Anguilla anguilla* spawn in a narrow latitudinal range from 23 to 30°N and from about 48 to 74°W, and (2) American eels *A. rostrata* spawn in a greatly overlapping area from 19.5 to 29.0°N and from 52 to 79°W. Small European leptocephali were caught from late February until mid-July and small American leptocephali from mid-February through April. Small leptocephali (7 mm or less long) of both species have been caught in the same net tow between late February and mid-April over about two-thirds of the area of spatial overlap. This indicates substantial spatiotemporal sympatry of spawning. Collections of small leptocephali of both species along north–south transects across the area of the North Atlantic Subtropical Convergence, a frontal zone with steep horizontal gradients of temperature and with limited horizontal mixing, show that spawning of both species occurs in and to the south of the frontal zone. Some feature of the frontal zone thus may serve as a common cue for adults of both species to cease migrating and to spawn. Most larvae of both species are not separated on a north–south axis as previously suggested. Rather, they are introduced into a similar and complex oceanographic regime; in this context, distribution of the two species on two separate continents becomes problematic. The absence of small specimens with numbers of myomeres intermediate between those typical of European and of American forms in collections from regions of spatiotemporal overlap in spawning is indicative of (1) reproductive isolation between the two forms and (2) genetic rather than environmental determination of myomere numbers in the two forms.

In the 25 years following his 1904 discovery of a leptocephalus of the European eel *Anguilla anguilla* west of the Faroes, the Danish biologist Johannes Schmidt accumulated records of more than 16,000 European eel leptocephali and about 2,400 American eel *A. rostrata* leptocephali, although many records were never actually used by him (Boëtius and Harding 1985a, 1985b). From the distribution of the smallest leptocephali collected prior to mid-1921 Schmidt (1922) concluded that the European eel spawns during spring in, and only in, the Sargasso Sea in the southwestern North Atlantic Ocean. He also concluded that the American eel spawns earlier in an overlapping area to the west. However, Schmidt's (1922) conclusions were based upon only 148 European leptocephali 10 mm or less long and only 21 American leptocephali 10 mm or less long

(Boëtius and Harding 1985a, 1985b), of which 18 of the latter were from one tow. Despite the limitations of his data, Schmidt (1922, 1923, 1925) stated his case so strongly that his ideas were largely accepted for 35 years, and little additional research was conducted on oceanic migration and spawning.

Researchers of fish migration were finally jolted from their complacency when Tucker (1959) proposed that (1) European eels do not succeed in returning to the Sargasso Sea to spawn but perish without reproducing; (2) American and European eels are not distinct species but merely ecophenotypes whose distinguishing characteristics are environmentally determined; and (3) the European eel populations are maintained entirely by reproduction of the American eel population. While Tucker's (1959) proposal generated a lively correspondence in the pages of *Nature* (D'Ancona and Tucker 1959; Jones and Tucker 1959; Deelder and Tucker 1960) and elsewhere (Bruun 1963) and stimulated considerable genetic research (see Williams and Koehn 1984), his conclusions have generally been rejected though not disproved. The value of Tucker's contribution

---

[1]Present address: Department of Epidemiology, University of North Carolina, Chapel Hill, North Carolina 27514, USA.

[2]Present address: Pêches et Océans Canada, Institute Maurice-Lamontagne, C.P. 1000, Mont Joli, Québec G5H 3Z4, Canada.

was his recognition that Schmidt's conclusions were based upon scanty and circumstantial data and, as recently stated (Williams and Koehn 1984), Tucker's ". . . criticisms of orthodox views need more attention than they have received."

Recent research based upon collections of leptocephali from the Sargasso Sea is allowing us to reconsider carefully Schmidt's conclusions and Tucker's proposal. This research includes a thorough but gentle review of the published and unpublished material collected by Schmidt (Boëtius and Harding 1985a; Harding 1985), examination of other historical material (Kleckner and McCleave 1985), and new field research by West German (Schoth and Tesch 1982, 1984; Tesch 1982b) and American (Kleckner et al. 1983; Wippelhauser et al. 1985) groups.

Our objectives in this paper are (1) to define the spawning areas of the American and European eels in space and time by assessing all the data available to date, and especially to assess the degree of sympatry and its implications for the migrations of leptocephali; (2) to present evidence that both species spawn in association with a persistent frontal zone in the Sargasso Sea, and especially to stress that this association contributes to the sympatry and inevitably has implications for migration of the adults; and (3) to consider the taxonomic status of the two "species" in an ecological context.

Spawning Regions and Seasons

Here we present evidence that spawnings of the American eel and European eel are partly sympatric and occur in the Sargasso Sea in winter and spring as Schmidt (1922) himself concluded. Our evidence, like Schmidt's, is circumstantial and is based upon the distribution of small leptocephali in time and space. Despite considerable effort (Post and Tesch 1982), adult eels have never been captured in the Sargasso Sea. Eel eggs have never been identified in plankton samples from the Sargasso Sea.

We have assembled records of 1,635 European leptocephali and of 728 American leptocephali 10 mm or less total length from various sources (Table 1). Nearly all of these small larvae were captured in Isaacs Kidd midwater trawls, multiple opening and closing nets (MOCNESS), opening–closing 2-m ring nets or 1- to 2-m open ring nets specifically fished to capture *Anguilla* leptocephali. Mesh size was generally 0.85 mm or less during investigations in the area and time of spawning and generally 2.0 mm or less in other investigations. We make the explicit assumption that spawning may occur anywhere within the limits of distribution of leptocephali 10 mm or less total length, but spawning may be more or less widespread (see below).

Spawning of European eels apparently occurs in a narrow latitudinal range from about 23 to 30°N but across a wide longitudinal range from about 48 to 74°W (Figure 1). Schmidt's (1922) distribution of small European leptocephali was extended from about 67 to 70.5°W by Schoth and Tesch (1982) and to about 74°W by us (unpub-

TABLE 1.—Sources of data used to determine distribution of leptocephali, 10 mm or less total length, of European and American eels.

Source number	Number of leptocephali				Source	Reference
	European eel		American eel			
	≤7 mm	>7 to 10 mm	≤7 mm	>7 to 10 mm		
1	29	119	2	19	Schmidt's material utilized in his classic 1922 paper	Boëtius and Harding (1985a, 1985b)
2	74	284	0	1	Later Schmidt material	Boëtius and Harding (1985b)
3	32	102	0	0	Other Danish historical material	Boëtius and Harding (1985b)
4	0	0	1	3	North American historical material	Kleckner et al. (1985); Kleckner and McCleave (1985)
5	103	320	37	144	Biologische Anstalt Helgoland, 1979 cruise	Tesch (1982b); Schoth and Tesch (1982)
6	2	2	137	131	University of Maine, 1981 cruise	Kleckner et al. (1985); Wippelhauser et al. (1985)
7	231	337	99	154	University of Maine, 1983 and 1985 cruises	Unpublished data of present authors
Total	471	1,164	276	452		

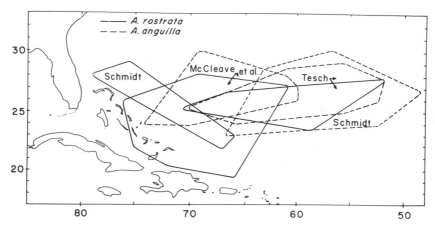

FIGURE 1.—Distribution of leptocephali, 10 mm or less total length, of the American eel *Anguilla rostrata* and the European eel *A. anguilla*. (Schmidt = sources 1 and 2 of Table 1; Tesch = source 5 of Table 1; McCleave et al. = sources 4, 6, 7 of Table 1.)

lished data). No extensions to the northerly, southerly or easterly limits defined by Schmidt (1922) have been made; however, lack of sampling effort has precluded easterly extensions.

American eel spawning occurs in a slightly broader latitudinal range, but with a similar northern limit: that is, from about 19.5°N to about 29°N. It, too, occurs across a wide longitudinal range (Figure 1). Schmidt (1922) did not illustrate the distribution of American leptocephali 10 mm or less long, but the 21 specimens in his collections were caught to the west of the locations of capture of most of his small European leptocephali (Figure 1). Our collections (Wippelhauser et al. 1985; present authors, unpublished data) and those of Schoth and Tesch (1982) expand the suggested area for spawning substantially, both latitudinally and longitudinally. Schoth and Tesch (1982) caught small American leptocephali as far east as they caught small European leptocephali (about 52°W).

Overlap in vertical distribution of small leptocephali of the two species is also virtually complete (Castonguay and McCleave 1987). No significant differences were observed in the vertical distribution of the two species during day or night at any time of year. Larvae less than 5 mm long were found between 50 and 350 m deep during both day and night. There is no evidence that they perform a diel vertical migration. Larvae 5–10 mm long were found mostly between 100 and 150 m during day and between 50 and 100 m during night, suggesting they vertically migrate. Castonguay and McCleave (1987) hypothesize that this shallow distribution of larvae less than 10 mm

long is indicative that spawning occurs in near-surface waters.

European leptocephali 10 mm or less long have been caught primarily in March and April both by Schmidt (Boëtius and Harding 1985b) and by recent workers (Schoth and Tesch 1982; present authors, unpublished data). We did capture four specimens on 27 February (Kleckner et al. 1985; Wippelhauser et al. 1985). Schmidt also captured small leptocephali in May, June, and as late as 20 July (Boëtius and Harding 1985b).

American leptocephali 10 mm or less long have been caught from mid-February (Kleckner et al. 1985; Wippelhauser et al. 1985) through April (Schoth and Tesch 1982; Boëtius and Harding 1985b; present authors, unpublished data).

Leptocephali 7 mm or less long of both species have also been captured in the same net tow in 34 instances, all on recent cruises (sources 5–7 of Table 1). These collections involve 113 American leptocephali, 173 European leptocephali, and 29 leptocephali identifiable only as *Anguilla*. Collections were made as early as 27 February and as late as 16 April and were distributed over much of the western three-quarters of the area of spatial overlap found for leptocephali 10 mm or less long (Figure 2). There is therefore considerable evidence in support of an argument that substantial spatiotemporal overlap exists in spawning of the two species. The small larvae caught in the same tow can reasonably be assumed to have traveled along similar trajectories and to reflect spawning by the two species at similar times and locations. If egg incubation time is about 2 d (Yamamoto and Yamauchi 1974) and the length at hatching is 2.9

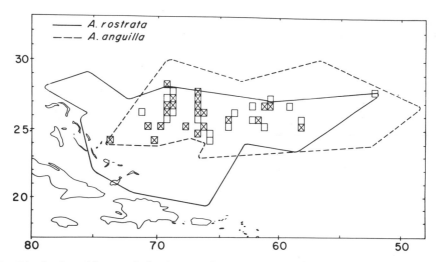

FIGURE 2.—Distribution of leptocephali, 10 mm or less total length, of the American and European eels and locations where leptocephali of both species 7 mm or less long (⊠) and 10 mm or less long (□) were caught in the same net tow. (Sources 5–7 of Table 1.)

mm (Yamamoto et al. 1975) as for the Japanese eel *Anguilla japonica* and the growth rate is 0.243 mm/d as for the American eel (Wippelhauser et al. 1985), leptocephali 7 mm long are about 19 d old (postfertilization) and those 10 mm long are about 31 d old.

The strength of conclusions concerning the spatial limits of spawning distributions must be tempered by the reality that the locations of capture of small leptocephali reflect the distributions both of fishing effort and of larvae. Schmidt (1922) explicitly recognized the problem and noted that to define the limits of spawning of the European eel ". . . it would be necessary to ascertain, not only where the youngest leptocephali were to be found, but also where they were not." However, Schmidt failed to heed his own advice, since, as his distribution of stations shows (Schmidt 1925), once he found small larvae he returned repeatedly to the same central area (Boëtius and Harding 1985a). When we consider sympatry, we have to add the temporal dimension to the spatial dimension with the same caution. In addition, the year-to-year variation in both spatial and temporal dimensions is unknown.

In a statistical reanalysis of Schmidt's (1922) data, Boëtius and Harding (1985a) argued that Schmidt did have sufficient data, both positive and negative, to define the northern limit of spawning of the European eel as about 30°N. However, they concluded that Schmidt had insufficient data to define eastern, western, or southern boundaries because of lack of effort outside his

closed curve, which defined the purported distribution of larvae 10 mm or less long. Our recent sampling (Kleckner et al. 1983; Wippelhauser et al. 1985; present authors, unpublished data) and that of Tesch (Schoth and Tesch 1982; Tesch 1982b) includes both positive and negative stations. These data have shown the northern limit of American eel spawning to be quite similar to that of the European eel (Figure 1). These collections have also added to our knowledge of the southerly limits to spawning of both species; forthcoming results from a 1981 cruise (Tesch 1982a) should add to this definition.

Spawning and the Subtropical Convergence Zone

Given the above, we suggest that the northern limits to spawning of both species are inherently more well defined than the southern or longitudinal limits. The definition occurs for biological and oceanographical reasons rather than for sampling reasons.

We have previously presented the hypothesis that adults of both Atlantic species of *Anguilla* cease migrating when they encounter or cross, from north to south, an extended frontal zone which meanders east–west across the Sargasso Sea at about 24–29°N latitude. We have provided preliminary supporting data for the American eel (Kleckner et al. 1983; McCleave and Kleckner 1985). The distribution of catches of small larvae of both species by Schoth and Tesch (1982), considered in conjunction with physical oceanographic data (Wegner 1982), seems also to support the hypothesis. Wegner (1982) observed that the catches of Schoth and Tesch (1982) were restricted to the convergence area and stated: "Perhaps the frontal zones belong to the area stimulating spawning of the migrating adult eels."

This frontal zone, located within the North Atlantic Subtropical Convergence, is marked by abrupt horizontal temperature, salinity, and density changes. It is persistent from year to year, although its exact position varies annually, seasonally, and even day to day (Voorhis et al. 1976; Leetma and Voorhis 1978; Voorhis and Bruce 1982). The frontal zone separates a permanently stratified, warm, saline surface water mass in the southern Sargasso Sea from a seasonally stratified, cooler, less-saline surface water mass in the northern Sargasso Sea (Katz 1969; Voorhis 1969; Leetma 1977; Wegner 1982). Mixing occurs in the frontal zone and creates an area with intermediate and distorted characteristics. Nevertheless, the front is distinct horizontally and vertically, and it is a shallow-water phenomenon (approximately the upper 500 m).

We conducted two cruises in 1983 and one in 1985 to the Sargasso Sea during late winter and early spring specifically to test the frontal-spawning hypothesis for both species. On these cruises, six transects in total were made along approximately north–south oriented axes in the frontal zone. At regular stations along the transects, leptocephali were sampled with standardized tows of an Isaacs Kidd midwater trawl (mouth opening, 8.7 m^2; mesh, 0.5 mm) fitted with a flow meter and a depth-transmitting pinger. Oblique tows to 300 m, lasting 2–3 h at 0.8–1.0 m/s, generally filtered about 5–10 $\times$ 10^4 m^3 of water.

Two transects made in March 1985 are particularly instructive because they were sufficiently long (~ 610 km) to pass clearly from northern Sargasso Sea water through the frontal zone into southern Sargasso water. On the first of these transects, which followed the 69°W meridian from 31 to 25.5°N, leptocephali of both species were abundant. Leptocephali were essentially restricted to the southern half of this transect, and both species were rather uniformly abundant there (Figure 3A). Specimens 5 mm or less long of one or both species were taken at stations 7 and 9–12 (Figure 3B). About half the American leptocephali and nearly all the European leptocephali were 10 mm or less long.

The leptocephali were abundant only in the

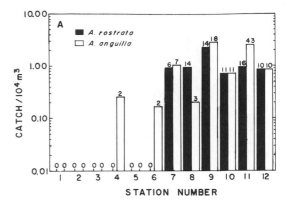

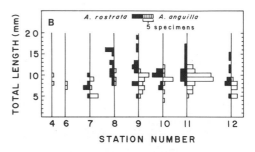

FIGURE 3.—(A) Catches of leptocephali of American and European eels (expressed as numbers of leptocephali per 10^4 m^3 of water filtered) along a 610-km transect (from 25.5°N, 69°W to 31°N, 69°W) across the frontal zone in the Sargasso Sea, 15–21 March 1985. North is to the left, south to the right. Numbers above the histogram bars are actual numbers of leptocephali caught. (B) Total lengths of leptocephali captured along the transect.

frontal zone and to its south. The frontal zone is indicated by a rapid increase of about 1.5°C in surface temperature between stations 6 and 7 (Figure 4A) and by deepening of isotherms in the upper 200 m between stations 6 and 7 and between 8 and 9 (Figure 4B). Salinity as well as temperature changes in the frontal zone are reflected in a density plot by a deepening of isopycnals in the upper 200 m at these stations (Figure 5).

Implications for Adult Migrations

If our hypothesis concerning the concentration of spawning in and south of the frontal zone is correct, it has clear implications for migrations of the adults. Migration, guided by presently unknown clues, apparently ceases when a specific oceanic feature, the frontal zone itself or the water mass to its south, is encountered. Although oceanic migration routes of both species are unknown, it is certain that most adults must migrate

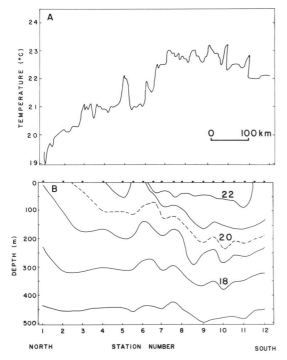

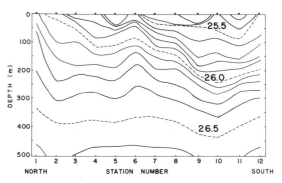

FIGURE 5.—Depths of isopycnals (plotted as sigma-*t*) along a 610-km transect across the frontal zone in the Sargasso Sea, 15–21 March 1985.

FIGURE 4.—Surface temperature (A) and depths of isotherms (B) along a 610-km transect across the frontal zone in the Sargasso Sea, 15–21 March 1985.

generally southward. Eels should thus encounter or cross the frontal zone from the north. This tendency would explain the apparently more precise northern limit to spawning and the common limit for both species (Figure 1). American eel adults which enter the southern Sargasso Sea directly from the continent to the west or from the islands of the Antilles arc to the south would encounter the southern water mass and would spawn without reaching the frontal zone, which may explain the broader latitudinal range of spawning of the American eel than of the European eel.

Kleckner et al. (1983) and McCleave and Kleckner (1985) have argued that the migration of adults occurs in the surface few hundred meters of the water column. The major physical distinctions between northern and southern water masses are restricted to the upper 500 m at most (Katz 1969; Pickard and Emergy 1982; Wegner 1982; Kleckner and McCleave, unpublished data).

Some feature of the surface waters south of the front or in the frontal zone probably serves as the cue to trigger cessation of migration. This feature is well offshore and over water some 5,000 m

deep. We have no evidence concerning the nature of the cue. While horizontal temperature gradients in the surface waters are high, the maximum being about 2°C/km (Voorhis 1969), such a temperature gradient is still small relative to eel length and probable swimming speed. Nevertheless, temperature may be a cue.

Perhaps a distinctive odor in the southern water mass serves as the recognition cue for returning adult eels, which were imprinted on the odor some years earlier as leptocephali. *Anguilla* leptocephali that are just beyond the oil-drop resorption stage have sensory cilia present in the olfactory epithelium (S. Egginton, personal communication), suggesting early development of olfaction. The olfactory acuity of subadult eels is amazingly high (Teichmann 1957, 1959), and preference for seawater over inland water by migrating adult eels is based upon olfaction (Hain 1975). Pankhurst and Lythgoe (1983) reported degeneration of the olfactory mucosa following artificial maturation of female European eels by hormone injections, but they were unable to say whether this was a normal or artifactual event.

Numerous potential sources of distinctive odors exist. Species composition of phytoplankton, zooplankton, and mesopelagic fishes all differ in near-surface waters of the northern and southern Sargasso Sea (Hulbert 1964; Colton et al. 1975; Backus et al. 1969, respectively). Dissolved free amino acids may accumulate in upper layers of the pycnocline in the Sargasso Sea (Liebezeit et al. 1980). Amino acids are known to be potent olfactory stimuli for many fishes, including the American eel (Silver 1979), and potent gustatory stimuli for many fishes, including the Japanese eel (Yoshii et al. 1979). There is also a chlorophyll-*a* maximum between 75 and 125 m deep in the

Sargasso Sea (M. Gilmartin, personal communication).

The hypothesis that spawning occurs in the frontal region provides a common behavioral mechanism for concentrating adults of both species for this purpose in an otherwise vast ocean. It also accommodates the observed differences in spawning area and time of the two species. Furthermore, the required concentration can occur without the need for precise migratory orientation (Leggett 1984; McCleave and Kleckner 1985).

The existence of such a common mechanism would also increase the degree of sympatry between the two species by concentrating them together—at least over part of the space–time axes of reproduction. Once having been concentrated by features of the frontal zone, olfaction might (also?) play a role in mate location or in species discrimination. Edel (1975) in an early study on artificial maturation of female American eels remarked on a unique "odor of ripeness" given off in the skin mucus. Sorensen and Winn (1984) showed that mature male American eels are attracted to mature females by olfaction and argued for the existence of a sex pheromone, perhaps a species-specific one.

The time seems appropriate for imaginative experiments on the possible role of olfaction in the final stages of migration, in mate location, and in reproductive isolation.

Implications for Leptocephalus Migration

The front hypothesis, coupled with the finding that small larvae of both species coexist along an east–west band (Figure 1), has implications for the migration of leptocephali. First, it negates the views of Tucker (1959) and Vladykov (1964) that spawning of the American eel must be much farther south than that of the European eel and that, as a consequence, the migration of the American species begins much farther south. Their arguments apparently formed the basis for Harden Jones's (1968) plotting of the hypothetical migratory drift of the two species in the north Atlantic from areas separated on a north–south axis (his Figure 21) and for his implication that a continental separation of the two species was based largely on drift from northerly versus southerly starting locations. Harden Jones's (1968) often-copied plot (e.g., Baker 1978) was based upon surface current hydrographic charts, not larval distribution data.

Secondly, the front hypothesis implies that many (or even most) larvae of the two species are introduced into the same oceanographic regime, though not necessarily at the same time, and that their early drift is similar and subject to the meandering and eddy variability characteristic of the frontal region (Voorhis et al. 1976; Leetma and Voorhis 1978; Gunn and Watts 1982; Voorhis and Bruce 1982; Wegner 1982). Given the present state of our knowledge, continental separation must be considered in the context of some east–west separation in spawning area, but with much overlap. In view of the extensive overlap in the distribution of larvae of the two species and the variability in water movements, statements about distribution to different parts of Europe from different parts of the spawning ground (Boëtius 1980), separation of species between Iceland and Greenland (Williams et al. 1984; Boëtius 1985), and movement of hybrids to intermediate geographic regions of Iceland and northern Europe (Williams and Koehn 1984) must be viewed with healthy skepticism.

Taxonomic Implications

Tucker's (1959) hypothesis that the American and European eels represent a single species rests squarely on the idea that the difference in mean numbers of myomeres or vertebrae between European and American "ecophenotypes" is produced by differences in temperature encountered by developing embryos during ascent in different parts of the spawning area (Tucker 1959). He felt that those phenotypes destined to become "American" were spawned to the south of those destined to become "European." If Tucker was correct, eel embryos developing under similar conditions should fail to show two distinct myomere distributions. We could restate this as a "null hypothesis": there is a unimodal distribution of myomere numbers among Atlantic *Anguilla* embryos which develop under the same environmental conditions.

Williams and Koehn (1984) also have argued that there is but a single species of Atlantic *Anguilla*, with the American and European forms representing two partly separate breeding populations. They made two points which are pertinent here. (1) Support for the recognition of two species would come from demonstration of intrinsic reproductive isolation, despite partial sympatry (Williams and Koehn 1984). The "null hypothesis" here is: there is no intrinsic reproductive isolation in north Atlantic *Anguilla*. (2) They argued that there is intergradation and appreciable gene flow from the American to the European population. This argument was based upon the presence of morphologically intermediate specimens (i.e., specimens with vertebral counts below the usual range for European eels) in geographically intermediate areas (Iceland and northern Europe) located thousands of kilometers from the spawning area. These intermediates were presumed to have migrated from a region of sympatry between the main centers of spawning of the two populations. In the present context the appropriate "null hypothesis" is: morphologically intermediate specimens are more likely to be produced in the region of sympatry.

Insofar as our assumption is correct that leptocephali of both species 7 mm or less long captured in the same net tow reflect spawning in sympatry and development under similar conditions, distributions of myomere numbers of these specimens can form the basis for tests of these "null hypotheses," at least in an informal sense. Under any of these null hypotheses, the distribution of myomeres of these small "sympatric" leptocephali

should converge toward a more central distribution than that exhibited by groups of leptocephali in which the probability of sympatric spawning is much lower. This convergence would be evident (1) as a higher mean myomere number for specimens assigned to the American form (100–110 myomeres) and a lower mean for those assigned to the European form (112–119 myomeres) and (2) in a higher proportion of specimens with the intermediate number of myomeres (111).

Our studies provide no evidence of convergence of myomere distributions (Table 2). For samples taken only during the spawning season, the frequency distributions of myomere counts of leptocephali 7 mm or less long of each species collected in the same net tow did not differ significantly from the frequency distributions for specimens 7 mm or less long not collected in the same tow (chi-square goodness of fit tests, both $P > 0.5$) or from the distributions of specimens 8 mm or longer from all nets (both tests $P > 0.1$). The distributions of myomeres of the 7-mm-or-less,

TABLE 2.—Frequencies of occurrence (FO, number of leptocephali) and percentage distributions of the total number of myomeres of *Anguilla* species in various subsets of data. All myomere counts were made in our laboratory, mostly by one of us (R. C. K., M. C.) or by G. S. Wippelhauser according to criteria of Kleckner and McCleave (1985) and Wippelhauser et al. (1985).

Number of myomeres	Winter–spring, both species, ≤7 mm, same net[a]		Winter–spring, both species, ≤7 mm, different nets[a]		Winter–spring, both species, ≥8 mm, all nets[a]		Summer–fall, both species, ≥15 mm, all nets[b]		Historical data, both species, all nets[c]	
	FO	%	FO	%	FO	%	FO	%	FO	%
Anguilla rostrata										
100							1	0.16		
101	1	1.35	1	0.68			0	0.00		
102	3	4.05	3	2.03	11	1.78	1	0.16	7	0.36
103	0	0.00	1	0.68	13	2.10	5	0.79	12	0.62
104	3	4.05	4	2.70	32	5.18	43	6.76	67	3.48
105	5	6.76	12	8.11	42	6.80	113	17.77	230	11.94
106	7	9.46	20	13.51	90	14.56	170	26.73	409	21.22
107	20	27.03	32	21.62	163	26.38	187	29.40	609	31.60
108	12	16.22	39	26.35	133	21.52	85	13.36	377	19.56
109	14	18.92	25	16.89	89	14.40	23	3.62	172	8.93
110	9	12.16	11	7.43	45	7.28	8	1.26	44	2.28
Anguilla sp.										
111	1		1		17		5		5	
Anguilla anguilla										
112	7	6.19	10	10.31	45	8.27	28	11.76	70	7.53
113	15	13.27	14	14.43	80	14.71	66	27.73	164	17.65
114	28	24.78	20	20.62	117	21.51	80	33.61	238	25.62
115	23	20.35	19	19.59	130	23.90	39	16.39	239	25.73
116	19	16.81	14	14.43	93	17.10	19	7.98	132	14.21
117	9	7.96	12	12.37	42	7.72	5	2.10	67	7.21
118	10	8.85	4	4.12	28	5.15	1	0.42	15	1.61
119	2	1.77	4	4.12	9	1.65			4	0.43

[a] Sources 6, 7 of Table 1.
[b] Unpublished data of present authors from cruises in July–August and September–October 1985, western Sargasso Sea.
[c] Source 4 of Table 1.

same-net group for both species were significantly different from both the 15-mm-or-longer, summer–fall group and the historical data group (Table 2) (all four tests, $P < 0.001$). However, there was no trend toward convergence because, in the 7-mm-or-longer group, high myomere counts were overrepresented for American eels and low myomere counts were underrepresented for European eels compared with expected values.

Mean myomere numbers within each species in the three subsets of data from the spawning season are not significantly different from one another (Table 3). The mean myomere number of the small specimens from the same nets for each species is intermediate between those of the other two groups; under the "null hypotheses" the mean for American eels should be higher, and the mean for European eels lower, than the means for the other two groups. The means for the summer–fall subset and the historical subset are lower than for the other groups for each species, and the rank-ordered means are the same for the five subsets within each species. However, the differences between the means for the two species are nearly the same for all five subsets.

Other aspects of the distributions, besides the mean, show similarities where divergences would be expected under the above-mentioned "null hypotheses." The distribution of American lepto-

cephali 7 mm or more long caught in the same nets as their European counterparts is just as skewed to the left as other distributions, and the distribution of European leptocephali similarly caught is as skewed to the right as others (Table 3). The skewness and leptokurtosis present in our distributions is characteristic of distributions in other studies as well (Schoth 1982). The frequency of occurrence of specimens with 111 myomeres is comparable among the data sets; it is not high in the group with highest probability of sympatric spawning (Table 2).

Comparini and Rodino (1980) showed separation of larvae of *Anguilla* in the Sargasso Sea into two distinct forms with respect to the malate dehydrogenase locus, but Williams and Koehn (1984) felt that the larvae were sampled over an area large enough to produce the two forms by simple allopatry. Comparini and Schoth (1982) published a fuller account of the electrophoretic and meristic studies made on 121 *Anguilla* leptocephali 7-25 mm long. By comparing records between Comparini and Schoth (1982) and Schoth and Tesch (1982) we found that 72 of the 121 came from stations where leptocephali 7 mm or less long of both species were collected together and 108 of the 121 came from where leptocephali 10 mm or less long of both species were collected together. These two papers were unavailable when Williams and Koehn (1984) went to press,

TABLE 3.—Sample statistics for distributions of numbers of myomeres of *Anguilla* leptocephali in various subsets of data. Skewness and kurtosis were tested for significance by t-tests ($P < 0.01**$) (Sokal and Rohlf 1981). Paired comparisons of means were based on the Games and Howell method (Sokal and Rohlf 1981). Within each species, means without a letter in common are significantly different ($P < 0.01$); means with a letter in common are not significantly different ($P > 0.05$).

Group	Category	N	Mean	Variance	Skewness	Kurtosis
	Anguilla rostrata					
1	Winter–spring, ≤7 mm, same net	74	107.270 zy	4.227	−0.958**	3.872**
2	Winter–spring, ≤7 mm, different nets	148	107.277 z	3.113	−0.903**	4.160**
3	Winter–spring, ≥8 mm, all nets	618	107.112 z	3.104	−0.617**	3.293**
4	Summer–fall, ≥15 mm, all nets	636	106.368 y	1.824	−0.116	3.573**
5	Historical data, all nets	1927	106.843 z	1.942	−0.194**	3.119**
	Anguilla anguilla					
1	Winter–spring, ≤7 mm, same net	113	114.965 z	2.927	0.335	2.464**
2	Winter–spring, ≤7 mm, different nets	97	115.092 z	3.340	0.139	2.537**
3	Winter–spring, ≥8 mm, all nets	544	114.789 z	2.716	0.300**	2.652**
4	Summer–fall, ≥15 mm, all nets	238	113.891 y	1.482	0.505**	3.065**
5	Historical data, all nets	929	114.517 z	2.054	0.278**	2.741**

but their existence greatly weakens the criticism.

Data from a variety of sources have been used in a previous section to demonstrate that spawning of the American and European eels occurs mainly along an east–west axis (Figure 1) and that there is a substantial region of sympatry, also along an east–west axis (Figure 2). There is no evidence from our work in the Sargasso Sea that European eel larvae are largely found north of American eel larvae (Figure 3; Kleckner and McCleave unpublished data); neither is there any such evidence from work of Schoth and Tesch (1982). Both studies show small larvae of the two forms mixed together in the frontal zone. This finding removes from consideration the major environmental cline which Tucker (1959) invoked to produce the disjunct distribution of myomere counts for Atlantic eels.

We have argued in agreement with Williams and Koehn (1984) that there is a region of overlap in spawning area and time between the two forms; indeed, we have inferred on the basis of data presented above that it is a greater overlap than many authors have suggested. We fully support, with data taken at sea, the statement of Williams and Koehn: "A resultant region of sympatry is likely to lie between the main centers of spawning. . . ." However, their theory that interbreeding and production of viable offspring occurs there requires the following: "Specimens of mixed parentage from this intermediate region would perhaps have an intermediate sort of larval dispersal that would put them in the geographically intermediate region of northern Europe. As returning adults they might have intermediate migratory mechanisms that would put them back in the intermediate spawning region where they might mate with each other or backcross. . . ."

Yet elsewhere in their paper, Williams and Koehn (1984) present evidence for near panmixia of both European and American forms, as do Avise et al. (1986) for American forms. Williams and Koehn (1984) consider larval distribution to be essentially random because of the highly variable nature of the ocean currents.

The arguments of Williams and Koehn (1984) in the preceding two paragraphs are incompatible. A simpler explanation supported by our findings is that (1) intrinsic reproductive isolation of some sort prevents viable interbreeding in the area and time of overlap of spawning in the Sargasso Sea, and (2) the difference in numbers of myomeres between the two forms is genetically rather than environmentally determined.

Acknowledgments

This research was supported by the National Science Foundation (grants OCE77-19440 and OCE82-08394) and the National Geographic Society (grants 2261-80 and 2940-84). This paper was written while the senior author was a visiting professor in the Department of Biology, McGill University, Montreal; the counsel of William C. Leggett and the financial support of the Natural Sciences and Engineering Research Council of Canada, the McGill University Faculty of Graduate Studies and Research, the University of Maine Center for Marine Studies, the Leopold Schepp Foundation, and the Eppley Foundation for Research are gratefully acknowledged. We appreciate the helpful criticisms of Paul Bentzen, Yves Delafontaine, George Rose, and especially William Leggett of an early draft of the manuscript.

References

Avise, J. C., G. S. Helfman, N. C. Saunders, and L. S. Hales. 1986. Mitochondrial DNA differentiation in North Atlantic eels: population genetic consequences of an unusual life history pattern. Proceedings of the National Academy of Sciences of the United States of America. 83:4350–4354.

Backus, R. H., J. E. Craddock, R. L. Haedrich, and D. L. Shores. 1969. Mesopelagic fishes and thermal fronts in the western Sargasso Sea. Marine Biology 3:87–106.

Baker, R. R. 1978. The evolutionary ecology of animal migration. Hodder and Stoughton, London, England.

Boëtius, J. 1980. Atlantic *Anguilla*. A presentation of old and new data of total numbers of vertebrae with special reference to the occurrence of *Anguilla rostrata* in Europe. Dana 1:93–112.

Boëtius, J. 1985. Greenland eels, *Anguilla rostrata* LeSueur, Dana 4:41–48.

Boëtius, J., and E. F. Harding. 1985a. A re-examination of Johannes Schmidt's Atlantic eel investigations. Dana 4:129–162.

Boëtius, J., and E. F. Harding. 1985b. List of Atlantic and Mediterranean *Anguilla* leptocephali: Danish material up to 1966. Dana 4:163–249.

Bruun, A. F. 1963. The breeding of the north Atlantic freshwater-eels. Advances in Marine Biology 1:137–169.

Caprio, J. 1982. High sensitivity and specificity of olfactory and gustatory receptors of catfish to amino acids. Pages 109–134 *in* T. J. Hara, editor. Chemoreception in fishes. Elsevier Scientific, Amsterdam, The Netherlands.

Castonguay, M., and J. D. McCleave. 1987. Vertical distributions, diel and ontogenetic vertical migrations and net avoidance of leptocephali of *Anguilla* and other common species in the Sargasso Sea. Journal of Plankton Research 9:195–214.

Colton, J. B., Jr., D. E. Smith, and J. W. Jossi. 1975. Further observations on a thermal front in the Sargasso Sea. Deep-Sea Research 22:433–439.

Comparini, A., and E. Rodinò. 1980. Electrophoretic evidence for two species of *Anguilla* leptocephali in the Sargasso Sea. Nature (London) 287:435–437.

Comparini, A., and M. Schoth. 1982. Comparison of electrophoretic and meristic characters of 0-group eel larvae from the Sargasso Sea. Helgoländer Meeresuntersuchungen 35:289–299.

D'Ancona, U., and D. W. Tucker. 1959. Old and new solutions to the eel problem. Nature (London) 183:1405–1406.

Deelder, C. L., and D. W. Tucker. 1960. The Atlantic eel problem. Nature (London) 185:589–592.

Edel, R. K. 1975. The induction of maturation of female American eels through hormone injection. Helgoländer Wissenschaftliche Meeresuntersuchungen 27:131–138.

Gunn, J. T., and D. R. Watts. 1982. On the currents and water masses north of the Antilles/Bahamas arc. Journal of Marine Research 40:1–18.

Hain, J. H. W. 1975. The behaviour of migratory eels, *Anguilla rostrata*, in response to current, salinity and lunar period. Helgoländer Wissenschaftliche Meeresuntersuchungen 27:211–233.

Harden Jones, F. R. 1968. Fish migration. Edward Arnold, London, England.

Harding, E. F. 1985. On the homogeneity of the European eel population (*Anguilla anguilla*). Dana 4:49–66.

Hulbert, E. M. 1964. Succession and diversity in the planktonic flora of the western North Atlantic. Bulletin of Marine Science of the Gulf and Caribbean 14:33–44.

Jones, J. W., and D. W. Tucker. 1959. Eel migration. Nature (London) 184:1281–1283.

Katz, E. 1969. Further study of a front in the Sargasso Sea. Tellus 21:259–269.

Kleckner, R. C., and J. D. McCleave. 1985. Spatial and temporal distribution of American eel larvae in relation to north Atlantic Ocean current systems. Dana 4:67–92.

Kleckner, R. C., J. D. McCleave, and G. S. Wippelhauser. 1983. Spawning of American eel, *Anguilla rostrata*, relative to thermal fronts in the Sargasso Sea. Environmental Biology of Fishes 9:289–293.

Kleckner, R. C., G. S. Wippelhauser, and J. D. McCleave. 1985. List of Atlantic *Anguilla* leptocephali: American material. Dana 4:99–128.

Leetma, A. 1977. Effects of the winter of 1976–1977 on the northwestern Sargasso Sea. Science (Washington, D.C.) 198:188–189.

Leetma, A., and A. D. Voorhis. 1978. Scales of motion in the subtropical convergence zone. Journal of Geophysical Research 83:4589–4592.

Leggett, W. C. 1984. Fish migrations in coastal and estuarine environments: a call for new approaches to the study of an old problem. Pages 159–178 *in* J. D. McCleave, G. P. Arnold, J. J. Dodson, and W. H. Neill, editors. Mechanisms of migration in fishes. Plenum, New York, New York, USA.

Liebezeit, G., M. Bolter, I. F. Brown, and R. Dawson. 1980. Dissolved free amino acids and carbohydrates at pycnocline boundaries in the Sargasso Sea and related microbial activity. Oceanologica Acta 3:357–362.

McCleave, J. D., and R. C. Kleckner. 1985. Oceanic migrations of Atlantic eels (*Anguilla* spp.): adults and their offspring. Contributions in Marine Science 27(supplement):316–337.

Pankhurst, N. W., and J. N. Lythgoe. 1983. Changes in vision and olfaction during sexual maturation in the European eel *Anguilla anguilla* (L.). Journal of Fish Biology 23:229–240.

Pickard, G. L., and W. J. Emery. 1982. Descriptive physical oceanography, 4th edition. Pergamon, Oxford, England.

Post, A., and F.-W. Tesch. 1982. Midwater trawl catches of adolescent and adult Anguilliform fishes during the Sargasso Sea eel expedition 1979. Helgoländer Meeresuntersuchungen 35:341–356.

Schmidt, J. 1922. The breeding places of the eel. Philosophical Transactions of the Royal Society of London, B: Biological Sciences 211:179–208.

Schmidt, J. 1923. Breeding places and migrations of the eel. Nature (London) 111:51–54.

Schmidt, J. 1925. The breeding places of the eel. Smithsonian Institution Annual Report 1924:279–316.

Schoth, M. 1982. Taxonomic studies on the 0-group eel larvae (*Anguilla* sp.) caught in the Sargasso Sea in 1979. Helgoländer Meeresuntersuchungen 35:279–287.

Schoth, M., and F.-W. Tesch. 1982. Spatial distribution of 0-group eel larvae (*Anguilla* sp.) in the Sargasso Sea. Helgoländer Meeresuntersuchungen 35:309–320.

Schoth, M., and F.-W. Tesch. 1984. The vertical distribution of small 0-group *Anguilla* larvae in the Sargasso Sea with reference to other anguilliform leptocephali. Meeresforschung 30:188–195.

Silver, W. L. 1979. Electrophysiological responses from the olfactory system of the American eel. Doctoral dissertation. Florida State University, Tallahassee, Florida, USA. (Not seen; cited in Caprio 1982.)

Sokal, R. R., and F. J. Rohlf. 1981. Biometry, 2nd edition. W. H. Freeman, San Francisco, California, USA.

Sorensen, P. W., and H. E. Winn. 1984. The induction of maturation and ovulation in American eels, *Anguilla rostrata* (LeSueur), and the relevance of chemical and visual cues to male spawning behaviour. Journal of Fish Biology 25:261–268.

Teichmann, H. 1957. Das Reichvermögen des Aales (*Anguilla anguilla* L.). Naturwissenschaften 44:242.

Teichmann, H. 1959. Über die Leistung des Geruchssinnes beim Aal (*Anguilla anguilla* L.). Zeitschrift für Vergleichende Physiologie 42:206–254.

Tesch, F.-W. 1982a. Further studies on eel larvae collections taken by R. V. "Friedrich Heincke" 1981 in the Sargasso Sea and during north Atlantic transects. International Council for the Exploration of the Sea C.M. 1982/M:3, Copenhagen, Denmark.

Tesch, F.-W. 1982b. The Sargasso Sea eel expedition 1979. Helgoländer Meeresuntersuchungen 35:263–277.

Tucker, D. W. 1959. A new solution to the Atlantic eel problem. Nature (London) 183:495–501.

Vladykov, V. D. 1964. Quest for the true breeding area of the American eel (*Anguilla rostrata* LeSueur). Journal of the Fisheries Research Board of Canada 21:1523–1530.

Voorhis, A. D. 1969. The horizontal extent and persistence of thermal fronts in the Sargasso Sea. Deep-Sea Research 16 (supplement):331–337.

Voorhis, A. D., and J. G. Bruce. 1982. Small-scale surface stirring and frontogenesis in the subtropical convergence of the western North Atlantic. Journal of Marine Research 40 (supplement):801–821.

Voorhis, A. D., E. H. Schroeder, and A. Leetma. 1976. The influence of deep mesoscale eddies on sea surface temperature in the north Atlantic subtropical convergence. Journal of Physical Oceanography 6:953–961.

Wegner, G. 1982. Main hydrographic features of the Sargasso Sea in spring 1979. Helgoländer Meeresuntersuchungen 35:385–400.

Williams, G. C., and R. K. Koehn. 1984. Population genetics of north Atlantic catadromous eels (*Anguilla*). Pages 529–560 *in* B. J. Turner, editor. Evolutionary genetics of fishes. Plenum, New York, New York, USA.

Williams, G. C., R. K. Koehn, and V. Thorsteinsson. 1984. Icelandic eels: evidence for a single species of *Anguilla* in the north Atlantic. Copeia 1984:221–223.

Wippelhauser, G. S., J. D. McCleave, and R. C. Kleckner. 1985. *Anguilla rostrata* leptocephali in the Sargasso Sea during February and March 1981. Dana 4:93–98.

Yamamoto, K., and K. Yamauchi. 1974. Sexual maturation of Japanese eel and production of eel larvae in the aquarium. Nature (London) 251:220–222.

Yamamoto, K., K. Yamauchi, and G. Moriaka. 1975. Pre-leptocephalic larvae of the Japanese eel. Bulletin of the Japanese Society of Scientific Fisheries 41:29–34.

Yoshii, K., N. Kamo, K. Kurihara, and Y. Kobatake. 1979. Gustatory responses of eel palatine receptors to amino acids and carboxylic acids. Journal of General Physiology 74:301–317.

American Fisheries Society Symposium 1:298–312, 1987

Marine Migration and Orientation of Ocean-Type Chinook and Sockeye Salmon

M. C. Healey and C. Groot

Department of Fisheries and Oceans, Fisheries Research Branch, Pacific Biological Station
Nanaimo, British Columbia V9R 5K6, Canada

Abstract.—The different species, and stocks within species, of Pacific salmon *Oncorhynchus* spp. undertake marine migrations of differing length and complexity. In this paper, we compare the marine migrations of ocean-type chinook salmon *Oncorhynchus tshawytscha,* exemplifying short-distance ocean migration, and sockeye salmon *O. nerka,* exemplifying long-distance ocean migration, with a view to assessing the sophistication of direction-finding mechanisms required for each type of migration. During their outward migration as juveniles to oceanic feeding grounds, both species apparently use compass orientation. During their homing migration, however, both species probably use a combination of compass and bicoordinate orientation until near the home stream mouth. Upon nearing the home stream both species apparently switch to orientation by local environmental cues. We conclude that the sophistication in direction- and goal-finding capabilities required for short- and long-distance migration, as represented by these two salmon species, does not differ significantly.

Anadromous forms of Pacific salmon *Oncorhynchus* spp. undertake some of the most extensive open-ocean migrations of any species known. Individual chum *O. keta* or sockeye *O. nerka* salmon, for example, may spend 5 or 6 years at sea (Healey 1986), during which time they roam over many thousands of square kilometers of the north Pacific Ocean (Neave 1964; French et al. 1976; Neave et al. 1976). Yet these fish are able to return with remarkable precision to their natal stream as adults to spawn (Quinn 1985). In contrast to these extensive migrations, individuals of some races of pink *O. gorbuscha* or chinook *O. tshawytscha* salmon may remain close to shore and within a few hundred kilometers of their natal stream throughout their ocean life (Major et al. 1978; Takagi et al. 1981). The variety of environmental conditions experienced by fish which display such different migratory habits, and the problems of direction and goal finding that they must solve during their ocean migrations, may be considerably different. In this paper, we contrast the ocean migrations of southern British Columbia stocks of ocean-type chinook salmon, exemplifying short-distance ocean migration, and sockeye salmon, exemplifying long-distance ocean migration. Finally, we speculate about the factors which govern the migration and homing behaviour of these species. Our working hypothesis is that short-distance migrators like ocean-type chinook salmon that do not move out of coastal waters can accomplish their migrations with less complex orientation mechanisms than can long-distance migrators like sockeye salmon that range hundreds of kilometers offshore.

Migration of Juveniles

Healey (1983) argued from ocean migratory patterns and other ecological characteristics that two races of chinook salmon, stream- and ocean-type, should be recognized. Stream-type chinook salmon migrate far offshore whereas ocean-type chinook salmon remain in coastal waters throughout their ocean life. Individual fish can be assigned to one of these two behavioural types by scale growth patterns. Ocean-type chinook salmon occur only in spawning populations south of about 56°N, but dominate in virtually all river systems from this latitude to the southern extremity of their range in California (Healey 1983).

Ocean-type chinook salmon enter the ocean when about 70–80 mm in fork length, usually during June or July of their first summer of life. After they leave their natal river, ocean-type chinook salmon remain close to shore and in sheltered waters for several months. For example, Healey (1980a, 1980b) reported high catches of juvenile ocean-type chinook salmon in the southern Strait of Georgia throughout the period June to November, after which catches declined. Immature ocean-type chinook salmon in their second ocean year are also abundant in the Strait of Georgia, as evidenced by sport fishery catches (Argue et al. 1983).

Sockeye salmon in southern British Columbia typically migrate seaward after 1 year in fresh water (Foerster 1968). Hartt (1980) and Hartt and Dell (1986) showed that juvenile sockeye, pink, and chum salmon in the eastern Pacific migrate northward along the coast in a narrow band after leaving their natal river. This moving band of juveniles extends 1,800 km from southern Vancouver Island to Yakutat in Alaska and persists for about 3 months (Figure 1A). Chinook salmon are also found in this band of juveniles, but they are invariably stream-type rather than ocean-type (Healey 1983).

Sockeye salmon smolts leaving the Fraser River can follow two routes out of the Strait of Georgia to join this band of fish: either south through Juan de Fuca Strait or north through Johnstone Strait (Figure 2). Most, if not all, apparently leave the Strait of Georgia via the northern route (Groot and Cooke, in press). Upon leaving the Fraser estuary most smolts proceed along the mainland coast northward but some are flushed west across the Strait of Georgia by the Fraser River plume and tidal currents towards the Gulf Islands (Figure 2). Once among the Gulf

Islands, these smolts turn north and migrate diagonally back across the strait to join up with the smolts that have moved directly north from the river mouth (Figure 2).

Sockeye salmon juveniles migrate through the Strait of Georgia, a journey of about 200 km, in about 30 d (Groot and Cooke, in press). To accomplish this, they must travel a minimum of 6–7 km/d. Similar rates of travel were observed for sockeye smolts migrating out of Babine Lake, which travelled an average of 5–8 km/d; individual schools travelled at rates of 24.5–30 cm/s during active migration (Johnson and Groot 1963; Groot 1972). Travelling at 24.5–30 cm/s, smolts in the Strait of Georgia must have swum at least 6–8 h each day on a direct course to cover the distance through the strait. Approximately this number of hours is spent in active migration each day by sockeye smolts in fresh water (Johnson and Groot 1963; Groot 1965, 1972).

During their first summer in the Gulf of Alaska, juvenile sockeye salmon continue to travel rapidly along the coast of North America. Over 10,000

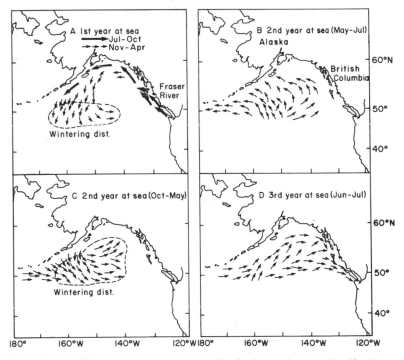

FIGURE 1.—Model of Fraser River sockeye salmon migration in the northeastern Pacific Ocean (modified from French et al. 1976). (A) First year to sea showing coastal band of juveniles migrating northwest and west along the coast and subsequent movement south to overwintering grounds. (B) Second year at sea showing north and westward movement during spring and summer. (C) Second year at sea showing eastward movement to overwintering grounds during the fall and winter. (D) Third year at sea showing return to the Fraser River as maturing adults.

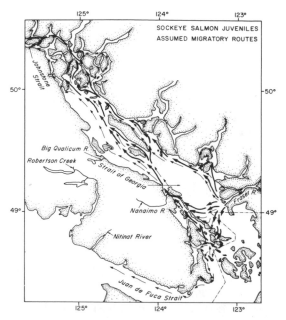

FIGURE 2.—Migratory routes of Fraser River sockeye salmon smolts in the Strait of Georgia on their way to the Pacific Ocean. Heavy arrows indicate major paths of movement; light arrows indicate minor paths. Light arrows in Juan de Fuca Strait indicate that we believe few sockeye salmon leave the Strait of Georgia by this route.

young sockeye salmon have been tagged at several sites along the west coast of North America and 11 of these were recovered in the Fraser River fishery 2 years later. Hartt (1980) estimated that, to cover the distances of 1,150 to 2,770 km between the Fraser River mouth and the tagging sites in southern Alaska, these fish must have travelled 13.7 to 25.9 km/d. The lengths of the fish at tagging averaged 20.8 cm. Travelling at their optimum swimming speed, which is about two body lengths per second for sockeye salmon of this size (Brett 1965), the fish must have swum on a direct course for 9–17 h/d to accomplish their migration from the Fraser River to the tagging site.

Thus, in contrast to ocean-type chinook salmon smolts, sockeye salmon smolts appear to migrate rapidly northward after leaving their natal river mouth. Observations in both the Strait of Georgia and other coastal areas of the Gulf of Alaska strongly suggest that juvenile sockeye salmon have a north to northwest directional orientation after reaching salt water (Hartt and Dell 1986; Groot and Cooke, in press)). This orientation will cause them to accumulate along the eastern shore of the Strait of Georgia and keep them close to shore as they move north.

Distribution and Dispersal of Immature Fish

Detailed information on the dispersal patterns of ocean-type chinook salmon after their first summer in the ocean is lacking. However, some important inferences may be made from general observations on the composition of the ocean troll catch of chinook salmon and from recaptures of chinook salmon tagged on the coastal fishing grounds. These general observations can now be augmented by information from specific populations tagged as juveniles and recaptured after one or more years at sea.

Ocean-type chinook salmon may spend up to 5 years in the ocean before they mature and return to their natal stream to spawn (Healey 1986). During that time, they may disperse as far west as 175°W and north to about 60°N (Healey 1983a). Chinook salmon are comparatively rare in offshore waters of the eastern half of the north Pacific Ocean, however (Manzer et al. 1965), and ocean-type fish are the smaller fraction of offshore catches (Healey 1983). On the other hand, ocean-type fish are abundant near the North American coast over the continental shelf (Figure 3), as evidenced by the large commercial troll catches of immature and maturing fish in these waters (Major et al. 1978; Healey 1983). In view of their abundance in coastal waters and scarcity offshore, ocean-type chinook salmon may be characterized as bound to the coast, even though some do disperse far offshore. Whether the ocean-type fish that migrate well offshore represent particular populations or particular genetic strains is not known.

Recoveries of chinook salmon tagged in the ocean at various locations along the North American coast provide specific information on the movement patterns and origins of fish from different parts of the coast. These data can only be interpreted in a qualitative way, as fishing effort and effort to recover tags differed among areas of the coast and tagging studies. In most instances, the greatest number of recaptures was from the tagging location, suggesting a considerable fidelity to location by chinook salmon captured in various parts of the coast (Figure 4). Aggregations of chinook salmon in particular locations of the coast and persistent differences in size and age of chinook salmon between nearby geographic locations are also known to occur (Healey 1986b). These observations suggest that ocean-type chinook salmon may be relatively sedentary during their immature phase in the ocean, a possibility that is supported by recent tag recovery information to be presented later.

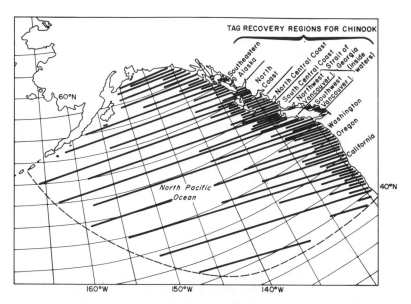

FIGURE 3.—Ocean distribution of ocean-type chinook salmon, and tag recovery regions for chinook salmon tagged in the ocean as immatures or at the time of seaward migration as smolts. The approximate western and southern limits of ocean distribution of ocean-type chinook salmon are shown by a dashed line. The density of bars within this region is intended to indicate the relative density of chinook salmon.

Chinook salmon tagged off southeastern Alaska were recaptured as far south as California and those tagged off California were recaptured as far north as southern British Columbia (Figure 4). Chinook salmon tagged at intermediate points along the coast were recaptured both north and south of the release point. Although the data are limited, it appears that fish captured north of the tagging site were captured only in the ocean troll fisheries whereas those captured south of the tagging site were captured in both ocean and river-mouth fisheries (Godfrey 1968). This suggests that immature fish moved north from

the tagging site whereas maturing fish did not. It also appears that the movement patterns of chinook salmon tagged in inside waters of British Columbia and Alaska may have been different from those tagged in outside waters since, in the former instance, most recaptures came from the area of tagging whereas, in the latter instance, recaptures were distributed over a much broader geographic area (Figure 4).

For many of the releases of tagged fish, records are available concerning the location of recaptures made in the year of tagging and in subsequent

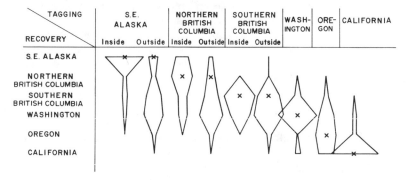

FIGURE 4.—Distribution of recoveries of chinook salmon tagged as immature fish in the ocean in various regions along the coast of North America. "Inside" refers to taggings done inside the coastal island chain (e.g., east of the Queen Charlotte Islands in northern British Columbia) and "outside" to taggings done outside the coastal island chain (e.g., west of the Queen Charlotte Islands). The width of the kite diagrams indicates the proportion of recaptures in each region. The "×" within each kite diagram indicates the tagging region.

years. There was no clear difference in distribution of chinook salmon recaptured in the year of tagging or in subsequent years. In particular, there was no evidence that the distribution of the main body of tagged fish moved either north or south along the coast in the years following tagging.

Keeping these general observations in mind, we can examine in more detail the ocean distribution of four stocks of ocean-type chinook salmon from southern British Columbia. The Big Qualicum River and Robertson Creek (Figure 2) have production hatcheries on them, and releases of tagged fish from these hatcheries have been on the order of 60,000 to 100,000 per year. The Nanaimo and Nitinat stocks (Figure 2) had no intensive hatchery rearing at the time that the taggings to be discussed here were made. The releases from these systems, with one exception, were of wild fry captured migrating downstream, held in pens and fed until about 60 mm fork length, then tagged and released. These releases were on the order of 10,000 to 20,000. The exception was the first hatchery release from the Nanaimo River which was comparable in size to the other hatchery releases. These four chinook salmon stocks were chosen to represent inside sheltered-water stocks (Big Qualicum and Nanaimo rivers), outside open-coast stocks (Robertson Creek and Nitinat River), wild stocks (Nanaimo and Nitinat rivers), and hatchery stocks (Robertson Creek and Big Qualicum River).

Chinook salmon catches from California to Alaska are now routinely sampled for the presence of tagged fish. The goal is to examine 20% of the catch from each major fishery. Tag recovery and tag decoding are the responsibility of each state in the USA and of the Department of Fisheries and Oceans in Canada, but information is shared among all fisheries agencies. The Canadian data base is currently up to date with respect to Canadian recoveries and most U.S. recoveries of Canadian tags. There are, as yet, a few unresolved errors in the data set. The information presented here, should, therefore, be regarded as preliminary, although substantial changes in the qualitative picture are unlikely.

We examined the 1977, 1978, and 1979 brood-year releases from Robertson Creek, totalling approximately 434,000 tagged smolts; the 1978 and 1979 brood-year releases from Nitinat River, totalling approximately 29,200 tagged smolts; the 1976 and 1977 brood-year releases from Big Qualicum River, totalling approximately 176,000 tagged smolts; and the 1979 and 1980 brood-year

releases from Nanaimo River, totaling approximately 105,000 tagged smolts. The total number of tagged fish released is not known absolutely as some fish lose the coded wire tags shortly after tagging, and this immediate tag loss was not always tested for. The numbers above are corrected for known tag loss. Releases of the 1978 and 1979 brood years from Robertson Creek were in two groups with separate tag codes, so that within-brood variation in recapture pattern could be investigated.

From recaptures and the proportion of the catch that was sampled, we calculated the total number of tags in the catch for each tagged group for six regions of the British Columbia coast and southeastern Alaska (Figure 3). We normalized total tags in the catch to a release of 100,000 tags and expressed the estimated recaptures as numbers of tagged fish of each stock per 1,000 chinook salmon in the ocean troll catch. This way of expressing the tag recoveries indicates the occurrence of each tagged stock relative to all other stocks in a particular region of the coast, and involves no assumptions about overall abundance of chinook in any region.

Robertson Creek chinook salmon were distributed from southwestern Vancouver Island to southeastern Alaska, but were relatively most abundant in north-central and northern British Columbia (Table 1). Alaskan recoveries of Robertson Creek chinook salmon are probably underestimated in this analysis, but it is doubtful that they would be greater than recoveries from northern British Columbia. Nitinat River chinook salmon had a similar distribution, although no recaptures were reported from the very intensive fishery off southwestern Vancouver Island, nor from southeastern Alaska (Table 1). That some Nitinat River chinook salmon migrate into Alaskan waters is demonstrated by a recovery made from a foreign trawling vessel operating in central Alaskan waters (A. C. Wertheimer and M. L. Dahlberg, National Marine Fisheries Service, Auke Bay, Alaska, unpublished report). The Nitinat fish appeared, however, to have their major distribution slightly south of Robertson Creek chinook salmon, although recaptures of Nitinat fish were too small for definitive analysis. The absence of Nitinat chinook salmon from catches off southwestern Vancouver Island is significant, since Nitinat River is tributary to this fishing area. Neither Robertson Creek nor Nitinat River chinook salmon were recorded from the Strait of Georgia troll fishery (Table 1).

TABLE 1.—Average estimated recoveries per 1,000 chinook salmon captured for releases of 100,000 tagged smolts from four river systems on Vancouver Island.

River system	Age at recapture[a]	Coastal region[a]						
		GS	SWVI	NWVI	SC	NC	N	AK
Robertson	0.1	0.0	0.0	0.0	0.0	0.0	0.0	0.0
	0.2	0.0	0.08	0.33	0.38	1.25	0.57	0.16
	0.3	0.0	0.02	0.29	0.41	1.05	0.47	0.22
	0.4	0.0	0.03	0.06	0.03	0.09	0.22	0.10
Nitinat	0.1	0.0	0.0	0.0	0.0	0.0	0.0	0.0
	0.2	0.0	0.0	0.0	0.99	0.0	0.0	0.0
	0.3	0.0	0.0	1.04	0.0	1.78	0.39	0.0
	0.4	0.0	0.0	0.09	0.0	0.72	0.51	0.0
Big Qualicum	0.1	0.18	0.0	0.0	0.0	0.0	0.0	0.0
	0.2	2.17	0.12	0.42	2.99	1.21	0.45	0.03
	0.3	0.31	0.08	0.14	0.54	0.65	0.12	0.01
	0.4	0.0	0.0	0.0	0.12	0.03	0.0	0.0
Nanaimo	0.1	1.52	0.02	0.0	0.10	0.0	0.0	0.0
	0.2	4.32	0.07	0.86	3.19	1.09	0.52	0.0
	0.3	0.0	0.0	0.03	3.34	0.39	0.03	0.0
	0.4	0.0	0.0	0.0	0.0	0.0	0.0	0.0

[a] GS = Strait of Georgia; SWVI = southwestern Vancouver Island; NWVI = northwestern Vancouver Island; SC = southern central coast; NC = north-central coast; N = north coast; AK = southeastern Alaska.
[b] European system: freshwater annuli are before the decimal point, marine annuli after.

Big Qualicum chinook salmon were distributed from the Strait of Georgia to southeastern Alaska, but their greatest relative abundance was in the Strait of Georgia and the south-central British Columbian coast (Table 1). Nanaimo River chinook salmon had a similar distribution except that none were recaptured from southeastern Alaska (Table 1).

The relative abundance of all stocks decreased with age in all recovery areas, and there were no major changes in the distribution of any stock with age. Older fish retained their abundance in northern recovery areas but declined in abundance in the southern recovery areas, however, so that the center of distribution of each stock moved slightly north with increasing age of fish (Table 1).

Although there was some variation between brood years in the relative abundance of each stock in the various fishing areas, distribution patterns were consistent from year to year, as demonstrated by the distribution of Robertson Creek chinook salmon at age 0.3 from different releases (Figure 5).[1] The variation in relative

---

[1]Salmon ages are presented in the European system. The numeral preceding the decimal point refers to annuli laid down in fresh water, that following the decimal point to annuli laid down in the ocean. Absence of a numeral either preceding or following the decimal point means that either freshwater or marine age was not determined.

abundance between releases within a brood year was usually as great as the differences between brood years. The apparent absence of recaptures from southeastern Alaska for the 1979 brood year is probably an error in the data base. Consequently, the distribution patterns indicated may be taken as representative of the four stocks under consideration (Table 1).

In contrast to chinook salmon, immature sockeye salmon from southern British Columbia wander widely in the Gulf of Alaska during their ocean residence. Little is known about what happens to immature sockeye salmon after October or November of their first ocean year, when they have reached Kodiak Island. Because they are found well to the south in the Gulf of Alaska the following spring, French et al. (1976) concluded that there is a general movement south and southwestward in autumn and winter (Figure 1A).

Around 10,409 age .0 and 28,430 age .1 sockeye salmon have been tagged in the north Pacific Ocean between 1956 and 1970 (French et al. 1976). Since sockeye salmon are believed to home accurately (Quinn 1985), the tagging locations of fish recaptured 1 or 2 years later in the Fraser River or its approaches provide information on the ocean distribution of immature Fraser River sockeye salmon.

The ocean distribution of immature Fraser River sockeye salmon extends into the Gulf of Alaska southward to 45°N, westward to 178°E,

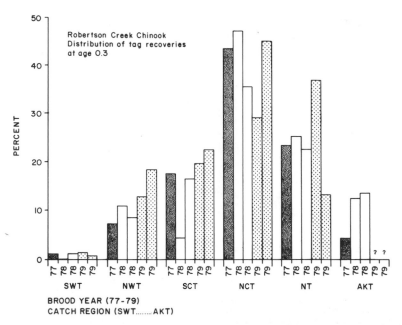

FIGURE 5.—Proportions of chinook salmon from Robertson Creek, British Columbia, recaptured at age 0.3 by trollers fishing in different tag recovery regions. The data comprise one release from the 1977 brood year, and two releases from each of the 1978 and 1979 brood years. Recovery regions include southwestern and northwestern Vancouver Island trolls (SWT, NWT), south-central and north-central trolls (SCT, NCT), northern troll (NT), and southeastern Alaska troll (AKT). Recaptures for the 1979 brood-year releases in the southeastern Alaska troll are uncertain.

and northward to the Aleutian chain, a distance of 6,600 km from the home river. The distribution of fish tagged at age .2 further suggests that immature Fraser River sockeye salmon move north and east in spring and summer (Figure 1B) then south and west in autumn and winter (Figure 1C), keeping generally north of the 15°C isotherm (French et al. 1976). The immature fish thus move in a large circle around the Gulf of Alaska.

Several tentative conclusions regarding the migratory behaviour of chinook and sockeye salmon as immatures appear possible. Sometime after entering the sea, probably late in their first or early in their second ocean year (i.e., before the fish are of legal size and vulnerable to harvest), ocean-type chinook salmon juveniles migrate northward along the coast from their natal stream. As a consequence of this migration, their ocean distribution is established, and that distribution does not change dramatically either seasonally or as the fish age. As was suggested for juvenile sockeye salmon, a north or northwest orientation during this migration would suffice to create such a distribution.

The open-coast chinook salmon stocks establish ocean distributions further north, and perhaps further offshore, than inside sheltered-coast stocks. It may be the open-coast stocks that account for the ocean-type chinook salmon captured offshore in high seas research cruises (Healey 1983).

Locally, chinook salmon congregate in particular areas as indicated by concentrations of fishing vessels during chinook salmon fisheries. The fact that chinook salmon tend to occur at depth rather than near the surface (Tayor 1969; Argue 1970) suggests that the areas in which they aggregate may be characterized by bottom topographic features, or oceanographic features below the mixed layer, that serve to congregate potential prey. Different sized fish may also have different habitat requirements, a possibility suggested because the size composition of the catch changes dramatically along the west coast of Vancouver Island (Healey 1986b). Furthermore, chinook salmon from each brood year that are destined to mature at an older age appear to occupy the most northerly parts of the stock's geographic distribution. This is indicated because, as a brood ages, it disappears from the southern parts of its distribution but not from the northern parts (Table 1).

Immature sockeye salmon, on the other hand,

are distributed far offshore and appear to migrate actively throughout their life in the ocean. Their seasonal movements carry them in a large circuit of the Gulf of Alaska once each year (Figure 1A–C). These movements appear to be, in part at least, governed by temperature, since sockeye salmon do not move south of the 15°C isotherm. Their migration as immatures may be a response to seasonal movements of greatest ocean plankton production and thus serves to keep the sockeye salmon in regions of good feeding. Whatever the motivation for their behaviour, sockeye salmon apparently are constantly on the move during their ocean residence whereas chinook salmon, after quickly establishing a coastal distribution, appear relatively sedentary.

Spawning Migration of Mature Fish

Maturing chinook salmon apparently migrate quickly from their ocean feeding area to their natal stream mouth. Older chinook salmon from Nitinat, Big Qualicum, and Nanaimo rivers and Robertson Creek were seldom captured in ocean fishing areas adjacent to each stock's spawning stream even though intensive fisheries occurred there. These older age-classes are, however, captured in river-mouth recreational fisheries. If maturing fish of the older age-classes had been resident in the ocean fishing areas for any appreciable time, they would surely have contributed significantly to the ocean fisheries.

More direct evidence on speed of migration comes from the recapturing of maturing fish tagged in the ocean. Parker and Kirkness (1956) reported the date of tagging and recapture for 53 chinook salmon tagged in southeastern Alaska and recaptured during the same year in river-mouth fisheries from northern British Columbia to Oregon. The average rate of travel of chinook salmon bound for different spawning rivers ranged from 11.5 to 25.1 km/d. These are minimum rates of travel since many of the fish were probably tagged before they had begun their homeward migration. The migration speeds of the 10 fastest fish ranged from 37.9 to 77.8 km/d and averaged 45.8 km/d. If we assume that these fish, most of which were in their fourth year of life, averaged 80 cm in length (Healey 1986b), and that their optimal cruising speed was about one body length per second (Brett 1983), then these chinook salmon were travelling at about two-thirds their optimal sustainable rate during homeward migration. The fastest fish was travelling faster than its optimal cruising speed.

Approximately 63,330 sockeye salmon aged .2 and older were tagged in open waters of the north Pacific Ocean between 1956 and 1970 under the auspices of the International North Pacific Fisheries Commission (French et al. 1976). Seven hundred twenty-four of these were recaptured in waters around Vancouver Island. These can be considered to be Fraser River fish, since 90% of the sockeye salmon caught in the fisheries in southern British Columbia and Washington state are produced in this river (Groot and Quinn, in press).

Maturing Fraser River sockeye salmon apparently move northeastward toward shore during May and June, then southeastward in July and August along southeastern Alaska and the Queen Charlotte Islands toward Vancouver Island (Figure 1D) (French et al. 1976).

Fraser River sockeye salmon approaching Vancouver Island can migrate north around the island through Queen Charlotte and Johnstone straits or south through Juan de Fuca Strait. The route that the adults choose varies between years (Figure 6). From 1953 to 1977, most of the fish migrated via the southern route (average 80%, range 65–90%). Since 1978, more sockeye salmon have migrated via the northern route (average 53%, range 22–81%) (Figure 6) (IPSFC 1954–1984; Groot and Quinn, in press). The proportion of fish utilizing the northern route correlated positively with the Fraser River discharge for the years 1953–1977 (Wickett 1977; Groot and Quinn, in press) and positively with sea-surface temperature along the British Columbia coast for the years 1978–1983 (IPSFC 1954–1984; Groot and Quinn, in press). These two factors are thought to be indicative of ocean and climate conditions that affect the winter distribution of maturing sockeye salmon prior to homeward migration (Groot and Quinn, in press).

Fraser River sockeye salmon entering the Strait of Georgia via the southern route travel mainly through Rosario and Haro straits and enter the River via the main channel (Figure 7) (Verhoeven and Davidoff 1962). Sockeye salmon entering the Strait of Georgia via the northern route travel along the Vancouver Island shore, in contrast to the juveniles which move out along the mainland shore. The fish may hold for a while in Johnstone Strait and Discovery Passage but, after entering the Strait of Georgia, sockeye salmon seem to follow a direct route, moving between Texada and Lasqueti islands, towards the Fraser River (C. Groot, K. Cooke, and B. Hungar, Pacific Biological Station, Nanaimo, unpublished data). Fish

PERCENT FRASER SOCKEYE USING NORTHERN PASSAGE

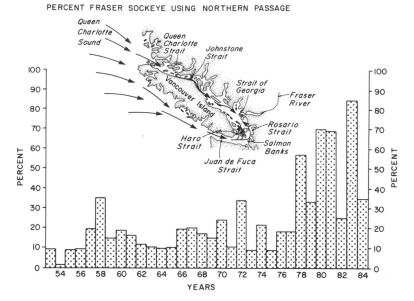

FIGURE 6.—Migratory routes of adult sockeye salmon returning to the Fraser River around Vancouver Island via the northern and southern routes. The bar graph indicates the proportion of the total run that used the northern route (modified from Groot et al. 1984).

migrating from the north are more likely to enter the Fraser River via the northern channels through the delta than those that migrate from the south (Verhoeven and Davidoff 1962).

The optimal swimming speed for maturing sockeye salmon is about 1.8 km/h, or 43 km/d (Brett 1983). Sockeye salmon migrating in coastal waters have been observed to swim about 2 km/h, or close to their optimal speed (Madison et al. 1972; Stasko et al. 1976). Groot and Quinn (in press) found that 23% of sockeye salmon tagged

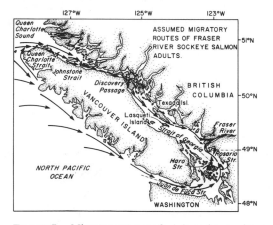

FIGURE 7.—Migratory routes of adult sockeye salmon through the Strait of Georgia and adjacent waters on their way to the Fraser River.

more than 1,000 km from the Fraser River migrated more than 45 km/d. These homing sockeye salmon must have swum day and night at their optimal swimming speed with almost perfect orientation to the home stream to account for their rate of travel.

Both chinook and sockeye salmon, therefore, appear to accomplish their homeward migration quickly. Their speeds of travel suggest virtually continuous swimming on a direct course from the ocean feeding area to the home stream. Relatively, however, sockeye salmon migrate further (several thousand kilometers) than chinook salmon (a few hundred to 1,000 km), and sockeye salmon travel faster. The homeward migration of chinook salmon is also along the shore, whereas sockeye salmon begin their migration well offshore in the Gulf of Alaska.

Discussion

Both chinook and sockeye salmon apparently undertake two directed and rapid marine migrations, the first as juveniles to establish an ocean distribution, the second as adults returning to their natal stream (Table 2). The possibility that the sophistication of direction-finding capability necessary to accomplish these migrations may differ among the species has not previously been considered for Pacific salmon.

TABLE 2.—Comparison of ocean migrations of ocean-type chinook and sockeye salmon from southern British Columbia.

Ocean-type chinook salmon	Sockeye salmon
(1) Remain in the vicinity of their natal stream during first summer at sea	(1) Undertake a directed migration north or northwest soon after entering the ocean
(2) Migrate north and establish a distribution along the coast within a few hundred to 1,000 km of their natal stream, probably during their first winter at sea	(2) Migrate south and west into the open waters of the Gulf of Alaska more than 1,000 km from their natal stream during their first winter at sea
(3) Maintain a relatively fixed coastal distribution throughout their ocean life	(3) Move continuously in a wide circle around the Gulf of Alaska throughout their ocean life
(4) Migrate rapidly along the coast from the ocean feeding area to their home stream when mature	(4) Migrate rapidly from the open Gulf of Alaska directly to their home stream when mature

Griffin (1955) defined three levels of direction-finding ability in animals. The first level, type 1, or piloting, is a simple reliance on visual or other landmarks within familiar territory. Animals possessing only this kind of direction-finding ability search in an undirected way in unfamiliar territory. The second level, type 2, is called compass or one-directional orientation. This is the ability to move in a particular compass direction even in unfamiliar territory by means of celestial or other reference cues. The third level, type 3, is true bicoordinate or goal orientation. Animals having this ability can navigate toward a specific geographic goal from an unfamiliar area. In general, type-2 orientation is performed by juveniles or young of the year who are migrating away from the breeding grounds for the first time. Goal orientation is apparently only performed by older animals who have previous experience of the goal (i.e., wintering or breeding grounds, Perdeck 1958). Goal orientation is often assumed to be involved in homing.

Juvenile chinook and sockeye salmon movements along the west coast of North America suggest a definite directional preference (north or northwest), which implies compass orientation. Experiments with juvenile sockeye salmon have shown that they are able to utilize compass orientation during their migration out of lakes as smolts (Johnson and Groot 1963; Groot 1965) and during their dispersal as fry into lakes (Brannon 1972; Quinn and Brannon 1982). Directional prefer-

ences of smolts and fry in lakes appear to be innate and involve the use of both the sun and the earth's magnetic field (Groot 1965; Brannon 1972; Quinn 1980) although other cues may also be important. Taylor (1986) has demonstrated that juvenile chinook are able to use geomagnetic and other universal cues to find a compass direction. In the marine environment, Healey (1967) found that juvenile pink salmon displayed directional preferences during migration through a coastal inlet and that they probably used the sun to find directions.

We conclude, from these and other observations (Groot 1965, 1982; Quinn 1980, 1982; Quinn and Brannon 1982), that Pacific salmon, like birds (Emlen 1975), can use a variety of mechanisms to find compass directions and that compass orientation (Griffin's type 2) is probably the direction-finding mechanism of juvenile sockeye and chinook salmon migrating north from their natal stream mouth. Thus, with respect to juvenile migration, we reject our working hypothesis that ocean-type chinook salmon require less sophisticated direction finding than sockeye salmon.

The homing migration of maturing adults from their feeding grounds can be divided into two phases: an ocean phase that carries the fish from offshore feeding grounds to the coast, and a nearshore phase that carries the fish along the shore to their river (Hasler 1966). Sockeye salmon clearly display both phases whereas ocean-type chinook salmon may display only the nearshore phase. Little is known about the ocean phase of sockeye salmon migration except that it is rapid, well directed, and well timed (Royce et al. 1968; French et al. 1976; Groot and Quinn, in press). The point at which sockeye salmon make landfall at the end of the ocean phase of their homing migration seems to be related to climatological and oceanographic conditions prior to or during this phase of the migration (Groot and Quinn, in press). When the Gulf of Alaska was warm, sockeye salmon made landfall at the north end of Vancouver Island and approached the Fraser River primarily via the northern route. When the Gulf of Alaska was cold, sockeye salmon were distributed further south, made landfall on the west coast of Vancouver Island, and approached the Fraser River primarily via the southern route (Groot and Quinn, in press). A specific compass orientation (Griffin's type 2) among returning adults could, therefore, account for the differences in landfall during warm and cold years.

After making landfall, Fraser River sockeye

salmon are able to locate their natal stream via either a northern or southern route around Vancouver Island. Since these fish left the Strait of Georgia primarily by the northern route (Groot and Cooke, in press), adults homing via the southern route are travelling a route with which they have no previous experience. Furthermore, even though some Fraser River water is flushed out through Juan de Fuca Strait, oceanographic conditions off the west coast of Vancouver Island are too complex for the fish simply to follow up the odour trail of the river. True bicoordinate navigation (Griffin's type 3) seems to be indicated in this case; however, a strong easterly compass orientation might also carry the fish into Juan de Fuca Strait and ultimately near enough to the Fraser River for odour trails to provide final guidance.

Chinook salmon returning to their natal streams on the east and west coasts of Vancouver Island face a somewhat similar problem. While a southeastward compass orientation would suffice to carry them south and east along the coast north of Vancouver Island, once they reach the north end of Vancouver Island they must be able to choose correctly the outside or the inside route to reach their home river. Since very few chinook salmon from Big Qualicum and Nanaimo rivers were captured on the west coast of Vancouver Island, and no chinook salmon from Nitinat River and Robertson Creek were captured on the east coast of the island, errors in choice of migration route must be rare. In our view, simple compass orientation would not be sufficient to prevent substantial errors in choice of route by these salmon. Some other directional or goal-finding system must be available to the fish. In the case of ocean-type chinook salmon the fish are retracing the route of their outward migration as juveniles, and they may, therefore, be using compass orientation to find general directions but depending on specific physical landmarks or other cues at critical choice points. A difficulty with this hypothesis is that it does not explain how the fish recognize critical choice points, since they ought to be unaware of the possibility of making an error. An alternative hypothesis is that both chinook and sockeye salmon employ true navigation (Griffin's type 3) even though the chinook salmon's direction-finding problem at first sight appears the simpler.

A number of investigators have concluded that there is no need to invoke goal orientation, or navigation, to explain the high-seas migration of Pacific salmon (Harden Jones 1968; Leggett 1977;

Able 1980). These authors based their conclusion, in part, on Saila and Shappy's (1963) Monte Carlo simulation of the salmon's return from the high seas. This simulation suggested that only a weak homeward orientation was required to produce rates of return that approximated the observed rates of return from high-seas tagging studies. Quinn and Groot (1984), however, argued that Saila and Shappy's (1963) assumptions about swimming speed, duration of migration, and return success were incorrect and resulted in substantial underestimation of the strength of orientation required for salmon homeward migration and did not explain the apparently well-directed, well-timed, and rapid movements in the open ocean.

So far there is no hard evidence that Pacific salmon are capable of goal orientation, but some further circumstantial evidence for sockeye salmon will strengthen the case for taking the possibility seriously. For example, 4–10 weeks before returning to their spawning streams, Bristol Bay sockeye salmon are spread across 3,700 km of ocean measured in an east–west direction. The peak of the spawning run passes through Bristol Bay between 2 and 9 July and 80% of the run occurs within a span of 9–22 d. Some sockeye salmon migrate to Bristol Bay from as far away as 2,200 km (either directly, if starting in the western north Pacific, or around the Alaskan peninsula, if starting in the eastern north Pacific) at speeds averaging 45–56 km/d (Hartt 1966; Royce et al. 1968; French et al. 1976). The sockeye salmon converge on the home area by swimming continuously at their optimal speed in a very direct migration, irrespective of whether their starting point in the ocean is east or west of Bristol Bay and of whether they can swim on a direct course or have to circumnavigate the Alaska Peninsula. Groot (1982) concluded that these fish must use bicoordinate orientation. Thus, with respect to the homing migration to the river mouth, we also reject our working hypothesis that ocean-type chinook salmon will require a less sophisticated guidance mechanism than sockeye salmon.

Migration in the coastal zone near to the river mouth may involve a different direction-finding mechanism and may be more akin to Griffin's type-1 orientation. There are few data on the behaviour of chinook salmon during this phase of their migration, but it seems likely that they behave similarly to sockeye salmon.

In the Strait of Georgia, home stream odours could aid sockeye salmon in finding the mouth of the Fraser River. Sonic tracking with depth-sensing tags (Quinn and terHart, in press) indicated that sockeye salmon moved through the Strait of Georgia in a highly directed way, either near the surface or around 15 m deep. Movement patterns became more complex, with large vertical and horizontal excursions from the migration path, when the fish passed channels and inlets on their way to the river mouth. This behaviour strongly suggested that the fish were searching and testing different water masses for odour cues (Quinn and terHart, in press).

Two hypotheses have been proposed in which odours are used for homing. The "imprinting hypothesis" (Hasler 1966; Hasler and Scholz 1983) proposes that specific odours emanating from the rocks, plants, and soil in the home stream system are learned by juvenile salmon during crucial development stages. Exposure to these imprinted odours stimulates upstream swimming in adult salmon (Johnsen and Hasler 1980). The "pheromone hypothesis" (Nordeng 1977; Stabel 1984) proposes that the homeward migration of adult salmon is directed by population-specific pheromone trails laid down by juveniles on their way to sea. Also, fish migrating later in the season may be guided by pheromones from adults that migrated earlier. The response to home stream odour is considered to be learned (Hasler 1966; Hasler and Scholz 1983) whereas the response to pheromones is considered to be innate (Nordeng 1977). If pheromones are part of the total bouquet of odours that juvenile salmon learn prior to emigration, then there is no basic difference between the two hypotheses (Selset and Doving 1980; Horrall 1981; Hara et al. 1984).

Behavioural and neurophysiological studies have shown that sockeye and coho salmon (*Oncorhynchus kisutch*) can recognize stock-specific odours (Groot et al. 1986; Quinn and Tolson 1986). However, most, if not all, juvenile sockeye salmon from the Fraser River take the northern route out of the Strait of Georgia, whereas the adults return via either the northern or the southern route, which is inconsistent with the pheromone hypothesis (Groot et al. 1986).

Evidence so far indicates that riverine and lake odours are more important for homing salmon (Hasler 1966; Hasler and Scholz 1983). Hara et al. (1965) demonstrated that chinook salmon are capable of smelling very dilute concentrations of their home stream water, while Groves et al. (1968) showed that chinook salmon in the Columbia River apparently used both olfaction and

vision in selecting their home tributary, although olfaction was the more important sense. Thus, olfaction and home stream odour appear to be important guidance mechanisms once the salmon are near their natal river, but how olfaction is actually used during coastal and riverine migration is still an open question.

An alternative to the olfaction hypotheses is that returning adults retrace the migratory route that they took as juveniles—that they recall all the twists and turns of their outward journey and replay this memory tape backwards on their return journey (Groot et al. 1984; Groot and Cooke, in press). For sockeye salmon, however, the outward migration path of juveniles can be fundamentally different from that of returning adults. It is conceivable, however, that adult chinook salmon could use this kind of a mechanism since their homing migration appears, in general, to retrace the outward migration of the juveniles.

In conclusion, the problems of orientation during migration appear not to be fundamentally different for chinook and sockeye salmon, even though sockeye salmon migrate much further. For both, compass orientation will suffice to guide their seaward migration whereas a more complicated mechanism appears necessary to explain their homing migration. For both, the oceanic and coastal phases of their homing migration are likely guided by different mechanisms than those that guide their final movements toward their natal river and spawning tributary. In our view, the most likely guidance mechanisms used by Pacific salmon are compass orientation (Griffin's type 2) during the outward migration to the ocean and a combination of compass and goal orientation (Griffin's types 2 and 3) during the homing migration back to the vicinity of the natal stream. Once near the natal stream they probably switch to following odour trails of their home tributary (Griffin's type 1). While we cannot disprove the hypothesis that returning adult chinook salmon retrace their outward migration path as juveniles by means of memory, we feel that it is more likely that sockeye and chinook salmon utilize similar orientation mechanisms during comparable phases of their marine migration.

References

Able, K. P. 1980. Mechanisms of orientation, navigation, and homing. Pages 283–373 *in* S. A. Gauthreaux, editor. Animal migration, orientation and navigation. Academic Press, New York, New York, USA.

Argue, A. W. 1970. A study of factors affecting exploitation of Pacific salmon in the Canadian gauntlet fishery of Juan de Fuca Strait. Canadian Department of Fisheries and Forestry, Pacific Region, Technical Report 1970-11.

Argue, A. W., R. Hilborn, R. M. Peterman, M. J. Staley, and C J. Walters. 1983. Strait of Georgia chinook and coho fishery. Canadian Bulletin of Fisheries and Aquatic Sciences 211.

Brannon, E. L. 1972. Mechanisms controlling migration of sockeye salmon fry. International Pacific Salmon Fisheries Commission Bulletin 21.

Brett, J. R. 1965. The relation of size to rate of oxygen consumption and sustained swimming speed of sockeye salmon (Oncorhynchus nerka). Journal of the Fisheries Research Board of Canada 22:1491–1501.

Brett, J. R. 1983. Life energetics of sockeye salmon, Oncorhynchus nerka. Pages 29–63 in W. P. Aspey and S. I. Lustick, editors. Behavioural energetics: the cost of survival in vertebrates. Ohio State University Press, Columbus, Ohio, USA.

Emlen, S. T. 1975. Migration: orientation and navigation. Pages 129–219 in D. S. Farner, J. R. King, and K. G. Parkes, editors. Avian biology, volume 5. Academic Press, New York, New York, USA.

Foerster, R. E. 1968. The sockeye salmon. Fisheries Research Board of Canada Bulletin 162.

French, R., H. Bilton, M. Osako, and A. Hartt. 1976. Distribution and origin of sockeye salmon (Oncorhynchus nerka) in offshore waters of the north Pacific Ocean. International North Pacific Fisheries Commission Bulletin 34.

Godfrey, H. 1968. Review of information obtained from the tagging and marking of chinook and coho salmon in coastal waters of Canada and the United States. Fisheries Research Board of Canada Manuscript Report 953, Ottawa, Canada.

Griffin, D. R. 1955. Bird navigation. Pages 154–197 in A. Wolfson, editor. Recent studies in avian biology. University of Illinois Press, Urbana, Illinois, USA.

Groot, C. 1965. On the orientation of young sockeye salmon (Oncorhynchus nerka) during their seaward migration out of lakes. Behaviour 14 (supplement): 1–198.

Groot, C. 1972. Migration of yearling sockeye salmon (Oncorhynchus nerka) determined by time-lapse photography of sonar observations. Journal of the Fisheries Research Board of Canada 29:1431–1444.

Groot, C. 1982. Modifications on a theme—a perspective on migratory behaviour of Pacific salmon. Pages 1–21 in E. L. Brannon and E. O. Salo, editors. Proceedings of the salmon and trout migratory behavior symposium. University of Washington, School of Fisheries, Seattle, Washington, USA.

Groot, C., and K. Cooke. In press. Are the migrations of juvenile and adult Fraser River sockeye salmon (Oncorhynchus nerka) in near-shore waters related? Canadian Special Publication of Fisheries and Aquatic Sciences 96.

Groot, C., L. Margolis, and R. Bailey 1984. Does the route of seaward migration of Fraser River sockeye salmon (Oncorhynchus nerka) smolts determine the route of return migration of adults? Pages 283–292 in J. D. McCleave, G. P. Arnold, J. J. Dodson, and W. H. Neill, editors. Mechanisms of migration in fishes. Plenum, New York, New York, USA.

Groot, C., and T. P. Quinn. In press. The homing migration of sockeye salmon to the Fraser River. U.S. National Marine Fisheries Service Fishery Bulletin 85.

Groot, C., T. P. Quinn, and T. Hara. 1986. Responses of migrating sockeye salmon (Oncorhynchus nerka) to population-specific odours. Canadian Journal of Zoology 64:926–932.

Grooves, A. B., G. B. Collins, and P. S. Trefethen. 1968. Roles of olfaction and vision in choice of spawning site by homing adult chinook salmon (Oncorhynchus tshawytscha). Journal of the Fisheries Research Board of Canada 25:867–876.

Hara, T. J., S. Macdonald, R. E. Evans, T. Marui, and S. Arai. 1984. Morpholine, bile acids and skin mucus as possible chemical cues in salmonid homing: electrophysiological re-evaluation. Pages 363–378 in J. D. McCleave, G. P. Arnold, J. J. Dodson, and W. H. Neill, editors. Mechanisms of migration in fishes. Plenum, New York, New York, USA.

Hara, T. J., K. Ueda, and A. Gorbman. 1965. Electroencephalographic studies of homing salmon. Science (Washington, D.C.) 149:884–885.

Harden Jones, F. R. 1968. Fish migration. Edward Arnold, London, England.

Hartt, A. C. 1966. Migrations of salmon in the north Pacific Ocean and Bering Sea as determined by seining and tagging, 1959–1960. International North Pacific Fisheries Commission Bulletin 19.

Hartt, A. C. 1980. Juvenile salmonids in the oceanic ecosystem—the critical first summer. Pages 25–58 in W. J. McNeil and D. C. Himsworth, editors. Salmonid ecosystems of the north Pacific. Oregon State University Press, Corvallis, Oregon, USA.

Hartt, A. C., and M. B. Dell. 1986. Early oceanic migrations and growth of juvenile salmon and steelhead trout. International North Pacific Fisheries Commission Bulletin 46:1–105.

Hasler, A. D. 1966. Underwater guideposts. University of Wisconsin Press, Madison, Wisconsin, USA.

Hasler, A. D., and A. T. Scholz. 1983. Olfactory imprinting and homing in salmon. Springer-Verlag, New York, New York, USA.

Healey, M. C. 1967. Orientation of pink salmon (Oncorhynchus gorbuscha) during early marine migration from Bella Coola River system. Journal of the Fisheries Research Board of Canada 24:2321–2338.

Healey, M. C. 1980a. The ecology of juvenile salmon in Georgia Strait, British Columbia. Pages 203–209 in W. J. McNeil and D. C. Himsworth, editors. Salmonid ecosystems of the north Pacific. Oregon State University Press, Corvallis, Oregon, USA.

Healey, M. C. 1980b. Utilization of the Nanaimo River estuary by juvenile chinook salmon, Oncorhynchus tshawytscha. U.S. National Marine Fisheries Service Fishery Bulletin 77:653–668.

Healey, M. C. 1983. Coastwide distribution and ocean migration patterns of stream- and ocean-type chinook salmon, *Oncorhynchus tshawytscha*. Canadian Field-Naturalist 97:427–433.

Healey, M. C. 1986a. Optimum size and age at maturity in Pacific salmon and effects of size selective fisheries. Canadian Special Publication of Fisheries and Aquatic Sciences 89:39–52.

Healey, M. C. 1986b. Regional and seasonal attributes of catch in the British Columbia troll fishery. Canadian Technical Report of Fisheries and Aquatic Sciences 1494:1–65.

Horrall, R. M. 1981. Behavioural stock-isolating mechanisms in Great Lakes fishes with special reference to homing and site imprinting. Canadian Journal of Fisheries and Aquatic Sciences 38:1481–1496.

IPSFC (International Pacific Salmon Fisheries Commission). 1954–1984. Annual Reports for the years 1953–1983. IPSFC, New Westminster, Canada.

Johnsen, P. B., and A. D. Hassler. 1980. The use of chemical cues in the upstream migration of coho salmon, *Oncorhynchus kisutch* Walbaum. Journal of Fish Biology 17:67–73.

Johnson, W. E., and C. Groot. 1963. Observations on the migration of young sockeye salmon *(Oncorhynchus nerka)* through a large, complex, lake system. Journal of the Fisheries Research Board of Canada 20:919–938.

Leggett, W. C. 1977. The ecology of fish migrations. Annual Review of Ecology and Systematics 8:285–308.

Madison, D. M., R. M. Horrall, A. B. Stasko, and A. D. Hasler. 1972. Migratory movements of adult sockeye salmon *(Oncorhynchus nerka)* in coastal British Columbia as revealed by ultrasonic tracking. Journal of the Fisheries Research Board of Canada 29:1025–1033.

Major, R. L., J. Ito, and H. Godfrey. 1978. Distribution and origin of chinook salmon *(Oncorhynchus tshawytscha)* in offshore waters of the north Pacific Ocean. International North Pacific Fisheries Commission Bulletin 38.

Manzer, J. I., T. Ishida, A. E. Peterson, and M. G. Hanavan. 1965. Salmon of the north Pacific Ocean, part 5. Offshore distribution of salmon. International North Pacific Fisheries Commission Bulletin 15.

Neave, F. 1964. Ocean migrations of Pacific salmon. Journal of the Fisheries Research Board of Canada 21:1227–1244.

Neave, T., T. Yonemori, and R. G. Bakkala. 1976. Distribution and origin of chum salmon in offshore waters of the north Pacific Ocean. International North Pacific Fisheries Commission Bulletin 35.

Nordeng, H. 1977. A pheromone hypothesis for homeward migration in anadromous salmonids. Oikos 28:155–159.

Parker, R. R., and W. Kirkness. 1956. King salmon in the ocean troll fishery of southeastern Alaska. Alaska Department of Fisheries Research Report 1:1–64.

Perdek, A. C. 1958. Two types of orientation in migrat-

ing starlings, *Sturnus vulgaris* L., and chaffinches, *Fringilla coeless* L., as revealed by displacement experiments. Ardea 46:1–37.

Quinn, T. P. 1980. Evidence for celestial and magnetic compass orientation in lake migrating sockeye salmon fry. Journal of Comparative Physiology 137:243–248.

Quinn, T. P. 1982. Intra-specific differences in sockeye salmon fry compass orientation mechanisms. Pages 79–85 *in* E. L. Brannon and E. O. Salo, editors. Proceedings of the salmon and trout migratory behavior symposium. University of Washington, School of Fisheries, Seattle, Washington, USA.

Quinn, T. 1985. Homing and the evolution of sockeye salmon *(Oncorhynchus nerka)*. Contributions in Marine Science 27(supplement):353–366.

Quinn, T. P., and E. L. Brannon. 1982. The use of celestial and magnetic cues by orienting sockeye salmon smolts. Journal of Comparative Physiology A, Sensory, Neural, and Behavioral Physiology 147:547–552.

Quinn, T. P., and C. Groot. 1984. Pacific salmon *(Oncorhynchus)* migrations: orientation versus random movement. Canadian Journal of Fisheries and Aquatic Sciences 41:1319–1324.

Quinn, T. P., and B. A. terHart. In press. Movements of adult sockeye salmon in British Columbia coastal waters in relation to temperature and salinity stratification: ultrasonic telemetry results. Canadian Special Publication of Fisheries and Aquatic Sciences 96.

Quinn, T. P., and G. M. Tolson. 1986. Evidence of chemically mediated population recognition in coho salmon *(Oncorhynchus kisutch)*. Canadian Journal of Zoology 64:84–87.

Royce, W. F., L. S. Smith, and A. C. Hartt. 1968. Models of oceanic migrations of Pacific salmon and comments on guidance mechanisms. U.S. Fish and Wildlife Service Fishery Bulletin 66:441–462.

Saila, S. B., and R. A. Shappy. 1963. Random movement and orientation in salmon migration. Journal du Conseil, Conseil International pour l'Exploration de la Mer 28:153–166.

Selset, R., and K. B. Doving. 1980. Behaviour of mature anadromous char *(Salmo alpinus* L.) towards odorants produced by smolts of their own population. Acta Physiologica Scandinavica 108:113–122.

Stabel, O. B. 1984. Homing and olfaction in salmonids: a critical review with special reference to Atlantic salmon. Biological Reviews of the Cambridge Philosophical Society 59:333–388.

Stasko, A. B., R. M. Horrall, and A. D. Hasler. 1976. Coastal movements of adult Fraser River sockeye salmon *(Oncorhynchus nerka)* observed by ultrasonic tracking. Transactions of the American Fisheries Society 105:64–71.

Takagi, K., K. V. Aro, A. C. Hartt, and M. B. Dell. 1981. Distribution and origin of pink salmon *(Oncorhynchus gorbuscha)* in offshore waters of the north Pacific Ocean. International North Pacific Fisheries Commission Bulletin 40.

Taylor, F. H. C. 1969. The British Columbia offshore

herring survey, 1968–1969. Fisheries Research Board of Canada Technical Report 140.

Taylor, P. B. 1986. Experimental evidence for geomagnetic orientation in juvenile salmon, *Oncorhynchus tshawytscha* Walbaum. Journal of Fish Biology 28:607–623.

Verhoeven, L. A., and E. B. Davidoff. 1962. Marine tagging of Fraser River sockeye salmon. International Pacific Salmon Fisheries Commission Bulletin 13.

Wickett, W. P. 1977. Relationship of coastal oceanographic factors to the migration of Fraser River sockeye salmon (*Oncorhynchus nerka* W.). International Council for the Exploration of the Sea, C.M. 1977/M:26, Copenhagen, Denmark.

American Fisheries Society Symposium 1:313–330, 1987

Influences of Origin, Life History, and Chance on the Atlantic Coast Migration of American Shad

MICHAEL J. DADSWELL AND GARY D. MELVIN[1]

Fisheries Research Branch, Department of Fisheries and Oceans, Biological Station
St. Andrews, New Brunswick E0G 2X0, Canada

P. JAMES WILLIAMS AND DAPHNE E. THEMELIS

Department of Biology, Acadia University, Wolfville, Nova Scotia B0P 1X0, Canada

Abstract.—Tag-return data and population discrimination studies indicate that three partially distinct aggregations of American shad *Alosa sapidissima* occur on the Atlantic coast of North America. Each aggregation consists of a varying proportion of fish originating from rivers in the north, central, and southern regions of the species' range. Group wintering sites are off Florida, in the Middle Atlantic Bight, and in the Scotian Shelf–Gulf of Maine region. Northern migration during summer terminates in the Bay of Fundy, the St. Lawrence estuary, and along the Labrador coast. After leaving wintering sites, prespawning adults select ocean isotherms of 13–18°C and migrate close inshore, probably to facilitate recognition of homing clues, while nonspawning American shad migrate offshore associated with isotherms of 3–15°C. Northward migration of prespawning adults is rapid (mean ± SD, 30.2 ± 14.3 km/d). After spawning, spent adults continue to migrate northward at a slower rate (8.8 ± 4.2 km/d). Although American shad from all regions are present throughout the summer in the Bay of Fundy, the proportion of northern fish there is greatest during June at lower temperatures (10–14°C); fish from the southern region are most numerous in July at higher temperatures (16–20°C). The course and direction of migration in the bay of Fundy is partly attributable to chance and partly to oceanographic and topographic clues. Chance apparently decides which tidal basin an individual fish first enters but, once it is committed, its migration is under strong behavioral constraints, probably controlled by residual current direction and coastline. Migration under these conditions is slower (3.6 ± 0.78 km/d) and is a lock-step process with a rigidly determined direction aligned to residual currents. After leaving the Bay of Fundy, American shad move to wintering sites. There may be a genetic component in their selection of these wintering sites.

Among diadromous fishes whose life cycles involve ocean migrations of thousands of kilometers, two strategies appear: utilization of large, open-ocean current structures or migration along coastal corridors (Leggett 1977b; McCleave et al. 1984). Open-ocean migrants usually exhibit semelparous life histories (*Oncorhynchus* spp.) and exploit large ocean gyres (Healey and Groot 1987; Reddin and Shearer 1987, both this volume). Drift models and orientation with magnetic, celestial, or solar navigation have been hypothesized to explain these migrations (Royce et al. 1968; Quinn 1982; Quinn and Groot 1984). Long-distance coastal migrants tend towards iteroparous life histories (species of *Alosa* and *Morone*) and make annual migrations back and forth along a particular coastline (Leggett and Whitney 1972; Boreman and Lewis 1987, this volume). Environmental

fluctuations, local currents, and olfactory clues have all been proposed as mechanisms controlling coastal migration (Leggett and Whitney 1972; Arnold and Cook 1984; Dodson and Dohse 1984).

American shad *Alosa sapidissima* are long-distance coastal migrants. Each spring American shad leave offshore wintering grounds and migrate north along the Atlantic coast, returning southward in fall (Talbot and Sykes 1958). Extreme ends of the migration are Florida (Williams and Bruger 1972) and Labrador (Dempson et al. 1983). During an average life span of 5 years at sea, an American shad may migrate over 20,000 km. Movement appears to be broadly controlled by climate, and postulated migration models require that the fish maintain themselves within "preferred" isotherms (Leggett and Whitney 1972; Neves and Depres 1979). However, direct evidence from field studies and tag returns suggest American shad cross thermal barriers, remain for extended periods in temperatures outside their

---

[1]Present address: National Hilsa Team, Freshwater Fisheries Research Station, Chanpur, Comilla, Bangladesh.

TABLE 1.—Summary of American shad tagging information, Atlantic coast of USA and Canada, 1946–1985.

Tagging site	Tag	Number tagged	Recaptures Number	Recaptures %	Life phase	Authors, agency
St. Lawrence estuary	Jaw	1,886	114	6.0	Ocean	Vladykov (1956)
Miramichi River	Dart	800	34	4.2	Spawning	Dadswell, Fisheries and Oceans
Annapolis River	Dart	5,074	288	5.8	Spawning	Melvin et al. (1986)
Bay of Fundy						
Cumberland Basin	Dart	7,790	459	5.9	Ocean	Dadswell, Fisheries and Oceans
Minas Basin	Dart	5,790	368	6.3	Ocean	Dadswell, Fisheries and Oceans
Saint John Harbour	Dart	638	39	6.1	Ocean	Dadswell, Fisheries and Oceans
Narraguagus River	Dart	583	11	1.9	Spawning	Maine Marine Resources
Gulf of Maine	Disk	601	43	7.1	Ocean	Talbot and Sykes (1958)
Connecticut River	Dart	18,374	383	2.1	Spawning	Leggett (1977a)
Hudson River	Disk	3,295	227	6.8	Spawning	Talbot and Sykes (1958)
Mid-Atlantic coast	Disk	3,241	1,154	35.6	Ocean	Talbot and Sykes (1958)
Delaware Bay	Disk	2,920	144	4.9	Ocean	White et al. (1969)
Chesapeake Bay	Disk	4,775	112	2.3	Spawning	Talbot and Sykes (1958)

preferred range, and migrate rapidly between regions regardless of currents and temperature (Dadswell et al. 1983; Melvin et al. 1986). Because of these discrepancies with the environmental-control model, we review the results of American shad tagging studies from the last 40 years, including new information. These data and results from recent population discrimination studies (Melvin 1984; Williams 1985) suggest that origin, life history, and chance play a role in American shad migration. The evidence also suggests that American shad alternate between extrinsic and intrinsic cues to direct migration, depending on their physiological state, and at times may use a bicoordinate navigation system with map, compass, and clock.

Aggregations of American Shad at Sea

Since 1945 there have been numerous tagging studies of American shad over the greater portion of their range (Vladykov 1956; Talbot and Sykes 1958; White et al. 1969; Leggett 1977a; Miller et al. 1982; Dadswell et al. 1983; Melvin et al. 1986). During this period, over 60,000 American shad were tagged and there were approximately 3,450 (5.7%) returns with usable information (Table 1). Three types of tags were used: FT1 dart, Petersen disk, and jaw straps. Return rates for all tag types were similar (5.1 ± 2.0%[2]) except for one case (35.6%) where the fish were recaptured soon after they were tagged in adjacent spawning rivers. These data suggest differential tag loss or mortality associated with tag type can be disregarded for migration studies.

Two patterns of movement were evident from tag returns. American shad tagged in or near spawning streams (Figure 1A, B) were recaptured over a wide area of the Atlantic coast but the majority of returns were in or near the river of tagging; there were few returns at other freshwater sites. These fish represent relatively homogeneous aggregations from a single river population. American shad tagged at oceanic sites were also recaptured over wide areas of the coast but returns were distributed relatively evenly over several freshwater sites (Figures 1C, D and 2A, B). Ocean aggregations represent a heterogeneous mixture of American shad from many rivers.

Although American shad populations mix in the sea over most of their range, at least from Chesapeake Bay to the St. Lawrence River (Figure 3), discrete aggregations exist seasonally at widely separated marine locations. During summer, aggregations occurred in the upper Bay of Fundy, the St. Lawrence estuary, and off Newfoundland and Labrador (Figure 4). During winter, three aggregations were observed—off Florida, in the Middle Atlantic Bight, and on the Scotian Shelf (Figure 4).

Aggregations of American shad in the Middle Atlantic Bight and the Bay of Fundy are well documented (Perley 1852; Leim 1924; Talbot and Sykes 1958; Neves and Depres 1979; Dadswell et al. 1983). Aggregations at the other sites are poorly known, but records of occurrence and tag returns have been persistent through time.

Summer occurrences of American shad off Newfoundland and Labrador were first reported during the 1930s and records, although few, have been consistent (Hodder 1966; Hare and Murphy 1974; Dempson et al. 1983). American shad tagged

---

[2]In this paper, all values in this form are means ± SD.

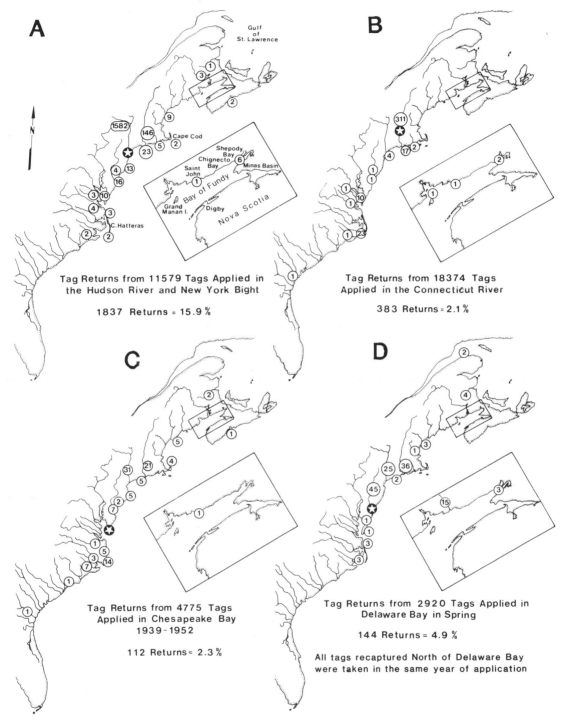

FIGURE 1.—Recapture localities for American shad tagged in USA sites during spring. Numbers in circles indicate total tags recaptured at a site; stars in circles represent tagging sites. Returns without accurate location information were not illustrated. Chesapeake Bay and Hudson River returns are from Talbot and Sykes (1958), Delaware Bay returns from Miller et al. (1982), and Connecticut River returns from W. C. Leggett (McGill University, unpublished data).

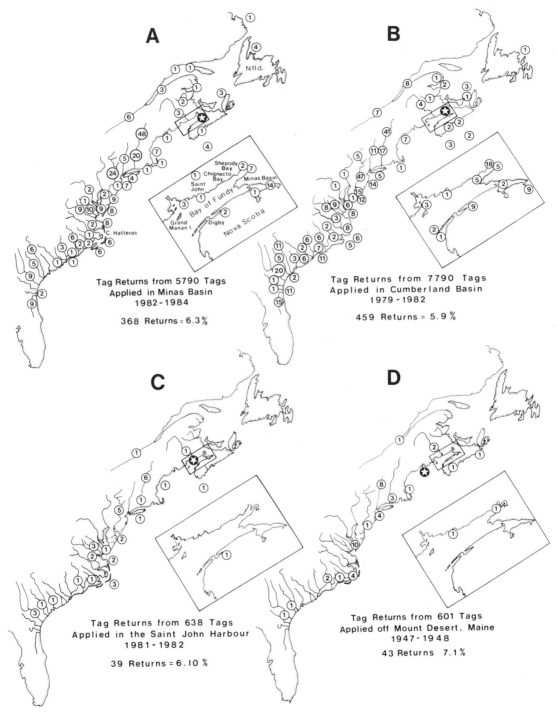

FIGURE 2.—Recapture localities for American shad tagged in the Bay of Fundy–Gulf of Maine during summer. Numbers in circles indicate total tags recaptured at a site; stars in circles represent tagging sites. Gulf of Maine returns are from Talbot and Sykes (1958).

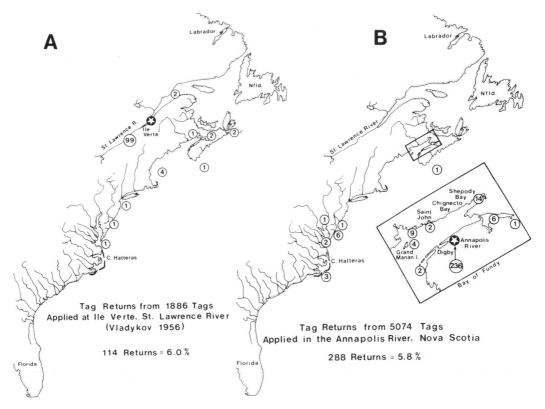

FIGURE 3.—Recapture localities for American shad tagged in the St. Lawrence estuary (Ile Verte) and the Annapolis River (after Vladykov 1956; Melvin et al. 1986).

in the inner Bay of Fundy were recaptured during subsequent years in the Newfoundland–Labrador region on a mean Julian day[3] of 182 (July 1) and on mean day 213 (August 1) off Nain, Labrador (Table 2). These returns coincide with the maximum abundance of American shad in the inner Bay of Fundy (Dadswell et al. 1983) and must represent a separate group. Similarly, American shad tagged in the inner Bay of Fundy 1–3 years previously had a mean recapture day of 180.5 (June 30) in the St. Lawrence estuary (Ile Verte; Table 2). In contrast, mean recapture day was 150.8 (May 31) for fish tagged in the Bay of Fundy and captured during subsequent years in the St. Lawrence River on the spawning grounds above Trois Rivières. Peak spawning activity in the St. Lawrence is late June (Vladykov 1950; Provost et al. 1984). It appears the St. Lawrence estuary and St. Lawrence River aggregations are two different groups. Vladykov (1956) found that American

shad tagged at Ile Verte were recaptured at distant sites in the sea (Figure 3). Annual occurrence of American shad in summer at the Ile Verte site and the similarity of the regional oceanographic conditions there to those of the inner Bay of Fundy (D'Anglejean 1981) suggest this site is another marine terminus for American shad migration. Further study at Ile Verte would clarify the situation.

Occurrence of American shad on the Scotian Shelf during winter is known both from catch records (Vladykov 1936) and tag recaptures (Vladykov 1956; Table 2). Trawl surveys (Department of Fisheries and Oceans, unpublished data), commercial catches (Maine Department of Fisheries), and tag returns (Table 2) indicate a persistent annual pattern. Mean Julian day of recapture for American shad tagged in the Bay of Fundy was 74.6 (March 15), which is the same date when aggregations were present off the Carolinas and in the Middle Atlantic Bight (Table 2). Oceanographic conditions at 100–200 m on the Scotian Shelf during winter (9–10°C; McLellan 1954) are

_____

[3]Julian day: day of the year counting from January 1 (day 1) to December 31 (day 365).

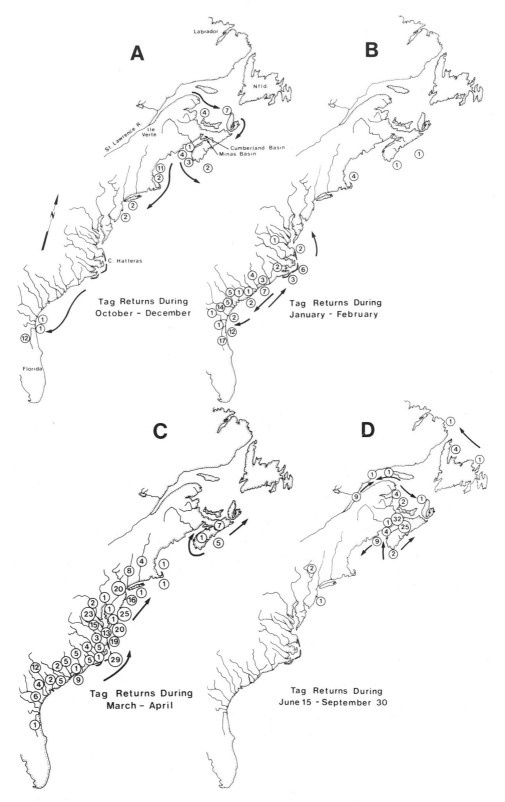

FIGURE 4.—Seasonal distribution of tag returns from American shad tagged in the bay of Fundy 1979–1985.

TABLE 2.—Mean recapture Julian day (calendar date) for American shad tagged in the inner Bay of Fundy and recaptured in marine waters off southern USA, the Scotian Shelf, the St. Lawrence estuary and river, and the Labrador coast.

Recapture site	Mean Julian day of recapture (calendar date)	Range	N
Mayport, Florida	17.0 (Jan 17)	Dec 29–Feb 8	13
Georgia coast	45.8 (Feb 15)	Feb 9–Mar 12	5
South Carolina coast	46.1 (Feb 15)	Jan 22–Feb 23	9
North Carolina coast (south of Cape Hatteras)	31.6 (Feb 1)	Jan 15–Feb 24	3
North Carolina coast (north of Cape Hatteras)	58.1 (Mar 1)	Feb 17–Apr 15	9
Scotian Shelf	74.6 (Mar 15)	Nov 11–Jun 10	9
St. Lawrence River	150.8 (May 31)	May 22–Jun 7	13
Inner Gulf of St. Lawrence	180.5 (Jun 30)	Jun 1–Jul 20	12
Newfoundland–Labrador	182.0 (Jul 1)	Jun 8–Jul 15	6
Nain, Labrador (Dempson et al. 1983)	213.0 (Aug 1)	Jul 24–Aug 18	4

within the preferred temperature range of American shad.

Fish tagged in the Bay of Fundy during summer were recaptured annually off Florida in winter. Northward movement of the mean Julian day of recapture in the southern USA (Table 2) and capture of American shad in the ocean off Georgia and Florida from November through January (Figure 4) suggest this aggregation is probably separate from the aggregation overwintering in the Middle Atlantic Bight.

Regional Origins of Aggregations

Tag returns indicate that American shad wintering in the Middle Atlantic Bight represent populations from Georgia to Québec (Figures 1, 3). Fish tagged in Delaware Bay in early spring were recaptured in rivers of the Bay of Fundy and Gulf of St. Lawrence a few weeks later (Table 3; White et al. 1969; Miller et al. 1982) and spawners tagged in Bay of Fundy rivers were recaptured the succeeding winter in the Middle Atlantic Bight (Melvin et al. 1986). Those tagged in Chesapeake Bay and Pamlico Sound in winter and early spring were recaptured in rivers south to Georgia during the same or subsequent years (Talbot and Sykes 1958).

The regional composition of the aggregation occurring off Florida during winter is unknown. There is no evidence to suggest American shad from populations north of Cape Hatteras winter with this group. Tag-return information for fish tagged in the Bay of Fundy was ambivalent. Mean Julian day for recapture was earliest both for Florida and for North Carolina south of Cape Hatteras, suggesting American shad migrated onshore, then moved from both northern and south-ern directions towards rivers in Georgia and South Carolina (Table 2).

American shad that overwinter on the Scotian Shelf appear to be mostly from northern populations. Vladykov (1956) and Melvin et al. (1986) found that fish tagged in Canadian rivers migrated to the Scotian Shelf in winter. Analysis of otoliths by appearance criteria (Williams 1985) indicated that 73% of 26 fish taken on the Scotian Shelf during winter (1981–1985) were of Canadian origin and 27% were from mid-Atlantic rivers.

The aggregation of American shad in the Bay of Fundy during summer consisted of individuals of populations from the entire Atlantic coast (Figure 5; Dadswell et al. 1983; Melvin 1984). Analysis of regional tag returns from rivers for 15-d tagging periods in the inner Bay of Fundy during summer indicated the majority of fish of northern origin (Bay of Fundy, Gulf of St. Lawrence) arrived during June and early July when water temperatures were 10–16°C (Figure 5). American shad originating from rivers south of Cape Cod (regions 1 and 2) were present throughout the summer but constituted the majority during July and August at temperatures of 16–20°C.

Population discrimination studies conducted in the upper Bay of Fundy coincident with the tagging study corroborated the seasonal representation of American shad from different regions. Melvin (1984) collected fish from 13 rivers spanning the species' reproductive range (Florida to Québec) and examined 10 meristic and 16 morphometric characters to develop linear discriminate functions (LDF). The functions were then used to assign fish of unknown origin captured in the Cumberland Basin to regions. Results of regional comparisons of seasonal trends of LDF

TABLE 3.—Ocean migration rate and mean Julian day of point arrival for pre- and postspawning adult American shad, Atlantic coast. Data are from White et al. (1969), Leggett (1977a), Squires (Maine Department of Marine Resources), and Dadswell (unpublished data).

Tag site	Recapture site	N	Mean Julian day of recapture	Days at large	Coastline traveled (km)	Migration rate (km/d)
		Prespawning American shad				
Virginia	Hudson River	2	120.5	9.0	512	56.9
Delaware Bay	Hudson River	25	127.8	19.7	350	17.8
Delaware Bay	Connecticut River	36	138.1	31.8	616	19.4
Delaware Bay	Saint John River	15	154.8	45.4	1,440	31.7
Delaware Bay	Miramichi River	4	168.3	64.0	2,210	34.5
Delaware Bay	Gaspé	2	153.0	57.5	2,500	43.5
New Jersey coast	Saint John River	3	162.0	38.0	760	20.0
Inner Bay of Fundy	Florida	18	362.6	155.9	2,800	17.5
Mean ± SD						30.2±14.3
		Postspawning American shad				
Delaware River	Long Island	1	158.0	30.0	448	14.9
Delaware River	Maine coast	1	200.0	64.0	1,092	17.0
Delaware River	Inner Bay of Fundy	2	236.0	130.0	1,500	11.5
Hudson River	Long Island	10	166.6	41.7	256	6.1
Hudson River	Rhode Island	5	173.6	48.6	448	9.2
Hudson River	Inner Bay of Fundy	1	237.0	106.0	1,350	12.7
Connecticut River	Long Island Sound	10	197.2	71.4		
Connecticut River	Block Island	5	215.8	18.0	84	4.7
Connecticut River	Rhode Island	3	214.3	24.0	112	4.7
Connecticut River	Maine coast	1	206.0	68.0	560	8.2
Connecticut River	Inner Bay of Fundy	2	223.0	109.0	1,022	9.4
Narraguagus River	Inner Bay of Fundy	1	191.0	39.0	430	11.0
Narraguagus River	Outer Bay of Fundy	2	234.5	90.0	660	7.3
Annapolis River	Inner Bay of Fundy	8	200.0	56.8	185	3.2
Annapolis River	Outer Bay of Fundy	8	244.0	117.1	455	3.9
Mean ± SD						8.8±4.2

classification were similar to those of tag returns (Figure 6). American shad from regions 3 and 4 (northern) were most abundant in early summer and abundances of region-1 and -2 fish (southern) peaked in mid-summer.

Using differences in ring zonation of otoliths collected from the same fish used by Melvin (1984), Williams (1985) divided Atlantic coast populations into three groups, Canadian (regions 3 and 4), mid-USA (region 2), and southern USA (region 1). Appearance criteria correctly distinguished regional affinity 93% of the time. When these criteria were applied to fish of unknown origin collected in the inner Bay of Fundy, the pattern of dominance by Canadian fish during early summer and by central and southern USA during mid-summer was again evident (Figure 7).

Origins of American shad in the summer aggregations in the St. Lawrence estuary and off Labrador are unknown. Tag information of Vladykov (1956) suggests some fish in the St. Lawrence aggregation may originate as far south as Chesapeake Bay (Figure 3). Until further tagging or population discrimination studies are conducted on these aggregations, their origins will remain uncertain.

Coastal Migration

The northward, inshore coastal migration of American shad each spring was postulated over a century ago (McDonald 1884) but was not demonstrated until the 1950s (Talbot and Sykes 1958). All American shad were thought to move north along the coastal corridor as a single group held together by selection of a preferred temperature range of 13–18°C (Leggett and Whitney 1972). However, Neves and Depres (1979) demonstrated that while some fish were migrating north within a few kilometers of the coast, another group was offshore along the continental shelf over depths of 50–200 m in temperatures of 3–15°C.

Tag returns indicated the majority of American shad migrating north alongshore in the mid-Atlantic region were probably prespawning adults, since most tag returns later during the same year

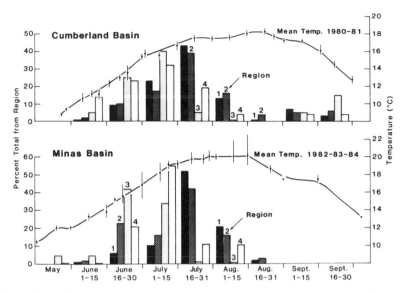

FIGURE 5.—Proportions of tag returns from rivers in Atlantic coast regions as percentages of total recaptures from each region in relation to period of tagging and temperature in Cumberland and Minas basins. Regions are (1) Florida–Cape Hatteras, (2) Cape Hatteras–Cape Cod, (3) Bay of Fundy, and (4) Gulf of St. Lawrence.

were from rivers (Table 3; Talbot and Sykes 1958; Miller et al. 1982). Offshore migrants were probably juvenile and nonspawning adults. Inshore migration of ripe adults, although bioenergetically inefficient because migration in the mid-Atlantic region is against countervailing currents (Bumpus and Lauzier 1965), nevertheless would be required to facilitate recognition of homing cues, especially olfactory ones (Dodson and Dohse 1984).

Data were unavailable for calculating offshore migration rates, but inshore migration rates could be determined with tag return information (Table 3). Prespawning American shad moved north rapidly, some traversing the 2,500 km from Delaware

72	17.3%	24.0%	26.1%	32.6%	Cape Hatteras South
250	20.5%	29.6%	27.3%	22.5%	Cape Cod South
214	30.3%	21.9%	19.1%	28.6%	Bay of Fundy
122	28.7%	22.3%	30.2%	18.8%	Gulf of St. Lawrence
Sample Number	June	July	Aug.	Sept.	

FIGURE 6.—Percentages of all American shad collected in the Cumberland Basin, Bay of Fundy (1979–1982), according to collection month and to region of origin as inferred from linear discriminate function analysis of meristic and morphological characteristics.

Bay to the Gulf of St. Lawrence in 60 d. Prespawning migration averaged 30.2 ± 14.3 km/d, similar to the theoretical optimum migration rate of 29 km/d (Leggett and Trump 1978). In contrast, postspawning adults had a mean northward migration rate of only 8.8 ± 4.2 km/d.

South of Cape Cod, prespawning American shad migrate close inshore (Leggett and Whitney 1972; Dadswell, unpublished data) but north of there, tag returns are fewer and the migratory corridor is less clear. Some fish perhaps migrate along the coast of Maine while others may migrate offshore around the edges of Georges Bank. Prespawning fish arrive at rivers south of Cape Cod at temperatures of 13–18°C (Leggett and Whitney 1972) but American shad move to northern rivers almost as quickly before ocean temperatures are above 10°C (Melvin et al. 1986).

Nonreproductive American shad migrating from their wintering site in the Middle Atlantic Bight (Neves and Depres 1979) must cross the Gulf of Maine during May and June, where a constant sub-surface temperature of 6°C prevails (Figure 8), to arrive annually at the inner Bay of Fundy during June and July (Table 4). When tag returns were grouped chronologically by Julian day, a counterclockwise migratory pattern was evident in the Bay of Fundy (Figure 9). Fish entered the bay during April and May on the Nova Scotia side and departed on the New Brunswick side from August to October.

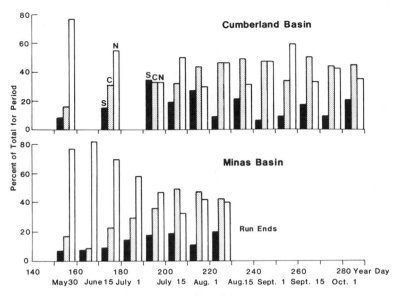

FIGURE 7.—Percentage regional representation by 10-d period for American shad collected in the Cumberland Basin (1979–1981) and Minas Basin (1982–1985), Bay of Fundy, as determined by otolith quality. Regions are (S) Florida to Cape Hatteras, (C) Cape Hatteras to Cape Cod, and (N) Canada.

In the inner bay, the run appeared to divide by chance, portions going to both the Minas and Cumberland basins (Figure 9). Evidences in support of this scenario were the similar regional compositions of the run in each basin (Figures 5, 7), the similar mean times of arrival in each basin (early run, Table 4; Dadswell et al. 1984b), and the similar distributions of tag returns from each site (Figure 2). In addition, postspawning fish tagged in the Annapolis River had an equal chance of recapture in either basin (Figure 10).

Once fish committed to a particular route, however, their migration pathway was rigid. American shad that migrated first to Cumberland Basin moved along the northern (New Brunswick) shore and left the Bay during August and September on either side of Grand Manan Island (Figure 11). Fish that moved first to Minas Basin, however, migrated through Cumberland Basin before leaving the Bay of Fundy by the same route (Figure 11). Several points of evidence support this scenario. Fish tagged in Cumberland Basin were never recaptured in Minas Basin during the same year, but those tagged in Minas Basin were recaptured in Cumberland Basin. There was a late abundance peak in Cumberland Basin but none in Minas basin (Table 4; Dadswell et al. 1983); the late abundance peak had a large portion of northern fish (Figures 5, 7). Fish tagged in the Annapolis River had a second, smaller peak period of

recapture in Cumberland Basin in late summer (Figure 10). When shoreline length was accounted for in this migration model, the migration rates of all recaptured American shad in the Bay of Fundy during the same summer were similar and averaged 3.6 ± 0.78 km/d (Table 5). Direction of movement was in the same direction as the residual current flow of the Bay of Fundy (Bumpus and Lauzier 1965).

American shad departed from the Bay of Fundy through the Gulf of Maine by two routes. One contingent followed the Maine coastline at approximately the 100-m depth (Figure 12) and passed Portland–Cape Ann in October and November (Dadswell, unpublished data). A lack of tag returns from inshore during fall (Figure 4) and results of trawl surveys (Neves and Depres 1979) indicated that migration further southward was largely offshore. Some of these fish, however, arrived off Florida and Georgia in inshore waters during November and December (Figure 4; Table 3). The other contingent left the Bay along the eastern shore of Grand Manan, passing Brier Island and southwestern Nova Scotia (Figure 12). This second contingent, which may have consisted largely of Bay of Fundy or northern fish, occupied the Scotian Shelf during winter (Figure 13). There they were probably joined by fish migrating south from the Gulf of St. Lawrence (Figure 3; Vladykov 1956) and Labrador.

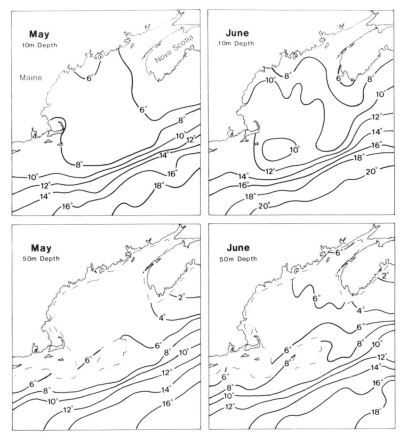

FIGURE 8.—Isotherms of subsurface temperature (10 m, 50 m) for the Gulf of Maine during May and June (after Colton and Stoddard 1972).

Tag returns of American shad tagged in the Bay of Fundy were used to assess the migratory pattern of the Scotian Shelf winter aggregation. After wintering on the shelf, fish moved onshore along eastern Nova Scotia; some probably migrated back to the Bay of Fundy, and others moved north to the Gulf of St. Lawrence around Cape Breton (Figure 13). The pathway for inward migration is not well documented but American shad were off the northern shore of the St. Lawrence estuary in June (Figure 13). Those fish departed the Gulf of St. Lawrence via its southern shore passing Baie de Chaleur, Prince Edward Island, and Cape Breton. This is the same direction and route as the main residual current flow (Bumpus and Lauzier 1965).

A summary by season of tag returns, occurrence records, and trawl survey information illustrates a pattern consistent with three winter sites and three summer terminus points for American shad during their annual migration along the Atlantic coast (Figure 14). During January–February, American shad are off Florida, the Middle Atlantic Bight, and Nova Scotia and entering streams to spawn from Florida to South Carolina. In March and April, movement is onshore and northward, both in the Middle Atlantic Bight and off Nova Scotia (Figure 4) and spawning runs are underway from North Carolina to the Bay of Fundy. By late June, American shad are concentrated in the inner Bay of Fundy, in the inner Gulf of St. Lawrence, and off Newfoundland (Table 2), but spawning fish are still upstream from the Delaware River to the St. Lawrence River. During autumn, American shad leaving the St. Lawrence estuary are captured across the southern Gulf of St. Lawrence but, at the same time, those departing the Bay of Fundy are found from Maine to Long Island and some are already off Florida and Georgia (Figure 4).

Discussion

In view of much of the information previously

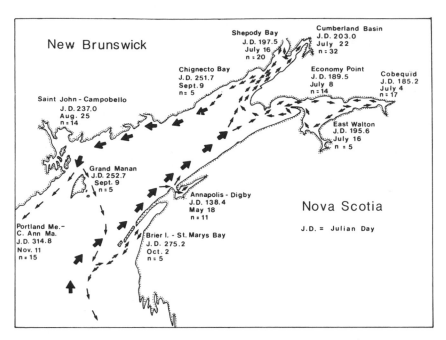

FIGURE 9.—Mean Julain day (J.D.) of recapture by site and proposed migratory routes for American shad in the bay of Fundy during summer, for all tag data pooled (Annapolis River, Minas Basin, Cumberland Basin, and Saint John Harbour).

available on American shad migration, an appropriate null hypothesis would have been that, in the sea, the fish are concentrated into a relatively small geographic area at any one time and that adults and juveniles are migrating together. McDonald (1884) was the first to state this hypothesis and empirical justification was provided by Talbot and Sykes (1958) and Leggett and Whitney (1972). Temperature was thought to provide the migratory clue (McDonald 1884; Leggett and Whitney 1972) and to regulate ocean swimming speed (Leggett 1977a). Neves and Depres (1979) questioned this hypothesis, stating "it would seem energetically wasteful for North Atlantic populations to follow the same shoreward route as do Middle and South Atlantic shad." However, they still proposed a temperature range in which migration occurred.

Results from 50 years of tagging, however, clearly indicate that American shad are not all concentrated into a relatively small geographic area at any one time, nor do they migrate together at the same rate. Instead, discrete aggregations occur in the sea at the same time at widely separated geographic locations. These aggregations move north and south along the Atlantic coast on a seasonal basis with considerable intermixing. The question remains: what cues or clues do the fish use to regulate when or where they move in the sea?

Although there is no doubt American shad move north and south seasonally, the evidence does not suggest that certain temperature levels provide the major cue for migration. Fish off Virginia experience a totally different suite of temperature stimuli from those wintering on the Scotian Shelf; however, fish from both these sites arrive at the Annapolis River to spawn during the same short time period (Melvin et al. 1986). A fish migrating from Delaware Bay in April to spawn in the Miramichi River in June will encounter ocean temperatures ranging from 10–12°C to 4°C (Colton and Stoddard 1972). Similarly, a fish leaving the inner Bay of Fundy in September and entering the St. John's River, Florida, in December to spawn would leave 18°C water (Dadswell et al. 1983), migrate through temperatures of 10–12°C in the Gulf of Maine (Colton and Stoddard 1972), and traverse water as warm as 20°C before arriving in Florida. In each case, the same behavioral response occurs under different and diverse temperature stimuli. Temperature change interacting with an additional stimulus such as photoperiod may initiate migratory behavior, but the timing of such behavior by different fish appears related to their origin or life history stage.

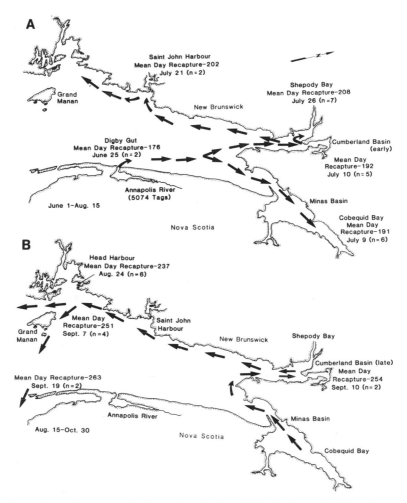

FIGURE 10.—Movements of postspawning American shad tagged in the Annapolis River, Bay of Fundy, during summer. (A) June 1–August 15: the population moves inward in the Bay of Fundy, divides into two approximately equal-sized groups, and moves to the heads of embayments. The Cumberland Basin contingent moves along the New Brunswick shore first. (B) August 15–October 30: the Minas Basin contingent moves into Cumberland Basin, then out of the Bay of Fundy along the New Brunswick shore.

Temperature appears to be a poor clue for migratory direction among fishes (Smith 1985). American shad selecting a broad temperature preference range of 13–18°C (Leggett and Whitney 1972) or 3–15°C (Neves and Depres 1979) cannot perceive which way to turn within this preferendum for directional movement. Why would a ripe fish offshore of Virginia in March take a westerly heading to arrive inshore when the isotherm gradient is north–south? Why would fish migrate westerly along the New Brunswick shore of the Bay of Fundy in late summer when this route takes them from "preferred" temperatures of 16–18°C to temperatures of 10–12°C? American

shad must cross the Gulf of Maine during May and June to arrive by the end of June in the upper Bay of Fundy (Dadswell et al. 1983). If migration is at depths of 10 m or more, either a constant temperature of 6°C prevails or movement is against a reverse thermocline. In all these cases, migration follows a set pattern and direction each year regardless of isotherm gradient or its presence or absence.

Since we cannot accept the null hypothesis concerning American shad migration or the keystone role that temperature was thought to play, what factors do influence or regulate migration? American shad have been shown to exhibit a high

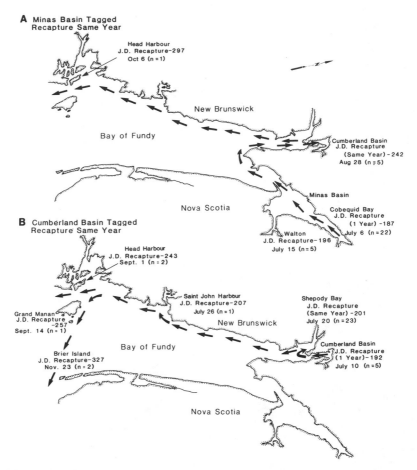

FIGURE 11.—Movements of American shad tagged in the upper Bay of Fundy during summer, determined from tag returns in the same year (returns 1 year later at tag sites are excluded). (A) Fish tagged in Minas Basin move to Cumberland Basin before leaving the bay on the New Brunswick shore. (B) Movements inferred from Cumberland Basin tag returns.

degree of homing to their probable streams of origin (Hollis 1948; Talbot and Sykes 1958; Carscadden and Leggett 1975; Melvin et al. 1986). If populations of fish are reproductively isolated to a sufficient degree and accumulate genetic adaptations to the local situation, then genetic control over migration may evolve. Recent work has indicated that origin may control the migration of homing salmon (Thorpe and Mitchell 1981; Quinn 1982; Brannon 1984; Healey and Groot 1987). Although all American shad populations are mixed together in the sea, different populations demonstrate behavior that suggests some intrinsic control of migration. The early and rapid migration of some fish south to Florida in the fall suggests that individuals know where they should go and when to arrive. American shad from the Annapolis River home to spawn from both south (Virginia) and east (Scotian Shelf). Homing from these two areas to the same locality implies navigation ability which overrides the different temperature and current conditions encountered along the two routes. Origin, then, appears to provide both cues and clues for migration.

Life history stage of American shad also appears to have some control over migration. Ripe fish migrate close inshore in spring, which may be a strategy to improve recognition of homing clues (Dodson and Dohse 1984), but nonreproductive fish apparently remain offshore (Neves and Depres 1979). Ripe fish migrate at a much faster rate than postspawning or feeding ones. Slower migration rate during feeding is one strategy to optimize growth (Ware 1975). Offshore residence of nonre-

TABLE 4.—Mean Julian day (calendar date) of tagging in Cumberland and Minas basins (Bay of Fundy) for American shad recaptured from regions on the Atlantic coast. Regions are the same as in Figure 5, river recaptures only.

	Cumberland Basin			Minas Basin		
Run	Returns	Mean day ±SD	Range	Returns	Mean day ±SD	Range
Region 1 (Florida–Cape Hatteras)						
Early	96	198.4±13.6 (Jul 17)	162–262	48	201.6±16.5 (Jul 20)	165–227
Late	9	250.9± 8.9 (Sep 8)				
Region 2 (Cape Hatteras–Cape Cod)						
Early	102	198.8±15.6 (Jul 17)	154–277	84	195.8±18.5 (Jul 15)	152–224
Late	17	251.7±15.2 (Sep 9)				
Region 3 (Bay of Fundy)						
Early	15	181.9±12.2 (Jul 1)	156–272	50	175.8±18.7 (Jun 25)	130–201
Late	5	253.4±21.2 (Sep 10)				
Region 4 (Gulf of St. Lawrence)						
Early	18	180.3±14.5 (Jun 29)	160–267	9	189.7±14.7 (Jul 9)	167–215
Late	4	240.2±28.4 (Aug 28)				

productive fish could be a result of ontogenetic changes in preference for temperature (McCauley and Huggens 1979) or light intensity (Loesch et al. 1982).

Movements of tagged American shad in the Bay of Fundy indicated there was an element of

TABLE 5.—Recaptures during the same year in the Bay of Fundy–Gulf of Maine for American shad tagged in the Annapolis River, Minas Basin, and Cumberland Basin.

Release site	Recapture location	N	Mean time at large (d)	Minimum migration distance (km)	Migration rate (km/d)
Annapolis	Minas	6	57.0	220	3.9
Annapolis	Cumberland	5	64.1	160	2.5
Annapolis	Shepody Bay	3	49.6	210	4.2
Annapolis	Saint John	2	71.0	360	5.1
Annapolis	Head Harbour	9	102.3	440	4.3
Annapolis	Grand Manan	4	132.0	470	3.6
Minas	Minas (gillnet)	9	5.1	15	2.9
Minas	Minas (weir)	16	18.7	40	2.1
Minas	Cumberland	5	68.6	195	2.8
Minas	Head Harbour	2	99.0	250	2.5
Minas	Gulf of Maine	7	112.0	625	5.6
Cumberland	Cumberland	33	5.4	30	5.5
Cumberland	Shepody Bay	12	13.9	50	3.6
Cumberland	Head Harbour	2	133.0	280	2.1
Cumberland	Gulf of Maine	3	138.0	430	3.1
Mean±SD					3.6±0.78

chance involved in migration, at least within confined coastal regions. Whether chance influences migration in the open ocean, leading fish east or west of Nova Scotia along the continental shelf, for example, will require further research to resolve.

In general, genetic or life history characteristics of American shad appear to influence behavior and to provide many of the cues for migration. On the other hand, when intrinsic factors do not influence or override external ones, some similar migratory patterns are obvious, suggesting use of external stimuli. Temperature change or some aspect of seasonality broadly influences migratory direction. During increasing temperatures and day length, fish move north; when these decrease, they move south. However, when they are within large semienclosed coastal regions, they follow the direction of residual currents and the coastline. American shad migrating in the Bay of Fundy and the Gulf of St. Lawrence move in the same direction as the residual current (Dadswell et al. 1983) and they do so even when in the smaller embayments (Tee 1975; Dadswell et al. 1984b). Feeding Atlantic herring *Clupea harengus harengus* in the Gulf of St. Lawrence are likewise known to follow the residual current direction (Winters and Beckett 1978). Fish are known to exploit selective tidal stream transport (Harden

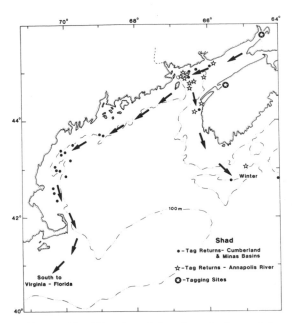

FIGURE 12.—Migration of American shad out of the Bay of Fundy in fall as indicated by tag returns. Many return localities were fixed accurately by fishermen using Loran navigation.

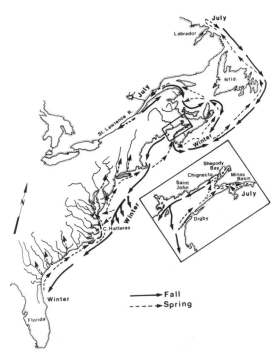

FIGURE 14.—General migration pattern and terminus points of American shad on the Atlantic coast of North America determined from seasonal distribution of tag returns, trawl surveys, and occurrence records.

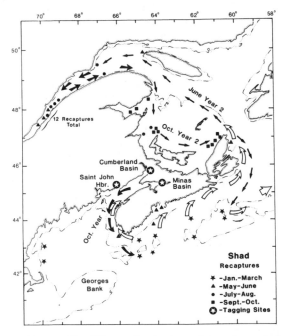

FIGURE 13.—Winter distribution of American shad tagged in the Bay of Fundy and recaptured on the Scotian Shelf, and subsequent (year-2) migration patterns determined from the chronological sequence of tag returns. Depth contour is 100 m.

Jones et al. 1978) and this behavior is thought to be energetically efficient (Weihs 1978). Whether fish can use the much more subtle residual currents for guidance clues is unproven but general observations suggest they may (Dadswell et al. 1984a). The lateral line system may provide the sensory ability to distinguish current or water movement direction in the absence of visual clues (Sutterlin and Waddy 1975).

Migration information for the American shad suggests this species may use a physiological optimizing strategy (Leggett 1977b) while it is nonreproductive but a bicoordinate system (Quinn 1982) when it must reach a specific goal at a certain time. Extrinsic factors related to ocean climate, seasonality, and currents may provide cues and clues for portions of the nongoal-oriented migration. Intrinsic cues and bicoordinate navigation appear to be important during goal-oriented migration.

Acknowledgments

We thank the many students who helped tag American shad. L. Linkletter, B. Bradford, and D. Carter assisted with tag return procedures. A.

Lupine, W. Leggett, and T. Squiers provided unpublished tag information for the Delaware, Connecticut, and Narraguasus Rivers, respectively. W. McMullon and F. Cunningham prepared the figures. R. Rulifson, R. Neves, J. Cooper, and M. Sinclair reviewed the manuscript and provided helpful suggestions.

References

Arnold, G. P., and P. H. Cook. 1984. Fish migration by selective tidal stream transport: first results with a computer simulation model for the European continental shelf. Pages 227–262 in J. D. McCleave, G. P. Arnold, J. J. Dodson, and W. H. Neill, editors. Mechanisms of migration in fishes. Plenum, New York, New York, USA.

Boreman, J., and R. R. Lewis. 1987. Atlantic coastal migration of striped bass. American Fisheries Society Symposium 1:331–339.

Brannon, E. L. 1984. Influence of stock origin on salmon migratory behavior. Pages 103–111 in J. D. McCleave, G. P. Arnold, J. J. Dodson, and W. H. Neill, editors. Mechanisms of migration in fishes. Plenum, New York, New York, USA.

Bumpus, D. F., and L. M. Lauzier. 1965. Surface circulation on the continental shelf off eastern North America between Newfoundland and Florida. American Geographical Society, Serial Atlas of the Marine Environment 7, New York, New York, USA.

Carscadden, J. E., and W. C. Leggett. 1975. Meristic differences in spawning populations of American shad (Alosa sapidissima). Evidence for homing to tributaries in the Saint John River, New Brunswick. Journal of the Fisheries Research Board of Canada 32:653–660.

Colton, J. B., and R. R. Stoddard. 1972. Average monthly sea-water temperatures Nova Scotia to Long Island 1940–1959. American Geographical Society, Serial Atlas of the Marine Environment 21, New York, New York, USA.

Dadswell, M. J., R. Bradford, A. H. Leim, D. J. Scarratt, G. D. Melvin, and R. G. Appy. 1984a. A review of research on fishes and fisheries in the Bay of Fundy between 1976 and 1983 with particular reference to its upper reaches. Canadian Technical Report of Fisheries and Aquatic Sciences 1256:163–294.

Dadswell, M. J., G. D. Melvin, and P. J. Williams. 1983. Effect of turbidity on the temporal and spatial utilization of the inner Bay of Fundy by American shad (Alosa sapidissima) (Pisces: Clupeidae) and its relationship to local fisheries. Canadian Journal of Fisheries and Aquatic Sciences 40(Supplement 1):322–330.

Dadswell, M. J., G. D. Melvin, P. J. Williams, and G. S. Brown. 1984b. Possible impact of large-scale tidal power developments in the upper Bay of Fundy on certain fish stocks of the northwest Atlantic. Canadian Technical Report of Fisheries and Aquatic Sciences 1256:577–600.

D'Anglejean, B. 1981. On the advection of turbidity in the Saint Lawrence middle estuary. Estuaries 4:2–15.

Dempson, J. B., L. J. LeDrew, and G. Furey. 1983. Occurrence of American shad (Alosa sapidissima) in northern Labrador waters. Naturaliste canadien (Québéc) 110:217–221.

Dodson, J. J., and L. A. Dohse. 1984. A model of olfactory-mediated conditioning of directional bias in fish migrating in reversing tidal currents based on the homing migration of American shad Alosa sapidissima. Pages 263–282 in J. D. McCleave, G. P. Arnold, J. J. Dodson, and W. H. Neill, editors. Mechanisms of migration in fishes. Plenum, New York, New York, USA.

Harden Jones, F. R., G. P. Arnold, M. G. Walker, and P. Scholes. 1978. Selective tidal stream transport and the migration of plaice (Pleuronectes platessa L.) in the southern North Sea. Journal du Conseil, Conseil International pour l'Exploration de la Mer 38:331–337.

Hare, G. M., and H. P. Murphy. 1974. First record of American shad (Alosa sapidissima) from Labrador waters. Journal of the Fisheries Research Board of Canada 31:1536–1537.

Healey, M. C., and C. Groot. 1987. Marine migration and orientation of ocean-type chinook and sockeye salmon. American Fisheries Society Symposium 1:298–312.

Hodder, V. M. 1966. Two further records of the American shad in Newfoundland waters. Transactions of the American Fisheries Society 95:228–229.

Hollis, E. H. 1948. The homing tendency of shad. Science (Washington, D.C.) 108:332–333.

Leggett, W. C. 1977a. Ocean migration rates of American shad (Alosa sapidissima). Journal of the Fisheries Research Board of Canada 34:1422–1426.

Leggett, W. C. 1977b. The ecology of fish migrations. Annual Review of Ecology and Systematics 8:285–308.

Leggett, W. C., and C. L. Trump. 1978. Energetics of migration in American shad. Pages 370–377 in K. Schmidt-Koenig and W. T. Keeton, editors. Animal migration, navigation and homing. Springer-Verlag, New York, New York, USA.

Leggett, W. C., and R. R. Whitney. 1972. Water temperature and migrations of American shad. U.S. National Marine Fisheries Service Fishery Bulletin 70:659–670.

Leim, A. H. 1924. The life history of the shad (Alosa sapidissima (Wilson)) with special reference to the factors limiting its abundance. Contributions to Canadian Biology 2:163–284.

Loesch, J. G., W. H. Driete, Jr., and E. L. Foell. 1982. Effects of light intensity on catchability of juvenile anadromous Alosa species. Transactions of the American Fisheries Society 111:41–44.

McCauley, R. W., and N. W. Huggins. 1979. Ontogenetic and non-thermal seasonal effects on thermal preferenda of fish. American Zoologist 19:267–271.

McCleave, J. D., G. P. Arnold, J. J. Dodson, and W. H. Neill, editors. 1984. Mechanisms of migration in fishes. Plenum, New York, New York, USA.

McDonald, M. 1884. The shad and alewifes. Pages 594–607 in G. B. Goode and 20 associate authors. The fisheries and fishery industries of the United States. U.S. 47th Congress, 1st Session, Senate Miscellaneous Document 124, Washington, D.C., USA.

McLellan, H. J. 1954. Bottom temperatures on the Scotian Shelf. Journal of the Fisheries Research Board of Canada 11:404–418.

Melvin, G. D. 1984. The usefulness of meristic and morphometric characters in discriminating populations of American shad (Alosa sapidissima) inhabiting Cumberland Basin, New Brunswick. Doctoral dissertation. University of New Brunswick, Fredericton, Canada.

Melvin, G. D., M. J. Dadswell, and J. D. Martin. 1986. Fidelity of American shad, Alosa sapidissima (Clupeidae), to its river of previous spawning. Canadian Journal of Fisheries and Aquatic Sciences 43:640–646.

Miller, J. P., F. R. Griffiths, and P. S. Thurston-Rodgers. 1982. The American shad (Alosa sapidissima) in the Delaware River basin. Delaware Basin Fisheries and Wildlife Cooperative, Trenton, New Jersey, USA.

Neves, R. J., and L. Depres. 1979. The oceanic migration of American shad, Alosa sapidissima, along the Atlantic coast. U.S. National Marine Fisheries Service Fishery Bulletin 77:199–212.

Perley, M. H. 1852. Reports on the sea and river fisheries of New Brunswick. Queens Printer, Fredericton, Canada.

Provost, J., L. Verret, and P. Dumont. 1984. L'alose savoureuse au Québec: synthèse des connaissances biologiques et perspectives d'aménagement d'habitats. Canadian Manuscript Report of Fisheries and Aquatic Sciences 1793.

Quinn, T. P. 1982. A model for salmon navigation on the high seas. Pages 229–237 in E. L. Brannon and E. O. Salo, editors. Proceedings of the salmon and trout migratory behavior symposium. University of Washington, School of Fisheries, Seattle, Washington, USA.

Quinn, T. P., and C. Groot. 1984. Pacific salmon (Oncorhynchus) migrations: orientation versus random movement. Canadian Journal of Fisheries and Aquatic Sciences 41:1319–1324.

Reddin, D. G., and W. M. Shearer. 1987. Sea-surface temperature and distribution of Atlantic salmon in the northwest Atlantic. American Fisheries Society Symposium 1:262–275.

Royce, W. F., L. S. Smith, and A. C. Hartt. 1968. Models of oceanic migrations of Pacific salmon and

comments on guidance mechanisms. U.S. Fish and Wildlife Service Fishery Bulletin 66:441–462.

Smith, R. J. F. 1985. The control of fish migration. Springer-Verlag, Heidelburg, West Germany.

Sutterlin, A. M., and S. Waddy. 1975. Possible role of the posterior lateral line in obstacle entrainment of brook trout (Salvelinus fontinalis). Journal of the Fisheries Research Board of Canada 32:2441–2446.

Talbot, G. B., and J. E. Sykes. 1958. Atlantic coast migrations of American shad. U.S. Fish and Wildlife Service Fishery Bulletin 58:473–490.

Tee, K. T. 1975. Tide-induced residual current in Minas Channel and Minas Basin. Doctoral dissertation. Dalhousie University, Halifax, Canada.

Thorpe, J. E., and K. A. Mitchell. 1981. Stocks of Atlantic salmon (Salmo salar) in Britain and Ireland: discreteness and current management. Canadian Journal of Fisheries and Aquatic Sciences 38:1576–1590.

Vladykov, V. D. 1936. Occurrence of three species of anadromous fishes on the Nova Scotian banks during 1935 and 1936. Copeia 1936:168.

Valdykov, V. D. 1950. Movements of Quebec shad (Alosa sapidissima) as demonstrated by tagging. Naturaliste canadien (Québec) 77:121–135.

Valdykov, V. D. 1956. Distant recaptures of shad tagged in Quebec. Naturaliste canadien (Québec) 83:235–248.

Ware, D. M. 1975. Growth, metabolism and optimal swimming speed of a pelagic fish. Journal of the Fisheries Research Board of Canada 32:33–41.

Weihs, D. 1978. Tidal stream transport as an efficient method for migration. Journal du Conseil, Conseil International pour l'Exploration de la Mer 38:92–99.

White, R. L., J. T. Lane, and P. E. Hamer. 1969. Population and migration study of major anadromous fish. New Jersey Department of Conservation and Economic Development Miscellaneous Report 3, Trenton, New Jersey, USA.

Williams, P. J. 1985. Use of otoliths for stock differentiation of American shad (Alosa sapidissima Wilson). Masters thesis. Acadia University, Wolfville, Canada.

Williams, R. O., and G. E. Bruger. 1972. Investigations on American shad in the St. John's River. Florida Department of Natural Resources Marine Research Laboratory Technical Series 66.

Winters, G. H., and J. S. Beckett. 1978. Migrations, biomass and stock interrelationships of southwest Newfoundland–southern Gulf herring from mark–recapture experiments. International Commission for the Northwest Atlantic Fisheries Research Bulletin 13:67–79.

American Fisheries Society Symposium 1:331–339, 1987

Atlantic Coastal Migration of Striped Bass

JOHN BOREMAN AND R. RHETT LEWIS[1]

National Marine Fisheries Service, Northeast Fisheries Center
Woods Hole, Massachusetts 02543, USA

Abstract.—A tagging and recapture data base for striped bass *Morone saxatilis* along the northeastern coast of the United States has been assembled by the American Littoral Society. The data base spans the period 1963–1985 and is composed of 27,674 tagging records and 2,559 recapture records. Results of the analyses are consistent with general conclusions of published studies of the migratory habits of anadromous striped bass along the Atlantic coast: (1) migration is northward along the coast in the spring and southward in the fall; (2) there is an apparent lack of coastal migration by stocks from southern North Carolina to Florida; (3) the majority of striped bass caught in northern waters are of Chesapeake Bay origin, with a lesser contribution by the Hudson River and North Carolina stocks; and (4) the contribution of the Hudson River stock to coastal fisheries is essentially northeastward from the mouth of the river.

Stocks of striped bass *Morone saxatilis* along the Atlantic coast from North Carolina to the Canadian Maritime Provinces undertake marine migrations. These coastal migratory stocks have supported important commercial and recreational fisheries in the Atlantic coastal states during the past 50 years (Koo 1970; Boreman and Austin 1985) and have also been the focus of public attention on issues such as power plant siting and operation (McFadden 1977; Barnthouse et al. 1984), highway siting (USDOT and USCOE 1984), estaurine pollution (Mansueti 1962; Coutant 1985), and interjurisdictional fisheries management (ASMFC 1981). With the recent substantial decline in production of the Chesapeake Bay and Roanoke River stocks (Boreman and Austin 1985), the coastal movement patterns of the contributing stocks have become a key issue in management of the coastal striped bass fisheries (ASMFC 1981).

Tagging programs involving anadromous striped bass along the Atlantic coast have been conducted from the 1930s to the 1980s (Table 1). Over 75,000 striped bass were tagged in these programs, and recoveries ranged from 4.1 to 41.8%. Conclusions based on analyses of these programs are that (1) migration is along the coast to the north in the spring and to the south in the fall (Vladykov and Wallace 1938, 1952; Merriman 1941; Chapoton and Sykes 1961; Clark 1968); (2) there is an apparent lack of coastal migrations by striped bass from southern North Carolina to

Florida (Raney 1957); (3) the majority of striped bass caught in northern waters are of Chesapeake Bay origin with a lesser contribution by striped bass originating in the Hudson River and the Roanoke River (Tiller 1950; Raney 1952; Mansueti 1961; Shcaefer 1968b; Berggren and Leiberman 1978; Van Winkle and Kumar 1982); (4) striped bass less than 2 years old do not migrate (Mansueti 1961; Koo 1970; Kohlenstein 1980, 1981); and (5) most of the striped bass that migrate along the coast are female (Bigelow and Schroeder 1953; Schaefer 1968a; Holland and Yelverton 1973; Oviatt 1977).

Porter and Saila (1969) determined that an analysis of combined tagging data on striped bass from the large number of uncoordinated tagging efforts did not result in substantial improvements in the predictive ability or in providing more valid inferences concerning migratory behavior. Conclusions from the individual tag and recapture studies were reinforced by their analysis of combined data.

Problems in inferring migratory patterns and stock composition from these tagging programs are related to either the limited geographic areas of tagging, the short periods of time during which the programs were conducted, or both. It is possible that a relatively strong year class in one of the contributing stocks may bias interpretation of tag recapture data. Van Winkle and Kumar (1982) determined that stock composition of a coastal fishery depends on the relative year-class strengths of the contributing stocks, the geographic location of the fishery, and the sex of the fish.

A tagging and recapture data base spanning

---

[1]Present address: National Urban Coalition, 1120 G Street, N.W., Washington, D.C. 20005, USA.

TABLE 1.—Summary of major tagging studies of anadromous striped bass along the Atlantic coast.

Study	Location of tagging	Tagging years	Number tagged	Percent recovered
Pearson (1933)	Maryland: Chesapeake Bay	1931	305	29.2
Merriman (1937, 1941)	Connecticut, New York, and North Carolina coasts	1936–1937	2,642	21.5
Vladykov and Wallace (1952)	Maryland and Virginia: Chesapeake Bay	1936–1937	3,352	31.9
Raney et al. (1954)	Massachusetts to Chesapeake Bay	1949–1952	9,320	8.5
Chapoton and Sykes (1961)	North Carolina and Chesapeake Bay	1955–1959	478	14.6
Hassler et al. (1981)	Roanoke River, North Carolina	1956–1980	11,141	28.6
Alperin (1966)	Long Island, New York	1956–1961	1,917	14.7
Massman and Pacheco (1961)	Virginia: Chesapeake Bay	1957–1958	2,429	27.8
Mansueti (1961)	Potomac River	1957–1958	1,103	37.9
Whitney (1961)	Lower Susquehanna River	1959	298	42.0
Nichols and Miller (1967)	Potomac River	1959–1961	8,973	37.3
Clark (1968)	Canada to Chesapeake Bay	1959–1963	6,679	7.8
Schaefer (1968b)	Long Island, New York	1961–1964	912	10.9
Grant et al. (1970)	Virginia: Chesapeake Bay	1968–1969	8,525	13.2
Holland and Yelverton (1973)	North Carolina coast	1968–1971	1,752	11.2
Ritchie and Koo (1973)	Maryland: Chesapeake Bay	1971–1972	1,818	27.0
Moore and Burton (1975)	Maryland: Chesapeake Bay	1972	1,726	41.8
Young (1980)	Long Island, New York	1976–1979	1,701	4.1
McLaren et al. (1981)	Hudson River, New York	1976–1977	5,219	Unknown
TI (1980, 1981)	Hudson River, New York	1977–1978	6,114	Unknown
Rulifson (unpublished data)	Upper Bay of Fundy, Canada	1985	1,180	11.0

years of relatively good and poor production from all contributing stocks over a wide geographic area may provide more useful insight into the coastal migratory pattern of striped bass. One such data base on striped bass has been assembled by the American Littoral Society (ALS) between 1964 and 1985, representing a geographic range from Canada to North Carolina. Austin and Custer (1977) used a limited portion of this data base to examine movement patterns of striped bass in Long Island Sound. In this paper, the ALS tagging and recapture data are used to examine the seasonality of striped bass movement along the coast and the relative contributions of the Chesapeake Bay, northern North Carolina, and Hudson River stocks to the mid-Atlantic and New England recreational fisheries.

Tagging Program

Between 1964 and 1983, 27,674 striped bass were released with dorsal loop tags by members of the American Littoral Society. Members purchased the tags in lots of 10 from the ALS; each tag had a corresponding index card that was filled out by the member when the tag was placed on a fish. Information contained on the index card included tag number, species of fish, date of tagging, location of release, name and address of tagger, and size of the tagged fish (usually reported as length in inches with no indication whether length meant fork length, total length, or standard length). When a tagged fish was recaptured, the tag was mailed to the ALS headquarters and the recapture information was published in the ALS publication *The Underwater Naturalist*. No reward was paid for the tag. Published recapture information includes the name of the person who caught the tagged fish and the location and date of the recapture. Until 1973, tag cards for the recaptured fish were discarded by ALS when the information was published.

To expedite data coding, tagging and recapture locations were categorized into 53 geographic regions. These regions were used to define the range of the coastal migratory stocks of striped bass from the Maritime Provinces of Canada to the Pamlico Sound in North Carolina. The 53 regions were combined into nine areas to expedite data analysis and interpretation (Figure 1; Table 2).

Sixty-seven percent of the tagged fish were released in area III and area V (Table 2). The peak years of tag releases were 1972 and 1973, when annual releases were close to 5,000 fish. The 1973

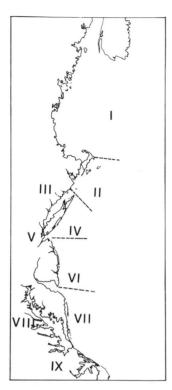

FIGURE 1.—Geographic areas used in analysis of American Littoral Society tag data.

peak in releases of tagged fish corresponded with the peak in the 1887–1983 time series of reported commercial landings of striped bass in Atlantic coastal states (Boreman and Austin 1985). However, the peak in releases may also have corresponded to a period when the most ALS members participated in the tagging program.

Overall, 97% of the tagged fish were released during April through November (Table 3); Long Island Sound was the only area where tagged fish were released during every month of the year. Seventy-seven percent of the fish released with tags were between 28 and 51 cm in length (Table 4); the overall length range was 3–127 cm.

Tag Recoveries

Altogether 2,559 tagged striped bass (9.2% of those tagged) were reported as recaptured from 1964 to 1985. We were able to trace 1,950 (77% of the reported recaptures) to a tagging record. The recaptured fish were well distributed among the geographic areas (Table 5); less than half (46%) of the fish were recaptured in the same area in which they were originally released.

The proportion of tagged fish that were recap-

tured varied widely among the tagging areas (Table 2). The highest recapture rate (15.2%) was for tagged fish released in Chesapeake Bay (area VIII), and the lowest rate (3.8%) was for tagged fish released in the Hudson River–Raritan Bay regions (Area V). A wide variation in recovery rates is also evident from the other striped bass tagging studies (Table 1). Recovery rates were generally higher for fish tagged and released in Chesapeake Bay (13–42%) than elsewhere along the coast (4–22%).

Lengths at tagging of recaptured fish are only available for fish released since 1973. A comparison of these lengths to lengths of all fish tagged during the same time period shows a distinct shift into the 41–51-cm size range for the recaptured (Table 4). This suggests a higher natural mortality, tagging-related mortality, higher tag loss by individuals less than 41 cm in length, or simply growth of the tagged fish. The difference may also be due to the minimum size regulations on the coastal fisheries, which were at least 41 cm for all coastal states (except Maine, Delaware, Maryland, Virginia, and North Carolina) during 1964–1981 (ASMFC 1981). A person who caught a tagged fish may have been reluctant to remove the tag if the fish was less than legal size.

The average number of days at large for a tagged striped bass was 243 d. The longest period a fish was at large was over 12 years (4,416 d). This fish was tagged and released along the coast of Maine in August 1973 and recaptured along the coast of northern New Jersey in September 1985. Number of tag recoveries versus days at large closely fit a negative exponential curve (slope = $e^{-0.0046}$; $\log_e$-transformed $r^2 = 0.925$; $P < 0.001$), suggesting an almost constant rate of loss of tagged individuals from the coastal migratory population (Figure 2).

Seasonality of Movement

Tag return data were combined over tagging years to examine general trends in the seasonal and geographic location of tag recaptures. The seasonal distribution of recaptures was consistent for tagged fish released in areas I–VIII (no fish were tagged in area IX) and is best represented by the seasonal distribution pattern for all tagging areas combined (Figure 3).

The recapture data reveal a pattern of northward movement along the coast in the spring, residence in the more northern areas during the summer months, southward movement along the coast in the fall, and winter residence in the more

TABLE 2.—Numbers of striped bass tagged by American Littoral Society members (1964–1983) and recaptured along the Atlantic coast (1964–1985).

	Tagging area	Number of taggers	Number tagged	Number recovered	Percent recovered
I	Canada Maritimes to Chatham, Massachusetts	195	2,812	303	10.8
II	Southern Massachusetts and Rhode Island	290	2,311	144	6.2
III	Long Island Sound	569	9,851	901	9.1
IV	Atlantic Ocean coast of Long Island	181	1,099	59	5.4
V	Hudson River–Raritan Bay	524	8,558	324	3.8
VI	Atlantic Ocean coast of New Jersey	418	2,363	128	5.4
VII	Delaware River; Maryland, Virginia, and North Carolina coasts	13	36	2	5.6
VIII	Chesapeake Bay and tributaries	29	644	98	15.2
IX	Roanoke River, Albermarle Sound, Neuse River, Tar River, and Pamlico Sound	0			
	Total	2,219	27,674	1,959	7.1

TABLE 3.—Monthly number of tagged striped bass released by American Littoral Society members in each geographic area, 1964–1983.

Month					Area					
	I	II	III	IV	V	VI	VII	VIII	IX	Total[a]
Jan	2	0	77	1	1	0	0	0	0	81
Feb	0	0	67	0	0	0	0	0	0	67
Mar	1	1	155	4	38	148	0	5	0	352
Apr	31	7	382	35	762	452	10	34	0	1,713
May	236	179	1,940	110	1,255	239	8	104	0	4,071
Jun	743	425	1,821	154	1,211	247	3	31	0	4,635
Jul	455	371	1,556	145	1,585	216	0	85	0	4,413
Aug	583	297	1,085	126	909	209	9	95	0	3,313
Sep	427	287	955	163	717	231	2	84	0	2,866
Oct	296	716	1,197	209	1,243	329	2	64	0	4,056
Nov	23	31	503	148	718	282	2	142	0	1,849
Dec	17	0	131	4	124	11	0	1	0	288
Total	2,814	2,314	9,869	1,099	8,563	2,364	36	645	0	27,704

[a] Does not include 30 fish for which information on month of tagging is unavailable.

southern areas. During the period of the tagging study, only New Jersey had seasonal limits (open 1 March to 31 December) on its coastal striped bass fishery (ASMFC 1981); thus, the possibility of the pattern being biased by regulated seasonality of fishing effort is minimal.

Stock Composition

The origin of striped bass stocks that contribute to fisheries along the Atlantic coast may be inferred from the ALS recapture data. The lack of experimental control over the tagging program prohibits an analysis of the proportion of fish from each contributing stock that is vulnerable to a given fishery. However, the ALS recapture data yield insights into the presence or absence of a stock in a given geographic location. Furthermore, since relative fishing effort could not be assessed in this study, results of this analysis should only be viewed in terms of the presence or absence or a given stock in a geographic region.

Potential stock origin locations are Chesapeake Bay (area VIII), the Hudson River above the Harlem River confluence (region 26 in area V), and northern North Carolina (area IX), based on conclusions of Tiller (1950), Raney (1952), Mansueti (1961), Schaefer (1968b), Berggren and Lieberman (1978), and Van Winkle and Kumar (1982). The traditional method of determining stock origin is tracing movements of tagged fish released in spawning areas. Since no fish were tagged in area IX, and relatively few fish (645) were tagged in area VIII, the number of fish tagged in a given area that were recaptured in an estuary of potential stock origin was tallied.

Striped bass recaptured in Chesapeake Bay were tagged in areas I–VIII (Table 6). Fish recaptured in the Hudson River were tagged in areas I–VI, and fish recaptured in northern North Carolina waters were tagged in areas I, II, III, and V. These data support the conclusion of McLaren et

TABLE 4.—Length-frequency distributions of striped bass tagged by American Littoral Society members, 1964–1983 and 1973–1983, and of recovered striped bass when they were tagged, 1973–1983.[a]

Length at tagging (cm)	Number of fish tagged		Number of fish recovered 1973–1983
	1964–1983	1973–1983	
<13	36 (0.1%)	12 (0.1%)	0
15–25	1,650 (6.0%)	1,077 (7.2%)	6 (0.5%)
28–38	9,988 (36.2%)	5,656 (37.9%)	284 (27.6%)
41–51	10,620 (38.5%)	5,770 (38.7%)	558 (54.3%)
53–64	3,036 (11.0%)	1,303 (8.7%)	106 (10.3%)
66–76	1,131 (4.1%)	452 (3.0%)	34 (3.3%)
79–89	556 (2.0%)	304 (2.0%)	21 (2.0%)
91–102	379 (1.4%)	227 (1.5%)	12 (1.2%)
104–114	137 (0.5%)	84 (0.6%)	6 (0.6%)
117–127	44 (0.2%)	33 (0.2%)	1 (0.1%)
Total	27,577 (100.0%)	14,918 (99.9%)	1,028 (99.9%)
Unknown length	97	79	76

[a] Lengths of recaptured fish at time of tagging are unavailable prior to 1973.

al. (1981) that the contribution of the Hudson River stock to the coastal fisheries is essentially northeastward from the mouth of the river. The data are also consistent with the general contention that at least three stocks may contribute to the coastal fisheries: Hudson River, Chesapeake Bay, and northern North Carolina.

The recovery of 18 tags in northern North Carolina waters provides evidence (albeit limited) that North Carolina stocks of striped bass may have contributed to northern coastal fisheries during the past two decades. In the 1930s, Merriman (1941) tagged 600 striped bass in the extreme eastern end of Albermarle Sound, North Carolina, of which 21 were recovered in Chesapeake Bay and along the coast as far north as Point Judith, Rhode Island. Holland and Yelverton (1973) tagged striped bass along the North Carolina coast and recovered tags in Albemarle Sound, Chesapeake Bay, and as far north as Maine. However, of over 11,000 striped bass tagged by Hassler et al. (1981) in the Roanoke River proper during 1956–1980 (Table 1), none of the 3,000+ recover-

ies were outside the bays and rivers of North Carolina. The authors concluded that the Roanoke River stock contributes to essentially a local fishery, and contributes little to fisheries in the north Atlantic areas.

The 45 recaptures of striped bass tagged in the Hudson River above the Harlem River confluence (region 26 in area V) were distributed as follows:

Area	Recoveries	Area	Recoveries
I	0	VI	1
II	0	VII	1
III	12	VIII	0
IV	5	IX	0
V	24		

Vladykov and Wallace (1952) and Raney (1952) suggested that the Hudson River may serve as overwintering grounds for some Chesapeake striped bass. Tagging studies in the Hudson River by McLaren et al. (1981) do not strongly support this conclusion; they recovered few tags from south of the New York Bight. The present study also does not support this conclusion, since none of the fish tagged and released in the Hudson River above New York Harbor were recovered in the Chesapeake Bay.

Discussion

Results of our analysis are consistent with general conclusions of published studies of the migratory habits of striped bass along the Atlantic coast. It is evident from the geographic distribution of tag recoveries that regulations intended to protect the Chesapeake stocks from excessive exploitation need to cover all coastal waters north of Chesapeake Bay, including the lower Hudson River and Raritan Bay area.

Austin and Custer (1977) outlined four major difficulties that are encountered when one attempts to use a sportfishing club tagging program to draw conclusions about movements of coastal migratory stocks. Three of these problems are evident in the ALS tagging program. The first problem stems from the geographic clustering of membership. The greatest concentration of ALS tagging as in the New York metropolitan area, and relatively few striped bass were tagged south of New Jersey. A closely related problem arises when particular members intensify their tagging efforts in a limited geographic location. The high tag-recovery rate of fish released in area VIII may be because most (88%) of the tagging in that area

TABLE 5.—Geographic distribution of recoveries of striped bass tagged by American Littoral Society members, 1964–1985.

Tag release area	Tag recovery area										Total
	I	II	III	IV	V	VI	VII	VIII	IX	Unknown	
I	98	54	19	25	19	13	22	36	4	13	303
II	8	32	30	12	4	8	22	20	3	5	144
III	15	31	465	133	45	29	74	69	10	30	901
IV	1	1	5	24	7	4	6	10	0	1	59
V	3	3	28	45	117	31	43	42	1	11	324
VI	5	10	14	7	17	28	19	24	0	4	128
VII	0	0	0	1	0	0	0	1	0	0	2
VIII	0	1	1	1	0	0	0	92	0	3	98
IX	0	0	0	0	0	0	0	0	0	0	0
Total	130	132	562	248	209	113	186	294	18	67	1,959

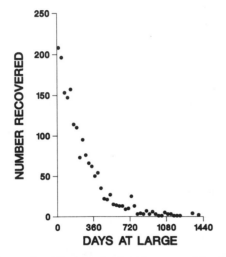

FIGURE 2.—Number of striped bass tagged by American Littoral Society members that were recovered versus days at large, in intervals of 30 d, 1964–1985.

was done by one of the 25 individuals who participated in the program, who may have been an above-average tagger. A third problem in using sport anglers as taggers is the potential to release predominantly "short" fish. Although the length frequency of tagged fish does not imply that ALS members tended to release smaller fish, the length frequency of the recaptured fish at the time they were tagged (Table 4) implies a tendency to return only tags from fish that were larger than the minimum legal size. The fourth problem identified by Austin and Custer (1977), which could not be assessed in the present study, arises because commercial catches cannot be screened as closely as sport catches for fish with tags. This may lead to a lower tag recovery rate in the commercial fisheries and an underestimate of the mortality imposed by those fisheries.

The coastal migratory pattern of anadromous stocks of striped bass is similar to the patterns of other anadromous species that migrate along the Atlantic coast. American shad *Alosa sapidissima* and river herrings (blueback herring *Alosa aestivalis* and alewife *Alosa pseudoharengus*) also exhibit the tendancy to move northward along the coast in the spring, reside in the more northern waters during the summer months, and return to southern waters during the fall and winter (Leggett and Whitney 1972; Neves and Depres 1979; Neves 1981). Striped bass are more restricted than American shad in their coastal migratory range: striped bass stocks from north of southern North Carolina are migratory, whereas American shad from stocks along the entire Atlantic coast have appeared in the Bay of Fundy during the summer months (Dadswell et al. 1986, 1987, this volume). Limited tagging data suggest that river herring stocks that appear in the Bay of Fundy may originate at least as far south along the Atlantic coast as North Carolina (Rulifson, unpublished data cited in Dadswell et al. 1986). Curtis (1971) reported that blueback herring tagged in South Carolina were recovered as far north as Cape Cod. Atlantic salmon *Salmo salar* stocks originating in Connecticut and maine appear off Labrador, Newfoundland, and Greenland during the spring, summer, and autumn fishing season, but do not range as far south along the Atlantic coast as the other anadromous species (A. Meister, personal communication). The southern limit to the migratory range of Atlantic salmon may be influenced by the lack of suitable spawning and nursery rivers south of Connecticut (Netboy 1968).

Acknowledgments

Three individuals made this paper possible. Derrick W. Bennett graciously offered the ALS tag-

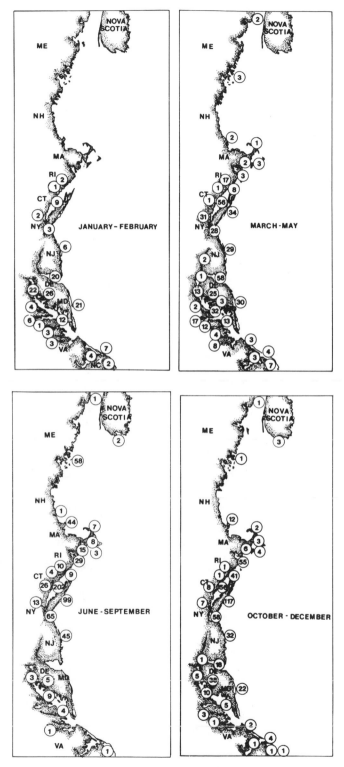

FIGURE 3.—Number of striped bass tagged by American Littoral Society members subsequently recovered along the Atlantic coast, 1964–1985.

TABLE 6.—Geographic distribution of striped bass tagged by American Littoral Society members that were recovered in the Hudson River, Chesapeake Bay, or northern North Carolina, 1964–1985.

Tag release area	Number recovered			
	Hudson River (region 26)	Chesapeake Bay (area VIII)	Northern North Carolina (area IX)	Total
I	4	36	4	44
II	1	20	3	24
III	17	69	10	96
IV	1	10	0	11
V	28	42	1	71
(Region 26ᵃ)	(11)	(0)	(0)	(11)
VI	3	24	0	27
VII	0	1	0	1
VIII	0	92	0	92
IX	0	0	0	0
Total	54	294	18	366

ᵃ Hudson River above the Harlem River confluence.

ging data base for research purposes. Pamela Carlsen accepted the tedious and frustrating task of assigning species and geographic zone codes to every card in the data base. Stanley McClain tracked down and reconstructed the striped bass tag recovery information. We are also indebted to the members of the American Littoral Society who participated in the coastwide tagging program.

Anne Richards, Anne Lange, Richard Hennemuth, and Roger Rulifson provided useful comments and suggestions on the manuscript. Susan Shepherd and Anne Richards assisted in preparation of the graphics and tables.

References

Alperin, I. M. 1966. Dispersal, migration and origins of striped bass from Great South Bay, Long Island. New York Fish and Game Journal 13:79–112.

ASMFC (Atlantic States Marine Fisheries Commission). 1981. Interstate fisheries management plan for striped bass. Fisheries Management Report 1, Washington, D.C., USA.

Austin, H. A., and O. Custer. 1977. Seasonal migration of striped bass in Long Island Sound. New York Fish and Game Journal 24:53–68.

Barnthouse, L. W., J. Boreman, S. W. Christensen, C. P. Goodyear, W. Van Winkle, and D. S. Vaughan. 1984. Population biology in the courtroom: the Hudson River controversy. BioScience 34:14–19.

Berggren, T. J., and J. T. Lieberman. 1978. Relative contribution of Hudson, Chesapeake, and Roanoke striped bass, Morone saxatilis, stocks to the Atlantic coast fishery. U.S. National Marine Fisheries Service Fishery Bulletin 76:335–345.

Bigelow, H. B., and W. C. Schroeder. 1953. Striped

bass Roccus saxatilis (Walbaum) 1792. U.S. Fish and Wildlife Service Fishery Bulletin 53:389–404.

Boreman, J., and H. M. Austin. 1985. Production and harvest of anadromous striped bass stocks along the Atlantic coast. Transactions of the American Fisheries Society 114:3–7.

Chapoton, R. B., and J. E. Sykes. 1961. Atlantic coast migration of large striped bass as evidenced by fisheries and tagging. Transactions of the American Fisheries Society 90:13–20.

Clark, J. R. 1968. Seasonal movements of striped bass contingents of Long Island Sound and the New York Bight. Transactions of the American Fisheries Society 97:320–343.

Coutant, C. C. 1985. Striped bass: environmental risks in fresh and salt water. Transactions of the American Fisheries Society 114:1–2.

Curtis, T. A. 1971. Anadromous fish survey of the Santee and Cooper system. South Carolina Wildlife Resources Department, Progress Report AFS 3-1 (July 1, 1970–June 30, 1970), Columbia, South Carolina, USA.

Dadswell, M. J., G. D. Melvin, P. J. Williams, and D. E. Themelis. 1987. Influences of origin, life history, and chance on the Atlantic coast migration of American shad. American Fisheries Symposium 1:313–330.

Dadswell, M. J., R. A. Rulifson, and G. R. Daborn. 1986. Potential impact of large-scale tidal power developments in the upper Bay of Fundy on fisheries resources of the northwest Atlantic. Fisheries (Bethesda) 11(4):26–35.

Grant, G. C., V. G. Burrell, Jr., C. R. Richards, and E. B. Joseph. 1970. Preliminary results from striped bass tagging in Virginia 1968–1969. Proceedings of the Annual Conference Southeastern Association of Game and Fish commissioners 23:558–570.

Hassler, W. W., N. L. Hill, and J. T. Brown. 1981. The status and abundance of striped bass, Morone saxatilis, in the Roanoke River and Albermarle Sound, North Carolina, 1956-1980. North Carolina Department of Natural Resources and Community Development, Division of Marine Fisheries, Special Scientific Report 38, Raleigh, North Carolina, USA.

Holland, B. F., Jr., and G. F. Yelverton. 1973. Distribution and biological studies of anadromous fishes offshore North Carolina. North Carolina Department of Natural and Economic Resources, Division of Commercial and Sport Fisheries, Special Scientific Report 24, Raleigh, North Carolina, USA.

Kohlenstein, L. C. 1980. Aspects of the population dynamics of striped bass (Morone saxatilis) spawning in Maryland tributaries of the Chesapeake Bay. Doctoral dissertation. Johns Hopkins University, Baltimore, Maryland, USA.

Kohlenstein, L. C. 1981. On the proportion of the Chesapeake Bay stock of striped bass that migrates into the coastal fishery. Transactions of the American Fisheries Society 110:168–179.

Koo, T. S. Y. 1970. The striped bass fishery in the Atlantic states. Chesapeake Science 11:73–93.

Leggett, W. C., and R. R. Whitney. 1972. Water temperature and the migrations of American shad. U.S. National Marine Fisheries Service Fishery Bulletin 70:659–670.

Mansueti, R. J. 1961. Age, growth, and movements of the striped bass, *Roccus saxatilis,* taken in size selective fishing gear in Maryland. Chesapeake Science 2:9–36.

Mansueti, R. J. 1962. Effects of civilization on striped bass and other estaurine biota in Chesapeake Bay and tributaries. Proceedings of the Gulf and Caribbean Fisheries Institute 14:110–136.

Massman, W. H., and A. L. Pacheco. 1961. Movements of striped bass tagged in Virginia waters of Chesapeake Bay. Chesapeake Science 2:37–44.

McFadden, J. T., editor. 1977. Influence of Indian Point unit 2 and other steam electric generating plants on the Hudson River estuary with emphasis on striped bass and other fish populations. Consolidated Edison Company of New York, New York, New York, USA.

McLaren, J. B., J. C. Cooper, T. B. Hoff, and V. Lander. 1981. Movements of Hudson River striped bass. Transactions of the American Fisheries Society 110:168–167.

Merriman, D. 1937. Notes on the life history of the striped bass. *Roccus lineatus.* Copeia 1937:15–36.

Merriman, D. 1941. Studies on the striped bass (*Roccus saxatilis*) of the Atlantic coast. U.S. Fish and Wildlife Service Fishery Bulletin 50(35).

Moore, C. J., and D. T. Burton. 1975. Movements of striped bass, *Morone saxatilis,* tagged in Maryland waters of Chesapeake Bay. Transactions of the American Fisheries Society 104:703–709.

Netboy, A. 1968. The Atlantic salmon. A vanishing species? Faber and Faber, London, England.

Neves, R. J. 1981. The offshore distribution of alewife, *Alosa pseudoharengus,* and the blueback herring, *A. aestivalis,* along the Atlantic coast. U.S. National Marine Fisheries Service Fishery Bulletin 79:473–485.

Neves, R. J., and L. Depres. 1979. The oceanic migration of American shad, *Alosa sapidissima,* along the Atlantic coast. U.S. National Marine Fisheries Service Fishery Bulletin 77:199–212.

Nichols, P. R., and R. V. Miller. 1967. Seasonal movements of striped bass, *Roccus saxatilis* (Walbaum), tagged and released in the Potomac River, Maryland, 1959–61. Chesapeake Science 8:102–124.

Oviatt, C. A. 1977. Menhaden, sport fish and fishermen. University of Rhode Island, Marine Technical Report 60, Kingston, Rhode Island, USA.

Pearson, J. C. 1933. Movements of striped bass in Chesapeake Bay. Maryland Fisheries 22:15–17.

Porter, J., and S. B. Saila. 1969. Cooperative striped bass migration study. Final Report, Contract 14-16-005, to U.S. Fish and Wildlife Service, Washington, D.C., USA.

Raney, E. C. 1952. The life history of the striped bass, *Roccus saxatilis* (Walbaum). Bulletin of the Bingham Oceanographic Collection, Yale University 14(1):5–97.

Raney, E. C. 1957. Subpopulations of the striped bass, *Roccus saxatilis* (Walbaum), in tributaries of Chesapeake Bay. U.S. Fish and Wildlife Service Special Scientific Report Fisheries 208:85–107.

Raney, E. C., W. S. Woolcott, and A. G. Mehring. 1954. Migratory pattern and racial structure of Atlantic coast striped bass. Transactions of the North American Wildlife and Natural Resources Conference 19:376–396.

Ritchie, D. E., and T. S. Y. Koo. 1973. Fish movements—Maryland study. Hydrographic and ecological effects of enlargement of the Chesapeake and Delaware Canal. Army Corps of Engineers, Philadelphia District Contract DACW-61-71-C-0062. Final Report, Philadelphia, Pennsylvania, USA.

Schaefer, R. H. 1968a. Sex composition of striped bass from the Long Island surf. New York Fish and Game Journal 15:117–118.

Schaefer, R. H. 1968b. Size, age composition and migration of striped bass from the surf waters of Long Island. New York Fish and Game Journal 15:1–51.

TI (Texas Instruments). 1980. 1977 year class report for the multiplant impact study of the Hudson River estuary. Report to Consolidated Edison Company of New York, New York, New York, USA.

TI (Texas Instruments). 1981. 1978 year class report for the multiplant impact study of the Hudson River estuary. Report to Consolidated Edison Company of New York, New York, New York, USA.

Tiller, R. E. 1950. A five-year study of the striped bass fishery of Maryland, based on analysis of scales. University of Maryland, Chesapeake Biological Laboratory, Publication 85, Solomons, Maryland, USA.

USDOT and USCOE (U.S. Department of Transportation and U.S. Army Corps of Engineers). 1984. Final supplemental environmental impact statement. Westside highway project. Volume 2—fisheries portion. Washington, D.C., USA.

Van Winkle, W., and K. D. Kumar. 1982. Relative stock composition of the Atlantic Coast striped bass population: further analysis. Oak Ridge National Laboratory, Environmental Sciences Division, Publication 1988, NUREG/CR-2563, ORNL/TM-8217, Oak Ridge, Tennessee, USA.

Vladykov, V. D., and D. H. Wallace. 1938. Is the striped bass (*Roccus lineatus*) of Chesapeake Bay a migratory fish? Transactions of the American Fisheries Society 67:67–86.

Vladykov, V. D., and D. H. Wallace. 1952. Studies of the striped bass. *Roccus saxatilis* (Walbaum), with special reference to the Chesapeake Bay region during 1936–1938. Bulletin of the Bingham Oceanographic Collection, Yale University 14(1):132–177.

Whitney, R. R. 1961. The Susquehanna fishery study, 1957–1960; a report of a study on the desirability and feasibility of passing fish at Conowingo Dam. Maryland Department of Research and Education, Contribution 169, Solomons, Maryland, USA.

Young, B. H. 1980. A study of the striped bass in the marine district of New York state II. April 1, 1976–March 31, 1979. U.S. National Marine Fisheries Service, Project AFC-9, Completion Report, Stony Brook, New York, USA.

American Fisheries Society Symposium 1:340–357, 1987

Spatial and Temporal Aspects of the Ocean Migration of Anadromous Arctic Char

J. B. DEMPSON

Fisheries Research Branch, Department of Fisheries and Oceans, Post Office Box 5667
St. John's, Newfoundland A1C 5X1, Canada

A. H. KRISTOFFERSON

Arctic Resource Assessment, Department of Fisheries and Oceans
Winnipeg, Manitoba R3T 2N6, Canada

Abstract.—Information on ocean migrations of fishes of the genus *Salvelinus* is more limited than for other salmonid genera. Part of the reason is related to the lower degree of anadromy exhibited by this group. The Arctic char *Salvelinus alpinus* has a complex life history including variability in migratory behaviour. Ocean migrations have been reported to be of short duration in localized coastal areas with populations showing a high degree of homing. These generalizations are examined with respect to temporal and spatial changes in the ocean distribution of marine migrant Arctic char, based on commercial catch records and tagging studies carried out in Labrador and in Cambridge Bay, Northwest Territories. Factors shown to influence distribution, movements, mixing of stocks, and duration at sea prior to upstream overwintering migration include local marine environmental conditions; availability of marine food resources; fish size, sex, and state of maturation; and proximity to other river systems.

The Arctic char *Salvelinus alpinus* has a Holarctic distribution of anadromous and resident freshwater forms. It is the most northerly distributed freshwater fish (Walters 1955) and is one of the few species known to occur naturally in systems where no other fish species are present (Johnson 1980). The phenotypic plasticity of Arctic char has allowed it to evolve a variety of life history tactics to cope with most cool, oligotrophic habitats (Barbour 1984). Barbour (1984) stated that the overall strategy for survival of the species is related to the variation exhibited in all life history parameters and the precise adaptation to individual habitats. Migratory behaviour is only one aspect in the complex life history of Arctic char in which the species exhibits a highly variable nature.

Migration by fishes has been considered as an adaptation for increasing a species' abundance by enhancing its growth, fecundity, and survival (Nikolsky 1963; Harden Jones 1968; Northcote 1978, 1984). In northern latitudes where Arctic char are most abundant, periodic migrations to the sea enable anadromous populations to take advantage of ample marine food resources. Most information on Arctic char migrations, however, pertains to movements and biological characteristics of populations moving to and from the sea (Johnson 1980; McCart 1980; Gyselman 1984; Dempson and Green 1985). The seaward movement coincides

with spring runoff and ice breakup in coastal rivers and consists of both first-time and repeat migrants; the larger Arctic char tend to enter the sea first. First-time migrants have spent 1–8 years in fresh water. Repeat migrants include both adults (maturing and nonmaturing) and juveniles. Both adults and juveniles, therefore, undergo several seaward migrations. Juvenile and adult groups show little overlap of their respective size distributions, and length distributions remain very stable over time even in populations where stock size has decreased (Johnson 1980; Dempson and Green 1985). There is also little overlap in the timing of adult and juvenile migrations either to or from the sea. This suggests that each group maintains an independent existence at sea, possibly moving in distinct groups or schools.

Arctic char are not known to overwinter at sea (Grainger 1953) and the return to fresh water follows a similar pattern: larger maturing fish enter early followed first by nonmaturing adults and then juveniles. Arctic char are iteroparous and adults mature on an intermittent basis (Dutil 1984). In some populations, the upstream run consists largely of nonmaturing fish, the majority of maturing individuals remaining in fresh water during the year in which they will spawn (Johnson 1980). Thus, some Arctic char possess a migratory strategy whereby they may forego annual marine migrations and subsequently spend 2 years or more in fresh water. Compared with Pacific salmon *Oncorhynchus* spp. and most Atlantic salmon *Salmo salar* populations, anadromous Arctic char have a shorter and more irregular period of marine residence.

Information on ocean migrations of Arctic char is rather limited in comparison with other salmonid species (Jensen and Berg 1977). Part of the reason may be that Arctic char have a lower degree of anadromy (Rounsefell 1958) and lower commercial importance; harvested stocks of anadromous Arctic char typically occur in extreme northern environments. Ocean migrations of Arctic char have been reported to be of short duration in localized coastal areas where populations show a high degree of homing (Yessipov 1935; Sprules 1952; Grainger 1953; Nielsen 1961; Le Jeune 1967; Moore 1975). This paper reviews these generalizations by examining temporal and spatial changes in the ocean distribution, movements, and abundance of anadromous Arctic char. Analyses of catch and effort data and tag recovery information are used in determining how geographical, environmental, and biological factors may influence the distribution, movements, and intermixing of stocks and the duration fish spend at sea prior to their upstream migration.

Methods

Sources of data and areas of investigation.— Major fisheries for anadromous Arctic char occur along the northern Labrador coast north of latitude 54°N (Dempson and Green 1985) and in the area of Cambridge Bay, Victoria Island, Northwest Territories (69°03′N, 105°10′W) (Kristofferson et al. 1984). Average commercial landings from 1979 to 1984 were 61 tonnes/year at Cambridge Bay and 206 tonnes/year for northern Labrador; 85% of the Labrador harvest occurred within the Nain fishing region (Figure 1). The Cambridge Bay fishery takes place in the estuaries or river mouths of seven rivers (Figure 2) using shore-set gill nets with stretched mesh sizes of 139–165 mm. It is targeted on either downstream migrants during spring or the upstream run later in summer (Kristofferson et al. 1984). In contrast, the northern Labrador fishery takes place entirely at sea during the summer using gill nets with stretched mesh sizes of 114 and 127 mm set from mainland or offshore island shorelines. The Nain fishing region has been subdivided into several geographical areas from which catch and effort data and tag recovery information can be obtained (Figure 1).

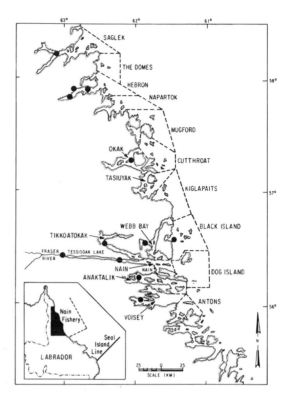

FIGURE 1.—Geographical separation of the Nain fishing region subareas from which Arctic char catch and effort data and tag recovery information were derived. Tagging locations (●) are also indicated.

Additional biological sampling of the Labrador fishery has been carried out to obtain information on food and feeding habits, sex ratio distribution, and degree of maturity of Arctic char at sea. Sex ratio data were also obtained from logbooks maintained by selected commercial fishermen.

In both regions, extensive tagging studies have been carried out in order to determine distribution patterns and the extent of intermixing of adjacent populations (Table 1). Floy spaghetti tags ($N = 6,195$) were used in the Cambridge Bay studies whereas Carlin tags ($N = 7,566$) with doubled stainless steel thread were used in Labrador. Arctic char examined in tagging studies were either outward migrants caught by angling or gillnetting during the spring (Labrador only), upstream migrants caught by angling or gillnetting or at counting fences during the summer and fall (Cambridge Bay and Labrador), or fish caught and released from gill nets at sea during the summer (Labrador only). All fish tagged and released were measured for fork length (mm). In the Cambridge Bay fishery, only fish greater than 400 mm fork

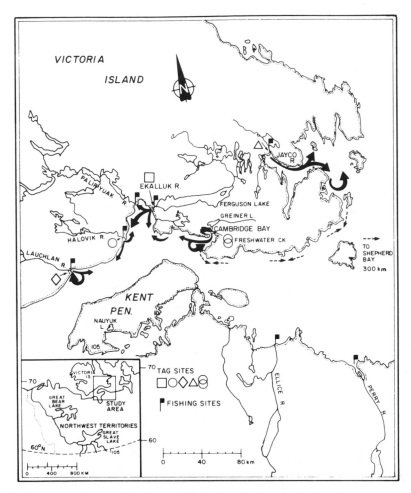

FIGURE 2.—The Cambridge Bay area, Northwest Territories, showing tagging locations, commercial fishing sites, and possible dispersal routes for Arctic char.

length were tagged. Recaptured fish were obtained from commercial and recreational fisheries either at sea or in river mouths and estuaries. Other tagged fish were caught as they returned back through counting fences.

Information on temperatures in the Hebron Fiord, northern Labrador, was obtained from Ryan thermographs set in approximately 5 m of water from July 17 to September 23, 1985. Sea temperature information for the Seal Island line in southern Labrador (Figure 1)—within the area defined by 52°42′N, 55°45′W; 53°42′N, 55°45′W; 53°30′N, 53°00′W; and 54°30′N, 53°00′W—was obtained from archived oceanographic data from the Marine Environmental Data Service, Ottawa, Canada. Lazier (1982) has shown that the southward-flowing water above the continental shelf between 52°N and 60°N could be represented by

one water mass. Ocean temperature data for this continental shelf area at a depth of 20 m were averaged over 113 stations for July–August between 1977 and 1985.

Data analyses.—Information from purchase slips for commercial landings of Arctic char by individual fishermen in Labrador included area where fish were caught, date, number of nets used, weights of fish landed, and total number of fish caught. Catch and effort data from the Nain stock unit were used in examining temporal and spatial changes in distribution and abundance of Arctic char caught at sea in the northern Labrador fishery. The Nain stock unit was divided into an inshore and an offshore zone. The inshore zone included the subareas Anaktalik Bay, Nain Bay, Tikkoatokak Bay, and Webb Bay; the offshore zone consisted of Dog Island and Black Island (Figure 1).

TABLE 1.—Summary of recoveries, from the first (R_1) to the seventh (R_7) year after tagging of tagged Arctic char released in various subareas of northern Labrador and Northwest Territories; R_0 represents recoveries during the same year of tagging. Codes: Sp = tagged during spring outward migration; U = tagged during upstream migration; S = tagged at sea during the summer.

Stock unit and subarea	Code	Years of tagging	Number tagged	Recaptures (number)								Total	% recaptured
				R_0	R_1	R_2	R_3	R_4	R_5	R_6	R_7		
Labrador													
Voisey													
Voisey Bay	S	1979–1984	331	22	38	13	2	1	0	0		76	23.0
Nain													
Anaktalik Bay	S	1979–1985	187	13	28	6	3	1	0	0		51	27.3
Nain Bay	Sp	1979–1985	1,213	221	112	37	14	3	0	0		387	31.9
Fraser River	U	1975–1979	829	7	111	56	33	23	8	4	1	243	29.3
Tikkoatokak Bay	Sp, S	1979–1985	1,272	373	153	31	8	0	0	0		565	44.4
Webb Bay	Sp	1979, 1984–1985	84	23	6	0	0	1	0	0		30	35.7
Offshore[a]	Sp, S	1980, 1981, 1984–1985	122	10	8	7	0	0	0			25	20.5
Total			3,707	647	418	137	58	28	8	4	1	1,301	35.1
Okak													
Okak Bay	S	1974, 1978–1980, 1984–1985	370	16	13	5	3	1	0	0	1	39	10.5
Hebron													
Hebron Fiord	S	1978–1980, 1982, 1984	411	8	28	18	8	3	0	2	0	67	16.3
Ikarut River (adults)	Sp, U	1981–1985	1,045	40	156	72	11	3				282	27.0
Ikarut River (juveniles)	Sp, U	1981–1985	1,054	5	44	5	1	0				55	5.2
River H-3	U	1981–1985	331	0	14	10	4	5				33	10.0
Total			2,841	53	242	105	24	11	0	2		437	15.4
Saglek													
Saglek Fiord	S	1978–1982	317	2	14	8	5	4	0	0	0	33	10.4
Labrador total			7,566	740	725	268	92	45	8	6	2	1,886	24.9
Northwest Territories													
Cambridge Bay													
Ekalluk River	U	1978–1979	1,621	3	428	100	69	54	20	13	3	690	42.6
Halovik River	U	1981	996	0	52	53	27	24				156	15.7
Lauchlan River	U	1983	995	0	128	38						166	16.7
Freshwater Creek	U	1982	808	9	94	47	13					163	20.2
Total			4,420	12	702	238	109	78	20	13	3	1,175	26.6
Jayco													
Jayco River	U	1980–1981	1,775	2	11	57	61	18	7			156	8.8
Northwest Territories total			6,195	14	713	295	170	96	27	13	3	1,331	21.5

[a] Offshore area includes Dog Island and Black Island.

Catch data were analysed to detect possible changes in the distribution of fish between inshore and offshore zones and to detect seasonal changes in abundance. Differences in abundance between zones and among weeks within zones were tested by Kruskal–Wallis one-way analyses of variance (Sokal and Rohlf 1969) of data from all weeks for years 1977–1985. Migratory timing, defined as abundance of fish as a function of time (Mundy 1982; Butt 1984), was examined by calculating the migratory time density from the cumulative weekly proportions of catch and catch-per-unit-effort data (CUE) by year from 1977 to 1985 and for the three time periods 1977–1979, 1980–1982, and 1983–1985. Empirical migratory time density for the time series of weekly proportions (P_t) was calculated by the method of Mundy (1982):

$$P_t = n_t/N;$$

n_t = abundance, catch, or CUE for time interval t;

N = total abundance, catch, or CUE.

The annual mean t ($\bar{t}$) over m weeks was then calculated as

$$\bar{t} = \sum_{t=1}^{m} t \cdot P_t;$$

the variance (S_t^2) was estimated from

$$S_t^2 = \sum_{t=1}^{m} (t - \bar{t})^2 P_t.$$

The grand mean for all years was just the average of all $\bar{t}$. Individual years could be compared with the 95% confidence interval about the grand mean and categorized as years of early, late, or average migration time (Mundy 1982; Butt 1984). All weekly intervals were subsequently converted into actual monthly dates. Effort data were expressed in terms of man-weeks of fishing following the method initiated by Coady and Best (1976).

Differences in the spatial and temporal distribution of Arctic char in the Nain stock unit were also examined by analysing tag recovery information. Adult Arctic char from two subareas, Nain Bay and Tikkoatokak Bay (Figure 1), were tagged and released each spring (May 25–June 12, 1979–1985) during the outward migrations. A greater proportion of the tagging was done after 1982 than before this date. Over the latter period (1982–1985), we wished to test the hypothesis that movement patterns of a specific fish stock did not differ among years. A categorical data-modelling procedure (Bishop et al. 1975; SAS 1985) was used to fit a log-linear model to the number of tag recoveries by subarea and year. The model included a term for numbers of fish caught because both effort and catch differed among subareas. All 4 years of data (1982–1985) were grouped and tag recoveries only during the same year of tagging (R_0) were analysed.

An estimate of the annual duration at sea was derived from recaptures of adult Arctic char tagged and released during the spring outward migration in Nain Bay and Tikkoatokak Bay,

Labrador. This was a minimum estimate because these fish were subsequently recaptured at sea in the commercial fishery. It is, however, useful for relative comparisons among years. A more direct estimate was obtained from gillnetted Arctic char tagged and released at the mouth of the Ikarut River, Hebron Fiord, Labrador (58°09′N, 63°05′W) (Figure 6) and in the immediate estuary during the outward migration from June 4 to 12, 1983. Recaptures of these fish occurred later that summer as they migrated upstream through the counting fence on the Ikarut River. The counting fence was located above the head of tide approximately 1.5 km upstream from the mouth.

Results

Altogether, 7,566 Arctic char were tagged and released in the northern Labrador area, and 1,886 (24.9%) were subsequently recaptured. The percentage recovery varied from a low of 5.2% for juveniles released in the Ikarut River, Hebron Fiord, to 44.4% for adults tagged in Tikkoatokak Bay (Table 1). These latter fish were tagged and released largely during the spring outward migration and were subsequently recaptured in the commercial fishery. Similarly, of 6,195 Arctic char tagged in the Cambridge Bay area, 1,331 (21.5%) were recaptured. The percentage recovery was similar to that observed in Labrador, ranging from 8.8% at Jayco River to 42.6% at Ekalluk River. In both regions, a few fish were recovered 6 and 7 years after tagging, but the majority (≥90%) were recaptured within 3 years of release (Table 1).

Temporal Distribution at Sea

Recaptures from the commercial fishery of Arctic char tagged during the spring outward migration in Nain Bay and Tikkoatokak Bay, Labrador (Figure 1), provided minimum estimates of the annual duration of stay in the sea. Differences were found between areas and among years (Table 2). In general, fish tagged and released in Nain Bay spent an average 57.1 d (8.2 weeks) at sea prior to recapture while those from Tikkoatokak Bay were at sea an average of 52.3 days (7.5 weeks). Maximum duration at sea prior to recapture was about 13 weeks for fish tagged in both subareas, although less than 30% of the fish were recaptured after 10 weeks at sea (Table 2).

Data obtained from tag recoveries at the Ikarut River counting fence indicated the average period at sea in 1983 was 65.8 d (9.4 weeks). The shortest period spent at sea was 32 d (recaptured July 13);

TABLE 2.—Minimum estimates of the annual duration of stay in the sea for Arctic char tagged during the spring outward migration in various areas in northern Labrador and recapture dates in the same year.

Release area	Year	Number tagged	Number recaptured	Mean date[a] of recapture	Number of days at sea prior to recapture		
					Mean	Maximum	% out >10 weeks
Nain Bay	1982	211	25	Jul 27	52.4	76	20
	1983	187	44	Jul 24	56.1	90	20
	1984	200	25	Jul 29	59.9	93	36
	1985	230	45	Aug 4	59.0	90	40
	1982–1985	828	139		57.1	93	29
Tikkoatokak Bay	1982	277	85	Jul 19	42.6	80	7
	1983	239	60	Jul 25	58.3	82	28
	1984	192	66	Jul 29	57.5	90	24
	1985	173	58	Aug 5	54.5	84	24
	1982–1985	881	269		52.3	90	20
Ikarut River, Hebron Fiord	1983	224	31	Aug 14	65.8	109	32

[a] Includes only those fish recaptured in the commercial fishery (Nain Bay, Tikkoatokak Bay releases) or at the Ikarut River counting fence, for which date of release and recapture were known.

the longest was 109 d (recaptured September 22). Fish tagged during the earlier period (June 4–6) spent about 13 d longer at sea than those tagged in the later period (June 10–12). However, the length of time a fish might have been in the river prior to passing through the counting fence on its return from the sea is unknown, nor it is known how long fish may have been at the mouth of the river or in the estuary prior to being tagged in the spring.

Table 3 summarizes the mean and annual migratory timing of Arctic char in northern Labrador based on catch and catch-per-unit-effort data for the Nain stock unit. In general, run timing was slightly later based on CUE data. The earliest run occurred in 1979 when, based on catch data, the mean date of migration was July 9 (July 13 if based on CUE data). Both dates were outside the 95% confidence limits for the grand mean. The latest runs were in 1984 and 1985 when the annual mean run timing was between August 1 and August 5. These figures fall outside of the confidence interval for the grand mean.

Based on either catch or CUE, data suggest that the timing of migration varied annually and that Arctic char were significantly more abundant at sea later in the summer during the last several years (1983–1985) than in the two previous time periods (Table 3; Figure 3). On average, for all years combined (1977–1985), 90% of the commercial catch was taken by August 12 and 50% by July 15.

TABLE 3.—Mean migratory timing by year for northern Labrador Arctic char based on catch and catch-per-unit-effort (CUE) data with a summary by time period, including 95% confidence intervals (CI) (after Mundy 1982).

Year	Mean date of catch (95% CI)		Duration of fishery
	Catch	CUE	
1977	Jul 18	Jul 22	Jul 1–Sep 17
1978	Jul 13	Jul 17	Jul 1–Sep 16
1979	Jul 9	Jul 13	Jun 20–Sep 2
1980	Jul 23	Jul 25	Jul 1–Sep 11
1981	Jul 14	Jul 17	Jun 22–Sep 12
1982	Jul 19	Jul 19	Jun 24–Sep 17
1983	Jul 28	Jul 30	Jul 1–Sep 16
1984	Aug 1	Aug 5	Jun 25–Sep 15
1985	Aug 4	Aug 4	Jun 26–Sep 19
1977–1979	Jul 14 (Jul 5–22)	Jul 21 (Jul 8–Aug 3)	
1980–1982	Jul 19 (Jul 8–30)	Jul 21 (Jul 8–Aug 1)	
1983–1985	Jul 31 (Jul 20–Aug 12)	Aug 3 (Jul 21–Aug 16)	
1977–1985	Jul 21 (Jul 14–28)	Jul 24 (Jul 18–30)	

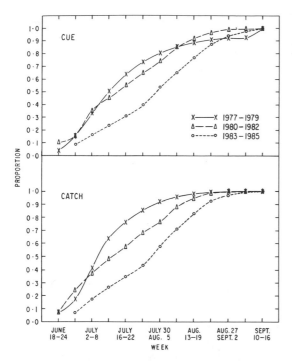

FIGURE 3.—Cummulative proportion of catch per unit effort (CUE) and catch as a function of time for Arctic char caught in the Nain stock unit of northern Labrador over three time intervals, 1977–1979, 1980–1982, and 1983–1985.

Analyses of annual and seasonal changes in abundance also provided information on temporal distribution of Arctic char in the northern Labrador area. Results of the Kruskal–Wallis analysis of variance indicated that there was a highly significant difference in abundance between inshore and offshore zones ($\chi^2 = 85.0$; df = 1; $P < 0.0001$; Figure 4). When zones were analysed separately, there was difference in abundance among weeks for both the inshore zone ($\chi^2 = 23.5$; df = 12; $P = 0.03$) and the offshore island zone ($\chi^2 = 41.0$; df = 12; $P < 0.0001$). Abundance initially increased as Arctic char moved into this area, then later decreased as the season advanced and the majority of fish were assumed to have returned to rivers located largely within the inner bay areas.

The temporal distribution of tag recoveries of Arctic char tagged and released during the spring in Nain Bay and Tikkoatokak Bay supports the above evidence based on CUE data for a seasonal movement of fish into the offshore island zone. The majority of tag recoveries in the offshore island zone occurred during late July to mid

August; this is after the peak recovery of tags from the inshore fishing areas (Figure 5).

Spatial Distribution at Sea

Results of tagging experiments in northern Labrador indicate little intermixing of populations from widely distributed areas along the 300-km length of coastline from Antons to Saglek Fiord. Only 1.3% of Arctic char tagged in the Voisey or Nain stock unit areas were recaptured north of Black Island and less than 0.2% recaptured south of Antons. Similarly, less than 1% of Arctic char tagged in the Okak, Hebron, or Saglek subareas were recaptured south of the Kiglapait subarea.

The same general observations apply to the Cambridge Bay area. Very little mixing occurred between Arctic char populations located east and west of Cambridge Bay. Only 10% of all fish tagged in either area were recovered in the other area. Some mixing, however, took place around Cambridge Bay itself.

On the basis of the actual distribution of tag recoveries, several stock units can be designated (Table 4). The Voisey stock unit consists of the inshore Voisey Bay subarea and the coastal Antons subarea. The Nain stock unit is made up of Anaktalik Bay, Nain Bay, Tikkoatokak Bay, and

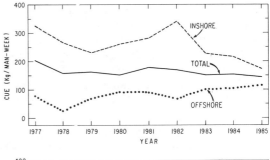

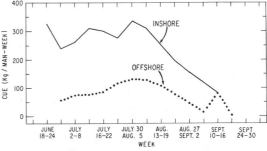

FIGURE 4.—Differences in the annual and seasonal abundance of Arctic char between the inshore and offshore island fishing zones of the Nain stock unit in northern Labrador.

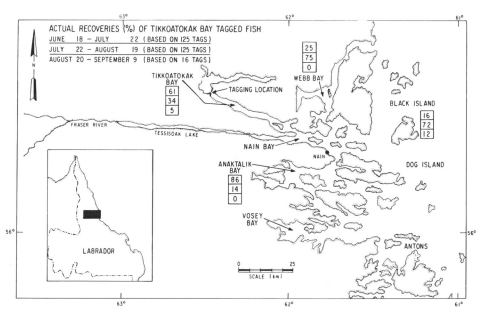

FIGURE 5.—Summary of the percent distribution of tag recoveries over three time periods for Arctic char tagged and released during the spring in the Tikkoatokak Bay subarea of the Nain stock unit in northern Labrador.

Webb Bay for the inshore zone and Dog Island and Black Island for the offshore island zone (Figures 1, 6). The Okak stock unit consists of the Okak Bay subarea and an offshore island or coastal component of the Cutthroat, Tasiuyak, and Kiglapait subareas. The remaining stock units are designated Hebron and Saglek (Table 4; Figure 6). Adjusting tag recoveries for numbers of fish caught or for fishing effort has little effect on the designated stock unit boundaries. Major differences, however, occur in the relative distribution of fish in inshore or offshore zones (Figure 7). Within the Nain stock unit subareas, adjusted values indicate more fish were apparently recaptured in the offshore zone, whereas the opposite was true for the Voisey stock unit. With respect to the Okak stock unit, the adjusted values indicate an inshore–offshore distribution of 75 and 16%, respectively, in contrast to the actual distribution of 61 and 33%.

Tag recovery information from the Cambridge Bay region suggests the existence of at least three stock units (Table 5). The Jayco River population forms one unit. The second unit includes populations from the Lauchlan, Halovik, Paliryuak, and Ekalluk rivers as well as Freshwater Creek. No tags were recovered from fisheries at the Perry and Ellice rivers (Figure 2), suggesting that Arctic char from Victoria Island do not migrate to these areas and may represent part of a third stock unit.

The longest distance travelled by an Arctic char tagged in northern Labrador was approximately 250 km. This fish was tagged June 6, 1985, at the head of Nain Bay and recaptured 71 d later at Makkovik Bay. Of all recaptures of Arctic char tagged during spring at Nain Bay, 95% were within a distance of 70 km and only 2.3% were 100 km or more away from the release site. Similarly, of the Arctic char recaptured after they were tagged and released at Tikkoatokak Bay during spring, 78% were within a 70-km distance and only 4.4% were caught more than 100 km away. Similar results were obtained at Cambridge Bay. One fish, however, was tagged in the Ekalluk River in 1979 and was recaptured in 1982 at Shepherd Bay, 550 km to the east. Overall, 85% of all Arctic char tagged were recaptured within 60 km and only 9% were recovered more than 100 km away. There was no evidence for a relationship between distance travelled and size of fish from either northern Labrador or Cambridge Bay. In Labrador, fish tagged during the spring outward migration appear to leave the immediate vicinity of the river mouths and distribute themselves throughout the bays and fiords, moving further away with the melting and retreating ice. In general, the data suggest that dispersal of Arctic char at sea in the Nain area is not extensive. Intermixing of local and adjacent populations does occur at sea, but there appears to be a

TABLE 4.—Percentage distribution of recoveries, by stock unit, of Arctic char tagged and released in various subareas of northern Labrador.

Tagging location, stock unit, and subarea	Number tagged	Length (mm) Mean	Length (mm) Range	Number recaptured[a]	Voisey In-shore	Voisey Off-shore	Voisey Total	Nain In-shore	Nain Off-shore[b]	Nain Total	Okak In-shore	Okak Off-shore[c]	Okak Total	Hebron	Saglek	Other
Voisey																
Voisey Bay	331	507	360–650	75	55	28	83	10	7	17	0	0	0	0	0	0
Nain																
Anaktalik Bay	187	481	319–680	47	0	2	2	77	19	96	0	2	2	0	0	0
Nain Bay	1,213	451	193–670	379	1	2	3	67	29	96	<1	<1	<1	0	0	<1
Fraser River	829	470	230–670	233	0	1	1	87	11	98	0	<1	<1	0	0	0
Tikkoatokak Bay	1,272	498	180–775	556	1	2	3	75	21	96	<1	1	1	0	0	0
Webb Bay	84	485	345–645	30		0	0	97	3	100	0	0	0	0	0	0
Offshore	122	446	276–573	23	0	4	4	30	57	87	0	9	9	0	0	0
Total	3,707	473	180–775	1,268	<1	2	2	75	22	97	<1	1	1	0	0	<1
Okak																
Okak Bay	370	474	270–688	33	0	0	0	0	6	6	61	33	94	0	0	0
Hebron																
Hebron Fiord	411	497	300–660	64	0	0	0	0	0	0	3	6	9	88	0	3
Ikarut River (adults)	1,045	467	300–725	281	0	0	0	0	<1	<1	1	3	4	94	0	1
Ikarut River (juveniles)	1,054	199	116–295	55	0	0	0	0	0	0	0	0	0	100	0	0
River H-3	331	378	125–710	33	0	0	0	0	0	0	0	6	6	91	0	3
Total	2,841	361	116–725	433	0	0	0	0	<1	<1	1	3	4	94	0	1
Saglek																
Saglek Fiord	317	487	230–690	33	0	0	0	0	0	0	0	0	0	9	88	3

[a] Includes only recaptures for which area of recovery was known.
[b] Offshore area includes Dog Island and Black Island.
[c] Offshore area includes Kiglapaits, Tasiuyak, Cutthroat, and Mugford.

tendency for mixing to occur more in the offshore island or outer coastal areas than in the inside bays (Figure 7).

Cambridge Bay Arctic char tagged during the upstream migration in the Ekalluk River in fall 1978 were recaptured the following spring in the Paliryuak, Halovik, and Lauchlan fisheries, suggesting that they entered the ocean and moved along the coast in a southwesterly direction (Figure 2). Ekalluk River Arctic char were also recaptured as they entered the mouth of Ekalluk River in the fall of 1979, presumably on their way back upstream to overwinter in this system. An identical pattern was observed again in 1980.

Although marine dispersal is generally not extensive, there is some evidence from tag recoveries that ocean movement patterns of specific stocks may vary from year to year. Spring tagging data from Nain Bay and Tikkoatokak Bay, Labrador (1982–1985), were analysed to test the hypothesis that movements in the ocean vary annually.

In the log-linear modelling results (Table 6), area refers to the different subareas within the Nain stock unit whereas state refers to categories of tagged or untagged fish. For both Nain Bay and

Tikkoatokak Bay, the major source of variation in the model is the area × year interaction. This interaction indicates that not only do numbers of fish caught differ among sites and years, but, from year to year, catch changes in different ways at different sites. The significant area × state interation indicates that the ratio of tagged to untagged fish differs among subareas. The year × state interaction indicates a significant difference in the ratio of tagged to untagged fish among years. This was significant only for Arctic char tagged during the spring in Tikkoatokak Bay. The likelihood ratio measures the three-factor interaction adjusted for the different numbers of fish caught in different subareas and years. The results indicate a significant three-way interaction for the Nain Bay subarea, suggesting that, for some stocks, movement patterns at sea vary annually. This is consistent with annual changes in the ocean distribution of these fish over the past 4 years. However, other alternative explanations are also consistent with the occurrence of such interactions. There was no significant difference within the Tikkoatokak subarea, indicating that the different distribution of tagged fish observed during

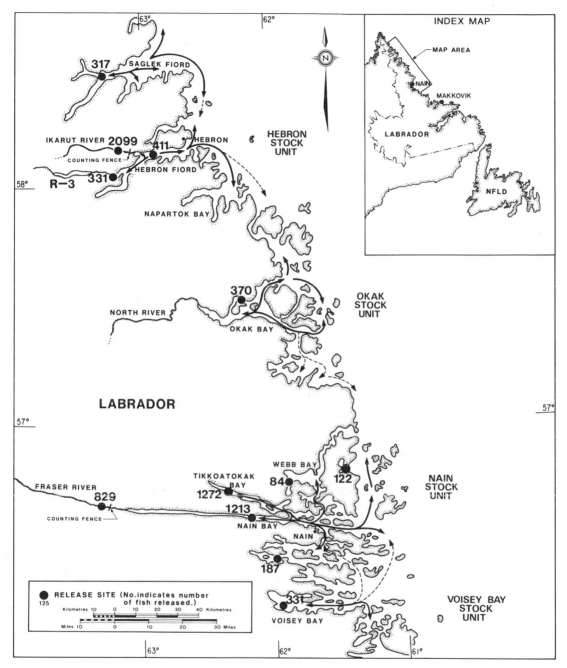

FIGURE 6.—General patterns of ocean movements of anadromous Arctic char in northern Labrador showing number of fish tagged and release locations. Dominant migrations are illustrated with solid continuous lines; fine broken lines represent minor movements.

the past several years was probably a result of different numbers of fish captured in the commercial fishery.

Recaptures of tagged Ikarut River Arctic char in the same system over several years (284 adults and juveniles) indicate that some returned to their previous overwintering stream. It is not known, however, if this stream was necessarily their natal stream. Recaptures in the second or subsequent years after tagging (years $R_2 - R_4$) were mostly

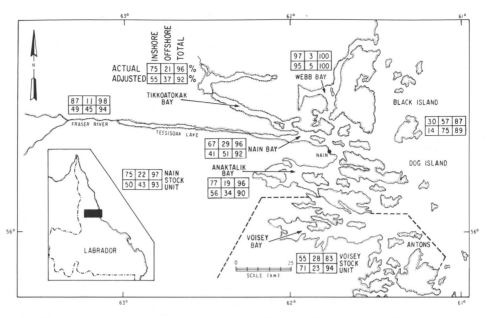

FIGURE 7.—Summary of actual and adjusted (by number of fish caught) tag recoveries from Arctic char released in various subareas of the Nain and Voisey stock units in northern Labrador and for the total Nain stock unit. Recapture values refer to the percent recovery in inshore or offshore zones of the stock unit to which the subarea was affiliated.

first-time returns (85%) and only 21 fish (20 adults and one juvenile) were recaptured two or three times. Five of the multiple recaptures had been absent 2 years before their second recovery. These data suggest that some fish either remain in the system for several years without migrating to sea or they utilize other rivers within the Hebron Fiord in the intervening years. The Ikarut River has virtually no accessible standing water so it is believed that the second reason is more probable. Two fish (one adult and one juvenile) tagged in the Ikarut River were recaptured in river R-3 (Figure 6) and six fish tagged on their upstream migration into river R-3 were subsequently recaptured in the Ikarut River. It should be noted that only the

Ikarut River has been monitored with a counting fence and no extensive fishing has been carried out in the other rivers within the Hebron Fiord.

There is also some evidence for homing of seaward migrants in the Cambridge Bay area. During the 1978 upstream migration in the Ekalluk River, 628 Arctic char were tagged and released. During the 1979 upstream migration, 19 of these were recaptured in the Ekalluk River commercial fishery and an additional 250 were observed migrating upstream at the counting fence in Ekalluk River. Thus, a minimum of 43% came back that year. Fifty-three of the tagged Arctic char were also recaptured in the 1979 spring fisheries at Paliryuak, Halovik, and Lauchlan rivers. Some of

TABLE 5.—Percentage distribution of recoveries, by stock unit, of Arctic char tagged and released in various rivers of the Cambridge Bay area, Northwest Territories.

Tagging location, stock unit, and subarea	Number tagged	Number recaptured	Percent recapture by fishing location								
			Ekalluk River	Paliryuak River	Halovik River	Lauchlan River	Cambridge Bay area	Ellice River	Perry River	Jayco River	Other
Cambridge Bay											
Ekalluk River	1,621	690	49	16	13	12	10	0	0	<1	<1
Halovik River	996	156	17	2	46	32	3	0	0	0	0
Lauchlan River	995	166	2	1	4	92	1	0	0	0	<1
Freshwater Creek	808	163	4	0	0	5	87	0	0	4	<1
Jayco											
Jayco River	1,775	156	0	0	1	0	6	0	0	93	0

TABLE 6.—Summary of results for the log-linear modelling procedure testing the hypothesis that ocean movements of a specific population varies annually for Arctic char tagged during the spring outward migration from both the Nain Bay and Tikkoatokak Bay subareas.

	Nain Bay subarea			Tikkoatokak Bay subarea		
Source	df	χ^2	P	df	χ^2	P
Area	5	176	0.0001	5	491	0.0001
Year	3	45	0.0001	3	81	0.0001
State	1	4,184	0.0001	1	3,957	0.0001
Area × year	15	17,423	0.0001	15	17,419	0.0001
Area × state	5	34	0.0001	5	79	0.0001
Year × state	3	5	0.1415	3	9	0.0231
Year × state × area	12	24	0.0198	11	18	0.0918

these fish could have been intercepted before returning to overwinter in the Ekalluk system.

Evidence for overwintering of Arctic char in different rivers was also obtained from the Cambridge Bay data. Four percent of tag recoveries in the Cambridge Bay area were from systems other than those the fish were migrating into when tagged. In 1983, 38 of the Arctic char tagged at the Ekalluk River in 1978–1979 were recaptured. Five (13%) of these were observed migrating up the Lauchlan River to overwinter. Similarly, 53 Arctic char tagged at the Halovik River in 1981 were recaptured in 1983. Two (3.8%) of these were observed migrating through the counting fence on the Lauchlan River during 1983. The Ekalluk and Lauchlan rivers are separated by 120 km while the Halovik and Lauchlan rivers are about 60 km apart (Figure 2). However, as for the Labrador situation, it is not known which was the natal stream of these fish.

Ecological and Environmental Data

Information on sex ratio distributions, obtained from logbooks completed by commercial fishermen, indicated differences in the proportion of female Arctic char between inshore and offshore zones of the Nain stock unit (Table 7). The data suggest that there may be a greater tendency for males to move further away into the offshore island areas, where their percentage was approximately 13% higher than in the inshore zone.

Subsamples were obtained in order to examine states of maturity of Arctic char in both zones (Table 7). Although sample size was small (1,368 fish) in comparison with numbers of fish sexed for the commercial logbooks, the sex ratios from the subsample were in general agreement with those from the logbooks. Large differences were observed in the percentage of mature fish between the two zones (Table 7). These data indicate that

maturing fish have a greater tendency to remain localized than the nonmaturing component.

The distribution of Arctic char at sea may also be influenced by their feeding habits. A broad comparison of stomach contents (Table 8) indicates that a substantial component of the diet of Arctic char in the Nain and Okak areas is made up of capelins *Mallotus villosus* and sand lances *Ammodytes* spp. This is in contrast to Arctic char in the Hebron and Saglek Fiords which feed more heavily on small sculpins (Cottidae) and invertebrates. In those areas where a substantial portion of the diet is represented by migratory prey species such as capelin, Arctic char could undergo more distant and variable feeding migrations into the offshore island areas (Dog Island, Black Island, and Cutthroat).

Some of the variability observed in the migratory timing of Arctic char in the Nain area (Table 3) can be explained by environmental conditions. Average July–August ocean temperatures at a depth of 20 m along the Seal Island line in southern Labrador were significantly correlated with annual migratory timing ($r = 0.78$; $P = 0.014$; Figure 8). Years of late migratory timing were associated with cold ocean temperatures. Only the ocean temperature information from 1983 ap-

TABLE 7.—Summary of sex ratio data for Arctic char from the inshore and offshore zones of the Nain stock unit, 1979–1985, with subsamples for determination of state of maturity.

	Male		Female		Total	
Data base	N	% mature	N	% mature	N	% female
Inshore zone	6,999		9,761		16,760	58.2
Subsample	315	40.0	555	62.9	870	63.8
Offshore zone	1,398		1,152		2,550	45.2
Subsample	248	15.7	250	26.8	498	50.2
Total	8,397		10,913		19,310	56.5
Subsample	563	29.3	805	51.7	1,368	58.8

TABLE 8.—Frequency of occurrence and contribution by weight of major food organisms found in stomach samples of Arctic char, for various areas in northern Labrador.

Area	N	Frequency of occurrence (%)				Contribution by weight (%)			
		Capelins	Sand lances	Sculpins	Invertebrates[a]	Capelins	Sand lances	Sculpins	Invertebrates
Nain region									
Inshore zone	224	35.5	10.5	18.3	18.6	69.0	5.4	10.3	1.8
Offshore zone	211	12.2	8.9	23.6	38.8	38.1	8.5	17.7	27.3
Okak Bay	130	10.0	24.4	26.3	23.9	28.8	31.6	21.5	6.9
Hebron–Saglek Fiord	87	0.3	3.5	23.4	58.9	0.4	0.8	82.2	10.0

[a] Amphipoda, euphausiacea, mysidacea, copepoda.

pears inconsistent with the other data (Figure 8).

Information on daily ocean temperatures were available from Hebron Fiord, northern Labrador, from July 17 to September 23, 1985. These data were examined in relation to the daily number of upstream migrant Arctic char recorded at the Ikarut River counting fence (Figure 9). There was an overall trend for a decrease in fiord temperatures from July through September. Daily fiord temperatures during July 17–31 averaged 7.6°C following which temperatures decreased to a mean of 3.0°C during August 1–15. September temperatures averaged 1.2°C. The wide daily fluctuations recorded were probably the result of wind conditions circulating colder water from lower depths.

Numbers of adult fish migrating upriver in 1985 fluctuated daily but 91% of the adult run was complete by August 30 (Figure 9). Fiord temperatures did not appear to be the primary trigger of upstream runs. Juveniles entered the river in several large peaks (Figure 9) and 94% of their run occurred after August 30. In some respects, these peaks appear to follow shortly after sharp decreases in fiord temperature, although similar temperature decreases in early August did not cause juveniles to leave the fiord. In general, the juvenile run is essentially over when fiord temperatures remain around 0°C.

Discussion

The wide distribution of commercial fishing activities for Arctic char and Atlantic salmon along the northern Labrador coast provides an opportunity to examine spatial and temporal aspects of the ocean movements of Arctic char. Insight into the fidelity of Arctic char to their natal rivers and their use of alternate rivers was obtained from tag recoveries in mouths or estuaries of rivers in the Cambridge Bay area of the Northwest Territories.

Our analyses of tagging data are in general agreement with observations from the literature regarding short residency of Arctic char at sea. Minimum estimates for the average length of time at sea in northern Labrador were 8–9 weeks. This is 2–3 weeks longer than the average period at sea reported by Johnson (1980) and Gyselman (1984) for Arctic char around Parry Bay, Northwest Territories, and what Mathisen and Berg (1968) reported for northern Norway. It is suggested that these differences are a result of regional environmental conditions which permit Arctic char to enter the sea earlier in the year in Labrador than in the Northwest Territories. Mean May and June

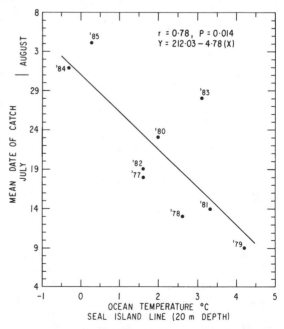

FIGURE 8.—Relationship between mean date of capture as derived from catch data for Arctic char in the Nain stock unit of northern Labrador, and July–August sea temperatures at the 20-m depth from the Seal Island line, 1977–1985.

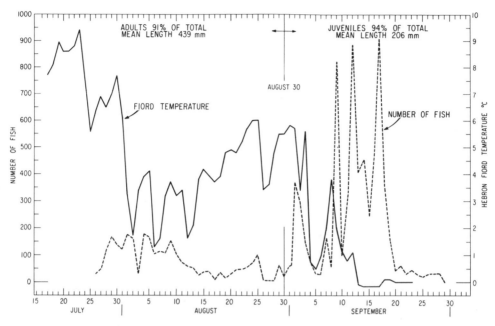

FIGURE 9.—Daily counts of upstream migrant Arctic char in Ikarut River, Labrador, in relation to sea temperatures obtained from the Hebron Fiord in 1985.

air temperatures from 1970 to 1979 at Cambridge Bay were −9.3 and 1.8°C; at Hopedale, Labrador (approximately 160 km south of Nain), corresponding temperatures were 1.2 and 6°C. Both our study and that of Johnson (1980) found that the period Arctic char spent at sea depended to some extent on the date at which fish migrated to the ocean; early outmigrants remaining at sea longer.

Based on 1 year of data, we found no evidence that ocean temperatures initiate movement of adult Arctic char from the ocean into Ikarut River, Labrador. River entry of juveniles followed shortly after periods of declining sea temperature in late August and September, which also has been observed for immature brook trout *Salvelinus fontinalis* in the Richmond Gulf area of Hudson Bay (Dutil and Power 1980).

Although these movements may be a tactic to avoid unfavorable winter sea conditions (Northcote 1978), not all juveniles leave the ocean with the first sharp decrease in sea temperatures. The juvenile run in Labrador lasts for about 1 month and, over 5 years (1981–1985) of observation at Ikarut River, it has been characterized by several large peaks in the upstream migration. Average winter temperatures in Hebron Fiord have been reported to be below −1.7°C (Nutt and Coachman 1956). Since salmonid fishes are unable to survive

prolonged subzero temperatures (Brett and Alderice 1958), Arctic char must leave the ocean to avoid freezing (Johnson 1980); thus their duration at sea may be limited by this factor, although most fish generally have returned to fresh water before sea temperatures fall to 0°C.

Ocean temperature has been cited as the limiting factor in the distribution of anadromous Arctic char in Norway. Jensen (1981) indicated that coastal water temperatures of 14°C at a depth of 4–5 m may act as a thermal barrier in the distribution of anadromous Arctic char into southern areas.

Analyses of commercial catch data were used to compare the timing of the relative abundance of Arctic char in the ocean feeding area of the Nain stock unit. Our results showed that, although the annual period at sea is short, there are significant differences among years. There is also evidence to indicate a possible relationship between time at sea and the marine environmental conditions. However, Mundy (1982) cautioned against use of univariate explanations of variability in migratory timing because it is difficult to describe multivariate phenomena with univariate models. Years of earlier migration timing in the fishery generally coincided with largest landings of Arctic char, a phenomenon also observed in catches of chinook salmon *Oncorhynchus tshawytscha* in the Yukon

River, Alaska (Mundy 1982).

Our analyses of tag recovery information showed that the majority of fish were recaptured within 70 km of their release site; this is in general agreement with the literature regarding limited dispersal of Arctic char at sea. Moore (1975) reported maximum distances Arctic char travelled at sea in the Cumberland Sound area of Baffin Island were 40–50 km and Nielsen (1961) reported a maximum distance of 62 km at west Greenland. However, not all Arctic char remain in close proximity to their native rivers as suggested by Grainger (1953) and Nielsen (1961). There is considerable mixing of populations from individual rivers or subareas during the ocean phase of their life history, although the intermixing of populations from widely distributed areas is minimal. There also appears to be variable immigration among adjacent river systems, as observed in other areas (Jensen and Berg 1977; Johnson 1980; Gyselman 1984). As a result, local stock units or complexes can often be identified for management purposes.

Jensen and Berg (1977) reported the longest distance travelled by an Arctic char in Norway was 940 km. Anadromous Arctic char tagged in Nauyuk Lake, Northwest Territories, have been recaptured 350–550 km away (Johnson 1980; Gyselman 1984). One fish tagged in Labrador was recaptured 250 km away in the same year in which it was released, a distance Gyselman (1984) indicated may be too great for Arctic char to travel in one summer.

In a review of the ecology of fish migrations, Leggett (1977) stated that tag recovery data derived from commercial catch records may provide more information on the distribution of fishing effort than on the distribution of fish. With this problem in mind, we used a log-linear modelling procedure to determine if there was evidence that movement patterns of a specific fish stock varied annually. This procedure, which removes the effect of different numbers of fish caught in different subareas and different ratios of tagged to untagged fish among subareas, indicated that, for one population, there is evidence of variable migration patterns year to year. This was also suspected by Jensen and Berg (1977). However, an alternative hypothesis is also consistent with the findings. Similar results would be observed if there were variation in the annual timing of the outward migration and fish migrating early (or late) tended to migrate to different areas. In our replicated tagging experiments during the spring,

we did not know which component of the total run we were tagging, so in some years we may have tagged proportionately more late-run fish than others.

Our results indicate that both the spatial and temporal distribution of Arctic char at sea may be influenced by the sex and maturation characteristics of the population. In this respect, Arctic char are no different from other salmonids. In some areas, particularly in the Northwest Territories, maturing fish do not go to sea during the year in which they will spawn. In other areas, such as northern Labrador, maturing fish appear to restrict their marine movements. More males and, in particular, more nonmaturing fish of both sexes were found in the more distant offshore island fishing areas. From observations on the upstream migrations of Arctic char, it was found that maturing fish, particularly females, are the first to leave the ocean (Johnson 1980; McCart 1980; Dempson and Green 1985). In the Ikarut River, Hebron Fiord, Labrador, 76% of maturing females and 62% of maturing males had entered the river by August 12. In contrast, 86% of nonmaturing adult females and 81% of males entered the river after August 12 over the period 1981–1985. While this would provide an advantage in selecting optimal spawning sections in rivers, it may also reflect changes in salinity tolerance with onset of maturation, as has been demonstrated in other *Salvelinus* species (Sutterlin et al. 1976; McCormick and Naiman 1984). This is also important from a management standpoint. In Labrador, Arctic char are generally iteroparous alternate-year spawners. In those areas where subtantial numbers of prespawners go to sea, it would be advantageous to restrict commercial fishing activities in those areas where these fish are most abundant.

Leggett (1984) reviewed studies on the relationship between ocean temperature and movements of fish and indicated that, in some cases, these relationships may be indirect and related to occurrence of preferred prey organisms. For example, the occurrence of winter flounder *Pseudopleuronectes americanus* in nearshore areas has been shown to be correlated with the presence of spawning capelins.

The movement of Arctic char at sea is largely a feeding migration. It is possible, therefore, that their temporal and spatial distribution would be influenced by the distribution of dominant prey organisms. Cold ocean temperatures around insular Newfoundland during the past several years have affected movements of capelins by delaying the inshore spawning migration and, in some cases, this has resulted in offshore spawning (W. H. Lear and G. H. Winters, Department of Fisheries and Oceans, St. John's, Newfoundland, personal communication). This may explain the increase in abundance of Arctic char in offshore island areas of the Nain stock unit during the past several years.

As outlined in the introduction, homing has been considered to be a general phenomenon in the migration of anadromous Arctic char and is a strategy used to optimize reproductive success by many salmonids (Northcote 1978). Arctic char have the capacity to home to their natal rivers but the behavioural pattern does not appear to be rigid (Johnson 1980). Our data and those of others (Jensen and Berg 1977; Jensen 1981; McCart 1980) clearly indicate the variability in the immigration of Arctic char and their utilization of available river systems. Jensen and Berg (1977) reported that 64% of tags recovered in freshwater had originated in other rivers. Perhaps it is only the nonspawning, overwintering components of the population that use "other" river systems, as Armstrong (1984) and Armstrong and Morrow (1980) have shown for Dolly Varden *Salvelinus malma*. Thus, a fish tagged in one river may have originated elsewhere and its recapture later in another system might reflect a return to its natal stream. In areas such as northern Labrador where several rivers of similar characteristics enter the same bay or fiord, the interchange among rivers may be expected to be higher than in other regions.

Straying has been proposed as an evolutionary alternative strategy to homing (Quinn 1984). Arctic char seem to utilize this tactic in continuously seeking alternative overwintering and perhaps spawning localities. Maturing fish have the capacity to home but may or may not always return to their natal streams. Johnson (1980) has stated that there are several biological advantages to this strategy for a species that lives in areas where environmental conditions can be rather unpredictable and extreme. Homing ensures distribution of reproductive effort in "successful" areas, whereas straying and overwintering in alternate systems allows for the exploration and colonization of new systems (Johnson 1980).

The anadromous Arctic char has adapted to take full advantage of both the freshwater and marine environments in which it survives. It is the only salmonid species to have successfully colonized the circumpolar region of the northern hemisphere. Its ocean migrations are simple, generally of short duration and in localized areas. However, migrations are complicated by their variable frequency, the influence of marine environmental conditions, and the different biological characteristics and maturation components of the sea-going population. Investigations are lacking on the distribution of juvenile Arctic char at sea. The biological characteristics of the components of populations that interchange among rivers need clarification. Information on ocean movements and marine environmental conditions would assist in understanding factors influencing the distribution and abundance of Arctic char at sea and how these could relate to catchability and to the success of coastal commercial fisheries.

Acknowledgments

We thank R. Porter, M. O'Connell, H. Lear, L. Johnson, and E. Gyselman for critically reading the manuscript and providing editorial advice. Jake Rice and Don Stansbury provided statistical assistance with the categorical data analyses. J. Lannon typed the manuscript.

References

Armstrong, R. H. 1984. Migration of anadromous Dolly Varden charr in southeastern Alaska—a manager's nightmare. Pages 559–570 *in* Johnson and Burns (1984).

Armstrong, R. H., and J. E. Morrow. 1980. The Dolly Varden charr, *Salvelinus malma*. Pages 99–140 *in* E. K. Balon, editor. Charrs: salmonid fishes of the genus *Salvelinus*. Dr. W. Junk, The Hague, The Netherlands.

Barbour, S. E. 1984. Variation in life history, ecology and resource utilization by Arctic charr *Salvelinus alpinus* (L.) in Scotland. Doctoral dissertation. University of Edinburgh, Edinburgh, Scotland.

Bishop, Y. M. M., S. E. Fienberg, and P. W. Holland. 1975. Discrete multivariate analysis: theory and practice. MIT Press, Cambridge, Massachusetts, USA.

Brett, J. R., and D. F. Alderice. 1958. The resistance of cultured young chum and sockeye salmon to temperatures below 0°C. Journal of the Fisheries Research Board of Canada 15:805–813.

Butt, A. 1984. An examination of the variability of migratory timing statistics estimated from catch and effort observations. Doctoral dissertation. Old Dominion University, Norfolk, Virginia, USA.

Coady, L., and C. W. Best. 1976. Biological and management investigations of the Arctic char fishery at Nain, Labrador. Canada Fisheries and Marine Service Technical Report 624.

Dempson, J. B., and J. M. Green. 1985. Life history of anadromous Arctic charr, *Salvelinus alpinus*, in the

Fraser River, northern Labrador. Canadian Journal of Zoology 63:315–324.

Dutil, J. D. 1984. Energetic costs associated with the production of gonads in the anadromous Arctic charr *(Salvelinus alpinus)* of the Nauyuk Lake basin, Canada. Pages 263–276 *in* Johnson and Burns (1984).

Dutil, J. D., and G. Power. 1980. Coastal population of brook trout, *Salvelinus fontinalis,* in Lac Guillaume-Delisle (Richmond Gulf) Quebec. Canadian Journal of Zoology 58:1828–1835.

Grainger, E. H. 1953. On the age, growth, migration, reproductive potential and feeding habits of the Arctic char *(Salvelinus alpinus)* of Frobisher Bay, Baffin Island. Journal of the Fisheries Research Board of Canada 10:326–370.

Gyselman, E. C. 1984. The seasonal movements of anadromous Arctic charr at Nauyuk Lake, Northwest Territories, Canada. Pages 575–578 *in* Johnson and Burns (1984).

Harden Jones, F. R. 1968. Fish migration. Edward Arnold, London, England.

Jensen, J. W. 1981. Anadromous Arctic char, *Salvelinus alpinus,* penetrating southward on the Norwegian coast. Canadian Journal of Fisheries and Aquatic Sciences 38:247–249.

Jensen, K. W., and M. Berg. 1977. Growth, mortality and migrations of the anadromous Arctic char, *Salvelinus alpinus* L., in the Vardnes River, Troms, northern Norway. Institute of Freshwater Research Drottningholm Report 56:70–80.

Johnson, L. 1980. The Arctic charr, *Salvelinus alpinus.* Pages 15–98 *in* E. K. Balon, editor. Charrs: salmonid fishes of the genus *Salvelinus.* Dr. W. Junk, The Hague, The Netherlands.

Johnson, L., and B. L. Burns, editors. 1984. Biology of the Arctic charr: proceedings of the International symposium on Arctic charr. University of Manitoba Press, Winnipeg, Canada.

Kristofferson, A. H., D. K. McGowan, and G. W. Carder. 1984. Management of the commercial fishery for anadromous Arctic charr in the Cambridge Bay area, Northwest Territories, Canada. Pages 447–461 *in* Johnson and Burns (1984).

Lazier, J. R. N. 1982. Seasonal variability of temperature and salinity in the Labrador current. Journal of Marine Research 40 (supplement):341–356.

Leggett, W. C. 1977. The ecology of fish migrations. Annual Review of Ecology and Systematics 8:285–308.

Leggett, W. C. 1984. Fish migrations in coastal and estuarine environments: a call for new approaches to the study of an old problem. Pages 159–178 *in* J. D. McCleave, G. P. Arnold, J. J. Dodson, and W. H. Neill, editors. Mechanisms of migration in fishes. Plenum, New York, New York, USA.

Le Jeune, R. 1967. The sea run Arctic char of George River. Quebec Service de la Faune, Bulletin 10:1–45. Translated from French: Fisheries Research Board of Canada Translation Series 4360, 1978, Ottawa, Canada.

Mathisen, O. A., and O. M. Berg. 1968. Growth rates of the char *Salvelinus alpinus* (L.) in the Vardnes River, Troms, northern Norway. Institute of Freshwater Research Drottningholm Report 48:177–186.

McCart, P. J. 1980. A review of the sytematics and ecology of the Arctic char, *Salvelinus alpinus,* in the western Arctic. Canadian Technical Report of Fisheries and Aquatic Sciences 935.

McCormick, S. D., and R. J. Naiman. 1984. Osmoregulation in the brook trout, *Salvelinus fontinalis*—II. Effects of size, age and photoperiod on seawater survival and ionic regulation. Comparative Biochemistry and Physiology A, Comparative Physiology 79:17–28.

Moore, J. W. 1975. Distribution, movements and mortality of anadromous Arctic char, *Salvelinus alpinus* L., in the Cumberland Sound area of Baffin Island. Journal of Fish Biology 7:339–348.

Mundy, P. R. 1982. Computation of migratory timing statistics for adult chinook salmon in the Yukon River, Alaska, and their relevance to fisheries management. North American Journal of Fisheries Management 2:359–370.

Nielsen, J. 1961. Preliminary results of tagging experiments with char, *Salvelinus alpinus* (L.), in Greenland. Meddelelser om Grønland 159(8):24–48.

Nikolsky, G. V. 1963. The ecology of fishes. Academic Press, London, England.

Northcote, T. G. 1978. Migratory strategies and production in freshwater fishes. Pages 326–359 *in* S. D. Gerking, editor. Ecology of freshwater fish production. Blackwell Scientific Publications, Oxford, England.

Northcote, T. G. 1984. Mechanisms of fish migration in rivers. Pages 317–355 *in* J. D. McCleave, G. P. Arnold, J. J. Dodson, and W. H. Neill, editors. Mechanisms of migration in fishes. Plenum, New York, New York, USA.

Nutt, D. C., and L. K. Coachman. 1956. The oceanography of Hebron Fjord, Labrador. Journal of the Fisheries Research Board of Canada 13:709–758.

Quinn, T. P. 1984. Homing and straying in Pacific salmon. Pages 357–362 *in* J. D. McCleave, G. P. Arnold, J. J. Dodson, and W. H. Neill, editors. Mechanisms of migration in fishes. Plenum, New York, New York, USA.

Rounsefell, G. A. 1958. Anadromy in North American Salmonidae. U.S. Fish and Wildlife Service Fishery Bulletin 58:171–185.

SAS (Statistical Analysis System). 1985. SAS users guide: statistics, 5th edition. SAS Institute, Cary, North Carolina, USA.

Sokal, R. R., and F. J. Rohlf. 1969. Biometry. W. H. Freeman, San Francisco, California, USA.

Sprules, W. M. 1952. The Arctic char of the west coast of Hudson Bay. Journal of the Fisheries Research Board of Canada 9:1–15.

Sutterlin, A. M., P. Harmon, and H. Barchard. 1976. The culture of brook trout in salt water. Canada Fisheries and Marine Service Technical Report 636.

Walters, V. 1955. Fishes of western arctic America and eastern arctic Siberia: taxonomy and zoogeography. Bulletin of the American Museum of Natural History 106:255–368.

Yessipov, V. K. 1935. Materials on the biology and fishery of the Arctic char (*Salvelinus alpinus* L.) on Novaya Zemlya. Trudy Arkticheskogo Instuta 17: 5–71. Translated from Russian: Fisheries Research Board of Canada Translation Series, 4436, 1978, Ottawa, Canada.

American Fisheries Society Symposium 1:358–363, 1987
© Copyright by the American Fisheries Society 1987

Life History, Distribution, and Seasonal Migration of Barramundi in the Daly River, Northern Territory, Australia

ROLAND K. GRIFFIN

Department of Industries and Development, Post Office Box 4160
Darwin, Northern Territory, 5794 Australia

Abstract.—Tagging and sampling of barramundi *Lates calcarifer* was undertaken in three phases between 1980 and 1984. Of 3,555 fish tagged, 544 were recaptured. Simultaneous sampling and tagging at two locations on the Daly River showed a generally downstream movement in July and August 1983. Tag recoveries from the commercial fishery were disproportionately high in August and September, possibly as a result of movement of fish downstream at that time. Large numbers of age-0+ fish were observed where a culvert had impeded upstream movement. Comparison of sizes of fish from upper and lower zones of the river suggested that those in upper freshwater zone are mostly small immature males and those in brackish estuarine areas are generally mature males or females derived from males by protandry. Several features of the life cycle of this catadromous, protandrous species are related to selection pressures such as spawning site access, spawning seasonality, food availability, cannibalism, and protection of breeding stock from poor seasonal conditions.

The barramundi *Lates calcarifer* (Bloch) is a large centropomid perch, growing to 150 cm total length (TL) and 40 kg. It is widely distributed through southeast Asia, Indonesia, India, Papua New Guinea, and northern Australia, where it inhabits rivers, lakes, billabongs (oxbow lakes), estuaries, and coastal waters. It is rarely found outside areas influenced by rivers and its life cycle appears dependent upon climatic factors which affect those regions.

Barramundi are protandrous hermaphrodites changing sex to female at 6–7 years of age (85–90 cm TL) or older (Moore 1979; Davis 1982). Barramundi are considered to be catadromous, generally spending their first years in the upper parts of rivers and moving down to the estuary to spawn when mature as males at about 3 years of age (60 cm TL, approximately). Most of these mature individuals probably remain in the tidal, brackish part of the river where they become females.

The coastal gill-net fishery, of which barramundi is the primary target species, is the second most important in the Northern Territory, being worth approximately two million Australian dollars annually (Grey and Griffin 1979; Rohan et al. 1981). Commercial fishing is conducted in the mouths of rivers and nearby coastal waters from February to October. There is a 4-month closed season from 1 October to 31 January and commercial netting is permitted only in lower estuarine and coastal waters.

The barramundi fishery and its management

have been reviewed by Grey and Griffin (1979) and Rohan et al. (1981). Barramundi is also a popular angling species and the recreational fishery is of considerable economic importance to the Northern Territory (Griffin 1982).

The climate of northern Australia is markedly seasonal with a typically dry winter (May–October) and wet summer (November–April). Most rainfall is from the northwest monsoon from December to March. Air and water temperatures rise rapidly as the season changes from dry to wet during August–October. Commercial fishermen have suggested that there is a "spawning run" during that period. As a closed season to protect spawning fish is in force from 1 October to 31 January, it was considered important to identify the existence and timing of seasonal movement. This paper examines the results of a series of tagging experiments and observations which were conducted to identify and define long- and short-term movements of barramundi.

Methods

Study Area

The principal study site was the lower 90 km of the Daly River southwest of Darwin (Figure 1). The Daly River has a catchment of 51,800 km^2 and a tidal length of 100 km, making it the third largest river in the Northern Territory and one of the largest in northern Australia (Anonymous 1975). River discharge is markedly seasonal; river heights in the monsoon season are 5–15 m above

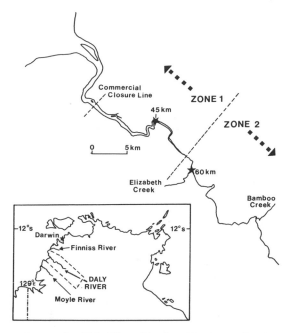

FIGURE 1.—Daly River, Northern Territory, showing main sampling sites. Inset shows the northern part of the Northern Territory.

dry season levels. During the monsoon season, many isolated sections of the river (including numerous billabongs) are joined by floodwaters for varying periods.

Tagging—General

Fish were captured in gill nets, seines, cast nets, and fyke nets and by angling. The success of each of these methods varied greatly with seasonal conditions and type of habitat.

Red FT-4 spaghetti tags (Floy Tag and Manufacturing, Seattle, Washington, USA) were attached to opercular bones with stainless steel wire. During 1982, the tags were modified by covering the tag legend with heat-shrunk plastic tubing to prevent abrasive damage to tag numbers. After 1983, fish larger than 35 cm TL were tagged with Floy FT-2 dart tags inserted below the first dorsal fins. Fishermen in the study area were aware of the tagging program and reporting of recaptured fish was considered to be complete. A reward was offered for return of tags and capture information.

Tagging Studies

Tagging studies have been divided into three phases, during which different aspects of seasonal movement and distribution were investigated.

Phase 1.—Barramundi were sampled in different habitats to assess distribution differences and seasonality of spawning activity beginning in October 1980 and continuing through 1984. Those fish not required for gonad or gut analysis were tagged and released. This work was supplemented from 1982 by releases made by anglers. Under this government-sponsored scheme (known as AMTAG), sportfishermen tagged and released barramundi (using Floy FT-2 dart tags) which were surplus to their requirements. Those released in the Daly River were included with the research taggings in analysis of the results of this phase of research.

Phase 2.—In July–August 1983, 1,678 barramundi were tagged and released at two locations on the tidal section of the Daly River (Figure 1); 770 at Cattle Yards, 45 km upstream, and 908 at Elizabeth Creek, 60 km upstream. All fish were captured with gill nets of either 12.7-, 15.2-, or 17.8-cm stretched mesh and tagged with modified opercular spaghetti tags.

Phase 3.—During March and April 1982–1985, barramundi were sampled at Bamboo Creek (Figure 1) where they were aggregated in a small pool (30 m diameter, approximately) below a culvert. Those fish, mostly age 0+ and 1+ (15–50 cm TL), were apparently attempting to move upstream but were prevented from doing so by the velocity of the water in the culvert pipe (approximately 3 m·s^{-1}). Prior to 1984, fish were marked with opercular spaghetti tags (age 1+) or by fin clips (age 0+). In 1984 and 1985, blue streamer shrimp tags (Hallprint, similar to Floy FTSL-73) were used on age-0+ fish and Floy FT-2 anchor tags on those aged 1+ or older.

Results

General

Capture in gill nets frequently resulted in injuries to fish and subsequent tagging mortality. Sixteen tagged fish were found that had apparently died from netting injuries and approximately 12.5% of early recaptures of fish caught for tagging by gill nets in phase 1 had lesions on the dorsal and ventral parts of the head or had scars from lesions which had recently healed.

Mean lengths of fish taken in 12.7-, 15.2-, and 17.8-cm-mesh gill nets in two broad zones of the Daly River (Figure 1) were compared (Table 1; Figure 2). Zone 1 ("lower") comprises brackish and marine tidal waters and zone 2 ("upper") comprises all nontidal fresh water as well as those

TABLE 1.—Total lengths of gillnetted barramundi from lower and upper zones (zones 1 and 2, respectively) of the Daly River. Asterisks indicate that means differ significantly between zones (*t*-test; $P > 0.01$).

Gill net mesh size (cm)	Lower zone			Upper zone		
	Mean total length (SD) (cm)	N		Mean total length (SD) (cm)	N	t
12.7	57.9 (7.65)	915		56.8 (5.81)	644	3.05*
15.2	71.2 (9.88)	849		67.4 (8.38)	342	6.28*
17.8	79.8 (10.88)	1,559		75.7 (8.41)	120	4.03*

TABLE 2.—Monthly proportions of commercial catch and commercial tag returns of barramundi, Daly River, 1981–1985.

Month	% catch	Tag returns[a] (%)
Feb	10.0	7 (9.6)
Mar	10.9	6 (8.2)
Apr	15.6	3 (4.1)
May	19.9	6 (8.2)
Jun	13.2	6 (8.2)
Jul	8.6	6 (8.2)
Aug	9.2	18 (24.7)
Sep	12.6	21 (28.8)
Total	100.0	73 (100)

[a] Total for the month, 1980–1985.

fresh waters affected by tidal action. For all three mesh sizes, the mean lengths of fish taken in zone 1 were significantly greater than in zone 2.

Phase 1

During phase 1, 1,762 barramundi were tagged, 1,465 during research operations and 297 by anglers. Of those, 148 (8.4%) have been recaptured. Analysis of commercial tag returns by month for the years 1982–1985 (Table 2) shows significant departures from the pattern of recaptures that would be expected from the monthly distribution of commercial catch for the same period. ($\chi^2 = 14.72$; $P < 0.05$). The apparently higher number of recaptures in August and September is interpreted as being the result of movement of fish into the commercial sector for the spawning season.

Phase 2

Of the 1,678 barramundi tagged in July–August during phase 2, 245 were recaptured by commer-

cial fishermen, 14 by anglers, and 151 by research personnel at three sites (Table 3). The pattern of research recaptures for those fish released at the two main sites suggested that a general downstream movement occurred, as only 8.2% of the fish tagged at km 45 were recaptured at km 60, whereas 50.8% of those tagged at km 60 were recaptured downstream at km 45. For those fish which were recaptured at the same site, the mean time between tagging and recapture was 3.6 d at km 60 and 7.2 d at km 45.

Twenty-two fish were captured three times. For nine of those, movement was progressively downstream, terminating with capture in the commercial fishery within 2 months of tagging. One fish moved first 14 km upstream in 1 d and was subsequently released and recaptured in the commercial fishery 52 km downstream. Another fish was captured four times, between 2 July and 16

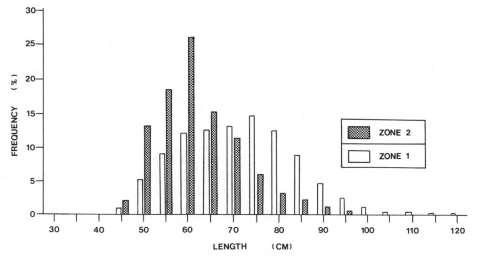

FIGURE 2.—Length-frequency distribution of barramundi from upper (zone 2) and lower (zone 1) zones of the Daly River.

TABLE 3.—Numbers of research recaptures of barramundi at three sites on the Daly River during phase 2.

Release site	Recapture site			Total recaptures
	km 45	km 51	km 60	
km 45	64 (87.7%)	3 (4.1%)	6 (8.2%)	73
km 51	7	6		13
km 60	33 (50.8%)	11 (16.9%)	21 (32.3%)	65
Total	104	20	27	151

August, the first and third times at km 60 and the second and fourth times at km 45. These latter two patterns of movement perhaps indicate that the 15-km distance between the two sites is within the range of normal movement. If the two sampling sites had been further apart, the pattern of movement might have been more conclusive.

The percentages of fish recaptured by commercial fishermen in successive 15-d periods following tagging was calculated (Table 4). These data suggest that the probability of capture of tagged fish increased from July through September as a consequence of the fish moving downstream into the commercial fishery. Coincidentally, the increase in recaptures is mirrored by an increase in water temperature over the same period ($r^2 = 0.94$). The sharp rise in water temperature which usually occurs in the latter part of August is a regular annual phenomenon associated with the change in weather patterns.

Only five upstream movements beyond the tagging area were recorded. Those fish moved from lower tidal areas (km 45–51) to upper tidal fresh waters (between km 60 and 87).

Phase 3

Altogether, 676 juveniles were captured at the Bamboo Creek culvert. Juvenile barramundi were found at this location during periods when floodwaters were receding, usually from March

TABLE 4.—Percentages of commercial recaptures of tagged barramundi in the lower Daly River by time period after tagging during phase 2.

Time period	% recaptured[a]	Temperature[b] (°C)
16 Jul–30 Jul	1.0	21.8
1 Aug–15 Aug	1.6	22.2
16 Aug–30 Aug	2.7	26.6
31 Aug–14 Sep	3.5	29.3
15 Sep–30 Sep	4.0	28.8

[a] Percentage of available tagged fish recaptured.
[b] Mean water temperature of the Daly River during those periods.

through to May. Most recoveries of tags from this site were made at the same location; a few of the recoveries were of dead fish and loose tags after the pool had dried out. None were recaptured upstream of the culvert but this result is not necessarily significant as sampling and fishing effort upstream was much less than below the culvert. No fish were observed to actually pass through the pipe.

One 44-cm (age-1+) fish, which was tagged on 20 February 1985 at km 87 was recaptured on 5 June 1985 a further 113 km upstream. This was the only recaptured fish recorded that had moved from tidal to nontidal waters.

Discussion

As with any mark–recapture experiment, assessment of movements of barramundi was biased by the distribution of fishing effort. Commercial fishing was restricted to the lower estuaries and adjacent coastal waters while recreational fishing occurred mainly in fresh waters and brackish upper tidal waters. Returns by recreational fishermen constituted only 15% of total returns. Most tagged fish were released in areas which were either between the areas of operation of the recreational and commercial sectors of the fishery or in popular recreational fishing areas. The combined effect of these factors was to present a picture of one-way movement of fish from fresh water to salt water.

The results of phase 1 and phase 2 of this work provide some evidence that the largely one-way movement of tagged barramundi was probably more than an artifact of sampling. The size differences observed in different zones of the river (Figure 2; Table 1) suggest that immature fish up to age 3 or 4 prefer upper fresh waters and mature fish (males and females) prefer brackish and estuarine tidal waters. Moore and Reynolds (1982) described movements of barramundi in Papua New Guinea. They found that 3- and 4-year-old fish migrated downstream to coastal spawning grounds some distance from the river mouth. Some fish then returned to the upper parts of the river and some remained in coastal waters. Young fish of the 0+ and 1+ age-classes were found to migrate upstream in the Fly River.

No such large-scale movement away from the Daly River was found in this study. Although there is considerable commercial fishing effort in the adjacent Moyle and Finniss rivers (Figure 1) no recaptures of fish tagged in the Daly were made in those areas. The greatest movement downstream was 92 km and upstream 113 km.

The downstream movement of barramundi which appears to take place in August and September in the Daly River is possibly triggered by the coincident rise in water temperature or increasing day length or some combination of these and other, unrecognized factors. A downstream movement at this time would accord well with observations of barramundi spawning activity in Australia and Papua New Guinea (Moore 1982; Russell and Garrett 1983, 1985; Davis 1985a; Griffin 1985).

In Papua New Guinea, barramundi spawning occurs in inshore waters adjacent to mangroves in salinities from 28 to 35‰ between October and February (Moore 1982). Davis (1985a) found barramundi larvae and early juveniles in Van Diemen Gulf from September through February; in the Norman River, Russell and Garrett (1983) found evidence of spawning from December through February. In Leanyer Swamp near Darwin, Griffin (1985) found juvenile barramundi of 10–14 mm in early September indicating that spawning had occurred in August.

The eggs of barramundi are pelagic and hatch within 24 h (Wongsomnuk and Manevonk 1973). Several workers (Moore 1982; Russell and Garrett 1983; Davis 1985a; Griffin 1985) found that post-larvae enter saline coastal swamps on high spring tides when about 5 mm TL, suggesting that these areas are important nursery areas. Young-of-the-year fish remain in these swamps or in adjacent floodplain areas as long as possible, leaving at around 20–30 cm or when water levels begin to fall (Moore 1982). They then move upstream in their first year and generally remain in the upper freshwater reaches until mature.

The observation that fish taken in fresh waters are smaller than those in brackish and marine waters provides additional evidence for the hypothesis that the upper fresh waters are used mainly by smaller (immature) fish. The existence of protandry in barramundi, most fish under 90 cm TL being males (Davis 1982; Moore 1982), combined with the observed low proportion of fish above that size in upper fresh waters (Figure 2) suggests that female and mature male barramundi prefer the lower, brackish, tidal habitat. The mechanisms for the evolution of protandry in barramundi can only be speculated upon; however, the advantages, in terms of total fecundity, in having the largest, oldest (and presumably, fittest) individuals being female is a most likely

reason. Davis (1984) found that the barramundi is extremely fecund; one fish of 124 cm contained 46 × 10^6 eggs. Such high fecundity may be necessary to ensure success in variable seasonal conditions. Given such a breeding strategy, it is interesting to relate that strategy to the apparently different habitat preferences of mature and immature individuals. Three possible reasons why such a significant behavioural adaptation may have evolved, in part to protect the evolutionary investment in large breeding stock, are considered.

Firstly, the adaptation would allow mature fish access to suitable spawning areas before there was enough flow in the river to allow access from upper fresh waters. This could be an important benefit if there were an advantage to be gained from early spawning. Davis (1985a) suggested that such a strategy could result in improved survival due to reduced cannibalism in the nursery swamps but also suggested, as did Griffin (1985), that lack of rainfall in early wet season months could negate that effect. Secondly, the presence of mature breeding stock mainly in tidal waters would effectively preclude them from the effects of environmental perturbations in fresh waters which occasionally cause major mortality of barramundi (Bishop 1980; Brown et al. 1982). Thirdly, separation of the juvenile and adult fish to some extent would minimize the opportunity for cannibalism which is known to occur at times. Davis (1985b) reported that cannibalism was common among barramundi in Van Diemen Gulf and Griffin (1985) reported a high incidence of predation on juveniles by adults in June and July 1981 at Daly River. Cannibalism of this nature appears to be related to seasonal abundance of juveniles in lower estuarine areas as swamps on adjacent floodplains dry out and small fish are forced out into the river. Availability of suitable food resources could also be a contributing factor to size-class separation. In estuarine waters, there exists a greater diversity of prey of a size suitable for barramundi of 60–130 cm TL, whereas prey availability in fresh waters is limited in both size and abundance, particularly in closed fresh waters.

Separation of juvenile and mature fish to some extent has important implications for fisheries managers because the commercial fishery operates only in estuarine waters preferred by mature fish and the recreational fishery is based mainly in freshwater areas apparently preferred by smaller immature fish. Because the barramundi is protandrous, the recreational sector rarely takes female fish. In a survey of anglers (Griffin 1982) it was found that the mean size of angler catches from the most popular fishing areas was 3.1 kg. Catches by anglers of fish greater than the size at which sex inversion occurs are not common and almost all such catches are from tidal waters.

The observations of upstream movement are particularly relevant in relation to artificial barriers which might impede migration. Kowarsky and Ross (1981) found, in a study of a weir and fishway on the Fitzroy River in central Queensland, that barramundi accumulated below the weir but very rarely negotiated the 15 steps of the fishway. Although there are few such structures in the Northern Territory, it is clear that planning for future water storages, causeways, etc. should take into account the effect on barramundi populations.

The results of this study, in combination with previously published information, are useful in assessing the impact of exploitation, both commercial and recreational, on stocks of barramundi. However, it is clear that before traditional population modelling methods or derivations of them can be applied with confidence to this species, many aspects of its life history, including seasonal movements and the effects of seasonal variations in climatic conditions on recruitment, must be further investigated.

References

Anonymous. 1975. Review of Australia's water resources, 1975. Australian Government Publishing Service, Canberra, Australia.

Bishop, K. A. 1980. Fish kills in relation to physical and chemical changes in Magela Creek (East Alligator River system, Northern Territory) at the beginning of the tropical wet season. Australian Zoologist 20:485–500.

Brown, T. E., A. W. Morley, N. T. Sanderson, and R. D. Tait. 1982. Report of a large fish kill resulting from natural acid water conditions in Australia. Journal of Fish Biology 22:335–350.

Davis, T. L. O. 1982. Maturity and sexuality in barramundi, *Lates calcarifer* (Bloch), in the Northern Territory and south-eastern Gulf of Carpentaria. Australian Journal of Marine and Freshwater Research 33:529–545.

Davis, T. L. O. 1984. Estimates of fecundity in Barramundi, *Lates calcarifer* (Bloch), using an automatic particle counter. Australian Journal of Marine and Freshwater Research 35:111–118.

Davis, T. L. O. 1985a. Seasonal changes in gonad maturity and abundance of larvae and early juveniles of barramundi, *Lates calcarifer* (Bloch), in Van Diemen Gulf and the Gulf of Carpentaria. Australian Journal of Marine and Freshwater Research 36:177–190.

Davis, T. L. O. 1985b. The food of barramundi, *Lates calcarifer* (Bloch), in coastal and inland waters of Van Diemen Gulf and the Gulf of Carpentaria, Australia. Journal of Fish Biology 26:669–682.

Grey, D. L., and R. K. Griffin. 1979. A review of the Northern Territory barramundi fishery. Northern Territory Department of Industrial Development, Fishery Report 1, Darwin, Australia.

Griffin, R. K. 1982. A survey of amateur angling for barramundi (*Lates calcarifer*) in the Northern Territory. Northern Territory Department of Primary Production, Technical Report 2, Darwin, Australia.

Griffin, R. K. 1985. The importance of mangrove/coastal wetland to three commercial fisheries in the Northern Territory; particularly for barramundi (*Lates calcarifer*). Pages 277–283 in K. N. Bardsley, J. D. S. Davies, and C. D. Woodroffe, editors. Coasts and tidal wetlands of the Australian monsoon region. Australian National University North Australian Research Unit, Mangrove Monograph 1, Darwin, Australia.

Kowarsky, J., and A. H. Ross. 1981. Fish movement up stream through a central Queensland (Fitzroy River) coastal fishway. Australian Journal of Marine and Freshwater Research 32:93–109.

Moore, R. 1979. Natural sex inversion in giant perch, *Lates calcarifer*. Australian Journal of Marine and Freshwater Research 30:803–813.

Moore, R. 1982. Spawning and early life history of barramundi, *Lates calcarifer* (Bloch), in Papua New Guinea. Australian Journal of Marine and Freshwater Research 33:647–661.

Moore, R., and L. F. Reynolds. 1982. Migration patterns of barramundi, *Lates calcarifer* (Bloch), in Papua New Guinea. Australian Journal of Marine and Freshwater Research 33:671–682.

Rohan, G., R. K. Griffin, and D. L. Grey. 1981. Northern Territory barramundi fishery review of management situation paper. Northern Territory Department of Primary Production, Technical Bulletin 49, Darwin, Australia.

Russell, D. J., and R. N. Garrett. 1983. Use by juvenile barramundi, *Lates calcarifer* (Bloch), and other fishes of temporary supralittoral habitats in a tropical estuary in northern Australia. Australian Journal of Marine and Freshwater Research 34:805–811.

Russell, D. J., and R. N. Garrett. 1985. Early life history of barramundi, *Lates calcarifer* (Bloch), in north-eastern Queensland. Australian Journal of Marine and Freshwater Research 36:191–201.

Wongsomnuk, S., and S. Manevonk. 1973. Results of experiments on artificial breeding and larval rearing of the sea bass (*Lates calcarifer*) (Bloch). Thailand Department of Fisheries, Contribution 5, Bangkok, Thailand.

American Fisheries Society Symposium 1:364–376, 1987

Marine Migrations of Atlantic Salmon from Rivers in Ungava Bay, Quebec

G. Power and M. V. Power

Department of Biology, University of Waterloo, Waterloo, Ontario N2L 3G1, Canada

R. Dumas and A. Gordon

Koksoak Research Centre, Makivik Corporation, Post Office Box 179
Fort Chimo, Quebec J0M 1C0, Canada

Abstract.—Historical as well as recent evidence indicates most Atlantic salmon *Salmo salar* from Ungava Bay rivers migrate beyond the confines of the bay. Timing of the marine migration is correlated with ice conditions and is restricted to a short, variable window of suitable sea temperatures. Temperatures as low as 1.0°C may be encountered during parts of the migration, suggesting that colder water is tolerated during migration than is selected for feeding and growth. Estimates of minimal swimming times from the northern tip of Labrador, assumed to be the last place to warm, suggest that migrants should arrive in all rivers at about the same time. Local knowledge supports this suggestion. Large smolt size in Ungava stocks may be a consequence of the short interval for exiting from the bay. Proportions of Atlantic salmon exhibiting different life histories, including estuary growth, mixed sea and estuary growth, and sea growth, varied in Koksoak catch samples during 1961–1969 and 1979–1985. Two hypotheses were considered to explain the observed shifts in life cycle. One, based on the stochastic effects of climate on the ease of passage through Ungava Bay, was discounted. The other, relating to estuary growth conditions, appeared more acceptable. During summer, estuary salmon grow at a rate approaching 0.2 cm/d and increase in condition at the same time. Estuary growth is similar from year to year. The estuary hypothesis is discussed in terms of Baker's general model of migration. The evidence fits the model very well and helps explain the paradox that, as fishing pressure in the Koksoak estuary has increased, so has the proportion of Atlantic salmon adopting an estuary life history.

Atlantic salmon *Salmo salar* were reported in Ungava Bay by the first traders to arrive in the area in 1830 and an August fishery was quickly established (Power 1976). Turner (1885), reporting on the fishery at Fort Chimo (Kuujjuaq), in the estuary of the Koksoak River, wrote that the fish came from the Atlantic Ocean and followed the coastline of Ungava Bay to the rivers. Power (1969) agreed with Turner's conclusion on the basis that marine growth of Ungava Atlantic salmon was similar to that of the species from other regions. In the absence of any direct evidence about marine migrations, it was assumed that the ice-cold waters of Ungava Bay were an unsuitable habitat for growing Atlantic salmon. Hudson Bay Company records showed that in years when ice conditions in Ungava Bay were bad enough to delay supply ships, Atlantic salmon were late entering the rivers (Power 1976). This theme was developed further by Power (1981) using evidence from studies of the distribution of Atlantic salmon on the high seas, which showed that few were caught when sea surface temperatures were below 2.0°C (May 1973), and information on sea surface temperatures in Ungava Bay

(Dunbar 1958). In Ungava rivers, smolt outmigration peaks in July but young fish are delayed in the estuaries by very low sea temperatures. In August, sea surface temperatures are between 2.0 and 4.0°C, the adult return migration begins, and the smolts can exit to the high seas. Many smolts remain in the estuaries until the thermal barrier between river and sea temperatures disappears in September. There is a well-defined short thermal window for migration, and timing must be precise.

Recent work on the Koksoak Atlantic salmon stock has shown that their migratory behaviour includes several alternative strategies (Robitaille et al. 1986). The entire life cycle can take place in fresh water; they can start life in the river, then migrate between river and estuary; they can migrate between river and estuary and then go to sea (occasionally they reverse the estuary–sea sequence); or they can have a more typical anadromous life cycle. The proportions of fish exhibiting different migratory strategies varies from year to year. In this paper, we consider two hypotheses that might explain the migratory behaviour of Ungava Atlantic salmon. The first assumes that the duration of suitable marine conditions for migration controls the proportion of distant marine migrants. The second explanation is based on Baker's (1978) model of migration which suggests that the quality of the estuarine habitat is the controlling factor. The migration model presented by Gross (1987, this volume) is a related model and equally suitable. The challenge, then, is to see how available data can contribute to our understanding of the migration patterns of Ungava Atlantic salmon and to identify what information can most easily be gathered to confirm or modify our interpretations.

Information Available

A considerable amount of information about the Atlantic salmon of Ungava Bay has accumulated in the last 35 years. Atlantic salmon occur in several rivers (Figure 1) but the principal runs are found in the Koksoak, Whale, and George rivers. Between 1947 and 1955, the Fisheries Research Board of Canada carried out an oceanographic study that included Ungava Bay, one aim of which was to investigate marine resources that could be used by the Inuit (Dunbar 1952; 1958). The Arctic Institute of North America and the Province of Quebec financed studies between 1956 and 1960. These provided a first description of the biology of Ungava Atlantic salmon stocks and were, in part, motivated by a desire to understand the impact of Inuit fishing on northern stocks (Power 1969). In 1961, the Industrial Development Branch of the federal Department of Northern Affairs and Natural Resources pro-

moted and financially backed a commercial salmon fishery by the Eskimo Cooperative at Fort Chimo (Kuujjuaq) (Power 1961). From 1961 to 1969, unpublished reports on the fishery gave details on the timing and composition of the run, the ages, lengths, and weights of various classes of Atlantic salmon caught, and fishing statistics on catch and effort. The fishery was centered on the Koksoak River, extending in some years to the Whale River. Social conditions and incentives changed during the next decade and the cooperative's interest in the fishery diminished.

Atlantic salmon fishing, however, continued for subsistence purposes much as it was practiced in other Ungava rivers, notably the Leaf and George rivers. During the 1970s, the James Bay hydroelectric scheme came into being and 29% of the discharge of the Koksoak River was diverted into the LaGrande River (MLCP and SAGE 1980). A variety of studies were launched including many carried out by consultants for Hydro-Quebec. Others completed by the Koksoak Research Centre of Makivik Corporation concerned Atlantic salmon harvests by subsistence and quasicommercial entrepreneurial fishermen. This information is beginning to appear in the literature (Côté and Babos 1984; Lapierre 1984; Robitaille et al. 1984a, 1984b, 1986) but much is still in manuscript form. These manuscripts, raw data provided by Makivik research department, personal communications, and direct observations, provide the information used in this paper.

Several terms are used in this paper for Atlantic salmon life history stages. *Grilse* are fish that have spent one winter at sea before returning. *Two-sea-winter salmon* have spent two winters at sea. *Previously spawned salmon* are returning to spawn for a second (or subsequent time). *Kelts* are anadromous Atlantic salmon that spawned the previous autumn. *Estuary salmon* are those which descend to the estuary as smolts and migrate between the estuary in summer and fresh water in winter (perhaps remaining in the lower river). They show very well-defined annuli, difficult to distinguish from spawning marks, and appear to spawn frequently. Some Atlantic salmon spend only the first postsmolt summer in the estuary and follow this with a year of normal sea growth (termed *mixed growth salmon*). Other combinations of habitat use occur but these are relatively uncommon and, for the purposes of this analysis, they have been lumped together as "other."

When Atlantic salmon have been examined, they have usually been caught by Inuit fishermen

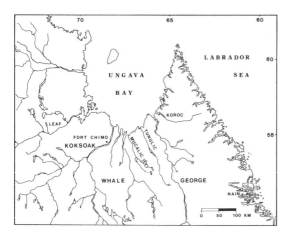

FIGURE 1.—Rivers discharging into Ungava Bay known to sustain stocks of anadromous Atlantic salmon. The largest runs occur in the Koksoak, Whale, and George rivers; smaller stocks are found in the Leaf, Mucalic, Tunulic, and Koroc rivers.

in 100- to 150-mm-mesh synthetic-fiber gill nets (multifilament nylon, monofilament nylon, and others) set at the surface from shore in tidal parts of river estuaries. Fork lengths (inches or centimeters in the original measurements) and weights (pounds or kilograms, obtained with spring balance or commercial scales; if fish had been eviscerated, their weights were multiplied by 1.2 to estimate whole-body fresh weights) were measured. Numbers of Atlantic salmon refer to sample sizes. Reference to the original sources provides more details on methodology.

Evidence that Atlantic Salmon Leave and Return to Ungava Bay

To our knowledge, only three Atlantic salmon tagged at distant points have been recaptured in Ungava. One was marked in October 1970 in west Greenland and recaptured in the Koksoak River in August of the following year (Power and Cressman 1975). Two were tagged off Nain, Labrador, in 1982; one was recaptured in 1983 in the George River and one in 1984 in the Koksoak River (Reddin and Dempson 1986). Among the fish tagged at Nain in 1982 and recaptured off the Labrador coast the same year, one had moved north and four south. It appears the stock off Nain in July and August is of mixed origin and includes some fish moving north towards Ungava Bay.

Circumstantial evidence of distant migration of at least a component of the Ungava stocks is provided by interceptions of Atlantic salmon along the supposed migratory route around the eastern shore of Ungava Bay and on the coast of northern Labrador. Power and Cressman (1975) reported on the characteristics of 74 Atlantic

salmon taken near Port Burwell in 1967 and concluded that most were of Ungava origin. They also noted previous catches of Atlantic salmon near the tip of Labrador. Since 1983, exploratory fishing at Killiniq (Port Burwell, at the northeast entry to Ungava Bay) with a variety of gears resulted in a few Atlantic salmon captures. Three fish were taken in 1983, 29 Atlantic salmon and one smolt in 1984, and a small unknown number in 1985 (Table 1). These are by-catches of fisheries for Atlantic cod *Gadus morhua* and Arctic char *Salvelinus alpinus*. In 1985, two Atlantic salmon were caught in gill nets set for Arctic char off the Koroc River (Table 1). These data are consistent with the theory that Ungava Atlantic salmon carry out regular migrations to distant marine feeding areas. They do not support a suggestion by Legendre and Legendre (1984) that these stocks confine their migrations to Ungava Bay.

Sea Ice and Atlantic Salmon

Ice cover during June through September was measured for the years 1964–1985 for the sea areas of Ungava Bay and the western Labrador Sea (Figure 2). As a working hypothesis, it was assumed that ice at the northern peninsula of Quebec and Labrador was correlated with a cold-water barrier to Atlantic salmon entering Ungava Bay through which the fish would not pass.

The percentage ice cover in areas 1–5 during 1977–1985 (Figure 2) was examined to see if there was a consistent pattern of distribution and critical areas from which the ice cleared late. Areas 2 and 3 along the eastern shore of Ungava Bay were often, but not consistently, the last to clear of ice; area 5 on the Labrador coast was never last. A

TABLE 1.—Atlantic salmon caught by boats operating out of Killiniq (Port Burwell) and off Koroc River, 1983–1985. Length is fork length; weight is round weight; age includes the year of capture as a full year. Types of salmon include 2-s-w for 2-sea-winter, 1-s-w for grilse, and "salmon" when sea age is not known. Condition factor = weight (g) × 100/(fork length, cm)^3. Killiniq data are from D. J. Gillis (personal communication).

Year and dates	Location	Type of salmon	Number	Mean length (cm)	Mean weight (kg)	Mean condition factor	Mean age (years)
1983							
Jul 23	Burwell harbour	2-s-w	1		4.8		
Aug 1	Jackson Island	2-s-w	2		4.8		
Aug 4–11	Ikkudliayak Fiord	"Salmon"	6–8				
1984							
Aug 7–10	Ekortiarsuk Fiord	"Salmon"	5				
Aug 30–Sep 16	Burwell harbour	2-s-w	22	77.3	5.46	1.17	8.14
Aug 31–Sep 15	Burwell harbour	1-s-w	7	61.4	2.72	1.17	7.00
Oct 3	Burwell harbour	Smolt	1	28.7	0.20	0.85	6.00
1985							
Aug 21	Koroc estuary	1-s-w	1	58.7	2.15	1.06	8.00
Aug 23	Koroc estuary	2-s-w	1	79.5	5.55	1.10	8.00

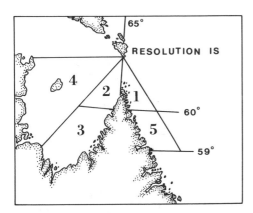

FIGURE 2.—Regions in Ungava Bay and northern Labrador Sea used to measure the percentage of ice cover at intervals during the summer.

better correlate with the time of arrival of anadromous Atlantic salmon in the rivers of Ungava Bay was percentage of ice cover in the entire bay, areas 2 through 4. This measure was less subject to variation due to wind-induced ice movement within the bay. Plots of cumulative percent ice cover in Ungava Bay against cumulative percent fresh-run anadromous Atlantic salmon catches (Figure 3) show a clear relationship. In 1964 and 1965, Atlantic salmon entered the Koksoak estuary before all ice had cleared from the bay but less than 20% of the catch was obtained before the ice had disappeared. Between 1966 and 1969, the fish did not arrive until the bay was clear of ice. During the years 1977 to 1985, some Atlantic

salmon were taken before all the ice had cleared, but 80% of the catch was taken later. In the summers of 1983 to 1985, the ice was late in disappearing, and, in each of these years, the fish were late in arriving.

To confirm the relationship between Atlantic salmon arrival and ice conditions, plots of cumulative ice cover against date were used to estimate the Julian day on which 50% ice cover remained each year. These data were correlated with the mean Julian day on which grilse and 2-sea-winter salmon occurred in the Koksoak River catch samples for the periods 1961–1969 and 1979–1985, the only years for which data were available (Figure 4). For 2-sea-winter salmon, $r = 0.88$, $P < 0.001$; for grilse, $r = 0.80$, $P < 0.002$. These are strong correlations between ice cover and Atlantic salmon arrival. It is probably not the ice which controls Atlantic salmon movement, but nearshore sea surface temperatures which are influenced by ice.

What temperatures are barriers for migration of Atlantic salmon in the sea is not certain. Power

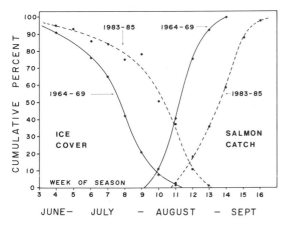

FIGURE 3.—The cumulative percentage of ice cover in Ungava Bay compared with the cumulative catch of grilse and 2-sea-winter Atlantic salmon in Inuit fisheries in the estuary of the Koksoak River. The interval 1964–1969 was a period of normal ice melt; 1983–1985 were years in which the ice disappeared late.

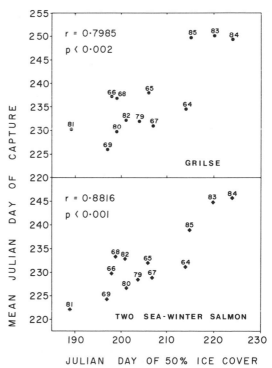

FIGURE 4.—The correlation between the Julian day on which ice cover was reduced to 50% and the mean Julian day of capture of grilse and 2-sea-winter Atlantic salmon as revealed by catch samples from the Koksoak fishery. Years are indicated by the last two digits.

(1981) suggested 2.0°C was the critical lower limit. May (1973) reported Atlantic salmon were rarely found at temperatures below 3.0°C; Reddin and Murray (1985) and Reddin and Shearer (1987, this volume) showed that the distribution of Atlantic salmon in the northwest Atlantic can be bounded by the 4.0°C isotherm and the species avoids water colder than this.

There is always the problem of scale of measurements when the migratory routes of fish are considered, and it is quite possible for nearshore temperatures in Arctic seas to considerably exceed reported oceanographic surface values. The importance of knowing the precise conditions encountered by migrating fish was emphasized in several recent publications (Lynn 1984; Westerberg 1984).

At Killiniq, which is assumed to be the critical area for Atlantic salmon migrating into and out of Ungava Bay, sea temperatures are consistently low. During August and September 1984, nearshore surface temperatures were less than 2.0°C (except for one value of 3.0°C on September 20). In 1985, they were less than 3.0°C. Temperatures generally declined with depth but temperature and salinity profiles showed temporal variability, implying tidal mixing and some instability in the water column. Both years were late ice years (Figure 4) and the salmon run was late (Table 2). Atlantic salmon were caught in water as cold as 1.0°C, at which temperature they were described as being "rather lethargic" (Gillis and Fife, personal communications).

South of Killiniq, the sea is warmer. Shore surface conditions off Koroc River in the southeastern bay were 6.0–8.5°C in July 1985, while salinities were 9–21.5‰. At this time, the bay was 75% ice covered and nearshore conditions were obviously affected by freshwater runoff.

These observations suggest temperatures tolerated during migration may be lower than those selected for feeding. Unless there is an unknown plume of warmer water, Ungava Atlantic salmon must, in some years, migrate through seawater as cold as 1.0°C. Conditions will vary from year to year depending on temperatures and conditions in Hudson Strait and the Labrador current. They may also be influenced by the flux of warm water into the Labrador Sea gyre from the Irminger current. The subject of annual variations in marine climate in the northwest Atlantic was reviewed in a Northwest Atlantic Fisheries Organization symposium in 1981 (Dunbar 1982; Trites 1982) and will not be discussed here except to note there is strong evidence of annual variations and of longer-term trends.

Swimming Speeds across Ungava Bay

Evidence available (Reddin and Dempson 1986) suggests Atlantic salmon returning to Ungava Bay probably accumulate in July along the Labrador coast, many as far south as Nain. They swim north in a nearshore wedge of warmer water to the tip of Labrador and, as soon as conditions allow,

TABLE 2.—Mean Julian day for appearance of grilse and 2-sea-winter Atlantic salmon in samples from Inuit catches in the Koksoak River estuary, 1961–1969 and 1979–1985.

	Grilse		2-sea-winter fish		
Year	Number sampled	Mean day of sample	Number sampled	Mean day of sample	Lag time for grilse (days)
1961	156	231.7	262	225.0	6.7
1962	507	237.6	614	228.2	9.4
1963	721	229.6	1095	224.8	4.8
1964[a]	327	234.7	2492	231.5	3.2
1965	619	238.1	922	232.0	6.1
1966	792	237.3	1015	230.0	7.3
1967	274	231.2	820	229.1	2.1
1968	319	237.1	581	233.6	3.5
1969	131	226.3	509	224.5	1.8
1979	89	232.1	179	228.6	3.5
1980	45	229.8	27	226.8	3.0
1981	98	230.3	138	222.4	7.9
1982	83	234.9	158	233.1	1.8
1983	97	250.3	185	245.2	5.1
1984	32	249.3	153	245.8	3.5
1985	31	249.8	108	239.4	10.4
Mean		236.3		231.3	5.0
(SD)		(7.5)		(7.0)	(2.7)

[a] Mixed sample, mostly Koksoak fish but includes some Whale River fish.

enter Ungava Bay and migrate in the warmest nearshore waters around the coast to southern rivers. Grilse arrive at the rivers a few days later than 2-sea-winter salmon (Table 2), which might be explained by their different swimming speeds.

Weihs (1984) estimated the swimming speed (m/s) of migrating salmon in the size range 0.3 to 0.7 m fork length (L, m) as $0.5 L^{0.43}$. Cook (1984) used similar speeds for migrating Atlantic salmon and quoted work in progress to the effect that the fish are able to maintain consistent direction. If it is hypothesized that the last place Atlantic salmon can experience adequate water temperatures for migration is Killiniq, the passage time of interest is that along the coast of Ungava Bay. The route presumed (Figure 5) allows fish to take advantage of the thermal channel along the coast; it is further assumed that the fish can maintain consistent direction for periods of time. The resulting esti-mates of passage times (Table 3) are minimal times. They take no account of the circulation in Ungava Bay, which is generally counter-clock-wise, or the very strong tidal currents, which are engendered by some of the highest tides in the

world and which flow strongly in both directions along the Coast (Koksoak estuary: 9.1 to 12.9 m for neap and spring tides; Canadian Hydrographic Service). A mean time lag of 5 d (16 years' data) between mean times of arrival of 2-sea-winter salmon and grilse in the Koksoak estuary catch samples (Table 2) is greater than the estimated half-day lag in swimming times along the pre-sumed route. A difference of 5 d requires a common starting point 3,000 km distant and mi-gration times of 51 and 56 d for 0.8-m-long 2-sea-winter salmon and 0.6-m-long grilse, respectively. Even if a common starting point at Nain were assumed, a mean difference of this magnitude would necessitate a circuitous route. Further, the calculations of swimming time take no account of temperature conditions and Atlantic salmon swimming at temperatures between 1.0 and 4.0°C may swim more slowly than Weih's formula indi-cates. A. L. Meister (Atlantic Sea Run Salmon Commission, personal communication) calculated the rate of Atlantic salmon travel from tag returns of U.S. fish at 15–80% of the swimming speeds we used for Table 3. Such rates fit more closely the observed time lag between grilse and 2-sea-winter salmon captures in the Koksoak fishery.

Estimated swimming speeds suggest there should be only minor differences in the time of arrival of Atlantic salmon in the various Ungava rivers. Such differences could only be detected by specifically planned simultaneous observations. Local knowledge and past field observations do not contradict the inference that Atlantic salmon arrive in all the rivers at about the same time.

Atlantic salmon smolts leaving Ungava Bay probably migrate in the opposite direction along the same route as the returning fish. If they follow the nearshore waters as far south as Nain before dispersing seaward, the distance covered could exceed 1,000 km. With a brief thermal window for migration, swimming speeds could be important. Swimming speed calculations extended to smaller fish are even more tentative, since they are out-side the range specified by Weihs (1984). Small fish are also much more likely to be affected by currents. Our calculations suggest that a 12-cm smolt might take 21 d to go from the Koksoak to Killiniq, whereas a 25-cm smolt could make the passage in 15 d (Table 3). Since many smolts do not leave the estuary of the Koksoak until late September when they have attained lengths of 30–35 cm (Power 1981), there is some support for the idea that a necessary characteristic of Ungava salmon stocks is large smolt size. If this argument

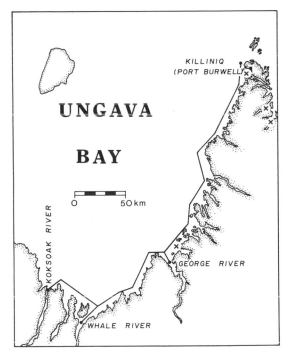

FIGURE 5.—The route chosen for estimation of mini-mal swimming times for smolts, grilse, and 2-sea-winter Atlantic salmon between Killiniq and the major Ungava rivers (Table 3). Crosses indicate places where Atlantic salmon have been captured since 1983 (Table 1).

TABLE 3.—Estimated swimming times for Atlantic salmon from Killiniq to major Ungava rivers based on the formula of Weihs (1982), the route in Figure 5, and no effects from currents. Fork lengths used in the calculations are given in parentheses.

				Time in days		
					Smolt	
Trajectory	Distance (km)	Grilse (65 cm)	2-sea-winter (80 cm)		(12 cm)	(25 cm)
Killiniq to Koksoak	365	6.8	6.3		21	15
Killiniq to Whale	325	6.1	5.6			
Killiniq to George	225	4.2	3.9			
George to Koksoak	140	2.6	2.4			
George to Whale	100	1.9	1.7			
Whale to Koksoak	40	0.7	0.7			

is accepted and applied to the Atlantic salmon stock in Hudson Bay (LeJeune and Legendre 1968), it may explain why this stock is isolated and has only a limited anadromous migration; the smolts cannot swim the distance to Atlantic feeding grounds in the time available.

Life History Variations

Atlantic salmon in Ungava Bay exhibit a wide variety of life histories within and among stocks. The terminology applied to these variations and stages has evolved as studies have proceeded. In 1960, recognized life cycles were those appropriate to more temperate areas. Seeming exceptions to these were forced into the accepted mold during the initial years of sampling of the Koksoak fishery. By 1965, it became apparent that the originally adopted categories were no longer adequate or acceptable. New categories were defined

to accommodate new interpretations of life history as seen on the scales (Côté and Babos 1984).

The proportion of Atlantic salmon exhibiting different life histories has varied considerably from year to year in the Koksoak catch samples (Table 4); this is the only stock for which there are several years of data. Two hypotheses can be considered to explain the observed variations. The first relates to conditions for migration in Ungava Bay, the second to conditions in the Koksoak estuary.

Marine Conditions

A hypothesis which might explain changes in the proportion of anadromous, mixed growth, and estuary salmon in the Koksoak River is that conditions for smolt migration vary from year to year and this influences the proportion of smolts trapped in the estuary. The argument regarding

TABLE 4.—Sample size and percentage of various life history classes of Atlantic salmon in Inuit catches in the Koksoak River estuary, 1961–1969 and 1979–1985.

Year	Sample size[a]	Grilse	2-sea-winter	Mixed growth	Estuary salmon	Previously spawned	Other types	Kelts[b]
1961	857	26.3	61.1	1.2	1.9	8.7	0.7	(30.9)
1962	1,371	39.8	48.2	5.3	2.3	4.4	0.0	(6.9)
1963	2,067	37.1	56.4	3.6	1.2	1.5	0.2	(6.4)
1964[c]	3,012	11.2	85.6	0.8	0.3	1.8	0.2	(3.5)
1965	1,751	38.3	57.1	3.0	0.4	0.9	0.3	(7.8)
1966	2,062	39.1	50.1	8.9	0.5	1.1	0.2	(1.6)
1967	1,694	22.1	66.3	6.1	3.0	1.6	0.9	(26.9)
1968	1,488	30.6	55.8	5.2	5.7	2.5	0.2	(30.0)
1969	1,378	15.8	61.4	3.6	15.6	3.1	0.5	(39.8)
1979	432	22.9	46.1	12.0	16.2	2.6	0.3	(5.4)
1980[d]	210	35.1	21.1	13.3	28.9	0.0	1.6	(38.8)
1981	547/411	23.8	33.3	14.6	25.5	2.2	0.5	(19.6)
1982	356/307	27.0	51.1	9.8	6.5	2.3	2.2	(8.4)
1983	373/301	32.2	60.5	4.3	1.0	1.7	0.3	(8.3)
1984	375/258	12.4	59.3	1.2	26.4	0.4	0.4	(10.1)
1985	311/205	15.1	52.2	15.1	16.6	0.7	0.3	(7.1)

[a] For 1981 to 1985, the percentages of kelts were calculated from the entire samples, the left totals; other percentages are for the period after sea-run salmon enter the fishery, and are based on the right totals, which exclude kelts.

[b] Kelts: calculated as percentages of total samples; other percentages were calculated from total samples less kelts.

[c] 1964: mixed sample, mostly Koksoak fish but including some Whale River fish.

[d] 1980: single fisherman's catch.

the necessity for large smolts in Ungava stocks implies that these smolts may be performing near the limits for successful passage. Stochastic variations in climate operating on this system would change the likelihood of movement away from the Koksoak and the duration of suitable conditions for migration. Smolts trapped one year might escape the following year and give rise to mixed growth salmon; otherwise they would remain estuary salmon. It is possible to test this hypothesis by attempting to correlate variations in life history with conditions in Ungava Bay (Figure 6).

When the window for migration is compared with life history categories in catch samples, there is no suggestion that years with short periods suitable for migration are followed 2–3 years later by marked increases in mixed growth and estuary salmon. The time lag allows a smolt to grow to catchable size in the estuary. Similarly, a mixed growth salmon trapped in the bay in year x is not available for capture until year $x + 2$. Statistical correlations between date of 50% ice melt, the period between this date and the start of the next freeze up, and the proportions of different life histories lagged 2–4 years are all nonsignificant.

Estuary Conditions

The Koksoak is the largest river emptying into Ungava Bay (mean annual discharge 2,500 m³s), draining 137,500 km² of central Quebec. It warms the estuary in summer to between 5.0 and 10.0°C. The shape of the estuary with a narrow neck and

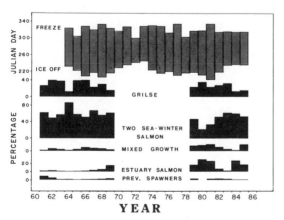

FIGURE 6.—The percentage of Atlantic salmon with different life histories in Koksoak catch samples, 1961–1969 and 1979–1985, and the estimated duration of suitable marine conditions for migration through Ungava Bay. The window for migration is approximately equal to the difference between ice off and the start of freezing, upper histogram.

expanded basins upstream, a large tidal zone (96 km long), and high tides all contribute to the recycling of nutrients and the productivity of the estuary. The estuary supports a large stock of anadromous brook trout *Salvelinus fontinalis*, which grow quickly and attain a large size (Power 1980). It attracts a stock or stocks of anadromous Arctic char from nearby rivers for feeding in early summer. Inuit fishermen take a variety of other species in subsistence fisheries including lake whitefish *Coregonus clupeaformis*, sculpins *Myoxocephalus* spp., and longnose sucker *Catostomus catostomus*. During July and August, large shoals of juvenile *sculpins* are common; other plentiful food items for Atlantic salmon include various amphipods and mysids as well as sand lances *Ammodytes* spp. and, at times, the polychaete *Nereis* sp.

A hypothesis concerning the estuary states that conditions vary from year to year; in years of high productivity, more Atlantic salmon remain in the estuary than in poorer years. Testing this hypothesis is difficult in the absence of measurements. Possible correlates of estuary productivity include summer temperatures at Fort Chimo, rainfall, and river discharge. However, none of these correlate with life history variations (Figure 6). A measure of the suitability of the estuary for Atlantic salmon is the growth rate of resident fish, but this cannot be assumed to correlate with life history variations since the latter depend on proportions of fish adopting various migration tracks, not on how well they grow.

The growth of Atlantic salmon in the Koksoak estuary was remarkably constant during 1982–1985 (Table 5). Smolts during the first summer grew at a rate of just over 1 cm every 5 d, the same value found by Robitaille et al. (1984b) for 1980. Estuary salmon during their second summer grew slightly less rapidly, about 1 cm every 6 d. Rather limited data indicate annual growth increments declined for older estuary salmon (Figure 7). Not only was growth rapid, but it was accomplished by an increase in condition factor. The exponents b in the length–weight (W) equation $W = aL^b$ were 3.98 (95% confidence limits, 3.88–4.07) in 1984 and 3.43 (3.08–3.77) in 1985. The 1984 exponent was significantly different from the 1985 one (t-test, $P < 0.05$). In addition, the standard error of the slope was much less in 1984 (0.0474 versus 0.3231). This difference was likely due to a larger sample and more accurate weighing in 1984 rather than to a real difference in growth.

During the 1960s, few estuary fish appeared in

TABLE 5.—Growth of Atlantic salmon in the Koksoak and Koroc river estuaries. Postsmolt ages are S.0+ for fish during the first summer in the estuary and S.1+ for those 1 year older. Fork lengths are regressed against Julian day. Periods of observation vary from July through September (see Figure 7). For the Koksoak, there were no significant differences between years for S.0+ and S.1+ smolts (t-test; $P > 0.05$). Koroc River S.0+ smolts had significantly slower growth than fish of similar age in the Koksoak River (t-test; $P < 0.05$).

Location	Year	Number	Slope (cm/d)	95% confidence limits	SE slope	t value	Intercept
			Age S.0+				
Koksoak	1982	17	0.189	0.074, 0.304	0.206	3.531	−15.137
Koksoak	1983	12	0.206	0.137, 0.275	0.031	6.543	−18.103
Koksoak	1984	12	0.214	0.054, 0.374	0.072	2.992	−21.449
Koroc	1985	19	0.045	0.013, 0.077	0.015	3.106	13.779
Koksoak	1982–1984	41	0.203	0.154, 0.251	0.024	8.551	−18.256
			Age S.1+				
Koksoak	1983	13	0.186	0.133, 0.239	0.024	7.813	4.755
Koksoak	1984	126	0.152	0.134, 0.170	0.009	16.754	11.160
Koksoak	1985	57	0.165	0.142, 0.189	0.012	13.866	10.070
Koksoak	1983–1985	196	0.157	0.145, 0.168	0.007	22.338	10.747

catch samples because all samples were drawn from the commercial harvest, the fish were caught in 140-mm-mesh nets, and the fish had been selected for shipping south for sale. Any small Atlantic salmon caught were undoubtedly consumed locally. Estuary salmon, older than two estuary summers, and mixed growth salmon were large enough to be taken and these appeared in the catches in 1968 and 1969. From the available data, it was not possible to reconstruct growth rates for estuary salmon during the 1960s. We are left with the conclusion that it is not possible to estimate past growing conditions in the Koksoak estuary.

Discussion

Baker (1978) provided a conceptual framework and basis for discussions of animal migration. His migration model divides the lifetime track of an organism into component movements, each of which can be considered in terms of its type, initiation, costs, advantages, and selection for migration threshold. An organism responds in a way which maximizes its potential reproductive success, S_p. This has two components: an action-dependent one, S_d, relating to the individual, and an action-independent one, S_i, relating to contributions by any progeny to future gene pools; $S_p = S_i + S_d$. For an individual, the suitability, h, of habitat H, is measured by its effect on reducing the action-dependent component of S_p. This does not change in an "ideal" habitat, but over the life span of the individual, it decreases from a maximum value to nil at death. The action-independent component of S_p is, of course, zero prior to reproduction. Migration from one habitat to an-

other becomes advantageous when $h_1 < h_2M$, where subscripts refer to habitats and M is the migration factor. The migration factor is the value of S_d at the time the individual arrives at H_2 had the organism remained in H_1 divided by the value of S_d upon arrival at H_2. The loss of S_d during migration is a measure of the migration cost. A term $\bar{E}$, the mean expectation of migration, is the mean of the product of all accessible habitat suitabilities and migration factors ($\bar{hM}$). Migration is advantageous when $h < \bar{E}$. An organism may have no prior knowledge of conditions in potentially available habitats but selection can act on correlates of target habitat suitabilities such as temperature, food supply, or population density so that appropriate migration thresholds become part of the species' repertoire of responses. Since deme density will, in most circumstances, cause h to vary, it will also change the mean expectation of migration $\bar{E}$ by varying the migration factor M. Once migration begins, densities will fall, initiating a corresponding change in h until $h = \bar{E}$ and the migration ceases. Under these circumstances, it is possible to arrive at an equilibrium position in which all or only a proportion, p, of the population migrates ($0 \le p \le 1$). A more thorough discussion of the model and its complexities was given by Baker (1978); its interest here is in how it can be applied to the migration patterns of the Koksoak Atlantic salmon stocks.

During the freshwater parr stage, there is a general downstream drift of the larger, older parr. In the lower Koksoak River, very few parr younger than 3+ years are found (Power 1969). This migration could be described either as a

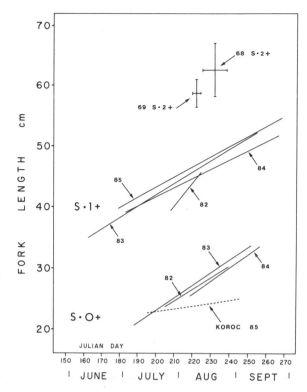

FIGURE 7.—Growth of Atlantic salmon in the Koksoak estuary. Years are indicated by the last two digits; S.0+, S.1+, and S.2+ represent Atlantic salmon in their first, second, and third years of estuary growth, respectively. The limits shown for the S.2+ fish are ± 1 SD. Equations and confidence intervals for the other lines are given in Table 5.

noncalculated removal migration or as a facultative removal migration in the terms of Baker (1978). In either case, the older parr move into larger and deeper habitats and this change of habitat is accompanied by an increased growth rate (Power 1969). The smolt stage of Atlantic salmon is characterized by an obligatory downstream migration which occurs, for Ungava Bay fish, between ages 3+ and 8+ years, when the fish are about 21 cm long. Smolts arrive in the estuary in July (Power 1981), where they are delayed by low temperatures in Ungava Bay. Many remain in this transition area, taking advantage of the warm river plume, until September, when the thermal barrier between river and sea disappears. The Koksoak estuary is clearly a new habitat in the terminology of Baker (1978), and the performance of the postsmolts in it can be best considered by reference to his migration model.

Two hypotheses were postulated to explain the variations in life history observed in catch samples of Koksoak River Atlantic salmon. The first was that changes in the timing and duration of suitable marine conditions for migration result in different numbers of smolts being trapped in the estuary from year to year. Such smolts would either become mixed growth salmon or estuary salmon. The catch samples, despite some shortcomings, leave no doubt that the proportions of Atlantic salmon showing different life histories have varied over the 16 years of observations. However, it has not been possible to correlate these changes with variations in ice-free periods in Ungava Bay or any other physical variable that might correlate with ease of passage through Ungava Bay; therefore the accidental trapping hypothesis seems untenable.

The alternative hypothesis was that conditions in the estuary vary from year to year and, in some years, are so good that some of the postsmolts grow beyond the migratory phase and terminate their seaward migration at this point. This hypothesis seems to have considerable merit, especially because it fits well into Baker's (1978) general model of migration and specifically into the effects of density on the stimulus to migrate.

The Koksoak estuary is a good habitat for Atlantic salmon during a brief period each year. Growth rates, such as those reported for smolts during the first summer and for older estuary salmon, are excellent and are achieved at the same time condition factors are increasing. The length increment of a grilse between smolt migration (21 cm) and return is about 40 cm, and a 2-sea-winter salmon adds another 20 cm to this during an additional year feeding at sea. Estuary fish grow at a rate which would allow them to achieve these sizes in about 200 and 350 d, respectively. Grilse are absent about 400 d and 2-sea-winter salmon about 765 d.

To fit variations in life history of Koksoak salmon into Baker's migration model, we may assume that various densities of smolts arrive in the estuary each summer and that conditions in the estuary are not constant both within and between years. An individual smolt leaves the estuary when the habitat suitability of the estuary, h_e, is less than E, its own particular expectation of migration. The mean expectation for the entire smolt migration, $\bar{E}$, is based on the cost of migration and the average benefits derived. The thresholds for migration are normally distributed over a range of values and keyed to the rate of food intake, rate of intraspecific encounters, or some other correlate of estuary suitability. During late summer (August), conditions in the Koksoak estuary are such that $h_e \cong h_m M$; h_m is probably relatively constant because of the size of the marine habitat, whereas M could vary with conditions of passage. As Baker (1978) argued, $\bar{E}$ has been selected and is built into the response strategy of the particular stock. In years when larger numbers of smolts are in the estuary, the advantage is tipped in favour of migration because of intraspecific competition for resources. As smolts depart, conditions improve for the remainder, but a smaller proportion remains than in years when the smolt output is small. Included in the measure of h_e are the effects of any interspecific competition for resources as well as variations in estuary productivity. The result is an equilibrium condition in which the proportion of anadromous migrants varies and the nonmigrants' potential reproductive success balances that of the migrants. Support for this comes from a greater incidence of iteroparity and a higher relative fecundity amongst estuary salmon (Robitaille et al. 1984a), which suggests they can make the same contribution to future generations as large 2-sea-winter salmon. Losers in this would seem to be the mixed growth salmon who run the risks and incur the costs of migration but return at a smaller size and hence are less fecund than 2-sea-winter females. Larger smolts tend to have higher survival rates (Lindroth 1985) and mixed growth salmon may well balance their contributions to future generations with those of estuary salmon and multi-sea-winter salmon if their large sizes at migration are associated with low marine mortality rates.

The above discussion becomes even more interesting when the Koksoak data are examined more closely. The growth data suggest that the estuary salmon maintain a growth rate that is constant from year to year. This could be considered a threshold value below which it is better to migrate than stay. The Koroc River postmolts clearly cannot maintain this and must migrate (Figure 6). The estuaries of the George and Whale rivers are more funnel shaped and open than that of the Koksoak, and estuary and mixed growth salmon seem rare there. The Leaf River estuary may operate more like the Koksoak in that there is a large semienclosed basin, Leaf Bay, at its mouth. A few large postmolts, 26.6–37.6 cm long, were caught there in 1963 (Power 1969). The critical factors are the size of the estuary and its suitability in relation to the size of the smolt run.

In northern rivers with large estuaries, the possibility for terminating seaward migration at this point exists. Such a habitat is an oasis of warm, productive water and a long migration is required to arrive in an area offering equal or better conditions. Smolt output tends to be low because of low productivity in the river ecosystems and because, in Ungava, stock selection has been for large smolt sizes. In southern rivers, the balance is different. Smolt runs are large relative to estuary space and there are not the same thermal and productivity gradients to cross in entering the sea.

Changes in the proportions of Koksoak salmon migrating beyond the estuary varied in the years 1961–1969 and 1979–1985. The proportion of fish appearing in catch samples that had followed estuary or mixed growth migration tracks was quite low until 1968 when it rose above 10%; in 1969 it was 19.2%. Commercial fishing began in 1961 with the purchase of new nets and opening of the Inuit cooperative's cleaning and packaging facility. Catches of Atlantic salmon must have increased considerably, but this cannot be documented. Most progeny of Atlantic salmon spawning in 1961 would have migrated seaward between 1965 and 1967; 2 or 3 years later they would have appeared in catches as either mixed growth or estuary salmon; 1 or 2 years later they would have appeared as grilse or 2-sea-winter salmon. If spawning escapement became greatly reduced with the advent of the fishery, then smolt output could have been reduced 4–6 years later if there were no compensatory adjustments in parr survival. According to the migration model, this would result in a greater proportion of smolts remaining in the estuary. Since the fishery continued with similar intensity to 1969, depressed stocks would have continued to produce small smolt runs and higher incidences of estuary salmon. There are no reliable records of what happened during the 1970s. Fishing effort seems to have declined somewhat until the latter part of the decade when harvest studies, in connection with the James Bay hydroelectric project, focussed attention on subsistence catches. Later, monies available under the hunter support program encouraged the purchase of new gear so that, by 1977 and through to 1981, Atlantic salmon harvests rose to a high level again (Gillis and Kemp 1983). During this period, speed boats and large outboard engines were purchased, which enabled Inuit to visit their nets more easily and quickly. At the same time, several cabins were constructed at fishing sites, enabling fishermen and their families to live there more comfortably all summer. These changes, combined with some entrepreneurial fishing operations, have combined to sustain a high level of fishing effort in the Koksoak estuary. This effort is not only directed at Atlantic salmon but also at other species which are potential competitors, such as anadromous brook trout and Arctic char. It is tempting to suggest that the drop in abundance of estuary salmon in 1982 and 1983 was related to reduced fishing 7 and 8 years previously, but this is speculative in the absence of catch records.

In conclusion, Baker's (1978) migration model provides a good conceptual framework for discussion of migration and life history of Ungava Atlantic salmon. The data available can be explained by reference to this model and the hypothesis relating to estuary habitat suitability fits best with our observations. This model explains the apparent paradox that estuary salmon have increased in abundance even though such fish are liable to capture in estuarine fisheries during most of their growing and feeding life, whereas sea migrants are only exposed to the nets during their passage through the estuary.

Acknowledgments

The data in this paper were collected over 25 years by many persons, all of whom we thank for their contributions. Rather than single out any individual for special mention, this paper is dedicated to John P. Gleave, who collected data from the Koksoak fishery in 1961 and 1962. He lost his life in a canoe accident in September 1962 returning from a search for salmon spawning areas. Over the years, support was provided by the Department of Indian and Northern Affairs, the National Research Council, the Natural Sciences and Engineering Research Council, the Makivik Corporation, and the Government of Quebec.

References

Baker, R. R. 1978. The evolutionary ecology of animal migration. Hodder and Stoughton, London, England.

Cook, P. M. 1984. Directional information from surface swell: some possibilities. Pages 79–101 in McCleave et al. (1984).

Côté, Y., and I. Babos. 1984. Caractéristiques scalimétriques des saumons du Koksoak (Ungava, Québec). Naturaliste canadien (Québec) 111:401–409.

Dunbar, M. J. 1952. The Ungava Bay problem. Arctic 5:4–16.

Dunbar, M. J. 1958. Physical oceanographic results of the "Calanus" expeditions in Ungava Bay, Frobisher Bay, Cumberland Sound, Hudson Strait and northern Hudson Bay, 1949–1955. Journal of the Fisheries Research Board of Canada 15:155–201.

Dunbar, M. J. 1982. Twentieth century marine climate change in the northwest Atlantic and subarctic regions. NAFO (Northwest Atlantic Fisheries Organization) Scientific Council Studies 5:7–15.

Gillis, D. J., and W. B. Kemp. 1983. The Koksoak River Fishery 1977–1981, a summary report. Makivik Corporation, Manuscript Report, Westmount, Canada.

Gross, M. R. 1987. Evolution of diadromy in fishes. American Fisheries Society Symposium 1:14–25.

Lapierre, S. 1984. The salmon of the Koksoak. Hydro-Quebec, Montreal, Canada.

Legendre, P., and V. Legendre. 1984. Postglacial dispersal of freshwater fishes in the Québec peninsula. Canadian Journal of Fisheries and Aquatic Sciences 41:1781–1802.

LeJeune, R., and V. Legendre. 1968. Extension d'aire du saumon d'eau douce (Salmo salar) au Québec. Naturaliste canadien (Québec) 95:1169–1173.

Lindroth, A. 1985. The Swedish salmon smolt releases in the Baltic. Norstedts Tryckeri, Stockholm, Sweden.

Lynn, R. 1984. Measuring physical-oceanographic features relevant to the migration of fishes. Pages 471–486 in McCleave et al. (1984).

May, A. W. 1973. Distribution and migration of salmon in the northwest Atlantic. International Atlantic Salmon Foundation Special Publication Series 4:373–382.

McCleave, J. D., G. P. Arnold, J. J. Dodson, and W. H. Neill, editors. 1984. Mechanisms of migration in fishes. Plenum, New York, New York, USA.

MLCP and SAGE (Ministere du Loisir, de la Chasse et de la Pêche and Societe d'Amenagement General de l'Environnement Ltee). 1980. Etude des populations de saumons du Fleuve Koksoak 2: effets possibles de la reduction de debit de la rivière Caniapiscau sur les populations de saumons. Societe d'Energie de la Baie James, Groupe d'Etude Conjoint Caniapscau-Koksoak. Manuscript report, Montreal, Canada.

Power, G. 1961. Salmon investigations on the Whale River, Ungava in 1960 and the development of an Eskimo fishery for salmon in Ungava Bay. Arctic 14:119–120.

Power, G. 1969. The salmon of Ungava Bay. Arctic Institute of North America Technical Paper 22.

Power, G. 1976. History of the Hudson's Bay Company salmon fisheries in the Ungava Bay region. Polar Record 18:151–161.

Power, G. 1980. The brook charr, Salvelinus fontinalis. Pages 141–203 in E. K. Balon, editor. Charrs: salmonid fishes of the genus Salvelinus. Dr. W. Junk, The Hague, The Netherlands.

Power, G. 1981. Stock characteristics and catches of Atlantic salmon (Salmo salar) in Quebec, and Newfoundland and Labrador in relation to environmental variables. Canadian Journal of Fisheries and

Aquatic Sciences 38:1601–1611.

Power, G., and D. Cressman. 1975. Atlantic salmon *(Salmo salar)* taken in the sea in north Labrador. Journal of the Fisheries Research Board of Canada 32:307–309.

Reddin, D. G., and J. B. Dempson. 1986. Origin of Atlantic salmon (*Salmo salar* L.) caught at sea near Nain, Labrador. Naturaliste canadien (Québec) 113:211–218.

Reddin, D. G., and J. J. Murray. 1985. Environmental conditions in the northwest Atlantic in relation to salmon catches at west Greenland. International Council for Exploration of the Sea, Anadromous Catadromous Fisheries Committee, C.M. 195/M:10, Copenhagen, Denmark.

Reddin, D. G., and W. M. Shearer. 1987. Sea-surface temperature and distribution of Atlantic salmon in the northwest Atlantic Ocean. American Fisheries Society Symposium 1:262–275.

Robitaille, J. A., Y. Côté, G. Hayeur, and G. Shooner. 1984a. Particularités de la reproduction du saumon atlantique *(Salmo salar)* dans une partie du réseau Koksoak, en Ungava. Canadian Technical Report of Fisheries and Aquatic Sciences 1313.

Robitaille, J. A., Y. Côté, G. Shooner, and G. Hayeur. 1984b. Croissance estuarienne du saumon atlantique *(Salmo salar)* dans le fleuve Koksoak, en Ungava. Canadian Technical Report of Fisheries and Aquatic Sciences 1314.

Robitaille, J. A., Y. Côté, G. Shooner, and G. Hayeur. 1986. Growth and maturation patterns of Atlantic salmon *(Salmo salar)* in the Koksoak River, Ungava, Québec. Canadian Special Publication of Fisheries and Aquatic Sciences 89:62–69.

Trites, R. W. 1982. Overview of oceanographic conditions in NAFO subareas 2, 3 and 4 during the 1970–79 decade. NAFO (Northwest Atlantic Fisheries Organization) Scientific Council Studies 5:51–78.

Turner, L. M. 1885. Fishes of Ungava district, Hudson's Bay Territory. Smithsonian Institute, Manuscript Report, Washington, D.C., USA.

Weihs, D. 1984. Bioenergetic considerations in fish migration. Pages 487–508 in McCleave et al. (1984).

Westerberg, H. 1984. The orientation of fish and the vertical stratification at fine- and micro-structure scales. Pages 179–203 in McCleave et al. (1984).

American Fisheries Society Symposium 1:377–388, 1987

Perspectives on the Marine Migrations of Diadromous Fishes[1]

THOMAS P. QUINN

School of Fisheries, WH-10, University of Washington, Seattle, Washington 98195, USA

WILLIAM C. LEGGETT

Department of Biology, McGill University, Montreal, Quebec H3A 1B1, Canada

Abstract.—Anadromous and catadromous fishes often migrate long distances in coastal and oceanic waters. While research has succeeded in describing the general features of the migrations (distribution, routes, and timing), the underlying proximate and ultimate factors affecting migrations are poorly understood. This paper advances the view that interpretation of descriptive information will generally benefit from insights derived from allied disciplines. Specifically, detailed information on fish distributions should be related to physical and biological characteristics of the ocean. General knowledge of currents, temperatures, and salinities and of distributions of prey, competitors, and predators must be refined and applied to migratory fish research. Migration reflects the internal state of the fish, including changes in hormones associated with osmoregulatory and reproductive physiology, and the preeminent biological needs of the fish at that time—such as predator avoidance, travel, growth, or reproduction. The influence of oceanographic features may vary substantially depending upon the motivational state of the fish involved. The proximate responses of the fish will, in turn, depend upon the evolutionary pressures that shaped the migratory pattern. These points are devloped and illustrated with reference to the ocean migrations of anadromous and catadromous species.

The spatial and temporal changes in distribution of diadromous fishes have been defined for several economically important species, though conspicuous gaps in information persist for even the best-studied ones. The movements of other species are known only vaguely. The process of studying fish migrations generally begins when the spawning and rearing areas for the species are located. The routes between those areas and the timing of movement can then be determined. Once the "bare bones" of the migration have been described, more sophisticated hypotheses can be proposed to explain the proximate (physiological and environmental) and ultimate (evolutionary: Gross 1987, this volume) factors influencing the migration and attendant aspects of the life history of the species.

This review will focus only on recent progress made by integrating data on the dynamics of the physical and biological environment with descriptive studies of migratory behavior. Physical features such as temperature, tides, currents, salinity, and frontal systems are important because they may limit spawning areas or times. Currents can help, hinder, or direct the migrations of adult fishes (Dodson and Leggett 1973), and can have a

major influence on the distribution of eggs and larval forms (Fortier and Leggett 1982; Power 1982). Biotic factors such as the abundance and patchiness of potential prey items, competitors, and predators may have both proximate and evolutionary influences on the seasonal and geographical patterns of spawning and feeding (Fortier and Leggett 1982; Frank and Leggett 1982, 1983a, 1983b). While oceanography will influence marine migrations in general, its impact on diadromous migrations is complicated by the marked changes experienced by the fish as they move between marine and freshwater habitats.

Rather than review the available descriptive studies on diadromous fish migrations, this paper (1) briefly examines the range of spawning and rearing environments used by diadromous fishes by way of illustrating that these animals are a subset of the much larger group of migratory fishes, (2) considers some of the constraints on the varied migratory strategies that derive from a basic definition of migration, and (3) reviews recent developments in migration research on sockeye salmon *Oncorhynchus nerka* and Atlantic eels *Anguilla* spp. that reflect the trend towards integration with oceanography.

Continuum of Migratory Life History Patterns

While the terms "anadromous" and "catadro-

---

[1]Contribution 711 from the School of Fisheries, University of Washington.

mous'' suggest distinct migratory strategies, examination of the life histories of fishes reveals a continuum of migratory patterns (McDowall 1987, this volume). In an extreme form of catadromy, American eels *Anguilla rostrata* and European eels *A. anguilla* spawn in an oceanographically defined environment and rear in rivers and lakes (Bozeman et al. 1985; McCleave et al. 1987, this volume). Migration to estuaries rather than to fresh water is a very common pattern shown by, for example, Atlantic menhaden *Brevoortia tyrannus,* spot *Leiostomus xanthurus,* Atlantic croaker *Micropogonias undulatus,* and the flounders *Paralichthys* spp. (Nelson et al. 1979; Miller e al. 1985). It has been estimated that nearly 80% of the commercial fisheries catch on the Atlantic and Gulf of Mexico coasts derives from species which spawn in the ocean but rear in estuaries (Miller et al. 1985). Some marine fishes spawn offshore but rear in nearshore areas rather than in estuaries. For example, sablefish *Anoplopoma fimbria* spawn over the north Pacific continental slope and juveniles migrate inshore to rear in inlets, bays, and sounds. They subsequently return to offshore waters where they exist as loosely defined stocks (Melteff 1983). The pelagic scombrids extend the continuum from high to low reliance on fresh or coastal waters for rearing to its extreme. In such fishes, migrations are not directed to specific geographical locations but to oceanic regions (Strasburg 1960; Harden Jones 1968; Miller 1979), and stocks may be difficult to identify (Laurs and Wetherall 1980).

Many fishes that live at sea migrate to nearshore, estuarine, or freshwater sites to spawn. Some amount of homing often occurs by these fishes, arrayed along a continuum towards anadromy. Herring *Clupea harengus* spawn demersal eggs on subtidal substrates. Wheeler and Winters (1984) reported an 81% average homing to the area of previous spawning by Atlantic herring *C. h. harengus* in Newfoundland, Canada. Hourston (1982) reported similar results with Pacific herring *C. h. pallasi* spawning along British Columbia. There is less evidence, however, that herring home to the site where they were spawned. A substantial period of juvenile residence at a site may be a prerequisite for subsequent homing (as in salmon, for example), but technical problems limit our ability to study homing in species with small larvae. American shad *Alosa sapidissima* and striped bass *Morone saxatilis* rear in broadly defined offshore waters and have predictable seasonal changes in distribution (Boreman and Lewis 1987, this volume; Dadswell et al. 1987, this volume), and they typically spawn in the lower reaches of large rivers (Mansuetti and Kolb 1953; Leggett 1976). Evidence indicates that these species home to their natal rivers (Carscadden and Leggett 1975; Berggren and Lieberman 1978; Melvin et al. 1986).

While the Salmonidae are famous for the extreme anadromy displayed by some members, a substantial range of anadromy exists in this group (Rounsefell 1958). Pink salmon *Oncorhynchus gorbuscha* generally do not feed in fresh water and tend to spawn in the lower reaches of rivers, sometimes within tidal influence. Freshwater residence by juveniles is very brief as they are physiologically adapted for seawater upon emergence from the redd and migrate to sea at once. Their marine migrations take them into the open ocean for a full year before they return to fresh water to spawn (Takagi et al. 1980). In contrast to pink salmon, coho salmon *O. kisutch* typically spend 1 year or more in fresh water prior to seaward migration and their marine migrations are often restricted to coastal waters (Godfrey 1965). The family also includes species which make only limited use of the ocean for rearing and which feed extensively in fresh water as adults (e.g., brook trout *Salvelinus fontinalis*) or are restricted to fresh water (lake trout *S. namaycush*). Other members of the family such as Dolly Varden *S. malma* and Arctic char *S. alpinus* may have complex patterns of migration between freshwater and coastal environments (Armstrong 1984; Dempson and Kristofferson 1987, this volume). While one might expect that extensive use of distant oceanic feeding grounds would be associated with shorter freshwater residence, no such tradeoff is evident. Sockeye salmon typically remain in fresh water for at least a year prior to seaward migration, and fully freshwater populations exist, yet their oceanic distribution is as broad as that of chum salmon *Oncorhynchus keta,* a species with limited freshwater residence (French et al. 1976; Neave et al. 1976). Within the family, iteroparous species are more often freshwater residents than semelparous ones (species transplanted into the North American Great Lakes are discounted here). Distances travelled at sea do not seem to vary systematically between semelparous and iteroparous species; Atlantic salmon *Salmo salar* and steelhead *S. gairdneri* migrate long distances, as do many of the Pacific salmon (*Oncorhynchus*) species.

A variety of fishes spawn in fresh water and

migrate within fresh water to the lower reaches of the river system or its estuary for rearing (e.g., shortnose sturgeon *Acipenser brevirostrum:* Buckley and Kynard 1985). There are, of course, many fishes which spawn in rivers and rear in lakes. Repeat spawning in the same site has been documented for white suckers *Catostomus commersoni* (Werner 1979), roach *Rutilus rutilus* (L'Abée-Lund and Vøllestad 1985), and many salmonids.

In contrast to the upstream spawning migration of many adult fishes, certain South American fishes migrate substantial distances downstream to spawn in the lower reaches of large rivers (reviewed by Lowe-McConnell 1975). This pattern is extended to include estuarine or coastal spawning by such species as the barramundi *Lates calcarifer* (Griffin 1987, this volume). A wide variety of species exhibit varying degrees of catadromy (McDowall 1987), and the use of offshore spawning areas, paired with longer freshwater residence, completes the continuum back to the anguillid eels.

Constraints on Migration

While definitions of migration vary, most researchers use the term to describe temporally and spatially coordinated movements of large numbers of animals. Temporal coordination consists of initiation and cessation of movement and cyclic patterns of activity during migration. Spatial coordination of animals' movements results from passive and active processes. For fishes, the water flow in rivers and the tidal, coastal, and oceanic currents are the primary sources of passive transport. Active movement has been divided by Griffin (1955) into three categories: piloting (use of remembered features or landmarks), orientation (maintenance of a compass heading), and navigation (goal-directed movement across unfamiliar areas). These distinctions provide a framework for evaluating the mechanisms underlying migration.

The migrations of diadromous fishes have the general characteristics described above but they also have three special features associated with the transition between marine and freshwater environments. First, the fishes experience marked changes in the water through which they move. Salinity, flow regime (velocity and directional characteristics), prey and predator communities, and many other features distinguish the environments which diadromous fishes experience in a relatively brief period of time. Second, because

the water is changing, the sensory mechanisms guiding migration are also likely to change as the fish move between a river and the ocean. Many mechanisms may be involved in fish migration (McCleave et al. 1984). The relative importance of these mechanisms probably changes with the environments. Third, the fishes themselves undergo substantial physiological changes as they prepare for larval metamorphosis or reproduction, and as they adjust to the new ionic environments. Thus, when we study diadromous migrants, we are studying fishes whose physiology and behavior are not fixed in time or space. Their changing motivational states are a major confounding factor in migration research.

Knowledge of marine migrations is usually inferred from changes in abundance over time and space and from mark–recapture studies. Data from such sources suffer the obvious limitation of being biased by the distribution of fishing effort (Leggett 1977). When migration is studied, the term's definition may serve as a useful focus for research directions: what are the proximate and ultimate factors influencing the temporal and spatial changes in fish distribution? Displacement results from the movement of the water and the movement of fish within the water. Thus, particular care must be used in determining the movement patterns of the water, the locomotor capacity of the fishes (Webb 1975; Weihs 1984, 1987, this volume) and the directedness of the movements. For example, recaptures of immature sockeye salmon on the high seas indicate relatively slow net movement (about 32 km/d: French et al. 1976). They probably do not actually swim slowly (Ware 1978) but their movements may not be highly directed, lowering net displacement. Maturing sockeye salmon, however, travel much more rapidly (up to 60 km/d and more: French et al. 1976; Groot and Quinn, in press) and their movements appear to be highly oriented (Quinn and Groot 1984).

Optimal feeding and spawning times in geographically distant regions require fishes to correctly time their migrations. Those that arrive on the spawning grounds too early or late may encounter inappropriate environmental conditions for spawning, the incubation of eggs, or larval development. The importance of population-specific spawning time for progeny survival has been illustrated by studies on sockeye salmon (Goodlad et al. 1974; Brannon, in press) and American shad (Leggett 1985).

Fishes that arrive on the spawning grounds

prematurely may be vulnerable to predation if concentrated in small areas, and this may favor individuals that mature en route to the spawning grounds rather than on site. The timing and orientation of migration is not only influenced by the window of ecologically acceptable spawning times but also by any costs of early departure from the feeding grounds such as smaller size at maturity, lower fecundity, smaller eggs, or some combination of effects. In general, environmental conditions in fresh water, especially water flow and temperature, are more locally variable and change more rapidly than do oceanic conditions. For this reason, migrations to freshwater and estuarine sites are likely to be more precisely timed and directed than migrations to oceanic regions.

Sockeye Salmon Migrations

The remainder of this paper will emphasize recent research on sockeye salmon and Atlantic eel migrations and illustrate the benefits of integrating such work with oceanography. Sockeye salmon commence marine migration in the spring, typically after 1 year in a lake. These salmon, known as smolts, enter a radically different physical and biological environment from their nursery lake or the river that they descended to reach the sea. In the case of British Columbia's Fraser River, most smolts enter the estuary between mid-April and late May, near the river's period of peak discharge (Thomson 1981). Depending upon the tide, the vertical profiles of temperature and salinity may vary considerably (Thomson 1981). The combined river and tidal velocities generally exceed the smolts' 24–34-cm/s swimming capacity. The smolts migrate north along the mainland and the east side of Vancouver Island (Healey and Groot 1987, this volume). Depending upon whether they enter the estuary on a flooding or ebbing tide, the smolts will encounter currents that will facilitate or hinder northward travel. Thus, their displacement seems to result from an interaction between their northward swimming and the relatively strong reversing currents. These fish experience dramatic decreases in surface temperature and increases in salinity as they leave the Strait of Georgia (Thomson et al. 1985), and must negotiate narrow channels with rapid, reversing tidal currents (up to 10–20 km/h in some areas). It is not known how the smolts respond to such tidal currents, but they reach the northern end of Vancouver Island and presumably join the band of juveniles migrating northward parallel to the coast (Hartt 1980).

Fraser River sockeye salmon generally spend 2½ years at sea, feeding over a large area (French et al. 1976) and subject to interannual variations in temperature and currents (Schumacher and Reed 1983; Tabata 1983, 1984; Mysak 1985) and in zooplankton biomass (Frost 1983) and species composition (Fulton and LeBrasseur 1985). Interannual changes in sockeye salmon distribution at sea are not sufficiently well documented to permit correlation with oceanic variations. However, the homeward migrations of maturing sockeye salmon show correlations with oceanic temperatures. Burgner (1980) reported that warm temperatures at sea were associated with early arrival of sockeye salmon to Bristol Bay, Alaska. Blackbourn (in press) also found that early arrival of Alaskan runs was correlated with warm oceanic conditions, but found the opposite pattern for populations returning to the Fraser River. Blackbourn (in press) proposed that the oceanic distribution is directly or indirectly affected by water temperature: the fish are farther north than usual when the waters are warm and farther south when cold (Figure 1). This model implies that sockeye salmon begin their homeward migration at a stock-specific date and at a fixed speed; return timing is affected chiefly by the distance to be travelled. In this model, the factors affecting oceanic feeding movements and distribution are essentially independent of the homeward migration from the high seas to coastal waters. However, Fujii (1975) presented evidence that cold, high-salinity water in the Aleutian passes can delay the entry of maturing sockeye salmon into Bristol Bay from the Gulf of Alaska. Entry into the bay occurred when the fronts were dissipated by tide and wind.

The assumption of fixed date of departure requires that sockeye salmon possess a precise timing mechanism. A mechanism based on day length presents problems for pelagic migrants with broad distributions because day length and rate of change of day length vary substantially with latitude. For example, Bristol Bay sockeye salmon might experience day lengths differing by as much as 150 min in June (Quinn 1982).

Not only run timing but migratory routes of sockeye salmon have been correlated with oceanographic conditions. The route taken by Fraser River sockeye salmon around Vancouver Island may be influenced by temperature, salinity, or river discharge (IPSFC 1984; Hamilton 1985;

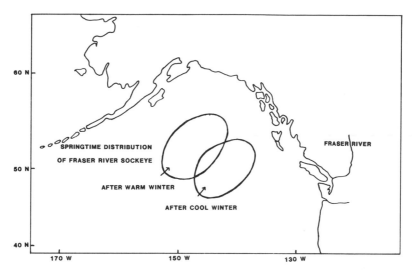

FIGURE 1.—A simple temperature displacement model proposed to explain the statistical relationship between oceanic temperatures and the timing of sockeye salmon runs to the Fraser River (from Blackbourn, in press).

Groot and Quinn, in press). Warm water temperatures have been associated with larger proportions of Fraser River sockeye salmon using the northern route. This is generally consistent with Blackbourn's (in press) model of more northerly distribution in warm years. Less is known about interannual variations in oceanic current patterns than is known about variations in temperature. However, Hamilton and Mysak (1986) proposed that there is a relationship between migrations of pink and sockeye salmon to the Skeena and Nass rivers in British Columbia and the appearance of a large current feature, the Sitka Eddy in the Gulf of Alaska.

Studies indicating the influence of temperature on fish distribution and migration are by no means restricted to sockeye salmon. Reddin and Shearer (1987, this volume) analyzed Atlantic salmon catch data and concluded that temperature and, to a lesser extent, food availability influence the oceanic distribution of this species. Dempson and Kristofferson (1987) correlated run timing of Arctic char with oceanic temperatures. Correlations, however, do not identify the link between the physical factors and fish migratory behavior. Ultimately, anadromous fishes probably go to sea because they can grow faster there than in fresh water. In order to realize this potential increase in growth, they must strike a balance between food availability and optimal temperature for food conversion. In this regard, correlations of fish distribution and temperature may represent either a direct effect of temperature on the fish, activating

preference or avoidance responses, or an indirect effect on prey abundance to which the fish respond. Attempts to model the responses of fishes to environmental conditions hold promise for explaining the feeding distributions of some species (Neill 1979, 1984). However, behavioral thermoregulation does not appear adequate, as a guidance mechanism, to explain the rapid movement of fishes through complex thermal regimes (Dadswell et al. 1987; Power et al. 1987, this volume; Groot and Quinn, in press). It is unlikely that temperature serves to direct rapid migrations, hence correlations with migratory routes and timing probably result from direct or indirect influences on feeding distribution prior to migration.

It has long been known that most salmon that leave fresh water as juveniles and enter the ocean never return. Since almost all of those that do return to fresh water spawn in their natal stream, it has been assumed that the rest die of natural causes or at the hands of fishermen. Harden Jones (1968) was skeptical of this explanation and proposed that a substantial number of salmon are lost at sea owing to disorientation. In an expansion of this position, Harden Jones (1984) noted that there is a region of the north Pacific Ocean from which no tagged salmon had been recovered in coastal areas. This region is oceanographically different from the northern regions where salmon are more abundant, being much less stratified, and he hypothesized that this feature makes homeward orientation difficult for salmon. While this hypothesis is intriguing, a more parsimonious explanation is that the absence of tag returns from this area was an artifact of natural, tag-induced, and fishing mortality. Most salmon in this region are immature and relatively small, and suffer higher rates of natural and tag-induced mortality than maturing salmon tagged farther north. Moreover, these salmon are primarily of Asian origin and, consequently, are very susceptible to the extensive Japanese drift-net fishery on the high seas. In recent years, this fishery has been reduced, and 69 salmon tagged in the area in question have since been recovered in coastal waters (C. Harris, University of Washington, personal communication). This example provides a cautionary note on the dangers of inferring too much about migration from tagging studies. While large tagging data sets (e.g., Hourston 1982; Wheeler and Winters 1984; Boreman and Lewis 1987; Dadswell et al. 1987; A. L. Meister, Atlantic Sea Run Salmon Commission, personal communication) generally serve as the basis for understanding migrations, they are almost always biased by nonrandom effort in tag application and recovery.

Some of the problems with conventional mark–recapture studies can be reduced by use of telemetry. A recent ultrasonic tracking study has indicated that sockeye salmon migrating to the Fraser River through coastal waters may experience 6–8°C changes in surface temperature and 2–4‰ changes in salinity over tens of kilometers in certain areas (Quinn and terHart, in press). Sockeye salmon were surface oriented in waters with little or no stratification (Figure 2). However, they often crossed the thermocline or halocline when one was present. No particular temperature or salinity was preferred; neither did the fish consistently prefer the warmest or least saline water available to them (Figure 3). Orientation to the thermocline is consistent with the findings of Westerberg (1982) and Døving et al. (1985) on Atlantic salmon. Westerberg (1984) proposed that salmon orient in estuarine systems by using the current shear at the thermocline as a reference for olfactory-based rheotactic responses to water from the home river. Alternative hypotheses (not all mutually exclusive) for orientation in regions with reversing tidal currents include the conditioning of rheotactic responses by olfaction (Dodson and Dohse 1984), the selective use of tidal currents (Arnold and Cook 1984), and the maintenance of a compass direction. Detailed, simultaneous records of current speed and direction and fish movement are needed to evaluate these hypotheses. One of the few tracking studies

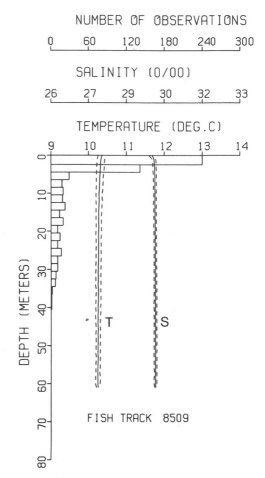

FIGURE 2.—Amount of time spent in relation to depth by a sockeye salmon (bars) tracked in waters with no vertical stratification of temperature (T) or salinity (S) (from Quinn and terHart, in press).

which recorded currents indicated that Atlantic salmon swimming speed and direction were quite constant, relative to the water. However, the reversing tidal currents caused the ground speed and direction to vary considerably (Smith et al. 1981; Hawkins and Urquhart 1983; Figure 4).

Atlantic Eel Migrations

The influence of oceanographic conditions on diadromous migrations is also well illustrated by studies on anguillid eels. Considerable progress has been made towards unravelling the complex migrations of these fishes in the Atlantic Ocean, and many of the principles may apply to the even more enigmatic Australasian eels as well (Jellyman 1987, this volume). The transport of larvae from the spawning grounds is strongly

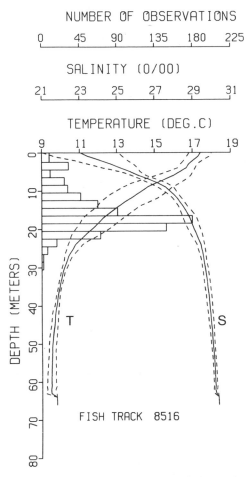

FIGURE 3.—Amount of time spent in relation to depth by a sockeye salmon (bars) tracked in waters with distinct vertical stratification of temperature (T) and salinity (S) (from Quinn and terHart, in press).

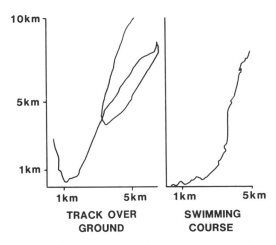

FIGURE 4.—Movement of a telemetered Atlantic salmon relative to the ground (left), and the actual swimming course of the fish (right) when currents were discounted (from Hawkins and Urquhart 1983).

influenced by the current regime in the area (Schoth and Tesch 1982; Kleckner and McCleave 1982, 1985), and can be modelled from a knowledge of currents (Power and McCleave 1982). However, detrainment from the Gulf Stream to the North American coast may involve active, oriented migration (Kleckner and McCleave 1985). One complex issue is how the larvae of European and American eels segregate themselves to their respective continents. Evidence indicates that the distributions of the leptocephali of the two species overlap considerably (McCleave et al. 1987). What current regimes or patterns of larval behavior ensure that the species remain separate? What selective pressures maintain these differences, as eels seem to be capable of inhabiting rivers from the coast of the Carib-

bean Sea to Greenland? Metamorphosis from leptocephalus to glass eel occurs in coastal waters, and young eels appear to use selective tidal stream transport to ascend rivers (McCleave and Kleckner 1982; Sheldon and McCleave 1985; McCleave and Wippelhauser 1987, this volume). The selective use of tidal currents for movement through estuaries or retention within them may be common to various fishes, but the actual manner in which it is accomplished is not yet clear.

After several years in fresh water, the American and European eels descend rivers, traverse estuarine and coastal waters, and migrate to the Sargasso Sea, their putative spawning grounds. Ultrasonic telemetry of European eels revealed that they swim deep (100–300 m: Tesch 1978a, 1978b), but many did not swim towards the Sargasso Sea (Tesch 1978a, 1978b, 1979) and there was no clear relationship between swimming depth and water conditions. Other tracking studies have led to the conclusions that eel migrations may be guided by avoidance of cold water (Westin and Nyman 1979), or by positive rheotaxis guided by electric currents induced by movement relative to the earth's magnetic field (Westerberg 1979). McCleave and Kleckner (1985) hypothesized that these guidance mechanisms need only produce a modest southerly bias in orientation to facilitate successful homing of American eels to the Sargasso Sea (a southwesterly bias is needed for European eels). Homing can, in principle, be achieved by the interplay of weak directional biases with the ocean circulation experienced by members of the two species. There may be no need to propose highly accurate orientation to explain the migration of eels. Conceptually, it is safer to assume relatively simple behavioral models to explain migration unless the data compel acceptance of sophisticated navigational mechanisms (Leggett 1984). However, natural selection exacts a severe penalty from fish whose movements are poorly coordinated with the environmental cycles and with other members of the population.

Whatever the oceanic orientation mechanism that leads eels towards their spawning grounds, some cue would seem necessary to terminate the migration. A persistent oceanic front oriented along the east–west axis of the Sargasso Sea at about 24–29°N latitude might signal an eel's arrival at its spawning site. The front, located in the North Atlantic Subtropical Convergence, has abrupt horizontal temperature and salinity changes in the upper 150–250 m of the water column (Voorhis 1969). Eels are believed to execute their southward migration in the upper mesopelagic or epipelagic zones. This vertical positioning would cause them to intersect and experience the physical and biological differences associated with the front (McCleave and Kleckner 1985; McCleave et al. 1987). McCleave et al. (1987) found the highest concentrations of newly hatched larvae in and to the south of the front over a large area along the east–west axis. This suggests that the front acts as the northern boundary of the spawning area and provides a signal to terminate the migration and commence spawning. The existence of the front may also play a role in concentrating eels in sufficient densities in the open ocean to achieve successful reproduction. McCleave et al. (1987) hypothesized that the unique biological community associated with the front may imbue the waters with a "bouquet" to which the leptocephali imprint, and to which the adults respond by terminating their migration and initiating reproduction.

In conclusion, the complex marine migrations of salmon and eels provide examples of the importance of oceanographic information in interpreting descriptive studies of migration. However, meaningful integration of oceanographic data with studies of fish movements is not a simple task. Data on physical features of the ocean must be collected on spatial scales which are appropriate to the movements of the fish (Leggett 1984). Moreover, the complex relationships between abiotic and biotic factors and fish migrations must be viewed with considerable care (Frank and Leggett 1985). The water is the fish's medium for life, its source of guidance information, and also a potential source of transportation. When migration is studied, the developmental state of the fish must be considered, as migratory behavior will be determined by the fish's motivation to respond to the myriad environmental variables that it can detect. Diadromy should be viewed as part of a continuum of migratory strategies for growth and reproductive success in fishes. Diadromy presents special problems in addition to those experienced by freshwater or marine species, but the value of examining migration in relation to the physical and biological environment is common to all studies of fish migration.

Acknowledgment

The authors gratefully acknowledge the Natural Sciences and Engineering Research Council of Canada (grants G-1485 and A-6513) for its contribution to the preparation of this paper.

References

Armstrong, R. H. 1984. Migration of anadromous Dolly Varden charr in southeastern Alaska—a manager's nightmare. Pages 549–570 in L. Johnson and B. L. Burns, editors. Biology of the Arctic charr: proceedings of the international symposium on Arctic charr. University of Manitoba Press, Winnipeg, Canada.

Arnold, G. P., and P. H. Cook. 1984. Fish migration by selective tidal stream transport: first results with a computer simulation model for the European continental shelf. Pages 227–261 in McCleave et al. (1984).

Berggren, T. J., and J. T. Lieberman. 1978. Relative contribution of the Hudson, Chesapeake and Roanoke striped bass, Morone saxatilis, stocks to the development of the Atlantic coast fishery. U.S. National Marine Fisheries Service Fishery Bulletin 76:335–345.

Blackbourn, D. J. In press. Sea surface temperature and the pre-season prediction of return timing in Fraser River sockeye. Canadian Special Publication of Fisheries and Aquatic Sciences.

Boreman, J., and R. R. Lewis. 1987. Atlantic coastal migration of striped bass. American Fisheries Society Symposium 1:331–339.

Bozeman, E. L., G. S. Helfman, and T. Richardson. 1985. Population size and home range of American eels in a Georgia tidal creek. Transactions of the American Fisheries Society 114:821–825.

Brannon, E. L. In press. Sockeye spawning time in relation to stream temperature and fry emergence. Canadian Special Publication of Fisheries and Aquatic Sciences.

Buckley, J., and B. Kynard. 1985. Yearly movements of shortnose sturgeons in the Connecticut River.

Transactions of the American Fisheries Society 114:813–820.

Burgner, R. L. 1980. Some features of ocean migration and timing of Pacific salmon. Pages 153–164 in W. J. McNeil and D. C. Himsworth, editors. Salmonid ecosystems of the north Pacific. Oregon State University Press, Corvallis, Oregon, USA.

Carscadden, J. E., and W. C. Leggett. 1975. Meristic differences in spawning populations of American shad, Alosa sapidissima: evidence for homing to tributaries in the St. John River, New Brunswick. Journal of the Fisheries Research Board of Canada 32:653–660.

Dadswell, M. J., G. D. Melvin, P. J. Williams, and D. E. Themelis. 1987. Influences of origin, life history, and chance on the Atlantic coast migration of American shad. American Fisheries Society Symposium 1:313–330.

Dempson, J. B., and A. H. Kristofferson. 1987. Spatial and temporal aspects of the ocean migration of anadromous Arctic char. American Fisheries Society Symposium 1:340–357.

Dodson, J. J., and L. A. Dohse. 1984. A model of olfactory-mediated conditioning of directional bias in fish migrating in reversing tidal currents based on the homing migration of American shad (Alosa sapidissima). Pages 263–281 in McCleave et al. (1984).

Dodson, J. J., and W. C. Leggett. 1973. Behavior of American shad (Alosa sapidissima) homing to the Connecticut River from Long Island Sound. Journal of the Fisheries Research Board of Canada 30:1847–1860.

Døving, K. B., H. Westerberg, and P. B. Johnsen. 1985. Role of olfaction in the behavioral and neuronal responses of Atlantic salmon, Salmo salar, to hydrographic stratification. Canadian Journal of Fisheries and Aquatic Sciences 42:1658–1667.

Fortier, L., and W. C. Leggett. 1982. Fickian transport and the dispersal of fish larvae in estuaries. Canadian Journal of Fisheries and Aquatic Sciences 39:1150–1163.

Frank, K. T., and W. C. Leggett. 1982. Coastal water mass replacement: its effect on zooplankton dynamics and the predator–prey complex associated with larval capelin (Mallotus villosus). Canadian Journal of Fisheries and Aquatic Sciences 39:991–1003.

Frank, K. T., and W. C. Leggett. 1983a. Multispecies larval fish associations: accident or adaptation? Canadian Journal of Fisheries and Aquatic Sciences 40:754–762.

Frank, K. T., and W. C. Leggett. 1983b. Survival value of an opportunistic life-stage transition in capelin (Mallotus villosus). Canadian Journal of Fisheries and Aquatic Sciences 40:1442–1448.

Frank, K. T., and W. C. Leggett. 1985. Reciprocal oscillations in densities of larval fish and potential predators: a reflection of present or past predation? Canadian Journal of Fisheries and Aquatic Sciences 42:1841–1849.

French, R., H. Bilton, M. Osako, and A. Hartt. 1976.

Distribution and origin of sockeye salmon (Oncorhynchus nerka) in offshore waters of the north Pacific Ocean. International North Pacific Fisheries Commission Bulletin 34.

Frost, B. W. 1983. Interannual variation of zooplankton standing stock in the open Gulf of Alaska. Pages 146–157 in W. S. Wooster, editor. From year to year: interannual variability of the environment and fisheries of the Gulf of Alaska and the eastern Bering Sea. University of Washington, Washington Sea Grant Program, Seattle, Washington, USA.

Fujii, T. 1975. On the relation between the homing migration of the western Alaska sockeye salmon, Oncorhynchus nerka (Walbaum), and oceanic conditions in the eastern Bering Sea. Memoirs of the Faculty of Fisheries, Hokkaido University 22:99–192.

Fulton, J. D., and R. J. LeBrasseur. 1985. Interannual shifting of the subarctic boundary and some of the biotic effects on juvenile salmonids. Pages 237–247 in W. S. Wooster and D. L. Fuharty, editors. El Niño north: Niño effects in the eastern subarctic Pacific Ocean. University of Washington, Washington Sea Grant Program, Seattle, Washington, USA.

Godfrey, H. 1965. Salmon of the north Pacific Ocean, part IX. Coho salmon. International North Pacific Fisheries Commission Bulletin 16.

Goodlad, J. C., T. W. Gjernes, and E. L. Brannon. 1974. Factors affecting sockeye salmon (Oncorhynchus nerka) growth in four lakes of the Fraser River system. Journal of the Fisheries Research Board of Canada 31:871–892.

Griffin, D. R. 1955. Bird navigation. Pages 154–197 in A. Wolfson, editor. Recent studies in avian biology. University of Illinois Press, Urbana, Illinois, USA.

Griffin, R. K. 1987. Life history, distribution, and seasonal migration of barramundi in the Daly River, Northern Territory, Australia. American Fisheries Society Symposium 1:358–363.

Groot, C., and T. P. Quinn. In press. The homing migration of sockeye salmon to the Fraser River. U.S. National Marine Fisheries Service Fishery Bulletin.

Gross, M. R. 1987. Evolution of diadromy in fishes. American Fisheries Society Symposium 1:14–25.

Hamilton, K. 1985. A study of the variability of the return migration route of Fraser River sockeye salmon (Oncorhynchus nerka). Canadian Journal of Zoology 63:1930–1943.

Hamilton, K., and L. A. Mysak. 1986. Possible effects of the Sitka Eddy on sockeye and pink salmon migration off southeast Alaska. Canadian Journal of Fisheries and Aquatic Sciences 43:498–504.

Harden Jones, F. R. 1968. Fish migration. Edward Arnold, London, England.

Harden Jones, F. R. 1984. A view from the ocean. Pages 1–26 in McCleave et al. (1984).

Hartt, A. C. 1980. Juvenile salmonids in the oceanic ecosystem—the critical first summer. Pages 25–57 in W. J. McNeil and D. C. Himsworth, editors. Salmonid ecosystems of the north Pacific. Oregon State University Press, Corvallis, Oregon, USA.

Hawkins, A. D., and G. G. Urquhart. 1983. Tracking fish at sea. Pages 103–166 in A. G. MacDonald and I. G. Priede, editors. Experimental biology at sea. Academic Press, London, England.

Healey, M. C., and C. Groot. 1987. Marine migration and orientation of ocean-type chinook and sockeye salmon. American Fisheries Society Symposium 1:298–312.

Hourston, A. S. 1982. Homing by Canada's west coast herring to management units and divisions as indicated by tag recoveries. Canadian Journal of Fisheries and Aquatic Sciences 39:1414–1422.

IPSFC (International Pacific Salmon Fisheries Commission). 1984. International Pacific Salmon Fisheries Commission Annual Report 1983.

Jellyman, D. J. 1987. Review of the marine life history of Australasian temperate species of Anguilla. American Fisheries Society Symposium 1:276–285.

Kleckner, R. C., and J. D. McCleave. 1982. Entry of migrating American eel leptocephali into the Gulf Stream system. Helgoländer Meeresuntersuchungen 35:329–339.

Kleckner, R. C., and J. D. McCleave. 1985. Spatial and temporal distribution of American eel larvae in relation to north Atlantic Ocean current systems. Dana 4:67–92.

L'Abée-Lund, J. H., and L. A. Vøllestad. 1985. Homing precision of roach Rutilus rutilus in Lake Arungen, Norway. Environmental Biology of Fishes 13:235–239.

Laurs, R. M., and J. A. Wetherall. 1981. Growth rates of north Pacific albacore, Thunnus alalunga, based on tag returns. U.S. National Marine Fisheries Service Fishery Bulletin 79:293–302.

Leggett, W. C. 1976. The American shad (Alosa sapidissima), with special reference to its migration and population dynamics in the Connecticut River. American Fisheries Society Monograph 1:169–225.

Leggett, W. C. 1977. The ecology of fish migrations. Annual Review of Ecology and Systematics 8:285–308.

Leggett, W. C. 1984. Fish migrations in coastal and estuarine environments: a call for new approaches to the study of an old problem. Pages 159–178 in McCleave et al. (1984).

Leggett, W. C. 1985. The role of migration in the life history evolution of fish. Contributions in Marine Science 27(supplement):277–295.

Lowe-McConnell, R. H. 1975. Fish communities in tropical freshwaters. Longman, London, England.

Mansuetti, R., and H. Kolb. 1953. A historical review of the shad fisheries of North America. Chesapeake Biological Laboratory, Publication 97, Solomons, Maryland, USA.

McCleave, J. D., G. P. Arnold, J. J. Dodson, and W. H. Neill, editors. 1984. Mechanisms of migration in fishes. Plenum, New York, New York, USA.

McCleave, J. D., and R. C. Kleckner. 1982. Selective tidal stream transport in the estuarine migration of glass eels of the American eel (Anguilla rostrata). Journal du Conseil, Conseil International pour l'Exploration de la Mer 40:262–271.

McCleave, J. D., and R. C. Kleckner. 1985. Oceanic migration of Atlantic eels (Anguilla spp.): adults and their offspring. Contributions in Marine Science 27(supplement):316–337.

McCleave, J. D., R. C. Kleckner, and M. Castonguay. 1987. Reproductive sympatry of American and European eels and implications for migration and taxonomy. American Fisheries Society Symposium 1:286–297.

McCleave, J. D., and G. S. Wippelhauser. 1987. Behavioral aspects of selective tidal stream transport in juvenile American eels. American Fisheries Society Symposium 1:138–150.

McDowall, R. M. 1987. The occurrence and distribution of diadromy among fishes. American Fisheries Society Symposium 1:1–13.

Melteff, B. R., editor. 1983. Proceedings of the international sablefish symposium. Alaska Sea Grant, Fairbanks, Alaska, USA.

Melvin, G. D., M. J. Dadswell, and J. D. Martin. 1986. Fidelity of American shad, Alosa sapidissima (Clupeidae), to its river of previous spawning. Canadian Journal of Fisheries and Aquatic Sciences 43:640–646.

Miller, J. M. 1979. Nearshore abundance of tuna (Pisces: Scombridae) larvae in the Hawaiian Islands. Bulletin of Marine Science 29:19–26.

Miller, J. M., L. B. Crowder, and M. L. Moser. 1985. Migration and utilization of estuarine nurseries by juvenile fishes: an evolutionary perspective. Contributions in Marine Science 27(supplement):338–352.

Mysak, L. A. 1985. On the interannual variability of eddies in the northeast Pacific Ocean. Pages 97–106 in W. S. Wooster and D. L. Fluharty, editors. El Niño north: Niño effects in the eastern subarctic Pacific Ocean. University of Washington, Washington Sea Grant Program, Seattle, Washington, USA.

Neave, F., T. Yonemori, and R. G. Bakkala. 1976. Distribution and origin of chum salmon in offshore waters of the north Pacific Ocean. International North Pacific Fisheries Commission Bulletin 35.

Neill, W. H. 1979. Mechanisms of fish distribution in heterothermal environments. American Zoologist 19:305–317.

Neill, W. H. 1984. Behavioral enviroregulation's role in fish migration. Pages 61–66 in McCleave et al. (1984).

Nelson, W. R., M. C. Ingham, and W. E. Schaff. 1979. Larval transport and year-class strength of Atlantic menhaden, Brevoortia tyrannus. U.S. National Marine Fisheries Service Fishery Bulletin 75:23–41.

Power, G., M. V. Power, R. Dumas, and A. Gordon. 1987. Marine migrations of Atlantic salmon from rivers in Ungava Bay, Quebec. American Fisheries Society Symposium 1:364-376.

Power, J. H. 1982. Advection, diffusion, and drift migrations of larval fish. Pages 27–37 in McCleave et al. (1984).

Power, J. H., and J. D. McCleave. 1982. Simulation of the North Atlantic ocean drift of Anguilla leptocephali. U.S. National Marine Fisheries Service Fishery

Bulletin 81:483–500.

Quinn, T. P. 1982. A model for salmon navigation on the high seas. Pages 229–237 *in* E. L. Brannon and E. O. Salo, editors. Proceedings of the salmon and trout migratory behavior symposium. University of Washington, School of Fisheries, Seattle, Washington, USA.

Quinn, T. P., and C. Groot. 1984. Pacific salmon (*Oncorhynchus*) migrations: orientation versus random movement. Canadian Journal of Fisheries and Aquatic Sciences 41:1319–1324.

Quinn, T. P., and B. A. terHart. In press. Movements of adult sockeye salmon in British Columbia coastal waters in relation to temperature and salinity stratification: ultrasonic telemetry results. Canadian Special Publication of Fisheries and Aquatic Sciences.

Reddin, D. G., and W. M. Shearer. 1987. Sea-surface temperature and distribution of Atlantic salmon in the northwest Atlantic Ocean. American Fisheries Society Symposium 1:262–275.

Rounsefell, G. A. 1958. Anadromy in North American Salmonidae. U.S. Fish and Wildlife Service Fishery Bulletin 58(131):171–185.

Schoth, M. and F.-W. Tesch. 1982. Spatial distribution of 0-group eel larvae (*Anguilla* sp.) in the Sargasso Sea. Helgoländer Meeresuntersuchungen 35:309–320.

Schumacher, J. D., and R. K. Reed. 1983. International variability in the abiotic environment of the Bering Sea and Gulf of Alaska. Pages 111–133 *in* W. S. Wooster, editor. From year to year: interannual variability of the environment and fisheries of the Gulf of Alaska and the eastern Bering Sea. University of Washington, Washington Sea Grant Program, Seattle, Washington, USA.

Sheldon, M. R., and J. D. McCleave. 1985. Abundance of glass eels of the American eel, *Anguilla rostrata*, in mid-channel and near shore during estuarine migration. Naturaliste Canadien (Review of Ecology and Systematics) 112:425–430.

Smith, G. W., A. D. Hawkins, G. G. Urquhart, and W. M. Shearer. 1980. Orientation and energetic efficiency in the offshore movements of returning Atlantic salmon *Salmo salar* L. Scottish Fisheries Research Report 21:1–22.

Strasburg, D. W. 1960. Estimates of larval tuna abundance in the central Pacific. U.S. Fish and Wildlife Service Fishery Bulletin 60(167):231–249.

Tabata, S. 1983. Commentary: interannual variability in the abiotic environment of the Bering Sea and the Gulf of Alaska. Pages 139–145 *in* W. S. Wooster, editor. From year to year: interannual variability of the environment and fisheries of the Gulf of Alaska and the eastern Bering Sea. University of Washington, Washington Sea Grant Program, Seattle, Washington, USA.

Tabata, S. 1984. Oceanographic factors influencing the distribution, migration, and survival of salmonids in the northeast Pacific Ocean—a review. Pages 128–160 *in* W. G. Pearcy, editor. The influence of ocean conditions on the production of salmonids in

the north Pacific. Oregon State University, Oregon Sea Grant Program, Corvallis, Oregon, USA.

Takagi, K., K. V. Aro, A. C. Hartt, and M. B. Dell. 1981. Distribution and origin of pink salmon (*Oncorhynchus gorbuscha*) in offshore waters of the north Pacific Ocean. International North Pacific Fisheries Commission Bulletin 40.

Tesch, F.-W. 1978a. Horizontal and vertical swimming of eels during the spawning migration at the edge of the continental shelf. Pages 378–391 *in* K. Schmidt-Koenig, and W. T. Keeton, editors. Animal migration, navigation, and homing. Springer-Verlag, Berlin, Germany.

Tesch, F.-W. 1978b. Telemetric observations on the spawning migration of the eel (*Anguilla anguilla*) west of the European continental shelf. Environmental Biology of Fishes 3:203–209.

Tesch, F.-W. 1979. Tracking of silver eels (*Anguilla anguilla* L.) in different shelf areas of the northeast Atlantic. Rapports et Procès-Verbaux des Réunion, Conseil International pour l'Exploration de la Mer 174:104–114.

Thomson, K. A., B. A. terHart, and P. Welch. 1985 CTD survey of the inside passage of British Columbia, June 1985. University of British Columbia, Department of Oceanography, Manuscript Report 45, Vancouver, Canada.

Thomson, R. E. 1981. Oceanography of the British Columbia coast. Canadian Special Publication of Fisheries and Aquatic Sciences 56.

Voorhis, A. D. 1969. The horizontal extent and persistance of thermal fronts in the Sargasso Sea. Deep-Sea Research 16(supplement):331–337.

Ware, D. M. 1978. Bioenergetics of pelagic fish: theoretical change in swimming speed and ration with body size. Journal of the Fisheries Research Board of Canada 35:220–228.

Webb, P. W. 1975. Hydrodynamics and energetics of fish propulsion. Fisheries Research Board of Canada Bulletin 190.

Weihs, D. 1984. Bioenergetic considerations in fish migration. Pages 487–508 *in* McCleave et al. (1984).

Weihs, D. 1987. Hydromechanics of fish migration in variable environments. American Fisheries Society Symposium 1:254–261.

Werner, R. G. 1979. Homing mechanism of spawning white suckers in Wolf Lake, New York. New York Fish and Game Journal 26:48–58.

Westerberg, H. 1979. Counter-current orientation in the migration of the European eel. Rapports et Procès-Verbaux des Réunion, Conseil International pour l'Exploration de la Mer 174:134–143.

Westerberg, H. 1982. Ultrasonic tracking of Atlantic salmon: I, movements in coastal regions; II, swimming depth and temperature stratification. Institute of Freshwater Research Drottningholm Report 60:81–120.

Westerberg, H. 1984. The orientation of fish and the vertical stratification at fine- and micro-structure scales. Pages 179–203 *in* McCleave et al. (1984).

Westin, L., and L. Nyman. 1979. Activity, orientation, and migration of Baltic eel (*Anguilla anguilla* L.).

Rapports et Procès-Verbaux des Réunion, Conseil International pour l'Exploration de la Mer 174:115–123.

Wheeler, J. P., and G. H. Winters. 1984. Homing of Atlantic herring (*Clupea harengus harengus*) in Newfoundland waters as indicated by tagging data. Canadian Journal of Fisheries and Aquatic Sciences 41:108–117.

American Fisheries Society Symposium 1:389, 1987

RECRUITMENT MECHANISMS

Preamble

RONALD J. KLAUDA

*The Johns Hopkins University, Applied Physics Laboratory Environmental Sciences Group,
Shady Side, Maryland 20764, USA*

Recruitment in fishes has traditionally been studied from different perspectives. It is, therefore, not surprising that several definitions of this concept can be found in the literature. Larval fish ecologists view recruitment as an ontogenetic ecological process which involves all early life stages from the egg through a fully developed juvenile. Fisheries managers view recruitment as the addition of new fish to a vulnerable (or catchable) population through growth among smaller size categories. Others view recruitment as the process whereby diadromous fishes shift residency between freshwater and marine habitats.

The common threads that weave through these and other views of recruitment suspend the array of abiotic and biotic environmental factors that alter rates of growth and mortality in fish populations and cause year-class variation. Attempts to rank the relative importance of abiotic versus biotic factors continue to spark heated debates among population dynamicists. Scientists tend to agree that both density-dependent and density-independent processes are important regulatory mechanisms for fish populations in general. But disagreement quickly emerges when discussion focuses on a single species or genus.

This section explores a major issue in fisheries science, the search for proximate causes of recruitment variability. The collection of papers envelop and integrate the physiological, behavioral, and ecological topics discussed in previous sections. This section is structured around the theme of comparisons that flows through this book and seeks commonalities and contrasts in recruitment mechanisms among an array of fish species and populations.

The papers included in this section offer geographic and phylogenetic diversity. The research interests of contributing authors are broad and varied. Their papers focus on diadromous fishes from the northern and southern hemispheres that represent seven families (Salmonidae, Perichthyidae, Clupeidae, Anguillidae, Plecoglossidae, Mugilidae, Prototroctidae) and three categories of diadromy (anadromy, catadromy, amphidromy). The final paper extends the discussion to nondiadromous fishes and compares recruitment variability in several marine and anadromous species.

American Fisheries Society Symposium 1:390–401, 1987

Causes of Variable Recruitment in a Small Atlantic Salmon Stock

E. Michael P. Chadwick

Fisheries Research Branch, Gulf Region, Department of Fisheries and Oceans
Moncton, New Brunswick E1C 9B6, Canada

Abstract.—Recruitment of Atlantic salmon *Salmo salar* in Western Arm Brook, a small Newfoundland river, was influenced by a combination of density-dependent and environmental factors. In fresh water, egg-to-smolt survival for eight out of 10 year classes was constant; 88% of the variation in year-class strength was explained by egg deposition; and mean annual growth rate, the size of age-4+ smolts (the predominant age-group), and the size a parr must achieve to become an age-4+ smolt were all negatively density dependent. Smolt age was not density dependent, but the percentage of age-3+ smolts was negatively correlated with air temperature in the first year of life. In the sea, survival was more variable than in fresh water and positively correlated with the size of smolts. When egg depositions were low, it appeared that one spawner produced about eight spawners in the next generation.

An important question for the fishery manager is by how much can we control recruitment or the rate young fish enter the exploitable stage of their life cycles? If recruitment is largely dependent on stock size or biological factors, then presumably it can be controlled by regulating harvest. By contrast, if recruitment is dominated by environmental factors, then at best it might be predicted but not controlled.

Atlantic salmon *Salmo salar* is a good species for studying the causes of recruitment. First, because they are anadromous, stocks are easily identified when adults return to their natal rivers. Second, because adults are large, vulnerable, and not numerous, it is often possible to count spawners and to estimate egg deposition. Third, number of juveniles or smolts can be estimated as they migrate downstream. Fourth, the migrations provide a convenient opportunity to obtain unbiased estimates of size, age, and sex structure of a stock, or at least of the migrants. Fifth, rivers are discrete habitats, this fact makes it possible to compare the productivity of different stocks or the productivity of the same stock over time. Finally, because the species is well studied, there is a great deal of background information for almost all aspects of its life history.

Because of the species' complicated life history in fresh water and the sea, the long migration routes, and the adverse climate of northern latitudes, one might expect that recruitment of Atlantic salmon would be largely controlled by the environment. The studies of Dunbar and Thomson (1979), Power (1981), Saunders et al. (1983), and Martin and Mitchell (1985) suggest the importance of factors like water discharge and ocean temperature in controlling recruitment. On the other side, because of the large size of spawners and their eggs (Alm 1959) and the incidence of repeat spawning for some stocks, it might be expected that recruitment would be independent of the environment and controlled by density-dependent factors. It has also been suggested that recruitment curves for this species are steeply dome-shaped (Elson 1975), a consequence of density dependence for biological characteristics like freshwater mortality (Gee et al. 1978), smolt age (Montgomery and Naiman 1981; Bielak and Power 1986), and precocity of male parr (Caswell et al. 1984).

The picture of recruitment of Atlantic salmon and other anadromous species may be confusing because we lack adequate data. Because it is difficult to measure mortality and growth of a population, we often draw conclusions regarding recruitment from scant information from juvenile surveys, tagging, catch statistics, infrequent biological samples, and correlations with environmental variables. These types of data may be neither comparable among years (Ludwig and Walters 1981), nor interchangeable among themselves, nor reliable for building a composite picture of any particular stock. Elliott (1984) has emphasized that long time series of data on abundance and characteristics of one discrete stock are necessary if we really want to understand the factors which control recruitment.

The objective of this paper is to examine recruitment in the small Atlantic salmon stock of Western Arm Brook, Newfoundland, which has been studied in its natural state for 15 years. The basic question is what are the density-dependent and environmental factors which influence recruitment or the production of smolts in Western Arm Brook? This question is divided into four specific parts. (1) Does egg deposition explain annual variation in numbers of smolts? (2) Are variations in size, age, and sex ratio of smolts density dependent? (3) Are growth and mortality rates of parr influenced by water discharge and temperature? (4) Are smolt numbers a good measure of subsequent recruits?

Methods

Western Arm Brook (Figure 1) is a pristine, fourth-order stream on the northwestern coast of Newfoundland (51°11'N, 56°46'W). The watershed is small (150 km²) and, because of its low relief and over 2,000 hectares of lakes, there are no large fluctuations in discharge. A fish-counting fence has been maintained with no washouts since 1971. Each year, fish in upstream and downstream migrations were completely counted, and biological attributes such as fork length, age, and sex were determined from random samples of Atlantic salmon smolts and adults. Complete data are available for 13 year classes, providing the longest and most complete time series of information on wild Atlantic salmon migrations in Canada, if not in the world (Chadwick 1981, 1982b).

Egg depositions for nine year classes were estimated from counts of spawners. Spawners were randomly sampled for sex and fork length and fecundity was calculated from a length–fecundity relationship (Chadwick 1982b). Over the range of the data set, egg depositions have varied sevenfold.

The influence of fish density on biological characteristics of smolts was tested with two indices of stock density: number of smolts in a year class

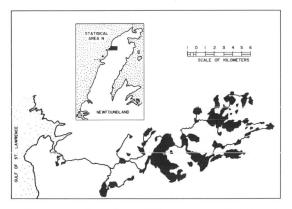

FIGURE 1.—Location of Western Arm Brook and statistical area N.

and moving 3-year average of smolt numbers adjusted to age 3+. The numbers of smolts were adjusted to age 3+ by assuming an annual survival rate of 40% (Evans et al. 1984). The moving 3-year average was used to account for possible competition among year classes that immediately preceded and followed an individual year class. Age and fork length (mm) were available for all year classes of smolts and adults; sex, weight (g), and condition were available for most year classes. Because smolts grew as they aged (Chadwick 1981), the analyses were restricted to age-4+ smolts, the predominant age-group. Correlations were also calculated between annual downstream migrations of Atlantic salmon parr and smolts and other fish species (Table 1).

Density dependence was also tested for estimates of eight growth and survival parameters. Six of these parameters provided best fits in a model of growth and smolting of parr in Western Arm Brook that accounted for the distributions of ages and lengths of smolts in 10 year classes 1968–1977 (Evans et al. 1984); values for the six parameters in the 1978–1980 year classes were fitted when recent data became available. These parameters were *SURV*, annual survival for parr older than age 3+; *MUG*, mean annual growth rate in fresh water; *SIGG*, standard deviation of *MUG*; *MUL*, mean criterion length of age-3+ smolts, or the size a parr must achieve to become an age-3+ smolt in the following year; *SIGL*, standard deviation of *MUL*; and, *MUL-OFFSET*, criterion length of age-4+ smolts.

The final two parameters, survival from egg to age 3+ and survival of smolts for 1 year at sea, were calculated as follows. The survival from egg to age 3+ was the number of smolts adjusted to age 3+ as a percentage of estimated egg deposition (Chadwick 1982b). Survival at sea was the sum of 20% of one-sea-winter (1SW) Atlantic salmon harvested in commercial fisheries of statistical area N (Chadwick 1984) and spawning escapement of 1SW salmon into Western Arm Brook as a percentage of the number of smolts which went to sea in the previous years. Western Arm Brook is one of the major Atlantic salmon rivers in statistical area N. Based on the relative size of its drainage basin, smolt production in Western Arm Brook was assumed to be 10% of the total for statistical area N (Chadwick 1984). About 50% of tagged kelts were recaptured in distant fisheries (outside statistical area N) and, therefore, it was assumed that harvest in these fisheries was equal to harvest in the home-water

TABLE 1.—Harvests (numbers of fish) of one-sea-winter (1SW) Atlantic salmon in fisheries of statistical area N, 1963–1985, and counts of migrating Atlantic salmon and other species in Western Arm Brook, 1971–1985.

| | 1SW Atlantic salmon | | | | Downstream migrants | | | | | | |
| | Fisheries in statistical area N | | Upstream migrants | | Atlantic salmon | | | Brook trout[a] | American eel[b] | Rainbow smelt[c] | American shad[d] |
Year	Recreational	Commercial	Returns	Spawners	Kelts	Smolts	Parr				
1963	908										
1964	1,449										
1965	1,771										
1966	1,977										
1967	2,011										
1968	2,223										
1969	2,748	792									
1970	2,913	2,104									
1971	2,018	1,047	937	732	185	5,734	434	135	97	108	3
1972	1,332	2,062	415	214	210	11,906	431	220	197	181	52
1973	2,648	8,428	827	380	95	8,484	250	429	97	365	5
1974	1,789	2,738	526	319	302	12,055	267	809	574	539	3
1975	2,716	3,667	640	394	201	9,733	122	851	92	607	0
1976	3,014	4,258	552	420	208	6,359	148	408	30	926	0
1977	2,413	3,922	376	351	498	9,640	358	373	65	354	12
1978	1,350	1,268	317	286	210	13,071	899	1,000	69	527	2
1979	3,281	6,814	1,576	1,576	1	9,400[e]	235	109	1	53	0
1980	1,651	6,919	470	433	898	15,675	1,292	847	139	339	0
1981	2,511	7,370	471	425	168	13,981	484	465	400	252	2
1982	2,156	10,799	467	391	299	12,477	1,065	600	325	105	1
1983	1,947	2,432	1,146	1,137	206	10,552	1,599	802	168	216	0
1984	1,753	2,766	238	123	719	20,653	2,204	662	226	149	2
1985	1,325	2,532	500[e]	164	111	13,417	886	247	332	168	6

[a] *Savelinus fontinalis.*   [b] *Anguilla rostrata.*   [c] *Osmerus mordax.*   [d] *Alosa sapidissima.*   [e] Estimated.

commercial fisheries of statistical area N (Chadwick et al. 1985).

The influence of environmental factors on annual variations in the previously mentioned biological characteristics was tested with several estimates of water temperature and discharge. These estimates included annual mean daily temperature; degree days greater than 7°C, the activity threshold of parr (Allen 1969); annual mean monthly discharge; and an index of summer discharge, the sum of mean monthly discharges for June, July, and August. Air temperatures were obtained from Environment Canada (various dates) at St. Anthony, 90 km northeast of Western Arm Brook; air temperatures above 0°C were highly correlated ($r = 0.91$; df $= 103$) to water temperatures in Western Arm Brook (Chadwick 1981). Water discharge data were available for Ste. Geneviève River (Anonymous 1985), which is adjacent to Western Arm Brook.

Yield, expressed as the number of next-generation spawners produced per spawner, was calculated two ways. In both, it was assumed in all years that spawners were 74% female and the average female spawner carried 3,390 eggs (unpublished data). Egg-to-smolt survival rates were calculated as described above, on the assumption that survival from age-3+ parr to age-4+ smolts was 40% (Evans et al. 1984). In one method, sea survival was calculated each year from harvest in the commercial fishery and from river escapement, as described above. The second method assumed that, because of annual variation in migration routes, interception rates by distant fisheries, and catchability in home-water fisheries, it was not possible to estimate sea survival from catch statistics and counts of escaping adults. Therefore, it was assumed that sea survival was a constant 17.4%. This estimate was calculated from a tagging study of adult Atlantic salmon in 1977 (Chadwick et al. 1985).

Results

Density-Dependent Factors

Eighty-eight percent of the variation in numbers of smolts from seven year classes (1973–1979) was explained by egg deposition (Table 2; Figure 2). The sizes of the 1972 and 1980 year classes were smaller than the large egg depositions would have predicted.

Fork length, weight and condition of age-4+ smolts declined as numbers of smolts increased (Table 2); the decline in fork length was significant. The latter relationship was particularly evident between fork length and the 3-year average number of smolts adjusted to age 3+ (Figure 3). This relationship was not linear; instead, fork

TABLE 2.—Summary of biological characteristics estimated for year classes of Atlantic salmon in Western Arm Brook, 1968–1981.

Year class	Egg deposition (thousands)	Survival, egg to age 3+ (%)	Number of all smolts, adjusted to age 3+		% of smolts actually age 3	Age-4+ smolts				Smolts counted	
			Annual number	Running 3-year mean		Fork length (mm)	Weight (g)	Condition[a]	% female	Mean age	Number
1967			16,800[b]								
1968			33,364	28,595	3	175	49	0.92	72.7	3.98	11,213
1969			35,621	30,658	4	173	47	0.90	69.7	4.13	10,835
1970			22,988	26,634	6	174				3.90	9,198
1971			21,292	20,024	7	174				3.93	8,164
1972	1,464	1.1	15,793	18,091	22	177				3.60	8,141
1973	428	4.0	17,189	20,136	6	174	49	0.91	81.9	3.94	6,074
1974	787	3.5	27,426	23,043	20	174	48	0.90	84.3	3.64	13,316
1975	667	3.7	24,515	29,099	20	179	51	0.88	73.0	3.64	11,855
1976	827	4.3	35,355	34,639	7	171	45	0.88	75.0	3.94	12,743
1977	870	5.1	44,046	37,299	14	170	45	0.90	78.5	3.78	18,136
1978	737	4.4	32,497	34,018	9	170	43	0.87	84.3	3.88	12,735
1979	572	4.5	25,510	38,317	6	167	42	0.89	86.8	3.97	8,578
1980	3,024	1.9	56,944	38,590	6	164	39	0.87	74.0	3.89	21,444
1981	866	3.8	33,315[b]			165			72.1		13,600[b]

[a]Condition = 10^5 weight/fork length^3.   [b]Rough estimate.

length was constant below a threshold number of 30,000 age-3+ smolts, and declined with number above the threshold. Year-class variations in smolt age and sex ratio were not correlated with smolt abundance.

Density dependence was also found in the estimated growth rates of parr and smolts. Three parameters in the model of Evans et al. (1984) were correlated with the average numbers of smolts adjusted to age 3+ (Table 3; Figure 4): mean growth rates of year classes *(MUG)* and the criterion length of age-4+ smolts *(MUL-OFFSET)* declined with an increase in abundance and standard deviation of mean growth rate *(SIGG)* and

the coefficient of variation in growth rate *(CV)* increased with abundance.

Two further correlations indicated density dependence. First, there was a significant positive correlation between the numbers of parr and smolts migrating downstream (Figure 5). Smolts and parr are easily distinguished in Western Arm Brook (Chadwick and Léger 1986), so the correlation was not a result of misidentifying parr as smolts. The second positive correlation was between fork length of smolts and fork length of 1SW Atlantic salmon which returned to the river (Figure 6). Although estimates of sea survival were weak, smaller smolts appeared to have lower sea survival (Figure 7), but this may have been related to environmental conditions at sea.

Environmental Factors

Out of 53 combinations tested, there were only two significant correlations between environmental factors and biological characteristics of smolts. First, the number of true age-3+ smolts as a percentage of total smolts adjusted to age 3+ (Table 2) was negatively correlated with both annual and winter mean daily temperatures (Table 4); that is, the proportion of age-3+ smolts was greatest in cold years (Figure 8). Second, the criterion size of age-4+ smolts was positively correlated ($P < 0.05$) with summer mean daily temperature ($r = 0.65$); this independent variable, together with the number of smolts adjusted to age-3+ explained 74% of the variation in *MUL-OFFSET* ($P < 0.01$)

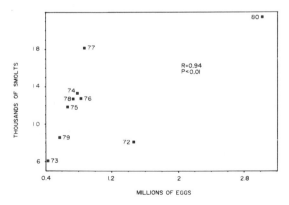

FIGURE 2.—Relationship between estimated egg deposition and year-class strength of Atlantic salmon smolts leaving Western Arm Brook, 1972–1980 year classes. The correlation coefficient R refers to the 1973–1979 year classes.

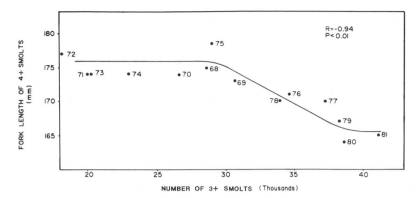

FIGURE 3.—Relationship between the abundance of Atlantic salmon smolts adjusted to age 3+ and the mean fork length of smolts leaving Western Arm Brook, year classes 1968–1981. The correlation coefficient (R) is for values above 28,000 smolts.

in a multiple linear regression. Environmental factors did not appear to influence growth rate.

In nine out of 10 year classes, survival in fresh water did not appear to be influenced by environmental factors. For the 1974–1979 and 1981 year classes, survival between eggs and age-3+ parr ranged between 3.5 and 5.1% with a coefficient of variation of 13% (Table 2). The lower survival of the 1980 year class was probably a result of the very large egg deposition. As explained in a previous paper, the lower survival of the 1972 year class was probably because of a very cold and dry winter during egg incubation (Chadwick 1982b).

The survival at sea was more variable than egg-to-smolt survival in fresh water. Mean sea survival was 11% and the coefficient of variation

was 40% (Table 5). Three smolt migrations, those of 1977, 1983, and 1984, resulted in less than half the average survival rate. As mentioned, there was some indication that survival rate was positively correlated with fork length of smolts (Figure 7). This correlation was improved when the 1977 migration was omitted ($r = 0.75$; $P = 0.01$). The year 1977 was recognized as a year of poor sea survival throughout the north Atlantic Ocean (Porter and Ritter 1984).

Yield

It is difficult to calculate yield because our estimates of sea survival are weak. If a constant annual sea survival of smolts is assumed, the Western Arm Brook Atlantic salmon stock has a

TABLE 3.—Summary of parameters providing best fits to the model of Evans et al. (1984) for each year class of Atlantic salmon smolts in Western Arm Brook; *SURV*, annual survival for parr older than age 3+; *MUL*, mean criterion length (mm) or the minimum length that a parr must attain before becoming a smolt, in this case an age-3+ smolt; *SIGL*, standard deviation of *MUL*; *OFFSET*, the amount by which the criterion length decreases with each successive year of parr age; *MUL-OFFSET*, criterion length to become an age-4+ smolt; *MUG*, mean annual growth rate (mm); *SIGG*, standard deviation of *MUG*; and *CV*, coefficient of variation of *MUG*.

Year class	Parameter							
	SURV	*OFFSET*	*MUL*	*SIGL*	*MUL-OFFSET*	*MUG*	*SIGG*	*CV*
1968	0.40	16	164	5.0	148	35.6	5.9	17
1969	0.95	12	162	11.1	150	35.3	8.2	23
1970	0.40	12	163	7.0	151	36.2	5.5	15
1971	0.40	6	160	5.0	154	35.0	5.8	17
1972	0.40	8	158	6.0	150	38.2	7.0	18
1973	0.45	18	167	6.5	149	35.5	7.0	20
1974	0.40	15	160	6.0	145	37.0	7.3	20
1975	0.40	−1	154	8.0	155	37.6	5.5	15
1976	0.40	14	162	7.0	148	33.8	8.0	24
1977	0.40	11	155	7.0	144	33.0	9.0	27
1978	0.40	22	162	5.2	140	32.0	9.4	29
1979	0.40	14	156	5.3	142	31.0	9.2	30
1980	0.40	15	156	5.6	141	31.5	6.9	22

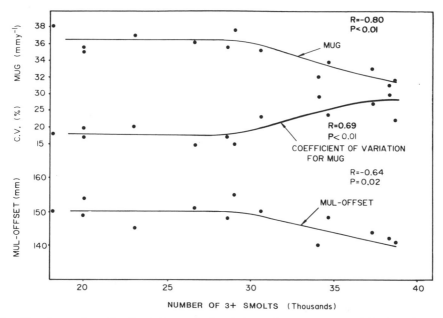

FIGURE 4.—Abundance of smolts adjusted to age 3+ in relation to three parameters of the Atlantic salmon growth model of Evans et al. (1984): *MUG*, mean annual growth rate in mm, and its coefficient of variation (100 × *SIGG/MUG*); and *MUL-OFFSET*, the criterion length (mm) to become an age-4+ smolt. The correlation coefficient (*R*) is for values above 28,000 smolts.

logistic stock–recruitment curve (Figures 2, 9). The curve is mostly linear up to an egg deposition of about one million eggs or 400 spawners; it implies that one spawner produces about eight adults. The asymptote occurs at egg depositions representing more than 1,000 spawners. For the highest egg deposition, which yielded the 1980 year class, one spawner produced three adults. There appears to be a nonlinear part of the curve near the origin, implying that, at very low egg

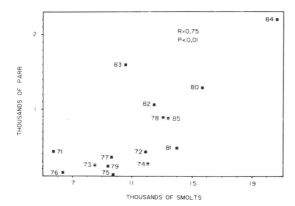

FIGURE 5.—Relationship between abundances of downstream-migrating Atlantic salmon parr and smolts in Western Arm Brook, 1971–1984.

depositions, stock productivity is less than eight adults per spawner (Figure 9).

If yearly estimates of sea survival (Table 5) are considered, the stock–recruitment curve is very different. In this case, the curve is sharply dome-shaped (Figure 9), and maximum yield is produced by about 500 spawners. The linear left limb of the curve suggests production of nearly 10 adults per spawner but at the highest egg deposition recorded in Western Arm Brook (for the 1980 year class), one spawner would produce only one adult. An assumption underlying this recruitment curve is that harvest in distant commercial fisheries was a constant proportion of harvest in home waters. It was also possible, however, that the poor sea survival of the 1980 year class was a result of adverse environmental conditions and not of poor survival of the smaller smolts. It is difficult to make a judgment about which recruitment curve is more correct until there are more data representing high egg depositions.

Discussion

At least for the Atlantic salmon stock in Western Arm Brook, recruitment could be controlled by regulating the number of adults which survive to spawn. At low stock density, one spawner

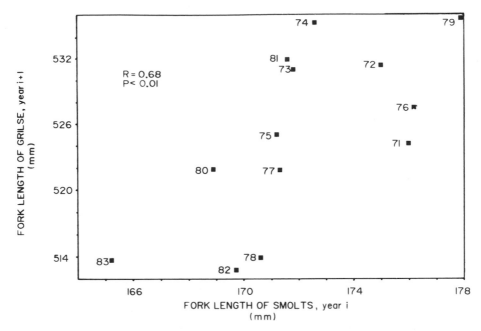

FIGURE 6.—Relationship between fork lengths of Atlantic salmon smolts and of one-sea-winter fish (grilse) returning the following year to Western Arm Brook. The year of the smolt migration is indicated.

clearly produced eight offspring. At higher stock density, the picture was less clear. Environmental factors, however, did not appear to greatly influence the production of smolts. This finding contrasts with the situation for most other fish species, whose survival at young ages is considered to be greatly influenced by environmental factors (for review, see May 1984). The size of smolts, not age or survival, declined at high stock densities and there was some indication that sea sur-

vival was also related to size of smolts. Perhaps smaller smolts were more vulnerable to environmental factors at sea, but there were not enough data to be certain of this.

It should be emphasized that Western Arm Brook was a good site to study recruitment. Each year, all smolts and adults were counted without error. The samples were taken randomly and, therefore, were representative of the stock. Finally, the river contains a single stock of Atlantic salmon, which is the predominant species. Of the 640 kg of fish biomass exported from the river each year, Atlantic salmon smolts represent 88% (Table 1), so interactions with other species or stocks are probably negligible. Unlike many other rivers, which have Atlantic salmon stocks with several sea ages and distinct early and late runs, Western Arm Brook has a stock entirely made up of 1SW fish, which enter the river in late summer.

Except for one year class, the relationship between eggs and smolts in Western Arm Brook (Figure 2) was different from the sharply domed curves described by Elson (1975) and Gee et al. (1978). Their curves apparently resulted from a high density-dependent mortality. Because mortality in Western Arm Brook was very constant, it might be useful to reexamine the previous studies to ensure that incomplete counts of recruits or

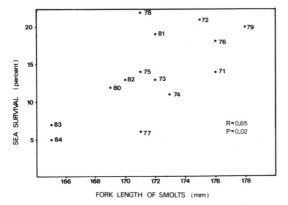

FIGURE 7.—Relationship between fork length of Atlantic salmon smolts in Western Arm Brook and their sea survival. The year of the smolt migration is indicated.

TABLE 4.—Mean fork lengths of Atlantic salmon smolts leaving Western Arm Brook and of one-sea-winter (1SW) fish returning to the river the following year in relation to environmental conditions near Western Arm Brook 1968–1982. Air temperatures for St. Anthony, 90 km north of Western Arm Brook, are from Environment Canada (various dates). Water discharge for Ste. Geneviève River, 15 km south of Western Arm Brook, are from Anonymous (1985).

Year (i)	Degree-days		Mean daily temperature (°C)			Water discharge		Fork length (mm)	
	>4°C	>7°C	Annual	Summer[a]	Winter[b]	Total annual (10^6 m^3)	Summer (m^3/s)	Smolts	1SW fish (year $i+1$)
1968	819	447	1.5	10.2	−6.2				
1969	977	579	2.9	11.3	−4.1				
1970	927	555	1.6	10.8	−5.9	299	10.7		
1971	955	576	1.6	10.9	−6.1	344	12.6	176	528
1972	745	414	−1.5	9.7	−10.3	307	15.0	175	524
1973	865	511	1.0	10.7	−8.3	253	11.4	172	531
1974	755	423	−0.4	9.9	−10.2	266	12.2	173	531
1975	959	597	0.6	11.4	−9.1	231	8.4	171	535
1976	875	508	0.4	10.6	−8.4	306	6.5	176	525
1977	824	475	1.7	10.1	−5.7	398	15.1	171	527
1978	790	465	0.5	9.9	−6.9	277	11.7	171	522
1979	963	552	1.8	10.9	−5.8	351	9.0	178	514
1980	681	338	0.7	9.2	−6.8	325	11.8	169	536
1981	846	460	2.4	10.1	−4.3	249	6.5	172	522
1982	796	470		10.2	−8.8	297	11.1	170	532
1983								165	513
1984								165	514

[a] Mean of June, July, August, September.
[b] Mean of January, February, March, April.

increased emigration of parr at high densities were not mistaken for mortality.

Smolt age of the Western Arm Brook stock was constant and appeared to be a fixed characteristic of this population. The model of Evans et al. (1984) predicted that smolt age would not change even at high stock density, which is what has been observed with the recent year classes. This result is useful for interpreting changes in smolt age which have been observed for other populations, for example, those in the Godbout River (Bielak and Power 1986) and Matamek River (Mont-

gomery and Naiman 1981). It is possible that changes in smolt age are not a result of some density-dependent phenomenon, but rather occur because stocks with different smolt ages have different vulnerabilities to exploitation. For example, a stock with predominantly age-4+ smolts will require more than twice as many eggs to produce the same number of smolts as a stock with predominantly age-3+ smolts; consequently, the stock with older smolt age would be more vulnerable to overexploitation. This hypothesis needs to be elaborated more completely and then tested.

The density-dependent decrease in smolt size and its possible implication for marine survival is also of interest. First, it is not a phenomenon unique to Western Arm Brook. Similar data for another 1SW salmon stock, Big Salmon River, Bay of Fundy (Jessop 1975), indicate that size of the predominant smolt age-group, age 3+, was negatively correlated with stock density (Figure 10). Stock density was estimated as the abundance of age-2+ parr, and a 40% survival was assumed between age-groups.

Second, many authors have described correlations between smolt size and sea survival rates for Atlantic salmon (Larsson 1977; Ritter 1977) and Pacific salmon (Peterman 1978; Bilton 1984), although Walters et al. (1978) cautioned that estimates of sea survival are poor. Thus, while it may

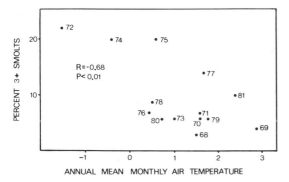

FIGURE 8.—Relationship between annual mean monthly temperatures (St. Anthony, Newfoundland) and the percentage of age-3+ Atlantic salmon smolts among all smolts (adjusted to age 3+) in Western Arm Brook. Year classes are indicated.

TABLE 5.—The yield or number of adult Atlantic salmon produced per spawner projected from assumptions that sea survival varied or remained constant for each of eight year classes from Western Arm Brook.

Year class	Number of spawners	Varying sea survival		Constant sea survival	
		Sea survival (%)	Yield per spawner	Sea survival (%)	Yield per spawner
1972	732	18	2	17	2
1973	214	6	3	17	8
1974	380	22	8	17	6
1975	319	20	7	17	7
1976	394	12	5	17	8
1977	420	19	10	17	9
1978	351	13	6	17	8
1979	286	7	3	17	8
1980	1,576	5	1	17	3

be true that smolt size declines with density in Western Arm Brook, it is not yet convincing that smaller smolts have reduced sea survival. The poor returns of Atlantic salmon in 1985, for example, were seen in all stocks along the west coast of Newfoundland, and most of these other stocks were below carrying capacity. Presumably, smolts from these other stocks would not

have been smaller than in previous years unless smolt size was influenced by some unidentified environmental factors.

A further consequence of reduced smolt size could be a change in sea age. It was shown in a previous paper that ovarian development of smolts was inversely correlated with sea age (Chadwick et al. 1986); some smolts from Western Arm Brook had well-developed yolk vesicles in their ovaries, while smolts from 2SW and 3SW stocks had none. In a more recent analysis (unpublished data), it was found that Western Arm Brook smolts with yolk vesicles (mean fork length, 176 mm) were significantly ($P < 0.01$) larger than those without vesicles in their ovaries (mean fork length, 155 mm). It is possible that a decline in smolt size could result in delayed maturity of Atlantic salmon. Because of the very high exploitation of 2SW salmon by commercial fisheries (90% or more: Pratt et al. 1974), it is very

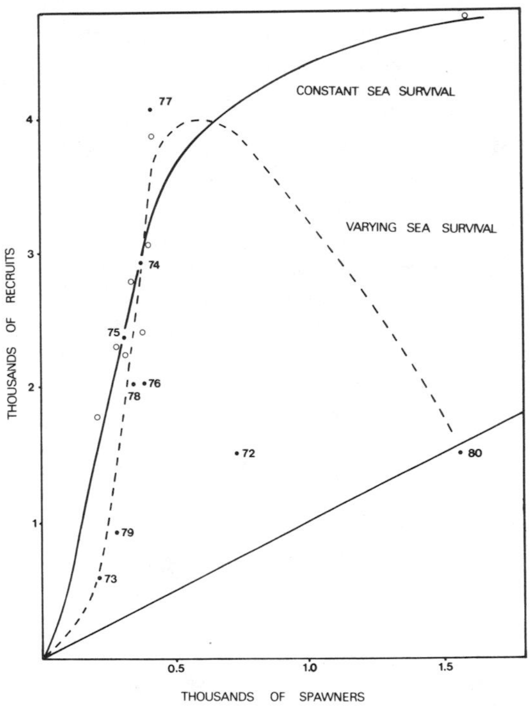

FIGURE 9.—Stock–recruitment relationship for Atlantic salmon in Western Arm Brook. The solid line and open circles are based on an assumption that sea survival was a constant 17.4%. The dashed line and solid circles reflect a presumption that sea survival could be calculated each year. Ricker's (straight) replacement line and year classes of recruits are also indicated.

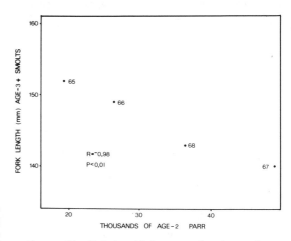

FIGURE 10.—Relationship between abundance of age-2+ Atlantic salmon parr and fork length of age-3+ smolts in Big Salmon River, New Brunswick. Data are from Jessop (1975). Year classes are indicated.

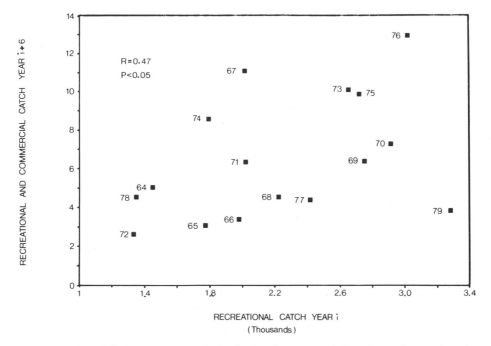

FIGURE 11.—Relationship between sport catch of Atlantic salmon, as an index of spawning stock, and sport plus commercial catch 6 years later, as an index of recruits, in statistical area N, Newfoundland.

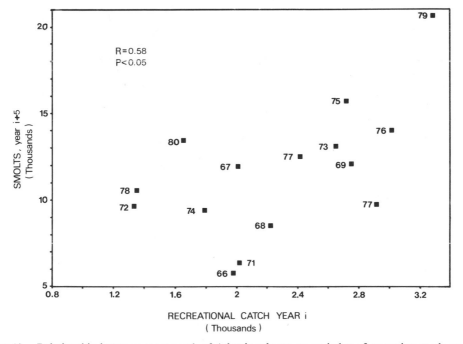

FIGURE 12.—Relationship between sport catch of Atlantic salmon, as an index of spawning stock, and smolts leaving Western Arm Brook 5 years later, as an index of recruits.

difficult to test this hypothesis in the field. The possibility that, in recent years, some of Western Arm Brook smolts have become 2SW salmon and not returned to the river cannot be discounted completely; it could explain the apparently low sea survival of smolts to 1SW salmon.

One may ask if it is necessary to count and randomly sample smolt migrations to understand recruitment. By themselves, counts of adults did not provide any index of recruitment. There was no correlation between spawning escapements on Western Arm Brook when they were lagged by 6 years. This result suggests that most of stock production was harvested in commercial fisheries outside the river and those adults which did survive to return to the river were not an adequate index of recruitment or production.

Catch data can also be used to measure stock and recruitment. There was a significant but weak correlation between sport catch (Moores et al. 1978), used as an index of spawning stock, and combined commercial and sport catches (Table 1) in statistical area N 6 years later, used as an index of recruitment (Figure 11). Sport catch (in statistical area N) was also correlated with the number of smolts migrating from Western Arm Brook 5 years later (Figure 12). Thus, sport catch may be a useful measure of spawning escapement, but, at best, catch data provide only a crude measure of recruitment.

In summary, it appears that recruitment of Atlantic salmon in Western Arm Brook is influenced differentially in the freshwater and marine phases of the life history. In fresh water, survival of eight out of 10 year classes was constant and variations in year-class strength were explained by egg deposition. Mean growth rates and fork lengths of age-4+ smolts were inversely correlated with density. In the sea, survival was more variable, but this observation may have resulted from an inability to account for commercial catches of Western Arm Brook fish or from adverse environmental conditions at least once every 5 years. Survival at sea may also be related to size of smolts. Below 500 spawners, it was clear that one spawner produced about eight subsequent spawners. There was not enough information to make a judgement about yields at higher egg depositions. Finally, it appears possible to discover the factors which control recruitment if we are able to study a stock in sufficient detail over long time periods.

Acknowledgments

I thank several people for their help: John Wright, who assisted with computer programming; Phyllis Collette, who typed several manuscript drafts; Ross Claytor and Max Blouw, for their careful reviews; and the comments of two anonymous referees which improved the clarity of the manuscript.

References

Allen, K. R. 1969. Limitations on production in salmonid populations in streams. Pages 3–18 in T. G. Northcote, editor. Symposium on salmon and trout in streams. H. R. MacMillan Lectures in Fisheries, University of British Columbia, Vancouver, Canada.

Alm, G. 1959. Connection between maturity, size and age in fishes. Institute of Freshwater Research Drottningholm Report 40:5–145.

Anonymous. 1985. Historical stream flow summary, Atlantic provinces to 1984. Inland Waters Directorate, Water Resources Branch, Ottawa, Canada.

Bielak, A. T., and G. Power. 1986. Independence of sea age and river age in Atlantic salmon from Québec north shore rivers. Canadian Special Publication of Fisheries and Aquatic Sciences 89:70–78.

Bilton, H. T. 1984. Returns of chinook salmon in relation to juvenile size at release. Canadian Technical Report of Fisheries and Aquatic Sciences 1245.

Caswell, H., R. J. Naiman, and R. Morin. 1984. Evaluating the consequences of reproduction in complex salmonid life cycles. Aquaculture 43:123–134.

Chadwick, E. M. P. 1981. Biological characteristics of Atlantic salmon smolts in Western Arm Brook, Newfoundland. Canadian Technical Report of Fisheries and Aquatic Sciences 1024.

Chadwick, E. M. P. 1982a. Dynamics of an Atlantic salmon stock (Salmo salar) in a small Newfoundland river. Doctoral dissertation. Memorial University of Newfoundland, St. John's, Canada.

Chadwick, E. M. P. 1982b. Stock–recruitment relationship for Atlantic salmon (Salmo salar) in Newfoundland rivers. Canadian Journal of Fisheries and Aquatic Sciences 39:1496–1501.

Chadwick, E. M. P. 1984. Prediction of 1SW Atlantic salmon returns, statistical area N, 1984. Canadian Atlantic Fisheries Science Advisory Committee, Research Document 83/84, Halifax, Canada.

Chadwick, E. M. P., and C. Léger. 1986. Avalaison des tacons (Salmo salar L.) dans une petite rivière de Terre-Neuve. Naturaliste canadien (Québec) 113: 55–60.

Chadwick, E. M. P., R. G. Randall, and C. Léger. 1986. Ovarian development of Atlantic salmon (Salmo salar) and age at first maturity. Canadian Special Publication of Fisheries and Aquatic Sciences 89:15–23.

Chadwick, E. M. P., D. G. Reddin, and R. F. Burfitt. 1985. Fishing and natural mortality rates for 1SW Atlantic salmon. International Council for the Exploration of the Sea, C.M. 1985/M:18, Copenhagen, Denmark.

Dunbar, M. J., and D. H. Thomson. 1979. West Greenland salmon and climatic change. Meddelelser om Gronland 202:1–19.

Elliott, J. M. 1984. Numerical changes and population regulation in young migratory trout *(Salmo trutta)* in a lake district stream, 1966–83. Journal of Animal Ecology 53:327–350.

Elson, P. F. 1975. Atlantic salmon rivers smolt production and optimal spawning—an overview of natural production. International Atlantic Salmon Foundation Special Publication Series 6:96–119.

Environment Canada. Various dates. Monthly record, Atmospheric Environment Service, Ottawa, Canada.

Evans, G. T., J. C. Rice, and E. M. P. Chadwick. 1984. Patterns in growth and smolting of Atlantic salmon *(Salmo salar)* parr. Canadian Journal of Fisheries and Aquatic Sciences 41:783–797.

Gee, A. S., N. J. Milner, and R. J. Hemsworth. 1978. The effect of density on mortality in juvenile Atlantic salmon *(Salmo salar)*. Journal of Animal Ecology 47:497–505.

Jessop, B. M. 1975. Investigation of the salmon *(Salmo salar)* smolt migration of the Big Salmon River, New Brunswick, 1966–72. Canada Fisheries and Marine Service Resource Development Branch Maritimes Region Technical Report Series MAR/T-75-1.

Larsson, P. O. 1977. Size dependent mortality in salmon smolt plantings. International Council for the Exploration of the Sea, C.M. 1977/M:43, Copenhagen, Denmark.

Ludwig, D., and C. J. Walters. 1981. Measurement errors and uncertainty in parameter estimates for stock and recruitment. Canadian Journal of Fisheries and Aquatic Sciences 38:711–720.

Martin, J. H. A., and K. A. Mitchell. 1985. Influence of sea temperature upon the numbers of grilse and multi-sea-winter Atlantic salmon *(Salmo salar)* caught in the vicinity of the River Dee (Aberdeenshire). Canadian Journal of Fisheries and Aquatic Sciences 42:1513–1521.

May, R. M., editor. 1984. Exploitation of marine communities. Life Sciences Research Reports 32.

Montgomery, W. L., and R. J. Naiman. 1981. Implications of changes in Atlantic salmon populations from the Matamek River, Québec. International Council for the Exploration of the Sea, C.M. 1981/0, Copenhagen, Denmark.

Moores, R. B., R. W. Penney, and R. J. Tucker. 1978. Atlantic salmon angled catch and effort data Newfoundland and Labrador 1953–77. Canada Fisheries and Marine Service Data Report 84.

Peterman, R. M. 1978. Testing for density-dependent marine survival in Pacific salmonids. Journal of the Fisheries Research Board of Canada 35:1434–1450.

Porter, T. R., and J. A. Ritter. 1984. Possible causes of low abundance of Atlantic salmon in Canada, 1983. International Council for the Exploration of the Sea, C.M. 1984/M:28, Copenhagen, Denmark.

Power, G. 1981. Stock characteristics and catches of Atlantic salmon *(Salmo salar)* in Québec, Newfoundland and Labrador in relation to environmental variables. Canadian Journal of Fisheries and Aquatic Sciences 38:1601–1611.

Pratt, J. D., G. M. Hare, and H. P. Murphy. 1974. Investigations of production and harvest of an Atlantic salmon population, Sandhill River, Labrador. Canada Fisheries and Marine Service, Resource Development Branch, Newfoundland Region, Technical Report Series NEW/T-74-1, St. John's, Canada.

Ritter, J. A. 1977. Relationships between smolt size and tag return rate for hatchery-reared Atlantic salmon *(Salmo salar)*. International Council for the Exploration of the Sea, C.M. 1977/M:27, Copenhagen, Denmark.

Saunders, R. L., E. B. Henderson, B. D. Glebe, and E. J. Loudenslager. 1983. Evidence of a major environmental component in determination of the grilse:larger salmon ratio in Atlantic salmon *(Salmo salar)*. Aquaculture 33:107–118.

Walters, C. J., R. Hilborn, R. M. Peterman, and M. J. Staley. 1978. Model for examining early ocean limitation of Pacific salmon production. Journal of Fisheries Research Board of Canada 35:1303–1315.

American Fisheries Society Symposium 1:402–416, 1987

Recruitment Mechanisms of Striped Bass and Atlantic Salmon: Comparative Liabilities of Alternative Life Histories

Paul J. Rago and C. Phillip Goodyear[1]

U.S. Fish and Wildlife Service, National Fisheries Center–Leetown, Box 700
Kearneysville, West Virginia 25430, USA

Abstract.—Naturally reproducing stocks of striped bass *Morone saxatilis* and Atlantic salmon *Salmo salar* have declined drastically in the last 20 years. These species face the common problems of anadromous fish, but have evolved very different solutions. Our purpose is to compare the relative sensitivities of these alternative solutions or life history strategies to decreases in conditional survival probabilities. Such decreases are relevant to the issues of increased fishing mortality or environmental contaminants. Eigenvalue analysis and Monte Carlo simulations of models by age (striped bass) or life stage (Atlantic salmon) suggested that striped bass are more sensitive than Atlantic salmon to fishing mortality. Striped bass recruitment is highly variable, and population persistence is contingent on the formation of strong year classes. The likelihood of formation of a strong year class diminishes rapidly as increases in fishing mortality decrease the average age of the population. Atlantic salmon have a more complex life history in which the durations of the freshwater and marine stages vary considerably. The persistence of Atlantic salmon populations hinges on demographic plasticity related to the chronological age at which maiden fish spawn. Repeated spawning is relatively unimportant. We use a model of alternative "lives" of Atlantic salmon to show that the selection for early age at smolting and decreased duration of the marine phase can be outcomes of increased fishing mortality alone. Annual variations in marine survival rates alter the relative fitness of various "lives" and act to maintain them in the population.

Striped bass *Morone saxatilis* and Atlantic salmon *Salmo salar* are highly prized recreational and commercial species, but naturally reproducing stocks of both species are depressed. Commercial landings of striped bass along the Atlantic seaboard of the United States declined from a peak of 6.7 kilotonnes (kt) in 1973 to 0.8 kt in 1983 (Boreman and Austin 1985). Similarly, commercial catches of Atlantic salmon in the north Atlantic Ocean declined from a peak of 12.7 kt in 1973 to 6.7 kt in 1984 (Anonymous 1985).[1]

The decline of both species spurred intervention by management to reduce fishing mortality. The measures applied included areal and seasonal closures of fisheries for both species, reductions in licensed effort for Atlantic salmon, and increases in the minimum legal size of striped bass. The plight of striped bass in the USA stimulated a congressionally mandated research program to identify the cause of causes of the decline (Public Law 96-118). The decline in Atlantic salmon provided impetus to the formation of the North Atlantic Salmon Conservation Organization (NASCO). This recently formed international body is attempting to resolve conflicts among salmon-producing and salmon-consuming nations.

The common problem of depression of stocks shared by Atlantic salmon and striped bass is usually ascribed to habitat degradation or excessive fishing mortality or some combination of these. Certainly, the elimination of habitats or access to them will cause populations to decline in proportion to the loss of available habitats. Extirpation of Atlantic salmon from southern New England was largely the result of dams that denied the fish access to suitable spawning habitats (Saunders 1981). Price et al. (1985) provided evidence for the decline in habitat quality for striped bass in Chesapeake Bay. In contrast to the effects of habitat destruction, the effects of fishing on recruitment are less easily understood (Paloheimo and Elson 1974).

Atlantic salmon and striped bass are phylogenetically distant and the geographic loci of their greatest abundance are widely separate. Both species face the common problems of anadromous fish but have evolved dramatically different solutions. We compare the relative sensitivities of these alternative solutions or life history strategies to decreases in conditional survival probabilities. Such decreases are relevant to the problems

---

[1]Present address: National Marine Fisheries Service, Southeast Fisheries Center, Miami Laboratory, Miami, Florida 33149, USA.

of increased fishing mortality or environmental contaminants. To facilitate this comparison, we use age-structured models for striped bass and life-stage-structured models for Atlantic salmon. The parameters in our models are realistic but do not define a particular population. Our analyses illustrate the comparative liabilities of two very different sets of adaptations to a common problem.

Methods

Description of Models

Striped bass.—From strictly a modeling standpoint, the life history of striped bass is straightforward. Adults migrate to natal areas (Morgan et al. 1973) in spring and commence spawning when water temperatures are near 15–18°C. The buoyant eggs (diameter, 1.0–1.5 mm) hatch in 29–80 h, depending on water temperature; larvae are 2.0–3.7 mm long at hatching at absorb their yolk over a period of 3 d (Setzler et al. 1980). Young striped bass spend 2–3 years in the estuary before joining the coastal migratory stocks. Maturation is a function of both size and age and is distributed over ages 2–4 for males and 3–6 for females. Spawning is believed to occur annually thereafter until a maximum age of 30 years or more is reached (Setzler et al. 1980).

These concepts are schematically and mathematically represented in Figure 1. The governing equation for the population is the classic Leslie projection matrix (Leslie 1945), a formalism repeatedly applied to striped bass in the literature (Christensen et al. 1977; Saila and Lorda 1977;

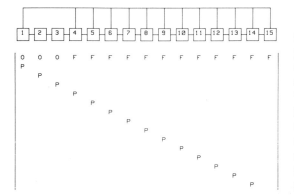

FIGURE 1.—Flow diagram and population projection matrix for striped bass. Numbers in the flow diagram designate age-group. In the projection matrix, F is age-specific fecundity and P is the probability of transferring to the next age-group.

DeAngelis et al. 1980; Heyde and Cohen 1985). Matrix elements in the first row of A_b are the numbers of age-0+ females produced by a female striped bass of each age; matrix elements along the principal subdiagonal are the probabilities of surviving from one age-class to the next. The population projection equation becomes

$$X_{t+1} = A_b X_t; \qquad (1)$$

X is a vector of the number of females in specific age-classes, t is year, and A_b is the projection matrix for striped bass.

Atlantic salmon.—The life cycle of Atlantic salmon is complex. Atlantic salmon may spend up to 6 years in fresh water before smolting and 3 years or more at sea before returning to spawn (Power 1981). Spent adults (kelts) remain in streams in the winter following spawning and may return to spawn after spending an additional winter at sea. The variable duration of the freshwater and marine phases means that a newly hatched egg can follow a variety of different "lives." The concept of "lives" was developed more fully by Lenski and Service (1982) and Rago and Dorazio (1984). In the following sections we illustrate the concept of "lives" for Atlantic salmon. We then show how "lives" can be condensed into a flow diagram and then a matrix model.

We adopt a somewhat simplified model of Atlantic salmon biology in which smolting occurs at either age 2+ or 3+ years and fish may mature after one to three sea winters (SW). Multiple spawning can occur twice for adults that mature after 1 SW, and once for 2-SW and 3-SW fish. We have assumed that kelts (K1 and K2) spend an additional winter at sea before spawning (i.e., the "long absence" repeat spawners of Allen et al. 1972). The combinations of two smolt years and three different times of maturation result in six possible life histories or "lives" (Table 1). We designate each "life" by the combination of age at smolting and the number of SW at first spawning. Thus "life" 3.2 refers to a 3-yer-old smolt that first spawns after two sea winters. This designation of a life is patterned after Murray's (1968) designation of age. A "life" simply indicates a unique path or branch (Table 1) from age 0+ to the previous spawner stage (PS1 or PS2). The probability of following a given life is equal to the product of probabilities along a given path. The sum of the probabilities of all "lives" is one.

The possibility of following different "lives" means that a cohort may reproduce anytime within chronological ages of 4–9 years; however the maximum number of spawnings for any "life" is limited to three in our model. The net effect of this life history pattern is to distribute the reproductive contributions of a year class over several years. Even if Atlantic salmon spawned only once (i.e., if they were semelparous), the reproduction of a year class would be distributed over 4 years (Table 1). Intuitively, it is evident that this is a "bet-hedging" strategy (Stearns and Crandall 1981) that spreads the risk of reproductive failure over several years. If probabilities of different lives are density dependent, it is also clear that much resiliency can be conferred on the population. An example of a density-dependent mechanism would be density-related schedules of smoltification (Chadwick et al. 1978).

The alternative paths followed by Atlantic salmon can be summarized in a flow diagram (Figure 2). Note that age is not preserved in this formulation; e.g., the 1-SW stage is composed of fish either 4 or 5 years old. Similarly, the PS2 stage can consist of fish 7, 8, or 9 years old. The paths in this diagram can be analyzed by various methods of loop analysis (see Caswell 1982a,

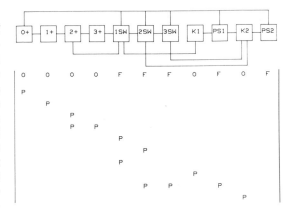

FIGURE 2.—Flow diagram and projection matrix for Atlantic salmon. Life stage abbreviations in the flow diagram are defined in Table 1. In the projection matrix, F is the life-stage-specific fecundity and P is the probability of transferring to the next life stage.

1982b) or econometrics (Evans and Dempson 1986).

Alternatively, the notational complexity can be reduced by expressing the flow diagram as the elements of a transition matrix (Figure 2). The nonzero elements below the principal subdiagonal relate to transfers to other life stages. The zero fecundity terms in the eighth and tenth columns of the first row correspond to the hiatus in reproduction by kelts after spawning. The matrix equation for the *life stages,* of Atlantic salmon is given by the equation

$$X'_{t+1} = A_s X'_t; \qquad (2)$$

X' is a vector of number of females in the life stages defined in Figure 2.

Parameter Estimation

Parameter estimation is always difficult for natural populations and must be based on a variety of data sources (e.g., Evans and Dempson 1986). A single population is rarely studied in sufficient detail to provide all the necessary parameters for a model. We have taken parameters for striped bass from Goodyear (1985), and those for Atlantic salmon from several sources—particularly from Murray (1968), Symons (1979), Chadwick (1982), and Buck and Hay (1984). For Atlantic salmon, we needed estimates of freshwater survival rates, smoltification schedules for parr, maturation rates for adults at sea, fecundity as a function of sea age, and the probability of successful respawning. Our liberal use of published data does not imply that we have defined the dynamics of a particular

TABLE 1.—Representation of Atlantic salmon biology as a set of alternative "lives." Each pathway designates a unique sequence of transition from freshwater to marine environments, duration at sea prior to first spawning, and repeat spawning. In the "Life" column, the number left of the decimal is age at smolting and the number to the right is the number of sea winters at first spawning.

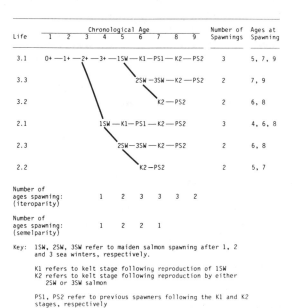

Key: 1SW, 2SW, 3SW refer to maiden salmon spawning after 1, 2 and 3 sea winters, respectively.

K1 refers to kelt stage following reproduction of 1SW
K2 refers to kelt stage following reproduction by either 2SW or 3SW salmon

PS1, PS2 refer to previous spawners following the K1 and K2 stages, respectively population; rather we have defined a "representative" population with reasonable parameters.

Maturation rates.—The mark–recapture data of Murray (1968) were used to derive estimates of the fraction of the marine population maturing, by sea age, for Atlantic salmon. The observed rates of return of marked fish reflect both total mortality and the fraction of the oceanic stock that matures. To separate these two effects, one must assume that annual survival at sea is constant and that all of the remaining adults mature after 3 SW. If T represents the total number of fish marked, and R_1, R_2, and R_3 the number of returns of 1-, 2-, and 3-SW Atlantic salmon, respectively, the expected numbers of returns can be described as follows:

$$R_1 = TSf_1;$$
$$R_2 = TS^2(1 - f_1)f_2;$$
$$R_3 = TS^3(1 - f_1)(1 - f_2)f_3; \qquad (3)$$

S is the annual survival rate at sea; f_1 is the fraction of the population alive at the end of one sea winter that matures; f_2 is the corresponding fraction of 2-SW fish that return. Note that an assumption that all 3-SW fish mature (i.e., $f_3 = 1$) results in a system of three equations in three unknowns—S, f_1, and f_2. To estimate these parameters, we used the total tag return data (pooled across years) of Murray (1968) for the Little Codroy River. To estimate the fraction maturing, we used recaptures from both trap counts and commercial fisheries in the Little Codroy estuary. We assumed that fish from this source were destined to spawn and therefore represented mature fish. The solution to equations (3) was simply attained by iteration on a computer. To estimate the maturation schedules for females, we adjusted the number of marked and recaptured fish by the female proportion of the marked smolts and recaptures, respectively. We further assumed an initial posttagging mortality of 90%. Adjustment factors and the solution to equations (3) are given in Table 2.

Murray (1968) also presented data on tag returns of previous spawners that can be used to estimate the probability that a spawning female in year i will return to spawn in year $i + 2$. If R_p is the number of tags recovered from previous spawners, the probability of a spawner returning to spawn again is R_p/T divided by the expected survival rate and the fraction maturing. We estimated this probability as

$$\text{Prob (respawning)} = \frac{R_p/T}{S^2f_1 + S^3(1 - f_1)f_2}. \qquad (4)$$

Other parameters.—Freshwater survival rates were taken from Symons (1979) for intermediate population densities of Atlantic salmon. Fecundity estimates for Atlantic salmon were derived by L. Stolte (U.S. Fish and Wildlife Service, personal communication). Sex ratios of returning Atlantic salmon were derived from data of Buck and Hay (1984). Initial survival of tagged Atlantic salmon was assumed to be 10%; this value was intended to include both handling mortality and initial marine mortality.

Eigenvalue Analyses

The elements of the transition matrices A_b and A_s, given in Figures 1 and 2, respectively, are nonnegative and real, so that by the Perron–Frobenius theorem (Sykes 1969) the matrices will have a single real root whose modulus exceeds those of all other roots. This property enables one to draw on a large body of theory related to Leslie matrix models (see Usher 1971). In all of our analyses of model properties, we have assumed a stable, nongrowing population. This was obtained by choosing a value of the first-year survival rate that sets the population intrinsic growth rate to zero (or, equivalently, the finite rate of increase to one) by the procedure of Vaughan and Saila (1976).

Matrix models enable the computation of the stable age vector and the reproductive value. We determined these iteratively using the method of Keyfitz (1968). The validity of the iterative approach was checked by use of a numerical analysis package on a microcomputer. Sensitivity of the matrix coefficients, expressed as the partial derivative of the finite rate of increase with respect to the model parameter, was computed by the general method of Caswell (1978).

Many biologists are familiar with the general properties of Leslie matrices and the equivalence

TABLE 2.—Tagging data of Murray (1968) used to estimate fraction of female Atlantic salmon maturing by sea winter (SW).

Variable	Number	Adjustment factor	Revised number	Estimated fraction mature
Tags released	61,242	0.1 × 0.8306	5,087	
Tags recovered				
1 SW	194	0.2103	412	0.08
2 SW	341	0.5927	202	0.66
3 SW	14	0.7143	10	1.00

of population growth rate and the dominant eigenvalue of the matrix A. Although the dominant eigenvalue (λ_1) defines the population's rate of growth, the trajectory that it follows is influenced by the subdominant eigenvalues ($\lambda_2, \lambda_3, \lambda_4 \ldots$). In particular, oscillations and the rate of convergence to the stable age structure are determined in part by the magnitude of the subdominant eigenvalues. In much the same way that an electronic signal can be decomposed into underlying frequencies, the eigenvalue set provides a measure of the population's response to perturbations. In human demography, the process of extracting the components of variation of a population projection matrix is known as spectral decomposition (Keyfitz 1968).

The Perron–Frobenius theorem (Sykes 1969) ensures that the moduli of all subdominant eigenvalues will be smaller than the dominant eigenvalue. Because the dominant eigenvalue is constrained to be 1.0 in our formulation, the real parts of all subdominant eigenvalues converge to zero when raised to powers. By De Moivre's theorem (Thomas 1972), a complex number, r, can be written as the product of an exponential part and the sum of a sine and cosine function. Then for the general complex root λ,

$$\lambda^n = \exp(-nr) \qquad (5)$$
$$= \exp[-n(x + iy)]$$
$$= \exp(-nx)[\cos(ny) + i \sin(ny)];$$

The real part of the complex root, x, corresponds to the rate of dampening and the imaginary part, y, governs the frequency and length of the waves. All of the eigenvalues contribute to the population's convergence to a new equilibrium. Thus, the convergence of a population with a high average modulus of the subdominant roots is slower than that of a population with a low average modulus.

Horst (1977a, 1977b), the first to examine the eigenvalue set for fish populations, used the set to compare responses to changes in mortality of the youngest age-groups for several marine species. Horst used an Argand diagram to plot the eigenvalue set. An Argand diagram simply allows for the graphical presentation of complex numbers in a two-dimensional plane in which the x-axis represents the real component and the y-axis represents the imaginary component. Rago (1980) suggested that the area enclosed by the eigenvalue set provides an index of a population's sensitivity to perturbations. As the subdominant eigenvalues diminish when the population is projected through

time (i.e., when the matrix is raised to successive powers), the area enclosed by the eigenvalues in the Argand plane approaches zero. The rate of convergence to zero can be a useful index of a population's dynamic response to an additional source of mortality (Rago 1980).

Results

Parameter Estimates

Parameters for striped bass and Atlantic salmon are summarized in Tables 3 and 4, respectively. These parameters were used for all simulations except when total survival rate of adult fish was varied.

Eigenvalue Analyses

Argand plane.—Large average moduli of the subdominant eigenvalues indicate that older age-groups contribute more than younger ones to the total reproductive effort. When this condition holds, convergence to a new stable structure is slow because of the lagged effects of previous reproductive success; i.e., older individuals continue to contribute heavily until replaced by younger cohorts that have survival and reproductive schedules different from those of their parents. The Argand diagram thus suggests how quickly a population should converge to a new age structure.

The overall pattern of λ for Atlantic salmon comprises five large moduli and several small λs. The Argand plot is more symmetrical for striped bass than for Atlantic salmon (Figure 3). When mortality increases, the subdominant eigenvalues shrink rapidly for striped bass but not for Atlantic salmon. This decrease implies that the contributions of older striped bass become less important. Thus, the population variability for striped bass

TABLE 3.—Age schedules of average fecundity for female striped bass used in the model simulations.

Age	Weight (kg)	Fecundity (eggs)	Age	Weight (kg)	Fecundity (eggs)
2	0.4		14	21.3	1.8×10^6
3	0.9		15	23.3	1.9×10^6
4	1.6	3.3×10^4	16	25.1	2.1×10^6
5	2.8	1.7×10^5	17	26.8	2.2×10^6
6	4.4	3.5×10^5	18	28.5	2.4×10^6
7	6.3	5.3×10^5	19	30.0	2.5×10^6
8	8.1	6.8×10^5	20	31.4	2.6×10^6
9	10.8	9.0×10^5	21	32.7	2.7×10^6
10	12.6	1.0×10^6	22	33.9	2.8×10^6
11	14.2	1.2×10^6	23	34.9	2.9×10^6
12	17.9	1.5×10^6	24	35.9	3.0×10^6
13	19.2	1.6×10^6	25	36.8	3.1×10^6

TABLE 4.—Summary of model parameters used for Atlantic salmon. SW is sea winter; PS is previous spawner; prob is probability.

Matrix element i,j	Description	Estimate
1,5	Fecundity of 1-SW salmon = female eggs × hatching survival × 1 (1 − exploitation rate in stream) × fraction maturing	$1,600(0.13)(1-0.5)(0.08)$
1,6	Fecundity of 2-SW salmon = female eggs × hatching survival × (1 − exploitation rate in stream) × fraction maturing	$3,700(0.13)(1-0.5)(0.66)$
1,7	Fecundity of 3-SW salmon = female eggs × hatching survival × (1 − exploitation rate in stream) × fraction maturing	$5,500(0.13)(1-0.5)(1.0)$
1,9	Fecundity of PS1 = female eggs × hatching survival × (1 − exploitation rate in stream) × fraction maturing	$3,700(0.13)(1-0.5)(1.0)$
1,11	Fecundity of PS2 = female eggs × hatching survival × (1 − exploitation rate in stream) × fraction maturing	$5,500(0.13)(1-0.5)(1.0)$
2,1	Stream survival 0+ to 1+	0.41
3,2	Stream survival 1+ to 2+	0.57
4,3	Stream survival × (1 − fraction smolting)	$0.57(1-0.33)$
5,3	Stream survival × fraction smolting × initial sea survival	$0.57(0.33)(0.1266)$
5,4	Stream survival × initial sea survival	$0.57(0.1266)$
6,5	Marine survival × (1 − fraction maturing after 1 SW)	$0.5(1-0.08)$
7,6	Marine survival × (1 − fraction maturing after 2 SW)	$0.5(1-0.66)$
8,5	Prob of 1-SW fish becoming kelt 1 = Prob of 1-SW fish respawning/marine survival × (1−instream exploitation rate)	$0.1824/0.5(1-0.05)$
9,8	Prob of Kelt 1 becoming PS1 = marine survival	0.5
10,6	Prob of 2-SW fish becoming kelt 2 = Prob of 2-SW fish respawning/marine survival × (1−instream exploitation rate)	$0.1824/0.5(1-0.5)$
10,7	Prob of 3-SW fish becoming kelt 2 = Prob of 2-SW fish respawning/marine survival × (1−instream exploitation rate)	$0.1824/0.5(1-0.5)$
10,9	Prob of PS1 becoming kelt 2 = Prob of 2-SW fish respawning/marine survival × (1−instream exploitation rate)	$0.1824/0.5(1-0.5)$
11,10	Prob of kelt 2 becoming PS2 = marine survival	0.50

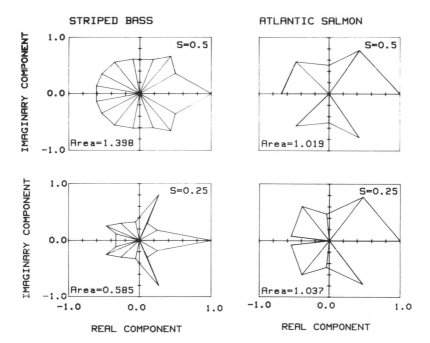

FIGURE 3.—Plots of eigenvalue sets in the complex plane for striped bass and Atlantic salmon under two different survival rates (S) for adults. Note the asymmetry of the Argand diagrams for Atlantic salmon. In Argand diagrams, the abscissa values are real numbers and the ordinate values are imaginary.

should increase with mortality. For Atlantic salmon, in contrast, the overall shape and area enclosed by the eigenvalues change little with changes in survival. This consistency suggests that most of the oscillatory properties of Atlantic salmon are not attributable to older age-classes. Rather, they appear to be due to the properties of the freshwater age-groups.

The convergence properties of the Argand diagram are illustrated in Figure 4. For striped bass, the convergence of the subdominant eigenvalues to zero is smooth and the rate of convergence increases as survival decreases. For Atlantic salmon, the pattern of convergence is similar initially, but becomes more variable as the number of time periods (matrix powers) increases (Figure 4). Striped bass are sensitive to decreased adult survival because the numbers of reproducing adults are severely reduced. When survival is high, the large number of reproducing age-groups buffers the population from change. When survival is low, it becomes a liability because of the

increased period of exposure to the high mortality rates before peak reproductive value is attained. Juvenile Atlantic salmon are not exposed to the decreased survival rates and, therefore, act as a buffer to changes imposed on older life stages.

Stable age structure.—The relative insensitivity of Atlantic salmon to changes in survival is illustrated by changes in the predicted stable life stage structure that develop at different survival rates (Figure 5). The percentage of older striped bass decreases rapidly as survival decreases. Atlantic salmon, in contrast, change little in overall life stage composition as sea survival decreases because the proportion of the population (numeric not biomass) that lives in the freshwater environment is large. Note also that the stable structure for Atlantic salmon does not monotonically decrease as it does in striped bass. This situation is a result of the pooling of ages in all life stages beyond age 3+.

Reproductive value.—The reproductive value

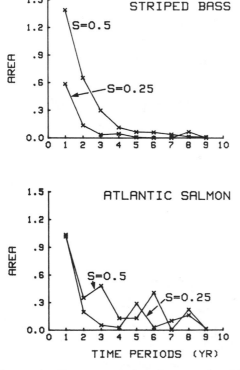

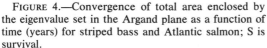

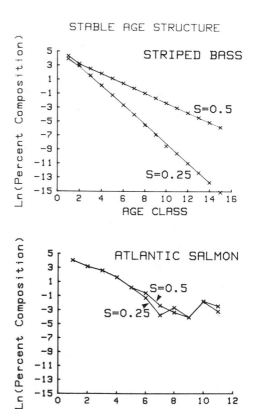

FIGURE 4.—Convergence of total area enclosed by the eigenvalue set in the Argand plane as a function of time (years) for striped bass and Atlantic salmon; S is survival.

FIGURE 5.—Stable age and life stage structures for striped bass and Atlantic salmon, respectively. Results are expressed in terms of $\log_e$ (percent composition) for adult survival rates (S) of 0.5 and 0.25 for each species.

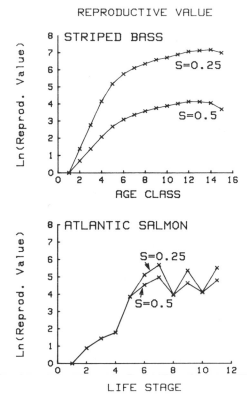

FIGURE 6.—Reproductive values of striped bass and Atlantic salmon by age-class and life stage, respectively, for adult survival rates (S) of 0.5 and 0.25 for each species.

of a life stage increases as survival decreases (Figure 6), partly because of the assumption of a constant population growth rate in which survival of the initial age-group exactly balances reduced adult fecundity. Thus, as adult survival decreases, the survival from egg to ages 0+ (Atlantic salmon) or 1 (striped bass) increases. Hence, the number of young produced per individual in a reproducing age-group must necessarily increase. The change in reproductive value in response to decreased survival is greater for striped bass than for Atlantic salmon because the effect is distributed over a larger number of age-groups.

Sensitivity analysis.—Caswell (1978) first demonstrated that the sensitivity of any element a_{ij} of a population projection matrix was the product of the stable age fraction (w_j) of the jth class and the reproductive value (v_i) of the ith class. Since reproductive value of the first age-group is defined as 1.0, the sensitivity to fecundity decreases with age because w_j decreases with j. Also, sensitivity to changes in fecundity is generally much less

than to changes in survival.

Striped bass are most sensitive to changes in survival before the onset of reproduction. When survival decreases, sensitivity coefficients are higher initially for the younger age-classes but the pattern reverses for older age-classes (Figure 7A). Atlantic salmon are most sensitive to survival terms related to the fraction smolting—particularly the fraction of age-2+ smolts (Figure 7B). This sensitivity is expected because the average age at first reproduction for the population decreases with average smolt age. Sensitivity coefficients related to the probability of successfully spawning for a second or third time were relatively small. Thus, processes affecting the distribution of ages for maiden Atlantic salmon are more important to population persistence than processes governing subsequent reproduction.

Sensitivity coefficients for changes in fecundity are much less than those related to survival. The change in population growth rate of striped bass populations in response to changes in fecundity will be greater when adult survival is high (Figure 7C). A similar pattern holds for Atlantic salmon (Figure 7D), but the magnitude of the changes is much less.

Contributions of Lives to Total Reproduction

The "lives" approach provides a convenient means of predicting the effects of fishing pressure. The total reproductive potential of the population composed of individuals following different lives depends on reproductive potential of the several lives and their frequency in the population. To illustrate how the relative advantage of a particular life changes with fishing pressure, we show the potential egg deposition for each life as a function of total annual survival (Figure 8). The bold line in Figure 8 shows the composite reproductive potential based on the parameters in Table 4.

Several general features are of import. First, the life with maximum reproductive potential shifts from life 2.3 at high sea survival to life 2.2 at intermediate sea survival and to life 2.1 at low sea survival. Second, the trajectories of egg deposition for 2-year-old smolts (lives 2.1, 2.2, 2.3) are consistently higher than those of the 3-year-old smolts (lives 3.1, 3.2, 3.3) except when sea survival is very low. When survival is low, the cost of spending an extra year in fresh water is less than the cost of spending an extra year of exposure to high mortality at sea. The advantage of life 2.3 drops rapidly as survival decreases, its curve

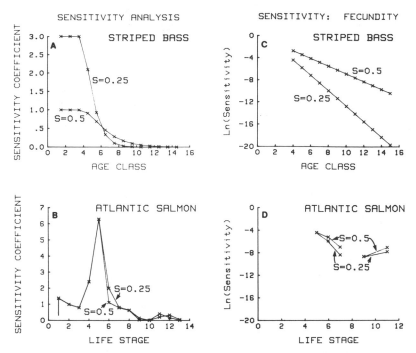

FIGURE 7.—Sensitivity coefficients of survival and fecundity elements of the respective population projection matrices for striped bass and Atlantic salmon. Coefficients were computed for adult survival rates (S) of 0.5 and 0.25 for each species.

falling below life 3.1 and even below 3.2. Even the 2.2 strategy falls below the 3.1 strategy at the lowest levels of survival tested (~27%/year). The advantage of the 3.1 strategy is that it keeps fish in a protected environment longer, and then allows a larger fraction to successfully spawn. Third, the transition points between lives, where the advantage of spending an extra year at sea to increase fecundity fails to offset the cost of increased mortality, are equal for the 2- and 3-year-old smolts.

The shifts in relative advantage among "lives" as survival changes suggest a mechanism for the maintenance of multiple life history strategies. If sea survival fluctuates, then the relative advantage of following a particular life also changes. Thus, the mixture of lives present in a population may reflect the recent history of variations in survival rates. Fishing mortality necessarily restricts the range of possible survival rates, thereby limiting the types of lives selected. Populations of Atlantic salmon in northern extremes should be more vulnerable to fishing than those in the south because they require a longer period in fresh water (Power 1981).

Selection for early maturation tends to decrease

yield because it decreases exposure to the fishery. If effort is increased to maintain yield (e.g., due to price changes, see Clark 1976; Strand et al. 1980), selection favors a further reduction in yield by selection for earlier maturation and increased residence time in fresh water. Thus a positive feedback loop with respect to yield is implicit (Figure 8) if the fishery responds to decreasing catch per unit effort by increasing effort. If there is any heritability of "lives," the foregoing fishing strategy accelerates changes in population structure with particularly ominous implications for both yield and the population.

It is not necessary to invoke a genetic mechanism for the shift toward shorter duration of life at sea. This shift is entirely a consequence of the differential survival of the various lives. To demonstrate a significant heritability effect—i.e., that the offspring of individuals following a particular life are more likely to follow the life of their parents—one must demonstrate that the rate of increase in earlier-maturing fish is greater than that predicted simply by chance alone (i.e., independent lives). Thus, forecasts with the model could provide a null hypothesis for assessing potential genetic change in Atlantic salmon pop-

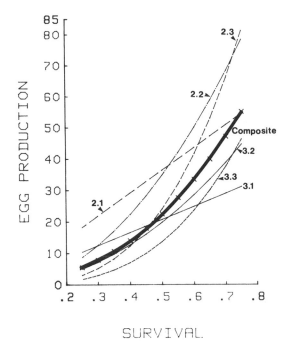

FIGURE 8.—Potential lifetime egg production per individual Atlantic salmon as functions of adult survival during various "lives." Lives are denoted by decimal values showing age at smolting (left) and number of sea winters at first spawning (right).

ulations. Such forecasts might help distinguish between the competing hypotheses of heritable age at first spawning (Schaffer and Elson 1975) and of environmentally determined maturation rates (Saunders et al. 1983).

Sensitivity of Population Structure to Fishing

We evaluated the sensitivity of both species to fishing on the basis of the amount of the compensatory increase in survival or fecundity that would be required to offset losses to fishing. In this analysis, we used the compensation ratio (Goodyear 1977, 1980) to measure the overall change in the survival and fecundity parameters that must occur to enable a population undergoing exploitation to stabilize at a new equilibrium. The compensation ratio (CR) is calculated as

$$CR = \frac{P_o}{P_e} ; \qquad (6)$$

P_o = potential fecundity per recruit for the unfished population;
P_e = potential fecundity per recruit for the exploited population.

Potential fecundity per recruit (P) is the maximum average lifetime production of eggs per recruit under optimum growth and natural mortality schedules. This definition incorporates the effect of density-dependent fecundity and adult survival. These density-dependent phenomena tend to decrease the actual average egg production per recruit at equilibrium below the levels that would exist at low population densities.

The potential fecundity per recruit is calculated as

$$P = \sum_{i=1}^{n} S_i E_i M_i F_i; \qquad (7)$$

S_i = maximum probability of survival from recruitment to age-class i;
E_i = maximum mean fecundity per mature female in age-class i;
M_i = maximum fraction of age-class i females that are mature;
F_i = fraction of age-class i that is female;
n = number of age-classes in the population.

The parameter values needed to solve for P in the unfished population (i.e., P_o) were taken from Tables 3 and 4 under the assumption that all density-dependent increases in growth and survival among adults have been fully used. Specifically, no further reduction in abundance would cause the recruits to have lower natural mortality rates, to mature earlier, or to increase fecundity.

To estimate P for the exploited population (i.e., P_e), one must reduce the survival of the recruited age-classes. The probability of a recruit surviving to age-class i (S_i) is simply the product of the annual total survival probabilities to which the recruit is exposed before entering the ith age-class. The total survival probabilities are higher in an unexploited population than in an exploited population. Thus, the value of P is higher for the unexploited population. The relationship simply reflects that the probability of an egg surviving to produce a recruit egg must be higher in the exploited population, if the stock is not tending toward extinction.

A minimum natural mortality rate of 0.15 was assumed for all striped bass beyond their first year of life, and for all Atlantic salmon beyond the smolt stage. Survival rates for Atlantic salmon parr were taken from Table 4, and mortalities of 0.75 and 0.25 were assumed to occur during the smolt and postspawning migrations to the ocean. The compensation ratio was evaluated for fishing mortality rates *(F)* from 0.01 to 1.2 for each species.

Fishing mortality has a more powerful effect on the reproductive value of striped bass recruits than of Atlantic salmon recruits (Figure 9). As a consequence, the exposure of striped bass to any given level of fishing requires a much greater density-dependent response than would be required from Atlantic salmon to permit persistence of the population. Clearly the life history strategy of striped bass is more sensitive than that of Atlantic salmon to changes in annual postrecruit mortality. Analyses thus far have focused on equilibrium characteristics of the life history strategies. We next examine population responses to varying survival rates of juvenile fish.

Population Sensitivity to Variable First-Year Survival

The relative sensitivity of population fecundity to environmentally induced variations in first-year survival provides a measure of the degree of protection imparted by the life history strategy adopted by the species. We evaluated the relative sensitivity of both life history patterns by simulating annual variations in first year survival as follows:

$$N_1 = s_0 N_0 e^{(sR_t + C)} ; \qquad (8)$$

R = random normal deviate;
s = standard deviation of the random term;
C = bias correction term to force the growth rate to unity.

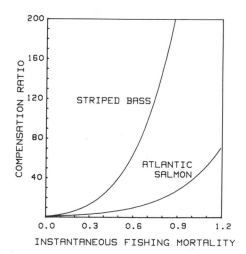

FIGURE 9.—Comparison of compensation ratios for striped bass and Atlantic salmon as functions of instantaneous fishing mortality rate.

This convention assumes that the underlying survival rate is lognormally distributed, an assumption that is consistent with observations of striped bass in Chesapeake Bay (Goodyear and Christensen 1984) and with an evaluation of the form of random variation in Pacific salmonids (Peterman 1981). The value of s was arbitrarily chosen to be 0.5, which is somewhat lower than the 0.719 estimated for the Chesapeake stock of striped bass by Goodyear and Christensen (1984). However, since our purpose is to evaluate the relative propagation of random noise in both life history strategies, the absolute value of s is not important.

The term C was computed by the iterative convergence scheme of Goodyear and Christensen (1984). It is required to eliminate the positive bias in the population growth rate that is associated with this form of random variation in survival. The relative effect of the random variation was assessed as the cumulative frequency distribution of 1,000 coefficients of variation (CV = SD/mean) of simulated annual egg deposition. Each CV was based on the last 50 years of a 75-year simulation. Separate frequency distributions were determined for both species for annual survival probabilities for recruits of 0.25, 0.5, and 0.75. We assumed that striped bass were recruited at age 1 and Atlantic salmon as postsmolts.

The density-dependent regulation of age at smolting has been investigated by many researchers, most recently by Evans et al. (1984). We assessed the effect of this mechanism on the propagation of random variation in Atlantic salmon by making the fraction of parr that become smolts at age 2 (M_2) a function of the abundance of parr (N) in the two preceding year classes, i.e.,

$$M_2 = 0.66(1 - f); \qquad (9)$$

f = minimum of 1 and $(N_2 + N_3)/d$;
$d = 2(N_2 + N_3)$ for the stable age distribution.

Thus, the fraction of parr that become smolts at age 2 is 0 at densities of preceding year classes that exceed twice that for the stable age distribution and 0.33 at the density of the stable age distribution, and approaches 0.66 as the sum of preceding year classes declines.

At survival rates of 0.75 and 0.50, the cumulative frequency distributions of CVs are considerably lower for striped bass than for Atlantic salmon (Figure 10). This observation demonstrates the stability imparted to the striped bass stock by the large numbers of age-classes that

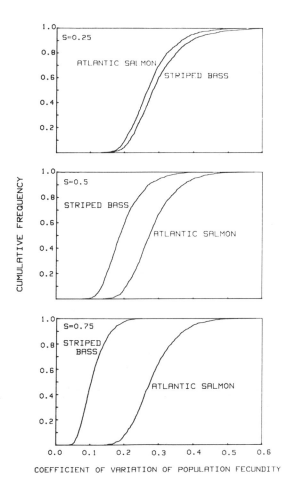

FIGURE 10.—Distributions of the coefficient of variation of population fecundity for striped bass and Atlantic salmon under adult survival rates (S) of 0.25, 0.5, and 0.75.

contribute to reproduction. As survival declines, the bulk of the reproductive effort is compressed into the first few reproducing age-classes and the population response to variable first-year survival increases. At a survival rate of 0.25, striped bass are more sensitive than Atlantic salmon to variable first-year survival at any of the survival rates examined (Figure 10).

Postrecruit survival rates have little effect on the propagation of variable first-year survival for Atlantic salmon; population stability actually increases slightly as survival decreases. If the fraction of age-2 parr that become smolts is density dependent, the propagation of variable survival is buffered and the corresponding variability in the population is reduced (Figure 11).

Discussion

Comparative analysis of life history strategies can be a useful tool for understanding population-specific (Fetterolf 1981) and species-specific (Garrod and Knights 1979; Pauly 1981) responses to fishing pressure. Two of the most important papers that address the intraspecific variation of anadromous fishes are by Leggett and Carscadden (1978: American shad *Alosa sapidissima*) and Schaffer and Elson (1975: Atlantic salmon). These authors have shown through comparisons of populations what experimentation could not: the roles of abiotic factors and their variations in the molding of life history strategies.

Striped bass are long-lived, highly fecund, and iteroparous (i.e., reproduce more than once). Recruitment varies widely and populations are often dominated by large year classes (Boreman and Austin 1985). The longevity of striped bass ensures that dominant year classes will have many years to contribute to reproduction. This acts to dampen the effects of variable recruitment induced by environmental variations and other factors. Thus striped bass "hedge their bets" (Stearns and Crandall 1981) by increasing the frequency of reproduction and number of offspring. The probability of population extinction is diminished by the reduced stakes associated wtih each reproductive event (Slobodkin and Rapoport 1974). Failures of individual year classes are balanced by the probability of strong year classes forming in other years.

Atlantic salmon probably inhabit a more variable environment than striped bass. Temperature ranges are certainly greater in northern streams than in the piedmont streams and rivers inhabited by striped bass. Moreover, the freshwater migrations of Atlantic salmon are more arduous than

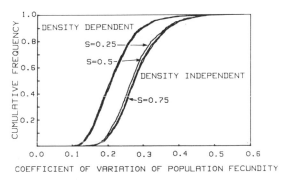

FIGURE 11.—Distributions of the coefficient of variation of population fecundity of Atlantic salmon under assumptions of density dependence and independence.

those of striped bass. For example, striped bass migrations generally range from 15 to 150 km upstream from the mouths of relatively low-gradient rivers in Chesapeake Bay (Hardy 1978), whereas Atlantic salmon regularly navigate up to 200 km in the St. John River, 190 km in the Miramichi River, and 320 km in the Tobique River (Schaffer and Elson 1975; Power 1981). Although Atlantic salmon may spawn repeatedly, their difficulties of migration, their fasting while resident in streams, and their return to sea place a high premium on successful reproduction. A succession of poor year classes would rapidly decimate the relatively short-lived Atlantic salmon if other "bet-hedging" mechanisms were not employed.

Atlantic salmon hedge their bets in a variety of ways. First, egg size is increased. This not only results in larger, more robust larvae, but also prolongs the period of transition to exogenous food resources. Second, the eggs are deposited in the benign environment of a gravel nest, protected from most vertebrate predators and sheltered from wide variations in temperature and oxygen. The importance of these mechanisms of increased parental investment are well known (e.g., Wootton 1979). The third, and perhaps most important, mechanism of risk aversion is the variable duration of residence in both fresh and salt water. A single year class can smolt over a period of several years and then remain at sea from one to over three years before returning to spawn. Thus, even if the likelihood of repeat spawning is negligible, a year class can reproduce over several years. Hence, the consequences of high mortality (in a single year) for population persistence are reduced. Density-dependent smoltification schedules will further buffer the variability in total population fecundity.

Results of our application of "lives" to Atlantic salmon support previous theoretical investigations of Schaffer and Elson (1975), Schaffer (1979), Caswell et al. (1984), and Myers (1984). The prediction of increased frequency of grilse spawners is obtained without invoking a genetic mechanism. To demonstrate a heritability component, one must first show that the rate of increase in grilse frequencies is greater than expected on the basis of a selection model alone. We extend the model of Caswell et al. (1984) to include a realistic formulation of multiple spawning. Multiple spawning was a relatively unimportant part of the population's potential fecundity. This was largely due to the low probability of a fish returning to spawn because of an interim year at sea. If we had assumed that kelts returned in the year following first reproduction ("short absence previous spawners," in the terminology of Allen et al. 1972), then multiple spawning might have contributed a larger share.

The persistence of Atlantic salmon populations hinges on demographic plasticity related to the chronological age at which maiden fish spawn. The advantages of being a large fecund female diminish rapidly as sea mortality rates increase. The large increase in population fecundity attributable to another year of feeding at sea becomes insufficient to compensate for the fewer fish returning to spawn. In contrast, striped bass rely on large year classes to ensure population survival. As sea mortality increases, the contributions of older age-classes rapidly decline and the period over which a strong year class can dominate the population's reproductive output diminishes. If the environmental variability to which striped bass have evolved remains consistent, the likelihood of subsequent strong year classes will decrease as fishing mortality increases.

Although neither Atlantic salmon nor striped bass exists in isolation, the task of assessing nonequilibrium multispecies associations rapidly exhausts available knowledge well before meaningful management recommendations can be made. At the recently held Dahlem Conference (May 1984), participants noted that most of the theoretical groundwork has not been laid for such an endeavor—much less the data requirements. Thus, comparisons among species and populations will continue to yield insights for some time to come.

We have used both deterministic and stochastic models to examine the behavior of populations at equilibrium. Implicit in this treatment is the assumption that populations retain the biological capacity to respond (and instantaneously at that!) to changes in survival rates. Even if this mechanism were possible, our analysis of eigenvalues demonstrates that the convergence to a new steady state, governed by such essential population features as longevity, age at first reproduction, number of reproducing age-groups, and so on, will lag the imposed change by several years. If the biological response to altered conditions also lags the stimulus, then the likelihood of long-term transient conditions is firmly established. For example, Goulden and Hornig (1980) experimentally examined the consequences of lagged changes in natality and mortality rates in *Daphnia* populations.

If delays in physiological responses alone are sufficient to generate transient conditions, then the superposition of territoriality, cannibalism, and competition guarantees it. For management, this means that extinction via fishing mortality could be in progress long before it is apparent in the normal time frame of management decisions. Perhaps we are fortunate that the need for extreme management actions in support of striped bass and Atlantic salmon has already been perceived.

Acknowledgments

We thank P. Eschmeyer, W. Van Winkle, G. Evans, and R. Klauda for their constructive reviews. R. Dorazio, J. Kitchell, and E. M. T. Chadwick reviewed an earlier draft of this paper.

References

Allen, K. R., R. L. Saunders, and P. F. Elson. 1972. Marine growth of Atlantic salmon (*Salmo salar*) in the northwest Atlantic. Journal of the Fisheries Research Board of Canada 29:1373–1380.

Anonymous. 1985. Report of meeting of the working group on north Atlantic salmon. International Council for the Exploration of the Sea, CM 1985/Assess:15, Copenhagen, Denmark.

Boreman, J., and H. M. Austin. 1985. Production and harvest of anadromous striped bass stocks along the Atlantic coast. Transactions of the American Fisheries Society 114:3–7.

Buck, R. J. G., and D. W. Hay. 1984. The relation between stock size and progeny of Atlantic salmon, *Salmon salar* L., in a Scottish stream. Journal of Fish Biology 23:1–11.

Caswell, H. 1978. A general formula for the sensitivity of population growth rate to changes in life history parameters. Theoretical Population Biology 14:215–230.

Caswell, H. 1982a. Optimal life histories and maximization of reproductive value: a general theorem for complex life cycles. Ecology 63:1218–1222.

Caswell, H. 1982b. Stable population structure and reproductive value for populations with complex life history parameters. Ecology 63:1223–1231.

Caswell, H., R. J. Naiman, and R. Morin. 1984. Evaluating the consequences of reproduction in complex salmonid life cycles. Aquaculture 43:123–134.

Chadwick, E. M. P. 1982. Stock–recruitment relationship for Atlantic salmon (*Salmo salar*) in Newfoundland rivers. Canadian Journal of Fisheries and Aquatic Sciences 39:1496–1501.

Chadwick, E. M. P., T. R. Porter, and P. Downton. 1978. Analysis of growth of Atlantic salmon (*Salmo salar*) in a small Newfoundland river. Journal of the Fisheries Research Board of Canada 35:60–68.

Christensen, S. W., D. L. DeAngelis, and A. G. Clark. 1977. Development of a stock–progeny model for assessing power plant effects on fish populations. Pages 196–226 *in* Van Winkle (1977).

Clark, C. W. 1976. Mathematical bioeconomics: the optimal management of renewable resources. John Wiley & Sons, New York, New York, USA.

DeAngelis, D. L., L. J. Svoboda, S. W. Christensen, and D. S. Vaughan. 1980. Stability and return times of Leslie matrices with density-dependent survival: applications to fish populations. Ecological Modelling 8:149–163.

Evans, G. T., and B. Dempson. 1986. Calculating the sensitivity of a salmonid population model. Canadian Journal of Fisheries and Aquatic Sciences 43:863–868.

Evans, G. T., J. C. Rice, and E. M. P. Chadwick. 1984. Patterns in growth and smolting of Atlantic salmon (*Salmo salar*) parr. Canadian Journal of Fisheries and Aquatic Sciences 41:783–797.

Fetterolf, C. 1981. Forward to the Stock Concept Symposium. Canadian Journal of Fisheries and Aquatic Sciences 38(12):iv–v.

Garrod, D. J., and B. J. Knights. 1979. Fish stocks: their life-history characteristics and response to exploitation. Symposia of the Zoological Society of London 44:361–382.

Goodyear, C. P. 1977. Assessing the impact of power plant mortality on the compensatory reserve of fish populations. Pages 186–195 *in* Van Winkle (1977).

Goodyear, C. P. 1980. Compensation in fish populations. Pages 253–280 *in* C. H. Hocutt and J. R. Stauffer, Jr., editors. Biological monitoring of fish. Lexington Books, Lexington, Massachusetts, USA.

Goodyear, C. P. 1985. Toxic materials, fishing, and environmental variation: simulated effects on striped bass' population trends. Transactions of the American Fisheries Society 114:107–113.

Goodyear, C. P., and S. W. Christensen. 1984. Bias-elimination in fish population models with stochastic variation in survival of the young. Transactions of the American Fisheries Society 113:627–632.

Goulden, C. E., and L. L. Hornig. 1980. Population oscillations and energy reserves in planktonic Cladocera and their consequences to competition. Proceedings of the National Academy of Sciences of the USA 77:1716–1720.

Hardy, J. D., Jr. 1978. Development of fishes of the mid-Atlantic Bight, volume 3. Aphredoderidae through Rachycentridae. U.S. Fish and Wildlife Service Biological Services Program FWS/OBS-78/12.

Heyde, C. C., and J. E. Cohen. 1985. Confidence intervals for demographic projections based on products of random matrices. Theoretical Population Biology 27:120–153.

Horst, T. J. 1977a. Effects of power station mortality on fish population stability in relationship to life history strategy. Pages 297–310 *in* Van Winkle (1977).

Horst, T. J. 1977b. Use of the Leslie matrix for assessing environmental impact with an example for a fish population. Transactions of the American Fisheries Society 106:253–257.

Keyfitz, N. 1968. Introduction to the mathematics of population. Addison–Wesley. Reading, Massachusetts, USA.

Leggett, W. C., and J. E. Carscadden. 1978. Latitudinal

variation in reproductive characteristics of American shad *(Alosa sapidissima)*: evidence for population specific life history strategies in fish. Journal of the Fisheries Research Board of Canada 35:1469–1478.

Lenski, R. E., and P. M. Service. 1982. The statistical analysis of population growth rates calculated from schedules of survivorship and fecundity. Ecology 63:655–662.

Leslie, P. H. 1945. On the use of matrices in certain population mathematics. Biometrika 33:183–222.

May, R. M., editor. 1984. Exploitation of marine communities. Springer-Verlag, New York, New York, USA.

Morgan, R. P., II, T. S. Y. Koo, and G. E. Krantz. 1973. Electrophoretic determination of populations of the striped bass, *Morone saxatilis,* in the upper Chesapeake Bay. Transactions of the American Fisheries Society 102:21–32.

Murray, A. R. 1968. Smolt survival and adult utilization of Little Codroy River, Newfoundland, Atlantic salmon. Journal of the Fisheries Research Board of Canada 25:2165–2218.

Myers, R. A. 1984. Demographic consequences of precocious maturation of Atlantic salmon *(Salmo salar)*. Canadian Journal of Fisheries and Aquatic Sciences 41:1349–1353.

Paloheimo, J. E., and P. F. Elson. 1974. Reduction in Atlantic salmon *(Salmo salar)* catches in Canada attributed to the Greenland fishery. Journal of the Fisheries Research Board of Canada 31:1467–1480.

Pauly, D. 1981. On the interrelationships between natural mortality, growth parameters, and mean environmental temperature in 175 fish stocks. Journal du Conseil, Conseil International pour l'Exploration de la Mer 39:175–192.

Peterman, R. 1981. Form of random variation in salmon smolt-to-adult relations and its influence on production estimates. Canadian Journal of Fisheries and Aquatic Sciences 38:1113–1119.

Power, G. 1981. Stock characteristics and catches of Atlantic salmon *(Salmo salar)* in Quebec, and Newfoundland and Labrador in relation to environmental variables. Canadian Journal of Fisheries and Aquatic Sciences 38:1601–1611.

Price, K. S., and seven coauthors. 1985. Nutrient enrichment of Chesapeake Bay and its impact on the habitat of striped bass: a speculative hypothesis. Transactions of the American Fisheries Society 114:97–106.

Rago, P. J. 1980. A matrix model for inshore Lake Michigan fish populations. Master's thesis. Colorado State University, Fort Collins, Colorado, USA.

Rago, P. J., and R. M. Dorazio. 1984. Statistical inference in life-table experiments: the finite rate of increase. Canadian Journal of Fisheries and Aquatic Sciences 41:1361–1374.

Saila, S. B., and E. Lorda. 1977. Sensitivity analysis applied to a matrix model of Hudson River striped bass population. Pages 311–332 *in* Van Winkle (1977).

Saunders, R. L. 1981. Atlantic salmon *(Salmo salar)* stocks and management implications in the Canadian Atlantic provinces and New England, USA. Canadian Journal of Fisheries and Aquatic Sciences 38:1612–1625.

Saunders, R. L., E. B. Henderson, B. D. Glebe, and E. J. Loudenslager. 1983. Evidence of a major environmental component in determination of the grilse:larger salmon ratio in Atlantic salmon *(Salmo salar)*. Aquaculture 33:107–118.

Schaffer, W. M. 1979. The theory of life-history evolution and its application to Atlantic salmon. Symposia of the Zoological Society of London 44:307–326.

Schaffer, W. M., and P. F. Elson. 1975. The adaptive significance of variations in life history among local populations of Atlantic salmon in North America. Ecology 56:577–590.

Setzler, E. M., and eight coauthors. 1980. Synopsis of biological data on striped bass, *Morone saxatilis* (Walbaum). NOAA (National Oceanic and Atmospheric Administration) Technical Report NMFS (National Marine Fisheries Service) Circular 433.

Slobodkin, L. B., and A. Rapoport. 1974. An optimal strategy of evolution. Quarterly Review of Biology 49:181–200.

Strand, I. E., V. J. Norton, and J. G. Adriance. 1980. Economic aspects of commercial striped bass harvest. Marine Recreational Fisheries 5:51–62.

Stearns, S. C., and R. E. Crandall. 1981. Bet-hedging and persistence as adaptations of colonizers. Pages 371–383 *in* G. G. H. Scudder and J. L. Reveal, editors. Evolution today. Proceedings of the second international congress of systematics and evolutionary biology. Carnegie-Mellon University, Hunt Institute for Botanical Documentation, Pittsburgh, Pennsylvania, USA.

Sykes, Z. M. 1969. On discrete stable population theory. Biometrics 25:285–293.

Symons, P. E. K. 1979. Estimated escapement of Atlantic salmon *(Salmo salar)* for maximum smolt production in rivers of different productivity. Journal of the Fisheries Research Board of Canada 36:132–140.

Thomas, G. B., Jr. 1972. Calculus and analytical geometry. Addison–Wesley, Reading, Massachusetts, USA.

Usher, M. B. 1971. Developments in the Leslie matrix model. Pages 29–60 *in* J. N. R. Jeffers, editor. Mathematical models in ecology. Blackwell Scientific Publications, Oxford, England.

Van Winkle, W., editor. 1977. Assessing the effects of power-plant-induced mortality on fish populations. Pergamon, New York, New York, USA.

Vaughan, D. S., and S. B. Saila. 1976. A method for determining mortality rates using the Leslie matrix. Transactions of the American Fisheries Society 105:380–383.

Wootton, R. J. 1979. Energy costs of egg production and environmental determinants of fecundity in teleost fishes. Symposia of the Zoological Society of London 44:133–159.

American Fisheries Society Symposium 1:417–429, 1987

Review of the Components of Recruitment of Pacific Salmon

RANDALL M. PETERMAN

Natural Resource Management Program, Simon Fraser University
Burnaby, British Columbia V5A 1S6, Canada

Abstract.—Large variability exists between years in abundance of recruits of Pacific salmon *Oncorhynchus* spp. Research on the components of recruitment (reproduction, survival, growth, and maturation) has identified numerous proximate causes of that variability. Recent work shows that marine survival and growth depend on fish abundance for some Pacific salmon species. New results are reported here for (1) growth of pink salmon *O. gorbuscha* in relation to marine zooplankton abundance and (2) covariation in marine survival among sympatric salmon stocks. A synthesis of the components of recruitment leads to the prediction that stock–recruit relations for Pacific salmon may commonly generate more than one potential equilibrium population. Such multiple equilibrium models have important implications for research and management.

The Pacific salmon *Oncorhynchus* spp. of North America are anadromous and semelparous. After emerging from gravel beds where eggs are spawned, salmon spend varying periods in fresh water before undergoing lengthy migrations to rearing areas in the Pacific Ocean. Mature adults migrate back to their natal freshwater habitat, reproduce, and die. Three species of Pacific salmon are harvested only as they mature and migrate back toward the coast: pink salmon *O. gorbuscha,* chum salmon *O. keta,* and sockeye salmon *O. nerka.* One prominent feature of data on abundance and biomass of these recruits is the large variability over time. Two- to 20-fold variations in abundance of recruits are quite common.

This large variability in recruitment of Pacific salmon has stimulated extensive research on its proximate causes. Understanding these causes should improve our ability to manage these stocks by providing better means of forecasting or better data on the best ways to enhance or harvest populations. In this paper, I review some of the recent research on the proximate causes of between-year variability in recruitment of Pacific salmon populations; readers may find reference to earlier works in the cited papers. I focus largely on the marine life phase because many density-dependent and density-independent causal mechanisms of variability in freshwater growth and survival have been widely understood since the 1950s and 1960s. As part of my review, I also add new results concerning two components of recruitment: survival (for pink and chum salmon) and growth (for pink salmon) in the ocean as affected by food supply. In the last section, I will show how a synthesis of the known components of recruitment leads to a prediction that salmon

stocks with two or more domains of population stability may be common. Stocks with these stability properties must be managed differently from the way they are under the current, single-equilibrium theories.

A Simple Approach: Stock and Recruitment

The first step in attempting to explain interannual variability in recruitment is usually to take into account the egg production which gave rise to that recruitment by fitting descriptive spawner–recruit (or stock–recruit) curves of some assumed form (Ricker 1954; Shepherd 1982). However, such fitted curves usually account for very little of the variation in recruitment. In addition, we now recognize that there are biases inherent in the fitting procedures caused by inaccurate and imprecise data, as well as by autocorrelations (Walters and Ludwig 1981; Walters 1985). Therefore, the average conditions described by these heuristic recruitment curves are of limited use to fisheries managers and researchers.

A more obvious approach to understanding that variability is to investigate not just egg production but all components which link spawners to the abundance of subsequent recruits: reproduction, survival, growth, and maturation. Ware (1980) did this for nonsalmonids by combining energetic components of these processes. Many other researchers have focused on intra- and interpopulation mechanisms which affect the population components of salmon recruitment. Those components are addressed below, after a description of the data used in my new analyses.

Data Sources

Salmon.—Pink salmon in the Fraser River,

British Columbia, spawn mainly in the fall. The resulting fry (newly hatched fish) migrate seaward the following spring at an average length of 35 mm (Healey 1980) or weight of 0.3 g and spend about 1.5 years at sea before maturing and migrating back to their spawning grounds at an average weight of 2.5 kg. This fixed 2-year life cycle contrasts with that of Fraser River chum salmon, which also go to sea at about 36 mm length (Healey 1980) but mature mainly during their third or fourth years at about 5.4 kg (Beacham and Starr 1982). Fraser River chum salmon data for brood years 1965–1979 were obtained from M. Farwell (Canada Department of Fisheries and Oceans, personal communication) for annual abundance of spawners, fry, and returning adults (catch plus escapement) by age. (Escapement refers to fish that "escape" the fishery and ascend the river to spawning grounds.) Fry abundances were updated estimates from samples taken at Mission, British Columbia, calculated by the standard International Pacific Salmon Fisheries Commission (IPSFC) method (J. Woodey, IPSFC, personal communication). These fry abundances were well correlated with those presented by Beacham and Starr (1982), which were calculated by a different method ($r = 0.75$; $P < 0.001$). Abundance data for Fraser River pink salmon spawners, fry, and returning adults (1961–1981) were drawn from IPSFC (1984). Weights of adult pink salmon (Table 1) were from purse seine samples in statistical area 20, where pink salmon catches are almost entirely from the Fraser River stock (Ricker 1982; IPSFC 1984). Only weight data for brood years 1957–1977 were used because the zooplankton data series used in part of the analysis ended in 1980, before the pink salmon from brood year 1979 returned.

Marine survival rate was calculated as R/F, where R is recruit abundance, or total number of adult fish maturing from a given brood class, and F is fry abundance for that brood class. Natural logs of R/F were used to normalize the variance (Peterman 1981). Recruits per spawner (R/S) were similarly transformed. In another analysis, catch and escapement data on the pink salmon population in statistical area 8 of the central British Columbia coast were used (Peterman 1977; Henderson and Charles 1984). The catches included those area-8 fish intercepted in the adjacent area-7 fishery. One stock, on the Bella Coola–Atnarko River, constituted 73% of area 8 pink salmon.

Zooplankton.—An index to the food supply of

pink salmon in the Gulf of Alaska was derived from zooplankton samples taken during 1956–1980 by the weather ship at ocean station P (50°N, 145°W) (Fulton 1983). These samples provide the longest continuous series of plankton density data for the north Pacific Ocean. The normal depth of samples was 150 m. In accordance with Fulton's (1983) recommendation, samples taken when the wire was out more than 180 m or less than 100 m were omitted, as were data taken when the wire angle was greater than 35° from the vertical, because these were likely unrepresentative of plankton over 150 m deep. Two types of sampling net were used but one part of the data series was rescaled to the SCOR net type (Fulton 1983). Zooplankton wet weight densities (mg/m^3) were calculated as the average of all daily observations in each 10-d period; missing 10-d averages were filled in by linear interpolation between observed points. Most of these filled-in points occurred prior to 1969. Zooplankton productivity measures were not available, so an index of the total annual zooplankton production was calculated as the 12-month sum of these average 10-d standing crop densities (Table 1). Less than 10% of the zooplankton weight in ocean station P samples was derived from euphausiids and amphipods; most was from copepods. While pink salmon do feed heavily on copepods during their first 8 months at sea, they consume mostly euphausiids, amphipods, squids, and fishes during the last segment of their ocean life (Takagi et al. 1981). Thus, the zooplankton abundance is only an indirect measure of food available to pink salmon.

TABLE 1.—Data used in analysis of weight-per-adult Fraser River pink salmon. Abundance is number of adult pink salmon in catch and escapement produced in each brood year; zooplankton densities are the 12-month sum (beginning 1 August of "brood year + 1") of zooplankton densities in each 10-d estimate. Last column is the third divided by the fourth column. Data sources given in text.

Brood year	Weight (kg)	Abundance (millions)	Zooplankton (mg/m^3)	Fish per zooplankton (thousands/[mg/m^3])
1957	2.376	6.460	3,762.5	1.72
1959	3.093	1.830	3,372.9	0.54
1961	2.299	5.326	1,699.0	3.13
1963	2.871	2.271	1,784.9	1.27
1965	2.413	12.850	5,067.3	2.54
1967	2.626	3.849	1,768.0	2.18
1969	2.268	9.707	2,761.6	3.52
1971	2.435	6.753	1,901.0	3.55
1973	2.721	4.867	2,216.5	2.20
1975	2.630	8.173	3,188.3	2.56
1977	2.190	14.100	3,565.0	3.96

Components of Recruitment: Covariation among Stocks

One way to increase our understanding of variability in the components of salmon recruitment such as growth, survival, or maturation is to examine how those variables are correlated among stocks which overlap in space and time during part of their life cycle. This approach is based on the known migration patterns of Pacific salmon (e.g., French et al. 1976; Takagi et al. 1981) whereby stocks that spawned and reared in fresh water thousands of kilometers apart migrate to similar regions in the Gulf of Alaska. During the period when these separate stocks inhabit a common environment, they are more likely to be exposed to similar levels of food, predators, and diseases than they are when they do not overlap. If these biological factors vary over a large spatial scale and if they have important effects on the components of recruitment, then we would expect those components to show high covariation among stocks and years.

An example of this approach is from a study of variability in mean age at maturity of Alaskan sockeye salmon, which typically varies from 4.0 and 6.0 years. By making pair-wise comparisons of stocks which migrated in the same years to ocean rearing areas, I found a highly significant pattern of covariation among stocks in the interannual variability of mean age at maturity (Peterman 1985). For example, unusually late age at maturity in one stock normally occurred simultaneously with delayed maturity in other stocks. Further analysis showed that most of the interannual variability in age at maturity was due to factors affecting growth during the first 1.5 years of marine life, out of a normal total of 2.5 years spent in the ocean, and that freshwater factors had a relatively minor influence (Peterman 1985).

This method of investigating patterns of covariation among stocks has also been used successfully by Ricker (1982) in examining body size of Pacific salmon and by Koslow (1984) and Shepherd et al. (1984) studying recruitment variability in marine fish species. The latter two papers documented evidence for a link between large-scale processes in the physical environment and variability in recruitment abundance.

Pink and Chum Salmon Results

In another example of this approach, I compared variability in marine survival rates and recruits per spawner of pink and chum salmon stocks from the Fraser River, British Columbia. About mid-April, both species migrate from fresh water to the ocean as fry. After spending 2–3 months in southern coastal waters of British Columbia (Healey 1980), these fish migrate northward up the coast in a narrow band and then move out into the Gulf of Alaska by early fall (Hartt 1980), where the two species of the same brood year overlap in their distribution (Neave et al. 1976; Takagi et al. 1981). However, after approximately 14–16 months of sympatry, the pink salmon migrate back toward fresh water (Takagi et al. 1981).

More than half of the interannual variability of Fraser River chum salmon appears to occur in the first 14–16 months at sea, when they are sympatric with Fraser River pink salmon. A significant correlation exists between the natural logarithm of marine survival rate ($\log_e$[surviving adults/fry entering the ocean]) for these two stocks from the same brood year ($r = 0.75$; $r^2 = 0.56$; $P = 0.032$; $N = 8$). This correlation is not an indirect effect of common freshwater events because the correlation between freshwater survival rates ($\log_e$[fry entering the ocean/spawner]) of those two stocks was not significant ($r = 0.17$; $P = 0.69$; $N = 8$). The significant correlation between marine survival rates of these two stocks, plus their lengthy sympatry, strongly suggests that most of the between-year variation in marine survival of Fraser River chum salmon year classes arises during the early ocean life stage from factors affecting the marine habitat shared by both species. This pattern exists even though Fraser River chum salmon remain at sea for an average of two more years after pink salmon from the same brood year return to fresh water.

This result is similar to those for sockeye salmon; most of the density-dependent component of marine survival of Babine Lake sockeye salmon occurs in the first 15 months of ocean life (Peterman 1982b). The largest part of the variability in mean age at maturity of sockeye salmon year classes also occurs during this early ocean period (Peterman 1985). These studies empirically substantiated a common assumption, that the first 1–1.5 years in the ocean are a major source of interannual variability in marine survival and maturation of some Pacific salmon species. Future research might, therefore, benefit from focusing on causal mechanisms during that portion of the life history.

Improved forecasting of adult abundance can also result from identification of common patterns of variation among species which mature at different ages. Because of their 2-year lifespan, adult pink salmon are enumerated 1 year before the first of the corresponding chum salmon brood matures at age 3. In the Fraser River pink and chum salmon case noted above, the correlation of 0.75 between marine survival rates of these two species permits a forecast of chum salmon brood class abundance from its fry abundance and the marine survival rate of pink salmon from the same brood year.

In cases where fry abundance is not known, such forecasts of adult chum salmon abundance may be possible from data on recruits per spawner, which are normally more readily available. For example, $\log_e(R/S)$ is significantly correlated between the Fraser River pink and chum salmon stocks ($r = 0.68$; $P = 0.029$; $N = 10$). A similar correlation was found between R/S of pink and chum salmon over a wide area of British Columbia (Anderson and Bailey 1974). As shown by the example of the Fraser River stocks, such a correlation may exist even if freshwater survival rates of pink and chum salmon are uncorrelated, as long as those stocks are sympatric for part of their marine life.

Discussion of Covariation

It is likely that this type of examination of common patterns of variation in the components of recruitment will provide valuable insights into survival, growth, and maturity for many species of anadromous and catadromous fishes. These groups of species are particularly well suited to this kind of analysis because different stocks spend only a part of their life cycle in the same habitat as other conspecific stocks. One can then define the portion of the life history in which most of the interannual variation in a variable such as survival occurs, thereby helping to focus research on the life stage critical for that component of recruitment and perhaps even identifying likely causal mechanisms.

There is another extremely promising extension to the exploration of patterns of covariation among stocks which are contiguously distributed during part of their life. By removing from each stock's data set the variation shown in common by the sympatric stocks, a "cleaned up" data set will remain (Shepherd et al. 1984). Such filtered data on abundance of recruits, for example, will increase the probability of detecting a significant stock–recruit relation (Shepherd et al. 1984) or

any other relation being tested which involves factors specific to the stock.

Components of Recruitment: Individual Stocks

Considerable research has been done on proximate causes of interannual variability in the components of recruitment. Major sources of variation in reproduction as well as in freshwater survival and freshwater growth were well documented for Pacific salmon by early workers. These processes are known to be affected by density-dependent mechanisms (e.g., competition and predation) as well as density-independent ones such as temperature and water flow (e.g., Neave 1953; Hunter 1959; Wilimovsky 1962; Killick and Clemens 1963; Ward and Larkin 1964; Foerster 1968; Simon and Larkin 1972; Alderdice et al. 1977; Meacham and Clark 1979). Recently, there has been growing interest in the effects of body size on salmonid reproductive success, beyond simple fecundity. Factors such as variable egg size, competition for redd sites, and depth of redds can cause large variation in initial abundance of a brood class of fry in ways not necessarily reflected by variation in abundance of spawners (Fowler 1972; van den Berghe and Gross 1984; Beacham and Murray 1985; several papers in Smith et al., in press).

These freshwater components of variability in recruitment of subsequent adults will not be addressed further. In the next sections, I review within-stock research on the marine components of survival and growth, as well as maturation.

Marine Survival

Marine survival rates of Pacific salmon are distributed lognormally (Peterman 1981), which contributes to the skewed distribution of recruit abundances seen on many stock–recruit plots. Most abundances are clustered at low levels, with occasional extremely high values.

Marine survival rate increases with larger body size at time of seaward migration (Ricker 1962a; Bilton et al. 1982), but survival rate decreases with increased stock abundance for Babine Lake sockeye salmon (Peterman 1982b; McDonald and Hume 1984). In this stock, most of the density-dependent component of marine mortality occurs during the first 15 months of ocean life. The early ocean life stage is also the period when the largest portion of total marine mortality occurs (Ricker 1976).

Predation by birds or salmonids can remove up to 85% of juvenile salmon as they leave fresh water (Parker 1968; Mace 1983; Wood 1984). Aggregation and functional responses of predators usually lead to nonlinear, depensatory mortality such that the highest percent mortality occurs at low abundance of juvenile salmon (Peterman and Gatto 1978; Mace 1983; Wood 1984).

Density-independent factors such as temperature and upwelling strength also cause variability in marine survival of salmon, and their complex interaction with density-dependent processes is covered by numerous papers included in McNeil and Himsworth (1980), Pearcy (1984), and Smith et al. (in press).

Marine Growth

Variability between years in adult body size of Pacific salmon affects biomass of catch and reproductive potential of spawners. Growth during the marine life phase is particularly important because over 98% of an individual salmon's final weight is gained in salt water. Pearcy (1984) contains several relevant papers.

Recent evidence shows that salmon weight is affected by size-selective fishing and by abundance of conspecifics. Coho salmon *O. kisutch* and pink salmon stocks in British Columbia have decreased significantly in size, apparently in response to the cumulative effects of size-selective fishing (Ricker 1981). The other *Oncorhynchus* species have not generally shown a consistent size trend, in some cases possibly because of confounding temperature trends (Ricker 1981, 1982). Age-specific adult body size of sockeye salmon from Bristol Bay, Alaska, is inversely related to abundance of those stocks and this relation is modified by temperature (Rogers 1980, 1984; Eggers et al. 1984). Age-specific body sizes of British Columbia sockeye salmon show not only a significant inverse relation with the abundance of their own stock, but also with the abundance of all Gulf of Alaska sockeye salmon (Peterman 1984). This latter abundance variable accounts for as much of the between-year variation in body size as the within-stock abundance (Peterman 1984). Thus, significant density-dependent interaction exists among sockeye salmon stocks which share a common ocean environment. Circumstantial evidence led to the hypothesis that the decreased size of adult sockeye salmon at high abundance was due to competition for food (Rogers 1980; Peterman 1984) and not to size-selective predation or disease mortality (Peterman 1984).

Pink salmon results.—Further evidence concerning density-dependent growth and food supply in the ocean comes from an analysis of pink salmon from the Fraser River, British Columbia. These fish have a fixed 2-year life cycle and are present in this river only in odd years. A significant inverse relation exists between mean adult weight of these pink salmon and their abundance at maturity (catch plus escapement) (IPSFC 1980, 1984; $r = -0.76$; $P = 0.007$; $N = 11$). This relation implies density-dependent growth within the Fraser River pink salmon population, although Ricker (1982) suggested that this might be a spurious correlation.

To further explore this relation, I included a measure of food supply in the analysis. Except for recent years, as described in the Data Sources section, I used the same body size and abundance data as Ricker (1982) and IPSFC (1984) (Table 1); these variables did not have significant linear time trends ($r = 0.27$, $P = 0.41$ and $r = 0.51$, $P = 0.11$, respectively). I used zooplankton densities sampled at ocean station P as an index of food supply for the pink salmon (Table 1). Mean annual zooplankton abundance at ocean station P shows as much as a threefold variation between years over 1956–1980 (Frost 1983). I calculated an index of competition in the marine life phase as the ratio of Fraser River adult pink salmon abundance to the zooplankton density summed over the final year the fish were at sea. This year began on 1 August of the year in which the fry went to sea. This ratio of fish per zooplankton therefore estimates the number of adult Fraser River pink salmon present in the Gulf of Alaska per unit zooplankton density.

There was a highly significant inverse correlation between adult body weight of pink salmon and the number of fish/zooplankton ($r = -0.86$, $P < 0.001$, $N = 11$; Figure 1). Adult weight decreased when there were more fish per unit food supply. Taking zooplankton into account increased the proportion of variation in adult weight accounted for compared with the simpler IPSFC (1984) relation, which used only fish abundance ($r^2 = 0.74$ with zooplankton; $r^2 = 0.57$ without). These results are consistent with the hypothesis that density-dependent growth, arising from competition for food, occurs in the marine environment of Fraser River pink salmon.

The single major outlier from the relation in Figure 1 is the 1957 brood-year weight, which was well below the expected value. Fish from that brood year migrated seaward in 1958 during the

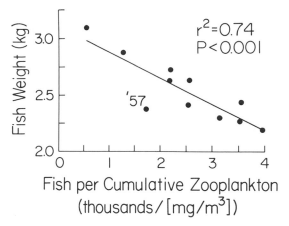

FIGURE 1.—Mean adult weight of Fraser River pink salmon for brood years 1957–1977 in relation to the ratio of Fraser River adult pink salmon abundance to cumulative annual 10-d mean zooplankton density at ocean station P.

1957–1958 El Niño event, which had a large impact on plankton in part of the north Pacific Ocean (Wooster and Fluharty 1985). During major El Niño events such as this one, warm southern waters penetrate further north along the British Columbia coast than normal, and these waters have low densities of zooplankton composed of small species (Fulton and LeBrasseur 1985). This unusual inshore body of water did not affect the ocean station P region (Figure 2), and my zooplankton data, therefore, do not reflect this anomalous coastal condition. Indeed, ocean station P zooplankton densities were slightly above the

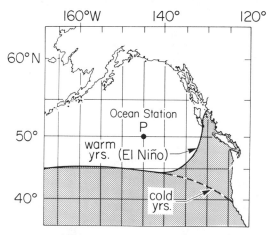

FIGURE 2.—Location of ocean station P and the boundary between subarctic waters and southern, zooplankton-poor waters in cold years or warm El Niño years (after Fulton and LeBrasseur 1985).

historical mean in 1958. I therefore hypothesize that the weight of adult pink salmon from the 1957 brood year was below that expected by the regression line of Figure 1 because the fish in that year experienced poorer early marine growth as they passed through coastal waters with low food density. My analysis includes only this one year in which an El Niño event was strong enough to affect plankton in the northeastern Pacific; the zooplankton sampling program at station P terminated after 1980. The 1982–1983 El Niño event, however, also produced unusually small adult pink salmon; those returning to the Fraser River in 1983 had the smallest mean size on record (1.86 kg: IPSFC 1984). Oregon coho salmon caught that year were also the smallest on record and Oregon chinook salmon *O. tshawytscha* were one-third below their historical mean weight (Pearcy et al. 1985). The r^2 increases dramatically (to $r^2 = 0.91$; $P < 0.001$) if the 1957 brood year point is eliminated from the correlation in Figure 1, as is justified because of the lack of effect of El Niño on waters at ocean station P.

The regression in Figure 1 accounts for 74% of the interannual variability in Fraser River pink salmon body weight, yet only the abundance of that pink salmon stock was included in the ratio of the independent variate. Because the r^2 is so high, other pink salmon stocks and other species competing for similar food apparently had relatively little effect on growth of Fraser River pink salmon. While Fraser River pink salmon represent 49% of all British Columbia pink salmon when they are present in odd years, they make up a much smaller, but unknown portion of the total planktivorous salmon population in the Gulf of Alaska, where their distribution overlaps those of chum, sockeye, and Alaskan pink salmon (French et al. 1976; Neave et al. 1976; Takagi et al. 1981).

If the hypothesis of competition for food is correct, then the tight fit in Figure 1 further implies that (1) Fraser River pink salmon are a relatively cohesive group during the period when final adult weight is most affected by food supply, and (2) high fish abundance relative to zooplankton density may cause a local depletion of zooplankton. To my knowledge, the only evidence of cohesiveness of a salmon stock in the open ocean was given by Pearcy (1984), who showed that 19 juvenile coho salmon from the Columbia River, Oregon, were caught in one purse seine haul 140 km and 31 days from their release from a hatchery. If Fraser River pink salmon remain as a relatively large but independent school, then their large numbers could cause a local decrease in zooplankton because the fish are concentrated in only the top 10 m of water (Takagi et al. 1981). The average abundance of Fraser River pink salmon fry is 305 million, and the fish migrate northward in a narrow 37-km-wide band along the coast (Hartt 1980). By early fall, just before they move westward into the Gulf of Alaska, they are 19–22 cm long (Hartt and Dell, in press). They could conceivably deplete the local food supply anywhere during their migration. Such a depletion would only be temporary at any location because of continuing fish migration and because zooplankton populations near the surface are replenished by reproduction and by vertical migration from deep waters (Miller et al. 1984). Previous modelling work (Walters et al. 1978) suggested that overgrazing of food by salmon was unlikely. However, as noted in that paper, results were highly contingent on assumed (but unknown) rates of vertical migration of zooplankton to the surface from the very large, dense deep-water populations.

Maturation

Like variation in growth, variability between years in the mean age of maturity of brood classes can also affect variation in abundance and biomass of recruits. Delayed maturity will cause maturing adults to be larger when they return toward fresh water, but there will be fewer fish remaining in the cohort owing to longer exposure to marine mortality. The net effect of these opposing processes depends on each specific situation (Bilton et al. 1982).

Variation in mean age at maturity is related to freshwater and saltwater growth, as well as to parental age composition. Larger size at ocean entry leads to earlier maturity in coho and sockeye salmon (Bilton et al. 1982; Peterman 1982a), as does faster growth early in marine life (reviewed by Peterman 1985). Abundance and biomass of salmon recruits will, therefore, be variable among years to the extent that freshwater and saltwater growth vary. In some *Oncorhynchus* species, there tends to be a positive correlation between age of spawners and age of their offspring; this could be due to a genetic or physiological maternal effect (Ricker 1972; Bradford and Peterman, in press; several papers in Smith et al., in press).

Discussion of Recruitment Components

Prior to the mid-1970s, most salmon biologists

held the view that survival and growth rates in the ocean were not dependent on stock abundance. However, the recent research reviewed here shows that density-dependent marine growth by sockeye and pink salmon exists, and density-dependent marine survival of sockeye salmon occurs. Aggregation responses of predators to high abundance of juvenile chinook and coho salmon also exist. These compensatory processes must, therefore, be accounted for in production forecasts for future salmonid enhancement facilities.

The empirical evidence also shows that most of the between-year variation in marine survival, marine growth, and mean age at maturity of brood classes arises from mechanisms operating during the earliest portion of ocean life. In the case of chum and sockeye salmon, this important period covers approximately the first 14–18 months that the fish are in the ocean. Future research on sources of interannual variability in recruitment processes should focus on this period.

The documented age-, size-, and density-dependent components of recruitment also have important implications for the stability properties of Pacific salmon and for the management of these fish. When these complex components are combined with those in fresh water, stock–recruit curves result which are much more complicated than normally assumed by a Ricker (1954) or Shepherd (1982) model. The last section deals with such a synthesis.

Synthesis: Multiple Equilibria

Ricker (1962b), Holling (1973), and Paulik (1973) showed how two or more nonlinear mortality processes combined in series could create a stock–recruitment curve with more stable points than the one exhibited by the standard Ricker (1954) model. The primary mechanism leading to multiple equilibria that was addressed in those early papers was depensatory predation mortality, in which the highest percent mortality was caused at low salmon abundance. Considerable empirical evidence shows that this type of predation mortality is common (Neave 1953; Peterman and Gatto 1978; Mace 1983; Wood 1984). We should, therefore, expect salmon populations to frequently exhibit population behavior which reflects more than one stable equilibrium point.

The best way to test this prediction would be to synthesize the components of recruitment described in previous sections into a combined recruitment model, one for each of several stocks, and determine if this model explained more of the variation in recruitment than the best Ricker model for those stocks. All of these components of recruitment have yet to be measured for a single stock, however; they have been observed piecemeal for many different stocks and species. It is possible, nevertheless, to postulate a set of components for one stock which have the same qualitative form as the processes observed for different stocks in the field. The resulting combined recruitment model would then represent a generic form which could be explored to illustrate how its behavior differs from the single-equilibrium Ricker model.

Example

To show this methodology, I use an extremely simple example in which there are only two density-dependent components of survival. A good representation of the egg-to-fry relation over a wide range of spawner abundance is provided by pink salmon in Sashin Creek, Alaska (Skud 1973; Figure 3). Subsequent predation mortality of these fry can be assumed to be either strictly depensatory, called type-II predation by Holling (1973) (Figure 4A, B), or compensatory at very low prey abundance but depensatory above that abundance, called type-III predation (Figure 4C). By making the simplest assumption that mortality subsequent to predation and up to maturity is density independent, the egg–fry stage and the fry–recruit stage can be combined to generate number of recruits. The resulting stock–recruit model for an unharvested stock is most easily distinguished from Ricker's (1954) standard model when plotted as R/S versus S (Figure 5). With

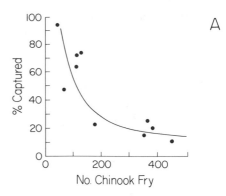

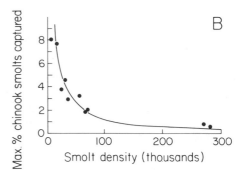

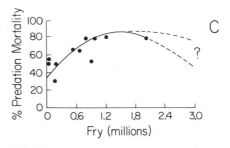

FIGURE 4.—Predation-induced mortality rates on juvenile salmon: (A) percentage of chinook salmon fry captured by Bonaparte's gulls during 5-min experiments (after Mace 1983); (B) maximum daily percent mortality of chinook salmon smolts due to merganser predation (after Wood 1984); (C) percent mortality of pink salmon fry per day due to the predator complex of coho salmon smolts and trout (after Peterman and Gatto 1978).

type-II predation, the new model has two crossovers of the equilibrium line $R/S = 1$, at S_1 and S_2, instead of only one (Figure 5). The abundance at S_1 is a stable equilibrium abundance, but the one at S_2 is unstable. Above S_2, $R/S > 1$, so the population increases away from S_2; below S_2, $R/S < 1$, so spawning abundance decreases away from S_2. Thus, in the case with type-II predation, a threshold spawner abundance, S_2, is created, below which the population will tend to move

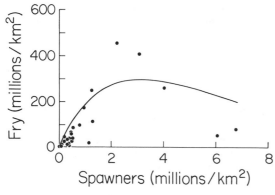

FIGURE 3.—Abundance of pink salmon fry in relation to spawner abundance for Sashin Creek, Alaska (data from Skud 1973).

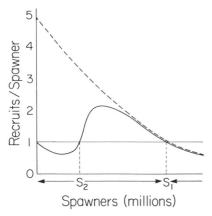

FIGURE 5.—Stock–recruitment curves replotted as recruit/spawner versus spawners for the standard Ricker (1954) model (dashed line) and a model combining the fry production curve in Figure 3 with a fry mortality function like the one in Figure 4A (solid line). Arrows indicate direction in which spawner abundance would tend to change in the absence of fishing (toward the stable abundance, S_1, and away from the unstable or "boundary" abundance, S_2).

toward extinction, even if harvesting is completely stopped. Only artificial enhancement of the population, or a beneficial stochastic event such as very good survival, could prevent the population from going extinct. With type-III predation (Figure 6), a critical spawner abundance

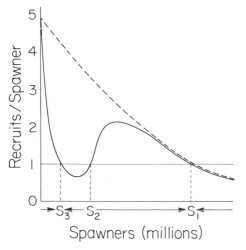

FIGURE 6.—Stock–recruitment curves replotted as recruits/spawner versus spawners for the standard Ricker (1954) model (dashed line) and a model combining the fry production curve in Figure 3 with a fry mortality function like the one in Figure 4C (solid line). Arrows indicate direction of change in spawner abundance in the absence of fishing.

also exists but, in this case, a population dropping below S_2 would not go toward extinction but toward a lower stable equilibrium, S_3, which would be very unproductive for harvesting. Elimination of harvest of a population which moved into this lower "domain of stability" would not permit it to recover to high population levels near the upper stable point; the population would be trapped at the low unproductive level until artificial enhancement or stochastic events raised its abundance above the boundary at S_2 (Figure 6).

The theory of models with more than one equilibrium point recognizes that stochastic events will prevent a population from ever reaching a stable equilibrium abundance. However, such stable points act as "attractors" towards which the population tends to move in a "noisy" trajectory (May 1977; Peterman 1977). While these models are deterministic, they still have utility in explaining some of the interannual variability in salmon recruitment, which has significant stochastic components as noted previously. For example, many salmon populations have failed to recover from overharvesting and have remained at unprecedented low abundances even after harvesting was greatly reduced. If a standard, single-equilibrium Ricker model were the true form for the stock–recruitment model, then such populations should have rebounded to higher abundance as long as an environmental change did not permanently decrease that single-equilibrium value at the same time as overharvesting occurred. The latter confounding effect of a time trend usually cannot be separated from the multiple-equilibrium explanation in most historical data. One major exception is the case of pink salmon in area 8, British Columbia.

Details of the area 8 stock are in Peterman (1977) and I only add recent data here (from Henderson and Charles 1984). In this situation, the even-year pink salmon stock occupies the same habitat as the odd-year stock but, with their fixed 2-year life cycle, even- and odd-year populations are genetically isolated. The odd-year Area 8 stock was overharvested in the early 1960s and stayed at about 11% of its mean historical abundance, despite drastic reduction in the exploitation rate to 14–43%, well below the 60–70% rate normally sustainable. This persistent low abundance cannot be explained by a deteriorating rearing habitat because there has been a "natural control": the abundance of the even-year stock has not shown a similar decrease and it is uncorrelated with abundance of the odd-year stock (r =

0.13; $P = 0.63$). The multiple-equilibrium model in Figure 6 describes this situation for the odd-year stock better than a single-equilibrium Ricker model. While no quantitative data exist on the predation components over a wide range of prey abundance, coho salmon smolts and rainbow trout *Salmo gairdneri* are known to prey heavily on pink salmon fry of area 8 (J. Greenley, Canada Department of Fisheries and Oceans, personal communication), and the potential exists for the type of relation shown in Figure 4C, which is from a stock with similar predators. Unlike the theoretical example of unharvested fish in Figure 6, the population in area 8 has been harvested. Therefore, to illustrate how the population fluctuated around the presumed equilibria, the different fishing mortalities applied to each brood class were taken into account by plotting the escapement, S_{t+2}, which resulted from each parental escapement, S_t (Figure 7). Those points that fell below the replacement level of $(S_{t+2}/S_t) = 1$ led to a decrease in S_t in the next generation, and those points above 1 led to an increase (Figure 7). When a recruitment curve similar to that in Figure 6 is overlaid on the data for the odd-year stock, the model appears consistent with the data (Figure 7). After being drastically reduced below a critical threshold spawner abundance, the spawning pop-

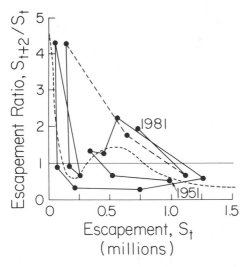

FIGURE 7.—Relative escapements of pink salmon progeny in year t + 2 plotted against parental escapements in year t, area 8, British Columbia. Sequence covers brood years 1951–1981. The curved broken line is a hypothetical stock–recruitment curve similar to the one in Figure 6. The straight broken lines connect points for years in which enhancement facilities operated (brood years 1975 and 1977).

ulation remained at low abundance for six generations, varying around the lower stable equilibrium of about 120,000 fish. Artificial enhancement of the 1975 and 1977 brood classes (Greenley, personal communication) helped to increase the spawner population sufficiently to get it back up to the more productive domain of stability surrounding the upper equilibrium spawner population of about 760,000 fish. The population has remained in this upper domain of stability in spite of exploitation rates as high as 71% and elimination of enhancement.

Conclusion

This example illustrates how more complex stock–recruitment curves could explain some of the temporal patterns of recruitment not explainable by the simpler Ricker model. Even more complex curves would result if all components of recruitment were incorporated, including growth. The growth component has had too little attention in studies of Pacific salmon recruitment; the focus has been on abundance of recruits alone, which assumes fish weight is not related to measurable variables. However, sufficient data now exist on sockeye and pink salmon to warrant explicit inclusion of growth into stock–recruitment analyses, as is done for many pelagic fishes. Another recommendation is to focus research effort on the components of recruitment of a small number of Pacific salmon stocks. Currently, research effort is being spread over many stocks with the result that all the components of recruitment are not known for any given stock; we therefore cannot empirically test the hypothesis of multiple equilibria for Pacific salmon.

While the evidence for multiple equilibria for Pacific salmon is weak and circumstantial, the empirical evidence is strong for insects, mammals, and other fishes (reviewed by May 1977; Peterman et al. 1979). There is no reason to expect that Pacific salmon will be any different, because their populations are subject to the same processes that give rise to multiple equilibria in other systems: predation (Noy-Meir 1975; Southwood and Comins 1976; Peterman 1977; Walters et al. 1980; Steele and Henderson 1984), parasitism and disease pathogenicity (Anderson 1979), competition (Gilpin and Case 1977), schooling and dispersal (Comins 1977; Clark and Mangel 1979), and fishing mortality (Peterman and Steer 1981), to give only a few examples.

By acknowledging that multiple equilibria are possible in *Oncorhynchus* populations, we can help to focus future research to gain improved management and understanding of recruitment variability.

Acknowledgments

I am grateful to Morley Farwell, John Fulton, and John Parslow, who provided data. Michael Bradford and Judith L. Anderson provided valuable discussion and comments; D. J. Garrod and Chris C. Wood made valuable suggestions which improved the manuscript. Funding was provided by the Natural Sciences and Engineering Research Council of Canada and by a Senior Scientist Fellowship from the Scientific Affairs Division of the North Atlantic Treaty Organization. The Southwest Fisheries Center of the U.S. National Marine Fisheries Service, La Jolla, California, kindly provided facilities during part of this project.

References

Alderdice, D. F., R. A. Bams, and F. P. J. Velsen. 1977. Factors affecting deposition, development and survival of salmonid eggs and alevins. A bibliography, 1965–1975. Canada Fisheries and Marine Service Technical Report 743.

Anderson, A. D., and D. D. Bailey. 1974. The return of chum salmon stocks to the Johnstone Strait–Fraser River study area, and prospects for 1974. Canada Fisheries and Marine Service, Technical Report Series PAC/T-14-15, Vancouver, Canada.

Anderson, R. M. 1979. The influence of parasitic infection on the dynamics of host population growth. Pages 245–281 in R. M. Anderson, B. D. Turner, and L. R. Taylor, editors. Population dynamics. Blackwell Scientific Publications, Oxford, England.

Beacham, T. D., and C. B. Murray. 1985. Effect of female size, egg size, and water temperature on developmental biology of chum salmon (Oncorhynchus keta) from the Nitinat River, British Columbia. Canadian Journal of Fisheries and Aquatic Sciences 42:1755–1765.

Beacham, T. D., and P. Starr. 1982. Population biology of chum salmon, Oncorhynchus keta, from the Fraser River, British Columbia. U.S. National Marine Fisheries Service Fishery Bulletin 80:813–825.

Bilton, H. T., D. F. Alderdice, and J. T. Schnute. 1982. Influence of time and size at release of juvenile coho salmon (Oncorhynchus kisutch) on returns at maturity. Canadian Journal of Fisheries and Aquatic Sciences 39:426–447.

Bradford, M. J., and R. M. Peterman. In press. Maternal size effects may explain positive correlations between age at maturity of parent and offspring sockeye salmon (Oncorhynchus nerka). Canadian Special Publication of Fisheries and Aquatic Sciences 96.

Clark, C. W., and M. Mangel. 1979. Aggregation and fishery dynamics: a theoretical study of schooling and the purse seine tuna fisheries. U.S. National Marine Fisheries Service Fishery Bulletin 77: 317–337.

Comins, H. N. 1977. The development of insecticide resistance in the presence of migration. Journal of Theoretical Biology 64:177–197.

Eggers, D. M., C. P. Meacham, and D. C. Huttunen. 1984. Population dynamics of Bristol Bay sockeye salmon, 1956–1983. Pages 200–225 in W. G. Pearcy, editor. The influence of ocean conditions on the production of salmonids in the north Pacific. Oregon State University, Sea Grant College Program, ORESU-W-83-001, Corvallis, Oregon, USA.

Foerster, R. E. 1968. The sockeye salmon, Oncorhynchus nerka. Fisheries Research Board of Canada Bulletin 162.

Fowler, L. G. 1972. Growth and mortality of fingerling chinook salmon as affected by egg size. Progressive Fish-Culturist 34:66–69.

French, R., H. Bilton, M. Osako, and A. C. Hartt. 1976. Distribution and origin of sockeye salmon (Oncorhynchus nerka) in offshore waters of the north Pacific Ocean. International North Pacific Fisheries Commission Bulletin 34.

Frost, B. W. 1983. Interannual variation of zooplankton standing stock in the open Gulf of Alaska. Pages 146–157 in W. S. Wooster, editor. From year to year. University of Washington, Washington Sea Grant Program, Seattle, Washington, USA.

Fulton, J. 1983. Seasonal and annual variations of net zooplankton at Ocean Station "P", 1956–1980. Canadian Data Report of Fisheries and Aquatic Sciences 374.

Fulton, J., and R. J. LeBrassuer. 1985. Interannual shifting of the subarctic boundary and some of the biotic effects on juvenile salmonids. Pages 237–247 in W. S. Wooster and D. L. Fluharty, editors. El Niño north: Niño effects in the eastern subarctic Pacific Ocean. University of Washington, Washington Sea Grant Program, Seattle, Washington, USA.

Gilpin, M. E., and T. J. Case. 1977. Multiple domains of attraction in competition communities. Nature (London) 261:40–42.

Hartt, A. C. 1980. Juvenile salmonids in the oceanic ecosystem—the critical first summer. Pages 25–57 in W. J. McNeil and D. C. Himsworth, editors. Salmonid ecosystems of the north Pacific. Oregon State University Press, Corvallis, Oregon, USA.

Hartt, A. C., and M. B. Dell. 1986. Early oceanic migrations and growth of juvenile Pacific salmon and steelhead trout. International North Pacific Fisheries Commission Bulletin 46.

Healey, M. C. 1980. The ecology of juvenile salmon in Georgia Strait, British Columbia. Pages 203–229 in W. J. McNeil and D. C. Himsworth, editors. Salmonid ecosystems of the North Pacific. Oregon State University Press, Corvallis, Oregon, USA.

Henderson, M. A., and A. T. Charles. 1984. Reconstruction of British Columbia pink salmon stocks (Oncorhynchus gorbuscha): 1970–1982. Part 1: Queen Charlotte Islands, north coast and central coast. Canadian Manuscript Report of Fisheries and Aquatic Sciences 1785.

Holling, C. S. 1973. Resilience and stability of ecological systems. Annual Review of Ecology and Systematics 4:1–23.

Hunter, J. G. 1959. Survival and production of pink and chum salmon in a coastal stream. Journal of the Fisheries Research Board of Canada 16:835–886.

IPSFC (International Pacific Salmon Fisheries Commission). 1980. IPSFC Annual Report for 1979.

IPSFC (International Pacific Salmon Fisheries Commission). 1984. IPSFC Annual Report for 1983.

Killick, S. R., and W. A. Clemens. 1963. The age, sex ratio and size of Fraser River sockeye salmon 1915 to 1960. International Pacific Salmon Fisheries Commission Bulletin 14.

Koslow, J. A. 1984. Recruitment patterns in northwest Atlantic fish stocks. Canadian Journal of Fisheries and Aquatic Sciences 41:1722–1729.

Mace, P. M. 1983. Bird predation on juvenile salmonids in the Big Qualicum estuary, Vancouver Island. Canadian Technical Report of Fisheries and Aquatic Sciences 1176.

May, R. M. 1977. Thresholds and breakpoints in ecosystems with a multiplicity of stable states. Nature (London) 269:471–477.

McDonald, J. G., and J. M. Hume. 1984. Babine Lake sockeye salmon (Oncorhynchus nerka) enhancement program: testing some major assumptions. Canadian Journal of Fisheries and Aquatic Sciences 41:70–92.

McNeil, W. J., and D. C. Himsworth, editors. 1980. Salmonid ecosystems of the north Pacific. Oregon State University Press, Corvallis, Oregon, USA.

Meacham, C. P., and J. H. Clark. 1979. Management to increase anadromous salmon production. Pages 377–386 in H. Clepper, editor. Predator–prey systems in fisheries management. Sport Fishing Institute, Washington, D.C., USA.

Miller, C. B., B. W. Frost, H. P. Batchelder, M. J. Clemons, and R. E. Conway. 1984. Life histories of large, grazing copepods in a subarctic ocean gyre: Neocalanus plumchrus, Neocalanus cristatus, and Eucalonus bungii in the northeast Pacific. Progress in Oceanography 13:201–243.

Neave, F. 1953. Principles affecting the size of pink and chum salmon populations in British Columbia. Journal of the Fisheries Research Board of Canada 9:450–491.

Neave, F., T. Yonemori, and R. G. Bakkala. 1976. Distribution and origin of chum salmon in offshore waters of the north Pacific Ocean. International North Pacific Fisheries Commission Bulletin 35.

Noy-Meir, I. 1976. Stability of grazing systems: an application of predator–prey graphs. Journal of Ecology 63:459–481.

Parker, R. R. 1968. Marine mortality schedules of pink salmon of the Bella Coola River central British Columbia. Journal of the Fisheries Research Board of Canada 25:757–794.

Paulik, G. J. 1973. Studies of the possible form of the stock and recruitment curve. Rapports et Procès-Verbaux des Réunions, Conseil International pour l'Exploration de la Mer 164:302–315.

Pearcy, W. G., editor. 1984. The influence of ocean conditions on the production of salmonids in the north Pacific. Oregon State University, Sea Grant College Program, ORESU-W-83-001, Corvallis, Oregon, USA.

Pearcy, W., J. Fisher, R. Brodeur, and S. Johnson. 1985. Effects of the 1983 El Niño on coastal nekton off Oregon and Washington. Pages 188–204 in W. S. Wooster and D. L. Fluharty, editors. El Niño north: Niño effects in the eastern subarctic Pacific Ocean. University of Washington, Washington Sea Grant Program, Seattle, Washington, USA.

Peterman, R. M. 1977. A simple mechanism that causes collapsing stability regions in exploited salmonid populations. Journal of the Fisheries Research Board of Canada 34:1130–1142.

Peterman, R. M. 1981. Form of random variation in salmon smolt-to-adult relations and its influence on production estimates. Canadian Journal of Fisheries and Aquatic Sciences 38:1113–1119.

Peterman, R. M. 1982a. Model of salmon age structure and its use in preseason forecasting and studies of marine survival. Canadian Journal of Fisheries and Aquatic Sciences 39:1444–1452.

Peterman, R. M. 1982b. Nonlinear relation between smolts and adults in Babine Lake sockeye salmon (Oncorhynchus nerka) and implications for other salmon populations. Canadian Journal of Fisheries and Aquatic Sciences 39:904–913.

Peterman, R. M. 1984. Density-dependent growth in early ocean life of sockeye salmon (Oncorhynchus nerka). Canadian Journal of Fisheries and Aquatic Sciences 41:1825–1829.

Peterman, R. M. 1985. Patterns of interannual variation in age at maturity of sockeye salmon (Oncorhynchus nerka) in Alaska and British Columbia. Canadian Journal of Fisheries and Aquatic Sciences 42:1595–1607.

Peterman, R. M., W. C. Clark, and C. S. Holling. 1979. The dynamics of resilience: shifting stability domains in fish and insect populations. Pages 321–341 in R. M. Anderson, B. D. Turner, and L. R. Taylor, editors. Population dynamics. Blackwell Scientific Publications, Oxford, England.

Peterman, R. M., and M. Gatto. 1978. Estimation of functional responses of predators on juvenile salmon. Journal of the Fisheries Research Board of Canada 35:797–808.

Peterman, R. M., and G. Steer. 1981. Relation between sport-fishing catchability coefficients and salmon abundance. Transactions of the American Fisheries Society 110:585–593.

Ricker, W. E. 1954. Stock and recruitment. Journal of the Fisheries Research Board of Canada 11:559–623.

Ricker, W. E. 1962a. Comparison of ocean growth and mortality of sockeye salmon during their last two years. Journal of the Fisheries Research Board of Canada 19:531–560.

Ricker, W. E. 1962b. Regulation of the abundance of pink salmon populations. Pages 155–211 in N. J. Wilimovsky, editor. Symposium on pink salmon.

University of British Columbia, Institute of Fisheries, Vancouver, Canada.

Ricker, W. E. 1972. Hereditary and environmental factors affecting certain salmonid populations. Pages 19–160 in R. C. Simon and P. A. Larkin, editors. The stock concept in Pacific salmon. H. R. MacMillan Lectures in Fisheries, University of British Columbia, Vancouver, Canada.

Ricker, W. E. 1976. Review of the rate of growth and mortality of Pacific salmon in salt water, and non-catch mortality caused by fishing. Journal of the Fisheries Research Board of Canada 33:1483–1524.

Ricker, W. E. 1981. Changes in the average size and average age of Pacific salmon. Canadian Journal of Fisheries and Aquatic Sciences 38:1636–1656.

Ricker, W. E. 1982. Size and age of British Columbia sockeye salmon (Oncorhynchus nerka) in relation to environmental factors and the fishery. Canadian Technical Report of Fisheries and Aquatic Sciences 1115.

Rogers, D. E. 1980. Density-dependent growth of Bristol Bay sockeye salmon. Pages 267–283 in W. J. McNeil and D. C. Himsworth, editors. Salmonid ecosystems of the north Pacific. Oregon State University Press, Corvallis, Oregon, USA.

Rogers, D. E. 1984. Trends in abundance of northeastern Pacific stocks of salmon. Pages 100–127 in W. G. Pearcy, editor. The influence of ocean conditions on the production of salmonids in the north Pacific. Oregon State University, Sea Grant College Program, ORESU-W-83-001, Corvallis, Oregon, USA.

Shepherd, J. G. 1982. A versatile new stock–recruitment relationship for fisheries and the construction of sustainable yield curves. Journal du Conseil, Conseil International pour l'Exploration de la Mer 41:76–80.

Shepherd, J. G., J. G. Pope, and R. D. Cousens. 1984. Variations in fish stocks and hypotheses concerning their links with climate. Rapports et Procès-Verbaux des Réunions, Conseil International pour l'Exploration de la Mer 185:255–267.

Simon, R. C., and P. A. Larkin, editors. 1972. The stock concept in Pacific salmon. H. R. MacMillan Lectures in Fisheries, University of British Columbia, Vancouver, Canada.

Skud, B. E. 1973. Factors regulating the production of pink salmon. Rapports et Procès-Verbaux des Réunions, Conseil International pour l'Exploration de la Mer 164:108–112.

Smith, H. D., L. Margolis, and C. Wood, editors. In press. Sockeye salmon: population biology and future management. Canadian Special Publication of Fisheries and Aquatic Sciences 96.

Southwood, T. R. E., and H. N. Comins. 1976. A synoptic population model. Journal of Animal Ecology 45:949–965.

Steele, J. H., and E. W. Henderson. 1984. Modelling long-term fluctuations in fish stocks. Science (Washington, D.C.) 224:985–987.

Takagi, K., K. V. Aro, A. C. Hartt, and M. B. Dell. 1981. Distribution and origin of pink salmon (Oncorhynchus gorbuscha) in offshore waters of the north Pacific Ocean. International North Pacific Fisheries Commission Bulletin 40.

van den Berghe, E. P., and M. R. Gross. 1984. Female size and nest depth in coho salmon (Oncorhynchus kisutch). Canadian Journal of Fisheries and Aquatic Sciences 41:204–206.

Walters, C. J. 1985. Bias in the estimation of functional relationships from time series data. Canadian Journal of Fisheries and Aquatic Sciences 42:147–149.

Walters, C. J., R. Hilborn, R. M. Peterman, and M. J. Staley. 1978. Model for examining early ocean limitation of Pacific salmon production. Journal of the Fisheries Research Board of Canada 35:1303–1315.

Walters, C. J., and D. Ludwig. 1981. Effects of measurement errors on the assessment of stock–recruitment relationships. Canadian Journal of Fisheries and Aquatic Sciences 38:704–710.

Walters, C. J., G. Steer, and G. Spangler. 1980. Responses of lake trout (Salvelinus namaycush) to harvesting, stocking and lamprey reduction. Canadian Journal of Fisheries and Aquatic Sciences 37:2133–2145.

Ward, F. J., and P. A. Larkin. 1964. Cyclic dominance in Adams River sockeye salmon. International Pacific Salmon Fisheries Commission Progress Report 11.

Ware, D. 1980. Bioenergetics of stock and recruitment. Canadian Journal of Fisheries and Aquatic Sciences 37:1012–1024.

Wilimovsky, N. J., editor. 1962. Symposium on pink salmon. H. R. MacMillan Lectures in Fisheries, University of British Columbia, Vancouver, Canada.

Wood, C. C. 1984. Foraging behavior of common mergansers (Mergus merganser) and their dispersion in relation to the availability of juvenile Pacific salmon. Doctoral dissertation. University of British Columbia, Vancouver, Canada.

Wooster, W. S., and D. L. Fluharty, editors. 1985. El Niño north: Niño effects in the eastern subarctic Pacific Ocean. University of Washington, Washington Sea Grant Program, Seattle, Washington, USA.

American Fisheries Society Symposium 1:430–440, 1987

Effect of Fall and Winter Instream Flow on Year-Class Strength of Pacific Salmon Evolutionarily Adapted to Early Fry Outmigration: A Great Lakes Perspective[1]

JOHN F. KOCIK AND WILLIAM W. TAYLOR

Department of Fisheries and Wildlife, Michigan State University
East Lansing, Michigan 48824, USA

Abstract.—Pink salmon *Oncorhynchus gorbuscha*, sockeye salmon *O. nerka*, and chum salmon *O. keta* are essentially ecological equivalents in their use of riverine habitat. These oncorhynchids are stream spawners that deposit their eggs in the early fall. The eggs incubate through winter, and emergence and outmigration of the juvenile salmon occur in early spring. Although these fish are transient in the riverine environment, the stream plays a critical role in controlling their production and year-class strengths by significantly influencing egg and alevin survival. In these early stages, survival is primarily a function of the quantity and quality of instream flow during the fall and winter in conjunction with redd superimposition and streambed overseeding. A model is proposed to explain the relationship between abiotic and biotic factors upon oncorhynchid recruitment, based on our knowledge of pink salmon in the Great Lakes and a review of literature pertaining to early-outmigrating oncorhynchids.

Pink salmon *Oncorhynchus gorbuscha* were inadvertently introduced into the Great Lakes watershed in 1956 (Nunan 1967). Like many introduced species, its range expansion and population growth have been rapid, and the pink salmon appears to be an established member of the Great Lakes ichthyofauna. The history of the pink salmon's range expansion and population growth in the Great Lakes has been well documented and will not be discussed (Schumacher and Hale 1962; Kwain and Lawrie 1981; Wagner and Stauffer 1982; Kwain 1987, this volume). However, the population dynamics of pink salmon stocks in the Great Lakes are poorly understood and present a complicated puzzle for investigators.

The abundance of pink salmon, at least in the United States waters of Lake Superior, has fluctuated greatly, and the mechanisms causing these irregularities are not clear. In Lake Superior, the 1970s represented a period of explosive population growth for pink salmon (Wagner and Stauffer 1982). By 1979, the pink salmon population was estimated to be 10–20 times larger than in past years (Wagner and Stauffer 1982). However, this phenomenal growth did not continue into the 1980s. The 1981 spawning run of pink salmon, which was expected to be the largest ever due to the large number of spawners observed in Lake

Superior tributaries in 1979 (the species typically has a 2-year life cycle), was nearly a complete failure (Bagdovitz et al. 1986). Lower numbers have continued to the 1985 spawning season, and the levels of abundance observed in the mid to late 1970s have yet to be repeated. In an effort to understand why these dramatic changes may have occurred, we began an investigation of the factors that may control year-class strength of pink salmon in the Great Lakes. An additional objective was to investigate the factors that control the production of early-outmigrating oncorhynchids in general and to determine common recruitment strategies, if any, of these fish.

Various life history strategies have evolved in the genus *Oncorhynchus* that have enabled these fish to become adapted to a variety of freshwater environments and to utilize these habitats to their fullest extent for spawning and incubation. Pink salmon, chum salmon *O. keta,* and sockeye salmon *O. nerka* are closely related phylogenetically and exhibit many similarities in their social, taxonomic, physiological, and genetic characteristics (Hoar 1976). These fish are termed early-outmigrating oncorhynchids because they utilize the stream or river exclusively for egg deposition and incubation, and they outmigrate soon after emergence. Even though these salmon are transient in lotic environments, the stream environment can be a dominant factor controlling year-class strength of these fish by determining their initial egg deposition and, ultimately, their freshwater survival. In order to understand those fac-

[1]Michigan Agricultural Experiment Station number 11950.

tors that influence year-class strength in early-outmigrating oncorhynchids and to contrast ocean and Great Lakes stocks, a general life history review is given.

Life History

Pacific Stocks

Pacific stocks of pink and chum salmon migrate directly to estuarine habitat upon emergence from their redds (Neave 1955; Hoar 1956; Simenstad et al. 1982a, 1982b). Pink salmon appear to be transient in the estuary whereas chum salmon may reside in the estuary for as little as 4 d but generally inhabit the estuary for approximately 1 month (Levy and Northcote 1982; Simenstad et al. 1982a, 1982b). The estuary is apparently the major rearing area for chum salmon juveniles, but pink salmon make only limited use of it (Levy and Northcote 1982). Pink salmon spend approximately 18 months in the ocean; chum salmon may reside there for 1–5 years (depending on the stock) before returning to their natal streams to spawn (Scott and Crossman 1973).

Sockeye salmon may migrate directly to the ocean upon emergence but more typically outmigrate to freshwater lakes where they reside for 1–3 years before smolting (Foerster 1968). Thus, lakes act as the major nursery area for sockeye salmon. After smoltification, sockeye salmon migrate to the ocean where they undertake extensive feeding migrations, lasting 1–4 years, before returning to their natal streams to spawn (Foerster 1968). Kokanee, landlocked sockeye salmon, do not outmigrate to the ocean but complete their entire life cycle in fresh water (Scott and Crossman 1973).

Some Pacific races of chinook salmon *O. tshawytscha* and coho salmon *O. kisutch* have also developed the strategy of using streams exclusively for incubation (Chapman et al. 1961; Scott and Crossman 1973). Chinook salmon that outmigrate early feed in estuaries for periods ranging from 6 to 189 d, depending on the size of the outmigrant (Simenstad et al. 1982a). In general, the smaller the fish is upon reaching the estuary, the longer the duration of estuarine residence (Simenstad et al. 1982a). Upon leaving the estuary, chinook salmon migrate to the open ocean or to bays, where they feed extensively for 1–5 years before returning to their native river to spawn.

Coho salmon that exhibit early outmigration have been called nomads because they are not considered to be actively migrating but rather to have been forced out of the riverine environment by the larger members of their cohort (Chapman 1962). Very little is known about the behavior and survival of these early-outmigrating coho salmon (Simenstad et al. 1982a).

Great Lakes Stocks

Great Lakes pink salmon migrate directly into the lacustrian environment upon emergence from their redds in early May and apparently do not reside in the freshwater marshes of the Great Lakes for any extended period of time (Kwain 1982; Bagdovitz et al. 1986). These fish generally reside in the lacustrian environment for approximately 15 months. However, substantial numbers of 3-year-old pink salmon have been noted in Lake Superior; these fish have resided in the lacustrian environment for an additional 12 months.

Collins (1971) reported that kokanee experimentally introduced into Lake Huron from 1964 to 1969 either outmigrated directly to the lake upon emergence or resided in the stream, feeding for a few weeks before outmigration. The kokanee then resided in the lake for 1–3 years before returning to the lotic environment for spawning. Although limited natural reproduction did occur, the kokanee population of Lake Huron decreased through the late 1970s and is now considered virtually extinct (J. Collins, Ontario Ministry of Natural Resources, personal communication).

Some Great Lakes chinook and coho salmon may also have adapted the strategy of early outmigration. Most chinook salmon in the Great Lakes appear to smolt and outmigrate after 2 or 3 months of stream rearing (Carl 1982; Seelbach 1985). We have, however, observed some chinook salmon outmigrating shortly after emergence in Lake Superior and Lake Huron tributaries. However, the survival rates of these fry (postemergent juveniles) upon reaching the lakes and the mechanism triggering their outmigration are still unknown.

Most Great Lakes coho salmon smolt after a year of stream residence, but Seelbach (1985) collected some coho salmon smolts that were outmigrating only 8 months after spawning. These smolts were collected after a fairly mild winter and Seelbach postulated that rapid growth during the first 2–3 months after emergence allowed these fish to smolt at an early age. Most of this cohort, however, remained in the riverine environment for an additional year of rearing.

After smolting, coho salmon spend 1–3 years in the lakes and chinook salmon reside there 1–5 years (Parsons 1973). Chinook and coho salmon generally return to their natal streams for spawning, but there seems to be a somewhat greater incidence of straying than in Pacific stocks (Scott and Crossman 1973).

Limiting Factors

Oncorhynchid populations are affected by a variety of factors during their life history. Oncorhynchids typically exhibit a type-III survivorship curve (Figure 1) with the greatest mortality occurring in the earliest stages of their life and a sharp decline in the curve due to death after spawning (Thompson 1959). The survival of oncorhynchids might be more precisely illustrated by a champagne glass type model (Figure 2). In this model, potential egg deposition is at the top of the "glass"; subsequent numbers in the cohort and, therefore, the shape of the glass are molded by the severity of the various limiting factors at each life stage. Although the glass can be severely narrowed at any life history stage, the majority of factors limiting year-class strength for these salmon have evolutionarily occurred during the first few months of life, hence the type-III survivorship curve. Limiting factors can be biotic or abiotic and are typically a combination of both.

Of all the habitats utilized by these oncorhynchids, the riverine environment is the most dynamic (Wickett 1958; Foerster 1968). This is due, in part, to the limited environmental buffering capacity of rivers because of their relatively small size as compared to other salmonid habitats. Due to their limited buffering capacity, lotic ecosys-

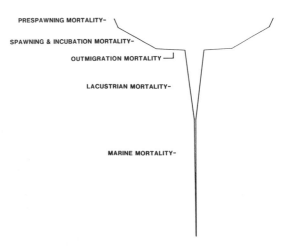

FIGURE 2.—Champagne glass model of an oncorhynchid population. Potential egg deposition is expressed by the width of the top of the glass and the shape of the glass downward is molded by the mortality rates at different phases of the salmon's life history. The survival rates used to generate this model are from Foerster (1968).

tems are often severely affected by meteorological conditions such as droughts, floods, severe winter conditions, unusual temperature extremes, etc. In addition, the relative immobility of the salmon at this life stage compounds these environmental effects. Short-term climatic changes would, therefore, have a greater effect upon a riverine system than a lacustrian, estuarine, or marine ecosystem. This is not to say that these larger ecosystems are not affected by environmental variables, for they are (e.g., El Niño) and often to a great magnitude (Barber and Chavez 1983; Cane 1983).

Not all riverine environments are equally dynamic in nature, however. Given the appropriate temperature and water quality conditions, streams with an annual base flow greater than 50% of the average annual daily flow are considered excellent for salmonid production, and streams with a base flow less than 25% are considered poor (Raleigh and Nelson 1985). Streams that are controlled by groundwater sources are often quite stable environments with relatively constant base flows and temperature regimes. In these streams, climatic conditions (abiotic) would probably play a lesser role in the establishment of year-class strength than would biotic factors (predation, competition, etc.).

Streams that are predominately controlled by the runoff of surface water experience highly variable flow and temperature regimes during

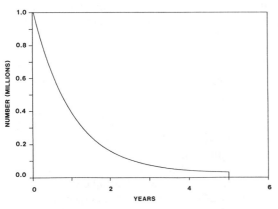

FIGURE 1.—Theoretical type-III survivorship curve based on average survival rates throughout the life history of sockeye salmon (after Thompson 1959).

oncorhynchid spawning and incubation. Egg deposition and survival would be dramatically affected by abiotic factors in these streams. The U.S. tributaries to Lake Superior are primarily characteristic of these types of streams. Thus, we feel that the characteristics of stream flow during spawning and incubation exert a major influence in determining year-class strength of Great Lakes pink salmon and possibly of other stocks of early-outmigrating oncorhynchids in systems where stream flows are variable. Evidence of the controlling factors in each ecosystem has been reported in the literature and is summarized in the following sections.

Riverine Ecosystems

Egg deposition.—The potential strength of a salmonid year class is, in part, a function of the number of eggs the brood stock can deposit. The full potential of an oncorhynchid spawning population is rarely realized due to factors that limit the number of eggs deposited in the gravel (i.e., available habitat, egg retention, redd superimposition, etc.). Thus, total potential egg deposition, in most situations, is primarily dependent upon the spawner biomass and the amount of available spawning habitat.

Spawner biomass determines the total number of ova that may be deposited. Intimately related to the biomass of spawners are sex ratio, fecundity, average weight, age at spawning, and other biological characteristics of the spawning population. These parameters are somewhat stable for a specific stock but may change over time due to environmental and fishing pressures (Ricker 1981). Although our model does not specifically deal with these biological characteristics, they must be kept in mind since changes in these characteristics can have a great effect upon the reproductive potential of a species (Ricker 1954).

The amount of available spawning habitat is controlled by the density-independent phenomenon of stream flow. Variation in water levels will affect passage of adults, predation upon adults, adult mortality, and general stress on adults (Wickett 1958). Thus, if low stream flow increases stress or increases spawner mortality, total potential egg deposition will decrease. Conversely, high stream flow may prevent upstream migration or may wash eggs out of the redd before the female can cover them (Hale et al. 1985; Raleigh and Nelson 1985). The result is similar to altering the number of eggs carried by the spawning population (Wickett 1958).

Instream flow also has a direct effect upon density-dependent factors related to egg deposition, two of the most important of these being egg retention and redd superimposition. Egg retention in the gonads of females upon the completion of spawning is generally quite low (1–5%: McNeil 1966; Foerster 1968). However, as the number of spawners in an area increases, the salmon become stressed, and the number of eggs retained by the females increases (Neave 1953).

Redd superimposition is essentially the digging up and displacement of redds constructed by early-spawning salmon by the subsequent redd-digging activity of salmon that spawn later. Superimposition generally occurs when spawning fish are temporally separated and a female cannot defend her redd. As the spawner abundance increases, an asymptotic relationship develops between the number of female spawners and the number of eggs deposited (Figure 3). This relationship assumes that redd sites are chosen in a random fashion (McNeil 1964). At the asymptote of this curve a 1:1 ratio of egg deposition to displacement exists, and no net gain occurs in the number of eggs deposited even though spawning is still underway (McNeil 1964). As the ascending limb of this curve approaches the asymptote, superimposition may be occurring at relatively high levels but is not yet detrimental to the number of eggs deposited. This can be explained by the degree of superimposition in the stream. Complete superimposition is essentially the same as the superimposition occurring at the asymptote

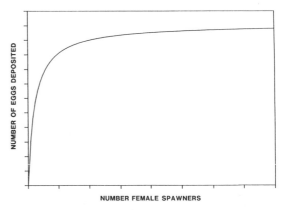

FIGURE 3.—Theoretical Beverton–Holt curve demonstrating the effect of spawner abundance upon egg deposition (based on Heard 1978). At the asymptote of the curve, displacement of eggs equals deposition and no net gain will be realized in the number of eggs deposited.

of the curve. Partial superimposition displaces only some of the eggs deposited by the earlier spawners; meanwhile, additional redd habitat is being used. Interspecific and interracial superimposition are additional factors that may also affect oncorhynchid populations in areas where different stocks are not spatially separated.

The net effect of both superimposition and increased egg retention is to reduce the number of eggs deposited into viable redds by the spawning population. The outcome can be important. Foerster (1968) reported egg retention in sockeye salmon to vary from 0.2 to 13.8%. Thus, an increase in spawner abundance could reduce potential deposition up to 13.6%. Further, using data on pink salmon from McNeil (1964), we estimated that superimposition could reduce effective egg deposition from 96% of potential at a density of 12.9 females/100 m² to 31% at a density of 330 females/100 m².

Egg survival.—The survival of eggs during the fall and winter incubation period is also intimately linked with stream flows. For the eggs and alevins to properly incubate, they need fresh water to deliver oxygen and remove wastes. Generally, the direct impact of stream flow upon the freshwater phase of oncorhynchid life history is in the form of a dome-shaped curve, as excessive or inadequate flows will each have a detrimental impact upon the stock–recruitment relationship (Wickett 1958).

Dewatering can vary in its detrimental effects upon salmon redds depending primarily upon the amount of residual flow, moisture retention and relative humidity, extremes of temperature, substrate composition and percent fines, dissolved oxygen, alevin behavior, and other species-specific characteristics such as egg size, depth of deposition, and rate of development (Becker and Neitzel 1985). The effects of a one-time dewatering, such as a natural period of low flow during incubation, depend primarily on the duration of the dewatering and the developmental phase of the salmon, since eggs are more resistant to dewatering than are the alevins (Becker et al. 1983).

High water can also be detrimental to incubating oncorhynchid eggs and alevins. Floods during the incubation stage can wash eggs and embryos out of redds prior to full development, damage them mechanically by shifting redd gravels, or suffocate them by imparting fine silts (Wickett 1958; McNeil and Ahnell 1964; Foerster 1968).

Another factor that greatly influences freshwa-

ter survival is streambed overseeding, defined by Heard (1978) "as an egg density in spawning bed gravels that leads to a significantly greater freshwater mortality than a lesser density would cause" (Figure 4). Low stream flows during spawning can influence overseeding by reducing the available habitat. The number of eggs deposited per unit area is probably not fixed, as the incubation capacity of the redds may depend upon interstitial waterflow. Oxygenated water from the stream is transported to the intergravel environment, delivering oxygen and removing nitrogenous wastes. Exchange of stream water and interstitial water is regulated by stream flow, gradient profile of the stream, composition of the gravel bed, gravel bed depth, and surface configuration of the gravel bed (Vaux 1962). Even in streams with substantial groundwater input, the flow of surface water is important to the delivery of oxygenated water through redds. Sheridan (1962) found that the major source of oxygenated water in salmon spawning riffles was the flowing stream, not groundwater. Thus, stream flow influences freshwater survival not only by regulating the amount of habitat available for spawning but also by influencing the physical and chemical environment of the intergravel system.

One mechanism through which overseeding influences freshwater survival is the degradation of intergravel water quality. Bailey et al. (1980) found that as egg densities increased in a hatchery experiment, the oxygen consumption rate increased, thus decreasing the amount of dissolved oxygen to levels stressful to the alevins. The levels of total ammonia (NH_3 and NH_4) also increased at high egg densities, but they did not

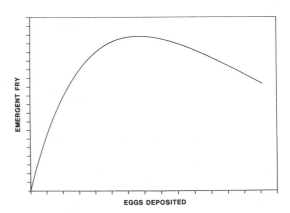

FIGURE 4.—Theoretical Ricker curve showing the effect of increased egg deposition upon the number of emergent fry (based on Ricker 1954; Heard 1978).

reach critical levels due to the low temperatures and pH of the water. In natural redd environments with warmer or more alkaline waters, a shift in total ammonia equilibria towards NH_3 may cause mortality or stimulate premature emergence of the fry (Rice and Bailey 1980a, 1980b).

The changes in dissolved oxygen and total ammonia concentrations observed under hatchery conditions would be compounded in the natural environment. The biological oxygen demand of detritus in the stream and the bacterial flora normally associated with incubating eggs would also affect the intergravel water quality (Bell et al. 1971). The presence of dead eggs in the substrate would also reduce the intergravel water quality. Dead salmon eggs and their associated microbial flora can use up to four times more oxygen than live eggs (Ellis 1970).

Dead eggs also may attract invertebrate egg predators (Ricker 1962) although the importance of these predators in population control is questionable. Although invertebrates have been noted to prey upon incubating eggs and alevins (Claire and Phillips 1968), most investigators have found invertebrates to be scavengers upon eggs and alevins that are already dead (Nicola 1968; Ellis 1970; Elliott and Bartoo 1981). If this is the case, invertebrate scavengers may actually play a cleansing role in interstitial areas of the redd, reducing the biological oxygen demand by removing dead and decaying eggs (Ellis 1970).

Wells and McNeil (1970) found that intergravel conditions influenced the development of oncorhynchids in a natural system. Their work at Sashin Creek, Alaska, showed that segments of a pink salmon population that utilized three distinctive segments of the stream had different growth and development rates. The uppermost stream section, which had the highest dissolved oxygen and coarsest spawning gravel, produced the largest and fastest-developing alevins. This area also supported the best survival between egg deposition and emergence (McNeil 1968). Thus, due to complex interactions between the incubating eggs, the redd ecosystem, and the stream flow, great variations in early survival rates can occur. Foerster (1968) reported that freshwater survival rates for sockeye salmon varied from 1% to 98.3%. Studies documenting the survival of pink and chum salmon during the incubation stage are numerous (Hunter 1959; McNeil 1966, 1968; Bams 1972; Heard 1978; Bailey et al. 1980); deposition-to-emergence survival for these species generally is between 0.88% (Hunter 1959) and 31% (McNeil 1966).

Timing of emergence.—Streambed overseeding can affect survival not only directly in the redd but indirectly by influencing the timing of fry emergence and subsequent movements to lacustrian or marine nursery areas. Fry that emerge prematurely due to excessive egg and alevin densities and the resultant poor water quality (Alderdice and Wickett 1958; Bailey et al. 1980; Kapuscinski and Lannon 1983) may be subjected to slow growth and higher marine and lacustrian mortality rates during their first weeks of life due to poorer feeding opportunities (Foerster 1968; Fedorov and Bogdanova 1979; Simenstad et al. 1982a), harsher environmental conditions (Bailey et al. 1976; Fedorov and Bogdanova 1979), or increased predation (Bams 1967; Parker 1971). Therefore, the timing of emergence, which depends upon riverine conditions, can directly influence survival of the fry in lacustrian and estuarine environments.

Freshwater rearing areas.—Oncorhynchid fry that feed in lotic systems for extended periods depend upon the productivity of the riverine environment. For early-outmigrating stocks, stream productivity may not be as critical because the stream does not act as a major rearing area. Riverine feeding by early-outmigrating oncorhynchid fry is limited; its extent depends on fry developmental stage, length of migration, and the availability of food (McDonald 1960; Foerster 1968; Mason 1974; Loftus and Lennon 1977). For most early-outmigrating oncorhynchids, riverine feeding is not a critical limiting factor because the fry are transient in rivers, and estuaries or lakes are the primary nursery areas.

For sockeye salmon, the lacustrian nursery habitat may act as the next limiting factor in their life history. Carrying capacity of nursery lakes is basically a function of habitat availability and the productivity of the lacustrian environment (Silliman 1970; Robinson and Barraclough 1978; McDonald and Hume 1984). The extent that the carrying capacity is utilized depends essentially on system-specific parameters: the fry production in river systems (McDonald and Hume 1984) connected to a specific lake; and the quality and quantity of available nursery habitat in that lake (Silliman 1970; Robinson and Barraclough 1978).

Estuarine and Marine Ecosystems

Estuaries are important to all oncorhynchids that have access to them (Simenstad et al. 1982a). All five North American oncorhynchids use estuarine food resources before moving to the open ocean, although pink and sockeye salmon use them less than the other species (Manzer 1969; Levy and Northcote 1982; Simenstad et al. 1982a).

The duration of estuarine residence is dictated by numerous biotic and abiotic factors. Fry developmental stage, food quantity and quality in the estuary, river discharge into the estuary, and estuarine topography are just some of the factors that determine estuarine residence (Iwamoto and Salo 1977). Marine mortality is typically highest during the first few weeks or months after young fish reach the marine environment (Ricker 1962; Foerster 1968; Peterman 1982; Bax 1983). In spite of their productivity and generally large size, estuaries and the open ocean have a limited carrying capacity for oncorhynchid populations (Simonova 1978; Healey 1979; Peterman 1984). The survival rate of oncorhynchids in marine ecosystems is typically less than 10% (Foerster 1968). Variations in these survival rates and their importance in oncorhynchid recruitment are reviewed by Peterman (1987, this volume).

Recruitment and Year-Class Strength

Although all environments encountered by oncorhynchids during their life history have a limited carrying capacity, we feel that the stream environment is the most important in determining the year-class strength. Support for this viewpoint comes not only from our limited studies of pink salmon in the U.S. waters of Lake Superior, but also from work by Wickett (1958), Hunter (1959), and Heard (1978) on the Pacific coast. Wickett (1958) found that fluctuations in riverine discharge can result in an eightfold variation in pink and chum salmon year-class strength, whereas ocean conditions caused only threefold variations in year-class strength.

Hunter (1959) analyzed the variation between freshwater and marine survival rates by calculating an index termed the range of variation (r.v.), which is the highest survival rate divided by the lowest survival rate. He found that fry survival in the stream ranged from 0.88 to 16.47% (r.v. = 18.72) for pink salmon and from 0.99 to 19.41% (r.v. = 19.61) for chum salmon; in contrast, ocean survival for these species ranged from only 0.7 to 5.2% (r.v. = 7.4) and 0.85 to 2.6% (r.v. = 3.1), respectively. One of the most graphic examples of the variation in freshwater survival is revealed through analysis of the 27-year data base for pink salmon in Sashin Creek, Alaska (Heard 1978).

There, variation in freshwater survival ranged from 0.06 to 21.75% (r.v. = 362.5) whereas marine survival ranged from 0.3 to 17.8% (r.v. = 59.33). Thus, even though oceanic survival varies, the greatest variation in survival clearly occurs in rivers. This variation is often a direct or indirect function of stream flow acting through processes such as bed overseeding and redd superimposition. A prime determinant in the year-class strength of early-outmigrating oncorhynchid stocks is the survival rate experienced in the riverine ecosystem.

In attempting to explain the collapse of the 1979 year class of pink salmon in the U.S. waters of Lake Superior, most evidence seems to point to a limiting factor during the species' early life history in streams. Instream flow, in most of these streams, is controlled by precipitation events and surface runoff. It appears that stream flow variation, a function of wet and dry years, has led to the variance in year-class strength observed in these waters. Initially (1957–1969), rainfall levels during spawning (August and September) were relatively low (Figure 5). During this period, the biomass of spawning pink salmon was also quite low since these fish were establishing their populations from the small initial stocking of Lake Superior; spawning runs occurred only in odd-numbered years. Rainfall levels in the early and mid 1970s were higher and the abundance and distribution of pink salmon dramatically increased. However, precipitation events changed in 1979. Extremely low rainfall at spawning during that year corresponded with the highest observed spawner abundance in many of the U.S. tributaries to Lake Superior. These two factors combined

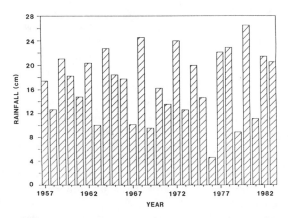

FIGURE 5.—Total rainfall during August and September from 1957 to 1983 at Marquette, Michigan. Data are from the U.S. Weather Bureau.

to provide excellent conditions for overseeding and superimposition that probably led to the collapse of the pink salmon population. The 1981 spawning and incubation period was again characterized by relatively dry weather that, combined with low spawner biomass resulting from the 1979 year-class failure, contributed to the continued decline of the odd-year run of pink salmon in Lake Superior. Of the U.S. tributaries to Lake Superior examined, only the Two Hearted River in Michigan did not experience a large decline in its pink salmon population. Two Hearted River, unlike other rivers, is controlled predominately by groundwater and does not experience great fluctuations in water level during the fall spawning period (W. J. Gruhn, Michigan Department of Natural Resources, personal communication). In addition, Two Hearted River is a much larger river system than most typical spawning streams utilized by pink salmon in the U.S. waters of Lake Superior. Thus, its main channel allows more spawning areas to remain watered in the event of decreased instream flow.

The even-year runs, which started circa 1976 (Kwain and Chappel 1978), continued to grow, although they remained at low levels, presumably due to low spawner biomass. Bagdovitz et al. (1986) found that outmigrating pink salmon fry in the Laughing Whitefish River were almost twice as abundant in the spring outmigration of the 1982 brood year as in the outmigration of the 1983 brood year. This relationship occurred despite the presence of more spawners in 1983 than in 1982. Bagdovitz (1985) theorized that mild winter temperatures and high water levels during the 1982 spawning and incubation period and low water levels and colder temperatures during the 1983 spawning and incubation period caused the difference in the observed survival rates. It is our opinion that there will be a change in year-class strength in Lake Superior, with the even-year runs beginning to dominate. The adult returns to the Laughing Whitefish River in 1984 and 1985 appear to support this theory. Although the spawning runs were low in both years, approximately 50 adult pink salmon spawned in 1984 whereas only seven were observed in 1985. Whether this even-year dominance will continue depends on future riverine environmental conditions during the fall and winter.

Summary

In this paper, we have synthesized information on the utilization of various habitat types throughout the life history of early-outmigrating oncorhynchids. Although variations in the environmental stability of each ecosystem encountered greatly influences the survival, growth, and recruitment of individual stocks, it is the riverine ecosystem that plays the principal role in determining the recruitment of oncorhynchid populations. The decline of the pink salmon stocks in the U.S. waters of Lake Superior appears to be a function of unstable stream environments in that area where the majority of tributaries are surface-water dominated. This phenomenon is probably not unique to the Great Lakes since salmon stocks utilizing short coastal streams of the Pacific coast may also be significantly impacted by changes in stream flow caused by climatic variations. Conversely, streams controlled by groundwater seepage or any constant water source would be capable of producing a relatively constant stock–recruitment relationship given sufficient spawner biomass from oceanic or lacustrian survival. In conclusion, although pink, chum, and sockeye salmon have distinctly different life history patterns, it appears that the quantity and quality of stream flow is a common factor controlling their population dynamics and recruitment.

Acknowledgments

The authors are indebted to Wilbert C. Wagner of the Michigan Department of Natural Resources for his continued support and assistance in many aspects of this study. Appreciation is also extended to Linda A. Kocik and Gary E. Whelan for their assistance in preparing this manuscript. This research was sponsored by the Michigan Sea Grant College Program (grants NA-80AA-D-00072, NA-80AA-D-SG045, and NA-86AA-D-SG043, project R/GLF-15).

References

Alderdice, D. F., and W. P. Wickett. 1958. A note on the response of developing chum salmon eggs to free carbon dioxide in solution. Journal of the Fisheries Research Board of Canada 15:797–799.

Bagdovitz, M. S. 1985. Ecology and life history of pink salmon in selected Michigan tributaries to Lake Superior. Master's thesis. Michigan State University, East Lansing, Michigan, USA.

Bagdovitz, M. S., W. W. Taylor, W. C. Wagner, J. P. Nicolette, and G. R. Spangler. 1986. Pink salmon populations in the U.S. waters of Lake Superior, 1981–1984. Journal of Great Lakes Research 12: 72–81.

Bailey, J. E., J. J. Pella, and S. G. Taylor. 1976. Production of fry and adults of the 1972 brood of pink salmon, *Oncorhynchus gorbuscha*, from gravel incubators and natural spawning at Auke Creek, Alaska. U.S. National Marine Fisheries Service Fishery Bulletin 74:961–971.

Bailey, J. E., S. D. Rice, J. J. Pella, and S. G. Taylor. 1980. Effects of seeding density of pink salmon, *Oncorhynchus gorbuscha*, eggs on water chemistry, fry characteristics, and fry survival in gravel incubators. U.S. National Marine Fisheries Service Fishery Bulletin 78:649–658.

Bams, R. A. 1967. Differences in performance of naturally and artificially propagated sockeye salmon migrant fry, as measured with swimming and predation tests. Journal of the Fisheries Research Board of Canada 24:1117–1152.

Bams, R. A. 1972. A quantitative evaluation of survival to the adult stage and other characteristics of pink salmon (*Oncorhynchus gorbuscha*) produced by a revised hatchery which simulates optimal natural conditions. Journal of the Fisheries Research Board of Canada 31:1379–1385.

Barber, R. T., and F. P. Chavez. 1983. Biological consequences of El Niño. Science (Washington, D.C.) 222:1203–1210.

Bax, N. J. 1983. Early marine mortality of marked juvenile chum salmon (*Oncorhynchus keta*) released into Hood Canal, Puget Sound, Washington, in 1980. Canadian Journal of Fisheries and Aquatic Sciences 40:426–435.

Becker, C. D., and D. A. Neitzel. 1985. Assessment of intergravel conditions influencing egg and alevin survival during salmonid redd dewatering. Environmental Biology of Fishes 12:33–46.

Becker, C. D., D. A. Neitzel, and C. S. Abernathy. 1983. Effects of dewatering on chinook salmon redds: tolerance of four development phases to one-time dewatering. North American Journal of Fisheries Management 3:373–382.

Bell, G. R., G. E. Hoskins, and W. Hodgkiss. 1971. Aspects of characterization, identification, and ecology of the bacterial flora associated with the surface of stream incubating Pacific salmon (*Oncorhynchus*) eggs. Journal of the Fisheries Research Board of Canada 28:1511–1525.

Cane, M. A. 1983. Oceanographic events during El Niño. Science (Washington, D.C.) 222:1189–1195.

Carl, L. M. 1982. Natural reproduction of coho salmon and chinook salmon in some Michigan streams. North American Journal of Fisheries Management 4:375–380.

Chapman, D. W. 1962. Aggressive behavior in juvenile coho salmon as a cause of emigration. Journal of the Fisheries Research Board of Canada 19:1047–1080.

Chapman, D. W., J. F. Corless, R. W. Phillips and R. L. Demory. 1961. Summary report, Alsea watershed study. Oregon Agricultural Experiment Station Miscellaneous Paper 110.

Claire, E. W., and R. W. Phillips. 1968. The stonefly *Acroneuria pacifica* as a potential predator on salmonid embryos. Transactions of the American Fisheries Society 97:50–52.

Collins, J. J. 1971. Introduction of kokanee salmon

(*Oncorhynchus nerka*) into Lake Huron. Journal of the Fisheries Research Board of Canada 28:1857–1871.

Elliott, S. T., and R. Bartoo. 1981. Relation of larval *Polypedilum* (Diptera: Chironomidae) to pink salmon eggs and alevins in an Alaskan stream. Progressive Fish-Culturist 43:220–221.

Ellis, R. J. 1970. *Alloperla* stonefly nymphs: predators or scavengers on salmon eggs and alevins? Transactions of the American Fisheries Society 99:677–683.

Fedorov, K. Ye., and L. S. Bogdanova. 1979. The growth and development of the larvae of the pink salmon, *Oncorhynchus gorbuscha*, under different temperature and feeding regimes. Journal of Ichthyology 18:568–576.

Foerster, R. E. 1968. The sockeye salmon, *Oncorhynchus nerka*. Fisheries Research Board of Canada Bulletin 162.

Hale, S. S., T. E. McMahon, and P. C. Nelson. 1985. Habitat suitability index models and instream flow suitability curves: chum salmon. U.S. Fish and Wildlife Service, Biological Report 82(10.108).

Healey, M. C. 1979. Detritus and juvenile salmon production in the Nanaimo estuary: I. Production and feeding rates of juvenile chum salmon (*Oncorhynchus keta*). Journal of the Fisheries Research Board of Canada 36:488–496.

Heard, W. R. 1978. Probable case of streambed overseeding—1967 pink salmon, *Oncorhynchus gorbuscha*, spawners and survival of their progeny in Sashin Creek, southeastern Alaska. U.S. National Marine Fisheries Service Fishery Bulletin 76:569–582.

Hoar, W. S. 1956. The behaviour of migrating pink salmon and chum salmon fry. Journal of the Fisheries Research Board of Canada 13:309–325.

Hoar, W. S. 1976. Smolt transformation: evolution, behavior, and physiology. Journal of the Fisheries Research Board of Canada 33:1234–1252.

Hunter, J. G. 1959. Survival and production of pink and chum salmon in a coastal stream. Journal of the Fisheries Research Board of Canada 16:835–886.

Iwamoto, R. N., and E. O. Salo. 1977. Estuarine survival of juvenile salmonids: a review of the literature. Report to Washington Department of Fisheries, Seattle, Washington, USA.

Kapuscinski, A. R. D., and J. E. Lannon. 1983. On density of chum salmon (*Oncorhynchus keta*) eggs in shallow matrix substrate incubators. Canadian Journal of Fisheries and Aquatic Sciences 40:185–191.

Kwain, W. 1982. Spawning behavior and early life history of pink salmon (*Oncorhynchus gorbuscha*) in the Great Lakes. Canadian Journal of Fisheries and Aquatic Sciences 39:1353–1360.

Kwain, W. 1987. Biology of pink salmon in the North American Great Lakes. American Fisheries Society Symposium 1:57–65.

Kwain, W., and J. A. Chappel. 1978. First evidence for even year spawning pink salmon, *Oncorhynchus gorbuscha*, in Lake Superior. Journal of the Fisheries Research Board of Canada 35:1373–1376.

Kwain, W., and A. H. Lawrie. 1981. Pink salmon in the Great Lakes. Fisheries (Bethesda) 6(2):2–6.

Levy, D. A., and T. G. Northcote. 1982. Juvenile salmon residency in a marsh area of the Fraser River estuary. Canadian Journal of Fisheries and Aquatic Sciences 39:270–276.

Loftus, W. F., and H. L. Lennon. 1977. Food habits of the salmon smolts, Oncorhynchus tshawytscha and O. keta, from the Salcha River, Alaska. Transactions of the American Fisheries Society 106:235–240.

Manzer, J. I. 1969. Stomach contents of juvenile Pacific salmon in Chatham Sound and adjacent waters. Journal of the Fisheries Research Board of Canada 26:2219–2223.

Mason, J. C. 1974. Behavioral ecology of chum salmon fry (Oncorhynchus keta) in a small estuary. Journal of the Fisheries Research Board of Canada 31:83–92.

McDonald, J. 1960. The behavior of Pacific salmon fry during their downstream migration to freshwater and saltwater nursery areas. Journal of the Fisheries Research Board of Canada 17:655–676.

McDonald, J., and J. M. Hume. 1984. Babine Lake sockeye salmon (Oncorhynchus nerka) enhancement program: testing some major assumptions. Journal of the Fisheries Research Board of Canada 41:70–92.

McNeil, W. J. 1964. Redd superimposition and egg capacity of pink salmon spawning beds. Journal of the Fisheries Research Board of Canada 21:1385–1396.

McNeil, W. J. 1966. Distribution of spawning pink salmon in Sashin Creek, southeastern Alaska, and survival of their progeny. U.S. Fish and Wildlife Service Special Scientific Report Fisheries 538.

McNeil, W. J. 1968. Migration and distribution of pink salmon spawners in Sashin Creek in 1965, and survival of their progeny. U.S. Fish and Wildlife Service Fishery Bulletin 66:575–586.

McNeil, W. J., and W. H. Ahnell. 1964. Success of pink salmon spawning relative to size of spawning bed materials. U.S. Fish and Wildlife Service Special Scientific Report Fisheries 469.

Neave, F. 1953. Principles affecting the size of pink and chum salmon populations in British Columbia. Journal of the Fisheries Research Board of Canada 9:450–491.

Neave, F. 1955. Notes on the seaward migration of pink and chum salmon fry. Journal of the Fisheries Research Board of Canada 12:369–374.

Nicola, S. J. 1968. Scavenging by Alloperla (Plecoptera: Chlorperlidea) nymphs on dead pink (Oncorhynchus gorbuscha) and chum (O. keta) salmon embryos. Canadian Journal of Zoology 46:787–796.

Nunan, P. J. 1967. Pink salmon in Lake Superior, Ontario. Ontario Fish and Wildlife Review 6(3–4):9–14.

Parker, R. R. 1971. Size selective predation among juvenile salmonid fishes in a British Columbia inlet. Journal of the Fisheries Research Board of Canada 28:1503–1510.

Parsons, J. W. 1973. A history of salmon in the Great Lakes, 1850–1970. U.S. Fish and Wildlife Service Technical Paper 68.

Peterman, R. M. 1982. Nonlinear relation between smolts and adults in Babine Lake Sockeye salmon (Oncorhynchus nerka) and implications for other salmon populations. Canadian Journal of Fisheries and Aquatic Sciences 39:904–913.

Peterman, R. M. 1984. Density-dependent growth in early ocean life of sockeye salmon (Oncorhynchus nerka). Canadian Journal of Fisheries and Aquatic Sciences 41:1825–1829.

Peterman, R. M. 1987. Review of the components of recruitment of Pacific salmon. American Fisheries Society Symposium 1:417–429.

Raleigh, R. F., and P. C. Nelson. 1985. Habitat suitability index models and instream flow suitability curves: pink salmon. U.S. Fish and Wildlife Service, Biological Report 82(10.109).

Rice, S. D., and J. E. Bailey. 1980a. Ammonia concentrations in pink salmon, Oncorhynchus gorbuscha, redds of Sashin Creek, southeastern Alaska. U.S. National Marine Fisheries Service Fishery Bulletin 78:809–811.

Rice, S. D., and J. E. Bailey. 1980b. Survival size and emergence of pink salmon, Oncorhynchus gorbuscha, alevins after short-term and long-term exposures to ammonia. U.S. National Marine Fisheries Service Fishery Bulletin 78:641–648.

Ricker, W. E. 1954. Stock and recruitment. Journal of the Fisheries Research Board of Canada 11:559–623.

Ricker, W. E. 1962. Regulation of the abundance of pink salmon populations. Pages 155–201 in N. J. Wilimovsky, editor. Symposium on pink salmon. H. R. MacMillan Lectures in Fisheries, University of British Columbia, Vancouver, Canada.

Ricker, W. E. 1981. Changes in average size and average age of Pacific salmon. Canadian Journal of Fisheries and Aquatic Sciences 38:1636–1656.

Robinson, D. G., and W. E. Barraclough. 1978. Population estimates of sockeye salmon (Oncorhynchus nerka) in a fertilized oligotrophic lake. Journal of the Fisheries Research Board of Canada 35:851–860.

Schumacher, R. E., and J. G. Hale. 1962. Third generation pink salmon, Oncorhynchus gorbuscha (Walbaum), in Lake Superior. Transactions of the American Fisheries Society 91:421–422.

Scott, W. B., and E. J. Crossman. 1973. Freshwater fishes of Canada. Fisheries Research Board of Canada Bulletin 184.

Seelbach, P. W. 1985. Smolt migration of wild and hatchery-raised coho and chinook salmon in a tributary of northern Lake Michigan. Michigan Department of Natural Resources, Fisheries Research Report 1935, Lansing, Michigan, USA.

Sheridan, W. L. 1962. Waterflow through a stream spawning riffle in southeastern Alaska. U.S. Fish and Wildlife Service Special Scientific Report Fisheries 407.

Silliman, R. P. 1970. Birectilinear recruitment curves to assess influence of lake size on survival of sockeye salmon *(Oncorhynchus nerka)* to Bristol Bay and forecast runs. U.S. Fish and Wildlife Service Special Scientific Report Fisheries 600.

Simenstad, C. A., K. L. Fresh, and E. O. Salo 1982a. The role of Puget Sound and Washington coastal estuaries in the life history of Pacific salmon: an unappreciated function. Pages 285–286 in E. L. Kennedy, editor. Estuarine comparisons. Academic Press, London, England.

Simenstad, C. A., W. J. Kinney, S. S. Parker, E. O. Salo, J. R. Cordell, and H. Beuchner 1982b. Prey community structure and trophic ecology of outmigrating juvenile chum and pink salmon in Hood Canal, Washington: a synthesis of three year's studies, 1977–1979. University of Washington, Fisheries Research Institute, Final Report, Seattle, Washington, USA.

Simonova, N. A. 1978. Population dynamics of Kamchatka River sockeye salmon *(Oncorhynchus nerka).* Journal of Ichthyology 18:722–733.

Thompson, W. F. 1959. An approach to population dynamics of the Pacific red salmon. Transactions of the American Fisheries Society 88:206–209.

Vaux, W. G. 1962. Interchange of stream and gravel water in a salmon spawning riffle. U.S. Fish and Wildlife Service Special Scientific Report Fisheries 405.

Wagner, W. C., and T. M. Stauffer. 1982. Distribution and abundance of pink salmon, *Oncorhynchus gorbuscha,* in Michigan, USA tributaries of the Great Lakes, 1967–1980. Transactions of the American Fisheries Society 111:523–526.

Wells, R. A., and W. J. McNeil. 1970. Effect of quality of spawning bed on growth and development of pink salmon embryos and alevins. U.S. Fish and Wildlife Service Special Scientific Report Fisheries 616.

Wickett, W. P. 1958. Review of certain environmental factors affecting the production of pink and chum salmon. Journal of the Fisheries Research Board of Canada 15:1103–1126.

American Fisheries Society Symposium 1:441–450, 1987
© Copyright by the American Fisheries Society 1987

Effect of Winter Severity on Steelhead Smolt Yield in Michigan: An Example of the Importance of Environmental Factors in Determining Smolt Yield

PAUL W. SEELBACH

Michigan Department of Natural Resources, Institute for Fisheries Research
Ann Arbor, Michigan 48109, USA

Abstract.—During 1981–1985, I examined the dynamics of a wild population of steelhead *Salmo gairdneri* in a Michigan tributary of Lake Michigan. Parr populations were monitored by electrofishing and emigrant populations with traps installed near the river mouth. The study river supported fall parr populations of 200,000 to 300,000 age-0+ and 80,000 age-1+ steelhead. Nearly all of the population smolted at age 2 and, despite consistent age-1+ parr production, annual smolt yield varied from 10,000 to 72,000. Variation in smolt yield was a consequence of variation in mortality during the presmolt winter. Overwinter mortality ranged from 13 to 90%. Overwinter mortality was significantly correlated with an index of the intensity of cold temperatures ($r^2 = 1.00$). In this river, where spawners were abundant and flow remained fairly constant throughout the year and from year to year, annual smolt yield was determined by the stream's carrying capacity for age-1+ parr and the severity of presmolt winter temperatures. Additional support for this idea was found in a correlation between the number of adults which returned from seven smolt cohorts and the index of intense cold ($r^2 = 0.54$). The above scenario is probably representative of the dynamics which determine smolt yield in a number of other productive Great Lakes steelhead rivers. Salmonid management efforts are often directed at determining the relationship between spawner abundance and smolt yield. Between fertilization and smolting, however, juvenile salmonids live through many stages, during which additional biological and environmental factors may act to define subsequent smolt yield. All potential factors need to be considered when attempts are made to explain variability in annual smolt yields.

Self-sustaining wild populations of steelhead *Salmo gairdneri* now exist in all five of the North American Great Lakes following this anadromous species' introduction from Pacific Ocean drainages (Biette et al. 1981). These populations are believed to be the sole or major source of the abundant adult steelhead which return each year to spawn in many river tributaries of the Great Lakes. Despite the importance of these populations, knowledge of their dynamics is limited. In particular, complete descriptions of smolt populations and of the dynamics affecting smolt yield are scarce due to the difficulty of adequately measuring smolt populations. (Smolts are juvenile steelhead which have undergone a physiological transformation in preparation for ocean life and are actively migrating downstream, in this case to a large lake.) Only Stauffer (1972), Hassinger et al. (1974), and Kwain (1983) have attempted to quantify the smolt yield of a major Great Lakes stream as well as to assess the parr population. (Parr are stream-dwelling juvenile steelhead which have not yet smolted.) Hassinger et al. and Kwain were not able to trap the entire smolt run because of flooding; Stauffer did not obtain actual population estimates of parr, nor did he test the actual

efficiency of his trapping scheme. Information on the dynamics of Pacific coast smolt populations has also been lacking; however, investigations of these processes are currently underway (personal communications, 1985, from F. H. Everest, U.S. Forest Service; T. H. Johnson, Washington Department of Game; C. J. Cedarholm, Washington Department of Natural Resources; B. R. Ward, British Columbia Ministry of Environment; and M. L. Murphy, U.S. National Marine Fisheries Service).

Smolt yield is a measure of both riverine production and future adult returns for wild steelhead populations. Fishery managers, therefore, desire consistent, maximal annual smolt yields. Studies of time-series data show, however, that smolt yield can be quite variable from year to year. In a given river, the maximum smolt yield is often as much as three to six times the minimum and, 35% of the time, annual values vary from the mean by ±0.5 times the mean (Table 1).

Possible causes of the observed variation in smolt yield can be placed into three categories: (1) random measurement errors, (2) biological factors, and (3) environmental factors (Hartman and Holtby 1982; Elliott 1984). Measurement errors

TABLE 1.—Variation in annual salmonid smolt yields.

Location	Species	Smolt yield fluctuation (max/min)	Percent of years where yield deviated ±0.5 times the mean (N)	Source
Michigan	Steelhead	6.6	33.3 (3)	This study
Michigan	Steelhead	11.6[a]	77.8 (9)	Stauffer (1972)
Washington	Steelhead	5.2	28.6 (7)	Loch et al. (1985)
Washington	Steelhead	3.0	42.9 (7)	Loch et al. (1985)
British Columbia	Steelhead	2.0	0.0 (9)	Lirette et al. (1985)
France	Atlantic salmon[b]	4.7	100.0 (2)	Bagliniere (1976)
Scotland	Atlantic salmon	1.9	12.5 (8)	Buck and Hay (1984)
Newfoundland	Atlantic salmon	3.8	22.2 (9)	Chadwick (1985)
Newfoundland	Atlantic salmon	1.7	10.0(10)	Murray (1968)
Maine	Atlantic salmon	12.8	60.0(10)	Baum and Jordan (1982)
Quebec	Atlantic salmon	4.9	37.5 (8)	Elson (1975)
Washington	Cutthroat trout[c]	4.8	57.1 (7)	Loch et al. (1985)
British Columbia	Coho salmon[d]	3.6	33.3(12)	Holtby and Hartman (1982)

[a] Represents data for age-2 smolts.   [b] *Salmo salar*.   [c] *Salmo clarki*.   [d] *Oncorhynchus kisutch*.

are difficult to completely eliminate; however, where constant sampling effort is maintained from year to year, the magnitude of these errors can be assumed to remain fairly constant. Biological factors include spawner abundance, predation, intraspecific competition, and interspecific competition. Environmental factors include fluctuating climatic factors such as precipitation and temperature and human-induced perturbations.

Many of the Great Lakes' more productive steelhead rivers lie in Michigan's northwestern lower peninsula and empty into Lake Michigan (Seelbach 1986). Very little information is available on the steelhead populations of these rivers or their dynamics. As part of a study of the characteristics and dynamics of a steelhead population in one of these rivers, I measured the complete smolt emigrations and assessed presmolt parr populations in the river during 1981–1984. In this paper, I describe the variability in smolt yield observed in my study and examine the effects of various factors on this variability.

Methods

This study was conducted on the Little Manistee River, a coldwater river which flows through forested areas of the northwestern portion of Michigan's lower peninsula. This river flows into Manistee Lake and subsequently into Lake Michigan near Manistee (Figure 1). The Little Manistee River is approximately 107 km long, with an average width of 13 m and an average depth of less than 1 m (although pools up to 2 m deep are common). The river drains an area of 58,818 hectares. Flow is fairly stable, averaging 5–6 $m^3 \cdot s^{-1}$, with peak flows reaching 12–14 $m^3 \cdot s^{-1}$. The average gradient is 0.16%. The primary bottom type is sand, although long stretches of gravel and small cobble exist. The river lies above porous sandy loam and, as a result, spring seepage occurs along most of the main stream. This seepage helps create the stable flow condition described above and keeps water temperatures below 21°C throughout the year.

Population estimates were obtained for steelhead parr during August and September 1981–1983 at 14 stations (Figure 1). The sampling stations, each approximately 100 m long, were selected so as to cover the range of habitat types which occurred along the length of the river. Parr were collected by electrofishing, and population estimates were calculated for each site by the removal method (Zippin 1958). In 1981, estimates for stations 8–13 were obtained from the Michigan Department of Natural Resources (MDNR); (stream survey records, 1981, Lansing). These were calculated by mark–recapture methods—the implications of this difference in methodology are

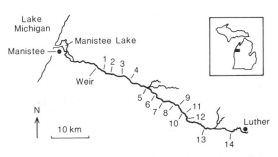

FIGURE 1.—Map of the Little Manistee River, showing location of the Michigan Department of Natural Resources weir and the 14 population survey stations.

discussed below. For a total estimate, the river, from its source near Luther to the MDNR weir, was divided into five sections by habitat type (defined by bottom type and gradient). Population estimates for each station were then expanded across the area of each section and the total number of fish in the river determined from stratified sampling equations (Schaeffer et al. 1979).

I examined the population estimates for bias between MDNR methods used in 1981 and those used in the present study. There was no sampling bias by method type for age-0+ parr, but MDNR estimates for age-1+ parr were below what would have been expected based on my sampling of other stations (Seelbach 1986). The total age-1+ parr population was estimated with a correction for this bias (Table 2).

Emigrant populations were monitored with modified inclined-screen traps installed at the MDNR weir (Seelbach et al. 1985; Figure 1). Traps were checked daily during April through June 1982–1984. Emigrants were identified as either true smolts or forced-emigrant presmolts (Seelbach 1986). Based on the published minimum smolt size of 140 mm and on coloration, I determined that presmolts constituted less than 2% of the total number of emigrants. It is possible that some presmolts migrated from the study river during other seasons, most likely during fall (fall emigrants have been found in some salmonid populations: Sopuck 1978; Ruggles 1980; and Youngson et al. 1983); however, no information on this is available. The remainder of this discussion focuses on true smolts, as these were believed to support nearly the entire returning adult population (Seelbach 1986). Smolt age was determined from length-frequency and scale analyses. The total number of smolts trapped was calculated for each age group by summing the daily catch totals. Total smolt yield was estimated for

each group by dividing the number trapped by the estimated trapping efficiency. Trapping efficiency was determined by releasing known numbers of marked smolts upstream of the traps and noting their recapture rate. Efficiency was approximately 42% in 1982 and 1983, but fell to 8% in 1984 due to high water.

As nearly all of the steelhead in the study river smolted by age 2 (Seelbach 1986), the percent of the previous fall's age-1+ parr population which smolted the following spring was equivalent to overwinter survival for this age-group. This calculation assumed that the number of presmolts which emigrated during the late fall and winter was negligible. If substantial numbers did emigrate, then survival would have been somewhat lower than reported here. If the number which emigrated was substantial and varied among years, then my analysis of the factors affecting survival would be invalid. Several pieces of evidence supported the above assumption for the study river (Seelbach1986). (1) Studies of the adult returns of marked smolts and of the scales of returning adults showed that at least 70–80% of the returning adults had come from river smolts. A substantial portion of the remaining fish were believed to be hatchery fish that strayed into the river from distant sources. Thus, there was little evidence for the existence of substantial numbers of fall presmolts. (2) In a year of high winter survival (1983–1984), smolts represented 90% of the previous fall's age-1+ parr populations. Because some winter mortality occurs, these data suggest that the number of fall presmolts was negligible. (3) The proportion of returning adults which had spent 1 year in the river prior to emigration (as determined from scale patterns) was the same for adults returning from the emigration years 1982 (severe winter) and 1983 (mild winter), suggesting that, if fall emigrants did exist

TABLE 2.—Numbers of parr and age-2 smolts, standing crop (fish per hectare in parentheses), and percent overwinter survival from age 1+ to age 2 (with 95% confidence limits) for steelhead in the Little Manistee River 1981–1984.

Winter year	Age-0+ parr	Age-1+ parr	Age-2 smolts	Percent overwinter survival to age-2 smolts
1981–1982	199,883 ± 10,689 (1,648 ± 88)	81,600 ± 6,635[a] (673 ± 55)	10,401 ± 1,677 (86 ± 14)	13 ± 2
1982–1983	322,416 ± 4,128 (2,658 ± 34)	80,172 ± 2,657 (661 ± 22)	51,180 ± 5,082 (422 ± 42)	64 ± 4
1983–1984	312,798 ± 3,450 (2,579 ± 28)	79,501 ± 2,600 (656 ± 21)	71,763 ± 17,941 (592 ± 148)	90 ± 23

[a] Estimate corrected for sampling bias.

(and survive to return), the proportion which emigrated each year was not variable.

Data on spawner abundance were from the MDNR (Little Manistee River weir reports, 1979–1982, Lansing). Climatic data were from the U.S. National Climatic Center (1970–1985). Groundwater data were from G. Huffman (U.S. Geological Survey, personal communication).

A more detailed description of these methods, and of the assumptions involved, may be found in Seelbach (1986).

Results

The Little Manistee River, above the fish weir, consistently supported fall populations of 200,000 to 300,000 age-0+ and 80,000 age-1+ steelhead. Standing crop averaged 2,295 age-0+ and 621 age-1+ fish/hectare (Table 2). Consistent annual age-1+ parr densities have also been reported for some other steelhead populations in both the Great Lakes and Pacific Coast regions (Taube 1975; Stauffer 1979; Everest et al. 1984; J. W. Peck, MDNR, personal communication). In contrast to the consistent age-1+ populations, the number of age-2 smolts which left the river each spring fluctuated between 10,000 and 72,000 (standing crop ranged between 86 and 592 fish/hectare) (Table 2). Survival through the second winter of life varied from 13 to 90%.

As age-2 smolts made up nearly 90% of the emigrant population, I will concentrate on the relationships which affected this group. The large variation in age-2 smolt yield observed in this study was due to fluctuations in survival through the presmolt winter. Overwinter survival to age-2 smolts showed strong, but not significant, linear relationships with indices of river flow and an excellent relationship with an index of the intensity of coldness (significant at $P < 0.01$). Indices were used because actual measurements of river flow and temperature were not available. Flow in the study river is heavily influenced by groundwater, and fall rainfall and well levels in winter were thought to be representative of winter groundwater levels. River temperatures are influenced by air temperatures (Evans 1973), and the index used was believed to reflect both the intensity and the duration of extremely cold river temperatures. This index was descriptive of the severity of winter conditions observed during the study years. During the winter of 1981–1982 (when the severity index was nearly twice that for 1983–1984), ice cover and frazil ice were prevalent in many areas of the study river—conditions

not found during the following two winters. Survival was related to (1) the amount of rainfall during the previous fall in nearby Cadillac, Michigan ($r^2 = 0.91$), and winter groundwater levels in nearby Irons, Michigan ($r^2 = 0.66$), and (2) the number of days during which the minimum air temperature was less than or equal to $-12°C$ (January–February) in Cadillac, Michigan ($r^2 = 1.00$; Figure 2). Total smolt yield was similarly related to fall rainfall, groundwater levels, and intensity of coldness ($r^2 = 0.87$, 0.72, and 1.00, respectively).

Additional factors which could potentially have affected smolt yield were considered and eliminated. Consistent methods were used throughout the study, so I assumed that measurement errors were not an important factor. Biological and environmental factors which might have affected the population prior to age 1+ had no effect, as evidenced by the consistent densities of age-1+ parr.

These biological factors included, notably, spawner abundance. The minimum number of spawners needed to produce maximum smolt yield was unknown. Using calculations similar to those of Elson (1975) for Atlantic salmon in New Brunswick and Johnson (1985) for steelhead in

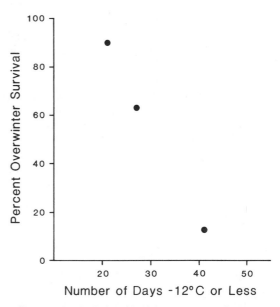

FIGURE 2.—Relationship between overwinter survival to age-2 smolts and the intensity of presmolt winter cold for steelhead in the Little Manistee River during 1982–1984. Intensity of cold is shown as the number of days with minimum air temperatures of $-12°C$ or less during January and February in Cadillac, Michigan.

Washington, I determined that the average spawner abundance in the study stream (approximately 7,000–10,000 fish during 1979–1982) was approximately two to four times higher than a conservative estimate of that needed to produce maximum smolt yields (Seelbach 1986).

Any effects of biological factors on the population between age-1+ parr and age-2 smolts were unknown; however, the strong statistical relationships found between winter severity indices and survival during this period suggested that the dominant factors were abiotic ones.

The correlation between smolt yield and winter severity found in this study was excellent, but it was the product of only three data points. Three points are the minimum required to perform regression analysis and do not typically produce relationships with high levels of significance. No other estimates of overwinter survival to smolting exist for comparison. The relationship found here is presented as a hypothesis which will require further testing. In an attempt to test this hypothesis using available data, I examined two independent population abundance data sets for evidence of this same relationship. In the first analysis, the number of adult steelhead returning to the Little Manistee weir each spring, analyzed by smolt cohort ($N = 7$), was linearly related to the intensity of cold during the presmolt winter ($r^2 = 0.54$; $P < 0.01$; Figure 3). In addition, in recent years adult returns to several nearby rivers have undergone fluctuations similar to those observed in the study river, suggesting some widespread climatic effect on population abundance (Seelbach 1986).

The second analysis involved 9 years of steelhead smolt yield data from the Black River, a tributary to northern Lake Michigan in Michigan's upper peninsula. Stauffer (1972) observed that fluctuations in yield of age-2 smolts were correlated with fluctuations in age-0+ parr and felt that this might be related to variable spawner abundance. I examined environmental conditions in relation to Stauffer's data and found a slight, though not significant at $P < 0.10$, correlation between age-2 smolt yield and the intensity of cold during the presmolt winter ($r^2 = 0.32$; the function used was $Y = \log_e a + b \log_e X$), similar in slope to that for the Little Manistee River. Further analysis revealed that 92% of the variability in Stauffer's data ($P = 0.01$) could be explained by a negative relationship between smolt yield and the number of extreme high-flow days each year. High flows typically occurred in spring during the spawning–hatching period. I do not believe this

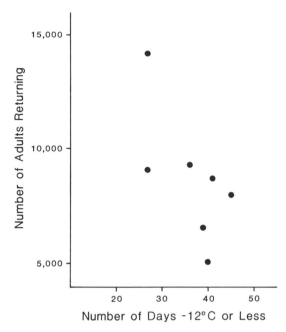

FIGURE 3.—Relationship between the number of maiden adult steelhead per smolt cohort returning to the Little Manistee River each spring during 1978–1986 and the intensity of cold during the presmolt winter. Intensity of cold is shown as the number of days with minimum air temperatures of $-12°C$ or less during January and February in Cadillac, Michigan.

demonstrated that cold during the presmolt winter was unimportant. Rather, cold may have been an important factor only to cohorts which had not already been reduced by factors such as limited spawners or flooding. Flooding may be an important factor in the Black River system, though not in the Little Manistee, as the Black River lies in a region where solid bedrock lies very close to the land surface and thus river flow is affected by pulses in surface runoff (Veatch 1933).

Discussion

The Little Manistee river is similar in many ways to several other productive Great Lakes steelhead rivers (these include, notably, several rivers in the northwestern part of Michigan's lower peninsula). These rivers all have extremely stable discharge patterns and abundant spawning populations. The results of this study suggest that, in rivers with these characteristics, smolt yield will be determined by the stream's carrying capacity for age-1+ parr and the severity of presmolt winter temperatures. Annual winter temperatures undergo large and frequent fluctuations in the Great Lakes region (Figure 4), so smolt yield from such rivers can be expected to fluctuate from year to year.

In contrast, in tributaries such as the Black River (described above for Stauffer's 1972 study), where flow is sensitive to surface water inputs, smolt yield may be related more to year-class strength as determined by flood conditions during the spawning–hatching stage. Factors which affect the population later in life, such as summer low flows or winter severity, may only have a major effect on the stronger year classes.

Several northern Great Lakes tributaries are subject to low water levels in some seasons (Knutilla 1970; Hassinger et al. 1974; Kwain 1983) and produce important numbers of age-1 presmolts. The dynamics leading up to the production of presmolts presumably parallels those discussed above for smolts. Strong year classes that are not limited by spawner abundance or flooding produce large numbers (as rearing habitat is filled to capacity), whereas weak year classes produce smaller numbers (Stauffer 1972).

In this study, an environmental factor played a major role in the determination of steelhead smolt yield. Other evidence that environmental factors determine smolt yield has been found in studies of time-series data on parr, smolts, and adult salmonids. Elliott (1984) and Frenette et al. (1984) related fluctuations in stream flow to fluctuations in parr densities. Hartman (1982) attributed a major increase in smolt production to mild winter

conditions, while Chadwick (1982) blamed severe winter conditions for one year's particularly low smolt yield. Huntsman (1931), Power (1981), Scarnecchia (1981), and Wood (1984) all found correlations between adult abundance and environmental conditions during the riverine life stages. In addition, these authors found that annual adult abundance patterns were consistent over broad geographical areas, suggesting a widespread climatic effect.

Environmental factors can affect mortality during several of the life stages of juvenile salmonids. Below are listed the various periods of life and evidence for environmental effects at each.

Spawning–hatching period.—Numerous authors have pinpointed environmental effects on mortality during this early period. Frenette et al. (1984) found that low flows during the incubation period were correlated with subsequent low parr densities. Chadwick (1982) reported that low flows and cold temperatures during incubation can drastically affect parr year-class strength. In contrast, flooding during this period can also result in low parr densities due either to a reduction in usable spawning area (fish cannot spawn where velocities are too high) or to displacement of fry (Brett 1951; Chapman and Bjornn 1969; Seegrist and Gard 1972; Hartman and Holtby 1982; Everest et al. 1984).

Summer periods.—In many rivers, late summer is a period of low flows. Low flows, and the resultant limited habitat, have been shown to limit parr densities in several instances (Havey 1974; Mason 1976; Hartman and Holtby 1982; Holtby and Hartman 1982; Elliott 1984; Frenette et al. 1984; Bottom et al. 1985; Johnson 1985). This may, in turn, limit smolt yields.

Winter periods.—Several authors have felt that smolt yield can be directly related to variable overwinter mortality (Bustard and Narver 1975; Mason 1976; Holtby and Hartman 1982; Everest et al. 1984). In regions where winter temperatures are moderate, overwinter mortality is usually related to the severity of winter flooding (Hartman 1965; Chapman and Bjornn 1969; Seegrist and Gard 1972; Bustard and Narver 1975; Holtby and Hartman 1982). In colder regions, cold temperatures and low flows have been related to overwinter mortality (Needham et al. 1945; Hassinger et al. 1974; Cunjak 1986). I suspect that cold temperatures are more important relative to other mortality factors in the colder regions of the steelhead's range. Shuter et al. (1980) felt that the influence of cold water temperatures on the mor-

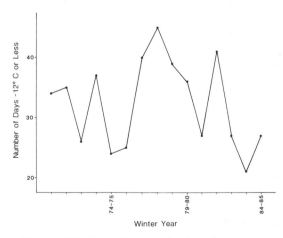

FIGURE 4.—Fluctuations in the intensity of winter cold during 1970–1985 in Cadillac, Michigan. Intensity of cold is shown as the number of days with minimum air temperatures of −12°C or less during January and February.

tality of smallmouth bass *Micropterus dolomieui* increased towards the northern edge of their range. Winter temperatures for Great Lakes steelhead are comparable to those at the northern extremes of the steelhead's native Pacific coast range (Figure 5).

The possible factors which cause overwinter mortality in salmonid parr populations include hypothermia, inadequate lipid reserves and subsequent starvation, predation, displacement by flooding, and physical damage from anchor ice and frazil ice (Brett and Alderdice 1958; Reimers 1963; Hartman 1965; Chapman and Bjornn 1969; DeVries 1971; Hassinger et al. 1974; Bustard and Narver 1975; Mason 1976; Riddell and Leggett 1981; Everest et al. 1984). As water temperatures drop below 5°C, the behavior of juvenile salmonids changes markedly (Meister 1962; Hartman 1963; Saunders and Gee 1964; Chapman and Bjornn 1969; Bustard and Narver 1975; Rimmer et al. 1983; Everest et al. 1984; Cunjak 1986; Heifetz et al. 1986). The fish become essentially inactive and take up hiding positions in log cover, in rock cover, and at the bottom of deep pools. This hiding behavior is believed to reduce the fish's

vulnerability to factors such as flooding, predation, and frazil ice. Hiding areas may also be refuges from colder areas of the stream. In spring-fed rivers, springs may serve in such a capacity (Cunjak 1986). Chapman (1966), Bustard and Narver (1975), and Mason (1976) concluded that, in some streams, the availability of overwinter refugia may be the critical factor limiting smolt production. Everest et al. (1984) found that steelhead concentrated in winter refuge areas and that these were limited to approximately 10% of the total stream area. Winter flow levels define the wetted area, and thus the potential overwinter refuge area, of streams. The severity and duration of winter environmental conditions may ultimately define the effective refuge area. The extent to which overwinter refuge area limits smolt yield will depend on the severity of winter conditions and will vary among years and among rivers.

For populations which spend more than one winter in the river, some evidence suggests that the presmolt winter is the critical winter, and that conditions during earlier winters have little effect on smolt yield (Everest et al. 1984). That variation in winter severity during the fish's first winter has no effect on age-1+ parr densities means either (1) that age-0+ fish use different refuge areas than age-1+ fish, and that these areas are not limiting, or (2) that, at low age-0+ densities, mortality rates are reduced so that populations of age-1+ fish reach carrying capacity within 6 to 7 months. Both of these are valid hypotheses, as age-0+ salmonids can burrow into small-sized gravel where larger ones cannot (Bustard and Narver 1975), and compensatory mechanisms are known to occur in salmonid populations (consider the extremely high mortalities of hatchery fish planted within a wild population: Cooper 1959).

The above review, though brief, demonstrates that environmental factors often can have a major effect on the determination of smolt yield. In a given situation, more than one environmental factor may be significant. For populations in which fish remain 2–4 years in the river, multiple summer- and winter-related factors come into play.

Management efforts are often directed at determining the number of spawners which will produce the maximum smolt yield. Consequently, although all of the above factors have been shown to influence smolt yield to some degree, management models typically focus only on the relationship between spawner abundance and smolt yield (Elson 1975; Symons 1979; Watt and Penney

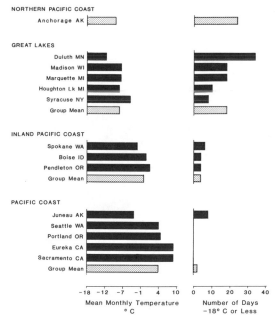

FIGURE 5.—Winter temperatures for various regions within the steelhead's range. Temperatures are shown as the mean monthly air temperature (°C) in January and February and the number of days with minimum air temperatures of −18°C or less during January and February (data from Ruffner and Bair 1977).

1980; Chadwick 1982; Buck and Hay 1984). The assumptions implicit in this are (1) that the effects of other biological factors and of environmental factors are small relative to the effect of spawner abundance, and (2) that the situations in which these additional factors have a major effect are rare and unpredictable and thus of little consequence in modeling efforts. As demonstrated by the information presented above, these assumptions are invalid for several salmonid populations. All potential factors need to be considered when attempts are made to explain variability observed in annual smolt yields.

Acknowledgments

Many people contributed to the collection of field data over a period of several years, and I am thankful to all for their assistance. Special thanks go to personnel of the MDNR's Institute for Fisheries Research and to the biologists and technicians of MDNR District 6. W. C. Latta and J. S. Diana provided guidance and encouragement throughout all phases of this research. R. D. Clark provided thoughtful discussions during the formulation of this paper. W. C. Latta, G. Power, and F. H. Everest reviewed the manuscript. This project was carried out as part of my doctoral studies in the School of Natural Resources, The University of Michigan, Ann Arbor.

References

Bagliniere, J. L. 1976. The downstream activity of the smolts in the Elle River, Normandie. Annales d'Hydrobiologie 7:159–177.

Baum, E. T., and R. M. Jordan. 1982. The Narraguagus River, an Atlantic salmon river management report. State of Maine, Atlantic Sea Run Salmon Commission, Bangor, Maine, USA.

Biette, R. M., D. P. Dodge, R. L. Hassinger, and T. M. Stauffer. 1981. Life history and timing of migrations and spawning behavior of rainbow trout (Salmo gairdneri) populations of the Great Lakes. Canadian Journal of Fisheries and Aquatic Sciences 38:1759–1771.

Bottom, D. L., P. J. Howell, and J. D. Rogers. 1985. The effects of stream alteration on salmon and trout habitat in Oregon. Oregon Department of Fish and Wildlife, Corvallis, Oregon, USA.

Brett, J. R. 1951. A study of the Skeena River climatological conditions with particular reference to their significance in sockeye production. Journal of the Fisheries Research Board of Canada 8:178–187.

Brett, J. R., and D. F. Alderdice. 1958. The resistance of cultured young chum and sockeye salmon to temperatures below 0°C. Journal of the Fisheries Research Board of Canada 15:805–813.

Buck, R. J. G., and D. W. Hay. 1984. The relationship between stock size and progeny of Atlantic salmon (Salmo salar L.) in a Scottish stream. Journal of Fish Biology 24:1–11.

Bustard, D. R., and D. W. Narver. 1975. Aspects of the winter ecology of juvenile coho salmon (Oncorhynchus kisutch) and steelhead trout (Salmo gairdneri). Journal of the Fisheries Research Board of Canada 32:667–680.

Chadwick, E. M. P. 1982. Stock–recruitment relationship for Atlantic salmon (Salmo salar) in Newfoundland rivers. Canadian Journal of Fisheries and Aquatic Sciences 39:1496–1501.

Chadwick, E. M. P. 1985. The influence of spawning stock on production and yield of Atlantic salmon, Salmo salar L., in Canadian rivers. Aquaculture and Fisheries Management 1:111–119.

Chapman, D. W. 1966. Food and space as regulators of salmonid populations in streams. American Naturalist 100:345–357.

Chapman, D. W., and T. C. Bjornn. 1969. Distribution of salmonids in streams, with special reference to food and feeding. Pages 153–176 in T. G. Northcote, editor. Symposium on salmon and trout in streams. H. R. MacMillan Lectures in Fisheries, University of British Columbia, Vancouver, Canada.

Cooper, E. L. 1959. Trout stocking as an aid to fish management. Pennsylvania State University, College of Agriculture Experimental Station Bulletin 663, State College, Pennsylvania, USA.

Cunjak, R. A. 1986. The winter biology of stream salmonids. Doctoral dissertation. University of Waterloo, Waterloo, Canada.

DeVries, A. L. 1971. Freezing resistance in fishes. Pages 157–187 in W. S. Hoar and D. J. Randall, editors. Fish physiology, volume 6. Environmental relations and behavior. Academic Press, New York, New York, USA.

Elliott, J. M. 1984. Numerical changes and population regulation in young migratory trout Salmo trutta in a Lake District stream, 1966–1983. Journal of Animal Ecology 53:327–350.

Elson, P. F. 1975. Atlantic salmon rivers, smolt production and optimal spawning: an overview of natural production. International Atlantic Salmon Foundation Special Publication Series 6:96–119.

Evans, E. 1973. Trout water quality. Michigan Department of Natural Resources, Michigan Water Resources Commission, Lansing, Michigan, USA.

Everest, F. H., J. R. Sedell, G. H. Reeves, and J. Wolfe. 1984. Fisheries enhancement in the Fish Creek basin—an evaluation of in-channel and off-channel projects, 1984. U.S. Forest Service, Annual Report to the Bonneville Power Administration, Division of Fish and Wildlife, Project 84-11, Portland, Oregon, USA.

Frenette, M., M. Caron, P. Julien, and R. J. Gibson. 1984. Interaction entre le debit et les populations de tacons (Salmo salar) de la riviere Matamec, Quebec. Canadian Journal of Fisheries and Aquatic Sciences 41:954–963.

Hartman, G. F. 1963. Observations on behavior of

juvenile brown trout in a stream aquarium during winter and spring. Journal of the Fisheries Research Board of Canada 20:769–787.

Hartman, G. F. 1965. The role of behavior in the ecology and interaction of underyearling coho salmon (Oncorhynchus kisutch) and steelhead trout (Salmo gairdneri). Journal of the Fisheries Research Board of Canada 22:1035–1081.

Hartman, G. F. 1982. Answer to question. Page 372 in G. F. Hartman, editor. Proceedings of the Carnation Creek workshop, a 10 year review. Malaspina College, Nanaimo, Canada.

Hartman, G. F., and L. B. Holtby. 1982. An overview of some biophysical determinants of fish production responses to logging in Carnation Creek, British Columbia. Pages 348–372 in G. F. Hartman, editor. Proceedings of the Carnation Creek workshop, a 10 year review. Malaspina College, Nanaimo, Canada.

Hassinger, R. L., J. G. Hale, and D. E. Woods. 1974. Steelhead of the Minnesota north shore. Minnesota Department of Natural Resources, Technical Bulletin 11, St. Paul, Minnesota, USA.

Havey, K. A. 1974. Effects of regulated flows on standing crops of juvenile salmon and other fishes at Barrows Stream, Maine. Transactions of the American Fisheries Society 103:1–9.

Heifetz, J., M. L. Murphy, and K. V. Koski. 1986. Effects of logging on winter habitat of juvenile salmonids in Alaskan streams. North American Journal of Fisheries Management 6:52–58.

Holtby, L. B., and G. F. Hartman. 1982. The population dynamics of coho salmon (Oncorhynchus kisutch) in a west coast rain forest stream subjected to logging. Pages 308–347 in G. F. Hartman, Editor. Proceedings of the Carnation Creek workshop, a 10 year review. Malaspina College, Nanaimo, Canada.

Huntsman, A. G. 1931. The maritime salmon of Canada. Biological Board of Canada Bulletin 21.

Johnson, T. H. 1985. Density of steelhead parr for mainstream rivers in western Washington during the low flow period, 1984. Washington State Game Department, Fisheries Management Division, Report 85-6, Olympia, Washington, USA.

Knutilla, R. L. 1970. Statistical summaries of Michigan streamflow data. U.S. Geological Survey and Michigan Department of Natural Resources, Water Resources Commission, Lansing, Michigan, USA.

Kwain, W. 1983. Downstream migration, population size, and feeding of juvenile rainbow trout. Journal of Great Lakes Research 9:52–59.

Lirette, M. G., R. S. Hooton, and W. R. Olmsted. 1985. A summary of wild steelhead smolt enumeration and habitat productivity studies at Quinsam River, 1976–1984. British Columbia Ministry of the Environment, Fisheries Technical Circular 67, Nanaimo, Canada.

Loch, J. J., M. W. Chilcote, and S. A. Leider. 1985. Kalama River studies final report, part 2. Juvenile downstream migrant studies. Washington Department of Game, Fisheries Management Division Report 85-12, Olympia, Washington, USA.

Mason, J. C. 1976. Response of underyearling coho salmon to supplemental feeding in a natural stream. Journal of Wildlife Management 40-775–778.

Meister, A. L. 1962. Atlantic salmon production in Cove Brook, Maine. Transactions of the American Fisheries Society 91:208–212.

Murray, A. R. 1968. Numbers of Atlantic salmon and brook trout captured and marked at the Little Codroy River, Newfoundland, counting fence and auxiliary traps, 1954–63. Fisheries Research Board of Canada Technical Report 84.

Needham, P. R., J. W. Moffett, and D. W. Slater. 1945. Fluctuations in wild brown trout populations in Convict Creek, California. Journal of Wildlife Management 9:9–25.

Power, G. 1981. Stock characteristics and catches of Atlantic salmon (Salmo salar) in Quebec, and Newfoundland and Labrador in relation to environmental variables. Canadian Journal of Fisheries and Aquatic Sciences 38:1601–1611.

Reimers, N. 1963. Body condition, water temperature and over-winter survival of hatchery-reared trout in Convict Creek, California. Transactions of the American Fisheries Society 92:39–46.

Riddell, B. E., and W. C. Leggett. 1981. Evidence of an adaptive basis for geographic variation in body morphology and time of downstream migration of juvenile Atlantic salmon (Salmo salar). Journal of the Fisheries Research Board of Canada 38:308–320.

Rimmer, D. M., U. Paim, and R. L. Saunders. 1983. Autumnal habitat shift of juvenile Atlantic salmon (Salmo salar) in a small river. Canadian Journal of Fisheries and Aquatic Sciences 40:671–680.

Ruffner, J. A., and F. E. Bair, editors. 1977. The weather almanac. Gale Research, Detroit, Michigan, USA.

Ruggles, C. P. 1980. A review of the downstream migration of Atlantic salmon. Canadian Technical Report of Fisheries and Aquatic Sciences 952.

Saunders, R. L., and J. H. Gee. 1964. Movements of young Atlantic salmon in a small stream. Journal of the Fisheries Research Board of Canada 21:27–36.

Scarnecchia, D. L. 1981. Effects of streamflow and upwelling on yield of wild coho salmon (Oncorhynchus kisutch) in Oregon. Canadian Journal of Fisheries and Aquatic Sciences 38:471–475.

Schaeffer, R. L., W. Mendenhall, and L. Ott. 1979. Elementary survey sampling. Duxbury Press, North Scituate, Massachusetts, USA.

Seegrist, D. W., and R. Gard. 1972. Effect of floods on trout in Sagehen Creek, California. Transactions of the American Fisheries Society 101:478–482.

Seelbach, P. W. 1986. Population characteristics and dynamics of wild steelhead in a Michigan tributary of Lake Michigan. Doctoral dissertation. University of Michigan, Ann Arbor, Michigan, USA.

Seelbach, P. W., G. R. Alexander, and R. N. Lockwood. 1985. A modified inclined-screen trap for catching salmonid smolts in large rivers. North American Journal of Fisheries Management 5:494–498.

Shuter, B. J., J. A. MacLean, F. E. G. Fry, and H. A. Regier. 1980. Stochastic simulation of temperature effects on first-year survival of smallmouth bass. Transactions of the American Fisheries Society 109:1–34.

Sopuck, R. D. 1978. Emigration of juvenile rainbow trout in Cayuga Inlet, New York. New York Fish and Game Journal 25:108–120.

Stauffer, T. M. 1972. Age, growth, and downstream migration of juvenile rainbow trout in a Lake Michigan tributary. Transactions of the American Fisheries Society 101:18–28.

Stauffer, T. M. 1979. Two-year cycles of abundance of age-0 rainbow trout in Lake Superior Tributaries. Transactions of the American Fisheries Society 108:542–547.

Symons, P. E. K. 1979. Estimated escapement of Atlantic salmon (Salmo salar) for maximum smolt production in rivers of different productivity. Journal of the Fisheries Research Board of Canada 36:132–140.

Taube, C. M. 1975. Abundance, growth, biomass and interrelationship of trout and coho salmon in the Platte River. Michigan Department of Natural Resources, Fisheries Research Report 1830, Ann Arbor, Michigan, USA.

U.S. National Climatic Center. 1970–1985. Climatological data—Michigan, 1970–1985. Asheville, North Carolina, USA.

Veatch, J. O. 1933. Agricultural land classification and land types of Michigan. Michigan State College, Agricultural Experiment Station, Special Bulletin 231, East Lansing, Michigan, USA.

Watt, W. D., and G. H. Penney. 1980. Juvenile salmon survival in the Saint John River system. Canadian Technical Report of Fisheries and Aquatic Sciences 939.

Wood, W. A. 1984. Trends in historic abundance and present status of natural stocks of north coastal Washington coho and chinook salmon. Pages 193–204 in J. M. Walton and D. B. Houston, editors. Proceedings of the Olympic wild fish conference. Peninsula College, Port Angeles, Washington, USA.

Youngson, A. F., R. J. G. Buck, T. H. Simpson, and D. W. Hay. 1983. The autumn and spring emigrations of juvenile Atlantic salmon, Salmo salar L., from the Girnock Burn, Aberdeenshire, Scotland: environmental release of migration. Journal of Fish Biology 23:625–639.

Zippin, C. 1958. The removal method of population estimation. Journal of Wildlife Management 22:82–90.

American Fisheries Society Symposium 1:451–454, 1987

Parent–Progeny Relationship for an Established Population of Anadromous Alewives in a Maine Lake

CLEMENT J. WALTON

Maine Department of Marine Resources, Marine Resources Laboratory
West Boothbay Harbor, Maine 04575, USA

Abstract.—The relationship between annual egg deposition and the production of juvenile anadromous alewives *Alosa pseudoharengus* in Damariscotta Lake, Maine, was examined during 8 years, from 1977 through 1984. Annual egg deposition varied by a factor of almost five, but numbers of juveniles emigrating from the lake were relatively constant and independent of egg deposition. The parent–progeny relationship in this established alewife population was asymptotic. Juvenile production in Damariscotta Lake appeared to be controlled by competition for zooplankton resources.

Spring migrations of anadromous alewives *Alosa pseudoharengus* into freshwater spawning habitats, and the summer and fall emigrations of juveniles from nursery areas, occur in numerous coastal watersheds in eastern North America. Anadromous alewives home to lakes, ponds, and slow-flowing streams to spawn. Abundance of spawning adults generally is positively correlated with surface area of the spawning and nursery habitats. Counts or numerical estimates of spawning alewives or juvenile emigrants have been reported by several investigators (Cooper 1961; Havey 1961, 1973; Tyus 1971; Saila et al. 1972; Huber 1974; Kissil 1974; Richkus 1974; and Rideout 1974). None of these studies demonstrated a consistent relationship between parental stock abundance and recruitment, although they confirmed an expected positive correlation between spawner abundance and numbers of juvenile emigrants at low stock levels. For example, Havey's (1973) study of juvenile alewife production in a Maine lake yielded a strong and positive linear relationship ($r^2 = 0.88$) between numbers of juvenile emigrants and numbers of adult immigrants 4 years later, and a weak but positive linear relationship ($r^2 = 0.52$) between $\log_{10}$ of female escapement from the fishery and $\log_{10}$ of numbers of juvenile emigrants. Brown (1972) demonstrated an inverse relationship between stock and recruitment for landlocked alewives in Lake Michigan, but Henderson and Brown (1985) found no such relationship for alewives in Lake Huron.

Part of the difficulty in studying stock and recruitment for anadromous alewives is that in some cases spawning run fish are representative of the spawning stock in the lake (Walton 1983), and in other cases (Libby 1981) they are not, a problem not evident in landlocked stocks. Immigrating adults and emigrating juveniles exhibit variability in abundance within and between sampling days; thus estimates derived from limited numbers of samples must be used with caution.

Year-class abundance of anadromous populations of alewives which spawn in Maine lakes appears to be established prior to emigration of juveniles from the freshwater nursery areas (Walton 1983). The capacities of Maine lakes to produce juvenile alewives are finite. Therefore, the relationship between spawning stock abundance and production of juveniles should be asymptotic at some range of spawner abundance (Beverton and Holt 1957) in established populations. In studying the numbers of juvenile alewives produced soon after introductions of spawning fish to new habitats, I observed a positive correlation between parents and progeny, a result similar to that observed by Havey (1973). In these cases of low spawner abundance, the production of juveniles apparently remained below the carrying capacity of the lakes until the spawning populations increased as the stock became established.

In this paper, I examine data collected on spring immigrations of mature alewives and summer–fall emigrations of juveniles from Damariscotta Lake, Maine, between 1977 and 1984. These data were used to explore the hypothesis that an asymptotic relationship exists between egg deposition and production of juvenile emigrants in an established and relatively stable alewife population.

Methods

Study area.—Damariscotta Lake is a large (18.06-km²) oligotrophic lake in Lincoln County,

Maine. The lake has traditionally supported the state's largest commercial alewife harvest (Walton 1983). Landlocked Atlantic salmon *Salmo salar,* brown trout *Salmo trutta,* lake trout *Salvelinus namaycush,* and smallmouth bass *Micropterus dolomieui* dominate the sport fishery. The lake also has substantial populations of landlocked white perch *Morone americana,* pumpkinseed *Lepomis gibbosus,* chain pickerel *Esox niger,* and brown bullhead *Ictalurus nebulosus,* as well as a seasonal population of alewives.

The alewife spawning run enters and the juvenile emigrants leave the lake through a stone pool-and-weir fishway that flows into the saline estuary of the Damariscotta River. The commercial fishery is conducted near the estuary end of the fishway with fixed concrete and steel traps. The fishery has been intensive for decades. Annual harvests remove up to 90–98% of the spawning run. The long-term average escapement is about 5% (Cating 1958; Walton 1983). Annual commercial harvests in recent years (1950–1984) averaged 1.3×10^6 fish, ranging from 0.1×10^6 to 2.7×10^6 fish.

Sampling procedures.—The commercial harvest of alewives was monitored each year by collecting daily samples of 50 or more fish selected randomly to estimate sex ratios and size distributions. Multiple daily catch samples demonstrated no significant differences in the precision of estimates derived from one, two, or three daily samples. The total weight of each daily harvest was divided by the weights of males and females from that day's catch to estimate numbers of fish harvested; daily estimates were summed to estimate total harvest.

Escapement was monitored with a counting trap at the lake end of the fishway. From 1977 through 1979, numbers of fish entering the lake were estimated by 24-h counts for two randomly selected days in each 5-d interval of the spawning run. The counting trap exit was closed at the start of each counting period and the fish were tallied and released into the lake at 2-h intervals. The trap was open during days when no counts were made. From 1980 through 1984, all fish entering the lake were counted with a Smith-Root model 602-A fish counter. This counter appeared to be affected by temperature changes and adjustments based on two or more daily visual counts were necessary to assure accuracy. Daily samples of at least 50 fish were collected at the counting trap; the fish were measured and sexed to estimate sex

ratios and size distributions.

The total number of females entering the lake each year was estimated by multiplying the mean number of fish per counting interval by the total number of possible counting intervals (1977–1979) or by summation of daily fish estimates (1980–1984). Confidence intervals (95%) for the estimates of total females entering the lake each year were derived from the formula given by Becker (1962).

Spawning run females entering the lake were measured but not weighed. Annual egg deposition was calculated from regressions of fecundity on total length derived from samples of 100 or more females from the commercial catch and applied to the length distributions of females leaving the trap and entering the lake. This method provided a reasonable approximation of the numbers of eggs spawned because repeated examinations of the ovaries of spent fish emigrating from the lake revealed little or no egg retention. Length measurement and fecundity estimate procedures were described by Walton (1983).

From the end of the adult spawning run (mid-June) until the start of the juvenile emigration (usually mid-July), the lake outlet was screened to prevent unmonitored juvenile emigration. From 1977 through 1980, the abundance of juveniles was estimated by volumetric counts (Havey 1973) of emigrants passing through a trap in the fishway. Confidence intervals (95%) for these juvenile estimates were derived from the formula given by Becker (1962). After 1980, juveniles were counted continuously with a Northwest Marine Technology model FC-1 counter. Counter accuracy was routinely monitored by passing a known number of juveniles through the counting head.

Results and Discussion

Sex ratios in the commercial harvest were not significantly different from 1:1 in all years ($P > 0.05$). However, for adults which escaped the fishery, passed through the fishway, and entered the lake, sex ratios ranged from 1.2:1 to 2.7:1, males to females (Table 1). The present study corroborated Libby's (1981) observations on the Damariscotta Lake alewife population and confirmed that poor passage conditions in the fishway inhibited the movements of larger and heavier fish and decreased the proportion of adult females which reached the lake.

During the study period, the estimated total numbers of fish in the annual harvests declined by an order of magnitude (Table 1). Reproductive

TABLE 1.—Statistics for adult and juvenile alewives in Damariscotta Lake, Maine, 1977–1984.

Year	Total fish harvested[a]	Fish entering the lake[b]	Male:female ratio in lake	Females entering the lake[c]	Estimated egg deposition (10^9)	Juvenile emigrants (10^3)[d]
1977	1,277,640	27,740	1.9:1	9,460±2,300	1.4	16,365±3,042
1978	909,490	53,180	1.6:1	20,580±3,720	3.2	14,823±4,505
1979	77,940	20,310	2.1:1	5,620±910	0.8	14,777±3,766
1980	844,240	43,865	2.3:1	13,470±1,360	2.1	10,082±4,100
1981	626,370	69,079	1.4:1	28,790±1,030	4.5	15,823
1982	330,210	56,653	1.2:1	25,930±1,070	4.1	14,991
1983	98,730	21,156	1.2:1	9,690±1,040	1.4	16,522
1984	231,410	39,561	1.7:1	14,860±610	2.2	14,477

[a] Estimates are rounded to the nearest 10 fish.
[b] Total counts of adults were recorded after 1979.
[c] Estimates ± 95% confidence intervals.
[d] Estimates ± 95% confidence intervals, 1977–1980; total counts of juvenile emigrants were recorded after 1980.

success, however, was not affected by this apparent stock decline. The fishway at Damariscotta Lake has small pools and provides passage for only a small portion of the fish making the spawning run (Libby 1981). There was no significant relationship between the number of fish in the spawning run (as total fish harvested) and the number of females which escaped the fishery and entered the lake ($r = -0.14$; $N = 8$; $P > 0.05$).

There was a positive and significant relationship between the number of females entering the lake and estimated egg deposition ($r = +0.69$; $N = 8$; $P < 0.05$). Annual mean total lengths of females entering the lake to spawn during the 8-year study ranged from 300.3 to 308.9 mm. Since fecundity varied with size in ripe female alewives, estimated egg deposition was assumed to be the best index of parental stock (Figure 1). There was no significant linear relationship ($P > 0.05$) between estimated egg deposition and number of juvenile emigrants ($r = 0.03$; $N = 8$; $P > 0.05$). Despite the

annual variability in estimated egg deposition, the numbers of juveniles produced remained relatively constant throughout the 8-year study (Table 1).

These data support the hypothesis that numbers of spawning females and numbers of juvenile emigrants are asymptotically related over the observed range of adult escapement at Damariscotta Lake. Havey (1973) reported a significant log-linear relationship between number of female spawners and number of juvenile emigrants in the Love Lake, Maine, alewife stock. Havey's average numbers of 0.7 female spawners and 407 juvenile emigrants per surface hectare of Love Lake were lower than the overall mean values I calculated for Damariscotta Lake: 1.3 females and 8,157 juvenile emigrants per hectare. Havey's Love Lake data are also consistent with the hypothesis of an asymptotic parent–progeny relationship for anadromous alewives because his positive correlation between numbers of females

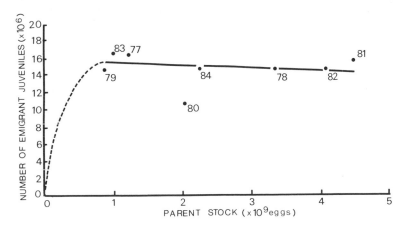

FIGURE 1.—Relationship between an index of parental stock abundance (estimated annual egg deposition) and numbers of emigrating juvenile alewives, Damariscotta Lake, Maine, 1977–1984 ($r = +0.03$; $P > 0.05$).

and juvenile emigrants occurred at relatively low levels of spawner abundance per surface area of the spawning and nursery habitat.

Walton (1983) suggested that competition for limited zooplankton resources may be the major factor affecting growth and survival of juveniles in established populations of anadromous alewives in Maine lakes. The asymptotic relationship between parents and progeny in Damariscotta Lake (Figure 1) is a reproduction curve of the form described by Ricker (1975) as representing a situation with an upper limit to the food supply where progeny survival is determined largely by competition. Beverton and Holt (1957) also associated an asymptotic reproduction curve with competition for food. Intraspecific competition during the freshwater phase of early juvenile growth may be an important factor affecting the reproductive success of the Damariscotta Lake population and other anadromous alewife stocks in the Gulf of Maine.

Acknowledgments

Assistance in the field and laboratory research for this paper was provided by Jan Barter, Sherry Collins, David Libby, David Sampson, Sally Sherman, Malcolm Smith, and Katharine Walton. Figure 1 was drafted by James Rollins. Ronald J. Klauda and an anonymous reviewer critically evaluated the manuscript and made important contributions to the final draft. Financial support for the research was provided by the U.S. National Marine Fisheries Service and the Maine Department of Marine Resources.

References

Becker, C. D. 1962. Estimating red salmon escapements by sample counts from observation towers. U.S. Fish and Wildlife Service Fishery Bulletin 61(192):355–369.

Beverton, R. J. H., and S. J. Holt. 1957. On the dynamics of exploited fish populations. Fishery Investigations, Series II, Marine Fisheries, Great Britain Ministry of Agriculture Fisheries and Food 19:1–533.

Brown, E. H., Jr. 1972. Population biology of alewives, *Alosa pseudoharengus*, in Lake Michigan, 1949–70. Journal of the Fisheries Research Board of Canada 29:477–500.

Cating, J. P. 1958. Damariscotta (Maine) alewife fishery. Commercial Fisheries Review 20(6):1–15.

Cooper, R. A. 1961. Early life history and spawning migration of the alewife, *Alosa pseudoharengus*. Master's thesis. University of Rhode Island, Kingston, Rhode Island, USA.

Havey, K. A. 1961. Restoration of anadromous alewives at Long Pond, Maine. Transactions of the American Fisheries Society 90:281–286.

Havey, K. A. 1973. Production of juvenile alewives, *Alosa pseudoharengus*, at Love Lake, Washington County, Maine. Transactions of the American Fisheries Society 102:434–437.

Henderson, B. A., and E. H. Brown. 1985. Effects of abundance and water temperature on recruitment and growth of the alewive (*Alosa pseudoharengus*) in South Bay, Lake Huron, 1954–82. Canadian Journal of Fisheries and Aquatic Sciences 42:1608–1613.

Huber, M. E. 1974. Adult spawning success and emigration of juvenile alewives (*Alosa pseudoharengus*) from the Parker River, Massachusetts. Master's thesis. University of Massachusetts, Amherst, Massachusetts, USA.

Kissil, G. W. 1974. Spawning of the anadromous alewife, *Alosa pseudoharengus*, in Bride Lake, Connecticut. Transactions of the American Fisheries Society 103:312–317.

Libby, D. A. 1981. Difference in sex ratios of the anadromous alewife, *Alosa pseudoharengus*, between the top and bottom of a fishway at Damariscotta Lake, Maine. U.S. National Marine Fisheries Service Fishery Bulletin 79:207–211.

Richkus, W. A. 1974. Factors influencing the seasonal and daily patterns of alewife (*Alosa pseudoharengus*) migration in a Rhode Island river. Journal of the Fisheries Research Board of Canada 31:1485–1497.

Ricker, W. E. 1975. Computation and interpretation of biological statistics of fish populations. Fisheries Research Board of Canada Bulletin 191.

Rideout, S. G. 1974. Population estimate, movement, and biological characteristics of anadromous alewives (*Alosa pseudoharengus* Wilson) utilizing the Parker River, Massachusetts in 1971–1972. Master's thesis. University of Massachusetts, Amherst, Massachusetts, USA.

Saila, S. B., T. T. Polgar, D. J. Sheehy, and J. M. Flowers. 1972. Correlations between alewife activity and environmental variables at a fishway. Transactions of the American Fisheries Society 101:583–594.

Tyus, H. M. 1971. Population size, harvest, and movements of alewives, *Alosa pseudoharengus* (Wilson), during spawning migrations to Lake Mattamuskett, North Carolina. Doctoral dissertation. North Carolina State University, Raleigh, North Carolina, USA.

Walton, C. J. 1983. Growth parameters for typical anadromous and dwarf stocks of alewives, *Alosa pseudoharengus* (Pisces, Clupeidae). Environmental Biology of Fishes 9:277–287.

American Fisheries Society Symposium 1:455–468, 1987
© Copyright by the American Fisheries Society 1987

Review of Recruitment Mechanisms of the American Shad: The Critical Period and Match–Mismatch Hypotheses Reexamined

VICTOR A. CRECCO AND THOMAS SAVOY

Connecticut Department of Environmental Protection, Marine Fisheries Office
Post Office Box 248, Waterford, Connecticut 06385, USA

Abstract.—We examined whether the critical period and match–mismatch hypotheses could explain recruitment variability of the American shad *Alosa sapidissima* in the Connecticut River. Previously published larval survivorship curves, feeding rates of larvae, zooplankton densities, and selected hydrographic and meteorological data from 1979 through 1984 were analyzed for interrelationships. Once a causal mechanism was established between river hydrography and year-class strength, several environment-dependent stock–recruitment models were developed to predict year-class variability from 1966 through 1980. All survivorship curves from 1979 through 1984 demonstrated that mortality rates were highest among first-feeding larvae, then declined steadily through juvenile development. There was also a strong inverse correlation between the mortality rates of first-feeding larvae from 1979 through 1984 and year-class strength, whereas the mortality rates of all other life stages showed weak correlations. These results are consistent with the two primary predictions from the critical period hypothesis. Mean monthly river flow, temperature, and total monthly rainfall data from 1967 through 1984 were all significantly correlated with the corresponding juvenile indices only for the month of June, when most American shad hatch in the Connecticut River. High June river flows were inversely related to the feeding success of first-feeding larvae from 1979 through 1984 and to year-class strength. These results are consistent with the primary predictions of the match–mismatch hypothesis. We developed several environment-dependent stock–recruitment models, incorporating density-dependent (parent stock size) and key density-independent factors (May and June river flows and monthly rainfall). These models explained 80–87% of the recruitment variability of the 1966–1980 year classes, indicating that year-class strength of American shad is regulated primarily by river flow and temperature conditions mediated by density-dependent processes.

The search for causal mechanisms behind recruitment variability has been a consistent theme of fish population studies in this century (Hjort 1926; Marr 1956; Cushing 1982). Most scientists agree that erratic fluctuations in recruitment of most fish stocks are due to differential larval mortality (Sharp 1980; Bakun et al. 1982), mainly caused by density-independent factors such as hydrographic and meteorological events (Gulland 1965; Lasker 1975; Nelson et al. 1977). It is still unclear, however, whether density-independent factors regulate larval mortality and recruitment alone or in combination with density-dependent processes (cannibalism, competition, and predation) as assumed by most stock–recruitment models (Ricker 1954; Beverton 1962; Shepard 1982).

Several hypotheses have been advanced to help clarify the biological pathways through which hydrographic and meteorological events influence fish egg and larval mortality and, ultimately, recruitment to the spawning stock (Hjort 1926; Hempel 1965; Lasker 1975; Cushing and Dickson 1976). The "critical period" (Hjort 1926) and "match–mismatch" (Cushing and Dickson 1976) hypotheses are two of the best known (May 1974) and most controversial (Marr 1956; Sinclair and Tremblay 1984). The critical period hypothesis predicts that year-class strength is established by two possible mechanisms: starvation of first-feeding larvae, and advection of larvae to unfavorable areas. The second mechanism, regarding the advection of larvae, was developed more extensively by the match–mismatch hypothesis, which invokes hydrographic events to control the timing of critical life cycle events, such as the advection of fish larvae towards or away from their food supply, as well as the coupling of fish eggs and larvae with key predators (Frank and Leggett 1982). The match–mismatch hypothesis furnishes the biotic and abiotic mechanisms by which the critical period effects might operate. Since these hypotheses are interrelated, we believe that the predictions from both should be rigorously tested. Moreover, if the key hydrographic factors that trigger high larval mortality can be identified, the ability to predict recruitment at some early life stage may be improved dramatically by the merger of important climatic variables with a stock–recruitment model (Parrish and Mac-Call 1978; Bakun 1984).

For this paper, we examined whether the critical period and match–mismatch hypotheses could explain larval mortality and recruitment variability for American shad *Alosa sapidissima,* based on previous statistical (Leggett 1977; Crecco et al. 1986) and integrated field studies (Crecco et al. 1983; Crecco and Savoy 1984, 1985b) in the Connecticut River. Once a causal relationship was established, the hydrographic and meteorological factors known to affect larval mortality and recruitment were incorporated with the Ricker stock–recruitment model to predict recruitment variability and measure density–dependent effects for the 1966–1980 year classes.

The American shad, an anadromous clupeid, is particularly suited for testing the critical period and match–mismatch hypotheses. Each female American shad broadcasts 200,000–500,000 ova each year in the freshwater portions of many east coast rivers of North America (Leggett 1969). A large proportion of the progeny dies during the egg and larval stages (Crecco et al. 1983). Thus, small annual changes in egg and larval mortality can lead to wide fluctuations in recruitment to the spawning stock. The timing and location of American shad migration and spawning and the subsequent production of eggs, larvae, and their food supply in the Connecticut River are closely linked to water temperature fluctuations from April through June (Leggett and Whitney 1972; Leggett 1976; Rosen 1982). When American shad larvae exhaust their yolk sac 3–5 d after hatching, they must feed on crustacean zooplankton (Rosen 1982; Crecco and Blake 1983), or death from malnutrition will ensue within 5 d (Wiggins et al. 1984). Intra-annual fluctuations in precipitation and river flow can influence the river temperature gradient and, perhaps, the synchrony between the production of larvae, their food supply, and their predators.

Larval and juvenile American shad forage within specific littoral habitats such as eddies and backwater areas (Watson 1968; Cave 1978) where river flow is greatly reduced. As a result, young American shad of various developmental stages can be sampled effectively from these habitats with a bag seine (Crecco et al. 1983), and accurate survivorship curves can be developed. Finally, accurate and long-term stock–recruitment data are available for American shad in the Connecticut River, as well as data for the associated environmental variables (Fredin 1954; Leggett

1976; Crecco et al. 1984) with which to develop environment-dependent stock–recruitment models.

Methods

Data Sources

American shad larvae were sampled during daylight hours in the Connecticut River with a 6.1-m plankton bag seine (2.4 m deep, wing and bag meshes of 0.505 mm, and 30-m lead ropes) from May 15 to July 20, 1979–1984. One seine haul was taken weekly at each of 8–12 fixed stations located between Enfield, Connecticut, and Turners Falls, Massachusetts (Figure 1). Further details on sampling and methods of estimating larval abundance from net samples were given by Crecco et al. (1983).

Juvenile American shad (40–90 mm total length, TL) were collected weekly from July 20 through October 15, 1979–1984 at seven fixed stations located below the Holyoke Dam (Figure 1). Juveniles were captured during daylight with a 15.2-m bag seine (4.8-mm mesh, 2.4 m deep, 2.4-m bag,

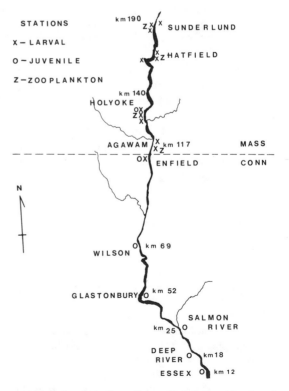

FIGURE 1.—Location of sampling stations for larval and juvenile American shad and zooplankton along the Connecticut River.

and 30-m lead ropes) as in the 1967–1978 juvenile surveys (Marcy 1976; Crecco et al. 1983). The annual index of year-class strength from 1979 to 1984 was the mean catch per seine haul from all stations and collection dates for that year. We assumed that the 1979–1984 indices reflect the relative success of those year classes given that the juvenile abundance indices from 1967 to 1979 were positively correlated ($r = 0.90$; $P < 0.001$) with the total number of virgin American shad from these year classes in the spawning populations (Crecco and Savoy 1985a).

We analyzed the stock–recruitment relationship of American shad based on the 1966–1985 population estimates of American shad lifted daily over the Holyoke Dam (Table 1). A thorough discussion of the methods by which population estimates were determined was presented by Crecco and Savoy (1985a). Only female American shad were used in the stock–recruitment analysis because the age structure and commercial landings of males are biased by gill-net selectivity and differential culling practices of commercial fishermen (Leggett 1976; Crecco et al. 1984). Recruitment estimates of female American shad from the 1966–1980 year classes (Table 1) were the total contribution of virgin females of those year classes in the 1970–1985 runs, based on the age-class structure from previous studies (Leggett 1976; Jones et al. 1976; Crecco et al. 1984).

The parent stock of female American shad from 1966 through 1980 was the annual population estimate for females minus that year's commercial catch. This procedure was necessary given that the main spawning areas (river km 75–190) are well upriver of the commercial fishing areas (Leggett 1976). An important sport fishery exists, but sport catches were not subtracted to estimate parent stock size because data on angler catches for the entire river are lacking from 1974 through 1981.

Critical Period Hypothesis

If the critical period hypothesis explains recruitment variability for American shad, the following predictions are expected. (1) The 1979–1984 larval survivorship curves should show that mortality rates are highest among first-feeding larvae (10–13 mm TL) and decline through late larval and juvenile development (May 1974; Fortier and Leggett 1985). (2) The mortality rates of first-feeding larvae should be inversely related to year-class strength (Gulland 1965).

We developed survivorship curves for American shad larvae and juveniles from 1979 to 1984 with the methods of Lough (1976) and Hewitt et al. (1985). The 42,000–180,000 seine-caught larvae and 800–2,300 juveniles taken each year were separated into 1- and 3-mm length groups, respectively. Because the plankton seine caught proportionally few yolk-sac larvae between 7 and 9 mm, the prolarvae were not included in the survivorship analysis. American shad prolarvae are only partially susceptible to seining as they are semi-

TABLE 1.—Recruitment of American shad based on Holyoke population estimates, Connecticut River. Explanatory variables are parent stock size, adjusted June temperatures, American shad lifted over Holyoke Dam, mean June and May flows, and adjusted May–June rainfall, 1966–1984.

Year	Recruitment	Parent stock size	June temperature (°C)	Shad lifted	June flow (m³/s)	May flow (m³/s)	May–June rainfall (mm)
1966	387,800	115,000	20.9	6,000	246	566	210
1967	222,000	167,000	21.4	6,000	437	964	228
1968	118,000	202,000	20.5	7,000	603	547	158
1969	245,000	384,000	21.2	14,000	375	1,005	148
1970	275,000	413,000	21.8	17,000	243	856	220
1971	491,000	424,000	21.1	20,000	203	1,175	207
1972	215,000	167,000	22.0	11,000	616	1,459	316
1973	154,000	111,000	20.6	5,000	534	897	203
1974	326,000	306,000	20.6	14,000	334	992	159
1975	280,000	247,000	21.8	23,000	379	627	180
1976	325,000	435,000	19.5	166,000	286	840	230
1977	620,000	157,000	22.4	112,000	250	542	257
1978	357,000	210,000	20.0	45,000	488	799	138
1979	441,000	247,000	20.8	87,000	448	905	74
1980	628,000	341,000	21.7	196,000	202	488	220
1981		293,000	20.8	143,000	313	513	118
1982		501,000	21.9	109,000	637	653	295
1983		423,000	20.3	185,000	336	1,137	122
1984		661,000	20.0	245,000	661	1,442	217

buoyant and remain in deep water (Marcy 1976).

A major criticism of early survivorship studies (Sette 1943; Ahlstrom 1954; Stevenson 1962) was that modes on length-frequency curves were used to convert length to age frequencies (Farris 1960; Dahlberg 1979). More reliable survivorship curves (Lough 1976; Hewitt and Brewer 1983; Miller and Stork 1984) have been developed since the discovery of daily growth increments on the otoliths of young fish (Pannella 1971; Brothers et al. 1976). In this study, we used the number of otolith increments to age 100–400 American shad larvae and 80–200 juveniles annually from 1979 through 1984. The relative distance between the otolith increments was also used to determine age-specific growth rates (mm/d) of larvae and juveniles. We assumed that the chronological ages from otolith increment counts accurately reflected the true ages of larvae and juveniles because a significant positive correlation ($r = 0.89$; $P < 0.001$) was found between the number of otolith increments and the true ages of 248 hatchery-reared American shad larvae (Savoy and Crecco 1987). The methods for otolith extraction, preparation, and back-calculation, as well as the criteria for counting daily increments were described by Crecco and Savoy (1985b) and Savoy and Crecco (1987).

The length–age relationships of American shad larvae and juveniles from 1979 to 1984 were always sigmoid-shaped and well described by the Gompertz model:

$$L_t = L_0 \exp(K)[1 - \exp(-At)]; \qquad (1)$$

L_t = total length (mm); t = estimated age (d) since hatching; L_0 = length at hatching (8.0 mm); K = growth rate at the inflection point; and A = rate of exponential decay. The average age (t) of each 1- and 3-mm length group in the survivorship curves was estimated by rearranging the Gompertz equation:

$$t = \log_e K/K - \log_e[L_t(L_0)]/A. \qquad (2)$$

Because larval and juvenile growth rates vary with age, the number of fish within each 1- and 3-mm length interval was standardized for growth differences by dividing abundance by the time (days) required to grow into the next interval. The slope of each age-frequency curve measured larval and juvenile mortality rates.

To test the prediction that mortality rates are highest among first-feeding larvae, each survivorship curve from 1979 to 1984 was separated into four length intervals: (1) 10–13 mm, reflecting

first-feeding larvae (Maxfield 1953); (2) 14–18 mm, intermediate-sized larvae; (3) 19–25 mm, larvae approaching metamorphosis; and (4) 40–80 mm, the length range of most juvenile American shad captured. Each length interval was transformed to age with the Gompertz equation (2), and instantaneous daily mortality rates (Z) were estimated for each age interval by an exponential model:

$$N_t = A \exp(-Z_t); \qquad (3)$$

N_t is number of larvae at age t. The daily mortality rate (M_t, %/d) was calculated by

$$M_t = 1 - \exp(-Z_t). \qquad (4)$$

If these data are consistent with the first prediction of the critical period hypothesis, mortality rates (M_t) among first-feeding larvae should be consistently higher than mortality rates for all other stages.

To examine the second prediction, that mortality among first-feeding larvae is inversely related to year-class strength, we examined how mortality rates of first-feeding larvae, mid-sized larvae, late larvae, and juveniles from 1979 through 1984 were correlated with the juvenile indices of abundance for those years. For our data to be consistent with the second prediction, we would expect that only mortality rates among first-feeding larvae would be inversely related to the juvenile indices.

Match–Mismatch Hypothesis

If the match–mismatch hypothesis provides the primary mechanism of high larval mortality of American shad, the following two outcomes are expected. (1) Only hydrographic and meteorological factors coincident with larval development should be related to American shad year-class strength. (2) Short-term fluctuations in one or more of the hydrographic factors should be related to year-class strength, larval feeding success, and food availability.

To examine the first prediction, the juvenile indices of abundance from 1967 to 1984 (Marcy 1976; Crecco 1985) were related to mean monthly river flows (m³/s), water temperatures (°C), and total monthly rainfall (mm) for all months. Empirical support for the hypothesis is provided if significant correlations were confined only to the month of June, when most American shad larvae hatch in the Connecticut River (Cave 1978; Crecco et al. 1983). These hydrographic and meteorological factors were chosen because river flows and temperatures were related to deviations from the stock–recruitment relationship (Leggett 1977), the rate at which American shad eggs and larvae grow and develop (Marcy 1976; Wiggins et al. 1984), and the timing and duration of American shad spawning (Leggett 1976). Long-term data on daily river flows, temperatures (U.S. Geological Survey 1967–1984) and total monthly rainfall (U.S. National Weather Service, Washington, D.C.) were recorded within the major spawning areas (km 89–140) for American shad (Crecco and Savoy 1984).

Each of the hydrographic and meteorological factors (x) were related to the juvenile indices (CPE) with exponential models,

$$CPE = a\exp(bx), \qquad (5)$$

and power models,

$$CPE = ax^b, \qquad (6)$$

by nonlinear least-squares regressions (SAS 1982). The use of nonlinear multiplicative models was justified, given that environmental factors usually affect the survival rate rather than the absolute number of recruits (Ricker 1975).

As for the second prediction, we evaluated the extent to which the feeding success of American shad larvae varied with short-term changes in zooplankton densities (numbers/m^3), river flows, and water temperatures from 1979 through 1984. Two or three replicate zooplankton samples were taken at each of four fixed stations weekly (Figure 1) with a 30-cm Clark–Bumpus plankton sampler (80-μm mesh) 1 m below the surface. Only cladocerans, copepods, and insects were counted because American shad larvae select for these taxa (Crecco and Blake 1983). The percentage of American shad larvae with zooplankton in their guts, defined as the feeding incidence, was determined for 30–60 first-feeding larvae (10–13 mm) chosen weekly May 15–July 15, 1979–1984 (Crecco 1985). Larger (>13-mm) larvae were not analyzed because their stomachs were usually full of food and, therefore, those larvae were not thought to be food limited. The overall mean feeding incidence and zooplankton density for each year were the mean weekly values weighted to the total number of 10–13-mm larvae caught in that week. The weekly values were weighted by the number of larvae caught weekly so that the overall mean feeding rate and zooplankton density reflected the overall coupling among larval feeding success, abundance, and food availability. Weekly changes of larval feeding incidence rates from 1979 through 1984 were related to corre-

sponding changes in zooplankton density, river flow, and temperature. The weighted mean feeding incidence rates and zooplankton densities from 1979 through 1984 were also related to the juvenile indices with linear regression methods.

Results

Critical Period Hypothesis

The shape of the larval and juvenile survivorship curves were similar from 1979 to 1984 (Figure 2). Mortality rates were highest (17–27%/d) among first-feeding larvae, then declined steadily throughout larval development (Table 2). This indicated that 60–80% of the larvae died shortly after feeding began, which is consistent with the first prediction of the critical period hypothesis.

A strong inverse relationship ($r = -0.63$; $P < 0.10$) was evident between the 1979–1984 mortality rates of first-feeding larvae and the juvenile indices (Table 2), but the correlations between the juvenile indices and mortality rates of older larvae (14–25 mm) and juveniles (40–80 mm) were weak and inconsistent. These results suggest that yearclass strength of American shad is established shortly after first-feeding larvae sustain catastrophic mortality (17–27%/d), which corroborates the second prediction of the critical period hypothesis.

Match–Mismatch Hypothesis

Mean monthly river flow, water temperature, and total monthly rainfall data from 1967 through 1984 were all significantly related to the corresponding juvenile indices only for the month of June (Table 3), during which most American shad larvae hatch and develop in the Connecticut River (Maxfield 1953; Cave 1978). Correlation coefficients for climatic data corresponding to the egg (April, May) and juvenile (July–October) periods, and all other months (November–March) were generally less than 0.40. Annual changes in yearclass strength of American shad during 1967 to 1984 were inversely related to mean June river flows and total June rainfall and positively related to June river temperatures. These results are consistent with the first prediction of the match–mismatch hypothesis, that recruitment variability for American shad is ultimately linked to hydrographic and meteorological events during larval development.

The relationship between the arcsine of the weekly larval feeding rate and weekly changes in mean river temperature was always positive and

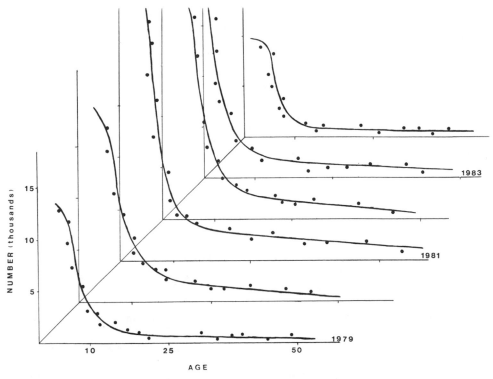

FIGURE 2.—Survivorship curves for seine-caught American shad larvae and juveniles between 7.0 and 80 mm, 1979–1984. Age is in days.

significant (Table 4). The relationship between larval feeding success and weekly fluctuations in mean June river flow was negative and statistically significant for all years except 1982. The relationships between larval feeding success and weekly changes in zooplankton density were inconsistent. There were significant positive correlations between feeding success and zooplankton in 1979 and 1983, strongly negative ones in 1981 and 1982, and only weakly positive ones in 1980

and 1984. That short-term changes in river temperature and flow were positively and negatively related, respectively, to the feeding success of American shad larvae is consistent with the second prediction of the match–mismatch hypothesis. Prolonged periods of low and stable river flows lead to a steady rise in water temperature and transparency. If favorable hydrographic events coincide with peak larval emergence of American shad, larvae would experience high survival and growth. By contrast, high river flows are likely to reduce water temperature and transparency, cause advection of larvae from their preferred habitat, and dissipate the microscale patches of river zooplankton (Beach 1960). These flow-driven effects lead to unfavorable feeding conditions, lower growth, and higher mortality rates of first-feeding larvae (Crecco and Savoy 1985b).

Although empirical support for the match–mismatch hypothesis based on statistical evidence alone may be questionable (Bakun and Parrish 1980), the match–mismatch hypothesis was further corroborated by the way zooplankton densities and larval feeding success rates varied be-

TABLE 2.—Age-specific daily mortality rates of larval and juvenile American shad in the Connecticut River, 1979–1984, and correlation coefficients between age-specific mortality and juvenile index.

Year or statistic	Juvenile index	Percent daily mortality			
		3–9 d	10–18 d	19–29 d	Juvenile
1979	19.6	17.2	11.7	3.0	1.9
1980	42.7	18.4	12.8	6.1	1.8
1981	16.0	26.4	4.9	6.4	2.0
1982	4.7	23.6	10.9	6.4	1.8
1983	26.3	18.1	5.7	7.3	1.5
1984	13.0	27.0	6.2	4.1	2.2
r		−0.63	0.32	0.17	−0.37

TABLE 3.—Correlation coefficients for power and exponential (exp) regressions of juvenile indices of American shad abundance (1967–1984) versus selected monthly climatic factors; a + denotes $r < 0.01$ and an asterisk (*) denotes a significant correlation ($P < 0.05$).

Month	Temperature (°C)		Connecticut River flow (m³/s)		Rainfall (mm)	
	Power	Exp	Power	Exp	Power	Exp
Jan	−0.132	−0.132	−0.260	−0.195	−0.138	+
Feb	−0.101	+	−0.280	−0.194	+	+
Mar	−0.251	−0.281	+	+	0.276	0.370
Apr	+	+	+	+	+	0.014
May	+	+	+	+	−0.146	−0.142
Jun	0.661*	0.658*	−0.769*	−0.760*	−0.612*	−0.706*
Jul	0.498	0.502	−0.490	−0.390	+	0.044
Aug	+	+	+	+	+	+
Sep	+	+	0.169	0.138	0.197	0.233
Oct	−0.121	−0.114	0.292	0.354	0.112	0.154
Nov	0.103	0.139	−0.118	+	+	+
Dec	−0.121	+	−0.162	−0.171	+	+

tween strong and weak year classes. There was a significant positive correlation ($r = 0.96$; $P < 0.01$) between the weighted mean feeding incidences of first-feeding larvae and year-class strength from 1979 through 1984 (Table 5). The relationship between mean zooplankton densities for May and June and year-class strength was also positive ($r = 0.90$; $P < 0.05$) and significant from 1979 through 1984. These data suggest that high June river flows and low river temperatures, such as in 1982 and 1984, reduce larval survival and, ultimately, recruitment to the spawning population. This coupling between biotic and abiotic factors provides a reasonable explanation for the lack of a parent–progeny relationship for American shad in the Connecticut River (Figure 3).

Climate–Fisheries Model

Having shown that hydrographic and meteorological factors during larval development influence American shad recruitment (R), we developed several environment-dependent stock–recruitment models (Parrish and McCall 1978; Stocker et al. 1985). These contained both density-dependent (parent stock) and density-independent factors (mean May and June river flow, temperature, and total May and June rainfall). These models were designed to predict recruitment from 1966 through 1980 and measure the potential interactions between density-dependent and density-independent processes. Climatic data for May were analyzed because, during some years, American shad egg production and larval

TABLE 4.—Linear regressions between the arcsine of the weekly percentage of larval American shad with ingested food (Y) and mean weekly Connecticut River water temperatures (°C), $\log_e$ mean river flows (m³/s), and mean weekly zooplankton densities (number/m³) from 1979 through 1983 (X values). Asterisks denote significant F values ($P < 0.05$*)

Year	Feeding % versus water temperature	Feeding % versus river flow	Feeding % versus zooplankton density
1979	$Y=-48.14+3.19X$ $r=0.854$; $F=16.18$*	$Y=81.40-11.14X$ $r=-0.786$; $F=9.67$*	$Y=-99.80+16.90X$ $r=0.925$; $F=35.94$*
1980	$Y=-69.48+4.34X$ $r=0.946$; $F=59.04$*	$Y=192.14-31.22X$ $r=-0.887$; $F=25.82$*	$Y=-17.90+5.63X$ $r=0.354$; $F=1.00$
1981	$Y=-64.63+3.87X$ $r=0.769$; $F=8.70$*	$Y=179.06-27.55X$ $r=-0.659$; $F=4.60$*	$Y=-99.20-12.90X$ $r=-0.636$; $F=4.07$*
1982	$Y=-56.30+3.54X$ $r=0.768$; $F=8.70$*	$Y=95.84-13.71X$ $r=-0.466$; $F=1.94$	$Y=87.20-12.20X$ $r=-0.633$; $F=4.68$*
1983	$Y=23.55+0.07X$ $r=0.927$; $F=51.01$*	$Y=6.00-0.03X$ $r=-0.866$; $F=22.19$*	$Y=252.10+15.01X$ $r=0.812$; $F=19.63$*
1984	$Y=-62.70+4.53X$ $r=0.921$; $F=50.63$*	$Y=211.00-18.28X$ $r=-0.833$; $F=18.56$*	$Y=-22.43+5.65X$ $r=0.405$; $F=1.43$*

TABLE 5.—Relationship among overall weighted mean zooplankton densities, weighted mean feeding incidences of larval American shad, and year-class strength (juvenile index) of American shad, 1979–1984, Connecticut River. Standard errors are in parentheses; correlation coefficients (r) are between year-class strength and zooplankton densities and feeding incidence.

Year or statistic	Juvenile index	Zooplankton density (number/m³)	Feeding incidence (%)
1979	19.6	1,041(214)	25.8(3.1)
1980	42.7	2,257(326)	37.6(4.3)
1981	16.0	841(186)	16.7(2.6)
1982	4.7	687(171)	14.6(3.0)
1983	24.9	897(184)	26.6(3.1)
1984	13.0	1,010(228)	19.4(3.3)
r		+0.90	+0.96

emergence in the Connecticut River may begin during late May (Marcy 1976; Cave 1978). The total parent stock size *(PS)* from 1966 to 1980 was divided into the number lifted *(LF)* into the Holyoke Dam impoundment, as indicated by annual counts at the fish lift (O'Leary et al. 1984), and those *(PB)* that spawned below the dam. This split was necessary because larvae produced within the Holyoke impoundment are geographically isolated from larvae produced below. Moreover, increasing the spawning habitat of adult American shad to include the Holyoke impoundment (river km 140–196) is expected to enhance reproductive success and American shad recruitment in future years (Leggett 1977; Moffitt et al. 1982).

We represented density-dependent effects in the model with the Ricker parent–progeny func-

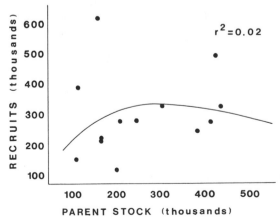

FIGURE 3.—Parent–progeny relationship for American shad based on the Holyoke recruitment data, 1966–1980.

tion for the total parent stock $(PS = PB + LF)$,

$$R_p = a(PS)\exp(bPS), \qquad (7)$$

and for parent stocks separately from above *(LF)* and below *(PB)* the dam,

$$Rp = a(PS)\exp(bPB + cLF); \qquad (8)$$

R_p = predicted recruitment of female American shad; a = exponent of density independence; b and c = exponents of density dependence. A stepwise regression method (Draper and Smith 1981) was used to select the most significant ($P <$ 0.05) climatic variables and initial parameter estimates in the nonlinear model. The linear form of the model was

$$\log_e(R/PS) = a + bPB + cLF + dX; \qquad (9)$$

X = one of the environmental factors. The final environment dependent stock–recruitment model was

$$R_p = a(PS)\exp(bPB + cLF)\exp(dX). \qquad (10)$$

The best least-square estimates of the exponents *(a, b, c, d)* and their standard errors were estimated from the nonlinear regression method (SAS 1982).

The colinearity among the environmental variables (May and June flow, rainfall, and temperature) was reduced by replacing one of the covariates (i.e., river temperature) with adjusted temperatures, defined as the geometric mean temperature from 1966 through 1984 plus the residuals of the linear regression of June river flow and temperature. This method was also used to remove the potential colinearity between total May and June rainfall and June flow.

We plotted the multiplicative residuals (R_p/R) for each model with predicted recruitment (R_p) and each explanatory variable *(PB, LF, X)*. Models that exhibited serial correlations between the residuals and the predicted recruitment or any explanatory variable were deleted from further analyses.

Mean June river flow together with parent stock sizes from above and below the impoundment *(PB, LF)* was the best three-variable model. This nonlinear model explained over 80% of the recruitment variability from 1966 through 1980 (Table 6). The exponents for density dependence *(PB, LF)* and June river flow differed significantly from zero. When recruitment between 1966 and 1980 was related only to parent stock size *(PS)*, this single-variable stock–recruitment model explained only 2.2% of the recruitment variability,

TABLE 6.—Environment-dependent stock–recruitment models for American shad in the Connecticut River, 1966–1980, incorporating density-dependent and density-independent variables. R_p = predicted recruitment; JFW = mean June flow; MFW = mean May flow; MJP = adjusted May–June rainfall; LF = American shad lifted over Holyoke Dam; PB = American shad below Holyoke Dam; PS = total parent stock size; SE = asymptotic parameter standard error.

Model	Parameter		SE	t statistic	Probability
Ricker model					
$R_p = 3.31(PS)\exp(-0.0031PS)$	$a =$	3.31	2.73	1.21	$P < 0.25$
$r^2 = 0.022$	$PS =$	-0.0031	0.0024	1.29	$P < 0.25$
Environment-dependent models					
$R_p = 11.75(PS)\exp(-0.0061PB$	$a =$	11.75	2.99	3.93	$P < 0.01$
$-0.0032LF)\exp(-0.0034JFW)$	$PB =$	-0.0061	0.0007	8.71	$P < 0.001$
$r = 0.822$	$LF =$	-0.0032	0.0009	3.56	$P < 0.01$
	$JFW =$	0.0034	0.0006	5.67	$P < 0.001$
$R_p = 11.32(PS)\exp(-0.0060PB$	$a =$	11.32	2.96	3.82	$P < 0.01$
$-0.003LF)\exp(-0.0032JFW)$	$PB =$	-0.006	0.0007	8.57	$P < 0.001$
$\exp(0.0006MFW)$	$LF =$	-0.003	0.0008	3.75	$P < 0.01$
$r^2 = 0.865$	$JFW =$	-0.0032	0.0007	4.57	$P < 0.001$
	$MFW =$	0.0006	0.0003	2.00	$P < 0.05$
$R_p = 10.28(PS)\exp(-0.0057PB$	$a =$	10.28	2.82	3.65	$P < 0.01$
$-0.0033LF)\exp(-0.0033JFW)$	$PB =$	-0.0057	0.0007	8.14	$P < 0.001$
$\exp(0.0025MJP)$	$LF =$	-0.0033	0.0009	3.67	$P < 0.01$
$r^2 = 0.835$	$JFW =$	-0.0033	0.0006	5.50	$P < 0.001$
	$MJP =$	0.0025	0.0011	2.27	$P < 0.05$

and the density-dependent exponent did not differ significantly from zero (Table 6; Figure 3). This indicated that density-dependent processes were present but overshadowed statistically by climatically induced variability in recruitment. The significant negative exponent for June flow confirms the predictions of the critical period and match–mismatch hypotheses that high and turbulent flows during June reduce the survival of first-feeding American shad larvae and their eventual recruitment to the spawning stock. The significant density-dependent exponent for parent stock above Holyoke (*LF*) is compatible with the hypothesis that adding more spawning area enhances the stability and recruitment potential to the spawning population (Moffitt et al. 1982).

Either mean May flow or total May–June rainfall was selected as a significant fourth variable, which, together with June flow and parent stock size, explained over 86% of the recruitment variability (Table 6). Neither mean May nor June river temperatures were significant in these models. The positive and significant exponents for May flow and May–June rainfall in the presence of June flow were unexpected and difficult to explain. The most reasonable explanation consistent with the match–mismatch hypothesis is that high May rainfall and flows depress May water temperature, thereby postponing the onset of American

shad spawning (Leggett and Whitney 1972) and larval hatching (Cave 1978) until mid-June, when low flow conditions improve the feeding success and survival rates of American shad larvae (Crecco et al. 1983; Crecco and Savoy 1984).

The three variable model, containing both parent stocks together ($PS = PB + LF$), June flow, and adjusted May–June rainfall, was used to examine how recruitment varied when June flow and parent stock size varied and May–June rainfall was held constant at the mean level (203 mm) from 1966 through 1980. The three-dimensional recruitment curve (Figure 4) showed that dominant year classes of American shad are associated with low June flows (50–100 m³/s) and moderate parent stock sizes (150,000–300,000 spawners), and that high parent stock sizes (500,000–700,000 spawners) are not advantageous due to the greater influence of density-dependent mortality. When parent stock dropped to low levels (10,000–50,000 spawners), low June flows were less effective in producing dominant year classes because the spawning stock approached the limits of its compensatory reserve. Lastly, high June flows (600–800 m³/s) caused year-class failure of American shad regardless of parent stock size, indicating that major climatic events overshadow the compensatory mechanism of the population. This analysis indicates that the emergence of dominant year classes is most likely when low June river flows (150–250 m³/s) are coupled with moderate-size parent stocks (150,000–300,000 spawners).

Discussion

The central theme of the critical period and match–mismatch hypotheses is that food availability and larval predation (Sinclair et al. 1985; Fortier and Leggett 1985) are the proximate determinants of year-class strength, whereas hydrographic events are the ultimate causes that drive the system (Legendre and Demers 1984). The results of this study indicate that temporal changes in river flow and temperature, coincident with early larval development, are the ultimate regulators of year-class strength of American shad in the Connecticut River and, undoubtedly, in other coastal rivers. Whether larval mortality is directly affected by predation, malnutrition, or some combination thereof cannot yet be determined with confidence due to the host of potential interactions. Climatic factors such as storm events are nonlinear time-dependent processes (Sharp 1980) that may sweep American shad larvae and their zooplankton prey from "safe sites" (Frank and Leggett 1985) to sites of low food density and, perhaps, of higher predator abundance. Close association of American shad larvae to eddy and backwater areas (Cave 1978) offers further support for this hypothesis. High and erratic river flows coincident with the peak of larval emergence may also reduce the transparency of the water and the ability of fish larvae to see prey (Theilacker and Dorsey 1980), reducing larval growth and enhancing predation. Low transparency can interfere with photosynthesis

and river phytoplankton production (Whitton 1980), causing the selective elimination of major larval prey such as filter-feeding cladocerans and copepods (Chandler 1937; Hynes 1970), leading to higher incidences of malnutrition among first-feeding larvae. Finally, because June water temperature and transparency are inversely related to June flows, it is uncertain whether the significant inverse relationships between weekly flow rate and larval feeding success for 1979–1984 (Table 4) are related directly to river turbidity, to increases in larval growth and metabolism resulting from rising temperatures (Crecco and Savoy 1985b), or to improved feeding conditions when visibility increases with falling water levels. Given the numerous biotic and abiotic pathways through which river flow can affect larval survival, we consider predation and starvation as proximate equivalents rather than discrete factors whose effect on larval mortality can be separated.

It is difficult to explain the poor relationships between weekly changes in zooplankton densities and larval feeding rates from 1979 to 1984 (Table 4). One explanation is that weekly zooplankton sampling was inadequate to detect short-term changes in larval feeding success and zooplankton availability. Another explanation, consistent with the match–mismatch hypothesis, is that larval mortality is not triggered directly by the absolute abundance of zooplankton, but rather by the successful temporal and spatial synchrony between climatic conditions that promote successful feeding and peak emergence of American shad larvae. Similarly, Lasker (1975) and Lasker and Smith (1977) also concluded that survival rates of larval northern anchovy *Engraulis mordax* de-

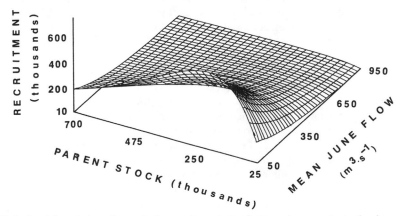

FIGURE 4.—Relationship of American shad recruitment to changes in parent stock size and mean June Connecticut River flow with May–June rainfall held constant (203 mm).

pended not so much on plankton density as on the timing and intensity of upwellings and the production cycle of larvae and their food supply. Evidence from other clupeoid-like fishes also indicated that hydrographic events were the ultimate factors influencing larval mortality and recruitment (Bakun 1973; Parrish and MacCall 1978; Sinclair et al. 1985).

The survivorship curves for American shad larvae showed that 65–80% of the larvae died during and shortly after larvae begin feeding, thus supporting the major prediction of Hjort's critical period hypothesis. There are no other published survivorship curves for natural populations of American shad larvae to which these data can be compared. Rearing experiments of American shad larvae showed that mortality rates were low for prolarvae, rose abruptly for first-feeding larvae, and then declined steadily as larvae approached metamorphosis (Wiggins et al. 1984). Although the mortality of first-feeding larvae (6–8%/d) under controlled hatchery conditions is much lower than mortality rates (17–26%/d) for wild American shad larvae, the shape of the survivorship curve for hatchery larvae is consistent with the predictions of the critical period hypothesis.

In this study, the overall success of our multiple regression models to accurately forecast ($r^2 = 0.80$–0.87) recruitment variability of American shad was attributed to our adherence to the empirical–statistical approach (Austin and Ingham 1978). In the empirical stage, the selection of river flows, temperature, and rainfall in the model was based on our rigorous examination of the critical period and match–mismatch hypotheses, whereby June hydrographic and meteorological factors were shown to affect American shad larval growth, survival, and year-class strength. In the statistical stage, the environment-dependent stock–recruitment models were developed by incorporating the key environmental factors with a Ricker parent–progeny function. This two-stage method, used here and elsewhere (Parrish and MacCall 1978; Leggett et al. 1984), represents an effective scientific protocol for predicting recruitment for other fish stocks subject to high environmental variability. This method is superior to the exploratory approach, whereby correlation analyses are applied to masses of recruitment and environmental data in the hope of discovering a statistical fit (Bakun 1984).

The relative importance of parent stock size (density-dependent factor) and climatic factors on American shad recruitment was clearly demonstrated by these multiple-regression models. Not only were the density-dependent exponents (b, c) significant in all the models, but the addition of parent stock size explained substantially more (10–25%) of the recruitment variability than models containing only climatic factors. These findings support the earlier contention (Leggett 1977; Yoshiyama et al. 1981) that density-dependent factors (competition and predation) exert a subtle but measurable influence on American shad recruitment, although their effects are obscured statistically by climatically induced variability (Nelson et al. 1977).

References

Ahlstrom, E. H. 1954. Distribution and abundance of egg and larval populations of the Pacific sardine. U.S. Fish and Wildlife Service Fishery Bulletin 56:83–140.

Austin, H. M., and M. C. Ingham. 1978. Use of environmental data in the prediction of marine fisheries abundance. Pages 3–108 in Climate and fisheries. University of Rhode Island, Center for Ocean Management Studies, Kingston, Rhode Island, USA.

Bakun, A. 1973. Coastal upwelling indices, west coast of North America, 1946–1971. NOAA (National Oceanic and Atmospheric Administration) Technical Report NMFS (National Marine Fisheries Service) SSRF (Special Scientific Report Fisheries) 671.

Bakun, A. 1984. Report of the working group on environmental studies and monitoring. FAO (Food and Agriculture Organization of the United Nations) Fisheries Report 291(1):41–54.

Bakun, A., J. Beyer, D. Pauly, J. G. Pope, and G. D. Sharp. 1982. Ocean sciences in relation to living resources. Canadian Journal of Fisheries and Aquatic Sciences 39:1059–1070.

Bakun, A., and R. H. Parrish. 1980. Environmental inputs to fishery population models for eastern boundary current regions. Pages 67–104 in Workshop on the effects of environmental variation on the survival of larval pelagic fishes. Intergovernmental Oceanographic Commission, IOC Workshop Report 28, Paris, France.

Beach, N. W. 1960. A study of the planktonic rotifers of the Oequeoe River system, Presque Isle County, Michigan. Ecological Monographs 30:339–357.

Beverton, R. J. H. 1962. Long-term dynamics of certain North Sea fish populations. Pages 242–259 in E. D. Le Cren and M. W. Holdgate, editors. The exploitation of natural animal populations. Blackwell Scientific Publications, Oxford, England.

Brothers, E. B., C. P. Matthews, and R. Lasker. 1976. Daily growth increments in otoliths from larval and adult fishes. U.S. National Marine Fisheries Service Fishery Bulletin 74:1–8.

Cave, J. R. 1978. American shad, *Alosa sapidissima*, larval distribution, relative abundance and movement in the Holyoke Pool, Connecticut River, Massachusetts. Master's thesis. University of Massachusetts, Amherst, Massachusetts, USA.

Chandler, D. C. 1937. Fate of typical lake plankton in streams. Ecological Monographs 7:445–479.

Crecco, V. A. 1985. Effects of hydrographic fluctuations on year-class strength of Connecticut River shad, *Alosa sapidissima*. Doctoral dissertation. University of Connecticut, Storrs, Connecticut, USA.

Crecco, V. A., and M. M. Blake. 1983. Feeding ecology of coexisting larvae of American shad and blueback herring in the Connecticut River. Transactions of the American Fisheries Society 112:498–507.

Crecco, V. A., and T. Savoy. 1984. Effects of fluctuations in hydrographic conditions on year-class strength of American shad *(Alosa sapidissima)* in the Connecticut River. Canadian Journal of Fisheries and Aquatic Sciences 41:1216–1223.

Crecco, V. A., and T. Savoy. 1985a. Density-dependent catchability and its potential causes and consequences on Connecticut River shad, *Alosa sapidissima*. Canadian Journal of Fisheries and Aquatic Sciences 42:1649–1648.

Crecco, V. A., and T. Savoy. 1985b. Effects of biotic and abiotic factors on growth and relative survival of young American shad in the Connecticut River. Canadian Journal of Fisheries and Aquatic Sciences 42:1640–1648.

Crecco, V. A., T. Savoy, and L. Gunn. 1983. Daily mortality rates of larval and juvenile American shad *(Alosa sapidissima)* in the Connecticut River with changes in year-class strength. Canadian Journal of Fisheries and Aquatic Sciences 40:1719–1728.

Crecco, V. A., T. Savoy, and L. Gunn. 1984. Population dynamics studies of American shad in the Connecticut River. Connecticut Department of Environmental Protection, Final Report AFC 13, Hartford, Connecticut, USA.

Crecco, V., T. Savoy, and W. Whitworth. 1986. Effects of density-dependent and climatic factors on American shad, *Alosa sapidissima*, recruitment: a predictive approach. Canadian Journal of Fisheries and Aquatic Sciences 43:457–463.

Cushing, D. H. 1982. Climate and fisheries. Academic Press, New York, New York, USA.

Cushing, D. H., and R. R. Dickson. 1976. The biological response in the sea to climatic changes. Advances in Marine Biology 14:1–122.

Dahlberg, M. D. 1979. A review of survival rates of fish eggs and larvae in relation to impact assessments. U.S. National Marine Fisheries Service Marine Fisheries Review 41(3):1–12.

Draper, N., and H. Smith. 1981. Applied regression analysis. John Wiley & Sons, New York, New York, USA.

Farris, D. A. 1960. The effect of three different types of growth curves on estimates of larval fish survival. Journal du Conseil, Conseil International pour l'Exploration de la Mer 25:294–306.

Fortier, L., and W. C. Leggett. 1985. A drift study of larval fish survival. Marine Ecology Progress Series 25:245–257.

Frank, K. T., and W. C. Leggett. 1982. Environmental regulation of growth rate, efficiency, and swimming performance in larval capelin, *Mallotus villosus*, and its application to the match/mismatch hypothesis. Canadian Journal of Fisheries and Aquatic Sciences 39:691–699.

Frank, K. T., and W. C. Leggett. 1985. Reciprocal oscillations in densities of larval fish potential predators: a reflection of present or past predation. Canadian Journal of Fisheries and Aquatic Sciences 42:1841–1849.

Fredin, R. A. 1954. Causes of fluctuations in abundance of Connecticut River shad. U.S. Fish and Wildlife Service Fishery Bulletin 54:247–259.

Gulland, J. A. 1965. Survival of the youngest stages of fish, and its relation to year-class strength. International Commission for the Northwest Atlantic Fisheries Special Publication 6:363–371.

Hempel, G. 1965. On the importance of larval survival for the population dynamics of marine food fish. California Cooperative Oceanic Fisheries Investigations Reports 10:13–23.

Hewitt, R. P., and Brewer, G. D. 1983. Nearshore production of young anchovy. California Cooperative Oceanic Fisheries Investigations Reports 24:235–245.

Hewitt, R. P., G. H. Theilacker, and N. C. H. Lo. 1985. Causes of mortality in young jack mackerel. Marine Ecology Progress Series 26:1–10.

Hjort, J. 1926. Fluctuations in the year classes of important food fishes. Journal du Conseil, Conseil International pour l'Exploration de la Mer 1:5–38.

Hynes, H. B. N. 1970. The ecology of running waters. University of Toronto Press, Toronto, Canada.

Jones, R. A., P. Minta, and V. A. Crecco. 1976. A review of American shad studies in the Connecticut River. Pages 135–164 *in* Proceedings of a workshop on American shad. U.S. National Marine Fisheries Service, Washington, D.C., USA.

Lasker, R. 1975. Field criteria for survival of anchovy larvae: the relation between inshore chlorophyll maximum layers and successful first feeding. U.S. National Marine Fisheries Fishery Bulletin 73:453–462.

Lasker, R., and P. E. Smith. 1977. Estimation of the effects of environmental variations on the eggs and larvae of Northern anchovy. California Cooperative Oceanic Fisheries Investigations Reports 19:128–137.

Legendre, L., and S. Demers. 1984. Towards dynamic biological oceanography and limnology. Canadian Journal of Fisheries and Aquatic Sciences 41:2–19.

Leggett, W. C. 1969. Studies on the reproductive biology of the American shad *(Alosa sapidissima)*. A comparison of populations from four rivers of the Atlantic seaboard. Doctoral dissertation. McGill University, Montreal, Canada.

Leggett, W. C. 1976. The American shad *Alosa sapidissima*, with special reference to its migrations and population dynamics in the Connecticut River. American Fisheries Society Monograph 1:169–225.

Leggett, W. C. 1977. Density dependence, density independence and recruitment in the American shad *(Alosa sapidissima)* population of the Connecticut River. Pages 3–17 *in* Proceedings of the conference on assessing the effects of power-plant induced mortality on fish populations. Oak Ridge National Laboratory, Energy Resource Development Administration, and Electric Power Resource Institute, Oak Ridge, Tennessee, USA.

Leggett, W. C., K. T. Frank, and J. E. Carscadden. 1984. Meteorological and hydrographic regulation of year-class strength in capelin *(Mallotus villosus)*. Canadian Journal of Fisheries and Aquatic Sciences 41:1193–1201.

Leggett, W. C., and R. R. Whitney. 1972. Water temperature and the migrations of American shad. U.S. National Marine Fisheries Service Fishery Bulletin 70:659–670.

Lough, R. G. 1976. Mortality and growth of Georges Bank–Nantucket Shoals herring larvae during the 1975–1976 winter period. International Commission for the Northwest Atlantic Fisheries, Research Document, Serial 4004 76/6/123, Dartmouth, Canada.

Marcy, B. C., Jr. 1976. Early life history studies of American shad in the lower Connecticut River and the effects of the Connecticut Yankee plant. American Fisheries Society Monograph 1:141–168.

Marr, J. C. 1956. The "critical period" in early life history of marine fishes. Journal du Conseil, Conseil International pour l'Exploration de la Mer 21:160–170.

Maxfield, G. H. 1953. The food habits of hatchery-produced pond-cultured shad *(Alosa sapidissima)* reared to a length of two inches. Chesapeake Biological Laboratory Publication 98, Solomons, Maryland, USA.

May, R. C. 1974. Larval mortality in marine fishes and the critical period concept. Pages 3–19 *in* J. H. S. Blaxter, editor. The early life history of fish. Springer-Verlag, Heidelberg, West Germany.

Miller, S. J., and T. Stork. 1984. Temporal spawning distribution of largemouth bass and young-of-the-year growth, determined from daily otolith rings. Transactions of the American Fisheries Society 113:571–578.

Moffitt, C. M., B. Kynard, and S. G. Rideout. 1982. Fish passage facilities and anadromous fish restoration in the Connecticut River. Fisheries (Bethesda) 7(6):2–11.

Nelson, W., M. Ingham, and W. Schaef. 1977. Larval transport and year class strength of Atlantic menhaden, *Brevoortia tyrannus*. U.S. National Marine Fisheries Service Fishery Bulletin 75:23–41.

O'Leary, J., B. Kynard, and J. Buckley. 1984. 1984 Connecticut River Basin anadromous fish studies. Massachusetts Cooperative Fishery Research Unit, Performance Report AFS-4-R-20, Amherst, Massachusetts, USA.

Pannella, G. 1971. Fish otoliths: daily growth layers and periodical patterns. Science (Washington, D.C.) 173:1124–1127.

Parrish, R. H., and A. D. MacCall. 1978. Climatic vari-ation and exploitation in the Pacific mackerel fishery. California Department of Fish and Game, Fisheries Bulletin 167.

Ricker, W. E. 1954. Stock and recruitment. Journal of the Fisheries Research Board of Canada 11:559–623.

Ricker, W. E. 1975. Computation and interpretation of biological statistics of fish populations. Fisheries Research Board of Canada Bulletin 191.

Rosen, R. A. 1982. Seasonal cycles, distribution, and biomass of young American shad *(Alosa sapidissima)* in the Holyoke Pool, Connecticut River. Doctoral dissertation. University of Massachusetts, Amherst, Massachusetts, USA.

SAS (Statistical Analysis Systems). 1982. SAS user's guide. SAS Institute, Cary, North Carolina, USA.

Savoy, T. F., and V. A. Crecco. 1987. Daily increments on the otoliths of larval American shad and their use in population dynamics studies. Pages 413–432 *in* R. Summerfelt and G. Hall, editors. Age and growth of fish. Iowa University Press, Des Moines, Iowa, USA.

Sette, O. E. 1943. Biology of the Atlantic mackerel, *Scomber scombrus* of North America. Part I: early life history; including the growth, drift, and mortality of the egg and larval populations. U.S. Fish and Wildlife Service Fishery Bulletin 38(50):149–237.

Sharp, G. D. 1980. Workshop on the effects of environmental variation on the survival of larval pelagic fishes. Pages 15–66 *in* G. D. Sharp, editor. Report of the workshop on effects of environmental variation on survival of larval pelagic fishes. Intergovernmental Oceanographic Commission, IOC Workshop Report 28, Paris, France.

Shepard, J. G. 1982. A versatile new stock–recruitment relationship for fisheries, and the construction of sustainable yields curves. Journal du Conseil, Conseil International pour l'Exploration de la Mer 40:67–75.

Sinclair, M., and M. J. Tremblay. 1984. Timing of spawning of Atlantic herring *(Clupea harengus harengus)* populations and the match-mismatch theory. Canadian Journal of Fisheries and Aquatic Sciences 41:1055–1065.

Sinclair, M., M. J. Tremblay, and P. Bernal. 1985. El Niño events and variability in a Pacific mackerel *(Scomber japonicus)* survival index: support for Hjort's second hypothesis. Canadian Journal of Fisheries and Aquatic Sciences 42:602–608.

Stevenson, J. C. 1962. Distribution and survival of herring larvae *Clupea pallasii* in British Columbia waters. Journal of the Fisheries Research Board of Canada 19:735–810.

Stocker, M., V. Haist, and D. Fournier. 1985. Environmental variation and recruitment of Pacific herring *(Clupea harengus pallasi)* in the Strait of Georgia. Canadian Journal of Fisheries and Aquatic Sciences 42(supplement 1):174–180.

Theilacker, G., and K. G. Dorsey. 1980. A review of larval fish behavior, physiology and their diversity. Pages 105–142 *in* G. D. Sharp, author. Report of the workshop on the effects of environmental variation on the survival of larval pelagic fishes. Intergovernmental Oceanographic Commission, IOC Workshop Report 28, Paris, France.

U.S. Geological Survey. 1967–1984. Water resources data, Connecticut, water years, 1966–1983. Water Resources Division, Hartford, Connecticut, USA.

Watson, J. F. 1968. The early life history of the American shad *Alosa sapidissima* (Wilson) in the Connecticut River above Holyoke, Massachusetts. Master's thesis. University of Massachusetts, Amherst, Massachusetts, USA.

Whitton, B. A. 1980. River ecology. University of California Press, Berkley, California, USA.

Wiggins, T. A., T. R. Bender, V. A. Mudrak, and J. A. Coll. 1984. The development, feeding, growth and survival of cultured American shad larvae through the transition from endogenous to exogenous nutrition. Pennsylvania Fish Commission, Benner Spring Fish Research Station, Special Publication, Bellefonte, Pennsylvania, USA.

Yoshiyama, R. M., W. Van Winkle, B. L. Kirk, and D. E. Stevens. 1981. Regression analysis of stock–recruitment relationships in three fish populations. Oak Ridge National Laboratory, Nuclear Regulatory Research, Research Report W-7405-eng-26, Oak Ridge, Tennessee, USA.

American Fisheries Society Symposium 1:469–482, 1987

Stock–Recruitment Relationship and Compensatory Mortality of American Shad in the Connecticut River

ERNEST LORDA

Northeast Utilities Service Company, Environmental Programs Department
Post Office Box 270, Hartford, Connecticut 06141, USA

VICTOR A. CRECCO

Connecticut Department of Environmental Protection, Marine Fisheries Office
Post Office Box 248, Waterford, Connecticut 06385, USA

Abstract.—We developed an environment-dependent stock–recruitment model for the American shad *Alosa sapidissima* in the Connecticut River to estimate total prerecruit mortality, compensatory mortality, and the fishing rate (u_s) at maximum sustainable yield (MSY). We also compared the compensatory mortality estimate of American shad to those of 19 other fish stocks to investigate how compensation related to mean population fecundity. Our four-variable model, including total parent stock size, stock sizes above and below the Holyoke Dam, and mean June river flow, explained over 80% of the recruitment variability from the 1966 to the 1980 year classes. The mean compensatory mortality rate (1.21) represented 20% of the mean prejuvenile mortality and 11% of the total prerecruit mortality. Compensatory mortality was much lower in the Holyoke impoundment than below the dam, mainly because of the low number of spawners lifted into the impoundment prior to 1976. Although our estimate of the exploitation rate (u_s) at MSY (59%) under average June flow conditions was considerably higher than present exploitation rates (20–25%), the u_s values varied between 40 and 80% when mean June river flow was allowed to vary. Compensatory mortality of American shad was higher than the compensatory mortality reported for less fecund clupeids. This is consistent with the hypothesis that the degree of compensation and stock stability among fish stocks increases with mean population fecundity.

It is widely believed that most fish populations can compensate for increased mortality by enhancing population growth and survival (McFadden 1977). Because compensation may involve an increase in birth and reduction in death rates as population density declines, the biological processes that bring about compensation are termed "density dependent." The existence of compensatory mortality has intuitive appeal and is a fundamental theory of fisheries science (Cushing 1975; Ricker 1975; Gulland 1977, 1983) because fish populations under low to moderate exploitation neither increase continually nor decline to extinction over the long term. Therefore, the degree to which fish populations can tolerate exploitation without recruitment failure may depend on the amount of compensatory mortality. Despite its potential importance, compensatory mortality is usually difficult to estimate accurately in natural populations (Goodyear 1980) because recruitment is subject to large measurement errors (Walters and Ludwig 1981) and density-independent factors.

Stock–recruitment theory (Ricker 1954; Beverton and Holt 1957) has been the object of renewed interest (Ware 1980; Shepherd 1982; Garrod 1982,

1983; Gulland 1983; Goodyear and Christensen 1984), and stock–recruitment models provide a convenient method for estimating prerecruitment compensatory mortality from a time series of recruitment and parent stock data. However, stock–recruitment curves have seldom provided reliable forecasts of recruitment because recruitment variability is often more related to environmental fluctuations than to parent stock size (Cushing 1977). Only recently have fisheries scientists attempted to combine stock–recruitment models with key environmental variables (Nelson et al. 1977; Parrish and MacCall 1978) shown by field studies (Lasker 1975; Frank and Leggett 1982) to directly affect prejuvenile mortality. Crecco and Savoy (1984) used this approach for American shad *Alosa sapidissima* in the Connecticut River, and they reported that high river flows reduced larval survival, resulting in an inverse relationship between recruitment and mean June river flow. Although Crecco et al. (1986) developed an environment-dependent stock–recruitment model containing June river flow, they did not use the model to estimate compensatory mortality, nor did they examine how river flow variation affects the fishing rate at maximum sustainable yield (MSY).

In this paper, we developed a four-parameter stock–recruitment model for American shad to estimate total prerecruit mortality, compensatory mortality, and the fishing rate (u_s) at MSY. Our compensatory mortality estimate was compared to those reported for 19 fish stocks (Cushing and Harris 1973) to examine how compensation and stock stability relate to mean population fecundity. We also investigated to what extent the expansion of American shad spawning habitat in the Connecticut River improved recruitment rates from 1976 through 1980. It should be noted that the term compensatory mortality is used synonymously with density-dependent mortality.

Methods

Data Sources

American shad have historically ascended the Connecticut River as far north as Bellows Falls (Stevenson 1898) at river km 280 (Figure 1). Following the construction of the Holyoke Dam in 1849, anadromous fishes were restricted to the lower 139 km of the river. Although attempts to restore anadromous fish to the upper river began as early as 1873, it was not until 1955 that American shad were able to spawn within the Holyoke impoundment (an additional 58 km) after a fish lift was constructed. As a result, between 5 and 10% of the annual parent stock was lifted into the Holyoke impoundment from 1955 through 1975. Improvements in the fish lift and the construction of a second lift in 1976 allowed 40–50% of each year's parent stock to spawn in the impoundment after 1976 (Moffitt et al. 1982).

Long-term data for American shad (Table 1) on parent stock, recruitment, and annual number of spawners lifted into the Holyoke impoundment and for associated environmental variables are available from 1966 to 1980 (Leggett 1976; Moffitt et al. 1982; O'Leary and Booke 1985; Crecco et al. 1986). Female American shad reach sexual maturity between 4 and 6 years of age, but 60% of the average year class attains maturity before age 6 (Leggett 1969). Therefore, total recruitment (R) of female American shad from the 1966–1980 year classes was the total number of virgin (first-time) female spawners of ages 4 through 6 in the 1970–1985 spawning runs calculated from their age structure from previous studies (Leggett 1976; Jones et al. 1976; Crecco et al. 1984). Only female American shad were used because the male age structure is biased by gill-net selectivity and dif-

ferential discard practices by commercial fishermen (Leggett 1976; Crecco et al. 1986). Virgin fish were identified during age and growth analyses by the lack of distinct spawning scars at the periphery of the scales (Leggett 1969).

Population size estimates of female American shad from 1970 through 1985 were derived from daily lift rates at the Holyoke Dam (Moffitt et al. 1982; O'Leary and Booke 1985). Major improvements in the Holyoke fish lift in 1969, 1975, and 1976 (Henry 1976) resulted in a progressive increase in the mean passage rates (number of fish per day) during the periods 1969–1974, 1975, and 1976–1985 following each fish lift improvement (Crecco and Savoy 1985a; Table 1). We developed weighting coefficients to reflect the increased efficiency of the lift after each improvement by dividing the mean passage rate from 1962 through 1968 by the mean passage rates from 1969 to 1974, 1975, and 1976 to 1985. The annual number of American shad entering the Connecticut River from 1970 through 1985 was estimated by (1) dividing the total number of American shad lifted annually by the number of days during which 99% of that total was passed, (2) multiplying the mean lift rate by the appropriate weighting coefficient (Crecco and Savoy 1985a), and (3) multiplying the weighted mean lift rate by 1,000 to scale this lift-based population estimate relative to the size of the population estimates based on commercial fishery data (Leggett 1976; Crecco et al. 1984). Finally, the annual number of female American shad was estimated by multiplying each year's total number of fish by the estimated proportion of female fish in that year's run.

The total parent stock size (P_t) of female American shad from 1966 to 1980 (Table 1) was the annual female population size minus that year's commercial catch (Crecco and Savoy 1985a). This total parent stock was partitioned into the parent stock (P_a) that spawned above the Holyoke dam, as indicated by annual counts at the lift (Moffitt et al. 1982; O'Leary and Booke 1985), and the parent stock (P_b) that spawned below ($P_b = P_t - P_a$). Many of the females lifted before 1976 had partially spawned because of delays at the fish lift. As a result, the average fecundity (185,600 eggs) of American shad lifted into the Holyoke impoundment between 1966 and 1975 was 31% lower (Foote 1976; Saunders 1981) than the average population fecundity (269,000 eggs) for the lower river (Leggett 1969). After 1975, the fish lift became fully automated and the average fecundity in the Holyoke impoundment

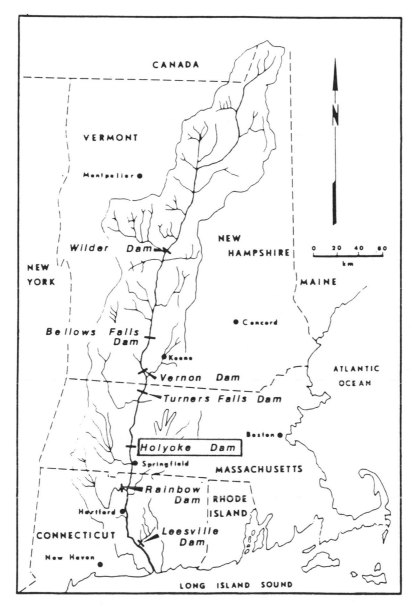

FIGURE 1.—The Connecticut River and its watershed with the location of fish passage facilities planned or in operation since 1955 (from Moffitt et al. 1982).

approached 269,000 eggs (Saunders 1981). To account for the lower fecundity in the Holyoke pool due to lifting delays, we reduced the female parent stock (P_a) in the Holyoke impoundment from 1966 through 1975 by 31%,

$$P_a' = (1 - 0.31) \times \text{(number of females lifted)},$$

whereas the corresponding parent stock below Holyoke Dam (P_b) was increased by an equivalent factor,

$$P_b' = P_b + (0.31 \times \text{number of females lifted}).$$

The mean June river flows (Table 1) were based on daily river flow rates (m^3/s) recorded in the Connecticut River by the U.S. Geological Survey near a major spawning area (river km 89) for American shad below the Holyoke Dam (Leggett 1977a).

To simplify the calculation of annual recruitment (R) in Table 1, we ignored the reproductive contribution of repeat spawners. Repeat spawners

TABLE 1.—Recruitment and parent stock data for American shad in the Connecticut River from 1966 through 1980, annual June river flows, and proportions (P_a/P_t) of parent stock lifted into the Holyoke impoundment (data sources: Leggett 1976; Moffitt et al. 1982; O'Leary and Booke 1985; Crecco et al. 1986).

| Year | Recruits (females, 10^3) (R) | Parent stock (females, 10^3) | | | Mean June river flow (m^3/s) (F) | Proportion of spawners above Holyoke (P_a/P_t) |
		Total (P_t)	Above Holyoke (P_a)	Below Holyoke (P_b)		
1966	388	115	4.1	110.9	246.1	0.036
1967	222	167	4.1	162.9	437.1	0.025
1968	118	202	4.8	197.2	603.4	0.024
1969	245	384	9.6	374.4	375.3	0.025
1970	275	413	11.7	401.3	244.0	0.028
1971	491	424	13.8	410.2	203.2	0.032
1972	215	167	7.6	159.4	616.4	0.045
1973	154	111	3.4	107.6	534.6	0.031
1974	326	306	9.6	296.4	334.8	0.031
1975	280	247	15.8	231.2	379.0	0.064
1976	325	435	166.0	269.0	286.7	0.382
1977	620	207	112.0	95.0	250.0	0.541
1978	357	210	45.0	165.0	489.0	0.214
1979	441	248	87.0	161.0	445.2	0.351
1980	628	341	196.0	145.0	201.3	0.575
Means	339	265.1	46.0	219.1	376.4	0.174[a]

[a] $\Sigma P_a/\Sigma P_t$.

have only represented 10–15% of the annual female spawning stocks in the Connecticut River between 1976 and 1984 (Crecco et al. 1984). By using only virgin spawners, our estimates of annual recruitment rates (R/P_t,), parent stock at replacement (P_r), and exploitation rate (u_s) at MSY were conservative because mean life-time fecundity of a recruit would increase by 10–15% if repeat spawners were included. Conservative estimates of the optimal rate of fishing (u_s) are desirable for relatively short-lived fishes, like the American shad, whose recruitment is affected by large and erratic environmental fluctuations.

Biological Basis and Mathematical Form of the Model

Catch per unit effort of juvenile American shad in the Connecticut River from 1967 through 1980 (Marcy 1976; Crecco and Savoy 1985a) was positively correlated ($r = 0.89$; $P < 0.01$) with the number of adult recruits from those year classes. As a result, year-class strength of American shad in the Connecticut River was assumed to be established prior to the juvenile stage (Leggett 1977). Moreover, Savoy and Crecco (unpublished) found that the relative abundance of 18–30-d-old larvae from 1979 through 1984 was closely correlated ($r = 0.88$; $P < 0.05$) with the juvenile indices for those years, suggesting that compensatory mortality is mainly confined to the egg and early larval stages. Therefore, we used the dome-shaped (Ricker 1954) stock–recruitment curve to describe compensatory mortality confined to an early life history stage when progeny abundance is still roughly proportional to the initial number of eggs. By contrast, the asymptotic Beverton and Holt stock–recruitment curve is more useful when density-dependent mortality (Harris 1975) takes place throughout the prerecruitment period (Cushing and Horwood 1977).

The mathematical form of our environment-dependent stock–recruitment model was

$$R = \alpha P_t \exp(-\beta_a P_a - \beta_b P_b)\exp(-\varphi F), \quad (1)$$

where the subscripts a and b refer to the stocks above and below Holyoke Dam, respectively; t refers to the total parent stock; R and P are thousands of female recruits and spawners; F is the mean June river flow (m^3/s); and α, β_a, β_b, and φ are model parameters. The biological meaning of these parameters is as follows: α is the annual rate of recruitment (recruits per spawner) in the absence of compensatory mortality and river flow effects; β_a and β_b are coefficients of instantaneous compensatory mortality; φ is the coefficient of instantaneous mortality associated with June river flows. Because R in equation (1) represents the sum of recruitment from above and below the Holyoke Dam, our model makes no assumptions about whether mature progeny produced in the Holyoke impoundment return there or spawn below the dam.

The model followed Ricker's original stock–recruitment equation ($R = \alpha P \exp[-\beta P]$), except that two compensatory mortality coefficients were used to describe separate stock-dependent processes above and below Holyoke Dam. In addition, June flow effects on total recruitment were represented by a multiplicative term ($\exp[-\varphi F]$ in equation 1), as suggested by Ricker (1975). The use of two compensatory (β) coefficients is justified for American shad in the Connecticut River inasmuch as the progeny produced above and below Holyoke Dam are geographically isolated by the dam until juvenile emigration begins. Moreover, the area of potential spawning habitat above the dam (70 km) is considerably smaller than the area (120 km) below. June river flow was chosen as the major environmental variable because it affects other environmental factors associated with survival of American shad eggs and larvae. Firstly, high June river flows may transport eggs and larvae to areas of low food density and high predator abundance (Crecco and Savoy, in press). Secondly, high river flows caused in June by storm events reduce water temperatures (Crecco and Savoy 1984), thereby delaying the development of eggs and larvae. Finally, high river flows increase turbidity, which may interfer with the ability of sight-feeding larvae to obtain food. These mechanisms are consistent with the significant ($r = -0.74$; $P < 0.01$) inverse correlation between recruitment and mean June river flow from 1966 through 1980 reported by Crecco and Savoy (1984).

Total prerecruit instantaneous mortality (Z) from equation (1) was estimated as

$$Z = -\log_e(R/E) = \log_e(f) - \log_e(\alpha^*) \\ + (\beta_a P_a) + (\beta_b P_b); \qquad (2)$$

f is the average number of female eggs per female spawner, E is total production of female eggs in thousands ($E = fP_t$), and α^* is the rate of recruitment (α) from equation (1) adjusted by the factor $\exp(-\varphi F)$ to account for June flow effects on recruitment. We reduced the mean fecundity (f) of American shad from above and below the Holyoke Dam by 25% to reflect average rates of egg retention and incomplete fertilization (Watson 1970; Reed and Russo 1976). For an assumed 1:1 sex ratio in progeny production, f in equation (2) was $(1 - 0.25)(269,000)(0.50) \cong 100,000$ female eggs per female spawner.

The instantaneous prerecruit mortality (Z) in equation (2) was partitioned into density-independent (Z_i) and compensatory (Z_c) components as follows:

$$Z_i = \log_e(f) - \log_e(\alpha^*); \qquad (3)$$

$$Z_c = Z_a + Z_b = (\beta_a P_a) + (\beta_b P_b); \qquad (4)$$

Z_a and Z_b are the compensatory mortalities above and below Holyoke Dam, respectively.

An estimate of the parent stock at replacement level (P_r) is needed to calculate the exploitation rate at MSY (Ricker 1954), so we derived a coefficient of compensatory mortality (β^*) for the entire parent stock (P_t) as:

$$\beta^* = (\beta_a P_a + \beta_b P_b)/P_t. \qquad (5)$$

Since equation (4) could now be rewritten as $Z_c = (\beta^*)P_t$, the parent stock at replacement (P_r) was estimated according to Ricker's (1954) derivation as

$$P_r = \log_e(\alpha^*)/\beta^*. \qquad (6)$$

The parent stock (P_s) for maximum sustainable yield was calculated from Hilborn's (1985) equation

$$P_s = [0.5 - 0.07\log_e(\alpha^*)]P_r, \qquad (7)$$

and the rate of exploitation (u_s) at MSY with Ricker's equation

$$u_s = \beta^* P_s. \qquad (8)$$

Unlike Ricker's original derivation of equation (6), in which both α and β were constants, our derived parameters (α^*) and (β^*) are variables. $\log_e(\alpha^*)$ is the instantaneous recruitment rate in the absence of compensatory mortality, and varies annually with the mean June river flow by

$$\log_e(\alpha^*) = \log_e(\alpha) - \varphi F. \qquad (9)$$

On the other hand, the derived coefficient of compensatory mortality (β^*) varies annually with the proportion of the parent stock (P_t) lifted into the Holyoke impoundment. In equation (5) β^* equals β_b in the absence of lifting ($P_a = 0$ and $P_b = P_t$) and equals β_a when the entire stock is lifted ($P_a = P_t$ and $P_b = 0$). Therefore, we derived the 1966–1980 mean values of $\log_e(\alpha^*)$ and β^* for equations (6) to (8), by using the 1966–1980 mean of F in equation (9) and the 1966–1980 means of P_a, P_b, and P_t in equation (5). The latter computation yielded the β^* value that corresponds to the average proportion of parent stock (P_t) lifted into the Holyoke impoundment from 1966 through 1980 (Table 1). It should be noted that equation (9) is only valid over the observed range of June river flows and does not imply that maximum recruitment occurs at zero flow. Although the optimal flow is unknown, it is probably close to the lowest mean June flow (179 m³/s) observed since 1929 (U.S. Geological Survey 1967–1985).

Estimation of Model Parameters, Mortalities, and Fishery Statistics

We estimated the four parameters α, β_a, β_b, and φ by fitting equation (1) to the 1966–1980 data (Table 1) using the nonlinear regression procedure NLIN in SAS (1982). Given the short time series (15 years) and the serial correlation usually present in stock–recruitment data, the final parameters were reestimated by the bias-reduction procedure known as "jackknifing" (Tukey 1958; Miller 1974). This procedure corrects first-order bias due to serial correlation and provides more realistic estimates of parameter variability in small-sample estimation problems (Miller 1974). The jackknife procedure can be applied to nonlinear regression problems (Miller 1974) and also provides standard errors for interval estimation and hypothesis testing (Miller 1974; Bissell and Ferguson 1975).

This technique involves the repeated estimation of the parameters according to usual regression methods, except that a different data point is left out each time. This process generates n sets of partial estimates (based on $n - 1$ observations) which are used to compute the final parameter estimates and their standard errors. When parameters are estimated simultaneously, it is also possible to obtain a jackknifed variance–covariance matrix (Miller 1974). Computational details for this and other applications of the jackknife can be found in Bissell and Ferguson (1975). For recent applications of the jackknife method to estimation problems in marine biology and fisheries, see Meyer et al. (1986) and Smith (1980), respectively.

Since the jackknife procedure can estimate the mean and standard error of general statistics containing several variables, we obtained jackknife estimates of our derived parameters β^* and $\log_e(\alpha^*)$ (equations 5 and 9), total prerecruit mortality (Z) and its components $(Z_i, Z_c, Z_a,$ and Z_b: equations 2, 3, and 4), parent stock at replacement $(P_r$: equation 6), parent stock at MSY $(P_s$: equation 7,) and exploitation rate at MSY $(u_s$: equation 8). The jackknife point estimates of these statistics represent their expected values (i.e., means) given the variation of parent stock size, June river flow, and proportion of spawners in the Holyoke impoundment from 1966 through 1980.

Finally, we used the cross-validation method (Geisser 1975; Efron 1982) to measure the magnitude and direction of bias in predicting annual recruitment with our model. This method is especially useful for validating model predictions when only a small data set is available for both parameter estimation and model validation. Briefly, the cross-validation method involves leaving out one data point at a time, fitting the model to the remaining points, and seeing how well the fitted model predicts the excluded point. The average of the prediction errors, each point being left out once, is the cross-validated measure of prediction error. Unlike the errors from a regression model fitted to all the data, where the average is always zero, the cross-validated mean error may be positive or negative depending on whether the model tends to over- or underestimate. In addition, the cross-validated mean error is a conservative measure of expected prediction error because the data points are not allowed to assist in their own prediction (Efron 1982).

Results

Environment-Dependent Stock–Recruitment Model

The fitted stock–recruitment model

$$R = 11.9 \, P_t \exp(-0.0033 \, P_a - 0.0049 \, P_b)\exp(-0.0026 \, F)$$

explained 80% ($R^2 = 0.80$) of the recruitment variability of American shad from 1966 through 1980 (Figure 2). The cross-validation analysis estimated the mean prediction error as +2,870 recruits (95% confidence interval, CI, about the mean, −50,000 to +56,000), indicating that the model tends to slightly overestimate recruitment. The jackknife estimates of the model parameters

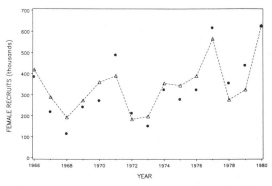

FIGURE 2.—Recruitment data (circles) and model predictions (triangles) of annual recruitment of American shad in the Connecticut River from 1966 through 1980. The model explained 80% of the annual recruitment variability ($R^2 = 0.80$).

$\log_e(\alpha)$, β_a, β_b, and φ, as well as the derived parameters $\log_e(\alpha^*)$ and β^*, were significantly different from zero (Table 2). The null hypothesis of no compensatory mortality during the recruitment period of American shad was rejected at $P < 0.01$ because the two compensatory parameters (β_a and β_b) tested separately were highly significant.

Although the existence of compensatory mortality was indicated by the model, the 1966–1980 recruitment data did not exhibit a convincing Ricker parent–progeny relationship (Figure 3). This is because about 50% of the recruitment variability of American shad is explained by annual fluctuations in June river flow (Crecco and Savoy 1984). According to Figure 3 (top), high June flows (>550 m^3/s) tend to cause year-class failure of American shad regardless of parent stock size, whereas low June flows (<250 m^3/s) tend to produce dominant year classes especially over the mid-range (100,000–300,000 spawners) of parent stock sizes. By contrast, recruitment was less sensitive to changes in the proportion (P_a/P_t) of spawners in the Holyoke impoundment (Figure 3, bottom). Only when the lifting rates exceeded 50% did subsequent recruitment show a noticeable increase. These results suggest that lifting 50–60% of the total annual spawning stocks into the Holyoke impoundment will enhance long-term recruitment by about 20%, but annual recruitment variability is modulated by hydrographic and meteorological events during the egg and larval stages.

In order to show the shape of the underlying parent–progeny relationship, we adjusted the 1966–1980 recruitment data for deviations of the annual mean June flows ($\bar{F}$) from the long-term mean flow ($F = 376.4$ m^3/s: Table 1) by

$$\text{adjusted } R = R\exp[\varphi(\bar{F} - F)]. \quad (10)$$

We also generated the expected recruitment curve of American shad for average flow and average proportion of spawners in the Holyoke impoundment from 1966 through 1980 by

$$R = \alpha^* P_t \exp(-\beta^* P_t); \quad (11)$$

α^* and β^* were the mean estimates of these parameters obtained from equations (9) and (5), respectively.

After the June flow variability effects were removed, the adjusted recruitment data exhibited a more pronounced decline at high parent stock sizes (Figure 4), which is consistent with the shape of the Ricker curve (equation 11). This suggests that the compensatory response of American shad is difficult to detect without accounting for flow-driven effects.

Prerecruitment Mortality Estimates

The compensatory mortalities for progeny in the entire river ($Z_c = 1.21$) and in the area below the Holyoke Dam ($Z_b = 1.07$) were significantly different from zero ($P < 0.01$; Table 3). By contrast, the compensatory mortality ($Z_a = 0.14$) for progeny in the Holyoke impoundment was not significant even though the corresponding compensatory coefficient (β_a) from the model was highly significant (Table 2). The lack of significance of Z_a was attributed to the wide range (4,000–196,000 female spawners) of parent stock sizes (P_a) in the Holyoke impoundment from 1966 through 1980, which increased the variance of Z_a. To investigate this hypothesis, the model parameters were reestimated with data from the 10 years (1966–1975) when the range of parent stock sizes lifted was only 4,000 to 14,000 females. We found that the estimate of β_a for this period of low lifting rates was not significant ($P > 0.05$), whereas estimate of β_b remained highly significant despite

TABLE 2.—Parameter estimates of the environment-dependent stock–recruitment model of American shad obtained by nonlinear regression and jackknife methods. Parameters $\log_e(\alpha^*)$ and (β^*) were derived for overall mean June Connecticut river flow and average proportion of parent stock in the Holyoke impoundment, respectively. The t-statistic corresponds to the null hypothesis that the jackknife estimates do not differ from zero.

Parameters	Regression estimates	Jackknife estimates	Jacknifed SE	t	P
Model (equation 1)					
α	12.19	11.90			
$\log_e(\alpha)$		2.48	0.314	7.9	<0.01
β_a	3.06×10^{-3}	3.29×10^{-3}	1.00×10^{-3}	3.3	<0.01
β_b	5.05×10^{-3}	4.86×10^{-3}	8.39×10^{-4}	5.8	<0.01
ϕ	2.59×10^{-3}	2.57×10^{-3}	8.41×10^{-4}	3.1	<0.01
Derived					
$\log_e(\alpha^*)$ (equation 5)		1.51	0.187	8.1	<0.01
β^* (equation 9)		4.59×10^{-3}	6.33×10^{-4}	7.2	<0.01

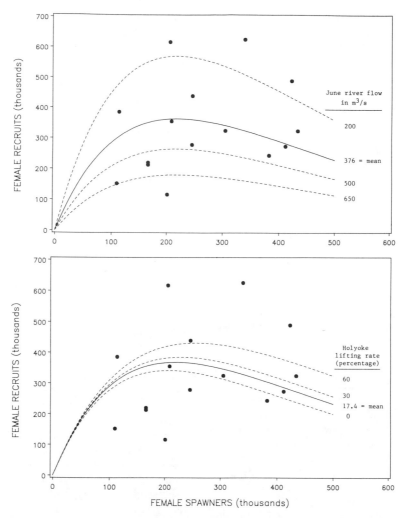

FIGURE 3.—**Top.** Recruitment data (circles) of American shad from 1966 through 1980, and recruitment curves generated by the model for various Connecticut River flows and constant average proportion of parent stock in the Holyoke impoundment ($\overline{P}_a/\overline{P}_t = 0.1734$). **Bottom.** Recruitment curves generated by the model for various proportions (P_a/P_t) of parent stock in the Holyoke impoundment and constant overall mean June river flow ($\overline{P} = 376.4$ m³/s).

the shorter time series (10 years). Since there were not enough data to estimate the model parameters for the high-lift years (1976–1980), our tentative conclusion was that compensatory mortality in the Holyoke impoundment had been negligible during the colonization period, but may have increased to a significant level when 100,000–200,000 female spawners entered the Holyoke impoundment annually after 1975.

The total prerecruit mortality (Z) was 11.22 (95% CI, 10.9 to 11.5: Table 3), leading to an average survival rate of about 13 mature American shad per 1,000,000 fertilized eggs. Since com-

pensatory mortality of American shad is largely confined to the egg and early larval stages (Crecco and Savoy, in press), we compared our estimate of compensatory mortality to the total prejuvenile mortality rates estimated directly on shad eggs and larvae from 1979 to 1984 (Savoy and Crecco, unpublished). Total mean compensatory mortality from the model ($Z_c = 1.21$) amounted to about 20% of the mean total egg and larval mortality of 5.94 (Table 4). This suggested that density-dependent processes may play a major role in regulating American shad recruitment to the juvenile stage during years of high egg production and low to

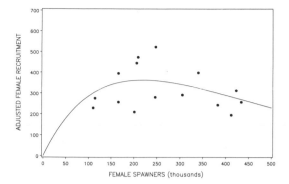

FIGURE 4.—Recruitment data (circles) for American shad adjusted for June Connecticut River flow variability (equation 10) and the recruitment curve generated by equation (11) for average June flow ($\bar{F} = 376.4$ m³/s) and mean proportion ($\bar{P}_a/\bar{P}_t = 0.1734$) of parent stock in the Holyoke impoundment.

moderate June river flows.

Fishery Statistics

The jackknife estimate of parent stock at replacement (P_r) was 326,100 female American shad (Table 3) and was about 23% higher than the overall mean parent stock size (265,000 spawners) from 1966 through 1980 (Table 1). This suggests that there is a substantial surplus of recruits for harvesting. Moreover, the overall mean recruitment (339,000 females) from 1966 through 1980 was close to the theoretical maximum recruitment, estimated as 361,000 spawners by Ricker's (1954) equation

$$R(\text{max}) = \alpha^*/2.72\beta^*, \qquad (12)$$

α^* and β^* being the 1966–1980 mean estimates of these parameters obtained from equations (9) and (5), respectively.

The parent stock size at MSY ($P_s = 128,000$

spawners) was far below the overall mean parent stock ($\bar{P} = 265,100$ spawners), resulting in a relatively high average rate of exploitation at MSY ($u_s = 0.59$; Table 3). Given that the current exploitation rates of females by the sport and commercial fisheries combined have not exceeded 0.20 to 0.25 (Crecco et al. 1984), these results suggest that a large potential surplus of recruits is not currently being harvested. One problem with our jackknife estimates of P_s and u_s (Table 3) is that they assume no variation in the annual June flow and proportion (P_a/P_t) of spawners in the Holyoke impoundment, because these statistics were derived with the 1966–1980 mean estimates of β^* and $\log_e(\alpha^*)$. This assumption is not realistic inasmuch as American shad recruitment varies greatly with annual fluctuations of June flow and, to a lesser extent, with annual changes in the percentage of the total spawning stock lifted into the Holyoke impoundment (Figure 3). To assess how the exploitation rate as MSY might be affected by simultaneous variation in June flows and lifting rates, we generated the response surface of u_s by evaluating equations (5) through (8) for various combinations of flows (from 200 to 600 m³/s) and lifting rates (0 to 60%). The ranges of these variables are similar to their actual ranges (Table 1). The response surface showed how American shad recruitment and fishing rate at MSY depend on climatic variability (Figure 5). When June river flows are low (200–250 m³/s) dominant year classes are produced, giving rise to a large surplus yield and high maximum exploitation rates ($u_s = 60$–70%) regardless of the proportion of spawners in the Holyoke impoundment. Yet, when mean June flows are high (500–600 m³/s), recruitment failure is likely to occur, leading to a precipitous drop in exploitation rates at MSY ($u_s = 40$–45%). This drop occurs indepen-

TABLE 3.—Jackknife mean estimates and confidence intervals (CI) of prerecruit instantaneous mortalities and fishery statistics of American shad in the Connecticut River (1966–1980). The t-statistic corresponds to the null hypothesis that the jackknife estimates do not differ from zero.

Parameter or statistic		Jackknife estimates	Jackknifed 95% CI	t	P
Instantaneous mortality[a]					
Z	Prerecruit (total)	11.22	10.92–11.52	80.0	<0.01
Z_i	Density-independent	10.01	9.61–10.41	53.6	<0.01
Z_c	Compensatory (total)	1.21	0.71–1.72	5.2	<0.01
Z_a	Compensatory (Holyoke impoundment)	0.14	−0.03–0.32	1.8	NS
Z_b	Compensatory (below Holyoke)	1.07	0.62–1.51	5.1	<0.01
Fishery statistics					
P_r	Parent stock at replacement	326.1	262–390	10.9	<0.01
P_s	Parent stock at MSY	128.8	104.6–152.9	11.4	<0.01
u_s	Exploitation rate at MSY	0.59	0.47–0.70	11.1	<0.01

[a] At mean parent stock level.

TABLE 4.—Mean instantaneous mortality rates of eggs and larval American shad in the Connecticut River from 1979 through 1984 (data source: Savoy and Crecco, unpublished).

	Mean instantaneous mortality		
Life stage and durations	Total	SE (total)	Daily
Eggs and yolk-sac larvae (2–3 d)	2.76	0.47	0.39
First-feeding larvae (day 3–9)	1.73	0.15	0.25
Middle larvae (day 10–18)	0.82	0.13	0.09
Late larvae (day 19–29)	0.63	0.07	0.06
Total prejuvenile (29 d)	5.94		0.21

dently of the proportion of spawners in the impoundment. These results illustrate the difficulty of setting maximum pemissible fishing rates for a species like the American shad, whose recruitment rates are so dependent on climatic variation.

Effect of Increasing the Shad Spawning Habitat

By adding the Holyoke impoundment as spawning grounds, potential American shad recruitment increased on average by 20–30% when parent stock sizes exceeded 200,000 female shad (Figure 3). We also compared the rates of recruitment (R/P_t) for the low-lift (1966–1975) and high-lift (1976–1980) periods. The R/P_t ratio increased from an average of 1.07 during the years when less than 4% of the spawning stock was lifted to 1.67 when 20–57% of the parent stock was lifted into the Holyoke impoundment. Although the average recruitment rate after 1975 was 56% higher than before 1975, the mean R/P_t ratios did not differ significantly due to the small sample size (5 years) after 1975.

Compensatory Mortality of Other Fish Stocks

Cushing and Harris (1973) estimated compensatory mortality rates for 19 fish stocks by fitting parent–progeny data to the Ricker stock–recruitment model. We compared the mean population fecundity (269,000 ova) and compensatory mortality for the American shad to those of the other 19 fish stocks. The compensatory mortality ($Z_c = 1.21$) of American shad was about the same as the average compensatory mortality of the flatfish group, exceeded that of a group of less fecund clupeids and of a salmonid group, and was lower than that of the highly fecund gadoid group (Table 5). This positive correlation between compensatory mortality and population fecundity ($r = 0.79$ for the 19 stocks plus the American shad) is consistent with the findings of Cushing and Harris (1973), suggesting that the high compensatory capacity of American shad is related to their higher fecundity as compared to other marine clupeids.

Discussion

The regulation of fish population numbers by compensatory mortality has received considerable attention in stock–recruitment theory, but except for density-dependent processes affecting

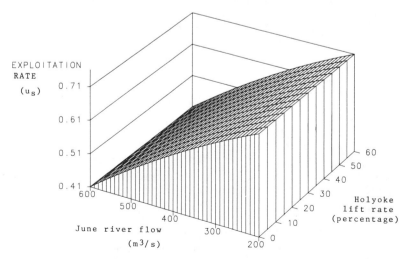

FIGURE 5.—Response surface of exploitation rate (u_s) of American shad at maximum sustainable yield to simultaneous variation in June Connecticut River flow and lifting rates at the Holyoke Dam.

TABLE 5.—Mean population fecundity and compensatory mortality $Z_c = \beta P$ of 19 fish stocks (Cushing and Harris 1973) and the American shad in the Connecticut River (this study).

Group	Number of fish stocks	Group means	
		Fecundity 10^3 eggs/female	Compensatory mortality
Salmonids[a]	6	2.8	0.78
Clupeids[b]	6	44.0	0.79
Flatfish[c]	3	186.7	1.20
American Shad	1	269.0	1.21
Gadoids[d]	4	775.0	1.75

[a] Pink salmon *Oncorhynchus gorbuscha*, chum salmon *O. keta*, sockeye salmon *O. nerka*.

[b] Pacific herring *Clupea harengus pallasi*, Atlantic herring *C. h. harengus*, Pacific sardine *Sardinops sagax*.

[c] Plaice *Pleuronectes platessa*, Pacific halibut *Hippoglossus stenolepsis*.

[d] Haddock *Melanogrammus aeglefinus*, Atlantic cod *Gadus morhua*.

growth and fecundity (Ware 1980), few empirical studies have attempted to measure the amount of compensatory mortality. We found that 20% of the prejuvenile losses of American shad could be attributed to compensatory mortality (Tables 3, 4), indicating that this species possesses a relatively high capacity for stabilization despite high environmental variability (Crecco and Savoy 1984). Compensatory mortality of American shad (Crecco and Savoy, in press; Savoy and Crecco, unpublished) and perhaps other marine clupeids (Cushing 1975), is largely confined to the embryonic and early larval stages. This suggests that the stability of the American shad population in the Connecticut river could be impaired by additional juvenile and postjuvenile mortality (Leggett 1977).

The biological pathways through which compensatory mortality operates in the presence of high environmental variability may be numerous and complex. Compensatory mortality among fish stocks may result from intra- and interspecific competition, cannibalism, and predation (Ricker 1954; Goodyear 1980). Cannibalism on American shad eggs and larvae can likely be ruled out because adults are not known to feed in fresh water (Walburg and Nichols 1967), and juveniles consume crustacean zooplankton and insects (Maxfield 1953; Domermuth 1976). High densities of American shad eggs and larvae might attract vertebrate and invertebrate predators, enhancing the encounter rate between predator and prey, and giving rise to strong density-dependent predation. In addition, the somatic growth rates of egg and larval predators may be related to prey densities (Hassell 1978), leading to density-dependent mortality of the prey and density-dependent growth of the predator. It is also possible that effects of river flow on egg and larval mortality would mediate the effects of predator-induced mortality. Previous studies (Marcy 1976; Crecco and Savoy 1985b, 1987) found that the rates at which American shad eggs and larvae grow and develop were inversely related to June river flows. Therefore, if the timing of peak egg and larval production is synchronous with storm events, the developmental rates of eggs and larvae would be slowed, thus prolonging their susceptibility to predation. Compensatory mortality among first-feeding larvae could result from malnutrition (Lasker 1975) only if grazing rates of larvae were capable of depleting river zooplankton abundance. However, spatial changes in zooplankton abundance appear to be more related to hydrographic events than to larval grazing rates (Crecco and Savoy 1984, in press), so malnutrition among first-feeding larvae would probably be a density-independent factor. Given the numerous ways in which hydrographic events can mediate the timing and magnitude of predation and starvation effects, it is unlikely that a single mechanism is responsible for the relatively high compensatory mortality of American shad ($Z_c = 1.21$).

Our estimate of compensatory mortality for American shad was larger than those of other clupeids but less than the compensatory mortality of highly fecund gadoids. We hypothesize that higher compensatory mortality for American shad relative to other marine clupeids is due to their relatively high fecundity (mean = 269,000 ova: Leggett 1976), which is consistent with the hypothesis of Cushing and Harris (1973) that compensatory mortality and the capacity for stabilizing abundance are greater among highly fecund fishes. This greater stability suggests that American shad populations in the Connecticut River and elsewhere are less vulnerable to recruitment failure due to overfishing than are less fecund marine clupeids.

Our estimate of exploitation rate at MSY ($u_s = 59\%$: Table 3) for average June flow conditions and proportion of spawners in the Holyoke impoundment was considerably higher than values (35–45%) recommended earlier (Leggett 1976; Crecco et al. 1984). They may be too optimistic for several reasons. Firstly, the model estimate of u_s assumes constant mean June river flow (376.4 m^3/s) and thus no climatically induced variability in recruitment. This was shown to be unrealistic given that u_s is highly sensitive to variation in recruitment due to river flows (Figure 5). This result underscores the problems of estimating maximum sustainable yield for a species like American shad that is subject to high environmental variability. Secondly, an implicit assumption of our stock–recruitment model was that commercial fishing mortality rates are not inversely related to population size (depensatory mortality). However, Crecco and Savoy (1985a) reported that the commercial gill-net fishery for American shad in the Connecticut River was depensatory, as did Peterman and Steer (1981) for chinook salmon *Oncorhynchus tschawytscha*. If commercial fishing for American shad is depensatory, exploitation rates will rise as the stock declines even when fishing effort remains constant. Furthermore, the population size of Connecticut River American shad underwent temporary recruitment failure from 1950 to 1957 (Fredin 1954; Leggett 1976) following a significant rise (45–55%) in commercial exploitation rates after World War II. The population size increased to its former levels within 5–10 years after the exploitation rates were reduced below 35% through vigorous management constraints (Leggett 1976; Crecco et al. 1984), so it would be unwise to raise exploitation rates towards our estimated MSY levels.

The detection of a statistically significant stock–recruitment relationship for most fish populations is usually difficult where the parent stock sizes seldom vary far from replacement levels (Cushing 1977) and climatically induced recruitment variability is high (Parrish and MacCall 1978). Our tentative conclusions that pre-1976 compensatory mortality for American shad was negligible in the Holyoke impoundment and that recruitment rates were nearly proportional to parent stock size are consistent with the findings of Gibson (1985) in the Pawcatuck River, Rhode Island. He also found that American shad recruitment was nearly proportional to parent stock size at the beginning of the Pawcatuck restoration program. We believe that similar interactions among recruitment, parent stock size, and climatic variability may be present in other rivers during their colonization, so our approach to assessing recruitment variability and compensation may be transferable to other anadromous fishes.

Finally, we would like to emphasize that American shad recruitment data from 1966–1980 included only 5 years (1976–1980) of high lifting rates (20–55%) at Holyoke Dam. It is likely that the compensatory mortality rates in the Holyoke

impoundment and below the dam will change as future year classes enter the spawning stock. Therefore, the contribution of compensatory mortality to total prerecruit mortality reported here should be reevaluated when more data become available.

Acknowledgments

We thank C. M. Moffitt, S. B. Saila, I. R. Savidge, and D. Welch for their constructive criticism of early drafts of this manuscript and many helpful comments.

References

Beverton, R. J., and S. J. Holt. 1957. On the dynamics of exploited fish populations. Fishery Investigations, Series II, Marine Fisheries, Great Britain Ministry of Agriculture Fisheries and Food 19.

Bissell, A. F., and R. A. Ferguson. 1975. The jackknife: toy, tool or two-edged weapon? Statistician 24(2):79–100.

Crecco, V., and T. Savoy. 1984. Effects of fluctuations in hydrographic conditions on year-class strength of American shad, *Alosa sapidissima*, in the Connecticut River. Canadian Journal of Fisheries and Aquatic Sciences 41:1216–1223.

Crecco, V. A., and T. F. Savoy. 1985a. Density-dependent catchability and its potential causes and consequences on Connecticut River American shad (*Alosa sapidissima*). Canadian Journal of Fisheries and Aquatic Sciences 42:1649–1657.

Crecco, V. A., and T. F. Savoy. 1985b. Effects of biotic and abiotic factors on growth and relative survival of young American shad, *Alosa sapidissima*, in the Connecticut River. Canadian Journal of Fisheries and Aquatic Sciences 42:1640–1648.

Crecco, V. A., and T. Savoy. 1987. Review of recruitment mechanisms of the American shad: the critical period and match–mismatch hypotheses reexamined. American Fisheries Society Symposium 1:455–468.

Crecco, V. A., and T. F. Savoy. In press. Effects of climatic and density-dependent factors on intra-annual mortality of larval American shad. American Fisheries Society Symposium 2.

Crecco, V., T. Savoy, and L. Gunn. 1984. The Connecticut River shad study, 1981–1983. Connecticut Department of Environmental Protection, Marine Fisheries Office, Project AFC-14, Final Report, Waterford, Connecticut, USA.

Crecco, V., T. Savoy, and W. Whitworth. 1986. Effects of density-dependent and climatic factors on American shad (*Alosa sapidissima*) recruitment: a predictive approach. Canadian Journal of Fisheries and Aquatic Sciences 43:457–463.

Cushing, D. H. 1975. Marine ecology and fisheries. Cambridge University Press, Cambridge, England.

Cushing, D. H. 1977. The problems of stock and recruitment. Pages 116–133 *in* J. A. Gulland, editor. Fish population dynamics. John Wiley & Sons, New

York, New York, USA.

Cushing, D. H., and J. G. K. Harris. 1973. Stock and recruitment and the problem of density dependence. Rapports et Procès-Verbaux des Réunions, Conseil International pour l'Exploration de la Mer 164:142–155.

Cushing, D. H., and J. W. Horwood. 1977. Development of a model of stock and recruitment. Pages 21–35 in J. H. Steele, editor. Fisheries mathematics. Academic Press, New York, New York, USA.

Domermuth, R. B. 1976. Summer foods of larval and juvenile American shad, Alosa sapidissima, juvenile blueback herring, Alosa aestivalis, and pumpkinseed, Lepomis gibbosus, in the Connecticut River between Holyoke and Enfield dams, 1972. Master's thesis. University of Massachusetts, Amherst, Massachusetts, USA.

Efron, B. 1982. The jackknife, the bootstrap and other resampling plans. Society for Industrial and Applied Mathematics, Regional Conference Series in Applied Mathematics, Monograph 38, Philadelphia, Pennsylvania, USA.

Foote, P. S. 1976. Blood lactic acid levels and age structure of American shad (Alosa sapidissima, Wilson) utilizing the Holyoke dam fishlift, Massachusetts, 1974 and 1975. Master's thesis. University of Massachusetts, Amherst, Massachusetts, USA.

Frank, K. T., and W. C. Leggett. 1982. Environmental regulation of growth rate, efficiency, and swimming performance in larval capelin, Mallotus villosus, and its application to the match/mismatch hypothesis. Canadian Journal of Fisheries and Aquatic Sciences 39:691–699.

Fredin, R. A. 1954. Causes of fluctuations in abundance of Connecticut River shad. U.S. Fish and Wildlife Service Fishery Bulletin 54:247–259.

Garrod, D. J. 1982. Stock and recruitment—again. Great Britain Ministry of Agriculture Fisheries and Food Directorate of Fisheries Research. Fisheries Research Technical Report 68.

Garrod, D. J. 1983. On the variability of year-class strength. Journal du Conseil, Conseil International pour l'Exploration de la Mer 40:46–54.

Geisser, S. 1975. The predictive sample reuse method with applications. American Statistical Association Journal 70:320–328.

Gibson, M. R. 1985. A preliminary analysis of factors controlling year class strength in Pawcatuck River shad. Rhode Island Division of Fish and Wildlife, Great Swamp Field Headquarters, Research Reference Document 85/1. West Kingston, Rhode Island, USA.

Goodyear, P. C. 1980. Compensation in fish populations. Pages 253–280 in C. H. Howatt and J. R. Stauffer, Jr., editors. Biological monitoring of fish. Lexington Books, Lexington, Massachusetts, USA.

Goodyear, P. C., and S. W. Christensen. 1984. On the ability to detect the influence of spawning stock on recruitment. North American Journal of Fisheries Management 4:186–193.

Gulland, J. A., editor. 1977. Fish population dynamics. John Wiley & Sons, New York, New York, USA.

Gulland, J. A. 1983. Fish stock assessment: a manual of basic methods. FAO/Wiley series on food and agriculture, volume 1. John Wiley & Sons, New York, New York, USA.

Harris, J. G. K. 1975. The effect of density-dependent mortality on the shape of the stock and recruitment curve. Journal du Conseil, Conseil International pour l'Exploration de la Mer 36:144–149.

Hassell, M. P. 1978. The dynamics of arthropod predator–prey systems. Princeton University Press, Princeton, New Jersey, USA.

Henry, S. M. 1976. Development of fish passage facilities for American shad at the Holyoke Dam on the Connecticut River. Pages 289–304 in R. St Pierre, editor. Proceedings of the workshop on American shad, University of Massachusetts, Amherst, Massachusetts. U.S. Fish and Wildlife Service, Northeast Region, Newton Corner, Massachusetts, USA.

Hilborn, R. 1985. Simplified calculation of optimum spawning stock size from Ricker's stock recruitment curve. Canadian Journal of Fisheries and Aquatic Sciences 42:1833–1834.

Jones, R. A., P. Minta, and V. A. Crecco. 1976. A review of American shad studies in the Connecticut River. Pages 1–162 in R. St Pierre, editor. Proceedings of the workshop on American shad, University of Massachusetts, Amherst, Massachusetts. U.S. Fish and Wildlife Service, Northeast Region, Newton Corner, Massachusetts, USA.

Lasker, R. 1975. Field criteria for survival of anchovy larvae: the relation between inshore chlorophyll maximum layers and successful first feeding. U.S. National Marine Fisheries Service Fishery Bulletin 73:453–462.

Leggett, W. C. 1969. Studies on the reproductive biology of the American shad (Alosa sapidissima). A comparison of populations from four rivers of the Atlantic seaboard. Doctoral dissertation. McGill University, Montreal, Canada.

Leggett, W. C. 1976. The American shad (Alosa sapidissima), with special reference to its migration and population dynamics in the Connecticut River. American Fisheries Society Monograph 1:169–225.

Leggett, W. C. 1977. Density dependence, density independence, and recruitment in the American shad (Alosa sapidissima) population of the Connecticut River. Pages 3–17 in W. Van Winkle, editor. Proceedings of the conference on assessing the effects of power-plant-induced mortality on fish populations. Pergamon, New York, New York, USA.

Marcy, B. C., Jr. 1976. Early life history studies of the American shad in the lower Connecticut River and the effects of the Connecticut Yankee plant. American Fisheries Society Monograph 1:141–168.

Maxfield, G. H. 1953. The food habits of hatchery-produced pond-cultured shad, Alosa sapidissima, reared to a length of two inches. Chesapeake Biological Laboratory Publication 98, Solomon's, Maryland, USA.

McFadden, J. T. 1977. An argument supporting the

reality of compensation in fish populations and a plea to let them exercise it. Pages 153–183 *in* W. Van Winkle, editor. Proceedings of the conference on assessing the effects of power-plant-induced mortality on fish populations. Pergamon, New York, New York, USA.

Meyer, J. S., C. G. Ingersoll, L. L. McDonald, and M. S. Boyce. 1986. Estimating uncertainty in population growth rates: jackknife vs. bootstrap techniques. Ecology 67:1156–1166.

Miller, R. G., Jr. 1974. The jackknife: a review. Biometrika 61:1–15.

Moffitt, C. M., B. Kynard, and S. G. Rideout. 1982. Fish passage facilities and anadromous fish restoration in the Connecticut River basin. Fisheries (Bethesda) 7(6):2–11.

Nelson, W., M. Ingham, and W. Schaef. 1977. Larval transport and year class strength of Atlantic menhaden *(Brevoortia tyrannus)*. U.S. National Marine Fisheries Service Fishery Bulletin 75:23–41.

O'Leary, J., and H. Booke. 1985. Connecticut River anadromous fish investigations. University of Massachusetts, Federal Aid in Fish Restoration, Project F-45-R-2, Performance Report, Amherst, Massachusetts, USA.

Parrish, R. H., and A. D. MacCall. 1978. Climatic variation and exploitation in the Pacific mackerel fishery. California Department of Fish and Game, Fish Bulletin 167:110.

Peterman, R. M., and G. J. Steer. 1981. Relation between sport-fishing catchability coefficients and salmon abundance. Transactions of the American Fisheries Society 110:585–593.

Reed, R. J., and A. J. Russo. 1976. American shad research in the Connecticut River, Massachusetts, 1976: I. Fecundity, egg retention, sex ratio, and age class composition. University of Massachusetts, Massachusetts Cooperative Fishery Research Unit, Final Report, Amherst, Massachusetts, USA.

Ricker, W. E. 1954. Stock and recruitment. Journal of the Fisheries Research Board of Canada 11:559–623.

Ricker, W. E. 1975. Computation and interpretation of biological statistics of fish populations. Fisheries Research Board of Canada Bulletin 191.

SAS (Statistical Analysis System). 1982. SAS user's guide: statistics. SAS Institute, Cary, North Carolina, USA.

Saunders, P. 1981. Case history: effects of anadromous fish passage at Holyoke Dam, Massachusetts on the population dynamics of American shad in the Connecticut River, 1970–1979. Master's thesis. University of Massachusetts, Amherst, Massachusetts, USA.

Shepherd, J. G. 1982. A versatile new stock–recruitment relationship for fisheries, and the construction of sustainable yields curve. Journal du Conseil, Conseil International pour l'Exploration de la Mer 40:67–75.

Smith, S. J. 1980. Comparison of two methods of estimating the variance of the estimate of catch per unit effort. Canadian Journal of Fisheries and Aquatic Sciences 37:2346–2351.

Stevenson, C. H. 1898. The restricted inland range of the shad due to artificial obstructions and its effect on natural reproduction. U.S. Fisheries Commission Bulletin 17:265–271.

Tukey, J. W. 1958. Bias and confidence in not-quite large samples. Annals of Mathematical Statistics 29:614. (Abstract.)

U.S. Geological Survey. 1967–1985. Water resource data, Connecticut, water years 1966–1984. Water Resources Division, Hartford, Connecticut, USA.

Walburg, C. H., and R. P. Nichols. 1967. Biology and management of the American shad and status of the fisheries. Atlantic coast of the United States, 1960. U.S. Fish and Wildlife Service Special Scientific Report Fisheries 550.

Walters, J. C., and D. Ludwig. 1981. Effects of measurement errors on the assessment of stock–recruitment relationships. Canadian Journal of Fisheries and Aquatic Sciences 38:704–710.

Ware, D. M. 1980. Bioenergetics of stock and recruitment. Canadian Journal of Fisheries and Aquatic Sciences 37:1012–1024.

Watson, J. F. 1970. Distribution and population dynamics of American shad *(Alosa sapidissima,* Wilson), in the Connecticut River above Holyoke Dam, Massachusetts. Doctoral dissertation. University of Massachusetts, Amherst, Massachusetts, USA.

American Fisheries Society Symposium 1:483–491, 1987

Factors Influencing Recruitment of the Atlantic Species of Anguillid Eels

CHRISTOPHER MORIARTY

Department of the Marine Fisheries Research Centre
Abbotstown, Castleknock, Dublin 15, Ireland

Abstract.—Fourteen species of anguilliform eels are present in the Sargasso Sea. Of these, the two *Anguilla* species are represented only by larvae in trawl samples, which suggests that *Anguilla* larvae make an active migration from the species' breeding area. There is an overall tendency for juvenile anguillid eels to migrate gradually upstream so that they reach all accessible watercourses; variation among populations and individuals is extreme. The success of the anguillid eel's stratagem for survival appears to be based in part on avoidance of predators, particularly the congers, and on high population densities of its own species. This is achieved at the cost of a long larval life, followed by the possibility of an exceptionally long subadult existence and the certainty of death after a single spawning. The degree of variation in habits among individuals enables the species to thrive in a wide range of biotopes, from the subarctic to the tropical, and from mountain streams to the depths of the sea.

Schmidt (1923) established that the two Atlantic species of *Anguilla,* European eel *A. anguilla* and American eel *A. rostrata,* spawn in tropical oceanic waters. Boetius and Boetius (1967) showed that the optimum temperature for metabolism of European eels is 25°C. These two observations suggest that these eels are best suited to warm water. In spite of this, fishery statistics show that more than half the catches of anguillid eels (family Anguillidae) are made in temperate waters (FAO 1984).

Fourteen species of anguilliform eels are found in the Sargasso Sea (Post and Tesch 1982). Twelve species are represented by juvenile or adult stages or both. The most abundant eel larvae present in the Sargasso are those of the two *Anguilla* species. Neither of these species, however, has been captured there as juveniles or adults. The presence of other anguilliform eels at all stages of their life cycle shows that it should be physically possible for *Anguilla* species to remain in the Sargasso Sea. The absence of any but larval *Anguilla* suggests an active emigration from the breeding area.

The evolutionary success of the *Anguilla* eels is clearly demonstrated both by the abundance of larvae in the breeding area and by the position of the immature stages in international catch figures. The total catch of the two Atlantic species of *Anguilla* is roughly equal to that of all the conger eels (Congridae), and none of the other eels merit separate treatment in the FAO figures.

The abundance and extensive geographical range of anguillid eels have apparently been achieved by the adoption of migratory habits which bring these fish not only to regions where the ambient temperature is far below the optimum for metabolism but also from highly saline nursery grounds to brackish- or freshwater habitats. Since these eels spawn only at the end of their lives, recruitment may fairly be considered to be in progress until the fish reach the "silver eel" stage, when feeding ceases and the spawning migration begins.

A major factor in recruitment success of anguillid eels appears to lie in the high degree of variability throughout their life cycles. This paper illustrates this variability, first through a review of studies on European eels undertaken within a limited geographical area (the Republic of Ireland), and secondly by reference to data on distribution and migration of the two species of *Anguilla* in the Atlantic Ocean.

The Irish data are important because, although the country's land area is small (67,860 km^2), its drainage systems exhibit a wide variety of trophic and physical conditions. The variations in the physiography of the river systems have presented European eels with a variety of situations likely to influence their migratory habits. The surveys have, moreover, demonstrated a very wide degree of variation in growth rate and feeding among populations which may be ascribed to the trophic state of the waters (Moriarty 1979). One final point of interest in the Irish data is that they have been collected by one worker applying constant sampling techniques.

Irish Data

Sampling Sites and Methods

Juvenile European eels in their first postlarval year are captured as they ascend elver passes at hydroelectric dams situated at the heads of estu-aries in the Rivers Erne and Shannon (Figure 1). The dam on the Erne at Ballyshannon blocks the entire river and it is believed that nearly all ascending eels are caught. The generators on the Shannon at Ardnacrusha are supplied by a head-race canal which carries the major proportion of

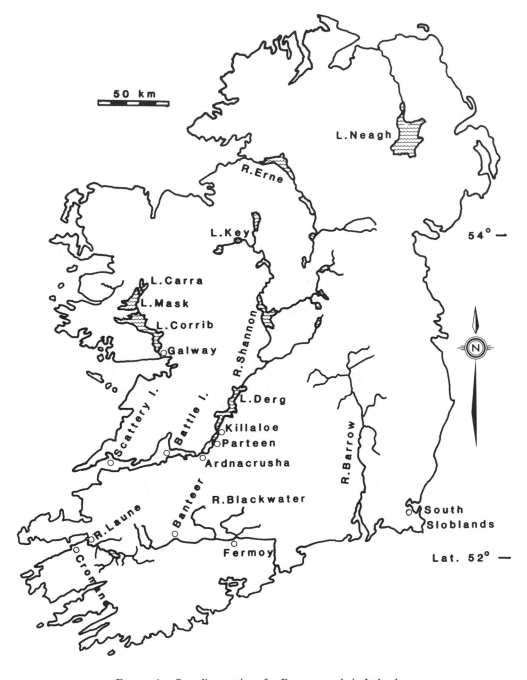

FIGURE 1.—Sampling stations for European eels in Ireland.

the water in the river. However, a substantial flow is maintained in the natural bed of the river. Young eels that have passed through the natural bed of the Shannon are captured in elver passes at a dam at Parteen, which blocks the entire river. These elver passes have been sampled on a monthly basis since 1973.

Details of the methods used in sampling juvenile eels in lakes and rivers were given by Moriarty (1972). Standard commercial "summer" fyke nets are used, each unit consisting of a pair of funnels joined mouth to mouth by a leader. The cod-end mesh is 11 mm knot-to-knot, and the maximum hoop size is 50 cm. Sampling takes place in July and August, and the nets are set in water between 3 and 4 m deep. The unit of effort is one such net fished overnight for one night only. Eel age is determined by reading burned otoliths (Christensen 1964). The validity of this technique was discussed by Moriarty (1983a).

Three river systems and one coastal lagoon have been selected as examples of the migratory patterns of the juvenile eels. With the exception of the eels in the Corrib system (Figure 1), the populations are unexploited. The Blackwater estuary is narrow with strong tidal currents. The freshwater section examined is a broad, slow lowland river. The Shannon estuary is broad and currents are slack. Parteen reservoir is steep sided and narrow in contrast to the lakes upstream, which are broad and have extensive areas of water less than 4 m deep. The Corrib system is one of three lowland lakes joined by very short rivers. Apart from the dam at Parteen, there are no major obstructions to the passage of eels in any of these river systems. The South Sloblands channel is an artificial lake of 100 hectares created by the construction of a sea wall. Its unique feature is that there are no inflowing streams and no natural outlet to the sea. Water leaves the channel either by seepage or by a pumped discharge at times of high rainfall.

Silver eels, caught by commercial nets near the sea on the Shannon and Corrib at Killaloe and Gallway, respectively, have been sampled since 1968 in the course of casual visits to the fisheries.

Upstream Migration

In the Shannon, it is believed that the majority of European eels in their first postlarval year migrate to the hydroelectric dam at Ardnacrusha, where they are trapped for transport upstream. The total annual catch at this point varied from 6,688 to 512 kg between 1977 and 1985. Attempts to correlate the annual variations in eel catch with water temperature, water flow in the river, time of arrival, and length of migration season have all failed. In the River Erne, even greater variation in total annual catch was observed over the same period, from 131 to 4,551 kg.

Details of the migration of juvenile eels at Parteen were given by Moriarty (1986). Most of the eels ascending the fish pass are small and age determinations of a subsample indicated that the majority had spent one winter in the 15-km stretch of river downstream. However, it is clear that many relatively large eels also take part in this active migration, the biggest taken in the course of sampling measured 50 cm. The maximum age determined for these upstream migrants was 10 years. These observations showed that an individual eel, after a more or less sedentary period as long as 10 years, may begin or continue migration farther upstream.

Juveniles

Data on length, age, and catch per unit effort of 12 samples of juvenile eels are presented in Table 1. The length of 45 cm highlighted in the table was selected because virtually all European eels longer than this are female; the age of 11 years was arbitrarily chosen. As distances from the mouths of rivers increased, the numbers of small and young eels and the catch per unit effort decreased. The situation is complicated because neither the lakes nor the different stretches of

TABLE 1.—Variations in length and age frequencies and population density (expressed as CUE, catch per fyke net fished for one night) of European eels according to position in Irish river systems.

River and position	Distance upstream (km)	% <45 cm long (N)	% <11 years old (N)	CUE
River Blackwater				
Estuary	0	65 (1,809)	78 (102)	4.2
Fermoy	30	56 (309)	21 (171)	8.6
Banteer	72	20 (50)	8 (47)	4.5
River Shannon				
Estuary (Battle Island)	0	39 (373)	48 (21)	7.2
Parteen Reservoir	15	59 (57)	63 (27)	1.1
Lake Derg	25	39 (271)	1 (259)	1.6
Lake Key	185	25 (365)	15 (256)	1.5
River Corrib				
Lake Corrib (south)	4	65 (390)	47 (331)	4.4
Lake Corrib (north)	30	48 (345)	28 (270)	1.3
Lake Mask	40	53 (127)	36 (116)	1.2
Lake Carra	50	45 (71)	34 (68)	0.5
South Sloblands				
Channel	0	62 (408)	61 (91)	15.6

river sampled provide similar habitats, but the overall pattern is clear. Extensive data from other watercourses in Ireland support the view that, with increasing distance from the coast, the numbers of eels and the proportions of young eels decrease.

The greatest population density, as indicated by catch per unit effort, was observed in the South Sloblands channel. It was nearly double that of the highest riverine and estuarine figures and more than three times those of any of the lakes. The channel was the only enclosed area into which postlarval eels had easy access but from which juveniles were unable to migrate upstream.

A long-term experiment begun in 1981 (Moriarty 1983b) involves monthly sampling in a bay approximately 1 km square in Lough Derg, the most downstream of a series of lakes on the River Shannon. Changes in length frequency and in catch per unit effort observed between months indicate that the European eel population of the bay is subject to change throughout the season. A regular feature of the changing length frequencies has been the presence of a high proportion of large specimens in April at the end of the eels' hibernation period. The recovery rate of tagged eels decreases throughout the season, supporting the view that the eel population in the bay is not sedentary.

These results contrast with observations made in Lough Key in the headwaters of the same river system (Moriarty 1974). Repeated netting at one point yielded a substantial catch on the first day, after which catches remained extremely small. In this case, it appears that the eels were not engaged in active movements comparable with those in Lough Derg.

Silver Eels

Figure 2 gives lengths at age (postlarval winters) for samples of silver eels from contiguous river systems caught in commercial fisheries close to the sea at Galway and Killaloe (Figure 1). The eels captured in these fisheries migrated from all waters in the respective river systems. They illustrate the variation in growth rate and age at maturity both within and between populations.

Differences in length at maturity between males and females are very pronounced at Killaloe, where the smallest female measurd 46 cm and males rarely measured more than 45 cm. Killaloe males ranged from 5 to 12 years old and from 38 to 47 cm long. Females, in contrast, were 46–98 cm long and 11–30 years old. Variation in length with age was so great that no significant correlations ($P > 0.05$) were observed in linear regressions of length on age within the samples. The Galway eels were much smaller, a situation long known to fishermen and fish merchants alike. The random sample of 36 specimens shown in Figure 2 gives

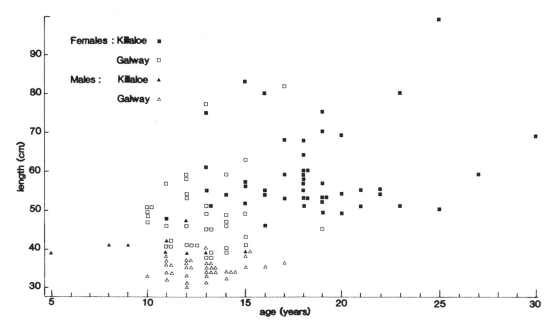

FIGURE 2.—Length at age of silver European eels in random samples from adjacent river systems in Ireland.

an age range for males from 10 to 17 years and a length range from 30 to 39 cm. In this case, the separation of males and females by size is incomplete. Females as small as 36 cm are plentiful, and 70% of the females sampled were less than 50 cm.

Perhaps the most remarkable feature of the data is that age and length at maturity appear to be independent of growth rate: the biggest silver eels from both populations were not the fastest growing and the oldest were not the biggest. One 15-year-old male measured only 39 cm, while a female of the same age attained 83 cm. The oldest silver eel was 30 years and measured 68 cm.

Sexual maturity depends to some extent on size, however. Maximum and minimum lengths for male European eels of 48 and 31 cm, and a minimum length for females of 37 cm, are well established (Tesch 1977). However, the variation within these limits makes it impossible to state categorically the age or length at which an eel will mature. In the examples given, broad generalizations are possible: the Galway eels grow more slowly and mature at smaller sizes than do those from Killaloe. Dietary differences between the respective populations of yellow eels were clearly demonstrated (Moriarty 1972, 1974), and there is no good reason to doubt that these explain much of the variation.

Interspecific Relationships

In the Shannon estuary, sampling took place at two points. The catch at Scattery Island, 12 km from the open sea, comprised 15 conger eels *Conger conger* and one European eel. At Battle Island, 48 km farther upstream, where salinity was much lower, conger eels were absent and European eels abundant. A catch similar to that at Scattery Island was made in the estuary of the River Laune. At Cromane, 4 km from the open sea, the catch comprised nine conger eels and no European eels, whereas 8 km farther upstream, at low salinity, the catch was 14 European eels and no conger eels. The stomach of one conger eel contained two European eels, giving direct evidence of predation on European eels by conger eels.

International Data

Predation on larval anguillid eels in the Sargasso Sea by other fishes appears to be minimal. In the spring of 1979, Appelbaum (1982) examined the stomach contents of about 1,000 pelagic fish representing 25 species. Leptocephali were found in only one of these species, the myctophid *Cera-*

toscopelus warmingii. Of 278 specimens examined, five contained one leptocephalus each. One of these could not be identified and might have been an anguillid, but the other four belonged to other families. There is thus no evidence of heavy predation on the anguillid larvae, in spite of their abundance.

Bottger (1982) conducted plankton hauls in the Sargasso Sea in 1979 using exceptionally fine-mesh nets (55 μm and 100 μm) to collect organisms small enough to serve as food for the young eel larvae. She concluded that the concentration of the potential food supply for larval fish appeared to be similar to the quantities available in other areas, such as the California current, well known for fish larval development.

Perhaps surprisingly, therefore, larval eels emigrate in very large numbers from a region where food is plentiful and the risk of predation appears to be small. They then migrate, eastwards or westwards depending on the species, across areas of ocean where productivity is extremely low (FAO 1981).

Migration of Unpigmented Eels

Migration of unpigmented eels in the sea takes place in winter at temperatures as low as 4.5°C (Deelder 1952) and invasion of fresh water usually begins at 9°C (Tesch 1977). It appears that temperature is more important in determining the beginning of entry to fresh water than is the date. This temperature is a few degrees below that at which the majority of juvenile eels begin to feed after their winter fasting period and may allow these small eels a measure of freedom from cannibalistic predation. It may also be significant that the immigration of glass eels in winter or early spring in northern Europe coincides with the period when the Atlantic mackerel *Scomber scombrus* and other pelagic piscivorous fish are feeding in offshore or warmer waters (Wheeler 1979).

Large populations of European eel are found in the North Sea (Aker and Koops 1979), in spite of the presence of many inflowing rivers in which substantial immigration of elvers may be observed. In such a case, there is no impediment to the movement of elvers into fresh water. Since downstream migration of subadult eels is extremely rare, it must be assumed that a proportion of the young eels remain in estuaries and possibly in the sea without invading inland waters.

Migration in Fresh Water

After arrival in fresh water, the young eels continue to show great variability in the extent to which they migrate further. This was shown in the case of the European eel by Deelder (1984) and Moriarty (1986) and in the case of the American eel by Liew (1982). Deelder described the active migration of European eels in their first freshwater summer as far upstream as 120 km in the Netherlands. Liew's study took place on the St. Lawrence River at the Moses–Saunders dam, 240 km upstream and it is not surprising that no American eels in their first freshwater year were found at this distance from the estuary.

The picture in general is that, as distance from the mouth of the river increases, the numbers of small eels, the numbers of young eels, and the population density all decrease. The important points in the context of recruitment are the evidence, on the one hand, of large eels being plentiful in estuaries and in the lowest reaches of the river systems and, on the other hand, the comparative scarcity of small eels in the upper reaches.

Ireland's longest river, the Shannon, extends 258 km. European eels are present throughout this river system and in all parts of Ireland except where high waterfalls impede their migration. Where rivers are longer, for example, the Rhine in Germany, eels are rare in the upper reaches. It is possible that the presence of milldams and weirs have reduced the extent of their migrations, in such large systems, but it seems likely that the majority of eels reach maturity without ever migrating to the highest accessible points of these rivers.

Observations in Lake Ontario gave similar results to the Lough Derg tag-and-release data. Hurley (1972) tagged and released American eels at different points in the Bay of Quinte, a long, narrow inlet. Recoveries of eels tagged at the downstream end of the bay were low, whereas those at the upstream end were relatively high. It appears from these results that many anguillid eels in the lower reaches of river systems or even of a narrow bay make frequent movements while those that reach upstream habitats are more sedentary.

Fishery Yields

The degree of variation among individuals and populations of anguillid eels has prevented any realistic assessment of the stocks (EIFAC 1985). However, annual catch figures are available and provide data on minimum annual yield which may be compared with data for other eels (FAO 1984). In the case of the northeastern Atlantic, the catch of European eels exceeds that of the larger and faster-growing conger eel; the total catch of *Anguilla* species is roughly equal to that of all the Congridae. North of latitude 50°N in Europe, the European eel catch is more than 10 times that of the conger eel.

Exposure to Predation

Substantial populations of European eel are found in the North Sea, where trawling has been in progress since 1964 (Aker and Koops 1979). Trawling for eels in the sea does not appear to take place in waters to the south. As far north as the Irish Sea, conger eels are caught in trawls but European eels are absent from the catches (Briggs and Warren 1982). Farther south, conger eels are caught in large quantities (FAO 1984). According to Wheeler (1979), conger eels are virtually absent from the North Sea. These observations suggest that coexistence of the two species is unusual; the conger eel's northward range ends well to the south of that of the European eel and the conger eel is unable to tolerate low salinities at any latitude. It appears that substantial populations of postlarval European eels may exist only where salinities or temperatures are too low for the conger eel.

Creutzberg (1961) showed that unpigmented eels in coastal waters may be found at all levels of the water column during incoming tides at night. When tides ebb at night, and at all stages of daytime tides, few elvers can be caught by plankton nets; most elvers move to the bottom and perhaps also burrow into the substrate. The nocturnal activity avoids the risk of predation by birds and perhaps also by those pelagic fishes which hunt by daylight.

Young eels continue to avoid light as they enter fresh water (Deelder 1952). The greatest numbers migrate from sunset to some time after midnight, when the intensity of migration decreases. Exceptions to this rule are frequent and there are many reports of migrations of enormous numbers in daylight. When migration of young European eels reaches its seasonal peak in Ireland's River Erriff, large numbers may be seen ascending damp moss at the edge of the waterfall in bright sunlight some hours before sunset. The numbers migrating, however, increase at dusk (Moriarty 1978).

Predation on the immigrating eels by birds, especially by gulls *Larus* spp., is heavy in the daytime. Predation on eels in their first freshwater season by larger eels may also be observed. As many as 50 newly arrived immigrants were found in the stomach of a large juvenile European eel (Moriarty 1978, 1982).

Discussion

Perhaps the most impressive feature of the life cycle of the two Atlantic anguillid eels is the diversity of behaviour exhibited within each species. The sole common feature is the confinement of the entire population to a single breeding ground. Thereafter, individualistic behaviour patterns seem to be the rule. Uniformity of breeding habit and diversity of individual behaviour is apparent also in the *Anguilla* species of the Southern Hemisphere (Bruton et al. 1987, this volume; Jellyman 1987, this volume).

The failure of any expedition to capture juvenile anguillid eels in the Sargasso Sea implies that the larvae migrate from the breeding ground, generally westwards for the majority of American eels and eastwards for European eels and a small number of American eels (Boetius 1976).

After metamorphosis, postlarvae of both species approach coastal waters, but large numbers may remain in the sea (Aker and Koops 1979). In such cases, some eels which have spent some time in brackish water may migrate downstream and adopt a fully marine life. Those postlarvae which leave the open sea continue to migrate through river estuaries, passing as they do so through populations of resident estuarine eels of both sexes and all sizes.

On arrival in fresh water, some of the elvers settle in the lower reaches of river systems, while others continue their journey for long distances. It appears that the presence of a lake close to the mouth of a river effectively inhibits progress upstream by the elvers. Those eels which settle in the lower reaches may remain there for periods of 10 years or more or may proceed upstream at any time between the observed extremes. This movement takes place throughout the summer, but the months of peak activity vary from year to year.

Many female eels and nearly all males reach the "silver" stage in the lower reaches of river systems. Others, in the course of a life span that may be as long as 35 years (Moriarty 1978), penetrate minor tributaries and lakes great distances from the sea. The presence of small and young eels

downstream with old and large eels upstream would be easy to explain, for instance, by reference to a negative reaction by older eels to increasing population pressure. A feature of eel populations is the continued presence of large eels at all points in any watercourse. Large populations of European eels inhabit purely marine conditions in spite of the general tendency for the species to be catadromous.

The Sargasso Sea is clearly a suitable habitat for anguilliform eels (Post and Tesch 1982) but the two species of *Anguilla* emigrate from it at an early stage in their life cycle. The nature of the mechanism whereby the larvae leave the breeding area is open to question. It may be entirely passive, depending on chance distribution in suitable currents. The possibility of swimming in a chosen direction exists, as does the selection of particular currents by means of vertical migrations. Whatever the mechanism, the larvae disappear from an area of high population density and are found in areas of the ocean where food is scarce. Migration to coastal waters leads once more to a concentration of the population. Returning to the ocean would bring the young eels back to a poor food supply, leaving as an alternative the invasion of brackish and fresh water.

In warm inshore waters where food is plentiful, anguillid eels are exposed to the risk of predation, particularly from conger eels. The conger eels themselves avoid predators by their burrowing habits and nocturnal activity. Presumably, the conger eels would thus compete with anguillid eels for habitat in addition to preying upon them. Anguillid eels therefore move to cool waters and ultimately to fresh water where the only important predatory fishes, in the case of European eels, are conspecific cannibals. Their nocturnal habits give anguillid eels a measure of protection from such diurnal piscivorous birds as cormorants *Phalacrocorax* spp.

However, in cool water, anguillid eels are less effective than coldwater fish in obtaining food; the frequency of empty stomachs in eel samples is unusually high, and growth rates lower, when compared with sympatric species (Moriarty 1972). The slow growth rate of these eels increases the period from postlarva to spawning adult and renders the eels liable to overcrowding. Therefore, they gradually migrate upstream to regions of decreased population pressure and less risk of competition and cannibalism.

The occupation of a single spawning ground leads to an infinite capacity for cross-fertilization, as demonstrated by Helfman et al. (1987, this volume). This militates against the evolution of specialized races including, for example, cold-water forms. The factor which compensates for this lack of specialization is the extent of divergence between the habits of individuals. Few species of fish, if any, can equal the anguillid eel's diversity of habitats. Within any given habitat, eels may be found which are fast growing, slow growing, largely piscivorous, or largely invertebrate feeders. The catadromous habit of anguillid eels, therefore, appears to be merely one of many forms of life-style within the species.

The effectiveness of this strategy may be seen in the fact that the two *Anguilla* species produce more larval young than all the other twelve Sargasso eels together. The yield of the Atlantic species of *Anguilla,* as judged by commercial catch data, is greater than that of the conger eels, which are both larger and faster growing. The essential element in the success of the *Anguilla* eels appears to be their extraordinary ability to accept an almost endless variety of habitats.

References

Aker, E., and H. Koops. 1979. On the trawl fishery on eels by the Federal Republic of Germany in the German Bight. Rapports et Procès-Verbaux des Réunions, Conseil International pour l'Exploration de la Mer 174:7–9.

Appelbaum, S. 1982. Studies on food organisms of pelagic fishes as revealed by the 1979 North Atlantic eel expedition. Helgoländer Meeresuntersuchungen 35:357–367.

Boetius, J. 1976. Elvers, *Anguilla anguilla* and *Anguilla rostrata,* from two Danish localities. Size, body weight, developmental stage and number of vertebrae related to time of ascent. Meddelelser fra Danmarks Fiskeri- og Havundersogelser 7:199–220.

Boetius, I., and J. Boetius. 1967. Studies on the European eel, *Anguilla anguilla* (L.). Meddelelser fra Danmarks Fiskeri- og Havundersogelser 4:339–405.

Bottger, R. 1982. Studies on the small invertebrate plankton of the Sargasso Sea. Helgoländer Meeresuntersuchungen 35:369–383.

Briggs, R. P., and P. Warren. 1982. Fishes trawled from the north Irish Sea by the research vessel "Clione" during April 1980. Irish Naturalists' Journal 20:440–442.

Bruton, M. N., A. H. Bok, and M. T. T. Davies. 1987. Life history styles of diadromous fishes in inland waters of southern Africa. American Fisheries Society Symposium 1:104–121.

Christensen, J. M. 1964. Burning of otoliths, a technique for age determination of soles and other fish. Journal du Conseil, Conseil International pour l'Exploration de la Mer 29:73–81.

Creutzberg, F. 1961. On the orientation of migrating elvers (*Anguilla vulgaris* Turt.) in a tidal area. Netherlands Journal of Sea Research 1:257–338.

Deelder, C. L. 1952. On the migration of the elver (*Anguilla vulgaris* Turt.) at sea. Journal du Conseil, Conseil International pour l'Exploration de la Mer 18:187–218.

Deelder, C. L. 1984. Synopsis of biological data on the eel *Anguilla anguilla* (Linnaeus) 1758. FAO (Food and Agriculture Organization of the United Nations) Fisheries Synopsis 80 (revision 1).

EIFAC (European Inland Fisheries Advisory Commission). 1985. Report of the 1985 working party on eel. FAO (Food and Agriculture Organization of the United Nations), Rome, Italy.

FAO (Food and Agriculture Organization of the United Nations). 1981. Atlas of the living resources of the seas. FAO, Rome, Italy.

FAO (Food and Agriculture Organization of the United Nations). 1984. Catches and landings. FAO Yearbook of Fishery Statistics 56.

Helfman, G. S., D. E. Facey, L. S. Hales, and E. L. Bozeman, Jr. 1987. Reproductive ecology of the American eel. American Fisheries Society Symposium 1:42–56.

Hurley, D. A. 1972. The American eel (*Anguilla rostrata*) in eastern Lake Ontario. Journal of the Fisheries Research Board of Canada 29:535–543.

Jellyman, D. J. 1987. Review of the marine life history of Australasian temperate species of *Anguilla.* American Fisheries Society Symposium 1:276–285.

Liew, P. K. L. 1982. Impact of the eel ladder on the upstream migrating eel *Anguilla rostrata* population in the St. Lawrence River at Cornwall: 1974–1978. Pages 17–22 *in* K. H. Loftus, editor. Proceedings of the 1980 North American eel conference. Ontario Ministry of Natural Resources, Fisheries Technical Report Series 4, Toronto, Canada.

Moriarty, C. 1972. Studies of the eel *Anguilla anguilla* in Ireland. 1. In the lakes of the Corrib System. Irish Fisheries Investigations Series A (Freshwater) 10.

Moriarty, C. 1974. Studies of the eel *Anguilla anguilla* in Ireland. 3. In the Shannon Catchment. Irish Fisheries Investigations Series A (Freshwater) 14.

Moriarty, C. 1978. Eels. Universe Books, New York, New York, USA.

Moriarty, C. 1979. Biological studies of the eel in Ireland. Rapports et Procès-Verbaux des Réunions, Conseil International pour l'Exploration de la Mer 174:16–21.

Moriarty, C. 1982. Behaviour and exposure to bird predation of elvers *Anguilla anguilla* following mass release. Irish Naturalists' Journal 21:220–221.

Moriarty, C. 1983a. Age determination and growth rate of eels *Anguilla anguilla* (L.). Journal of Fish Biology 23:257–264.

Moriarty, C. 1983b. A population study of the eel *Anguilla anguilla* in Meelick Bay, Lough Derg. Fisheries Bulletin (Dublin) 7.

Moriarty, C. 1986. Riverine migration of young eels *Anguilla anguilla* (L.). Fisheries Research (Amsterdam) 4:43–58.

Post, A., and F.-W. Tesch. 1982. Midwater trawl catches of adolescent and adult anguilliform fishes during the Sargasso Sea eel expedition 1979. Helgoländer Meeresuntersuchungen 35:341–356.

Schmidt, J. 1923. The breeding places of the eel. Philosophical Transactions of the Royal Society of London 211:179–208.

Tesch, F.-W. 1977. The eel. Chapman and Hall, London, England.

Wheeler, A. 1979. The fishes of the British Isles and north-west Europe. Michigan State University Press, East Lansing, Michigan, USA.

American Fisheries Society Symposium 1:492–506, 1987
© Copyright by the American Fisheries Society 1987

Switching of Size and Migratory Pattern in Successive Generations of Landlocked Ayu

KATSUMI TSUKAMOTO

Ocean Research Institute, University of Tokyo, Nakano-ku, Tokyo, 164 Japan

RIKIZO ISHIDA

Tokai Regional Fisheries Research Laboratory, Chuo-ku, Tokyo, 104 Japan

KENJI NAKA

Shiga Prefectural Fisheries Experimental Station, Hikone, Shiga, 522 Japan

TAKESHI KAJIHARA

Ocean Research Institute, University of Tokyo, Nakano-ku, Tokyo, 164 Japan

Abstract.—Juveniles of landlocked ayu *Plecoglossus altivelis* in Lake Biwa, Japan, differentiate into small "residents," large "spring migrants," and intermediate "summer migrants." Residents remain in the lake until spawning in autumn and migrants enter inlet streams from early spring until midsummer. The objects of this study were to (1) examine the mechanism of such differentiation in size and migratory pattern and (2) determine the triggering mechanism of upstream migration of the ayu. During both larval recruitment and upstream migration of juveniles, the age and size increased with the time of migration or recruitment; i.e., the timing of migration did not depend on a fixed age or size. Fish with earlier birth dates or larger growth rates (or both) recruited or migrated earlier. Spring migrants consisted of early born fish. Fish remaining in the lake in June were late born or early born with extremely poor growth, and would differentiate into summer migrants and residents. Thyroid activity was lower in summer migrants than in lake residents. These observations suggested that birth date, growth rate, and endocrinological conditions caused the differentiation of migratory patterns. Since small residents apparently spawn earlier than large migrants, their progeny should be early born and migrate early to become large migrants. Conversely, the progeny of large migrants would be born late, would likely become small residents, and would in turn produce early born, early migrating progeny. Thus, switching of size and migratory pattern would occur in successive generations. Three conditions seem necessary for the upstream migration that would sustain this pattern: age and size peculiar to the migration time; endocrinological development to an appropriate state; and changes in environmental factors such as temperature, fish density, or starvation to trigger the migration. These three steps must be filled in specific order.

What drives fishes upstream? The mechanism of upstream migration is one of the most interesting subjects in the study of fish migration. Most diadromous fishes migrate to spawn. Their migration is accompanied by various physiological and ecological changes in maturation, social behavior, feeding habit, etc. These apparent changes related to spawning may mask the nature of the endogenous drive for "movement." Therefore, amphidromous species, which show diadromous migration without any relation to spawning, may be good material for the study of migration.

The ayu *Plecoglossus altivelis* is an amphidromous salmonoid fish with a life span of only 1 year. This is an important species for game fishing as well as fish culture. Ayu spawn adhesive eggs in gravel along the lower reaches of rivers. In autumn, newly hatched larvae, 6 mm long, drift downstream to the sea and spend the winter months there (Iwai 1962). The juveniles (about 60 mm long) start an upstream migration in spring and grow to a length of 150–300 mm by the end of summer, feeding on algae adhering to rocks. In autumn, mature fish spawn and then die. This typical amphidromous pattern is preserved in landlocked populations that are known from Lake Biwa and several other lakes in Japan.

In the landlocked population of Lake Biwa, however, there are differences among fish groups with respect to body size, migration pattern, and reproductive characteristics (Azuma 1970, 1973a, 1973b, 1973c). Such differences in migratory pattern also can be seen in Arctic char *Salvelinus alpinus* (Nordeng 1961), Dolly Varden *Salvelinus malma* (Maekawa 1984), brown trout *Salmo trutta* (Jonsson 1985), sockeye salmon *Oncorhynchus nerka* (Ricker 1938), and masu salmon *Oncorhynchus masou* (Kubo 1980). Differentiation among the ayu in Lake Biwa varies from that in other species since the habitat is restricted to the lake and its inlet streams. If we distinguish Lake Biwa ayu by time of their upstream migration, they may be roughly divided into three groups: (1) spring migrants, which go upstream in spring (March–May) and grow large (to about 150 mm) in the inlet streams of the lake; (2) summer migrants, which start the migration in summer (June–August); and (3) residents, which remain in the lake throughout their lives until their terminal spawning migration to lower stream reaches in late summer or early autumn. Residents mature at small sizes (about 80 mm, called dwarfism by Azuma 1973c). Both migrants and residents spawn in the same inlet streams but in different reaches. Examination of the differences between migrants and residents in the landlocked population may help to clarify the migration mechanisms of amphidromous fish. Furthermore, the Lake Biwa fish do not have the problem of changing osmoregulation faced by their marine counterparts, which may simplify interpretation of migration patterns.

Many biological developments are size dependent. Size is, however, a function of age, and we also should examine age as a factor controlling the motivation for migration. Although the ages at migration have been examined for salmon, a time scale measured in years is too coarse for good analysis of the effects that annual changes in environmental factors have on ontogeny, especially for short-lived fish like the ayu. The discovery of daily growth increments on fish otoliths (Pannella 1971) has provided fisheries biologists with new levels of information (Radtke and Dean 1982), and this technique has been applied advantageously to the ayu (Tsukamoto and Kajihara, in press). We determined the age in days for fish in our study and compared the age, size, birth date, growth rate, and thyroid activity of larvae and juveniles of behaviorally and morphologically differentiated groups in order to clarify the mechanisms by which migratory patterns vary among landlocked ayu. We also determined the role of birth date and growth rate in the upstream migrations of marine amphidromous stocks, and we present a "triple jump hypothesis" for the triggering mechanism of upstream migration.

Methods

Experimental design.—The study consisted of four parts. During (1) recruitment of larval and (2) upstream migration of juvenile landlocked ayu in Lake Biwa, the ages, sizes, birth dates, and growth rates of the fish were examined. The results were compared with those obtained during (3) upstream migrations of amphidromous marine stocks to confirm analogies of habitat transition. Lastly, factors causing (4) migratory pattern differentiation in the lake stock were determined from analyses of birth date, growth rate, and thyroid activity.

Larval recruitment of landlocked fish.—In Lake Biwa, samples of larval ayu were taken on three nights at the time of each new moon in October, November, and December 1982, during routine cruises of the *Biwako-maru* of Shiga Prefectural Fisheries Experimental Station (Figure 1; Table 1). A square-frame larval net (1 × 2 m at the mouth, 10 m long, and 0.68-mm mesh in the 2-m-long cod end) was towed 28 times in each sampling period, 500–1,000 m offshore where the bottom was 30–70 m deep. Each tow was conducted at a speed of 1.6 m/s and the net fished mainly in the 7–8 m layer from the surface. Ten fish were randomly collected from each sample of a tow and were preserved in 70% ethanol. After standard lengths were measured, sagitta otoliths were extracted and daily growth increments were counted by the method described below.

Upstream migration of landlocked fish.—Juvenile ayu which ascended the River Ado from Lake Biwa were trapped with a commercial fish weir about 500 m upstream from the river mouth (Figure 1). From April to July 1982, about 30 fish were collected monthly (Table 1) and preserved in 70% ethanol for age determination and examination of meristic characters. Fish ascending River Ado in March 1982 were scarce during the early period of the migration season. Therefore, a March 1982 sample was taken from the nearby River Chinai, and March 1983 ascendants in the Ado were analyzed as well.

Upstream migration of amphidromous fish.— Juvenile ayu migrating upstream from the sea were collected from two rivers about once every 2 weeks in spring. In the River Yabe, flowing to the Ariake-kai (Figure 1), fish were sampled three times with a dip net at the fishway of a little dam about 7 km upstream from the river mouth (Table 1). A beach seine was used to collect four samples just inside the mouth of River Tenryu, flowing to

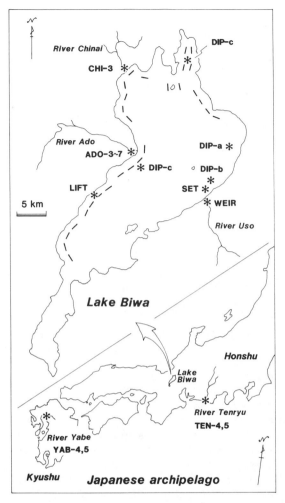

FIGURE 1.—Locality maps for the ayu study. Asterisks show places where juvenile fish were sampled; sample codes are given nearby. Each bar along the coast of Lake Biwa represents a larval-net tow during the *Biwako-maru* cruise.

the Enshu-nada (Figure 1). Samples were fixed in 70% ethanol and age was determined from otoliths.

Migratory patterns of landlocked fish.—Four types of fishing gear were used to assess migration patterns of Lake Biwa ayu. Weirs ("yana" in Japanese) were used as described above to capture upstream migrants. A set net with trap ("eri") was used to catch fish moving along the coast about 0–500 m offshore. A large push-type lift net ("oisade-ami") was used to collect fish in shallow water (<1 m) near the beach where they sometimes schooled in small numbers (or appeared without schooling behavior). Finally, a dip

net ("okisukui," 1×2 m at the mouth) was mounted on the bow of a powerful boat driven rapidly into the center of a high-density ayu school, or pod ("maki"), in the lake. Swarming of ayu juveniles was a remarkable behavior of the dwarf type observed both offshore in central parts of the lake and near shore from early summer to fall (Naka and Mizutani 1974). Both the DIP-a and DIP-c samples (Table 1) included fish from several schools, but DIP-b was a sample from a single school. Samples for age determination were preserved in 70% ethanol, those for histological analysis of the thyroid gland in 10% formalin. Details of each sample are listed in Table 1.

Age determination.—Based on daily growth increments on sagitta otoliths, the ages of ayu could be easily and accurately determined within a 2% error even for fish 300 d old (Tsukamoto and Kajihara, in press). A pair of sagittae were mounted in Euparal on a glass microscope slide. All rings outside a 15-μm radius were counted through a light microscope with two sets of arrow image projectors (Nikon Teaching Head) or with a camera lucida at 600× magnification. Sagittae have radii of about 15 μm at hatching with 2–7 embryonic increments. The mean of the counts by two readers was accepted as the age when the counts agreed within 5%. Birth dates and catch dates were expressed as Julian dates, which were used in all statistical analyses.

Growth rate.—Body length was closely related to the sagitta radius for larval and juvenile ayu, and the radius increased linearly with fish age (Tsukamoto and Umezawa, unpublished). From these observations, it could be assumed that the growth of the ayu before the upstream migration was roughly linear. Thus we simply calculated the growth rate of each fish from the estimated age and the difference between body length at sampling and mean body length at hatching.

Histology of the thyroid gland.—Thyroid gland activity was compared among WEIR, SET, DIP-a, and DIP-b samples. The head and chest of preserved juveniles were imbedded in paraffin, sectioned in a frontal (horizontal) plane at thicknesses of 5 μm, and stained with hematoxylin and eosin. The height of epithelial cells of a thyroid follicle was measured on the orthogonal axis set arbitrarily in the section where the area of the follicle was observed to be maximum among the consecutive sections; four measurements within a follicle were averaged, and these were, in turn, averaged over 10 thyroid follicles per fish.

Meristic characters and body form.—Soft

TABLE 1.—Samples examined in the age analysis of ayu.

Sample code	Sampling date	Number of fish	Standard length (mm)[a]	Gear	Locality	Behavior
			Larval recruitment			
OCT	Oct 17–18, 1982	229	22.2±3.7	Larva net	Lake Biwa	?
NOV	Nov 13–14, 1982	186	25.5±2.2	Larva net	Lake Biwa	?
DEC	Dec 13–14, 1982	170	28.8±2.9	Larva net	Lake Biwa	?
			Upstream migration of landlocked fish, Lake Biwa			
ADO-3	Mar 16, 1983	31	84.4±5.4	Weir	River Ado	Upstream migration
CHI-3	Mar 24, 1982	30	69.6±3.4	Weir	River Chinai	Upstream migration
ADO-4	Apr 13, 1982	25	71.1±2.6	Weir	River Ado	Upstream migration
ADO-5	May 11, 1982	28	74.9±3.5	Weir	River Ado	Upstream migration
ADO-6	Jun 15, 1982	22	79.1±4.1	Weir	River Ado	Upstream migration
ADO-7	Jul 20, 1982	3	80.8±5.0	Weir	River Ado	Upstream migration
			Upstream migration of amphidromous fish			
TEN-4a	Apr 6, 1982	19	60.6±9.7	Seine	River Tenryu	Upstream migration
TEN-4b	Apr 20, 1982	19	54.5±9.0	Seine	River Tenryu	Upstream migration
TEN-5a	May 4, 1982	18	54.8±6.9	Seine	River Tenryu	Upstream migration
TEN-5b	May 14, 1982	20	56.8±8.8	Seine	River Tenryu	Upstream migration
YAB-4	Apr 20, 1982	30	69.0±5.4	Dip net	River Yabe	Upstream migration
YAB-5a	May 4, 1982	28	70.2±10.9	Dip net	River Yabe	Upstream migration
YAB-5b	May 17, 1982	29	70.3±8.7	Dip net	River Yabe	Upstream migration
			Behavioral differentiation			
WEIR	Jun 19, 1984	29	75.3±6.9	Weir	River Uso	Upstream migration
SET	Jun 20, 1984	30	72.2±5.8	Set net	Lake Biwa	?
DIP-a	Jun 19, 1984	30	69.5±4.6	Dip net	Lake Biwa	Schooling in the lake
DIP-b	Jun 19, 1984	30	91.9±5.0	Dip net	Lake Biwa	Schooling in the lake
DIP-c	Jun 15, 1984	22	70.5±5.6	Dip net	Lake Biwa	Schooling in the lake
LIFT	Apr 5, 1984	17	48.9±8.1	Lift net	Lake shore	?

[a] Mean±SD.

X-ray photos were taken of fish in samples ADO-3, -5, and -6 and WEIR, SET, and DIP-a. Numbers of vertebrae, and of dorsal and anal fin pterygiophores were counted for each fish. Body height and standard length were measured with slide callipers.

Data analysis.—Least-squares regressions were obtained for the relationships between catch date and biological variables in each sample such as age, size, birthdate, and growth rate and for the logarithmic relationships between standard length and body height. *F*-tests were used in covariance analyses to test for significant differences between two slopes; *t*-tests were used to test the significance of differences in means of variables between migrants and residents. Biological parameters of monthly samples and the height of follicular epithelial cells of migrants and residents were compared by χ^2 tests.

Results

Larval Recruitment of Landlocked Fish

Both age and size of ayu larvae in Lake Biwa increased with catch date ($P < 0.001$), and monthly samples differed significantly ($P <$ 0.001). The minimum age and size (standard length) of all samples in October were 22 d and 14.5 mm, respectively; the maxima in December were 102 d and 40.0 mm (Figure 2). Regressions between age and size for each monthly sample were different from each other ($P < 0.001$). The mean birth date of each monthly sample was different from the others ($P < 0.001$). The relationship between birth date and catch date was significant ($P < 0.001$). This showed that the earlier a fish hatched, the earlier it recruited to the sampling ground (Figure 3).

The growth rate, as a whole, decreased with birth date ($P < 0.001$); i.e., the earlier a fish was born, the better it grew (Figure 4). Furthermore, the growth rate also decreased with catch date. For fish born during September 18–21, for example, growth rates shown by October, November, and December samples were 0.55, 0.40, and 0.32 mm/d; for those of fish born during September 22–25, rates were 0.54, 0.40, and 0.31 mm/d respectively ($P < 0.001$). For fish with roughly the same birthdate, the individuals with the greater growth rate recruited to the larval habitat earlier than those with a lesser growth rate.

These results suggested (1) that a considerable

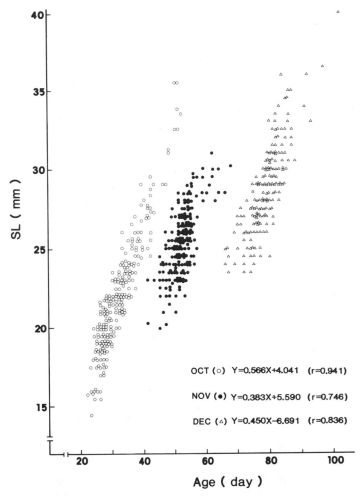

FIGURE 2.—Relationships between age *(X)* and standard length *(SL, Y)* of ayu larvae recruited into a Lake Biwa nursery habitat, October–December 1982.

portion of fish in a monthly cohort might have moved out of the study area and that new fish were recruited to it in successive months, i.e., that use of the nursery habitat was transient; (2) that birth date and growth rate determined the time of the recruitment; and (3) that fish age and size were peculiar to the time of recruitment, although the problems of net avoidance and mesh size might have caused a slight sample bias.

Upstream Migration of Landlocked Fish

Both age and size of juvenile ayu caught by the Ado weir were linearly correlated with the time of upstream migration ($P < 0.001$; Figure 5). Successive ages at migration time were different one from another ($P < 0.005$) except between the two March samples (one of them from River Chinai)

and between May and June ($P > 0.1$). Size showed a similar tendency except for the March 1983 datum (Figure 5). The minimum age and size at migration were 193 d (mean of ADO-3) and 84.4 mm (mean of CHI-3). Clear correspondence between mean birth date and the time of upstream migration was observed (Figure 6). The earlier a fish was born in autumn, the earlier it started upstream in spring ($P < 0.001$).

Upstream Migration of Amphidromous Fish

In the amphidromous marine populations of ayu associated with the Rivers Tenryu and Yabe, age at upstream migration also increased with the time of migration ($P < 0.001$). In neither river, however, did size increase with the time of migration ($P > 0.05$), which might have been due to the

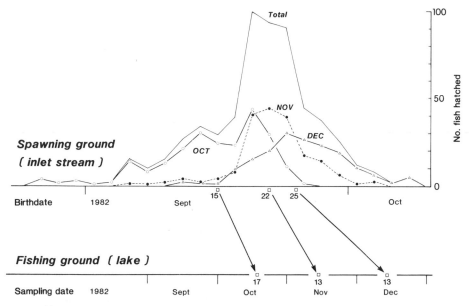

FIGURE 3.—Distributions of birth dates of ayu in a spawning tributary to Lake Biwa, as calculated from samples of larvae taken in the lake during October–December 1982. Dates along the birth date axis are mean hatching dates calculated from the corresponding samples dated along the bottom axis.

short sampling periods (38 and 27 d in the Tenryu and Yabe, respectively). The minimum ages at migration were 150 and 180 d and the minimum sizes were 54.5 and 69.0 mm in the River Tenryu and the River Yabe, respectively. The age and size of ayu in the Tenryu were smaller than those of the Yabe at the same time of migration ($P <$ 0.01), perhaps because of the differing distances between sampling site and river mouth. For both rivers, there were clear correspondences between

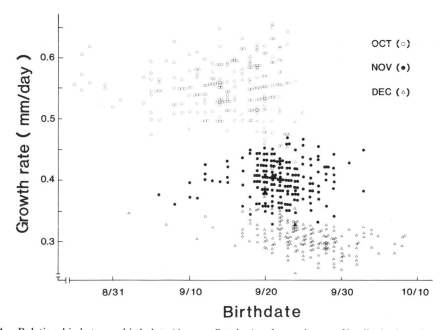

FIGURE 4.—Relationship between birth date (August–October) and growth rate of landlocked ayu larvae sampled from Lake Biwa during October–December 1982.

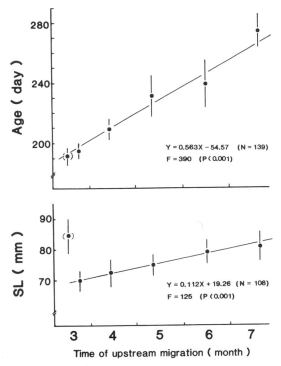

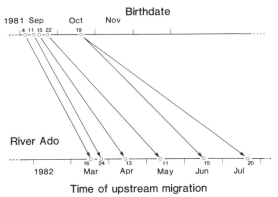

FIGURE 6.—Correspondence between mean birth date of juvenile ayu and the time of their migration from Lake Biwa to the weir on the River Ado. (The March 24 sample was from the River Chinai; the March 16 sample was taken in the Ado during 1983.)

FIGURE 5.—Changes in mean age and standard length (SL) of juvenile ayu with the time of their upstream migration to the River Ado weir, April (month 4) to July (month 7) 1982. The dots in parentheses represent the earliest fish going upstream in March 1983. The other March sample was from the River Chinai in 1982. Vertical bars are standard deviations. In the equations, X (time of upstream migration) is measured in Julian days from January 1 of the previous year.

birth date and the time of upstream migration ($P <$ 0.005; Figure 7), similar to that of the landlocked population (Figure 6). Mean birthdate of the Yabe population was earlier than that of the Tenryu population ($P < 0.001$). Growth rate decreased with the time of migration in both rivers ($P < 0.05$; Figure 8); furthermore, the regression for the Tenryu was lower in elevation than that for the Yabe ($P < 0.001$), though the slopes did not differ significantly ($P > 0.05$).

Migratory Patterns of Landlocked Fish

The six samples of Lake Biwa ayu examined for migratory patterns all had late birth dates in the latter half (October–November) of the spawning season (Table 2). Except for DIP-b with larger size fish and LIFT with a much earlier catch date, the other four groups did not differ greatly in their age, size, birth date, or growth rate, although some combinations differed. Fish in DIP-b, repre-

senting a high-density school of large fish, had an especially late mean birth date ($P < 0.01$) and a much larger growth rate ($P < 0.01$) compared with other groups. Fish in group LIFT had a larger variance in age, size, and birth date than those in the other five groups ($P < 0.05$), although their growth rate was roughly the same as the others, except DIP-b fish. This suggested that group LIFT consisted of fish with various histories but commonly with small growth rates.

Fish in groups SET and DIP-a, -b, and -c remained in the lake until June, whereas those in ADO-3, -4, and -5 and CHI-3 (Table 1) went upstream as spring migrants. The relationships

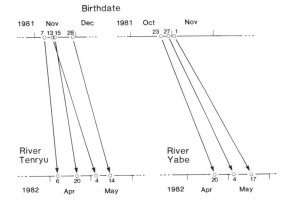

FIGURE 7.—Correspondence between mean birth date of amphidromous ayu and the time of their upstream migrations to the lower reaches of the Rivers Tenryu and Yabe.

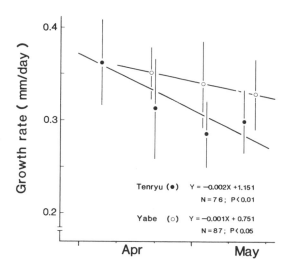

Tenryu (●) Y = −0.002X +1.151
N = 7 6 ; P⟨0.01

Yabe (○) Y = −0.001X + 0.751
N = 87 ; P⟨0.05

Time of upstream migration

FIGURE 8.—Relationships between mean growth rate of amphidromous ayu and the time of their upstream migration in the Rivers Tenryu and Yabe. Vertical bars are standard deviations. In the equations, X (time of upstream migration) is measured in Julian days from January 1 of the previous year.

between birth date and growth rate (Figure 9) for these two behaviorally different types suggested the following conclusions. (1) Most of the fish born in the early half (August–September) of the spawning season became spring migrants. (2) The fish remaining in the lake in June consisted mainly of late-born (October–November) fish and partly of early born fish with extremely poor growth; these would differentiate into summer migrants and residents. Although 35% of the LIFT group was born in the earlier half of the spawning season, these fish might have remained in the lake after April (catch date) since their growth rates were low (Table 2).

The mean height of follicular epithelial cells (HFEC) in the thyroid glands of WEIR summer migrants was significantly lower than it was in the SET, DIP-a, and DIP-b fish that remained in the lake ($P < 0.05$), but did not differ among the latter three groups ($P > 0.05$; Table 3). The HFEC variance for WEIR fish was greater than for SET and DIP-a fish ($P < 0.05$), but not significantly different from that of the large DIP-b fish. The large WEIR variance stemmed from the frequency distribution of HFEC measurements, which had a mode less than 7 μm and a tail that placed 20% of the means above 11 μm. Fish in the latter 20% had follicles with very scanty colloid

TABLE 2.—Age, birth date, size, and growth rate of ayu in behaviorally differentiated groups, Lake Biwa. All were sampled in mid-June except sample LIFT was taken in April (see Table 1).

Sample code	Age (d)[a]	Mean birth date	Standard length (mm)[a]	Growth rate (mm/d)[a]
WEIR	249±17	Oct 14	75.3±6.9	0.27±0.03
SET	254±15	Oct 10	72.2±5.8	0.25±0.02
DIP-a	256±13	Oct 7	69.5±4.6	0.24±0.02
DIP-b	230±12	Nov 2	91.9±5.0	0.36±0.03
DIP-c	249±20	Oct 9	70.5±5.6	0.27±0.03
LIFT	175±30	Oct 12	48.9±8.1	0.25±0.02

[a] Mean±SD.

and high epithelium, whereas colloid volumes of the modal follicles did not differ greatly from those of other groups. These results showed that fish going upstream had thyroid follicles that were hypofunctioning, or were hyperactive with little hormone reserve, in contrast to the groups remaining in the lake, which had both high thyroid activity and much reserve. In addition, the rela-

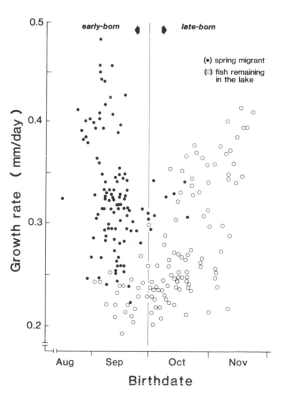

FIGURE 9.—Relationship between birth date and growth rate of juvenile Lake Biwa ayu. Solid circles represent fish that migrated upstream during March–May. Open circles represent fish that stayed in the lake until June.

TABLE 3.—Thyroid activity of behaviorally differentiated groups of ayu, Lake Biwa.

Sample code	Number of fish	HFEC[a] (μm)	Standard length (mm)[b]	Body weight(g)[b]
WEIR	20	8.4±3.3	90.7±9.8	8.9±3.2
SET	20	11.4±2.1	82.7±10.5	7.3±3.0
DIP-a	11	12.1±1.7	74.1±6.1	5.0±1.4
DIP-b	9	11.0±2.1	94.0±5.4	10.4±2.0

[a] Mean±SD of height of follicular epitherial cells (HFEC).
[b] Mean±SD.

tion between size and HFEC of samples in Table 3 was not significant ($P > 0.05$).

There were no significant differences among nonmigrants, spring migrants, and summer migrants for three meristic characters, the numbers of vertebrae and dorsal and anal fin pterygiophores ($P > 0.05$; Table 4). Slopes of regressions between the logarithms of standard length and body height were not significantly different from one another ($P > 0.05$) but their elevations differed among WEIR, SET, and DIP-a data ($P < 0.05$; Figure 10) and between ADO-6 and the two groups, ADO-3 and -5 ($P < 0.01$; Figure 10).

Discussion

Migratory Patterns of Landlocked Ayu

Azuma (1970, 1973a, 1973b, 1973c) classified the landlocked ayu in Lake Biwa into four groups (A–D in Table 5) based on the differences in morphological and ecological features. He suggested that the Lake Biwa fish were undergoing intraspecific differentiation, although its degree is not advanced. The most important difference between his hypothesis and our results is the correspondence we found between birth date and the time of upstream migration; Azuma suggested, in contrast, that fish hatching early remained in the

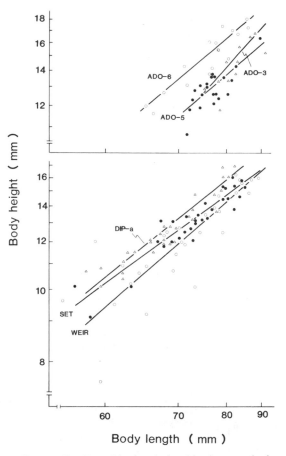

FIGURE 10.—Logarithmic relationships between body length and body height for Lake Biwa ayu collected at the River Ado weir (top) and for a behaviorally differentiated group collected in June (bottom). Sample codes along the lines correspond to those in Figure 1; triangles, solid circles, and open circles indicate ADO-3, -5, and -6 in top and DIP-a, SET, and WEIR in bottom, respectively.

TABLE 4.—Meristic characters and adjusted mean of body height in groups of juvenile ayu with different migration patterns in Lake Biwa.

Sample code	Number of fish	Standard length[a] (mm)	Number of vertebra[a]	Number of pterygiophore[a] Dorsal[b]	Anal[c]	Body height (mm)	Migration pattern
				Time-series analysis			
ADO-3	11	82.5±4.8	60.5±0.7	10.1±0.3	15.0±0.4	10.9	Spring migrant
ADO-5	21	76.9±4.2	60.6±0.5	10.2±0.5	15.1±0.5	10.9	Spring migrant
ADO-6	16	76.6±6.9	60.4±0.8	10.3±0.4	14.9±0.6	11.5	Summer migrant
				Group analysis			
WEIR	30	72.3±9.3	60.3±0.6	10.2±0.4	14.8±0.7	11.0	Summer migrant
SET	30	73.9±7.2	60.5±0.7	10.2±0.4	14.7±0.7	11.2	Nonmigrant
DIP-a	30	69.2±6.9	60.4±0.8	10.1±0.5	14.9±0.6	11.4	Nonmigrant

[a] Mean±SD. [b] Interneural spine. [c] Interhemal spine.

TABLE 5.—Correspondence of terminology for landlocked ayu used by Azuma (1973c) and in this study.

This study		Azuma (1973c)					
Terminology	Sample code	Terminology	Birth date	Migration (time)	Adult size	Body form	Number of fin rays[a]
Stream population							
Spring migrant	ADO-3,4,5, CHI-3	A: Early ascending group	Late (Oct–Nov)	Feeding upstream migration (Feb–Mar); spawning downstream migration (Sep–Oct)	Large (>100 mm)	Running water type	D: more A: more
Summer migrant	ADO-6,7, WEIR	B: Late-ascending group	Intermediate (Sep–Oct)	Feeding upstream migration (May–Jul); spawning downstream migration ? (Sep)	Intermediate (75–85 mm?)	Intermediate type	D: less A: less
Lake population							
Resident (Autumn migrant)	Dip-a,b,c? SET? LIFT?	C: Group of small size	Early (Aug–Sep)	Spawning upstream migration (Aug–Sep)	Small (dwarf) (60–80 mm)	Standing water type	D: more A: less
		D: Group of large size	?	?	Large (110–120 mm?)	Standing water type	D: more A: less

[a] D = dorsal; A = anal.

lake and the late-hatching fish went upstream in spring (Table 5). Azuma emphasized the seasonal segregation of spawning among the four groups, associated with changes in water temperature (Figure 11), which might cause the morphological differences. We could not find the differences in meristic characters among fish resident in the lake and spring and summer migrants, although the fish showed significant differences in body forms which agree with Azuma's (1973a) distinction

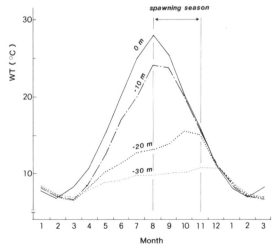

FIGURE 11.—Annual changes in water temperature (WT) of Lake Biwa at the surface and at depths of 10, 20, and 30 m.

between standing water type and running water type (Table 5). And as he pointed out, there was good correspondence between behavior and body height: migrants had less body height than fish in the lake (Figure 10, bottom) and the earlier the migrants had the lower the body height (Figure 10, top). It was noteworthy, however, that there was no such morphological difference ($P > 0.05$) between ADO-6 summer migrants in 1982 and DIP-a fish remaining in the lake in 1984, suggesting that there is no absolute relation between body form and migratory pattern. The differences in regression elevation did not seem to be substantial (Huxley 1932) and body form changes easily with environmental conditions (Kafuku 1966; GFES 1978). It was known that the rate of body height increase diminishes among fish inhabiting shallow water (Maruyama and Ishida 1978). Consequently, the apparent correspondence between behavior and body form shown in Figure 10 may be derived from short-term effects of habitat transition or accidental differences in feeding condition. Moreover, enzyme variation was not significant between residents and spring migrants (Nishida and Takahashi 1978; SFES 1982). Variation in body form might merely result from differences in environmental conditions and not from genetic isolation. Although segregation of spawning seasons exists and spawning areas of migrants and lake residents are located in different reaches of a stream, these factors do not maintain spatial isolation of larvae in the lake. A mark–recapture study, in which an isozyme was used as a genetic marker, showed that the released fish spread widely through the lake and seemed to mix completely with the wild larvae (SFES 1983). It was apparent in the present study that larvae hatched at the same spawning season did not necessarily recruit at the same time into and out of a habitat, but that fish with the same growth rate did move together (Figure 4); general correspondence existed between birth date and catch date, however (Figure 3).

Eggs and larvae can experience quite different temperatures at the beginning and the end of a spawning season; temperatures can decline about 13°C over this interval both at the stream spawning ground and at the lake surface (Figure 11). Temperature affects not only somatic development but also food abundance, and thus might also change the ontogeny of behavioral characteristics such as feeding, schooling, and vertical migration. We found that the growth rate of ayu, which integrates all these factors, affects the time of the recruitment (Figure 4). In addition, it was apparent that the chance match or mismatch of ayu larvae to the patchiness of food also influences the growth rate regardless of birth date. The maximum size of larvae observed in their habitat, 35–40 mm standard length, agrees with the size at

which stomach development is completed (Yamazaki 1986). At this same size, jumping behavior develops rapidly, which is closely related to the behavior of upstream migration (Uchida 1986). Although the mesh size of a net seriously affects the lower size limit of a sample, the minimum size and age of the larvae sampled in the lake roughly coincided with the minima (13 mm, 21 d) of larvae of the amphidromous population collected in the surf zone (Tsukamoto, et al. unpublished). These results suggest that ayu must make transitions in behavior or habitat at lengths of about 15 and 35 mm and that the grounds where we sampled larvae in the lake are a habitat peculiar to a certain period of their life history.

The process of differentiation among landlocked ayu might be summarized as follows. Most of the early hatched fish recruit early into the larval habitat in the lake and go upstream early as spring migrants (Figure 12). Late-born fish and early born fish with poor growth recruit late to the larval habitat, remain in the lake until the end of spring and afterwards, and separate into summer migrants and residents according to their endocrinological conditions. A quantitative analysis, however, was extremely difficult since commercial fishing effort in the lake was high for every stage except early larvae and mature fish, and a considerable portion of each group seemed to be caught before each upstream migration. Spawning

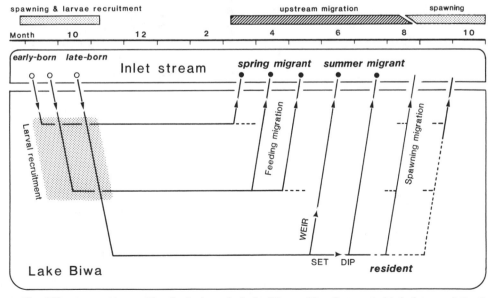

FIGURE 12.—Migratory patterns of landlocked ayu in Lake Biwa, with reference to birth dates and the times of recruitment and upstream migration.

ayu that had been resident in the lake throughout the summer before finally moving upstream in early autumn were not dealt with in this study because the accuracy of age determination decreased for fish over 300 d old (Tsukamoto and Kajihara, in press). Analysis of this group by scanning electron microscopy is a subject remaining for the future.

The spawning season of small residents is earlier (1 month or more) than that of large migrants. Thus, the progeny of small residents must be born early and so go upstream early to be large migrants. That is, small residents would produce large migrants in the next generation (Figure 13). On the other hand, large migrants mature late and their progeny, with late birth dates, have the potential to remain in the lake and become small residents. Thus, there would be cyclic switching in size and migratory pattern in successive generations.

Bilton (1971) presented a similar hypothesis on alternation of age and size at return in successive generations of sockeye salmon. Precisely speaking, however, there is an intermediate type of summer migrant between small residents and large migrants of the ayu. Early born fish with poor growth rates remain in the lake (Figure 9). Growth, and thus migratory pattern, might be determined by chance availability of food. Therefore, the genes of some small residents and large migrants would be well mixed through successive generations, contrary to the isolation between even-year and odd-year spawning populations of pink salmon *Oncorhynchus gorbuscha* (Ishida 1966). In conclusion, it was not genetic isolation but the differences in birth date, growth rate, and endocrinological condition that caused the size and migratory pattern differences in landlocked ayu in Lake Biwa.

According to the categories of heterochrony (Gould 1977), small residents would belong to the

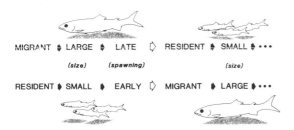

FIGURE 13.—Cyclic switching of fish size and migratory pattern in successive generations of landlocked ayu in Lake Biwa.

class of progenesis and large migrants roughly to that of hypermorphosis, where the age at maturation of amphidromous fish (1 year) is standardized. Switching of categories of heterochrony in successive years must be a remarkable phenomenon. At present, however, we do not have sufficient knowledge to explain it. It might be said that the ayu is an evolutionarily "flexible" species.

Triggering Mechanism for Upstream Migration

Various biological phenomena depend on age or size, such as development of various organs, metamorphosis, maturation (Alm 1959), and smoltification (Kato 1983). Various environmental conditions weaken the close relationships between age or size and biological developments by modifying the developmental time table. On the other hand, size is closely related to age as a function of time. Differentiation of the ayu stomach depends on both age and size (Yamazaki 1986). Development of jumping behavior by ayu, which is closely related to migration behavior, seems to be controlled by both age and size (Uchida 1986). Age and size cannot be separated in biological development. As in the case of maturation (Alm 1959), it appears that there must be minimum necessary conditions of both age and size for upstream migration by ayu. These conditions seem to be about 130 d and 50 mm for amphidromous marine populations and 180 d and 60 mm for the landlocked population. Although the cause of the age and size differences between these two populations is still unclear, the landlocked fish spawn 1–2 months earlier than the marine ones. Furthermore, environmental conditions such as water temperature, salinity, and food abundance may affect the age and size at migration.

Some of the results obtained for the ayu agree with those from studies of salmonid fishes. The age and size at return varies greatly in species such as chum salmon *Oncorhynchus keta* (Semko 1954; Sano 1966), sockeye salmon (Bilton 1971), Arctic char (Nordeng 1961), and brown trout (Jonsson 1985). Among fish born in the same year, it is apparent that the age that salmon or trout return to spawn increases with the year they migrate from the nursery stream. The correspondence is 1:1 on the yearly scale with which these fish typically are aged. A closer comparison with the ayu results cannot be made because of the differences in time scale. Sockeye salmon returning at age 5 were smaller and showed a faster growth rate than those returning at age 6 (Egorova, unpublished: cited in Hanamura 1966). This finding is consistent with our results; ayu size increased with the migration time and fish with larger growth rates started their migrations earlier. However, change in size at migration should be considered carefully; in our study, for example, the earliest migrants one year were larger than later migrants the preceding year (Figure 5). Hotta (1953) reported that size decreased with the time of migration of an amphidromous marine ayu population. It was unclear whether or not this was due to differences in year, area, or population.

Landlocked and amphidromous marine ayu showed some commonalities in our study. In both situations, migration or habitat transition required a minimum age or size, but did not start at a fixed age or size. Fish with the earlier birth date or the faster growth rate migrated or recruited earlier; i.e., the birth date and the growth rate had the potential to determine the timing of migration or habitat transition. Thus, the age and size peculiar to the migration time seemed to be necessary conditions for upstream migrations by ayu (Figure 14). Birth date and growth rate determined the age and size at migration. This process could be a fundamental first step in the triggering mechanism of migration.

Although the three groups of Lake Biwa ayu (WEIR, SET, and DIP-a; Table 2) had roughly the same conditions of age, size, birth date, and growth rate, some went upstream and the others remained in the lake. Some of the fish remaining in the lake (DIP-b) had greater size and growth rate than summer migrants (WEIR), but did not themselves migrate. This result suggested that the age, size, birth date, and growth rate were not sufficient conditions for the initiation of migration, although they were apparently necessary ones. Thyroid activity seemed to be involved in the migration of ayu (Honma and Tamura 1963). Plasma thyroid hormone (T_4) level in juveniles going upstream in an artificial river was higher than that in fish going downstream (Tsukamoto et al. in press). For coho salmon *Oncorhynchus kisutch,* it was also confirmed that the timing of downstream migration coincided with a T_4 surge at new moon (Grau et al. 1981). Behavioral differentiation of the late-born ayu into summer migrants and lake residents seemed to be associated with differences in endocrinological condition. Recent analysis with radioimmunoassay showed that the plasma T_4 levels of WEIR, SET, and DIP-a fish were 4.8, 10.1, and 3.3 ng/mL, respec-

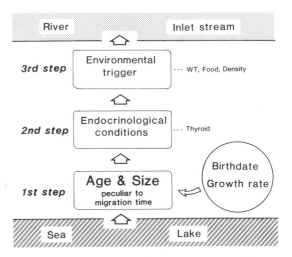

FIGURE 14.—Diagram of triggering mechanisms for upstream migrations of ayu; WT is water temperature.

tively (Tsukamoto et al., unpublished). Comparisons between the histological results and plasma T_4 levels showed that SET and DIP-a were in quite different states although they had similar heights of follicular epitherial cells. The DIP-a fish might have reached a preparatory stage for migration, with high activity of the thyroid but without the T_4 surge. The SET fish seemed to be in a state just before or during migration with the T_4 surge in the blood, whereas WEIR fish showed a state of exhaustion both histologically and in actual plasma T_4 level. Thus, the endocrinological condition must be satisfied as the second step for migration (Figure 14).

Environmental cues are well known to play an important role as a final trigger of migration (Smith 1985). Upstream migration of the ayu was stimulated by a rise in river temperature (Kusuda 1963; Tanizaki 1966). An increase in water temperature facilitated the jumping activity of ayu in the laboratory (Uchida 1986). Light also may control aspects of ayu migration as it does for salmon (Hoar 1953). Experiments confirmed that increases in fish density facilitate both upstream movements and jumping behavior of ayu (Tsukamoto et al. 1985). Furthermore, starvation seems to drive the ayu upstream (Uchida 1986). These lines of evidence show that environmental factors apparently act on the upstream migration as a final trigger (third step). Thus, we propose that the upstream migration of ayu does not occur until all three steps are accomplished in a specific order like a "triple jump."

Acknowledgments

We express our gratitude to F. Hosokawa and A. Umezawa for their technical assistance in otolith observation, and to M. Oya for her help in histological examination. The staff of Shiga Prefectural Fisheries Experimental Station and S. Imakyurei generously provided materials for this study. We also thank M. Okiyama for his advice in the analysis of meristic characters. Thanks to R. J. Klauda and E. L. Cooper for reading the manuscript. This study was partly supported by a Grant-in-Aid for Scientific Research (60129035) from the Ministry of Education, Science and Culture, Japan.

References

Alm, G. 1959. Connection between maturity size and age in fishes. Institute of Freshwater Research Drottningholm Report 40:5–145.

Azuma, M. 1970. Studies on the variability of the landlocked ayu-fish, *Plecoglossus altivelis* T. and S., in Lake Biwa. I. On the mode of distribution and some body form variation at early phases of development. Japanese Journal of Ecology 20:63–76.

Azuma, M. 1973a. Studies on the variability of the landlocked ayu-fish, *Plecoglossus altivelis* T. and S., in Lake Biwa. II. On the segregation of population and the variations in each population. Japanese Journal of Ecology 23:126–139.

Azuma, M. 1973b. Studies on the variability of the landlocked ayu-fish, *Plecoglossus altivelis* T. and S., in Lake Biwa. III. On the differences in the process of maturation, spawning habits, and some morphological features of each population. Japanese Journal of Ecology 23:147–159.

Azuma, M. 1973c. Studies on the variability of the landlocked ayu-fish, *Plecoglossus altivelis* T. and S., in Lake Biwa. IV. Considerations on the grouping and features of variability. Japanese Journal of Ecology 23:255–265.

Bilton, H. T. 1971. A hypothesis of alternation of age of return in successive generations of Skeena River sockeye salmon *(Oncorhynchus nerka)*. Journal of the Fisheries Research Board of Canada 28:513–516.

GFES (Gifu Prefectural Fisheries Experimental Station). 1978. The effect of stocking of reared juveniles of the ayu. Japan Fisheries Agency, Freshwater Fisheries Laboratory and Research Division, Final Report of 1972–1976, Tokyo, Japan.

Gould, S. J. 1977. Ontogeny and phylogeny. Belknap Press of Harvard University Press, Cambridge, Massachusetts, USA.

Grau, E. G., W. W. Dickhoff, R. S. Nishioka, H. A. Bern, and L. C. Folmar. 1981. Lunar phasing of the thyroxine surge preparatory to seaward migration of salmonid fish. Science (Washington, D.C.) 211:607–609.

Hanamura, N. 1966. Salmon of the north Pacific Ocean, part 3. A review of the life history of north Pacific salmon, 1. Sockeye salmon in the Far East. International North Pacific Fisheries Commission Bulletin 18:1–27.

Hoar, W. S. 1953. Control and timing of fish migration. Biological Reviews of the Cambridge Philosophical Society 28:437–452.

Honma, Y., and E. Tamura. 1963. Studies on the endocrine glands of the salmonid fish, the ayu, *Plecoglossus altivelis* Temminck and Schlegel. V. Seasonal changes in the endocrines of the landlocked form, the koayu. Zoologica (New York) 48:25–31.

Hotta, H. 1953. On the ecology of the ayu juvenile. Japanese Journal of Ichthyology 3:15–20.

Huxley, J. S. 1932. Problems of relative growth. Methuen, London, England.

Ishida, T. 1966. Salmon of the north Pacific Ocean, part 3. A review of the life history of north Pacific salmon, 2. Pink salmon in the Far East. International North Pacific Fisheries Commission Bulletin 18:29–39.

Iwai, T. 1962. Studies on the *Plecoglossus altivelis* problems: embryology and histophysiology of digestive and osmoregulatory organs. Bulletin of the Misaki Marine Biological Institute Kyoto University 2:1–101.

Jonsson, B. 1985. Life history patterns of freshwater resident and sea-run migrant brown trout in Norway. Transactions of the American Fisheries Society 114:182–194.

Kafuku, T. 1966. Morphological differences between domesticated common carp and wild ones. Bulletin of Freshwater Fisheries Research Laboratory (Tokyo) 16:71–82.

Kato, T. 1983. Studies on maturation and the smoltification in pond cultured masu salmon, *Oncorhynchus masou*. Pages 1–12 *in* Progress reports on masu salmon production 3. Japan Fisheries Agency, Marine Ranching Program, Tokyo, Japan.

Kubo, T. 1980. Studies on the life history of the "masu" salmon *(Oncorhynchus masou)* in Hokkaido. Scientific Reports of the Hokkaido Salmon Hatchery 34:1–95.

Kusuda, R. 1963. An ecological study of the anadromous "ayu", *Plecoglossus altivelis* T. and S.—II. Seasonal variations in the composition of the anadromous ayu schools in the river Okumo, Kyoto. Bulletin of the Japanese Society of Scientific Fisheries 29:822–827.

Maekawa, K. 1984. Life history patterns of the miyabe charr in Shikaribetsu Lake, Japan. Pages 233–250 *in* L. Johnson and B. Burns, editors. Biology of the Arctic charr: proceedings of the international symposium on Arctic charr. University of Manitoba Press, Manitoba, Canada.

Maruyama, T., and R. Ishida. 1978. Effect of water depth of the pond on the growth and body form of the ayu. Bulletin of Freshwater Fisheries Research Laboratory (Tokyo) 28:211–219.

Naka, K., and E. Mizutani. 1974. Studies on the schooling of ayu-fish, *Plecoglossus altivelis* T. and S., on the surface of Lake Biwa. Research Report of Shiga Prefectural Fisheries Experimental Station 25:52–63 (Hikone, Japan).

Nishida, M., and Y. Takahashi. 1978. Enzyme variation in populations of ayu, *Plecoglossus altivelis*. Bulletin of the Japanese Society of Scientific Fisheries 44:1059–1064.

Nordeng, H. 1961. On the biology of char in Salangen, north Norway. I. Age and spawning frequency determined from scales and otoliths. Nytt Magasin for Zoologi (Oslo) 10:67–123.

Pannella, G. 1971. Fish otoliths: daily growth layers and periodical patterns. Science (Washington, D.C.) 173:1124–1126.

Radtke, R. L., and J. M. Dean. 1982. Increment formation in the otoliths of embryos, larvae, and juveniles of the mummichog, *Fundulus heteroclitus*. U.S. National Marine Fisheries Service Fishery Bulletin 80:201–215.

Ricker, W. E. 1938. "Residual" and kokanee salmon in Cultus Lake. Journal of the Fisheries Research Board of Canada 4:192–218.

Sano, S. 1966. Salmon of the north Pacific ocean, part 3. A review of the life history of north Pacific salmon, 3. Chum salmon in the Far East. International North Pacific Fisheries Commission Bulletin 18:41–57.

Semko, R. S. 1954. The stocks of West Kamchatka salmon and their commercial utilization. Izvestia TINRO 41:3–109.

SFES (Shiga Prefectural Fisheries Experimental Station). 1982. Study on the propagation of the landlocked ayu. SFES, Report of 1981 research by grant of Japanese Fisheries Agency, Hikone, Japan.

SFES (Shiga Prefectural Fisheries Experimental Station). 1983. Study on the propagation of the landlocked ayu. SFES, Report of 1982 research by grant of Japanese Fisheries Agency, Hikone, Japan.

Smith, R. J. F. 1985. The control of fish migration. Zoophysiology 17.

Tanizaki, R. 1966. Catch of the ayu and water temperature during the season of upstream migration. Physiology and Ecology 14:33–38.

Tsukamoto K., and T. Kajihara. In press. Age determination of ayu with otolith. Bulletin of the Japanese Society of Scientific Fisheries 53.

Tsukamoto, K., T. Otake, and K. Aida. In press. Plasma thyroxine concentration and upstream migratory behavior of the ayu. Bulletin of the Japanese Society of Scientific Fisheries 54.

Tsukamoto, K., K. Uchida, Y. Murakami, M. Endo, and T. Kajihara. 1985. Density effect on jumping behavior and swimming upstream in the ayu juveniles. Bulletin of the Japanese Society of Scientific Fisheries 51:323.

Uchida, K. 1986. Behavioral study on characteristics of the upstream migration of the ayu, *Plecoglossus altivelis*. Doctoral dissertation. University of Tokyo, Tokyo, Japan.

Yamazaki, Y. 1986. Feeding habit of the amphidromous ayu. Master's thesis. University of Tokyo, Tokyo, Japan.

American Fisheries Society Symposium 1:507–518, 1987
© Copyright by the American Fisheries Society 1987

Factors Affecting Recruitment and Survival of Mugilids in Estuaries and Coastal Waters of Southeastern Africa

STEPHEN J.M. BLABER

CSIRO Division of Fisheries Research, Post Office Box 120
Cleveland, Queensland 4163, Australia

Abstract.—More than 40 species of grey mullet, Mugilidae, occur in the coastal waters of the Indian and western Pacific oceans. Most are euryhaline (to salinities of approximately 1‰) and enter estuaries; at least 10 species occur commonly in fresh water. All grey mullet species spawn in the sea. The migratory behaviour, spawning times, and size at recruitment into estuaries of the 15 species of southeastern Africa are reviewed and compared. Spawning occurs in the nearshore zone during the rainy season. Larvae apparently locate estuaries by following turbidity gradients and currents. Spawning during rainy periods, when river discharge is maximal, increases the likelihood that fry will successfully locate nursery grounds. In this regard, recent evidence indicates that many species have turbidity preferenda, which may help to separate ecologically similar and sympatric species. Mugilid larvae initially feed on zooplankton, but all species investigated show a similar sequence of changes in diet upon entering estuaries. At 10–15 mm standard length, they change from feeding on surface zooplankton to selecting vertically migrating zooplankters on the bottom; at 10–20 mm, they shift from zooplankton in the benthos to meiobenthos; finally, at 15–45 mm, they shift to the adult iliophagous habit of ingesting sand grains and microbenthos. Juveniles frequent shallow, quiet-water areas and it is probable that the change from planktonic, macrophagous carnivory to benthic, microphagous omnivory can only occur in sheltered areas. Once iliophagous, various species feed on substrata of different grain sizes, further reducing interspecific interactions. The roles of predators, including other fish species, birds, and reptiles, are considered in relation to the behavioural and physiological survival strategies of juvenile mullet. Movement of young mullet into shallow water reduces predation by piscivorous fishes, but makes juveniles more accessible to avian predators. Mortality from predation may also be affected by diurnal and seasonal changes in swimming fitness mediated by respiratory and haematological changes. Although, for most species, recruitment to estuaries or fresh water in the life cycle may not be obligatory, such areas provide the most suitable conditions for growth and survival.

Grey mullet (Mugilidae) are among the most abundant fishes in shallow coastal waters and estuaries of the tropics and subtropics. The family consists of some 95 species (Nelson 1984), of which more than 40 occur in the Indian and western Pacific oceans. Many species are closely related and ecologically similar, and their relatively uniform morphology has led to generic confusion. Between 10 and 16 genera are currently recognized (Thomson 1966; Nelson 1984).

Almost all species are euryhaline and habitually frequent low-salinity estuarine waters; most, however, do not occur in salinities below 1‰. About 10 species commonly occur in fresh water and a few, such as *Myxus capensis* in Africa and *Myxus petardi* in Australia, spend most of their life in fresh water. The most ubiquitous species, *Mugil cephalus,* is found circumtropically, inhabiting rivers, estuaries, the open sea, and hypersaline lagoons of up to 80‰ (Whitfield et al. 1981). In contrast, some species are highly endemic: *Valamugil robustus* and *Liza luciae,* for example,

occur in and adjacent to only a few estuaries of Natal and Mozambique. Despite such differences, the feature shared by almost all species is that they are catadromous and must spawn in the sea. This habit dominates their life history, causing regular migrations, changes of environment, and exposure to a variety of potential mortality factors. In this paper, spawning, migrations, orientation and navigation, changes in feeding ecology, and predation are reviewed in relation to survival strategies of mullet. Particular emphases are placed on southeastern Africa and the relative importance of recruitment to estuaries and fresh water.

Migrations, Spawning Times, and Recruitment

Fifteen species of mullet occur in southeastern Africa (Table 1), of which five are endemic, nine range widely throughout the Indo-Pacific region and one, *Liza dumerili,* is found on both the east and west African coasts. With the possible exception of *Liza vaigiensis* and *Valamugil parmatus*

TABLE 1.—Species of Mugilidae occurring in southeastern Africa and biological factors relevant to their distribution and recruitment. Data were drawn largely from Smith (1965), Wallace (1975), Blaber (1977), Blaber and Whitfield (1977), and the author's records; U = unknown.

Species	Geographical range[a]	Catadromous in south-eastern Africa	Salinity range ‰	Spawning sites	Spawning periods	Period of recruitment into estuaries	Minimum size (mm)[b] at recruitment	Preferred adult substratum (mm)	Gonad maturation stage reached in estuaries and fresh water[c]
Crenimugil crenilabis	ST/T,IP	No	2–35	Lagoons	Jun[d]	Aug–Oct	28	0.25	Very rare in Africa
Liza alata	ST/T,IP	Yes	0.7–35	Inshore marine	U	Jul–Jan	14	0.5–1.0	U
Liza dumerili	WT/T,Af	Yes	0.7–72	Inshore marine	Jun–Nov	Aug–Nov	13	0.25–1.0	IV
Liza luciae	ST,E	Yes	30–36	U	U	U	U	U	U
Liza macrolepis	ST/T,IP	Yes	0.7–72	Inshore marine	May–Dec[a]	Jul–Mar	10	0.25–0.5	IV
Liza richardsoni	WT/T, E	Yes	0.5–35	Inshore marine	Sep–Mar	Jan–Jun	11	0.125–0.25	
Liza tricuspidens	WT/ST, E	Yes	4–35	Inshore marine	Aug–Nov	Nov–Jan	17	0.5–1.0[f]	U
Liza vaigiensis	T,IP	No	35	Marine	U	U	U	U	Not recorded in estuaries
Mugil cephalus	Te/T,WW	Yes	0–80	Inshore marine	May–Sep	Jun–Dec	15	0.25–0.5	IV
Myxus capensis	WT/ST,E	Yes	0–35	Inshore marine	Apr–May	Aug–Dec	10	0.125–0.5	III in fresh water, IV in estuaries
Valamugil buchanani	ST/T,IP	Yes	0.7–60	Inshore marine	Oct–Dec	Oct–Jul	10	0.125–0.25	IV
Valamugil cunnesius	ST/T,IP	Yes	0.7–65	Inshore marine	Nov–Jun	Jan–Jul	11	0.125–0.25	IV
Valamugil parmatus	T,IP	No	35	U	U	U	U	U	Not recorded in estuaries
Valamugil robustus	ST,E	Yes	0.7–39	Marine	U	Sep–May	11	0.125–0.25	IV
Valamugil seheli	T,IP	No	5–35	Marine	U	Sep–Feb	9	0.125–0.25	U

[a] Te = temperate; WT = warm temperate; ST = subtropical; T = tropical; IP = Indo-Pacific; Af = west and east Africa; E = endemic; WW = worldwide.
[b] Standard length.
[c] After Davis (1977).
[d] Not recorded in Africa, data for Pacific from Helfrich and Allen (1975).
[e] Jun–Feb in India (Luther 1963).
[f] Main food is filamentous algae, few sand grains.

(which are very rare), and *Liza luciae* (which is restricted to the St. Lucia system of Natal), all species have been recorded in estuaries in low salinities (Table 1). *Mugil cephalus* and *Myxus capensis* are the only species that commonly occur in fresh water (Bok 1979; Bruton et al. 1987, this volume). The former is also common in estuaries and the sea, but the latter is mainly confined to fresh waters when adult.

All available data indicate that species found in rivers and estuaries of southeastern Africa migrate to the sea to spawn (Wallace 1975; Van der Horst and Erasmus 1978; Whitfield 1980b). Spawning has not been recorded in estuaries or fresh water, although the gonads of most species reach an advanced state of development just prior to emigration to the sea (Wallace 1975; Table 1).

Of the two species occurring in fresh water, *Mugil cephalus* reaches advanced sexual development in fresh water, whereas *Myxus capensis* shows very limited gonad development (Bok 1979). According to Bok (1979), the limited sexual development of *M. capensis* in fresh water may be an adaptation to a catadromous life history: the centre of distribution of *M. capensis* is the southeastern Cape, a region of low and spasmodic rainfall with long periods of low river flow and short, high-intensity floods. Thus, fish are trapped in isolated stretches of river for extended periods, during which time vitellogenesis would be a waste of energy. The gonads only begin ripening once the fish have migrated to the estuary and have a clear run to the spawning grounds in the sea. Under similar isolated conditions, the gonads of

M. cephalus ripen at the spawning season but are resorbed if the fish is confined to fresh water. The spawning grounds are close inshore, immediately beyond the surf zone (Day et al. 1981), although the precise sites are largely unknown. There is indirect evidence that *M. cephalus* in southeastern Africa may spawn at least 3 km from shore (Bok 1984).

There are also few data from other areas of the world. *Mugil cephalus* in the USSR and the USA was reported to spawn at night, offshore over "deep" water (Dekhnik 1953; Arnold and Thompson 1958). Helfrich and Allen (1975) observed *Crenimugil crenilabis* spawning at night in shallow water within atoll lagoons. *Liza vaigiensis* and *L. oligolepis* (=*Valamugil parmatus*) were seen in dense schools in nearshore areas of the Arabian Sea during the monsoon, a phenomenon probably connected with spawning (Moazzam and Rizvi 1980).

Only *M. cephalus* has been recorded in large prespawning aggregations in estuaries and rivers (Wallace 1975; Whitfield and Blaber 1978a). Large numbers of fish with ripe gonads school in estuary mouths before moving into the sea, a phenomenon noted throughout the species' worldwide range (Thomson 1963; Apekin and Vilenskaya 1978). The spawning run of *M. cephalus* may occur regularly, such as at St. Lucia in Natal where, since at least 1968, the fish have appeared at the estuary between April 12 and May 12 (Natal Parks Board, unpublished records).

Recorded spawning periods along the coastline from Mozambique to the Cape are shown in Table 1. Species that range along most of the coast spawn later in the south; *Liza dumerili,* for example, spawns between June and November in Natal (Wallace 1975) and between January and February in the Cape (Van der Horst and Erasmus 1978). Most species spawn from winter to early summer. There are few data on spawning stimuli, although the above data and Thomson (1966) suggested that temperature is the most important factor; a variety of optimum temperatures have been reported, particularly for widespread species such as *M. cephalus*.

With regard to recruitment success and survival, there are critical periods in the early life history at the egg and larval stages. The eggs are vulnerable to environmental conditions and predation. Those of most species are small (0.5–1.0 mm diameter: Thomson 1966) and pelagic. Lee and Menu (1981) demonstrated that the optimal salinity range for hatching of *M. cephalus* was 30–40‰ with a peak at 35‰. Several authors (Tang 1964; Kuo et al. 1973) have shown that the fertilized eggs of *M. cephalus* must stay in suspension in order to develop and that they sink in standing water. There is sufficient water movement in the sea to prevent the eggs sinking to the bottom. In the relatively calm waters of estuaries, however, a combination of lack of water movement, less depth, and (usually) lower specific gravity would cause the eggs to touch bottom, thereby inhibiting development (Kuo et al. 1973). In terms of predation, in southeastern Africa the eggs of Mugilidae are an important food item for Ambassidae, a family of small fishes that are abundant in the inshore waters of the Indo-Pacific region (Martin and Blaber 1983). Natarajan and Patnaik (1968) concluded that predation by *Ambassis gymnocephalus* on mugilid eggs in the Lake Chilka region of India significantly affects recruitment to the mullet fishery.

Two critical periods are reported for the larvae of *M. cephalus* and *Liza macrolepis:* at age 3 d, when the mouth is formed and feeding begins; and at age 11–12 d, when the larvae assume a fish-like shape, develop scales, and attain sustained swimming powers (Liao et al. 1971; Kuo et al. 1973; Chaudhuri et al. 1977; James et al. 1983). Postlarvae appear in lagoons, estuaries, and mangrove systems at lengths of 10–15 mm (standard length, SL; Table 1) corresponding to ages of between 4 and 6 weeks (Kuo et al. 1973; Thomson 1966). Recruitment occurs mainly in the summer, which is the rainy season, when the rivers are flowing and the mouths of "closed" estuaries are open (Day et al. 1981). Similar recruitment patterns linked to the rainy season or monsoon periods, when river discharge is greatest, have been recorded throughout the Indo-Pacific region (Sarojini 1958; Kowtal 1976; De Silva 1980; Potter et al. 1983).

Migration into Estuaries

The recruitment of postlarval mullet to river systems from the sea depends upon their successfully locating an estuary mouth and proceeding in the right direction. The literature on fish migration is extensive, but very little of it is concerned with "first-time" navigation of postlarvae. In the recent review of oceanic and estuarine transport of fish eggs and larvae, Norcross and Shaw (1984) stated that "spawning often takes place close to gyral, upwelling, or other directional circulations." The spawning grounds of mugilids lie in the vicinity of estuary mouths (Wallace 1975);

hence the distance between spawning grounds
and nursery areas is short. In Natal, at least, the
eggs and larval stages are likely to be retained in
inshore waters due to current systems in the area
(Wallace and Van der Elst 1975).

In order to enter an estuary, the larvae must
arrive adjacent to the mouth, either by swimming
actively towards the estuary or by depending
passively on local currents. Although virtually
nothing is known of the behaviour of postlarval
mullet in the sea, sufficient ecological data are
available to erect a model of the mechanisms
involved in the migration into estuaries (Figure 1).

During the spawning period, rivers are typically
flowing strongly, decreasing the salinity and increasing the turbidity of the sea (Cyrus 1985) at
considerable distances from the estuary mouth.
These gross perturbations of the vertical stratification of the sea may provide the "cue" (sensu
Harden Jones 1984) for larval orientation. Detection of changes in the complex microstructure of
the water in such perturbed areas has been suggested as one mechanism that facilitates orientation (Westerberg 1984).

Once the mullet locate an estuary, several
"clues" (sensu Harden Jones 1984) are available
to them to assist orientation. Salinity reduction
may not be one of them, for recent experimental
evidence (Cyrus 1985) indicates that juvenile *Liza
macrolepis*, *L. dumerili*, *Valamugil cunnesius*,
and *V. buchanani* do not react uniformly to salinity gradients, a finding that is supported by field
observations of postlarvae of these species in

southern Africa, nor do *Liza vaigiensis*, *L. dussumieri*, and *M. cephalus* in Australia when they
enter hypersaline systems (Blaber et al. 1985;
Blaber, in press). Temperature is also an unlikely
clue, as thermal gradients in estuaries are irregular and highly variable (Cyrus 1985).

Turbidity, however, may be an important clue
as most species of mullet show a preference for
waters with a turbidity higher than that in the sea
(Blaber and Blaber 1980; Cyrus 1985). Turbidity
gradients such as shown in Figure 2 occur along
the lengths of many Natal, Australian, and southeast Asian estuaries and extend into the sea
(Blaber 1981, in press; Cyrus 1985). Also, there
exists within most estuaries a vertical gradient
from relatively low turbidity on the surface to high
turbidity on the bottom (Figure 2). Under experimental conditions, larvae of *Liza macrolepis* and
Mugil cephalus avoid strong illumination and congregate in places of low light intensity or high
water turbidity (Liao 1975; James et al. 1983;
Cyrus 1985). In order to find maximum turbidities,
or lowest light intensities, larvae in the mouth of
an estuary must move towards the bottom. That
they do this is well established in relation to their
changeover from pelagic to benthic feeding. In
addition, however, it enables them to take advantage of the stronger tidal movement of water
inwards that occurs close to the bottom, particularly during the periods of strong river flow. The
various strategies whereby fish larvae utilize tidal
currents for transport have recently been reviewed by Leggett (1984) and Norcross and Shaw

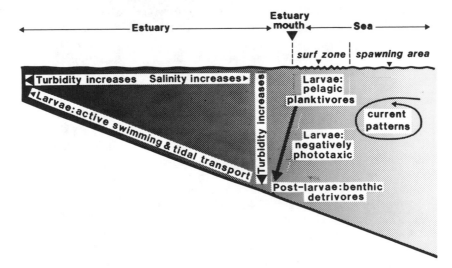

FIGURE 1.—Mechanisms involved in the migration of postlarval mullet into open estuaries during the rainy
season.

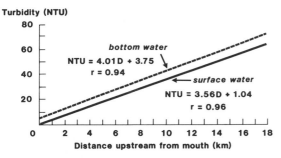

Turbidity (NTU)

FIGURE 2.—The relationship between turbidity and distance (D) from the mouth for surface and bottom waters on a rising tide at St. Lucia estuary, Natal (after Cyrus 1985). NTU = nephelometric turbidity units.

(1984). Selective tidal-stream transport has been shown to be an important mechanism for migration in European flatfish (Greer Walker et al. 1978) and eels (McCleave and Kleckner 1982) as well as for penaeid prawn larvae in estuaries of the Gulf of Carpentaria (Staples 1980). These organisms achieve movement into the estuary by passively drifting on the flood tide and settling on the ebb. It is probable that postlarval mullet also use such a mechanism to aid their active movement upstream. Postlarval mullet are commonly observed entering estuary mouths on the flooding tide (Whitfield 1980b; Torricelli et al. 1982).

Once well into an estuarine system, however, juvenile mullet spread throughout shallow water areas (Thomson 1966; Blaber 1978) and penetrate the furthest reaches; some species enter fresh water. This active movement appears to take place primarily in shallow waters along the edges of estuaries, where currents are slow or nonexistent (Blaber 1978; Whitfield and Blaber 1978a) and the juveniles avoid deep water areas. The clues for continued upstream movement are obscure but may relate to turbidity and salinity preferenda (Cyrus 1985).

Changes in Feeding Ecology during Recruitment

The feeding habits of juvenile mullet change when they recruit to the estuarine environment (Blaber and Whitfield 1977; De Silva and Wijeyratne 1977; Chan and Chua 1979). Mugilid larvae initially feed on zooplankton, but all species investigated show a similar sequence of changes in diet upon entering estuaries: at 10–15 mm (SL) they change from feeding on surface-dwelling zooplankton to vertically migrating zooplankters on the bottom; at 10–20 mm, they change from

zooplankton in the benthos to meiobenthos; and finally, at 15–45 mm, they shift to the iliophagous habit of ingesting sandgrains and microbenthos. It is probable that the change from being planktonic macrophagous carnivores to benthic microphagous omnivores can only occur in sheltered areas (Blaber and Whitfield 1977). Only in shallow waters are vertically migrating zooplankters available on the substratum (Grindley 1981), although they are available as surface plankton during part of their diel migration. Consequently, each change in the feeding habit of mullet, from zooplankton at the surface to zooplankton on the bottom, or from zooplankton on the bottom to meiobenthos, involves little or no change in prey type. The change to iliophagous feeding takes place gradually with the ingestion of increasing quantities of substratum (Blaber and Whitfield 1977).

The transitions in diet are closely linked with the mechanism for migration into estuaries and a change from a pelagic to a benthic mode of life. As the fish move closer to the substratum where they benefit from tidal transport, vertically migrating zooplankters are the only ones available. The switch in food from zooplankton to benthos, particularly microbenthos, may be caused by the paucity of the former and the abundance of the latter in most Indo-Pacific estuaries. Standing stocks of zooplankton in most southeastern African estuaries are low (Blaber et al. 1981), whereas the substratum is rich in organic matter and has a high biomass of benthic animals (Day 1981). Several studies have shown that the energy value of the benthos and bottom detritus in Natal estuaries is at least two orders of magnitude greater than that of the zooplankton (Whitfield 1980a; Blaber et al. 1984). It is probable that the large biomass of adult and juvenile mugilids in estuaries is permitted only by the large resource of energy contained in the substratum. It is evident, therefore, that the survival of juvenile mullet recruiting to estuaries depends upon sequential changes in diet.

Factors such as salinity and turbidity vary markedly in estuaries, but ways in which they may influence feeding ecology have not been thoroughly investigated. That they may do this indirectly through limiting effects on prey organisms is documented (Boltt 1975; Bruton 1985), but laboratory studies show that salinity levels may directly alter the growth and food intake of juvenile mullet. De Silva and Perera (1976) showed that food intake by *M. cephalus* was salinity dependent, and highest at 30‰. They also showed, however, that conversion efficiencies were greatest at salinities of less than 10‰, because the rate of digestion was slower at low salinities. They concluded that possibly both intake and digestion are related to the metabolic cost of osmoregulation. It is unfortunate that no comparable metabolic data are available for other mullet species, since such data might shed light on the influence of physiological mechanisms on the distribution and ecology of mugilids.

Predators

The tolerance of mugilids to abiotic environmental extremes suggests that biotic factors are likely to be of greater importance in population regulation. Estuaries and fresh waters provide an abundance of suitable prey, so food availability is probably not a limiting factor. Mortality from fish, bird, and reptile predation, however, may be very high.

Published information on species of fish in estuaries of southeastern Africa that include mugilids in their diet is summarized in Table 2. In most species, mullet do not form a predominant part of their food. By frequenting shallow water areas, juvenile mullet avoid large predatory fish, which, in any case, have reduced numbers in most estuaries (Blaber 1980). Major (1978) found that juvenile *M. cephalus* less than 50 mm SL occur seasonally in estuarine intertidal areas in Hawaii at a time when there are the most low tides and the fewest high tides. Water temperatures in these shallow waters are close to the lethal limits for the species, but the tidal situation allows increased time for feeding in areas where there are no predators. By the time the fish reach 50 mm, the tidal situation has changed and allows predators access to the shallow areas at low tide. This coincides with a reduction in the tolerance of *M. cephalus* to high temperatures. Major (1978) also considered that the schooling habit increases the chances of survival of individual mullet.

Although adult mullet are generally safe from fish predation in estuaries, some important exceptions exist. Prespawning schools of *M. cephalus* that migrate annually from the St. Lucia system of

TABLE 2.—Summary of published data on fish predation on Mugilidae in estuaries and rivers of southeastern Africa.

Predator	Prey (L.=Liza)	Percent frequency in diet	Prey stage[a]	Area	Reference[b]
Argyrosomus hololepidotus	*L. dumerili*	0.5	J, A	Cape	4
	L. richardsoni	2.1	J, A	Cape	4
	Mugil cephalus	2.6	J, A	Cape	4
	Myxus capensis	0.3	J, A	Cape	4
	Mugilidae	1.0	J, A	Natal	6
Caranx ignobilis	Mugilidae	3.0–11	J	Natal	2, 6
Caranx melampygus	Mugilidae	3.0	J	Natal	2
Caranx papuensis	Mugilidae	2.0	J	Natal	2
Caranx sexfasciatus	*L. macrolepis*	2.0	A	Natal	2
	Valamugil cunnesius	1.0	A	Natal	2
	Mugilidae	3.0	J	Natal	2
Carcharhinus leucas	*Mugil cephalus*	100.0[c]	A	Natal	3
Elops machnata	*L. dumerili*	2.4	?	Cape	4
	Mugilidae	19.0	?	Cape	4
	Mugilidae	1.0	J, A	Natal	6
Lichia amia	*L. dumerili*	0.3	?	Cape	4
	L. richardsoni	4.8	?	Cape	4
	Mugil cephalus	4.8	?	Cape	4
	Mugilidae	43.0[d]	A	Natal	6
Monodactylus falciformis	Mugilidae	1.9	J	Cape	4
Platycephalus indicus	*L. richardsoni*	7.1	?	Cape	4
Pomatomus saltatrix	*L. richardsoni*	4.2	?	Cape	4
	Mugil cephalus	8.3	?	Cape	4
	Mugilidae	3.0	J, A	Natal	5
Sphyraena barracuda	Mugilidae	7.0–12.0	J	Natal	1
Sphyraena jello	Mugilidae	7.0	J	Natal	1
Tachysurus feliceps	Mugilidae	1.7	?	Cape	4
Tylosurus leiurus	Mugilidae	4.5	J, A	Natal	6

[a] J = juvenile; A = adult.
[b] 1 = Blaber (1982); 2 = Blaber and Cyrus (1983); 3 = Bruton (1977); 4 = Marais (1984); 5 = Van der Elst (1976); 6 = Whitfield and Blaber (1978c).
[c] Restricted period during prespawning aggregations of prey.
[d] Sample size was only 11.

Natal are heavily preyed on by the shark *Carcharhinus leucas* (Bruton 1977). Sharks gather in large numbers at the narrow mouth of the estuary and decimate the tightly packed schools of mullet. They also prey extensively on large migrating and spawning schools of mullet in other areas of the world; according to Kesteven (1942), sharks are regularly seen in attendance on migrating *M. cephalus* in Australia, and *C. leucas* has been recorded feeding on *M. cephalus* in Louisiana (Darnell 1958). Helfrich and Allen (1975) documented *Carcharhinus melanopterus* attacking a spawning school of *Crenimugil crenilabis* in the Pacific. Cech and Wohlschlag (1982), working on *M. cephalus* in Texas, suggested that physiological changes are relevant to ecological strategies for avoiding such predators. During the warmest months and the autumn spawning period, *M. cephalus* develop enhanced haemoglobin concentrations which, correlated with changes in respiration and gill ventilation rates, provide for more rapid sustained swimming (4.9–9.3 body lengths) during the spawning season. It is likely that this increased aerobic fitness helps, among other things, to reduce mortality from predatory fishes during the period that the mullet are in coastal waters for spawning.

Piscivorous birds are probably the most important predators of mugilids in southeastern Africa. Whitfield (1978) found a high correlation between densities of fish and avian predators. In southern Africa, fry, juvenile, and adult mugilids are preyed on by a variety of birds using differing hunting strategies. Preference for shallow waters may aid small mullet in avoiding fish predators, but it renders them particularly vulnerable to wading birds. As mullet also swim mainly in the top 30 cm of the water column (Whitfield and Blaber 1978b), both juveniles and adults are available to swimming and diving birds. Table 3 summarizes the data on bird predation on mullet in Natal estuaries, where mullet form the most important food of cormorants, herons, and fish eagles. Although energy intake data are few, the little information published suggests that mullet are a primary food source. For example, *M. cephalus* and *Valamugil buchanani* form 61% and 15%, respectively, of the calorific intake of the cormorant *Phalacrocorax carbo* in the Kosi estuary system (Jackson 1984). Resource partitioning by water depth, capture method, and prey size ensures that all sizes of mullet are taken. White pelicans *Pelecanus onocrotalus* feed on pre- and postspawning schools of *M. cephalus* in the St. Lucia estuary, and upwards of 200 kg of fish/d are consumed by over a thousand birds in a period of 1 to 2 weeks (Whitfield and Blaber 1979a). The high number of piscivorous birds, which is clearly related to fish densities, indicates that the birds have a major effect on estuarine mullet populations in southeastern Africa.

Similar results were reported by Lenanton et al. (1984) from the Peel–Harvey system of Western Australia and by Wells (1984) from New Zealand, particularly with regard to cormorant predation. Herons were also shown to be important predators of mullet in Bengal (Mukherjee 1971) and Florida (Hutton and Sogangeres-Bernal 1959).

TABLE 3.—Summary of published data on bird predation on Mugilidae in the estuaries and rivers of Natal, South Africa.

Predator	Hunting method	Prey	Standard length range of prey (mm)	% Frequency	Reference[a]
Phalacrocorax carbo	Swimming	*Liza macrolepis*	54–177	8	1
		Mugil cephalus	68–190	56	1
		Valamugil buchanani	47–246	32	1
		Mugilidae	20–200	22	3
Phalacrocorax africanus	Swimming	Mugilidae	20–60	5	3
Ardea cinerea	Wading	Mugilidae	20–100	37	3
Ardea goliath	Wading	Mugilidae	40–300	33	3
Egretta alba	Wading	Mugilidae	20–180	19	3
Ceryle rudis	Diving	*Liza macrolepis*	23–57	58	1
		Mugilidae	20–60	14	2
Haliaeetus vocifer	Diving	*Mugil cephalus*	240–540	58	2
Hydroprogne tschegrava	Diving	Mugilidae	60–250	7	2
Pelecanus onocrotalus	Swimming	*Mugil cephalus*	300	100[b]	3

[a] 1 = Jackson (1984); 2 = Whitfield and Blaber (1978b); 3 = Whitfield and Blaber (1979a).
[b] Restricted period during pre- and postspawning aggregations of prey.

Crocodiles *Crocodylus niloticus* in southeastern Africa are important predators of larger mullet in some estuaries. Together with sharks and pelicans, they feed extensively on mullet, particularly during spawning migrations (Whitfield and Blaber 1979b). Based upon aerial counts of crocodiles and an assumed average daily intake of 1.1 kg/crocodile, it was estimated that 3.9 tonnes of *M. cephalus* were consumed in the 8-day spawning run at St. Lucia, Natal, in 1976 (Whitfield and Blaber 1979b).

In summary, mullet are exposed to different groups of predators at each stage of their lifecycle. As eggs, larvae, and postlarvae forming part of the plankton in the sea, they are consumed by planktivorous fishes and possibly by invertebrates. As juveniles in shallow estuaries and fresh water, they are preyed upon by birds. As adults moving in schools from estuaries to the sea to spawn and returning after spawning, they are vulnerable to large predators, both at the estuary mouth and at the spawning sites. With our present state of knowledge, it is not possible to quantify the mortality at each stage. The relative importance of each to recruitment success is, therefore, unknown.

Dependence on Estuaries or Fresh Water

Most grey mullet species in the Indo-Pacific region have similar migration patterns into estuaries and fresh water, although there are exceptions. Species such as *Crenimugil crenilabis* and *Valamugil parmatus* occur mainly in the sea. Interspecific competition in estuaries is reduced by a superabundance of food, differential recruitment, substrate preferences, and the extent of penetration into fresh water. Possibly food is more plentiful in estuaries than in fresh water, and Bok (1979) suggested that adult *Myxus capensis*, which, unlike most mullet, spend most of their life in fresh water in southeastern Africa, may be excluded from estuarine areas by competition from other mullet species.

Since all species spawn in the sea, movement from estuaries and fresh water into the sea is obligatory, and mortality from predation a direct consequence. However, to what extent is the estuarine–freshwater phase obligatory? It is impossible to estimate with any certainty what proportions of the life cycle are spent in different environments, but the evidence suggests that, for the majority of species, marine phases are short and confined to the larval stage and spawning periods. By maximizing their time in estuaries and

fresh water, mullet can take advantage of rich, detritus-based food resources while avoiding an array of predators in the sea. Mugilidae is only one of several families of coastal fishes that use estuaries as nursery areas (Day et al. 1981). However, the degree to which mullet stocks depend upon estuaries can only be ascertained by comparing the occurrence of the various species in estuaries, fresh water, and the sea. Information on this subject is scattered and often conflicting. Juveniles of most species are rarely reported from clear oceanic waters of depths greater than 1–2 m. The occurrence of adult *Crenimugil crenilabis*, *Liza vaigiensis*, *Valamugil buchanani*, and *Mugil cephalus* in shallow marine environments is well documented (Thomson 1966; Van der Elst 1982; Blaber et al. 1985). These four species, the largest of the mullets, are probably the least vulnerable to fish predators in the sea. *Mugil cephalus* and *V. buchanani* reach 60 cm and 125 cm, respectively (Smith 1965; Van der Elst 1982). Russell (1983) stated that *C. crenilabis*, *Liza dussumieri*, *L. vaigiensis*, *M. cephalus* and *Myxus elongatus* are uncommon or rare on the Great Barrier Reef. However, the last four are abundant in adjacent estuarine areas of the mainland of Queensland (Grant 1982). Thomson (1966) found no evidence that a freshwater phase is obligatory for *Mugil cephalus*, but he did not take account of the juvenile phase. Martin and Drewry (1978), in a comprehensive review of data on *M. cephalus*, stated that this species is apparently restricted to shallow water during a discrete trophic (feeding) phase: "Trophic phase adults typically in freshwater in Australia, estuarine elsewhere but readily entering freshwater."

Given that juveniles of most mullet species are seldom seen outside estuarine or freshwater areas, and that such areas provide the major portion of suitable environments for feeding, it is reasonable to state that an estuarine phase is obligatory for the juveniles, at least. A decision upon this question is important from a fisheries standpoint because estuaries in most parts of the world, particularly the Indo-Pacific, are being degraded by pollution and industrial development. Mullet form the basis of important fisheries throughout the Indo-Pacific, and the world catch (mostly Indo-Pacific) increased from 49,000 tonnes in 1962 to 179,000 tonnes in 1981 (FAO 1982). It is likely that such an increase in catch has been possible, despite widespread environmental degradation of estuaries through pollution and industrial development, because mullet are tolerant of such factors as low oxygen levels (<5 mg $\cdot$ L^{-1}: Blaber et al. 1984). In studies of polluted estuaries and rivers in Natal, Whitfield (1980a) and Blaber et al. (1984) showed that the food chain from benthic floc (detritus) to iliophagous fish remained viable, even in conditions of organic pollution and an impoverished invertebrate fauna. Mugilids dominate the fish fauna of these estuaries, and the food chain from detritus to mullet accounts for most of the energy in terms of standing stocks. Mullet are particularly well adapted to a migratory life cycle and are among the most resilient of fishes, so the greatest factor influencing their survival may be the loss of estuarine environments. Further quantitative data are urgently required on mortality rates at the different life history stages in sea, estuary, and fresh water in order to pinpoint at which times these important species are most vulnerable to human pressures, such as pollution and fishing.

Acknowledgments

I thank the many students and staff of Rhodes University and the University of Natal for their assistance. My contributions to the research would not have been possible without the financial support of the South African National Committee for Oceanographic Research (CSIR), the University of Natal, the World Wildlife Fund, the Oppenheimer Trust, and the Natal Parks Board. I am grateful to Ron Thresher and Tim Davis (CSIRO) for their constructive criticisms of the manuscript.

References

Apekin, V. S., and N. I. Vilenskaya. 1978. A description of the sexual cycle and the state of the gonads during the spawning migration of the striped mullet, *Mugil cephalus*. Journal of Ichthyology 18:446–456.

Arnold, E. L., and J. R. Thompson. 1958. Offshore spawning of the striped mullet *Mugil cephalus* in the Gulf of Mexico. Copeia 1958:130–132.

Blaber, S. J. M. 1977. The feeding ecology and relative abundance of mullet (Mugilidae) in Natal and Pondoland estuaries. Biological Journal of the Linnean Society 9:259–275.

Blaber, S. J. M. 1978. The fishes of the Kosi system. Lammergeyer 24:28–41.

Blaber, S. J. M. 1980. Fishes of the Trinity Inlet system of North Queensland with notes on the ecology of fish faunas of tropical Indo-Pacific estuaries. Australian Journal of Marine and Freshwater Research 31:137–146.

Blaber, S. J. M. 1981. The zoogeographical affinities of estuarine fishes in south east Africa. South African Journal of Science 77:305–307.

Blaber, S. J. M. 1982. The ecology of *Sphyraena barracuda* (Osteichthyes: Perciformes) in the Kosi system with notes on the Sphyraenidae of other Natal estuaries. South African Journal of Zoology 17:171–176.

Blaber, S. J. M. In press. The ecology of fishes of estuaries and lagoons of the Indo-Pacific with particular reference to south east Africa. *In* A. Y. Arancibia, editor. Fish community ecology in estuaries and coastal lagoons: towards an ecosystem integration. Universidad Nacional Autonoma de Mexico Press, Mexico City, Mexico.

Blaber, S. J. M., and T. G. Blaber. 1980. Factors affecting the distribution of juvenile estuarine and inshore fish. Journal of Fish Biology 17:143–162.

Blaber, S. J. M., and D. P. Cyrus. 1983. The biology of Carangidae in Natal estuaries. Journal of Fish Biology 22:373–393.

Blaber, S. J. M., D. P. Cyrus, and A. K. Whitfield. 1981. The influence of zooplankton food resources on the morphology of the estuarine clupeid *Gilchristella aestuarius*. Environmental Biology of Fishes 6:351–355.

Blaber, S. J. M., D. G. Hay, D. P. Cyrus, and T. J. Martin. 1984. The ecology of two degraded estuaries on the north coast of Natal. South African Journal of Zoology 19:224–240.

Blaber, S. J. M., and A. K. Whitfield. 1977. The feeding ecology of juvenile Mugilidae in south east African estuaries. Biological Journal of the Linnean Society 9:277–284.

Blaber, S. J. M., J. W. Young, and M. C. Dunning. 1985. Community structure and zoogeographic affinities of the coastal fishes of the Dampier region of north west Australia. Australian Journal of Marine and Freshwater Research 36:247–266.

Bok, A. H. 1979. The distribution and ecology of two mullet species in some freshwater rivers in the eastern Cape, South Africa. Journal of the Limnological Society of Southern Africa 5:97–102.

Bok, A. H. 1984. The demography, breeding biology and management of two mullet species (Pisces: Mugilidae) in the eastern Cape, South Africa. Doctoral dissertation. Rhodes University, Grahamstown, South Africa.

Boltt, R. E. 1975. The benthos of some southern African lakes. Part V: the recovery of the benthic fauna of St. Lucia Lake following a period of excessively high salinity. Transactions of the Royal Society of South Africa 41:295–323.

Bruton, M. N. 1977. The biology of *Clarias gariepinus* (Burchell, 1822) in Lake Sibaya, KwaZulu, with emphasis on its role as a predator. Doctoral dissertation. Rhodes University, Grahamstown, South Africa.

Bruton, M. N. 1985. The effects of suspensoids on fish. Hydrobiologia 125:221–241.

Bruton, M. N., A. H. Bok, and M. T. T. Davies. 1987. Life history styles of diadromous fishes in inland waters of southern Africa. American Fisheries Society Symposium 1:104–121.

Cech J. J., and D. E. Wohlschlag. 1982. Seasonal patterns of respiration, gill ventilation, and hematological characteristics in the striped mullet, *Mugil cephalus* L. Bulletin of Marine Science 32:130–138.

Chan, E. H., and T. E. Chua. 1979. The food and feeding habits of greenback grey mullet, *Liza subviridis* (Valenciennes), from different habitats and at various stages of growth. Journal of Fish Biology 15:165–171.

Chaudhuri, H., R. M. Bhowmick, G. V. Kowtal, M. M. Bagchi, R. K. Jana, and S. D. Guptha. 1977. Experiments in artificial propagation and larval development of *Mugil cephalus* L. in India. Journal of the Inland Fisheries Society of India 9:30–41.

Cyrus, D. P. 1985. The influence of turbidity on fish distribution in Natal estuaries. Doctoral dissertation. University of Natal, Pietermaritzburg, South Africa.

Darnell, R. M. 1958. Food habits of fishes and larger invertebrates of Lake Pontchartrain, Louisiana, an estuarine community. Publications of the Institute of Marine Science, University of Texas 5:353–416.

Davis, T. L. O. 1977. Reproductive biology of the freshwater catfish *Tandanus tandanus* Mitchill, in the Gwydir River, Australia. I: structure of the gonads. Australian Journal of Marine and Freshwater Research 28:139–158.

Day, J. H. 1981. The estuarine fauna. Pages 147–178 *in* J. H. Day, editor. Estuarine ecology with particular reference to southern Africa. A. A. Balkema, Rotterdam, The Netherlands.

Day, J. H., S. J. M. Blaber, and J. H. Wallace. 1981. Estuarine fishes. Pages 197–221 *in* J. H. Day, editor. Estuarine ecology with particular reference to southern Africa. A. A. Balkema, Rotterdam, Netherlands.

Dekhnik, T. V. 1953. Reproduction of *Mugil cephalus* in the Black Sea. Comptes Rendus, (Doklady) de l'Academie des Sciences de l'URSS 93:201–204.

De Silva, S. S. 1980. Biology of juvenile grey mullet: a short review. Aquaculture 19:21–36.

De Silva, S. S., and P. A. B. Perera, 1976. Studies on the young grey mullet, *Mugil cephalus* L. I. Effects of salinity on food intake, growth and food conversion. Aquaculture 7:327–338.

De Silva, S. S., and M. J. S. Wijeyratne. 1977. Studies on the biology of young grey mullet, *Mugil cephalus* L. II. Food and feeding. Aquaculture 12:157–167.

FAO (Food and Agriculture Organization of the United Nations) 1982. FAO Yearbook of Fishery Statistics.

Grant, E. M. 1982. Guide to fishes. Department of Harbours and Marine, Brisbane, Australia.

Greer Walker, M., F. R. Harden Jones, and G. P. Arnold. 1978. The movement of plaice (*Pleuronectes platessa* L.) tracked in the open sea. Journal du Conseil, Conseil International pour l'Exploration de la Mer 38:58–86.

Grindley, J. R. 1981. Estuarine plankton. Pages 117–146 *in* J. H. Day, editor. Estuarine ecology with particular reference to southern Africa. A. A. Balkema, Rotterdam, The Netherlands.

Harden Jones, F. R. 1984. A view from the ocean. Pages 1–26 *in* J. D. McCleave, G. P. Arnold, J. J. Dodson, and W. H. Neill, editors. Mechanisms of migration in fishes. Plenum, London, England.

Helfrich, P., and P. M. Allen. 1975. Observations on the spawning of mullet, *Crenimugil crenilabis* (Forskal), at Enewetak, Marshall Islands. Micronesica 11:219–225.

Hutton, R. F., and F. Soganderes-Bernal. 1959. Studies on the trematode parasites encysted in Florida mullets. Florida Board of Conservation Marine Research Laboratory Special Scientific Report 1:1–88.

Jackson, S. 1984. Predation by pied kingfishers and whitebreasted cormorants on fish in the Kosi estuary system. Ostrich 55:113–132.

James, P. S. B. R., V. S. Rengaswamy, A. Raju, G. Mottanraj, and V. Gandhi. 1983. Induced spawning and larval rearing of the grey mullet *Liza macrolepis* (Smith). Indian Journal of Fisheries 30:185–202.

Kesteven, G. L. 1942. Studies on the biology of Australian mullet. I. Account of the fishery and preliminary statement of the biology of *Mugil dobula* Gunther. Australia Commonwealth Scientific and Industrial Research Organization Bulletin 157.

Kowtal, G. V. 1976. Studies on the juvenile fish stock of Chilka Lake. Indian Journal of Fisheries 23:31–40.

Kuo, C. M., Z. H. Shedhdah, and K. K. Milisen. 1973. A preliminary report on the development, growth and survival of laboratory reared larvae of the grey mullet, *Mugil cephalus* L. Journal of Fish Biology 5:459–470.

Lee, C. S., and B. Menu. 1981. Effects of salinity on egg development and hatching in grey mullet *Mugil cephalus* L. Journal of Fish Biology 19:179–188.

Leggett, W. C. 1984. Fish migrations in coastal and estuarine environments: a call for new approaches to the study of an old problem. Pages 159–178 *in* J. D. McCleave, G. P. Arnold, J. J. Dodson, and W. H. Neill, editors. Mechanisms of migration in fishes. Plenum, London, England.

Lenanton, R. C. J., I. C. Potter, N. R. Longeragan, and P. J. Chrystal. 1984. Age structure and changes in abundance of three important species of teleost in a eutrophic estuary (Pisces: Teleostei). Journal of Zoology (London) 203:311–327.

Liao, I. C. 1975. Experiments on the induced breeding of the grey mullet in Taiwan from 1963–1973. Aquaculture 6:31–58.

Liao, I. C., Y. J. Lu, T. L. Huange, and M. C. Lin. 1971. Experiments on induced breeding on the grey mullet *Mugil cephalus* L. Aquaculture 1:15–34.

Luther, G. 1963. Some observations on the biology of *Liza macrolepis* (Smith) and *Mugil cephalus* L. (Mugilidae) with notes on the fishery of grey mullets near Mandapam. Indian Journal of Fisheries 10:642–666.

Major, P. F. 1978. Aspects of estuarine intertidal ecology of juvenile striped mullet, *Mugil cephalus* in Hawaii. U.S. National Marine Fisheries Service Fishery Bulletin 76:299–314.

Marais, J. F. K. 1984. Feeding ecology of major carnivorous fish from four eastern Cape estuaries. South African Journal of Zoology 19:210–223.

Martin, T. J., and S. J. M. Blaber. 1983. The feeding ecology of Ambassidae (Osteichthyes, Perciformes) in Natal estuaries. South African Journal of Zoology 18:353–362.

Martin, F. D., and G. E. Drewry. 1978. Development of fishes of the Mid-Atlantic Bight, volume 6. Stromateidae through Ogcocephalidae. U.S. Fish and Wildlife Service Biological Services Program FWS-OBS-78/12.

McCleave, J. D., and R. C. Kleckner. 1982. Selective tidal stream transport in the estuarine migration of glass eels of the American eel (Anguilla rostrata). Journal du Conseil, Counseil International pour l'Exploration de la Mer 40:262–271.

Moazzam, M., and S. H. N. Rizvi. 1980. Fish entrapment in the seawater intake of power plant at Karachi coast. Environmental Biology of Fishes 5:49–57.

Mukherjee, A. K. 1971. Food habits of the water-birds of the Sunderban 24—Parganas District, West Bengal, India. Journal of the Bombay Natural History Society 68:37–64.

Natarajan, A. V., and S. Patnaik. 1968. Occurrence of mullet eggs in gut contents of Ambassis gymnocephalus. Journal of the Marine Biological Association of India 9:192–194.

Nelson, J. S. 1984. Fishes of the world. John Wiley & Sons, New York, New York, USA.

Norcross, B. L., and R. F. Shaw. 1984. Oceanic and estuarine transport of fish eggs and larvae: a review. Transactions of the American Fisheries Society 113:153–165.

Potter, I. C., N. R. Loneragan, R. C. J. Lenanton, P. J. Chrystal, and C. J. Grant. 1983. Abundance, distribution and age structure of fish populations in a western Australia estuary. Journal of Zoology (London) 200:21–50.

Russell, B. C. 1983. Annotated checklist of the coral reef fishes in the Capricorn–Bunker Group, Great Barrier Reef, Australia. Great Barrier Reef Marine Park Authority, Townsville, Australia.

Sarojini, K. K. 1958. Biology and fisheries of the grey mullets of Bengal. II. Biology of Mugil cunnesius Valenciennes. Indian Journal of Fisheries 5:56–76.

Smith, J. L. B. 1965. The sea fishes of southern Africa. Central News Agency, Cape Town, South Africa.

Staples, D. J. 1980. Ecology of juvenile and adolescent banana prawns, Penaeus merguiensis, in a mangrove estuary and adjacent offshore area in the Gulf of Carpentaria. I. Immigration and settlement of postlarvae. Australian Journal of Marine and Freshwater Research 31:635–652.

Tang, Y. A. 1964. Induced spawning of striped mullet by hormone injection. Japanese Journal of Ichthyology 12:23–28.

Thomson, J. M. 1963. Synopsis of biological data on the grey mullet Mugil cephalus Linneaus 1758. Australian Commonwealth Scientific and Industrial Research Organization Division of Fisheries and Oceanography Synopsis 1.

Thomson, J. M. 1966. The grey mullets. Oceanography and Marine Biology an Annual Review 4:301–335.

Torricelli, P., P. Tongiorgi, and P. Almansi. 1982. Migration of grey mullet fry into the Arno River: seasonal appearance, daily activity, and feeding rhythms. Fisheries Research (Amsterdam) 1:219–234.

Van der Elst, R. P. 1976. Game fish of the east coast of southern Africa. I. The biology of the elf, Pomatomus saltatrix (Linneaus), in the coastal waters of Natal. Oceanographic Research Institute (Durban) Investigational Report 44:1–59.

Van der Elst, R. P. 1982. A guide to the common sea fishes of southern Africa. C. Struik, Cape Town, South Africa.

Van Der Horst, G., and T. Erasmus. 1978. The breeding cycle of male Liza dumerili (Teleostei: Mugilidae) in the mouth of the Swartkops estuary. Zoologica Africana 13:259–274.

Wallace, J. H. 1975. The estuarine fishes of the east coast of South Africa. III. Reproduction. Oceanographic Research Institute (Durban) Investigational Report 41:1–51.

Wallace, J. H., and R. P. Van der Elst. 1975. The estuarine fishes of the east coast of South Africa. IV. Occurrence of juveniles in estuaries. V. Biology, estuarine dependence and status. Oceanographic Research Institute (Durban) Investigational Report 42:1–63.

Wells, R. D. S. 1984. The food of the grey mullet (Mugil cephalus L.) in Lake Waahi and the Waikato River at Huntly. New Zealand Journal of Marine and Freshwater Research 18:13–19.

Westerberg., H. 1984. The orientation of fish and the vertical stratification at fine and micro-structure scales. Pages 179–203 in J. D. McCleave, G. P. Arnold, J. J. Dodson, and W. H. Neill, editors. Mechanisms of migration in fishes. Plenum, London, England.

Whitfield, A. K. 1978. Relationship between fish and piscivorous bird densities at Lake St. Lucia. South African Journal of Science 74:478.

Whitfield, A. K. 1980a. A quantitative study of the trophic relationships within the fish community of the Mhlanga estuary, South Africa. Estuarine and Coastal Marine Science 10:417–435.

Whitfield. A. K. 1980b. Factors influencing the recruitment of juvenile fishes into the Mhlanga estuary. South African Journal of Zoology 15:166–169.

Whitfield, A. K., and S. J. M. Blaber. 1978a. Distribution movements and fecundity of Mugilidae at Lake St. Lucia. Lammergeyer 26:53–63.

Whitfield, A. K., and S. J. M. Blaber. 1978b. Feeding ecology of piscivorous birds at Lake St. Lucia. Part I. Ostrich 49:185–198.

Whitfield, A. K., and S. J. M. Blaber. 1978c. Food and feeding ecology of piscivorous fishes in Lake St. Lucia, Zululand. Journal of Fish Biology 13:675–691.

Whitfield, A. K., and S. J. M. Blaber. 1979a. Feeding ecology of piscivorous birds at Lake St. Lucia. Parts II and III. Ostrich 50:1–20.

Whitfield, A. K., and S. J. M. Blaber. 1979b. Predation on grey mullet (*Mugil cephalus* L.) by *Crocodylus niloticus* at St. Lucia, South Africa Copeia 1979:266–269.

Whitfield, A. K., S. J. M. Blaber, and D. P. Cyrus. 1981. Salinity ranges of some southern African fish species occurring in estuaries. South African Journal of Zoology 16:151–155.

American Fisheries Society Symposium 1:519–530, 1987

Speculations on the Evolution of Life History Tactics of the Australian Grayling

Tim M. Berra

Department of Zoology, The Ohio State University, Mansfield, Ohio 44906, USA

Abstract.—The Australian grayling *Prototroctes maraena* presents a good example of an amphidromous life cycle. Spawning takes place in the freshwater midreaches of the Tambo River, Victoria, during late April–early May (fall). Eggs are scattered over gravel, where they remain demersal and nonadhesive. The newly hatched larvae are presumably swept downstream to brackish water where they remain for about 6 months. During November (spring) juveniles ascend to the midreaches of the river where they spend the rest of their lives. Most (88%) grayling die before depositing a third annulus on their scales. The largest fish examined during an 11-month study of 1,479 specimens was 253 mm fork length. Males may spawn during their first year, whereas females appear to require 2 years in fresh water. The oldest fish collected had five annuli and well-developed gonads. Mature females produce an average of 47,000 eggs (0.9 mm diameter) and have a gonadosomatic index (GSI, gonad weight as a percentage of body weight) of about 27% near spawning time. Mature males develop breeding tubercles on the scales and fin rays when the GSI reaches 5.7%. As much as 14% of a ripe male's body weight may be testis at spawning time. The breeding season of this schooling species is short and synchronized; gonadal development begins in mid-March, reaches a peak in late April, and declines by early May. The bouyancy of grayling larvae insures that they will be swept downstream to a warmer and less variable marine or brackish habitat. The apparent decline–abundance cycles in grayling populations may reflect the species' complex life cycle and high fecundity. Several difficult environmental years in succession (typical of Australia's drought–flood cycles) could decimate the grayling population. The survivors could explosively repopulate during succeeding favorable years due to high fecundity and the spawning of 1-year-old males. It is suggested that the driving force molding the grayling life cycle is a response to the bottleneck of habitat variability. The structural, physiological, and behavioral aspects of grayling life history reflect a genetic memory of the environmentally unfavorable conditions and provide a tactic for surviving highly variable conditions.

Three characteristics typify the Australian freshwater fish fauna due to its long isolation from other continents: (1) it is depauperate, (2) it is derived from marine ancestors, and (3) it is highly endemic (Berra 1981). Australia occupies almost the same total area as does the United States minus Alaska. However, due to a lack of rainfall over much of this area, Australia is inhabited by relatively few freshwater fishes. The Australian fauna contains fewer than 200 species (Merrick and Schmida 1984) compared with over 760 species found in U.S. fresh waters (Lee et al. 1980).

The Australian grayling *Prototroctes maraena* (Figure 1) is a peculiar salmoniform fish found only in southeastern Australia. It is currently considered the sole member of the subfamily Prototroctinae within the family Retropinnidae, which includes the Australian and New Zealand smelts (Nelson 1984). Previously, it had been classified in its own family, Prototroctidae (McDowall 1976) or in the Aplochitonidae (Greenwood et al. 1966). *Prototroctes maraena* is the only extant species, and, until recently, its life history was virtually unknown. The New Zealand grayling, *P. oxyrhynchus,* has not been collected since 1923 and is presumed to be extinct (McDowall 1978).

The Australian grayling occurs in coastal rivers of southeastern Australia from about the latitude of Sydney to approximately 200 km west of Melbourne, as well as around the coast of Tasmania (Bell et al. 1980; Figure 2). It was the subject of an intensive 11-month study in 1979 in which major aspects of its life history were elucidated (Berra 1982, 1984; Berra and Cadwallader 1983; Berra et al., in press).

This paper is divided into two parts. A description of the Australian grayling life history is followed by unabashed speculation on the evolution of the species' life history tactics.

Australian Grayling Life History

Study Site and Methods

The site chosen for the 11-month field study was the Tambo River, a clear, gravel-bottomed stream of alternating pools and riffles flowing

FIGURE 1.—Australian grayling from the Tambo River (A and B) and Tasmania (C). Specimens are listed from top to bottom. (A) Male aged 3+, 196 mm FL (fork length); female aged 2+, 190 mm FL; 24 April. (B) Male aged 3+, 220 mm FL; female aged 2+, 186 mm FL; male aged 2+, 184 mm FL; 15 June. (C) Larva 51 mm FL; 15 October.

through granite bedrock about 300 km east of Melbourne, Victoria (Figure 2). The river drains into Lake King, an estuary open to the sea only at Lakes Entrance. Brackish water penetrates upstream as far as Tambo Upper, above which is fresh water. The collection localities ranged in elevation from 40 m at Ramrod Creek to 300 m at Haunted Stream (Figure 2). The vegetation over most of the area below 500 m is dry, open scle-

rophyll. Water temperature ranged from 5 to 26°C during 1979 and the pH was about 8. The water was clear and tea colored, and dissolved oxygen was not limiting. Water chemistry was documented by Berra (1984) and Graham et al. (1978).

The plan was to sample the Tambo River at numerous sites almost daily for about 1 year. Thus, the Australian grayling population could be monitored for time and place of spawning, age and growth, food habits, and many life history variables. Australian grayling were collected with gill nets, seines, fyke nets, electrofishing gear, and rotenone. From January through November 1979, 1,479 Australian grayling were collected and examined. Details of the study were published by Berra (1982).

Size, Age, and Growth

The largest Australian grayling taken was an age-5+ female of 253 mm fork length (FL). The smallest was 73 mm FL. The maximum weight recorded during this study was 186 g for both a male and a female taken in November. Size increased from January until May. Growth ceased during the winter months (June, July, August) and resumed in September. There was no difference in the length–weight relationship between the sexes (Berra and Cadwallader 1983). Based upon examination of scale annuli and length-frequency distribution, most (88%) Australian grayling belonged to the 1+ and 2+ age-class (Table 1). Fish aged 3+ and 4+ made up 11% of the collection. Less than 1% reached 5+. By counting circuli after the last annulus, it was determined that an annulus was formed on the scale by October (Berra and Cadwallader 1983).

Gonadosomatic Index and Spawning Season

By sampling continuously throughout the year, it was possible to pinpoint the time of spawning. Table 2 shows how the gonadosomatic index (GSI = weight of gonad as a percentage of body weight) changed with time. Australian grayling reached their peak of gonadal development in April when the testis averaged 10.7% and the ovary averaged 23% of total body weight of fish older than 1+. Both males and females have only a left gonad. Maturation is dramatic and highly synchronized between the sexes.

In 1979, the peak of gonadal development occurred on 24 April. Males caught that day were oozing milt, and eggs were easily expressed from swollen females. These ripe fish were taken by gill nets from a deep pool between riffles in the

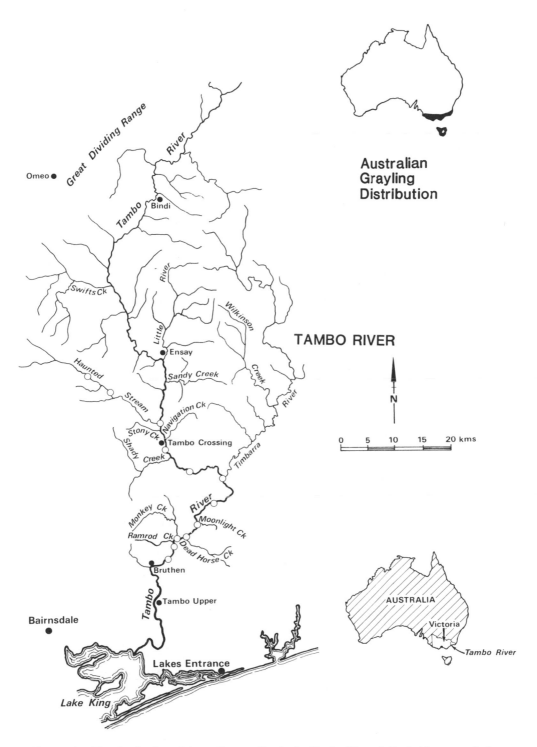

FIGURE 2.—The distribution of Australian grayling in the Tambo River, indicated by open circles.

TABLE 1.—Fork length range, number of fish, and percentage of individuals in each year class of Australian grayling from the Tambo River, 1979.

Annuli	Fork length range (mm)	Number	Percent of total
1	73–142	298	44.7
2	133–200	289	43.3
3	183–234	39	5.9
4	197–230	37	5.5
5	223–253	4	0.6

freshwater midreaches of the Tambo River at Stony Creek. The water temperature was 13°C. The first spent fish were taken on 1 May and only spent fish were collected after the first week of May. Thus, the 1979 spawning season in the Tambo River was inferred to be approximately a 2-week period from late April to early May.

Other rivers with different temperature regimens may produce different spawning seasons. Likewise, other years may also yield a somewhat different spawning date in the same river.

Body fat was extensive in February and decreased as the gonads enlarged, presumably utilized in gonadal growth. Fat deposits were again noticeable when growth resumed in October and November (spring).

In its undeveloped state, the testis consisted of transparent, compressed anterior and posterior lobes connected by a thin testicular filament (Figure 3A). Histology showed no sperm in the lumen of the narrow seminiferous tubules (Berra 1984). By mid-March (Figure 3B), both lobes were milky white and enlarged as was the connecting filament, due to migration of spermatogenic cells into it. Tubule diameter increased, sperm heads were in the center of the lumen, and the tubule wall was very thin. By mid-April, the two lobes were in contact, and the testis filled the body cavity by 24 April (Figure 3C), at which time the fish was very deep-bodied (Figure 1A). Histology revealed that the lumen of the seminiferous tubules was packed with sperm, tubule diameter was at its greatest, and the walls were very thin.

The females underwent a similar developmental cycle. In February, the ovary was ribbon-like with an expanded anterior end and a tapered posterior tip (Figure 3D). By late March, the ovary was filled with many tiny yellow eggs (Figure 3E). Enlargement continued until late April, when the ovary completely filled the coelom (Figure 3F; Berra 1984).

There was no sign of postspawning mortality or a spawning migration. The sex ratio, based upon dissection of 597 fishes, was 56:44 (335 males to 262 females), significantly different from 50:50 (Berra and Cadwallader 1983).

Fecundity and Age

Adult females caught between late March and early May had a mean of 47,000 eggs averaging only 0.86 mm in diameter (Table 3). All of these ripe females had more than one annulus on their scales. Females of age 1+ apparently do not spawn. Such is not the case with the males. On 10 April, 14 males age 1+ were caught. Five of these (36%) had a GSI of 5.7–9.1%. Apparently, some age-1+ males contribute to spawning, whereas none of the seven age-1+ females in that collection had a developed ovary. The five age-1+ males with the substantial GSI had breeding tubercles (illustrated by Berra 1982, 1984), whereas the nine with a nil GSI lacked tubercles. Tubercles appear only on males and only when the GSI reaches 5.7%; they decline in size and number after late June, and are completely gone by September.

Attempts to artificially fertilize the eggs from ripe fish caught on 24 April failed; however, this experiment confirmed Saville-Kent's (1886) observation that the eggs are demersal and nonadhesive.

Natural History

Field observations showed that Australian grayling is a schooling species. The fish can be observed in groups picking on algae-covered rocks throughout the year, but especially from October to March. Their diet consists of algae and insect larvae (Berra et al., in press), which they scrape from rocks with comb-like teeth and process in a rather long (for a salmoniform fish), looped gut. Gastrointestinal tracts were full throughout the year. It was assumed that food was not a limiting factor.

An unusual aspect of this fish is that it smells like a cucumber. Indeed, Australian grayling were called "cucumber herring" by turn-of-the-century naturalists. This skin odor is due to the presence of the chemical trans-2-cis-6-nonadienal (Berra et al. 1982). The same molecule is found in cucumbers.

Eleven native species and one exotic (*Salmo trutta*) were taken in the Australian grayling portion of the river (Berra 1982). Only the eels *Anguilla reinhardti* and *A. australis* could be considered predators on adult Australian grayling, and it is doubtful that this predation is important.

TABLE 2.—Monthly size and gonadosomatic index (GSI)[a] of Australian grayling from the Tambo River. Year classes 2–5 are pooled.

Month (1979)	Annuli	Total N	Fork length (mm), mean(range)	Weight (g), mean(range)	GSI[a] Males Mean(range)	N	GSI[a] Females Mean(range)	N
Jan	1	34	82(73–92)	5(3–8)	0.06(0.04–0.09)[b]			
	2–4	7	197(160–221)	99(45–135)	0.07(0.03–0.11)	6	0.40	1
Feb	1	0						
	2–3	4	191(169–211)	84(58–110)	0.12(0.06–0.18)	2	0.55(0.52–0.58)	2
Mar	1	13	107(88–119)	14(17–18)	1.96(0.02–4.42)	4	0.68(0.66–0.70)	2
	2–4	4	181(166–197)	72(51–82)	4.7(3.13–6.09)	3	9.7(5.82–13.52)	2
Apr	1	43	119(107–131)	19(13–24)	3.29(0.01–9.13)	23	0.19(0.05–0.53)	18
	2–4	12	189(166–217)	91(50–122)	10.7(9.05–12.6)	3	23.34(15.36–27.72)	7
May	1	75	125(111–137)	20(15–30)	0.89(0.01–10.78)	37	0.18(0.02–0.47)	28
	2–4	32	188(174–219)	75(58–116)	3.13(0.47–12.58)	13	8.27(0.57–31.41)	19
Jun	1	23	127(116–137)	21(18–26)	0.04(0.01–0.24)	9	0.24(0.05–0.50)	13
	2–4	20	194(173–225)	83(57–124)	1.65(0.40–3.15)	12	1.01(0.71–1.28)	8
Jul	1	28	129(113–141)	22(14–31)	0.02(0.01–0.09)	8	0.33(0.05–0.64)	16
	3	1	234	137			9.30	1
Aug	1	50	128(118–141)	20(16–36)	0.04(0.01–0.69)	28	0.44(0.12–0.89)	21
	2–5	14	198(185–253)	87(56–161)	0.31(0.26–0.41)	7	0.98(0.51–3.24)	7
Sep	1	11	133(121–142)	24(18–34)	0.01	5	0.54(0.36–0.87)	6
	2–4	14	203(177–230)	92(55–122)	0.23(0.17–0.30)	6	2.35(0.41–12.28)	7
Oct	1	1	116	11			0.03	1
	2–4	136	150(144–227)	40(15–149)	0.1(0.00–0.27)	80	0.23(0.00–1.09)	55
Nov	1	22	107(83–121)	10(4–14)	0.03(0.02–0.05)	9	0.10(0.02–0.50)	13
	2–5	126	152(112–229)	45(12–148)	0.05(0.01–0.34)	79	0.42(0.01–3.45)	47
	c	533	150(115–250)	38(13–186)				

[a] GSI is gonad weight as a percentage of body weight.
[b] Both sexes combined.
[c] Fish not aged.

One rotenone sampling of 300 m of stream in November yielded 641 Australian grayling.

Life Cycle

On the basis of data gathered during the 11 months of this study, the presumed diadromous life cycle of the Australian grayling is described as follows (Figure 4). Spawning takes place in the freshwater midreaches of the Tambo River from late April to early May. Large numbers of tiny, demersal, nonadhesive eggs settle in the interstices of the gravel bottom. After hatching, the larvae are presumably swept downstream to brackish waters in the estuary or sea in May. It is not known if the young remain in Lake King, or if they are passively transported or actively migrate to the sea from the estuary. The young spend about 6 months in the brackish water, then return in October–November to spend the rest of their lives, 5 years at most, in fresh water.

Four lines of circumstantial evidence support the idea that the larvae are swept downstream to brackish water. (1) Continual sampling of the midreaches of the Tambo River with a variety of gear failed to yield any larval or juvenile Australian grayling, even though Australian smelt *Retropinna semoni* as tiny as 15 mm were captured. (2)

The smallest preserved specimen of a grayling is a 51-mm FL, unpigmented larva taken from the mouth of the Arthur River, Tasmania, in 2.2% brackish water (Bell et al. 1980). (3) Saville-Kent (1886) described the 6.5-mm larvae as "remarkably slender and bouyant and swimming toward the surface . . ." This behavior would facilitate dispersal downstream by the current. (4) Juvenile Australian grayling (83–121 mm FL) suddenly appeared in the freshwater reaches of the Tambo River in November (Table 2).

This life cycle fits the definition of the term "amphidromous" coined by Myers (1949) and defined as "diadromous fishes whose migration from fresh water to the sea, or vice-versa, is not for the purpose of breeding, but occurs regularly at some other definite stage of the life cycle."

Two Australian fishes in the salmoniform family Galaxiidae, *Galaxias brevipinnis* and *G. truttaceous,* have a similar life cycle involving an autumn, freshwater spawning by highly fecund females that produced small eggs, followed by freshwater hatching, passive dispersal of larvae downstream to the sea, and migration of juveniles into fresh water about 6 months later (Cadwallader and Backhouse 1983; Merrick and Schmida 1984).

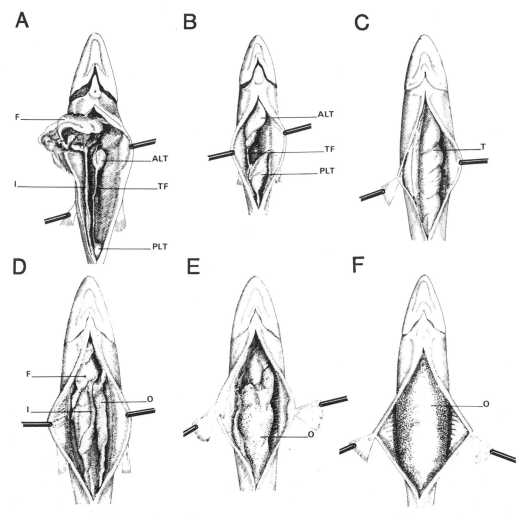

FIGURE 3.—Development of Australian grayling gonads. A–C, testis; D–F, ovary. A and D, 15 February; B, 13 March; C and F, 24 April; E, 29 March. ALT = anterior lobe; TF = testicular filament; PLT = posterior lobe; F = fat; I = intestine; O = ovary. Drawn from slides of actual specimens.

Speculations on the Evolution of Life History Traits

It is one thing to describe the life history of an animal like the Australian grayling. It is quite another thing to explain the evolution of that life history, as will be attempted below. Let us begin with the caveat that evolution via natural selection produces the best *possible* adaptations, not the best *imaginable* ones. In other words, organisms evolve within a certain historical context, and natural selection will do the best it can with what it is given in that context.

Egg Scattering

A question that one might ask is why do Aus-

tralian grayling scatter thousands of eggs? Why not adopt a more protective tactic of nest building or mouth brooding? The evolutionary context offers an answer. Balon (1985a, 1985b, and papers cited therein) has classified reproductive styles of fishes into a system of guilds which represent evolutionary trends from three ethological categories: nonguarding, guarding, and live breeding. Nonguarders are the most primitive and are divided into open-substratum egg scatterers and brood hiders. The open-substratum egg scatterers are subdivided into seven guilds. The Australian grayling life history described above fits into the second guild, called "rock and gravel spawners with pelagic larvae" (litho-pelagophils). This is

TABLE 3.—Fecundity and egg diameter of Australian grayling from the Tambo River in 1979. Each row represents one female.

Date (1979)	Fork length (mm)	GSI[a] (%)	Estimated number of eggs	Egg diameter (mm)	
				Mean	Range
28 Mar	185	13.5	26,918	0.79	0.60–0.90
11 Apr	217	15.4	54,003	0.76	0.60–0.95
12 Apr	169	27.7	55,372	0.86	0.75–0.96
24 Apr	190	27.2	64,966	0.94	0.67–1.30
24 Apr	185	25.2	47,560	0.88	0.76–0.95
24 Apr	189	23.7	42,858	0.83	0.61–0.96
24 Apr	192	22.4	43,730	0.88	0.60–1.02
24 Apr	183	21.8	30,876	0.84	0.59–1.00
1 May	189	28.4	62,720	0.87	0.76–0.96
1 May	183	27.3	45,000	0.96	0.91–1.02
1 May	188	27.1	59,474	0.79	0.65–0.94
1 May	194	31.4	66,865	0.89	0.75–1.20
2 May	178	24.3	35,666	0.85	0.75–1.00
8 May	174	22.1	25,121	0.86	0.70–1.10
Average	187	24.1	47,224	0.86	

[a] GSI is gonadosomatic index, gonad weight as a percentage of body weight.

the most common fish reproductive pattern and is the ancestral condition. It also agrees with the most likely hypothesis of chordate origins from a paedomorphic tunicate larva (Balon 1985a). It is not surprising that a relatively primitive fish (salmoniform) should retain an ancestral reproductive tactic. Balon (1985a) suggested that, with the invasion of fresh water by marine ancestors, the scattering of eggs on river gravel enhanced survival because invertebrate predators were relatively few compared to those in marine environments. There are a few examples of primitive fishes with advanced egg care systems (e.g., coelacanth *Latimeria latimeria*), but the implications of Balon's system, which is not meant to be a taxonomic classification, are that hiding a clutch of eggs represents an advancement and guarding the eggs is a further advancement. Brooding the eggs, as done by cichlids in the mouth or by seahorses in a pouch, insures even greater survival of the young. Retaining the eggs and giving birth to live young represents the ultimate in zygote care. So, Australian grayling scatter eggs because their ancestors did it, and the environmental pressure has not selected otherwise.

Brackish Water Phase

Another question that might be asked is, why should Australian grayling spend their first 6 months or so in brackish or marine waters? When one considers that all Australian freshwater fishes except the lungfish *Neoceratodus fosteri,* and perhaps the osteoglossids *Scleropages* spp., are derived from marine ancestors (Berra 1981), it is

not surprising that some vestiges of marine influence are retained. An estuary or the sea would be a more uniform habitat for the growing larvae and juveniles and would keep them out of the low winter temperature of the river until they have grown to a size at which they can swim back into the freshwater midreaches.

The eggs of the Australian grayling contain several oil droplets. In the ancestral marine situation, the eggs may have been buoyant. In fresh water, they are demersal, which protects them from displacement by the rapid current. The buoyant condition of the larvae causes the young to be swept downstream by the current. The environmental conditions more or less ensure that there is a brackish or marine phase even if it is not a physiological necessity.

r- and K-selection

Why are the eggs so tiny and numerous? These two questions are, of course, intimately related to one another and to r- and K-selection, terms coined by MacArthur and Wilson (1967). K-selection refers to traits of delayed reproduction, small clutches, parental care, and small reproductive effort that produce a few large offspring. On the other hand, r-selection refers to characteristics such as early age at first reproduction, large clutch size, no parental care, and large reproductive effort that results in numerous, small offspring (Stearns 1976).

Female Australian grayling averaging about 187 mm FL produced about 47,000 eggs of less than 0.9-mm average diameter (Table 3). This is a large

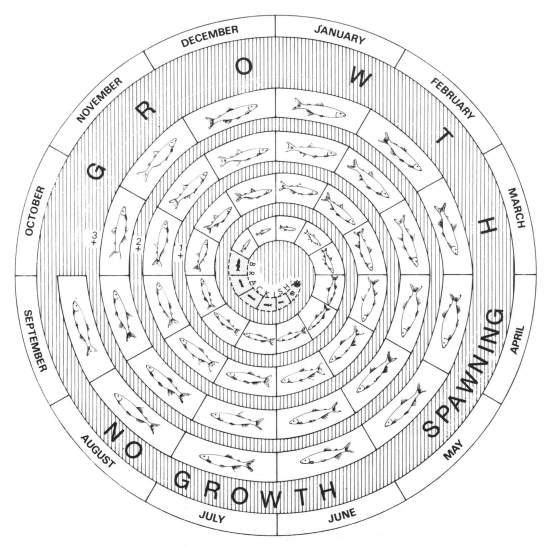

FIGURE 4.—Life cycle of the Australian grayling.

number for a fish that size. Since no mature age-1+ females were collected, it may be conjectured that the females have a delayed maturity in which more of their available resources are channelled into somatic growth. Thus, they are larger at their later maturation, which is likely to result in a gain in fecundity (Stearns and Crandall 1985). Some males, on the other hand, contribute to spawning their first year. These small but ripe males may represent an alternative reproductive strategy similar to the cuckholders among sunfish and jacks among salmon (Gross 1984). If these precocial "sneak spawners" are reproductively successful, this may result in an "evolutionary stable strategy" (Maynard Smith 1982; Gross

1984). Do the precocial grayling males pay the ultimate price for spawning the first year? Have they invested so much energy in gonadal development and sperm production that they do not survive to spawn in succeeding years? Further studies may shed light on these questions.

Australian grayling appear to be highly *r*-selected in some respects, which insures that they can repopulate an area rapidly after decimation by a harsh environmental year. Even though most (88%) Australian grayling die after age 2+, the remaining 12% provide a safety margin, insuring that there will be some individuals alive and ready to release large numbers of eggs after several unfavorable years in succession, a common occurrence in Australia. This minimizes the probability of extinction.

Environmental Variability

Before delving into the literature on environmental variation and life history tactics, it would seem appropriate to document the variability of the Tambo River as a habitat. Australia is the driest continent except for the polar regions (Warner 1977), but the southeast coast, south of the Great Dividing Range in Victoria, is one of the best and most uniformly watered areas of the continent (Warner 1977). Even here, however, serious droughts and tremendous floods affect the rivers. The Tambo River is at the western edge of a region of Victoria called East Gippsland. The climate of East Gippsland is influenced by strong meteorlogical depressions off the New South Wales coast which can bring heavy rain and severe flooding at any time of the year (Linforth 1969).

Annual rainfall in the Tambo River area is about 760–890 mm depending upon altitude. The rainfall in East Gippsland can vary greatly from month to month, depending upon east-coast depressions. On a seasonal basis, however, the difference between the median rainfall (rainfall which is not exceeded on 50% of the occasions) and the mean rainfall is very small except in autumn, which happens to be the Australian grayling breeding season. Linforth (1969) compiled the following East Gippsland rainfall figures from 1913 through 1965: in summer (December–February), the median and mean rainfalls were 188 mm; in autumn (March–May), the median was 173 mm, the mean 189 mm; in winter (June–August), the median was 184 mm, the mean 185 mm; and in spring (September–November), the median was 204 mm, the mean 206 mm.

East Gippsland has one of the most reliable rainfalls in Victoria, but drought is by no means rare. The area had at least 19 major droughts from 1882 through 1965 which lasted from 5 to 38 months and averaged 10 months. No regularity in the incidence of drought can be found, and its prediction by statistical means is not possible (Linforth 1969). McMahon (1979) concluded that annual streamflow in Australian rivers is so variable that white noise is a better predictor of streamflow than previous stream discharge records. He stated that 76% of streamflow can be explained by a white noise model as opposed to any form of autoregression model.

A strong east-coast depression can produce a great amount of rainfall very quickly. For example, Lakes Entrance, near the mouth of the Tambo River, has had seven 24-h rainfalls in excess of 76 mm from 1947 through 1966. The highest rainfall on record for a 24-h period was 129 mm, recorded in May. Buchan, near the headwaters of the Tambo River, has had six 24-h rainfalls in excess of 76 mm, and a maximum of 215 mm was recorded in July (Linforth 1969).

Examination of two recent years will show how variable streamflow in the Tambo River can be. Estimates made at the gauging station at Ramrod Creek (Figure 2) showed that, for the period July 1976 through June 1977, flow was 35% below the long-term mean. For the period July 1977 to June 1978, the flow was 126% above the mean (Graham et al. 1978). The very high streamflow for 1977–1978 was due to the much-greater-than-average rainfall in June 1978. The departures from average streamflows were +79% for June–September 1977, −78% for October–February 1978, +503% for March–June 1978, and +655% for June 1978 (Graham et al. 1978).

The Australian grayling life history study was carried out in 1979. This was an unusual year in that the river level fluctuated very little. Local residents said that flooding the previous year, 1978, was extensive and that the river level was up to 10 m higher than in 1979.

Life Histories in a Varying Environment

Life history traits that are most successful in a varying environment have been dealt with by Cohen (1966), Murphy (1968), Mountford (1971), Schaffer (1974), and Stearns (1977), among others. Murphy (1968) felt that iteroparity (reproducing several times in a lifetime) was an evolutionary response to uncertain survival from zygote to first maturity. Schaffer (1974) contended that environmentally induced variations in reproductive success favored reduced breeding in iteroparous species, greater longevity, and a longer reproductive life. He was careful to point out that fluctuating environments do not always favor greater reproductive effort. Schaffer (1974) felt that what influenced the adaptive response was the age specificity of the mortality (immatures or adults? constant or fluctuating?).

Stearns (1977) provided support for the idea that environmental fluctuations that resulted in highly variable juvenile mortality would lead to a K-selected strategy of delayed maturity, smaller reproductive effort, and greater longevity. Noakes and Balon (1982) seemed to be saying the opposite when they hypothesized that flooding should lead to earlier maturation, increased fecundity, and smaller eggs—in other words, *r*-selection.

The recent mathematical model builders have broadly rejected *r*- and *K*-selection as an explanatory system and have concentrated on age- and size-specific models (Law 1979; Michod 1979; Charlesworth 1980; Stearns and Crandall 1981). Searns (1982) suggested four reasons for this. (1) The predictions of *r*- and *K*-selection have been tested at least five times without success. (2) Classification systems based on *r*- and *K*-selection fail for about half of the data. (3) It is not clear how one can move logically from the assumption of density-dependent population regulation to the prediction of delayed maturity, long life, and few large young. (4) If one applied density-dependent increases in mortality rates (they should be *K*-selecting) equivalently to all age-classes, the predicted phenotype would be classified as *r*-selected (Charlesworth 1980). This suggests that the crucial issues are not mode of population regulation, but age-specific and size-specific changes in birth and death rates (Stearns 1982).

As with most traits, there is likely a genetic and an environmental component to age and size at maturity. However, Stearns and Crandall (1985) felt that neither age nor size are the traits under selection but, rather, that selection operates on the shape of the age–size maturation trajectory.

Is it possible that, within a single species, both *r*- and *K*-selection can be in operation? Given that Australian grayling habitat fluctuates seriously and unpredictably, and assuming that the periodic floods and droughts increase juvenile (or egg) mortality rather than adult mortality, can it be said that the Australian grayling life history exhibits some *r*- and *K*-selected traits? Large numbers of eggs, small egg size, and some precocious males are *r*-selected features. But, repeated spawnings over a several-year life span (iteroparity) and "delayed" maturity of females and most males until age 2+ could be considered *K*-selected traits. Does this mean that the Australian grayling is ready for any eventuality?

Before the studies of grayling life history (Berra 1982, 1984; Berra and Cadwallader 1983; Berra et al., in press), this species was considered one of the rarest and most endangered of Australian fishes (Lake 1971). How can a species as abundant as suggested by Table 2 be considered rare and endangered? Berra (1982) suggested that the cycle of alternate scarcity and abundance was a reflection of either "bad" or "good" Australian grayling years. Past authors must have based their conclusions of scarcity on the results of environmentally harsh years which depressed Australian grayling numbers. Given the life cycle described in the first section of this paper, Australian grayling mortality could be very high. Most of these fish die before a third annulus is added, and many eggs or young must perish on the way to brackish water during a severe flood or drought. On the other hand, when conditions improve, rapid repopulation is possible due to high fecundity, some age-1+ male breeders, and the relatively long lives (5+ years) of some adults.

An Explanation

The driving force shaping this life cycle appears to be a response to the bottleneck of habitat variability. The Australian grayling's life history has been shaped by floods and droughts, which are stochastic events extrinsic to the biology of the animal. These physical influences may decimate the population, but Australian grayling can recover rapidly, given a few good environmental years, due to their life history adaptations. This idea can be compared to Schoener's (1982) hypothesis that "during lean times, strong directional selection resulting from interspecific competition produces in each species adaptations most suited for resources used relatively exclusively by the species."

Neither competition nor predators are immediately obvious as important pressures in the life history of the Australian grayling, although sources of mortality and evidence of density-dependent growth and survival have not been investigated. During times of severe drought or flooding (lean times) selective pressures would favor those individuals with just those life history adaptations shown by the Australian grayling: high fecundity, early reproductive age of some males, juvenile development in a less perturbable environment (such as an estuary), and iteroparity. The structural, physiological, and behavioral aspects of Australian grayling life history reflect a genetic memory of the bottleneck of environmentally unfavorable conditions.

Acknowledgments

Steven Stearns, Zoologisches Institut, Switzerland, read an early draft of this paper and helpfully suggested many of the life history references. Mart R. Gross of Simon Fraser University, Burnaby, Canada, commented on the implications of precocial males. P. L. Cadwallader of the Victoria Fisheries and Wildlife Service and D. M. Ware of the Department of Fisheries and Oceans, Nanaimo, Canada, reviewed the manuscript and provided many helpful comments. John Las Gourgues of the Victoria Ministry for Conservation drew the figures.

References

Balon, E. K. 1985a. Patterns in the evolution of reproductive styles in fishes. Pages 35–53 *in* G. W. Potts and R. J. Wootton, editors. Fish reproduction. Academic Press, London, England.

Balon, E. K., editor. 1985b. Early life histories of fishes. Dr. W. Junk, Dordrecht, The Netherlands.

Bell, J. D., T. M. Berra, P. D. Jackson, P. R. Last, and R. D. Sloane. 1980. Recent records of the Australian grayling *Prototroctes maraena* Gunther (Pisces: Prototroctidae) with notes on its distribution. Australian Zoologist 20:419–431.

Berra, T. M. 1981. An atlas of distribution of the freshwater families of the world. University of Nebraska Press, Lincoln, Nebraska, USA.

Berra, T. M. 1982. Life history of the Australian grayling, *Prototroctes maraena* (Salmoniformes: Prototroctidae) in the Tambo River, Victoria. Copeia 1982:795–805.

Berra, T. M. 1984. Reproductive anatomy of the Australian grayling *Prototroctes maraena* Gunther. Journal of Fish Biology 25:241–251.

Berra, T. M., and P. L. Cadwallader. 1983. Age and growth of Australian grayling, *Prototroctes maraena* Gunther (Salmoniformes: Prototroctidae), in the Tambo River, Victoria. Australian Journal of Marine and Freshwater Research 34:451–460.

Berra, T. M., A. Campbell, and P. D. Jackson. In press. Diet of the Australian grayling. *Prototroctes maraena* Gunther (Salmoniformes: Prototroctidae), with notes on the occurrence of a trematode parasite and black peritoneum. Australian Journal of Marine and Freshwater Research 38.

Berra, T. M., J. F. Smith, and J. D. Morrison. 1982. Probable identification of the cucumber odor of the Australian grayling *Prototroctes maraena*. Transactions of the American Fisheries Society 111:78–82.

Cadwallader, P. L., and G. N. Backhouse. 1983. A guide to the freshwater fish of Victoria. Victorian Government Printing Office, Melbourne, Australia.

Charlesworth, B. 1980. Evolution in age-structured populations. Cambridge University Press, Cambridge, England.

Cohen, D. 1966. Optimizing reproduction in a randomly varying environment. Journal of Theoretical Biology 12:119–129.

Graham, W. A. E., R. K. Herbert, and A. J. Schalken. 1978. Gippsland regional environmental study. Input stream assessment, 2 volumes, 1 and 2. State Rivers and Water Supply Commission, Melbourne, Australia.

Greenwood, P. H., D. E. Rosen, S. H. Weitzman, and

G. S. Myers. 1966. Phyletic studies of teleostean fishes, with a provisional classification of living forms. Bulletin of the American Museum of Natural History 131:339–456.

Gross, M. R. 1984. Sunfish, salmon, and the evolution of alternative reproductive strategies and tactics in fishes. Pages 55–75 *in* G. W. Potts and R. J. Wootton, editors. Fish reproduction. Academic Press, London, England.

Lake, J. S. 1971. Freshwater fishes and rivers of Australia. Nelson, Melbourne, Australia.

Law, R. 1979. Optimal life histories under age-specific predation. American Naturalist 114:399–417.

Lee, D. S., C. R. Gilbert, C. H. Hocutt, R. E. Jenkins, D. E. McAllister, and J. R. Stauffer, Jr. 1980. Atlas of North American freshwater fishes. North Carolina State Museum of Natural History, Raleigh, North Carolina, USA.

Linforth, D. J. 1969. The climate of East Gippsland. Proceedings of the Royal Society of Victoria 82:27–36.

MacArthur, R. H., and E. O. Wilson, 1967. The theory of island biogeography. Princeton University Press, Princeton, New Jersey, USA.

Maynard Smith, J. 1982. Evolution and the theory of games. Cambridge University Press, Cambridge, England.

McDowall, R. M. 1976. Fishes of the family Prototroctidae (Salmoniformes). Australian Journal of Marine and Freshwater Research 27:641–659.

McDowall, R. M. 1978. New Zealand freshwater fishes. Heinemann, Auckland, New Zealand.

McMahon, T. A. 1979. Hydrologic characteristics of Australian streams. Monash University Department of Civil Engineering, Civil Engineering Research Report 3/1979:1–79.

Merrick, J. R., and G. E. Schmida. 1984. Australian freshwater fishes. Published by Merrick, Macquarie University, School of Biological Sciences, North Ryde, Australia.

Michod, R. E. 1979. Evolution of life histories in response to age-specific mortality factors. American Naturalist 112:531–550.

Mountford, M. D. 1971. Population survival in a variable environment. Journal of Theoretical Biology 32:75–79.

Murphy, G. I. 1968. Pattern in life history and the environment. American Naturalist 102:391–403.

Myers, G. S. 1949. Usage of anadromous, catadromous and allied terms for migratory fishes. Copeia 1949:89–96.

Nelson, J. S. 1984. Fishes of the world, 2nd edition. John Wiley & Sons, New York, New York, USA.

Noakes, D. L. G., and E. K. Balon. 1982. Life histories of tilapias: an evolutionary perspective. Pages 61–82 *in* R. S. V. Rullin and R. H. Lowe-McConnell, editors. The biology and culture of tilapias. International Center for Living Aquatic Resource Management, Manila, Phillippines.

Saville-Kent, W. 1886. [No title.] Papers and Proceedings, Royal Society of Tasmania, cv–cvi.

Schaffer, W. M. 1974. Optimal reproductive effort in

fluctuating environments. American Naturalist 108:783–790.

Schoener, T. W. 1982. The controversy over interspecific competition. American Scientist 70:586–595.

Stearns, S. C. 1976. Life-history tactics: a review of the ideas. Quarterly Review of Biology 51:3–47.

Stearns, S. C. 1977. The evolution of life history traits: a critique of the theory and a review of the data. Annual Review of Ecology and Systematics 8:145–171.

Stearns, S. C. 1982. The emergence of evolutionary and community ecology as experimental sciences. Perspectives in Biology and Medicine 25:621–648.

Stearns, S. C., and R. E. Crandall. 1981. Quantitative predictions of delayed maturity. Evolution 35:455–463.

Stearns, S. C., and R. E. Crandall. 1985. Plasticity for age and size at sexual maturity: a life-history response to unavoidable stress. Pages 13–33 in G. W. Potts and R. J. Wootton, editors. Fish reproduction. Academic Press, London, England.

Warner, R. F. 1977. Hydrology. Pages 53–84 in D. N. Jeans, editor. Australia: a geography. Sydney University Press, Sydney, Australia.

American Fisheries Society Symposium 1:531–546, 1987

Comparison of Recruitment Variability and Life History Data among Marine and Anadromous Fishes

B. J. Rothschild and Gerard T. DiNardo

University of Maryland, Center for Environmental and Estuarine Studies
Chesapeake Biological Laboratory, Solomons, Maryland 20688 USA

Abstract.—This paper compares indices of recruitment variability for marine and anadromous fishes and examines the relationship of recruitment variability to the life history and morphological characteristics: relative fecundity, egg size, incubation time, size at hatching, duration of the yolk-sac larva stage, eye development, and mouth development. These relationships are examined via two-way classifications (high or low) based on each datum's position relative to the median value (greater or less than) for the recruitment indices and life history traits. It appears that the observed relationships can be explained by examining the spawning strategies of marine and anadromous fishes, particularly how they relate to the placement of reproductive material in salubrious conditions. Among anadromous fish, the environment-sampling process relies upon the adults as the primary samplers for salubrious environmental conditions. Conversely, among marine fish the task of sampling the environment for salubrious conditions is left to the individual eggs and larvae.

The most important tasks in fishery science usually relate to recruitment prediction or control. These tasks are difficult because the sources of recruitment variability are not well understood owing to their great complexity. To continue to unravel this complexity, it is necessary to examine the problem from as many perspectives as possible.

It has been believed for a long time, particularly with regard to marine fish, that recruitment variability is related to variability in larval survival (Hjort 1914). It is further believed that variability in larval survival owes to the feeding success of larval fish. It has been argued that feeding success is affected by the fragility of larvae, many of which hatch without pigmented eyes or functional mouth parts (Fabre-Domergue and Bietrix 1896; Hjort 1914; Lasker 1975—see, however, Marr 1956 and Rothschild 1986 for discussions of the "critical period"). A comparison of marine and anadromous larvae leaves one with the impression that, at hatching, anadromous fish are ontogenetically more advanced than marine fish—they are accordingly less "fragile" and should not, all other things being equal, be as susceptible to vagaries in food supply; as a consequence, the variability in their recruitment time series should be less than that of marine fish.

This paper examines these assertions. We examine the indices of recruitment variability for marine and anadromous fishes and the relation of recruitment variability to life history and morphological characteristics often linked to larval fragil-
ity and survival. These include the aforementioned eye and jaw development as well as other morphological indices (e.g., Blaxter and Hunter 1982): relative fecundity, egg diameter, hatching size; and temporal indices (e.g., Shepherd and Cushing 1980; Beverton and Holt 1957) thought to be related to the larva's susceptibility to predation: egg incubation time and duration of the yolk-sac larval stage.

Methods

Recruitment data were assembled from 30 marine and 25 anadromous stocks for which more than 10 years of data were available. Tables 1 and 2 give the coefficients of variation of recruitment time series (CVR), which are intended to serve as indices of recruitment variability for each of the 55 stocks. The CVRs are arrayed in rank order in Appendices 1 and 2.

Life history data on relative fecundity, egg size, incubation time, size at hatching, duration of yolk-sac larval stage, eye development, and mouth development at hatching were also assembled. The data associated with each trait were likewise arrayed in rank order facilitating estimation of a median value for each trait (Appendices 1–3). Because each population of the same species has essentially the same reported life history traits, "ties" exist in the vicinity of the median value. In these instances, each tied value was assigned at random to be either greater or less than the median.

Availability of a median CVR and a median for

TABLE 1.—Statistical description of recruitment in 25 anadromous fish stocks. Age is the age of fish at time of recruitment estimate, period is the time series length in years, mean is the average of the recruitment estimates, SD is the standard deviation and CV is the coefficient of variation (SD/mean).

Stock number	Species	Area	Source[a]	Age	Period	Mean	SD	CV
1	American shad *Alosa sapidissima*	Head of Chesapeake Bay, Maryland	A	0	1962–1984	1.0[c]	2.1	2.10
2	American shad	Potomac River, Maryland	A	0	1962–1984	2.2[c]	3.0	1.36
3	American shad	Connecticut River, Connecticut	B	4–6	1940–1971	134.5[d]	33.8	0.25
4	Blueback herring *Alosa aestivalis*	Head of Chesapeake Bay, Maryland	A	0	1962–1982	56.2[c]	159.6	2.84
5	Blueback herring	Potomac River, Maryland	A	0	1962–1982	29.8[c]	34.9	1.17
6	Blueback herring	Pamunkey River, Virginia	C	0	1972–1982	298.0[e]	411.6	1.38
7	Alewife *Alosa pseudoharengus*	Head of Chesapeake Bay, Maryland	A	0	1962–1982	10.4[c]	21.5	2.07
8	Alewife	Potomac River, Maryland	A	0	1962–1982	5.4[c]	7.0	1.30
9	Alewife	Pamunkey River, Virginia	C	0	1972–1982	14.0[e]	15.5	1.11
10	White perch *Morone americana*	Chesapeake Bay, Maryland	A	0	1962–1984	17.5[c]	14.2	0.81
11	Striped bass *Morone saxatilis*	Head of Chesapeake Bay, Maryland	A	0	1962–1984	13.8[c]	10.3	0.75
12	Striped bass	Potomac River, Maryland	A	0	1962–1984	6.3[c]	7.5	1.19
13	Striped bass	Sacramento–San Joaquin estuary, California	D	0	1959–1976	68.0[c]	24.9	0.37
14	Pink salmon (odd-year stock) *Oncorhynchus gorbuscha*	Prince William Sound, Alaska	E	2	1940–1971	5,331.6[d]	3,934.0	0.74
15	Pink salmon (even-year stock)	Prince William Sound, Alaska	E	2	1940–1971	5,673.1[d]	3,161.6	0.56
16	Pink salmon (odd-year stock)	Kodiak area, Alaska	E	2	1952–1970	5,176.1[d]	4,016.1	0.77
17	Pink salmon (even-year stock)	Kodiak area, Alaska	E	2	1952–1970	8,917.0[d]	3,708.8	0.42
18	Sockeye salmon *Oncorhynchus nerka*	Chignik area, Alaska	E	4–7	1949–1971	1,066.7[d]	498.6	0.47
19	Sockeye salmon	Karluk River, Alaska	E	4–7	1887–1953	2,278.5[d]	1,225.8	0.54
20	Sockeye salmon	Columbia River, Oregon	E	4–7	1938–1974	141.7[d]	85.5	0.60
21	Chum salmon *Oncorhynchus keta*	Prince William Sound, Alaska	E	3–5	1952–1971	642.0[d]	327.8	0.51
22	Chinook salmon *Oncorhynchus tshawytscha*	Sacramento–San Joaquin estuary, California	F	[b]	1967–1978	66.2[f]	46.8	0.71
23	American shad	Sacramento–San Joaquin estuary, California	F	[b]	1967–1978	1,932.7[f]	1,668.3	0.86
24	Longfin smelt *Spirinchus thaleichthys*	Sacramento–San Joaquin estuary, California	F	[b]	1967–1978	17,139.0[f]	28,077.6	1.64
25	Delta smelt *Hypomesus transpacificus*	Sacramento–San Joaquin estuary, California	F	[b]	1967–1978	835.8[f]	459.1	0.55

[a] Source: (A) Boone (1980); Maryland Department of Natural Resources, personal communication; (B) Crecco (1978); (C) Loesch and Kriete (1982); (D) Chadwick et al. (1977); (E) INPFC (1962; 1974); (F) Stevens and Miller (1983).

[b] No ages reported; recruitment estimates are based upon total number of young fish.

[c] Recruitment estimated as the average number of juveniles per tow.

[d] Recruitment estimated as total number in thousands.

[e] Recruitment estimated as a weighted catch per unit effort.

[f] Recruitment estimated as a trawl index ($\times 10^4$).

each life history trait enabled each datum to be classified as being either greater than or less than the median. The classification also enabled a two-way classification of CVRs and life history traits, each datum being classified as to whether it was greater than or less than the median CVR and the median value for the particular life history trait.

An important methodological consideration relates to the quality of the data. It is important first to take note of qualifications that are inherent in any large mass of recruitment and life history data

collected and analyzed by a large number of authors in a variety of ways.

(1) Recruitment data tend to be inherently noisy and hence real differences among estimates can be obscured by sampling or other procedural error.

(2) The number of observations in each time series is not particularly large and hence real differences may be masked.

(3) Techniques for estimating recruitment for anadromous and marine fish differ. Recruitment to anadromous stocks is generally estimated from

TABLE 2.—Statistical description of recruitment in 30 marine fish stocks. Age is the age of fish at time of recruitment estimate, period is the time series length in years, mean is the average of the recruitment estimates, SD is the standard deviation and CV is the coefficient of variation (SD/mean).

Stock number	Species	Area	Source[a]	Age	Period	Mean	SD	CV
1	Butterfish *Peprilus triacanthus*	NW Atlantic Ocean	A	0	1968–1983	127.0[d]	93.9	0.74
2	Atlantic croaker *Micropogonias undulatus*	York River, Virginia	B	0	1954–1977	20.7[d]	34.2	1.65
3	Spot *Leiostomus xanthurus*	Chesapeake Bay	C	0	1962–1984	8.3[d]	8.6	1.04
4	Atlantic mackerel *Scomber scombrus*	NW Atlantic Ocean	D	1	1963–1983	0.8[d]	0.9	1.12
5	Atlantic herring *Clupea harengus harengus*	Gulf of Maine	E	1	1947–1978	2,053.6[e]	1,420.3	0.69
6	Pacific sardine *Sardinops sagax*	California	F	2	1930–1962	3,541.9[e]	3,958.4	1.12
7	Atlantic menhaden *Brevoortia tyrannus*	Western Atlantic Ocean	G	1	1955–1975	3,362.0[e]	2,927.2	0.87
8	Gulf menhaden *Brevoortia patronus*	Gulf of Mexico	H	1	1964–1976	16,367.1[e]	5,351.7	0.33
9	Haddock *Melanogrammus aeglefinus*	North Sea	I	3	1955–1973	1,129.7[f]	1,800.0	1.59
10	Sole *Solea solea*	North Sea	J	2	1931–1971	94.7[e]	111.1	1.17
11	Plaice *Pleuronectes platessa*	North Sea	J	2	1945–1971	414.9[e]	191.5	0.46
12	Yellowtail flounder *Limanda ferruginea*	Southern New England	K	[b]	1944–1965	22.8[e]	15.6	0.68
13	Capelin *Mallotus villosus*	Labrador	L	2	1966–1978	59,000[e]	37,900	0.64
14	Saithe *Pollachius virens*	North Sea	M	1	1961–1978	265,372[f]	157,683	0.59
15	Anchovy *Engraulis capensis*	South Africa	N	0	1964–1976	56,030,770[f]	15,411,700	0.27
16	Silver hake *Merluccius bilinearis*	Georges Bank	O	1	1955–1973	1,207,453[f]	874,699	0.72
17	Pilchard *Sardinops ocellatta*	South Africa	N	3	1950–1975	13,673,500[f]	10,354,600	0.76
18	Atlantic cod *Gadus morhua*	North Sea	P	1	1963–1977	232,937[f]	146,880	0.63
19	Chub mackerel *Scomber japonicus*	California	Q	1	1928–1968	74,044.5[g]	70,921.4	0.96
20	Whiting *Gadus merlangus*	North Sea	P	1	1963–1978	1,333,274[f]	651,530	0.49
21	Atlantic cod	Georges Bank	R	1	1960–1973	24,766[f]	6,302	0.25
22	Atlantic cod	NE Arctic Ocean	S	1	1962–1977	1,011,370[f]	774,546	0.77
23	Haddock	Georges Bank	T	1	1931–1973	72,231[f]	73,039	1.01
24	Haddock	NE Arctic Ocean	S	1	1962–1978	273,897[f]	356,238	1.30
25	Atlantic herring	Norway	U	1	1950–1969	13,734,900[f]	19,059,000	1.39
26	Atlantic herring	Georges Bank	V	2	1963–1974	1,743,079[f]	1,040,054	0.60
27	Peruvian anchovy *Engraulis ringens*	Peru–Chile	W	[c]	1960–1978	306,200[e]	199,600	0.65
28	Petrale sole *Eopsetta jordani*	NE Pacific Ocean	X	4–7	1939–1958	4,025.4[h]	2,497.5	0.62
29	Yellowfin sole *Limanda aspera*	Bering Sea	Y	3	1964–1978	7,481.5[e]	3,354.2	0.45
30	Pacific halibut *Hippoglossus stenolepis*	North Pacific Ocean	Z	3	1935–1971	140,165.7[e]	53,859.2	0.38

[a] Source:
(A) Waring and Anderson (1984)
(B) Norcross and Austin (1981)
(C) Maryland Department of Natural Resources, personal communication
(D) Anderson (1984)
(E) Anthony and Fogarty (1985)
(F) Troadec et al. (1980)
(G) ASMFC (1981)
(H) Ahrenholz (personal communication)

(I) Sahrhage and Wagner (1978)
(J) Holden (1978)
(K) Sissenwine (1974)
(L) Leggett et al. (1984)
(M) ICES (1979c)
(N) Newman and Crawford (1980)
(O) Anderson (1977)
(P) ICES (1979b)
(Q) Parrish and MacCall (1978)

(R) Serchuk et al. (1978)
(S) ICES (1979a)
(T) Clark and Overholtz (1979)
(U) Dragesund et al. (1980)
(V) Anthony and Waring (1980)
(W) Pauly and Tsukayama (1983)
(X) Ketchen and Forrester (1966)
(Y) Wakabayashi (1984)
(Z) Hoag and McNaughton (1978)

[b] No ages reported; recruitment estimates are based upon entry into the fishable stock at approximately 238 g.
[c] No ages reported; recruitment estimates based upon entry into the 4-cm size class.
[d] Recruitment estimated as the average number of juveniles per tow.
[e] Recruitment estimated as total number ($\times 10^6$).
[f] Recruitment estimated as total number.
[g] Recruitment estimated as biomass ($\times 10^3$ pounds).
[h] Recruitment estimated as number of fish per 100 h of trawling.

observations, while recruitment to marine stocks is generally estimated from solving the catch equation iteratively. Since the latter methodology may contain statistical problems that concern linkages among years, it is possible that estimates of recruitment variability deduced from catch equation analyses might contain spurious variability—as might be suggested by the hint of relationship between the CVRs and number of sample years for marine fish in Figure 1.

(4) Estimation of recruitment for marine and anadromous fish may reckon recruitment to occur at different ages although the effects of this possible source of difference are not certain.

(5) Data may include trend as well as nontrend variability.

(6) Some of the data points are highly correlated in the sense that data from salmon populations, for example, will tend to be more alike than data from independent, unrelated stocks. This would mean that the results of the analysis would depend on the balance of the kinds of populations studied.

To be sure, the exercise of obtaining recruit-

ment time series and measurements on various life history variables is eclectic. We do not know the extent to which existent data are representative of marine and anadromous fish. Further, we cannot be sure, without much more extensive analysis, that the data used here are representative of those data that are actually available. For this reason, it is necessary to exercise care in making quantitative statistical interpretations, or in extending inferences beyond the data at hand. On the other hand, if these data are taken for what they are, interesting and useful comparisons can be made which may lend insights into the direction of future data acquisition or research. Accordingly, the data are not embellished with statistical analyses, which could be misleading, for or against a particular hypothesis (even if the statistical tests were nonparametric), as the disparateness of the sources would generate concern regarding the meaning of significance levels. Thus, we simply present the analyses and our impressions, which, we believe, raise important questions.

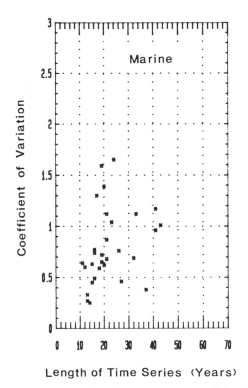
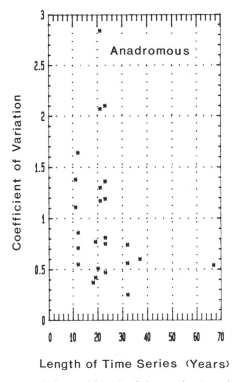

FIGURE 1.—Relationship between the coefficient of recruitment variation and length of time series (years) for marine and anadromous fish.

Results

Coefficients of Recruitment Variation

The median coefficients of variation for marine and anadromous fish are 0.70 and 0.77, respectively, based on data in Tables 1 and 2. Hence, as shown in Figure 2, recruitment time series for anadromous fish tend to be more variable than for marine fish.

This comparison requires further inspection of the data, as it appears that sources of variability in marine and anadromous fish may differ. For example, it appears, as is the case for many range-related statistics, that a relation may exist between the CVR and the length of the time series, particularly for marine fish (Figure 1). If this is true, then the CVRs would need to be adjusted to account for differences in sample size. Another problem involves the particular variability of a single group of fish. The alosids appear to contribute much of the CVR variation among anadromous fish (Figure 3). To compare CVRs among families, consider as a point of reference CVRs greater or less than 0.75. The salmonids and the

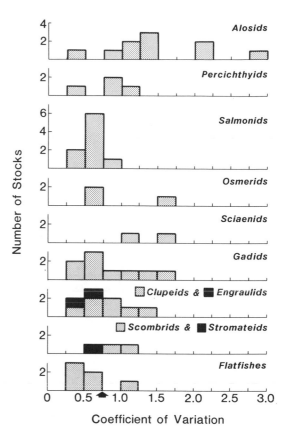

FIGURE 3.—Histograms of the coefficient of recruitment variation (CVR) for marine and anadromous fish grouped by family. The arrow on the abscissa marks CVR = 0.75.

flatfishes exhibit coefficients of variation that are mostly less than 0.75 while the alosids, percichthyids, sciaenids, gadids, clupeids, and scombrids exhibit more coefficients of variation greater than 0.75.

We conclude from the data at hand that recruitment of marine fish is no more or less variable than recruitment of anadromous fish. Rather, recruitment variability appears to depend mostly on taxonomic family or group.

Life History Attributes

The median values for life history attributes for marine and anadromous fish are displayed in Figure 4. Marine fish have a higher relative fecundity, longer duration of the yolk-sac larval stage, and a longer egg incubation time than anadromous fish, whereas anadromous fish have larger eggs and larger size at hatching. It is worth emphasizing that the egg diameter metric tends to minimize

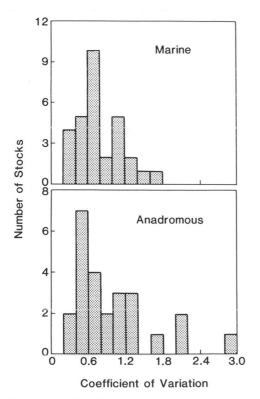

FIGURE 2.— Distribution of the coefficients of recruitment variation (from Tables 1, 2) for marine and anadromous fish.

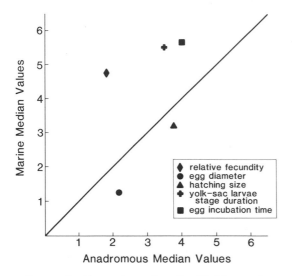

FIGURE 4.—Comparison of median life history characteristics for marine and anadromous fish species. Median relative fecundity values were multiplied by 0.01.

the differences in egg size. A more appropriate metric would be egg volume, a function of the cube of diameter, which would emphasize differences in the sizes of the egg.

The differences identified in Figure 4 should not be regarded as differences among independent characteristics. For example, relative fecundity and egg size are clearly correlated. Rather, Figure 4 characterizes in a somewhat quantitative way a set of differences between those anadromous and marine fish for which we have data.

Recruitment Variability and Life History Traits

Relative fecundity.—The two-way classification between CVR and relative fecundity (number of eggs per gram of body weight) in marine and anadromous fish is shown in Figure 5. The median relative fecundities for marine and anadromous fish are 475 and 167, respectively. Among anadromous fish, it appears that variation in recruitment is related to variation in relative fecundity. Species with high relative fecundities exhibit high recruitment variability, while species with low relative fecundities exhibit low variability. Among marine fish, in contrast, it does not appear that variation in recruitment is related to variation in fecundity. High recruitment variability is observed in species with high and low relative fecundities. Hence, it appears that marine and anadromous fish have different CVR–fecundity

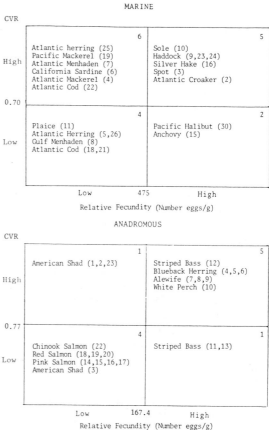

FIGURE 5.—Two-way classification of relative fecundity (number of eggs/g of fish) and the coefficient of recruitment variation (CVR) for marine and anadromous fish stocks. Values in the upper right corner of each cell represent the total number of species per cell. The stock numbers in parentheses after each species are those of Table 1 and 2 and Appendices 1 and 2.

relationships.

Egg diameter.—The two-way classification between CVR and egg diameter (mm) in marine and anadromous fish is shown in Figure 6. Median egg diameters of marine and anadromous fish are 1.25 and 2.18 mm, respectively. Among anadromous fish, small-egg species exhibit high recruitment variability, while large-egg species appear to exhibit low variability. Among marine fish, in contrast, there does not appear to be any relationship between CVR and egg diameter. Again, the response of recruitment variability to egg diameter appears to be different in marine and anadromous fish. Since fecundity and egg diameter are usually reciprocal, it is not surprising that a positive relation between CVR and fecundity is coupled

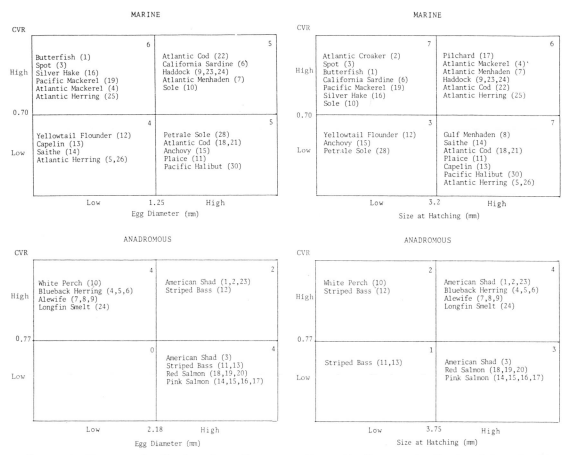

MARINE

CVR

High

Butterfish (1)
Spot (3)
Silver Hake (16)
Pacific Mackerel (19)
Atlantic Mackerel (4)
Atlantic Herring (25)

Atlantic Cod (22)
California Sardine (6)
Haddock (9,23,24)
Atlantic Menhaden (7)
Sole (10)

0.70

Low

Yellowtail Flounder (12)
Capelin (13)
Saithe (14)
Atlantic Herring (5,26)

Petrale Sole (28)
Atlantic Cod (18,21)
Anchovy (15)
Plaice (11)
Pacific Halibut (30)

Low   1.25   High

Egg Diameter (mm)

MARINE

CVR

High

Atlantic Croaker (2)
Spot (3)
Butterfish (1)
California Sardine (6)
Pacific Mackerel (19)
Silver Hake (16)
Sole (10)

Pilchard (17)
Atlantic Mackerel (4)
Atlantic Menhaden (7)
Haddock (9,23,24)
Atlantic Cod (22)
Atlantic Herring (25)

0.70

Low

Yellowtail Flounder (12)
Anchovy (15)
Petrale Sole (28)

Gulf Menhaden (8)
Saithe (14)
Atlantic Cod (18,21)
Plaice (11)
Capelin (13)
Pacific Halibut (30)
Atlantic Herring (5,26)

Low   3.2   High

Size at Hatching (mm)

ANADROMOUS

CVR

High

White Perch (10)
Blueback Herring (4,5,6)
Alewife (7,8,9)
Longfin Smelt (24)

American Shad (1,2,23)
Striped Bass (12)

0.77

Low

American Shad (3)
Striped Bass (11,13)
Red Salmon (18,19,20)
Pink Salmon (14,15,16,17)

Low   2.18   High

Egg Diameter (mm)

ANADROMOUS

CVR

High

White Perch (10)
Striped Bass (12)

American Shad (1,2,23)
Blueback Herring (4,5,6)
Alewife (7,8,9)
Longfin Smelt (24)

0.77

Low

Striped Bass (11,13)

American Shad (3)
Red Salmon (18,19,20)
Pink Salmon (14,15,16,17)

Low   3.75   High

Size at Hatching (mm)

FIGURE 6.—Two-way classification of egg diameter (mm) and the coefficient of recruitment variation (CVR) for marine and anadromous fish stocks. Values in the upper right corner of each cell represent the total number of species per cell. The stock numbers in parentheses after each species are those of Tables 1 and 2 and Appendices 1 and 2.

FIGURE 7.—Two-way classification of size at hatching (mm) and the coefficient of recruitment variation (CVR) for marine and anadromous fish stocks. Values in the upper right corner of each cell represent the total number of species per cell. The stock numbers in parentheses after each species are those of Tables 1 and 2 and Appendices 1 and 2.

with a negative relation between CVR and egg diameter in anadromous fish.

Size at hatching.—The two-way classification between CVR and size at hatching (mm) in marine and anadromous fish is shown in Figure 7. Median sizes at hatching among marine and anadromous fish are 3.2 and 3.75 mm, respectively. The data suggest that variability in marine fish recruitment declines as size at hatching increases. No particular relationship is evident between the CVR and size at hatching in anadromous fish.

Egg incubation time.—The two-way classification between the CVR and egg incubation time (days) in marine and anadromous fish is shown in Figure 8. Median incubation times among marine and anadromous fish are 5.65 and 4 d, respec-

tively. The CVR appears to be related to egg incubation time in both marine and anadromous fish. Among anadromous fish, species with short incubation times exhibit high variability, while species with long incubation times exhibit low variability. Among marine fish, species with short incubation times tend to exhibit higher variability, while species with long incubation times tend to exhibit lower variability.

Duration of yolk-sac larva stage.—The two-way classification between the CVR and the duration of the yolk-sac larva stage (days) in marine and anadromous fish is shown in Figure 9. Median yolk-sac larva stage durations among marine and anadromous fish are 5.5 and 3.5 d, respectively. As the duration of the yolk-sac larva stage in-

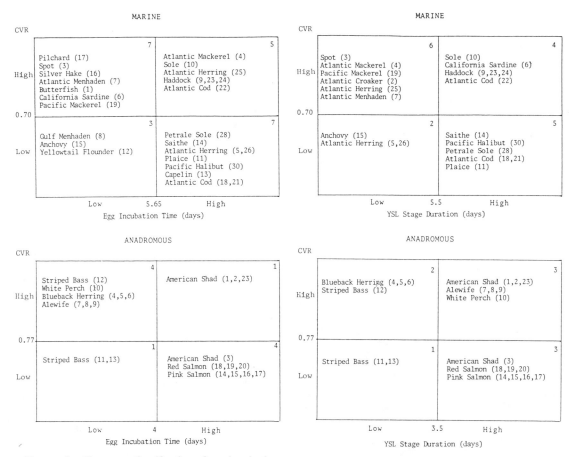

FIGURE 8.—Two-way classification of egg incubation time (days) and the coefficient of recruitment variation (CVR) for marine and anadromous stocks. Values in the upper right corner of each cell represent the total number of species per cell. The stock numbers in parentheses after each species are those of Tables 1 and 2 and Appendices 1 and 2.

FIGURE 9.—Two-way classification of yolk-sac larva (YSL) stage duration (days) and the coefficient of recruitment variation (CVR) for marine and anadromous fish stocks. Values in the upper right corner of each cell represent the total number of species per cell. The stock numbers in parentheses after each species are those of Tables 1 and 2 and Appendices 1 and 2.

creases, recruitment variability appears to decrease for marine fish. For the anadromous fish, there does not appear to be any relationship between duration of the yolk-sac larva stage and the CVR.

Eye pigmentation and mouth development.— The two-way classification between the CVR and eye pigmentation in marine and anadromous fish is presented in Figure 10. Among marine fish, there does not appear to be any relationship between eye development and the CVR. Among anadromous fish, species with unpigmented eyes appear to exhibit high variability, while species with pigmented eyes exhibit low variability. The relationship between mouth development and the coefficient of variation for marine and anadro-

mous fish is presented in Figure 11. Among marine fish, there does not appear to be any relationship between mouth development and the CVR. Among anadromous fish, species with an undeveloped mouth tend to exhibit high variability, while species with a developed mouth exhibit low variability.

Discussion

Recruitment variability in anadromous fish appears to be greater than that of marine fish. This conclusion may result from an artifice which owes to the alosids representing a major source of variability. Suppose though, that recruitment variability in marine and anadromous fish is actually similar. This supposition would mean that,

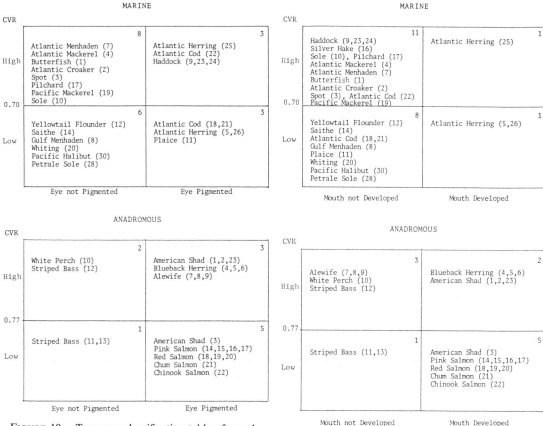

FIGURE 10.—Two-way classification table of eye development (pigmented or not pigmented) and the coefficient of recruitment variation (CVR) for marine and anadromous fish stocks. Values in the upper right corner of each cell represent the total number of species per cell. The stock numbers in parentheses after each species are those of Tables 1 and 2 and Appendix 3.

FIGURE 11.—Two-way classification of mouth development and the coefficient of recruitment variation (CVR) for marine and anadromous fish stocks. Values in the upper right corner of each cell represent the total number of species per cell. The stock numbers in parentheses after each species are those of Tables 1 and 2 and Appendix 3.

because the marine and anadromous fish in our sample differ in life history traits (i.e., the marine fish represented in our sample have a greater relative fecundity, egg incubation time, and yolk-sac larva stage duration than anadromous fish, whereas anadromous fish have larger egg diameter and size at hatching than marine fish), life history traits do not affect recruitment variability.

This consequence, however, may be too superficial. Important relationships appear to exist between recruitment variability and aggregate samples of both marine and anadromous fish. Indeed, the important sources of variability appear to be more related to each family than to whether or not the fish is marine or anadromous.

Three sets of comparisons between marine and anadromous fish recruitment variability and life-history characteristics seem warranted. The first relates to factors that are more or less correlated with the egg size, the second relates to time-dependent developmental factors, and the third relates to the morphological development of the larvae.

With regard to egg size factors, we observe that relative fecundity, egg diameter, and size at hatching should be correlated because highly fecund fish tend to have smaller eggs and smaller larvae. The data suggest that marine and anadromous fish are different; the CVR in marine fish does not appear to be related to either relative fecundity or to egg diameter, whereas the CVR in anadromous fish appears to be positively correlated with fecundity and negatively correlated with egg diameter. Any relation between CVR and size at hatching is not particularly strong. These results suggest that the relatively large differences among populations in egg size or egg volume tend to be minimized by hatching time; i.e., egg size differences tend to be much larger than larval size differences.

These distinctions regarding egg size differences between marine and anadromous fish may, however, be a function of the much greater range of egg sizes in anadromous fish compared to marine fish. In other words, if the range of egg sizes in marine fish were sufficiently great, then perhaps we would expect to see a relatively low recruitment variability in large-egged marine fish. (In actuality, some marine fish such as the Pacific halibut or the Greenland halibut *Reinhardtius hippoglossoides* have very large eggs; the Pacific halibut has a low CVR; we have not analyzed Greenland halibut recruitment variability.) Put another way, what would happen to the CVR if marine fish had large eggs or anadromous fish had small eggs?

With regard to temporal phenomena, the data suggest that the CVR declines as egg incubation time increases for both marine and anadromous fish, whereas there is an implication that the CVR declines as the yolk-sac larva duration increases in marine fish but not in anadromous fish. A decline in CVR with increased stage duration for yolk-sac larvae seems counterintuitive, particularly if we consider these early stages, as is customary in the literature, to be vulnerable to predation death (Beverton and Holt 1957; Shepherd and Cushing 1980). One of the largest recorded year classes of plaice in the North Sea occurred during an exceptionally cold winter. Because of depressed water temperatures, the egg stage was unusually long and apparent survival of the larva was unusually high. What is the advantage, at least with respect to CVR, of an extended duration of the yolk-sac larva stage or of egg incubation?

Finally, with respect to morphological characters, the CVR does not seem to be related to larva eye pigmentation. Rather, eye pigmentation at hatching seems to be more characteristic of anadromous fish than of marine fish. Likewise, mouth development does not seem to be related to marine fish CVR. This characteristic seems to be more a function of the anadromous fish environment rather than the marine fish environment. Why do marine fish tend to have poorly developed eyes and mouth structure at hatching, in contrast to anadromous fish, and why are these indices of fragility uncorrelated with CVR?

One can only speculate. It appears that the differences in CVRs and life history traits can be best studied by distinguishing among large- and small-egged fish and associating these traits with the anadromous and marine environments, respectively. As pointed out by Rothschild (1986), the high fecundity of most fish species functions to enable each egg or larva to sample the environment for salubrious living conditions (at least, ample food and minimal predation). The nature of this sampling process varies among different populations. For example, yellowfin tuna *Thunnus albacares* allocate their eggs to almost the entire tropical Pacific Ocean during many months of the year. Bristol Bay sockeye salmon allocate their eggs to redds in a brief 21-d period during the summer. Herring in the north Atlantic spawn in several specific locations at specific times, but the populations are so diverse that at least one population spawns in each month of the year.

There are many ways of classifying these spawning strategies. In developing such a classification, it is helpful to think of any strategy as developing the most efficient search process to enable the eggs and larvae to find salubrious conditions. Taking this into account, we can think of a large-egg, anadromous fish strategy and small-egg, marine fish strategy. In the large-egg strategy, the environment sampling process relies upon the adults as the primary samplers for salubrious conditions whereas, in the small-egg strategy, the eggs and larvae are the primary samplers.

These strategies are necessitated by the nature of the marine and anadromous environments. Although differences are a matter of degree, the anadromous environment is spatially restricted, is more tightly coupled to atmospheric conditions, and has less spatial patchiness of food, relative to the time of spawning and the ambit of larvae, than the marine environment. As a consequence of these conditions, spawning anadromous fish have, in the course of evolution, become much more precise with regard to the placement of eggs in salubrious conditions, particularly as the anadromous time–space conditions are fairly restricted. In contrast, the patchy nature of the marine environment and the often large temporal and spatial advective movement of eggs and larvae, as well as the vast areas in which eggs and larvae of any population exist, limit the ability of spawning marine fish to adequately sample the environment for salubrious conditions for the eggs and larvae (herring are an exception); hence, the sampling task is left to the individual eggs and larvae.

This scenario provides a rationale for why

longer periods of egg incubation and yolk-sac larva durations seem to reduce rather than increase the CVR, contrary to the literature. While it is true that these very young life history stages are particularly vulnerable, it is also true that, in the marine environment, increasing the duration of the early stages increases the efficiency of the sampling process, and that the concomitant increased dispersal of eggs and larvae may function to reduce mortality on eggs and larvae from predation. But clearly there is a trade-off for species that pass through these life stages quickly: a decrease in the time eggs and larvae are vulnerable to predation might be accompanied by a search procedure which is inefficient in finding food or avoiding predation.

Extending this scenario, we suggest that small size and lack of development in the early life stages of marine fish is consistent with the opportunity for greater dispersal and a more efficient search procedure for salubrious conditions. However, greater dispersal in the anadromous fish environment, coupled with imprecise temporal and spatial deposition of eggs and larvae, would result in conditions which are not salubrious for the eggs and larvae.

We can conclude from these observations that anadromous fish have become more specialized than marine fish, require more suitable environmental conditions per egg, and are, therefore, more highly tuned to particular environmental conditions which, when varied, could cause considerable stress to the population. Populations compensate for stress in two ways: by short-run changes in the variability of population dynamics, and by seemingly longer-run changes in genetic constituency. We could reason that compensation for natural or anthropogenic environmental change might be most difficult for the more highly tuned populations.

In terms of population dynamics, it appears that the separation between anadromous and marine fish is somewhat artificial. Each population within these two categories has a large variety of traits that separate it from every other population. These traits may be classified according to mechanisms that stabilize or "average" recruitment variability. An appropriate way to classify these traits would be according to the stabilizing or averaging process that dampens recruitment variability. The high-fecundity fish dampen recruitment variability through a sampling of the environment by large numbers of eggs and larvae. The low-fecundity fish dampen variability by spawning few eggs in conditions that are more favorable for survival. The management implications are that there is relatively little that can be done to control variability in high-fecundity fish, whereas control of recruitment of low-fecundity fish by control of parent stock seems to have a high degree of feasibility.

Acknowledgments

We thank Edward Houde and William Richkus for providing comments.

References

Anderson, E. D. 1977. Assessment of the Georges Bank silver hake stock. U.S. National Marine Fisheries Service, Northeast Fisheries Center, Woods Hole 77-21, Woods Hole, Massachusetts, USA.

Anderson, E. D. 1984. Status of the northwest Atlantic mackerel stock—1983. National Marine Fisheries Service, Northeast Fisheries Center, Woods Hole Laboratory Reference Document 83-40, Woods Hole, Massachusetts, USA.

Anthony, V. C., and M. J. Fogarty. 1985. Environmental effects on recruitment, growth, and vulnerability of Atlantic herring (Clupea harengus harengus) in the Gulf of Maine region. Canadian Journal of Fisheries and Aquatic Sciences 42 (Supplement 1): 158–173.

Anthony, V. C., and G. Waring. 1980. Assessment and management of the Georges Bank herring fishery. Rapports et Procès-Verbaux des Réunions, Conseil International pour l'Exploration de la Mer 177:72–111.

ASMFC (Atlantic States Marine Fisheries Commission). 1981. Fishery management plan for Atlantic menhaden Brevoortia tyrannus (Latrobe). ASMFC, Washington, D.C.

Beverton, R. J. H., and S. J. Holt. 1957. On the dynamics of exploited fish populations. Fishery Investigations, Series II, Marine Fisheries, Great Britain Ministry of Agriculture Fisheries and Food 19.

Blaxter, J. H. S., and J. R. Hunter. 1982. The biology of the clupeoid fishes. Advances in Marine Biology 20:1–223.

Boone, J. G. 1980. Estuarine fish recruitment survey—July 1, 1979 through June 30, 1980. Maryland Department of Natural Resources, Federal Aid in Fish Restoration, Project F-27-R-6, Performance Report, Annapolis, Maryland, USA.

Chadwick, H. K., D. E. Stevens, and L. W. Miller, 1977. Some factors regulating the striped bass population in the Sacramento-San Joaquin estuary, California. Pages 18–35 in W. Van Winkle, editor. Proceedings of the conference on assessing the effects of power-plant induced mortality on fish populations. Pergamon, New York, New York, USA.

Clark, S. H., and W. J. Overholtz. 1979. Review and assessment of the Georges Bank and Gulf of Maine haddock fishery. U.S. National Marine Fisheries

Service, Northeast Fisheries Center 79-05, Woods Hole, Massachusetts, USA.

Crecco, V. 1978. Population dynamics of the American shad (Alosa sapidissima) in the Connecticut River, 1940–1977. Connecticut Department of Environmental Protection, Marine Region, Hartford, Connecticut, USA.

Culley, M. 1971. The pilchard; biology and exploitation. Pergamon, New York, New York, USA.

Dragesund, O., J. Homre, and O. Ulltang. 1980. Biology and population dynamics of the Norwegian spring spawning herring. Rapports et Procès-Verbaux des Réunions, Conseil International pour l'Exploration de la Mer 177:43–71.

Fabre-Domergue, and E. Bietrix. 1896. La periode critique post-larvaire des poissons marins. Annales des Science Natural, Zoologie.

Fahay, M. P. 1983. Guide to the early stages of marine fishes occurring in the western north Atlantic Ocean, Cape Hatteras to the southern Scotian Shelf. Journal of Northwest Atlantic Fishery Science 4.

Forrester, C. R., and D. F. Alderdice. 1967. Preliminary observations on embryonic development of the petrale sole (Eopsetta jordani). Fisheries Research Board of Canada Technical Report 41.

Fritzsche, R. A. 1978. Development of fishes of the mid-Atlantic Bight: an atlas of egg, larval and juvenile stages, volume 5. Chaetodontidae through Ophidiidae. U.S. Fish and Wildlife Service Biological Services Program FWS/OBS-78/12.

Hardy, J. D., Jr. 1978a. Development of fishes of the mid-Atlantic Bight: an atlas of egg, larval and juvenile stages, volume 2. Anguillidae through Syngnathidae. U.S. Fish and Wildlife Service Biological Services Program FWS/OBS-78/12.

Hardy, J. D., Jr. 1978b. Development of fishes of the mid-Atlantic Bight: an atlas of egg, larval and juvenile stages, volume 3. Aphredoderidae through Rachycentridae. U.S. Fish and Wildlife Service Biological Services Program FWS/OBS-78/12.

Hart, J. L. 1973. Pacific fishes of Canada. Fisheries Research Board of Canada Bulletin 180.

Hjort, J. 1914. Fluctuations in the great fisheries of northern Europe viewed in the light of biological research. Rapports et Procès-Verbaux des Réunions, Conseil International pour l'Exploration de la Mer 20:1–228.

Hoag, S. H., and R. J. McNaughton. 1978. Abundance and fishing mortality of Pacific halibut, cohort analysis, 1935–1976. International Pacific Halibut Commission Scientific Report 65.

Holden, M. J. 1978. Long-term changes in landings of fish from the North Sea. Rapports et Procès-Verbaux des Réunions, Conseil International pour la l'Exploration de la Mer 172:11–26.

Hunter, J. R., and C. A. Kimbrell. 1980. Early life history of Pacific mackerel, Scomber japonicus. U.S. National Marine Fisheries Service Fishery Bulletin 78:89–101.

ICES (International Council for the Exploration of the Sea). 1979a. Report of the Arctic fisheries working group. ICES, CM 1979/G:20, Copenhagen, Denmark.

ICES (International Council for the Exploration of the Sea). 1979b. Report of the North Sea round fish working group. ICES, CM 1979/G:7, Copenhagen, Denmark.

ICES (International Council for the Exploration of the Sea). 1979c. Report of the saithe (coalfish) working group. ICES, CM 1979/G:6, Copenhagen, Denmark.

INPFC (International North Pacific Fisheries Commission). 1962. The exploitation, scientific investigation and management of salmon (genus Oncorhynchus) stocks on the Pacific coast of Canada in relation to the abstention provisions of the North Pacific Fisheries Convention. International North Pacific Fisheries Commission Bulletin 9.

INPFC (International North Pacific Fisheries Commission). 1974. Additional information on the exploitation, scientific investigation, and management of salmon stocks on the Pacific coasts of Canada and the United States in relation to the abstention provisions of the North Pacific Fisheries Convention. International North Pacific Fisheries Commission Bulletin 29.

Jones, P. W., F. D. Martin, and J. D. Hardy, Jr. 1978. Development of fishes of the mid-Atlantic bight: an atlas of egg, larval and juvenile stages, volume 1. Acipenseridae through Ictaluridae. U.S. Fish and Wildlife Service Biological Services Program FWS/OBS-78/12.

Ketchen, K. S., and C. R. Forrester. 1966. Population dynamics of the petrale sole, Eopsetta jordani, in waters off western Canada. Fisheries Research Board of Canada Bulletin 153.

Lasker, R. 1975. Field criteria for survival of anchovy larvae: the relation between inshore chlorophyll maximum layers and successful first feeding. U.S. National Marine Fisheries Service Fishery Bulletin 73:453–462.

Leggett, W. C., K. T. Frank, and J. E. Carscadden. 1984. Meteorological and hydrographic regulation of year-class strength in capelin (Mallotus villosus). Canadian Journal of Fisheries and Aquatic Sciences 41:1193–1201.

Loesch, J. G., and W. H. Kriete, Jr. 1982. Anadromous fisheries research, Virginia, anadromous fish project, 1982. College of William and Mary, School of Marine Science, Virginia Institute of Marine Science, Gloucester Point, Virginia, USA.

Marr, J. C. 1956. The "critical period" in the early life history of marine fishes. Journal du Conseil, Conseil International pour l'Exploration de la Mer 21:160–170.

Martin, F. D., and G. E. Drewry. 1978. Development of fishes of the mid-Atlantic bight: an atlas of egg, larval and juvenile stages, volume 6. Stromateidae through Ogcocephalidae. U.S. Fish and Wildlife Service Biological Services Program FWS/OBS-78/12.

McPhail, J. D., and C. C. Lindsey. 1970. Freshwater fishes of northwestern Canada and Alaska. Fisheries Research Board of Canada Bulletin 173.

Newman, G. G., and R. J. M. Crawford. 1980. Population biology and management of mixed-species pelagic stocks of South Africa. Rapports et Procès-Verbaux des Réunions, Conseil International pour l'Exploration de la Mer 177:279–291.

Norcross, B. L., and H. M. Austin. 1981. Climate scale environmental factors affecting year class fluctuations of Chesapeake Bay croaker *Micropogonias undulatus*. Virginia Institute of Marine Science Special Scientific Report 110.

Parrish, R. H., and A. D. MacCall. 1978. Climatic variation and exploitation in the Pacific mackerel fishery. California Department of Fish and Game, Fish Bulletin 167.

Pauly, D., and I. Tsukayama. 1983. On the seasonal growth, monthly recruitment and monthly biomass of Peruvian anchoveta *(Engraulis ringens)* from 1961 to 1979. FAO (Food and Agriculture Organization of the United Nations) Fisheries Report 291:987–1004.

PSEG (Public Service Electric and Gas Company). 1982a. Alewife *(Alosa pseudoharengus):* a synthesis of information on natural history, with reference to occurrence in the Delaware River and estuary and involvement with the Salem nuclear generating station. Salem Nuclear Generating Station 316(b) Demonstration, Appendix 4, Newark, New Jersey, USA.

PSEG (Public Service Electric and Gas Company). 1982b. American shad *(Alosa sapidissima):* a synthesis of information on natural history, with reference to occurrence in the Delaware River and estuary and involvement with the Salem nuclear generating station. Salem Nuclear Generating Station 316(b) Demonstration, Appendix 3, Newark, New Jersey, USA.

PSEG (Public Service Electric and Gas Company). 1982c. Atlantic croaker *(Micropogonias undulatus):* a synthesis of information on natural history, with reference to occurrence in the Delaware River and estuary and involvement with the Salem nuclear generating station. Salem Nuclear Generating Station 316(b) Demonstration, Appendix 8, Newark, New Jersey, USA.

PSEG (Public Service Electric and Gas Company). 1982d. Blueback herring *(Alosa aestivalis):* a synthesis of information on natural history, with reference to occurrence in the Delaware River and estuary and involvement with the Salem nuclear generating station. Salem Nuclear Generating Station 316(b) Demonstration, Appendix 6, Newark, New Jersey, USA.

PSEG (Public Service Electric and Gas Company). 1983a. Spot *(Leiostomus xanthurus):* a synthesis of information on natural history with reference to occurrence in the Delaware River and estuary and involvement with the Salem nuclear generating station. Salem Nuclear Generating Station 316(b) Demonstration, Appendix 7, Newark, New Jersey, USA.

PSEG (Public Service Electric and Gas Company). 1983b. Striped bass *(Morone saxatilis):* a synthesis of information on natural history, with reference to occurrence in the Delaware River and estuary and involvement with the Salem nuclear generating station. Salem Nuclear Generating Station 316(b) Demonstration, Appendix 9, Newark, New Jersey, USA.

PSEG (Public Service Electric and Gas Company). 1984. White perch *(Morone americana):* a synthesis of information on natural history, with reference to occurrence in the Delaware River and estuary and involvement with the Salem nuclear generating station. Salem Nuclear Generating Station 316(b) Demonstration, Appendix 10, Newark, New Jersey, USA.

Rothschild, B. J. 1986. Dynamics of marine fish populations. Harvard University Press, Cambridge, Massachusetts, USA.

Russell, F. S. 1976. The eggs and planktonic stages of British marine fishes. Academic Press, London, England.

Sahrhage, D., and G. Wagner. 1978. On fluctuations in the haddock population of the North Sea. Rapports et Procès-Verbaux des Réunions, Conseil International pour l'Exploration de la Mer 172:72–85.

Serchuk, F. M., P. Wood, and B. E. Brown. 1978. Atlantic cod *(Gadus morhua):* assessment and status of the Georges Bank and Gulf of Maine stocks. U.S. National Marine Fisheries Service, Northeast Fisheries Center, Woods Hole Laboratory Reference 78-03, Woods Hole, Massachusetts, USA.

Shepherd, J. G., and D. H. Cushing. 1980. A mechanism for density-dependent survival of larval fish as the basis of a stock-recruitment relationship. Journal du Conseil, Conseil International pour l'Exploration de la Mer 39:160–167.

Sissenwine, M. P. 1974. Variability in recruitment and equilibrium catch of the southern New England yellowtail flounder fishery. Journal du Conseil, Conseil International pour l'Exploration de la Mer 36:15–26.

Stevens, D. E., and L. W. Miller. 1983. Effects of river flow on abundance of young chinook salmon, American shad, longfin smelt and delta smelt in the Sacramento–San Joaquin river system. North American Journal of Fisheries Management 3:425–437.

Thompson, W. F., and R. Van Cleve. 1936. Life history of the Pacific halibut, 2. Distribution and early life history. International Pacific Fisheries Commission Report 9.

Troadec, J. P., W. G. Clark, and J. A. Gulland. 1980. A review of some pelagic fish stocks in other areas. Rapports et Procès-Verbaux des Réunions, Conseil International pour l'Exploration de la Mer 177:252–277.

Wakabayashi, K. 1984. Estimates of biomass and yield for yellowfin sole in the eastern Bering Sea. International North Pacific Fisheries Commission Bulletin 42:65–72.

Waring, G. T., and E. D. Anderson. 1984. Status of the northwestern Atlantic butterfish stock—1983. National Marine Fisheries Center, Woods Hole Laboratory Reference Document 83-41, Woods Hole, Massachusetts, USA.

Appendix 1

Ranked order of the coefficient of recruitment variation and values of life history characteristics for stocks of anadromous species used in the contingency tables. The reference number (in parentheses) for each stock is the one used in Table 1.

Coefficent of variation of recruitment			Egg diameter (mm)			Relative fecundity (number of eggs/g of fish)		
0.25	American shad	(3)	0.92	White perch	(10)	0.6	Chinook salmon	(22)
0.37	Striped bass	(13)	1.04	Blueback herring	(4)	0.85	Sockeye salmon	(18)
0.42	Pink salmon	(17)	1.04	Blueback herring	(5)	0.85	Sockeye salmon	(19)
0.47	Sockeye salmon	(18)	1.04	Blueback herring	(6)	0.85	Sockeye salmon	(20)
0.51	Chum salmon	(21)	1.1	Alewife	(7)	0.86	Pink salmon	(14)
0.54	Sockeye salmon	(19)	1.1	Alewife	(8)	0.86	Pink salmon	(15)
0.55	Delta smelt	(25)	1.1	Alewife	(9)	0.86	Pink salmon	(16)
0.56	Pink salmon	(15)	1.2	Longfin smelt	(24)	0.86	Pink salmon	(17)
0.60	Sockeye salmon	(20)	3.15	American shad	(1)	167.41	American shad	(1)
0.71	Chinook salmon	(22)	3.15	American shad	(2)	167.41	American shad	(2)
0.74	Pink salmon	(14)	3.15	American shad	(3)	167.41	American shad	(3)
0.75	Striped bass	(11)	3.15	American shad	(23)	167.41	American shad	(23)
0.77	Pink salmon	(16)	3.15	Striped bass	(11)	195.91	Striped bass	(11)
0.81	White perch	(10)	3.15	Striped bass	(12)	195.91	Striped bass	(12)
0.86	American shad	(23)	3.15	Striped bass	(13)	195.91	Striped bass	(13)
1.11	Alewife	(9)	4.7	Sockeye salmon	(18)	666.65	Blueback herring	(4)
1.17	Blueback herring	(5)	4.7	Sockeye salmon	(19)	666.65	Blueback herring	(5)
1.19	Striped bass	(12)	4.7	Sockeye salmon	(20)	666.65	Blueback herring	(6)
1.30	Alewife	(8)	6.0	Pink salmon	(14)	777.69	Alewife	(7)
1.36	American shad	(2)	6.0	Pink salmon	(15)	777.69	Alewife	(8)
1.38	Blueback herring	(6)	6.0	Pink salmon	(16)	777.69	Alewife	(9)
1.64	Longfin smelt	(24)	6.0	Pink salmon	(17)	911.1	White perch	(10)
2.07	Alewife	(7)						
2.10	American shad	(1)						
2.84	Blueback herring	(4)						

Egg incubation time (days)			Hatching size (mm)			Yolk-sac larval stage duration (days)		
2	Striped bass	(11)	2.6	White perch	(10)	2.5	Blueback herring	(4)
2	Striped bass	(12)	2.85	Striped bass	(11)	2.5	Blueback herring	(5)
2	Striped bass	(13)	2.85	Striped bass	(12)	2.5	Blueback herring	(6)
2.5	White perch	(10)	2.85	Striped bass	(13)	3	Striped bass	(11)
3.6	Blueback herring	(4)	3.75	American shad	(1)	3	Striped bass	(12)
3.6	Blueback herring	(5)	3.75	American shad	(2)	3	Striped bass	(13)
3.6	Blueback herring	(6)	3.75	American shad	(3)	3.5	American shad	(1)
4	American shad	(1)	3.75	American shad	(23)	3.5	American shad	(2)
4	American shad	(2)	3.75	Blueback herring	(4)	3.5	American shad	(3)
4	American shad	(3)	3.75	Blueback herring	(5)	3.5	American shad	(23)
4	American shad	(23)	3.75	Blueback herring	(6)	3.5	Alewife	(7)
4	Alewife	(7)	3.75	Alewife	(7)	3.5	Alewife	(8)
4	Alewife	(8)	3.75	Alewife	(8)	3.5	Alewife	(9)
4	Alewife	(9)	3.75	Alewife	(9)	4.0	White perch	(10)
55	Sockeye salmon	(18)	7.0	Longfin smelt	(24)	95	Pink salmon	(14)
55	Sockeye salmon	(19)	18.93	Sockeye salmon	(18)	95	Pink salmon	(15)
55	Sockeye salmon	(20)	18.93	Sockeye salmon	(19)	95	Pink salmon	(16)
95.5	Pink salmon	(14)	18.93	Sockeye salmon	(20)	95	Pink salmon	(17)
95.5	Pink salmon	(15)	20	Pink salmon	(14)	100	Sockeye salmon	(18)
95.5	Pink salmon	(16)	20	Pink salmon	(15)	100	Sockeye salmon	(19)
95.5	Pink salmon	(17)	20	Pink salmon	(16)	100	Sockeye salmon	(20)
			20	Pink salmon	(17)			

Appendix 2

Ranked order of the coefficient of recruitment variation and values of life history characteristics for stocks of marine species used in the contingency tables. The reference number (in parentheses) for each stock is the one used in Table 2.

Coefficent of variation of recruitment			Egg diameter (mm)			Relative fecundity (number of eggs/g of fish)		
0.25	Atlantic cod	(21)	0.75	Butterfish	(1)	181	Plaice	(11)
0.27	Anchovy	(15)	0.80	Spot	(3)	300	Atlantic herring	(5)
0.33	Gulf menhaden	(8)	0.9	Yellowtail flounder	(12)	300	Atlantic herring	(25)
0.38	Pacific halibut	(30)	0.91	Silver hake	(16)	300	Atlantic herring	(26)
0.45	Yellowfin sole	(29)	1.03	Capelin	(13)	304	Chub mackerel	(19)
0.46	Plaice	(11)	1.1	Chub mackerel	(19)	375	Atlantic menhaden	(7)
0.49	Whiting	(20)	1.15	Saithe	(14)	380	Gulf menhaden	(8)
0.59	Saithe	(14)	1.17	Atlantic mackerel	(4)	400	Pacific sardine	(6)
0.60	Atlantic herring	(26)	1.2	Atlantic herring	(5)	450	Atlantic mackerel	(4)
0.62	Petrale sole	(28)	1.2	Atlantic herring	(25)	475	Atlantic cod	(18)
0.63	Atlantic cod	(18)	1.2	Atlantic herring	(26)	475	Atlantic cod	(21)
0.64	Capelin	(13)	1.3	Petrale sole	(28)	475	Atlantic cod	(22)
0.65	Peruvian anchovy	(27)	1.35	Atlantic cod	(18)	528	Sole	(10)
0.68	Yellowtail flounder	(12)	1.35	Atlantic cod	(21)	550	Haddock	(9)
0.69	Atlantic herring	(5)	1.35	Atlantic cod	(22)	550	Haddock	(23)
0.72	Silver hake	(16)	1.4	Pacific sardine	(6)	550	Haddock	(24)
0.74	Butterfish	(1)	1.45	Haddock	(9)	699	Pacific halibut	(30)
0.76	Pilchard	(17)	1.45	Haddock	(23)	718	Silver hake	(16)
0.77	Atlantic cod	(22)	1.45	Haddock	(24)	1256	Anchovy	(15)
0.87	Atlantic menhaden	(7)	1.45	Anchovy	(15)	1291	Spot	(3)
0.96	Chub mackerel	(19)	1.61	Atlantic menhaden	(7)	1624	Atlantic croaker	(2)
1.01	Haddock	(23)	1.95	Sole	(10)			
1.04	Spot	(3)	1.95	Plaice	(11)			
1.12	Atlantic mackerel	(4)	3.2	Pacific halibut	(30)			
1.12	Pacific sardine	(6)						
1.17	Sole	(10)						
1.30	Haddock	(24)						
1.39	Atlantic herring	(25)						
1.59	Haddock	(9)						
1.65	Atlantic croaker	(2)						

Egg incubation time (days)			Hatching size (mm)			Yolk-sac larval stage duration (days)		
1.5	Pilchard	(17)	1.21	Atlantic croaker	(2)	0.5	Spot	(3)
2	Spot	(3)	1.5	Spot	(3)	1.75	Atlantic mackerel	(4)
2	Silver hake	(16)	1.72	Butterfish	(1)	2.2	Chub mackerel	(19)
2	Gulf menhaden	(8)	2.75	Yellowtail flounder	(12)	2.5	Anchovy	(15)
2	Atlantic menhaden	(7)	2.84	Anchovy	(15)	3.0	Atlantic croaker	(2)
2.5	Butterfish	(1)	3.0	Pacific sardine	(6)	3.5	Atlantic herring	(5)
2.5	Pacific sardine	(6)	3.0	Petrale sole	(28)	3.5	Atlantic herring	(25)
3.13	Chub mackerel	(19)	3.1	Chub mackerel	(19)	3.5	Atlantic herring	(26)
3.96	Anchovy	(15)	3.1	Silver hake	(16)	4.0	Atlantic menhaden	(7)
5	Yellowtail flounder	(12)	3.1	Sole	(10)	5.0	Sole	(10)
6.3	Atlantic mackerel	(4)	3.2	Gulf menhaden	(8)	5.5	Pacific sardine	(6)
8.5	Petrale sole	(28)	3.2	Pilchard	(17)	9	Saithe	(14)
11	Sole	(10)	3.5	Atlantic menhaden	(7)	10	Haddock	(9)
12	Saithe	(14)	3.61	Atlantic mackerel	(4)	10	Haddock	(23)
12.5	Atlantic herring	(5)	4.0	Haddock	(9)	10	Haddock	(24)
12.5	Atlantic herring	(25)	4.0	Haddock	(23)	10	Pacific halibut	(30)
12.5	Atlantic herring	(26)	4.0	Haddock	(24)	10	Petrale sole	(28)
12.5	Plaice	(11)	4.0	Saithe	(14)	11	Atlantic cod	(18)
13	Haddock	(9)	4.5	Atlantic cod	(18)	11	Atlantic cod	(21)
13	Haddock	(23)	4.5	Atantic cod	(21)	11	Atlantic cod	(22)
13	Haddock	(24)	4.5	Atlantic cod	(22)	12	Plaice	(11)
14	Pacific halibut	(30)	6.5	Plaice	(11)			
15	Capelin	(13)	6.5	Capelin	(13)			
15	Atlantic cod	(18)	6.78	Pacific halibut	(30)			
15	Atlantic cod	(21)	7.0	Atlantic herring	(5)			
15	Atlantic cod	(22)	7.0	Atlantic herring	(25)			
			7.0	Atlantic herring	(26)			

Appendix 3

Presence or absence of eye pigmentation and mouth development in marine and anadromous fish larvae at hatching, used in the contingency tables. An × indicates eyes pigmented or mouth developed; a 0 indicates eyes not pigmented or mouth not developed.

Species	Source[a]	Eye pigmented	Mouth developed
Anadromous			
Alewife	A, B	×	0
Blueback herring	A, C	×	×
American shad	A, D	×	×
Striped bass	E, F	0	0
White perch	E, G	0	0
Pink salmon	H, I	×	×
Sockeye salmon	H, I	×	×
Chum salmon	H, I	×	×
Chinook salmon	H, I	×	×
Marine			
Atlantic herring	A, J	×	×
Atlantic menhaden	A, J	0	0
Atlantic mackerel	K	0	0
Yellowtail flounder	J, L	0	0
Butterfish	J, L	0	0
Atlantic croaker	M	0	0
Spot	J, N	0	0
Saithe	J, O	0	0
Pilchard	P	0	0
Atlantic cod	J	×	0
Chub mackerel	K, Q	0	0
Gulf menhaden	R	0	0
Haddock	J	×	0
Sole	S	0	0
Plaice	S	×	0
Whiting	S	0	0
Silver hake	J	0	0
Pacific halibut	T	0	0
Petrale sole	U	0	0

[a] Source:

(A) Jones et al. (1978)	(H) McPhail and Lindsey (1970)	(O) Hardy (1978a)
(B) PSEG (1982a)	(I) Hart (1973)	(P) Culley (1971)
(C) PSEG (1982d)	(J) Fahay (1983)	(Q) Hunter and Kimbrell (1980)
(D) PSEG (1982b)	(K) Fritzsche (1978)	(R) Blaxter and Hunter (1982)
(E) Hardy (1978b)	(L) Martin and Drewry (1978)	(S) Russell (1976)
(F) PSEG (1983b)	(M) PSEG (1982c)	(T) Thompson and Van Cleve (1936)
(G) PSEG (1984)	(N) PSEG (1983a)	(U) Forrester and Alderdice (1967)

American Fisheries Society Symposium 1:547–549, 1987
© Copyright by the American Fisheries Society 1987

FUTURE DIRECTIONS

Perspectives and New Directions for Research on Diadromous Fishes

ROGER A. RULIFSON

Institute for Coastal and Marine Resources and Department of Biology
East Carolina University, Greenville, North Carolina 27858, USA

Research on anadromous and catadromous (diadromous) fishes has been historically focused primarily on species of commercial or recreational value. Regional and international agencies responsible for managing stocks and monitoring commercial and sport fisheries have funded many of these studies, their major goal being to improve fishery management practices. Researchers funded by these agencies are often constrained to present results related only to the objectives of the funding agency. Consequently, basic scientific information gathered about a particular diadromous species, although published in the scientific literature, is seldom compared with information published about the same or other diadromous species in other regions of the world. These comparisons are crucial in revealing differences and similarities in life history strategies. This problem exists on a global scale. Although migration routes of diadromous fishes often cross international boundaries, ongoing research programs in one country may be relatively unknown to researchers in another country. As a result, efforts in one country to enhance or monitor diadromous stocks may be impeded because of fishery practices involving the same stocks in another country. Additionally, research on a diadromous species in the northern hemisphere may be unknown to fisheries scientists studying related species in the southern hemisphere.

In the 1980s, investigators still face the prospect that more funding will be available for research on specific management objectives than for basic scientific endeavors. Many researchers thus will continue to focus on one species or geographic location. Basic scientific issues are usually presented in the primary literature, but much agency-sponsored research is published in specialized journals or technical reports (the so-called "grey literature"). These specialized reports often contain information which could stimulate new ideas

and further our basic understanding of one or several closely related diadromous species, but dissemination of these data to other researchers is often poor. The need for a widely disseminated, peer-reviewed work that addresses general theories of diadromy and compares life history strategies among several species is evident.

With these thoughts in mind, an informal and spontaneously organized workshop was held during the "Common Strategies" symposium to provide a forum for interested attendees to exchange concerns and ideas about diadromy. A major objective was to summarize and include the discussion as part of the symposium proceedings. Most of the concepts and ideas brought forth centered around six major topics: (1) standardization of terminology through efforts to identify and describe basic biological processes common to diadromous fishes; (2) conservation of gene pools during stock restoration efforts; (3) the role of hatcheries in stock restoration and enhancement efforts, and the ethics associated with these programs; (4) the bioenergetics of diadromy; (5) the community ecology of habitats supporting diadromous species; and (6) the evolutionary significance of diadromy. This paper summarizes the general line of thought expressed by the workshop participants and strives to motivate scientists to seek solutions to these problems.

A diversity of perspectives on the concept of diadromy, apparent among workshop participants and throughout the four-day symposium, restricts our ability to develop standard terminology for describing certain notable biological processes. For example, salmon researchers have developed special terminology for various phases of salmonid life cycles such as parr, smolt, and kelt. "Smoltification" describes the process of metamorphosis from the parr to smolt stage, which prepares the young salmon for transition to the marine environment. The young of most nonsalmonid species also undergo a process similar to smoltification, which can only be described as a rigid set of physiological adaptations that prepares them for a dramatic osmotic change in their external environment. However, there is no standard terminology for this set of preparatory changes for any diadromous species except the Salmonidae. Even salmon experts disagree on the exact set of physiological changes referred to as "smoltification," and this was evident in the opinions expressed during the workshop. Indeed, no consensus was reached on whether or not a problem existed. However, a concerted effort should be made to define and understand the basic physiological processes underlying the diadromous life cycles so that common terminology can be defined to aid in the comparison and integration of information among species and geographical regimes.

An exciting area of diadromy to be further explored and clarified is the concept of homing and navigation. Little information exists on the number and types of diadromous species having the ability to home or navigate. Several species can navigate (i.e., use "map and compass") to find their way back to a coastline and suitable habitat for spawning, but they may not exhibit homing. Fish may come back to a general region—even the same river—but this phenomenon does not imply that homing was involved. Cooperative efforts among researchers are needed to identify those species able to home or navigate. Grouping diadromous fishes based on these abilities or inabilities may shed some light on the evolutionary development of these behavioral phenomena.

Worldwide, people working to preserve or enhance diadromous fish populations through stocking programs should consider using natal strains to conserve gene pools. The mixing of stocks with nonnative strains has been given little attention until recently, but it is of great concern in the USA, Canada, and South Africa. For example, 65 million striped bass *Morone saxatilis* have been stocked in coastal tributaries of the Gulf of Mexico, USA, since 1965 to enhance the sport fishery. Less than 1% of these fish were of Gulf of Mexico origin; the remainder were from Chesapeake Bay or South Carolina stocks. There are distinct differences among these strains of fish. Gulf of Mexico striped bass are endemic, riverine, and relatively nonmigratory. Chesapeake Bay strains are migratory by nature and were stocked into Gulf coast rivers in an attempt to produce stocks

that would migrate into coastal waters to grow, then return to the rivers as adults and contribute to the fishery. It was assumed that stock size (and viability of the sport fishery) would increase if fish were used that would exploit coastal oceanic waters. These stocking programs have been only moderately successful, however, because the northern strains from Chesapeake Bay have not adjusted well to the higher temperatures of Gulf coast rivers. The numbers of stocked northern fish now far exceed the remnant populations of native striped bass, and the resultant mixing of the gene pools during spawning may well spell the demise of endemic striped bass stocks in these waters. Similar threats to native stocks from diversion of water and fish from one geographic location to another are widespread. Such problems have already been addressed in New Zealand, where introducing nonnative strains into streams is illegal. Even so, the prospect of losing genetic diversity is not appreciated by the public, and destruction of a gene pool is not readily apparent even to the most informed layman.

A topic directly related to the preservation of diadromous fish stocks is the role of hatcheries in restoration and enhancement efforts. In the past, stocking programs have generally considered only the cost:benefit ratio. Recently, however, the ethics of stocking programs have been questioned. Are stocking programs employed to save a population or to preserve or enhance a fishery? If the latter goal is important, should stocking efforts be at levels high enough to create a "put-and-take" fishery for commercial and recreational fishermen? What level of stocking effort remains in harmony with the environment; i.e., is overstocking detrimental? Are there evolutionary processes taking place in stocked populations that might change the fecundity and growth rates of both wild and stocked fish? These questions easily provoke speculation, but it is quite difficult to obtain useful information with which to answer them properly.

An experience in the Soviet Union was discussed. Large numbers of chum salmon *Oncorhynchus keta* were transplanted from one stream to another and effects of the stocking activity on catches and stock size were monitored for 10 years. Stock size decreased to about 5% of its original level as a consequence of introducing nonnative strains. Examination of the gene pool revealed a shift in the population toward characteristics of the introduced strain. Documented studies of this nature are usually difficult to come by but should be rigorously pursued before major fish stocking or transplantation programs are implemented.

Another issue that requires examination is the community ecology of habitats supporting diadromous fishes. Many studies focus on certain aspects of diadromous species during the freshwater portion of the life cycle, but few address the importance of these migratory species in the ecology of the habitat. What are the processes that regulate cohabitation with nonanadromous species during the freshwater phase of the life cycle? Certainly studies have documented the deleterious effects on indigenous fishes from introducing or establishing salmonid populations in new habitats. Nevertheless, additional studies should be undertaken to examine the bioenergetics of habitats supporting diadromous fish stocks. Once diadromous fishes enter the ocean migration phase of the life cycle, specific life history patterns become quite speculative. Is there an ecological advantage to migrating long distances, or are ocean migrations merely the result of a wandering process? Further studies are needed on the ways fish may optimize their use of residual currents and isotherms to conserve energy.

The evolutionary mechanism for diadromy and its significance remain unanswered. In his keynote address, Robert McDowall noted that the families of fishes with the greatest proportions of diadromous species are ancient in evolutionary terms. Thus, the assumption that diadromy has emerged recently is questionable. It is usually believed, with support from the fossil record, that morphological evolution progresses from simple to complex. Is it appropriate to extend this presumption to behavioral patterns such as diadromy or residency? What happens to evolutionary theory and how would the various data fit if the presumed direction of adaptation was reversed? Suppose diadromy was the original life style and residency a later evolutionary stage. The new migratory population of brown trout *Salmo trutta* that has appeared in Poland may then represent a reversion caused by environmental stress. This argument could also be extended to other species. Is this scenario correct? Comparing the data against such a hypothesis may improve our understanding of diadromy and perhaps provide new directions to explore.

One of the easiest steps in learning more about common and diverse strategies in diadromy would be to establish a coordinated international effort through a central group or agency to identify diadromous species and characterize their life history patterns. Since a large portion of information on diadromous species remains buried in the "grey literature," a central group could act as a clearing house and depository for these reports. Abstracts about each data base could also be provided to interested parties.

American Fisheries Society Symposium 1:550–561, 1987

ABSTRACTS OF POSTER PAPERS

Development of Nursery Systems for Rearing Shortnose Sturgeons

T. I. J. SMITH, W. E. JENKINS, W. D. OLDLAND, AND R. D. HAMILTON

Marine Resources Research Institute, South Carolina Wildlife and
Marine Resources Department
Post Office Box 12559, Charleston, South Carolina 29412, USA

Shortnose sturgeons *Acipenser brevirostrum* range from Canada to Florida and are listed as an endangered species in the United States. During 1985, a cooperative state–federal program focused on development of nursery systems for production of stockable-sized juveniles. Mortality was high (80%) during the first 2–3 months of tank rearing trials with several groups of fry even though various disease control agents and differing culture techniques were used. When the fish reached 180 mm total length (30 g; 4–5 months in age), mortality essentially ceased. Indoor intensive tank systems were more suitable than ponds for producing juveniles of 25–50 mm total length.

Growth and survival of advanced fingerlings in indoor tanks were similar among groups with initial population densities ranging from 5.4 to 118.4 fish/m^2 of tank bottom area. A standing crop of 17.2 kg/m^3 was attained at the highest population density, and overall feed conversion rate for all advanced fingerlings fed a soft-moist trout ration was 1.4. Mean fish size at the conclusion of the study was 332.8 mm total length (148.2 g; age, 264 d). Nine hundred eighteen advanced fingerlings were produced and 596 of these were released as part of a stock rehabilitation effort. The remaining fish were retained for grow out to adult size under culture conditions.

How Are Anadromous Salmonid Life Histories Linked to Freshwater Residency?

J. A. HUTCHINGS AND D. W. MORRIS

Department of Biology, Memorial University, St. John's, Newfoundland A1B 3X9, Canada

Patterns of covariation in salmonid life history traits reflect differences in the degree of anadromy among salmonid life histories. Principle components analysis conducted on eight life history traits for 29 forms of salmonids defined three factors: degree of anadromy, size at maturity, and rate of early development. The primary factor ranked salmonids from large, early maturing, semelparous individuals bearing few, large eggs (anadromous form) to the opposite suite of characters in small, iteroparous individuals (nonanadromous form). Body size did not affect patterns of covariation in life histories. Principal components analyses performed separately on the traits of anadromous and nonanadromous salmonids yielded marked differences in fecundity and iteroparity. Egg size increased with degree of anadromy among genera, although the relationship was not as strong within genera. Time spent in fresh water prior to the initial seaward migration explained 45% ($P < 0.01$) of the variation in anadromous salmonid life histories, suggesting that early juvenile stages strongly influence patterns of covariation among salmonid life history traits. Variations in egg size and egg number, and their effects on early juvenile survival and development, reflect differing degrees of anadromy and iteroparity among salmonid life histories.

Wilder Fish Ladder with a Hydroturbine as a Fish-Attracting Water System

A. J. MILLETTE

New England Power Company, 25 Research Drive, Westborough, Massachusetts 01581, USA

Fish ladders and hydroelectric power generation have historically competed for water from available streamflow. This is no longer true at New England Power Company's "Wilder Fish Ladder," due to the innovative inclusion of a 3,200-kW hydroturbine (waterwheel) within the fishway's attraction-water delivery system. For a fish ladder to be effective, migrating fish must be attracted to the fishway entrance. To attract fish, a large volume of "attraction" flow is added to the relatively small fishway flow just inside the fishway entrance, and the combined flow discharges to the tailrace as a plume, which attracts upstream-migrating fish such as Atlantic salmon *Salmo salar* and American shad *Alosa sapidissima*. The common methods of providing attraction flow are pumped flow lifted to the fishway from the tailrace and gravity flow dropping from the forebay pond. Both options are net users of power, since pumps consume electric power and gravity flow uses water which has the potential to generate electricity. With the gravity flow option, the water's energy ("head") must be dissipated before being added to the fishway flow. At Wilder Dam, a 17-m head had to be dissipated. Two options were studied: energy-dissipating valves and chambers; and a small hydroturbine. Both did the job; however, the energy-dissipating valve is an energy waster, whereas the hydroturbine drives a 3,200-kW hydroelectric generator, producing economic benefits that offset its cost. The fishway turbine–generator has the additional benefits of providing year-round low-flow augmentation at peak generating efficiency and increased base-load generation during high-flow periods.

Larval Migration of Amphidromous Ayu: Application of Otolith Tagging to a Mark–Recapture Study on Eggs and Larvae

K. TSUKAMOTO*, K. MOCHIZUKI**, T. OTAKE*, Y. YAMAZAKI*
M. OKIYAMA*, AND T. KAJIHARA*

**Ocean Research Institute, University of Tokyo, Minamidai, Nakano-ku, 164 Tokyo, Japan
and **University Museum, University of Tokyo, Hongo, Bunkyo-ku, 113 Tokyo*

In order to obtain knowledge of the early life history of amphidromous ayu *Plecoglossus altivelis*, an otolith-tagging method for eggs and larvae was used in a mark–recapture study. Serious mass mortality (99.9%) was suggested during downstream migration in autumn. The experiment on dispersion of larvae from a river mouth suggested that marked fish were passively transported by the tidal current. Preliminary analysis showed that one marked larva (24.0 mm) was found out of 1,569 larvae examined 2 months after release in 1984 and two larvae (16.2 and 18.5 mm) out of 134 fish 40 d after release in 1985. No larvae were caught more than 4 km offshore, while many larvae of various ages and sizes occurred in the surf zone. These findings suggest that the ayu disperse and remain in nearshore coastal waters throughout the marine portion of their life cycle.

Life History Aspects of the South African Catadromous Mullet

A. H. BOK

*Amalinda Nature Conservation Station, Post Office Box 12043
Amalinda, East London 5252, South Africa*

Myxus capensis, the freshwater mullet, is endemic to the southern and southeastern coasts of South Africa and occurs in the freshwater reaches of rivers and lagoons. A recent study showed *M. capensis* to be a catadromous species which has adapted its life history in response to an unstable riverine environment. *Myxus capensis* spawns at sea and the young fry migrate through the estuaries and move upstream into freshwater reaches of rivers on the southeastern coast of South Africa. The adult fish return to their marine spawning grounds 3–6 years later when maximum size is reached and large energy reserves, in the form of fat deposits, have accumulated. Migration into fresh water appears to be a typical feeding migration designed to increase abundance through changes in growth and fecundity. *Myxus capensis* displays several life history tactics characteristic of migratory fish species which are thought to increase population fecundity by increasing the number of large females and hence maximizing egg production. The sex ratio is in favour of females, and females grow faster than males; they reach a larger ultimate size and remain longer than males in the freshwater feeding areas. Comparative life history data on the estuarine-dependent mullet *Mugil cephalus*, which also penetrates into fresh water in this region, helped to assess the adaptive significance of the life history tactics of *Myxus capensis*. Human-induced habitat changes in recent years have markedly reduced the numbers of *M. capensis* in virtually all rivers within its range. The erection of barriers to upriver migration has prevented access to large stretches of its previous habitat and almost completely eliminated *Myxus capensis* from certain rivers.

Intermediate Salinities Stimulate Growth in a Wild Population of Anadromous Brook Trout

P. O. STEELE* AND A. M. STEELE**

**Department of Zoology, University of Western Ontario, London, Ontario N6A 5B7, Canada
and **Department of Neuropathology, Victoria Hospital, London, Ontario N6A 5B7*

Anadromous salmonids exhibit a six-fold increase in growth rates under laboratory conditions in isomotic waters (5–10‰ NaCl). This phenomenon has not been documented in wild populations. A study of an anadromous population of brook trout *Salvelinus fontinalis* in the Hudson Bay lowlands of Ontario indicates that fish of the Sutton River exhibit dramatic growth rates when inhabiting the cold (−1 to +5°C) isosmotic waters of Hudson Bay during summer months. Physiological evidence (mucous cell activity, skin colouration, elongated shape) suggests that high growth rates are due to elevated levels of growth hormone maintained by osmoregulation in an isosmotic environment. Radioimmunoassays confirmed that brook trout entering the Sutton River had elevated concentrations of growth hormone. In some fish, these concentrations were an order of magnitude higher than those in individuals resident in the river for three or more days. It is hypothesized that the transient increases of hormones, such as growth hormones, that accompany the fish's transition to seawater, particularly during smoltification, may be prolonged by maintaining the fish at isosmotic salinities.

Thermal Adaptations in Alaskan Chinook and Sockeye Salmon

C. V. BURGER

U.S. Fish and Wildlife Service, National Fishery Research Center, 1011 East Tudor Road
Anchorage, Alaska 99503, USA

Salmon spawning areas and times were compared in several Alaskan streams that produce multiple runs of chinook salmon *Oncorhynchus tshawytscha* and sockeye salmon *O. nerka*; the objective was to determine the factors that affect their spawning times and distribution. The populations compared were Kenai River chinook salmon (4-year study) and sockeye salmon in the Russian, Brooks, and Karluk rivers (literature review). Our study of 188 radio-tagged chinook salmon (1979–1982) in the Kenai River confirmed that an early run occurred each May and June and that the fish spawned primarily in two tributaries; fish in a late run (July and August) spawned in the river's main stem. Once this distribution was known, peak spawning times were determined. Spawning peaked during August in tributaries (six streams) influenced by lakes but during July in tributaries (three streams) having no lake influences. The moderating effects of lakes may have increased fall and winter temperatures of downstream waters, enabling successful reproduction for later-spawning fish because hatching and emergence could be completed in a shorter time. The occurrence and the time of spawning (late August) of the late run is unique among chinook salmon stocks in south-central Alaska. This behavior may have developed only because two large lakes (Kenai and Skilak) directly influence main stem spawning areas. Multiple runs of sockeye and coho salmon *O. kisutch* in the Kenai River provide further evidence—late-run sockeye and coho salmon spawn immediately downstream of Kenai and Skilak lakes. Multiple runs of sockeye salmon also exist in each of the Russian, Brooks, and Karluk rivers and their spawning areas are well documented. Early-run salmon in the Russian River spawn near its headwaters (no lake influence), but the late-run fish spawn downstream of Upper Russian Lake. Brooks River sockeye salmon spawn in five tributaries upstream of Brooks Lake (early run) and in the river below Brooks Lake (late run). Early-run sockeye salmon in the Karluk River drainage spawn in 12 tributaries to Karluk Lake, none of which are lake fed. The Karluk late run, however, spawns in Lower Thumb, O'Malley, and Karluk rivers, all of which are lake influenced. Partial streamflow records for the Karluk drainage demonstrate that temperature in Falls Creek (used by early-run spawners) decreases to 0°C for about 2 months during winter. Temperatures in Lower Thumb and Karluk rivers, however, do not fall below 1–2°C during winter. These data support our argument that differences in spawning times in lake-influenced areas are temperature related. We hypothesize that salmon have adapted to thermal regimes in the home stream and that selection has occurred for stock-specific run times that insure the presence of adults at spawning areas just prior to the optimum spawning period. This strategy promotes emergence times that enhance survival of fry. The occurrence of multiple runs insures optimum use of habitat and species abundance. If run timing is now genetically controlled, and if the various spawning groups in a drainage are isolated stocks that have adapted to predictable stream temperatures, there are implications for stock-transplantation programs. If migration and spawning times of indigenous stocks are predetermined for local environmental conditions, the implications associated with changes in temperature regimes resulting from hydroelectric and other types of riverine development must also be considered.

Time-Series Analysis of Discharge, Turbidity, and Juvenile Salmon Outmigration in the Susitna River, Alaska

S. S. HALE

Alaska Department of Fish and Game, Susitna River Aquatic Studies Program
Anchorage, Alaska 99501, USA

During 3 years of study of juvenile salmon outmigration from the middle reach of the Susitna River, a correspondence was noted between peaks of river discharge and peaks of outmigration. Discharge peaks can have a positive effect on salmon survival rate by facilitating outmigration and reducing predation but can also have a negative effect by displacing fry downstream from what would otherwise be their rearing areas. Two large hydroelectric dams proposed for a region above the salmon-rearing areas would markedly change the downstream discharge, temperature, and turbidity regimes. Box–Jenkins models were developed for the 1983 and 1984 time series of river discharge, turbidity, and outmigration rates of chinook salmon *Oncorhynchus tshawytscha* and sockeye salmon *O. nerka* fry to better understand the forces that shape the series and to statistically describe natural conditions. First-order autoregressive terms were a strong component in all time series examined. About 74% of the variance in discharge and 85% of the variance in turbidity for one day were explained by the values of each on the previous day. This percentage was 44% for chinook salmon outmigration and 43% for sockeye salmon outmigration; the lower numbers indicated the effect of behavioral decisions on biological time series. Fish have a greater tendency to move in pulses than do parcels of water or suspended sediments, partly because discharge events provide an environmental cue that operates on all subgroups of the outmigrating population. Although the patterns of the time-series plots of chinook salmon outmigrations were different between the 2 years, the underlying stochastic processes which generated these series were the same. The placement of a large reservoir in the system would likely change the nature of these processes by filtering out high-frequency events. Bivariate transfer-function models were constructed for turbidity and salmon outmigration rates that explain present values in terms of previous values as well as past values of discharge.

Habitat Suitability Index Curves for Anadromous Fishes

J. H. CRANCE

Division of Biological Services, U.S. Fish and Wildlife Service, 2627 Redwing Road
Fort Collins, Colorado 80526, USA

The Delphi technique was used to develop habitat suitability index curves for striped bass *Morone saxatilis*, American shad *Alosa sapidissima*, Atlantic sturgeon *Acipenser oxyrhynchus*, and shortnose sturgeon *A. brevirostrum*. At least eight experts served as panelists for each species. Each Delphi exercise was conducted by correspondence and consisted of four or five rounds. Water velocity, depth, temperature, and substrate were the primary habitat variables evaluated. Activities considered were migration, spawning, and incubation; larvae, juveniles, and adults were considered as primary life stages. Sixty-three index curves were developed for the four fish species. Each index curve depicts the optimal range of a variable for a life stage or activity of each species and, when applicable, the upper and lower limits of the variable that are suitable. For example, the panel of experts for Atlantic sturgeon reached a consensus that water velocities ranging from 46 to 76 cm/s are optimal for spawning by this species and that velocities of 6 cm/s or lower and 107 cm/s or higher are unsuitable for spawning.

Extended Freshwater Residence Prior to Spawning: The Influence of Water Velocity and Temperature on Swimming Capacity and Its Role in Controlling the Upstream Migration of Anadromous Coregonines of James Bay, Quebec

L. BERNATCHEZ AND J. J. DODSON

Departement de Biologie, University Laval, Quebec G1K 7P4, Canada

Anadromous lake whitefish *Coregonus clupeaformis* and ciscoes *C. artedii* leave their feeding grounds in James Bay to enter the Eastmain River as early as mid-July and migrate 27 km upstream. The majority of these fish traverse 6 km of rapids from mid-August to mid-September when mean water temperature declines from 17 to 10°C. Such an early migration results in an extended residence of 6–10 weeks on the spawning grounds without feeding. Spawning occurs when water temperature falls below 5°C. In order to explain such costly energetic and apparently nonadaptive behavior, we hypothesized that low water temperature and high current speed encountered in rapids may represent an important environmental constraint on the migration of ciscoes and lake whitefish. The influence of these factors on metabolism and swimming capacity may be a major factor controlling the timing of the reproductive migration of both species. We tested the influence of temperature and water velocity on metabolic rate and swimming capacity of both species using respirometry techniques. Values of metabolic scope for activity coupled with the net energetic cost of swimming showed that these coregonines were not good performers compared to most salmonids. The maximum oxygen consumption, aerobic scope for activity, and maximum sustained swimming speed for lake whitefish were maximal at 12°C and minimal at 5°C. Swimming endurance of lake whitefish decreased logarithmically with swimming speed and was reduced at low temperature. The distance traversed before fish became fatigued at any swimming speed was minimal at 5°C. Our results suggest that migrating at low temperature may increase potential mortality before spawning. The results support the hypothesis that the combined effect of high water velocities and low ambient temperature on coregonine swimming capacity may be a more important factor than specific spawning temperature in the timing of their early reproductive migrations.

Biochemical and Genetic Analysis of American Shad Migrating into the Chesapeake Bay

E. N. SISMOUR AND R. S. BIRDSONG

Old Dominion University, Norfolk, Virginia 23508, USA

Seven enzymes extracted from heart and liver tissues of American shad *Alosa sapidissima* were examined by electrophoresis. The fish were captured during three intervals of migration into Chesapeake Bay and once from the Nansemond River, a tributary of the James River. Loci encoding malate dehydrogenase and nonspecific esterase were polymorphic. The esterase polymorphism served as a biochemical marker for an analysis of American shad migration. A statistically significant change of the predominating esterase genotypes within the migration occurred over time. The migration appears to be composed of multiple, genetically divergent spawning populations. The change in genetic composition may result from the congregation of James River stocks in the study area prior to their entry into fresh water. Alternatively, some populations may enter Chesapeake Bay in advance of others. High homozygosity from a collection made in the Nansemond River was attributed to sampling a smaller gene pool of individuals that had segregated from the main migration.

Behavior of Adult Blueback Herring Migrating Upstream through Lock 2 of the Erie Canal

W. A. KARP*, P. NEALSON*, D. J. LISPI**, AND Q. ROSS**

*BioSonics, Incorporated, 4520 Union Bay Place NE, Seattle, Washington 98105, USA, and
**New York Power Authority, 10 Columbus Circle, New York, New York 10019, USA

Hydroacoustic techniques were used to observe movements of adult blueback herring *Alosa aestivalis* immediately upstream and downstream of the first lock on the Erie Canal at Waterford, New York, in May 1985. Objectives were to document fish movements in response to lockages, to develop recommendations for modified lock operations, and to evaluate hydroacoustic techniques for monitoring fish passage. At the lower gates, estimates of fish passage into the lock increased with duration of opening. At the upper gates, a pulse of fish was generally observed to move out of the lock immediately after the gates opened, and duration of opening did not appear to influence rate of fish passage from the lock into the canal. Fish were observed to move downstream, away from the lock gates, to avoid turbulence created by water dumping during the initial stages of drawdown. Upstream fish passage might be enhanced by decreasing the rate of water dumping and prolonging the period that the downstream gates are held open. Increasing the frequency of lockages during dawn and dusk and when boat traffic is light might enhance upstream migrations.

Why Do So Few Anadromous Populations Minimize the Energetic Cost of Their Upstream Migrations?

L. BERNATCHEZ AND J. J. DODSON

Department de Biologie, Universite Laval, Quebec G1K 7P4, Canada

Students of fish migratory behavior have generally accepted that minimizing energetic cost per unit distance is the major criterion that anadromous migrants seek to optimize during upstream migration. In order to test this general theory, we documented from the literature the energetic expenditures and travel speeds of 16 anadromous fish populations involving 10 species observed during their upstream migrations. In addition, a series of parameters that characterized fish migratory behavior and the spawning river were calculated for each population. In all cases, the total cost of migration was important and remained relatively constant, varying by a factor of five. The length of the migration varied by a factor of 36. In most cases, the cost per unit distance is not minimized and migratory strategy does not conform to theoretical optimal strategy. The energetic efficiency of migration increases exponentially with migration length. Energy expenditure per unit distance approaches the theoretical minimum only in situations where river harshness leads to the exhaustion of energy reserves, which is the case for chum salmon *Oncorhynchus keta*, chinook salmon *O. tshawytscha*, and the Fraser River stocks of sockeye salmon *O. nerka*. We suggest that greater migration distance may lead to higher migratory efficiency by promoting selection for larger body size, more accurate upstream orientation, and least costly travel speeds. Minimizing the probability of death from exhaustive swimming during the upstream migration may be more important than energetic efficiency in determining migratory behavior of anadromous species.

Variation in Life History, Ecology, and Resource Utilization by Arctic Char in Scotland

S. E. BARBOUR

*Department of Fisheries and Oceans, Post Office Box 550, Station M
Halifax, Nova Scotia B3J 2S7, Canada*

A study was made of three populations of Arctic char *Salvelinus alpinus* from different habitats. Differences were found in morphology, feeding habits, growth, energetics, and reproductive tactics. A pelagic planktivorous, rather than benthic, life history was adopted by populations in competition with other salmonids. Measurements showed morphological coincidence with these life styles. Growth rate in body length was similar among the populations but growth in weight was related to the productivity of the habitat. Final body size was determined by the onset of sexual maturity. Large, deep, lowland fjord-like lochs produced larger, heavier Arctic char than a smaller, less-temperate hill loch and a mesoeutrophic Hebridean loch. Body resources, expressed as values for fish of a standard size, were greater in the lowland loch population. These fish invested more resources in somatic sexual dimorphism whereas the hill fish invested more in gonad tissue. The age at maturity and fecundity were greater among the lowland fish but egg size was smaller. The size of offspring at the onset of feeding was directly related to egg size. It is hypothesized that the requirements for yolk to ensure alevin survival may initiate adaptation of the life history. The lowland Arctic char (hypermorphic, large, old, and fecund with small but variable egg size) resemble the root stock of postglacial colonization. Large egg size, early maturity (with its demographic advantages), and small body size with reduced fecundity represents a chain of responses to more stringent environments.

Preliminary Analysis of Life History Strategies in Northern Fishes with Special Reference to Three Species of Ciscoes

R. E. DILLINGER, JR., J. M. GREEN, AND T. P. BIRT

Department of Biology, Memorial University, St. John's, Newfoundland A1B 3X9, Canada

Life history theory predicts that with increasing latitude, fish will maximize fitness in a variable environment by increasing total life span and age at maturity while decreasing brood size. This prediction has been confirmed for several species of marine fish. We tested this prediction using information on the life history tactics of six species of sympatric coregonine fishes from the Alaskan and Canadian arctic coasts. Emphasis was placed on three closely related species—*Coregonus autumnalis*, *C. laurettae*, and *C. sardinella*—and these were contrasted with *C. nasus*, *C. pidschian*, and *Prosopium cylindraceum* with data from our present field work and from previous studies done by others. As predicted by life history theory, growth decreased and life span and age at maturity increased with increasing latitude for all six species. Similarly, the number of broods, fecundity, and egg size decreased with increasing latitude for *C. autumnalis* and *C. sardinella*. However, fecundity increased with increasing latitude for *C. nasus*, *C. pidschian*, and *P. cylindraceum*. An increase in the number of broods was also exhibited by *C. nasus*. These results do not follow the predictions of life history theory.

Pigmentation, Size, and Upstream Migration of Elvers and Young American Eels in a Coastal Rhode Island Stream

A. J. HARO

Department of Zoology, University of Rhode Island, Kingston, Rhode Island 02881, USA

Progressive pigmentation of American eel *Anguilla rostrata* elvers in a coastal Rhode Island stream was essentially identical to that described for European eels *A. anguilla* and proceeded rapidly in fresh water. Elvers arriving earlier in the season were larger than those arriving later, paralleling studies of European elvers. Mean total length of elvers collected in 1984 was significantly larger than in 1982 or 1983. The main migration occurred during April and May and was related to decreasing flow rates and increasing stream temperature. The main concentration of elvers required about 1 month to ascend 200 m above the tidal zone. The relatively slow initial migration of elvers in this section of the stream is attributed to high stream gradient and the absence of tidal influence. Some elvers were able to migrate 2.5 km upstream of the tidal zone by August or September, but age-2+ yellow eels were more abundant than age-1+ elvers in these upstream areas, suggesting that American eels continue upstream migration as age 2+ or older yellow eels.

The Return Migration of Adult Atlantic Salmon to the Aberdeenshire Dee, Scotland

A. D. HAWKINS

Department of Agriculture for Scotland, Marine Laboratory, Aberdeen AB9 8DB, Scotland

Adult Atlantic salmon *Salmo salar* return to some Scottish east-coast rivers throughout the year. Fish may return to the Aberdeenshire Dee as early as January, or as late as October, to spawn in November or December. The fish returning early in the spring tend to be larger multi-sea-winter fish, while those returning in late summer and autumn tend to be grilse (one-sea-winter fish). In recent years, there has been a tendency for the spring run to decline and for some increase in the number of fish entering in the autumn. The freshwater movements of fish entering the river at different times of the year were studied by radio tracking. Atlantic salmon entering the river moved quickly through the estuary and lower parts of the river; they stopped for only short periods until they reached upstream holding pools, where they slowed and stopped for longer periods, sometimes spending many months at these locations. Spring fish moved farther upstream before stopping than fish entering later in the year. In October, the fish left their holding pools and moved short distances upstream to the spawning grounds. Females moved to particular spawning grounds and remained there, showing little further movement from day to day. Subsequently, they moved downstream and out to sea. Males moved back and forth along a stretch of river, from one spawning area to another, and appeared to stay longer on the spawning grounds. Many males died following spawning. The early entry of fish to the river cannot be seen as an adaptation which simply allows fish more time to complete their journey upstream. Though the journey to the higher tributaries is long, fish are generally able to move to the head of the river within several weeks under the good flow conditions which generally prevail in the Aberdeenshire Dee. It is suggested that the long time period spent in holding pools, especially by fish returning early and moving upstream, represents an attempt to reserve a place in a suitable holding position close to the spawning grounds. There may be pressure on fish originating in the higher tributaries to return earlier than others simply to ensure access to the limited holding positions available in the higher parts of the river. Early arrival, followed by a long-term stay in the river, may be a more feasible strategy for larger multi-sea-winter fish than it is for grilse.

Human Impact on the Diadromous Fish Fauna in the Meuse River Basin: A Historical and Geographical Analysis

G. T. HOUVENAGHEL

Universite Libre de Bruxelles, Belgium

In the continental waters of western Europe, where human impact on the environment has occurred for nearly 2,000 years, the diadromous fish fauna has been drastically reduced in species diversity, population numbers, and geographical range. This is particularly the case with sturgeons, shad, salmon, and eels, upon which important fisheries have been based. Historical and geographical data of such declines are given for the Meuse River, which flows from the northeastern part of France to the North Sea through Belgium and the Netherlands, giving a full ecological gradient from the salmonid zone upstream to the estuarine and tidal zone. The diadromous fish species are sea lamprey *Petromyzon marinus*, river lamprey *Lampetra fluviatilis*, European sturgeon *Acipenser sturio*, allice shad *Alosa alosa*, twaite shad *Alosa fallax*, Atlantic salmon *Salmo salar*, brown (sea) trout *Salmo trutta*, houting *Coregonus oxyrhynchus*, European flounder *Platichtys flesus*, smelt *Osmerus eperlanus*, and European eel *Anguilla anguilla*. Among them, the sea trout is the only species that is increasing; these fish were found in the lower Meuse in 1979 and progressed upstream to reach Belgian waters in 1983–1984. All the other species are in regression and some, like houting, shads, sturgeon, lampreys, and possibly flounder, have been extirpated, although some are still encountered in the tidal zone. In the estuarine zone, a connection with the delta region has been completely reshaped. Smelt, once heavily fished, are now poorly represented. The European sturgeon disappeared around 1850 because of reduction of mudflats and marsh areas. For the species with long migrations, data indicate that regression began in the 1920–1930s, corresponding to the building of large dams on the lower river. The low efficiency of the fishways explains the sudden decline of lampreys, salmon, houting, and shads. The reduction of the diadromous fish fauna in the Meuse River results from important changes in the environment (reduction of bottom area, changes in water speed and quality, reduction of the estuarine mixing zone) due to hydraulic management (diking, bank shaping, dams), which reduce migration recruitment and spawning. Alteration of water quality due to industrial and urban development affects larval and juvenile development while overexploitation reduces the population of adults during their migration to the spawning grounds.

Blood Coagulation Is Inhibited in Cold-Adapted Anadromous Brook Trout

P. O. STEELE* AND A. M. STEELE**

*Department of Zoology, University of Western Ontario, London, Ontario N6A 5B7, Canada and **Department of Neuropathology, Victoria Hospital, London, Ontario N6A 5B7

Blood clotting time in fish is prolonged at low temperatures. For some species, clotting may require 90 s at very low temperatures ($-2°C$). The mechanism responsible for prolonging coagulation at low temperatures is not known. In cold-adapted anadromous brook trout *Salvelinus fontinalis*, coagulation was completely inhibited during the return migration into the Sutton River from Hudson Bay. This inhibition occurred regardless of river water temperature or fish maturity. At present, we have not determined how blood coagulation is inhibited. One possible mechanism under investigation involves the action of a proteolytic enzyme, plasmin, on plasma fibrinogen and on the excessive amounts of growth hormone characterizing this population.

Time of Migration and Growth of Two Introduced Strains of Atlantic Salmon in a Southern New England Stream

R. D. ORCIARI, D. MYSLING, AND G. LEONARD

Connecticut Department of Environmental Protection, Bureau of Fisheries
Western District Headquarters, Harwinton, Connecticut 06791, USA

An evaluation of stocking unfed Atlantic salmon fry *Salmo salar* for producing smolts in the wild was carried out in Sandy Brook, a third-order tributary in the Connecticut River system. The Connecticut River was historically the southern limit of Atlantic salmon spawning in North America. Due to the species' extirpation from this river, it was necessary to introduce other strains for study. The closest viable population of Atlantic salmon exists in the Penobscot River, Maine. In 1982 and 1984, eggs were obtained from this stock. Icelandic-strain eggs were obtained in 1981 and 1983 due to the unavailability of Penobscot eggs. Smolts were captured each spring at a weir set 0.4 km above the mouth of Sandy Brook. Age and growth of smolts were determined separately for each group of fish sampled over sequential 5-d periods. Smolt runs, composed of fish aged 1+ to 3+, commenced in late April and early May. However, Penobscot age-1+ smolts migrated earlier than Icelandic age-1+ smolts. Weighted mean dates of migration were May 7 and May 21 for Penobscot and Icelandic age-1+ smolts, respectively. Spring growth increments of smolts, determined by measuring the zone of widely spaced circuli between the last annulus and the outer edge of the scale, increased as the run progressed. On the average, the spring growth increment was less for Penobscot smolts (21 mm) than for Icelandic age-1+ smolts (36 mm). Perhaps, by migrating earlier, Penobscot smolts may have had less opportunity to undergo rapid spring growth while in Sandy Brook. Presmolt critical length, represented by the lower 95% spread limit (one tail) of average smolt length at last annulus formation, was greater for Penobscot (114 mm) than for Icelandic (85 mm) age-0+ parr. Average total length was also greater in Penobscot (157 mm) than in Icelandic (145 mm) age-1+ smolts. At age 2+, smolts exhibited similar growth trends between strains, but differences were not as great as with age-1+ smolts. Resulting differences between strains of Atlantic salmon suggest that smolt growth and migration are, in part, genetically influenced. Icelandic age-0+ fish are capable of transforming into age-1+ smolts at a smaller size, due to their greater spring growth during the forthcoming spring and smaller average length as smolts. Icelandic parr would produce considerably more smolts than the same number of equal-sized Penobscot parr. However, increased production of late-migrating Icelandic smolts may have management value if the fish must encounter unfavorable water conditions and active predators.

Effects of Dietary Hormone Treatments in Reducing Large Variances in Growth Rates of American Eels

G. DEGANI* AND M. L. GALLAGHER**

*Galilee Technological Center, Israel, and **The Institute for Coastal and Marine Resources
East Carolina University, Greenville, North Carolina 27834, USA

Factors critical to the growth of elvers (glass eels) as they enter fresh water are largely unknown. The initial period is characterized by high mortality rates and major differences in growth rates among individuals. Reported growth rates of European eels *Anguilla anguilla* vary by as much as 120 times, and variations in reported rates of growth of *Anguilla japonica* were so extreme that dietary growth studies were difficult to carry out without a careful selection process. We have found growth rates of American eels *Anguilla rostrata* also to vary over a wide range. Our objective was to determine if systemic hormone deficiencies could account for the large differences in growth rates commonly seen in wild populations. Effects of dietary addition of 17-methyltestosterone (MT), 3,3′,5-triiodo-L-thyronine (T3), and bovine growth hormone (bGH) on growth, food conversion, and percent total body protein in these elvers were investigated. Both MT (1 mg/kg) and bGH (2 and 10 mg/kg) significantly increased the mean weight of elvers. Although higher concentrations of MT (10 mg/kg) increased mean body weight, the increases were not significant. The effects of MT were more pronounced in normally developing elvers than in slowly developing elvers. Reduction of water temperature had a much stronger influence on weight gain of slowly developing elvers receiving MT than on normally developing American eels receiving MT. A significant increase was found in the mean weight of slow-growing elvers receiving diets containing 20 mg T3/kg and held in the low-water-turnover system. A significant increase was also found in the weight of slow-growing elvers receiving diets containing 40 or 60 mg T3/kg and held in the high-water-turnover system. There was no significant difference in survival among all experimental groups. Food conversion was improved by both MT and bGH. In general, food conversion by slowly developing elvers was lower than food conversion by normally developing elvers. Total body protein of elvers was significantly related to body weight in all treatments, but not related to hormone levels when elvers were fed T3 or bGH. Total body protein was significantly lower ($P < 0.05$) in elvers receiving MT. These results indicate that bGH, T3, and MT generally increase growth in American eels at all growth rates. However, the failure of all hormones to increase slow-growing elver growth rates to a normal level, as well as the lower response of slow-growing elvers to these treatments, indicates that hormone deficiencies do not account for the large differences in growth rates.